THE CONSTRUCTION LAW LIBRARY FROM WILEY LAW PUBLICATIONS

CONSTRUCTION LITIGATION: REPRESENTING THE OWNER (SECOND EDITION)
Robert F. Cushman, Kenneth M. Cushman, and Stephen B. Cook, Editors

CONSTRUCTION LITIGATION: STRATEGIES AND TECHNIQUES
Barry B. Bramble and Albert E. Phillips, Editors

CONSTRUCTION RENOVATION FORMBOOK
Robert F. Cushman and John W. DiNicola, Editors

CONSTRUCTION SCHEDULING: PREPARATION, LIABILITY, AND CLAIMS
Jon M. Wickwire, Thomas J. Driscoll, and Stephen B. Hurlbut

CONSTRUCTION SUBCONTRACTING: A LEGAL GUIDE FOR INDUSTRY
PROFESSIONALS
Overton A. Currie, Neal J. Sweeney, and Randall F. Hafer, Editors

DESIGN PROFESSIONAL'S HANDBOOK OF BUSINESS AND LAW
Robert F. Cushman and James C. Dobbs, Editors

DRAFTING CONSTRUCTION CONTRACTS: STRATEGY AND FORMS FOR
CONTRACTORS
Samuel F. Schoninger

FEDERAL CONSTRUCTION CONTRACTING
James F. Nagle

HANDLING FIDELITY, SURETY, AND FINANCIAL RISK CLAIMS (SECOND EDITION)
Robert F. Cushman, George L. Blick, and Charles A. Meeker, Editors

HAZARDOUS WASTE DISPOSAL AND UNDERGROUND CONSTRUCTION LAW
Robert F. Cushman and Bruce W. Ficken, Editors

LEGAL GUIDE TO AIA DOCUMENTS (THIRD EDITION)
Werner Sabo

1992 DIRECTORY OF CONSTRUCTION INDUSTRY CONSULTANTS
Wiley Law Publications, Editors

1992 WILEY CONSTRUCTION LAW UPDATE
Overton A. Currie and Neal J. Sweeney, Editors

PROVING AND PRICING CONSTRUCTION CLAIMS
Robert F. Cushman and David A. Carpenter, Editors

SWEET ON CONSTRUCTION INDUSTRY CONTRACTS (SECOND EDITION)
Justin Sweet

TROUBLED CONSTRUCTION LOANS: LAW AND PRACTICE
Stanley P. Sklar, Editor

CONSTRUCTION CONTRACTOR'S HANDBOOK OF BUSINESS AND LAW

SUBSCRIPTION NOTICE

This Wiley product is updated on a periodic basis with supplements to reflect important changes in the subject matter. If you purchased this product directly from John Wiley & Sons, Inc., we have already recorded your subscription for this update service.

If, however, you purchased this product from a bookstore and wish to receive (1) the current update at no additional charge, and (2) future updates and revised or related volumes billed separately with a 30-day examination review, please send your name, company name (if applicable), address, and the title of the product to:

Supplement Department
John Wiley & Sons, Inc.
One Wiley Drive
Somerset, NJ 08875
1-800-225-5945

CONSTRUCTION CONTRACTOR'S HANDBOOK OF BUSINESS AND LAW

Robert F. Cushman, Esquire

G. Christian Hedemann, Esquire

Peter J. King

Editors

Wiley Law Publications

JOHN WILEY & SONS, INC.

New York • Chichester • Brisbane • Toronto • Singapore

Copyright © 1992 by John Wiley & Sons, Inc.

Chapter 4 copyright © 1985 by Robert F. Cushman.

Library of Congress Cataloging-in-Publication Data

ISBN 0-471-55300-9 (cloth edition)
ISBN 0-471-57838-x (paper edition)

Printed in the United States of America

10 9 8 7 6 5 4 3 2 1

PREFACE

The complexity of today's sophisticated construction projects often leads to poor coordination between designers and contractors, and between contractors and owners. Add to this the pressure of today's economy to get the most bang for the least buck and blend into the mixture the ever-present ingredient of time constraint, and no one can fail to see why claims by and against contractors are increasing at an alarming rate. Even with the increasing use of alternative dispute resolution, the construction industry remains, and will continue to be, controversial and adversarial.

To survive in this litigious economic climate, contractors, subcontractors, and material suppliers must continue to address their organizational, operational, performance procedures; their contract documents; and their collection procedures; and must adhere to the laws and regulations of federal and state governments with acumen and current wisdom.

In this handbook we have selected knowledgeable, articulate, and recognized authorities to address and give guidance to these recurring and important issues. Each of our 31 chapters presents a matter of significant consequence.

We believe we have assembled the most distinguished group of authorities ever to jointly author a book in the field of construction law. Each chapter has been written wisely, practically, and skillfully. The book should prove to be a welcome addition to the working library of the entire construction community and may make the difference between a successful construction firm and a financial disaster.

January 1992

ROBERT F. CUSHMAN
Philadelphia, Pennsylvania

G. CHRISTIAN HEDEMANN
Irvine, California

PETER J. KING
Chicago, Illinois

ABOUT THE EDITORS

Robert F. Cushman is a partner in the international law firm of Pepper, Hamilton & Scheetz and a recognized specialist and lecturer on all phases of construction and real estate law. He serves as legal counsel to numerous trade associations and construction, development, and bonding companies. Mr.Cushman is editor and coauthor of several books about construction, including the following John Wiley publications: *Construction Litigation: Representing the Contractor; Construction Litigation: Representing the Owner* (2d ed.); *Architect and Engineer Liability; Claims Against Design Professionals; Construction Defaults: Rights, Duties, and Liabilities; Construction Failures;* and *Proving and Pricing Construction Claims.* A member of the Pennsylvania bar, he is admitted to practice before the United States Supreme Court and the court of appeals for the Federal Circuit. Mr. Cushman has served as executive vice president and general counsel to the Construction Industry Foundation, as counsel to the American Construction Owners Association, and as regional chairman of the Public Contract Law Section of the American Bar Association. He is permanent chairman of the Andrews Conference Group's Construction Litigation and Hazardous Waste superconferences. Mr. Cushman is a charter member of the American College of Construction Attorneys.

G. Christian Hedemann is vice president and general counsel of Fluor Daniel, Inc., Irvine, California, one of the leading engineering, construction, operations, and maintenance companies in the world. He previously worked for Bechtel, Stone & Webster, and in private practice where he was a litigator. He received his B.A. and J.D. degrees from the University of Colorado at Boulder.

Peter J. King is a partner in the Chicago, Illinois, office of Arthur Andersen & Company's Litigation Services practice, with a special focus on managing strategic litigation information. His areas of specialty include construction litigation, the reinsurance industry, environmental litigation, and risk management. Mr. King has held firm leadership positions in London, Tehran, Canada, and the United States. He joined the firm's London office in 1971 after earning his B.S. degree in economics from the London School of Economics, where he later taught undergraduate and graduate accounting. He is a fellow of The Royal Institute of Chartered Accountants of England and Wales.

SUMMARY CONTENTS

DETAILED CONTENTS

Stephen G. Walker, Esquire
Ronald L. Shumway, Esquire
Stephen D. Butler, Esquire
Bechtel Corporation
San Francisco, California

Chapter 7   Contracting with the Material Supplier

Richard A. Holderness, Esquire
Graham & James
San Francisco, California

PART I

ORGANIZATION AND FINANCES

CHAPTER 1

FORM OF OPERATION OF THE CONSTRUCTION ORGANIZATION

James W. Fouch

James W. Fouch is a principal in the Special Services Division of Arthur Andersen's Chicago, Illinois, office. He is a registered professional engineer with a B.S. in industrial engineering from Purdue University. He has approximately 20 years of experience in construction, including consulting on construction claims litigation and construction project management. Mr. Fouch's background in construction claims litigation includes substantial consulting on delay and disruption claims, as well as contract reviews for project owners, construction managers, contractors, and architect/engineers. He also has been involved in numerous construction contract management assignments representing construction project owners for many different facilities, including electric power plants, gas pipelines, mass transit, commercial building, and waste treatment.

§ 1.1   Foundation of the Construction Business

Although the construction business can be seen in large new buildings, new plant facilities, and massive pieces of equipment, most of all construction is a reflection of people. The construction business is a people business. This fact is emphasized most dramatically by the names and owners of the construction companies. Many construction companies still bear their founders' names and are run as family-owned businesses. For a construction company's chief executive officer (CEO) to attend and participate in key project meetings or presentations is not unusual and often is expected.

The people of a construction company are assembled into organizational units that are similar to those of other businesses. Typically, the three primary organizational units that report to the CEO are operations, marketing, and administration.

§ 1.2   Marketing Organizational Unit

Within the marketing organizational unit reside the estimators, including the chief estimator, whose primary function is to obtain profitable work. In order to accomplish this objective, the marketing organization, as shown on **Figure 1–1**, is responsible for identifying desirable projects and qualifying the contractor as a potential bidder for desirable projects. The prequalification requirements can differ significantly between private and public construction work.

§ 1.3   —Public Construction Projects

Public construction projects normally are formally announced and all qualified bidders are permitted to submit quotations. These quotations generally are of a fixed-price form, either lump sum (a single price for the entire specified project) or perhaps unit prices for estimated quantities of work (for example, price per linear foot of six-inch diameter ductile iron pipe). The marketing organization's responsibility is to identify potential projects, submit qualification information, and obtain the request for proposal (RFP) information, including specifications and bid drawings.

After the contractor's marketing organization has received the RFP information, the risks and opportunities associated with the proposed project are evaluated. There are numerous reasons why the contractor's marketing

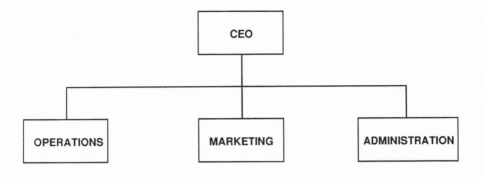

Figure 1–1. Construction company functions.

organization may decide not to submit a bid for a particular project. These may include any of the following reasons or others not mentioned:

1. The contractor is too busy and has insufficient project management personnel available to manage the project properly.
2. The construction project owner or the owner's project management representatives have a very poor reputation concerning project coordination and businesslike relationships with their contractors.
3. The project involves specialized construction procedures with which the contractor is unfamiliar or lacks experience.

4. The project is located in a construction market in which the contractor has not worked previously and involves potentially difficult union relationships.

5. The contractor expects an inordinate amount of competition, which significantly decreases its probability of being the successful bidder.

All of the above reasons are legitimate explanations for declining to bid a project. Unfortunately, if the first reason (too busy) does not exist, many contractors ignore or do not properly consider the other high risk concerns identified above.

Upon deciding to bid a project, the contractor's marketing organization begins the hectic activity of putting together what is sought to be a winning bid. The chief estimator must first decide what work the contractor will perform and what work will be subcontracted. Drawing and specification packages are sent to all potential subcontractors. Meanwhile, the contractor's estimators begin the process of determining the quantities of work involved in the project. This process is known as *taking off* the quantities of work from the drawings.

After the quantities of work have been determined, the estimators price the work using historical data that has been accumulated from numerous previous projects. Adjustments are made by the estimators to reflect unique project conditions, such as weather, congested working conditions, and accelerated schedule. The extent of field overhead (general conditions) required to manage the project is estimated and included with the contractor's scope of work.

Subcontractor bids are received by the chief estimator, normally at the last minute, and are integrated into the contractor's bid. While the hectic estimating and bid preparation activity is ongoing, the chief estimator evaluates the construction marketplace to determine the competitive nature of the bidding process and recommends a profit markup. The construction company's management reviews the bid prepared by the marketing organization and frequently adjusts the recommended profit markup to reflect the construction company's desire to be the winning bidder.

§ 1.4 —Private Construction Projects

In private construction projects, more negotiation normally is involved and the lowest bidder is not necessarily the successful bidder. Price is obviously an important consideration; however, other important considerations (for example, contractor's proposed project management team, contractor's prior successful projects for the construction project owner, and contractor's reputation for filing claims) also weigh heavily in the construction project owner's decision about which bidder will be awarded the contract.

Under special circumstances, the construction project owner might decide not to bid a project, but instead to negotiate with one selected contractor. The situation generally only occurs because the selected contractor is viewed as having special qualifications, not possessed by other contractors, for performing the project. Obviously, this is the most desirable set of circumstances from the contractor's standpoint. The contractor's marketing organization is responsible for cultivating relationships with potential construction project owners that may result in a negotiated contract award.

§ 1.5 Operations Organizational Unit

The operations organizational unit is responsible for managing and performing the construction work obtained by the marketing organizational unit. The operations organizational unit is organized by construction project with a project team assigned to each construction project. The size and complexity of the construction project dictates the size of the project team. The functions performed by the project team (see **Figure 1–1** in **§ 1.2**) include overall project management, project engineering, and construction supervision.

§ 1.6 —Project Management Function

A contractor's project management function is responsible for controlling and managing the construction project's scope, schedule, and cost. This function has primary responsibility for the success of the project from the contractor's standpoint and is indirectly responsible for the success of the project from the standpoint of all other parties involved with the project, including the construction project owner and the contractor's subcontractors.

Interface with owner and subcontractors. The contractor's project manager is the primary interface with the construction project owner and the subcontractors. As such, the contractor's project manager is responsible for reporting project status concerning schedule and cost, when a cost reimbursable contract is in force, to the construction project owner. The contractor's project manager, with support from the contractor's scheduling staff, coordinates the project schedule and initiates corrective action when schedule delays occur.

Submitting pay applications. The contractor's project manager also prepares the periodic (normally monthly) payment applications that are submitted to the construction project owner. This effort involves determining the contractor's percentage of completion for work performed by the contractor and reviewing the percentage of completion information included on subcontractor invoices. On larger construction projects, the contractor's area or craft superintendents develop the billing information and submit it to the contractor's project manager to be included in the payment application. The contractor's project manager reviews a draft (pencil copy) payment application with the construction project owner and makes any agreed to changes to the payment application as a result of this review. The revised payment application is submitted to the construction project owner along with appropriate lien waivers from subcontractors and material suppliers. The contractor's project manager is responsible for coordinating the timely receipt of lien waivers to support the periodic payment application request.

Approving payments. When payment is received by the contractor from the construction project owner, the contractor's project manager approves payments to subcontractors and material suppliers. The contractor's project manager sometimes uses payment to the subcontractors and material suppliers as leverage for improved performance on the project.

§ 1.7 —Project Engineering Function

The timely submittal of payment applications and aggressive billing by the contractor's project manager are keys to maintaining a positive cash flow on a project. Even more important to maintaining a positive cash flow is the recognition of changes to the work scope and timely processing of change order requests.

Handling changes. The contractor's project engineering staff is responsible for identifying any changes to the contract documents, including the construction drawings, that would increase the contractor's cost for performing the construction work. When a change is identified by the contractor's project engineering staff, or any other member of contractor's project team, the cost of the change is estimated and appropriate supporting documentation is accumulated. The contractor's project manager submits the change order request to the construction project owner for approval. Typically, change order requests involve negotiation between the construction project owner and the contractor. The contractor's project manager represents the contractor in these negotiations. Change order requests normally also involve the contractor's subcontractors and material suppliers. Thus, the contractor's project manager must interface with the subcontractors and material suppliers to obtain pricing information and documentation to be included in the contractor's change order request.

Coordinating submittals and obtaining permits. In addition to reviewing the construction drawings for changes to the bid drawings, the contractor's project engineering staff also is responsible for coordinating shop drawing submittals by the contractor's subcontractors and material suppliers. Shop drawings approved by the construction project owner's architect or engineer are required prior to the fabrication and shipment of equipment and material to be included in the construction project. The contractor's project engineering staff also coordinates the receipt of spare parts, technical manuals, operating procedures, and warranty documents from the contractor's subcontractors and material suppliers. In addition, the contractor's project engineering staff interfaces with local government agencies to obtain any permits that are the contractor's responsibility to obtain or provide.

§ 1.8   —Construction Supervision Function

The majority of a contractor's construction project work force is involved in the direct construction activities. The contractor has superintendents who are responsible for managing the construction work. On small construction projects, the contractor often combines the construction management and coordination function and the project management function so that the construction superintendent performs both of these functions with oversight from corporate operations management.

Managing and coordinating work force.   Many contractors perform some portion of the construction work with their own work force of construction craftsmen. Most general contractors began as civil construction contractors, so the work that they perform tends to be related to civil construction work, including concrete and formwork. Thus, the contractor must supervise and manage the work performed by its own crews while coordinating the construction work performed by subcontractors. Obviously, the contractor is more concerned about the work performed by its own work force, because the contractor assumes the cost, schedule, and quality risks associated with its own work. Whereas, most of these risks, with the exception of schedule coordination, are transferred to the subcontractors for work that the subcontractors are performing.

Maintaining equipment yard.   Many contractors maintain a construction equipment yard where they store construction equipment (for example, cranes, bulldozers, and scaffolding) that they use on the construction projects. Having its own construction equipment can provide an additional revenue source or competitive advantage for a contractor as opposed to renting construction equipment from a rental firm. The management of the construction equipment yard is the responsibility of the operations organizational unit because the construction equipment yard supports all projects for which the operations organizational unit is responsible. A construction equipment yard represents a large investment for a contractor and therefore can influence bidding decisions. A contractor does not want construction equipment sitting idle in the construction equipment yard while the contractor is making payments on the equipment. Thus, a contractor may bid a project for little or no profit just to keep its construction equipment investment working. A similar bidding decision may occur if a contractor has operations personnel not assigned to current projects.

§ 1.9   Administration Organizational Unit

The administrative organizational unit of a construction company (see **Figure 1–1** in **§ 1.2**) includes the functions of accounting, management information systems, legal, and human resources.

§ 1.10   —Accounting Function

The accounting function is responsible for numerous activities related to the contractor's finances, including collecting accounts receivable, managing the payroll, paying the bills, financial reporting, management reporting and cost accounting, cash management, tax preparation, and risk management.

Accounts Receivable

Collecting cash for work performed is the responsibility of the accounts receivable function. Payments received are primarily from construction project owners, although occasionally payments from subcontractors for backcharges are received. Outstanding accounts are monitored on a regular basis and potential delinquent accounts are identified. This monitoring usually is performed utilizing an accounts receivable listing, which groups the outstanding account balances according to the number of days that they are past due. At least monthly, all accounts receivable information is updated so that the aged accounts receivable report will be current, complete, and accurate. The accounts receivable activity is responsible for identifying potential uncollectible accounts early, so that necessary corrective action may be taken.

Payroll Management

Payroll management ensures payroll amounts are disbursed for authorized hours worked at an authorized wage rate. In addition, payroll management maintains appropriate documentation to support gross payroll amounts, withholding amounts, and usually accrued vacation hours. Inputs to the payroll function include time cards or reports, wage or salary authorizations, authorizations for payroll deductions, and tax withholding requirements. For many employees, the latter three items are updated infrequently and can be carried forward each pay period without reviewing each wage rate or deduction. These items usually are reviewed in total each pay period through the use of hash totals or reasonableness tests. Time cards or reports, however, must be reviewed for proper approval each pay period and the associated hours input into the payroll system. Gross payroll, withholding, and net pay are calculated and the payroll checks generated after all payroll information has been input to the payroll system. The calculated payroll amounts are reviewed for reasonableness prior to disbursing checks. Often contractors outsource their payroll processing. The outsourced tasks may include input of the authorized hours, maintenance of authorized wage rates and deductions, and processing of the payroll data and payroll check generation. It is important to note that outsourcing some of the payroll tasks does not relieve the contractor's accounting function of its overall payroll management responsibilities.

Accounts Payable Function

Paying the contractor's bills is the responsibility of the accounts payable function. The accounts payable function performs this responsibility by issuing checks. However, a check for payment is not issued until an authorized check signer, as designated by the contractor's management, has signed the check. Prior to signing a check, the designated check signer reviews supporting documentation accumulated by the accounts payable function. This documentation is usually comprised of:

1. An approved purchase order or referenced contract, including the agreed upon price, to ensure the goods or services were requested
2. An invoice that has been tested for clerical accuracy
3. A receiving slip, if applicable, to ensure the quantity of goods invoiced were actually received.

Prior to payment, these documents are compared to ensure that the amounts invoiced were actually ordered and received, and have been invoiced at the agreed price. The accounts payable function notes any discount terms associated with an invoice so that payment occurs in time to receive any contractual discount, if so desired. To maximize cash flow, the accounts payable function does not make a payment until the due date on the invoice. This monitoring activity normally is performed through the use of a computer system by the accounts payable function.

Cash Management Function

Cash management is crucial to the financial health of a construction company. Construction companies want to avoid financing the materials and labor used in construction. This can be accomplished through timely billing of the construction project owner and achieving payment terms with the construction project owner, material suppliers, and subcontractors that will allow the cash to be collected from the construction project owner before making payment to material suppliers and subcontractors.

Payment of subcontractors generally does not present cash flow problems because subcontractor billings usually are submitted to the construction project owner along with the general contractor's billings. The general contractor remits the subcontractor's portion of the billing when payment is received from the construction project owner. Potential cash flow problems can develop if the contract terms for the subcontractor and general contractor are different. For example, if the general contractor has a lump sum contract and the subcontractor has a time and materials contract, the subcontractor potentially could be due more monies from the general contractor than the general contractor will receive from the construction project owner.

Most construction contracts have a retention percentage stipulated in the contract that allows the construction project owner to retain a percentage of the amounts billed by the general contractor as an assurance that the remaining work will be performed in accordance with the contract documents. Contractors generally apply retainage to subcontractors and material suppliers consistent with the retainage on the contractor's billing. Contractors also attempt to offset excess retainage with earned profit so that the contractor does not experience a negative cash flow on a project.

Cash flow problems are an indicator to a contractor's management that potential problems exist with the management of the project. Cash flow problems may be an indication of administrative failures by the operations organizational unit to recognize or process change orders in a timely fashion. This situation can fester into serious future disputes between the construction project owner and contractor. Cash flow problems also can be an early indicator of serious future construction cost overruns. Thus, the cash management function provides an important early warning as part of the overall project management controls.

General Accounting

The contractor's general accounting function exists to reconcile the accounts receivable, accounts payable, other asset and liability accounts, and the cash accounts. The timely reconciliation of the company's bank accounts is an important control for the safeguarding of the contractor's assets. This important task often is neglected and results in cash flow problems or financial reporting problems due to accounting errors or irregularities. The information generated by the accounts receivable, accounts payable, and cash management functions cannot be relied on if the cash or bank accounts have not been reconciled.

Financial Reporting

Accounting information can be summarized in different ways to support different financial reporting needs. Banks, bonding companies, customers, and vendors may require financial statements prepared in accordance with generally accepted accounting principles (GAAP). These reports usually are prepared yearly and include two years of balance sheets, income statements, statement of cash flows, notes to the financial statements, and other financial information. Preparation of these reports often is outsourced to a public accounting firm that assists the company in preparing the statements in conjunction with a year-end financial audit.

Management Reporting

The accounting information also is summarized in a manner to facilitate management reporting. An objective of management reporting is to measure the actual performance of a crew, manager, or project against some standard or budget. The management reporting system is designed to capture information at the lowest level of detail, by task and by crew, in order to make information available for measuring performance. The detailed information is summarized in a hierarchical manner along the lines of responsibility (functional reporting) and along a separate hierarchical breakdown of the work (work breakdown structure). Construction company management uses the performance measurement information to identify potential project cost or schedule problems so that corrective action may be initiated if required.

Tax Matters

Accounting information is also important for filing tax returns. The financial statements prepared in accordance with GAAP are often the starting point for computing taxable income. However, because of differences between reporting for financial purposes and tax purposes, several adjustments must be made to the financial statements to compute taxable income. This should be done on a quarterly basis so that the appropriate quarterly tax is paid. Often, not enough effort is put into the quarterly income tax estimates and, instead, an amount that is too high is paid in order to reduce the risk of incurring an underpayment penalty. This situation may strain cash flow and cause the company to incur unnecessary interest costs.

Although federal income taxes remain the major tax burden for a contractor, state and local taxes have been increasing due to reduced federal funding. If a contractor operates in more than one state and has multistate filings, a minimum level of detailed financial information must be maintained for each state. Because of the complexities associated with federal, state, and local taxes, a contractor's tax work is often outsourced to a public accounting firm.

Risk Management

Contractors face significant risk from various sources. The management of the risks generally resides within the accounting function. Risks from perils such as theft, fire, flood, and wind are insurable. Other risks, such as bid risk, economic cycles, and environmental risk, often are not insurable and may be controlled best through education. In many cases, a risk management specialist may be required to monitor insurance coverage and awareness programs and to assess the trade-off between risks and the cost of alleviating the risks.

In addition to the common property damage insurance and auto liability insurance, contractors are required by law to carry Workers' Compensation insurance and generally also carry general liability insurance and builders' risk insurance.

Workers' compensation.   The nature of the work in the construction industry exposes workers to a higher risk of injury than in most other businesses. Workers' Compensation costs are directly related to the number of injuries that a contractor's workers incur. Most contractors have a function that is responsible for managing workers' compensation cost. Costs are minimized by accumulating information as to injuries by worker, type of injury, how the injury was incurred, and who was supervising the worker. From such information, management is able to isolate problem tasks, problem workers, or problem supervisors and take corrective action.

Safety programs.   Many times injuries can be prevented if proper precautions are taken. Implementing a safety program that outlines safety policies and procedures for day-to-day operations and high-risk tasks reduces injuries by increasing the level of awareness. Safety programs usually include visual reminders, awards for the most consecutive days without injuries, meetings or safety boards to communicate potential problems and identify safety procedures, and newsletters to inform all personnel of potential hazards and the recommended safety procedures. The reporting and reviewing of injury information, combined with a coordinated safety program, can reduce a contractor's workers' compensation costs substantially.

General liability insurance.   General liability insurance protects the insured from an accident arising out of the insured's business activity. General liability insurance does not provide coverage for employee injuries (workers' compensation), loss to the insured's own property (property damage insurance), or automobile liability (automobile insurance). General liability insurance usually excludes damages from pollutants, product liability, and business risks.

Builders' risk.   Builders' risk insurance covers the contractor's interest in a building under construction, alteration, or repair. The risk of loss does not transfer from the contractor to the owner until completion of the work. If the construction project is destroyed prior to completion, the contractor is responsible for any rebuilding expenses necessary to satisfy the contract.

Uninsurable risks.   Uninsurable risks are best controlled through employee education. In addition, the costs of insurance for insurable risks may be reduced through employee education. Safety programs that monitor accidents and increase employee awareness are an important part of any risk management program.

§ 1.11   —Management Information Systems

Historically, the management information systems (MIS) function for contractors resided within the accounting function because the primary function of the computer was to generate accounting and other financial information. More recently, contractors have been using computers to do much more, including bid preparation estimating, maintaining historical information on construction project owners and subcontractors, scheduling, and measuring project performance. As other functions become more dependent on computer operations, all functions may be served better if computer operations are made a separate function independent of accounting. This may help alleviate one function from monopolizing computer resources and also create segregation of duties, which enhances the control environment.

The MIS function can be divided into the areas of (1) operations, (2) system programming, (3) application programming, (4) data management, and (5) security. Operations is responsible for executing programs, generating output, and maintaining the hardware. System programming maintains the operating system software and network communications. Application programming maintains the programs that compute, summarize, and print the data as requested by the user functions (such as accounting, estimating, and project management). Data management is responsible for the input of large amounts of data and review of the input for completeness and accuracy. Security is responsible for passwording data files and programs to ensure that only authorized users have access. Estimating reports, financial information, and computer programs are examples of computer resources that should be restricted to a few authorized users. Ideally, a different individual would be responsible for each computer function to enhance controls. Due to cost restraints, however, such segregation of duties usually is not feasible.

§ 1.12 —Legal Function

The legal function for a contractor primarily involves the development and review of contracts. The construction business is run by contracts, as the term *construction contractor* implies. The general contractor has a contract with the construction project owner that establishes the scope of work to be performed, the time frame within which the work is to be performed, and the method by which the general contractor's payment for the work will be calculated. Numerous additional requirements or agreements are included in the general contractor's contract that support the primary agreements as to scope, schedule, and cost. All of these requirements or agreements are reviewed from a legal perspective before the general contractor signs the contract.

Although the construction project owner has leverage over the general contractor as to the form of contract to be used between the construction project owner and the general contractor, the general contractor has leverage over subcontractors and to a lesser extent material suppliers as to the form of contract that will be used between those parties. Thus, a major responsibility of the legal function is to draft the general contractor's contract forms and review exceptions taken by subcontractors and material suppliers to assure that the exceptions, which represent requested changes, do not detract from the intent of the contract documents.

The legal function also plays an active role in obtaining bonds from a surety. The three principal bonds involved in a construction project are the bid bond, performance bond, and payment bond. A *bid bond* protects the construction project owner from a contractor's failure to accept a project for an amount that was contractually agreed upon through a competitive bidding process. A *performance bond* protects the construction project owner from a contractor's failure to perform all obligations as agreed to in the contract. A *payment bond* protects the construction project owner from having to make additional payments to subcontractors or material suppliers if the contractor fails to pay subcontractors or material suppliers after the construction project owner has satisfied all payment obligations to the general contractor.

The construction project owner specifies the need for bid, performance, and payment bonds. The contractor's bonding capacity can be a limiting factor in obtaining new work. Therefore, the legal function works very closely with the contractor's surety to keep the contractor's bonding capacity at the maximum level possible.

The legal function also gets involved with contractual disputes between the contractor and the construction project owner or the contractor and subcontractors or material suppliers. The legal function is responsible for litigating claims brought by the contractor or against the contractor. Many contractors do not maintain permanent legal staffs, but instead outsource their legal work to private law firms.

§ 1.13   —Human Resources Function

The human resource function is responsible for maintaining or facilitating the communication of information related to fringe benefits, performance appraisals, and government reporting.

Rising health insurance premiums and post-retirement benefits have focused more attention on fringe benefits in recent years. It is becoming more important to perform reviews of the fringe benefit package in order to minimize cost and at the same time offer a competitive benefits package. Such reviews are often outsourced to firms with experts in fringe benefits. Obtaining and documenting employee benefit information, and coordinating the filing of claims also is part of managing fringe benefits.

Human resources often serves as the agent for collecting performance information on employees from one or many sources. Performance information for each employee is summarized in a standard format so that decisions can be made concerning salary increases, bonuses, promotions, or layoffs.

Human resources also is responsible for gathering and reporting statistics to government agencies. An example of this responsibility is the periodic submittal of equal employment opportunity statistics. Also, many public construction projects require specific involvement of minority business enterprises (MBE); the human resources function accumulates statistics and calculates the percentage of MBE participation and periodically reports the information to the construction project owner.

§ 1.14   Organizational Cost Constraints

Most construction projects are bid with a very small profit percentage. A profit markup of two to five percent of estimated direct construction costs, including subcontractor and material supplier costs, is normal for a general contractor. The profit markup is not truly profit because the markup must offset the contractor's home office overhead. The marketing and administrative organizational units represent the bulk of a contractor's home office overhead. Costs related to the contractor's CEO and operations management personnel located at the corporate office also would normally be included in the home office overhead.

Given the small profit margins that contractors achieve on projects, and noting that the contractor is not guaranteed a profit, successful contractors operate with very lean organizations. All the functions described in **Chapter 1** must be performed; however, it is not unusual for one person to perform multiple functions. For example, project managers who are not currently assigned to a project assist the marketing department in preparing bid estimates.

§ 1.15   Keys to a Successful Organization

Because the lifeline of a construction company is its ability to obtain profitable work, the marketing organization is a high profile function within a contractor's organization. Equally important is a contractor's ability to deliver a construction project on schedule, to the quality defined in the contract documents, and within a contractor's cost constraints. Thus, a contractor's project manager responsible for project operations can make the difference between the success or failure of a project. Too many project failures will result in a contractor no longer being in business. The administration functions generally are viewed by contractors as areas in which overhead costs can be squeezed and administrative failures are not considered to have the same effects on a contractor's bottom line as do project failures. These are probably shortsighted views that are not shared by the more successful contractors.

Although discussion has emphasized functions and responsibilities within a construction organization, the people who perform the functions and constitute the primary organizational units clearly make the difference between successful contractors and unsuccessful contractors.

CHAPTER 2

TAXES AND ACCOUNTING IN THE CONSTRUCTION INDUSTRY

Michael C. Stokke

Michael C. Stokke is a tax partner in the Minneapolis/Saint Paul, Minnesota, office of Arthur Andersen. His areas of specialty include the construction and real estate industries. He attended the University of Wisconsin, Eau Claire, graduating with a B.B.A. in accounting and also holds an M.B.A. degree from the University of Minnesota. Mr. Stokke is a member of the Arthur Andersen firmwide construction industry tax team, secretary/treasurer of the Twin Cities Area Chapter of Construction Financial Management Association, and serves as the chairman of the National Construction Financial Management Association Tax Committee. Mike is a CPA and a member of the Texas and Minnesota Society of CPAs.

§ 2.1   Historical Background

The construction industry historically has faced a unique range of taxation issues resulting from the uncertainty and timing of project revenues. Although most taxpayers use either the cash or accrual method of accounting to report income and expenses, contractors have been entitled to elect alternative methods of accounting for long-term contracts.[1] Beginning with the Tax Reform Act of 1986, however, the range of accounting methods available to contractors has been reduced significantly. As a result, tax accounting has become more complex, and cash flows have been negatively impacted. The taxpayer's understanding of the evolution of these tax and accounting method changes is important when preparing for an examination by the Internal Revenue Service (IRS) or state taxing authority.

Prior to 1986, neither the Internal Revenue Code of 1939 nor the Internal Revenue Code of 1954 included any specific statutory language regarding the use of special long-term contract methods of accounting. Although the

---

[1] For a discussion of tax planning issues from the perspective of the owner/developer, *see* Construction Owner's Handbook of Property Development (R. Cushman & P. King eds., John Wiley & Sons 1992).

Code provided no guidance, Treasury regulations recognized the use of the completed contract method (CCM) and percentage-of-completion method (PCM) as early as 1918. Although the early regulations provided little guidance for application of these methods, several courts agreed that long-term contract methods of accounting were allowable, thus providing some assurance to taxpayers that CCM and PCM were appropriate tax accounting methods.[2]

During the early 1970s, the Treasury Department (Treasury) issued and withdrew several versions of proposed regulations dealing with accounting for long-term contracts. Eventually finalized in January of 1976,[3] the significant elements of the regulations included the adoption of a final completion and acceptance standard for measuring the timing of income recognition and the separate set of costing rules for contracts accounted for under CCM.[4]

With the enactment of the Tax Equity and Fiscal Responsibility Act of 1982 (TEFRA), Congress began to reduce the deferral benefits available from the use of CCM by directing Treasury to modify the regulations to clarify the determination of contract completion, clarify segregation and aggregation rules, and address the allocation of costs to extended period long-term contracts.[5] The changes in the regulations were proposed March 13, 1983, and issued in final form on January 6, 1986.[6]

Prior to the Tax Reform Act of 1986, CCM was the accounting method most commonly used by contractors. Congress, however, perceived abuse in the application of this method because the recognition of income was deferred until the contract was complete. Legislators made several unsuccessful attempts to curtail the benefits derived from deferring income under CCM. It was not until the Reagan administration, however, when the United States government was in great need of increased tax revenue, that the completed contract method became an easy tax reform target.

As part of the Tax Reform Act of 1986, in scattered sections of 26 U.S.C., Congress moved to eliminate CCM and introduced a new accounting method called the *percentage-of-completion capitalized cost method* (PCCM), intended as the mechanism to phase out the use of CCM. In general, PCCM requires a contractor who was previously using a method other than PCM to utilize PCM for an established percentage of each item

---

[2] *See* Badgley v. Commissioner, 59 F.2d 203 (2d Cir. 1932); James C. Ellis, 16 B.T.A. 1225 (1929).

[3] T.D. 7397, 1976-1 C.B. 115.

[4] Treas. Reg. § 1.451-3 (1976).

[5] Tax Equity and Fiscal Responsibility Act of 1982, Pub. L. No. 97-248, § 229, 96 Stat. 324, 493 (1982). (codified as amended in scattered sections of 26 U.S.C.).

[6] T.D. 8067, 1986-1 C.B. 218. Treasury finalized the following regulations on that date: §§ 1.451-3, 1.446-1(c)(2)(ii), 1.451-5(b), 1.471-10, and 1.471-11(c).

of revenue or cost related to long-term contracts entered into after February 28, 1986. The percentage of a long-term contract required to be accounted for under PCM has been increased with each tax act since 1986. The Revenue Reconciliation Act of 1989 requires that 100 percent of all contracts entered into after July 11, 1989, be accounted for under PCM.

One of the most significant changes contained in the Tax Reform Act of 1986 is the modification of the cost allocation rules. Generally, all direct and indirect construction period costs must now be capitalized into the basis of the building and depreciated over the applicable recovery period rather than currently deducted as under prior rules.

These rules require that general and administrative costs that are directly attributable to the performance of specific contracts be allocated to the contract. In addition, employee benefits and a broader range of what constitutes construction period interest also must be allocated.

In addition to the tax law changes directly affecting the statutorily accepted methods of accounting, the Tax Reform Act of 1986 imposed the look-back requirement. This rule requires that, upon completion of a contract, the taxpayer recalculate the yearly contract income for each contract accounted for under PCM (including the PCM portion required under PCCM). To the extent that tax was over- or underpaid in the years the contract was being performed, the taxpayer is required to either pay interest to or receive interest from the government on such under- or overpayment. This rule has added enormous administrative complexity to tax accounting for long-term contracts.

Through the application of the extended period long-term contract cost allocation rules, virtual elimination of CCM in 1989, and the imposition of the look-back requirement, contractors have far fewer income deferral opportunities available today. However, some advantage remains for those contractors who have an understanding of the requirements and their exceptions. The purpose of this chapter is to provide the reader with an understanding of the requirements and ideas for maximizing any remaining benefits.

LONG-TERM CONTRACT METHODS OF ACCOUNTING

§ 2.2   Definition of Long-Term Contract

Before determining the proper method of accounting for a contract, it is necessary to establish whether the agreement is a *long-term contract* as defined by the Internal Revenue Code (the Code). A long-term contract, generally, is a contract for the manufacture, building, installation, or construction of property not completed within the same tax year that the taxpayer entered into the contract.[7] Prior regulations defined a long-term contract as one that covered a period of more than 12 months from the date the contract was entered into until completion.[8] This requirement was dropped and the present regulations do not prescribe any required length of time for a contract to be long-term.

The designation of a contract as long-term, therefore, no longer depends on the contract's length but rather depends on its relationship to the taxpayer's year-end. A contract qualifies as long-term if it merely spans the taxpayer's fiscal year. For example, a contract entered into on October 1, 1990, by a calendar year taxpayer and completed on January 31, 1991, is considered a long-term contract even though the contract took only four months to complete.

In the case of a contract in which not all the activities qualify, by definition, for long-term contract reporting (for example, contract services that are neither building, installation, construction, nor manufacturing), the IRS may segregate the contract into qualifying and nonqualifying activities. For example, when a taxpayer entered into contracts providing for engineering, procurement, construction management services, and actual construction, the IRS held that a long-term contract method could be applied only to the actual construction portion. Those portions of the contract related to the nonconstruction activities had to be "carved out" and accounted for separately under a non-long-term contract method.[9]

The taxpayer's reasonable belief that a contract would be completed during the tax year is not relevant in determining whether a contract is long-term.[10] A contract that meets the definition set forth in the Code is considered long-term and subject to the long-term contract requirements regardless of the taxpayer's reasonable belief or expectations when the taxpayer entered into the contract.

For contracts entered into after June 21, 1988, activities performed by a taxpayer who is related to another taxpayer who is performing a long-term contract must be accounted for as a long-term contract.[11] This is true regardless of whether such activities by themselves constitute long-term contracts. The requirement effectively forces certain taxpayers to change their methods of accounting regardless of whether their current accounting methods clearly reflect income.

---

[7] I.R.C. § 460(f)(1) (codified in 26 U.S.C.).

[8] Treas. Reg. § 1.451-3(a) (1957).

[9] Priv. Ltr. Ruls. 82-40-097, 83-08-005 (completed contract method); 86-23-001 (percentage-of-completion method).

[10] I.R.S. Notice 89-15, 1989-1 C.B. 634 (Q&A 3).

[11] Id. (Q&A 8).

§ 2.3   Completed Contract Method

Under CCM, all revenues and costs related to a contract are deferred until the contract is completed. This method provides that the gross contract price is not included in income and associated costs are not deducted until the year the contract is completed. As described in § **2.1**, the availability of CCM has been severely curtailed following the enactment of the Tax Reform Act of 1986.

The justification of allowing the deferral of income under CCM focuses on the risk inherent in building, installation, and construction contracts. The presence of this risk makes it difficult if not impossible for a contractor to determine while the contract is still in process the extent to which profit is derived from the contract.[12] Therefore, income is not considered realized until contract completion.

The two principal advantages of CCM are (1) precise matching of income with expense and (2) deferral of the recognition of income. CCM, however, possesses obvious disadvantages when a contract produces a loss because the recognition of the loss is deferred as well.

Currently, CCM is allowed only to the extent of the non-PCM portion of contracts accounted for under PCCM for contractors meeting the small contractor exception (as described in § **2.10**), or any home construction contract entered into after June 22, 1988.[13]

A home construction contract is a construction contract in which 80 percent of the estimated total contract costs (as of the close of the taxable year in which the contract was entered into) are attributable to the construction of dwelling units in buildings containing four or fewer dwelling units. These costs include the improvements to real property directly related to such dwelling units.[14]

§ 2.4   Percentage-of-Completion Capitalized Cost Method

PCCM was created in the Tax Reform Act of 1986 as a vehicle for phasing in the required use of PCM. Under PCCM, an established percentage of each item of revenue and each item of cost is taken into account under PCM. The remaining percentage is taken into account at the time such item would be taken into account using the taxpayer's normal method of accounting for long-term contracts, that is, the method used on or before February 28, 1986. This phasein of PCM was accomplished by legislated

---

[12] Rev. Rul. 70-67, 1970-1 C.B. 117.

[13] I.R.C. § 460(e).

[14] *Id.* § 460(e)(6)(A).

reductions of the allowed percentage that was not required to be accounted for under PCM.

For a long-term contract entered into after February 28, 1986, but before October 13, 1987, a contractor using PCCM reports 40 percent of net income from the contract under PCM. Assuming the contractor previously used CCM, the remaining 60 percent of the contract would be accounted for under CCM.

For contracts entered into after October 13, 1987, the Revenue Act of 1987, at Public Law No. 100-203, 101 *Statutes at large* 1330-382 (1987) (codified in scattered sections of 26 U.S.C.) increased the portion of a contract required to be accounted for under PCM from 40 percent to 70 percent. The percentage was again increased from 70 percent to 90 percent by the Technical and Miscellaneous Revenue Act of 1988 (TAMRA), at Public Law No. 100-647, 100 *Statutes at large* 3342 (1988), for contracts entered into after June 20, 1988. PCCM was generally repealed for most contracts by the Revenue Reconciliation Act of 1989, at Public Law No. 101-239, 103 *Statutes at large* 2106 (1989), thus requiring 100 percent use of PCM. Except for contracts specifically allowed to continue PCCM or some other method, the repeal of PCCM was effective for all contracts that resulted from the acceptance of a bid made on or after July 11, 1989, or for outstanding bids, if those bids could be altered or revoked at any time on or after July 11, 1989. Taxpayers having home construction contracts (described in § 2.3) and qualified ship contracts were allowed either to continue some form of PCCM or to use some other acceptable alternative. Taxpayers having residential construction contracts are allowed to use 70/30 PCCM rather than 90/10. A residential construction contract is one that would otherwise be a home construction contract but for the limitation on the number of dwellings contained in a single building.[15]

Contractors using PCCM must apply extended-period, long-term contract cost allocation rules (see § 2.15) to the percentage of the contract accounted for under PCM. Contractors who use CCM for the remaining percentage must apply the extended period allocation rules to that part as well.

Because PCCM was intended to spread the financial impact of converting from prior accounting methods to PCM, for example, CCM to PCM, contractors who used PCM prior to February 28, 1986, are not allowed to change to PCCM unless the consent of the Commissioner of Internal Revenue (the Commissioner) is obtained.[16]

---

[15] *Id.* § 460(e)(6)(B).

[16] I.R.S. Notice 89-15, 1989-1 C.B. 634, 637 (Q&A 14).

§ 2.5   Percentage-of-Completion Method

The Revenue Reconciliation Act of 1989 effectively repealed CCM by requiring the use of PCM for contracts entered into on or after July 11, 1989.[17] Home construction contracts and entities meeting the small contractor exception (see § **2.10**) are exempt from this requirement.[18]

PCM is more complex than CCM in determining income because the amount of income that is recognized under PCM depends on the estimated total cost of the contract. Thus, to the extent cost estimates vary from actual costs, recognized income will vary from actual income. However, the look-back requirement described in § **2.20** compensates for any economic impact of estimates that vary from actual cost.

Under PCM, the portion of the gross contract price that corresponds to the percentage of the entire contract completed during the taxable year must be included in gross income for the taxable year.[19] Except for purposes of applying the look-back method, any income under a contract, to the extent not previously included in gross income, shall be included in the gross income for the taxable year following the taxable year in which the contract was completed.[20]

Under this ratio, extended period long-term contract costs must be used to determine the percentage of completion. Prior to the addition of special long-term contracting rules contained in the Tax Reform Act of 1986, contractors using PCM could compute their completion percentage based either on the cost completion method or the physical completion method. The statute now requires the use of the cost completion method for contracts entered into after February 28, 1986.[21]

The cost completion method is based on a ratio of costs incurred with respect to the contract as of the end of the tax year to the total contract costs.[22] Prior law allowed the contractor to use any method of cost comparisons so long as the method was used consistently with respect to the contract and clearly reflected income.[23] The change in rules, however, may not result in dramatic differences in the recognition of income unless extended-period costs are a significant part of the total allocable costs.

To determine when costs are incurred for purposes of computing the percentage of completion, the "all events test" of I.R.C. § 461 is applied, as

---

[17] I.R.C. § 460(a).

[18] *Id.* § 460(e)(1).

[19] *Id.* § 460(b).

[20] *Id.* § 460(b)(1)(B).

[21] *Id.* § 460(b).

[22] *Id.* § 460(b)(1)(A).

[23] Treas. Reg. § 1.451-3(c)(2), T.D. 7397, 1976-1 C.B. 115, 116.

modified by I.R.C. § 461(h). The test applies regardless of the taxpayer's overall method of accounting.[24]

§ 2.6   Simplified Percentage-of-Completion Calculation

A simplified method of computing PCM was made available with I.R.S. Notice 87-61.[25] Under the simplified method, only certain costs are included in calculating both the costs allocated to the contract and the total estimated contract costs. This ratio then determines the percentage of completion. The simplified cost-to-cost method is less complex than the more comprehensive normal method because fewer costs must be included in the calculation. Under this method, the only costs used in the calculation are direct material, direct labor, and depreciation, amortization, and cost recovery allowances on equipment and facilities directly used to construct or produce the subject matter of the contract.[26]

The taxpayer must elect to use this simplified method and its use may not be revoked without the consent of the Commissioner. Election of this method subsequent to the first tax year ending after February 28, 1986, is a change of accounting method also requiring the consent of the Commissioner. Consent was not required to elect this method during the first tax year ending after February 28, 1986, but an election statement was required to be filed with the return for that tax year.[27]

§ 2.7   Electing the Ten Percent Method

For contracts entered into on or after July 11, 1989, there is an exception to the use of PCM. A contractor may elect not to recognize income and deductions under a long-term contract for any tax year if, at the end of the tax year, less than 10 percent of the total estimated costs of the contract have been incurred.[28] When 10 percent of the estimated contract costs are incurred (the 10 percent year), income and deductions deferred from previous years are recognized.[29]

---

[24] I.R.S. Notice 89-15, 1989-1 C.B. 634.

[25] I.R.S. Notice 87-61, 1987-2 C.B. 370.

[26] *Id.*

[27] *Id.*

[28] I.R.C. § 460(b)(5).

[29] *Id.*

If made, the election applies to all of the contractor's long-term contracts entered into during the tax year the election is made and all subsequent tax years.[30] This election can be revoked only with the consent of the Commissioner. The election also applies for purposes of the look-back requirement.[31] This means that if, after applying the look-back requirement, the actual 10 percent year is different from the 10 percent year determined based on estimated contract costs, the income and expenses must be reallocated to the contract based on the actual 10 percent year. This election is not available for taxpayers who use the simplified method of allocating contract costs described in § **2.6**.[32]

OTHER LONG-TERM CONTRACT ACCOUNTING METHOD ISSUES

§ 2.8   Electing or Changing an Accounting Method

Whichever long-term method of accounting is selected, the taxpayer must elect such method in the tax return for the first taxable year in which performance of a long-term contract begins.[33] Notification of the election must be given to the IRS by attaching to the tax return a statement meeting the requirements of I.R.S. Notices 87-61, 1987-2 C.B. 370, and 88-61, 1988-1 C.B. 547. Once elected, the same long-term contract method must be used for all long-term contracts in the same trade or business.[34]

Unless specifically allowed by statute to change to a different method of accounting, a taxpayer must first obtain the consent of the Commissioner.[35] Consent of the Commissioner is obtained by filing IRS Form 3115, Application for Change in Accounting Method, pursuant to the guidelines contained in Revenue Procedure 84-74, 1984-2 C.B. 736. To prevent the double counting of income or deductions resulting from a change in accounting method, the taxpayer is required to calculate an adjustment to reverse any duplicated amounts.

If the new accounting method is to be PCM, the change in method may be automatic and special rules allow a contractor to use a "cutoff" method rather than calculating an adjustment.

---

[30] *Id.* § 460(b)(5)(C).

[31] *Id.* § 460(b)(5)(D)(ii).

[32] *Id.* § 460(b)(5)(D)(i).

[33] Treas. Reg. § 1.451-3(a)(2).

[34] *Id.* § 1.451-3(a)(1).

[35] I.R.C. § 446(e); Treas. Reg. § 1.451-3(f).

A contractor has the ability to change retroactively to PCM for the following:

(1) all items under all long-term contracts entered into by the taxpayer after June 20, 1988; or

(2) all items under all long-term contracts entered into by the taxpayer after October 13, 1987; [or]

(3) all items under all long-term contracts entered into by the taxpayer after February 28, 1986.[36]

This election is to be made in the taxpayer's federal return for the first taxable year ending after June 20, 1988, for which the taxpayer is required to account under I.R.C. § 460 for long-term contracts. The election is made by attaching a statement to the return. An amended return for any affected tax year also must be filed.

If a taxpayer failed to comply with the long-term contract requirements for contracts entered into after February 28, 1986, and must change methods to comply, the requirements of Revenue Procedure 84-74 do not apply and Form 3115 need not be completed.[37] Under I.R.S. Notice 89-15, the Commissioner grants such taxpayers consent to change methods in order to conform to the statutory requirements. Such taxpayers may correct their methods of accounting by filing amended returns for all open tax years that include post-February 28, 1986, contracts.[38] If the taxpayer's failure to comply relates to a closed year, Form 3115 is required.[39]

§ 2.9 Severing and Aggregating Contracts

When necessary to more clearly reflect income, the regulations allow one agreement to be treated as several contracts or several agreements to be treated as a single contract.[40] The regulations provide that contracts will be severed or aggregated based on a determination made after a review of all facts and circumstances.[41] These rules are generally effective for contracts entered into after December 31, 1982.

The regulations contain a restriction that allows only the Commissioner, not the taxpayer, to sever or aggregate contracts.[42] The restriction apparently was intended to prevent taxpayers from using subsequent changes in

---

[36] I.R.S. Notice 89-15, 1989-1 C.B. 634, 645 (Q&A 47).

[37] *Id.* at 634 (Q&A 13).

[38] *Id.*

[39] *Id.*

[40] I.R.C. § 460(f)(3).

[41] Treas. Reg. § 1.451-3(e)(1)(ii).

[42] *Id.* § 1.451-3(e)(1)(i)(A).

agreements to achieve more favorable tax results. A strict reading of the language in the regulation, however, forces the taxpayer into a form-over-substance position that would prevent a taxpayer from treating a series of interdependent agreements as a single long-term contract. Notice 89-15 alters this regulation by stating that the taxpayer can use the same rules in making severing or aggregating determinations.[43] The notice provides that future regulations may require that the taxpayer attach a statement to its return for the first year contracts are severed or aggregated.[44]

As a general rule, the regulations provide that one agreement will not be severed and thus treated as several agreements unless the contract calls for separate delivery or acceptance of segments of the contract, or unless there is no business purpose for entering into a single contract. However, separate delivery or acceptance does not require severance.[45] In addition, the regulations provide that a factor possibly evidencing lack of a business purpose exists if the agreement covers two or more subject matters, none of which is the primary subject matter of the contract.[46]

Many of the fact patterns that raise segregation issues involve the existence of an option or change order. To the extent a change order does not increase the subject matter of a contract (for example, more units or another building), the change order will be considered part of the original contract and not segregated.[47] Therefore, in planning an option to increase the quantity of items covered by a contract, the contractor should consider including the option amount in the original contract quantity. The purchaser then has the option to decrease, rather than increase, the quantity and the contractor may avoid segregation of the option or change order as a separate contract.

Several agreements are not aggregated unless aggregation is a customary commercial practice or there is no business purpose for entering into several agreements rather than one agreement.[48] A factor evidencing that two agreements should be aggregated exists when a reasonable business person would not have entered into one of the agreements but for the existence of the other.[49]

The regulations provide examples to illustrate when segregation and aggregation are appropriate.[50] When a single contract called for the construction

---

[43] I.R.S. Notice 89-15, 1989-1 C.B. 634 (Q&A 38).

[44] *Id.*

[45] Treas. Reg. § 1.451-3(e)(2)(iii).

[46] *Id.* § 1.451-3(e)(2)(v).

[47] *Id.* § 1.451-3(e)(2)(viii).

[48] *Id.* § 1.451-3(e)(2)(vi).

[49] *Id.* § 1.451-3(e)(2)(vii).

[50] *Id.* § 1.451-3(e)(2).

of three houses in different locations, each completed in a subsequent tax year with a price allocable between them, the contract would be severed.[51] However, when the first three floors of a ten-story office building were completed and occupied, with the remaining floors to be completed and accepted in the following year, the contract would not be severed despite separate acceptance.[52] In this case, the contract would not be severed because there is no business purpose for separate contracts. The last construction example involved the same building, but the owner and contractor modified the first agreement by entering into a second agreement to stop construction at three floors and to complete the building at some unspecified date.[53] In this case, separate acceptance and business purpose justify severance of the modified agreement into separate contracts.

§ 2.10   Exception for Small Contractors

The Tax Reform Act of 1986 created an exception to the requirements of PCCM, PCM, the look-back requirements, and cost allocations for small contractors.[54] The small contractor, however, is subject to the interest allocation rules.

The small contractor exception applies if the following two conditions are met:

1. the contractor's average gross receipts for the three years preceding the year in which the contract began are less than $10 million; and
2. the contract is for the construction or improvement of real property, and the contract is expected to be completed within two years of its starting date.[55]

In determining whether a contractor meets the $10 million gross receipts test, the receipts of other businesses must be included if certain conditions exist.[56] During the three years preceding the year in which the contract began, all trades or business, including any predecessors under common control with the contractor and all members of any controlled group of which the contractor is a member, must be included in calculating the contractor's gross receipts. For this purpose, a controlled group exists when

---

[51] Treas. Reg. § 1.451-3(e)(2) (Example 1).

[52] Id. § 1.451-3(e)(2) (Example 4).

[53] Id. § 1.451-3(e)(2) (Example 5).

[54] I.R.C. § 460(e)(1).

[55] Id. § 460(e)(1)(B).

[56] Id. § 460(e)(2).

members are connected through stock ownership with a common parent whose interest is more than 50 percent.[57]

In addition, contractors who enter construction contracts through pass-through entities, such as partnerships, joint ventures, and corporations, also are subject to attribution rules that allocate receipts based on ownership interest.[58]

§ 2.11   Disposal of an Incomplete Contract

The tax implications of disposing of an incomplete contract are driven by the facts and circumstances in every case. The circumstances can vary from corporate or partnership distributions to sale of an interest, transfers to corporations and partnerships, corporate liquidations, or corporate reorganizations. In most cases, effective tax planning can help to minimize the tax impact.

Many fact patterns can result in the treatment of disposal of an incomplete contract as a sale, consequently creating a taxable event. To discuss each of these is beyond the scope of **Chapter 2**, but the taxpayer should be aware that the issue requires proper tax planning. For example, when a taxpayer assigns a contract entered into before March 1, 1986, the assignee must account for such contract under the long-term contract rules unless none of the terms of the contract are changed in connection with the assignment and the assignee agrees to perform all of the assignor's remaining obligations under the contract and becomes entitled to all remaining payments. In this case, the assignee may account for the contract under its normal long-term contract method.[59]

§ 2.12   Accounting for Loss Contracts

In the case of a loss contract, PCM is more advantageous than CCM. Just as CCM defers income, it also defers recognition of a loss.

Under PCM, all costs incurred during the taxable year with respect to a long-term contract must be deducted.[60] Under CCM, costs merely represent deferred expenditures that are to be treated as part of the cost of the particular contract and are not allowed as a deduction until the year in

---

[57] *Id.* § 460(e)(3).

[58] *Id.* § 460(e)(2)(C).

[59] I.R.S. Notice 89-15, 1989-1 C.B. 634, 637 (Q&A 10).

[60] Treas. Reg. § 1.451-3(c)(3).

which the contract is completed and the contract price is reported as gross income.[61]

§ 2.13   Contract Completion

The regulations provide that a long-term contract shall not be considered "completed" until final completion and acceptance have occurred.[62]

> Final completion and acceptance of a contract for federal income tax purposes is determined from an analysis of all the relevant facts and circumstances, including the manner in which the parties to the contract deal with each other and with the subject matter of the contract, the physical condition and state of the readiness of the subject matter of the contract, and the nature of any work or costs remaining to be performed or incurred on the contract.[63]

Final completion and acceptance is determined without regard to the contractor's obligation to supply other items that do not represent the primary subject matter of the contract.[64] In the case of a long-term contract with more than one subject matter, the additional units that do not represent the primary subject matter of the contract are not considered in determining completion.

The regulations provide examples that illustrate the determination of contract completion for a construction contract. When a building was completed in late 1984, but minor deficiencies required correction in the following year, the contract is considered complete for tax purposes in 1984.[65] In this case, the parties have dealt with each other in a manner that indicates final completion and acceptance has occurred. When a building was completed in late 1984 but the retainage was not released until the architect's certificate of completion was received in the subsequent year, the contract is considered complete for tax purposes in 1984.[66] Finally, when a shopping center was opened to the public and the parking lot was only 75 percent complete in 1985, the contract for its construction is considered complete for tax purposes in 1985.[67]

Any use of the primary subject matter of the contract by the purchaser (except for testing) is a factor to be considered in establishing the manner in

---

[61] *Id.* § 1.451-3(d)(1).

[62] *Id.* § 1.451-3(b)(2)(i)(A).

[63] *Id.* § 1.451-3(b)(2)(i)(B).

[64] *Id.* § 1.451-3(b)(2)(ii).

[65] *Id.* § 1.451-3(b)(2)(C) (Example 1).

[66] Treas. Reg. § 1.451-3(b)(2)(C) (Example 2).

[67] *Id.* § 1.451-3(b)(2)(C) (Example 4).

which the parties deal with each other and the subject matter of the contract.[68] As a practical matter, when the customer requires a test period following construction, contract language should specify that acceptance does not occur until successful test completion.

The timing of contract completion has an economic impact only on taxpayers using CCM. Any economic impact under PCM is eliminated through its mechanism of proportionate revenue recognition each year.

§ 2.14   —Disputed Contracts

The regulations contain an elaborate set of rules regarding the effect of contract claims and disputes on final completion and acceptance. Three categories of regulations govern:

1. When the dispute arises out of a claim made by the purchaser[69]
2. When the dispute arises out of a claim made by the taxpayer/ contractor[70]
3. When the dispute arises out of claims by both the purchaser and contractor.[71]

The rules provided for each type of dispute apply only when the subject matter of the contract has been tendered and the contract has been substantially completed.

COST CAPITALIZATION FOR A CONSTRUCTION CONTRACT

§ 2.15   Allocation of Costs in General

One of the more significant provisions of the Tax Reform Act of 1986 is the change in the rules governing cost allocation.[72] The extensive cost allocation procedures that applied to extended period long-term contracts (that is, contracts with an expected duration of more than three years) are made applicable to all contracts.

---

[68] *Id.* § 1.451-3(b)(2)(i)(B).

[69] *Id.* § 1.451-3(d)(2).

[70] *Id.* § 1.451-3(d)(3).

[71] *Id.* § 1.451-3(d)(4).

[72] I.R.C. § 460(c)(1).

The extended period long-term contract cost allocation rules are not new to contractors. The rules were first introduced in TEFRA with final regulations published by Treasury in January 1986.[73] The rules require that the direct and indirect costs directly attributable to the performance of specific contracts be allocated to the contract rather than currently deducted.[74]

§ 2.16   —Direct Costs

Direct material costs and direct labor costs must be treated as costs properly allocable to a long-term contract and capitalized. Direct material costs include those costs of materials that become an integral part of the subject matter of the long-term contract and those materials that are consumed in the ordinary course of building, constructing, or manufacturing the subject matter of the contract. The elements of direct labor costs include such items as shift differential, vacation pay, holiday pay, sick pay, payroll taxes, and payments to a supplemental unemployment benefit plan paid or incurred on behalf of the employees engaged in direct labor.[75]

§ 2.17   —Indirect Costs

Indirect costs include all costs other than direct material and labor costs. All indirect costs that provide a direct benefit to the performance of a contract must be allocated to the contract.[76] The regulations recognize that a certain type of cost may directly benefit a contract even though the same type of cost also benefits other activities of the taxpayer.[77] In this situation, the taxpayer must establish a reasonable method to distinguish between the proper amount attributable to the contract and the amount attributable to the taxpayer's other activities.

The regulations list specific examples of indirect costs that must be allocated.[78] The regulations also identify costs that are not required to be allocated, including the expenses associated with unsuccessful bids; marketing, selling, and advertising expense; and, costs attributable to strikes.[79]

---

[73] Treas. Reg. § 1.451-3(d)(6).

[74] *Id.*

[75] *Id.* § 1.451-3(d)(6)(i).

[76] *Id.* § 1.451-3(d)(6)(ii).

[77] *Id.*

[78] *Id.*

[79] Treas. Reg. § 1.451-3(d)(6)(iii).

§ 2.18 —General and Administrative Costs

If a general or administrative department (for example, centralized payroll) incurs costs that directly benefit, or are incurred by reason of, a long-term contract, the cost of the function is allocable to the contract.[80] The regulations require that the cost of functions directly benefiting more than one department must be allocated to contracts based on a factor or relationship that reasonably relates the cost of incurring the service to the benefits received by a contract.[81]

The regulations provide that the taxpayer may allocate indirect costs on either the direct-reallocation method, step-allocation method, or any other method authorized by cost accounting principles.

Direct-reallocation method.   Under the direct-reallocation method, the direct and indirect costs of service departments are allocated to production departments and then from the production departments to particular contracts. This method ignores benefits provided by one service department to other service departments.[82]

Step-allocation method.   Under the step-allocation method, a sequence of allocations is made, beginning with the allocation to other service and production departments of the total costs of service departments providing services to such other departments. Each department's costs (including those reallocated) are allocated to contract activities and other production activities not related to contract activities. The costs attributable to contract activities are then allocated to specific contracts.[83] Although the step-allocation method is initially more complex and time-consuming, it is generally more accurate and provides a more favorable capitalization policy for both current and future periods. Much of the implementation work associated with step-allocation need only be performed once because the same assumptions are used from year to year.

§ 2.19 Construction Period Interest

After the Tax Reform Act of 1986, interest costs paid or incurred during the production period relating to specified property must be allocated to

---

[80] *Id.* § 1.451-3(d)(9).

[81] *Id.* § 1.451-3(d)(9)(ii).

[82] *Id.* § 1.451-3(d)(9)(iii)(A).

[83] *Id.* § 1.451-3(d)(9)(iii)(B).

the contract.[84] In order for interest to be allocable to the contract, the property must meet at least one of the following:

1. The property is real property or property with a class life of at least 20 years
2. The estimated production period for the property exceeds two years or
3. The estimated production period exceeds one year and the cost exceeds $1,000,000.[85]

The amount of interest required to be capitalized with respect to any property should include interest on any indebtedness directly attributable to production expenditures and interest on other indebtedness to the extent that the taxpayer's interest costs could have been reduced if production expenditures had not been incurred. Some nonconstruction interest costs also are assigned to the construction period, provided those costs could have been reduced if the construction had not taken place and the debt had been repaid instead.[86] This approach is referred to as the *avoided cost theory.*

Contractors should be aware that the interest capitalization rules apply to a contractor's "net" production expenditures. Temporary regulations under I.R.C. § 263A provide a position supporting the allocation of interest to a contract only to the extent that the interest is undercollected.[87] That is, interest costs attributable to payments made to a contractor are generally subject to capitalization by the customer. The contractor need only capitalize interest with respect to indebtedness relating to the excess of its accumulated contract costs over the accumulated payments received by the contractor during the year.[88]

LOOK-BACK REQUIREMENT

§ 2.20   Look-Back Rules in General

Recognizing that the actual profit on a contract allocable to a given year varies from the PCM or PCCM estimates used in calculating and reporting

---

[84] I.R.C. §§ 460(c)(3), 263A(f).

[85] *Id.* § 263A(f)(1)(B).

[86] Temp. Treas. Reg. § 1.263A-1T(b)(2)(iv)(B) (1987).

[87] *Id.* § 1.263A-1T(b)(2)(iv)(C).

[88] *See* the Senate Report to the 1986 Act, 5 Rep. No. 99-313, 99th Cong., 2d Sess. at 145 (1986).

income for the year, the Tax Reform Act of 1986 established a look-back requirement. This look-back requirement is intended to offset the time value of money effects of using estimates during the life of the contract that differ from the actual amounts determined after completion of the contract.

The requirement is effective for contracts entered into after February 28, 1986, using either PCM or PCCM.[89] For contracts reporting under PCCM, the look-back requirement applies only to the percentage reported under PCM.[90] A de minimis exception is available for smaller contracts and contractors. The look-back rules do not apply to a contract if: the gross contract price of the contract does not exceed the lesser of $1 million or 1 percent of the taxpayer's average annual gross receipts for the three preceding taxable years; and the contract is completed within two years of contract commencement.[91]

Under the look-back requirement, taxpayers are required to pay interest if tax liability is deferred as a result of underestimating the total contract price or overestimating the total contract cost as compared to actual price and cost at completion. Interest owed is treated as an increase to the contractor's income tax except for purposes of computing any underpayment of estimated tax penalty. Interest due the IRS is to be reported on Form 8697, Interest Computation Under the Look-Back Method for Completed Long-Term Contracts, which must be attached to the income tax return filed for that year.

A taxpayer is entitled to receive interest if its tax liability is accelerated by overestimating the total contract price or underestimating total contract cost. To receive a refund of look-back interest, Form 8697 is to be filed separately from the income tax return.

Interest required to be paid under the look-back requirement is treated as interest expense for purposes of computing taxable income, and interest received is treated as taxable interest income.

Generally, widely-held pass-through entities, such as partnerships, S corporations, and trusts, specifically are allowed to compute look-back interest at the entity level rather than at the partner, shareholder, or beneficiary level.[92] If, however, the pass-through entity is closely-held, look-back interest may not be calculated at the entity level.[93] A pass-through entity is closely-held if at any time during the taxable year 50 percent or more of the beneficial interest is held directly or indirectly by five or fewer persons.[94]

---

[89] Treas. Reg. § 1.460-6(b)(5) (1990).

[90] Id. § 1.460-6(b)(1).

[91] Id. § 1.460-6(b)(3).

[92] I.R.C. § 460(b)(4)(A).

[93] Id. § 460(b)(4)(B).

[94] Id. § 460(b)(4)(C)(iii).

§ 2.21 —Normal Computation of Interest

Form 8697 allows two methods, normal and simplified, for the computation of look-back interest. Under the normal method, the amount of look-back interest charged or credited to a taxpayer is determined in three steps. The first step requires the reapplication of PCM to all contracts that are completed or adjusted during the filing year using the actual contract price and cost. This reapplication of PCM establishes the amount of taxable income that would have been reported if actual rather than estimated price and cost data had been used. In the second step, the taxpayer recomputes the tax liability resulting from the reapplication of PCM for each year affected by the contract. The taxpayer then compares the tax liability for each year resulting from the reapplication of PCM using actual price and cost with the tax liability that was reported in previous returns using price and cost estimates. This calculation must be performed for regular tax and the alternative minimum tax. Any difference is designated a hypothetical underpayment or overpayment. The final step applies the rate of interest on overpayments under I.R.C. § 6621 to the hypothetical underpayment or overpayment for each tax year. Interest is computed from the due date of original return to the due date of the return for the filing year.[95]

Considerable complexity arises in step two of the normal computation when taxable income must be recalculated for each year affected by the contract. This complexity is compounded when the taxpayer must recompute the tax liability multiple times for the same year in which the look-back method had been previously applied.

The regulations provide a *delayed reapplication method* that, if elected, may reduce the number of times the look-back method is required to be reapplied for postcompletion adjustments to a taxpayer's long-term contracts.[96] This method allows the taxpayer to wait until the cumulative amount of adjustments to either the contract price or contract costs reaches a threshold of 10 percent of these amounts prior to adjustment or, if less, $1 million. A reapplication of the look-back method must be made, regardless of reaching the thresholds, five years after the most recent application of the look-back method or, if earlier, the year in which the taxpayer reasonably believes the contract is finally settled and closed.[97]

---

[95] Treas. Reg. § 1.460-6(c)(1).

[96] § 1.460-6(e).

[97] *Id.*

§ 2.22   —Simplified Method of Computing Interest

The regulations provide a simplified approach to the calculation of look-back interest.[98] The simplified marginal impact method follows the normal method, but uses an assumed marginal tax rate for the taxpayer rather than the actual tax rates required in step two. The regulations require that the simplified method be used with respect to income from domestic long-term contracts of widely held partnerships, S corporations, or trusts.[99] C corporations, individuals, and owners of closely-held pass-through entities may elect the simplified method. Owners of widely-held pass-through entities also may elect the simplified method with respect to income from foreign contracts. However, when not mandatory, the simplified method for pass-through entities is applied at the owner level instead of the entity level.[100]

Although use of this simplified method may reduce the administrative burden of making look-back calculations, its use may result in a reduced refund. The simplified method imposes an overpayment ceiling, providing that the net hypothetical overpayment of tax is limited to the taxpayer's total federal income tax liability reduced by overpayments resulting from previous applications of the look-back requirement.[101] There is no corresponding limit on interest the contractor may owe the IRS.

OTHER TAX CONSIDERATIONS

§ 2.23   Alternative Minimum Tax

The Tax Reform Act of 1986 drastically changed the old law of the corporate add-on minimum tax. In calculating an entity's alternative minimum tax (AMT), the AMT rate is applied to an income base equal to regular taxable income plus or minus adjustments, including the use of PCM for all long-term contracts, plus preferences. AMT income then is reduced by an exemption amount that is gradually reduced to zero at higher income levels. The resulting AMT amount is payable to the extent it exceeds the taxpayer's regular tax.

The PCM adjustment required by the AMT calculation is of special concern to small contractors. This adjustment equals the difference between

---

[98] Treas. Reg. § 1.460-6(d).

[99] *Id.* § 1.460-6(d)(4)(i).

[100] *Id.* § 1.460-6(d)(4)(ii).

[101] *Id.* § 1.460-6(d)(2)(iii).

taxable income or loss reported for regular tax purposes utilizing a method other than PCM and that calculated under PCM. It is important to note that contractors who qualify under the small contractor exception, and are not required to use PCM because of the administrative burden, must use PCM for AMT purposes.[102]

Home construction contracts, also exempt from PCM, need not apply PCM for AMT purposes after September 30, 1990.[103] Under prior law, only the home construction contracts of small contractors were exempt.

§ 2.24   Retainages and Holdbacks

All amounts that a taxpayer is or will be entitled to receive from a customer under the contract must be included in total expected contract revenues. This includes amounts such as retainages and holdbacks that the customer has contracted to pay only upon satisfactory completion of the contract.[104]

§ 2.25   Awards and Incentives

Payments, such as award fees and incentive payments, are to be included in total expected contract revenues at the time and to the extent that the taxpayer can reasonably predict that the corresponding performance objectives will be met.[105]

§ 2.26   Costs Incurred Prior to Binding Contract

Under PCM, the taxpayer is not required to include any amount in gross income in any taxable year ending prior to the date that a contract is entered into, even if costs allocable to the contract are incurred in such a taxable year. In the subsequent year, all such costs are to be allocated to the contract and taken into account in determining the completion percentage. Thus, such costs are considered in determining the amount of contract revenue required to be taken into account in the subsequent taxable year.[106]

---

[102] I.R.C. § 56(b)(3).

[103] Revenue Reconciliation Act of 1989, Pub. L. No. 101–239, 103 Stat. 2106 (1989).

[104] I.R.S. Notice 89-15, 1989-1 C.B. 634, 642 (Q&A 27).

[105] *Id.* at 642 (Q&A 29).

[106] *Id.* (Q&A 29).

§ 2.27 Reimbursable Amounts Incurred

All reimbursements should be included in the total contract price in determining the amount included in gross income in the taxable year under PCM. Similarly, reimbursed costs allocable to the contract that have been incurred by the taxpayer are treated as contract costs in determining the percentage of completion for the taxable year for which such costs are incurred.[107]

---

[107] *Id.* (Q&A 31).

CHAPTER 3

INSURANCE FOR CONSTRUCTION IN THE 1990s

Thomas G. Cole
John W. Rucker, Jr.

Thomas G. Cole is a senior vice president with CIGNA Corporation in Philadelphia, Pennsylvania. He joined INA, a CIGNA subsidiary, in 1959 and has held various underwriting and marketing positions. He also has been the chief operating officer for another major insurance carrier. Throughout his career Mr. Cole has specialized in developing property, casualty, and marine coverages for contractors and the construction industry.

John W. Rucker, Jr., is vice president of underwriting with the CIGNA Corporation in Philadelphia, Pennsylvania. A veteran of twenty-nine years in the insurance industry, he has specialized in developing property, casualty, and marine coverages for contractors and the construction industry. Mr. Rucker earned the Chartered Property Casualty Underwriter (CPCU) designation in 1976. He is a member of the Society of CPCU's and instructs in that program for the Insurance Society of Philadelphia.

§ 3.1   Introduction

How does a contractor involved in construction manage insurable risk? The answer to that question is the major thrust of this chapter. Presented is an overview of applicable insurance issues for executives and owners of construction-related companies.

Construction operations have exposures that differ from other business risks. Therefore, special treatment is necessary for these exposures. The principal differences and the impact of the differences are the following.

1. A contractor can obtain work in several different ways. A client may contact the contractor directly to negotiate for the work to be done or the contractor may bid for the work based on the client's specifications. Because each contract has its unique requirements and characteristics, the exposures to loss, and their treatment, are subject to considerable change over time.

2. Unlike fixed location risks, contractors work from jobsite to jobsite. This constant change of locations requires a broad and flexible risk

management and insurance program in order to deal efficiently with changing exposures.

3. Normally, multiple contractors or subcontractors are performing various work activities at a construction site. The many activities, some performed simultaneously, create a changing exposure. This increases the need for a risk manager or other insurance professional who continually monitors the contractor's risk.

The material presented in **Chapter 3** is designed to give a practical understanding of the insurance issues that individuals in the construction industry and their professional advisers may need to address.[1] Because one major uninsured loss can devastate a contractor's business, it is important to understand exposure to loss and how it may be reduced or eliminated as well as how insurance coverages are designed to transfer the risk.

§ 3.2 Workers' Compensation Basics

Because construction is labor-intensive, and the contractor's employees are exposed to a variety of injuries, a major risk exposure is workers' compensation. State law requires employers to promptly pay statutory workers' compensation and occupational disease benefits. In most states, contractors can purchase a workers' compensation and employers' liability policy from an insurance company. However, in six states (Nevada, North Dakota, Ohio, Washington, West Virginia, and Wyoming), contractors must purchase workers' compensation from monopolistic state funds and supplement the coverage with employers' liability coverage from an insurance company. The United States Chamber of Commerce publishes an annual summary of workers' compensation requirements titled *Analysis of Workers' Compensation Laws*. It covers requirements in the 50 states, District of Columbia, Puerto Rico, United States Virgin Islands, Guam, and American Samoa, and Canadian provinces as well as requirements created by the Federal Employees' Compensation Act, Longshore and Harbor Workers' Compensation Act, Canadian Government Employees' Compensation Act, and the Merchant Seamen's Compensation Act.

In some states, contractors who are individual owners or copartners do not receive protection under workers' compensation laws because they may be considered employers rather than employees. In such cases, individuals may need separate accident and health insurance to compensate them for work-related injuries. Officers in corporations usually are eligible for the

---

[1] *See generally* Deutsch, Kerrigan & Stiles, Construction Industry Insurance Handbook (John Wiley & Sons 1991).

same benefits as other employees. The contractor must check the law in the state(s) where the contractor operates to identify the current impact.

§ 3.3   —Coverage Extensions

Every state in which the contractor has employees working or domiciled should be shown on the workers' compensation policy. However, a coverage extension in the form of an all-states endorsement is recommended if the contractor works in, has principal operations in, or hires employees from multiple states. The all-states endorsement provides for insurance in the states not listed in the policy.

If employees work on or near navigable streams or waterways, a separate endorsement entitling them to United States Longshore and Harbor Workers' Compensation may be added to a policy. If contractors are involved with bridge, dam, or pier work, or their employees are involved with loading or unloading a vessel, the contractors need this separate endorsement for proper protection.

In addition, a contractor with employees who are members of the crew of a vessel that operates on navigable rivers, streams, or other bodies of water may be subject to the Jones Act.[2] In this case, the contractor needs a policy endorsement that provides maritime voluntary compensation along with legal protection.

A typical workers' compensation policy includes a limit for employers' liability. This coverage protects the contractor and provides defense for a common law action against the contractor as a result of employee injuries. The contractor may select a limit per accident for this coverage.

§ 3.4   —Limits of Liability

Coverage for payment of statutory benefits to injured employees has no specific policy limit. Whatever the state law provides in the way of medical care, rehabilitation, lost time, permanent disability, or other conditions will be paid on behalf of the employer.

§ 3.5   —Other Employer Exposures

The general contractor may be subject to workers' compensation exposures from subcontractors' employees. This exposure occurs when the subcontractors fail to provide coverage for their workers. The general contractor

---

[2] *See* 46 U.S.C. § 688 (1988).

can guard against assuming this exposure by insisting in the subcontract that workers' compensation insurance be provided by the subcontractor. Additionally, evidence of this coverage in the form of an insurance certificate should be obtained from the subcontractor. The certificates of insurance should be made available to the general contractors' workers' compensation insurer to preclude a premium charge for the subcontractors' exposures.

Another possible additional exposure for any contractor is the employment of minors. Some states add a penalty of double or triple the normal compensation benefits should a minor be injured on the job. The contractor should check applicable state laws as well as require proof of age for younger employees.

§ 3.6 Liability Exposures

The liability exposures of a contractor involve the general public and employees of material suppliers to the jobsite as well as employees of other contractors. These people may be injured or have their property damaged as a result of something for which the contractor is responsible. **Sections 3.7 to 3.10** outline the main areas of insurance coverage designed to protect the contractor faced with legal responsibility for such injuries and damages.

§ 3.7 —Commercial General Liability

Commercial general liability (CGL) covers all kinds of bodily injury or damage to the property of others except that covered under workers' compensation or automobile coverage. This is the standard form available from most insurance companies and protects the majority of contractors.

A contractor may have to add other parties to liability insurance coverage as construction projects change. To do so, a contractor needs separate endorsements, called *Additional-Insured-Owners, Lessees,* or *Contractors,* to the policy, which amend the CGL's "Who Is Insured" provision. Liability that the additional insureds may incur because of the contractor's work will then be covered.

Basic Exclusions

CGL contains certain exclusions that either require additional premium for coverage, are covered elsewhere, or are generally uninsurable. Those of particular interest to contractors include the following.

Intentional injury.   Bodily injury or property damage that is inflicted on purpose by the contractor is not covered unless it is the result of a reasonable use of force to protect an individual or property.

Insured contracts.   Another exclusion precludes coverage for the assumption of all liability under any contract or agreement unless the liability either is assumed under an *insured contract* or is liability that the contractor would have by virtue of the absence of a contract or agreement. An insured contract includes:

1. A lease of premises
2. A side track agreement
3. An easement or license agreement except for construction or demolition operations on or within 60 feet of a railroad
4. An obligation required by ordinance to indemnify a municipality except in connection with work for a municipality
5. Elevator maintenance agreements
6. Tort liability assumed by the contractor to pay for bodily injury or property damage to a third party or organization. Tort liability is that imposed by law in the absence of any contract or agreement.[3]

An insured contract does not include:

1. Indemnity agreements between the contractor and architects, engineers, or surveyors for injury or damages arising out of failure to prepare maps, drawings, change orders, or surveys, and failure to give instructions or failure to give proper directions or instructions
2. Contracts in which the contractor assumes the liability from rendering professional services as an architect, engineer, or surveyor
3. Contracts that indemnify the other party for damage by fire to a premises rented or loaned to the contractor.[4]

Pollution liability.   Pollution damages and cleanup costs are excluded from CGL coverage. Pollution coverage may be available to cover damages from leakage of underground storage tanks, including coverage available for environmental cleanup costs, legal liability to third parties, and court costs. The cost of corrective action related to an escape of petroleum from underground petroleum tanks can be very expensive. Separate pollution coverage limits may be needed to comply with Environmental Protection Agency

---

[3] *Commercial General Liability Coverage Form* (Insurance Services Office, Inc., 1982, 1984).

[4] *Id.*

(EPA) requirements. The local EPA office should be contacted to determine current requirements.

Autos, aircraft, and watercraft. For the most part, CGL excludes claims arising out of the ownership, maintenance, or use of autos, aircraft, or watercraft. Other policy forms are available for these exposures.

Mobile equipment. Mobile equipment is excluded only while used for pre-arranged racing or stunting or while being transported by an automobile.

Property damage. Several exclusions eliminate or restrict coverage for damage to or loss of use of (1) property the contractor might own, occupy, rent, or control; (2) completed projects; or (3) impaired property.

Damage to the product. Excluded from coverage is property damage to "your product," arising out of it or any part of it. However, real property is not included in the definition of *your product*. Therefore, work performed by the contractor on dwellings, buildings, and structures is covered under CGL.

Damage to the work. This excludes coverage for property damage to "your work" arising out of it or any part of it and included in the products-completed operations hazard. The exclusion applies only to work within the products-completed operations hazard and does not apply if a subcontractor performed the damaged work or the work out of which the damage arises. For example, if a subcontractor's faulty wiring causes an entire building to burn and the general contractor is sued for the entire loss by the building owner, the general contractor's CGL policy should cover the contractor's liability for the entire amount of the loss, including the cost of the failed wiring. If, instead, the loss had originated in work performed by the general contractor, the general contractor would be covered only for damage to work actually performed by subcontractors; there would be no recovery for any work performed by the general contractor.

Property not physically insured. Another exclusion from CGL applies to property damage on impaired property or property that has not been physically injured, arising out of a defect, deficiency, inadequacy, or dangerous condition in "your product," or "your work," or a delay or failure by the contractor or anyone acting on the contractor's behalf to perform a contract or agreement in accordance with its terms. This exclusion does not apply to the loss of use of other property arising out of sudden and accidental physical injury to "your product" or "your work" after it has been put to its intended use. The CGL form defines *your work* and *your product* and should be reviewed for applicability to the contractor.

Occurrence versus claims-made policies.   CGL may be issued on either an occurrence or claims-made form. Since its introduction in 1986, the claims-made form of CGL has been sold on a limited basis by most insurance companies. For most contractors, the occurrence form is readily available. It is important, however, to understand how the features of these two forms apply.

Triggering events.   The trigger of the occurrence form is bodily injury or property damage that occurs during the policy period. For example, if someone is insured by the contractor's completed work during the 1990 policy period, the occurrence policy in effect at that time applies to the loss whether the claim is made against the contractor in 1991 or some later year. On the other hand, the trigger of the claims-made form is the first making of a claim against the contractor during the policy period. For example, if someone is insured during the 1990 policy period of a claims-made policy but does not make a claim against the contractor until after the policy is renewed in 1991, the claim is covered under the 1990 policy only. This assumes that the injury occurred after the retroactive date stated in the 1991 policy. The retroactive date is an extremely important feature of the claims-made form.

Types of limits.   Although the same types of limits are included in both the occurrence and claims-made versions of CGL form, they may apply quite differently in the case of latent injury claims. It can be held that certain types of injury or damage "occurred" continuously from the time the victim was first exposed to whatever caused the bodily injury until disease or damage ensued, possibly many years later. The contractor sued by a victim would be covered under all occurrence policies in effect during the years the bodily injury or property damage was occurring. This is called *stacking of limits.* This type of recovery is possible because occurrence-type policies cover bodily injury that take place during the policy period. A claims-made CGL policy does not cover claims for bodily injury that occurred before any retroactive date shown in the policy. The policy in effect when bodily injury occurred does not cover the injury unless claim is first made during the policy period or during an extended reporting period for that policy.

Basic tail reporting period.   The claims-made CGL form can have two types of extended reporting periods: the *basic tail* and the *supplemental tail.* The basic tail covers claims first made against the insured up to five years after the end of the policy period for injury or damage that occurred after the policy's retroactive date and before the end of the policy's expiration date. However, the injury or damage must be claimed as an occurrence that the insured reported to the insurance company within 60 days after the end of the policy period. Claims first made after the policy expires for injury resulting from an occurrence that has not been reported to the insurance company are covered under the basic tail only if the claim is first made within 60 days after the end of the policy period. When a claim for an occurrence is first made, the claim triggers coverage for all other subsequent claims that might arise from the same occurrence.

Supplemental tail reporting period.   The contractor can purchase the supplemental tail for an addition premium. In doing this, the contractor coverts the claims-made form to an occurrence form, which is subject to supplemental aggregate limits. These limits apply to claims first made during the supplemental reporting period. This insurance is excess over other applicable insurance. Because most contractors' operations do not involve significant latent injury or damage exposures, occurrence CGL forms are readily available.

§ 3.8   —Personal Injury Liability

In doing business, a contractor may take action against someone who the contractor believes has harmed the contractor. If in that process, the contractor subjects the individual to false arrest, detention or imprisonment, or malicious prosecution, the wronged party can claim personal injury. Such a claim also can be made for wrongful entry into, or eviction of an individual from, a room, dwelling, or premises that the person occupies. Personal injury liability insurance gives the contractor coverage in these circumstances.

Personal injury liability insurance also covers oral or written publication by the contractor of material that slanders or libels a person or organization, disparages a person's or organization's goods, products, or services, or violates a person's right of privacy.

Coverage usually is excluded in the case of publication of material, such as when the contractor says or writes or directs someone else to say or write statements with the knowledge that the statements are false.

§ 3.9   —Professional Liability

Certain activities of contractors may be construed as professional in nature and therefore may not be subject to standard CGL policy protection. Contractors who conduct design and build activities or engineering projects may be subject to professional liability claims as mentioned earlier. General liability policies normally exclude professional liability coverage whenever the contractor performs architectural or engineering services. Although a general liability policy covers a contractor's liability for third-party bodily injury and property damage arising from conditions on the contractor's premises or the contractor's operations, a professional liability policy covers claims based on allegations that the contractor was professionally negligent.

The most common professional liability exposure is when the contractor is involved in the specifications and design of the project. Also, claims may be based on failure to render architectural and engineering services. Both types of claims can be covered under a professional liability policy.

An endorsement may be added to the CGL to exclude the kind of work performed by an architect, engineer, or surveyor. Additionally, as explained in § 3.7, liability the contractor assumes for preparing, approving, or failing to approve maps, drawings, opinions, reports, surveys, change orders, designs, or specifications is excluded. Whenever the contractor is involved in these activities or contractually assumes responsibility for them, a professional liability exposure exists, and the contractor should purchase an architects' and engineers' professional liability policy.

§ 3.10   —Vendor's Liability

Vendor's liability may be extended to a contractor by a manufacturer when that contractor distributes or installs a product of the manufacturer. This coverage provides the contractor with protection against bodily injury or property damage arising out of the manufacturer's product. For example, a heating and air-conditioning contractor might install a specific brand of air conditioner. The manufacturer of the air conditioners may extend their general liability policy to protect the distributor-installer (contractor) against losses resulting from the units. The contractor should check for the availability of this protection from the manufacturers of products for which the contractor acts as a vendor.

§ 3.11   Automobile Liability

The commercial automobile liability policy or business automobile policy covers the contractor's automobiles and automobiles under long-term lease. It provides protection for injury or damage caused by an occurrence and arising from the ownership, maintenance, or use of automobiles anywhere in the United States, its territories, possessions, or Canada. This policy also permits coverage for vehicles operated by the named insured under long-term lease, when the lessee provides primary insurance and the lessor is named as an additional insured. With hired automobiles, the coverage is for the named insured but does not extend to the lessor.

Employers' nonownership liability covers the named contractor for business use of automobiles individually owned by employees or firm members. However, the coverage does not normally cover partners. Employers' nonownership liability, which is excess over any applicable primary coverage the vehicle owner may have, protects the contractor if the employee has no insurance or when limits prove to be inadequate. It does not protect the vehicle owner, who has an obligation to insure the automobile.

Although the contractor is automatically protected for employees' use of their own vehicles on company-related business, the contractor should confirm that employees who regularly use their automobiles are adequately insured.

The commercial automobile policy may be extended to include medical-payments coverage. This provides for reimbursement of reasonable medical expenses incurred by occupants of an insured automobile. The insurance is not applicable to employees eligible for workers' compensation benefits. Therefore, contractors should be aware that medical payments coverage usually is not included on trucks if all occupants will be employees.

Based on individual state laws and requirements, no-fault automobile benefits may be applicable to the contractor's commercial automobile policy. This coverage is designed to modify or restrict tort liability so that first-party benefits are payable under the contractor's own policy, regardless of fault. Depending on state law, a limited amount of injury or damage is payable. If the bodily injury or property damage exceeds a specified threshold, however, normal tort liability actions are permitted.

§ 3.12   —Automobile Physical Damage

Physical damage to owned vehicles as well as vehicles under long-term lease is normally covered as part of the commercial automobile policy.

The insured perils may include comprehensive coverage that is a type of all-risk coverage and includes any accidental damage to the vehicle other than damage caused by a collision. The vehicle may be insured on an actual cash value basis or alternatively on a stated amount basis. If the actual cash value basis is selected, the amount recovered in the event of a total loss is the current market value of the vehicle.

Stated perils coverage may be purchased as an alternative. The specific perils of fire, theft, windstorm, hail, earthquake, explosion, flood or rising waters, riot, civil commotion, malicious mischief, and vandalism may be insured at a premium savings over comprehensive coverage.

Collision damage to owned or long-term-leased vehicles is available at deductibles ranging from $50 to $1,000 or more.

Fleet automatic coverage is available for five or more insured vehicles. A fleet automatic endorsement is available without additional charge to include changes and additions to the automotive schedule without the need to endorse midterm.

§ 3.13   Excess Liability

Both commercial general liability and commercial automobile liability are written as primary policies with limits usually in the maximum range $1 million to $2 million. A contractor will likely need higher limits and a specific excess policy, or should consider an umbrella liability policy.

Umbrella Liability Policy

Umbrella coverage provides excess limits for the same or broader hazards insured under the primary policies. For those hazards omitted or excluded in the primary liability policy, umbrella policies provide coverage in excess of a self-insured retention or deductible. This retention is usually $10,000 or $25,000.

An important provision of most umbrella liability policies is the maintenance of the primary liability coverage. The contractor must keep the primary liability coverage listed in the umbrella policy in effect during the umbrella's policy period and at the underlying limits shown. The umbrella insurer only responds when the loss is above the limits that should have been maintained. Failure to do so may result in the umbrella insurer responding to a loss as though the primary liability policy with its limits is in force. This condition can cause serious loss if the contractor has lowered the limits on the primary coverage, canceled it entirely, or has different policy periods for the primary coverage and the umbrella policy.

Following Form Excess Policy

As an alternative to an umbrella policy, a contractor may purchase specific "following form" liability coverage. In this case, the excess policy provides no coverage broader than the primary policies, and merely extends the limits to whatever level is needed. This generally makes the following form excess policy less expensive.

§ 3.14   Builders' Risk

Construction contracts normally identify who is responsible for securing insurance to protect the property under construction, materials being used in the construction, and equipment being installed. An owner or the general contractor can purchase the coverage, but if neither party is specified, the purchase is the owner's responsibility. The contract's provisions should be checked to see who is responsible.

Regardless of who purchases the coverage, those involved in the construction project, such as the general contractor, subcontractors, and sub-subcontractors, have a stake in the amount and kind of coverage provided.

A builders' risk policy typically provides protection on an all-risk basis, that is, all perils are covered unless specifically excluded. Although forms from most insurance companies are similar, some vary in the coverage provided automatically and in what may be added by endorsement. A careful review should be made to assure that the following areas of exposure are addressed:

1. Buildings or structures during the course of construction, including foundations, sidewalks, and below-grade valves, should be the primary property covered.

2. Property destined to become part of the structure, including equipment, machinery, and fixtures, while at the jobsite, designated for delivery to the jobsite, or in transit, also should be covered.

3. Property at the jobsite incidental to construction, such as temporary structures, should be included. In this area, it is typical for scaffolding, building forms, and certain mobile equipment to be excluded from the builders' risk coverage but included in contractors' equipment policy forms.

Builders' risk insurance can be written on a specific basis, which applies to the projects for which it is purchased, or on a blanket basis for multiple construction projects.

In addition, builders' risk coverage may be purchased on a completed value or reporting form basis. With completed value builders' risk coverage, the project has full coverage from its inception date to its completion date, up to the limits purchased. If the project's value escalates beyond the value originally contemplated, limits should be increased accordingly.

On the other hand, if a reporting form is chosen, then the insured must report the values in place on the project on a monthly basis. As the value goes up, the premium increases. An honesty clause in this reporting form means that if the reported value is too low, any loss paid under the form will be scaled down in accordance with the underreported value. If the property of subcontractors is included in the builders' risk policy, the value of the subcontractor's property must be included in the contract price.

Listing all subcontractors and the general contractor as named insureds on the builders' risk policy is a good idea to prevent insurer subrogation against the subcontractors for damage to insured property. Doing this, however, requires a determination of responsibility for the payment of the premium, the timely notice of losses, and the preparation of loss documents.

Contractors can request a waiver of subrogation, whereby they ask insurers to give up the right to recover losses from a third party that may cause losses. This must be done before any loss occurs, but the waivers usually only apply on losses covered by the builders' risk policy. In seeking waivers in transactions in which several parties are involved, the best practice is to get waivers from all parties.

The duration of coverage clause in the typical builders' risk policy specifies when the insurance will end, although the definition of completion of a project is not always clear-cut. Because builders' risk contracts are tailor-made to fit particular projects, this definition can be spelled out.

Although the typical builders' risk policy is a comprehensive contract, the following areas should be investigated and added to the policy (if not already included) whenever an exposure exists.

Error in design.   Resultant damage from error, omission, or deficiency in design, specifications, workmanship, or materials. This wording is usually included in the policy without a specific premium charge or additional premium.

Debris removal.   This includes all expenses incurred for removal of debris resulting from an insured loss.

Automatic inflation update.   Beginning with the start of construction, limits are increased automatically and directly with any increase in building cost modifiers published by a recognized appraisal company.

Testing.   Although the construction project may essentially be complete, this option would extend the coverage while mechanical, electrical, or other testing is conducted. A separate premium charge usually is appropriate.

Additional expenses.   Loss of income, license fees, interest on loans, and other soft costs may be incurred or may escalate as a result of the delay caused by a covered loss at the jobsite. An additional premium is typically charged for these extensions.

§ 3.15   Installation Floater

For some projects, full builders' risk coverage is not necessary, or may not be extended to cover the subcontractors' interest. In these cases, contractors and subcontractors need to protect their materials, supplies, and equipment to be installed in the project. An installation floater is designed to accomplish this, providing coverage for damage to machinery, prefabricated or preassembled equipment, and fixtures or building supplies until they are installed, tested, and accepted. The equipment and materials are covered in transit or while stored at the jobsite for installation by the contractor.

§ 3.16 Transportation Floater

Building supplies, fixtures, and equipment may be purchased by a contractor or subcontractor without being designated for installation on a special job or project. When this occurs, and the contractor or subcontractor has an ownership interest in these supplies, it will be necessary to protect them while they are being transported. The protection is accomplished through purchase of a transportation floater.

Also known as transit insurance, this type of coverage protects owners of property against damage to their property while in the course of transit by carriers or by their own vehicles. Insurance may be arranged to cover incoming and outgoing shipments by various modes of transportation, including truck, train, airplane, or vessel. Transportation floaters ordinarily do not cover imports or exports for the ocean portion of their transit.

§ 3.17 Contractors' Equipment

Contractors have a financial interest in, and dependence on, the tools of their trade, whether the tools are small hand tools or million dollar pieces of heavy equipment. Contractors' equipment insurance can be used to insure virtually any type of machinery, tools, and equipment. Equipment designed for use principally on public roads is not eligible for the coverage.

Coverage can be purchased for named perils such as fire, lightning, and windstorm. Alternatively, all-risk coverage can be written to insure against all risks of physical loss, except those specifically excluded. For the former, the burden of proof is on the insured that a loss falls within one of the named perils. With all-risk coverage, the insurer must prove that a loss falls within an exclusion; otherwise there is coverage.

Contractors' equipment floaters can be written on a scheduled or a blanket basis. Small tools and equipment can be blanketed even though larger valued equipment is scheduled. If equipment changes frequently, the contractor may find it difficult to keep the equipment schedule up-to-date. Writing the equipment floater on a blanket basis avoids this problem.

Coverage provided by equipment floaters varies depending on specific insurance company forms. Therefore, it is important to review the following list to make sure that the contractors' needs are properly protected:

1. Most contractors' equipment floaters are written on an actual cash value basis. If replacement cost coverage is written, it is normally more expensive.

2. Contractors who loan or rent equipment to others should be sure that their equipment floaters provide coverage in those situations.

3. Equipment that is rented or leased from others may be included automatically. The contractor should investigate the reporting provisions and limits that may be applicable.

4. Many equipment floaters exclude or restrict coverage for booms, derricks, or cranes while in use. Restrictions may apply concerning loss arising from the weight of the load that exceeds the registered capacity of the equipment, or loss arising from the maintenance, repair, or servicing or such equipment. These limitations should be removed if possible.

5. The floater may be extended to cover the contractor's loss of income when the equipment is damaged and cannot be used.

6. The floater may be extended to cover rental expense for substitute equipment that may temporarily replace damaged equipment.

§ 3.18   Contractors' Other Property

A contractor also has real and personal property that requires protection under standard insurance forms. The following are the more important exposure areas for which policy provisions and extensions or options are available. The contractor should review these areas for specific applicability.

Buildings.   Property (buildings and their contents) owned by the contractor or owned by others but in the care, custody, or control of the contractor may need insurance protection.

Newly-acquired buildings.   Contractors often acquire buildings during construction for temporary use. Most policies have newly-acquired property provisions. The automatic limit provided, and time required to report this property under standard policy forms, should be reviewed.

Valuable records.   Contractors frequently have a need to protect valuable papers and records such as drawings and blueprints. The replacement value of the material should be identified and specifically insured.

Business interruption and extra expense. Contractors' loss of income and extra expense needed to remain in operation after a loss to real or personal property is a very important exposure area. Both business interruption and extra expense insurance are readily available in standard property forms. An additional premium, however, will be charged.

Data processing. Today, economies of scale and technical advances have made electronic data processing (EDP) an affordable option for even the smallest contractor. An EDP floater can be purchased to insure data processing hardware, software, and media. The floater also may cover extra expense to continue data processing operations following damage to the system.

§ 3.19   Additional Insureds

Contractors may be requested to add others with whom they are associated in business arrangements to their liability policies. Extending additional insured coverage to people receiving goods and services from the contractor protects those people from tort actions that might be brought against the contractor. This additional insured endorsement may be used when a hold-harmless clause is not requested or is not appropriate. Liability policies usually do not require anyone to pay any additional premiums for the attachment of the additional-insured endorsement.

Additional insureds also can be employees of the contractor. If a claim should be filed individually, naming, for example, a supervisor who is not an executive officer, director, or stockholder, no primary defense coverage would be available to that employee. Therefore, the insured has a choice about whether to buy certain coverage extensions, higher limits of liability, or new policy forms in preparation for a possible loss to that employee.

§ 3.20   Certificates of Insurance

Certificates of insurance show evidence that the person providing the certificate has appropriate insurance. Most often certificates are used to indicate that the certificate provider has insurance that covers contractual liability.

A larger, well-known company can use a generalized letter of coverage stating that it has a complete risk and insurance program that will provide coverage or protection needed by the contractor.

Although the insurance company agrees to provide notice of cancellation of the underlying policy to a certificate holder, the certificate is not a contractual obligation that the company must meet.

Although most insurance companies provide certificate holders with 10 days' notice prior to cancellation, the contractor should attempt to get an extension of this time period to 30 days, because making other arrangements for coverage may take that long.

Certificates dealing with workers' compensation should designate the states in which coverage applies. If the certificate indicates that all states are included, something is amiss, because the monopolistic fund states mentioned in § 3.2 cannot be included.

If the certificate holder needs United States Longshore and Harbor Workers' Act coverage or has operations in various countries, the certificate should attest to those coverages.

The contractor should have procedures for carefully monitoring certificates of insurance. Procedures might include reviewing the certificates received from subcontractors and the expiration of coverage as shown on the certificates.

§ 3.21   Key Thoughts

The key ingredients to proper insurance coverage for the contractor are knowing the contractor's risks, managing the risks, reducing the risks where and when possible, and obtaining adequate coverage. The contractor's insurance program should be monitored on a continuous basis. Understanding the risks presented by the contractor helps ensure that the contractor has a properly designed and maintained insurance program.

CHAPTER 4

JOINT VENTURES AND CONSORTIUMS

G. Christian Hedemann
Mark S. Strukelj

G. Christian Hedemann is vice president and general counsel of Fluor Daniel, Inc., Irvine, California, one of the leading engineering, construction, operations, and maintenance companies in the world. He previously worked for Bechtel, Stone & Webster, and in private practice where he was a litigator. He received his B.A. and J.D. degrees from the University of Colorado at Boulder.

Mark S. Strukelj is senior counsel in the law department of Fluor Daniel, Inc., Irvine, California, an international engineering and construction company. He advises Fluor Daniel in all aspects of engineering and construction contract law, project financed transactions, and related matters. Mr. Strukelj previously practiced general business law, primarily in the areas of tax and real estate. He obtained his undergraduate degrees at Loyola Marymount University and his law degree at Loyola Law School. Mr. Strukelj is a member of the California Bar Association.

FORMING THE ENTERPRISE

§ 4.1 Nature of Joint Venture or Consortium

The joint venture and consortium have always played important roles in the construction industry, and their use as convenient, flexible vehicles to achieve varied objectives in diverse contexts, both in the United States and internationally, is common. The consortium also has been used as a mechanism to facilitate cooperative efforts among multiple parties. Although many times the terms "joint venture" and "consortium" are used interchangeably, there are differences between the two entities.

Joint Venture

This chapter broadly uses the term *joint venture* to mean a business alliance of limited duration formed by two or more unrelated businesses or professional entities for the purpose of furnishing engineering, consulting, procurement, construction, and construction management services by consolidating the skills and resources of the participants.[1] The definition also includes the joint venture of a longer duration formed with the purpose of developing expertise or sales in a prospective, attractive market without being tied to a specific project.

A joint venture often has the legal attributes of a partnership, although the participants frequently provide in their agreement that for legal purposes a partnership is not being formed. Clearly, the main inspiration for the attempt to avoid acquiring partnership status is an aversion to assuming joint liability for each of the other participants' acts. Although it is possible to bind a client in a contract to the notion that joint liability does not exist, thus requiring the client to seek redress from each of the individual joint venturers, the joint venturers' exposure to third parties is commonly, and probably unavoidably, on a joint and several basis. For this reason, the legal distinction between partnerships and joint ventures is rarely made. The "*incidents* of both relationships are in all important respects the same, and courts freely apply the provisions of the Uniform Partnership Act [to joint ventures] where they are appropriate."[2]

A joint venture is sometimes distinguished from a partnership in a nonlegal way in that a joint venture is thought to be formed for a specific project while a partnership is intended to be formed to pursue a general or continuing business enterprise. In this sense, the phrase "joint venture" may be more appropriate for a construction project because the alliance typically dissolves after the project is completed. When dealing with the United States government in a joint venture, each participant may use its own approved accounting system rather than have the joint venture accounting system separately approved, as is the case with a true legal partnership.[3]

---

[1] The word *participant* is used to refer to an entity planning to form a joint venture or consortium with another entity.

[2] *See* Witkin, *Partnerships,* Summary of California Law, ch. XIII, § 17 (9th ed. 1989).

[3] *See* A. Paul Ingrao, *Joint Ventures: Their Use in Federal Government Contracting,* 20 Pub. Contract L.J. 3 (1991) [hereinafter Ingrao]; *see also* Matanuska Valley Bank v. Arnold, 223 F.2d 728 (9th Cir. 1955).

Consortium

The term *consortium* connotes to nonlawyers a business relationship in which the participants desire to combine their efforts and skills without the opportunity to share in the profits and losses or economic gain and loss of the enterprise and without the risks associated with a joint enterprise. This often requires discrete scopes of work with no overlap or interrelation of functions. It also requires the client to agree to deal with each of the participants individually (that is, several, but not joint, liability), which many clients are unwilling to do. To avoid third-party liability, subcontracts and purchase orders would be entered into in the name of the responsible participant, not in the name of the consortium.

A consortium is not an entity but is a contractual relationship between the consortium members. Like a joint venture, a consortium is established to execute a specific project. However, the consortium is distinguished from a joint venture in that the consortium members generally do not have a joint interest in the subject matter of the venture (for example, the project to be constructed), do not share in the profits or losses of the venture, and do not undertake any fiduciary duty toward each other unless expressly agreed to under the consortium agreement.[4]

§ 4.2   Selecting a Venture Partner

The factors brought to bear in selecting a joint venture or consortium partner are legion. Clearly, experience and judgment play predominant roles. In selecting a partner, however, the initial enthusiasm must be tempered with sober awareness of the need to interact compatibly throughout the term of the alliance and to weather the day-to-day challenges of the operations and changing conditions of the participants. Often one of the participants will have a more dominant bargaining position than the others; in such cases experience suggests that flexibility and forbearance in the use of that bargaining power assist in securing a workable relationship in the long term.

Often, participants choose each other on the basis of earlier experiences in which favorable impressions were formed. The concern that a potential partner will gain an advantage or will be trained as a competitor in an area in which the partner does not presently compete is balanced against the

---

[4] *See* Milton, *International Consortium: Definition, Purpose and the Consortium Agreement,* 3 Fordham Int'l L.J. 121 (1979–80). Milton defines an *international consortium* as "a temporary contractual relationship of two or more business entities of different nationalities, formed for the purpose of executing, jointly and severally, a specific contract, usually involving complex civil engineering, for the supply of goods and/or services." *Id.*

advantages of working together, acquiring experience in areas in which each partner may lack the requisite strengths.

Loosely speaking, the selection of partners in joint ventures may even encompass a prime contractor-subcontractor relationship. "Teaming," in United States government parlance, often entails a prime contractor-subcontractor structure.

§ 4.3   Reasons to Form Enterprise

Although engineering and construction companies decide to form a joint venture or consortium for reasons that often are unique, some factors in addition to the acquisition of experience and strength reoccurringly bear on this decision.

§ 4.4   —Pooling Resources and Sharing Risks

A fundamental reason for teaming with other participants is the need to bring together the technical resources to enable the team to furnish the kind and magnitude of services which each participant would not be able to provide individually. It also allows the participants to share and allocate among themselves extraordinary risks that may be involved.[5] A notable example is the consortium of companies formed several decades ago to build the Hoover Dam. Through a joint venture, the performance of services and risks associated with that performance can be allocated to the participant with the technical expertise to perform those services and manage such risks.

Sometimes the complete shifting of risks is not desired. For example, one participant may have primary responsibility to engineer a facility with the other participant having the responsibility to construct it. Although duties have been specifically assigned to each participant, the parties can agree to share the risks that may arise from the provision of those services.

In a consortium, although the participants typically allocate risks based upon the individual scopes of work of the participants, if gaps arise after the project is initially allocated among the participants, the consortium agreement could require a proportionate sharing of the costs of any items not anticipated during that initial allocation.

When participants perform services as a joint venture on United States government projects, government regulatory requirements also must be considered in establishing and operating the joint venture.[6]

---

[5] See Segal, *Joint Adventures—The Sharing of Losses Dilemma,* 181 U. Miami L. Rev. 429 (1963–1964).

[6] See Ingrao, 20 Pub. Contract L.J. at 3.

§ 4.5 —Meeting Legal Requirements

Many countries have enacted laws that require engineering and construction companies (among others) to form a joint venture or consortium, which might not otherwise be necessary, on the basis of strictly technological or business judgment. In an international context, such laws require foreign engineering and construction companies to enter into associations with one or more local firms to maximize utilization of often underemployed local talent (or some protected class) and to provide an incentive (or compulsion) for foreign firms to impart their technology and know-how to local firms in order to decrease the country's dependence on foreign expertise in the future.[7] The regulations governing United States work, requiring contractors to utilize minority, small, or women-owned contractors in performing such services, have a similar objective.

§ 4.6 —Business or Political Judgment

Aside from the need to form a joint venture or consortium to consolidate technical or financial resources, or to comply with applicable laws, engineering and construction companies may decide, on the basis of business or political judgment, that it would be advantageous from a marketing standpoint to form an association of some sort. For instance, one of the participants may be a sales representative or a source of knowledge of local business and political conditions.

§ 4.7 —Financing and Materials Supply

With the significant role that financing plays in many major projects, joint proposals may offer a substantive financing component. In such cases, financing institutions ordinarily are constrained by banking regulations and business risk factors to avoid being deemed as a joint venturer with either the borrower or the engineer/contractor. Moreover, laws in the United States that govern investment advisers may prohibit licensed financial advisers from forming a joint venture with unlicensed partners. When the proposal calls for the manufacture and supply of materials for incorporation into the project, a manufacturer of some of the materials may be a member of the joint venture offering a turnkey package. In fact, such a

---

[7] *See* Franko, *International Joint Ventures in Developing Countries: Mystique and Reality,* 6 Law & Pol. Int'l Bus. 315 (1974); *Contractors Fight Forced Joint Ventures,* Eng'g News Record, Feb. 12, 1976, at 49.

manufacturer of materials also may be instrumental in obtaining financing for the project.[8]

§ 4.8 Form of Enterprise

The joint venture and consortium often are legally based on a written agreement between participants setting forth the terms on which participants agree to work together, including the participants' respective obligations, rights, and liabilities. Unlike the often cumbersome formality of the corporation, the joint venture/consortium agreement may be amended quite simply to accommodate the developing needs of the participants and to reflect changes in the project or the client's wishes.

§ 4.9 —Liability Considerations

In recent years, as the magnitude of projects has increased and the associated legal liability has reached menacing proportions, companies in the engineering and construction industries have attempted to limit the liability to minimize the risks to which they are exposed. Because under partnership law each of the participants may be liable for the acts of each of the other participants, and because one or more of the participants may be a company with substantial assets and significant activities unrelated to the joint venture, this concern is real and bears upon the choice of the legal form of the joint venture.[9]

Typically the joint venture/consortium agreement expressly excludes such joint liability. Nevertheless, a third party looking at the enterprise from the outside may not perceive or be on notice that liability is several. Furthermore, joint venturers may not desire to share the risks of the joint venture equally. Although a participant may be willing to share in the profits (or losses) generated by the joint venture, that participant's appetite may not be the same for other types of risks. For example, most participants will not accept the liability arising from a participant's unauthorized acts. Therefore, whether operating in a joint venture or a

---

[8] *See* United States v. Penn-Olin Chem. Co., 378 U.S. 158, 84 S. Ct. 1710 (1964), *on remand,* 246 F. Supp. 917 (D. Del. 1965), *aff'd per curiam,* 389 U.S. 308, 88 S. Ct. 502 (1967) (describing further reasons for which joint ventures are formed).

[9] *See* Ingrao, 20 Pub. Contract L.J. at 3. In the context of United States government contracting, provisions of suspension and disbarment apply equally to all participants when fraud, criminal activity, or other improper conduct is imputed if the conduct is on behalf of joint venture or with knowledge of participants.

consortium form, the participants often limit their liability through appropriate cross-indemnification from their coparticipants.[10]

§ 4.10   —Subsidiary Corporation as Participant

One response to the joint liability problem inherent in a joint venture/consortium is the formation by each of the participants of a subsidiary corporation whose sole purpose is to carry out the participants' activities in the venture. In such a case, the venture would consist of the subsidiaries, which would operate according to the terms of the joint venture/consortium agreement as though the parents had been the participants, with the goal that the subsidiaries would protect the parents from liability. Of course, a subsidiary of any company should always observe the corporate niceties of separateness and independence to avoid exposing its parent to liability for the subsidiary's acts, thereby defeating the purpose of forming the subsidiary.

§ 4.11   —Corporation

The participants may conclude for liability considerations that it is best to form a corporation, the stock of which is held by the participant/shareholders, which would have the effect of isolating the shareholders from liability arising out of the project. As a further insulation, the newly formed corporation, possessing minimal assets and capabilities, might execute subcontracts for substantially all of its project services to individual participant/shareholders so that each of the subcontractors would be liable only for its own actions. However, as discussed in § **4.13**, classification as a corporation may give rise to a double tax—a tax at the corporate entity level and a tax at the participant level. Some states have enacted legislation to allow participants to operate as a "limited liability company" (LLC), which provides a participant with limited liability (equal to its capital investment) with the income pass-through and special allocation attributes of a partnership.[11]

Although there may be advantages to the use of an LLC (for example, partnership status for United States tax purposes with treatment as a corporation in a foreign country), the LLC has important drawbacks, such as

---

[10] See § **4.9** for further discussion of cross-indemnification among participants.

[11] *See* Burke & Sessions, *The Wyoming Limited Liability Company: An Alternative to Sub S and Limited Partnerships?*, 50 J. Tax'n 232 (1981); Johnson, Comment, *The Limited Liability Act*, 11 Fla. St. U. L. Rev. 387 (1983); Ribstein, *Limited Liability and Theories of the Corporation*, 50 Md. L. Rev. 80 (1991).

unclear status at the state level, limitations on transferability of interests, and limited duration. Clearly, choosing this form of doing business will depend upon the needs of the participant and the facts and circumstances of the particular transaction.

In a foreign context, it is worth noting that some countries are less than punctilious in viewing a subsidiary as separate from its parent. In a United States setting, establishing a corporation in which the percentage of ownership precludes consolidation on the parent's books may attract additional taxation at the subsidiary level.[12]

Shareholders' agreement and voting trusts.   When a corporation or its equivalent is used, a shareholders' agreement or voting trust is often executed, defining the rights and obligations of the participant/shareholders and setting forth the bases upon which the company will be operated and the project managed. Such an agreement would be in addition to, but should complement, the legal mechanisms built into the articles of incorporation and bylaws of the company, and would contain project-related details similar to those usually found in joint venture/consortium agreements.

Restrictions on use of shareholders' agreements and voting trusts. Many countries and states have laws that restrict the enforceability of shareholders' agreements or voting trusts, particularly when the agreement confers upon one of the shareholders a degree of control and management that is disproportionate to its actual ownership of the corporation, or dispossesses some of the shareholders of their rights at law. In addition, some jurisdictions have laws that render unenforceable any agreement that attempts to give irrevocable authority to manage a corporation to persons other than officers or directors. The laws restricting use of shareholders' agreements or voting trusts naturally also apply to provisions in the articles of incorporation and bylaws having a similar effect. This may be problematic when management and control of the project is important to one of the participants providing most of the expertise, reputation, or financial resources to the joint venture and when that participant does not or cannot legally own a controlling interest of the stock. Such a participant may wish to maintain final authority with respect to project management decisions, and in such cases the provisions of the shareholders' agreement must be drafted with a view toward those laws. In some countries, there may be comparable restrictions on the enforceability of some control provisions set forth in partnership-type agreements.

---

[12] *See generally* Crestol, Hennesay & Rua, The Consolidated Tax Return (1988).

§ 4.12   Scope of Fiduciary Duties

Participants must be aware of the fiduciary relationship that is created between themselves and the joint venture/consortium, to a greater or lesser degree depending on the form of the alliance and applicable law. As discussed in **§ 4.1**, a consortium relationship generally does not in and of itself create a fiduciary responsibility among the consortium participants. However, the terms of the consortium agreement may contractually give rise to such a relationship.

Generally, when a fiduciary relationship exists, each participant may have a duty to disclose all information within the participant's knowledge relating to the business of the joint venture/consortium. To mitigate this duty, the participants can specify the nature of the information to be disclosed to the other participants and provide that all other types of information are not subject to disclosure.

Participants also may have an obligation not to self-deal to the detriment of the joint venture/consortium participants. Even if the joint venture agreement is silent on the subject, all dealings with the joint enterprise by any participant may have to be kept at arm's length to avoid a claim by the other participants that the self-dealing participant obtained an unfair competitive advantage.

Finally, participants may be constrained legally to offer business opportunities arising out of the joint venture's activities to the joint venture and not take personal advantage of those opportunities. To mitigate this duty, participants can specify in the joint venture agreement the scope of the business opportunities each participant must make available.[13]

§ 4.13   Tax Considerations

A joint venture may be treated for tax purposes as a partnership if it has partnership traits.[14] Tax law defines a *partnership* as "a syndicate, group, pool, joint venture, or other unincorporated organization through or by means of which any business, financial operation, or venture is carried on,

---

[13] *See* Design Professional's Handbook of Business and Law, ch. 4 (R. Cushman & J. Dobbs eds., John Wiley & Sons 1991); Witkin, *Partnerships,* Summary of California Law, ch. XIII, §§ 18–21 (9th ed. 1989); Meinhard v. Salmon, 249 N.Y. 458, 164 N.E. 545 (1928); J. Carter, R. Cushman & C. Hartz, The Handbook of Joint Venturing, ch. 2, at 37 (1988).

[14] Under certain circumstances, for example in the co-ownership of property, a partnership is not necessarily created. *See* Treas. Reg. §§ 1.761-1(a) (as amended in 1972) and 301.7701-3(a) (1960). However, for purposes of discussing the tax consequences of a joint venture and because joint ventures are classified as partnerships under the tax law, the term "partnership" is used for clarity.

and which is not, within the meaning of [The Internal Revenue Code], a corporation or trust of estate."[15]

Partnerships accordingly are defined in the negative. In making a determination, the court considers all of the facts and circumstances surrounding the relationship that evidence the parties' business purpose when joining together to conduct business.[16] A conclusory statement in the agreement that the relationship is not a partnership is not dispositive.

Various factors are considered to determine whether a business entity is a partnership: the intent to share in profits or losses or both, joint ownership of capital, joint participation in management, joint contribution of services, existence of a partnership (joint venture) agreement, and the filing of partnership tax returns. In any event, an objective to carry on business for profit is typically an essential characteristic of a partnership.[17]

A consortium in the engineering and construction industry is usually set up to avoid having the legal characteristics of partnership status. One participant may provide the consortium engineering services or equipment supply, while the other party provides construction (that is, each participant's scope of work is discrete). Each participant can agree to perform its services individually or provide equipment, earn the profit related to that task, and accept the associated risk attributable to that individual scope of work. Although the parties are working together to complete a common project, their interests on the project and other interests are separate and distinct. The end result is that each party receives its allocable share of the project profits based on its allocable share of the overall scope of work and each party would bear the burden of its individual profits for tax purposes. In addition, liability, to the extent possible, is several, but not joint.

Partnership Not Taxable in United States

In the United States, a partnership ordinarily does not constitute a taxable entity separate and apart from the participants, although it usually must file an informational return. On the return, income or loss is computed as if the partnership were an individual taxpayer, disregarding various personal exemptions and deductions.[18] Accordingly, in most cases profits,

---

[15] See I.R.C. § 761(a) (codified in 26 U.S.C.). For cases defining joint ventures, see, e.g., Tompkins v. Commissioner, 97 F.2d 396 (4th Cir. 1938); S&M Plumbing Co. v. Commissioner, 55 T.C. 702 (1971); Podell v. Commissioner, 55 T.C. 429 (1970).

[16] See Carriage Square, Inc. v. Commissioner, 69 T.C. 119 (1977).

[17] See Rev. Rul. 55-606, 1955-2 C.B. 489. Cf. Brannen v. Commissioner, 78 T.C. 471, aff'd, 722 F.2d 695 (11th Cir. 1984) (in which profit motive was not determinative).

[18] See I.R.C. § 703(a). Regarding the treatment of limited liability companies as partnerships for tax purposes, see Rev. Rul. 88-76, Sept. 2, 1988, I.R.B. 1988-38; Priv. Ltr. Rul. 89-37-010 (June 16, 1989); Priv. Ltr. Rul. 90-30-013 (Apr. 25, 1990); Priv. Ltr. Rul. 90-52-039 (Oct. 1, 1990); Priv. Ltr. Rul. 91-190-029 (Feb. 7, 1991).

losses, deductions, special allocation items, credits, and tax preferences directly pass through to the individual participants and, subject to certain limitations, must be declared for tax purposes (in the taxable year in which the taxable year of the partnership ends) on the respective participant's income tax returns, whether or not cash or other property is distributed or losses are covered by contributions.[19] Each participant's share of profits, losses, deductions, credits, and tax preferences is reflected in that individual return and is consistent with the treatment of those items in the partnership return.[20]

Corporation Status

Potential participants in a joint venture should be aware of the possibility that the venture will be treated for tax purposes as a corporation. Internal Revenue Code Regulations delineate six characteristics of a business enterprise that distinguish corporations from other entities recognized by the Internal Revenue Code:

1. Associates;
2. An objective to carry on a business enterprise and share in its profits;
3. Continuity of life;
4. Centralization of management;
5. Limited liability; and
6. Free transferability of interest.[21]

Because "associates" and "an objective to carry on a business enterprise and share profits" are common characteristics for both corporations and partnerships, only the remaining four characteristics are evaluated for purposes of business entity classification. Equal weight is given to each characteristic.[22] So long as the joint venture enterprise lacks at least two of the four remaining characteristics, it will be classified as a partnership.[23]

Characterization for United States Tax Purposes

There are innumerable foreign variants of business entities other than the corporation or partnership, and the United States will characterize those

---

[19] *See* I.R.C. §§ 702(a)-(b), 706(a); Temp. Treas. Reg. § 1.704-1T (1988).

[20] *See* I.R.C. §§ 702(b), 6222; Treas. Reg. § 1.702-1(a) (as amended in 1991); Bell, Leola v. Commissioner, 219 F.2d 442 (5th Cir. 1955).

[21] *See* Treas. Reg. § 301.7701-2(a)(1) (as amended in 1983).

[22] *See* Rev. Rul. 88-76, 1988-2 C.B. 360.

[23] *See* Treas. Reg. § 301.7701-2(a)(3) (as amended in 1983).

entities for tax purposes according to its own criteria, not according to the law of the place in which the entity is formed. For instance, the *limitada* may be taxable in the United States as a corporation notwithstanding its partnership attributes in the country of its formation.[24] In many countries (for example, Argentina and Colombia), the *limitada* is not a corporation, and its members are taxed in the same manner as members of a partnership are taxed in the United States. However, because that entity has the attributes of a corporation under United States tax law, it is treated as a corporation for United States tax purposes.

Partnership May Be Taxable Outside the United States

In many countries other than the United States, a partnership is often a taxable entity, thus potentially giving rise to double taxation of the partnership, and possibly a withholding tax on profit remittances paid to the participant. In such situations, the participants may decide that this lack of tax benefit makes the limited liability aspects of a corporation more attractive than the traditional (in the United States) partnership form.

Foreign Taxation Checklist

The following is a checklist of some of the tax issues that may be involved in the selection of a joint venture form outside the United States:

_____ The differences, if any, in tax rates applicable to locally-formed companies and those applicable to domestically-qualified branches of foreign corporations

_____ The differences in tax rates, if any, on dividends payable by a local company to its foreign parent (often withheld by the payor subsidiary and sometimes exigible whether or not payment is actually made or legally permissible) and the tax rates on remittances of profits by branches to the home office

_____ The need for a United States participant in a domestic joint venture corporation doing business abroad to have a part of the subsidiary joint venture's earnings included on its parent's consolidated tax return

_____ The effect of any applicable tax treaties on the rate of taxation of the joint venture

---

[24] *See* Abbott Lab. Int'l Co. v. United States, 160 F. Supp. 321 (N.D. Ill. 1958) *aff'd per curiam,* 267 F.2d 940 (7th Cir. 1959). *See also* Aramo-Stiftung v. Commissioner, 172 F.2d 896 (2d Cir. 1949).

_____ The creditability of foreign taxes paid by the participants, considering especially the individual needs of the participants regarding the timing of the use of foreign tax credits[25]

_____ The "controlled foreign corporation," subpart F, and foreign personal holding company provisions of the Internal Revenue Code[26]

_____ The potential effect of laws that disallow deduction of certain kinds of expenses for purposes of calculating net income

_____ Tax holidays or incentives that may be available

_____ The effect of withholding taxes that may be levied on payments made by the joint venture to the participants for subcontracted services or profit remittance, and whether this is an expense to be borne by the joint venture or the participant.

The scope of **Chapter 4** does not permit a more extensive treatment of the tax issues (for example, tax basis of partnership assets, the individual partner's tax basis of its partnership interest, special allocations, and capital accounts) as they relate to a partnership structure. Although the partnership structure offers flexible structuring to fit the particular needs of the participants, the nuances of partnership taxation should be considered carefully by any prospective participant before venturing down the partnership road.[27]

§ 4.14   Antitrust Considerations

Although antitrust enforcement activity in the restraint of trade area in the United States has diminished in recent years, any participant entering a joint venture or consortium should consider the potential antitrust impact of the laws of any country with which the contemplated venture is connected.

In the United States, it has been clear for many years that the joint venture and the consortium fall within the purview of the antitrust laws.[28] In

---

[25] *See* Pugh & Thomas, *Income Tax Aspects of Joint Ventures Abroad,* Private Investors Abroad—Problems and Solutions in International Business in 1975, at 275 (1976) [hereinafter Pugh & Thomas].

[26] I.R.C. §§ 951–964, 951–972; Pugh & Thomas, Private Investors Abroad—Problems and Solutions in International Business in 1975, at 289–296.

[27] For a more complete treatment, *see* I.R.C. §§ 701–761; McKee, Nelson & Whitmore, Federal Taxation of Partnerships and Partners, (2d ed. 1990); Wigner, *Joint Venture with Corporate Participants Including Questions on Characterization as an Association,* 22 N.Y.U. Tax. Inst. 611 (1964); Pugh & Thomas Private Investors Abroad—Problems and Solutions in International Business in 1975, at 275.

[28] *See* United States v. Penn-Olin Chem. Co., 378 U.S. 158. Landes, *Harm to Competition: Cartels, Mergers, and Joint Ventures,* 52 Antitrust L.J. 625 (1983); Handler, *Emerging*

this connection, the engineering and construction industry has come under the scrutiny of antitrust enforcement agencies in a number of contexts.[29] This complex subject is further complicated by the fact that the scope of United States laws governing anticompetitive abuses often extends into international transactions.[30]

In addition to being cognizant United States law, participants in a joint venture or consortium also must be mindful of international laws that may restrict anticompetitive activities. For instance, with the elimination of European Economic Community (EEC) borders, joint cooperating enterprises may find they are subject to EEC competition law, which focuses on practices that restrict competition or abuse a "dominant" position within the EEC.[31] The EEC competition law is in addition to other applicable law and regulations in the particular member states.

Although antitrust issues are rarely a concern for the vast majority of joint enterprises in the engineering and construction industry, the following are a number of preliminary United States antitrust considerations applicable to the joint venture and consortium.[32] No attempt has been made to be comprehensive.

Eliminating a competitor.   A joint venture or consortium is evaluated for restraint of trade purposes according to the standards applicable to

---

Antitrust Issues: Reciprocity and Joint Ventures, 49 Va. L. Rev. 433 (1963); Pitofsky, *Joint Ventures Under the Antitrust Laws: Some Reflections on the Significance of Penn-Olin,* 82 Harv. L. Rev. 1007 (1969); Backman, *Joint Ventures and the Antitrust Laws,* 40 N.Y.U. L. Rev. 651 (1965); Bradley, *The Legal Status of Joint Ventures Under the Antitrust Laws: A Summary Assessment,* 21 Antitrust Bull. 453 (1976); Ingrao, 20 Pub. Contract L.J. at 3. *See generally* Von Kalinowski, 10 Antitrust L. & Trade Reg. § 71 (1975); U.S. Dept. of Justice, Antitrust Guide Concerning Research Joint Ventures (1980).

[29] *Cf.* United States v. Halliburton Corp., No. 73-1806, (S.D.N.Y. June 30, 1976) and United States v. Bechtel, No. C-76-99, (N.D. Cal. Jan. 5, 1979); Collusive Bidding and Related Practices, 2 Trade Reg. Rep. (CCH) § 4680; *Trustbusters Widen the War on Contractors,* Bus. Wk., Oct. 25, 1982 (regarding bid rigging). *See Case C: Joint Bidding,* U.S. Justice Dep't Antitrust Division, Antitrust Guide for International Operations (1977).

[30] *See* Kellison, *Joint Ventures Abroad and Per Se Antitrust Violations,* 1 Cal. W. Int'l L.J. (1970); Joelson & Griffin, *Multinational Joint Ventures and the U.S. Antitrust Law,* 15 Va. J. Int'l L. 487 (1975).

[31] *See* John Riggs & Anthony Giustini, *Joint Ventures Under EEC Competition Law,* 46 Bus. Law. No. 3 (May 1991).

[32] In the rare case in which a proposed joint venture or consortium has attributes that may give rise to an antitrust concern, potential participants may request the United States Justice Department to review in advance the proposed joint enterprise and render an opinion as to the Justice Department's present enforcement intention under the United States antitrust laws. *See* 28 C.F.R. pt. 50.6; *see, e.g.,* Bus. Rev. Letter No. 57 (1972), Chicago Bridge & Iron & Gen. Elec. Co., 1976 Trade Reg. Rep. (CCH) ¶ 50,194 (concerning a joint venture to fabricate nuclear reactor pressure vessels).

mergers. Because each enterprise often is formed by agreements between competitors, one operative factor in an antitrust analysis is whether the participants would have been able or willing to perform the object of the joint enterprise alone.[33] If they could have individually competed for the project, it may be argued that competition is restrained by the fact that a competitive factor in the market has been eliminated. Alternatively, the combined forces of the participants may be said to give the new joint enterprise a dominance in the market that it has not gained by superior skill and industry, thus unfairly damaging other competitors without this advantage.

Discouraging new entrants.   The size of one or more of the participants in the relevant geographical or product market is considered in antitrust analysis in determining whether the merger might discourage other potential competitors from entering that relevant market.

Territorial divisions, exclusivity, and covenants not to compete.   It may be important for the participants to agree contractually that they will not compete with the joint enterprise in a geographical or product area in which the joint enterprise will operate. In addition, participants often desire to cooperate on any exclusive basis through the joint venture or consortium. Care should be used in drafting such provisions to assure consistency with antitrust laws.[34]

Illegal tying and patent abuse.   Antitrust law generally prohibits the practice of conditioning the sale of one product, on which the seller has a patent or a distinct competitive advantage, to the concurrent sale of another product, over which the seller has no advantage, thereby giving the seller an unfair competitive advantage in the market for the second product.[35] This

---

[33] *See* United States v. Penn-Olin Chem. Co., 378 U.S. 158. *See also* United States v. National Elec. Ass'n, 1956 Trade Cas. (CCH) ¶ 68,534; Commonwealth Edison v. Federal Pac. Elec. Co., 1962 Trade Cas. (CCH) ¶ 70,488; United Nuclear Corp. v. Combustion Eng'g Inc., 302 F. Supp. 539, 555 (E.D. Pa. 1969). *See generally Merger Guidelines of the Department of Justice—1982,* 2 Trade Reg. Rep. (CCH) ¶ 4500.

[34] *See* Continental T.V., Inc. v. GTE-Sylvania, 433 U.S. 36, 97 S. Ct. 2549 (1977), *on remand,* 461 F. Supp. 1046 (N.D. Cal. 1978), *aff'd,* 694 F.2d 1132 (9th Cir. 1982); United States v. Arnold Schwinn & Co., 388 U.S. 365, 87 S. Ct. 1856 (1967), *on remand,* 291 F. Supp. 567 (N.D. Ill. 1968), *dismissed,* 442 F. Supp. 1366 (N.D. Ill. 1977), *overruled by* Continental T.V., Inc., 433 U.S. 36; White Motor Co. v. United States, 372 U.S. 253, 83 S. Ct. 696 (1963).

[35] *See Patent Licensing Practices—Antitrust Division Reappraisal,* 1981-5 Trade Reg. Rep. (CCH) ¶ 50,434; Fortner Enters. v. United States Steel Corp., 394 U.S. 495, 89 S. Ct. 1252 (1969); United States Steel Corp. v. Fortner Enters., 429 U.S. 610 (1977).

principle may apply to the situation in which one of the participants is furnishing financing, patented process technology, or materials for a project, which are either unavailable in the open market, or which are offered at terms that are substantially better than those available in the open market, and the purchase of those services is tied to the sale of the nonunique services offered by the joint enterprise.

SUGGESTIONS FOR DRAFTING THE AGREEMENT

§ 4.15   General Considerations

Numerous issues must be raised and resolved when drafting joint venture and consortium agreements. Obviously, resolution of those issues and the formal structure established will be based in each case on the particular variables involved, including the country or state in which the project is located or the work is to be performed.

In any event, it will probably be necessary to draft at least one agreement setting forth the participants' expectations regarding the joint enterprise, and the methods by which the project itself will be managed, including the obligations and rights of each of the participants. When submitting a proposal, it is often convenient to execute a brief statement of understanding (sometimes called a "Heads of Agreement Protocol," "Statement of Principles," "Memorandum of Understanding," and the like) that contains the basic outline of the important deal points, deferring the execution of a more extensive agreement until the proposal is accepted. If the corporate form or its equivalent is used, the participant/shareholders' agreement should relate directly to the formal mechanisms built into the articles of incorporation and bylaws. If services are to be performed in more than one country (for example, home office engineering and on-site construction work), two or more separate agreements with the client might be embodied in the overall agreement. If the services provided by the individual participants are to be functionally isolated from those of the others, having a master agreement containing general provisions, with subsidiary agreements with individual participants, may be helpful. **Sections 4.16** to **4.35** describe some of the features often found in joint venture and consortium agreements.[36]

---

[36] *See generally* Note, *Joint Venture Corporations: Drafting the Corporate Papers,* 78 Harv. L. Rev. 393 (1964); Birrell, *International Joint Ventures,* Private Investors Abroad— Problems and Solutions in International Business, at 241 (1976).

§ 4.16   Limitation on Use of Names

The agreement may provide that the right to use the name of the participants is limited to the joint venture/consortium and, upon termination of
the joint venture/consortium, that the right also terminates. In the event
one of the participants withdraws or is expelled, provision should be made
regarding continued use of the joint venture/consortium name. Those provisions may be fortified by a "mutual hold harmless" provision by which
each party indemnifies the other against damages caused by unauthorized
use of the individual participant's name. In countries in which trade name
protection is not adequate, consideration might be given to liquidated damages, or the execution of a separate license agreement with the joint ven-
ture/consortium, that would govern use of the name.

§ 4.17   Specification of Purpose

The agreement should specify the purpose for which the joint enterprise is
being formed. It is usually prudent to specify with some precision the
perimeters of the effort to distinguish the joint venture/consortium activities from other activities of the participants on their own behalf. There
may be a number of contingencies to the validity of the joint venture/con-
sortium, which should be listed, such as continued approval by government or client and approval by all parties of the terms negotiated into the
prime contract.

§ 4.18   Obligations of Participants

The obligations of the participants should be set forth clearly. In this regard,
the proposal or contract for the project in some cases may be made a part of
the agreement. The agreement also should clarify whether the venture itself
will hire personnel to perform the services or whether the participants will
be required to furnish such personnel, either by way of a seconding agreement or subcontract. Any special obligations to disclose and utilize patents
or secret processes should be spelled out.

§ 4.19   Restrictions on Use of Assets

Generally, assets are not contributed to or are not jointly owned by the
participants in a consortium. In the case of a joint venture or if assets are

owned by a consortium, however, the agreement should generally restrict the use of assets to the specified purposes of the joint venture/consortium. Similar restrictions might be placed on the ability of the participants to individually use the assets of the other participants other than as authorized in the joint venture/consortium agreement. The method of receiving and distributing funds should be set forth.

§ 4.20 Mechanism for Management and Control

One of the most important and potentially controversial features of the agreement is the mechanism for management and control of the joint enterprise and of the project in which the joint venture/consortium is involved. The procedure is dealt with in many different ways but often involves the following pattern.

Board decides policy. A board or managing committee composed of representatives of the participants may be given responsibility for policy and broad-based management decisions, and this board would in turn appoint management personnel. The procedures by which the board meets and decides issues should be set forth, including the place, time, and notice requirements of the meetings and, in a multinational setting, the language of deliberation. The number of the matters that must be submitted to the board, or that require unanimous consent, generally depends on the degree of responsibility and authority that the participants are willing to confer on the executive personnel carrying out the board's decisions.

Sponsoring participant. One of the participants may be designated as sponsor for purposes of maintaining overall project direction and implementing the decisions of the board. To ensure a mechanism for comprehensive project management and coordination, the agreement may refer in general terms to the methods by which decisions regarding staffing the project team will be made. Those matters can be specifically delegated to the sponsoring participant or left to the decision of the board.

Impasse breaking. The agreement may provide that in the event of an impasse regarding a decision affecting the project, one of the participants may act without the consent of the other in certain specified areas. For instance, in the interest of continuity the sponsor could be authorized to take certain actions relating to the project without the consent of the board. The danger of paralysis caused by a deadlock should be balanced against the efficiency of having one of the participants proceed to complete the project.

§ 4.21   Interests and Contributions

In the case of the joint venture, the percentage of the participation interest in and contribution to the joint venture by each of the participants should be stated. This statement should include the methods by which working capital, including funds to cover losses, will be originally and subsequently required to be contributed by the participants. The joint venture agreement may provide that profits and losses be shared in proportion to the participation percentages of the participants or on some other basis, if so agreed. It should be noted that distributions disproportionate to a participant's ownership interest may give rise to adverse tax consequences. Special tax saving clauses might be introduced to avoid those results. Often the percentage of joint venture interests is made subject to adjustment to reflect a level of effort by each participant that varies from the original allocation of interests.

The participants may wish to place some limit on the amount of working capital that they may be obligated to contribute. In cases in which contributions involve more than one currency, the value of the contributions should be clarified in the agreement, and if the participants agree that noncash capital contributions may be made, such as the value of services or patents and processes, a limitation (for instance, a minimum cash requirement) might be appropriate. Ordinarily, the participants restrict the right to transfer interests in the joint venture, and specify the degree, if any, by which a participant may subcontract its obligations. Finally, the agreement should state whether the fee will be divided according to a predetermined rate or on some other basis.

§ 4.22   Basis of Compensation

If one of the participants will individually perform services or furnish some of its employees, or if, in the case of a joint venture, contributions to the capital of the joint venture are to be made in part by the value of the services of one of the participants, then the commercial basis on which such services will be performed should be specified.[37] When one of the participants will perform services to the joint venture or consortium by way of a subcontract, on a cost basis, it is necessary to clarify whether part of the fee, as contrasted to reimbursable costs, will be passed along to that participant. Considerable detail should be devoted to the description of

---

[37] *See* I.R.C. §§ 61, 721 *et seq.*; Treas. Reg. § 1.721-1(b)(i) (1956) (regarding the tax treatment of such services).

compensation terms because the potential for disputes is great. All customary charges for overhead and special rates and surcharges should be described clearly. In long-term arrangements, rates should be subject to adjustment when increased costs can be substantiated.

§ 4.23   Distributions of Cash

A joint venture agreement should specify the time at which distributions of cash available from the joint venture to the participants will be made. If several contingent liabilities are involved, the participants may wish to defer cash distributions until those liabilities are discharged. If one of the participants has a unique need with regard to the timing or place of a distribution for tax purposes, or if potential currency conversion problems exist, it may be advisable to specify the timing, place, and currency of such distributions.

§ 4.24   Methods of Calculating Profit

In joint ventures, ambiguities in defining profit may arise over the appropriateness of special deductions, including contingency reserves, allocation for business development expenses, insurance premiums, employee benefits, and programs to be maintained individually by the participants' project support services (such as data processing, soils analyses, in-house economic analysis, and the services of the legal, insurance, and finance departments). Losses from prior years naturally should be recouped before any profit in the current year is deemed to exist. If the applicable tax laws allow special accounting methods that cause a different definition of profit than would result using generally accepted accounting principles, then the selected method should be stated.

§ 4.25   Limitation of Liability

Generally under a joint venture form, the liability of each participant in a joint venture is joint. Joint venture agreements usually set forth provisions limiting liability between the participants similar to the provisions contained in agreements with the clients of the participants. Frequently, a joint venture agreement provides that each of the participants indemnifies the other participants for any liability arising out of activities of the participants that are unrelated to the joint venture (for example, floating liens against one of the participants that encumber joint venture assets). When one of the participants brings specialized services to the joint venture, such as patented process technology or materials or financing services, it may be appropriate, on the one hand, for the participant supplying the specialized service or product to limit its liability to the other participants. On the other hand, the other participants may require that the participant furnishing such services hold the other participants harmless against liability arising out of these special activities. Use of an indemnity agreement also may be beneficial in the consortium setting, depending on the circumstances and the relative risks taken on by the participants without that indemnity. In any event, the usefulness of an indemnification by a participant is only as good as the financial strength of that participant.

§ 4.26 Right to Follow-Up Business and to Competition

Participants in a joint venture or consortium often feel that each participant should be prohibited from competing individually against the joint venture/consortium or the other participants with respect to business that is a follow-up to the project that is the object of the venture, or at least that some sort of right of first refusal should be allowed.

One of the practical disadvantages with such a restriction is that a particular client may find one of the participants unacceptable for some reason, thus foreclosing the project involved to all of the other participants. But in another context, if one of the participants has proprietary data or processes that are disclosed to the other participants on the project, it may be unfair to allow the other participants thereafter to bid individually on other jobs that utilize those data or processes.

A provision restricting follow-up business may cut both ways. For instance, during the course of construction, the client may perceive that one of the participants is making more significant contributions to the project than the other participants and may ask the participant to bid individually on follow-up work closely allied to the original project, without the other participants. If a contractual provision forbidding such activity exists, the participant having superior skill and industry may be unable to free itself from the association of a participant who does not contribute. Nevertheless, the participant who does in fact contribute to the success of the project and who may have played a role in developing new techniques, but whose role may not be known to the client, would have no protection of its rights in the business opportunity that developed in part as a result of its efforts.

Even in the absence of contractual provisions, as noted in § 4.12, a fiduciary obligation may be imposed by law or under an agreement on each of the participants, prohibiting one of the participants from individually participating in business opportunities that were developed through the efforts of the joint venture or consortium.[38]

§ 4.27   Inventions and Secrecy

The right of the participants to inventions developed during the course of performing the project services must be addressed. This right is a matter of negotiation, and, unless one of the participants has a strong proprietary position in information to which the invention relates, it may be resolved by sharing ownership according to the participation percentages of the participants or by giving each a royalty-free license, with or without the right to sublicense. Additionally, participants often wish to provide that each will keep the proprietary information of the others confidential.

§ 4.28   Confidentiality of Information

Participants often disclose confidential or proprietary information to co-participants at the inception or during the term of the joint venture or consortium. Typically, the contributing participant desires to maintain the confidentiality of that information. Accordingly, the joint venture or consortium agreement should contain a confidentiality provision that obligates each participant and the joint enterprise to maintain the confidentiality of the information and to return the information upon termination of the venture.

The confidentiality provision should describe the nature of the information to be maintained in confidence. The confidentiality provision should extend to the officers and employees of each participant. Also, the contributing participant should consider whether the duration of the confidentiality restrictions should continue throughout the term of the joint enterprise/consortium, or whether the duration should be longer or shorter than that term.

§ 4.29   Methods of Conduct

When legal or ethical conflicts may exist, some benefit may come from stating that certain specified norms will be observed, particularly regarding such matters as public disclosure of policies and payments to agents. To

---

[38] *Cf.* Meinhard v. Salmon, 249 N.Y. 458, 164 N.E. 545 (1928).

attempt to protect other participants from the illegal or unethical activities of one participant, the agreement should contain language emphasizing that all laws will be obeyed and the highest ethical standards observed. In addition, a cross-indemnity should be considered and labor relations policies should be clarified.

§ 4.30   Contracting Methods

The participants may have individual contractual policies that potentially conflict. For instance, one of the participants may be willing to accept more liability for a project than the other participant. Alternatively, although one participant may require the client to provide advance funds and mobilization payments, the other participant may be willing to use its own funds until payment is received from the client. In short, contractual policies differ among companies as do business policies, and in the interest of good client relations, it is often advisable to decide in advance on certain fundamental contractual issues so the joint venture or consortium may deal with the client through a consistent approach.

In an international joint venture or consortium, services related to a project frequently are performed in more than one country, but the joint venture or consortium participates only in the country where the project is located. This scenario may be the case when a project is located in a less-developed country and one of the participants is a national of the country. If the enterprise anticipates that a participant will individually perform services directly for the client, such as worldwide procurement or home office engineering, without the participation of the other participants, this fact, together with division of fee implementation, should be considered.

§ 4.31   Duration and Termination

The joint venture or consortium ordinarily exists for the term of the project unless otherwise terminated by mutual agreement or the withdrawal or expulsion of one of the participants. If one of the participants becomes insolvent, or breaches the joint venture/consortium agreement, or for other valid factors becomes unacceptable as a participant, the other participants may wish to have the right to take action necessary to ensure the continued success of the project in the name of the joint venture or consortium without the insolvent or breaching participant's consent. Such action may include replacing the unacceptable participant with another capable substitute (specifying the basis of compensation, if any) and ceasing all further distributions to the breaching participant. Obviously, any withdrawal has an impact on the ability of the joint venture or consortium to perform and, from the client's point of view, a change in the complexion of the joint venture or consortium may be a material change justifying termination or other damages. Also, the agreement should specify which provisions, if any, survive termination of the agreement.

§ 4.32 Preformation Expenses

The participants likely will incur expenses in advance of or collateral to the formation of the joint enterprise, such as costs for business development and legal efforts. The participants either agree to bear those expenses themselves—even though the expenses may directly contribute to the fortunes of the joint venture—or, in the case of a joint venture, agree that the expenses form a part of the capital contribution of the participants if the project is awarded.

§ 4.33 Accounting and Auditing

Each participant of a joint venture should have the right to audit the records of the joint venture as well as the records of the participants as they relate to services performed for the joint venture. Generally, such audit rights are not necessary for a consortium, although in a cost reimbursable setting the client typically will want audit rights. Participants may agree that a certified public accountant firm unrelated to the participants will prepare, keep, and audit such books and records, or one of the participants may perform one or more of those functions. In any case, the agreement should provide where the bank accounts will be located, who will be authorized to receive and disburse funds, and where the books of account will be stored. In the multinational setting, the currencies to be maintained should be stated specifically.

§ 4.34 Handling Taxes

If the joint venture is a partnership for tax purposes, responsibility for the preparation and filing of the joint venture's tax forms should be described clearly. Also, the participants should consider whether a "tax matters partner" should be designated.[39] Each participant may wish to retain certain

---

[39] *See* I.R.C. § 6231. Generally, all partnerships must designate a "tax matters partner." However, a *small partnership* (defined as a partnership with 10 or fewer partners that has no special allocations among the partners) is excluded unless that partnership elects to be treated as a partnership for purposes of I.R.C. § 6231.

notice and participation rights concerning any anticipated or ongoing tax dispute. In the event a tax matters partner is designated, that partner receives tax notices on behalf of the other partners, keeps all partners informed of administrative and judicial proceedings at the partnership level, and has certain rights relating to the audit of and settlement of adjustments to the partnership tax return.

§ 4.35   Governing Law and Arbitration

Increasingly, multinational joint venture and consortium agreements specify the law to govern interpretations of the applicable agreements and resulting disputes and agree to submit all disputes to arbitration. This practice may be problematic if the involvement of any third parties is desired, such as the client who is not a party to such an agreement and who would therefore be beyond the reach of the arbitration tribunal. On the other hand, the confidential, relatively informal nature of arbitration proceedings may be attractive for both the multinational and the domestic joint venture and consortium. When arbitration is chosen by participants in an international setting, and one of the participants is a national of the country where the project or client is located, it is important to ascertain whether that country has laws that enforce agreements to arbitrate outside that country. Arbitration in a neutral country is appropriate and often is considered fair.

The governing law and applicable rules for arbitration (if appropriate) should be stated. If the laws of the country where the project is located may not uphold key management or other provisions of the agreement, then a law that would validate those provisions should be selected.

PART II

CONTRACTING AND PROCUREMENT

CHAPTER 5

CONTRACTING WITH THE OWNER

Albert E. Phillips
Robert L. Crewdson

Albert E. Phillips is a senior partner of Phillips, Hinchey & Reid, an Atlanta, Georgia, law firm specializing in construction matters. Mr. Phillips is immediate past-chairman of the National Institute of Municipal Law Officers' (NIMLO) Section of Local Government Contracts and Procurement, and he currently serves as a member of the American Bar Association's Forum Committee on the Construction Industry, its Public Contract Law Section, the Construction Litigation Committee, and the Committee on Fidelity & Surety Law. He also serves as a member of the American Arbitration Association's Panel of Construction Arbitrators and has lectured extensively on the prevention, handling, and resolution of construction disputes.

Robert L. Crewdson is a senior associate in the law firm of Phillips, Hinchey and Reid, a construction law firm in Atlanta, Georgia. He graduated Phi Beta Kappa from the University of the South, received an M.A. in history from the College of William and Mary, and his law degree from the University of Virginia. Mr. Crewdson concentrates his practice in the area of construction law, representing owners, contractors, and sureties in all phases of the construction process. He has authored several articles in the field of construction law and has lectured before several organizations on construction issues.

§ 5.1   Risk Allocation Concerns

The contract documents that form the basis for the relationship between the general contractor and the owner contain a package of rights acquired by the owner and a separate package of rights acquired by the contractor. For each right or entitlement so acquired, the opposite party has a corresponding duty. With respect to its rights and duties, the contractor is concerned primarily with the allocation of various risks between the parties. Most states, localities, and the federal government require that public construction contracts be awarded on the basis of competitive bidding, with the contract being awarded to the lowest responsible and responsive bidder. When competitive bidding is the method of contractor selection, the owner generally specifies the contract terms in advance, and therefore also specifies the allocation of risks. Under those circumstances, the contractor's only mechanism for protecting itself from undesirable risks is to refrain from bidding. In the real world, however, there is never a lack of bidders, as many contractors seem more than willing to bid competitively for public projects, despite the risks.

In contrast, private owners have the flexibility to negotiate their contracts, to award them after competitive bidding, or to utilize some combination of both methods. In many instances, the owner identifies, or prequalifies, a group of selected contractors and seeks competitive bids. Regardless of the manner in which contracts are awarded, the contractor should be alert to the contractual provisions that allocate the risks involved in the upcoming project. The owner must accept certain risks, for example, the risk of having funds available at the time required to pay for the construction in accordance with the contract. Similarly, except for design-build contracts, the owner accepts the risk that its design plans and specifications may not be completely accurate or adequate for the purpose intended.

On the other hand, the contractor assumes the risk of providing the management, supervision, and guidance necessary to assure completion of the project on time, within the budgeted price, and in accordance with the plans and specifications. There are other risks, not as readily apparent as those noted above, that should be viewed as major concerns for the contractor. The first category of risk is that over which neither party has control, such as weather, changes in economic and market conditions (for example, inflation), labor strikes or unrest, and material shortages. The second category involves risks that, in fairness, should be borne by the owner; however, the owner frequently attempts to shift these risks onto the contractor. Included in this category of risks are owner-caused delays and disruptions, and varying or differing site conditions.

Although most contractors seek to insulate themselves from the effect of these risks, many risks wind up being borne by the contractor, and must be dealt with accordingly. Therefore, when negotiating a contract with the owner, the contractor must be concerned with far more than the price, the completion dates, and the basic description of the work to be done. The allocation of the described risks, and the resulting losses encountered by the parties to the contract when those risks become reality, could result in disaster for the contractor.

§ 5.2   Competitive Bidding Procedures

When competitive bidding procedures are used by private owners, the private owner normally reserves the right to reject the lowest bid and to contract with any bidder at the owner's discretion. In other words, no contractual relationship exists until the bid is accepted.[1] Therefore, a rejected

---

[1] Upton v. Fidelity Standard Life Ins. Co., 185 So. 2d 297 (La. Ct. App. 1966).

low bidder has no remedy against the private owner for rejection of the lowest bid.[2] However, if the private owner fails to reserve a right of rejection in its invitation for bids, and uses language indicating a commitment to award the contract to the lowest bidder, the low bidder whose bid is rejected may have a remedy in contract law based on the theory of promissory estoppel.[3] If the owner rejects the low bidder, or all bids, in bad faith, or in furtherance of a scheme to obtain estimates from the bidders at no cost, the low bidder may have a right to recover its bidding expenses.[4]

As noted in § 5.1, most states and localities have public bidding statutes. The requirements of the statutes vary from state to state. State and local public owners generally are required by law to award construction contracts on the basis of competitive bidding, with the award going to the lowest responsible, responsive bidder. Most state competitive bidding statutes allow the governmental entity a broad discretion to reject any or all bids.[5] Yet it is generally agreed that such discretion may not be exercised arbitrarily or capriciously.[6] For instance, the violation of a mandatory statutory procedure for the alteration of a price contained in a bid requires that the bid be rejected.[7]

§ 5.3 —Responsibility Factor

Public owners are required to award contracts to "the lowest responsible bidder."[8] The *responsibility* of the contractor is determined by reference to its judgment, skill, experience, financial resources, personnel, facilities, equipment, and integrity.[9] These criteria are admittedly subjective, particularly in the areas of judgment, skill, and integrity. Nevertheless, public bodies generally are accorded broad latitude in assessing the responsibility of the contractor. In fact, a court has held that public authorities have not only the right but also the duty to inquire into the responsibility of the

---

[2] Universal By-Prods., Inc. v. City of Modesto, 43 Cal. App. 3d 145, 117 Cal. Rptr. 525 (1974); North Cent. Utils., Inc. v. Walker Community Water Sys., Inc., 506 So. 2d 1325 (La. Ct. App. 1987).

[3] Swinerton & Walberg Co. v. Englewood, 40 Cal. App. 3d 98, 114 Cal. Rptr. 834 (1974).

[4] Milton v. Hudson Sales Corp., 152 Cal. App. 2d 418, 313 P.2d 936 (1957).

[5] Istari Constr., Inc. v. City of Muscatine, 330 N.W.2d 798 (Iowa 1983).

[6] Law Bros. Contracting Corp. v. O'Shea, 79 A.D.2d 1075, 435 N.Y.S.2d 812 (1981).

[7] J.L. Manta, Inc. v. Richard B. Braun, 393 N.W.2d 490 (Minn. 1986) (involving $6 change in $300,000 bid).

[8] *See, e.g.,* Poling v. Roman, 86 N.J. Super. 484, 207 A.2d 219 (1965); Capasso v. L. Pucillo & Sons, 132 N.J. Super. 542, 334 A.2d 370 (1974).

[9] Federal Elec. Corp. v. Fasi, 56 Haw. 57, 527 P.2d 1284 (1974); Suburban Restoration Co. v. Jersey City Hous. Auth., 179 N.J. Super. 479, 432 A.2d 564 (1981).

proposed contractors.[10] Once a determination is made that the contractor lacks responsibility, the decision is normally conclusive and nonappealable, absent a showing that the public entity abused its discretion or committed fraud.[11]

§ 5.4   —Responsiveness Issue

Although the responsibility of the contractor relates to its integrity and ability to complete the public construction project, the "responsiveness" of the contractor is determined by the conformance of the material elements of the contractor's bid to the invitation for bids.[12] Thus, the bidder is not permitted to respond to the bid invitation by suggesting material changes in the proposed contract documents or by otherwise proposing to vary the details of the proposed project. The contractor must bid the precise work called for in the bidding documents without condition.[13] If the bidder has not unequivocally agreed to perform the exact work reflected in the contract documents, or if the bidder has omitted or substituted certain items, the bid will be considered unresponsive and must be rejected.[14] However, there is recent authority that an "immaterial irregularity" in the bid (that is, lack of written signature although the bid bond was signed) may be considered an "informality," and waivable by the public owner.[15]

§ 5.5   —Bid Mistakes

It is not unusual for contractors to make mistakes in their bids, either because of mathematical errors, clerical mistakes, errors in judgment, or

---

[10] Donald F. Begraft, Inc. v. Borough of Franklin Bd. of Educ., 133 N.J. Super. 415, 337 A.2d 52 (1975).

[11] Sellitto v. Cedar Grove Township, 133 N.J.L. 41, 42 A.2d 383 (Sup. Ct. 1945); Old Dominion Dairy Prods., Inc. v. Brown, 471 F. Supp. 300 (D.D.C. 1979), rev'd on other grounds, 631 F.2d 953 (D.C. Cir. 1980).

[12] See, e.g., The Model Procurement Code for State and Local Governments, 1979 A.B.A. Sec. Pub. Cont. L. § 33-101(7).

[13] City of Rochester v. EPA, 496 F. Supp. 751 (D. Minn. 1980).

[14] Albert F. Ruehl Co. v. Board of Trustees, 85 N.J. Super. 4, 203 A.2d 410 (1964); Claus v. Babiarz, 40 Del. Ch. 500, 185 A.2d 283 (1962); George Harms Constr. Co. v. Borough of Lincoln Park, 161 N.J. Super. 367, 391 A.2d 960 (1978); Albert Elia Bldg. Co. v. Sioux City, 418 F. Supp. 176 (N.D. Iowa 1976); J. Turco Paving Contractor, Inc. v. City Council, 89 N.J. Super. 93, 213 A.2d 865 (1965); Remsco Assocs., Inc. v. Raritan Township Mun. Utils. Auth., 115 N.J. Super. 326, 279 A.2d 860 (1971).

[15] Farmer Constr. Ltd. v. State, 98 Wash. 2d 600, 656 P.2d 1086 (1983). See also Jensen & Reynolds Constr. Co. v. Alaska Dep't of Transp. & Pub. Facilities, 717 P.2d 844 (Alaska 1986).

simply the failure to conduct a proper site investigation prior to bidding. Bid mistakes come in many forms, and the type of mistake made is important. What happens when the contractor submitting the low bid contends that it has made a mistake in its bid and seeks to withdraw it? Several established principles guide a determination of the contractor's rights and responsibilities in these circumstances.

First, the contractor must demonstrate to the owner's reasonable satisfaction that it did, in fact, make an error in its bid.[16] Moreover, the mistake must relate to a material element of the contract and must be so substantial that enforcement of the bid would be unconscionable.[17]

Second, the nature of the mistake must be examined. The law generally allows a contractor to withdraw its bid, or correct it, if the mistake is one of fact (a misunderstanding of contract requirements), or is clerical in nature (typographical errors). However, withdrawal of the bid or corrections to the bid will not be permitted if the mistake is one of judgment, that is, misjudging the labor time required to perform a required task in a tightly confined space.[18] Nonetheless, it is important that the contractor notify the owner of the mistake before the contract award is made based on the low bid.[19]

In addition, courts occasionally hold that the contractor seeking to withdraw its bid must be free of negligence in making the mistake, and must have investigated the costs that were contained in its bid diligently. If the contractor has not done so, the contractor may be denied the right to withdraw the bid.[20] However, clerical mistakes may not constitute negligence on the part of the contractor, unless the contractor's negligence is extreme and its conduct demonstrates a total absence of diligence.

Although bid mistakes should be discovered and brought to the owner's attention prior to award of the contract, in some instances the contractor will be granted an upward equitable adjustment in its contract price, even

---

[16] T.P.K. Constr. Corp. v. O'Shea, 407 N.E.2d 1331, 430 N.Y.S.2d 34 (1980).

[17] Naugatuck Valley Dev. Corp. v. Acmat Corp., 10 Conn. App. 414, 523 A.2d 924 (1987).

[18] Balaban-Gordon Co. v. Brighton Sewer Dist. No. 2, 41 A.D.2d 246, 342 N.Y.S.2d 435 (1973); Derouin's Plumbing & Heating, Inc. v. City of Watertown, 71 A.D.2d 822, 419 N.Y.S.2d 390 (1979); Dick Corp. v. Associated Elec. Coop., Inc., 475 F. Supp. 15 (W.D. Mo. 1979); Peter Kiewit Sons' Co. v. Washington State Dep't of Transp., 30 Wash. App. 424, 635 P.2d 740 (1981); Wallace Indus. Constructors v. Louisiana Elec. Coop., Inc., 348 F. Supp. 675 (M.D. La. 1972), aff'd, 472 F.2d 1407 (5th Cir. 1973).

[19] Town of LaConner v. American Constr. Co., 21 Wash. App. 336, 585 P.2d 162 (1978); Lassiter Constr. Co. v. School Bd., 395 So. 2d 567 (Fla. Dist. Ct. App. 1981).

[20] State v. Hensel Phelps Constr. Co., 634 S.W.2d 168 (Mo. 1982); Board of Water & Sewer Comm'rs v. Spriggs, 274 Ala. 155, 146 So. 2d 872 (1962); A.J. Colella, Inc. v. County of Allegheny, 391 Pa. 103, 137 A.2d 265 (1958); Town of LaConner v. American Constr. Co., 21 Wash. App. 336, 585 P.2d 162 (1978); Lassiter Constr. Co. v. School Bd., 395 So. 2d 567 (Fla. Dist. Ct. App. 1981).

if the mistake is not discovered until after performance has begun.[21] Relief of this nature is extraordinary, however, and is granted only when the mistake is of substantial proportion, when the damage to the contractor would be enormous if it were not rectified, and when the benefit to the owner would be unconscionable. Statutes have now been enacted in a few states to provide relief to contractors for mistakes contained in bids on public projects.

§ 5.6   —Bid Protests

The federal government has issued detailed procedures for filing bid protests; however, states and localities have been slow to follow suit. If the state or local owner refuses the protest of a contractor, the contractor is typically relegated to the courts for relief.[22] The Supreme Court of Connecticut has recently observed that there "is a growing trend for courts to permit one who has been aggrieved by a refusal to award a public contract pursuant to lowest responsible bidder provisions to also vindicate the public interest by challenging such arbitrary or capricious action by government officials."[23] It should be recognized, however, that state and local public contracts funded in whole or in part by the federal government are subject to federal regulations concerning bid protests, and contractors may be forced to litigate such disputes before the Comptroller General and in the federal court system.[24]

§ 5.7   —Bid Bonds

Public owners, and some private owners, require bidders to submit a bid bond, or cash security, with their sealed bid. The amount of the bond is typically a percentage of the bid price, usually between 5 and 15 percent. The liability of the bid bond surety, and therefore of the contractor, is

---

[21] *See* Long v. Inhabitants of Athol, 192 Mass. 497, 82 N.E. 665 (1907).

[22] Paul Sardella Constr. Co. v. Braintree Hous. Auth., 3 Mass. App. Ct. 326, 329 N.E.2d 762 (1975), *aff'd,* 371 Mass. 235, 356 N.E.2d 249 (1976). *See* Gulf Oil Corp. v. Clark County, 94 Nev. 116, 575 P.2d 1332 (1978); Funderburg Builders, Inc. v. Abbeville County Memorial Hosp., 467 F. Supp. 824 (D.S.C. 1979); Haughton Elevator Div. v. Louisiana, 367 So. 2d 1161 (La. 1979); Zurenda v. Commonwealth, 46 Pa. Commw. 67, 405 A.2d 1124 (1979); American Totalisator Co. v. Seligman, 489 Pa. 568, 414 A.2d 1037 (1980); K.S.B. Technical Sales Corp. v. New Jersey Dist. Water Supply Comm'n, 150 N.J. Super. 533, 376 A.2d 203 (1977).

[23] Spiniello Constr. Co. v. Town of Manchester, 189 Conn. 539, 456 A.2d 1199 (1983).

[24] Qonaar Corp. v. Metropolitan Atlanta Rapid Transit Auth., 441 F. Supp. 1168 (N.D. Ga. 1977).

triggered in the event that the contractor fails or refuses to execute the contract after it has been awarded to the contractor as the low bidder, or if the contractor fails to provide required performance and payment bonds. In either situation, the owner is permitted to award the contract to the next lowest bidder, or rebid the entire project. Typically, the owner will not receive as low a price as the contractor's initial bid and, in those cases, the contractor and its surety usually will be obligated to pay the owner the difference between the owner's original low bid and the price at which the owner ultimately has to pay for a contract.[25] The owner also may be entitled to any additional expenses incurred as a result of having to obtain another contractor, including the expense of rebidding the project.[26]

Exceptions to the foregoing rules of damage are contained in statutes of certain jurisdictions, which specify a fixed amount of damage to be awarded under the bid bond (such as its entire sum) if the contractor fails to execute the contract.[27] In those cases, forfeiture of the entire penal sum of the bond is deemed to be the owner's liquidated damages.[28] Of course, private bid bonds can, by their terms, accomplish the same result. If the contractor has an established line of credit with its surety, the surety company typically will write the bid bond at no cost to the contractor.

§ 5.8 Basic Agreement Provisions

Obviously, all terms and provisions of the construction contract are important. Generally, the overall parameters for the project are set forth in a basic contract document; other important provisions may be contained in separate general, special, and supplementary conditions. **Sections 5.9** and **5.10** focus on the key provisions normally contained in the basic agreement.

§ 5.9 —Proper Project Description

The agreement usually contains a terse description of the project that identifies, in the broadest terms, the work to be performed. The contractor must pay attention to this provision to ensure that the work contemplated by the contractor, which has been bid or negotiated, is the same as that described in the agreement. For example, if a project is to be constructed in phases, and the proposed contract is intended to cover one particular phase, this fact should be spelled out clearly in the project description. If this fact

---

[25] Board of Educ. v. Saver-Williams Co., 16 Ohio App. 2d 7, 258 N.E.2d 605 (1979).

[26] *See* A.J. Colella, Inc. v. County of Allegheny, 391 Pa. 103, 137 A.2d 265 (1958).

[27] City of Merrill v. Wenzel Bros., 88 Wis. 2d 676, 277 N.W.2d 799 (1979).

[28] City of Lake Geneva v. States Improvement Co., 45 Wis. 2d 50, 172 N.W.2d 176 (1969).

is not delineated clearly, the owner may subsequently contend that the contractor agreed to perform the entire project for the price stated in the agreement. Similarly, any agreement to utilize used materials, or employ other "shortcuts," should be expressly included in the project description in order to prevent subsequent disputes.

§ 5.10   —Contract Price

The contract provision setting forth the contract sum often seems to be the least controversial, and simplest to draft, of all contract provisions. It is not unusual, however, for the parties to agree verbally to one price, while inserting something entirely different into the contract. For example, the statement: "The base price shall be $1 million," without additional language, leaves unclear what additions to the base price may be contemplated. The contract that specifies that the agreed price constitutes a "guaranteed maximum" must further specifically define the parties' understanding as to what costs are compensable to the contractor under the guaranteed maximum. If the price, or compensable costs, are expressed as units, it is important that the units used be clearly defined and that any estimated total price based upon the estimated totals of all units be reflected as an estimate only.

If the contractor is responsible for providing the contract language and permits the contract to contain ambiguous language, the contractor risks an adverse interpretation of the meaning of the contract, as ambiguities generally are construed against the party drafting the part of the agreement containing the ambiguity.[29] On the other hand, if the owner is responsible for the ambiguity, the contractor nevertheless runs the risk of an adverse interpretation, on the theory that the contractor was the knowledgeable party that should have caught the ambiguity, if the contractor indeed felt that any such ambiguity existed.

§ 5.11   Terms of Payment

In setting forth terms to be included in the contract, the parties may adopt one or more of the customary compensation formats, including:

1. **Lump sum.** The contractor agrees to furnish all materials and perform all work necessary to complete the entire contract for a fixed price.
2. **Unit price.** The parties identify each of the major work tasks and divide the tasks into units of measure, such as cubic yards, tons, or

---

[29] Glassman Constr. Co. v. Maryland City Plaza, Inc., 371 F. Supp. 1154 (D. Md. 1974).

square feet. As to each task, an agreed price is established for performance of one unit (the *unit price*). The contractor then is paid the agreed unit price for performance of every unit of each task required to complete the contract.

3. Cost plus a fixed fee. The owner reimburses the contractor for the cost of the work, and the contractor receives a predetermined lump sum fee for the contractor's services.

4. Cost plus a percentage fee. The contractor is reimbursed for the cost of the work and receives a percentage of the total cost as the contractor's fee.

5. Cost plus a fee (either fixed or percentage) with a maximum. The parties agree that the contractor will receive the cost of the work as well as a fee, but that the sum of the two shall not exceed a predetermined maximum amount.

Relation of Compensation to Risk Assumption

The principal problem addressed by each compensation format is the allocation of risks inherent in construction. The lump sum basis of compensation requires the contractor to assume the risk of most of the unknown variables. It proceeds on the assumption that the contractor is the expert. The theory posits that the contractor is better qualified to determine what its cost will be, and, to the extent that unforeseen problems arise, is in a better position to control those problems and the ensuing costs. This approach also permits the owner to quantify its construction costs at the outset and make plans accordingly.

Agreed unit prices are used as the basis for payment when the required work quantities are unknown to the parties at the time the contract is signed. Highway and bridge construction often are performed on the unit price basis. A unit price contract is essentially a variation of the lump sum contract, in that each unit is really a miniature lump sum agreement.

The cost plus a fixed fee method provides that the owner will pay the actual, reasonable cost of the work performed and materials supplied, and the contractor will receive a predetermined fee for the contractor's services. In this situation, the owner assumes the risk of loss or gain that may result from unforeseen circumstances. The contractor's corresponding risk is eliminated as to most items; however, the contractor's profit is capped by the fixed fee.

Each arrangement for compensation has its purpose and its particular benefits and drawbacks. In the final analysis, considerations of risk allocation and attendant economic realities generally determine the basis of compensation that is agreeable to the parties. Payment of the contract sum can be made on any basis acceptable to both parties. Although every contractor would like to be paid the entire contract price in advance, every owner would prefer payment long after the project is completed. The issue is a practical one—the time value of money.

Pay Requests and Retainage

Traditionally, the contractor is paid on a monthly basis after it submits to the architect or engineer an itemized pay request reflecting the materials furnished and work performed during the payment period. The architect or engineer reviews the pay request with regard to the quality and quantity of the work, makes any modifications it deems necessary, and certifies the pay request to the owner as being proper for payment. Normally, some portion of the amount earned is retained by the owner as additional security for the ultimate completion of the project. Retainage is typically set at 10 percent of the value of the work in place, and may be reduced to 5 percent (or less) as work progresses satisfactorily, and the danger to the owner of untimely completion or default diminishes. In fact, some state and federal agencies require that retainage be reduced when a public construction project reaches the 50 percent completion level and the project is progressing satisfactorily.[30]

To the extent that there is room for negotiation, the subject of retainage is one that should be discussed thoroughly between the contractor and the owner. The amount of money designated as retainage represents an amount that has been earned by the contractor. It is the contractor's money. The owner's sole basis for holding the money is as security, or collateral, to insure the contractor's timely completion of the work in accordance with contract requirements. During the time that work is being done, the contractor, to the extent of the funds withheld as retainage, must finance the project at its own expense.

It is therefore in the contractor's interest to seek (1) the lowest possible percentage to be retained and (2) the greatest possible reduction in retainage at the earliest possible time. Further, the contractor should seek an agreement with the owner for the latter to invest all amounts withheld as retainage in an interest-bearing account, and to pay the interest to the contractor as it is earned (or, at the very least, upon the payment of retainage). Similarly, it is incumbent upon the contractor to ensure that the payment provisions include a requirement that the owner pay interest on overdue amounts at the highest possible legal rate. In this way, the contractor may recover its loss of use of the funds; in addition, the possibility of an interest penalty may motivate the owner to make payment in a timely manner.

---

[30] Ga. Code Ann. § 13-10-2 (Michie Supp. 1991).

§ 5.12   Time for Performance

Most construction contracts provide for the time for performance either by allowing a specified number of calendar or workdays, or by designating that completion shall be achieved on or before a specified date. If the time for performance is expressed as a specific number of days, the contractor must ensure that the work can be performed during the allotted time, and that the beginning of the allotted time is triggered by a discrete event, such as the issuance of a written "notice to proceed." If the completion date is expressed as a date certain (for example, on or before December 14, 1992), the contractor must have this requirement conditioned upon issuance of a notice to proceed on or before a date certain, and in sufficient time for completion of the work.

The contractor also should insist upon provisions for extensions of time for all delays caused by conditions over which the contractor has no control. Such delays include delays occasioned by the owner or the owner's representatives, by acts of God, by the weather, by acts of governmental bodies, and by acts of other third parties over whom the contractor has no control and for whom the contractor is not responsible. The failure to reach agreement on the allocation of these risks could cause the contractor significant financial loss.

§ 5.13   Scheduling Requirements

In addition to establishing a date for substantial or final completion (and, in many instances, milestone completion dates), some owners require the contractor to furnish the owner with a project schedule generated through the use of the critical path method (CPM) or other scheduling techniques. Some owners require that the contractor employ a scheduling consultant. Others may be satisfied with submission of a simple bar chart. In rare cases, an owner may want to supply its own schedule and require the contractor to follow it.

Traditionally, it has been the contractor's right to utilize whatever scheduling approach it desires, the contractor's only commitment to the owner being to meet the deadlines set forth in the contract. As owners have become more sophisticated and, in many instances, more interested in maintaining current, updated information on job progress, they have begun to require more scheduling information and effort from the contractor than in the past.

From the contractor's perspective, its utilization of the time allowed for completion should be uniquely within the contractor's province. The contractor should not be held in default, or otherwise be deemed in breach of its contract, in the event a particular item of work is not completed by the discrete date shown on a detailed schedule. Although the owner may be entitled to information as to the progress of its project, the owner should have no contractual right regarding a failure to meet such discrete target dates in a detailed schedule. It is clearly in the contractor's interest to maintain as much control of the scheduling function as it can and to exclude as many scheduling requirements as possible from the contract.

However, when the owner insists on dictating the project schedule or insists that the contractor hire a scheduling consultant of the owner's choosing, the contractor should insist that the contract expressly state that the owner is providing the schedule. In the event the schedule provided by the owner is either inadequate or inaccurate, the resulting damage to the contractor and the project is the responsibility of the owner, as opposed to that of the contractor.

§ 5.14   Liquidated Damages

A failure by the contractor to complete the project within the specified time, without excuse, may create liability on the part of the contractor to the owner for breach of the timely completion clause of the contract. The damages may take the form of actual or liquidated damages, or both, depending on the contract terms used. Most contracts include a liquidated damages provision that assesses the contractor a predetermined amount for each unexcused day past the completion date. A liquidated damages clause introduces certainty into the contract, as both parties have notice of the amount for which the contractor will be liable, and to which the owner will be entitled, if the project is completed late. The imposition of liquidated damages generally is considered to be most useful when the actual damage to the owner will be difficult to ascertain, and the parties can agree in advance to an approximate amount. Such liquidated damages provisions generally are enforced by the courts, so long as the amount set as liquidated damages is not patently unreasonable.[31]

To the extent that the contract proposed by the owner contains a liquidated damages clause, the contractor should have the amount of such daily liquidated damages set as low as possible. This effort serves two functions. First, it is clearly in the contractor's economic interest for the liquidated damages rate to be minimal. Second, if a minimal rate can be negotiated, the existence of the clause effectively insulates the contractor from exposure for actual damages, which may far exceed the liquidated damages allowed under the contract. Liquidated damages that are set extremely high may be set aside by the courts as constituting a forfeiture or penalty against

---

[31] Leasing Servs. Corp. v. Justice, 673 F.2d 70 (2d Cir. 1982); Wilson v. Clarke, 470 F.2d 1218 (1st Cir. 1972); Restatement (Second) of Contracts § 346(1) (1981).

the contractor.[32] However, courts apparently have not yet held that a liqui-dated damages clause was too low, and therefore created a windfall for the contractor. Thus, to the extent that there is room for negotiation with the owner, the diligent contractor may be rewarded by effectively minimizing its liability for delay, while also insulating itself from potentially disastrous actual damages that could be incurred by the owner.

§ 5.15   Implementation of Changes

Due to changing needs, changing economic conditions, state of the art ad-vances concerning the project, and other factors, the owner may desire to implement modifications in the contractor's work as originally defined. It has long been recognized that the owner needs a mechanism to permit it to implement such changes after the contract has been executed, or, indeed, even after the work is partially complete. Absent such a mechanism, the owner is bound to the original design and the contractor is under no obliga-tion to accept any changes. On the other hand, given adequate compensa-tion and additional time in which to perform the work as changed, most contractors have no objection to such changes; in fact, many welcome them as an opportunity to earn additional profit or to reduce anticipated losses.

Almost all current form construction contracts contain a "changes" clause, which provides that the owner may require changes in the work, including additions, deletions, or modifications, as long as the changes are within the general scope of the project as contemplated by the parties at the time of executing the original contract.[33] What constitutes a change within the scope of the original contract may be a subjective matter.[34] By agreeing in advance to complete such changes, the contractor agrees to be bound by any such change orders.

Changes Clause Provisions

From the contractor's perspective, several important elements should be included in the changes clause.

Determining compensation.   First, and most importantly, the changes clause should provide a method for determining equitable compensation for the contractor, in the event that the contractor and owner are unable to

---

[32] *See* 5 Williston, A Treatise on the Law of Contracts § 776 (3d ed. 1961).

[33] *E.g.,* AIA Doc. A201, General Conditions of the Contract for Construction, para. 12.1.2 (1976), para. 7.3.1 (1987).

[34] *See* Peter Kiewit Sons' Co. v. Summit Constr. Co., 442 F.2d (8th Cir. 1969); Wunderlich Contracting Co. v. United States, 351 F.2d 956 (Ct. Cl. 1965).

reach agreement as to payment. For example, the clause may provide that, in the absence of an agreement concerning compensation for a change order, the contractor shall be entitled to the costs it reasonably incurred in implementing the change order, together with a specified percentage of that cost for overhead and profit.

Extending time.   The changes clause also should provide for an extension of all time deadlines that may be equitably indicated because of the change. In some instances, the contract time may not need to be extended. The change may not involve additional work, or may involve additional work that can be performed concurrently with work originally included in the agreement. Nevertheless, the changes clause should be broad enough to provide for time extensions when appropriate.

Adjusting price.   It is highly desirable that the changes clause reserve the contractor's right to seek an equitable adjustment in the contract price if the change impacts the contractor's ability to perform *unchanged* work. Although the contractor may be able to estimate the direct cost of performing change order work accurately, its ability to estimate the impact that such work will have on unchanged work may not be as great. In fact, there may be instances in which, despite having taken precautions, the contractor is unable to determine accurately the impact of a series of changes on the unchanged work. Absent contract language clearly reserving the contractor's right to make a subsequent request for these impact costs, the contractor could waive its right to compensation for these costs, or be deemed to have included such costs in the agreed change order price, thereby precluding any subsequent recovery of additional costs incurred by the contractor.

Implementing changes.   It is also important to the contractor that the changes clause designate how a change order is to be authorized. In some cases, an architect, engineer, construction manager, or other owner representative may verbally direct the contractor to proceed with changed work in the absence of any written directive from the owner. Proceeding in good faith, the contractor may incur significant costs, simply to have the owner disavow any such change as being implemented without the owner's authority. Thus, the carefully worded changes clause must set forth the procedure for implementing changes expressly, and give the contractor some protection from a claim of having performed the changed work on a volunteer basis.

§ 5.16   Differing Site Conditions

In most instances, the contractor receives a set of plans and specifications from the owner, and undertakes to construct the project according to those documents for a specific price. Most contracts include requirements that the contractor grade, tunnel, excavate, or otherwise negotiate conditions at or below the surface of the earth. However, it is not uncommon for the contractor to encounter conditions (such as rock or water) that were not readily discernible at the construction site prior to the execution of the contract. Similarly, the contractor that is engaged to renovate, modernize, or rehabilitate an existing structure may encounter conditions within the structure that were not ascertainable prior to construction. In both situations, the contractor may incur additional, unanticipated expense in performing different, and more extensive or difficult, tasks than originally contemplated. The contractor, having had no reason to include the cost of addressing the unforeseen condition in its fixed price, obviously does not wish to perform this extra work for free. On the other hand, the owner that has sought to cap its exposure with a lump sum contract does not want to increase its project cost. However, the question remains: who bears the risk for a condition at the site that is different than what the contractor reasonably expected and bid upon?

Claims due to differing site conditions usually arise in two primary forms: (1) the actual conditions are concealed or unknown and are at variance with those indicated in the contract or (2) although not in conflict with the contract, the conditions are concealed or unknown and could not have been reasonably anticipated by the contractor at the time it prepared the bid and executed the contract. Many standard form contracts contain differing site condition clauses, such as that contained in one of the American Institute of Architects (AIA) documents. Subparagraph 12.2.1 of AIA Document A201, for example, generally provides that the contract sum will be adjusted equitably between the parties if the contractor encounters concealed conditions or unknown conditions that vary from what is indicated in the contract documents. That clause further provides for an adjustment in the contract sum if conditions are encountered by the contractor that materially differ from conditions typically inherent in the type of project being constructed.[35]

The 1987 edition of the A201 form provides that the architect will make an initial determination of whether the contract sum should be adjusted because of differing site conditions. Subparagraph 4.3.6 provides, for instance, that the party observing the conditions that vary from those indicated in the contract documents, or that differ from conditions usually found in work of the character being performed, must give notice to the other party within 21 days of observing the conditions. Under this provision, the architect is then charged with the responsibility of investigating

---

[35] AIA Doc. A201, General Conditions of the Contract for Construction, para. 12.2.1 (1976).

the conditions to determine whether they are differing conditions and whether an increase in the contractor's cost and the time required for performance of the work has occurred.[36]

If the contractor demonstrates that the circumstances fall within the differing site conditions clause, the contractor generally is entitled to an equitable adjustment in the contract price, assuming that the contractor timely notifies the owner. The notice requirement allows the owner to alter its plans or otherwise obviate the necessity for the increased expense.

Beyond question, the contractor needs the protection afforded by a differing site conditions clause similar to that contained in the AIA documents. The clause provides the framework for the contractor to be compensated for work previously unforeseen, while allowing the contractor to refrain from "padding" its contract price with contingencies in order to avoid the risk of loss to which it otherwise may be exposed.

Unfortunately for general contractors, many owners, and particularly public owners, omit such differing site conditions clauses (also frequently referred to as changed conditions clauses) and insist that the contractor bear the risks that such conditions pose. This stringent approach usually includes broad disclaimers by the owner, which specify that any subsurface or other investigative information provided to the contractor must not be relied upon by the contractor, and obligates the contractor to handle any conditions encountered at its own expense. The notion that the contractor will include a contingency for this risk is widely espoused but carries dubious weight when the project is one submitted to competitive bidding and is otherwise attractive from the contractor's point of view.

Clearly, the contractor that can convince the owner to omit such a broad allocation of risk to the contractor is in a better position to receive equitable treatment from the owner if differing site conditions are encountered. However, even when no differing site conditions clause exists, the contractor may be entitled to recover from the owner because the owner is deemed to warrant the adequacy and completeness of its plans and specifications.[37] Plans and specifications not containing accurate information about the condition of the construction site may be deemed inadequate and inaccurate.[38] Nevertheless, courts continue to hold that the contractor that agrees to perform required site work is not relieved of that obligation merely

---

[36] *Id.* para. 4.3.6.

[37] United States v. Spearin, 248 U.S. 132 (1918).

[38] Pittman Constr. Co. v. Housing Auth., 169 So. 2d 122 (La. Ct. App. 1964); Ridley Inv. Co. v. Croll, 56 Del. 208, 192 A.2d 925 (1963). *See also* Annotation, *Ridley Investment Co. v. Croll—Summary of Decision*, 6 A.L.R.3d 1389 (1963); Annotation, *Construction Contractor's Liability to Contractor for Defects or Insufficiency of Work Attributable to the Latter's Plans and Specifications*, 6 A.L.R.3d 1394 (1966).

because it encounters unanticipated difficulties or increased expenses.[39] Therefore, an appropriate changed conditions clause is imperative.

§ 5.17 Delay Issues in General

If the owner, or someone for whom the owner is responsible (for example, the architect or engineer), delays the contractor's performance on the project, the contractor's cost of performance is inevitably increased. The delays may occur as the result of many situations over which the owner or its representatives have control. For example, access to the site may be delayed, owner-supplied equipment may not be delivered in a timely manner, owner decisions may be tardy, the architect's approval of shop drawings or other submittals may be untimely, and legitimate requests for information may go unanswered for unreasonable periods of time. There is probably no limit to the number of causes that foreseeably may delay the contractor's performance.

When delay occurs, it costs the contractor money, regardless of who causes the delay. Every time-related aspect of the project impacts cost. The contractor's field office overhead continues longer than originally anticipated. Insurance policies remain in effect for a longer period, with additional premiums. The need for temporary facilities may be extended at additional cost. In an inflationary economy, almost every expense of the contractor increases when it is incurred at a later point in time.

§ 5.18 —Owner-caused Delay

Principles of equity certainly dictate that the contractor ought to be entitled to compensation for any and all additional costs incurred as a result of owner-caused delays. Further, it is equally compelling that those same principles of equity provide for an extension of the contractor's time for completion of the work to account for the effect of the delay, and an exception to the requirement of paying delay damages to the owner that were occasioned by owner-caused delays.

In the absence of contract language to the contrary, these equitable principles create a right to recover damages against the owner. In the absence of express contract language, courts frequently hold that the owner undertook an implied contractual duty not to hinder or interfere with the contractor's ability to prosecute the work in a timely and efficient manner, and find the

---

[39] W.H. Lyman Constr. Co. v. Village of Gurnee, 84 Ill. App. 3d 28, 403 N.E.2d 1325 (1980); Pinkerton & Laws Co. v. Roadway Express, Inc., 650 F. Supp. 1138 (N.D. Ga. 1986).

owner in breach of that implied duty and in breach of the construction contract.[40]

§ 5.19   —No Damages for Delay Clause

For a number of reasons, owners, and especially public owners, have, during the past few years, increasingly embraced the concept of a no damages for delay clause in an effort to insulate themselves from paying delay damages to the contractor. These clauses generally provide that if the contractor is delayed due to the acts or omissions of the owner, or of someone for whom the owner is responsible, the contractor shall receive an extension of time equal to the period of delay as the sole compensation for the delay. The clause further provides that the contractor expressly waives any right it might otherwise have to any compensation, except for the time extension.

No damages for delay clauses have been litigated in many contexts and in many jurisdictions. They generally are given effect and enforced if the delay is foreseeable and there is no active wrongdoing on the part of the owner.[41] Although courts have not found these clauses to be in violation of public policy, they are closely scrutinized due to their intrinsic harshness.[42] If the clause conflicts with other contract provisions, it may be disregarded.[43]

Exceptions to Enforcement

As a result of the tendency of many courts to strictly construe no damages for delay clauses, several exceptions to enforcement of the clauses have developed. When the delay at issue was not contemplated by the parties in the no damages for delay clause, or when delay constitutes an abandonment of the contract, the contractor may recover damages.[44] In addition, if the

---

[40] *See* Lewis-Nicholson, Inc. v. United States, 550 F.2d 26 (Ct. Cl. 1977); United States v. Guy H. James Constr. Co., 390 F. Supp. 1193 (M.D. Tenn. 1972).

[41] B.J. Harland Elec. Co. v. Granger Bros., 24 Mass. App. Ct. 506, 510 N.E.2d 765 (1987); Phoenix Contracting Corp. v. New York City Health & Hosp. Corp., 118 A.D.2d 477, 499 N.Y.S.2d 953 (1986); Peter Kiewit Sons' Co. v. Iowa S. Utils. Co., 355 F. Supp. 376 (S.D. Iowa 1973); Gottlieb Contracting, Inc. v. City of N.Y., 86 A.D.2d 588, 446 N.Y.S.2d 311 (1982); M.A. Lombard & Son Co. v. Public Bldg. Comm'n, 101 Ill. App. 3d 514, 428 N.E.2d 889 (1981); Ace Stone, Inc. v. Township of Wayne, 47 N.J. Super. 431, 221 A.2d 515 (1966).

[42] F.D. Rich Co. v. Wilmington Hous. Auth., 392 F.2d 841 (3d Cir. 1968).

[43] Shintech, Inc. v. Group Constructors, Inc., 688 S.W.2d 144 (Tex. Ct. App. 1985).

[44] Ace Stone, Inc. v. Township of Wayne, 47 N.J. Super. 431, 221 A.2d 515 (1966); Peter Kiewit Sons' Co. v. Iowa S. Utils. Co., 335 F. Supp. 376 (S.D. Iowa 1973); Blake Constr. Co. v. C.J. Coakley Co., 431 A.2d 569 (D.C. 1981); City of Houston v. R.F. Ball Constr. Co., 570 S.W.2d 75 (Tex. Ct. App. 1978); People *ex rel.* Wells & Newton Co. v. Craig, 232

contractor can prove the owner is guilty of bad faith, or of active interference with the contractor's work, the no damages for delay clause will not be enforced.[45] An example of "active interference" is provided by a decision of the United States Court of Appeals for the Eighth Circuit. In that case, a railroad company owner contracted with a bridge builder to construct a bridge, when the owner had knowledge that the substructure was not yet ready for construction. The contractor, who had made many time-critical commitments upon receipt of the owner's notice to proceed, was delayed in starting for approximately 170 days. In response to the contractor's delay claim, the owner asserted the no damages for delay clause. The court held the owner liable and found that the exculpatory clause did not cover an act of the owner that amounted to active interference.[46]

On the other hand, the State of New York has taken a contrary view of the owner's active interference when a no damages for delay clause exists.[47] In that case, the owner hired the contractor to perform mechanical work under an $8 million contract. The contract contained a clause providing that only a time extension, and no delay damages, would be allowed in the event of owner-caused delay. The contractor sued the owner for delay and attempted to overcome the no damages for delay clause by proving the owner's active interference. The state's highest court reversed a verdict in favor of the contractor, and held that even the owner's active interference would not subject it to liability for delay unless such interference was willful, malicious, or in bad faith.[48]

After the *Kalisch-Jarcho* decision, the New York Court of Appeals recognized the following four exceptions to the enforceability of a no damages for delay clause:

1. Delays caused by the owner willfully or in bad faith
2. Unanticipated delays
3. Delays constituting abandonment of the project by the owner
4. Delays resulting from the breach of a fundamental contract obligation by the owner.[49]

N.Y. 125, 133 N.E. 419 (1921); *see* Hawley v. Orange County Flood Control Dist., 211 Cal. App. 2d 708, 27 Cal. Rptr. 478 (1963).

[45] Coatesville Contractors & Eng'rs, Inc. v. Borough of Ridley Park, 509 Pa. 553, 506 A.2d 862 (1986); John E. Green Plumbing & Heating Co. v. Turner Constr. Co., 500 F. Supp. 910 (E.D. Mich. 1980); Hallett Constr. Co. v. Iowa State Highways Comm'n, 261 Iowa 290, 154 N.W.2d 71 (1967); Allow-Howe Specialities Corp. v. United States Constr., Inc., 611 P.2d 205 (Utah 1980).

[46] United States Steel v. Missouri Pac. Ry., 668 F.2d 435 (8th Cir. 1982). *See also* United States Indus. v. Blake Constr. Co., 671 F.2d 539 (D.C. Cir. 1982).

[47] Kalisch-Jarcho, Inc. v. City of N.Y., 58 N.Y.2d 377, 448 N.E.2d 413, 461 N.Y.S.2d 746 (1983).

[48] *Id. See also* Edwin J. Dobson v. New Jersey, 218 N.J. Super. 133, 526 A.2d 1156 (1987).

[49] Corinno Civetta Constr. Corp. v. City of N.Y., 493 N.E.2d 905, 502 N.Y.S.2d 681 (1986).

In any event, the contractor carries the burden of overcoming the clause by proving, with sufficient evidence, the owner's bad faith, active interference, negligence, or unforeseeable conditions.[50]

Equitable considerations require that the contractor notify the owner of the delay condition, and that the owner be given the opportunity to remove the cause of delay, or acceleration, in order to limit its liability. Absent acts by the owner sufficient to waive the required notice, a requirement that the contractor promptly notify the owner of the contractor's claim generally is enforced.[51]

Finally, it appears that the inherent harshness of the no damages for delay provision is becoming noticed by the legislatures of certain states and, as a result, many states are beginning to prohibit such clauses as being contrary to public policy. Thus, at least three states have prohibited or limited the application of no damages for delay clauses.[52] In those states, the contractor's position should be improved measurably, as the no damages for delay provision is eliminated or severely limited.

§ 5.20   Dispute Resolution

How will differences of opinions on a project, which escalate into disputes, be resolved? Will the architect or engineer be the initial arbiter of the dispute? If all else fails, will the dispute be submitted to arbitration or will it wind up in a court of law? Pending the ultimate resolution of the dispute, what are the contractor's rights and obligations concerning further performance?

Many standard form construction contracts provide that the owner's representative or the architect and engineer, shall be the initial arbiter of disputes between the owner and the contractor. Although exceptions can be found, such clauses are not beneficial to the contractor and, when possible, should be eliminated. In most instances, the owner's representative feels pressured to support the owner's position, and at the conclusion of the dispute resolution process, the contractor will not have received a favorable consideration of its position. Even if pressure from the owner does not impact the architect or engineer's decision, there remains the appearance and suspicion of bias because the owner pays the architect or engineer.

---

[50] Dickinson Co. v. Iowa State Dep't of Transp., 300 N.W.2d 112 (Iowa 1981).

[51] Central Pa. Indus., Inc. v. Commonwealth, 25 Pa. Commw. 121, 358 A.2d 445 (1976); Blankenship Constr. Co. v. North Carolina State Highway Comm'n, 28 N.C. App. 593, 222 S.E.2d 452 (1976); Keith v. Burzynski, 621 P.2d 247 (Wyo. 1980).

[52] See, e.g., Cal. Pub. Cont. Code § 7102 (West 1991); Wash. Rev. Code Ann. §§ 4.24.360–.380 (West Supp. 1983).

§ 5.21   —Agreeing to Arbitrate

In the context of most disputes, the advantages to the contractor of arbitration greatly outweigh any disadvantages, and, similarly, the disadvantages of having to proceed through the judicial system greatly outweigh any advantages it may confer upon the general contractor. From the contractor's perspective, arbitration is a relatively quick, informal means of obtaining a decision concerning its dispute with the owner. The decision is made after the dispute has been heard by one or more arbitration panel members that generally have substantial knowledge of construction issues. Rights of appeal are severely limited; as a result, the ability of the owner to delay the final resolution of the dispute is limited. Similarly, delay tactics frequently employed in the courtroom arena are conspicuously absent from the arbitration process.

On the other hand, it is often suggested that any agreement to arbitrate should include an agreement for limited discovery. Without such an agreement, all parties are susceptible to a potential "trial by ambush." Although limited discovery probably is more beneficial to the contractor than to the owner, it is ultimately in neither party's interest that the dispute be resolved by any means other than the full and complete disclosure to the arbitration panel of all relevant facts by both parties. Because arbitration is permitted as a means of resolving the claim only upon the agreement of both parties, it is strongly suggested that any such agreement contain a procedure by which all parties obtain adequate, although limited, discovery.

§ 5.22   —Continuing to Prosecute Work

Many construction contracts require the contractor to continue prosecuting the work, pending final resolution of any existing disputes. Although there is nothing inherently wrong with this concept, in practice such an obligation can work to the substantial detriment of the contractor. For example, in the event the owner wrongfully fails to make payment to the contractor when payment is due, the contractor that is obligated to continue prosecuting the work may be forced to finance the job to its completion. This circumstance is sufficient to cause financial ruin to many contractors and substantial difficulty to many more. Any obligation to continue the work pending resolution of a dispute should likely be tempered by a provision permitting the contractor to suspend work under certain extreme circumstances, pending resolution of the dispute. Such circumstances would depend on the particular situation and should be tailored by the parties to function in an equitable manner.

For example, in one situation an owner and a contractor agreed that, in the event that the contractor in good faith believed payment in excess of $1 million was being wrongfully withheld by the owner, the contractor would be entitled to suspend performance pending final resolution of the dispute. The agreement further provided that if the contractor prevailed in the amount of $1 million or more, the contractor, in addition to being entitled to the funds withheld together with interest thereon, would be entitled to an extension of time to complete the work equal to the suspension as well as all delay damages occasioned by the suspension. If, on the other hand, resolution of the dispute concluded that the contractor was entitled to less than $1 million or nothing at all, then the contractor would be entitled to no extension of time, would recover nothing from the owner, would pay liquidated damages for the delayed completion, and would not be entitled to any interest on the funds properly withheld. This is but one example of an available method by which the contractor may temper the normal obligation to prosecute the work pending resolution of a dispute.

§ 5.23 Suspension of Work

Although not found in all construction contracts, many contracts contain a suspension of work clause, which provides the owner with the right to suspend the contractor's performance. Such clauses usually provide that the contractor shall be entitled to additional compensation, and any additional time necessary in which to complete the work because of the suspension.

A typical suspension of work clause is contained in ¶ 15.1 of the National Society of Professional Engineers (NSPE) General Conditions, published by the Engineers' Joint Contract Documents Committee (EJCDC). That paragraph generally provides that an owner may, without cause, suspend work on the project for a period of time not to exceed 90 days, simply by notifying the contractor and design professional in writing. The notice, under this provision, would include a specified date for resumption of the work. The contractor is also entitled to an increase in the contract sum and an extension of the time for performance under the NSPE General Conditions clause.[53]

Another example is found in AIA Document A201. Article 14 of the document provides that the owner may, without cause, suspend the work for any period of time the owner may desire. Again, the contractor is entitled to an increase in the contract sum, including profit on the increased costs. Of course, the contractor is not entitled to an adjustment in the contract sum if the contractor simultaneously causes the project to be suspended for another reason or fails to meet other deadlines for filing the claim adjustment.[54]

---

[53] EJCDC, Standard General Conditions of the Construction Contract, ¶ 15.1 (1990).

[54] AIA Doc. A201, General Conditions of the Contract for Construction, paras. 14.3.1, 14.3.2 (1987).

It should be noted that the 1987 edition of the AIA General Conditions is qualified by subparagraph 14.1.1, which provides that the contractor may terminate the contract if the work is stopped for a period of 30 days through no act or fault of the contractor (or those for whom the contractor is responsible), and if repeated suspensions constitute "in the aggregate more than 100 percent of the total number of days scheduled for completion, or 120 days in any 365-day period, whichever is less."[55]

Whatever suspension of work clause may be included, the contractor must ensure that the contract entitles the contractor to compensation resulting from the suspension, and that the contractor is likewise entitled to an extension of time for completion. Furthermore, suspension beyond a reasonable period of time under the circumstances should not be allowed, and the contractor should be allowed to terminate the project in that situation.

§ 5.24　Contract Termination

In the absence of contract language to the contrary, each party is permitted to terminate a construction contract in the event the other party breaches any of its material terms. Nevertheless, given the complexities of the construction process, it is preferable to delineate the termination rights of both parties so that (1) uncertainty is eliminated to a large degree and (2) fair warning is given to the defaulting party such that, when possible, the default may be cured and a potential dispute avoided. Certainly it is not in the interest of either party that contract terminations be commonplace and satisfactory completion the exception.

Thus, the contractor should be sure that its agreement with the owner provides a clear basis for terminating the work if the owner's acts or omissions constitute a material breach of the owner's obligations. For example, the owner's repeated failures to make payment to the contractor in a timely manner may constitute a material breach.[56] In the same vein, the owner's failure and refusal to cooperate with the contractor, and to permit the contractor's performance without hindrance, may constitute grounds for termination.

On the other hand, before the owner is allowed to terminate the contractor's right to proceed, it is only fair that the owner be obligated to give the contractor notice of the claimed breach or default and an opportunity to cure. Procedures clearly setting forth the rights and obligations of both parties in a termination situation permit an orderly procedure for terminating the project, and create an alternative to the chaos and confusion that may result in the absence of such provisions.

---

[55] *Id.* para. 14.1.1.

[56] Burras v. Canal Constr. & Design Co., 740 N.E.2d 1362 (Ind. Ct. App. 1984).

§ 5.25   Frequently Used Contract Forms

A number of organizations and entities have published standard forms of agreement for use by contractors. These groups include the American Institute of Architects (AIA), the National Society of Professional Engineers (NSPE), the Associated General Contractors of America (AGC), the federal government, and many state governments. Although the contractor may have little choice concerning government projects, more flexibility and negotiation may be available when dealing with private owners and developers, and with contract forms promulgated by private entities.

Obviously, the forms used more frequently than any other are those published by the AIA. The forms of the NSPE, though somewhat different in language, are very similar to the AIA forms in substance. Forms promulgated by the AGC are more contractor-oriented and, when utilized, probably benefit the contractor more than any other standard form of agreement.

Both the AIA and the NSPE forms generally are fair and equitable to the general contractor. Nevertheless, no two construction projects are identical. It is highly recommended that, to the extent possible, the contractor review whatever form is sought to be employed. Regardless of how standard a form appears to be, a contractor should attempt to ensure that the concepts discussed in **Chapter 5** are adequately employed for the protection of the contractor.

CHAPTER 6

CONTRACTING WITH THE SUBCONTRACTOR

Stephen G. Walker
Ronald L. Shumway
Stephen D. Butler

Stephen G. Walker is senior counsel of Bechtel Corporation in San Francisco, California, in the legal department's claims group. He received a degree in civil engineering from the Catholic University of America, followed by a law degree from Duquesne University, where he was a law review editor. He is admitted to the bars of Pennsylvania, New York, and California, and is a registered professional engineer in Pennsylvania. Mr. Walker is a member of the American Bar Association's Forum on the Construction Industry and the Construction Contracts Committee of the American Society of Civil Engineers. He is also on the panel of arbitrators of the American Arbitration Association and its Northern California Construction Industry Advisory Committee. He speaks and writes frequently about construction law topics.

Ronald L. Shumway is currently acting as claims counsel in Eurotunnel's London office, seconded there from the Bechtel Corporation Legal Department in San Francisco, California. He is a graduate of Brigham Young University, and received his J.D. from the Duke University School of Law, where he was an editor on the *Duke Law Journal*. Mr. Shumway is a member of the American Bar Association's Forum Committee on the Construction Industry, the Legal Advisory Committee of the Associated General Contractors of California, and speaks frequently on construction topics.

Stephen D. Butler is principal counsel in Bechtel Corporation's Legal Department in San Francisco, California. He is head of the Litigation Group and is responsible for managing Bechtel's litigation. He is a graduate of the University of Arizona, having received degrees in economics and law. He was a member of the editorial board of the *Arizona Law Review*. Mr. Butler is a member of the American Bar Association's Forum on the Construction Industry, the Center for Public Resources Construction Industry Task Force, and a member of the Construction Industry Panel of Arbitrators of the American Arbitration Association.

INTRODUCTION

§ 6.1 Background for Subcontracting

Subcontractors are a necessary part of the construction process, particularly in building construction, in which as much as 90 percent[1] of the work may be performed by subcontract. Despite the necessity of tight coordination and teamwork among the prime contractor and its subcontractors, tension inevitably will exist, expressed in terms of changes in contract and field conditions, disputes over real or imagined contract ambiguities,

---

[1] The prime contract may limit the amount of subcontracting.

undercapitalized or financially-strapped businesses, socioeconomic policies, and differences in approaches to dispute resolution.

Although disputes can be minimized by following established rules and practices, they can never be eliminated altogether. This chapter is intended to develop an acquaintance with these rules and practices, including an equitable approach to risk sharing.[2]

§ 6.2   —Parties to the Process

The parties essential to a discussion of the subcontracting process include the owner, the prime contractor, and the subcontractor. Under some circumstances suppliers are considered as, or have rights correlative to, subcontractors, and to that limited extent suppliers will be discussed in this chapter.[3] Subcontractors of tiers below the level of the first tier (the subcontractor who contracts directly with the prime contractor) also will be discussed and the distinction between first tier and other tiers made when essential to the issue under discussion.

Other affected parties include the design professional, equipment lessors, suppliers, employees, sureties, and lending institutions. All may have rights and obligations that may be asserted or imposed during the tenure of the contractor-subcontractor relationship; thus all may have to be considered when evaluating courses of action as problems arise.

Subcontractors. A *subcontractor* generally is defined as one who has a contract directly with a prime contractor to take a part of the permanent work at the site.[4] A prime contractor is one who contracts directly with one holding title to (or the right to possession of) the property on which an

---

[2] Although this chapter is intended to provide comprehensive treatment of subcontract formation issues, particularly as seen from the viewpoint of the prime contractor, a recent book in the Wiley Construction Law Library covers the entire subcontracting area and encompasses the subcontractor's position as well. *See* Construction Subcontracting: A Legal Guide for Industry Professionals (O. Currie et al. eds., John Wiley & Sons 1991).

[3] Supplier relationships and formation issues are discussed in **Ch. 7.**

[4] Royal Indem. Co. v. Kenny Constr. Co., 528 F.2d 184, 190 (7th Cir. 1975) (citing 17 C.J.S. *Contracts* § 11 (1963)); Richard v. Illinois Bell Tel. Co., 66 Ill. App. 3d 455, 383 N.E.2d 1242 (1978) (interpreting Illinois statute); Yellow Pine Lumber v. Insurance Co. of N. Am., 687 F. Supp. 545, 547 (W.D. Okla. 1988) (citing Clifford F. MacEvoy Co. v. United States *ex rel.* Calvin Tomkins Co., 322 U.S. 102, 64 S. Ct. 890 (1944) (defines subcontractor in Miller Act context)); see **Ch. 21.**

improvement is built.[5] A sub-subcontractor is one who performs part of the work of the subcontractor.[6]

Suppliers.   A *supplier* generally is defined as one who sells tangible goods or materials, or produces equipment, that are consumed or incorporated in the work at the project site, but who performs no work at the site.[7] Furnishing engineers or technicians to oversee installation of equipment normally does not, by itself, convert a supplier into a subcontractor, but even minimal on-site activity may be a factor when considered with other indicia of subcontractor status. However, suppliers of a contractor's capital equipment are not considered material suppliers.[8]

Application of Definitions

These definitions become important when construing the rights of the various parties to the construction process in a variety of contexts, particularly when interpreting a statute that uses these terms. Consequently, there is no general agreement on the precise meaning of the terms.[9]

Sometimes the definitions are difficult to apply, particularly when a statutory meaning differs from traditional concepts. A supplier who furnishes a substantial part of a subcontractor's requirements in accordance with the project plans and specifications may be a subcontractor for mechanic's lien or payment bond purposes in some states.[10] An off-site

---

[5] Battcock v. Duvall, 118 N.H. 81, 382 A.2d 916 (1978) (interpreting New Hampshire statute); Richard v. Illinois Bell Tel. Co., 66 Ill. App. 3d 455, 383 N.E.2d 1242 (1978) (interpreting Illinois statute); Cal. Bus. & Prof. Code § 7026 (West Supp. 1991) (definition under contractor license law).

[6] Schroeder v. C.F. Braun & Co., 502 F.2d 235 (7th Cir. 1974); Indianapolis Power & Light Co. v. Southeastern Supply Co., 146 Ind. App. 554, 257 N.E.2d 722 (1970) (citing Nash Eng'g Co. v. Marcy Realty Corp., 222 Ind. 396, 54 N.E.2d 263 (1944) (interpreting Illinois statute)).

[7] Socar, Inc. v. St. Paul Fire & Marine Ins., 288 S.C. 827, 341 S.E.2d 822 (Ct. App. 1986); Safeco Ins. Co. of Am. v. W.B. Browning Constr., 886 F.2d 807 (6th Cir. 1989); Cal. Bus. & Prof. Code § 7052 (West Supp. 1991).

[8] Continental Casualty Co. v. Clarence L. Boyd Co., 140 F.2d 115 (10th Cir. 1944).

[9] Dupree v. Gaubert Indus., Inc., 277 F. Supp. 321 (W.D. La. 1967).

[10] Piping Specialties Co. v. Kentile, Inc., 229 Cal. App. 2d 586, 40 Cal. Rptr. 537 (1964) (citing *Theisen v. County of L.A.,* 54 Cal. 2d 170, 352 P.2d 529, 5 Cal. Rptr. 161 (1960) (supply contract that was 6.67% of subcontract was substantial; however, supplies were standard items and not designed and manufactured especially for the project, thus making the supplier a "materialman" under California mechanic's lien statute)); Hub Elec. Co. v. Aetna Casualty & Sur. Co., 400 F. Supp. 77 (E.D. Mich. 1975) (supplier who furnished fixtures to electrical subcontractor was considered a subcontractor under Michigan payment bond statute).

concrete supplier in the vicinity of the jobsite may be a supplier for some purposes but not for others.[11]

The distinction between supplier and subcontractor is more than merely academic because entirely different laws apply to the two. Briefly, the Uniform Commercial Code (UCC) governs the purchase and sale of goods (which is the essence of the prime contractor-supplier relationship), and the common or civil law governs the relationship between the prime contractor and the subcontractor.

§ 6.3   —Current Contracting Atmosphere

Any current discussion of subcontracting should be considered against a backdrop of (1) tight competition, both at the prime contractor and subcontractor levels; (2) unrelenting political use of construction to further social and economic policies; (3) the general reputation of the prime contracting community given by subcontractors (whether or not fairly deserved) for sharp practices, such as bid shopping; and (4) a worldwide economy still in a slump after the public and private free-spending era of the 1950s, 1960s, and 1970s.

CONTRACT FORMATION

§ 6.4   Formation of Subcontract

As with the creation of any contract, a valid and binding subcontract requires at least two competent parties, a meeting of the minds, consideration, and lawful subject matter. For the most part, in dealing with construction contracting, the competency of the parties and the legality of the subject matter rarely are contested.

Subcontracts are entered into through bidding, negotiation, or a combination of both. The manner in which the prime contract is formed may influence the decision about which subcontracting method is used, and in some cases subcontracting will be dictated by state law. Generally, however, a prime contractor is free to choose any method.

---

[11] Dupree v. Gaubert Indus., Inc., 277 F. Supp. 321 (W.D. La. 1967) (off-site concrete supplier who delivered concrete directly into forms not a subcontractor for purposes of Louisiana lien law); 29 C.F.R. § 5.2(1)(2) (1990) (under Davis-Bacon Act, batch plant is part of the "site of the work" if it is "dedicated exclusively, or nearly so, to performance of the contract or project, and [is] so located in proximity to the actual construction location that it would be reasonable to include [it]"); see also **Ch. 21**.

§ 6.5   Bidding Process in General

Solicitation of quotes from several prospective subcontractors is perhaps the most time-honored method of determining price. Occasionally a single subcontractor may be selected to negotiate a contract without obtaining bids from others, perhaps because of lack of competition or the desire to preserve a long-standing relationship. Usually, however, competitive bids result in the lowest price.

§ 6.6   —Enforcement of Quotes by Contractor

Under traditional contract principles, one party who wishes to enter into a contract with another makes an offer to the other party, who has the option of accepting or refusing the offer.[12] Another variation is for one party to make an offer, with the other party having the option of accepting by beginning the performance required under the contract.[13] In either case, the party who makes the offer may withdraw that offer prior to acceptance of the offer.[14]

Construction subcontracting, however, does not fit neatly into traditional forms of contracting. When a subcontractor quotes a price for a portion of the work to be performed by the prime contractor, it is normally given just prior to the prime contractor's bid to the owner, that is, before the contractor knows whether it is the low bidder. Because of the need for time for the owner's consideration of its bids and the protests and controversies that sometimes occur, particularly in connection with public bidding, some time may pass before the contractor is in a position to accept the subcontractor's price.

Because of these economic considerations, and contrary to normal contracting principles, the majority rule is that a subcontractor may not withdraw its quote or offer prior to the passage of a reasonable time after the submission of the contractor's bid.[15] However, the contractor must have reasonably relied on the price in formulating its bid.[16] These principles are also

---

[12] E.A. Farnsworth, Farnsworth on Contracts § 3.3 (1990).

[13] *Id.*

[14] *Id.*

[15] Drennan v. Star Paving, 51 Cal. 2d 408, 333 P.2d 757 (1958); Restatement (Second) of Contracts § 87(2) cmt. e, illus. 4 (1981).

[16] Drennan v. Star Paving, 51 Cal. 2d 408, 333 P.2d 757 (1958); Restatement (Second) of Contracts § 87(2) cmt. e, illus. 4 (1981); Montgomery Indus. Int'l, Inc. v. Thomas Constr. Co., 620 F.2d 91 (5th Cir. 1980); Preload Technology, Inc. v. A.B.&J. Constr. Co., 696 F.2d 1080 (5th Cir.), *reh'g denied,* 703 F.2d 557 (5th Cir. 1983); MacIsaac & Menke Co. v. Freeman, 194 Cal. App. 2d 327, 15 Cal. Rptr. 48 (1961).

part of some statutory and other legal mechanisms that have been put in place over the years.

Anti-Bid-Shopping Procedures

The rule that the subcontractor's offer remains valid is not reciprocal, the contractor not being similarly bound to take the subcontractor's quote. This lack of reciprocity can (and subcontractors assure often does) lead to abuses while the prime contractor tries to get subcontractors to lower prices, improve their quotes, or make other concessions. These activities are collectively referred to as "bid shopping."

Largely as a result of lobbying by subcontractor groups, and supported by public agencies who believe that bid shopping is pervasive and results in higher construction costs, statutes have been enacted in several states to eliminate or greatly curtail the practice of bid shopping on public works projects. In addition, some agencies have resorted to bidding mechanisms that also are designed to ensure that adequate competition and an acceptable quality of work are brought to public projects. The federal government, however, has not joined in this effort.

The trade-off in these schemes is that subcontractors are bound by their bids for a certain period after the opening of the general bids by the public owner.[17] This tends to balance the relative advantages otherwise given to subcontractors if they were permitted to withdraw their bids after the prime contractor included them in its general bid to the owner and before the contractor had the opportunity to accept the sub-bids.[18]

Sublisting. The most common form of anti-bid-shopping scheme is the "subcontractor listing" procedure. It requires that the prime contractor list in its bid the names of all subcontractors whose prices are above a stated de minimus percentage of the total contract bid price.[19] The successful prime contractor is bound to enter into subcontracts with the listed subcontractors for the work, subject to a few specified "defaults," such as a subcontractor's failure to obtain a performance bond (if made a condition of acceptance of

---

[17] *See* Drennan v. Star Paving, 51 Cal. 2d 408, 333 P.2d 757 (1958); Restatement (Second) of Contracts § 87(2) cmt. e, illus. 4 (1981).

[18] A subcontractor that refuses to perform in accordance with its quote is liable for damages for breach of contract, measured by the difference between the quote and the price that the contractor must pay to another subcontractor for the same scope and time of performance. Preload Technology, Inc. v. A.B.&J. Constr. Co., 696 F.2d 1080 (5th Cir.), *reh'g denied,* 703 F.2d 557 (5th Cir. 1983).

[19] *See, e.g.,* Cal. Pub. Cont. Code § 4104 (West Supp. 1991).

the subcontractor's quote).[20] The penalties for violation of sublisting laws can be severe. For example, California provides a monetary penalty of up to 10 percent of the subcontract price as well as termination of the prime contract.[21] Violation is also punishable by sanctions under the state contractor licensing law, including fines and suspension or revocation of license.[22] Lastly, a subcontractor whose bid is wrongfully refused may have an independent right to lost profits from the contractor.[23]

Separate bidding.   Another method to prevent bid shopping requires that the names of sub-bidders be submitted directly to the owner. In one state, bids for several subtrades are filed directly with the public agency.[24] The bids of general contractors are submitted a couple of weeks later and must name a sub-bidder from the previously filed sub-bids for each trade.[25] Whoever violates the provisions of the sub-bid law is subject to fine and imprisonment.[26]

Another state requires that the three principal subtrades (electrical, mechanical, and HVAC) bid directly to the public owner, in the same manner as the general contractor.[27] The successful prime contractor then is assigned the responsibility for coordination of the successful three trades along with its own subcontractors.

---

[20] Depending on local statute, other reasons that may excuse the contractor from the obligation to enter into a subcontract may include the subcontractor's failure to execute a contract based on the subcontractor's bid; the insolvency or bankruptcy of the subcontractor; the failure of the subcontractor to perform; the listing of the subcontractor as the result of a clerical error; the subcontractor's failure to be licensed as required by statute; or the determination by the awarding authority that the subcontractor's performance is unsatisfactory. *See, e.g.,* Cal. Pub. Cont. Code § 4107.5 (West Supp. 1991).

[21] Cal. Pub. Cont. Code § 4110 (West Supp. 1991).

[22] *Id.* § 4111. For specific penalties, *see, e.g.,* Cal. Bus. & Prof. Code §§ 7028.3, 7090, 7095, 7099 (West Supp. 1991).

[23] Southern Cal. Acoustics Co. v. C.V. Holder, Inc., 71 Cal. 2d 719, 456 P.2d 975, 79 Cal. Rptr. 319 (1969) (en banc).

[24] Mass. Gen. L. ch. 149, § 44F(1) (1991); *see generally id.,* §§ 44A–H.

[25] *Id.* § 44F(3).

[26] *Id.* § 44J(7).

[27] N.Y. Gen. Mun. Law § 101 (McKinney 1989 & Supp. 1991). Recognizing the savings that could be gained by allowing a general contractor to subcontract the work of these three crafts, the New York City Board of Education was exempt from this statute for its recent five-year capital improvement program. N.Y. Pub. Auth. Law § 1735.1 (McKinney 1989 & Supp. 1991). Predictably, much criticism has been levied against this system by subcontractor and labor organizations. Brown, *Pact Frees $600 Million,* 221 Engineering News-Record 12 (1988).

Promissory Estoppel

Even without anti-bid-shopping laws, subcontractor quotes made to a prime contractor prior to the prime contractor's bid to the owner are generally enforceable for a period of time subsequent to the opening of bids by the owner. The legal doctrine that is the basis for this enforcement is called promissory estoppel,[28] and it had its first recognized application to a construction dispute in a 1958 California case.[29] The doctrine has been accepted in almost every state,[30] with few exceptions.[31]

To be able to enforce a pre-bid quote from a subcontractor, the contractor must use the quote in the development of its bid to the owner.[32] When the contractor is awarded the prime contract, it has a reasonable period from the opening of the bids within which to tell the subcontractor that its quote has been accepted.[33]

Care must be taken not to provide the subcontractor with an opportunity to renege on an improvident bid. For example, evidence of bid shopping could be construed as an indication that the contractor did not rely on the subcontractor's bid. Alternatively, waiting too long to accept the

---

[28] An excellent discussion of this legal doctrine and its practical application to the subcontract formation process is contained in Hughes, *Negotiation between Contractor and Subcontractor,* I Constr. L. Manual 143 (1983) (Associated General Contractors of California); see § **6.48**.

[29] Drennan v. Star Paving, 51 Cal. 2d 408, 333 P.2d 757 (1958).

[30] Restatement (Second) of Contracts § 87(2) (1981); Janke Constr. Co. v. Vulcan Materials Co., 386 F. Supp. 687 (W.D. Wis. 1974), *aff'd,* 527 F.2d 772 (7th Cir. 1976); N. Litterio & Co. v. Glassman Constr. Co., 115 U.S. App. D.C. 335, 319 F.2d 736 (D.C. Cir. 1963).

[31] Home Elec. v. Hall & Underdown Heating & Air Conditioning, 86 N.C. 521, 358 S.E.2d 539 (1987). This case was favorably discussed in S. Sigfreid & M. Lawrence, *Home Electric v. Hall & Underdown Heating & Air Conditioning: Mutuality Remains the Only Solution to the Construction Bidding Problem,* 9 Constr. Law., No. 4, at 3 (Nov. 1989), and drew spirited rebuttal in F. Hughes and W. Hurley, *Home Electric/Hall versus Drennan/Star Paving: Mutuality Is No Substitute for Equity,* 10 Constr. Law., No. 3, at 25 (Aug. 1990), followed by strong support in E. Rowe & A. Gwyn, *Home Electric v. Star Paving Promissory Estoppel Debate: The Rules of Offer and Acceptance Have Not Been Abandoned,* 11 Constr. Law. No. 1, at 6 (Jan. 1991).

[32] *See* Drennan v. Star Paving, 51 Cal. 2d 408, 333 P.2d 757 (1958); Montgomery Indus. Int'l, Inc. v. Thomas Constr. Co., 620 F.2d 91 (5th Cir. 1980); Preload Technology, Inc. v. A.B.&J. Constr. Co., 696 F.2d 1080 (5th Cir.), *reh'g denied,* 703 F.2d 557 (5th Cir. 1983); MacIsaac & Menke Co. v. Freeman, 194 Cal. App. 2d 327, 15 Cal. Rptr. 48 (1961). Should the existence of the quote and its contents ever become an issue, the quote should be in writing and should contain the essential elements of the deal, including whether the furnishing of a performance bond or other security is part of the basis of the bargain.

[33] Davies v. Langin, 203 Cal. App. 2d 579, 21 Cal. Rptr. 682 (1962). What is "reasonable" is a question of fact, dependent on the nature of the contract. Turner v. Mendenhall, 95 Idaho 426, 510 P.2d 490 (1973).

subcontractor's bid will fuel an argument that a "reasonable" waiting period has passed. What is reasonable may vary according to the circumstances; the statutory period in one state for supplier quotes is no later than 90 days from the time of the offer.[34]

Another way to give a subcontractor an excuse to withdraw its offer is to refuse to negotiate. Typically, the subcontractor's quote was given over the telephone; after receiving the award, the contractor then sends its form of subcontract to the successful subcontractor, who may balk at some provisions that the subcontractor claims are not part of the deal. Unless the contractor has conditioned receipt of an offer on the subcontractor's acceptance of the prime contractor's subcontract form, the contractor will have to be prepared to negotiate the terms and conditions with the subcontractor.

Confirmation of Offer

Enforcement of supplier quotes is just as important as enforcement of quotes from subcontractors. The rules are discussed more fully in **Chapter 7**. Some differences do arise, one example being California's version of the UCC,[35] which requires that the contractor make a written confirmation of the supplier's quote to keep it in force during the bidding and award period. Because the distinction between a subcontractor and a supplier is sometimes blurred, a contractor could face a tough decision concerning whether to list a firm that has quoted for work (as a subcontractor) or to confirm the offer in writing (as a supplier).

Aside from the enforcement of quotes, the negotiation process with suppliers is based entirely on the UCC. This process is often called "the battle of the forms," and the rules that govern it, also covered in **Chapter 7**, are considerably different than those for negotiation of subcontracts.

§ 6.7   —Enforcement of Quotes by Subcontractor

As described in § **6.6**, public agencies can wield significant power to force a contractor to use subcontractor quotes on public works projects. In certain instances, however, the subcontractor itself may be able to sue to recover damages when it is not awarded a subcontract, despite the award of the contract to the contractor and the use by the contractor of the subcontractor's price in the contractor's bid.

Breach of statutory duty.   Some states have permitted a subcontractor to recover lost profits and other damages on the ground that the general

---

[34] Cal. Uniform Com. Code § 2205(b) (West Supp. 1991).

[35] *Id.*

contractor breached a duty imposed by law, that is, it violated the sublisting laws. The courts have ruled that, in addition to the penalties provided by statute, the forsaken subcontractor is entitled to recover as if there had been a breach of an agreement that had as its basis the subcontractor's quote.[36]

Agreement.   A subcontractor also might seek to enforce its quote on the basis that the general contractor had promised, expressly or impliedly, to give the subcontractor the job if its quote were low and the general contractor were awarded the project.[37] To avoid disputes over whether such a promise was made, the contractor should be careful not to provide any information to the prospective subcontractor about the ranking or amount of the sub-bids. The law of promissory estoppel requires only notification to the successful subcontractor (not necessarily determined by the lowest price) within a reasonable time after the general bids are opened. Any comment or action that might lead the subcontractor to think it has been awarded the work should be avoided.

§ 6.8   —Presence of Bid Mistakes

Just as occasionally happens after a contractor submits a bid to an owner, a subcontractor may claim that its bid price was the result of a clerical or mathematical (but not judgmental) error. If the contractor should have been alerted to this fact because of an obvious disparity in the prices of the first and second low bidders, the subcontractor is entitled to rescind its bid. When this disparity should be obvious depends on each circumstance.[38]

The subcontractor's right to withdraw its bid in this situation becomes problematical for the prime contractor, who generally is unable to increase its bid price to the owner. It is important, then, to try to minimize the chance of post-bid rescission by being alert during the bidding stage to significant sub-bid disparities. At times this may be difficult, when quotes

---

[36] Southern Cal. Acoustics Co. v. C.V. Holder, Inc., 71 Cal. 2d 719, 456 P.2d 975, 79 Cal. Rptr. 319 (1969) (en banc).

[37] Electrical Constr. & Maintenance Co. v. Maeda Pac. Corp., 764 F.2d 619 (9th Cir. 1985).

[38] In Norcross v. Winters, 209 Cal. App. 2d 207, 25 Cal. Rptr. 821 (1962), the disparity between $4,800 (the low bid) and $7,991 (second-low) was not significant enough to put the contractor on notice of a mistake. The court did say, however, that the opposite result in the lower court also would have been upheld on appeal. The same result obtained in H.W. Stanfied Constr. Corp. v. Robert McMullin & Son, 14 Cal. App. 3d 840, 92 Cal. Rptr. 669 (1971), undoubtedly influenced by the fact that the contractor gave the subcontractor an opportunity to raise its bid price (from $9,384 to $13,261). When the subcontractor later complained that this higher price was still mistaken (compared with a second-low price of $18,500), the court held the subcontractor bound to its bid.

may vary because of the pricing of different scopes, such as because of differences in estimating. For example, some contractors may include staging, crane picks, or housekeeping; others may not.

§ 6.9   Statute of Frauds

One element of contract formation that attracts little attention but is deserving of mention is the requirement that certain contracts be in writing. Commonly known by lawyers as the Statute of Frauds, the law in virtually every state is that contracts relating to land transactions must be in writing and signed by the party against whom the contract is sought to be enforced.[39] This statute also applies to the sale of goods in excess of a stated amount, usually $500, as well as to contracts that will not be performed within one year of their making.[40]

Construction contracts (and, by extension, subcontracts) are not contracts that relate to an interest in land,[41] nor are they generally considered to be for the sale of goods.[42] However, a subcontract that is anticipated to be performed more than a year from the time of its making would come within the Statute of Frauds and, therefore, must be in writing.[43]

Notwithstanding the Statute of Frauds formalities, developments in the law seem to favor enforcement of oral contracts: those based on alleged conversations between the parties and coupled with conduct by the party to be charged, consistent with the notion of a contract and (perhaps) detrimental change of position by the party seeking to enforce the alleged promise.[44]

---

[39] Corbin, 2 Corbin on Contracts § 396 (1950 & Supp. 1991); 72 Am. Jur. 2d *Statute of Frauds* § 44 (1974 & Supp. 1991).

[40] Corbin, 2 Corbin on Contracts §§ 444–459, 467–497 (1950 & Supp. 1991); 72 Am. Jur. 2d *Statute of Frauds* § 3 (1974 & Supp. 1991); U.C.C. § 2-201 (1962).

[41] Schroeder v. Cedar Rapids Lodge No. 304, 242 Iowa 1297, 49 N.W.2d 880 (1951); Burns Bros. Plumbers, Inc. v. Groves Venture Co., 412 F.2d 202 (6th Cir. 1969); Corbin, 2 Corbin on Contracts § 476 n.32 (1950 & Supp. 1991).

[42] *Id.*

[43] Dove Sheet Metal, Inc. v. Hays Heating & Plumbing Co., 249 F. Supp. 366 (N.D. Fla. 1966).

[44] A well-publicized example of this tendency by the courts—and not even a construction case—is the famous Lee Marvin "palimony" case, in which the California Supreme Court held that an oral promise between an unmarried couple to share equally the property accumulated while they lived together constituted an enforceable express agreement. The court also held that courts may employ the doctrine of quantum meruit, or equitable remedies, when warranted by the facts of the case. Marvin v. Marvin, 18 Cal. 3d 660, 557 P.2d 106, 134 Cal. Rptr. 815 (1976).

CONTRACT TERMS

§ 6.10 Contract Terms in General

Many disputes arise during performance over contract terms that were ambiguous or unclear because of careless drafting, inattention to detail, or failure to appreciate the significance of the terms. Plenty of disputes will arise over the application of the terms to the facts that arise during performance; however, an understanding of the principal risk-sharing provisions and care in drafting will help to minimize disagreement over the meaning of the terms themselves.

Some prime contractors and subcontractors have drafted standard forms or use those developed by industry groups.[45] Because most contracting parties accept some negotiation of the form proffered, it is still necessary to understand the purpose of each clause in the contract. In addition, because changes in the law may affect any standard document, having the form periodically reviewed by an attorney is a wise practice.

Sections 6.11 and 6.12, then, discuss the principal risk-sharing clauses of most subcontracts. Examples of some commonly-used language are given to show how construction risks can be allocated. It should be emphasized, however, that these clauses are offered only as examples of the points discussed and not necessarily as complete expressions of the matters of which they are a part. Use of these clauses should be made with the advice of an attorney, preferably one experienced in construction law.

§ 6.11   —Apportionment of Risk

The concept of the parties' attempt to apportion the risks of the work and services to be performed under a subcontract has little meaning when the terms are one-sided. Contractors who must flow down onerous prime contract clauses or who have dominant bargaining power may impose significant risks on a subcontractor. Nonetheless, whether a contractor agrees to negotiate these risks or not, it is important to understand the nature of the risk either being passed on or retained.

When negotiating risk-apportioning clauses, one approach to determine whether acceptance of a risk is reasonable is to determine who is in the best position to control and evaluate the risk. If neither party is in any better position than the other, the party with the least bargaining power is likely to assume the risk.

---

[45] See § 6.48.

§ 6.12   —Complete Flow-Down of Risk

Regardless of how the risks are apportioned, the contractor must assure that the risks assumed under the prime contract that are to be passed on to subcontractors are done so completely, so as not to leave work that may remain unpriced. Many contractors have subcontracted portions of the work to subcontractors, only to find later that the subcontract document did not entirely do the job. There are two principal mechanisms to accomplish this transfer, or flow-down:[46] incorporation by reference of the prime contract terms, or a stand-alone, carefully-tailored subcontract.

Incorporation of Prime Contract Provisions

The easiest way to transfer risk from the prime contract to a subcontract is by simply referring by name or other designation to those clauses and documents in the prime contract for which the contractor wants the subcontractor to be responsible.[47] This can be done generally or specifically, usually a combination of both. For example, a general incorporation clause might state:

> Subcontractor hereby agrees to undertake to the contractor all of the responsibilities that the contractor has undertaken to the owner under the prime contract in connection with the work to be performed under this subcontract, and is similarly entitled to all of the rights that the contractor has against the owner.

This type of clause usually is effective to bind the subcontractor to broad prime contract rights and obligations, such as those in the general and special conditions. Because of the breadth of this language, however, it is often necessary to include references to specific portions of the prime contract. For example, specific reference usually is made to that portion of the technical specifications that the subcontractor will perform.

Other provisions are needed, of course. If the contractor wants to deviate from the payment provisions of the prime contract, a payment clause should be included specifically in the subcontract. Other provisions requiring special treatment should be dealt with similarly.

Stand-alone Subcontract

Subcontracts that stand alone, that is, that contain all of the obligations of the subcontractor without reference to the prime contract, are more

---

[46] For an in-depth discussion of flow-down issues, *see* T. Gary, *Incorporation by Reference and Flow-Down Clauses,* 10 Constr. Law. No. 3, at 1 (Aug. 1990).

[47] *Id.*

difficult to draft than those relying on incorporation by reference. This is because of the need to make sure that every obligation for which the subcontractor is to be responsible has been covered specifically. Despite the risk, some contractors, for example, those who perform a substantial amount of private work, who prefer not to permit their subcontractors to know the terms of their deals with owners, attempt to draft a subcontract that is all-inclusive.

Owner-required Flow-Down

Occasionally the choice to exercise the degree and manner of flow-down is not left entirely to the contractor. Some prime contracts, notably those of the federal government, dictate the flow-down of certain clauses. In a negotiated prime contract, a contractor may seek to remove this obligatory flow-down because of what is perceived as the owner's interference with the contractor's right to contract freely with its subcontractors.[48]

When such flow-down is required, the contractor must examine the terms of the prime contract to determine how the flow-down is to be accomplished. For example, one federal clause provides, in relevant part, the following concerning notice and assistance regarding patent and copyright infringement:

> The Contractor agrees to include, and require inclusion of, this clause in all subcontracts at any tier for supplies or services (including construction and architect-engineer subcontracts and those for material, suppliers, models, samples, or design or testing services) expected to exceed the dollar amount set forth in 13.000 of the Federal Acquisition Regulation (FAR).[49]

Flow-down of this type of clause usually is accomplished simply by including a general incorporation clause described in § **6.12**.[50] Nevertheless, another type of federal clause, regarding special prohibition on employment, seems to require more, providing that "[t]he Contractor agrees to include the substance of this clause, including this paragraph (e), appropriately modified to reflect the identity and relationship of the parties, in all subcontracts exceeding $25,000."[51] A provision like this requires more specific

---

[48] See § **6.30** for a discussion of mandatory flow-down of payment and retention clauses.

[49] FAR 52.227-2(c) (Apr. 1984).

[50] The American Bar Association Section of Public Contract Law has produced model subcontract clauses for federal work. Entitled *Model FAR-Compatible Provisions for Subcontracts under Federal Government Fixed-Price Construction Contracts,* the publication recognizes that "broad flow-down provisions may not in all cases satisfy government requirements or adequately assure that subcontracts reflect the extent to which the parties intend subcontractor rights and obligations to reflect the federal requirements."

[51] DFARS 52.203-7001 (Apr. 1987) (from Department of Defense FAR Supplement).

treatment of the flow-down obligation. It generally means that the clause needs to be substantially copied in the subcontract itself.[52]

As a practical matter, enforcement of mandatory flow-down provisions is rarely initiated by owners. The issue is more likely to be raised by subcontractors who may want the benefit of, say, a payment provision that is more favorable in the prime contract than that in the subcontract. They will likely prevail, inasmuch as they would be considered third-party beneficiaries of the prime contract clause.[53] A complaint to the owner would probably be effective as well.

§ 6.13 Protection with Bonding

Protection against a subcontractor's default should be a part of every contractor's risk management program. The unexpected and precipitous insolvencies of some of the industry's largest subcontractors[54] should be enough to encourage the development of a standard policy that requires bonding or other form of equivalent security in every case. Exceptions should be addressed at the highest levels of management after careful consideration of the circumstances.

Surety bonds are the most common form of security device. They are relatively inexpensive in relation to the financial harm against which they protect, uniformly accepted by contractors in the United States, relatively easy to obtain by subcontractors with established businesses, and sufficient in most cases to provide the required protection. From the subcontractor's viewpoint, bonds are preferable to other security devices that give the contractor more leverage in the resolution of disputes.[55]

Types of Bonds

The principal types of bond security are payment and performance bonds. The premium usually is the same, whether one or both types of bond are required. Thus, even if the prime contract requires only a performance bond, the contractor should ask for both bonds from its subcontractors.

---

[52] The ABA model form of subcontract is in accord.

[53] Bates & Rogers Constr. Corp. v. Greeley & Hansen, 109 Ill. 2d 225, 486 N.E.2d 902 (1985); Pennsylvania Supply Co. v. National Casualty Co., 152 Pa. Super. 217, 31 A.2d 453 (1943).

[54] It doesn't take an old-timer to recall the major financial problems, and in some cases bankruptcies, suffered by such well-known firms as Paul Hardeman, Fischbach & Moore, Lord Electric, and Howard P. Foley. *See, e.g., SPW Corp. Goes Bankrupt,* 214 Engineering News-Record 120 (1985), for a story about the bankruptcy of Sam P. Wallace.

[55] See discussion at **§ 6.15.**

Payment bonds.   A payment bond secures the subcontractor's obligation to pay for the labor and materials furnished to the project by or for the subcontractor. The advantage to the contractor is that this obligation extends to the lowest subtier, just as the contractor's own payment bond protects the owner from payment default at any tier.

Performance bonds.   A performance bond gives a financial guarantee of the subcontractor's obligation to complete performance in accordance with the terms of the subcontract. Because the performance obligation includes payment of labor and material, this bond covers the labor and material payment obligation if a payment bond is not furnished. Nevertheless, because the penal sum of the bond limits the payment obligation of the surety, labor and material payment claims would have to be satisfied out of the same pot as other performance claims.

Most performance obligations, including warranty obligations, are covered by a performance bond. A performance bond is not an insurance policy, however, and thus its coverage does not include insured obligations.

Language of Bond

No matter how routine the process of documenting the receipt of bonds from subcontractors may become, a review of the bond's wording always is important. In fact, the occasional subtle changes in wording should suggest that the form of bond receive the attention of counsel or an insurance professional.

Examination of Surety

As with the bond language, the surety should be examined carefully. Certain companies have immediate name recognition, but checking the financial responsibility of the surety against respected industry sources is important. One source is the *A.M. Best Company Key Rating Guide.* Published semi-annually, it contains two types of rating: Classes 1 through 15, and C through A+, with the highest rating being 15/A+.

Another source is published annually by the United States Treasury Department[56] and contains those sureties who are approved as sureties on bonds furnished by government contractors. However, the government disclaims any guarantee of the creditworthiness of any of the listed sureties. A more immediate (and probably more reliable) source of surety reliability is the contractor's own broker or surety.

---

[56] The list is published each July in the Federal Register and contains the bond qualifying limits for each listed surety.

§ 6.14 —Exceptions to Bonding

Every contractor should have a well-developed policy to address a subcontractor's inability or failure to furnish a bond.[57] Two questions arise: (1) Are alternate forms of security available? (2) If not, should the subcontractor be permitted to perform the work? Considerations involving the first question are dealt with in § 6.15.[58] Whether a subcontractor should be retained in the absence of adequate security, however, requires an in-depth analysis of the circumstances.[59]

Any investigation into the subcontractor's affairs should be conducted against a backdrop of skepticism. After all, the inability to obtain a bond is almost always related to financial problems. Therefore, the increased risk of default must be considered in evaluating the subcontractor's low price. In addition, it is always helpful to keep in mind what the surety industry calls the *Four Cs:* character (reputation), capacity (to perform the work), credit, and capital (to finance the work).

Several areas should be examined before the contractor agrees to accept an unbonded subcontractor. One area is the difference between the subcontractor's bid and that of the next low sub-bidder. A subcontractor who starts the project with a deficit is more likely to have financial problems than if performance were under a sound bid, problems that will undoubtedly exacerbate the financial conditions that led to unbondability in the first place.

The subcontractor's work on other projects as well as the availability of assets that might be used in conjunction with some of the bonding alternatives discussed in § 6.15 may be a fruitful source of information about performance or financial problems. Defective work, delays, large claims, significant bid disparities, and poor quality of backlog are just a few of the signals that might forewarn the contractor of pervasive difficulties.

Audited financial statements, reviewed by a competent financial analyst, should disclose trends in business, backlog, credit lines, taxes, the amount and type of loans, encumbered assets, mortgages and other security devices, and the character and timing of accounts receivable. An inquiry should be made of the makeup of accounts receivable because standard accounting practice is to recognize the probable recovery value of claims, even though several years may pass before that value is finally realized.

The subcontractor's reputation among banks, owners, contractors, and suppliers should not be overlooked. If the subcontractor is a union firm, the

---

[57] For in-depth treatment of the subject concerning exceptions to bonding, *see* R. Shumway & S. Walker, *Practical Alternatives When Your Subcontractor Client Cannot Bond,* 8 Constr. Law. No. 3, at 30 (Aug. 1988).

[58] See §§ 6.15 through 6.18.

[59] This discussion presumes that acceptance of the subcontractor's quote was predicated on a promise at the time the work was quoted that bonds would be furnished if required. See § 6.6.

trustee of the health and welfare fund would likely not be reluctant to provide information about the subcontractor's payment status, particularly if the record is unsatisfactory.

§ 6.15   Protection with Other Security Devices

Although bonding is the preferable method to secure a subcontractor's payment and performance obligations, other devices may be available when bonding is not feasible or desired. Because they deviate from the norm, however, the instruments that are the vehicles of these alternative methods should be examined by counsel.

§ 6.16   —Letters of Credit

One of the most acceptable bonding alternatives is the letter of credit, often referred to as an "L/C". A *letter of credit* is a bank's promise to pay an amount on demand up to the limit of the letter if the prime contractor alleges that the conditions upon which payment is to be made are fulfilled. An unconditional letter of credit is simply a letter of credit with no conditions attached: the bank must pay if the contractor so demands.

From the contractor's viewpoint, the letter of credit instrument is in many ways even preferable to a bond. Although a surety usually takes the position of its principal in a dispute (at least until its principal is proven wrong or the principal's financial stability is in question), and thus the alleged default is not promptly cured, the issuing bank on an unconditional letter of credit has an absolute obligation to pay on demand. This "on demand" feature of the letter of credit is disadvantageous to subcontractors: the amount of the letter of credit is a liability on the subcontractor's balance sheet.

Another characteristic of letters of credit is a notice provision whereby the contractor must give the subcontractor advance warning of an intent to call in the letter of credit. Even without the notice, however, the contractor must be able to demonstrate that the grounds upon which a call on the letter is made are valid. Just because the subcontractor files for bankruptcy protection does not insulate the contractor from inquiry, particularly if the trustee or debtor in possession believes it can recover from the contractor.

§ 6.17   —Escrow and Security Agreements

Various forms of escrow arrangements or security agreements also can provide substitute security for the prime contractor. In an *escrow arrangement,* certain assets of the subcontractor (usually cash or marketable securities) are handed over to a third person (usually a bank), who is given the authority to hold the assets pursuant to written instructions signed by each party. The instructions provide, for example, that the subcontractor may not retrieve any of the assets until the subcontract has been fully performed. In the event of the subcontractor's default, all or part of the assets are to be turned over to the contractor, who may sell them to satisfy the debt.

A *security agreement* has its basis in the UCC and allows the subcontractor to grant a security interest[60] in specified assets, which can include everything from personal property to a right to receive money in the future. To be effective against other potential creditors, the security interest must (1) be "perfected"[61] by filing a financing statement with a specified government functionary (most often the secretary of state, but sometimes others as well, such as a county clerk); and (2) hold a priority ahead of other creditors, either by being filed earlier than other secured interests, or having some other priority granted by the UCC, such as a purchase money security interest.[62]

When real estate is the asset given to secure the subcontractor's performance, a mortgage or deed of trust (depending on the practice in the jurisdiction) is the instrument signifying the contractor's security. Rights and remedies vary, but, in general, a default by the subcontractor will allow the contractor to follow certain steps to sell the property, retain sufficient proceeds to retire the debt, and turn over everything remaining to the subcontractor.

§ 6.18   —Financial Controls

Involvement in the subcontractor's purse strings will provide protection to some extent against improper disbursement of project-related revenue. None of the customary methods are fool-proof, either singly or in combination. But they do remind the subcontractor of the contractor's continuing monitoring of the subcontractor's performance and payment obligations.

Retention.   One possible control that must be exercised carefully is increased or prolonged retention, at least when statutory limits are not imposed. Because in building construction a 10 percent retention likely

---

[60] *See* U.C.C. § 9-201.

[61] *See, e.g.,* U.C.C. §§ 9-203, 9-204, 9-302.

[62] U.C.C. § 9-107. This priority can be made to apply to the contractor who provides, in some form or other, mobilization or other advance payment that allows the subcontractor to commence its portion of the work. In this way, the contractor's right to the tangible results of that advance payment can come ahead of banks and other lenders of the subcontractor.

contains not only anticipated profit but also overhead, the subcontractor's working capital is somewhat diminished even under normal industry retention practices. Accordingly, increasing the retention only worsens the subcontractor's cash flow and may prevent any opportunity at all for satisfactory performance on the project.

Control of payments. Another fiscal measure is to control payments to known sub-subcontractors and material suppliers by direct or joint payment. Direct payments give better assurance that potential lien and payment bond claimants have been paid, but care must be taken to avoid unwittingly admitting direct responsibility for these payments, particularly when a creditor does not have lien or payment bond protection. In any event, the contractor should obtain lien waivers and releases from each of the payees.

Right to audit. Finally, most of the alternatives to bonding cannot be properly implemented or monitored unless the subcontract provides for the contractor's right to audit the books and records of the subcontractor at any time during performance of the work. The audit rights should be broad and should include all books and records of the business, including those at the home office.

All of these alternatives to bonds require active participation of the subcontractor's counsel, and call for an unusual blend of construction law and commercial expertise so that the interests of both parties are balanced. An overreaching contractor unwittingly may so financially cripple the subcontractor as to prevent performance, thereby causing the exact problem the contractor wanted to avoid.

§ 6.19 Establishment of Labor Policies

Construction labor law[63] is a very specialized area that, even when confined to the prime contractor-subcontractor relationship, requires substantial understanding and experience to be able to deal adequately with the issues that can arise.[64] Nevertheless, general advice can be given about some of the more common labor clauses usually appearing in subcontracts.

Two principal areas of concern are labor harmony and the obligation to obey federal, state, and local laws regulating the employment of workers, including prevailing wage and safety laws. However, these issues must be

---

[63] See **Chs. 11** and **12** for discussion of related labor law issues.

[64] *See, e.g.,* C. Morris, The Developing Labor Law, Chs. 4, 26 (2d ed. 1983).

evaluated against a backdrop of the prime contractor's own labor policies. If the contractor is union, for example, its ability to accept proposals from, say, a nonunion subcontractor may be affected.

§ 6.20   —Maintenance of Labor Harmony

One of a prime contractor's most important concerns on a jobsite is maintaining labor harmony. Few jobsite disputes can disrupt a job more and have more long-term repercussions than one stemming from labor contract interpretations or jurisdictional conflicts. A subcontract clause that anticipates these disputes and provides a mechanism for their resolution will go a long way toward mitigating adverse impact on jobsite relations and productivity.

Union Issues

Many issues arise when the prime contractor is signatory to collective bargaining agreements. A straightforward way to ensure compliance with these agreements is to require the subcontractor to comply with the provisions of the agreements executed by the contractor or on its behalf (for example, by a trade association or project owner). In particular, work assignment, jurisdictional and other dispute settlement, and hiring clauses are important.

An oft-encountered requirement in union agreements is the obligation to make union trust fund payments for the fringe benefits of the union employee. Because many laws impose upon prime contractors the responsibility for the trust fund payments of their subcontractors,[65] it is important that the requirement for payments be flowed down in the subcontract.

Because obligations under labor agreements usually flow down to the lowest subcontract tier, a union contractor must require that the subcontractor further flow down the labor clause provisions into its subtiers. Failure to do so may make it difficult to require subtiers to comply without additional compensation or other concessions.

Open Shop Issues

Open shop issues may arise when a union contractor contemplates the use of nonunion subcontractors, or when a nonunion contractor wants to solicit

---

[65] 40 U.S.C. § 276a (1988); 40 U.S.C. §§ 270a–d (1988); Sherman v. Carter, 353 U.S. 210, 77 S. Ct. 793 (1957); Cal. Civ. Code §§ 3111, 3158, 3181 (Deering Supp. 1991).

quotes from union subcontractors. Both circumstances are problematical, but the implementation of the former is more difficult than the latter.

A clause in a labor agreement that impinges on the flexibility of a union prime contractor to subcontract with open shop firms is a so-called "wall-to-wall" subcontracting clause in the labor agreement. The courts generally have upheld the effectiveness of such clauses, which prohibit a union prime contractor from contracting with a nonunion subcontractor, even if the crafts hired by that subcontractor are different from those with whom the prime contractor has agreements.[66]

In the absence of a wall-to-wall prohibition, a union contractor should impose a requirement on the nonunion subcontractor that its employees work in harmony with other workers on the project, some of whom might be union trades. Failure to maintain harmony will give the contractor the right to terminate the subcontract.

A nonunion subcontractor generally is free to subcontract to a union firm.[67] Nonetheless, a labor harmony clause as described should be included in each subcontract, union and nonunion, so that the contractor has the ability to quell labor disturbances.

§ 6.21   —Payment of Prevailing Wages

Both the federal government and virtually every state have laws that require the payment of minimum wages on public projects.[68] Like the clause in the labor agreement used by unions to enforce the payment to health and welfare trust funds through several subtiers of subcontractors, governments can look to the prime contractor for the prevailing wage deficiencies of its subcontractors of any tier.[69]

In addition to prudent business practices that strive to weed out financially-irresponsible subcontractors, subcontract clauses are needed to impose the obligation of paying prevailing wages to covered workers. One way to see that the clause is being adhered to is to require certified payrolls. Additionally, to minimize the risk that lower tiers might default in paying the minimum wage set by law, the subcontract should require the further flow-down of this clause in lower tier subcontracts.

---

[66] Connell Constr. Co. v. Plumbers Local 100, 421 U.S. 616, 95 S. Ct. 1830 (1975).

[67] Id.

[68] Federal projects are governed by the Davis-Bacon law, 40 U.S.C. § 276a (1988). California's requirements are found at Cal. Lab. Code § 1774 (West Supp. 1991).

[69] 40 U.S.C. § 276a (1988); Cal. Lab. Code § 1775 (West Supp. 1991). Of course, the contractor can recover from delinquent subcontractors on whose behalf it makes payments and incurs penalties. See, e.g., Cal. Lab. Code § 1729 (West Supp. 1991).

§ 6.22   Time-related Responsibilities

One of the most common contract disputes is over the responsibility for delay in performance of the work. Although this handbook deals with the practical considerations that arise once the dispute over delays has arisen,[70] it is important to address delay issues in the subcontract. Understandably, of course, much of what is dictated to the subcontractor is flow-down from the prime contract. But many issues arise that are independent of the prime contractor's obligations to the owner.

§ 6.23   —Material Obligations

The concept of materiality in contracts generally refers to the degree of importance of a contract clause or level of responsibility of one of the parties.[71] It recognizes that, although all obligations contained in a contract must be fulfilled, some requirements are more important than others. For example, the duty to complete the work on time becomes a material obligation when the contract contains a time is of the essence clause.

When time is of the essence, a subcontractor's failure to complete the work in a timely manner is a material breach of contract.[72] However, provisions that set forth the damages for which a subcontractor is responsible for late completion have ameliorated the effect of time is of the essence clauses.[73] Consequently, a contractor may not invoke the usual remedies for material breach of contract because the damages for such breach already have been agreed to.[74]

---

[70] See **Ch. 21**.

[71] Restatement (Second) of Contracts § 241 (1981) lists five circumstances that are significant in determining whether a breach of contract is material:
1. Extent of injury to the nonbreaching party
2. Extent to which the injured party can be compensated
3. Extent to which the breaching party will suffer forfeiture
4. Likelihood that the breaching party will cure the default or breach
5. Extent to which the breaching party evidences good faith and fair dealing.

[72] General Sprinkler Corp. v. Loris Indus. Developers, Inc., 271 F. Supp. 551 (D.S.C. 1967); City of Larkspur v. Marin County Flood Control Dist., 168 Cal. App. 3d 953, 214 Cal. Rptr. 689 (1985).

[73] Vermont Marble Co. v. Baltimore Contractors, Inc., 520 F. Supp. 922 (D.D.C. 1981).

[74] *Id.*

§ 6.24   —Delay Provisions

The extent to which a subcontractor should be responsible for delays to the work should be at least coextensive with the contractor's obligation to the owner for delays to the project as a whole. A subcontract provision that attempts to enumerate the delays for which a time extension will be granted runs the risk of either being too broad, entitling the subcontractor to relief that is not similarly granted to the contractor under the prime contract, or too narrow, requiring damages or acceleration for the subcontractor-caused delays that the owner does not require of the prime contractor.

A contractor with an aggressive schedule who plans to complete the project early (and has estimated a corresponding reduction of overhead in its bid) may not want to flow down all of the excusable delay provisions of the prime contract. If this strategy is augmented by holding the subcontractor to the prime contractor's schedule, the likelihood of successful early completion is enhanced.

§ 6.25   —Damages for Late Completion

Like the imposition of time requirements, it is important to pass through to the subcontractor, to the extent that the subcontractor is responsible for the delay, the damages that the contractor may be liable for in the prime contract for late completion. If the prime contract is silent about the amount of damages, a general flow-down clause is sufficient to accomplish the transfer of this liability. If a stated amount for each day of delay, usually called liquidated damages,[75] is provided, then that amount should be passed through to the subcontractor.

In addition to flowing down the owner's damages from the prime contract, the contractor must make sure that it asserts the right to recover its own damages resulting from the subcontractor's inexcusable delays. The parties may agree on a liquidated amount; because of the fluctuation of the contractor's overhead during the course of performance, however, the contractor might prefer to provide for general delay damages liability.

Both owner and contractor damages resulting from the subcontractor's unexcused delays, whether or not liquidated, can be made to be the subcontractor's responsibility through a clause like the following:

> For any unexcused delay to the prime contract work for which the subcontractor is responsible, the subcontractor shall be liable to the contractor for all damages, including consequential and liquidated damages, sustained by the contractor or for which the contractor is or may be liable to the owner or others.

---

[75] See **Ch. 24** for a discussion of liquidated damages.

The other side of the coin is the issue of the subcontractor's entitlement to damages when its work is delayed through the acts or omissions of the owner or the contractor. The contractor should make sure that the subcontractor's right to damages for delay caused by the owner, if any, should be no greater than the contractor's right to recover those damages directly from the owner. Thus the flow-down should parrot the language of the prime contract.

For contractor-caused delays, whether the contractor should exculpate itself from the subcontractor's right to damages is a business judgment. A contractor would be hard-pressed to disclaim such delay damages when, at the same time, it is asserting a right to delay damages when the subcontractor is late. One way to avoid the issue is to maintain silence in the subcontract and leave the determination to prevailing law. For those who prefer predictability, however, it is better to address the issue expressly.

§ 6.26   —No Damages for Delay Clause

A *no damages for delay* clause[76] is one in which one party disclaims responsibility for damages for delays that the party causes to the other party. When the owner disclaims such damages, all the contractor can do is flow down this provision, and leave to the subcontractor (and perhaps to the contractor itself as well) the argument about the ineffectiveness of such a clause. However, a contractor who wishes to impose such a limitation on the subcontractor's right to recover damages for contractor-caused delays should be aware of the reluctance with which most courts enforce no damages for delay clauses.[77]

§ 6.27   —Following a Project Schedule

Responsibility for meeting completion dates is monitored by an accurate and well-maintained schedule. Two competing issues arise: (1) the subcontractor's responsibility to follow the contractor's schedule and (2) the contractor's disclaimer of the subcontractor's right to rely on the project schedule. Generally, the contractor cannot have it both ways.

Correlative to the subcontractor's obligation to follow a schedule is its right to rely on the schedule as well. A contractor who shows a conservative schedule to an owner and a more aggressive schedule to a subcontractor is only asking for trouble. Because the critical path (the shortest activity path from commencement of the work through completion) is shorter for the

---

[76] An in-depth discussion of this subject is contained in **Ch. 20.**

[77] *Id.*

latter schedule, the subcontractor may be entitled to a time extension (and maybe even damages) for a delay that would be off the critical path on the more conservative schedule.

Good contract (and subcontract) administration is facilitated with a contract clause that binds the subcontractor to the project schedule furnished to the owner. Such a clause also requires the subcontractor to furnish information about the progress of the work and to notify the contractor when any act or occurrence causes a change in the logic or duration of the schedule. A clause that accomplishes these objectives follows:

> Subcontractor shall be bound by, and shall be entitled to a copy of, the project schedule and any updates furnished by contractor to owner. Subcontractor shall provide schedule information about its work to contractor for inclusion in the contractor's schedule. Subcontractor shall report promptly to contractor any changes in work sequence or logic or the duration of any of its activities.

§ 6.28   Payment Policy Issues

No contract issue between a prime contractor and a subcontractor is more loaded with controversy than payment. Pay when paid clauses, prompt payment provisions, withholding provisions, and lien waivers provide fodder for disputes during negotiation of the subcontract terms.

A discussion of these issues requires a balancing of the interests of both parties, which means that what might be appropriate in one negotiation may not be in another. In other words, although a contractor might have a stated policy with respect to various payment issues, that policy might have to be reexamined when circumstances require.

§ 6.29   —Pay When Paid Clause

Many subcontract forms contain a provision that attempts to condition the contractor's obligation to pay for the subcontractor's work on receipt of payment from the owner for that work.[78] Whether such a clause is effective or not depends on its language. Because courts are reluctant to uphold all but the most well-drafted clauses, a contractor must consider whether it is worth the subcontractor's resistance during negotiation of the subcontract and possible perception by subcontractors of unfairness to include a clause that, in the end, might not accomplish the contractor's purpose.

The contractor's rationale for using such a clause is that it is not in the position of a banker; it cannot be responsible for the financial vagaries of the

---

[78] See also **Ch. 19.**

marketplace. The subcontractor, on the other hand, is at least two steps removed from the source of funding; thus the contractor is in a better position to evaluate the creditworthiness of the owner. In addition, nonpayment can result from the contractor's own financial problems, or from the owner's withholding, for many reasons other than the fault of the subcontractor.

If a contract is properly managed and payments are closely followed, the risk of nonpayment from the owner to either the contractor or the subcontractor should be the amount of work performed during any pay period. Most prime contract payment clauses provide 30 days between receipt of an invoice and payment to the contractor. If payment is not timely received, the contractor may be able to take immediate steps to assure payment without incurring further risk.[79]

A compromise and fair position is to limit the subcontractor's risk of nonpayment solely to the insolvency, bankruptcy, or financial inability of the owner. Arguably, today it is just as easy for a subcontractor to evaluate the ability of an owner to pay as it is for the contractor to make the evaluation. A clause that would accomplish the desired results would be along the following lines:

> All payments to subcontractor shall be made _____ days after receipt by contractor of payment from owner that encompasses the work performed by subcontractor for which payment is to be made. Contractor's liability to subcontractor for any such payment is absolutely contingent upon receipt of payment from owner. However, when payment from owner is delayed or otherwise not forthcoming for reasons beyond the control of and without the fault of subcontractor, except when nonpayment is the result of the owner's bankruptcy, insolvency, or financial inability, subcontractor shall nonetheless be entitled to payment.

§ 6.30   —Retention

Good financial management requires that some amount of money be withheld from the subcontractor from each pay requisition. Besides the fact that the owner will be withholding some percentage of the contractor's own progress payments (a portion of which, of course, belongs to each subcontractor who has performed work during the period for which payment is made), the contractor needs to make sure that a sum of ready cash is available both as protection against monetary loss from subcontractor deficiencies in payment and performance (particularly if the subcontractor is not bonded) and as an incentive to the subcontractor to perform the work timely and completely.

---

[79] See **Ch. 15** for a discussion of the contractor's remedies against the owner in the event of nonpayment.

Contract Provisions

Retention (sometimes also called retainage) is so well-entrenched in the construction industry that arguments over its use generally revolve around the amount of retention and the circumstances of its cessation and ultimate release. The percentage of withholding by the owner from the prime contractor usually is the standard against which the subcontractor's percentage is measured, and the diminution and release of retention often is based on the prime contract provisions as well.

A decision to withhold a percentage different from that under the prime contract may well be based on legitimate business considerations. For example, suppose the prime contract requires withholding retention of 10 percent of each progress payment, with cessation of such withholding upon 50 percent completion of the project if satisfactory progress has been made. Full payment of the retention is to be made upon substantial completion, less an amount sufficient to protect the owner against completion of punch list work.

When a subcontractor is unable to obtain a bond, the contractor often is tempted to increase the retention amount and withholding period.[80] A warning has been given against unduly increased and prolonged retention as a cure for nonbondability.[81] In the same way, a clause that gives the contractor the right to increase retention or to delay its release during the subcontractor's performance may be of little help when it is needed. Otherwise satisfactory performance often falters for lack of cash flow, making it ill-advised for the contractor to stifle the flow of money.

Retention of 10 percent of the subcontractor's payment requisition is consistent with industry standards. A better way to increase the contractor's protection against deficiencies in performance than to increase the retention amount is to defer the release of retention until substantial or final completion. A contractor always can waive this written requirement in specific cases, and its use normally will not unduly impinge upon the subcontractor's cash flow. However, the contractor should expect that the subcontractor's cost of capital during this deferred period will be included in the subcontract price.

Statutory Requirements

In some states, a contractor's freedom to negotiate retention provisions is limited by laws that circumscribe the scope of retention. For example, one

---

[80] See § **6.14.**
[81] See § **6.18.**

state restricts subcontractor retention to 5 percent of the subcontract amount on public projects.[82]

In addition to the amount of retention, a few states require that even the subcontractor has the right to furnish securities in lieu of retention[83] or to have the retention placed in an interest-bearing account, with the earnings to accrue to the account of the subcontractor.[84]

§ 6.31   —Periodic Payment Provision

Periodic payments, that is, those made during the course of the performance of the work and prior to final payment, generally lag by a few days the payment from the owner to the contractor.[85] This well-recognized practice helps the contractor to maintain a positive cash flow. Nevertheless, restrictions in its use may be imposed by statute. In any event, prior to making a periodic payment, the prudent contractor will want to ensure that the subcontractor has paid all labor and material suppliers that have bond or lien rights against the project or the contractor (directly or indirectly).

Statutory Requirements

The last few years have brought a wave of legislation that has restricted the length of time within which contractors can hold a subcontractor's money after receipt from the owner. Generally labelled *prompt payment statutes* (a name also given to similar recent statutes that apply to payments from owners to contractors) and applying mostly to public projects, they impose interest penalties for late payment of undisputed amounts.[86] Limitations may be placed on the amount of withholding permitted for disputed sums.[87]

---

[82] Wash. Rev. Code § 60.28.010 (3) (1990).

[83] *Id.* § 60.28.010 (4).

[84] *Id.* §§ 60.28.010 (2)(b), (3).

[85] The AGC Doc. 600, standard Subcontract for Building Construction, para. 5.2.5 (1984) provides that payments to the subcontractor shall be made no later than seven days after receipt of payment by the contractor from the owner. The AIA Doc. A401, Standard Form of Agreement between Contractor and Subcontractor, para. 11.3 (1987) provides three working days between receipt of payment from the owner and payment to the subcontractor.

[86] 31 U.S.C. § 3904 (b) (Supp. 1991); N.Y. State Fin. Law § 139-f.2 (McKinney 1989 & Supp. 1991); Cal. Pub. Cont. Code § 10262.5 (West Supp. 1991) (public works); Cal. Civ. Code § 3260 (West Supp. 1991) (private works).

[87] Cal. Pub. Cont. Code § 10262.5 (West Supp. 1991) (public works); Cal. Civ. Code § 3260(b) (West Supp. 1991) (private works).

These laws, however, do not proscribe the contractor's use of reasonable means to assure that statutory claimants have been paid.[88] They also usually permit the contractor to withhold amounts pursuant to subcontract provisions pertaining to, for example, uncorrected defective work.[89]

Partial Lien Releases and Waivers

During the making of periodic payments, the cautious contractor will want protection against the subcontractor's failure to flow money down to its employees, suppliers, lower-tier subcontractors, and a host of other potentially troublesome creditors of the subcontractor, some known, some unknown, and some unknowable.[90]

One reasonable protection against some (but clearly not all) of those creditors can be obtained by requiring regular lien releases and waivers, not only from the subcontractor, but also from lower-tier subcontractors and suppliers.[91] Many prime contracts require a certification (and sometimes partial lien releases and waivers) that all of the prime contractor's labor and material has been paid for; the contractor often passes the same requirement to its subcontractors to be sure that payments for their labor and material will not have to be made twice.

This well-established procedure puts a financially-pressed subcontractor in the position of having to certify payment to those covered by the partial lien release and waiver when, often as a practical matter, it is the very payment for which certification is being made that is needed to pay for labor and material covered by the certification. In response to a case that struck down a waiver reciting that payment had been received from the prime contractor (when in fact it had not), California passed a statutory scheme

---

[88] Cal. Pub. Cont. Code § 10262.5(b) (West Supp. 1991).

[89] *Id.*

[90] A regularly-updated list of these creditors will help identify some knotty problems that can arise when claims arise late in the project, when payments from the prime contractor may be ahead of the subcontractor's actual performance. Although early notice from a potential creditor is helpful to a contractor (e.g., Cal. Civ. Code §§ 3097 (private works), 3098 (public works) (within 20 days of first furnishing labor or material)), under some statutes notice need not be given until after performance has been completed (e.g., 40 U.S.C. § 270b(a); Cal. Civ. Code § 3091 (both within 90 days of last performing labor or furnishing material for action against payment bond)). For further examples, *see* R. Shumway & S. Walker, *Practical Alternatives When Your Subcontractor Client Cannot Bond,* 8 Constr. Law. No. 3, at 30, n.13 (Aug. 1988).

[91] The date of lower tier releases obviously will lag the prime contractor-subcontractor payment cycle by some necessary amount, but the date through which lower tiers are "paid in full" should be in the neighborhood of 30 days after the subcontractor is paid. Anything older than 60 days represents an unacceptable risk to the prime contractor and should set off alarm bells in the contractor's financial controls.

that dictates the form of waiver and release to be used, depending on whether payment is conditional (upon receipt of and successful negotiation of the payment) or unconditional (after receipt of the payment).[92]

As a matter of contract administration, the contractor should never forget that lien waivers and releases are only part of a system for monitoring the payment and performance activities of the subcontractor.

§ 6.32   —Final Payment Requirements

Considerations for final payment are much the same as those for periodic payments; however, they take on more seriousness, for no further opportunity exists to maintain a ready supply of cash for correcting later-discovered defective work, paying legitimate project-related debts, or satisfying any other unfulfilled obligation under the subcontract.

Statutory Requirements

Statutory requirements for final payment generally are the same as those for periodic payments, which are usually based on the passage of a specific time period after the contractor receives payment from the owner.[93] However, because most final payments to the contractor are designed to be made no earlier than the latest time for laborers and material suppliers of any tier to file liens or claims, the contractor usually is protected by these statutes as well.

Final Lien Releases and Waivers

The principal distinction between lien releases and waivers for final payment and those for periodic payments is the finality of the former. Although the distinction seems a bit obvious, this is the point in the project when a subcontractor is faced with either pursuing claims or executing a final release and accepting final payment.

It is still at the contract formation stage, however, when the contractor must decide what a subcontractor may be permitted to do at project closeout: reserve its right to pursue its claims, while still receiving final payment? Or make the choice between pursuing its contractual rights and forgoing—for the time being—its right to final payment?

---

[92] Cal. Civ. Code § 3262 (West Supp. 1991).

[93] For federal contracts the period is 7 days. 31 U.S.C. § 3904 (Supp. 1991). In California, the contractor must pay the subcontractor within 10 days from receipt of payment from a public or private owner. Cal. Pub. Cont. Code § 10262.5(a) (West Supp. 1991); Cal. Civ. Code § 3260(d) (West Supp. 1991).

To a large extent these issues can be decided by simply flowing down the project closeout provisions of the prime contract. Many owners allow a contractor to reserve its right to pursue its claims, as long as the owner has been notified previously of those claims prior to final payment.[94] In many cases, though, the prime contract is silent, and most owners will permit the contractor to give a reservation of right along with the final lien release and waiver. Leaving the issue unaddressed in the subcontract also has merit.

§ 6.33   Coordination of the Work

Under the law, the contractor usually is charged with the responsibility for coordinating the work of its subcontractors.[95] This implied obligation usually is sufficient to make the contractor liable to its subcontractors for damages incurred as a result of the acts of another subcontractor. A typical scenario is when one subcontractor delays the work of other subcontractors who might claim against the prime contractor to recover their delay damages.

The responsibility for coordinating the work of subcontractors can be negated by a subcontract clause that deflects this liability to the subcontractor responsible for the deficient performance. Such a clause might read as follows:

> Contractor shall not be liable to subcontractor for any delays caused by the work of any other subcontractor. However, this clause is not intended to prohibit subcontractor from seeking damages incurred as a result of any such delay directly from the subcontractor causing the delay.

Note that pursuant to the clause recommended at § 6.25, the subcontractor is required to protect the contractor from claims brought by other subcontractors resulting from the subcontractors' delay to their work.

§ 6.34   Insurance in General

A contractor must be cognizant of both owner requirements for insurance and those that arise because of the subcontracting relationship.[96] This is to

---

[94] AIA Doc. A201, General Conditions of the Contract for Construction, para. 9.10.4 (1987), provides in part: "Acceptance of final payment by the Contractor, a Subcontractor or material supplier shall constitute a waiver of claims by that payee except those previously made in writing and identified by that payee as unsettled at the time of final Application for Payment."

[95] *See* Annotation, *Building and Construction Contracts: Prime Contractor's Liability to Subcontractor for Delay in Performance,* 16 A.L.R.3d 1252 § 2 (1967 & Supp. 1991).

[96] See Ch. 3 for a discussion of some of the broad insurance issues related to this paragraph.

say, a certain amount of flow-down must be accompanied by an assessment of the subcontractor and the nature of the work that it will perform.

An owner familiar with construction risks will require the contractor to furnish at least three types of insurance: workers' compensation, automobile liability, and commercial general liability.[97] Some owners will include aircraft insurance; almost all will include United States Longshore and Harborworkers' Compensation Insurance if any part of the project is to be performed on or near a navigable waterway of the United States.

Most of these owner-required insurances should be passed on to subcontractors. Workers' compensation, which is required by virtually every jurisdiction, should be specified in the minimum statutory limits in the subcontract.

Commercial general liability insurance should be required, though the appropriate limits may vary. Larger subcontracts should contain liability limits approximating those required in the prime contract. Subcontracts in smaller amounts may permit lower limits, but in each case the potential risk should be evaluated. A minimum of $1 million, combined single limit, commercial general liability insurance usually is recommended.

Automobile insurance also should be required of a subcontractor with limits as stated in the prime contract.

When not furnished by the owner, builders' risk insurance usually is required of the prime contractor. However, requiring a subcontractor to provide builders' risk insurance is duplicative of the prime contractor's coverage and is, therefore, unnecessary.

§ 6.35   —Specific Insurance Provisions

A number of provisions should be included in the subcontract's insurance section, regardless of the owner's requirements. One such provision, requiring a 30-day notice from the insurance company that the next premium is due,[98] or that the policy has been canceled or modified, gives the contractor the opportunity to monitor the subcontractor's renewal and, if necessary, pay the required premium (and backcharge the subcontractor accordingly) to make sure that the insurance remains in force.

Another important provision requires the subcontractor's insurer to waive its subrogation rights. This means that the insurance company may not attempt to recover from any insured under the policy payments made as a result of the negligence or act of that insured. This allows, in effect, complete protection of all insureds under any policy to which the subrogation waiver applies.

---

[97] Prior to 1986, this was called comprehensive general liability insurance. The coverage provided under each differs in that the current commercial policy includes broad form comprehensive general liability, which was an endorsement under the former policy.

[98] Payments should be made annually.

The following are examples of provisions that require the notice and waiver of subrogation described above:

> Contractor and subcontractor waive all rights against each other and each insured for any loss or damage to the extent covered under any builders' risk or equipment or property insurance applicable to the work.

> The certificate of insurance furnished by subcontractor to contractor shall provide that no cancellation or modification of the policy shall be effective without 30 days prior written notice to contractor.

§ 6.36 Scope of Indemnity Protection

Indemnity, a difficult area of the law even for lawyers, is an important risk-transfer (and risk-avoidance) vehicle for contractors. In its simplest form, an indemnity clause provides contractual protection to one party (the indemnitee) from damages arising from the acts or omissions of the other party (the indemnitor).[99] The scope of the clause as regards the number of indemnitees and the conduct of the indemnitor may vary from clause to clause. For example, a prime contract indemnity clause may require the contractor to protect the owner and its representatives (and sometimes its consultants) from the acts and negligence of the contractor and its subcontractors.

The subcontract must flow down the indemnity obligations of the prime contract, with the contractor added as an indemnitee. In addition, the scope of the clause should be examined to make sure that the desired protection is achieved.

This indemnity protection should cover at least two areas: protection from claims of the subcontractor's employee and protection from the claims of a third party, both of whom are injured (in their person or in their property) because of the subcontractor's operations. The protection may extend to more than negligence or acts or omissions. Knowledge of prevailing law and care in drafting to encompass the extended protections are critical requirements. For example, the State of Washington requires a specific waiver of the sole remedy provisions of its workers' compensation law for a subcontract indemnity agreement to effectively protect against suits against the contractor by the subcontractor's employees.[100]

Indemnity clauses usually exclude from the indemnitor's obligations damages flowing from the sole negligence of the indemnitee (the contractor). This usually means that the subcontractor must defend and indemnify the prime contractor who is only partially responsible for the damage.

---

[99] See **Ch. 26** for a discussion of the circumstances in which a broad indemnity clause as that suggested here will be narrowly construed to limit the effect of the clause.

[100] Brown v. Prime Constr. Co., 102 Wash. 2d 235, 684 P.2d 73 (1984).

These clauses are strictly construed,[101] however, and in a few states even indemnification for partial negligence is unenforceable.[102]

It cannot be emphasized too strongly that, because of the exactness with which an indemnity clause must be drafted, consultation with an experienced attorney about the drafting or interpretation of such a clause is advisable.

§ 6.37   Rules Governing Dispute Resolution

Contract provisions that set forth the rules governing disputes between the prime contractor and its subcontractors are not something to be left to be worked out at the time a dispute arises. Fundamental questions must be determined in advance, some of which are dictated by the relationship between the prime contractor and the owner. To say the least, the parties usually are more in a frame of mind to approach dispute mechanisms rationally at the time of contract formation than when the parties are embroiled in a dispute.

Two types of disputes may arise between the contractor and a subcontractor: those that involve interpretation of the prime contract (assuming proper flow-down of the prime contract provisions) or the acts or omissions of the owner, and those that involve the interpretation of the subcontract or the acts or omissions of the contractor or the subcontractor. Each may be treated differently under the subcontract with respect to the procedures that govern their resolution.

§ 6.38   —Consistency with Prime Contract

Although the contractor may have a preferred method of dispute resolution, the principal consideration in the choice of a dispute resolution clause in a subcontract is the method of resolving disputes under the prime contract. Disputes that arise involving prime contract interpretation or the owner's breach of its prime contract obligations tend to occur more frequently than those between the contractor and the subcontractor. The two

---

[101] Southern Pac. Co. v. Gila River Ranch, Inc., 9 Ariz. App. 570, 454 P.2d 1010, *vacated,* 105 Ariz. 107, 460 P.2d 1 (1969); Guy F. Atkinson Co. v. Schatz, 102 Cal. App. 3d 351, 161 Cal. Rptr. 436 (1980).

[102] *See* N.Y. Gen. Oblig. Law § 5-322.1 (McKinney 1989 and Supp. 1991), which prohibits indemnification for the indemnitee's negligence, "whether such negligence be in whole or in part." Contrast with Cal. Civ. Code § 2782 (Deering Supp. 1991), which prohibits such indemnification only for the indemnitee's "sole negligence or willful misconduct," thus permitting indemnity for the indemnitee's partial negligence in California. *See generally* 13 Am. Jur. 2d *Building and Construction Contracts* § 141 (1964 & Supp. 1990).

primary reasons for this emphasis on the prime contract's disputes clause are to avoid inconsistent decisions and to pass claims through to the owner.

Avoiding Inconsistent Decisions

A contractor who includes a dispute resolution clause in a subcontract that is different from that in the prime contract runs the risk of inconsistent decisions under each procedure. These inconsistent results could even require double payment for the same issue if neither the owner nor the subcontractor were bound to a decision under the other's procedure.

For example, suppose the subcontractor that installed underground utilities for a building project claims that unsuitable soil increased the cost and time of performance of its work. Because the subcontract contains an arbitration clause, the subcontractor files a demand in arbitration against the contractor after trying unsuccessfully to resolve the dispute.

Because the dispute really involves conditions that are the responsibility of the owner under the prime contract, the contractor needs to draw the owner into the arbitration. Assume, however, that the prime contract does not contain an arbitration clause but rather requires resolution of disputes through litigation. Thus, in all probability because arbitration is consensual, the contractor cannot compel the owner to participate in the arbitration.

If the contractor loses the arbitration, it might try to recover against the owner in litigation. However, the fact that the contractor lost the arbitration and had to pay the subcontractor is not in and of itself relevant in the court proceeding to determine whether the owner has liability. In fact, the court could well find that the owner is not liable, thus preventing the contractor from recovering what it paid to the subcontractor.

Had the prime contract contained an arbitration clause, however, the contractor could have filed an arbitration demand against the owner after the subcontractor filed against the contractor. It is likely that either a contract provision[103] or a court[104] would provide for consolidation of the arbitrations and, as a result, the responsibilities of all parties could be resolved in one proceeding.

Pass-Through Claims

Another reason that the subcontract disputes provision should be consistent with the prime contract is to ensure that subcontractor disputes arising

---

[103] See AIA Doc. A201, General Conditions of the Contract for Construction, para. 4.5.5 (1987); Doc. A401, Standard Form of Agreement between Contractor and Subcontractor, para. 6.2 (1987).

[104] See Cal. Civ. Proc. Code § 1281.3 (West Supp. 1991) (court has discretion to order consolidation of arbitrations when common issues of law and fact and separate arbitration agreements exist, and the disputes arise from the same or related transactions).

from the acts or decisions of the owner or its representative can be passed through the prime contractor to the owner. This is more than simply a way to satisfy the need to avoid inconsistent decisions; it directs the request for relief to the party with ultimate responsibility for the actions about which complaint is made—the owner.

Though flow-up of subcontractor disputes involving the owner is common practice, care must be exercised not only in the drafting of a clause to implement this intention, but also in the preparation of subcontract close-out documents, particularly the final release.[105] Generally, flow-up is effective as long as the prime contractor has an obligation to the subcontractor to provide a vehicle for pressing the subcontractor's claims against the owner and to pay such sums as the owner pays to the contractor with respect to the subcontractor's claims.[106]

Below is a sample clause to effectuate the flow-up of subcontractor claims:

> Subcontractor agrees to be bound by and to follow the claims procedures of the prime contract with respect to claims of the subcontractor for which the owner is responsible. Contractor agrees to present such of subcontractor's claims that are timely presented and are in compliance with the procedures of the prime contract and with applicable law and, subject to the payment provisions of this subcontract, to pay to subcontractor such amounts as contractor receives from the owner on account of subcontractor's claims.

This clause does nothing more than set forth the subcontractor's obligation to pass disputes through the prime contractor to the owner when the owner is responsible. When the time comes actually to prosecute a claim, other details need attention, and often a separate written agreement will be made between the contractor and the subcontractor to resolve these other issues that arise during the disputes process.

§ 6.39   —Claims Against Prime Contractor

The contractor obviously has more flexibility in determining the dispute procedure for claims solely with a subcontractor. If the subcontract is silent on this issue, litigation is the forum available to the parties, absent a later

---

[105] See **Ch. 21**.

[106] *See* Severin v. United States, 99 Ct. Cl. 435 (1943), *cert. denied,* 322 U.S. 733 (1944); Board of County Comm'rs v. Cam Constr. Co., 300 Md. 643, 480 A.2d 795 (1984) (discussing evolution of the *Severin* doctrine and citing J.L. Simmons Co. v. United States), 158 Ct. Cl. 393; 304 F.2d 886 (1962). One recent case, however, did not permit flow-up because the prime contractor had not admitted liability to the subcontractor for its claim. APAC-Virginia, Inc. v. Virginia Dep't of Highways & Transp., 9 Va. 450, 388 S.E.2d 841 (1990). For further discussion, see **Ch. 21**; Sweet, Legal Aspects of Architecture, Engineering and the Construction Process § 32 at 655 (4th ed. 1989).

agreement to submit the dispute to some other procedure. However, frustration with the expense and delays in litigation has led to the increased use of alternative dispute resolution (ADR) procedures.[107]

As stated in § 6.37, it is important that the parties consider a dispute procedure, if it is to be other than litigation, at the time of contract formation. It is then that the parties are more likely to have an objective evaluation of the best procedure under the circumstances. It is not a mark of weakness or of pessimism about the success of the project for the parties to provide for a rational approach to resolve their disputes, as disputes are almost inevitable in construction projects.

§ 6.40   —Forum Selection Considerations

As with other flow-down issues, the place in which owner-related disputes are to be pursued should be the same as that specified in the prime contract. For prime contractor-subcontractor issues, however, forum selection can be an important consideration.[108]

Forum selection simply means determining the site in which the parties want the resolution of the dispute to take place. For example, the contractor may want to make sure that any suit by the subcontractor during the period of performance is brought near the project, where all the records and personnel are located that might be needed in defense of the action. On the other hand, the contractor might want dispute resolution to occur near the contractor's principal place of business, where the senior executives who are likely to participate in the process reside.

To make an informed choice, the contractor first needs to be aware of the rules that may be applied if no forum is specified. Of course the rules will depend on the process (litigation or ADR) selected, either in the contract (ADR) or by default (litigation) if no process is specified in the contract. If the process is specified in the contract, the forum generally also is specified. If the process is left to litigation, and no forum is specified in the contract, then the court rules on jurisdiction and venue will determine the forum.

§ 6.41   —Applicable Law for Disputes

As with forum selection, the law to be applied to disputes between the prime contractor and the subcontractor should not be overlooked.[109] Even

---

[107] See **Ch. 23** for a discussion of various ADR techniques.

[108] Sometimes the clause appears in a "miscellaneous provisions" section of a subcontract.

[109] *Id.*

if the contractor chooses to leave the subcontract silent on this issue, the decision to do so should be made intelligently. The parties should consider, and hopefully agree, on the applicable law for contract disputes because failure to do so can leave the unwary party at the mercy of the other party and its arguments on the applicable law. Rather than add this dispute to the existing dispute, the parties should agree on applicable law at the outset.

§ 6.42   —Recovery of Attorneys' Fees

Attorneys' fees[110] generally are not recoverable unless provided by contract or statute.[111] A contract provision stipulating that only one party to the contract is entitled to attorneys' fees is looked upon by the courts with disfavor, leading some states to legislate parity for the party who is not expressly granted the same right to attorneys' fees as the other party.[112]

Inasmuch as the law tends toward an equitable approach to entitlement to attorneys' fees, a subcontract provision that provides attorneys' fees to the prevailing party will almost certainly be upheld.[113] Such a provision might read simply as follows:

> In any dispute between the parties under the provisions of this subcontract that results in arbitration (if permitted by the subcontract or agreed to by the parties) or litigation, and that is a dispute for which an attorney is used, the prevailing party in such proceeding is entitled to recover from the other the costs, fees, and expenses of such proceeding, including reasonable attorneys' fees.

Although it is difficult to do, the parties may wish to define the term *prevailing* party rather than leave it to arbitrator or the court.[114]

---

[110] *Id.*

[111] United States *ex rel.* Micro-King Company v. Community Science Technology, Inc., 574 F.2d 1292 (5th Cir. 1978) (attorneys' fees permitted by contract); Gergora v. R.L. Lapp Forming, Inc., 619 F.2d 387 (5th Cir. 1980) (attorneys' fees permitted by statute).

[112] California Civil Code § 1717(a) (West Supp. 1991) provides in part as follows:

> In any action on a contract, where the contract specifically provides that attorney's fees and costs, which are incurred to enforce that contract, shall be awarded either to one of the parties or to the prevailing party, then the party who is determined to be the party prevailing on the contract, whether he or she is the party specified in the contract or not, shall be entitled to reasonable attorney's fees in addition to other costs.

[113] Many state statutes that govern the rights of subcontractors and suppliers to payment provide that attorneys' fees may be recovered by a prevailing claimant. *See, e.g.,* Cal. Civ. Code § 3250 (West Supp. 1991).

[114] California Code of Civil Procedure § 1021.1 sets forth the basis for an award of attorneys' fees following the rejection of a settlement offer. Some of the considerations for

§ 6.43   Miscellaneous Contract Provisions

Miscellaneous provisions usually get little attention, relegated as they are to the end of the subcontract. Nevertheless, it is wrong to ignore the issues contained in these provisions. They do not involve significant elements of risk transfer, but they merit consideration here.

§ 6.44   —Assignment of Rights and Obligations

In the absence of a contractual prohibition, either party to a contract may freely assign its rights and benefits under that agreement.[115] A party may retain the performance of its contractual obligations or it may assign those as well. Both the contractor and the subcontractor may have reasons to preserve their respective rights to assign both rights and obligations, but the subcontractor usually has the most to gain from such an assignment.

The contractor's freedom to assign its rights usually is limited in the prime contract. Therefore, an assignment provision in the subcontract usually deals with the subcontractor's assignment rights. A contractor who permits a subcontractor to assign its obligations freely defeats its efforts in carefully selecting the subcontractor in the first place. If a subcontractor gets into financial difficulties, assignment of part or all of the remaining performance requirements under the subcontract should be permitted only with the consent of the prime contractor, who should take the opportunity to review the experience and financial capability of the assignee.[116]

The right to assign benefits should be viewed circumspectly as well. Typically, a subcontractor in financial trouble attempts to assign its right to payment to a financial institution who holds a secured interest in the subcontractor's receivables. Although seemingly harmless, this practice injects a new party into jobsite relationships and requires that the contractor deal on payment issues with one who does not always understand construction procedures and practices. For example, a contractor with a backcharge

---

the court in determining the reasonableness of an offer might have application in deciding whether a party is prevailing. They are (1) the reasonableness of a party's failure to accept a settlement offer (the statute has seven criteria for determining "reasonableness"); (2) the amount of damages and other relief sought versus the results obtained; (3) any settlement efforts made by the parties; and (4) the existence of a party's bad faith or abuse of the legal process.

[115] 6 Am. Jur. 2d *Assignments* § 9 (1963 & Supp. 1991), citing Restatement (Second) of Contracts § 317(2) (1963).

[116] If the contractor permits the assignment, the original subcontractor should continue to be held to the underlying obligation. The contractor also should obtain security for the assignee's promise to perform.

against a subcontractor who has assigned payment rights to a bank will not enjoy having to explain to the bank's representative why jobsite, division, and home office overhead are all legitimate elements of delay damages.

A short and simple provision that adequately protects the contractor's discretion to permit assignment of subcontractual rights and obligations by the subcontractor is as follows:

> A subcontractor shall not assign any of its rights or obligations under this subcontract, including any portion of the work or payment therefor, without the written consent of contractor.

§ 6.45   —Parties' Successors in Interest

Most contracts contain a provision that makes the agreement binding on the parties' successors in interest, that is, those who, subsequent to the execution of the contract, may succeed to all or a part of the rights of a party to the agreement. A successor in interest might be the buyer of one of the firms who is a party to the subcontract, but it also might be a financial institution who takes control of a failing company (who may already be in default under the subcontract). The following clause ensures that the successor in interest complies with the requirements of the subcontract:

> Contractor and subcontractor bind each other and their successors and assigns with respect to the contractor's and subcontractor's respective obligations under this subcontract.

§ 6.46   —Inclusion of Integration Clause

An integration clause is one that attempts to confine the intent and expressions of the parties to the four corners of the subcontract. A typical clause is as follows:

> This subcontract (the documents comprising which having been described previously) represents the entire agreement between the parties, supersedes all prior oral and written agreements, negotiations, and representations, and may be modified only by written agreement of contractor and subcontractor.

An integration clause serves its purpose only if the contractor has good subcontract administration. A clause like the one above excludes, for example, any precontract clarifications of the parties or the subcontractor's written quote (unless specifically incorporated in the subcontract).

The courts will ignore an integration clause when necessary to resolve an ambiguity in the contract. In that case, a party is permitted to refer to prior writings or statements, called parol evidence, to show what the parties intended by the ambiguous language.[117]

§ 6.47   —Precedence of Documents

Prime contracts usually contain a clause that lists the contract documents according to a priority that must be followed whenever an inconsistency between the documents must be resolved. Because many (if not most) contract interpretation issues involve the prime contract documents, it is better to rely on the general flow-down provision in the subcontract to establish the same document precedence as in the prime contract, rather than to insert what might turn out to be a conflicting specific precedence provision.

§ 6.48   Construction Industry Forms

The construction industry has been inundated with forms published by many diverse organizations. Each organization has found existing forms inadequate for its own purposes, and so each form differs from the others in both risk-sharing philosophy and type of application.

Many of the industry organizations have published subcontract forms. Sometimes it is helpful to see what one organization has done, or what the industry as a whole has done, in its approach to risk sharing under a particular clause. These organizations, their current addresses and telephone numbers, and their form information are listed below for reference.

1. American Bar Association, Section of Public Contract Law, 750 North Lake Shore Drive, (312) 988-5000 (Form: *Model FAR-Compatible Provisions for Subcontracts Under Federal Government Fixed-Price Construction Contracts*)

2. Associated General Contractors of California, 3095 Beacon Boulevard, West Sacramento, CA 95691, (916) 371-2422 (Form AGCC-2, *Long Form Standard Subcontract; AGCC-3, Short Form Standard Subcontract*)

3. Associated General Contractors of America, 1957 E Street, N.W., Washington, D.C. 20006, (202) 393-2040 (Form: No. 600, *Standard Subcontract Agreement for Building Construction*; No. 601,

---

[117] California law, for example, even permits parol evidence when an ambiguity is not otherwise apparent from the face of the document (i.e., when needed to prove the fact of the ambiguity itself). Pacific Gas & Elec. Co. v. G.W. Thomas Drayage Co., 69 Cal. 2d 33, 442 P.2d 641, 69 Cal. Rptr. 561 (1968).

Subcontract for Use on Federal Construction; No. 603, *Short Form Subcontract*)

4. American Institute of Architects, 1735 New York Avenue, N.W., Washington, D.C. 20006, (202) 626-7300 (Form: AIA Document A401, *Standard Form of Agreement Between Contractor and Subcontractor* (1987)).

CHAPTER 7

CONTRACTING WITH THE MATERIAL SUPPLIER

Richard A. Holderness

Richard A. Holderness is head of the Construction Law Department of Graham & James, an international law firm in San Francisco, California. His practice focuses on advising owners, contractors, and subcontractors on all aspects of construction contracts, including contract drafting and interpretation, bidding problems, bid protests, differing site conditions, extra work requirements, change order problems, payment disputes, design deficiencies, delay claims, and performance problems. Mr. Holderness' practice encompasses private, local public agency, state, and federal construction contracts. He represents clients in litigation in state and federal courts, private arbitration, and other dispute resolution procedures mandated by the particular construction contracts.

§ 7.1 Introduction to Contracting Differences

Although contractors rarely make fine distinctions between contracting with subcontractors and contracting with material suppliers, most contractors recognize the obvious differences. Contractors generally recognize that subcontractors perform work at the project site and that material suppliers furnish no labor, supplying only the material or equipment.

Contractors also generally recognize that contracting with a material supplier usually involves a purchase order and contracting with a subcontractor usually involves a subcontract.

Beyond those obvious differences, few contractors distinguish between subcontractors and material suppliers or understand the significance of the differences. Fortunately, the similarities between contracting with subcontractors and contracting with material suppliers exceed the differences, so that contractors do not have to play by two completely different sets of rules during construction of a project. Nevertheless, the differences are important, and unless a contractor understands the differences, it will be handicapped in contracting with material suppliers.

§ 7.2 Mechanic's Liens and Public Works Bonds

The mechanic's lien and public contract bond rights of a material supplier may be more limited than those of a subcontractor. Statutes creating mechanic's liens and the requirement for public works bonds impose limitations on the availability of the rights, and those limitations may be more severe for material suppliers than for subcontractors.

A typical limitation is privity of contract. Generally, mechanic's lien and public works bond rights are available only to those in privity of contract with the prime contractor or in privity of contract with a direct subcontractor, but not a material supplier, to the prime contractor.[1] This limitation may create an anomaly in which a material supplier to a direct subcontractor to

---

[1] *See, e.g.,* 40 U.S.C. §§ 270a–270d (1988).

the prime contractor may have bond rights, but a material supplier to a direct material supplier to the prime contractor may not.[2]

Because the limitations on the availability of rights under mechanic's liens and public works bonds generally are created by statute, the statutes in the jurisdiction in which the project is being constructed should be consulted to determine the limitations that may apply. In its contract with the material supplier, the prime contractor may attempt to impose further limitations on the material supplier or have the material supplier waive its rights; however, further limitations on the rights, or waivers of the rights, may be prohibited by the statute creating the rights.[3]

§ 7.3 Application of Uniform Commercial Code

Contractors usually are not familiar with the Uniform Commercial Code (UCC) because it is not perceived to govern their businesses. When a contractor enters into a contract with a material supplier, however, the UCC, as adopted in the state whose law applies to the contract, governs the contract.

Unless a contractor recognizes that its contract with a material supplier is governed by the UCC, it could be in for some surprises. Fortunately, some of those surprises may be pleasant because the UCC provides extensive warranties about the material supplied and extensive remedies for breach of those warranties. Consequently, at times, the contractor will want the UCC to apply.

At first glance, it would seem that a contractor should have no difficulty determining if a particular contract is governed by the UCC. If the contract is with a material supplier, the contract is governed by the UCC. But determining if the contract is with a material supplier is more difficult than it would appear on the surface.

§ 7.4 —Commercial Contracts for Sale of Goods

The definition of a *material supplier* would seem obvious, but certain factors complicate that definition.

UCC Definition of Goods

By its own terms, the UCC applies only to commercial contracts for the sale of goods.[4] U.C.C. § 2-105 defines *goods* to mean "all things (including

---

[2] *Id.*

[3] *See* Cal. Civ. Code § 3262.

[4] *See* U.C.C. Art. 2 (1989).

specially manufactured goods) which are moveable at the time of identification to the contract for sale."

If anything, a construction project is not movable. A construction contract is for the furnishing of skilled construction services to build a project. It is not a sale of goods. Manufacturers, wholesalers, and merchants sell goods; contractors build structures. Because a construction contract involves the rendering of services and is not a sale of goods, the UCC would not seem to apply.

Combination of Goods and Services

Most construction contracts involve a combination of services and goods, however, and that combination as well as the use of subcontracts may create confusion about the exact type of contract a particular construction contract may be. A typical construction contract involves the use of skilled construction labor to assemble various goods and materials, such as concrete, steel, glass, and wood, into a finished structure. Much of the work is performed by subcontractors, who typically supply both labor and material.

Some subcontractors supply more labor than material, and some supply more material than labor. Does the UCC apply to one subcontract or the other or both? Courts in various parts of the country have wrestled with this question and unfortunately, the answers that they have given appear inconsistent.

§ 7.5   —Inconsistency among Court Decisions

The courts that have analyzed whether the UCC applies to a construction contract have reached varying conclusions, providing no clear test that can be applied consistently to determine if the UCC will apply to a particular contract.

At one extreme, a contract purely for the sale of goods, involving no labor, would be governed by the UCC. At the other extreme, a contract purely for the furnishing of services, involving no goods, would not be governed by the UCC. But when labor is supplied as part of a contract that also involves the sale of goods, the clarity rapidly disappears.

Most subcontracts involve both the furnishing of goods and the installation of those goods. The HVAC subcontractor furnishes and installs HVAC equipment and related ductwork; the structural steel subcontractor furnishes and erects the structural steel; the plumbing subcontractor furnishes and installs piping; the electrical subcontractor furnishes and installs conduit and wiring; the drywall subcontractor furnishes and installs drywall.

In each subcontract, the proportion of labor and material may vary but each involves a combination of labor and material.

Different courts have developed different tests to determine if the UCC applies to particular contracts that involve a combination of goods and services. Unfortunately, the tests are so broad and inconsistent that they provide little guidance to a contractor trying to determine if a particular contract is governed by the UCC.

In the end, three general conclusions can be derived from these tests:

1. The facts of the particular contract are critical to the determination of whether the UCC will apply

2. Many contracts that would appear to be construction contracts not governed by the UCC are determined by the courts to be governed by the UCC

3. Courts increasingly may be willing to apply the UCC to construction contracts because the purpose of the UCC is to achieve uniformity in commercial transactions, representing the best of modern commercial practices.[5]

§ 7.6 —Purpose of Uniform Commercial Code

The purpose of the UCC was described by one court when it determined that the UCC governed a contract for the construction of a large water tank:

> [T]he scope of coverage of "goods" is not to be given a narrow construction but instead should be viewed as being broad in scope so as to carry out the underlying purpose of the Code of achieving uniformity in commercial transactions. The Code, which by its own terms is to be liberally construed, should be uniformly applied to achieve its purposes.[6]

The rationale of this case could justify applying the UCC to all construction cases. The courts have not gone that far yet, but the inconsistency in their decisions makes it difficult to determine the extent to which they will go in the future. Perhaps the best ways to analyze both what the courts are doing presently and where they may be headed is to look at some of the tests that various courts have employed in analyzing whether particular construction contracts are governed by the UCC and then to look at the particular fact situations that courts have held to be governed by the UCC.

---

[5] *See* Pittsburgh-Des Moines Steel Co. v. Brookhaven Manor Water Co., 532 F.2d 572 (7th Cir. 1976).

[6] *Id.* at 580.

§ 7.7   Evaluation of Construction Contracts

The "tests" used to evaluate construction contracts are nothing more than classifications of a range of widely differing court decisions. The tests can provide only very general factors for consideration and methods of analysis for determining whether a particular contract will be governed by the UCC. Having been applied by different courts in different parts of the country on an almost case-by-case basis, the tests cannot be used as black-and-white litmus tests.

If the amount of equivocation in this discussion is disconcerting, that is because the law is evolving, and a contractor would run a great risk if it blindly relied on one test or another or even a combination of tests. The various rules should provide nothing more than general guidance, and each contract should be analyzed carefully and individually to determine if the UCC will apply.

§ 7.8   —Predominant Purpose Test

The predominant purpose test may be the easiest test to understand, but also may be the most difficult to apply. The test first recognizes that many construction contracts involve a combination of goods and services and then looks to the "predominant purpose" of the contract to determine if the UCC will apply. The test is described by a leading case as follows:

> The test . . . is not whether [the contracts] are mixed, but, granting that they are mixed, whether their predominant factor, their trust, their purpose, reasonably stated, is the rendition of service, with goods incidentally involved (e.g., contract with artist for painting) or is a transaction of sale, with labor incidentally involved (e.g., installation of a water heater in a bathroom).[7]

The test sounds deceptively simple, but determining the predominant purpose of a particular contract and whether the contract is the rendition of service, with goods only incidentally involved, or is the sale of goods, with labor only incidentally involved, can be difficult. The amount of labor involved is important but not determinative. A contract involving substantial amounts of labor still can be governed by the UCC if the predominant purpose of the contract is the furnishing of equipment or material, even if the furnishing of equipment or material involves substantial installation labor.[8]

---

[7] Bonebrake v. Cox, 499 F.2d 951, 960 (8th Cir. 1974).

[8] *Id.* at 951.

§ 7.9   —Analysis of Contract and Business Features

Some courts do not apply a test but instead balance or analyze various factors to determine whether a particular contract is governed by the UCC. The difference between the decisions of these courts is that they give varying importance to certain of the various factors. The decisions by these courts are hard to categorize, but generally they can be organized as follows.

Contractual language.   Some courts, primarily those in Illinois, rely almost exclusively on the language of the contract. Under this approach, if the parties to the contract are described in the contract as "owner" and "contractor" and the contract required "design" and "construction" of a structure, the contract would be considered a contract for services not governed by the UCC.[9] Conversely, if the parties were described as "buyer" and "seller" and the contract involved a "sale" rather than "design" and "construction," the contract probably would be considered a sale of goods governed by the UCC.[10]

Pricing structure.   The pricing structure of a contract can be an important factor, but it is usually not the sole factor considered. Under this approach, the value of the material furnished is one of the factors to be considered in determining if the UCC applies to the contract.[11] This approach may be similar to the predominant purpose test, but instead of trying to determine the predominant purpose, this approach balances various factors, one of which is the value of the materials, to determine if on balance the contract is for the sale of goods governed by the UCC.

Seller's business.   Another factor that some courts consider is the nature of the seller's business. If the "seller" primarily is a service entity that acquires materials only when needed for installation pursuant to a particular contract, a court may be more inclined to find that a contract with that entity is not for the sale of goods governed by the UCC.[12]

Division of contract.   A small minority of courts have tried to divide contracts into parts that are covered by the UCC and parts that are not. The resulting confusion is obvious, and few courts have adopted this approach. Nevertheless, the approach demonstrates the contortions courts are going

---

[9] *See* Nitrin, Inc. v. Bethlehem Steel Corp., 35 Ill. App. 3d 577, 342 N.E.2d 65 (1976).

[10] *Id.*

[11] *See* Coakley & Williams, Inc. v. Shatterproof Glass Corp., 706 F.2d 456 (4th Cir. 1983).

[12] *See* Ranger Constr. Co. v. Dixie Floor Co., 433 F. Supp. 442 (D.S.C. 1977).

through in their attempts to determine the applicability of the UCC to contracts that commonly are not perceived as contracts for the sale of goods.

§ 7.10   —Examination of All Relevant Factors

Although this chapter has attempted to artificially organize the differing approaches used by various courts into categories, the reality is that many courts are engaging in a multifaceted analysis of the unique terms of each particular contract to determine if the contract is governed by the UCC.

Courts increasingly are inclined to analyze all relevant factors of a particular contract to determine if it is governed by the UCC. The greater the number of factors considered by the courts during their analyses, the greater the uncertainty of the result and the greater the unpredictability of gauging future contracts.

Although the extent of the labor and services required by a particular contract will continue to be an important part of the analysis conducted by the courts, all other relevant factors also will be considered, and those factors will vary with the terms of each contract.

Few generalizations can be safely derived from the increasingly sophisticated analyses being conducted by the courts other than the general conclusions reached by looking at the extremes. At one extreme, the inclusion of a minor amount of labor or services incidental to the furnishing of material or equipment probably will not exclude the contract from the application of the UCC. At the other extreme, the inclusion of a minor amount of material or equipment in a contract predominantly for the furnishing of labor or services probably will not cause the contract to be governed by the UCC. Between the extremes, a determination about UCC applicability to construction contracts is a matter of degree, and all relevant factors must be considered.

§ 7.11   Expansion of UCC Applicability

Because the UCC was formulated and has been enacted by almost all states for uniformity and as representing the best of modern commercial practices,[13] courts may be willing to expand the applicability of the UCC to almost all contracts, thus promoting such purposes.[14] In fact, some courts apply the principles of the UCC even when they find that the UCC does not apply to the contract. This approach is probably a reflection of the UCC as

---

[13] *See* Pittsburgh-Des Moines Steel Co. v. Brookhaven Manor Water Co., 532 F.2d 572 (7th Cir. 1976).

[14] *Id.* at 580.

representing the best of modern commercial practices; courts are inclined to apply those practices as reflected in the UCC even when the UCC may not directly govern the contract.

One court found that the UCC did not apply to a contract for the installation of a sewer, but concluded that its failure to apply did not preclude the application to the contract of the UCC's policies and reasons.[15] Another court applied an implied warranty of fitness to a contract for the design and installation of an electrical system, although the UCC did not apply to the contract.[16] Yet another court found that the state's adoption of the UCC established a legislative policy that should be applied to analogous construction contract cases.[17]

Although this approach may be discomforting to contractors who are unaccustomed to the operation of the UCC, the expansion of UCC applicability to a wider range of what contractors consider to be "subcontracts" provides to the contractor extensive warranties and remedies that might not otherwise be available and may place the contractor in a better position than the contractor would have been in without the UCC.

Federal Government Procurement Contracts

In addition, the expanding application of the UCC is evidenced by federal government procurement contracts, which courts have found to be governed by the UCC. The courts have applied the UCC on the basis that it represents the best in modern decision and discussion about commercial transactions, especially when no contradictory legal authority exists.[18] This rationale would justify expanding the UCC to cover a wide range of contracts. Nevertheless, if contrary federal legal authority exists, the UCC will not supplant that authority.[19]

§ 7.12   —Typical Construction Contract Cases

One way to appreciate both the different approaches used by the courts and the application of the UCC to what would appear to be construction contracts is simply to list a variety of cases that analyze the applicability of the UCC to contracts that involve varying degrees of construction work. Such listing may not be scientific, but it demonstrates the increasing willingness

---

[15] Semler v. Knowling, 325 N.W.2d 395 (Iowa 1982).

[16] Air Heaters, Inc. v. Johnson Elec., Inc., 258 N.W.2d 649 (N.D. 1977).

[17] Link-Belt Co. v. Star Iron & Steel Co., 65 Cal. App. 3d 24, 135 Cal. Rptr. 134 (1976).

[18] See Reeves Soundcraft Corp., ASBCA No. 9030, 1964 B.C.A. (CCH) ¶ 4,317.

[19] See Machlett Lab., Inc., ASBCA No. 16194, 73-1 B.C.A. (CCH) ¶ 9,929 (1973).

of courts to apply the UCC broadly to contracts commonly viewed as construction contracts to which the UCC would not seem to apply.

The construction of a large water tank would commonly be viewed as a traditional construction contract to which the UCC would not apply, but a court found that the construction of the tank involved the sale of goods, not services, and was governed by the UCC.[20] The court made the interesting observation that: "In the present case, while the finished tank was scarcely one to be taken off the shelf, we are unaware of any authority that specially manufactured small dies should be goods and a very large tank not so classified." Carried to its logical extreme, the rationale of this case would abolish any distinction between construction contracts and manufacturing or sales contracts. Construction contracts would be viewed as a type of manufacturing or sales contract, with the only distinguishing features being the size of the object manufactured and the custom manufacturing of the object at the site.

Another court found that the design and construction of flooring materials for carnival equipment constituted goods and was covered by the UCC.[21] Still another held that the furnishing, installation, and maintenance of a computer system, including customized software, is governed by the UCC.[22]

The fact that the preceding two cases involve contracts to which the UCC applies may not be surprising to a contractor. Both sound as though they involved the manufacture and sale of goods. But what about a contract for the furnishing, pouring, and finishing of concrete? The contract sounds like a traditional construction contract, not a contract for the manufacture and sale of goods. But a court found that a contract for the sale of concrete and the labor to pour and finish the concrete was a sale of goods.[23]

Another court found that the building and installation of grain bins was governed by the UCC.[24] In addition, according to one court, the UCC applies to a contract for the installation of a roof.[25] A more understandable result is when a court found that a defective gas fitting supplied as part of contract to install a water heater was a "good."[26]

---

[20] Pittsburgh-Des Moines Steel Co. v. Brookhaven Manor Water Co., 532 F.2d 572 (7th Cir. 1976).

[21] Aluminum Co. of Am. v. Electro Flow Corp., 451 F.2d 1115 (10th Cir. 1971).

[22] Triangle Underwriters, Inc. v. Honeywell, Inc., 457 F. Supp. 765 (E.D.N.Y. 1978), *aff'd in relevant part, rev'd in part*, 604 F.2d 737 (2d Cir. 1979).

[23] Port City Constr. Co. v. Henderson, 48 Ala. App. 639, 266 So. 2d 896 (1972).

[24] Meeker v. Hamilton Grain Elevator Co., 110 Ill. App. 3d 668, 442 N.E.2d 921 (1982).

[25] Mennonite Deaconess Home & Hosp., Inc. v. Gates Eng'g Co., 219 Neb. 303, 363 N.W.2d 155 (1985).

[26] Worrell v. Barnes, 87 Nev. 204, 484 P.2d 573 (1971).

Another court allowed a subcontractor sued by a prime contractor to assert a defense allowed by the UCC that one party can demand adequate assurance of the other party's ability to perform, even though the subcontract involved a combination of goods and services.[27] By applying the predominant purpose test, yet another court determined that the predominant purpose of a contract was the purchase of an air conditioning system and that the installation labor was only peripherally involved.[28]

Some courts have simply ruled that the UCC does not apply to contracts involving construction. A good example is a contract that involved furnishing the labor and material for the installation of flooring in a medical facility under construction. The court concluded that the contract was for construction, not for the purchase and sale of goods.[29] About the only difference between this case and the one that involved a contract for furnishing the labor and material for pouring and finishing concrete, to which the court ruled the UCC applied, is that the courts are different.

Other courts have held that a caulking contract involves the rendering of services, not the sale of goods, and is not governed by the UCC,[30] that a construction contract for a mail processing center is primarily for services,[31] and that the UCC implied warranties do not apply to the construction and sale of a house.[32]

This inconsistency among various courts in different parts of the country provides no comfort to a contractor looking at a subcontract and trying to determine if the UCC applies, especially if no court in the contractor's state has addressed the issue of the applicability of the UCC to contracts similar to the one at which the contractor is looking. No easy solution exists for the contractor in such a predicament. The contractor should not be surprised if and should prepare itself for the possibility that a court eventually will find that the UCC applies to a certain contract, whether the application of the UCC is good or bad for the contractor in the particular situation.

§ 7.13 Advantages of UCC Application

For a contractor entering into a contract with a material supplier or subcontractor that will be governed by the UCC, the UCC provides many advantages. Although contractors usually are unfamiliar with the UCC, many UCC provisions are favorable to the "buyer," or contractor. If a dispute

---

[27] Ellis Mfg. Co. v. Brant, 480 S.W.2d 301 (Tex. 1972).

[28] Meeks v. Bell, 710 S.W.2d 789 (Tex. Ct. App. 1986).

[29] Ranger Constr. Co. v. Dixie Floor Co., 433 F. Supp. 442 (D.S.C. 1977).

[30] Decatur N. Assocs. v. Builders Glass, 180 Ga. App. 862, 350 S.E.2d 795 (1986).

[31] Boddie v. Litton Unit Handling Sys., 118 Ill. App. 3d 520, 455 N.E.2d 142 (1983).

[32] Miller v. Spencer, 732 S.W.2d 758 (Tex. Ct. App. 1987), dictum.

arises with a material supplier or a subcontractor that is furnishing a combination of labor and material, the contractor may find it wise to argue for the application of the UCC to the disputed contract because of the advantages that the UCC bestows on the contractor. Contractors should not be adverse to the UCC simply because they are not accustomed to it.

Some of the favorable provisions are codifications or restatements of traditional legal concepts; other provisions are modern concepts or modernized versions of older concepts. A few of the more important provisions for contractors will be discussed in §§ **7.14** through **7.20**.

§ 7.14 —Implied Warranties

The UCC establishes two important implied warranties: the implied warranty of merchantability[33] and the implied warranty of fitness for a particular purpose.[34] As the names imply, these warranties are not created by contract language or by express promises or statements but are implied by the UCC in commercial transactions to which the UCC applies. The warranty of merchantability is implied in all commercial transactions to which the code applies, and the implied warranty of fitness for a particular purpose is implied when two conditions specified by the UCC are satisfied.

Implied Warranty of Merchantability

The implied warranty of merchantability generally provides that the goods must be fit for the ordinary purposes for which they are used, must pass without objection in the trade, and must be of fair average quality.[35] According to the warranty, the goods must be of a quality comparable to that generally acceptable in that line of trade.

The implied warranty of merchantability is an important warranty because it is a broad warranty requiring that the goods be fit for their intended purposes and be of at least average quality. If express warranties are lacking, this warranty establishes important minimum requirements for the goods.

Breach of warranty. To establish a breach of the implied warranty of merchantability, the buyer (contractor) must establish the following: (1) a merchant sold the goods; (2) the goods were not merchantable at the time of sale; (3) the goods caused injury and damages to the buyer or the buyer's

---

[33] U.C.C. § 2-314.

[34] *Id.* § 2-315.

[35] *Id.* § 2-314.

property; (4) the injury and damages were caused by the defective nature of the goods; and (5) the buyer gave notice of the injury to the seller.[36]

Disclaimer of warranty.   Warranties can be disclaimed or waived, and the implied warranty of merchantability is no exception. However, the UCC specifies the requirements for an enforceable disclaimer of the warranty. Any disclaimer of the warranty of merchantability must contain conspicuous language specifically mentioning the word *merchantability.*[37] *Conspicuous* is defined to mean something that is written so that a reasonable person ought to have noticed it.[38] In its usual effort at commercial reasonableness, the UCC then provides alternative, less formal methods for disclaiming liability for warranties, including the warranty of merchantability. Those alternative methods include contract language to the effect that the goods are being sold "as is," "with all faults," or "as they stand."[39] If properly used, these alternative methods disclaim all warranties. The disclaimer cannot be unconscionable, even if it technically complies with the requirements of the UCC. If it is unconscionable, the disclaimer will not be enforced.[40]

Warranty of Fitness for Particular Purpose

The warranty of fitness for a particular purpose is narrower and more specific than the implied warranty of merchantability; but for construction contracts, it may be more important. The warranty is created when (1) the seller at the time of contracting has reason to know the particular purpose for which the goods are required and (2) the buyer (contractor) is relying on the seller's skill or judgment to select or furnish suitable goods.[41]

Many times, contractors have to rely on the ability of certain subcontractors or material suppliers to achieve certain results with their products. The warranty of fitness for a particular purpose makes those subcontractors and material suppliers liable for the failure of the products to achieve the desired results if they knew the purpose for which products were required and if the contractor was relying on the skill or judgment of the subcontractors or material suppliers to furnish suitable products. One court has added the

---

[36] F.E. Meyers Co. v. Pipe Maintenance Servs., Inc., 599 F. Supp. 697, 703 (D. Del. 1984); *see also* 1 White & Summers, Uniform Commercial Code § 9-7 (3d ed. 1988).

[37] U.C.C. § 2-316(2); *See* A&M Produce Co. v. FMC Corp., 135 Cal. App. 3d 473, 186 Cal. Rptr. 114 (1982); Steele v. Gold Kist, Inc., 186 Ga. App. 569, 368 S.E.2d 196 (1988).

[38] U.C.C. § 1-201(10); *see* A&M Produce Co. v. FMC Corp., 135 Cal. App. 3d 473, 186 Cal. Rptr. 114 (1982).

[39] *See* K&M Joint Venture v. Smith Int'l, Inc., 669 F.2d 1106 (6th Cir. 1982).

[40] A&M Produce Co. v. FMC Corp., 135 Cal. App. 3d 473, 186 Cal. Rptr. 114 (1982).

[41] U.C.C. § 2-315; Guaranteed Constr. Co. v. Gold Bond Prods., 153 Mich. App. 385, 395 N.W.2d 332 (1986).

requirement that the seller have reason to know that the buyer (contractor) is relying on the seller's skill and judgment.[42]

Implied warranty. Contractors must remember that the warranty of fitness for a particular purpose is an implied warranty. No special contract language is necessary to create the warranty. The warranty is created not by contract language, but by the circumstances of the seller knowing of the particular purpose for the goods and of the buyer's reliance on the seller's skill or judgment. If those circumstances are present, the warranty is created and becomes an implied part of the contract.

More strict warranty. As stated, this warranty may be more important for contractors than the implied warranty of merchantability because many contractors need material, equipment, or products that are technically suitable for a very specific purpose. Many goods that are perfectly "merchantable" will not meet the more strict requirement that they be fit for a particular purpose, especially if that purpose is a technical construction requirement.[43] To ensure that the warranty is created, a contractor should inform the seller that the contractor is relying on the seller's skill and judgment to select or furnish suitable goods required for the particular purpose.

Disclaimer of warranty. The warranty can be disclaimed more easily than the implied warranty of merchantability, probably because the warranty of merchantability is considered to be a more fundamental, safety-net-type warranty applicable to all commercial transactions, while the implied warranty of fitness for a particular purpose is a specific warranty narrowly focused on the requirements of a particular transaction. The implied warranty of fitness for a particular purpose may be disclaimed by general language.[44] The UCC does not specify or limit the language that may be used, but it does suggest that the following language would be adequate: "[T]here are no warranties which extend beyond the description on the face hereof."[45]

Design specifications waive both implied warranties. Neither the implied warranty of merchantability nor the implied warranty of fitness for a particular purpose applies if the contractor provides detailed specifications, which it usually receives from the owner, and requires the subcontractor or material supplier to comply with those specifications. Comment 9 to U.C.C. § 2-316 provides an explanation of the exclusion of the implied warranties if detailed specifications are provided:

---

[42] Barrington Corp. v. Patrick Lumber Co., 447 So. 2d 785 (Ala. Civ. App. 1984).

[43] *See* County of Henepin v. AFG Indus., 726 F.2d 149 (8th Cir. 1984).

[44] U.C.C. § 2-316 cmt. 4.

[45] *Id.* § 2-316.

The situation in which the buyer [contractor] gives precise and complete specifications to the seller is not explicitly covered in [the section about excluding warranties], but this is a frequent circumstance by which the implied warranties may be excluded. The warranty of fitness for a particular purpose would not normally arise since in such a situation there is usually no reliance on the seller by the buyer. . . . [T]he implied warranty of merchantability is displaced by the express warranty that the goods will comply with the specifications. Thus, where the buyer gives detailed specifications as to the goods, neither of the implied warranties as to quality will normally apply to the transaction unless consistent with the specifications.[46]

If the contractor requires the subcontractor or material supplier to comply with detailed specifications, the implied warranties of merchantability and fitness for a particular purpose do not apply, but the subcontractor or material supplier is required to comply with those detailed specifications.

§ 7.15   —Express Warranties

As the name implies, express warranties are express statements or express promises. According to the UCC, express warranties are created when the seller makes statements of fact or promises, including descriptions, or provides samples or models relating to the goods, and those statements, promises, samples, or models become the basis of the bargain between the parties.[47] Formal words such as "warrant" or "guarantee" are not required to create the warranty, and the seller is not required to have a specific intention to create a warranty.[48]

Distinction Between Implied Fitness and Express Warranties

The point at which the implied warranty of fitness for a particular purpose ends and an express warranty begins is not always clear. Although one warranty is implied and the other is express, in an actual transaction, the distinction between the two types of warranties may be extremely faint, as demonstrated by a case in California.

In that case, a supplier of steel tubing told the subcontractor responsible for installing a home heating system that the tubing was suitable for the required system. The court held that the supplier's statements about the suitability of the tubing constituted an express warranty based on the predecessor to California's version of U.C.C. § 2-313.[49]

---

[46] *Id.* cmt. 9.

[47] *Id.* § 2-313(1).

[48] *Id.* § 2-313(2); *see* Neville Constr. Co. v. Cook Paint & Varnish Co., 671 F.2d 1107 (8th Cir. 1982).

[49] Eichler Homes, Inc. v. Anderson, 9 Cal. App. 3d 224, 87 Cal. Rptr. 893 (1970).

The result in the case is not surprising, but shows the fine line between an express warranty and an implied warranty of fitness for a particular purpose. In the case, the tubing supplier expressly stated that the tubing was suitable when it was informed of the nature of the required heating system, a statement that created an express warranty. However, if the supplier was told that the subcontractor was relying on the supplier to select and furnish tubing that was suitable for the heating system and the supplier made no statement about the suitability of the tubing for the system, then an implied warranty of fitness for particular use probably would have been created. The statement by the supplier is what created an express instead of implied warranty.

Disclaiming Express Warranties

Disclaiming an express warranty is extremely difficult, and should be. Allowing a seller to make express statements or promises about the goods it is selling, upon which the buyer relies in deciding to purchase the goods, and then allowing the seller to disclaim responsibility for those statements or promises would be extremely unfair.[50]

A good example of a situation in which a court would not allow a seller to disclaim responsibility for express statements about the goods it sold involved the manufacturer and the distributor of a drill rig. The manufacturer and the distributor had disseminated a sales brochure that described the capabilities of and detailed specifications for the drill rig. The brochure also contained the following disclaimer language:

> We reserve the right to amend these specifications at any time without notice. The only warranty applicable is our standard written warranty. We make no other warranty expressed or implied and particularly make no warranty of suitability for any particular purpose.[51]

The purchaser of a drill rig sued the manufacturer and distributor for breach of express warranty, and the manufacturer and distributor asserted the disclaimer language as a defense. The court held that the statements and warranties in the brochure could not be disclaimed or excluded, and explained its holding as follows: "[W]hen a product has been expressly described by its manufacturer as having certain detailed capacities under certain conditions, it would be both unfair and unreasonable to construe the [disclaimer] language as negating the express description."[52]

---

[50] See Potter v. MCP Facilities Corp., 471 F. Supp. 1344 (E.D.N.Y. 1979); Fundin v. Chicago Pneumatic Tool Co., 152 Cal. App. 3d 951, 199 Cal. Rptr. 789 (1984).

[51] Fundin v. Chicago Pneumatic Tool Co., 152 Cal. App. 3d 951, 199 Cal. Rptr. 789 (1984).

[52] Id. at 958, 199 Cal. Rptr. at 794.

§ 7.16   —Limitation of Remedies

A seller may limit its exposure to breach of warranty claims by appropriate language in the contract or purchase order.[53] What is the difference between a disclaimer of liability and a limitation of remedy? A *disclaimer of liability* for a warranty attempts to totally disclaim liability for the warranty. In essence, the seller attempts to say that it is not liable for a particular warranty. A *limitation of remedy* does not attempt to disclaim liability for a particular warranty but instead attempts to limit or constrict the remedy, or what the purchaser is entitled to recover, if the warranty is breached.

A sophisticated seller will not attempt to disclaim liability for an express warranty because the disclaimer will probably be unsuccessful, but will instead attempt to limit the remedy available to the purchaser if the warranty is breached.

Creation of Limitation of Remedy

The limitation of remedy can be created by provisions in the contract or purchase order that limit the extent of the seller's liability if the goods are found to be defective or unsuitable.[54]

A typical limitation is that the purchaser's remedy for defective goods is limited to repair or replacement by the seller. Although this limitation may seem to be fair and adequate on the surface, a contractor should be wary of such a limitation because it could exclude liability for additional or consequential damages caused by the defect in the goods. Under such a limitation, a seller's liability may be limited to repairing or replacing the defective goods, while the contractor's liability could be for all damages caused by the defective goods, which could be hundreds of times greater than the cost of repairing or replacing the defective goods.[55]

Limitation on the Limitation

A limitation of remedy cannot be unconscionable.[56] The doctrine of unconscionability is discussed in **§ 7.19**, but in essence, a limitation of remedy cannot be so one-sided as to be unconscionable under the circumstances existing at the time of the making of the contract.[57]

An example of a limitation of remedy that was found unconscionable is a case in which a large corporation's sale of weight and sizing equipment to

---

[53] U.C.C. § 2-719.

[54] *Id.*

[55] *See* Lincoln Pulp & Paper Co. v. Dravo Corp., 445 F. Supp. 507 (D. Me. 1977).

[56] U.C.C. § 2-302.

[57] *Id.* cmt. 1.

a small farming company was accomplished pursuant to the corporation's standard form sales contract that contained an exclusion of liability for consequential damages. The court found the exclusion to be unconscionable and unenforceable.[58]

A contractor should not rely on the doctrine of unconscionability to protect itself against limitations of remedy. The availability of the doctrine depends on the facts of each case and, consequently, the success of the unconscionability argument is extremely difficult to predict. Rather than relying on the doctrine of unconscionability, a contractor should be alert to any limitation of remedy in any subcontract or purchase order, and either delete the limitation if possible or attempt to negotiate a reasonable limitation that fairly addresses the seller's responsibility for the goods, material, or equipment it is furnishing.

§ 7.17   —Duty to Deal in Good Faith

Under the UCC, parties to a contract have an implied duty to cooperate in good faith to fulfill their contractual obligations.[59] The UCC provides that "every contract or duty . . . imposes an obligation of good faith in its performance or enforcement."[60]

Construction contracts rely heavily on the cooperation of all parties involved in the construction process, and that cooperation usually must extend over a substantial period of time. Contractors and their subcontractors usually are allowed broad discretion to select appropriate construction means, methods, and techniques to fulfill their contractual obligations successfully. Because of the extended cooperation necessary for a construction project and because of the broad discretion allowed the various contractors and subcontractors, the UCC's requirement that the parties cooperate in good faith is critically important for construction contracts.

Under the UCC, a party that is allowed discretion to perform the details of the contract must exercise that discretion reasonably and in good faith or be held liable for the failure to do so.[61] In an extreme situation, if both parties fail to cooperate in good faith, that failure can void their contract.[62]

---

[58] A&M Produce Co. v. FMC Corp., 135 Cal. App. 3d 473, 186 Cal. Rptr. 114 (1982).

[59] *See* Balfour, Guthrie & Co. v. Gourmet Farms, 108 Cal. App. 3d 181, 166 Cal. Rptr. 422 (1980); Marquette Co. v. Norcem, Inc., 114 A.D.2d 738, 494 N.Y.S.2d 511 (1985).

[60] U.C.C. § 1-203.

[61] *See* Admiral Plastics Corp. v. Trueblood, Inc., 436 F.2d 1335 (6th Cir. 1971).

[62] *Id.*

§ 7.18   —Course of Dealing and Usage of Trade

The separate but related concepts regarding course of dealing and usage of trade are important to contractors. The concept of *course of dealing* refers to a series of previous transactions between parties through which the parties have established a basis of understanding for interpreting each other's expressions and conduct; the concept of *usage of trade* refers to trade customs or practices that are observed regularly enough to justify an expectation that they will be observed in a particular transaction.

Contractors commonly enter into numerous contracts with certain subcontractors and material suppliers for different projects over a period of several years, and the experience from those contracts establishes certain understandings between the parties about interpreting what they say and what they do.

Trade customs and practices play an important role in construction contracts, and contractors certainly expect subcontractors and suppliers to be aware of and to comply with those customs and practices.

Although the concepts were not invented by the UCC, under the UCC, a course of previous dealing and trade practices can be used to clarify or explain the express terms of a contract. The concepts essentially are a codification of the rule that a previous course of dealing and generally known trade customs can be used to explain or interpret ambiguities in a contract.

Course of dealing.   The UCC defines *course of dealing* to mean "a sequence of previous conduct between the parties to a particular transaction which is fairly to be regarded as establishing a common basis of understanding for interpreting their expressions and other conduct."[63]

Usage of trade.   The UCC defines *usage of trade* to mean "any practice or method of dealing having such regularity of observance in a place, vocation or trade as to justify an expectation that it will be observed with respect to the transaction in question."[64]

Application of the Concepts

The concepts essentially are used to interpret the contract, although the interpretation may go far beyond merely interpreting an occasional ambiguous word.

---

[63] U.C.C. § 1-205(1).
[64] *Id.* § 1-205(2).

Adding terms to contract. Under the UCC, course of dealing and usage of trade can add to the express terms of a contract.[65] These terms can be added even if the contract is unambiguous and complete on its face.[66] Some of the terms that courts have added to the express terms of a contract include the requirement to repay freight (added by course of dealing);[67] product available as condition of performance (added by course of dealing and usage of trade);[68] and term that wheat need not be grown on seller's land (added by usage of trade).[69]

Giving meaning to language. Course of dealing and usage of trade also may give a particular meaning to contractual language.[70] The particular meaning given by courts to contract language includes varying contract quantity by custom and usage, even when one of the parties had no actual knowledge of the custom;[71] defining cancellation rights by usage of trade;[72] determining quality of items and time for delivery by standards in the industry;[73] and supplementing "engineer's measure" by definitions from usage of trade.[74]

Disclaiming implied warranty. Course of dealing or usage of trade can operate to disclaim an implied warranty.[75] Courts have found that course of dealing or usage of trade could exclude or modify an implied warranty of fitness between a seller and a buyer when tags attached to bags of seed limited the seller's liability;[76] a 62-year course of dealing could exclude the UCC implied warranties;[77] and trade usage could exclude warranties for used farm equipment.[78]

---

[65] *Id.* §§ 1-205(3)–(4), 2-208.

[66] *Id.* § 2-202 cmt. 1; Nanakuli Paving & Rock Co. v. Shell Oil Co., 664 F.2d 772 (9th Cir. 1981).

[67] Neal Cooper Grain Co. v. Texas Gulf Sulphur Co., 508 F.2d 283 (7th Cir. 1974).

[68] Arcon Constr. Co. v. South Dakota Cement Plant, 349 N.W.2d 407 (S.D. 1984).

[69] Colley v. Bi-State, Inc., 21 Wash. App. 769, 586 P.2d 908 (1978).

[70] U.C.C. §§ 1-205(3), 2-202.

[71] Balfour, Gutherie & Co. v. Gourmet Farms, 108 Cal. App. 3d 181, 166 Cal. Rptr. 422 (1980).

[72] Sunbury Textile Mills, Inc. v. Commissioner, 585 F.2d 1190 (3d Cir. 1978).

[73] J.A. Jones Constr. Co. v. City of Dover, 372 A.2d 540 (Del. 1977).

[74] Rose Stone & Concrete v. County of Broome, 76 A.D.2d 998, 429 N.Y.S.2d 295 (1980).

[75] U.C.C. § 2-316(3)(c).

[76] Agricultural Servs. Ass'n v. Ferry-Morse Seed Co., 551 F.2d 1057 (6th Cir. 1977).

[77] Standard Structural Steel Co. v. Bethlehem Steel Corp., 597 F. Supp. 164 (D. Conn. 1984).

[78] Spurgeon v. Jamieson Motors, 164 Mont. 296, 521 P.2d 924 (1974).

Reasonableness controls.   The UCC provides that express terms, course of dealing, and usage of trade are to be construed as consistent with one another whenever possible. Nevertheless, if construing them as consistent produces an unreasonable result, express terms control both course of dealing and usage of trade. As between course of dealing and usage of trade, course of dealing prevails over usage of trade.[79]

§ 7.19   —Unconscionability in Contracts

The UCC allows courts to refuse to enforce an unconscionable contract or to limit or refuse to enforce an unconscionable clause in a contract.[80] Oddly, the UCC does not define *unconscionability* but instead provides a broad test to be used in evaluating whether a contract or clause is unconscionable:

> The basic test is whether, in light of the general background and the needs of the particular case, the clauses involved are so one-sided as to be unconscionable under the circumstances existing at the time of the making of the contract.[81]

As stated by the test, unconscionability is determined by the circumstances existing at the time the contract is formed, by deciding whether, under those facts and circumstances, the contract or the clause was unconscionable. Subsequent facts and circumstances, regardless of how unfair or unconscionable, are not relevant to the determination of unconscionability.[82]

In addition, the UCC provides as follows about unconscionability:

> (1) If the court as a matter of law finds the contract or any clause of the contract to have been unconscionable at the time it was made the court may refuse to enforce the contract, or it may enforce the remainder of the contract without the unconscionable clause, or it may so limit the application of any unconscionable clause as to avoid any unconscionable result.
>
> (2) When it is claimed or appears to the court that the contract or any clause thereof may be unconscionable the parties shall be afforded a reasonable opportunity to present evidence as to its commercial setting, purpose, and effect to aid the court in making the determination.[83]

Again, to determine unconscionability, a court looks back to the time the contract was formed and determines if the contract or the clause was

---

[79] U.C.C. § 1-205(4); *see* Southern Concrete Servs. v. Mableton Contractors, 407 F. Supp. 581 (N.D. Ga. 1975).

[80] U.C.C. § 2-302.

[81] *Id.* cmt. 1.

[82] *See* A&M Produce Co. v. FMC Corp., 135 Cal. App. 3d 473, 186 Cal. Rptr. 114 (1982).

[83] U.C.C. § 2-302.

unconscionable at that time. The parties are allowed to present evidence about the contract's commercial setting, purpose, and effect to assist the court in determining whether the contract was unconscionable.

Because a court looks at the facts and circumstances existing at the time the contract is formed, the determination of unconscionability is accomplished on a case-by-case basis, and the predictability of the determination is uncertain at best. Consequently, relying on "unconscionability" to justify a failure to perform a contract or to adhere to a clause of a contract can be extremely risky. What appears to be unconscionable to one party may be merely a hard bargain to the other party, and to the court. Therefore, unconscionability is not a panacea to cure every difficult contract or difficult clause.

Unconscionability versus Fraud

Unconscionability is not fraud. Unconscionability entails a bargain that is too unfair or too one-sided; fraud entails an intentional concealment or misrepresentation of material facts. Unconscionability is driving too hard a bargain; fraud is cheating while driving the bargain. Both unconscionability and fraud may excuse performance, but fraud also may allow the defrauded party to recover damages caused by the fraud.

§ 7.20 —Commercial Impracticability of Performance

The UCC excuses performance of a contract if its performance has become impractical because of an unexpected supervening event. The UCC provides that no breach of contract occurs "if performance as agreed has been made impracticable by the occurrence of a contingency the nonoccurrence of which was a basic assumption on which the contract was made or by compliance in good faith (with applicable laws)."[84]

The UCC requires (1) an unexpected supervening event that (2) makes performance of the contract impracticable. Both factors are required. An unexpected supervening event with only a minor impact on performance does not excuse that performance; extreme difficulty or expense in performing the contract not caused by an unexpected supervening event does not excuse performance.

By way of a generalized example, the UCC explains that a seller may be excused from timely delivery of goods when performance has become commercially impracticable because of unforeseen supervening

---

[84] *Id.* § 2-615.

circumstances not within the contemplation of the parties at the time of contracting.[85]

Determining Impracticability

What is impracticable? At one extreme, it is less than impossible: performance is possible, but from a commercial standpoint, it is impracticable.[86]

At the other extreme, a slight increase in cost does not constitute commercial impracticability. As stated by one court, commercial impracticability does not arise "merely because performance cannot be achieved under the most economical means."[87]

But where between the two extremes does commercial impracticability lie? Two California cases provide some guidance. Neither was decided under the UCC, but both analyzed commercial impracticability (or "extreme impracticability") as a form of impossibility of performance as a defense to performance of a construction contract.

In one case, unexpected conditions increased the cost of performing the work by about 10 to 12 times, and the court found that the increased cost constituted extreme impracticability and excused performance of the work.[88]

In the other case, unexpected conditions increased the cost of a drilling contract from $3.50 per foot to $5.00 per foot, and the court found that the increased drilling cost was merely an unforeseen difficulty that would not excuse performance.[89]

The burden of proving commercial impracticability is on the party relying on impracticability to excuse its performance. An example is an oil producer attempting to use commercial impracticability to excuse its performance. The court required the oil producer to prove that pipeline breakdowns and acts of government were not caused by the oil producer and that the producer could not have avoided the problems by reasonable efforts to prevent them.[90]

Like unconscionability, commercial impracticability is a risky excuse for not performing a contract. What may appear to the nonperforming party to be extreme commercial impracticability may appear to be nothing more than commonly expected difficulty to the other party and to the court. An

---

[85] *Id.* § 2-615 official cmt.

[86] *See* Restatement (Second) of Contracts § 261 (   ); Natus Corp. v. United States, 371 F.2d 450 (Ct. Cl. 1967); Aluminum Co. of Am. v. Essex Group, 499 F. Supp. 53 (W.D. Pa. 1980).

[87] Natus Corp. v. United States, 371 F.2d 450, 456 (Ct. Cl. 1967).

[88] Mineral Park Land Co. v. Howard, 172 Cal. 289, 156 P. 458 (1916).

[89] Kennedy v. Reece, 225 Cal. App. 2d 717, 37 Cal. Rptr. 708 (1964).

[90] Nissho-Iwai Co. v. Occidental Crude Sales, Inc., 729 F.2d 1530 (5th Cir. 1984).

unexpected supervening event to one party may be a commonly expected event to the other. An extreme increase in cost to one party may be a reasonable and modest increase to the other.

§ 7.21 Final Words of Caution

Contractors generally believe that the UCC does not apply to their business. They believe that the UCC applies to companies that manufacture or sell products. They see a clear distinction between their own type of business and the business of manufacturers and sellers of products, to whom the UCC applies.

The distinction is not as clear as many contractors believe. Their business is truly different than that of a company that manufactures and sells 500 million bite-sized crackers per year, but the UCC is broader than most contractors believe and might be broad enough to encompass both bite-sized crackers and the furnishing and placement of concrete.

The UCC is not totally foreign to the construction process. Purchase orders for material or equipment have been governed by the UCC since its inception. What may be foreign to contractors is the possibility that the breadth of the UCC may encompass a much wider range of contracts involved in the construction process than is commonly believed.

When a contractor tries to identify the contracts to which the UCC applies, it may have to include a wider range of contracts than those few purchase orders that involve only the purchase of material or equipment and absolutely no labor. Any contract that involves a combination of labor and material is a candidate for application of the UCC, and the more predominant the material portion of the contract, the more likely a court will find that the UCC applies.

The widening application of the UCC to what are commonly believed to be construction contracts not subject to the UCC is not necessarily bad news for contractors because the UCC gives to contractors more than it takes away. Nevertheless, if the UCC does govern a contract, the contractor must be aware of its own rights and remedies and what is required to perfect those rights and remedies. The contractor also must be aware of what the UCC requires of the contractor so that the contractor does not jeopardize its position by failing to perform as required, especially if the required performance is not expressly specified in the contract but instead is found in the UCC, such as good faith and fair dealing.

Contracting with the material supplier is not uniquely difficult once the fundamentals of the UCC are understood, but believing that the UCC applies only to purchase orders and never to subcontracts could create unique difficulties.

CHAPTER 8

FEDERAL GOVERNMENT CONTRACTING

Richard McKim Preston
Dean W. Fischer*

Richard McKim Preston is the managing partner of the construction group in the Washington, D.C., office of the national law firm of Seyfafth, Shaw, Fairweather & Geraldson. He holds a B.A. and J.D., cum laude, from Washington & Lee University and an M.A., cum laude, from Fairleigh Dickinson University. Mr. Preston specializes in the resolution of national and international construction disputes involving both governmental and private parties. In addition, he advises in the negotiation and administration of complex construction contracts. He regularly serves as an arbitrator for the American Arbitration Association in adjudicating construction disputes.

Dean W. Fischer is the partner in charge of Arthur Andersen's Government Contracts Group in the Chicago, Illinois, office. He specializes in federal government contracting, consulting with clients on a variety of contracting compliance, regulatory, and accounting issues. He graduated from Valparaiso University with a B.S. degree in accounting. His background is primarily in the manufacturing and construction industries, including consulting with and auditing high technology, multi-national defense contractors. Mr. Fischer is a member of the American Institute of Certified Public Accountants, the Illinois CPA Society, the National Contract Management Association, and the American Defense Preparedness Association.

*Assisted by Kevin P. Connelly of Seyfarth, Shaw, Fairweather & Geraldson and Steven J. Young of Arthur Andersen & Co.

185

OVERVIEW

§ 8.1   Introduction to Government Contracting

Federal government construction projects offer tremendous opportunities for construction contractors, especially during lean times in commercial construction. Although the potential for significant business exists in the federal arena, such opportunity does not exist without its costs. Construction contractors with no experience in contracting with the federal government may be shocked by the maze of statutory, regulatory, and contractual obligations to which they subject themselves in contracting with the federal government. It is essential that the contractor understand how the system works and the extent of its obligations in order to include in its bid the hidden costs of performing a government contract. This knowledge is also essential to avoid violating regulations and contractual terms, which violations may result in the contractor's incurrence of contractual, civil, and even criminal penalties.

The purpose of this chapter is to highlight some of the differences between federal government construction contracting and the commercial construction environment. In addition, the chapter details some of the significant obligations that are part of the price of obtaining federal government contracts.

To accomplish this purpose, a brief overview of the government contracting regulatory system is provided, followed by the identification of key provisions often found in solicitations, and subsequently incorporated in awarded contracts, and a discussion of the background and ramifications of these provisions. The chapter concludes by focusing on certain issues of which contractors should be aware during performance of government contracts.

§ 8.2   Federal Acquisition Regulation System

A contractor entering into its first federal government contract finds itself regulated by the Federal Acquisition Regulation System. This system is codified in the Federal Acquisition Regulation (FAR),[1] and in the acquisition regulations of individual agencies, which are intended to implement and supplement the FAR. The largest of these agency supplements is the Department of Defense (DOD) FAR Supplement.[2] In addition, the General Services Administration (GSA) FAR Supplement is of particular relevance to construction contractors, given the increasingly significant role GSA plays in federal construction contracts.[3] The system can be thought of as

---

[1] The FAR is published in Title 48, Chapter 1 of the Code of Federal Regulations (CFR).

[2] The DOD FAR Supplement (DFARS) is published in Title 48, Chapter 2 of CFR.

[3] The GSA FAR Supplement is published in Title 48, Chapter 5 of CFR.

the contractor's bible because, not only does the FAR set forth the rules and procedures on which the game of government contracting is played, but also it establishes a code of acceptable and unacceptable behavior, and prescribes penalties for unacceptable behavior.

Although the concept of rules and regulations in government contracting has been around for decades, the FAR is relatively young. In 1984, the FAR replaced the Defense Acquisition Regulation (DAR), the Federal Procurement Regulation (FPR), and the NASA Procurement Regulation (NASA PR) as the primary regulation governing government contracts. Contracts that the government awarded based on solicitations issued prior to April 1, 1984, generally are still subject to these precursors to the FAR.

The FAR is maintained by the Defense Acquisition Regulations (DAR) Council and the Civilian Agency Acquisition Council (CAAC). These councils also are responsible for preparing and issuing revisions to the FAR. However, many of the revisions to the FAR that have significant consequences are mandated by acts of Congress.

A government contractor will find many of the FAR clauses incorporated into its contract solely by reference to the applicable FAR citation. These "incorporated-by-reference" clauses have the same force and effect on the contractor as if their entire text had been repeated verbatim in the contract. For this reason and others, it is essential that a potential government contractor become familiar with the FAR. Ignorance of the complicated and onerous rules and regulations set forth within the FAR undoubtedly will lead to significant legal problems. The remainder of this chapter in large part pertains to an overview of the substance and ramifications of some of the major clauses that a construction contractor may expect to find in a federal government construction contract.

SOLICITATION

§ 8.3   Responding to the Solicitation

A contractor's first detailed involvement in a federal procurement action often is in responding to a solicitation. Through the solicitation, the government identifies to potential offerors what the government seeks to procure. The solicitation also contains the contractual provisions that govern performance of the contract. As discussed in § 8.2, the solicitation often does not set forth the contractual provisions in full, but rather consists of references to contract clauses, which are set forth in full in the FAR, or in the supplementary agency regulation. These provisions, which are incorporated by reference into the solicitation as well as into the subsequently awarded contract, have the same force and effect as if they were set forth in full in the solicitation and contract.

§ 8.4   Background on Truth in Negotiations Act

In some instances construction contractors find themselves subject to the Truth in Negotiations Act (TINA)[4] and its implementing regulations in the FAR.[5] These provisions, which in certain situations require contractors to share their cost or pricing data with the government for purpose of negotiations, will be completely foreign to a contractor that is used to working in a commercial environment.

The requirements of TINA grew out of a federal government purchasing system that procures many unique goods and services. As a result, government procurement personnel often cannot identify two or more qualified sources to fulfill their requirements. Without two or more competing suppliers, the government procurement personnel cannot rely on independent price competition between the suppliers to ensure that the prices proposed are fair and reasonable. In cases in which they cannot rely on competitive or market forces to ensure the reasonableness of pricing, government personnel employ a cost-based pricing approach. Under this approach, the government arrives at a price by requiring the contractor, in accordance with TINA and its implementing regulations, to provide details about estimated costs to perform the contract plus its proposed profit. The government and contractor personnel then negotiate a price based on the information furnished. These types of contracts normally are referred to as "sole source pricing actions" or "cost-based pricing actions." It should be emphasized that TINA is essentially a submission requirement, in that it requires the contractor to provide cost or pricing data to the government, while not requiring the contractor's offered price to equate to that data. However, TINA does have the effect of leveling the playing field for price negotiations.

§ 8.5   —Application of TINA to Contracts

TINA applies only to "negotiated" contracts over a certain dollar threshold. The current thresholds for the application of this Act are as follows: (1) DOD contracts, subcontracts, and contract changes with a price effect of $500,000 or more;[6] and (2) Civilian agency contracts, subcontracts, and

---

[4] 10 U.S.C. § 2306a (1988), as amended by National Defense Authorization Act for Fiscal Year 1991, Pub. L. No. 101-510, § 803, 104 Stat. 1485, 1589–1591 (1990), and by Persian Gulf Conflict Supplemental Authorization & Personnel Benefits Act of 1991, Pub. L. No. 102-25, § 704, 105 Stat. 75, 118.

[5] *See* FAR subpt. 15.8.

[6] 10 U.S.C. § 2306a(a).

contract changes with a price effect of $100,000 or more. (This threshold is expected to be raised to $500,000 by the end of 1992.)[7]

TINA further provides for exemptions from its requirements when certain conditions are met, even if the value of the procurement exceeds the dollar threshold of the Act. The exemptions depend on how the government seeks to procure goods and services. The government uses two methods of obtaining bids and proposals under federal contracts: (1) sealed bidding and (2) negotiated procurements. The regulations describe sealed bidding as a "method of contracting that employs competitive bids, public opening of bids, and awards."[8] All sealed bids, regardless of dollar value of the awarded contract, are exempt from the requirements of TINA.[9] Contracting by negotiation is the second method of contracting used by the government. The regulations define negotiations in the negative stating that "any contract awarded without using sealed bidding procedures is a negotiated contract."[10]

TINA and its implementing regulations exempt certain negotiated contracts from TINA's requirements. The regulations identify three cases in which negotiated procurements are exempt from the requirements of TINA. Negotiated contracts are exempt from TINA when proposed prices are:

(1) Based on adequate price competition;
(2) Based on established catalog or market prices of commercial items sold in substantial quantities to the general public;
(3) Set by law or regulation.[11]

Construction contracts rarely are based on established catalog or market prices and prices set by law or regulation. Therefore, **Chapter 8** does not discuss these exemptions, except to state that when applicable, the contractor often must claim the exemption by filling out Standard Form 1412.[12]

The FAR defines *adequate price competition* as existing if:

(i) Offers are solicited;
(ii) Two or more responsible offerors that can satisfy the Government's requirements submit priced offers responsive to the solicitation's expressed requirements; and
(iii) These offerors compete independently for a contract to be awarded to the responsible offeror submitting the lowest evaluated price.[13]

---

[7] FAR 15.804-2.

[8] *Id.* 14.101.

[9] 10 U.S.C. § 2306a(a).

[10] FAR 15.101.

[11] 10 U.S.C. § 2306a(b)(1); FAR 15.804-3(a).

[12] FAR 15.804-3(e).

[13] *Id.* 15.804-3(b).

Accordingly, the initial pricing of many construction contracts is exempt from the requirements of TINA even when the dollar threshold for applicability of the Act is exceeded because the government generally obtains adequate price competition to ensure that the price it receives is fair and reasonable. As a result, no cost information is required to support the reasonableness of the contractor's price.

However, the pricing of changes under the Changes clause that are in excess of the thresholds is subject to TINA because these change orders are not priced under a competitive bid process. Therefore, even when TINA is not applicable to the initial contracting action, it is in the best interest of construction contractors to understand the requirements of TINA for pricing and negotiating contract change orders.

§ 8.6   —Basic Requirements of TINA

TINA requires a contractor to disclose all of its cost or pricing data to the government prior to and during price negotiations. The regulations define *cost or pricing data* as "all facts, as of the date of price agreement, that prudent buyers and sellers would reasonably expect to affect price negotiations significantly. Cost or pricing data are factual, not judgmental, and are therefore verifiable."[14]

There have been several board of contract appeals cases that define more fully what constitutes cost or pricing data.[15] These cases are beyond the scope of a general overview. However, a practical method of determining whether information may constitute cost data is to decide whether the information represents verifiable, factual information of which the contractor would like to be cognizant if the contractor were in the government's position in negotiating a contract price. If the answer to this question is yes, the information probably should be disclosed to the government.

It is often difficult for a commercial company to understand the federal government requirement that the company surrender its superior position during price negotiations. However, a contractor has a contractual obligation to meet the disclosure requirements of TINA. Furthermore, the government requires the contractor to certify that its cost data disclosures are current, accurate, and complete as of the date of price agreement.[16] Note that the government is only entitled to one certificate, and the contractor

---

[14] *Id.* 15.801.

[15] *See, e.g.,* Texas Instruments, Inc., ASBCA No. 23678, 87-3 B.C.A. (CCH) ¶ 20,195 (1987) (computer generated reports containing certain product run costs were considered cost and pricing data); Grumman Aerospace Corp., ASBCA No. 27476, 86-3 B.C.A. (CCH) ¶ 19,091 (1986) (contractor's draft narrative analyzing subcontractor quote constituted cost or pricing data).

[16] FAR 15.804-4.

should submit that certificate as soon as practicable after price agreement is reached.[17]

§ 8.7 —Price Adjustments for Violations

TINA allows the government to recover the price effects of noncurrent, incomplete, or inaccurate cost data disclosures by the contractor without requiring the government to prove any intent to mislead on the part of the contractor.[18] The simple failure to disclose is enough in and of itself. The Price Reduction for Defective Cost or Pricing Data clause gives the government the right to execute a unilateral price reduction to the contract for the estimated price effect of noncurrent, inaccurate, or incomplete cost or pricing data disclosures made by the contractor (commonly referred to as defective pricing).[19] As a practical matter, a contractor is better off disclosing cost or pricing data before the date of price agreement and before the contractor begins the work required under the contract. At that time, the contractor has a strong negotiating position in establishing the price effect of the cost data because the government has not received the services it requires. If the government discovers noncurrent, inaccurate, or incomplete disclosures during a subsequent audit of the contract, the discovery can result in a costly dispute. Furthermore, the contractor will be at a disadvantage when negotiating the price effect of the undisclosed cost data if the government already has received the services required under the contract.

§ 8.8 —Subcontractor Flow-Down Provisions

As is the case with various contractual requirements incorporated through the FAR clauses, prime contractors and higher tier subcontractors should *flow down* the requirements of the following FAR clauses when applicable:

1. Price Reductions for Defective Cost or Pricing Data (FAR 52.215-22)
2. Price Reductions for Defective Cost or Pricing Data—Modifications (FAR 52.215-23)
3. Subcontractor Cost or Pricing Data (FAR 52.215-24)
4. Subcontractor Cost or Pricing Data—Modifications (FAR 52.215-25).

---

[17] *Id.*

[18] 10 U.S.C. § 2306a(d); FAR 52.215-22.

[19] FAR 52.215-22, 52.215-23.

It should be noted that prime contractors are liable for defective cost or pricing data furnished by their subcontractors.[20] By flowing down the appropriate clauses, contractors provide themselves with a contractual remedy against the offending subcontractor. The same exemptions and thresholds discussed in § 8.5 for prime contractors also are applicable to subcontractors. Furthermore, if a prime contract or higher tier subcontract is exempt from the requirement of TINA, the lower tier subcontracts also are exempt.

The prime contractor or higher tier subcontractor must perform price and cost analysis of subcontractor cost or pricing data and disclose the results of the analysis as part of its proposal. In addition, if the subcontract (or subcontract modification) exceeds the following thresholds, the prime subcontractor is required to submit cost or pricing data to the government:

1. $1,000,000 or more.
2.   Both more than $100,000 ($500,000 for DOD) and more than 10% of the prime contractor's proposed price.
3.   Considered to be necessary for adequately pricing the prime contract.[21]

It is important to determine whether TINA requirements are applicable to a specific contract. Contractors should note that the government sometimes requests cost or pricing data even when the submission is not mandated by TINA. In such instances, contractors are advised to oppose the imposition of these nonmandatory TINA requirements given the complexity of TINA and the serious consequences that may befall a contractor as a result of TINA violations.

§ 8.9   Procurement Integrity Provisions

As noted in § 8.2, many revisions to the FAR are mandated by Congress. Congressionally-mandated revisions to the FAR often have resulted from Congressional attempts to correct perceived improper business activities. For example, Congress passed legislation in November 1988 known as the "procurement integrity provisions" to deal with perceived problems in the trafficking of procurement information between government officials and prospective federal contractors,[22] which provisions did not become

---

[20] *See* Lockheed Aircraft Corp. v. United States, 193 Ct. Cl. 86, 432 F.2d 801 (1970).

[21] FAR 15.806-2(a).

[22] The procurement integrity provisions are set forth at § 27 of the Office of Federal Procurement Policy Act Amendments of 1988, Pub. L. No. 100-679, 102 Stat. 4063, as amended in § 814 of Pub. L. No. 101-189, 103 Stat. 1495-1498 and in § 815 of Pub. L. No. 101-510, 104 Stat. 1720 (codified at 41 U.S.C. § 423).

effective until December 1, 1990. The FAR contains extensive regulations implementing the requirements of the procurement integrity provisions.[23]

The Office of Federal Procurement Policy Act, as well as the implementing provisions in the FAR, prohibit the following actions on the part of contractors competing for the award of a prime contract or subcontract:

1. Offering, giving, or promising any money, gratuity, or thing of value to a procurement official;

2. Offering or even discussing future employment or business opportunities with a *procurement official,* defined as a government official who has participated substantially and personally in: (a) drafting, reviewing, or approving the specification or the statement of work; (b) preparing purchase requests; (c) preparing or issuing the solicitation; (d) evaluating bids or proposals; (e) selecting sources; (f) negotiating the contract or contract modification; or (g) reviewing or approving the award of a contract or contract modification;

3. Soliciting or obtaining, directly or indirectly, from a government official prior to the award of a contract proprietary or source selection information regarding that procurement.[24]

In addition, the Act and the regulations prohibit an individual or contractor who obtains authorized or unauthorized access to proprietary or source selection information from disclosing that information to any individual not authorized to receive such information.[25]

The Office of Federal Procurement Policy Act and the FAR prohibit a federal agency from awarding a contract or executing a modification in excess of $100,000 until the agency receives appropriate written certifications from the contractor.[26] The FAR requires the certificate to be signed by the individual responsible for the preparation of the company's bid or offer and requires the individual to certify that to the best of the individual's knowledge and belief there has been no violation or possible violation of the procurement integrity provisions as implemented by the FAR. In addition, the individual must certify that, to the best of the individual's knowledge and belief, each officer, employee, agent, representative, and consultant who participated personally and substantially in the preparation or submission of the contractor's bid or offer, or in the modification of the contract, has certified to the company that he or she is familiar with the procurement integrity provisions, will comply with them, and will report any violation or possible violations of them to the company official that signed the

---

[23] FAR 3.104.

[24] 41 U.S.C. § 423(a); FAR 3.104-3(a), 3.104-4(h)(1).

[25] *Id.* § 423(d); FAR 3.104-3(c).

[26] *Id.* § 423(e); FAR 3.104-9.

company's certification.[27] A bidder's failure to submit the solicitation's *Certificate of Procurement Integrity* renders its bid nonresponsive.[28]

The Office of Federal Procurement Policy Act and the regulations contain severe penalties for violation, providing for cancellation of the procurement or disqualification of an offeror if the government has not awarded the contract or executed the contract modification.[29] If the government has already awarded the contract or executed the contract modification, the Act and implementing regulations provide for the following administrative sanctions: (1) appropriate contractual remedies, such as profit recapture as provided for in the FAR Price or Fee Adjustment for Illegal or Improper Activity clause; and (2) voiding or rescission of the contract or contract modification.[30]

In addition, the FAR provides for referral of the matter to the agency's suspension and debarment official.[31] Further, individuals and companies that engage in conduct prohibited by the procurement integrity provisions may be subject to the imposition of civil fines of up to $100,000 or $1,000,000, respectively.[32] The procurement integrity provisions additionally provide for imprisonment of individual violators for a period not to exceed five years.[33] As has been shown, the provisions impose significant restrictions on contractors, which a contractor should be aware of prior to submitting an offer.

§ 8.10   Byrd Amendment Provisions

Federal government contractors are now subject to additional cost prohibitions and reporting requirements when they attempt to influence a member of Congress or a federal employee with respect to a contract award. Legislation enacted in 1989, popularly called the "Byrd Amendment" after its drafter, Senator Robert Byrd (D-W. Va.), prohibits an awardee of a federal contract, grant, loan, or cooperative agreement from using "appropriated funds" to attempt to "influence" a member of Congress or an officer or employee of any federal agency in connection with a contract award or modification.[34] The Byrd Amendment is the first provision to impose both

---

[27] *Id.*

[28] Spence Bros., B-243766, 91-1 CPD ¶ 428.

[29] 41 U.S.C. § 423(h)(1); FAR 3.104-11(d)(1).

[30] *Id.* § 423(g); FAR 3.104-11(d)(2).

[31] FAR 3.104-11(d)(3).

[32] 41 U.S.C. § 423(i).

[33] *Id.* § 423(j).

[34] The Byrd Amendment is set forth in § 319 of the Department of the Interior and Related Agencies Appropriations Act for Fiscal Year 1990, Pub. L. No. 101-121, 103 Stat. 750 (1990) (codified at 31 U.S.C. I.R.C. § 1352).

sweeping prohibitions and broad reporting requirements relating to lobbying efforts directed at awards of federal contracts. The prohibition on the
use of federal appropriated funds only applies to influencing activities in
connection with a specific, covered federal action.[35] It does not apply to
activities related to legislation and regulations for a program as distinguished from a specific, covered federal action.[36]

Subpart 3.8 of the FAR, entitled "Limitations On The Payment Of Funds
To Influence Federal Transactions," implements the requirements of the
Byrd Amendment. Contract clauses as well as the certification require-
ments are set forth at FAR 52.203-11 and 52.203-12.

The law requires contractors that "request or receive" a federal contract
to certify that they used no appropriated funds for a prohibited purpose.[37]
Profits and fees earned under federal contracts are not considered appropriated funds.[38]

The Byrd Amendment further establishes reporting requirements even
when contractors engage individuals to influence contract awards with
sources other than appropriated funds.[39] In such instances, the contractor
must file a disclosure statement that identifies:

1. To whom payments were made or are to be made
2. The amount of the payment
3. The purpose of the payment
4. How the payment was or will be made.[40]

The Byrd Amendment requires the contractor to file its certification and
disclosure (1) with each "submission that initiates agency consideration of
such person," (2) upon award of a contract exceeding $100,000 if there has
been no prior filing, or (3) quarterly with respect to any "material change"
in the accuracy of information previously disclosed.[41] Subcontractors at all
tiers are required to file a certification and disclosure statement to the next
higher tier subcontractor, up to the prime contractor, who must then file
the disclosures with the agency.[42]

The prohibition against use of appropriated funds does not apply to
(1) payment of "reasonable compensation" to a contractor's officers or

---

[35] 55 Fed. Reg. 24,540, 24,542 (June 15, 1990); see Canaveral Maritime, Inc., B-238356.2,
90-2 CPD ¶ 41.

[36] 55 Fed. Reg. 24,540, 24,542 (June 15, 1990).

[37] 31 U.S.C. § 1352(b)(2)(c); FAR 3.803(a).

[38] 55 Fed. Reg. 24,540, 24,542 (June 15, 1990).

[39] 31 U.S.C. § 1352(b)(2).

[40] Id.

[41] Id. § 1352(b)(4); FAR 3.803(b).

[42] FAR 3.803(d).

employees for legislative or agency lobbying activities not directly related to a contract award; or (2) payment of either "reasonable compensation" to officers or employees, or "reasonable payment" to a nonemployee consultant, for professional or technical services rendered directly in the preparation, submission, or negotiation of any bid, proposal, or application, or for "meeting requirements imposed by or pursuantto law" as a condition for receiving an award.[43]

There is no reporting requirement for payment of reasonable compensation to officers or employees of a contractor, or for payments to nonemployee consultants who perform identical, nonprohibited professional or technical service for which the use of appropriated funds is permitted. However, the FAR limits the definition of exempted *professional and technical services* to "advice and analysis directly applying any professional or technical discipline," such as "drafting of a legal document accompanying a bid or proposal," and "technical advice . . . on the performance or operational capability of a piece of equipment."[44] The regulations exclude from the definition of exempted professional and technical services, "communication with the intent to influence," and communication that advocates one proposal over another.[45] In both of the latter instances, (1) the use of appropriated funds is prohibited and (2) the disclosure requirements are applicable even when other than appropriated funds are used.

Civil penalties for noncompliance, that is, violation of the prohibition or failure to file or amend a disclosure, including a certification, are significant and range from $10,000 to $100,000 for each noncompliance. Furthermore, a contractor may be liable even if its violation is not knowing or willful. It should be noted that even unsuccessful offerors are subject to both the requirements and the penalties. Penalties are enforced through the Program Fraud Civil Remedies Act.[46] The government also reserves its other rights and remedies, which include criminal prosecution, suspension, and debarment.

§ 8.11   Other Improper Practices under FAR

In addition to the FAR provisions pertaining to procurement integrity and to the Byrd Amendment, the FAR sets forth additional regulations pertaining to improper business practices. These provisions place additional restrictions, and in some instances certification requirements, on contractors, with the possibility of a contractor's incurrence of significant penalties in

---

[43] 31 U.S.C. § 1352(e)(2); FAR 3.802(c)(2).

[44] FAR 3.802(c)(2)(B)(II), 52.203-12(b)(3)(ii)(B).

[45] *Id.*

[46] Pub. L. No. 99-509, §§ 6101–6104, 100 Stat. 1874, 1934 (1986).

the event of violation. **Sections 8.12** through **8.15** deal with some of the more significant provisions.

§ 8.12   —Independent Price Determination

With a few minor exceptions, the FAR requires the inclusion of the Certificate of Independent Price Determination clause, set forth at 52.203-2, in solicitations when the government anticipates awarding a firm-fixed-price contract or fixed-price contract with economic price adjustment.[47] The FAR then requires an offeror to certify as follows:

1. The contractor arrived at its offer independently, without engaging in discussions relating to its prices, the intention to submit an offer, or the methods or factors used to calculate the offered prices with other offerors or competitors
2. The contractor has not and will not disclose its offered price to any other offeror or competitor before bid opening (sealed bid) or contract award (negotiated procurement), unless required by law
3. The contractor has not and will not attempt to induce another contractor to either submit or not submit an offer in order to restrict competition.[48]

§ 8.13   —Contingent Fee Arrangements

The FAR prescribes policies and procedures that restrict contingent fee arrangements for soliciting or obtaining government contracts. The FAR requires contracting officers to include in all solicitations the Covenant Against Contingent Fees clause found at FAR 52.203-5 and in most solicitations the Contingent Fee Representation and Agreement clause found at FAR 52.203-4.[49]

The contractor warrants that it has not entered into an agreement with a party other than a "bona fide" employee or agency, in accordance with which the contractor pays the party a contingent fee for obtaining the contract.[50] If the contractor breaches this warranty, the government has the right to annul the contract without incurring any liability to the contractor,

---

[47] FAR 3.103-1.

[48] *Id.* 52.203-2(a).

[49] *Id.* 3.404(b), (c).

[50] *Id.* 52.203-5(a).

or to deduct from the contract price, or otherwise to recover, the full amount of the contingent fee.[51]

§ 8.14   —Anti-Kickback Provisions

Subpart 3.502 of the FAR implements the provisions of the Anti-Kickback Act of 1986.[52] Under the Anti-Kickback Act and implementing regulations, a *kickback* can be defined as offering or providing anything of value for the purpose of improperly obtaining or rewarding favorable treatment in connection with a contract.[53]

The Act and its implementing regulations prohibit any person from (1) providing, attempting to provide, or offering to provide any kickback; (2) soliciting, accepting, or attempting to accept any kickback; or (3) including, directly or indirectly, the amount of any kickback in the contract price.[54] The scope of the regulations are wide, and a contractor need not be awarded the contract to fall within the control of the statute.

The Anti-Kickback Act and the FAR require contractors to implement procedures designed to prevent and detect possible kickback violations.[55] The FAR further requires the contractor to report even possible violations to the Inspector General, the head of the agency, or the Department of Justice (DOJ).[56] Contractors are further required to cooperate fully with any federal agency investigating a possible violation.[57] The contractor is also required to flow down the anti-kickback clause in its subcontractors.[58]

§ 8.15   —Offer or Gift of Gratuity

The FAR further requires the contracting officer to include the Gratuities clause, found at 52.203-3, in most federal contracts.[59] The clause provides the government with the right to terminate a contract, if after a hearing, the government determines that a contractor or its agent offered or gave a gratuity (for example, an entertainment or gift) to an officer, official, or employee of the government with the intent to obtain a contract or favorable

---

[51] *Id.*

[52] 41 U.S.C. §§ 51–58.

[53] *Id.* § 52; FAR 3.502-1.

[54] 41 U.S.C. § 53; FAR 3.502-2.

[55] FAR 52.203-7(c)(1).

[56] *Id.* 52.203-7(c)(1)–(2).

[57] *Id.* 52.203-7(c)(3).

[58] *Id.* 52.203-7(c)(5).

[59] *Id.* 3.202.

treatment under a contract.[60] In addition, under certain circumstances, the government may obtain from the contractor exemplary damages of not less than 3 times nor more than 10 times the cost of the gratuity.[61]

§ 8.16   Socioecomonic Policies for Contractors

Through the FAR, the government imposes numerous social policies, disguised as contract regulations, on contractors. **Sections 8.17** through **8.21** discuss some of the policies implemented by contract clause that construction contractors may be required to satisfy.

§ 8.17   —Davis-Bacon Act

The FAR clause found at 52.222-6 imposes Davis-Bacon Act requirements on contractors. The regulations provide that the contractor will pay all laborers and mechanics employed or working on the site of the work unconditionally and not less than once a week, and that the contractor will deduct from the paychecks only those deductions allowed by the regulations of the Department of Labor.[62] The FAR prohibits contractors from computing wages at rates less than those contained in the wage determinations of the Secretary of Labor, which wage determinations should be attached to the contract.[63] Contractors are responsible for ensuring that the government-furnished wage determination is current. The Supreme Court has held that the government is not liable for increased costs incurred by a contractor due to the contractor's reliance on a noncurrent wage determination attached to the solicitation.[64] Indeed, the Davis-Bacon Act "requirement that the contractor pay not less than the specified minima presupposes the possibility that the contractor may have to pay higher rates."[65]

The regulations further prohibit, with minor exceptions for apprentices and trainees, the contractor's payment to laborers and mechanics of less than the appropriate wage rate and fringe benefits in the wage determination for the classification of work actually performed.[66] The regulations

---

[60] *Id.* 52.203-3(a).

[61] FAR 52.203-3(c).

[62] *Id.* 52.222-6(a).

[63] *Id.* 52.222-6.

[64] United States v. Binghamton Constr. Co., 347 U.S. 171, 178, *reh'g denied,* 347 U.S. 940 (1954).

[65] *Id.* at 178; R.G. Brown, Jr. & Co., IBCA No. 241, 61-2 B.C.A. (CCH) ¶ 3,230, at 16,741 (1961).

[66] FAR 52.222-6(a).

also require the contractor to post the Davis-Bacon poster at all times at the site of the work in a prominent and accessible place where it can be easily seen by the workers.[67]

The contracting officer is required to include the Davis-Bacon Act clause in all solicitations and contracts for construction in the United States in excess of $2,000.[68]

§ 8.18   —Work Hours and Safety Standards

The FAR requires the incorporation of the Contract Work Hours and Safety Standards Act—Overtime Compensation clause, set forth at 52.222-4,[69] in all construction solicitations and contracts when the contract may require or involve the employment of laborers or mechanics and the value of the contract exceeds $2,000.[70] This provision requires the payment of overtime at a rate of not less than one and one-half times the basic rate of pay for all hours worked in excess of 40 hours in the workweek.[71]

The regulations provide that the contractor will be liable for unpaid wages for violation of the Contract Work Hours and Safety Standards Act as well as for liquidated damages to the United States.[72] The contracting officer is authorized to withhold from payments to the contractor under any of the prime contractor's federal contracts a sum equal to unpaid wages and liquidated damages.[73]

The regulations further require contractors and subcontractors to maintain payroll records that demonstrate the contractors' and subcontractors' compliance with the regulations for a period of three years after completion of the contract.[74] Contractors are further required to flow these provisions down to subcontractors.[75]

§ 8.19   —Equal Opportunity

In general, construction contractors find the Equal Opportunity clause, set forth at FAR 52.222-26, contained in their contract. The regulations

---

[67] *Id.*

[68] *Id.* 22.407(a)(1).

[69] 40 U.S.C. §§ 327–333.

[70] FAR 22.305.

[71] *Id.* 52.222-4(a).

[72] *Id.* 52.222-4(b).

[73] *Id.* 52.222-4(c).

[74] FAR 52.222-4(d).

[75] *Id.* 52.222-4(e).

prohibit contractors from discriminating against any employee or applicant for employment because of race, color, religion, sex, or national origin.[76] The regulations require that contractors comply with Executive Order No. 11,246.[77] The contractor further agrees to provide to the contracting agency or the Office of Federal Contract Compliance Programs (OFCCP) access to the contractor's books, records, and accounts. This access is provided as determined necessary by these government entities to determine the contractor's compliance with the applicable equal opportunity rules.[78]

If the government determines that the contractor is in violation of the equal opportunity provisions, the government may cancel, terminate, or suspend the contract, in whole or in part, and may declare the contractor ineligible for further government contracts.[79] The contractor is also required to flow down the provisions of the clause to its subcontracts.[80]

§ 8.20   —Drug-Free Workplace

Over the past few years, the U.S. government has taken aggressive action to require that contractors who contract with the federal government take action to ensure a drug-free workplace. In November 1988, Congress enacted the Drug-Free Workplace Act (DFWA), which requires government contractors as well as recipients of federal grants to maintain a drug-free workplace.[81] Also in 1988, the Defense Acquisition Council published an interim rule regarding a drug-free work force for companies that contract with DOD.[82] In early 1989, the Federal Acquisition Counsel published an interim rule in the FAR, establishing a subpart to implement the Drug-Free Workplace Act of 1988.[83]

The FAR provisions in large part mimic the requirements of the DFWA. The FAR provisions are applicable to contracts valued at $25,000 or more.[84] However, the provisions do not apply to contracts or those parts of contracts to be performed outside the United States, its territories, and its possessions.[85]

---

[76] Id. 52.222-26(b)(1).

[77] 3 C.F.R. 167 (Supp. 1965), 30 Fed. Reg. 12,319 (1965); FAR 52.222-26(b)(6).

[78] Id. 52.222-26(b)(8).

[79] Id. 52.222-26(b)(9).

[80] Id. 52.222-26(b)(10).

[81] Pub. L. No. 100-690, § 5151, 102 Stat. 4181, 4304 (1988) (codified at 41 U.S.C. §§ 701–707).

[82] DFARS 223.7500–7504.

[83] FAR 23.500–506.

[84] Id. 23.501, 23,505.

[85] Id. 23.501(a), 23.505(c).

If subject to the FAR provisions, an offeror, by the submission of its offer, certifies that it will take certain designated steps in an attempt to keep illegal drugs out of the workplace. To be eligible for award, the offeror must agree to take the following actions:

1. Publish a statement notifying its employees that the contractor prohibits in its workplace the unlawful manufacture, distribution, dispensing, possession, or use of a controlled substance. This statement also must specify the actions that will be taken against employers for violation of such prohibition.

2. Establish an ongoing drug-free awareness program that provides information to employees regarding (a) danger of workplace drug abuse; (b) contractor's policy of maintaining a drug-free workplace; (c) the existence of any available drug counseling, rehabilitation, and employee assistance programs; and (d) potential penalties to the employee for workplace drug abuse violations.

3. Provide employees with a copy of the published statement and inform employees in writing that abiding by the requirements of the statement as well as notifying the contractor in writing within five calendar days of a conviction under a criminal drug statue is a condition of continued employment.

4. Notify the contracting officer within 10 calendar days after receiving notice of an employee's drug conviction, which notice shall include the position of the convicted employee.

5. Take action against the convicted employee within 30 calendar days from receipt of notice of the conviction, which action may include requiring the employee to participate satisfactorily in a drug abuse assistance or rehabilitation program, or in the alternative, taking appropriate personnel action against the employee, up to and including termination.

6. Make a good faith effort to maintain a drug-free workplace.[86]

Failure to provide the certification renders the offeror unqualified and ineligible for award.[87] Failure to live up to the certification can result in more onerous consequences, such as suspension of contract payments, termination of a contract for default, or suspension and debarment.[88] Particular instances in which these penalties may be appropriate include those in which: (1) the contractor has submitted a false certification; (2) the contractor has failed to comply with its certification; or (3) the contractor has

---

[86] *Id.* 23.504.

[87] *Id.* 52.223-5(d).

[88] FAR § 23.506(a).

failed to make a good faith compliance effort, as indicated by the number of contractor employees who have been convicted of criminal drug statute violations that occurred in the workplace.[89]

Note that neither the DFWA nor the FAR requires that a contractor test employees for illegal drug use on either a random or reasonable suspicion basis. Similarly, there is no requirement that contractors start drug counseling programs, or include such programs as a fringe benefit. Nor is there any requirement that contractors take any action as a result of an employee's substance abuse outside the workplace.

§ 8.21 —Buy American Act

Of particular importance to construction contractors are the FAR's Buy American Act provisions. The Buy American Act imposes stringent restrictions on a federal contractor's choice of construction materials. These restrictions need to be understood by the contractor before bidding a contract.[90] Regulations implementing the Buy American Act require all construction materials to be manufactured in the United States, unless specifically exempted from the Act's coverage.[91] Also, in order to satisfy the definition of a *domestic construction material,* the cost of the construction material's components mined, produced, or manufactured in the United States must exceed 50 percent of the cost of all its components.[92]

The regulations implementing the Buy American Act define a *construction material* as any article, material, or supply brought to the construction site for incorporation into the building or work.[93] Boards of contract appeals have interpreted this requirement to mean that if items are brought separately to the construction site at which they will be installed, rather than as a complete unit ready for installation, each item constitutes a separate construction material and must on its own satisfy the Buy American Act requirements.[94] However, if the items are brought to the construction site already integrated into a preassembled unit that will be installed at the site, the preassembled unit rather than each individual item in the unit, constitutes the construction material.[95]

---

[89] *Id.*

[90] 41 U.S.C. §§ 10a–10c.

[91] FAR 25.202.

[92] *Id.* 25.201.

[93] *Id.*

[94] *See, e.g.,* Allen L. Bender, Inc., ASBCA No. 38068, 89-3 B.C.A. (CCH) ¶ 22,092, at 111,098; George Hyman Constr. Co., ASBCA No. 13777, 69-2 B.C.A. (CCH) ¶ 7,830, at 36,389.

[95] *See, e.g.,* Mid-American Elevator Co., B-237282, 90-1 CPD ¶ 125.

Prior to a bidding deadline, a contractor may request a waiver from the Buy American Act requirement that only domestic construction material be used. Such a request may be granted if the authorized government officials determine that the cost of the domestic construction material would be unreasonable, or the construction material is not mined, produced, or manufactured in the United States in sufficient and reasonably available quantities of a satisfactory quality.[96] Note that the contractor cannot simply make its own determination that the cost of procuring necessary products or goods in the United States is too high and deliver noncompliant Buy American Act materials, but instead must request the government to make that determination.[97]

PERFORMANCE

§ 8.22   Contract Administration in General

Once a contract is awarded, there are a number of unique requirements that might affect administration of the contract. These provisions may have a significant cost impact on a contractor's performance, and if they are not carefully complied with could easily result in allegations of procurement fraud. Contractors should be aware of the following requirements established under the regulations.

§ 8.23   Cost Principles of FAR

Part 31 of the FAR pertains to cost principles that are applicable to certain government contracts. The stated scope of FAR part 31 is as follows:

> This part contains cost principles and procedures for (a) the pricing of contracts, subcontracts and modifications to contracts and subcontracts whenever cost analysis is performed and (b) the determination, negotiation or allowance of cost when required by a contract clause.[98]

As a result, contracts or contract modifications subject to the requirements of TINA as well as cost reimbursement contracts entered into with the federal government are subject to the cost principles set forth in part 31.

The cost principles deal with two primary issues: allocability of costs to the contract and allowability of costs. The regulations only provide rather

---

[96] FAR 25.202.

[97] M.S.I. Corp., VACAB No. 503, 65-2 B.C.A. (CCH) ¶ 5,203, at 24,450.

[98] FAR 31.000.

general guidance regarding the allocability of cost to cost objectives (such as contracts or modifications). The basic principle is that costs should be allocated based on the benefits received or other equitable relationships.[99] However, the regulations provide very specific guidance regarding the allowability of specific types of costs under federal government contracts. The government has determined for a variety of reasons, including public policy and some sense of fairness, that it will not pay contractors certain types of costs. These designated costs are said to be unallowable and are discussed in FAR 31.205. The contractor is responsible for identifying those costs and excluding them from any billings, claims, or proposals applicable to federal government contracts.[100] As a result, construction contractors have an obligation, when subject to the cost principles, to scrub any direct or indirect cost proposals, claims, or billings to the government to eliminate unallowable costs.

The regulations discuss 51 specific types of costs. Some of the more significant or troublesome unallowable cost types include advertising and public relations costs, bad debts, contributions, entertainment costs, interest, travel costs in excess of government per diems, lobbying costs, and alcoholic beverages costs. Prior to submitting cost information to the federal government, construction contractors should review the cost principles to ensure that the contractors have properly segregated and excluded unallowable costs.

All interest costs are unallowable for federal government contracting purposes.[101] However, the government does allow an imputed interest cost called *facilities capital cost of money.* This imputed cost is determined by multiplying the net book value of the company's tangible capital assets by an interest rate established by the Secretary of the Treasury. The specific guidelines for calculating facilities capital cost of money are discussed in detail in the FAR.[102]

In addition to the general allowability provisions of the cost principles, there are specific cost principles for construction and architectural engineering contracts.[103] These provisions deal specifically with charges for construction equipment, predetermined schedules of construction equipment use rates, equipment rental costs, and rental and other costs incurred in acquiring the temporary use of land, structures, and facilities.

---

[99] *See id.* 31.201-4.

[100] *Id.* 31.201-6.

[101] *See id.* 31.205-20.

[102] *See id.* 30.414, 31.205-10.

[103] *See id.* 31.105.

§ 8.24   Cost Accounting Standards

Public Law No. 91-379 requires certain national defense contractors and subcontractors to comply with cost accounting standards (CAS), to disclose in writing, and to follow consistently their cost accounting practices.[104] Most construction contracts are exempt from the requirements of CAS because the contracts are awarded based on price competition. Therefore, **Chapter 8** does not discuss the requirements of these standards in detail.

However, if a contractor is awarded a contract that includes the clauses associated with CAS, the company will be required to meet various requirements. First, if certain thresholds are met, the contractor may be required to complete a *Cost Accounting Standards Board Disclosure Statement*.[105] This statement provides the government with a detailed description of the contractor's method of accounting for costs under government contracts. Second, contractors performing CAS-covered contracts must propose and account for costs consistent with their disclosed or established cost accounting practices.[106] If a contractor does not comply with this consistency requirement or if a contractor changes its cost accounting practices, contract price adjustments may be required on CAS-covered contracts currently being performed by the contractor even if the contract was awarded on a fixed-price basis. Finally, if certain thresholds are met, the contractor's accounting system must account for its costs in accordance with 19 specific cost accounting standards.[107]

The application of the thresholds discussed can be relatively complex. In addition, some of the specific cost accounting standards require a high degree of expertise to interpret and implement. Finally, the thresholds and various standards currently are under review for revision. Therefore, if a construction contractor determines that one or more of its contracts are subject to the requirements of CAS, the contractor should seek the assistance of individuals with experience in this area.

§ 8.25   Time-Charging Issues

Historically, one of the more common areas of concern for government contractors is the accurate reporting of direct labor costs. Construction contractors often are not affected by the problems that have plagued

---

[104] Defense Production Act Amendments, Pub. L. No. 91-379, § 103, 84 Stat. 796 (1970); FAR 30.101(a).

[105] *See id.* 30.202-1.

[106] *See id.* 52.230-6.

[107] *See id.* 30.201-2(a).

government contractors in this area because their direct labor personnel are dedicated to one contract for an extended period of time, rather than working on several contracts each pay period.

Nevertheless, certain circumstances could arise in which construction direct labor personnel could work on various cost objectives in the same pay period. For example, the contractor may be performing various unpriced modifications to the contract, and the contractor's direct labor personnel may record their time separately for each unpriced modification in order to support the subsequent pricing. In this case, the direct labor reporting accuracy would have a direct impact on the pricing of contract modifications. Another common case occurs when a contractor is performing a lump sum job and is given some time and material work on the same job. Obviously, accurate reporting of labor between the lump sum work and the time and material work is critical to accurate billing. Yet another example occurs when a contractor accounts for project management cost as a direct cost and a project manager works on two or more contracts concurrently. In this case, the accuracy of the cost accounting by contract would be impacted directly by the integrity of the project manager's direct labor reporting. If a construction contractor relies on direct labor reporting records as the basis of pricing contracts or modifications to the government, the contractor must ensure that it has adequate internal controls over the integrity of the direct labor reporting.

§ 8.26   Audit and Record Retention

Another important aspect to contracting with the federal government is its contractual right to audit. A specific clause, Audit-Sealed Bidding, is incorporated in all sealed bid contracts expected to exceed $100,000.[108] This clause gives the government the right to audit the books and records associated with the pricing of cost based modifications to the contract. Other clauses, the Examination of Records by Comptroller General clause and the Audit-Negotiations clause, are incorporated in all negotiated contracts in excess of $10,000.[109] These clauses give the government the right to audit records pertinent to the contract or pertinent to the cost-based pricing of the contract or contract modifications.

These clauses require the contractor to retain pertinent records for established periods of time to allow the government to perform its audits. As a result, construction contractors may have a contractual obligation to retain records related to federal contracts for a specified period of time. The clauses provide for a general retention period of three years after final

---

[108] FAR 52.214-26.

[109] *Id.* 52.215-1, 52.215-2.

payment under the contract. However, FAR subpart 4.7 provides certain more specific guidance regarding record retention. The topics covered in this subpart include calculation of the retention period, specific retention periods, and microfilming records. If a construction contractor is subject to the audit clause requirements, it should compare its record retention policy to the provisions of subpart 4.7 to ensure compliance with its contractual obligations. Construction contractors also should be aware that signing government contracts probably gives the government substantial audit rights related to the companies' books and records.

§ 8.27 Value Engineering

In government contracts, contractors are required to perform strictly in accordance with the specifications and statement of work. In some instances, contractors develop ideas that allow the work to be done at a lower cost if changes can be made to the specifications or statement of work. Such changes require prior government approval. At one time, contractors had no incentive to propose such cost savings ideas because government approval of the ideas would also result in the issuance of a deductive change order, which reduced the contract amount by the cost of the deductive work as well as reduced profit.

To encourage contractors to submit cost savings ideas, the government initiated the value engineering program. Contractors who submit value engineering change proposals (VECPs) (cost reduction proposals) that are accepted by the government are entitled to share with the government in the cost savings that result from the proposal. The FAR defines a *value engineering change proposal* as a proposal that requires a change to the contract and results in reducing the overall projected cost to the agency without impairing essential functions or characteristics.[110] Proposed changes solely to the deliverable end item quantities or solely to the contract type cannot constitute VECPs.[111]

VECPs may result in both acquisition and collateral savings. *Acquisition savings* generally may be defined as savings in the cost of the contractor's performance of the contract, while *collateral savings* generally result from savings to the government of related costs, such as logistic, operation, or maintenance costs. The contractor's share of acquisition savings is determined by subtracting government costs from instant contract savings and multiplying the result by 55 percent for fixed price contracts and 25 percent for cost reimbursement contracts.[112] The contractor also is entitled to

---

[110] *Id.* 48.001.

[111] *Id.*

[112] *Id.* 52.248-3(f).

20 percent of any projected collateral savings determined to be realized in a typical year of use after first subtracting any government costs not previously offset.[113]

The FAR requires the contracting officer to insert the Value Engineering Construction clause in construction solicitations and contracts when the contract amount is estimated to be $100,000 or more.[114] The FAR prohibits the inclusion of the clause in an incentive-type construction contract.[115]

§ 8.28   Protection of Whistle-blowers

Federal contractors increasingly are being presented with the problem of handling employees who have "blown the whistle" on what they consider to be improper, inappropriate, or fraudulent activities on the part of the contractor. When the whistle-blower has made allegations to an authorized official of the DOD or DOJ, federal statute as well as recently promulgated regulations in the DOD FAR Supplement drastically constrain the defense contractor's right to fire or discipline the whistle-blower.

The Defense Acquisition Improvement Act of 1986 mandates that an employee of a defense contractor may not be discharged, demoted, or otherwise discriminated against as a reprisal for disclosing to a member of Congress or authorized DOD or DOJ official information regarding a substantial violation of law involving the competition for, negotiation of, or performance of a defense contract.[116] Aggrieved individuals may file a complaint with the DOD Inspector General (IG), which the IG is required to investigate unless the IG determines the complaint is frivolous.[117] The Defense Acquisition Improvement Act had no enforcement or remedial provisions. However, in § 837 of the fiscal year 1991 DOD Authorization Act,[118] Congress expanded the protection provided whistle-blowers and added enforcement and remedial provisions. The DAR Council has recently promulgated a new subpart 203.71 to the DOD FAR Supplement to implement the provisions of § 837 of the DOD Authorization Act.

Subpart 203.71 of the DOD FAR Supplement applies to all contracts exceeding $500,000, with a limited exception for commercial items, not applicable generally to construction contracts.[119] The regulations provide

---

[113] *Id.* 52.248-3(g).

[114] FAR 48.202.

[115] *Id.*

[116] 10 U.S.C. § 2409(a).

[117] *Id.* § 2409(b).

[118] Pub. L. No. 101-510, § 837, 104 Stat. 1485, 1616 (1990) (codified at 10 U.S.C. § 2409a).

[119] DFARS 203.7101.

protection for a contractor's employee who discloses information to an appropriate government official, information that the employee reasonably believes evidences a violation of any federal law or regulation relating to defense procurement or the contract. The regulations mandate that defense contractors not discharge or otherwise discriminate against the employee (with respect to compensation or terms and conditions of employment) as a result of that disclosure.[120] Aggrieved individuals file complaints with the Director of the Defense Logistics Agency.[121] If the Director determines after investigation that a violation has occurred, the Director may issue separately or in combination any of the following:

1. An order directing the violating defense contractor to take action to correct the violation

2. An order directing the violating contractor to reinstate the complainant to the position held when discharged, together with compensation (including back pay), benefits, and other terms and conditions of the aggrieved employee's employment

3. At the request of the aggrieved employee, an assessment against the contractor of an amount equaling all costs and expenses (including attorneys' fees and expert witness fees) reasonably incurred by the aggrieved party in bringing the complaint.[122]

The Director has the right to file an action for the enforcement of the orders in federal district court.[123] Contractors may seek review of these orders in the federal court of appeals.[124] Contractors also are required to inform all employees of the employees' rights under 10 U.S.C. § 2409a and subpart 203.71.[125] However, it does not appear that individuals have a private right of action under the whistle-blower statute.[126]

In addition to the above, courts have determined that the Occupational Safety and Health Act as well as analogous state laws protect employees who report statutory violations from adverse action against the employees by their employers.[127]

---

[120] *Id.* 203.7103.

[121] *Id.* 203.7104(a).

[122] *Id.* 203.7100.

[123] *Id.* 203.7106(c).

[124] *Id.* 203.7106(a).

[125] DFARS 252.203-7004(d).

[126] Mayo v. Questech, Inc., 727 F. Supp. 1007 (E.D. Va. 1989).

[127] Kilpatrick v. Delaware County Soc'y for Prevention of Cruelty to Animals, 632 F. Supp. 542 (E.D. Pa. 1988).

§ 8.29   Termination for Convenience

Through the use of the termination for convenience clause, the government reserves for itself the right to terminate a contract at any time for practically any reason. If a termination for convenience occurs, the contractor has the right to be made whole for the cost incurred to date plus a reasonable profit on the work performed. However, no anticipatory profits can be awarded under a federal government termination for convenience.[128] As a result, a construction contractor accepting federal government contracts must consider the additional risk of having a large portion of its business base withdrawn by the customer at any time.

A general overview of the steps in a termination for convenience is as follows:

1. The government makes a decision that it no longer requires the product or services required under the contract.

2. The procuring contracting officer (PCO) issues a notice of termination for convenience and the government appoints a termination contracting officer (TCO).

3. The TCO is responsible for directing the contractor to stop work; to take action to terminate all subcontracts; to segregate and dispose of termination inventory, special tooling, and equipment; and to prepare the necessary forms. Upon notice by the TCO, the contractor must stop work on the terminated portion of the contract immediately. If the contractor continues to incur costs on a terminated contract after the notice of termination, the government may not be required to reimburse the contractor for those costs.

4. Immediately upon receipt of the termination notice, the prime contractor terminates all subcontracts being performed or associated with the terminated portion of the contract.

5. The TCO and the contractor meet to discuss the termination and to agree on the steps required to protect and preserve the property in which the government has or may acquire an interest.

6. The contractor notifies the TCO in writing of any legal proceedings against the contractor generated out of any subcontract or other commitment related to the terminated portion of the contract.

7. The contractor settles all outstanding liabilities and claims resulting from the termination of subcontracts and obtains any approvals or ratifications required by the TCO under the provisions of the FAR. The contractors may obtain the authority from the TCO to settle subcontract claims up to $25,000.

---

[128] FAR 49.202(a).

8. The contractor submits its settlement proposal and supporting schedules. Costs incurred both internally and by outside experts to prepare the settlement proposal can be recovered separately in the proposal as settlement costs of the termination.

9. The contractor disposes of the termination inventories directed by the TCO.

10. The Defense Contract Audit Agency is called in to perform an audit of the claim amount if it is significant.

11. The TCO and contractor negotiated the settlement proposal.

12. If the two parties cannot negotiate a settlement, the TCO issues a unilateral determination of the settlement amount. The contractor can appeal the final decision of the TCO through the disputes process.

Generally speaking, contractors receive their costs incurred to date on terminated contracts plus a reasonable profit. However, there are certain unique considerations in the determination of the cost recoverable under a terminated contract. First, if the government estimates that the contractor would have been in a loss position at the conclusion of the contract, a pro rata share of that loss is allocated to the work done to date.[129] That pro rata share is disallowed as a recoverable cost under the termination for convenience.

If the contractor estimates that it would have incurred a loss under a terminated contract, it should determine whether that loss is associated with (1) poor estimating under the original contract proposal or (2) the existence of unadjudicated change orders that are not reflected in the current contract price. If a loss is generated by inaccurate cost estimates in the original contract proposal, there is very little the contractor can do to avoid a cost disallowance related to the pro rata share of that loss. However, if the loss is generated by unadjudicated changes, the contractor should take the required steps to ensure that the contract price used in the loss contract determination is increased for the cost and profit associated with those changes.

For the most part, the allocability and allowability of costs under terminations for convenience are controlled by cost principles. However, there are certain special cost considerations unique to terminations for convenience. For example, there are certain costs directly associated with the settlement of the termination that can be accounted for as direct costs of the termination even though the contractor has established practices to account for those costs as indirect. In addition, as discussed in § 8.29, the costs of outside experts, such as accountants and lawyers hired to assist in the termination proposal preparation, are allowable as direct costs of the settlement.

---

[129] *See id.* 49.203.

Furthermore, unamortized deferred start-up costs remaining under the contract are fully allowable as long as the contract, taken as a whole, would have been profitable.

Due to the unique accounting and cost considerations associated with terminations for convenience, a less experienced contractor should consider enlisting the assistance of outside experts to assist in the contractor's preparation of the termination for convenience settlement proposal.

§ 8.30   Termination for Default

A termination for default is the result of some action or inaction on the part of the contractor that results in a failure to meet its contractual obligations. If a contractor fails to meet its contractual obligation, the government may terminate the contract for default.[130] Under a termination for default, the contract generally recovers no cost incurred under the contract and almost certainly is liable for additional damages and reprocurement cost incurred by the government. Thus, default terminations can have severe financial consequences. Some of the reasons the contract may be terminated for default include:

1. Failure to meet the required schedules.
2. Failure to satisfy the stated performance requirements in the contract. This failure must be sufficient to prevent the item from being used for its intended purpose.
3. Failure to satisfy other provisions of the contract including the contract clause representations and certifications.

If the government intends to terminate a contract for default for any reason other than failure to meet the completion schedule, it will notify the contractor of its intent through the issuance of a show cause notice or cure letter and provide the contractor with a reasonable period of time to cure the alleged defects and show why it should not be terminated. If a contractor receives notice from the government that indicates its intent to terminate for default, the contractor should consider hiring a skilled government contracts attorney to attempt to avoid the termination for convenience, as the termination for default could lead to a loss of all costs incurred to date by the contractor and to potential claims by the government for the government's damages and reprocurement costs.

---

[130] *See id.* 52.249-10.

PART III

REGULATORY AND LABOR ISSUES

CHAPTER 9

STATE AND FEDERAL OSHA COMPLIANCE

Robert D. Moran

Robert D. Moran is a Washington, D.C., lawyer and management consultant with a practice confined to advising and representing business and industry throughout the country in OSHA-related matters. In 1970 he headed the task force that planned the implementation of the Occupational Safety and Health Act and the formation of OSHA. He then served a six-year term on the U.S. Occupational Safety and Health Review Commission and was its first chairman. He is listed in both *Who's Who in America* and *Who's Who in American Law.*

§ 9.1   Overview of the OSH Act

The Occupational Safety and Health Act (OSH Act)[1] became effective on April 28, 1971, and remains today almost exactly the same as it was at that time. The only change made during its first 20 years was a 1990 sevenfold increase in the maximum allowable penalty for each OSH Act violation.[2]

The law was enacted in an effort to reduce workplace injuries and illnesses by establishing standards that would enhance safe and healthful working conditions in places of employment throughout the United States. It applies to every employer engaged in a business affecting commerce who has employees, except employers covered under other existing occupational safety and health laws (such as the Federal Coal Mine Health and Safety Act) and under § 274 of the Atomic Energy Act of 1954 as amended.[3]

---

[1] P. L. No. 91-596, 84 Stat. 1590, 29 U.S.C. § 651 (1988).

[2] Originally the maximum penalty was $1,000 for a serious or nonserious violation, $10,000 for a willful or repeated violation, and $1,000 per day for failure to correct a previously established violation within the time allowed. The current maximums are $7,000 for serious or nonserious violations, $70,000 for willful or repeated violations, and $7,000 per day for a failure-to-correct.

[3] OSH Act § 4(b)(1), 29 U.S.C. § 653(b)(1). The exclusion has been the subject of considerable litigation. See U.S. Air, Inc. v. OSAHRC, 689 F.2d 1191 (4th Cir. 1982); Inspection of Norfolk Dredging Co., 783 F.2d 1526 (11th Cir. 1986).

The OSH Act applies in all 50 states, the District of Columbia, Puerto Rico, the Virgin Islands, American Samoa, Guam, and other U.S. territories.[4] Federal and state employees are specifically excluded from coverage, but the Act permits the adoption of measures extending substantially similar requirements to them.[5]

The Act is administered and enforced by the United States Department of Labor's Occupational Safety and Health Administration (OSHA) but it permits each of the states and territories to assume the responsibility for administration and enforcement within its own borders.[6] Twenty-three of them have done so.[7]

§ 9.2   Duties of Employers and Employees

In general, the duty of each employer under the OSH Act is threefold:

1.   Furnish each of its employees a place of employment, free from recognized hazards that are causing, or are likely to cause, death or serious physical harm[8]
2.   Comply with the occupational safety and health standards promulgated under the Act[9]
3.   Observe OSHA recordkeeping and reporting regulations.[10]

Each of the duties is explained in §§ 9.3 through 9.5.

The duty of each employee is to comply with the occupational safety and health standards, and all rules, regulations, and orders issued pursuant to the OSH Act that are applicable to their own actions and conduct.[11]

Employers who fail to comply with their obligations can be penalized by the government, but there is no government sanction against noncomplying employees.[12]

---

[4] OSH Act § 4(a), 29 U.S.C. § 653(a).

[5] *Id.* § 3(5), 29 U.S.C. § 652, excludes federal, state, and local agencies from the definition of the term *employer.* However, other sections of the OSH Act authorize the federal and state governments to adopt occupational safety and health programs for the benefit of their employees. *Id.* §§ 18, 19, 29 U.S.C. §§ 667, 668.

[6] *Id.* § 18, 29 U.S.C. § 667.

[7] Alaska, Ariz., Cal., Haw., Ind., Iowa, Ky., Md., Mich., Minn., Nev., N.M., N.C., Or., P.R., S.C., Tenn., Utah, Vt., V.I., Va., Wash., and Wyo.

[8] OSH Act § 5(a)(1), 29 U.S.C. § 654(a)(1).

[9] *Id.* § 5(a)(2), 29 U.S.C. § 654(a)(2).

[10] *Id.* § 8(c), 29 U.S.C. § 657(c).

[11] *Id.* § 5(b), 29 U.S.C. § 654(b).

[12] Atlantic & Gulf Stevedores v. OSAHRC, 534 F.2d 541 (3d Cir. 1976).

§ 9.3 —General Duty Clause

Congress intended that the OSH Act be enforced principally through specific standards that would tell employers what they must do to achieve a safe and healthful working environment. However, Congress added § 5(a)(1), the so-called "general duty clause," in order to fill gaps that might exist in the standards. The clause was not expected to be cited very much and was intended to cover only hazardous conditions that are obvious and admitted by all concerned, but for which no specific standard then existed.

Although it appears that more employers have been cited under the general duty clause than Congress contemplated, the courts have curtailed the use of the clause to some extent by imposing a number of requirements that must be proved before a general duty clause violation can be established.[13] As a result, it is not enough to simply show that a workplace hazard existed that caused death or serious physical harm to an employee. The proof that the Secretary of Labor must produce includes:

1. Identification of particular measures that the employer should have had in effect at the time the hazardous condition was present
2. Indication that such measures would be effective in counteracting the hazard
3. Evidence that it would be feasible to put such measures into effect.

In the words of the Court: "[T]he Secretary [of Labor] must be constrained to specify the particular steps a cited employer should have taken to avoid citation, and to demonstrate the feasibility and likely utility of those measures.[14]

§ 9.4 —Occupational Safety and Health Standards

Shortly after the OSH Act went into effect, the Secretary of Labor, under the authority Congress delegated to that position, adopted thousands of occupational safety and health standards.[15] In subsequent years, additional

---

[13] The leading case on general duty clause enforcement is National Realty & Constr. Co. v. OSAHRC, 489 F.2d 1257 (D.C. Cir. 1973). The rule of that case has been followed innumerable times. *See, e.g.,* Secretary of Labor v. Cerro Metal Prods. Div., 12 O.S.H. Cas. (BNA) 1821 (1986), and cases cited therein.

[14] *National Realty & Constr. Co. v. OSAHRC,* 489 F.2d 1257, 1268 (D.C. Cir. 1973).

[15] 36 Fed. Reg. 10,466–10,714 (May 29, 1971). All OSHA standards are now codified in 29 C.F.R.

standards have been added. Some standards have been revised while others have been revoked. The Secretary's authority to adopt standards is a continuing one. Thus, new standards can be adopted in the future.

Job safety and health standards generally consist of rules for avoidance of hazards that have been proven by research and experience to be harmful to personal safety and health. The standards supposedly constitute an extensive compilation of wisdom. They sometimes apply to all employers, as do fire protection standards, for example. A great many standards, however, apply only to workers while engaged in specific types of work—such as driving a truck or handling compressed gases.

Two of the many thousands of occupational safety and health standards are listed below in order to demonstrate the form of such standards.

Example number one. "Aisles and passageways shall be kept clear and in good repair, with no obstruction across or in aisles that could create a hazard."[16]

Example number two. "Employees working in areas where there is a possible danger of head injury from impact, or from falling or flying objects, or from electrical shock and burns, shall be protected by protective helmets."[17]

Another occupational safety and health standard (the hazard communication standard) is discussed in **§§ 9.24** through **9.28**.

It is the obligation of all employers and employees to familiarize themselves with the standards that apply to them and to observe the standards at all times.[18] Because all OSHA standards are not equal, their interpretation, application, scope, and validity depend on a number of different factors. One of those factors is the particular provision of law under which they were adopted.

Adoption of Standards

The OSH Act provided the Secretary of Labor with authority to adopt standards in three different ways. That authority appears in §§ 6(a), 6(b), and 6(c) of the Act.[19] The Secretary made use of all of that authority in the past but today the § 6(a) authority no longer exists and the § 6(c) authority has been so circumscribed by court decision that it has virtually fallen into disuse. Each of those three provisions will be discussed in sequence.

---

[16] 29 C.F.R. § 1910.23(b).

[17] *Id.* § 1926.100(a).

[18] 29 U.S.C. § 654.

[19] *Id.* §§ 655(a), (b), (c).

Section 6(a) standards. The authority under § 6(a) to adopt standards no longer exists, but during the time it existed, it was the basis for adopting most of the standards that are in effect today. It was limited to the adoption as OSHA standards of certain "national consensus standards" and "established Federal standards" that were in effect on December 29, 1970, the OSH Act's enactment date. Both of those kinds of *standards* are defined in the law itself.[20] No notice-and-comment rulemaking procedures were required for standards adopted under § 6(a). The reason for that unusual leeway was to permit OSHA[21] to get so-called "start-up" standards on the books as quickly as possible. To prevent the abuse of such power, the authority to adopt § 6(a) standards was restricted to consensus and established federal standards, and the power to adopt the standards as OSHA standards lasted for only two years,[22] expiring on April 28, 1973. Nevertheless, the Secretary of Labor made considerable use of the authority under § 6(a), 29 U.S.C. § 655(a), during the two-year period it existed and the vast majority of OSHA standards that are currently in effect were adopted under the section.

Section 6(b) standards. This is the authority for the adoption of all OSHA standards promulgated after April 28, 1973, except emergency temporary standards authorized by § 6(c). It requires that advance notice of the intent to promulgate a standard must be published in the Federal Register, and the public must be given an opportunity to comment on the proposal as well as request a hearing thereon, before the proposal can be adopted as an OSHA standard. Section 6(b), 29 U.S.C. § 655(b), is one of OSH Act's most detailed provisions and it has been the subject of considerable litigation.[23] Any OSHA standard that is adopted today must be promulgated under § 6(b) if it is to remain in effect for longer than six months.

---

[20] *See id.* § 652(9), 652(10).

[21] The Occupational Safety and Health Administration (OSHA) is an agency of the United States Department of Labor. The OSH Act gave rulemaking and enforcement authority to the Secretary of Labor. The Secretary then created OSHA, to be headed by an Assistant Secretary, and delegated statutory authority to that official. *See* 29 C.F.R. §§ 1910.2(b), 1910.4.

[22] For a discussion of the Secretary's OSH Act § 6(a) authority and its limitations, *see* Diebold Inc., v. Marshall, 585 F.2d 1327 (6th Cir. 1978). That decision also held that a standard adopted under § 6(a) cannot be interpreted to impose requirements that the standard's source did not impose. *Id.* at 1332. That is an important distinction because the usual rule is that the agency that promulgates a regulation may interpret it and that courts will defer to an agency's reasonable interpretation of its own regulations. Martin v. OSAHRC, 111 S. Ct. 1171 (1991).

[23] Two Supreme Court cases contain detailed discussion of OSH Act § 6(b): Industrial Union Dep't v. American Petroleum Inst., 448 U.S. 607 (1980), and American Textile Mfrs. Inst. v. Donovan, 452 U.S. 490 (1981).

Section 6(c) standards.   This authority is very limited and rarely used. It permits the adoption of "emergency temporary standards" in those situations in which the Secretary of Labor makes a satisfactory finding that: (1) a "grave danger" exists as a result of employee exposure to toxic substances, harmful physical agents, or "new hazards" and (2) an emergency standard is necessary to protect employees from such danger.[24] No notice-and-comment rulemaking is required, but a § 6(c) standard, 29 U.S.C. § 655(c), will automatically expire six months after adoption unless, prior thereto, it is promulgated under § 6(b) procedures.

Variances from standards.   The Secretary of Labor, upon an employer application therefor, is authorized to grant (1) temporary variances from standards in order to give the employer sufficient time to come into compliance if the employer can show a need and a protective plan of action,[25] and (2) variances without time limits if the Secretary finds that an employer is using safety measures that are as safe as those required by a standard. Affected employees must be given notice of each such application and an opportunity to participate in the variance-issuance process.[26]

§ 9.5   —Recordkeeping and Reporting Requirements

In order to accurately describe the nature of the occupational safety and health problem and the employer's activities in implementing its purposes, the OSH Act authorizes OSHA to adopt regulations requiring employers to create and maintain records and to make periodic reports. The best known regulation of that kind requires each employer to maintain an accurate record of work-related deaths, injuries, and illnesses;[27] however, there are literally hundreds of OSHA recordkeeping and reporting requirements.[28]

The OSH Act states that the records are to be made available to the Department of Labor and to the Department of Health and Human Services, either of which may require periodic reports thereon.[29] Nevertheless, some

---

[24] The difficulty of establishing the existence of those conditions is demonstrated by two decisions that invalidated OSHA attempts to adopt emergency temporary standards: Florida Peach Growers Ass'n v. Department of Labor, 489 F.2d 120 (5th Cir. 1974), and Asbestos Info. Ass'n v. OSHA, 727 F.2d 415 (5th Cir. 1984).

[25] 29 U.S.C. § 655(b)(6).

[26] 29 U.S.C. §§ 655(b)(6), 655(d).

[27] 29 C.F.R. pt. 1904.

[28] They are listed in a book coauthored by the writer. *See* Moran & Moran, The OSHA 500 (1991).

[29] OSH Act § 8(c), 29 U.S.C. § 657(c). *See also id.* § 24(a), 29 U.S.C. § 673(a). The injury/illness recordkeeping regulations are in 29 C.F.R. pt. 1904. *See id.* §§ 1904.1–.15.

judicial decisions hold that such records need not be disclosed in the absence of compulsory process.[30]

The OSH Act authorizes the adoption of regulations that require employers to promptly advise any employee exposed to potentially toxic materials or harmful physical agents of the same as well as the corrective action being undertaken.[31] The Secretary of Labor, in cooperation with the Secretary of Health and Human Services, is authorized by the Act to issue regulations in this area that shall provide employees or their representatives with an opportunity to observe such monitoring or measuring, and to have access to the records thereof and to all records that indicate their own exposure to toxic materials or harmful physical agents.[32]

The Act also authorizes the Secretary of Labor to adopt regulations requiring employers to conduct their own periodic inspections and to keep their employees informed of their protections and obligations under the law through posting of notices or other appropriate means. The information that employers may be required to give their employees also may include the provisions of applicable standards.[33]

§ 9.6   State Participation

The OSH Act encourages states to assume the fullest responsibility for the administration and enforcement of their occupational safety and health laws by providing the states with monetary grants to help them adopt and enforce OSH standards within their own borders.[34] A specific disclaimer of federal preemption is included in order to permit any state agency or court to assert jurisdiction under state law over any occupational safety or health issue with respect to which no federal standard is in effect.[35]

Any state may assume responsibility for the development and enforcement of occupational safety and health standards under the Act if such state

---

[30] See Secretary v. Taft Broadcasting Co., 12 O.S.H. Cas. (BNA) 1264 (1985), aff'd sub nom McLaughlin v. Kings Island Div., Taft Broadcasting Co., 849 F.2d 990 (6th Cir. 1988).

[31] OSH Act § 8(c)(3), 29 U.S.C. § 657(c)(3). Similar provisions appear in id. § 6(b)(7), 29 U.S.C. § 655(b)(7). Such requirements are included in various OSHA standards. See, e.g., 29 C.F.R. § 1926.58(n) (the recordkeeping requirements of the asbestos standard for the construction industry).

[32] Id. The implementing regulation is 29 C.F.R. § 1910.20.

[33] OSH Act § 8(c)(1), 29 U.S.C. § 657(c)(1). For an example of that, see 29 C.F.R. § 1910.1025 (the OSHA lead standard). It includes a requirement that the employer shall assure that each employee is informed of "[t]he content of this standard and its appendices." Id. § 1910.1025(l)(1)(v).

[34] OSH Act § 2(b)(11), 29 U.S.C. § 651(b)(11).

[35] Id. § 18(a), 29 U.S.C. § 667(a).

submits an approved plan for so doing to the Secretary of Labor.[36] The Secretary may approve such a plan under the following conditions.

1. An agency of the state must be designated or created to carry out the plan.
2. Standards (and enforcement thereof) must be provided that create safe and healthful employment at least as effective as that otherwise provided for under the OSH Act.
3. There must be adequate provisions for rights of entry and inspection of workplaces.
4. Enforcement capacity must be demonstrated.
5. Adequate funds for administration must be assured.
6. Effective and comprehensive job safety and health programs for all public employees within the state must be established to the extent permitted by the particular state's law.
7. The state, and employers within the state, must make such reports as may be required by the Secretary of Labor.[37]

The Secretary is obligated to make a continuing evaluation of the manner in which each state plan is being carried out and to withdraw approval of the plan whenever there is a failure to comply substantially with any provision thereof.[38]

In accordance with those provisions, twenty-one states and two territories currently administer and enforce the OSH Act.[39] For all intents and purposes, employers in those states are only subject to their state OSHA agency. The federal OSHA people play virtually no role at all there. The jurisdictions currently have the authority to inspect private employers, cite them, adjudicate contested enforcement actions, and adopt binding occupational safety and health standards and regulations. For the most part, OSHA itself does not do any of that in those places.

There are two additional states (Connecticut and New York) in which only state and local government agencies are within the state's OSHA authority. In all of the remaining states and territories, the state government plays no part in OSHA administration or enforcement except to provide consultative services upon request.

Although it was contemplated at the time the OSH Act was enacted that it would create uniformity of occupational safety and health requirements throughout the nation, that result has not occurred.

---

[36] *Id.* § 18(b), 29 U.S.C. § 667(b).

[37] *Id.* § 18(c), 29 U.S.C. § 667(c).

[38] *Id.* § 18(f), 29 U.S.C. § 667(f).

[39] See § **9.1**.

Most of the state-plan states adopt the OSHA standards verbatim, but the states can—and sometimes do—interpret and apply the standards differently. In addition, a number of state and local laws have been adopted in recent years that impose OSHA-type requirements on employers. Courts generally have construed such laws in such a manner that they have been shielded from preemption challenges based upon the Federal Supremacy Clause of the United States Constitution.[40]

One state (California) has been particularly active in this regard. In January 1991, it adopted a new Corporate Criminal Liability Act that requires employers to provide prompt notification of certain workplace hazards to both the state's OSHA agency, CAL/OSHA, and to affected employees.[41] Corporate managers who fail to do so can receive a three-year jail sentence and a $25,000 fine. A corporation can get a $1 million fine for such an offense. Many expect that other states will adopt similar provisions. Later in 1991, California adopted legislation that requires all employers doing business within the state to adopt a detailed, written injury/illness prevention program.[42] Other states may follow with similar legislation.

§ 9.7   Enforcement

Compliance with OSHA standards, with the recordkeeping requirements, and with the OSH Act's general duty clause is enforced by means of on-site inspection of worksites by a force of approximately 2,500 state and federal OSHA inspectors who are stationed at more than 100 different locations around the country.

The OSH Act authorizes the inspectors to enter without delay, and at any reasonable times, any establishment covered by the Act to inspect the premises and all pertinent conditions, structures, machines, apparatus, devices, equipment, and materials therein, and to question privately any employer, owner, operator, agent, or employee.[43] However, if the employer does not consent to such an inspection voluntarily, the inspection cannot be conducted unless OSHA obtains a warrant authorizing the inspection.[44] OSHA is also authorized to issue subpoenas to aid its inspections.[45]

---

[40] *See, e.g.,* Manufacturers Ass'n of Tri-County v. Knepper, 801 F.2d 130 (3d Cir. 1986), *cert. denied,* 484 U.S. 815 (1987) (upholding most provisions of Pennsylvania "right to know" law); Ohio Mfrs. Ass'n v. City of Akron, 801 F.2d 824 (6th Cir. 1986), *cert. denied,* 484 U.S. 801 (1987) (holding that a city "right to know" ordinance was preempted by OSH Act but only to extent that it covered worker safety and health).

[41] Cal. Penal Code § 387 (West 1991).

[42] Cal. Lab. Code § 6314.1 (West 1991).

[43] OSH Act §§ 8(a), (f), 29 U.S.C. §§ 657(a), (f).

[44] Marshall v. Barlow, Inc., 436 U.S. 307 (1978).

[45] OSH Act § 8(b), 29 U.S.C. § 657(b).

The OSH Act permits the employer and a representative authorized by its employees to accompany the inspector during the physical inspection of any workplace for the purpose of aiding such inspection.[46]

The Secretary of the Department of Health and Human Services (HHS) also is authorized to make inspections and question employers and employees in order to carry out those functions assigned to HHS under the Act.[47] That HHS authority is implemented by one of its subordinate agencies, the National Institute of Occupational Safety and Health (NIOSH). For additional discussion of that authority, see § 9.14 below.

§ 9.8   —Citations and Proposed Penalties

When an employer is believed to be in violation of the OSH Act as a result of an OSHA inspection, the employer is issued a written citation describing the specific nature of the violation. The citation must fix a reasonable time for abatement of the violation, and each citation (or copies thereof) must be posted by the employer prominently at or near each place where a violation referred to in the citation occurred. Notices, in lieu of citations, may be issued for de minimis violations that have no direct or immediate relationship to safety or health.[48]

If OSHA believes that the cited violation should be penalized, OSHA must notify the employer by certified mail of the penalty that it proposes to assess. The employer then has 15 working days within which to notify OSHA that it wishes to contest the citation or proposed assessment of penalty or both.[49]

If a cited employer fails to notify OSHA within such time that the employer intends to contest the citation or proposed assessment of penalty, the citation and the assessment shall be final, provided no employee files an objection to the time the citation allowed the employer to abate the cited violation (see § 9.21 on abatement).

If the employer notifies OSHA within such time that the employer does wish to contest, OSHA must certify the matter to the Occupational Safety and Health Review Commission and the Commission shall afford an

---

[46] *Id.* § 8(e), 29 U.S.C. § 657(e).

[47] *Id.* § 20(b), 29 U.S.C. § 669(b). That authority has been used in the past to conduct a so-called "health hazard evaluation" as set forth in *id.* § 20(a)(6), 29 U.S.C. § 669(a)(6). *See* Establishment Inspection of Keokuk Steel Castings, 493 F. Supp. 842 (S.D. Iowa 1980); General Motors Corp. v. NIOSH, 636 F.2d 163 (6th Cir. 1980).

[48] OSH Act §§ 9(a), (b), 29 U.S.C. §§ 658(a), (b).

[49] *Id.* §§ 10(a), (c), 29 U.S.C. §§ 659(a), (c). It is OSHA's current practice to use a single document that contains both the citation and the notification of proposed penalty. In OSHA's early days, the citation and proposed penalty were contained in separate documents.

opportunity for a hearing.[50] The Commission has the power to affirm, modify, or vacate any contested citation or proposed penalty. Orders of the Commission are final 30 days after issuance. Review of Commission orders may be obtained in the United States Court of Appeals.[51]

The foregoing procedures do not apply in the listed state-plan states.[52] Each of them employs varying adjudicatory systems when one of their citations is contested.

§ 9.9 —Occupational Safety and Health Review Commission

The OSH Act created the Occupational Safety and Health Review Commission (OSHRC) as an independent agency of the federal government and gave it only one function—to hear and decide contested OSHA citations and penalty proposals.[53] The Commission is a two-tiered court system. At the lower level, it has a number of administrative law judges (ALJs) who hear cases and issue rulings. The ALJ decisions can be reviewed and changed by the three-member presidentially-appointed Commission. Commission decisions can be appealed to the United States Courts of Appeal.[54]

The OSH Act provides that those who contest OSHA citations and penalty proposals are entitled to a fair and impartial hearing and decision on the contested matters. They receive just that from OSHRC. Its record over the first 20 years of its existence is one of impeccable fairness and impartiality between employers and OSHA. A count of reported decisions shows that OSHRC has fully sustained the OSHA charges in approximately one-fourth of its cases and has fully sustained the contesting employer in approximately one-third of its cases. In the remaining cases, some issues were decided in the employer's favor and others in OSHA's favor.

Perhaps more important than the win/loss record is the fact that all of OSHRC's decisions are in writing and contain detailed reasons why a particular disposition is being made.

At the hearings conducted by Commission ALJs, the burden of proof is on OSHA to prove the validity of all citations that the employer has

---

[50] *Id.* § 10(c), 29 U.S.C. § 659(c).

[51] *Id.* §§ 11(a), (b), 29 U.S.C. §§ 660(a), (b).

[52] See § **9.1.**

[53] OSH Act §§ 2(b)(3), 12, 29 U.S.C. §§ 651(b)(3), 661.

[54] *See id.* §§ 10(a), (c), 29 U.S.C. §§ 659(a), (c). An ALJ decision that is not ordered to be reviewed by the members of OSHRC will thereby automatically become a decision of OSHRC. It can then be appealed to the appropriate court of appeals in exactly the same manner.

contested. When OSHA does not carry that burden—and it often does not—the citation will be vacated.

No matter how much adverse evidence OSHA presents to a Commission ALJ about an employer, OSHRC will not impose any sanction or penalty greater than that set forth in the contested OSHA citation and penalty proposal. In other words, the "maximum sentence" an employer can receive in an OSHA enforcement proceeding is that listed on the citation and penalty proposal the employer received after the OSHA inspection. If the cited employer does not contest, the citation requirements listed and penalty proposed are exactly what the employer receives.

When an employer does contest, OSHRC is empowered to impose:

1. The same sanction the employer would have received if it did not contest
2. Something less than that
3. No sanction at all.

The employer who contests an OSHA citation may walk away scot-free as many employers have done and the employer may even be partially reimbursed for the fees and expenses incurred in contesting the citation.[55]

The jurisdiction of OSHRC does not exist in those places in which a state runs the OSHA program.[56] Each such state establishes its own adjudicatory system. The systems vary from one such state to another, but few, if any of them, extend the same assurances of impartiality and due process to those who contest state OSHA citations as OSHRC does for those contesting federal OSHA citations.

§ 9.10   —Abatement of Condition

Each OSHA citation must prescribe a reasonable time for elimination or abatement of the condition constituting the alleged hazard.[57] However, that time limit does not begin to run until a final order of OSHRC, if the citation is contested by the employer in good faith and not solely for delay or avoidance of penalties.[58]

Employees (or representatives of employees) also have the right to object to the period of time fixed in the citation for the abatement of a violation if,

---

[55] *See* Equal Access to Justice Act, 5 U.S.C. § 504 (1990), which, among other things, authorizes reimbursement of the fees and expenses incurred by small businesses in defending against unjustified OSHA citations.

[56] See § 9.1.

[57] OSH Act § 9(a), 29 U.S.C. § 658(a).

[58] *Id.* §§ 10(b), 17(d), 29 U.S.C. §§ 659(b), 666(d).

within 15 days after a citation is issued, an employee files a notice of contest with OSHA alleging that an unreasonable time was allowed for abatement. Review procedures similar to those discussed in **§ 9.8** apply when such a notice is filed.[59]

A failure-to-abate violation of the OSH Act exists in those situations in which the time for correction of a violation has been established (either as a result of a previously uncontested citation, or of the settlement or final adjudication of a prior contested citation), but the employer fails to abate within that time. In such a case, OSHA notifies the employer by certified mail of such failure and of the proposed penalty. The notice and assessment is final unless the employer contests the same by filing a notice of contest with OSHA within 15 working days.[60] A failure-to-abate notification is essentially the same as a citation (but higher penalties are authorized) and an employer who contests the notification receives the same kind of hearing and adjudication discussed above.

When an employer is under an abatement order for any reason and can establish that, despite a good faith effort to comply with the abatement requirements, abatement has not been completed because of factors beyond the employer's reasonable control, OSHA can grant an extension. If OSHA does not do so, the employer is entitled to a hearing before OSHRC, which can issue an order affirming or modifying the abatement requirement.[61]

§ 9.11   —Penalties for Violations

Except in those rare instances when OSHA does not seek a monetary penalty, citations and failure-to-abate notices are accompanied by proposed penalties. If left uncontested, those proposals become fines and must be paid. If contested, however, the penalty proposals have no force or effect. OSHRC, after a hearing, decides what penalty, if any, will be assessed. The amount of penalty authorized depends on the nature of the violation.

Willful or repeated violations may incur fines of up to $70,000 for each violation, while serious or nonserious violations may incur fines up to $7,000 for each violation.[62] Any employer who fails to correct a previously established violation within the time period prescribed, may be penalized up to $7,000 for each day the violation exists.[63]

The OSH Act also authorizes criminal penalties. A willful first violation by an employer that results in the death of any employee is punishable by a

---

[59] See § **9.8**.

[60] OSH Act § 10(b), 29 U.S.C. § 659(b).

[61] *Id.* § 10(c), 29 U.S.C. § 659(c). The procedures for invoking this process are set forth in 29 C.F.R. § 2200.37.

[62] OSH Act §§ 17(a), (b), (c), 29 U.S.C. §§ 666(a), (b), (c) (as amended, Nov. 1990).

[63] *Id.* § 17(d), 29 U.S.C. § 666(d) (as amended, Nov. 1990).

fine of up to $10,000 or imprisonment for up to six months. A second or subsequent conviction carries a penalty of up to $20,000 and up to one year in prison. Similar penalties are also included in the Act for false official statements and for giving unauthorized advance notice of inspections to be conducted under the Act.[64]

The Act does not preempt state and local criminal law. Consequently, a state or local district attorney can bring charges of murder, assault, battery, and similar charges against an employer for acts or omissions that cause death, injury, or illness to an employee.[65] Cases of that kind began to appear with some regularity in the late 1980s and early 1990s.

§ 9.12   Imminent Dangers

Any condition or practice in any place of employment that causes a danger to exist that could reasonably be expected to cause death or serious physical harm immediately, or before the imminence of such danger can be eliminated through normal enforcement procedures, may be restrained by order of a United States District Court upon petition of the Secretary of Labor. If the Secretary arbitrarily or capriciously fails to seek action to abate an imminent danger of such kind, a mandamus action to compel the Secretary to act may be maintained in the United States District Court by any employee who may be injured by reason of such failure. An OSHA inspector who concludes that imminent danger conditions or practices exist in any place of employment is obligated to inform the affected employees and employers of the danger and tell them that the inspector is recommending to the Secretary of Labor that injunctive relief be sought. The inspector may also post warning notices at the worksite.[66]

§ 9.13   Employee Protection from Harassment

No person may discharge or in any manner discriminate against any employee because the employee causes OSHA to inspect the employer's business, exercises any right under the OSH Act, files a complaint or other proceeding, or testifies or is about to testify in any proceeding under the Act. Any employees who believe that they have been discharged or otherwise discriminated against in violation of this provision may, within 30 days of such action, file a complaint with OSHA. The Secretary of Labor is authorized to investigate the matter and to bring action in the United States

---

[64] *Id.* §§ 17(e), (f), (g), 29 U.S.C. §§ 666(e), (f), (g).

[65] *See, e.g.,* New York v. Pymm, 14 O.S.H. Cas. (BNA) 1297 (N.Y. App. Div. 1989).

[66] OSH Act § 13, 29 U.S.C. § 662. *See also* 29 C.F.R. § 1903.13.

District Court for appropriate relief. The Secretary must notify the complainant of the action on the complaint within 90 days of its receipt.[67]

For a fuller discussion of this provision, see *Marshall v. Whirlpool Corporation*,[68] and the Supreme Court decision that affirmed the result reached in that case, *Whirlpool Corporation v. Marshall*.[69]

§ 9.14   National Institute for Occupational Safety and Health

A continuing program of research in the field of occupational safety and health, including the psychological factors involved, and the development of innovative methods, techniques, and approaches for dealing with occupational safety and health problems is the responsibility of the National Institute for Occupational Safety and Health (NIOSH), an organization created by the OSH Act as part of HHS.

NIOSH is authorized to conduct such research and experimental programs as are necessary for the development of criteria for new and improved occupational safety and health standards and, on the basis of such research and experimentation, recommend new or improved OSHA standards to the Secretary of Labor.

NIOSH also may require employers to do the following:

1. Measure, record, and make reports on the exposure of employees to potentially toxic substances or harmful physical agents that might endanger the employees' safety or health

2. Establish programs for medical examinations and tests as may be necessary to determine the incidence of occupational illness or the susceptibility of employees to such illnesses

3. Conduct such special research experiments and demonstrations as are necessary to explore new problems, including those created by new technology in occupational safety and health that may require ameliorative action beyond that which is otherwise provided in the operating provisions of the OSH Act

4. Conduct research into the motivational and behavioral factors relating to the field of occupational safety and health.

A part of this program is the publication annually of a list of all known toxic substances and the concentrations at which toxicity is known to occur, and industry-wide studies on chronic or low-level exposure to a broad

---

[67] OSH Act § 11(c), 29 U.S.C. § 660(c).

[68] 593 F.2d 715 (6th Cir. 1979).

[69] 445 U.S. 1 (1980).

variety of industrial materials, processes, and stresses on the potential for illness, disease, or loss of functional capacity in aging adults.

Upon the written request of any employer or authorized representative of employees, NIOSH is authorized to conduct on-site investigations in order to make determinations on whether any substance normally found in the place of employment has potentially toxic effects. That process, which has been used many times, is known as a "health hazard evaluation." The determinations made by NIOSH as the result of such an evaluation are printed in a report that is then submitted to both the employer and the affected employees as soon as possible. NIOSH has also made it a practice to submit such reports to OSHA. Resulting OSHA inspections and citations sometimes follow.

The OSH Act further provides that information obtained by the Department of Labor and HHS under the research provisions of the law is to be disseminated to employers and employees and organizations thereof.[70]

§ 9.15 Compliance and Noncompliance

The OSH Act is not a building code. Its sole purpose is to protect employees from workplace hazards. Thus, the simple existence of a condition that is not in compliance with an OSHA standard (such as the absence of perimeter guarding from an open-sided floor 10 stories above the ground) is not a violation unless at the time of that condition's existence there are employees who are endangered as a result of that condition's existence. The resulting risk of employee harm (if any) must be more than a mere possibility. There must be a significant risk of harm. No OSHA standard can be interpreted to embrace slight risks of harm.[71]

There are a number of other elements that must be proved before an OSHA violation can be established. Each of them will be discussed briefly in §§ 9.16 through 9.23. Each of the elements of proof discussed is based on legal principles that have been developed in contested citation cases. Whenever an employer contests an OSHA citation, the burden is on OSHA to prove each of the elements of proof.

§ 9.16   —Jurisdiction

It must be proved that the cited employer is "engaged in commerce" in order to establish that the employer is covered under the OSH Act.[72] In

---

[70] OSH Act §§ 20, 22, 29 U.S.C. §§ 669, 671.

[71] Pratt & Whitney Aircraft v. Secretary of Labor, 649 F.2d 96, 104 (2d Cir. 1981) (relying on Industrial Union Dep't v. American Petroleum Inst., 448 U.S. 607 (1980)).

[72] Secretary v. Burk Well Serv. Co., 12 O.S.H. Cas. (BNA) 1598 (1985).

most cases the cited employer will admit that fact. If admitted, OSHA need not produce evidence to establish jurisdiction. If the cited employer does not do business across state lines (a rather rare situation), the employer should deny the allegation in OSHA's complaint that the employer is "engaged in commerce."[73] OSHA must then introduce evidence to prove that point. If it does not, the citation will be vacated.

§ 9.17 —Applicability

OSHA has the burden of proving that the requirement of law under which it proceeds applies to the cited condition.[74] It is not unusual for an OSHA inspector to overlook the fact that many OSHA standards apply only when certain conditions exist, or only to certain jobs, employees, or employers. For example, 29 C.F.R. § 1926.400(c)(2) applies to "electrical installation used on the jobsite" (emphasis added). A citation for violating the provision because an accident was caused by contact with a public power line that simply crossed above the worksite, but was not used there, would be vacated because OSHA would be unable to prove its applicability to the particular condition it cited.

It should be noted in this regard that the OSHA standards regulating "general industry"[75] are applicable to construction work in some cases. The rule of thumb applied by OSHA is this: if an OSHA inspector observes a hazardous condition or practice at a construction worksite, but there is no construction standard regulating that condition, the inspector will issue a citation under the "general industry" standard that regulates that condition. The authority for that OSHA practice is stated in 29 C.F.R. § 1910.5(c): any standard shall apply according to its terms to any employment and place of employment in any industry, even though particular standards are also prescribed for that industry.

Thus, OSHA can cite an employer in the construction industry for noncompliance with a general industry standard in those situations in which there is no applicable construction standard that regulates the cited condition or practice.

---

[73] When an employer contests an OSHA citation, various pleadings must then be filed with OSHRC. The first one is known as the *complaint*. It must be filed by the Secretary of Labor. The employer must then file an *answer* to the complaint. *See* the Rules of Procedure codified in 29 C.F.R. § 2200.1–.108. For the most part, there are no comparable procedural rules in those states that have their own OSHA plans.

[74] Secretary v. Clement Food Co., 11 O.S.H. Cas. (BNA) 2120, 2123 (1984).

[75] OSHA has adopted some standards that apply specifically to particular industries. For example: "construction" (29 C.F.R. pt. 1926), "agriculture" (29 C.F.R. pt. 1928), and "maritime" (29 C.F.R. pt. 1915). OSHA also has many standards that have been grouped under the rather misleading designation "general industry" (29 C.F.R. pt. 1910).

§ 9.18   —Noncompliance

OSHA must prove the existence of the particular facts that it alleged in the citation.[76] For example, if it cites a noise violation because "employees were subjected to excess noise," proof that employees were in an area where airborne noise exceeded the permissible limits would not establish that allegation if those employees were wearing earmuffs that insulated them from the noise. It must be shown that the employees could hear the excessive noise levels.

There are also many standards that permit alternative means of compliance, one of which provides that "[e]very temporary floor opening shall have standard railings *or* shall be constantly attended by someone."[77] Proof of the absence of a standard railing around such a floor opening would not establish noncompliance with that standard. OSHA would have to prove noncompliance with both alternatives to establish a violation of that standard.

§ 9.19   —Employee Endangerment

It must be proved that at least one employee was endangered as a result of the cited employer's failure to comply with the cited standard.[78] For example, a citation for violation of 29 C.F.R. § 1910.28(a)(17), which requires that each scaffold have a screen as protection against tools and materials that the workers standing on it might drop, was vacated—even though the employer admitted to the absence of a screen—because there were no employees under the scaffold at the time of the alleged violation (although pedestrians were there).[79] There was no proof of *employee* endangerment.

The sole purpose of the OSH Act is to protect employees from workplace conditions that could be harmful to them as they engage in their work.[80] As

---

[76] Secretary v. Armor Elevator Co., 1 O.S.H. Cas. (BNA) 1409 (1973).

[77] 29 C.F.R. § 1910.23(a)(7) (1990) (emphasis added).

[78] The term *endangerment* is used in this discussion. Sometimes the case law will use the terms "employee exposure," "access to hazard," or "significant risk of harm to employees."

[79] Secretary v. City Wide Tuckpointing Serv. Co., 1 O.S.H. Cas. (BNA) 1232 (1973).

[80] The United States Supreme Court has emphasized that: "[A] workplace can hardly be considered 'unsafe' unless it threatens the workers with a significant risk of harm." Industrial Union Dep't v. American Petroleum Inst., 448 U.S. 607, 642 (1980). OSHRC requires that, before it can affirm any contested citation, OSHA must present sufficient evidence to support a finding that it is reasonable to predict or anticipate that employees will be, are, or have been at risk as a result of the factual condition constituting the alleged violation. Secretary v. Carpenter Contracting Corp., 11 O.S.H. Cas. (BNA) 2027, 2030 n.3 (1984).

has been stated in § **9.15,** the Act is not a building code or a law requiring employers to operate their businesses in whatever manner the rulemakers may desire. Consequently, proof of noncompliance with an OSHA standard is not enough to establish a violation thereof.

There must also be proof that, as a result of the employer's failure to comply with the standard, one or more employees was exposed to a significant risk of harm. "A violation of this Act is not established unless there is evidence that employees of respondent have been exposed to hazard *as a result of* noncompliance with the requirements of an occupational safety and health standard . . . . The burden of so establishing is a part of [OSHA's] prima facie case."[81]

§ 9.20   —Employer Knowledge

OSHA must prove that the condition or practice that caused the citation to issue was known to the cited employer. That is an essential element of OSHA's case in chief.[82] The employer-knowledge requirements are directed not to the law but to "the physical conditions which constitute a violation."[83] "[A]n inference of employer knowledge cannot be drawn from the mere presence of the violative condition at the worksite."[84]

There are many reasons for the requirement for employer knowledge, not the least of which is that: "[f]undamental fairness would require that one charged with and penalized for violation be shown to have caused, or at least knowingly acquiesced in, that violation."[85]

To carry this element of its burden of proof, it is not enough for OSHA to simply establish that a foreman or supervisor created or knew of the non-complying condition or practice when that person was acting contrary to company policy. As was stated by the Court of Appeals for the Third Circuit:

> [T]he Secretary may not shift to the employer the ultimate risk of non-persuasion in a case where the inference of employer knowledge is raised only by proof of a supervisor's misconduct (footnote 9 omitted). The participation of the company's own supervisory personnel may be evidence that an employer could have foreseen and prevented a violation through the exercise

---

[81] Secretary v. Bechtel Corp., 2 O.S.H. Cas. (BNA) 1336, 1337 (1974) (emphasis added).

[82] Pennsylvania Power & Light Co. v. OSAHRC, 737 F.2d 350, 357 (3d Cir. 1984).

[83] Secretary v. Columbian Art Works, Inc., 10 O.S.H. Cas. (BNA) 1132, 1133 (1981).

[84] Secretary v. Prestressed Sys., Inc., 9 O.S.H. Cas. (BNA) 1864, 1869 (1981).

[85] Secretary v. L.E. Myers Co., 12 O.S.H. Cas. (BNA) 1609, 1615 (1986).

of reasonable diligence, but it will not, standing alone, end the inquiry into foreseeability.[86]

In such cases, an employer will be "excused from responsibility for acts of its supervisory employees" upon a showing "that the acts were contrary to a consistently enforced company policy, that the supervisors were adequately trained in safety matters, and that reasonable steps were taken to discover safety violations committed by its supervisor."[87] When the citation is based on an accident, evidence that such an accident was a rare occurrence or had never happened before would be an indication of lack of employer knowledge.[88]

It is frequently difficult for OSHA to prove employer-knowledge at a construction worksite where conditions change from minute to minute. In order to establish the element, OSHA must prove "how long" the cited condition existed. When such proof does not exist, OSHRC has held that it cannot find that the employer knew or, with the exercise of reasonable diligence, could have known of that condition.[89]

§ 9.21   —Abatement Time

OSHA must prove that the calendar date listed on the citation for correction of the noncomplying condition was "reasonable." That rule also applies when the time for abatement listed on the citation is stated as "immediately."[90]

§ 9.22   —Feasibility

It is fairly well-known that, in cases alleging violation of the noise standard and standards limiting airborne exposure to toxic substances, OSHA must

---

[86] Pennsylvania Power & Light v. OSAHRC, 737 F.2d 350, 358 (3d Cir. 1984). The court added at footnote 9 that: "In so holding we join the federal courts of appeals that have previously addressed this issue. *See* Mountain States Tel. & Tel. v. OSHRC, 623 F.2d 155, 158 (10th Cir. 1980); Ocean Elec. Corp. v. Secretary of Labor, 594 F.2d 396, 402–403 (4th Cir. 1979); Horne Plumbing & Heating Co. v. OSHRC, 528 F.2d 564, 570–571 (5th Cir. 1976)." *Id.*

[87] Western Waterproofing Co. v. Marshall, 576 F.2d 139, 144 (8th Cir. 1978).

[88] *See* Marshall v. L.E. Myers. Co., 589 F.2d 270, 272 (7th Cir. 1978); Cotter & Co. v. OSAHRC, 598 F.2d 911 (5th Cir. 1979); Secretary v. FMC Corp., 12 O.S.H. Cas. (BNA) 2008, 2010 (1986).

[89] Secretary v. Novak & Co., 11 O.S.H. Cas. (BNA) 1783, 1784 (1984).

[90] Atlas Roofing Co. v. OSAHRC, 430 U.S. 442, 466 (1977); Secretary v. Gilbert Mfg., 7 O.S.H. Cas. (BNA) 1611, 1613 (1979).

prove both the technological and economic feasibility of the particular engineering or administrative controls it proposes.[91] That burden of proof also applies in other types of cases. For example, in a case involving extensive analysis of the OSHA standard providing for the guarding of machines, the Court of Appeals for the Sixth Circuit held that: "[W]here a standard imposes a duty without specifying the *means* of compliance, the Secretary has the burden of establishing the existence of a specific and technologically feasible means of compliance as an element of his showing that a violation has occurred."[92]

A citation for noncompliance with 29 C.F.R. § 1910.132(a) based on the employer's failure to require its employees to wear safety shoes was vacated because OSHA did not prove economic feasibility.

> [T]he rule to be applied is one of reasonableness and feasibility, and the financial impact of a particular requirement on an employer is not to be left entirely out of account, although it goes without saying that an employer is not to be permitted to tolerate a foreseeable hazard simply because the elimination of it may be costly.[93]

§ 9.23   —Likely Utility

It must be shown that OSHA's proposed method of abatement will, if put into effect, eliminate or materially reduce the allegedly hazardous condition or practice. That element of proof is always required in general duty clause cases, but the same principle also applies in other kinds of cases even though it may be labeled differently. For example, after restating the rule that noise controls will not necessarily be economically infeasible merely because they are expensive, one court stated: "But neither will controls be economically feasible merely because the employer can easily (or otherwise) afford them. In order to justify the expenditure, there must be a reasonable assurance that there will be an appreciable and corresponding improvement in working conditions."[94] In other words, in order for OSHA to

---

[91] Some of the cases so holding are: Secretary v. Sherwin-Williams Co., 11 O.S.H. Cas. (BNA) 2105 (1984); Secretary v. GAF Corp., 9 O.S.H. Cas. (BNA) 1451 (1981); RMI Co. v. Secretary of Labor, 594 F.2d 566 (6th Cir. 1979); Texas Indep. Ginners Ass'n v. Marshall, 630 F.2d 398, 414 (5th Cir. 1980); Champlin Petroleum Co. v. OSAHRC, 593 F.2d 637, 640 (5th Cir. 1979) (burden is on Secretary to demonstrate both the feasibility and the likely utility of the proposed control measures). *See also* Mountain States Tel. & Tel. Co. v. OSAHRC, 623 F.2d 155, 158 (10th Cir. 1980); Bristol Steel & Iron Works v. OSAHRC, 601 F.2d 717, 723 (4th Cir. 1979) (Commission erred in placing burden of proving infeasibility on cited employer).

[92] Diebold, Inc. v. Marshall, 585 F.2d 1327 (6th Cir. 1978).

[93] United Parcel Serv. v. OSAHRC, 570 F.2d 806, 812 (8th Cir. 1978).

[94] RMI Co. v. Secretary of Labor, 594 F.2d 566, 573 (6th Cir. 1979).

establish an abatement method, it must be proved that such method will actually abate the hazard resulting from the cited condition or practice.

§ 9.24   Hazard Communication Standard

OSHA has thousands of standards, but few of them have provoked as many citations or as much litigation as the standard adopted in an effort to control chemicals used on the jobsite: the OSHA hazard communication standard (HCS).[95] It is probably the most significant job safety and health regulatory action ever adopted. Its purpose is to alert workers to the existence of potentially dangerous substances in the workplace and the proper means and methods to protect themselves against the substances. Numerous states and some local governments have enacted substantially similar provisions. They are popularly known as "Right to Know" laws.

HCS is completely different from ordinary OSHA standards that obligate an employer to prevent (or minimize) workplace hazards through such means and methods as mandatory limitations on noise levels and airborne contaminants, or guarding requirements for machinery and elevated workstations. HCS does not impose mandatory limitations or requirements to abate hazardous conditions. It requires rather that *information* be developed, obtained, and provided. That is also true of state and local right to know laws.

HCS requires the communication of information on "hazardous chemicals" that are present in the workplace. There are few, if any, jobs today that do not involve such substances. They are present everywhere. Household cleaning materials, photocopy equipment, paint, correction fluid, medicines, even drinking soda. Those substances may seem innocuous to some individuals, but under HCS they are hazardous chemicals.

The OSHA standard went into effect for manufacturers in 1985 and, two years later, it was applied to all other employers. It requires each employer to do the following:

1. Adopt its own written hazard communication program
2. Keep a material safety data sheet (MSDS) for each product containing a hazardous chemical that is on its premises
3. Provide its employees with training and education on those chemical hazards
4. Make sure that proper warning labels are in place.

---

[95] The standard is codified at five different places in the Code of Federal Regulations. The text of each of the five is identical. Therefore, the subsections and appendix references will be the same no matter which CFR text is consulted. The five places in Title 29, C.F.R. where the standard appears are: §§ 1910.1200, 1915.99, 1917.28, 1918.90, and 1926.59.

It does not matter what the employee does or where the employee works. Office workers, retail employees, and persons who are not normally thought of as doing work with chemicals must receive the same protection as those who work with dangerous explosives and deadly chemicals.

§ 9.25   —Material Safety Data Sheet

An MSDS is essentially a technical bulletin, usually two to four pages in length (but sometimes much longer), that contains information about a hazardous chemical or a product containing one or more hazardous chemicals, such as its composition, its chemical and physical characteristics, its health and safety hazards, and the precautions for safe handling and use.[96]

The MSDS is the centerpiece of HCS. Labels are keyed to it and the employee training and information requirements are based on it. The MSDS serves as the primary vehicle for transmitting detailed hazard information to both employers and employees.

Each employer that is required to prepare an MSDS or to have one available is also obligated to submit a copy to the local fire department, emergency planning committee, and the state emergency response commission. A list of the chemicals for which MSDSs exist may be submitted as an alternative. The foregoing requirements are not part of HCS, however. They are imposed by a statute administered by the Environmental Protection Agency.[97]

§ 9.26   —Written Hazard Communication Program

Employers must develop, implement, and maintain at the workplace a written, comprehensive hazard communication program that includes provisions for container labeling, collection and availability of material safety data sheets, and an employee training program.[98] The program also must contain a list of the hazardous chemicals in each work area, the means the

---

[96] An MSDS must be prepared or obtained by each manufacturer, distributor, or importer for every product that contains a hazardous chemical. A copy must be provided to each purchaser of the product. The HCS does not include a list of all chemicals for which an MSDS must be prepared. It requires, rather, that manufacturers must conduct a "hazard determination" of their products to see if they contain any hazardous chemicals. HCS ¶ (d).

[97] The Emergency Planning and Community Right-to-Know Act (EPCRA), passed in 1986 as part of the Superfund Amendments and Reauthorization Act (SARA). The reporting requirements appear in 42 U.S.C. §§ 11,021–11,023, and the implementing regulations appear in 40 C.F.R. pt. 370.

[98] HCS ¶ (e).

employer will use to inform employees of the hazards of nonroutine tasks (for example, the cleaning of reactor vessels), and the hazards associated with chemicals in unlabeled pipes. If the workplace has multiple employers on-site (for example, a construction site), HCS requires those employers to ensure that information regarding hazards and protective measures be made available to the other employers on-site, when appropriate.

The written program does not have to be lengthy or complicated, but it must be readily available to employees and their designated representatives, and be provided to OSHA and NIOSH representatives when they request it.

§ 9.27   —Labels and Other Forms of Warning

Chemical manufacturers, importers, and distributors must ensure that containers of hazardous chemicals leaving the workplace are labeled, tagged, or marked with the identity, appropriate hazard warnings, and the name and address of the manufacturer or other responsible party.

Each container of hazardous chemicals that is stored or used at the workplace must be labeled, tagged, or marked with the identity of the hazardous chemicals contained therein, and must show hazard warnings appropriate for employee protection.[99]

The hazard warning can be any type of message, words, pictures, or symbols that convey the hazards of the chemical(s) in the container. Labels must be legible, in English (plus other languages, if desired), and prominently displayed.

There are several exceptions to the requirement for individual container labels:

1. Employers can post signs or placards that convey the hazard information if there are a number of stationary containers within a work area that have similar contents and hazards.

2. Employers can substitute various types of standard operating procedures, process sheets, batch tickets, blend tickets, and similar written materials for container labels on stationary process equipment if they contain the same information and are readily available to employees in the work area.

3. Employers are not required to label portable containers into which hazardous chemicals are transferred from labeled containers so long as they are intended only for the immediate use of the employee who makes the transfer.

4. Employers are not required to label pipes or piping systems.

---

[99] HCS ¶ (f).

§ 9.28   —Employee Information and Training

Employers must establish a training and information program for employees exposed to hazardous chemicals in their work area at the time of initial assignment and whenever a new hazard is introduced into their work area.[100]

At a minimum, the information that employees must be given includes the following:

1. Existence of the hazard communication standard and the requirements of the standard
2. Location and availability in the employee's workplace of the written hazard communication program, the list of hazardous chemicals, and the required MSDS forms
3. Operations in work areas where hazardous chemicals are present.

The employee training plan must consist of the following elements:

1. How the hazard communication program is implemented in that workplace, how to read and interpret information on labels and the MSDS, and how employees can obtain and use the available hazard information.
2. The hazards of the chemicals in the work area. (The hazards may be discussed by individual chemical or by hazard categories such as flammability.)
3. Measures employees can take to protect themselves from the hazards.
4. Specific procedures put into effect by the employer to provide protection, such as engineering controls, work practices, and the use of personal protective equipment (PPE).
5. Methods and observations—such as visual appearance or smell—workers can use to detect the presence of a hazardous chemical to which they may be exposed.

§ 9.29   OSHA's Ergonomic Guidelines

An OSHA effort to reduce the incidence of carpal tunnel syndrome and related cumulative trauma disorders (CTDs) among employees crystallized in late August 1990 with its publication of ergonomic guidelines for the meatpacking industry.[101] OSHA has announced that similar guidelines for

---

[100] HCS ¶ (h).

[101] The OSHA ergonomic guidelines were published by the United States Department of Labor in a pamphlet entitled *Ergonomics Program Management Guidelines for*

all employers will soon follow and that: "Ergonomics will be the major OSHA issue of the 1990s."[102]

Prior to issuance of the guidelines, OSHA had cited numerous employers under the general duty clause, 29 U.S.C. § 654(a)(1), because of employee CTDs. That practice is due to continue in the future.

The guidelines have not been adopted under required rulemaking procedures and are therefore not enforceable standards, rules, or regulations.[103] Nor are they an interpretation of the general duty clause.[104] They are simply suggestions made by OSHA that employers can either accept in full or in part or even totally reject. Whether OSHA will attempt to impose any kind of sanction against those employers who totally ignore the guidelines remains to be seen.

§ 9.30   —Checklist of Likely Substantive Provisions

The substantive provisions of OSHA's ergonomic guidelines are complex, extensive, pervasive, and are likely to prove to be expensive for employers. Although ergonomic guidelines covering all employers have not yet been published, they are virtually certain to contain the same provisions that have been written into the ergonomic settlement agreements that OSHA negotiated with Chrysler, IBP, and a number of other employers that received § 5(a)(1) citations in recent years based upon employee CTD. Similar provisions were contained in the ergonomic guidelines for meatpacking plants that OSHA issued on August 30, 1990.

Here is a list of 14 things that the guidelines are expected to tell employers to do:

_____ Adopt a written ergonomic program for each workplace that includes goals and timetables for reducing CTD by both medical treatment and changes in the way the work is done. The focus of the program

---

Meatpacking Plants. OSHA 3123 (1990). The pamphlet is available from any OSHA area office or from OSHA's Office of Information and Consumer Affairs, United States Department of Labor, Room N3637, 200 Constitution Avenue, NW, Washington, DC, 20210.

[102] Deputy Assistant Secretary of Labor Alan C. McMillan, Speech to the American Meat Institute, Cincinnati, Ohio (Dec. 3, 1989) (unpublished).

[103] The OSH Review Commission has consistently held that guidelines for implementing the Act "do not have the force and effect of law." Secretary v. FMC Corp., 5 O.S.H. Cas. (BNA) 1707, 1710 (1977). Pronouncements by the Secretary "that have not been promulgated as rules or regulations have *no binding legal effect* on either the Secretary or the Commission." Secretary v. Bristol Meyers Co., 7 O.S.H. Cas. (BNA) 1039 n.1 (1978) (emphasis added).

[104] The meatpacking guidelines include the disclaimer that: "Failure to implement these guidelines is not a violation of the General Duty Clause."

must be "to make the job fit the person not to force the person to fit the job."[105] The program must be regularly reviewed by top management with the results of that review committed to writing.

_____ Reduce or eliminate (1) faulty workstation layout; (2) improper work methods; (3) improper tools, including those that vibrate too much; and (4) job design problems like work flow, line speed, material handling, worker's posture, amount of force required, lifting methods, repetition rate, and work/rest regimens.

_____ Conduct periodic surveys of all jobs in order to identify the matters listed above that are to be reduced or eliminated.

_____ Conduct an annual survey of employees to determine the extent of their symptoms or complaints of CTD.

_____ Hire ergonomic professionals. Invest them with responsibility and sufficient resources to analyze all jobs and recommend changes.

_____ Hire health care providers. Give them sufficient authority and resources to rectify all reports of CTD complaints and symptoms.

_____ Establish safety and health committees and empower them to order needed changes.

_____ Monitor "CTD trends" by periodic review of sign-in logs at the company's health care facility, the OSHA-200 logs, workers' compensation claims, and individual employee medical records.

_____ Educate and train employees on ergonomic hazards, CTDs, and how to avoid them. Encourage them to report their early signs and symptoms of CTD and suggest changes in the way the work is done. Require that all employee reports, complaints, and suggestions be investigated by management and the results thereof reported back to the employee. Involve employees in all aspects of the company's ergonomic program. Provide for a suitable "break-in" period prior to employee assignment to production jobs.

_____ Commit adequate resources to accomplish the goals of the ergonomic program, and require rigorous adherence by management to sound medical practice recommendations.

_____ Establish a medical monitoring program that includes adequate medical treatment for CTDs, light duty assignments, medical removal of employees who have CTD, and sufficient rest periods for employees.

_____ Require that accomplishment of ergonomic goals receive the same management commitment and priority as production, and that the job performance of all managers be assessed accordingly.

---

[105] U.S. Dep't of Labor, OSHA 3123, Ergonomics Program Management Guidelines for Meatpacking Plants (1990) (cover of pamphlet).

____ Require that all scheduled and contemplated business expansion and changes in physical plant, materials, and equipment be reevaluated to ensure that they will contribute to the goals of the ergonomic program.

____ Keep detailed records on all of the matters mentioned above and record all CTD conditions on the OSHA-200 Form as occupational illnesses.

§ 9.31   —Industries to Be Covered

OSHA's efforts to stamp out CTDs will not be confined to manufacturing and construction jobs where the vast majority of its inspection activity has been concentrated in the past. The office, retail, and service industry environment will receive its share of attention as the result of a growing concern that hazardous repetitive motion is required to operate copiers, computers, word processors, laser scanners, and similar types of equipment.

Employers who want to avoid OSHA citations for "ergonomic hazards" will be well-advised to adopt their own written ergonomic program now, if they have not already done so. There have been a number of reports that OSHA inspectors will leave employers with existing ergonomic programs alone and concentrate their efforts in this field on those employers with no written plans for addressing ergonomics and CTDs.

CHAPTER 10

CURRENT FEDERAL AND STATE ANTIDISCRIMINATION LAWS

John B. McLeod

John B. McLeod is a partner with the law firm of Haynsworth, Marion, McKay & Guérard in Greenville, South Carolina. After graduating from Wofford College and Duke University Law School, he served as a law clerk to a federal circuit judge and spent four years on active duty in the Army Judge Advocate General's Corps. During the course of his private practice, Mr. McLeod has represented numerous employers in the area of employment and products liability litigation.

FEDERAL LAWS AGAINST DISCRIMINATION

§ 10.1   Title VII of Civil Rights Act of 1964

The primary federal law on the subject of discrimination is Title VII of the Civil Rights Act of 1964. This statute prohibits discrimination in employment on the basis of race, color, sex, religion, or national origin.[1] In addition, sexual harassment as well as discrimination on the basis of pregnancy is forbidden by this statute. Title VII applies to employers who have at least 15 employees during each working day in each of 20 or more calendar weeks in the current or preceding year.[2] It also applies to employees of federal, state, and local governmental units.

Title VII is enforced by a federal agency, the Equal Employment Opportunity Commission, and also may be enforced by state agencies in states that have antidiscrimination statutes. A victim of discrimination is required to file an administrative charge with both state and federal agencies within a specified period of time after the alleged discrimination has occurred. The enforcement agency investigates the charge of discrimination and makes a

---

[1] 42 U.S.C. §§ 2000e–2000e-16 (1988).

[2] *Id.* § 2000e(b).

finding as to whether or not it believes discrimination has occurred. Once this determination has been reached or more than 180 days have passed since the filing of the charge of discrimination, the employee may be issued a so-called *Notice of Right to Sue* that allows the employee to bring a lawsuit in state or federal court within 90 days.

If a lawsuit is brought, the charge of discrimination is decided by a judge rather than a jury.[3] The burden of proof is on the employee to prove discrimination on the part of the employer. This burden can be met by direct evidence of discrimination (which is quite difficult to come by) as well as by indirect or circumstantial evidence.[4] For instance, an employee may meet the burden of going forward by establishing a prima facie case, in which the employee establishes that he or she was a member of a protected group, an adverse employment action was taken against the employee, the employee was qualified for the job, and the employee was replaced by someone outside of the protected group or the position remained open.[5]

In addition to proving intentional discrimination, employees also may attempt to establish discrimination under the so-called "disparate impact" theory, in which an otherwise neutral employment practice, such as a test, is shown to have a disproportionate impact upon a protected group. For instance, the United States Supreme Court has ruled that an employer's requirement of a high school diploma, which was not shown to be job-related, violated Title VII because it excluded a greater number of blacks from employment.[6] In addition, subjective decision making in matters of hiring and promotion also may be examined under the disparate impact analysis.[7] In cases involving this theory of discrimination, statistical evidence is generally employed to show differences between the number of employees in a certain protected group and the number that would be expected in the absence of discrimination.[8] In a recent decision, however, the Supreme Court has emphasized that a discrimination plaintiff must, first of all, compare the racial composition of the jobs in question and the racial composition of the qualified population in the relevant labor pool; then, the plaintiff must also identify the specific employment practice that is allegedly responsible for the disparity and prove that the practice has caused exclusion of the group to which the plaintiff belongs.[9] In applying this

---

[3] Lehman v. Nakshian, 453 U.S. 156 (1981); Shah v. Mt. Zion Hosp. & Medical Ctr., 642 F.2d 268 (9th Cir. 1981).

[4] Robinson v. Montgomery Ward & Co., 823 F.2d 793 (4th Cir. 1987), *cert. denied,* 484 U.S. 1042 (1988).

[5] Texas Dep't of Community Affairs v. Burdine, 450 U.S. 248 (1981); McDonnell Douglas Corp. v. Green, 411 U.S. 792 (1973).

[6] Griggs v. Duke Power Co., 401 U.S. 424 (1971).

[7] Watson v. Fort Worth Bank & Trust, 108 S. Ct. 2777 (1988).

[8] Hazelwood Sch. Dist. v. United States, 433 U.S. 299 (1977).

[9] Wards Cove Packing Co. v. Atonio, 490 U.S. 642, 109 S. Ct. 2115 (1989).

analysis, a court recently held that, although an examination for promotion to lieutenant in the police department appeared to exclude more blacks than whites, the police department justified this disparity by establishing that the examination was related to the knowledge required for the position.[10]

In the event of an adverse determination by the court, the employer may be required to pay back pay—and possibly front pay—to the employee and may be required to reinstate the employee in the job or a job for which promotion was sought.[11] In addition, the employer will be required to pay the reasonable attorneys' fees and expenses incurred by the employee in pursuing administrative and judicial remedies.[12] Expenses and fees may include the costs of copying necessary documents, taking depositions, and traveling; in addition, the attorneys' fee award may be multiplied based upon various factors.[13] In that regard, it is not unusual for the attorneys' fees to exceed the amount of back pay awarded to an employee.

Personnel Policies and Procedures

Although the statute itself does not specifically regulate employment practices, employers must ensure that their personnel policies and procedures do not result in discrimination.

Application forms.   Although the law does not prohibit application forms that contain questions about an applicant's race, color, religion, sex, or national origin, the use of such questions may result in liability for discrimination if they have an adverse impact on a certain protected group. The best guideline in deciding what questions to ask on an application form is a determination about whether the questions have a legitimate relationship to the requirements of the job for which employment is sought.[14] Inquiries about an applicant's credit ratings, arrest records, or military discharge may be discriminatory in their impact upon a minority group.[15]

Physical and mental requirements.   Although employers are allowed to impose physical and mental requirements for a particular job, it is important to make certain that these requirements are job-related and do not

---

[10] Police Officers for Equal Rights v. City of Columbus, 916 F.2d 1092 (6th Cir. 1990).

[11] 42 U.S.C. § 2000e-5(g); Albemarle Paper Co. v. Moody, 422 U.S. 405 (1975).

[12] 42 U.S.C. § 2000e-5(k); New York Gaslight Club, Inc. v. Carey, 447 U.S. 54 (1980).

[13] King v. Palmer, 906 F.2d 762 (D.C. Cir. 1990).

[14] See Uniform Guidelines on Employee Selection Procedures, 29 C.F.R. § 1607 (1990).

[15] Carter v. Gallagher, 452 F.2d 315 (8th Cir. 1971), cert. denied, 406 U.S. 950 (1972); Gregory v. Litton Sys., Inc., 316 F. Supp. 401 (C.D. Cal. 1970), aff'd as modified, 472 F.2d 631 (9th Cir. 1972).

disqualify women and minorities at a rate disproportionate to that of majority groups disqualification.[16] By the same token, employers are allowed to use tests to determine an applicant's qualifications for a particular job; however, it is important that such tests have been "validated"—a validity study should be performed to determine if the measures of work behavior or performance are related to the job in question.[17]

Promotion decisions.   In addition to hiring practices, employers may be held liable for discrimination in promotions. It is important that promotion decisions not be based on any forbidden stereotypes, such as femininity or lack thereof.[18] If an applicant in a particular protected group is qualified for a promotional vacancy and the position is offered to a nonprotected group member, the employer will have a difficult time in establishing that discrimination was not a factor in the promotion decision.[19] Moreover, it is important that the employer not give conflicting reasons for denying a promotion to a member of a protected group and that company policies on promotions be followed.[20] As final considerations, a company's failure to post notice of job openings may be proof of discrimination[21] and failure to afford training opportunities to minority group members also may be a factor indicating unlawful discrimination.[22] Nevertheless, problems such as absenteeism, customer complaints, refusal to perform job duties, and refusal to work overtime are valid reasons on which to base a denial of promotion.[23]

Disciplinary termination.   The area of disciplinary termination presents the greatest potential exposure to liability for employers. An employer may terminate an employee for violating company policies without exposure as long as the policies are enforced fairly, without regard to race, color, sex, religion, or national origin.[24] Employers have been held liable when nonprotected group members were not disciplined for the same offenses as minority members.[25] Protected group members may be terminated for

---

[16] Griggs v. Duke Power Co., 401 U.S. 424 (1971).

[17] 42 U.S.C. § 2000e-2(h); Guardians Ass'n of the N.Y. City Police Dep't v. Civil Serv. Comm'n, 630 F.2d 79 (2d Cir. 1980), *cert. denied*, 452 U.S. 940 (1981).

[18] Hishon v. King & Spaulding, 467 U.S. 69 (1984).

[19] Monroe v. Burlington Indus., 784 F.2d 568 (4th Cir. 1986).

[20] Alvardo v. Board of Trustees, 928 F.2d 118 (4th Cir. 1991).

[21] Brown v. Gaston County Dyeing Mach. Co., 457 F.2d 1377 (4th Cir.), *cert. denied*, 409 U.S. 982 (1972).

[22] Ramsey v. American Air Filter Co., 772 F.2d 1303 (7th Cir. 1985).

[23] Mallory v. Booth Refrigeration Supply Co., 882 F.2d 908 (4th Cir. 1989).

[24] Moore v. City of Charlotte, 754 F.2d 1100 (4th Cir. 1985), *cert. denied*, 472 U.S. 1021 (1985).

[25] Dushon v. Cajon Co., 791 F.2d 43 (6th Cir. 1986).

unsatisfactory job performance as long as there is adequate documentation and the employer does not present unsupported reasons for the termination.[26] It is difficult, however, to justify a discharge allegedly for poor job performance when a favorable performance evaluation has been given to the employee in the recent past.[27]

§ 10.2 —Religious Discrimination

Title VII prohibits religious discrimination unless an employer is able to demonstrate that it is unable to reasonably accommodate the employee's religious observance or practice without undue hardship on the employer's business.[28] Under Title VII, an employer is prohibited from discriminating on the basis of an applicant's or employee's religion in hiring, discipline, and termination matters; by the same token, the employer is required to accommodate its employees' religious practices unless such accommodation results in the imposition of undue expense or inconvenience upon the employer.

For instance, Title VII was violated when an employer's performance evaluations were motivated by religious feelings on the part of the employee's supervisors.[29] On the other hand, the discharge of a government hospital chaplain was upheld because his evangelical preaching style interfered with his ability to carry out his duties as a counselor at a Veteran's Administration Hospital.[30] Ironically enough, a Title VII violation was found due to an employer's erroneous belief that an employee was a member of a particular religion.[31]

More difficult problems arise regarding the employer's duty to accommodate the religious practices of its employees. The usual situation is one in which the employee refuses to work on the employee's Sabbath, including Saturdays. The courts have been very strict in requiring employers to make efforts to accommodate the religious practices of their employees. For instance, Title VII was violated by the discharge of an employee who refused to work on Sunday because of religious beliefs.[32] After noting that the

---

[26] Dale v. Chicago Tribune Co., 797 F.2d 458 (7th Cir. 1986), *cert. denied,* 479 U.S. 1066 (1987).

[27] Chipollini v. Spencer Gifts, Inc., 814 F.2d 893 (3d Cir. 1987), *cert. denied,* 483 U.S. 1052 (1987); Monroe v. Burlington Indus., Inc., 784 F.2d 568 (4th Cir. 1986).

[28] 42 U.S.C. § 2000e-(j) (Supp. III 1991).

[29] Stoller v. Marsh, 682 F.2d 971 (D.C. Cir. 1982), *cert. denied,* 460 U.S. 1037 (1983).

[30] Baz v. Walters, 782 F.2d 701 (7th Cir. 1986).

[31] Compston v. Borden, Inc., 424 F. Supp. 157 (S.D. Ohio 1977).

[32] EEOC v. Ithaca Indus., Inc., 849 F.2d 116 (4th Cir.) (en banc), *cert. denied,* 488 U.S. 924 (1988).

burden is on the employer to offer accommodation, the court pointed out that the employer had "made no specific effort" to accommodate the employee. Despite the fact that the employer had a general policy of using volunteers to work on Sunday before directing any employee to work on that day, the court pointed out that this policy was simply for the convenience of the employees and not for reasons of religion.

The Supreme Court has held that an employer is not required to accept a method of accommodation that is preferred by the employee and that the employer need not show that each of the employee's alternative accommodations would result in undue hardship.[33] In another case, the Supreme Court found in favor of an employer even though the employer could have filled the plaintiff's Saturday shift from other available personnel (requiring overtime pay) or could have arranged for a "swap" between the plaintiff and another employee.[34] After noting that there were no volunteers for Saturday work and that the company's seniority provisions would have to be violated to accommodate the plaintiff, the Supreme Court held that the employer had met its obligations under Title VII.[35]

The Equal Employment Opportunity Commission has issued *Religious Discrimination Guidelines* to assist employers in their attempts to accommodate employees for religious reasons. These alternatives include voluntary substitutes, swaps, and flexible scheduling as well as lateral transfers and change of job assignments. The guidelines encourage employers to publicize policies regarding accommodations and voluntary substitution, and to utilize floating or optional holidays as well as staggered work hours or policies that permit employees to use compensatory time to make up for time lost due to the observance of religious practices.[36]

Undue Hardship

The lower federal courts have taken a practical approach to what constitutes *undue hardship.* For instance, undue hardship has been found when an employer would have been required to violate its seniority system by transferring the employee to a different shift.[37] In addition, it has been held that an employer is not required to adopt alternatives proposed by the

---

[33] Ansonia Bd. of Educ. v. Philbrook, 479 U.S. 60 (1986).

[34] Trans World Airlines, Inc. v. Hardison, 432 U.S. 63 (1977).

[35] The Equal Employment Opportunity Commission has taken the position, however, that the employer does not meet its burden of establishing an "undue hardship" by the "infrequent payment of premium wages for a substitute or the payment of premium wages while a more permanent accommodation is being sought." 29 C.F.R. § 1605.2(e) (1990).

[36] 29 C.F.R. §§ 1605.1–1605.3 (1990).

[37] Rohr v. Western Elec. Co., 567 F.2d 829, 830 (8th Cir. 1977).

employee when the employer's proposal effectively eliminates any conflict with the employee's religious observances.[38] Moreover, undue hardship has been found when an employee insisted upon reading the Bible at work.[39] On the other hand, in a rather bizarre decision, it was held that an employer had a duty to attempt accommodation of an employee's occasional use of a hallucinogenic drug even though the employee wanted to be a tractor-trailer driver.[40]

§ 10.3   —Sexual Harassment

In addition to the usual forms of discrimination, employers have been held liable under Title VII for sexual harassment on the job even though no actual adverse action was taken against an employee. Sexual harassment can take two forms: the so-called *quid pro quo* (in which sexual favors are sought) and the *hostile work environment* theory (intolerable working conditions as a result of sexually-related conduct).

A good example of the quid pro quo form of sexual harassment is a cause of action in which a secretary alleges that she was denied a raise and fired because she "rebuffed sexual advances by her male supervisor."[41] In that case, the court found that the employee had established an employer policy of compelling female employees to submit to sexual advances by their male supervisors and sent the case back for trial.

A hostile working environment may be found in situations involving offensive language, nude pinups, and offensive sexual conduct. To establish a hostile working environment claim, an employee must prove that the conduct in question is unwelcome, that the harassment is based upon sex, that the harassment is sufficiently pervasive or severe so as to create an abusive working environment, and that there is a basis for holding the employer liable.[42]

The courts have gone to opposite extremes in deciding whether or not a hostile working environment case has been made out. In one recent decision, a court held that sexually explicit pinups of nude and partially nude women as well as sexual jokes and remarks created a sexually hostile working environment for female welders in a shipyard.[43] In another case, a

---

[38] Postal Workers, S.F. Local v. Postmaster Gen., 781 F.2d 772 (9th Cir. 1986).

[39] Gillard v. Sears, Roebuck & Co., 32 Fair Empl. Prac. Cas. (BNA) 1274 (E.D. Pa. 1983).

[40] Toledo v. Nobel-Sysco, 892 F.2d 1481 (10th Cir. 1989), *cert. denied,* 110 S. Ct. 2208 (1990).

[41] Garber v. Saxon Business Prods., 552 F.2d 1032 (4th Cir. 1977).

[42] Meritor Sav. Bank v. Vinson, 477 U.S. 57 (1986); Paroline v. Unisys Corp., 879 F.2d 100 (4th Cir. 1989), *modified on other grounds,* 900 F.2d 27 (4th Cir. 1990) (en banc).

[43] Robinson v. Jacksonville Shipyards, Inc., 55 Empl. Prac. Dec. (CCH) ¶ 40,535 (M.D. Fla. 1991).

hostile working environment was established when the employee demonstrated a consistent pattern of verbal and physical conduct of a sexual nature that took place in the employee's office, such as sexually-oriented games and intimate touching between the supervisor and his female subordinates.[44]

An employer may be held liable for sexual harassment only when the employee proves that the employer had "actual or constructive knowledge of the existence of a sexually hostile working environment and took no prompt and adequate remedial action."[45] Although it is important for an employee to have complained of offensive sexual conduct to the employer, it is not necessary to establish that the employer actually knew of the offensive conduct.[46] An employee may succeed by showing that complaints about the harassment were lodged with the employer or that the harassment was so pervasive that employer awareness may be inferred.[47] However, an employer also may be held liable if it had knowledge that a worker had previously harassed employees other than the plaintiff.[48]

Employers should have a published policy prohibiting sexual harassment.[49] Once a complaint of sexual harassment is received, a prompt investigation should be conducted.[50] In the event that a claim of sexual harassment is found to be justified, an employer should take some form of disciplinary action, including termination, against the employee causing the harassment.[51]

Unless an employee is forced to quit as a result of sexual harassment, the damages to be awarded are nominal. In the event, however, that an employee establishes a case of constructive discharge, the back pay award may be considerable. In order to prevail on the theory of constructive discharge, an employee must prove that the working conditions were so intolerable that the employee had no choice but to quit and that the employer intended

---

[44] Spencer v. General Elec. Co., 697 F. Supp. 204 (E.D. Va. 1988) (only nominal damages awarded because no proof of lost job opportunities).

[45] Swentek v. USAIR, Inc., 830 F.2d 552 (4th Cir. 1987); Katz v. Dole, 709 F.2d 251, 256 (4th Cir. 1983).

[46] Meritor Sav. Bank v. Vinson, 477 U.S. 57 (1986).

[47] Katz v. Dole, 709 F.2d 251, 255 (4th Cir. 1983); Swentek v. USAIR, Inc., 830 F.2d 552, 558 (4th Cir. 1987).

[48] Paroline v. Unisys Corp., 879 F.2d 100, 107 (4th Cir. 1989), *modified on other grounds,* 900 F.2d 27 (4th Cir. 1990) (en banc); Yates v. Avco, 819 F.2d 630 (6th Cir. 1987).

[49] Meritor Sav. Bank v. Vinson, 477 U.S. 57 (1986).

[50] Swentek v. USAIR, 830 F.2d 552, 558 (4th Cir. 1987); Barrett v. Omaha Nat'l Bank, 726 F.2d 424 (8th Cir. 1984); *compare* Katz v. Dole, 709 F.2d 251, 254 (4th Cir. 1983) (employer held liable because of supervisor's failure to take action against verbal harassment).

[51] Yates v. Avco Corp., 819 F.2d 630 (6th Cir. 1987) (demotion of harasser insufficient); Paroline v. Unisys Corp., 879 F.2d 100, 108–09 (4th Cir. 1989), *modified on other grounds,* 900 F.2d 27 (4th Cir. 1990) (en banc) (warning of termination insufficient).

to force the employee to quit.[52] In that regard, an employer's failure to correct known intolerable working conditions may support a claim of constructive discharge.[53]

§ 10.4 —Pregnancy Discrimination

In 1978, Congress enacted the Pregnancy Discrimination Act requiring employers to treat pregnant employees in the same fashion as other employees who are disabled.[54] Under this statute, female employees who actually are disabled as a result of pregnancy or childbirth must be afforded the same benefits and leave time as any other employee who is temporarily disabled. On the other hand, policies that require an employee to take mandatory leave at a certain date prior to the expected birth of a child have been held to be illegal unless the employer can demonstrate that pregnancy causes a risk of serious harm to other people because it adversely affects the female employee's ability to carry out the requirements of her job or that the pregnancy causes a serious risk of harm to the female employee herself.[55]

Essentially, this statute requires that pregnancy-related disability leave simply be treated like any other disability leave. For instance, an employer does not violate the Act by refusing to hire a pregnant applicant who is not going to be on the payroll long enough to accrue sick leave and vacation time to cover her expected four- to six-week leave of absence following childbirth because the employer would not hire any applicant who was going to be out on leave for that period of time before training was completed.[56] Nevertheless, an employer that guarantees reinstatement to employees who are on nonpregnancy leave also must guarantee reinstatement to an employee who takes time off for childbirth.[57] Female employees who are out on pregnancy-related leave must be allowed to accumulate seniority in the same fashion as other employees who are on disability leave.[58]

---

[52] Bristow v. Daily Press, Inc., 770 F.2d 1251, 1255 (4th Cir. 1985), *cert. denied,* 475 U.S. 1082 (1986).

[53] Holsey v. Armour & Co., 743 F.2d 199, 209 (4th Cir. 1984), *cert. denied,* 470 U.S. 1028 (1985).

[54] 42 U.S.C. § 2000e-(k) (1988).

[55] Cleveland Bd. of Educ. v. LaFleur, 414 U.S. 632 (1974) (pre-Pregnancy Act decision finding school district's mandatory leave policy unconstitutional); Burwell v. Eastern Air Lines, 633 F.2d 361 (4th Cir. 1980), *cert. denied,* 450 U.S. 965 (1981); Levin v. Delta Air Lines, 730 F.2d 994 (5th Cir. 1984).

[56] Marafino v. St. Louis County Circuit Court, 537 F. Supp. 206 (E.D. Mo. 1982), *aff'd per curiam,* 707 F.2d 1005 (8th Cir. 1983).

[57] EEOC v. Western Elec. Co., 28 Fair Empl. Prac. Cas. (BNA) 1122 (M.D.N.C. 1982); *In re* South W. Bell Tel. Co. Maternity Benefits Litig., 602 F.2d 845 (8th Cir. 1979).

[58] Nashville Gas Co. v. Satty, 434 U.S. 136 (1977).

Although mandatory maternity leave policies violate the statute, an employer generally is not required to allow a nondisabled employee to take voluntary maternity leave; however, the courts have upheld state statutes that require employers to grant pregnancy leave to disabled pregnant employees for a specified period of time.[59] In addition, an employer may not have a policy that restricts pregnancy leave to a certain period of time unless a similar restriction is applied to other types of medical leaves.[60]

Over the years, the courts have wrestled with the dilemma confronting an employer who attempts to prevent female employees from working in a hazardous area. In the past, the courts allowed an employer to exclude women of childbearing years from toxic environments if the employer demonstrated that such restrictions were reasonably required to protect the health of unborn children.[61] However, the United States Supreme Court has now ruled that so-called "fetal protection policies" are prohibited by the Pregnancy Discrimination Act.[62] In a case dealing with a battery manufacturer who had a policy that no woman could be hired for or allowed to transfer into jobs having excessive lead levels unless she provided medical documentation of sterility, the Supreme Court rejected the employer's arguments about the possibility of injuries to the unborn fetus and, therefore, the "business necessity defense" did not apply. In reaching this result, the Supreme Court stated that the Pregnancy Discrimination Act made it clear that the decision to become pregnant or to work while either being pregnant or capable of becoming pregnant was reserved for each individual female and not for the employer.

§ 10.5   Civil Rights Act of 1866

A statute that was enacted shortly after the Civil War provides in part that all persons shall have the same right to make and enforce contracts as do white citizens.[63] Over 100 years after the enactment of this law, the United States Supreme Court held that this statute provided "a federal remedy against discrimination in private employment on the basis of race."[64] Despite the language about "race," this same statute has been held to prohibit

---

[59] California Fed. Sav. & Loan Ass'n v. Guerra, 479 U.S. 272 (1987) (California); Miller-Wohl Co. v. Commissioner of Labor & Indus., 692 P.2d 1243 (Mont. 1984).

[60] Maddox v. Grandview Care Ctr., 607 F. Supp. 1404 (N.D. Ga. 1985), aff'd, 780 F.2d 97 (11th Cir. 1986).

[61] Wright v. Olin Corp., 697 F.2d 1172 (4th Cir. 1982).

[62] International Union, UAW v. Johnson Controls, Inc., 111 S. Ct. 1196 (1991).

[63] 42 U.S.C. § 1981 (Supp. III 1991).

[64] Johnson v. Railway Express Agency, Inc., 421 U.S. 454, 460 (1975).

discrimination against Jewish people,[65] Arabs,[66] and aliens[67] as well as discrimination due to interracial marriages or associations.[68] Although § 1981 does not prohibit employment discrimination on the basis of membership in the Ku Klux Klan,[69] it does prohibit racial discrimination against whites.[70] The Supreme Court has limited the effect of § 1981 to situations involving hiring and promotions and has not extended it to claims of racial harassment.[71] Therefore, it has been held specifically that this statute does not apply to claims of discriminatory discharge.[72]

Title VII and § 1981 differ both in the type of proof required to establish discrimination and in the remedies available to successful plaintiffs. For instance, unlike disparate impact cases under Title VII, § 1981 requires proof that an employer intentionally discriminated against the employee.[73] However, once discrimination is established, the remedies available to a plaintiff under § 1981 are far more attractive than those under Title VII. For instance, a successful § 1981 plaintiff not only may recover back pay, but also may recover compensatory damages for mental or emotional distress, injury to reputation, and humiliation[74] as well as punitive damages (which may far exceed any back-pay award).[75] Although § 1981 claims may be filed much later than those under Title VII, § 1981 does not involve the Equal Employment Opportunity Commission's investigative and conciliatory procedures.[76]

§ 10.6   Age Discrimination in Employment Act

The Age Discrimination in Employment Act (ADEA) prohibits employers from discriminating against individuals over the age of 40 years on the basis of their age.[77] The statute provides no cap on the age of individuals

[65] Shaare Tefila Congregation v. Cobb, 481 U.S. 615 (1987).

[66] St. Francis College v. Al-Khazraji, 481 U.S. 604 (1987).

[67] Ramirez v. Sloss, 615 F.2d 163 (5th Cir. 1980); *but see* Bhandari v. First Nat'l Bank of Commerce, 887 F.2d 609 (5th Cir. 1989), *cert. denied,* 110 S. Ct. 1539 (1990).

[68] Parr v. Woodmen of the World Life Ins. Co., 791 F.2d 888 (11th Cir. 1986).

[69] Bellamy v. Mason's Stores, Inc., 508 F.2d 504 (4th Cir. 1974).

[70] McDonald v. Santa Fe Trail Transp. Co., 427 U.S. 273 (1976).

[71] Patterson v. McLean Credit Union, 491 U.S. 164, 109 S. Ct. 2363 (1989).

[72] Gonzalez v. Home Ins. Co., 909 F.2d 716 (2d Cir. 1990).

[73] Cooper v. Federal Reserve Bank, 467 U.S. 867, 875 (1984).

[74] Rosemond v. Cooper Indus. Prods., 612 F. Supp. 1105 (N.D. Ind. 1985); McCrary v. Runyon, 515 F.2d 1082 (4th Cir. 1975), *aff'd,* 427 U.S. 160 (1976); Fisher v. Dillard Univ., 499 F. Supp. 525 (E.D. La. 1980).

[75] Johnson v. Railway Express Agency, Inc., 421 U.S. 454 (1975); Block v. R.H. Macy & Co., 712 F.2d 1241 (8th Cir. 1983).

[76] Long v. Ford Motor Co., 496 F.2d 500 (6th Cir. 1974).

[77] 29 U.S.C. §§ 621–33a (Supp. III 1991).

protected by the ADEA, except for high-paid executives over the age of 65 who are entitled to a retirement benefit of at least $44,000 per year.[78]

The federal courts have held that an alleged victim of age discrimination must prove that age was a "determining factor" in the adverse employment decision in the sense that "but for" the employer's motive to discriminate against the victim because of age, the adverse employment action would not have been taken.[79] In that regard, the plaintiff must prove that it was "reasonably probable" rather than "merely possible," that the employer would not have discharged the plaintiff but for plaintiff's age.[80] A plaintiff must carry the initial burden of proof that plaintiff's job performance was at a level that met the employer's legitimate expectations and that, following the adverse employment decision, the plaintiff was either replaced by someone of comparable qualifications who was younger or that there was some evidence that the employer did not treat age neutrally in making the adverse employment decision.[81] Although proof of a replacement under the age of 40 is not always required, the courts have generally found no proof of discrimination when the replacement is over the age of 40.[82]

Defense to charge.   The usual defense to a charge of age discrimination is that the employee was not performing the employee's job in a satisfactory manner. As long as this reason is believable, the courts usually accept the employer's explanation of unsatisfactory job performance and rule in the employer's favor.[83] The plaintiff always has the burden of establishing that plaintiff was performing up to the employer's legitimate requirements.[84] In promotion cases, plaintiffs have lost their claims of age discrimination by their failure to prove that they were as qualified as those who were promoted.[85] It is important to bear in mind that the ADEA does not require that employers give special treatment to employees over the age of 40 years; all that is required is that such employees not be the subject of discrimination because of their age.[86]

Discharges of employees have been upheld for deliberate violation of company policies and management directions, particularly when the

---

[78] *Id.* § 631.

[79] Lovelace v. Sherwin-Williams Co., 681 F.2d 230 (4th Cir. 1982); Loeb v. Textron, Inc., 600 F.2d 1003 (1st Cir. 1979).

[80] Fink v. Western Elec. Co., 708 F.2d 909, 915 (4th Cir. 1983).

[81] Herold v. Hajoca Corp., 864 F.2d 317, 320 (4th Cir. 1988), *cert. denied,* 490 U.S. 1107, 109 S. Ct. 3159 (1989); Gill v. Rollins Protective Servs. Co., 773 F.2d 592 (4th Cir. 1985), *modified,* 788 F.2d 1042 (4th Cir. 1986).

[82] McLawhorn v. John W. Daniel & Co., 924 F.2d 535, 538 (4th Cir. 1991).

[83] Huhn v. Koehring Co., 718 F.2d 239, 244 (7th Cir. 1983).

[84] Douglas v. Anderson, 656 F.2d 528, 531 (9th Cir. 1981).

[85] Young v. Lehman, 748 F.2d 194, 198 (4th Cir. 1984).

[86] Williams v. General Motors Corp., 656 F.2d 120, 129 (5th Cir. 1981), *cert. denied,* 455 U.S. 943 (1982).

personnel file of the employee contains a number of written reprimands.[87] A claim of age discrimination also has been rejected when the employer established that the discharged employee did not meet production goals and that personality conflicts between the employee and the supervisor were severe.[88]

Ageist remarks.   In many cases, age discrimination plaintiffs base their claims upon alleged "ageist" remarks made by their employers. Although it is best to avoid making any references to a person's age or to the fact that someone is approaching retirement age, such remarks generally have been excluded by the courts. For instance, references to "young turks" and "young lions" have been held inadmissible as not being evidence of age discrimination.[89] Nevertheless, age discrimination has been established when an older employee was discharged without written warning or counseling and the supervisor had asked about the employee's age and retirement intentions.[90] Recently, a company was held liable for age discrimination when it refused to hire a 60-year-old applicant with over 30 years of experience in the industry on the ground that the applicant was "overqualified." The court found that denying work to an older job applicant because of "too much experience, training or education is simply to employ a euphemism to mask the real reason for refusal, namely, in the eyes of the employer, the applicant is too old."[91]

Reduction in work force.   The possibility of age discrimination is of particular concern in situations in which it is necessary for a company to institute a reduction in force. When older employees are affected by such layoffs, the courts have found liability when the ratio of younger employees to older employees is greater than before the reduction in force and the younger employees are less qualified than the older employees.[92] On the other hand, age discrimination has not been found even though statistics showed that an employer's work force has undergone an overall reduction in age.[93] Employers who attempt to reduce expenses by terminating higher paid employees run the risk of being held liable for age discrimination, particularly

---

[87] Bohrer v. Hanes Corp., 715 F.2d 213, 218–19 (5th Cir. 1983), *cert. denied,* 465 U.S. 1026 (1984).

[88] Clements v. General Accident Ins. Co. of Am., 631 F. Supp. 1477, 1479 (E.D. Mo. 1986), *vacated,* 821 F.2d 489 (8th Cir. 1987).

[89] Haskell v. Kaman Corp., 743 F.2d 113, 118 (2d Cir. 1984); Staniewicz v. Beechan, Inc., 687 F.2d 526, 528 (1st Cir. 1982).

[90] Hamilton v. 1st Source Bank, 895 F.2d 159, 162 (4th Cir.), *modified in part,* 928 F.2d 86 (4th Cir. 1990) (en banc).

[91] Taggart v. Time Inc., 924 F.2d 43, 47–48 (2d Cir. 1991).

[92] Duke v. Uniroyal, Inc., 928 F.2d 1413 (4th Cir. 1991).

[93] Brown v. M&M/Mars, 883 F.2d 505, 511 n.3 (7th Cir. 1989).

when the affected employees are in the protected group.[94] Employers may avoid liability for considering the higher labor costs associated with older employees as long as the decision to lay off employees is based on individual employment costs and individual ability.[95] In fact, a court has upheld the discharge of an older employee on the basis of economic necessity by pointing out that the employee could not require a trier of the fact to "second guess management's decision."[96] In addition, an employer who is undergoing a reduction in force is under no obligation to transfer an older employee and discharge another employee simply because that employee was younger than the plaintiff.[97]

Remedies.   A successful age discrimination plaintiff is entitled to a variety of remedies. If deemed appropriate by the court, reinstatement to the former job may be ordered, although a reinstatement order should not require the "bumping" of a plaintiff's successor who is innocent of discrimination.[98] In addition, an employee may be awarded back pay, which can consist not only of lost wages and pension benefits but also of insurance and vacation benefits.[99] Successful plaintiffs also have been allowed to recover so-called "front pay" for future lost wages when reinstatement is not deemed appropriate.[100] If the court finds that the discrimination was "willful" within the meaning of the ADEA (that is, the employer knew or showed reckless disregard for whether or not its employment decision was prohibited by the ADEA), liquidated damages in twice the amount of actual damages may be awarded.[101] Of course, attorneys' fees also are awarded to successful age discrimination plaintiffs and, on occasion, to successful employers.[102] Damages for pain and suffering may not be recovered in an action under the ADEA.[103]

---

[94] Metz v. Transit Mix, Inc., 828 F.2d 1202, 1206–08 (7th Cir. 1987); Leftwich v. Harris-Stowe State College, 702 F.2d 686, 691 (8th Cir. 1983).

[95] Mastie v. Great Lakes Steel Corp., 424 F. Supp. 1299, 1306–07 (E.D. Mich. 1976); Duncan v. El Paso Prods. Co., 40 Empl. Prac. Dec. (CCH) ¶ 36,186 (W.D. Tex. 1985).

[96] Nash v. Jacqueline Cochran, Inc., 548 F. Supp. 676, 681 (S.D.N.Y. 1982).

[97] Sahadi v. Reynolds Chem., 636 F.2d 1116 (6th Cir. 1980).

[98] Goldstein v. Manhattan Indus., Inc., 758 F.2d 1435, 1448 (11th Cir.), *cert. denied,* 474 U.S. 1005 (1985); Spagnuolo v. Whirlpool Corp., 717 F.2d 114, 122 (4th Cir. 1983).

[99] Kolb v. Goldring, Inc., 694 F.2d 869 (1st Cir. 1982); Bleakley v. Jekyll Island-State Park Auth., 536 F. Supp. 236, 245 (S.D. Ga. 1982); Fariss v. Lynchburg Foundry, 588 F. Supp. 1369, 1371 (W.D. Va. 1984), *aff'd,* 769 F.2d 958 (4th Cir. 1985).

[100] Duke v. Uniroyal, Inc., 928 F.2d 1413 (4th Cir. 1991); Fite v. First Tenn. Prod. Credit Ass'n, 861 F.2d 884 (6th Cir. 1988).

[101] Trans World Airlines, Inc. v. Thurston, 469 U.S. 111, 126 (1985).

[102] Herold v. Hajoca Corp., 864 F.2d 317, 322 (4th Cir. 1988), *cert. denied,* 490 U.S. 1107, 109 S. Ct. 3159 (1989); Nemeroff v. Abelson, 704 F.2d 652, 660 (2d Cir. 1983).

[103] Fiedler v. Indianhead Truck Line, Inc., 670 F.2d 806 (8th Cir. 1982).

Releases. One method of defeating an age discrimination claim is to obtain a release from an employee about to be terminated. Such releases have been upheld by the courts as long as some form of severance pay is provided by the employer and the employee's waiver of employee rights is knowing and voluntary.[104] Such releases must comply with the strict requirements of the Older Workers Benefit Protection Act.[105]

§ 10.7 Americans with Disabilities Act

On July 26, 1992, the provisions of the Americans with Disabilities Act (ADA) regarding discrimination in employment against disabled individuals will go into effect.[106] The requirements of this part of the ADA will first apply to businesses that have 25 or more employees; however, the coverage of the ADA will be extended to employers with 15 or more employees on July 26, 1994.[107]

The ADA prohibits discrimination against a qualified individual with a disability in virtually all aspects of the employment relationship, including job application procedures, hiring, promotions, compensation, employee training, and other terms, conditions, and privileges of employment.[108]

A *qualified individual with a disability* is a person who, with or without "reasonable accommodation," can perform the "essential functions" of a particular job.[109] The ADA does not protect discrimination on the basis of homosexuality, bisexuality, transvestism, transsexualism, pedophilia, exhibitionism, voyeurism, compulsive gambling, kleptomania, or pyromania.[110] Although current users of illegal drugs are not protected under the ADA,[111] the statute does protect a qualified individual who has completed a supervised drug rehabilitation program successfully or who has otherwise been rehabilitated successfully and is no longer using illegal drugs.[112] Oddly enough, an employee who is erroneously regarded as using illegal drugs is protected.[113]

---

[104] Duke v. Uniroyal, Inc., 928 F.2d 1413 (4th Cir. 1991); O'Shea v. Commercial Credit Corp., 930 F.2d 358 (4th Cir. 1991); Runyan v. National Cash Register Corp., 787 F.2d 1039 (6th Cir.) (en banc), *cert. denied,* 479 U.S. 850 (1986).

[105] 29 U.S.C. § 626(f).

[106] 42 U.S.C. §§ 12,101–213 (Supp. III 1991). *See generally* H.H. Perritt, Americans with Disabilities Act Handbook (2d ed. John Wiley & Sons 1991).

[107] *Id.* § 12,111(5).

[108] *Id.* § 12,112(a).

[109] *Id.* § 12,111(8).

[110] *Id.* § 12,211(a) & (b)(1) to (2).

[111] *Id.* § 12,211(b)(3).

[112] 42 U.S.C. § 12,114(b)(1)–(2).

[113] *Id.* § 12,114(b)(3).

Physical or Mental Impairment

To be protected by the ADA, an employee or applicant must have a "physical or mental impairment that substantially limits one or more major life activities, a record of such an impairment, or [be] regarded as having such an impairment."[114] Under regulations promulgated by the Equal Employment Opportunity Commission, a *physical or mental impairment* includes any physiological disorder or condition, cosmetic disfigurement, or anatomical loss affecting one or more of several body systems or any mental or psychological disorder.[115] For instance, an individual with epilepsy would be considered to have an impairment even if the symptoms were completely controlled by medicine.[116] A physical or mental impairment also includes orthopedic injuries; vision, speech, and hearing impairment; cerebral palsy; muscular dystrophy; multiple sclerosis; HIV infection; cancer; heart disease; diabetes; mental retardation; emotional illness; and learning disabilities.[117]

In cases arising under the Rehabilitation Act of 1973 (upon which the ADA is based), the courts have dealt with the problem of determining who is suffering from an impairment within the protection of that statute. For instance, it has been held that an individual who suffered from "acrophobia" (fear of heights) was not handicapped.[118] A court also has held that a person with a congenital back problem was impaired under the Rehabilitation Act.[119] On the other hand, a court found that the term "impairment" must be used in a commonsense fashion and, therefore, that a left-handed individual was not considered to be impaired.[120]

Major life activity.   Not only must an impairment be present, but also this impairment must involve a *major life activity,* a term that has been defined to include such functions as caring for oneself, performing manual tasks, walking, seeing, hearing, speaking, breathing, and learning as well as working.[121] In cases arising under the Rehabilitation Act, the courts have held that certain impairments always "substantially limit a major life activity,"

---

[114] *Id.* § 12,102(2).

[115] 29 C.F.R. § 1630.2(h) (1991) (proposed).

[116] 56 Fed. Reg. 8592 (Feb. 28, 1991).

[117] S. Rep. No. 116, 101st Cong., 2d Sess. 22 (1989).

[118] Forrisi v. Bowen, 794 F.2d 931, 935 (4th Cir. 1986).

[119] E.E. Black, Ltd. v. Marshall, 497 F. Supp. 1088, 1103 (D. Haw. 1980).

[120] Torres v. Bolger, 610 F. Supp. 593, 596 (N.D. Tex. 1985), *aff'd,* 781 F.2d 1134 (5th Cir. 1986).

[121] 29 C.F.R. § 1630.2(i) (1991) (proposed).

for example, blindness,[122] deafness,[123] paranoid schizophrenia,[124] and manic depression.[125] On the other hand, although the court found that an individual who was cross-eyed was impaired, the court held that this impairment did not substantially limit the individual's ability to work because the individual was able to perform all previous work assignments.[126]

Essential functions. In any event, a disabled individual must be able to perform the essential functions of the job in question. The term *essential functions* means job tasks that are fundamental and not marginal.[127]

Reasonable accommodation. The ADA requires that an employer make efforts toward a "reasonable accommodation" to an individual's disability.[128] An *accommodation* is any modification or adjustment in the work environment or in the way things are done customarily that enables an individual with a disability to enjoy equal employment opportunities. Reasonable accommodation may require job restructuring, modification of work schedules, reassignment to vacant positions, acquisition or modification of equipment or devices, adjustment or modification of examinations, training materials, or policies as well as provisions for qualified readers or interpreters as appropriate.[129] Employers are only obligated to make reasonable accommodations to the "known" physical or mental limitations of a qualified individual with a disability. Therefore, the employee/applicant must request a certain form of accommodation. Although the preference of an individual with a disability is to be given primary consideration in deciding upon the appropriate form of accommodation, the choice of accommodation remains in the discretion of the employer.[130] When one or more alternatives are available for accommodation, the employer may choose the one that is least expensive or easiest for the employer to implement as long as it provides a meaningful employment opportunity.[131]

Undue hardship. The failure to provide reasonable accommodation may be excused when the employer is able to establish that the proposed

---

[122] Brown v. Sibley, 650 F.2d 760 (5th Cir. 1981).

[123] Strathie v. Department of Transp., 716 F.2d 227 (3d Cir. 1983).

[124] Franklin v. United States Postal Serv., 687 F. Supp. 1214 (S.D. Ohio 1988); Doe v. New York Univ., 666 F.2d 761 (2d Cir. 1981).

[125] Gardner v. Morris, 752 F.2d 1271 (8th Cir. 1985).

[126] Jasany v. United States Postal Serv., 755 F.2d 1244 (6th Cir. 1985).

[127] 42 U.S.C. § 12,111(8).

[128] *Id.* § 12,112(b)(5).

[129] *Id.* § 12,111(9).

[130] 56 Fed. Reg. 8600 (Feb. 28, 1991).

[131] S. Rep. No. 116, 101st Cong., 2d Sess. 34–35 (1989).

accommodation would impose an undue hardship on its business. Under the ADA, the term *undue hardship* is defined as any action requiring significant difficulty or expense.[132] In deciding whether an undue hardship results, certain factors may be taken into consideration, such as the nature and cost of the accommodation required, the overall financial resources of the employer, the impact of the accommodation on the operation of the business, the number, type, and location of the employer's facilities, and the number of persons employed at the facility.[133]

Benefits.   In regulations promulgated by the Equal Employment Opportunity Commission, the Commission states that employees with disabilities must be given the same type of health insurance coverage that is given to other employees, although preexisting condition exclusions are permissible. In addition, employers may offer health insurance policies that limit coverage for certain procedures or treatments to a specified number per year even though such provisions may have an adverse effect upon those with disabilities. Moreover, an employer is not required to have a paid sick leave policy and may even reduce the number of paid sick days if the reduction applies to all employees.[134]

Remedies.   Individuals who feel that they have been discriminated against in violation of the ADA may bring a lawsuit that, if successful, could result in reinstatement to their former jobs, promotion, back pay (and possibly front pay) as well as an award of attorneys' fees.[135] In the event that an employer prevails in an ADA lawsuit, the employer may recover its attorneys' fees and expenses only in the event that the court determines that the individual's case was frivolous, unreasonable, or groundless.[136]

§ 10.8   Equal Pay Act

A federal law, known as the Equal Pay Act, prohibits discrimination in the payment of wages based on the sex of employees.[137] Accordingly, employers are required to pay equal wages to employees of different genders for jobs that require equal skill, effort, and responsibility and that are performed under similar working conditions unless one of four exceptions is

---

[132] 42 U.S.C. § 12,111(10)(A).

[133] *Id.* § 12,111(10)(B).

[134] 56 Fed. Reg. 8598 (Feb. 28, 1991).

[135] 42 U.S.C. § 12,117(a).

[136] H.R. Rep. No. 485, 101st Cong., 2d Sess., pt. 2, at 140.

[137] 29 U.S.C. § 206(d)(1) (1988).

applicable.[138] The statute does not require an employee to prove that the jobs are "identical;" rather, it is sufficient for the employee to establish that the jobs are "substantially equal."[139]

In order to meet this standard, it is necessary to view the job as a whole and to look at the characteristics of the jobs being compared over a full work cycle.[140] The employee must prove that the jobs had a "common core" of tasks and that a "significant portion" of the jobs is identical.[141] In making the critical comparison, the courts look to actual job requirements and performance and not simply to the job titles.[142]

If an employee demonstrates that the employee is receiving lower wages for "substantially equal work," the employer then has the burden of proving that the wage differential resulted from (1) a seniority system, (2) a merit system, (3) a system that measures earnings by quantity or quality of production, or (4) a differential based on "any factor other than sex."[143] These exceptions are narrowly construed by the federal courts.[144] For instance, a merit system is not required to be in writing; however, it must be an organized and structured procedure whereby employees are evaluated systematically according to predetermined criteria. In addition, the employees must be aware of the policy and it must not be based upon sex.[145] Although differences in experience, training, or ability of employees of different genders can justify differences in their salaries,[146] an employer who places great weight on subjective factors, such as experience, may be held liable for paying female employees lower salaries, particularly when higher goals were set for the female employees than the male employees.[147]

Employers are allowed to pay a higher salary to a male employee if his experience and ability made him the best person for the available job and a higher salary was required to hire him initially.[148] On the other hand, employers may not use a so-called "market rate" defense on the ground that less money is required to attract female employees. Such an approach

---

[138] *Id.* § 206(d)(1).

[139] Brennan v. Prince William Hosp. Corp., 503 F.2d 282, 291 (4th Cir. 1974), *cert. denied,* 420 U.S. 972 (1975).

[140] 29 C.F.R. § 1620.14 (1991).

[141] Brewster v. Barnes, 788 F.2d 985, 991 (4th Cir. 1986).

[142] Orahood v. Board of Trustees, 645 F.2d 651, 654 (8th Cir. 1981).

[143] 29 U.S.C. § 206(d)(1).

[144] EEOC v. Whitin Mach. Works, Inc., 635 F.2d 1095, 1097 (4th Cir. 1980).

[145] Brennan v. Victoria Bank & Trust Co., 493 F.2d 896, 901 (5th Cir. 1974); Hodgson v. Brookhaven Gen. Hosp., 436 F.2d 719, 726 (5th Cir. 1970).

[146] EEOC v. Aetna Ins. Co., 616 F.2d 719, 725 (4th Cir. 1980).

[147] Keziah v. W.N. Brown & Son, 888 F.2d 322 (4th Cir. 1989).

[148] Horner v. Mary Inst., 613 F.2d 706, 714 (8th Cir. 1980).

would serve to perpetuate the historic employment discrimination in wages suffered by females in the work force.[149]

One of the most troublesome areas under the Equal Pay Act involves executive and management positions. Due to the nature of these types of positions, it is difficult for the courts to compare the duties of the jobs in order to determine whether or not they are substantially equal. This difficulty in comparison is particularly true when such jobs are "highly specialized and require distinct skills," such as jobs in the computer programming and accounting areas.[150] For instance, it has been held that a female director of institutional studies did not meet the equal work standard in comparing her job with that of a male assistant comptroller of a college.[151] In another case, a female tax auditor failed to establish that she was engaged in work that was substantially equal to that of federal revenue agents.[152]

Employers should ensure that there are descriptions for various jobs or guidelines in place for determining salaries for their employees. In the absence of such policies or guidelines, the courts tend to review "the totality of the circumstances, not merely job comparisons" when management positions are involved.[153] For instance, a court decided that an "employer does all that the Act requires in the course of complying with reasonable procedures for establishing wages based on work, skill, effort, responsibility, qualification, seniority and the like, without regard to gender."[154]

Employers who violate the Equal Pay Act are subject to liability for the pay differential for a period of at least two years or for a period of three years if the violation is proved to be "willful."[155] In addition, it is possible that the employer could be required to pay front pay for a period of time.[156] Liquidated damages in twice the amount of the back pay awarded will be assessed against an employer unless the employer establishes that it acted in good faith and with reasonable grounds to believe it was not violating the law.[157] Although it has also been held that conformity to industry practices

---

[149] Corning Glass Works v. Brennan, 417 U.S. 188 (1974); Hodgson v. Brookhaven Gen. Hosp., 436 F.2d 719 (5th Cir. 1970); Futran v. Rain Radio Co., 501 F. Supp. 734 (N.D. Ga. 1980).

[150] Soble v. University of Md., 778 F.2d 164, 167 (4th Cir. 1985).

[151] Orahood v. Board of Trustees, 645 F.2d 651 (8th Cir. 1981).

[152] Edmondson v. Simon, 497 F. Supp. 411 (N.D. Ill. 1980).

[153] Roesel v. Joliet Wrought Washer Co., 596 F.2d 183, 185 (7th Cir. 1979).

[154] Ososky v. Wick, 704 F.2d 1264, 1268 (D.C. Cir. 1983).

[155] 29 U.S.C. § 255(a) (1974).

[156] Thompson v. Sawyer, 678 F.2d 257 (D.C. Cir. 1982), cert. denied, 104 S. Ct. 1308 (1984).

[157] 29 U.S.C. §§ 216(b), 260 (1988).

is not enough to establish the required good faith,[158] one court has held that reliance upon a legal opinion is sufficient to meet this standard.[159]

§ 10.9   Executive Order 11,246

Executive Order 11,246 prohibits job discrimination based on race, color, religion, sex, or national origin by employers who have service, supply, use, or construction contracts with the federal government as well as by contractors and subcontractors performing under federally-assisted construction contracts.[160] Employers who do business with the government are required to commit themselves to an equal opportunity clause, to take affirmative action to employ minorities, and to comply with the regulations promulgated by the Secretary of Labor.[161] Contracts involving $10,000 or less are exempt from the requirements of Executive Order 11,246.[162]

The equal opportunity provision of Executive Order 11,246 requires covered employers to commit themselves to refrain from discriminating against employees or applicants for employment on the basis of race, color, religion, or national origin. In addition, covered employers are required to take affirmative action to ensure that applicants and employees are not discriminated against on the foregoing grounds.[163]

The most burdensome requirement of Executive Order 11,246 is the promulgation and implementation of an *affirmative action plan.* This requirement is imposed on contractors with 50 or more employees who, among other things, have a contract of $50,000 or more with the government.[164] An affirmative action plan has a number of requirements directed toward increasing the number of females and minorities in the employer's work force. However, the critical part of an affirmative action plan is the *utilization analysis,* in which the contractor's employment of females and minorities is compared to the availability of such groups in the local job market. The utilization analysis consists of a work force analysis, an availability analysis, and a utilization determination.[165]

Executive Order 11,246 is enforced by the Office of Federal Contract Compliance Programs of the United States Department of Labor. Compliance officers from that division are empowered to conduct audits of

---

[158] Thompson v. Sawyer, 678 F.2d 257, 282 (D.C. Cir. 1982).

[159] Hill v. J.C. Penney Co., 688 F.2d 370 (5th Cir. 1982).

[160] 42 U.S.C. § 2000 note (Supp. III 1991); Exec. Order No. 11,246, 30 Fed. Reg. 12,319 (Sept. 24, 1965), *reprinted as amended in* 42 U.S.C. § 2000(e) note.

[161] *Id.* § 2000e note, § 202.

[162] 41 C.F.R. § 60-1.5(a)(1) (1990).

[163] 42 U.S.C. § 2000 note, § 202.

[164] 41 C.F.R. §§ 60-2.1(a), 50-1.40(a) (1990).

[165] *Id.* § 60-2.11 (1990).

government contractors to determine their compliance with Executive Order 11,246.[166] In addition, individuals may file complaints with the Office of Federal Contract Compliance Programs if they feel that an employer has violated the Executive Order.[167] The Office of Federal Contract Compliance Programs may conduct an investigation and a hearing, and sanctions may be imposed, including cancellation of the contract.[168] One court has indicated that back pay may be awarded to victims of discrimination in addition to other sanctions.[169]

§ 10.10   Retaliatory Discharge under Federal Law

In addition to the laws prohibiting various forms of discrimination, employees also may be protected for filing complaints about discrimination or becoming a whistle-blower who makes safety complaints. A number of federal statutes protect employees and former employees from retaliation for enforcing their rights under discrimination laws (or assisting others in doing so) and also protect employees who make complaints about safety violations or corporate misconduct.

For example, Title VII of the Civil Rights Act of 1964 prohibits retaliation against those who oppose discrimination or even participate in the Title VII enforcement process.[170] Employees claiming retaliation under this provision must establish that there is a causal connection between engaging in the protected activity and the adverse employment decision.[171] One of the best ways to establish the required causal connection is to show that there was a short period of time between the protected activity and the adverse personnel action.[172] Of course, the mere fact that an employee has engaged in a protected activity does not insulate the employee from discipline or discharge for such things as insubordination or poor job performance.[173]

In addition, the Fair Labor Standards Act prohibits the discharge of or discrimination against an employee "because such employee has filed any complaint or instituted or caused to be instituted any proceeding under or related to the Act or has testified or is about to testify in any such proceeding."[174] Although the actual filing of a formal complaint with the

---

[166] 42 U.S.C. § 2000e note, § 206.

[167] 41 C.F.R. § 60-1.21 (1990).

[168] *Id.* § 60-1.26 (1990).

[169] United States v. Duquesne Light Co., 423 F. Supp. 507 (W.D. Pa. 1976).

[170] 42 U.S.C. § 2000e-3(a) (1988).

[171] McKenna v. Weinberger, 729 F.2d 783, 791 (D.C. Cir. 1984).

[172] Donnellon v. Fruehauf Corp., 794 F.2d 598 (11th Cir. 1986).

[173] Brown v. Delta Air Lines Inc., 522 F. Supp. 1218 (S.D. Tex. 1980), *aff'd,* 673 F.2d 1325 (5th Cir. 1982).

[174] 29 U.S.C. § 215(a)(3) (Supp. III 1991).

Department of Labor is not required, the employee must prove that the "immediate motivating factor" for the adverse employment decision was the employee's assertion of statutory rights under the Fair Labor Standards Act.[175] In fact, an employee who simply complains to management about a potential violation of the Fair Labor Standards Act is protected from discharge even if there are other grounds for discharging the employee.[176]

A number of statutes protect employees who make complaints about alleged safety violations. For instance, the Occupational Safety and Health Act (OSH Act) prohibits discrimination against any employee for filing a complaint, instituting a proceeding, testifying in a proceeding, or exercising a right under the OSH Act, which regulates safety in the workplace.[177] However, the employee does not have the right to bring a private lawsuit under this provision because the enforcement of the provision is the responsibility of the Secretary of Labor.[178] Employees who work for power companies that operate nuclear power plants are encouraged to become whistle-blowers by the provisions of the Energy Reorganization Act.[179] This provision, however, does not apply to government contractors at government atomic energy facilities.[180]

On the other hand, a sailor is not protected from bringing safety complaints to the attention of the sailor's employer.[181] By the same token, an airline employee has no right to sue the airline for retaliation for making safety complaints.[182] However, a truck driver who is fired for making safety complaints is protected by § 405 of the Surface Transportation Assistance Act of 1982.[183]

§ 10.11   Federal Law Update: Civil Rights Act of 1991

On November 2, 1991, President Bush signed into law the Civil Rights Act of 1991[184] despite his earlier complaints that it was a "Quotas" bill. Perhaps the greatest change that will be caused by this statute is the addition of

---

[175] Hayes v. McIntosh, 604 F. Supp. 10 (N.D. Ind. 1984).

[176] Brennan v. Maxey's Yamaha, Inc., 513 F.2d 179, 181 (8th Cir. 1975).

[177] 29 U.S.C. § 660(c) (Supp. III 1991).

[178] Taylor v. Brighton Corp., 616 F.2d 256 (6th Cir. 1980).

[179] 42 U.S.C. § 5851 (Supp. III 1991).

[180] Adams v. Dole, 927 F.2d 771 (4th Cir. 1991).

[181] Meaige v. Hartley Marine Corp., 925 F.2d 700 (4th Cir. 1991).

[182] Pavolini v. Bard-Air Corp., 645 F.2d 144 (2d Cir. 1981).

[183] 49 U.S.C. § 2305 (1988).

[184] Pub L. No. 102-166, 105 Stat. 1071.

awards of compensatory and punitive damages in the event discrimination has been found. Under previous legislation, such as Title VII of the Civil Rights Act of 1964, remedies were limited to back pay, front pay, and reinstatement. Significantly, the new remedies will apply to the employment provisions of the Americans With Disabilities Act due to go into effect in July of 1992. Compensatory damages may include awards for emotional pain and suffering, inconvenience, mental anguish, loss of enjoyment of life, and other nonmonetary damages. Punitive damages may be awarded if an employee demonstrates that an employer discriminated with malice or reckless indifference to the employee's federally protected rights. Another very significant departure from prior law is that the parties have a right to a jury trial in the event the employee seeks compensatory or punitive damages. The addition of this new right may result in very large damages awards because of jury sympathy for employees.

Apparently President Bush's concerns about quotas were met by the compromise bill. The new law requires an employer, in cases of unintentional discrimination, to establish that a challenged employment practice is "job related for the position in question and consistent with business necessity."[185] This part of the statute should be of little concern to most employers because it is generally involved in class action lawsuits.

There are a number of other changes made by the Civil Rights Act of 1991 that will impact the methods by which employers implement their personnel policies. The result of this legislation will be to cause employers to think very carefully before taking any adverse employment action against a person in a protected group. Nevertheless, employers can protect themselves by establishing fair personnel practices and ensuring that any adverse personnel decisions are carefully reviewed before they are put into effect.

STATE LAWS AGAINST DISCRIMINATION

§ 10.12   Overview of State Antidiscrimination Laws

It is very important to recognize that some states have enacted antidiscrimination laws that go well beyond the coverage of federal law. Coverage of these laws is subject to constant revision, however, due to the ongoing tension between the assertion of rights by the various protected groups and the employer's traditional right to control personnel decisions without outside

---

[185] Pub. L. No. 102-166, § 105(a).

interference. As of this writing, some states have enacted statutes prohibiting discrimination on the following grounds:

1. Marital status
2. Criminal arrest or conviction records
3. Sexual orientation
4. Political affiliation
5. Family responsibilities or obligations
6. Educational level
7. Applicant referral status
8. Organizational affiliations
9. Reproductive considerations
10. Military status
11. Personal appearance, including physical characteristics such as weight or height
12. Medical condition (including results of certain AIDS tests)
13. Status as recipient of public assistance
14. Citizenship or place of birth
15. Affiliations with protected groups
16. Activities in pursuit of enforcement of laws or civil rights.

The statutes discussed in §§ **10.13** through **10.28** are most likely to be encountered in Mid-Atlantic, New England, and Far Western states. Also, the statutory protections discussed may apply only to certain groups (in some cases, only to public employees); but lobbying for extensions continues and those making employment decisions involving persons who might belong to any of the following classes would be well-advised to confirm the current status of the applicable state law.

§ 10.13   Marital Status

Statutes proscribing discrimination based on marital status generally prohibit adverse action based on the status of an employee as married, single, widowed, divorced, or because of the employee's marriage or termination of marriage to another person. States with such statutes include Alaska[186] and the District of Columbia,[187] which includes within its definition of marital status pregnancy and parenthood.

---

[186] Alaska Stat. § 18.80.220 (1986).
[187] D.C. Code Ann. § 1-2512(a) (1981).

§ 10.14   Criminal Arrest or Conviction Records

Statutes prohibiting discrimination based on criminal or conviction records proscribe adverse action based on conviction of criminal offenses, or on a determination that the applicant or employee lacks good moral character based on such conviction. Under the law of New York, for example, a statutory presumption of rehabilitation is created by release from the penal system,[188] for which the burden of rebuttal is placed on the employer. Employment may be denied only when there is a showing of a direct adverse relationship between the criminal act and the employment sought, or when such employment would create an unreasonable risk to the general public.[189]

§ 10.15   Sexual Orientation

Statutes prohibiting discrimination based on sexual orientation proscribe adverse action based on status of male or female homosexuality, heterosexuality, or bisexuality, either by practice or by preference.[190] In addition to preference or practice, the status of being identified as having such an orientation is protected under statutes like those of Massachusetts,[191] and of having a history of such a preference, practice, or identification is protected in Wisconsin.[192] Nevertheless, even liberal statutes such as enacted by Massachusetts may have limitations, such as the exclusion of persons whose sexual orientation involves minor children as sex objects.[193]

§ 10.16   Political Affiliation

Discrimination based on political affiliation may be prohibited in situations in which the person is affected adversely due to membership or identification with a political party. Some states broaden this classification to include the holding of political beliefs.[194] Political affiliation also may be defined not only by the status of endorsing a political party, in the present or the past, but also by the status of lack of political affiliation.[195]

---

[188] Meth v. Manhattan & Bronx Surface Transit Operating Auth., 521 N.Y.S.2d 54 (App. Div. 1987).

[189] Id.

[190] D.C. Code Ann. § 1-2512(a) (1981).

[191] Mass. Ann. Laws ch. 151B, § 3.6 (Law. Co-op 1988).

[192] Wis. Stat. Ann. § 111.32 (13m) (West 1988).

[193] Mass. Ann. Laws ch. 151B §§ 3.6, 3.9, 4.1, 4.2, 4.3, 4.15 (Law. Co-op 1988).

[194] Colo. Rev. Stat. § 24-50-111 (1989).

[195] D.C. Code Ann. § 1-2502(25) (1981).

§ 10.17   Family Responsibilities or Obligations

Discrimination based on parenthood is unlawful in jurisdictions such as Connecticut and the District of Columbia. The protection afforded in such jurisdictions may be limited to discrimination in preemployment inquiries, however. For example, in Connecticut information relating to an applicant's pregnancy, childbearing or rearing age or plans, reproductive potential, birth control, or family responsibilities may not be considered absent a direct bona fide employment qualification.[196] Family responsibilities also may include the status of being a contributor to the support of dependents, under laws such as those in the District of Columbia.[197]

§ 10.18   Educational Level

Although educational level is rarely recognized as constituting a protected status, Colorado and Pennsylvania have enacted statutes prohibiting discrimination based on educational level in some instances. In Colorado, public employment competitive examinations may not discriminate according to educational level, with some exceptions.[198] In Pennsylvania, discrimination may not be based on the holding of a high school equivalency certificate rather than a diploma.[199]

§ 10.19   Applicant Referral Status

The only state that prohibits discrimination based on "applicant referral status" is Colorado.[200] Protection of this category extends to applicants who are not referred for employment by a private employment agency, which status arguably results from unlawful screening by employment agencies, as well as to the unavailability of access to private employment agencies due to cost.

§ 10.20   Organizational Affiliations

Several states have enacted statutes prohibiting discrimination against persons due to organizational affiliation, which in practice generally applies to

---

[196] Conn. Gen. Stat. Ann. § 46a-60(a)(9) (West 1958).

[197] D.C. Code Ann. § 1-2502(12) (1981).

[198] Colo. Rev. Stat. § 24-50-112(3)(b) (1989).

[199] Pa. Stat. Ann. tit. 43, § 955 (1990).

[200] Colo. Rev. Stat. § 24-34-402(1)(g) (1989).

labor union membership. Colorado prohibits "unjust discrimination practices" by labor organizations,[201] and Pennsylvania prohibits discrimination in public employment based on membership in or activity on behalf of labor organizations.[202]

§ 10.21   Reproductive Considerations

The concept of discrimination based on sex has been extended by statute in Connecticut to include considerations related to pregnancy, childbearing capacity, sterilization, fertility, and related conditions.[203] The asking of questions regarding such factors, for example on employment applications, also is prohibited.[204]

§ 10.22   Military Status

Several states have enacted prohibitions against discrimination on the basis of various types of military status. National Guard obligations, status as a veteran, status as having been unfavorably discharged, and status as a disabled veteran are classifications that may be protected. Wisconsin, for example, prohibits discrimination based on membership either in the national guard or a state reserve defense force.[205] Illinois specifically prohibits discrimination against persons discharged from the armed forces "unfavorably," but such protection does not extend to those discharged dishonorably.[206]

§ 10.23   Personal Appearance

Very few states have enacted protections against discrimination based on the personal appearance classification. Only the District of Columbia has enacted a statute specifically prohibiting discrimination based on *personal appearance,* which is defined as the outward bodily appearance of any person, regardless of sex, including the manner or style of dress or personal grooming, including, but not limited to, hair style or beards.[207]

---

[201] *Id.* § 8-3-102(1)(d).

[202] Pa. Stat. Ann. tit. 71, § 741.905a (1990).

[203] Conn. Gen. Stat. Ann. § 46a-51(17) (West 1958).

[204] Conn. Gen. Stat. § 46a-60(a)(9) (1958).

[205] Wis. Stat. Ann. §§ 111.31(1), 111.31(2), 111.31(3), 111.321 (West 1988).

[206] Ill. Rev. Stat. ch. 68, § 1-103(P) (1989).

[207] D.C. Code Ann. § 1-2502(22) (1981).

The rationale for this protection is evidently that such personal choices may be representative of race, national origin, or religion, which also are protected categories. Only Michigan has prohibited discrimination based on a person's weight,[208] and only Michigan and Kansas have prohibited discrimination based on height.[209] Even in those states, however, some reasonable restrictions based on job requirements are allowed, such as in Kansas where minimum height requirements may be imposed for fire-fighters and law enforcement or security officers.[210]

§ 10.24   Medical Condition

Wisconsin is an example of a state that bars discrimination based on medical condition, including on results of certain AIDS tests.[211] In that state, discrimination is outlawed simply on the basis of having taken an AIDS test, regardless of the result.[212]

§ 10.25   Status as Recipient of Public Assistance

At least two states have prohibited discrimination based on the receipt of public assistance. Minnesota prohibits discrimination against those receiving federal, state, or local medical or other assistance, including subsidies and rental assistance or supplements.[213] North Dakota prohibits discrimination based on similar categories.[214]

§ 10.26   Citizenship or Place of Birth

Discrimination based on citizenship is prohibited in Colorado[215] and Minnesota.[216] The latter state extends the protected classification to include not only the birthplace of the individual but also the birthplace of lineal ancestors.[217]

---

[208] Mich. Stat. Ann. § 37.2102(1) (Callaghan 1990).

[209] Id.; Kan. Stat. Ann. § 44-1110 (1990).

[210] Kan. Stat. Ann. § 44-1110 (1990).

[211] Wis. Stat. Ann. § 103.15(2)(b) (West 1988).

[212] Id.

[213] Minn. Stat. Ann. § 363.01 subd. 42 (West 1988).

[214] N.D. Cent. Code § 14-02.4-02.18 (1990).

[215] Colo. Rev. Stat. § 24-34-402(1)(a) (1989).

[216] Minn. Stat. Ann. § 43A.01 subd. 2 (West 1988).

[217] Id.

§ 10.27   Affiliations with Protected Groups

Oregon is among several states that have enacted statutes prohibiting discrimination not only against members of protected groups but also against anyone affiliated or associated with one of those groups (which includes many of the protected groups discussed in §§ **10.12** through **10.27**).[218]

§ 10.28   Retaliatory Discharge under State Law

As with those statutes just discussed that protect those persons affiliated with protected groups, persons who actively pursue enforcement of certain laws (particularly civil rights laws) are afforded special protection in some states. For example, Minnesota protects from discrimination persons who join or participate in the activities of a local fair employment agency.[219] Oregon prohibits discrimination based on participation in a workers' compensation hearing or based on report of a public health violation.[220]

---

[218] Or. Rev. Stat. § 659.030(1)(a) (1953).

[219] Minn. Stat. Ann. § 363.01 subd. 23 (West 1988).

[220] Or. Rev. Stat. §§ 659.410, 659.035(1) (1953).

CHAPTER 11

CONSTRUCTION LABOR LAW ISSUES OF THE 1990s

William F. Hoefs
Charles S. Birenbaum

William F. Hoefs is a senior partner in the San Francisco, California, law firm of Thelen, Marrin, Johnson & Bridges' Labor and Employment Relations Practice Group. Mr. Hoefs received his undergraduate and law degrees from the University of Wisconsin, Madison. He is a member of the Wisconsin and California Bar Associations. He has a distinguished record as a trial attorney in state and federal court, where he has defended employers in discrimination, wrongful termination, and other employment-related litigation. He lectures in labor and employment law at California community colleges and is frequently asked to speak as an expert at conferences and seminars.

Charles S. Birenbaum is a partner in the San Francisco, California, law firm of Thelen, Marrin, Johnson & Bridges' Labor and Employment Relations Practice Group. He is a graduate of Oberlin College and Georgetown University Law Center, and is a member of the California bar. Mr. Birenbaum specializes in representation of management in matters involving organized labor. He regularly litigates at the National Labor Relations Board, United States Department of Labor, in arbitration and in federal and state courts. He frequently lectures and writes on labor and employment law and was a member of the adjunct faculty at Santa Clara University Law School, where he taught labor law.

§ 11.1   Introduction

Employers in the construction industry have received a great deal of attention from government, labor organizations, special interest groups, and academe over the industry's labor and employment relations. Even the seminal blueprint for labor peace embodied in the original National Labor Relations Act (NLRA),[1] was amended in 1959 to provide for the unique nature of employment in the construction industry.[2] The attention directed at the construction industry's labor and employment relations in the 1980s reflected controversy in a broad range of issues—from safety and health to the economic struggle between the open shop and unionized sectors. These controversies will continue to impact construction employers in the 1990s.

Numerous forces are at work in the development of labor law issues: new statutory obligations acquired in the 1980s and 1990s requiring judicial interpretation; organized labor's methodology to preserve and expand the union sector causing employers to rethink the union/nonunion strategies

---

[1] NLRA, 29 U.S.C. §§ 151–169 as amended.

[2] *Id.* § 158(f).

for their companies; population demographics and the changing nature of
the American work force requiring close examination of employment practices created in decades of ample labor supply in a more homogeneous labor
pool.

This chapter addresses various labor law issues for construction and engineering firms of the 1990s: union organizing through powerful corporate
campaigns; laws impacting prehire agreements and union elections at construction employers; picketing to coerce execution of prehire agreements;
preemption of employee wrongful discharge lawsuits by federal laws; plant
closing and mass layoff laws as they impact construction employers; drug
and alcohol testing; and cutting edge issues on the relationship between
multiemployer trust funds and construction employers.[3] This sampling of
critical issues for the construction employer supplements issues treated separately in other chapters of this book[4] and many other labor law issues that
will surface this decade through new legislation and operation of administrative agencies, arbitrators, courts, and collective bargaining.

§ 11.2   Top-Down Union Organizing of Construction Firms

Union membership in the building and construction trades continues its
decline from the post-World War II years.[5] The building and construction
trades' labor organizations have experienced difficulty with double breasting, the employer practice whereby a unionized company creates a separate
business entity to perform construction work nonunion, and with the fierce
competition in construction. The efficacy of picketing has likewise diminished over the years. Changes in law also have not helped organized labor's
cause. For example, minority contracting requirements on public sector jobs
have caused unionized contractors to retain small, nonunion, minority-
owned subcontractors for work on public projects.

To counter the forces at play against organized labor, unions have turned
to strategies for top-down organizing. *Top-down organizing* forces management recognition of organized labor without resort to picketing or more
traditional organizing among an employer's work force. Rather than seeking an election conducted by the National Labor Relations Board (NLRB)

---

[3] See §§ **11.2–11.7.**

[4] See **Chs. 10** and **12.**

[5] In a recent study by the Bureau of Labor Statistics (BLS), the BLS found that the total
number of construction industry employees who were union members dropped from
1,145,000 to 1,073,000 between 1989 and 1990. As a percentage of all those employed
in the construction industry, union members represented only 21.0% of the work force
in 1990, compared with a figure representing 21.5% of the work force in 1989. Daily
Lab. Rep. (BNA) No. 26, at B-10 (Feb. 7, 1991).

under the laws empowering such proceedings,[6] unions bypass that cumbersome process by forcing an employer to sign a union agreement in return for cooperation in the planning and certification stages of a project. These sorts of pressures are commonly referred to as *corporate campaigns.*

§ 11.3 —Corporate Campaign Tactics

Union corporate campaign tactics, deployed with much planning and resource, include the following kinds of activities:

1. Coalition building with other groups, environmental, neighborhood, or otherwise, for anti-employer campaigns
2. Intense lobbying with legislators and appointed or civil service government officials
3. Intervention in regulatory or licensing proceedings in an effort to use government or judicial procedure to thwart company goals
4. Product boycotts
5. Opposition to applications for government funds or grants
6. Environmental law challenges
7. Media and local advertising or leafleting against company presence and initiatives
8. Opposition to acquisition of real estate or other company interests
9. Economic and political campaigns directed at creditors, stockbrokers, stock analysts, shareholders, or investors in an effort to convince them that the company may falter during union organizing or strike activity
10. Organizing shareholders for proxy fights
11. Assistance to competitors
12. Threats to businesses or customers that support the employer.[7]

Unions frequently deploy only one or two of the listed tactics for the necessary effects on an employer. For example, if an agency holds hostage a necessary prerequisite to business until an employer recognizes a union, there may be no need to engage in other coercive tactics. One might expect a government official to exercise more restraint in this situation, but officials frequently do not perceive meddling in a company's private labor relations as inappropriate. Moreover, agency officials may know that a company that

---

[6] NLRA, 29 U.S.C. § 159 (1988); 29 C.F.R. §§ 101, 102 (1991).

[7] *See generally* C. Perry, Union Corporate Campaigns 1 (1987). Fletcher, *The Corporate Campaign—Labor's Ultimate Weapon Or Suicide Bomb* 65 N.C. L. Rev. 85 (1986); Jarley & Maranto, *Union Corporate Campaigns: An Assessment,* 43 Indus. & Lab. Rel. Rev. 505, 506–07 (1990).

must return to a government agency for future endeavors may not take legal recourse against the agency or its employees for fear of retribution later.

The costs of unions of corporate campaigns may be carried by their members. Unions may deduct money from employee dues or may set up industry funds with union employers for the purpose of union organizing.

Government Involvement in Labor Disputes

One of the corporate campaign tactics causing the most concern is the increase in union pressure on the legislative process. Through extensive lobbying efforts, unions have been able to influence new laws on both the national and local levels. Such laws may increase union power by conditioning receipt of government benefits on an employer's union recognition or acceptance of wage and benefit levels set by unions in their contracts rather than by free market forces.

Recent case law has provided employers with some guidance on methods to defeat this type of union and government behavior. In 1986, the United States Supreme Court addressed government interference in labor disputes in a case involving the taxi industry. In *Golden State Transit Corp. v. Los Angeles*,[8] the plaintiff, which operated taxicabs under the Yellow Cab name, applied to the City of Los Angeles for renewal of its operating franchise. After approval from the City's board of transportation, but while the renewal application was still pending with the City Council, the plaintiff transit company entered a labor dispute with the International Brotherhood of Teamsters.[9]

In an effort to pressure the employer, over the next two months Teamsters representatives urged for and received extensions of the renewal decision. Quickly, "the labor dispute and the franchise renewal issue had become clearly intertwined."[10] Rather than deny the application outright, however, the City Council conditioned further consideration of renewal upon settlement of the labor dispute.[11] When the employer did not buckle to City pressure, the City Council rejected the franchise application by a vote of 11 to 1.[12] The employer sued in federal court. The United States Supreme Court first considered the employer's right to receive an injunction restraining the City from its action.

The Court found that the City Council's actions were forbidden by the NLRA.[13] The Court recognized Congressional intent behind the NLRA to

---

[8] 475 U.S. 608 (1986) [hereinafter Golden State I].

[9] *Id.* at 609–10.

[10] *Id.* at 610.

[11] *Id.* at 611.

[12] *Id.*

[13] *Id.* at 618.

leave the collective bargaining arena open to the free play of economic forces between unions, employers, and their workers.[14] The City Council's actions effectively threw the City's weight behind the union and increased the union's comparative economic power by placing conditions on the franchise license—a matter not tied to labor negotiations. Consequently, the City's interference was preempted by the NLRA, and an injunction was appropriate to restrain the City's action.[15] In a subsequent hearing of the same case, the Court also found that Golden State Transit could recover monetary damages from the City.[16]

In *Associated Builders & Contractors v. Massachusetts Water Resources Authority,*[17] decided in May 1991, a similar issue in the construction industry was resolved by a federal court. In that case, the public sector defendant, the Massachusetts Water Resources Authority (MWRA), was responsible for cleanup of the Boston Harbor at an estimated cost of $6.1 billion over a 10-year period.[18] At the suggestion of its consulting engineers, the MWRA entered into a prehire agreement with local unions in an attempt to secure labor peace for the duration of the project.[19] This agreement required that all subcontractors on the project comply with its provisions.[20] The plaintiff, a trade association representing over 18,000 nonunion contractors, sought to enjoin MWRA from enforcing the agreement in the bidding process.[21]

Although the United States Court of Appeals for the First Circuit recognized that such prehire agreements are valid for private sector employers in the construction industry, the court nevertheless held that MWRA's agreement was preempted by the NLRA.[22] Government agencies acting in the capacity of a general contractor may not require adherence to an otherwise valid prehire agreement, because the government's action impermissibly interferes with federal rights to bargain with unions or to remain free from organized labor.

In addition to requiring the use of union labor through the licensing process and in the capacity of general contractor, local governments have used their legislative power to further union goals.

---

[14] Golden State I, 475 U.S. at 614.

[15] *Id.* at 615–18.

[16] Golden State Transit Corp. v. Los Angeles, 493 U.S. 103 (1989) [hereinafter Golden State II].

[17] 935 F.2d 345 (1st Cir. 1991).

[18] *Id.* at 347.

[19] *Id.*

[20] *Id.* at 347–48.

[21] *Id.* at 348.

[22] *Id.* at 355. The dissenters felt that MWRA operated as a general contractor in this circumstance, and should be allowed to enter a prehire agreement as would a private employer. Had this not been a construction industry case, the dissenters would have agreed with the majority. *Id.* at 360 (Breyer, C. J., Campbell, J., dissenting).

In *Associated Builders & Contractors v. Baca,*[23] the United States District Court for the Northern District of California considered county and municipal ordinances that conditioned the issuance of building permits for certain large private construction projects on agreement to pay the generally prevailing per diem wages to construction workers.[24] These wages are determined by the California Department of Industrial Relations by evaluating collective bargaining agreements and the results of individual negotiations.[25] Consistent with *Golden State I,* the Court recognized a congressional intent to protect the collective bargaining process and to ensure that the government is not "a party to the negotiations."[26] Because the government significantly interfered with private collective bargaining negotiations, these regulations were held preempted by the NLRA.[27] Thus, although union methods of exerting economic power may have diversified in recent years, governmental entities frequently are precluded from using their licensing, regulatory, or legislative authority to coerce employers in labor disputes.

Violation of Laws

Union corporate campaigns could violate other laws as well. The form of the campaign dictates the issues raised by it. For example, federal antitrust laws outlaw combinations or conspiracies in restraint of trade.[28] The law exempts legitimate union activity from antitrust liability,[29] but the courts have held unions liable for a variety of activities. A union may lose its protection under antitrust laws if it engages in activities that are neither lawful nor in pursuit of legitimate union objectives.[30] Conspiring with nonunion groups or persons for illegal boycotts, price-fixing, or violence may destroy the union exemption.[31] Antitrust penalties may be quite significant.

The NLRA also may prohibit union corporate campaign activities unrelated to government action. Unions regularly violate provisions of the NLRA that prohibit coercive measures designed to force employers to cease doing business with each other, normally referred to as unlawful

---

[23] 769 F. Supp. 1537, (N.D. Cal. 1991).

[24] *Id.* at 1540.

[25] *Id.*

[26] *Id.* at 1544.

[27] *Id.* at 1545. The court also held that these regulations were preempted by ERISA, because the prevailing wage calculation included reference to employee benefits, and by the Contracts Clause in the United States and California Constitutions, because the regulations substantially impaired existing collective bargaining agreements. *Id.* at 1547.

[28] Sherman Act, 15 U.S.C. §§ 1–7 (1988).

[29] Clayton Act, 15 U.S.C. §§ 12–17 (1988); 29 U.S.C. § 52 (1988).

[30] United States v. Hutcheson, 310 U.S. 469, 502–03 (1940).

[31] Allen-Bradley Co. v. Local 3, Elec. Workers, 325 U.S. 797, 809–10 (1945).

"secondary activity."[32] Unlawful secondary activity could form the basis for a lawsuit to recover monetary damages.[33] Other provisions of the NLRA protect workers from coercive conduct designed to retaliate against the workers for their antiunion sympathies.[34]

The Racketeer Influenced and Corrupt Organizations Act (RICO)[35] has been applied to labor organizations. The statute prohibits any person employed or associated with an enterprise from interfering or participating in the affairs of the enterprise through "a pattern of racketeering activity." The unauthorized use of union funds for illegal activity, such as violence or destruction of property, may result in a RICO violation.[36]

When government plays a role in a labor organization's corporate campaign, state action raises the possibility of constitutional law claims against the government and the union if the union is acting under color of state law. State as well as federal constitutions may apply. An employer may analyze whether the government agency has violated the employer's guarantee of due process[37] or equal protection of the laws.[38] For example, conducting business on an ongoing basis is a "property right" that the state may not destroy without due process of law. Unauthorized, irregular, or illegal state action in support of a labor organization, which results in denial of a license, project certification, or other prerequisite to business, may violate the due process clause of the Constitution. Similarly, if the government applies laws or regulations in a discriminatory or arbitrary manner between different classifications of employers or within a classification, there may be a violation of the equal protection clause. Government action pegged to union organizing or labor goals raises serious questions about the legitimacy of distinctions between unionized and nonunion employers.

State laws may apply to corporate campaigns as well. Most states permit companies to sue in tort for interference with prospective business advantage or contract. Tort damages could include punitive damages to sanction a union or other enterprise for violating an employer's rights. Actions also may arise for defamation (libel and slander), abuse of process, fraud, or

---

[32] NLRA, 29 U.S.C. §§ 158(b)(4)(i)(ii), (e) (1988).

[33] Labor-Management Relations Act, 29 U.S.C. § 187 (1988).

[34] NLRA, 29 U.S.C. §§ 157, 158(b)(1)(A) (1988).

[35] RICO, 18 U.S.C. §§ 1961–1968 (Supp. 1989).

[36] *Id.* at § 1961(i); United States v. Thordarson, 646 F.2d 1323 (9th Cir.), *cert. denied,* 454 U.S. 1055 (1981). The judicial consent decree now controlling Teamster special elections was possible through application of antiracketeering laws. *See, e.g.,* United States v. International Brhd. of Teamsters, 728 F. Supp. 1032 (S.D.N.Y.), *aff'd,* 907 F.2d 277 (2d Cir. 1990). On the other hand, at least one court has held that violations of the NLRA alone do not form the basis of a RICO lawsuit. Petrochem Insulation v. Pipe Trades Council, 137 L.R.R.M. (BNA) 2194 (N.D. Cal. 1991).

[37] U.S. Const. amend. XIV, § 1.

[38] *Id.*

negligent misrepresentation. Unions may raise preemption and First Amendment defenses to these actions. Many courts will permit a lawsuit anyway if the lawsuit will not interfere with the operation of federal statutory law.

Some states may maintain statutes regulating conduct in business affairs. For example, the State of California maintains a law that prohibits conduct offending any established public policy or that is "immoral, unethical, oppressive, unscrupulous or substantially injurious to customers." This broad language could apply to union attempts to disrupt business for organizational purposes.[39]

In sum, a battery of legal theories, many untested in the arena of organized labor, exist for defensive measures in a corporate campaign. Lawsuits in the 1990s will further define the effectiveness of legal routes to a union-free environment.

§ 11.4   Modifications in Law after *Deklewa*

Law on prehire agreements, the right to picket construction projects for organizational purposes, and construction employer election law will evolve in the 1990s as a consequence of modifications in law by the NLRB in the 1980s. **Sections 11.5** through **11.8** address the law on prehire agreements and organized labor's right to picket for organizational purposes.[40] The picketing at issue here is directed at an employer in an effort to force the employer to sign a prehire agreement. **Section 11.9** addresses the evolution of craft *bargaining unit law*—the law applied to create voting groups of workers for organizing purposes—as the building construction trade unions file for more elections at the NLRB.

§ 11.5   —Background on Prehire Agreements

Since 1959, Congress has recognized that national labor policy must reflect the uniquely temporary, transitory, and sometimes seasonal nature of construction industry employment.[41] In that year, Congress amended the

---

[39] Cal. Bus. & Prof. Code §§ 17200–17208 (West Supp. 1991). *See* Allied Grape Growers v. Bronco Wine Co., 203 Cal. App. 3d 432, 249 Cal. Rptr. 872 (1988) (applying § 17200 to a labor dispute).

[40] For a discussion of picketing for secondary objectives—to force employers to cease doing business with each other—*see* **Ch. 12**; *See also* H. Perritt, Labor Injunctions (John Wiley & Sons 1986 & Supp. 1992).

[41] S. Rep. No. 187, 86th Cong., 1st Sess. 27 (1959), *reprinted in* 1 NLRB, Legislative History of the Labor-Management Reporting and Disclosure Act of 1959, at 423 (1959) [hereinafter LMRDA Legislative History].

NLRA to allow construction industry employers to enter prehire agreements (contracts negotiated between labor unions and construction contractors prior to NLRB certification or even the hiring of the on-site workers).[42] Because most construction jobs are temporary, there is generally little time to hold a certification election to determine union representation. Prehire agreements allow construction employers to enter union labor contracts without a NLRB election or other proof that the union enjoys the support of a majority of employees in an appropriate craft unit. Such prehire agreements are entered before construction, providing contractors an opportunity to plan for labor costs in project bidding.

Prior case law held that because prehire agreements were entered without a showing of majority support, they were terminable at will.[43] These sorts of agreements were called "8(f) agreements" to reflect the section of the NLRA authorizing them. Yet, the 8(f) agreement could be transformed magically into an agreement that was not terminable at will under a legal rule labeled the "conversion doctrine." Once majority status in the appropriate craft was obtained on the job, the NLRB held that the § 8(f) relationship between the bargaining parties "converted" into a traditional "§ 9" relationship. Section 9 relationships exist after a union victory in an election or after voluntary recognition by the employer. Voluntary employer recognition is only allowed after the union shows majority support in an appropriate craft unit. In a § 9 relationship, both parties have an affirmative duty to bargain with each other over mandatory subjects of bargaining; an employer may not walk from a contract at will.[44] In 1987, however, the NLRB substantially changed this doctrine with its decision in *John Deklewa & Sons.*[45]

§ 11.6   —NLRB's *Deklewa* Decision

From 1960 to 1983, John Deklewa & Sons (Deklewa) agreed to a series of successive prehire agreements between the Ironworker Employers Association of Western Pennsylvania (Association) and the Ironworkers Union (Union).[46] Three years after joining the Association, however, Deklewa resigned and notified the Union that it was repudiating the agreement.[47]

---

[42] 29 U.S.C. § 158(f)(1988); *see also* LMRDA Legislative History at 424.

[43] *See* R.J. Smith Constr. Co., 191 N.L.R.B. 693 (1971), *enforcement denied sub nom.* Operating Eng'rs Local 150 v. NLRB, 480 F.2d 1186 (D.C. Cir. 1973).

[44] This affirmative duty to bargain stems from §§ 8(a)(5), 8(d), and 8(b)(3) of the Act.

[45] John Deklewa & Sons, 282 N.L.R.B. 1375 (1987), *enforced sub nom.* International Ass'n of Bridge, Structural & Ornamental Iron Workers Local 3 v. NLRB, 843 F.2d 770 (3d Cir.), *cert. denied,* 488 U.S. 889 (1988) [hereinafter Deklewa].

[46] 843 F.2d at 771–72.

[47] *Id.* at 772.

Deklewa then subcontracted some ironwork to a nonunion employer in violation of the prehire agreement.[48] The NLRB held that Deklewa committed an unfair labor practice by unilaterally repudiating the prehire agreement before its expiration, but that Deklewa was not obligated to bargain with the Union after contract expiration even though a majority of employees desired Union representation.[49]

In coming to this conclusion, the NLRB set forth the following basic and deceptively simple principles concerning prehire agreements:

(1) a collective-bargaining agreement permitted by Section 8(f) shall be enforceable under law for its full term;

(2) such agreements will not bar the processing of valid petitions for an employee election;

(3) in processing such petitions, the appropriate unit normally will be the single employer's employees covered by the agreement even if the employer is part of an association's multi-employer unit; and

(4) upon the expiration of such agreements, the signatory union will enjoy no presumption of majority status, and either party may repudiate the 8(f) bargaining relationship.[50]

From these general principles, some basic rules become apparent. Employers no longer are allowed to terminate their prehire contracts midterm and continue business nonunion. An employer may obtain the right to midterm contract termination through a bona fide election. When an election is held in a multiemployer unit, the NLRB has declared that it will find a single employer unit appropriate for the election.[51] Because elections are an approved method of repudiating prehire contracts midterm, the NLRB no longer requires a showing of employee disaffection by "objective considerations" to justify an election. Instead, the employer need only show that it is bound by an 8(f) agreement. If an election is held, it will determine the future relationship between the union and the employer. If the union loses the election because it cannot garner a majority of those casting votes, the 8(f) relationship is ended and the employer has no affirmative duty to bargain with the union or to follow a contract for the remainder of its term. If, on the other hand, the union wins the election, it is certified as the exclusive bargaining representative of employees in the bargaining unit, and the contract is enforceable for its term. An election victory also creates a bargaining duty that survives the prehire agreement's expiration. Finally, if no election is held and there is no voluntary recognition of a union, a prehire

---

[48] *Id.*

[49] *Id.*

[50] Deklewa, 282 N.L.R.B. 1375, 1385–86.

[51] *Id.* at 1385.

agreement is binding until it expires; after expiration, either party may walk away from the relationship.

Most federal circuit courts of appeal that have addressed prehire agreements since *Deklewa* have adopted the NLRB's new interpretation of the NLRA, although some have refused to apply it retroactively.[52] The *Deklewa* decision clarified the general relationship between employer and union during a prehire contract, but it left several issues undecided.[53] Three evolving areas of law under *Deklewa* involve picketing, multi-employer contracts, and bargaining unit theory.

§ 11.7 —Picketing after *Deklewa*

In *Deklewa,* the NLRB declared that during and after the term of a valid prehire agreement, signatory employers are immune from "any coercive union efforts, including strikes and picketing, to compel the negotiation and/or adoption of a successor agreement."[54] It did not, however, consider coercive union efforts before a prehire agreement is signed. In the recent case of *NVE Constructors, Inc. v. NLRB,*[55] decided in February 1991, the

---

[52] Corson & Gruman Co. v. NLRB, 899 F.2d 47 (D.C. Cir. 1990) (citing *Deklewa* with approval, but holding on procedural grounds); C.E.K. Indus. Mechanical Contractors, Inc. v. NLRB, 921 F.2d 350 (1st Cir. 1990) (adopting *Deklewa,* but not retroactively); Benson v. Brower's Moving & Storage, Inc., 907 F.2d 310 (2d Cir.), *cert. denied,* 111 S. Ct. 511 (1990) (citing *Deklewa* with approval); United Bhd. of Carpenters Local 953 v. Mar-Len, Inc., 906 F.2d 200 (5th Cir. 1990) (adopting *Deklewa,* but not retroactively); Fox Painting Co. v. NLRB, 919 F.2d 53 (6th Cir. 1990) (same); NLRB v. Bufco Corp., 899 F.2d 608 (7th Cir. 1990) (applying *Deklewa* retroactively); Mesa Verde Constr. Co. v. Northern Cal. Dist. Council of Laborers, 861 F.2d 1124 (9th Cir. 1988) (adopting *Deklewa,* but not retroactively); Plumbers Local 72 v. Payne, 850 F.2d 1535 (11th Cir. 1988) (citing *Deklewa* with approval, but not deciding the issue); Abbott v. Goodwin, 15 Or. App. 132, 804 P.2d 485, *opinion modified on other grounds,* 106 Or. App. 716, 809 P.2d 716, *reviewed denied,* 311 Or. 482, 813 P.2d 1064 (1991) (adopting *Deklewa,* but not retroactively).

[53] *See generally* Pleasure, *Construction Industry Labor Law: Contract Enforcement After Deklewa and Consumer Boycotts After DeBartolo and Boxhorn,* 10 Indus. Rel. L.J. 40, 46–47 (1988).

[54] 282 N.L.R.B. 1375, 1386 (1987). *Deklewa* does not provide a definitive answer to whether a union can picket to enforce an existing prehire agreement. Under the Supreme Court's pre-*Deklewa* decision in NLRB v. Iron Workers Local 103 (Higdon Contracting Co.), 434 U.S. 335 (1978), union picketing to enforce a prehire agreement was held unlawful when the union had not attained majority status. Now that prehire agreements cannot be repudiated mid-term, the kind of picketing proscribed in *Higdon* may be lawful.

[55] 934 F.2d 1084 (9th Cir. 1991). This holding followed another NLRB decision, Ryan Heating Co., 297 NLRB No. 91 (1990), which recognized that a minority union in the construction industry may picket for recognition for a reasonable time period up to 30 days. *Id. See also* International Bhd. of Painters Local 203, 298 NLRB No. 45 (1990); International Union of Operating Eng'rs Local 12, 298 NLRB No. 89 (1990).

Court of Appeals for the Ninth Circuit in California reviewed the NLRB's position that recognitional and organizational picketing by a minority union in the construction industry did not violate the NLRA. In this case, a local laborer's union picketed the construction site where NVE Constructors, Inc. (NVE) was a general contractor.[56] Because the union had not been recognized as the bargaining representative of NVE's 20 employees, the purpose of the picket was to "obtain a contract either by authorization [of the employees] or the contractor's signing a prehire agreement voluntarily."[57] NVE missed important material deliveries because of the picketing, which ended when NVE filed unfair labor practice charges.[58]

After recognizing that the NLRB's interpretations of the NLRA normally are accorded considerable deference,[59] the court upheld the NLRB's dismissal of NVE's complaint. The court agreed with the NLRB that a union may picket for prehire representation for up to 30 days without requesting a certification election.[60]

The NLRB also has held that a threat to picket is lawful when picketing does not occur and the union has not violated the 30-day rule. In *International Union, United Mine Workers, (Hatfield Dock & Transfer)*,[61] a union organizer attempted to obtain voluntary recognition and, when unsuccessful, stated that "he had done all he could to keep the pickets from shutting down the employer."[62] No picketing occurred either before or after this statement was made.[63] The NLRB interpreted the NLRA as prohibiting threats to picket only when the union already has picketed for a reasonable period of time without filing a petition for election.[64] In other words, only after a union has picketed for a reasonable period of time, not to exceed 30 days and without a petition for election, will additional picketing or picketing threats be unlawful.[65]

These decisions have enhanced the availability of picketing as an economically coercive tactic in a union's effort to secure prehire agreements. The decisions will no doubt be the subject of debate in other federal courts and may, in time, reach the United States Supreme Court. Practically, an

---

[56] 934 F.2d 1084, 1085 (9th Cir. 1991).

[57] *Id.*

[58] *Id.*

[59] *Id.* at 1086.

[60] *Id.* at 1087.

[61] 302 NLRB No. 44 (1991).

[62] *Id.,* slip op. at 3.

[63] *Id.*

[64] *Id.,* slip op. at 4.

[65] *Id.,* slip op. at 7. The NLRB does prohibit recognitional picketing when an employer does not employ any employees on the job. Cleveland Bldg. & Constr. Trades Council (Aetos Constr., 297 NLRB No. 47 (1989). Such conduct violated the provisions of the NLRB requiring an election petition after a period of picketing.

employer may dual or multi-gate a project to isolate picketing for organizational purposes. General contractors suffering the annoyance of a subcontractor's battle with organized labor will have an opportunity to isolate the subcontractor on its own gate. Nonetheless, work stoppages will occur when there is no notice of a labor dispute and work commences on the project. Combined with pressure from corporate campaigns on a project manager, general contractor, or an owner, unpredictable work stoppages or threats of picketing may augment an organizing drive's efficacy.

§ 11.8   —Multiemployer Prehire Contracts

As stated in § **11.6**, *Deklewa* defined the principle that an employer is bound to an 8(f) prehire agreement for its term, but upon expiration, no further duty accrues to recognize and bargain with the union.[66] The law on multiemployer bargaining and the significance of association membership are implicated by this change in *Deklewa*. Employers are no longer required to continue the bargaining relationship in a multiemployer forum once the contract is properly terminated for the individual employer. Yet, employers still are bound to the terms of the contracts they sign for the term of those contracts. The trick is ensuring sufficient flexibility in the contract to comport with company goals. Employers sometimes jeopardize rights they would ordinarily have under *Deklewa* if the contract limits their rights.

For example, in *Fortney & Weygandt, Inc.,*[67] a contractor signed a letter of assent in which he agreed to accept and become a party to a collective bargaining agreement between the union and the Associated General Contractors (AGC), of which he was not a member. The AGC master agreement contained a yearly renewal provision: the contract automatically renewed absent 60-days written notice of termination by either party.[68] When the contractor and union had no contact for almost a year and a half, the contractor notified the union of its intent to repudiate the agreement.[69] The NLRB held that the contractor's letter of assent made him a party to the agreement such that he was bound to the automatically renewed contract.[70]

In a similar case, the United States Court of Appeals for the First Circuit agreed with a NLRB decision that an employer was bound by the terms of an old multiemployer contract even though the contract was superseded by a new contract between the association and union.[71] In that case the

---

[66] *See* John Deklewa & Sons, 282 N.L.R.B. 1375 (1987).

[67] 298 NLRB No. 131 (1990).

[68] *Id.,* slip op. at 2.

[69] *Id.,* slip op. at 3.

[70] *Id.,* slip op. at 6.

[71] C.E.K. Indus. Mechanical Contractors v. NLRB, 921 F.2d 350, 356 (1st Cir. 1990).

defendant, C.E.K. Industrial Mechanical Contractors, Inc. (CEK), signed a collective bargaining agreement between a multiemployer association and Plumbers and Gasfitters Local 54, although CEK did not become a member of the association.[72] The agreement ran for a two-year period and provided for a one-year automatic renewal unless either party provided 60-days written notice to the other of an intent to terminate the contract.[73] The court agreed that, as a signatory to the agreement, CEK was a party to that agreement such that the automatic renewal provision applied.[74] The association had negotiated a new contract, but because CEK was not a member of the association and had not delegated bargaining authority to the association, it was not bound to the new agreement.[75] Yet, CEK had not served timely notice with respect to the prior agreement, and that contract was automatically renewed for one year.[76]

Interest Arbitration Provisions

Of particular concern should be agreements that contain an interest arbitration provision. Such provisions generally require that disputes arising out of the failure of the parties to negotiate a renewal of the agreement will be submitted to arbitration. In *Sheetmetal Workers Local Union No. 20 v. Baylor Heating & Air Conditioning,*[77] the United States Court of Appeals for the Seventh Circuit held that an individual employer signatory to a multiemployer collective bargaining agreement was required to submit to arbitration pursuant to that agreement, even after the employer had validly repudiated the prehire contract.[78] Although the contractor's repudiation of the prehire agreement was valid, the interest arbitration clause survived that termination.[79] This decision followed a decision by the United States Court of Appeals for the Ninth Circuit that held that an employer is bound by voluntarily accepted interest arbitration provisions of a prehire agreement.[80] Because courts are willing to hold individual signatories of a multiemployer prehire agreement to interest arbitration clauses, even after a valid termination of the agreement, contractors should scrutinize carefully any multiemployer collective bargaining agreement they enter.

---

[72] *Id.* at 352.

[73] *Id.*

[74] *Id.* at 356.

[75] *Id.*

[76] *Id.*

[77] 877 F.2d 547 (7th Cir. 1989).

[78] *Id.* at 555.

[79] *Id.*

[80] Sheet Metal Workers Local 206 v. R.K. Burner Sheet Metal Inc., 859 F.2d 758 (9th Cir. 1988).

Contractors should note that *Deklewa* does not alter another aspect of terminated prehire agreements that will no doubt cause a great deal of litigation in the 1990s—the duty to arbitrate contract violations after contract expiration. In *Litton Financial Printing Division v. NLRB,*[81] the United States Supreme Court addressed whether a dispute over layoffs occurring well after expiration of a collective bargaining agreement is arbitrable under the agreement. The Court ruled that an employer layoff after expiration of an agreement containing a seniority clause was not arbitrable, because a number of factors supporting the layoffs other than seniority, aptitude, and ability, occurred after expiration.[82] Had the employer based its layoff decisions only on matters that arose before contract expiration, such as seniority alone, the Court would have ruled otherwise. The Court stated that postexpiration arbitration is limited to "matters and disputes arising out of the relation governed by [the] contract."[83] A postexpiration dispute arises under the contract "only where it involves facts and occurrences that arose before expiration, where an action taken after expiration infringes a right that accrued or vested under the agreement, or where, under normal principles of contract interpretation, the disputed contractual right survives expiration of the remainder of the agreement."[84]

Although *Deklewa* provides a construction employer the right to walk from a union relationship after contract expiration, under *Litton,* a union may grieve and arbitrate matters after post expiration as long as the grievance satisfies the *Litton* test.

§ 11.9 —Bargaining Units in Multiemployer Environment

Because *Deklewa* terminates the conversion doctrine, many employers have the option to select nonunion status after a contract lawfully expires. In many cases, unions have decided to seek a § 9 relationship through employee elections conducted by the NLRB at the employer. Construction industry statistics indicate that building and construction trade unions win most of these elections.[85] One reason for union success in the election arena

---

[81] 111 S. Ct. 2215 (1991) [hereinafter Litton].

[82] *Id.* at 2225–26.

[83] *Id.* at 2224.

[84] *Id.* at 2225.

[85] In the most recent analysis of NLRB data by BNA Plus, the research division of the Bureau of National Affairs, the data revealed that, of those industries with 100 or more representation elections during the January through June, 1990 time period, unions in the construction industry had the highest success rate. During that period, construction unions won 96 of 169 R-elections for a 56.8% win ratio. In second place were the health-care unions (55.4%), followed by retail (50.0%), transportation, communication,

is the law utilized by the NLRB in selection of appropriate bargaining units, law that will continue to develop now that construction industry elections are more popular.

Many issues arise as to the appropriate bargaining unit for a construction employer: voting eligibility of employees on layoff and who work for other employers from time to time; the temporary nature of a project; the possibility of a multilocation unit; the possibility of a multicraft unit, for example, mixing laborers and carpenters in one unit; the possibility of technical or highly-skilled employees falling into a unit with less-skilled craft workers; and other issues. The unit may determine the outcome of the election and, significantly, if the employer ultimately loses an election, the size of a labor dispute and the extent of an employer's labor costs under a final agreement.

Notwithstanding *Deklewa,* the NLRB attempts to follow longstanding precedent in this area. Since 1961, the NLRB has recognized that the construction industry presents unique difficulties in determining proper bargaining units. In that year, the NLRB addressed voting eligibility of employees on layoff. The Board decided that all employees in the relevant craft unit who had been employed for at least 30 days in the 12-month period preceding the election eligibility date have a sufficient continuing interest in working conditions to warrant their participation in an election.[86] Alternatively, employees who have failed to receive 30 days of employment in the year immediately preceding the eligibility date for the election but who have worked some that year and at least 45 days in the past two years also may participate in the election.[87]

This law creates a huge pool of support for a union recently signatory with an employer. For example, an employer with a number of employees hired off the street may lose an election because the NLRB will count votes from union members who worked for the employer at least 45 days in the last two years of operation. Consequently, an employer may need to argue at the NLRB that its operations have changed significantly or that various factors justify inclusion in the unit of employees at other locations or in other crafts.

In *P.J. Dick Contracting,*[88] for example, the NLRB defined a bargaining unit encompassing 11 counties.[89] When determining an appropriate bargaining unit, the NLRB first considers the petitioning union's preference. The employer's preferences are then scrutinized. In considering the parties'

---

and utilities (44.2%), and manufacturing (42.1%) unions. Daily Lab. Rep. (BNA) No. 69, at D-3 (Apr. 10, 1991).

[86] Daniel Constr. Co., 133 N.L.R.B. 264 (1961).

[87] *Id.*

[88] 290 N.L.R.B. 150 (1988) [hereinafter P.J. Dick].

[89] *Id.* at 151.

positions, the NLRB reviews "community of interest" factors, such as the following:

1. Similarity of skills, functions, and working conditions among employees in the parties' preferences
2. Centralization of control over labor relations
3. Degree of employee transfer among the employer's construction sites
4. Extent of the parties' bargaining history.[90]

Since *Deklewa,* the NLRB has placed great deference on the parties' bargaining history.[91] Indeed, in *P.J. Dick,* prior bargaining history was the determinative factor in finding the 11-county bargaining unit appropriate.[92] For multilocation bargaining history to be determinative, however, the original bargaining unit must be one that the NLRB would have found appropriate in an initial unit determination.[93] If the multiemployer bargaining unit is one that the NLRB would not have certified, the parties then are free to reassess the scope of the new bargaining unit using traditional community-of-interest criteria.[94]

Bargaining unit law is extremely complex. The law will develop in this area as construction and engineering employers litigate unit issues at the NLRB.

§ 11.10   Collective Bargaining Agreements to Avoid Lawsuits

The 1980s will stand as a decade when the marriage between plaintiffs' personal injury attorneys and employment law was consummated by the development of wrongful discharge litigation. Individuals or classes of employees found relief from various employment-related injuries by suing employers under a wide range of theories: employees have successfully alleged breach of contract, express and implied; breach of a covenant of good faith and fair dealing implied into every contractual arrangement; intentional or negligent infliction of emotional distress; fraud or negligent misrepresentation; termination in violation of public policy; defamation; invasion of privacy; and other claims, both court-created and statutory.[95] Construction

---

[90] *Id.*

[91] *Id.*

[92] *Id.*

[93] Arrow Uniform Rental, 300 NLRB No. 29 (1990), slip op. at 9.

[94] *Id.*

[95] *E.g.,* Foley v. Interactive Data Corp., 47 Cal. 3d 654, 765 P.2d 373, 254 Cal. Rptr. 211 (1988); Tameny v. Atlantic Richfield Co., 27 Cal. 3d 167 610 P.2d 1330, 164 Cal. Rptr. 839 (1980).

and engineering employers are regularly subject to these sorts of lawsuits. One defense to many of these claims, which may be asserted by a union contractor, falls under the nomenclature of "preemption." The law of preemption is rapidly developing and will impact construction employers in the 1990s.

What is preemption? Why is it significant to construction and engineering employers? Preemption is the notion that one law supercedes another sufficiently to eliminate the other from potential use. The most common form of preemption involves federal law priority over state law. For example, in the context of the collective bargaining agreement, employees may be precluded from asserting state law claims by the Labor Management Relations Act (LMRA), which states that: "[s]uits for violation of contract between an employer and a labor organization representing employees in an industry affecting commerce . . . may be brought in any district court of the United States having jurisdiction of the parties."[96] The upshot of LMRA preemption is that a wrongful discharge case may be dismissed by a court that finds the only relief available for an employee is under a collective bargaining agreement. This may result in an employee's lost opportunity to receive large punitive and compensatory damage awards under state law in lieu of limited back pay and reinstatement awards under a union contract.

§ 11.11   —Supreme Court Treatment of LMRA Preemption

The Supreme Court has considered the issue of LMRA preemption frequently in the past decade. In general, the Court has determined that state law causes of action will be preempted unless they are "independent" of the collective bargaining agreement such that their resolution does not require interpretation of the collective bargaining agreement.[97]

The United States Supreme Court first considered this issue in *Allis-Chalmers Corp. v. Lueck.*[98] This case concerned the bad-faith handling of an insurance claim under a disability plan that was included in a collective bargaining agreement.[99] Bad-faith handling of such a claim was considered a tort under state law.[100] The Court decided that "state-law rights and obligations that do not exist independently of private agreements, and that as a result can be waived or altered by agreement of private parties, are preempted by those agreements."[101] As an example of an independent right,

---

[96] 29 U.S.C. § 185(a) (1988).

[97] Lingle v. Norge Div. of Magic Chef, Inc., 486 U.S. 399, 407 (1988).

[98] Allis-Chalmers Corp. v. Lueck, 471 U.S. 202 (1985).

[99] *Id.* at 203.

[100] *Id.*

[101] *Id.* at 213.

the Court noted that the LMRA does not grant the parties to a collective bargaining agreement the ability to contract for what is illegal under state law.[102] Violation of such a state law would not be preempted by the LMRA. However, state contract or tort law that is intrinsically related to the nature and existence of the collective bargaining agreement is preempted by the LMRA.[103] In this case, the state law is related to the underlying contract, because the determination of what is reasonable performance of the contractual obligation requires interpretation of the collective bargaining agreement.[104]

In 1987, the Court decided two other cases that impacted the area of LMRA preemption. The Court first considered whether a state-law tort claim that a union had breached its duty to provide members with a safe workplace was sufficiently independent to the collective bargaining agreement to withstand LMRA preemption.[105] The Court found that the state-law duty to provide a safe workplace rested on the employer.[106] Consequently, any duty placed on the union must have come from the underlying collective bargaining agreement. The state-law tort against the union was, therefore, not sufficiently independent of the agreement to avoid preemption.

Shortly thereafter, the Court considered the preemptive effect of the LMRA on individual employee contracts.[107] In a case against Caterpillar, the plaintiffs alleged that Caterpillar had breached individual employment contracts with the plaintiffs when it terminated their employment during a time period when a collective bargaining agreement also covered their employment.[108] The Court determined that the individual employment contracts were valid because they were entered at an earlier date when the employees were not covered by the collective bargaining agreement, and that breach of contract claims based on those individual contracts may arise under state law.[109] Therefore, the individual claims were not dependent upon an interpretation of the collective bargaining agreement such that they would be preempted by the LMRA.[110]

During the next term, the Court decided another case in which the plaintiff's state-law claims were not preempted by the LMRA. In *Lingle v. Norge Division of Magic Chef, Inc.,* the Court held that an employee's state-law

---

[102] *Id.* at 212.

[103] *Id.* at 216.

[104] Allis-Chalmers Corp. v. Lueck, 471 U.S. at 217.

[105] International Bhd. of Elec. Workers v. Hechler, 481 U.S. 851, 853 (1987).

[106] *Id.* at 859.

[107] Caterpillar, Inc. v. Williams, 482 U.S. 386 (1987).

[108] *Id.* at 394.

[109] *Id.* at 396.

[110] *Id.* at 397.

claim for retaliatory discharge was not preempted.[111] In *Lingle,* the plaintiff had been discharged for filing an allegedly false workers' compensation claim.[112] Ultimately, however, this discharge was ruled in error, and the plaintiff was reinstated with full back pay.[113] In the meantime, plaintiff filed a complaint for the tort of retaliatory discharge.[114] After evaluating the underlying cause of action, the Court unanimously reversed the dismissal of her claim, because the factual inquiries for the claim did not turn on the meaning of any provision of a collective bargaining agreement.[115]

In 1990 the Court reaffirmed the preemption doctrine in holding a wrongful death action preempted.[116] In *United Steelworkers v. Rawson,* the plaintiffs alleged that the union acted negligently in performing its duties as a member of a safety committee required by a collective bargaining agreement.[117] After evaluating the elements of the state-law claim, the Court recognized that the alleged duty was assumed by the union in a collective bargaining agreement, and was not a duty of reasonable care owed by the union to every person in society.[118] In holding this claim preempted, the Court reaffirmed that "[p]re-emption by federal law cannot be avoided by characterizing the Union's negligent performance of what it does on behalf of the members of the bargaining unit pursuant to the terms of the collective bargaining contract as a state-law tort."[119]

§ 11.12 —Lower Court Preemption Rulings

Following Supreme Court precedent, federal circuit courts of appeal have found a variety of state-law tort claims preempted by the LMRA. For example, the court in *Saunders v. Amoco Pipeline Co.* held a state-law wrongful termination claim preempted by the LMRA, notwithstanding that the plaintiffs were not union members.[120] The plaintiffs were bound by the terms of a collective bargaining agreement because they worked in covered bargaining units, although they were not union members.[121] Their lack of union membership was irrelevant. Because the collective bargaining

---

[111] 486 U.S. 399 (1988) [hereinafter Lingle].

[112] *Id.* at 401.

[113] *Id.* at 402.

[114] *Id.*

[115] *Id.* at 407.

[116] United Steelworkers v. Rawson, 110 S. Ct. 1904 (1990).

[117] *Id.* at 1907.

[118] *Id.* at 1910.

[119] *Id.* at 1911.

[120] 927 F.2d 1154 (10th Cir. 1991).

[121] *Id.* at 1156.

agreement between the company and its employees provided a grievance and arbitration procedure through which employees could challenge their termination, the state-law wrongful termination claim was preempted.[122]

Other jurisdictions have held a variety of state-law claims to be preempted. These claims include slander,[123] invasion of privacy,[124] infliction of emotional distress,[125] and breach of the implied covenant of good faith and fair dealing.[126] Similarly, the doctrine of preemption has been applied to a federal racketeering claim, which was preempted by the Railway Labor Act.[127]

As at the Supreme Court level, however, not all claims are preempted. For example, the United States Court of Appeals for the Ninth Circuit held that a state claim for handicap discrimination was not preempted by the LMRA.[128] In *Ackerman,* the plaintiff was terminated upon the expiration of her disability benefits after she left work with a bronchial infection and aggravated asthma.[129] The court evaluated the underlying state law, and recognized that this antidiscrimination law did not refer to the terms of any collective bargaining agreement.[130] Accordingly, the plaintiff's claim did not require the interpretation of a collective bargaining agreement and was independent of that agreement for LMRA preemption purposes.[131] In the same circuit, the court held that a claim for assault and battery was not preempted, because the conduct underlying the claim was illegal under state law.[132] Similarly, a parallel claim for intentional infliction of emotional distress was not preempted, because the type of behavior in the case could not have been contemplated by a collective bargaining agreement.[133]

It appears that few, if any, state-law claims for wrongful termination are immune from LMRA preemption challenges. A state-law cause of action will be preempted if its resolution depends on the interpretation of a collective bargaining agreement. If, however, the employer's actions are illegal under state law or violate a duty owed to society independent of the collective bargaining agreement, the state-law claim for wrongful termination

---

[122] *Id.*

[123] Willis v. Reynolds Metals Co., 840 F.2d 254 (4th Cir. 1988).

[124] *Id.;* Schlacter-Jones v. General Tel., 936 F.2d 435 (9th Cir. 1991); Tombrello v. USX Corp., 763 F. Supp. 541 (N.D. Ala. 1991).

[125] Willis v. Reynolds Metals Co., 840 F.2d 254 (4th Cir. 1988); McCormick v. AT&T Technologies, Inc., 934 F.2d 531 (4th Cir. 1991); Douglas v. American Info. Technologies Corp., 877 F.2d 565 (7th Cir. 1989).

[126] Newberry v. Pacific Racing Ass'n, 854 F.2d 1142 (9th Cir. 1988).

[127] Hubbard v. United Airlines, Inc., 927 F.2d 1094 (9th Cir. 1991).

[128] Ackerman v. Western Elec. Co., 860 F.2d 1514 (9th Cir. 1988) [hereinafter Ackerman].

[129] *Id.* at 1516.

[130] *Id.* at 1517.

[131] *Id.*

[132] Galvez v. Kuhn, 933 F.2d 773, 777 (9th Cir. 1991).

[133] *Id.* at 779.

will not be preempted. As state wrongful discharge law evolves, preemption litigation will evolve with it, particularly as unions and employers modify their agreements to cover new terms and conditions of employment. As discussed in § 11.19, the changes have already occurred in the drug and alcohol testing area.

§ 11.13   Worker Adjustment and Retraining Notification Act

The Worker Adjustment and Retraining Notification Act (WARN)[134] and United States Department of Labor (DOL) regulations interpreting the Act[135] have created ambiguous obligations for construction employers, which will ultimately find their way to courts for resolution.

WARN requires employers of 100 or more workers to give 60-days advance notice of a plant closing or a mass layoff. There are no industry exceptions to this statute.[136] A *plant closing* is defined as a permanent or temporary shutdown of a single site of employment, or one or more facilities or operating units within a single site of employment, that results in 50 or more employees losing their jobs during a 30-day period.[137] A *mass layoff* is defined as a reduction in force, which is not the result of a plant closing, that results in loss of employment for six months or longer of one third of the work force, if that is more than 50 employees, or 500 employees, whichever is less.[138] *Loss of employment* means termination or layoff exceeding six months or a reduction in hours of work of more than 50 percent during each six-month period.[139]

An employee has not experienced an employment loss if: (1) the closing or layoff is the result of the relocation or consolidation of part or all of the business, and (2) the employer offers to transfer the employee to a different site of employment within a reasonable commuting distance with no more than a six-month break in employment, or (3) the employer offers to transfer the employee to another site, regardless of distance, with no more than a six-month break and the employee accepts within 30 days of the offer or of the closing or layoff, whichever is later.[140]

Employers may order a plant closing or mass layoff before the conclusion of the 60-day period if the employer (1) was actively seeking capital or business that, if obtained, would have allowed it to avoid or postpone

---

[134] 29 U.S.C. §§ 2101–2109 (1988).

[135] 20 C.F.R. §§ 639.1–.10 (1991).

[136] 29 U.S.C. §§ 2101(a), 2102(a); 20 C.F.R. §§ 639.4, 639.5 (1991).

[137] *Id.*

[138] 20 C.F.R. § 639.3(f) (1991).

[139] *Id.*

[140] *Id.* §§ 639.3(f), 639.5(b) (1991).

the shutdown, and (2) reasonably and in good faith believed that giving the required notice would have precluded it from obtaining the sought capital or business.[141]

Employers also may order a plant closing or mass layoff with less than 60-days notice if the closing or layoff is caused by business circumstances that were not reasonably foreseeable as of the time that notice would have been required.[142] It should be noted that under the "unforeseeable business circumstances" section, notice must still be given; however, it can be less than 60 days. In the language of the statute, the employer must give "as much notice as is practicable . . . and a brief statement of the basis for reducing the notification period."[143]

Particularly important to construction employers, the WARN Act does not apply to the closing of a temporary facility or to a layoff due to the completion of a particular project or undertaking if the employees were hired with the understanding that they were being employed for the duration of that project or undertaking.[144] Nor does the Act apply if the closing is caused by a strike or lockout not intended to evade the requirements of the Act.[145]

The statute provides that written notice must go to:

1. Each representative of the affected employees or, if there is none, to each employee
2. The chief elected official of the unit of local government where the site is located
3. The state dislocated worker unit.

Congress did not prescribe the content of the written notice, but it did require the DOL to do so.[146]

The law is enforced in federal court by civil actions by employees or their representatives; employees may sue on behalf of a class. The government has no enforcement authority. This means that the DOL has no legal standing in any enforcement action. In addition, it will not issue advisory opinions about specific cases. Regulations by the government are merely interpretative. Therefore, they may be given some deference by the courts but not complete deference. Finally, WARN expressly prohibits a federal court from entering any order restraining a plant closing or a mass layoff.[147]

---

[141] Id.

[142] Id. § 639.9(b) (1991).

[143] 29 U.S.C. § 2102(b) (1988).

[144] Id. § 2103(1); 20 C.F.R. § 639.5(c) (1991).

[145] Id.

[146] 29 U.S.C. § 2102(a) (1988); 20 C.F.R. §§ 639.6, 639.7 (1991).

[147] 29 U.S.C. §§ 2104–2107 (1988).

The court may award back pay and lost fringe benefits for up to a maximum of 60 days. Damages are reduced by any sums paid to employees voluntarily for the period of violation. A prevailing party also is entitled to costs and reasonable attorneys' fees. Violation of the obligations to give notice to local government causes an additional fine of $500 per day of violation.[148] The statute contains no statute of limitations nor does it address the question of whether or not a jury trial is available. The answer to the question of the availability of trial by jury will turn on whether the courts will conclude that the damages sought are equitable in nature.

§ 11.14   —Problems under WARN for Construction Companies

The courts will address many issues under WARN in the 1990s. A few of the issues of interest to construction companies are as follows:

1. Whether the "temporary" employment exemption applies to employees on a project with no set completion date or completion dates many years into the future, such as long-term maintenance contracts or construction projects with such a long term that employees acquire a reasonable expectation of continued employment

2. Whether employees "secunded" or "leased" to another employer and who usually are reassigned upon completion of a project should be counted in a mass layoff calculation when it becomes clear that they will no longer be needed or whether the "unforeseen business circumstances" rule will apply to them

3. What evidence will be sufficient to establish temporary employment, for example, whether written contracts with all construction craft workers should be utilized and whether these should become part of collective bargaining agreements

4. What evidence will satisfy courts examining whether a strike or lockout is for the purpose of evading the statute's requirements.

Only a handful of cases have been decided since the law's enactment. *Solberg v. Inline Corp.*[149] considered the applicability of the WARN Act to projects under six months in duration. In Solberg, 300 workers who were hired between January and March of 1989 were subsequently laid off between May and October of the same year due to Inline's loss in May of a major contract. Six employees who were terminated in June and July filed suit against Inline for not providing the 60-day notice required under the

---

[148] *Id.* § 2104(a).

[149] 740 F. Supp. 680 (D. Minn. 1990).

WARN Act. The court, however, held that the Act did not require an employer to give notice to "part-time employees," which was unambiguously defined in the Act as those employees who worked less than 20 hours per week or had been employed for less than six months. As none of the six Inline employees had been working for over six months when they were discharged, the company had no obligation to give them notice.[150]

Another case addressed whether laid off workers must be counted in the determination of the size of an employer's work force at the time of a layoff. The question before the district court in *Damron v. Rob Fork Mining Corp.*[151] was whether workers, who had been laid off more than 10 years before the plant closing, could be added to the number of employees affected so that the employees could claim protection under the WARN Act. The WARN Act only covers those businesses that employ more than 100 full-time employees. The district court held that the laid off workers could not be added because they had no "reasonable expectation of [being] recall[ed]."[152] In reaching this conclusion, the court considered three criteria developed by the NLRB: "(1) the past experience of the employer; (2) the employer's future plans; (3) the circumstances of the layoff, including what the employees were told as to the likelihood of a recall."[153] As the employees were unable to show that the company had a record of laying off workers and eventually hiring them all back, or that those workers laid off 10 years ago could still reasonably think they would be recalled, the court refused to apply the 60-day notice rule to the closing of the mine.[154]

A United States District Court in Massachusetts, however, did apply the 60-day notice rule to a company that employed only 76 employees at the time of the mass layoff. The court held in *United Electrical Radio & Machine Workers v. Maxim, Inc.*[155] that the number of people employed when a mass layoff occurs is not relevant to a determination of a WARN Act violation. The only pertinent date is the day on which the 60-day notice should have been given. If on that date the company employs more than 100 workers, regardless of whether that number was only maintained for one day, the employer is required to notify its employees of a layoff 60 days in advance.[156]

These decisions are examples of the numerous issues under the WARN Act presented to the courts in the few years subsequent to passage. Obviously, many decisions under WARN are anticipated in the 1990s. Many of

---

[150] *Id.* at 684–86.

[151] 739 F. Supp. 341 (E.D. Ky. 1990), *aff'd,* 1991 WL 150778 (6th Cir. 1991).

[152] *Id.* at 344.

[153] *Id.*

[154] *Id.* at 344–45.

[155] Not reported in F. Supp; *see* 5 Individual Empl. Rights Cas. (BNA) 629 (D. Mass. 1990).

[156] *Id.* at 630.

the new decisions will bear on construction employer liability under the plant closing/mass layoff law.

§ 11.15   Drug Testing Programs

In the 1990s, drug and alcohol testing programs are being instituted by employers for both preemployment applicant screening and the screening of current employees. Although the tests are expensive, they may dramatically reduce the use of these substances in the workplace.

Construction employers have many reasons for instituting drug and alcohol screening programs. The most important concern about drug and alcohol use is its potentially great impact on worker safety. Drug and alcohol use also may impact employee on-the-job productivity, absenteeism, and employee medical costs. Drug use could even introduce crime to the workplace, for example, where employees might begin to sell illegal drugs to support their habit.

§ 11.16   —Drug-Free Workplace Act

Laws have cropped up in several regulated industries requiring drug testing or programs closely related to testing. One example is the Drug-Free Workplace Act of 1988,[157] which regulates federal contractors. Although the Act does not mandate testing, it requires federal government contractors and employers receiving federal grants to certify the drug-free condition of their employees, which has led to an enormous increase in drug and alcohol testing by those contractors.[158] In a recent survey by the American Management Association, 63 percent of the 1633 companies surveyed are now

---

[157] 41 U.S.C. §§ 701–707 (1988).

[158] Specifically, to be eligible for contract awards or grants, the contractors and grantees must agree to:

1. Publish and distribute to all employees a policy prohibiting the manufacture, distribution, possession, or use of illegal drugs in the workplace
2. Establish a drug awareness program
3. Inform employees that they must report to their employer any drug-related criminal convictions and notify the appropriate federal agency regarding such convictions
4. Take appropriate personnel acting against employees convicted of a drug-related criminal offense
5. Make a good faith effort to maintain a drug-free workplace.

There is no specific mention of drug testing in the Act, but an employer's good-faith effort might be questioned if an unusually high number of employee drug-related convictions is reported and the employer maintains no drug-testing program.

engaged in some form of employee drug testing, while 54.4 percent screen job applicants for drugs.[159] The 63 percent figure represented a 22 percent increase over the previous year, which may be attributed to the Drug-Free Workplace Act and to recent Supreme Court decisions approving drug testing,[160] and to the recent implementation of Department of Transportation regulations mandating the testing of drivers in that industry as well as similar regulations in other industries.[161]

Although there has not been much litigation by employers objecting to the legality of the Drug-Free Workplace Act, employers who have decided to drug test because of the Act have been challenged on their implementation of such tests by employees under many different constitutional, statutory, and common law theories.[162] Because of these numerous employee challenges, employers covered by the Act may begin to challenge the Act itself in order to clarify its nebulous requirement that an employer make a "good faith" effort to maintain a drug-free workplace. Other litigation may include the extent of good faith efforts required under the Act.

---

[159] Daily Lab. Rep. (BNA) No. 68, at A-2 (Apr. 9, 1991).

[160] In *Skinner* and *Von Raab,* the United States Supreme Court analyzed the applicability of Fourth Amendment protections to government employers who enacted preemployment drug screening programs. In National Treasury Employees Union v. Von Raab, 489 U.S. 656 (1989), the Supreme Court held that the United States Customs Service did not violate the Fourth Amendment by requiring employees to submit to a drug test. The Court balanced drug testing's intrusiveness into privacy against its promotion of legitimate government interests, finding the government's intent to deter drug use in the service responsible for enforcement of drug laws to be sufficiently compelling to overcome the standard Fourth Amendment requirement that an employer have particular suspicion before engaging in a "search." *Id.* at 667–77.

Similarly, in Skinner v. Railway Labor Executives Ass'n, 489 U.S. 602 (1989), decided the same day as *Von Raab,* the Court upheld the use of drug tests required by the Federal Railroad Administration—drug tests for employees involved in train accidents or violation of certain safety standards. The Court found that legitimate government interests again created a special need that justified departure from normal requirements. *Id.* at 624. Because the industry was public transportation, the Court held that the need for safety was a compelling factor justifying the tests.

[161] *See* Daily Lab. Rep. (BNA) No. 68, at A-2 (Apr. 9, 1991). *See also* Daily Lab. Rep. (BNA) No. 204, at C-1 (Oct. 22, 1990), in which David Robb, aide to William Bennett in the Office of National Drug Control Policy, and Mark A. de Bernardo, executive director of the Institute for a Drug-Free Workplace, claim that the majority of Fortune 500 companies have instituted drug-testing policies in the wake of *Skinner* and *Von Raab.*

[162] The Drug-Free Workplace Act has only been mentioned in one federal court case, Georgia Power v. International Bhd. of Elec. Workers Local 84, 707 F. Supp. 531 (N.D. Ga. 1989), *aff'd,* 896 F.2d 507 (1990). In *Georgia Power,* a public utility terminated a drug user who was eventually reinstated by an arbitrator to his position as an auxiliary equipment operator. The utility petitioned the district court to vacate the award as against the "well defined and dominant" public policy supporting the "war on drugs." Citing the Drug-Free Workplace Act, among other laws, the court held that the arbitrator's decision must be vacated. *Id.* at 536–40.

§ 11.17 —Nonunion Employers

Nonunion employers may implement drug and alcohol testing subject to state and federal constitutional employee protections and potential liability under various tort laws.

On the constitutional front, it is well recognized that, unlike the public or publicly-regulated employers who were the subjects of contention in the recent federal court cases approving drug testing, purely private employers are not subject to federal constitutional, that is, Fourth Amendment, requirements. Nevertheless, certain state constitutions do restrict the actions of private employers. For example, under Article I, § 1 of the California Constitution, a right of privacy has been established in the private sector.[163] In *Luck v. Southern Pacific Transportation Corp.,*[164] the California Court of Appeal considered lawfulness of random drug testing under Article I, § 1 of the California Constitution. After determining that the state constitution applied to the private sector employer, the court decided that the appropriate legal test was the "compelling interest" test, for example, whether a compelling employer interest outweighs the intrusion into an employee's express right to privacy as embodied in the California Constitution.[165]

The *Luck* court found that the plaintiff, a computer programmer, had no direct safety duties and no responsibility for rail operations. In fact, the plaintiff could only impact rail safety in an attenuated fashion if one of the plaintiff's programs eventually led to a problem.[166] There was no immediacy to the threat of danger, as with the rail employees or federal agents handling guns in federal court cases approving of drug testing of those employees. Consequently, the court found that a random drug test of the computer programmer in a non-safety-sensitive job was not permissible. The court indicated, "the testing cannot be upheld absent a clear, direct nexus between the employees' duties and the nature of the feared harm."[167]

Luck should serve notice to all private, nonunion employers that drug testing programs may not be upheld by state courts when the testing has no

---

[163] Cal. Const. art. I, § 1.

[164] 218 Cal. App. 3d 1, 267 Cal. Rptr. 618 (1990) [hereinafter Luck].

[165] *Id.* at 21. The court decided to use a "compelling interest" test, tougher than the Fourth Amendment "legitimate interests" test.

[166] *Id.*

[167] *Id.* at 23. *See also* Semore v. Pool, 217 Cal. App. 3d 1087, 266 Cal. Rptr. 280 (1990), in which the California Fourth District Court of Appeal held that a plaintiff claiming termination in violation of public policy based on a refusal to take a pupillary examination might be able to state a constitutional claim.

relation to an on-the-job safety concern or some other legitimate business concern.[168]

Nonunion employees also may allege contract or tort law claims as a response to an employer's drug tests. A popular cause of action in the event of an employee's termination for refusal to submit to a drug test is a wrongful discharge claim. In most states, all employment relationships are "at-will" unless a contrary written agreement exists between employer and employee. Some states allow exceptions to the at-will doctrine. For example, in California,[169] an employee may argue that, refusal to submit to a drug test does not satisfy the definition of *good cause* and: (1) the employer orally promised to discharge only upon "good cause"; or (2) the surrounding facts and conduct (such as longevity of service, commendations, assurances, and company policies and practices) created an implied-in-fact promise that the employee would not be terminated without good cause. Using this attack, a wrongful discharge contract claim might be viable in response to employer drug testing.

A popular tort law claim against an employer for administering a drug test is intentional or negligent infliction of emotional distress.[170] When the testing is observed, a court might find that the employer tested in an unreasonable manner. In *American Federation of Government Employees v. Sullivan,*[171] the United States District Court for the District of Columbia made it clear that it believed observed testing should be restricted to only those situations in which there was a prior history of sample tampering by the employee in question. If other courts follow *Sullivan,* the manner in which an employee is tested could be used against employers to litigate an emotional distress claim successfully.

Another tort claim that could be asserted against an employer who administers drug testing is the tort of invasion of privacy. The *Restatement (Second) of Torts* § 652A states:

(1) One who invades the right of privacy of another is subject to liability for the resulting harm to the interests of the other.

(2) The right of privacy is invaded by:
    (a) Unreasonable intrusion upon the seclusion of another (§ 652B).

---

[168] For a more detailed examination of the employer's need to limit employment testing to job-related factors, *see* C. Birenbaum, Employment Screening Techniques: Advantages and Pitfalls (Dec. 6, 1991) (unpublished manuscript, submitted for inclusion in materials from New York University's 44th National Conference on Labor).

[169] Pugh v. See's Candies, 116 Cal. App. 3d 311, 326–29, 171 Cal. Rptr. 917 (1981). *See also* Foley v. Interactive Data Corp., 47 Cal. 3d 654, 765 P.2d 373, 254 Cal. Rptr. 211 (1988).

[170] *See* Kelley v. Schlumberger Tech. Corp., 849 F.2d 41 (1st Cir. 1988) (court upholds jury verdict for emotional distress claim based on discharge of employee who failed urinalysis).

[171] 744 F. Supp. 294 (D.D.C. 1990) [hereinafter Sullivan].

The *Restatement (Second) of Torts* § 652B also states:

One who intentionally intrudes physically *or otherwise* upon the solitude or seclusion of another or his private affairs or concerns is subject to liability to the other for the invasion of his privacy, if the intrusion would be highly offensive to a reasonable person (emphasis added).

Although there are no reported cases involving a privacy tort claim against an employer for imposing drug testing, the state constitutional cases lead to the conclusion that this tort claim might be viable, especially if the manner of testing is especially intrusive. One case involving the privacy tort illustrates this potential cause of action. In *O'Brien v. Papa Gino's of America, Inc.,*[172] the employer required an involuntary polygraph test to determine if an employee was a drug user. Following the polygraph test results, the employee was discharged. The court held that polygraphing to determine the employee's drug-free status invaded the employee's privacy.[173] A similar argument might be made against an employer for conducting an intrusive drug and alcohol test.

An employer also could be liable for defamation if it releases drug test results to the public or to other prospective employers. Although truth is a defense to defamation, if the employer characterizes the employee in communications with third parties as a "drug addict" after just one positive test, then the employer exposes itself to potential liability.[174]

In the 1990s, nonunion employees faced with the increased likelihood of employer-mandated drug testing will probably increase their legal assault on the practice. Countless theories may arise on the subject. Employers may even violate antidiscrimination laws if drug testing policies adversely impact minorities.

§ 11.18   —Union Employers

Unionized construction employers must recognize that they have several additional obligations related to the drug and alcohol testing issue. First, implementation of certain screening techniques may be a mandatory subject of bargaining. For bargaining purposes, there is a distinction between employee screening versus applicant screening. Second, the unionized employer should examine obligations under collective bargaining agreements, which may impact the use of any screening technique.

---

[172] 780 F.2d 1067 (1st Cir. 1986).

[173] *Id.* at 1075–76.

[174] *See* Houston Belt & Terminal Ry. v. Wherry, 548 S.W.2d 743 (Tex. Ct. App.), *appeal dismissed,* 434 U.S. 962 (1977).

Current Employees

In *Johnson-Bateman Co.,*[175] the NLRB determined that absent a clear and unmistakable waiver by the union, drug testing of current employees by private sector employers in a § 9 relationship is a mandatory subject of bargaining. Some courts may provide limited exceptions to bargaining obligations when safety concerns arise,[176] but the majority of unionized employers should be concerned with the duty to bargain upon the implementation of a new employee drug testing program if they are in a § 9 relationship.

Critically, because *Deklewa*[177] has ensured that most construction employers are in an 8(f) relationship, *Johnson-Bateman Co.* may not apply to them. A construction employer that is in an 8(f) relationship under *Deklewa* has no mandatory duty to bargain over anything outside the existing prehire agreements with building and construction trade crafts. Many employers unilaterally implement drug testing programs in the construction industry without bargaining. One danger in this approach is that unions could call strikes or other protests to challenge new programs. Bargaining over a drug program also may become a condition to contract renewal.

Employment Applicants

The unionized construction employer need not be as concerned if it wishes to implement screening devices of job applicants. In *Star-Tribune,*

---

[175] 295 NLRB No. 26 (1989). Note, however, Consolidated Rail Corp. (Conrail) v. Railway Labor Executives Ass'n, 109 S. Ct. 2477 (1989), in which the Supreme Court held that an employer may unilaterally implement drug testing without bargaining if such action is "justified" by the collective bargaining agreement. In *Conrail,* decided under the Railway Labor Act (RLA), the employer required periodic medical examinations and return-to-duty physical exams, which justified the new drug testing as an implied contract term.

[176] *See* Local 194A v. Bridge Comm'n, 572 A.2d 204 (N.J. Super. Ct. App. Div. 1990) (drug testing is nonnegotiable when bridge operation affects public safety); Brotherhood of Maintenance of Way Employees v. Burlington N. R.R., 802 F.2d 1016 (8th Cir. 1986) (unilateral implementation of post-accident testing by employers is a "minor dispute" under the RLA); *see also* Local 346, IBPO v. MLRC, 391 Mass. 429, 462 N.E.2d 96 (1984) (police officers have no right to bargain over drug testing).

[177] See § **11.3** and John Deklewa & Sons, 282 N.L.R.B. 1375 (1987), *enforced sub nom.* International Ass'n of Bridge, Structural & Ornamental Iron Workers, Local 3 v. NLRB, 843 F.2d 770 (3d Cir. 1988), *cert. denied,* 488 U.S. 889 (1988). *Deklewa* has removed most construction employers from § 9 relationships acquired after "conversion" on projects initiated with prehire agreements. Consequently, most construction employers are in § 8(f) relationships when there is no duty to bargain over subjects that are not covered by contract.

A Division of Cowles Media, [178] the NLRB ruled that preemployment drug and alcohol testing of job applicants is not a mandatory subject of collective bargaining, because job applicants are not "employees" within the collective bargaining obligations of the NLRA. Similarly, by virtue of the employee definition, the NLRB may not deem other types of preemployment screening as mandatory subjects of bargaining.

Collective Bargaining Agreement Obligations

The unionized construction employer may find that collective bargaining agreements with the labor organizations representing its workers prohibit or otherwise affect the right to submit employees to drug and alcohol testing. Many agreements permit reasonable rule formulation by an employer, which may include the express right to conduct drug and alcohol testing. Other agreements may provide for "cooperation" in "safety and health" matters, which could be interpreted to permit drug and alcohol testing.

Arbitrators consider numerous elements in cases that concern the implementation of drug testing programs, including express contract language, past practice, negotiation history, and public policy. Most arbitrators find a breach of contract when an employer unilaterally implements a program and no express authorization for testing can be found in the contract. [179]

On the other hand, collective bargaining agreements that permit the employer to enact and conduct testing programs will be enforced by arbitrators. [180] The culmination of recent negotiations has resulted in several collective bargaining agreements that contain drug-testing provisions. As a first example, Boeing Company recently negotiated a collective bargaining agreement with the Teamsters and the Seattle Professional Engineering Employees Association, which includes a drug testing program. The program provides for drug and alcohol testing of employees upon "reasonable suspicion," followed by a rehabilitation program and random testing if the initial test yields a positive result. [181]

Another example of a recent drug-testing agreement between employer and union occurred in St. Louis, where local plumbing contractors and the Plumbers Union agreed to adopt a drug testing policy that provides for

---

[178] 295 NLRB No. 63 (1989).

[179] *E.g.,* Phillips Indus., Inc., 90 Lab. Arb. Rep. (BNA) (1988) 222 (DeLeone, Arb.) (no contract waiver); *Laidlaw Transit,* 89 Lab. Arb. Rep. (BNA) (1987) 540 (Allen, Arb.) (contract does not reference drug testing).

[180] *E.g.,* Jim Water Resources Inc., 88 Lab. Arb. Rep. (BNA) (1987) 1254 (Nicholas Arb.) (rejecting bashful kidney syndrome as an excuse from testing requirements).

[181] Daily Lab. Rep. (BNA) No. 231, at A-2 (Nov. 30, 1990).

testing of employees suspected of work-site drug use. Under the plan, managers were given the authority to determine when such tests were appropriate. The union leaders claimed that they agreed to such a plan to protect workers from the potential danger of drug-abusing coworkers.[182]

A third example of recent drug-testing agreements may be found in the nationwide substance abuse policy of the Sheet Metal and Air Conditioning Contractors' National Association and the Sheet Metal Workers International Association. In their policy, the union and employer association agreed to conduct drug and alcohol testing when a contractor is required to conduct such testing in order to bid on a project and when probable cause exists to test an employee. The agreement also permits preemployment testing of workers who are not current union members and requires local association chapters and unions to establish employee assistance programs.[183]

Finally, a drug and alcohol testing agreement recently was announced by the Massachusetts Water Resources Authority and the Boston Building Trades Council for the Boston Harbor cleanup project. Under the agreement, all construction workers employed on the project are subject to some form of drug and alcohol testing, including preemployment testing for all workers, and testing after certain accidents upon "reasonable suspicion."[184] All four of these agreements should serve as examples of what may be achieved with unions in the area of drug-testing programs.

§ 11.19   —Section 301 Preemption

As discussed in §§ 11.10 through 11.12 the preemption doctrine will cause a great deal of litigation in the 1990s. This is true in the drug-testing arena. Federal courts recently have held that many state constitutional or tort law claims raised against employers for drug and alcohol screening are preempted by § 301 of the LMRA. For example, in *Stikes v. Chevron, USA, Inc.,*[185] an employee filed a lawsuit claiming the company violated his constitutional right to privacy after the employer searched his vehicle pursuant to company policy. The court held that the employee's expectation of privacy was rooted in the contractual terms of his employment, thus, the LMRA preempted the state constitutional law claim.

In another case, *Jackson v. Liquid Carbonic Corp.,* the United States Court of Appeals for the First Circuit held that claims under Massachusetts law for violation of the right to privacy due to drug testing were preempted

---

[182] Daily Lab. Rep. (BNA) No. 3, at A-15 (Jan. 4, 1991).

[183] Daily Lab. Rep. (BNA) No. 104, at A-9 (May 30, 1991).

[184] Daily Lab. Rep. (BNA) No. 152, at A-2 (Aug. 7, 1991).

[185] 914 F.2d 1265 (9th Cir. 1990).

by § 301 of the LMRA, because the plaintiffs' expectations of privacy turned on union concessions during collective bargaining.[186]

§ 11.20   Multiemployer Trust Fund Issues

Many unresolved issues arise under the Employee Retirement Income Security Act (ERISA)[187] that may be addressed in the decade of the 1990s. Multiemployer trust funds are primarily governed by ERISA. Yet, there is the ever-present question about the interplay between trust funds, unions, and employers, and about the forum in which disputes between these parties will be decided. Another issue that will continue as a force in the 1990s is the scope of ERISA preemption of state law requirements for trust funds. A third issue involves the continuing attempts by trust funds to preserve their solvency by denying benefits to fund participants. Finally, there is the question of what new benefits trust funds and unions will propose to employers in the coming decade.

§ 11.21—Resolving the Statutory Conflict

Trust funds, with union consent, have long attempted to circumvent the NLRB's primary jurisdiction by commencing federal court actions under ERISA that seek trust fund contributions as the result of an employer's alleged violation of the NLRA. This trust fund ploy forces NLRA issues away from the jurisdiction of the NLRB and provides federal courts with opportunities to second-guess NLRB resolutions of labor disputes.

In *Laborers Health & Welfare Trust Fund v. Advanced Lightweight Concrete Co.,*[188] the United States Supreme Court set the initial guiding rule on the interplay between the NLRA and ERISA. In *Advanced Lightweight Concrete,* a trust fund sued to collect benefit contributions allegedly due after contract expiration. The trust fund contended that the defendant employer did not bargain in good faith under the NLRA, and therefore that contributions were due and owing until the bargaining duty was satisfied

---

[186] 863 F.2d 111 (1st Cir. 1988). *See also* Laws v. Calmet, 852 F.2d 430 (9th Cir. 1988) (suspended concrete mixer/driver's suit against drug-testing employer alleging invasion of privacy through drug test preempted, because privacy rights of driver were inextricably intertwined with collective bargaining agreement); Utility Workers v. Southern Cal. Edison Co., 852 F.2d 1083 (9th Cir. 1988) (union suit against employer alleging violation of California State constitutional rights due to unilateral implementation of drug testing program preempted, because resolution of claim was "substantially dependent" on analysis of collective bargaining agreement).

[187] 29 U.S.C. §§ 1001–1461 (Supp. 1989).

[188] 484 U.S. 539 (1988) [hereinafter Advanced Lightweight Concrete].

under the NLRA. The trust fund expressly relied on ERISA jurisdiction to justify a federal court's ability to rule on the NLRA issue.[189] The Supreme Court rejected the trust fund's jurisdictional argument, affirming a decision to dismiss the case for lack of jurisdiction. The Court reasoned that the federal courts should defer to the NLRB on duty-to-bargain issues under the NLRA rather than determine the matter under the ERISA enforcement statutes relied on by the trust fund. Because the labor law issues concerning bargaining were not as the heart of ERISA, but were central to the NLRA, the Court held that such NLRA issues were resolved more appropriately by the NLRB.[190]

Despite this ruling, the jurisdictional boundaries between the province of ERISA and that of the NLRA remain essentially blurred. Other contractual duties that an employer may owe to a trust fund under a collective bargaining agreement could conflict with the employer's statutory duties under the NLRA, yet the forum in which these matters should be resolved remains in question. Courts have handled these matters in varied ways since *Advanced Lightweight Concrete,* not always following the Supreme Court's decision. In *Diduck v. Kaszycki & Sons Contractors, Inc.,*[191] a union member brought suit for contributions that an insolvent employer failed to make to pension and insurance funds while the employee was a beneficiary. Because the named employer, Kaszycki, was insolvent, the plaintiff asserted that a joint venture, Trump-Equitable—which had contracted with Kaszycki for demolition work—was also liable for the payments under a joint employer theory. Despite the impassioned dissent of Circuit Judge Van Graafeiland, who cited *Advanced Lightweight Concrete* for the proposition that federal courts should not be deciding NLRA issues under the guise of ERISA jurisdiction, the majority of the United States Court of Appeals for the Second Circuit failed to address this jurisdictional problem, and reversed the lower court's summary judgment decision in favor of the Trump defendants.[192]

Other federal courts have simply distinguished *Advanced Lightweight Concrete* by interpreting it narrowly. In *United Food & Commercial Workers v. Harris-Teeter,*[193] a union and several employees brought suit under ERISA against an employer for its denial of the employees' request to participate in a benefit plan. The employer asserted an *Advanced Lightweight Concrete* defense, claiming that the court had no jurisdiction to hear the matter. The court rejected that argument, contending that unlike the plaintiffs in *Advanced Lightweight Concrete,* these plaintiffs were merely seeking

---

[189] *Id.* at 545–49.

[190] *Id.* at 552–53.

[191] 874 F.2d 912 (2d Cir. 1989) [hereinafter Diduck].

[192] *Id.* at 920–22.

[193] 716 F. Supp. 1551 (W.D.N.C. 1989) [hereinafter Harris-Teeter].

enforcement of the plan under ERISA, not vindication of some right created by the NLRA.[194]

In *Benson v. Brower's Moving & Storage, Inc.,*[195] the court again distinguished *Advanced Lightweight Concrete.* The *Benson* case involved an action under ERISA by pension funds against an employer for delinquent contributions. The court held that the defendants reliance on *Advanced Lightweight Concrete* was misplaced, because the pension funds were suing only for amounts due during the years covered by the collective bargaining agreement, not amounts allegedly due because of some NLRA principle binding the employer after the agreement's expiration.[196]

Finally, in *Scotto v. Brink's Inc.,*[197] a court again circumvented the *Advanced Lightweight Concrete* decision in order to rule in favor of a trust fund that was seeking benefit contributions from an employer for vacation and sick pay earned before the expiration of a collective bargaining agreement. Like the *Benson* court, the *Scotto* court held that the *Advanced Lightweight Concrete* defense did not apply because the fund was seeking contributions that accrued prior to the contract's expiration. Because no NLRA principles had to be addressed—no unfair labor practice or joint employer theory needed to be ruled on—the court could rule in favor of the trust fund based on its ERISA jurisdiction.[198]

The *Diduck, Harris-Teeter, Benson,* and *Scotto* cases illustrate that there are many unresolved issues that must be addressed by the federal courts in order to mark clearly the jurisdictional boundaries between ERISA and the NLRA, issues that should be addressed in the decade of the 1990s.

§ 11.22   —ERISA Preemption

Another area in which legal principles are evolving is ERISA preemption. By definition, ERISA preempts "any and all State laws insofar as they may now or hereafter relate to any employee benefit plan."[199] ERISA preemption of state laws makes sense in that employers should not be obligated to satisfy conflicting requirements of state employment laws.

Courts have interpreted the ERISA preemption theory as requiring a two-step analysis. First, in order to be preempted, the plan referenced by

---

[194] *Id.* at 1558–59.

[195] 726 F. Supp. 31 (E.D.N.Y. 1989), *aff'd,* 907 F.2d 310 (2d Cir.), *cert. denied,* 111 S. Ct. 511 (1990) [hereinafter Benson].

[196] *Id.* at 35.

[197] 751 F. Supp. 335 (E.D.N.Y. 1990) [hereinafter Scotto].

[198] *Id.* at 338–39.

[199] 29 U.S.C. § 1144(a) (1988). The United States Supreme Court has recognized the "conspicuous breadth" of ERISA preemption under this clause. FMC Corp v. Holliday, 111 S. Ct. 403, 407 (1990).

the state law must be an ERISA "plan." Second, the state law must "relate to" the ERISA plan in question.

First Step of Analysis

The first prong of the analysis—determining that the plan is an ERISA plan—was explained by the United States Supreme Court in *Fort Halifax Packing Co. v. Coyne.*[200] In *Fort Halifax,* an employer closed its poultry plant and laid off most of the employees working at the plant. The Maine Director of the Bureau of Labor Standards then filed suit to enforce the provisions of a state statute that required employers, in the event of plant closing, to pay employees not covered by a severance pay agreement a one-time lump-sum severance amount. The employer sought to invoke ERISA preemption of the state statute in order to escape compliance. The Court very carefully drew the distinction that, in this particular case, the Maine statute did not establish an employee benefit "plan." The one-time lump-sum payment required no administrative scheme and no need for financial coordination and control, which are normally necessary when periodic payments are made under an ERISA plan. Therefore, the statute was not preempted by ERISA.[201]

In contrast, the Court has explained that if the state law regulates a series of benefit payments creating a scheme that conflicts with federal law, such as the New Jersey statute that prohibited offsetting workers' compensation payments against pension benefits in *Alessi v. Raybestos-Manhattan, Inc.,*[202] the Court will preempt such statutes because they address employee benefit plans.

Despite the breadth of the ERISA preemption clause, the Court has recognized a limit on the scope of covered ERISA plans, specifically when the state law regulating ERISA plans involves insurance. Under ERISA, preemption is limited by § 514(b)(2), which expressly preserves any state law "which regulates insurance, banking, or securities."[203] In *Metropolitan Life Insurance Co. v. Massachusetts,*[204] the Court addressed the savings clause as applied to a Massachusetts requirement for certain minimum mental health benefits under a general health insurance policy or specific employee health care plans. The insurer contended that because the health care plan was regulated by ERISA, the state minimum benefits law was preempted by ERISA. The Court disagreed, citing the insurance savings clause. Referencing cases that have defined "insurance" under the McCarran-Ferguson

---

[200] 482 U.S. 1 (1987) [hereinafter Fort Halifax].

[201] *Id.* at 11–13.

[202] 451 U.S. 504 (1981).

[203] 29 U.S.C. § 1114(b)(2)(B) (1988).

[204] 471 U.S. 724 (1985) [hereinafter Metropolitan Life].

Act,[205] the Court held that the state statute in question was definitely an insurance statute because it involved regulating the spreading of risk. Therefore, the Court concluded, all mandated-benefit laws such as the Massachusetts statute should be saved from preemption by the savings clause.[206]

Another United States Supreme Court case, *Pilot Life Insurance Co. v. Dedeaux*,[207] also addressed the insurance "savings" provision of ERISA as it related to ERISA preemption. In *Pilot Life*, a permanently disabled employee filed a claim in Mississippi federal district court against his employer, alleging "bad-faith" tort and breach of contract claims under Mississippi common law for the employer's improper processing of his benefits under an ERISA-regulated welfare benefit plan. Using the *Metropolitan Life* factors to determine whether a state common law "relates to" insurance, the Court reasoned that: (1) the Mississippi common law of bad faith did not have the effect of spreading policyholder risk; and (2) the common law was not specifically directed to the insurance industry, because it applied to all contract cases.[208] The court also found that Congress intended solely an ERISA-based federal remedy for all complaints concerning the processing of a claim for benefits under an ERISA-regulated plan.[209] The Court held that the common law bad faith claim did not fall within the insurance savings clause of ERISA and was preempted.[210]

Various federal and state courts have applied the *Pilot Life* ruling to individual state statutes addressing the improper processing of ERISA-regulated employee benefits, with often conflicting and confusing results. For example, in *Kanne v. Connecticut General Life Insurance Co.*,[211] plaintiffs brought suit under California Insurance Code § 790.03(h) seeking compensatory and punitive damages for the insurer's failure to properly process a group health insurance claim. Under the traditional first prong of ERISA preemption analysis, the U.S. Court of Appeals for the Ninth Circuit determined that the plan in question was regulated by ERISA. The second part of the analysis required a determination of whether the insurance savings clause applied to the California statute. Citing *Pilot Life*, the court held that despite the fact the statute might affect policyholder risk, and the fact that the statute was directed solely at

---

[205] 15 U.S.C. §§ 1011–1015 (1988).

[206] 471 U.S. 724, 741–43.

[207] 481 U.S. 41 (1987) [hereinafter Pilot Life].

[208] *Id.* at 50–51.

[209] *Id.* at 56.

[210] *Id.* at 57. In a companion case to *Pilot Life*, Metropolitan Life Ins. Co. v. Taylor, 481 U.S. 58 (1987), the Court also held that when such preempted common law causes of action are filed in state court, they are removable to federal court under § 502(a)(1)(B) of ERISA.

[211] 859 F.2d 96 (9th Cir. 1988), *cert. denied*, 109 S. Ct. 3216 (1989) [hereinafter Kanne].

insurance, any cause of action under the statute was still preempted by ERISA. The court reasoned that preemption was required because *Pilot Life* determined that Congress intended that the "civil enforcement provisions of ERISA § 502(a) be the exclusive vehicle for actions by ERISA-plan participants and beneficiaries asserting improper processing of a claim for benefits."[212]

Other courts, notably the California Court of Appeal for the Fourth District in *Rizzi v. Blue Cross,*[213] have agreed with the *Kanne* analysis that California Insurance Code § 790.03(h) claims are preempted by ERISA under *Pilot Life*. Other federal courts, notably the United States District Court for the Northern District of California in *Graves v. Blue Cross,*[214] in a case decided *after Kanne,* have ignored this interpretation of California Insurance Code § 790.03(h), and have concluded that § 790.03 is a state law regulating insurance within the meaning of the savings clause. Consequently, the area of law involving possible ERISA preemption of state statutes that address the processing of employee benefits should be ripe for further litigation in the 1990s.

Second Step of Analysis

The second prong of the preemption test, whether the state law "relates to" an ERISA plan, is more difficult to interpret for employers, because the Court interprets the "relate to" language on a case-by-case basis. The case of *Ingersoll-Rand Co. v. McClendon,*[215] addressed this issue most recently, interpreting whether a state law cause of action for wrongful discharge should be preempted by ERISA. In *Ingersoll-Rand,* an employee sued his employer for wrongful discharge under state law tort and contract theories, alleging that the principal reason for his termination was the company's desire to avoid contributing to his pension fund. The company moved for summary judgment, which was granted by the trial court, on the grounds that ERISA preempted the employee's state law claim. After the Texas Supreme Court reversed, the United States Supreme Court reversed again, holding that summary judgment was correctly granted, because the Texas cause of action specifically referenced an ERISA plan. The Court concluded that "there would be no cause of action if there is no plan," thus summary judgment in favor of defendants was proper.[216] *Ingersoll-Rand*

---

[212] *Id.* at 100 (quoting Pilot Life, 481 U.S. at 56).

[213] 206 Cal. App. 3d 380, 253 Cal. Rptr. 541 (1988), *cert. denied,* 110 S. Ct. 78 (1989).

[214] 688 F. Supp. 1405, 1409–12 (N.D. Cal. 1988).

[215] 111 S. Ct. 478 (1990) [hereinafter Ingersoll-Rand].

[216] *Id.* at 484–85.

illustrates that not only does ERISA preempt state laws relating to ERISA plans, but also the preemption clause applies to attempts to litigate ERISA-related questions in state court.

Another example of ERISA preemption's impact on the construction industry in the state of California is *Operating Engineers v. Weiss Bros.*[217] There, an apprenticeship program committee brought a breach of contract action against a construction company for the company's failure to pay wages and benefits under an employee benefit plan agreement and for failing to hire apprentices as required by California Labor Code § 1777.5. Labor Code § 1777.5 in effect required contractors on public projects who have not signed collective bargaining agreements to be bound by the relevant apprenticeship standards for certain covered trades. The trial court sustained the company's demurrer and dismissed the case based on its determination that ERISA preempted the breach of contract claim.

The Third Appellate District affirmed, following *Hydrostorage v. Northern California Boilermakers,* [218] in concluding that the apprenticeship standards promulgated by the statute qualified as an ERISA "plan," and that Labor Code § 1777.5 related to the plan in question. The court noted that ERISA preempts any attempt under state law to enforce the terms of an ERISA plan. Therefore, because the statute related to and purported to regulate the apprenticeship standards, it was preempted by ERISA.[219] As certiorari on this case was recently denied by the United States Supreme Court, the courts have made it clear that states may not attempt to regulate nonsignatory employers by requiring them to contribute to ERISA-type trust funds.

Another significant ruling is the case of *Carpenters Southern California Administration Corp. v. El Capitan Development Co.*[220] In *El Capitan,* trust funds brought an action against the El Capitan Development Company to foreclose trust fund liens for unpaid contributions pursuant to state law that provides for the enactment of such liens. The California Supreme Court determined that the lien laws were designed specifically to affect an ERISA-regulated employee benefit plan, providing trust funds under collective bargaining agreements with a mechanic's lien remedy not provided by Congress. Therefore, the statute "related to" an ERISA plan and the plaintiffs' claim under that statute was held preempted.[221]

---

[217] 221 Cal. App. 3d 867, 270 Cal. Rptr. 786 (1990), *cert. denied,* 111 S. Ct. 1337 (1991).

[218] 891 F.2d 719 (9th Cir. 1989).

[219] 221 Cal. App. 3d at 876–81.

[220] 53 Cal. 3d 1041 811 P.2d 296, 282 Cal. Rptr. 277 (1991) *petition for cert.* (Sept. 18, 1991) [hereinafter El Capitan].

[221] *Id.* at 1049–54.

§ 11.23   —Using Funds to Advance
Social or Union Goals

Another issue that appears headed for increased litigation in the 1990s is the controversy over continuing attempts by multiemployer trust funds to earmark monies for the advancement of social, political, or union goals, rather than for the strict benefit of plan participants and beneficiaries. For example, trustees may amend their plans to prejudice participants who decide to work for nonunion companies or they may limit fund investments to unionized companies. There are several legal courses of action that may be taken in response to these trust fund attempts to manipulate funds.

First, ERISA itself provides some protections for plan participants from manipulative trustees. Under ERISA, the trustees are required to manage the fund for the sole and exclusive benefit of participants and beneficiaries.[222] Trustees must exercise the care and skill "that a prudent man" would exercise under like circumstances,[223] and manage the fund in accordance with the documents governing the trust.[224]

Plan participants have certain specific rights under ERISA, including the following:

1. The right to receive notice six months prior to the reduction of accrued benefits under any amendment

2. The right to be informed of any new "break-in-service" rules that will interrupt vested benefits

3. The right to petition the Department of Labor for further assistance and information when appropriate

4. The right to the required revision of the pension plan explanation pamphlet every five years if amendments have been made[225]

5. The right to bring suit alleging improper plan administration[226]

6. The right to be free from discharge, fine, discrimination, or coercion for exercising any right under a covered plan or under the terms of ERISA.[227]

---

[222] 29 U.S.C. § 1104 (1988).

[223] *Id.* at § 1104(a)(1)(B).

[224] *Id.*

[225] 29 U.S.C. § 1425 (Supp. 1989).

[226] *Id.* at § 1132(a). Suits to enforce the rights of employees under a collectively-bargained pension fund also may be brought under § 301 or § 302 of the Taft-Hartley Act. *See, e.g.,* Smith v. Evening News Ass'n, 371 U.S. 195 (1962) (breach of contract claim if benefits unilaterally changed).

[227] 29 U.S.C. §§ 1140–1141 (1988).

Second, although the plan participants may sue the trust funds for alleged improper use of funds under an ERISA theory, the contributing employer also may sue the trust funds to challenge administration of employer contributions.[228]

One key area of litigation during the decade will be challenges to trust fund decisions to cancel benefits for those employees leaving the union fold.

Various other theories may find their way into court as a consequence of trust fund investments or restrictions. Breach of fiduciary duty by the trustees, violations of the NLRA provisions that prohibit discrimination on the basis of union or antiunion sympathy, and perhaps even criminal law allegations may arise in the wake of trust fund manipulation.

§ 11.24   Necessity for Proper Planning

Labor and employment planning for construction and engineering employers will evolve with developments in the law. The scope and complexity of legal developments places employers in perilous positions, particularly smaller employers without the resources to track legal changes. Proper planning should provide a competitive edge for those employers that desire to reduce the probability of labor and employment liability.

---

[228] LMRA § 302(e), 29 U.S.C. § 186(e) (1988). *See* Employing Plasterers Ass'n v. Plasterers, 279 F.2d 92 (7th Cir. 1960).

CHAPTER 12

HOW TO GO DOUBLE BREASTED AND WHY

Melvin Hutson

Melvin Hutson is a partner in the law firm of Thompson, Mann & Hutson in Greenville, South Carolina. He and his firm represent management in employment, labor, and related legal matters. A substantial portion of his practice is devoted to the construction industry. Hutson is the past chairman of the National AGC Labor Lawyers' Council. He is also active in the American Bar Association where he is currently serving as co-chair of the Litigation Section's Committee on Labor Litigation.

§ 12.1   Divided Construction Market

In the decades between 1960 and 1980, open shop construction developed to the point that it dominated major parts of the construction industry in large geographic areas. By 1984, a nationwide survey determined that union construction accounted for no more than 30 percent of the total market.[1] Nevertheless, the 30 percent of construction done under union contracts included some of the largest and most sought-after projects.

The union response to this steep decline in the percentage of work performed under union contracts has taken many forms, including picketing, organization of drives, legal challenges directed at contractors, and actual or threatened boycotts against owners. Additionally, the building trades unions have made numerous attempts to induce changes in the labor laws that would restrict open shop. Sometimes the union response has been effective, as when Toyota changed the construction of its new auto assembly plant in Kentucky from open shop to union built.[2] At other times, union efforts have failed.

§ 12.2   Strategies for Serving a Divided Market

One constant result of the union response is that the attempts to stem union losses have made it more difficult than ever for a single company of any significant size to serve both the union and open shop sectors of the industry. Although double breasting is one of the strategies that has been adopted by a large number of organizations attempting to meet the demands of both sectors, it is certainly not the only strategy.

Some organizations have responded to the demands by merely ignoring their union obligations. According to the president of the building trades union, very small contractors often work nonunion despite being parties to union contracts. The contractors rarely are challenged because they are both too small and too numerous for the unions to afford to attack them.[3] Nevertheless, casebooks are filled with examples of small contractors that have been challenged successfully.

Many speciality contractors with traditional union ties have found that they can continue to meet their market needs by continuing to work

---

[1] Herbert R. Northrup, *Open Shop Construction Revisited,* Major Industrial Research Studies, No. 62 (Wharton School Indus. Research Unit, Univ. of Pa. 1984).

[2] *See* Richard Koenig, *Toyota Learns to Live with the U.S. Unions,* Wall St. J., Feb. 25, 1987, at 12.

[3] *See* Robert A. Georgine, President of the Building and Construction Trades Department, AFL-CIO, Testimony before the Subcommittee on Labor-Management Relations of the Committee on Education and Labor, United States House of Representatives, in Support of H.R. 281 (Mar. 4, 1987) (duplicated copy at 5).

exclusively union. Open shop jobs of significant size are rarely 100 percent nonunion. Almost all of them include at least some subcontractors working under union agreements. Dual gate systems generally have been effective in isolating these contractors from picketing or from other protests that may take place at the open shop entrances. As a result, the contractors have worked successfully on jobs that were largely nonunion.

Dual gates have been less effective on jobs in which union contractors predominate. Nevertheless, some open shop contractors have been able to compete successfully for work on some predominately union jobs. The opportunity to do so is limited severely by the prevalence of contract clauses that prohibit union contractors from subcontracting work to any company that is not bound to the same union agreement.

Other open shop contractors have used "project agreements" successfully to perform work that would otherwise have gone to a union contractor. This alternative frequently is impractical because of the expense and difficulty associated with obtaining a project agreement.

Each of these alternatives has obvious limitations. As a result, contractors seeking to serve both the union and open shop sectors of their industry frequently have elected to become double breasted.

§ 12.3   Double Breasting Defined

Double breasting is the practice by which a single owner has two or more companies (known as *double breasted* or *dual shop*), one of which operates union while the other operates nonunion. Typically, these separate companies seek to serve different markets, although some operate side by side, building similar projects in the same geographical area.

§ 12.4   Risks Involved in Double Breasting

Attempts at double breasting present substantial legal problems. Under the National Labor Relations Act (NLRA),[4] the existence of separate corporate identities does not, by itself, protect related companies from a determination that they constitute a "single employer." Such a holding can have severe consequences, including:

1. The loss of secondary boycott protection (that is, a union legally engaging in a strike against or picketing company A because of some dispute the union has with company B)

---

[4] 29 U.S.C. §§ 151–169.

2. The potential for both companies to be held jointly liable for unfair labor practices of one company
3. The possibility that the union contracts of one company will be applied to all companies in the related group.

However, the general presumption under the labor laws is that corporations are separate and distinct entities with the concomitant protection of limited liability.[5] As a result, multiple companies are treated as a single employer only when it is established that nominally separate corporations actually are operated as a single integrated business enterprise.[6] Thus, it is possible for a single owner to meet the demands of the union and open shop sectors of the construction industry through two separately managed companies.

§ 12.5   Determining Single Employer Status

The general considerations for determining whether related companies constitute a single employer were established many years ago. In 1965 in the case of *Radio Union v. Broadcast Service of Mobile, Inc.*, the United States Supreme Court said: "The controlling criteria, set out and elaborated in Board decisions, are interrelation of operations, common management, centralized control of labor relations and common ownership."[7] Nevertheless, no precise standard exists for determining whether or not a group of companies constitute a single employer. In *Operating Engineers v. NLRB (Peter Kiewit Sons' Co.)*, the Court of Appeals for the District of Columbia Circuit has stated:

> [We] conclude that "single employer" status, for purposes of the National Labor Relations Act, depends upon all the circumstances of the case, that not all of the "controlling criteria" specified by the Supreme Court need be present; that, in addition to the criterion of common ownership or financial control, the other criteria, whether or not they are present at the top level of management, are "controlling" indicia of the actual exercise of the power of common ownership or financial control; and that the standard for evaluating such exercise of power is whether, as a matter of substance, there is the "arm's" length relationship found among unintegrated companies.[8]

As the Court indicated, some general observations are possible on how future determinations will be made in single employer cases. First, no

---

[5] Alkire v. NLRB, 716 F.2d 1014, 1018 (4th Cir. 1983).

[6] United Tel. Workers v. NLRB, 571 F.2d 665, 667 (D.C. Cir. 1978).

[7] 380 U.S. 255, 85 S. Ct. 876 (1965).

[8] 518 F.2d 1040, 1045, 90 L.R.R.M. (BNA) 2321 (D.C. Cir. 1975), *vacated on other grounds*, 425 U.S. 800, 96 S. Ct. 1842 (1976).

precise formula for a double-breasted operation can be written. The decision-maker looks at the facts of each individual case and weighs all the factors in any decision on single employer status. Second, the factor of financial control or ownership is not controlling. Commonly-owned companies can be "separate employers." Finally, the decisions regarding single employer status are based primarily on the exercise of power and authority as opposed to the existence of power or the potential for the exercise of authority. An examination of the four individual factors illustrates the weight given to each.

§ 12.6   —Financial Control or Common Ownership

Financial control or common ownership is the factor that almost always is found to be present in double-breasted contracting arrangements because the basic concept is common ownership of separate businesses. As noted in § 12.5, however, the factor is not controlling.[9]

The special significance of financial control or common ownership is that some union contracts, by their specific terms, apply to all businesses owned or financially controlled by the employer signing the union contract. The National Labor Relations Board (NLRB) has struggled for many years with cases relating to whether these provisions are enforceable.[10] At present, the effect of contract clauses that bind all commonly-owned businesses is largely unknown.

§ 12.7   —Centralized Control of Labor Relations

The NLRB has made the following statement concerning the common control of labor relations:

> A critical factor in determining whether separate legal entities operate as a single employing enterprise is the degree of common control of labor relations policies. Thus, the Board has found common ownership not determinative where requisite common control was not shown, and the Board has held with court approval that such common control must be actual or active, as distinguished from potential control.[11]

---

[9] *See, e.g.,* Local 259, UAW (Stamford Motors, Inc.), 221 NLRB No. 97, 90 L.R.R.M. (BNA) 1729 (1975).

[10] Painters Dist. Council, 299 NLRB No. 86, 135 L.R.R.M. (BNA) 1217 (1990).

[11] Peter Kiewit Sons' Co., 206 N.L.R.B. 562, 84 L.R.R.M. (BNA) 1356 (1973), *rev'd,* 518 F.2d 1040, 90 L.R.R.M. (BNA) 2321 (D.C. Cir. 1975), *vacated,* 425 U.S. 800, S. Ct. 1842 (1976); Gerace Constr., Inc., 193 N.L.R.B. 645, 78 L.R.R.M. (BNA) 1367 (1971). *See also* Joe Robertson & Son, Inc., 174 N.L.R.B. 1073, 70 L.R.R.M. (BNA) 1396 (1969); Bel-Air Door, 150 N.L.R.B. 481, 58 L.R.R.M. (BNA) 1109 (1965); Los Angeles

The NLRB made this statement on actual or active control in the *Peter Kiewit* case in 1973, and has held the position for many years, continuing to express the same view since that time.

In an illustrative case involving Vulcan Materials Co., the Court of Appeals for the District of Columbia Circuit held that two divisions of Vulcan (the Mideast Division and the Chattanooga Division) were separate employers under the NLRA and entitled to the protection of the secondary boycott laws. After discussing the fact that Vulcan's manager of industrial relations, Carl Whitten, and Vulcan's manager of manpower planning and development, Robert Majors, had assisted the divisions and participated in negotiations, the Court said:

> Although the ultimate power to control both Mideast and Chattanooga resides in Vulcan, in fact that power has not been exercised; on the contrary each division exercises final and independent control over its operations, including its labor relations. The services of Whitten and Majors were advisory only and were furnished only at the invitation of the presidents of Mideast and Chattanooga, who made all final decisions. In short, the evidence justifies the finding that the divisions are operated as autonomous enterprises, under the doctrine of *American Fed. of Television and Radio Artists v. N.L.R.B.,* 149 U.S. App. D.C. 272, 462 F.2d 887 (1972), and *Los Angeles Newspaper Guild, Local 69 v. N.L.R.B.,* 443 F.2d 1173 (9th Cir. 1971), *enfg.* 185 NLRB No. 25 (1970), *cert. denied,* 404 U.S. 1018, 92 S. Ct. 681, 30 L. Ed. 2d 666 (1972).[12]

This case is consistent with the overwhelming weight of precedent, which indicates that high level or potential control of labor relations is insignificant. Potential control is a factor to be weighed, but the important point is actual day-to-day control over wages, hours, and working conditions.

§ 12.8   —Common Management

The question of whether two companies are under common management is similar to the issue of centralized control of labor relations in that the most important question is whether the day-to-day management of the companies is the same. In the Cook Construction Company case, illustrating how

---

Newspaper Guild, Local 69 (Hearst Corp.), 185 N.L.R.B. 303, 75 L.R.R.M. (BNA) 1014 (1970), *enf'd,* 443 F.2d 1173, 77 L.R.R.M. (BNA) 2895 (9th Cir. 1971); Miami Newspaper Printing Pressmen's Local No. 46 v. NLRB, 322 F.2d 405, 53 L.R.R.M. (BNA) 2629 (D.C. Cir. 1963); Frank N. Smith Assocs., 194 N.L.R.B. 212, 78 L.R.R.M. (BNA) 1603 (1971).

[12] Teamsters Local 391 v. NLRB (Chattanooga Div. Vulcan Material Co.), 543 F.2d 1373, 1376 (D.C. Cir. 1976).

common management can result in a single employer status finding, both corporations had the same president, vice-president, secretary, headquarters building, and telephone system, and three quarters of the supervisors and employees were employed interchangeably by the two corporations. Furthermore, the same officials determined labor policies for the two corporations.[13]

In a similar example, the NLRB held that a corporation and partnership constituted a single employer within the meaning of the NLRA when

1. The owner of the corporation had control over operations, financial affairs, and labor relations of both entities
2. These entities did not deal at arm's length with each other
3. The partnership was unable to function without aid and control of the corporation
4. The owner operated the partnership under the owner's personal state license
5. The owner gave home residence, and later corporation's address, as partnership's address
6. The owner occasionally supervised partnership employees and partnership employees reported to the corporation's office for work assignments
7. The owner shifted work from the union employees at the partnership to nonunion employees at the corporation to avoid honoring the collective bargaining agreement.[14]

The corporation as well as the partnership was ordered to recognize and bargain with the union, to abide by the existing union contracts, and to pay back wages and benefits to the affected employees.

A good example of separate management is found in a case in which the Court of Appeals for the District of Columbia Circuit held that separate operating divisions of the Hearst Corporation were separate employers for labor relations purposes.[15] The Court stated:

> [T]he ultimate power to control each division belonged to Hearst, since each division manager was answerable to Hearst. As the Board correctly held, however, the test is not whether an unexercised power to control exists. "There must be in addition such actual or active common control, as

---

[13] Cook Constr. Co., 203 N.L.R.B. 41, 83 L.R.R.M. (BNA) 1043 (1973).

[14] Burgess Constr. Corp., 227 N.L.R.B. 765 (1977), enf'd, 596 F.2d 378 (9th Cir.), cert. denied, 444 U.S. 940 (1979).

[15] Television & Radio Artists v. NLRB (Hearst Corp.), 462 F.2d 887, 80 L.R.R.M. (BNA) 2001 (D.C. Cir. 1972).

distinguished from merely a potential, as to denote an appreciable integration of operations and management policies."[16]

The court based its decision on the following facts:

1. The two divisions were competitors, dealing with each other at arm's
    length
2. The head of each division exercised final and independent control
    over the respective division with the exception of decisions requiring
    capital expenditures in excess of $10,000
3. Each division made its labor relations decisions independently, with-
    out seeking the counsel of the other.

In concluding that each division was independently managed, the Court
noted, "they have had complete discretion in the areas of management policy, labor relations, production, purchasing and all other aspects of planning and operation which might touch on labor's interest in this dispute."[17]
    These cases represent the extremes in the area of common management.
Between the two extremes, there have been numerous instances in which
the issue of common management has been considered. In these cases, the
common test applied is whether actual control over day-to-day operations is
exercised independently or jointly.
    In one case illustrating how the NLRB applies the various tests, the
issue was whether a company had committed unfair labor practices by
refusing to recognize the unions it bargained with as the representatives of
the employees of its open shop subsidiary. The NLRB found that the owners and managers of the parent company were the prime movers in organizing the open shop company and that they retained potential control
over it. The subsidiary's principal management official had initially consulted with the parent company on policy matters, but over time he assumed more independent responsibility, and he was in complete charge of
day-to-day operations. Because the open shop subsidiary's management
had actual control over its operations and employees, the NLRB held that
the two companies were separate employers. These companies had some
common directors, they shared a bookkeeper, and one company rented
office space, tools, and equipment from the other. Nevertheless, they were
separate employers because actual control over operations and employees
was separate. The details of the relationship between these companies are
described at length in the decision.[18]

---

[16] *Id.* at 892 (citations omitted).

[17] *Id.*

[18] Gerace Constr., Inc., 193 N.L.R.B. 645, 646, 78 L.R.R.M. (BNA) 1367 (1971).

Another 1971 case involved the issue of whether the contractors committed an unfair labor practice when the second company refused to apply the union contracts of the first company. Even though the same person was president of both companies and owned 70 to 75 percent of the stock of each, the NLRB dismissed the charge. It found that the two companies did not bid on the same jobs and that labor relations matters and day-to-day problems were handled separately.[19]

The cases demonstrate once again that the NLRB looks at the facts of each case and applies its general criteria without resorting to any specific formula.

In an evaluation of the common management test, it should be recognized that an important consideration when one company has committed unfair labor practices is whether those violations directly affect the employees of another company.[20]

§ 12.9   —Interrelation of Operations

By using the term *interrelation of operations,* the NLRB and the courts mean that they look to see whether the work performed by one company is an essential and integral step in the other company's daily operations. For example, the NLRB has held that two construction companies constituted a single employer when (1) one person owned 90 percent of each company, (2) the companies performed the same services in the same market, and (3) one company's operation depended almost entirely on facilities, equipment, administrative, engineering, sales, and clerical support by the other with the absence of any arm's length relationship.[21] The nonunion company had to abide by the union contract and to pay back wages and benefits to its employees according to that contract.

Similarly, in a non-construction-industry case, the NLRB held that a newspaper production company and a photo engraving company were a single employer.[22] The engraving company was located in the same building with the other company where it produced photo engraving plates used by the production company in the publication of two newspapers. The engraving company derived one third of its income from and devoted one half of its man-hours worked to the newspaper production company, and the managers of the businesses met daily to discuss the quality of newspapers printed.

---

[19] Frank N. Smith Assocs., Inc., 194 N.L.R.B. 212, 78 L.R.R.M. (BNA) 1603, 1604 (1971).

[20] NLRB v. Gibraltar Indus., Inc., 307 F.2d 428, 51 L.R.R.M. (BNA) 2029 (4th Cir. 1962).

[21] Harrisburg Drywall & Constr. Corp. & Al Bryant Assocs., Inc., 260 N.L.R.B. 128 (1982).

[22] Newspaper Prod. Co., 205 N.L.R.B. 738, 84 L.R.R.M. (BNA) 1186 (1973).

Likewise in *NLRB v. Jordan Bus Co.*,[23] the United States Court of Appeals in Denver upheld an NLRB decision that two separately-owned companies were a single employer because:

1. Single bus routes were run partly under the franchise of one company and partly under the franchise of the second
2. Bus drivers occasionally serviced an entire route and were paid partly by one company and partly by another
3. Four of the seven drivers employed by one company worked part-time for the other company
4. One company's supervisor indirectly supervised employees of the other company and served as dispatcher for both companies.

The Court stated:

> The Board was of the opinion that the functional integration, physical proximity, and degree of common management demonstrated by the foregoing facts warranted a finding that Jordan and Denco are a single employer. This finding is clearly supported by substantial evidence. To be sure, the two companies are separately owned. But this factor is not controlling, and indeed is the factor usually given least weight by the Board. See the Board's statement of policy reproduced in Sakrete of Northern California, Inc. v. N.L.R.B., 9 Cir., 332 F.2d 902, footnote 4. The Board usually stresses the factors tending to show operational integration, as it did in this case. And, we think the evidence shows a sufficient community of operations, labor relations, and management to support the finding in this case. See Hirsch Broadcasting Co., 116 NLRB 1780.[24]

This case and others on the issue show that it is very difficult for an employer to establish that separate parts of an integrated operation are separate employers for labor relations purposes.

§ 12.10   Alter Ego Determination

The separate employer principles outlined in §§ 12.5 to 12.9 do not protect a company that is created to avoid or evade its owner's union contracts. Companies or other entities employed for that purpose are declared "alter egos" and all the contractual or other legal obligations of the original company are applied to the new company.

The United States Supreme Court has held that an alter ego determination may be appropriate when a change in business operations is merely a

---

[23] NLRB v. Jordan Bus Co., 380 F.2d 219, 65 L.R.R.M. (BNA) 2550 (10th Cir. 1967).

[24] 380 F.2d at 222 (footnotes omitted).

"disguised continuance of the old employer," especially when it is found that the change was "a disguise intended to evade" the labor laws.[25] The NLRB continues to make alter ego findings in such situations. For example, in *Crawford Door Sales Co.*,[26] the NLRB found that, as the owner of the company approached retirement, he and his son completed a plan to allow the son's successor company to be nonunion. After starting a new company, the son held meetings with employees of the old concern, offering them a "take it or leave it" proposition for employment with the new nonunion company. The NLRB held that the new company was an "alter ego," bound to the same union obligations despite the fact that ownership was different.

Although common ownership is not essential to an alter ego finding, the NLRB has found an alter ego relationship in the absence of common ownership only when both companies were wholly owned by the same family or almost totally owned by the same individual,[27] or in cases in which the older company continued its control over the business allegedly sold to the new organization.[28] The NLRB reports contain numerous other cases in which new companies that were formed to evade obligations under a union contract were held to be alter egos.[29]

The effect of an alter ego determination is well-established. Each company is equally liable for remedying the other company's unfair labor practices and for paying any obligations incurred under union contracts.

§ 12.11   Effects of Single Employer Finding

Two companies that are not alter egos still may be found to constitute a "single employer" based on (1) interrelations of operations, (2) centralized control of labor relations, (3) common management, and (4) common ownership. Two or more companies that constitute a single employer lose the protection of the secondary boycott laws, but the union contracts of one company are not necessarily imposed on the others.

The U.S. Supreme Court has held that the question of whether the union contracts of one company are enforceable against a related entity is to be decided separately from the question of whether the two entities are independent enough to invoke the protection of the secondary boycott laws. The Court said that the determining factor in whether the union contracts will be extended to the nonunion group is whether, in the NLRB's view, a

---

[25] Southport Petroleum Co. v. NLRB, 315 U.S. 100, 106, 62 S. Ct. 452 (1942).

[26] 226 N.L.R.B. 1144 (1976).

[27] Nelson Elec. v. NLRB, 638 F.2d 965 (6th Cir. 1981).

[28] McAllister Bros., 278 N.L.R.B. 601 (1986), *enf'd*, 819 F.2d 439 (4th Cir. 1987).

[29] *See, e.g.*, Apex Decorating Co., 275 N.L.R.B. 1459 (1985); Advance Elec., Inc., 268 N.L.R.B. 1001 (1984); Campbell-Harris Elec., Inc., 263 N.L.R.B. 1143 (1983).

single bargaining unit is appropriate.[30] In the *South Prairie Construction* case, for example, the NLRB determined that separate bargaining units were appropriate because the union and nonunion employees did not share a common "community of interest."[31] The decision was based, in part, on the long history of separate operations and the history of independent determination of wages, hours, benefits, and other terms and conditions of employment.[32]

On the other hand, the NLRB has not hesitated to order the extension of a contract to unorganized employees when it finds, in a separate determination, that a single bargaining unit is appropriate.[33]

§ 12.12   Challenges to Double Breasted Operations

Legal challenges to the separate employer status of related companies in a double-breasted operation may be made in several forums. The traditional forum is the NLRB (see § 12.13); however, legal challenges also have been made through arbitration under the contract terms of the union company[34] and directly through the courts.[35]

§ 12.13   —Charges before National Labor Relations Board

The traditional route for questioning single employer status is a challenge before the NLRB. An unfair labor practice charge alleging that the nonunion company is violating § 8(a)(5) of the NLRA by refusing to recognize the union or the union contracts of the affiliated companies is the traditional form of such a challenge. The issue also could be raised in other types of unfair labor practice charges as well as in a defense to a secondary boycott charge filed by the company.

---

[30] South Prairie Constr. Co. (Peter Kiewit Co.) v. Local 627, Int'l Union of Operating Eng'rs, 425 U.S. 800, 96 S. Ct. 7842 (1976).

[31] South Prairie Constr., 231 N.L.R.B. 76 (1977), *enf'd*, 595 F.2d 844 (D.C. Cir. 1979).

[32] *Id.*

[33] *See, e.g.,* DMR Corp. & Harrill Elec. Contractors, Inc., 258 N.L.R.B. 1063, 108 L.R.R.M. (BNA) 1217 (1981); Better Bldg. Supply Corp. & Evergreen Roofing, Inc., 259 N.L.R.B. 469, 108 L.R.R.M. (BNA) 1381 (1981); Al Bryant, Inc., Harrisburg Drywall & Constr. Corp. & Al Bryant Assocs., Inc., 260 N.L.R.B. 128, 109 L.R.R.M. (BNA) 1284 (1982), *enf'd*, 711 F.2d 543 (3d Cir. 1983).

[34] *See, e.g.,* IBEW Local 323 v. Coral Elec. Corp., 576 F. Supp. 1128 (S.D. Fla. 1983).

[35] *See, e.g.,* Cuyahoga Wrecking Corp. v. Laborers Int'l Union, 644 F. Supp. 878 (W.D.N.Y. 1986).

If the related companies have not properly maintained their independence, the placing of a picket complaining about the nonunion operation at one of the union companies sites could be effective. To get the picket removed, the company would need to file secondary boycott charges with the NLRB, asking that agency to seek an injunction against the picketing. If the NLRB decided that the related companies were a single employer, it could refuse to act. The union company might have other options under a no strike clause or in a damage suit, but the company's options would be limited severely.

The NLRB is not the only forum in which a legal challenge could be made against a double-breasted company, but it is a very important setting. The NLRB has played a key role in the development of the law on this topic. Its decisions and the tests or standards it uses have been followed consistently.

§ 12.14   Requests for Information

As part of its legal obligation to bargain in good faith, a union contractor may be required to provide information to its unions. It is now established that, in certain circumstances, the negotiators must supply information about a related nonunion operation. In a case involving the Associated General Contractors of California, the NLRB required the bargaining group to reveal a full list of its membership, including nonunion members. The union said it was attempting to evade the contract by diverting work to sham nonunion companies.[36]

In a case involving a single employer, the union requested information relating to the business relationship of a construction company and its affiliate corporation.[37] The union demonstrated a reasonable basis for believing that the construction company was operating an alter ego operation through the affiliate. Therefore, the NLRB decided that the union was entitled to the information.

The standard for judging whether information must be produced is very favorable to the unions. In the *Corson & Gruman Co.* case,[38] the union requested information from Corson and Gruman based on suspicions that the company was transferring work to related nonunion companies. The union's belief was based solely on general concerns expressed by members and no objective evidence was available. Based on the liberal,

---

[36] Associated Gen. Contractors, 242 N.L.R.B. 891 (1979), *enf'd*, 633 F.2d 766 (9th Cir. 1980), *cert. denied*, 452 U.S. 915 (1981).

[37] Pence Constr. Co., 281 N.L.R.B. 322 (1986).

[38] Corson & Gruman Co., 278 N.L.R.B. 329, 121 L.R.R.M. (BNA) 1325 (1986), *enf'd*, 124 L.R.R.M. (BNA) 2560 (4th Cir. 1987).

discovery-type standard by which relevancy is to be judged, NLRB found that the union had demonstrated a reasonable basis to suspect that a contract violation had occurred. The union, therefore, proved that it was entitled to information.

§ 12.15   Checklists for Separate Employer Identity

The following items have been viewed by the NLRB as indicating that two commonly-owned businesses were separate employers for purposes of the NLRA. None of these factors, by themselves, were controlling. In each case the NLRB weighed all the indicators present in making its determination.

_____ Separate corporate structure or separate legal entity status
_____ Separate companies engaged in different types of business, such as highway construction and commercial construction
_____ Separate offices, phone numbers, and stationery
_____ Separate tax returns, when possible
_____ Independent bidding and solicitation of work (neither business being dependent on the other for work)
_____ Separate books and records
_____ Separate capital and credit
_____ Separate employee compensation plans
_____ Separate workers' compensation insurance contracts, if possible
_____ Absence of competition for business
_____ Separate bank accounts
_____ Absence of daily communications on routine matters
_____ Separate budgeting responsibility and separate spending authority (within overall limits)
_____ Absence of a line of personnel progression between companies
_____ Independent authority to set wages and conditions of employment
_____ Independent authority to negotiate collective bargaining agreements and otherwise deal with labor matters
_____ Payment for exchanged equipment or services at fair market value
_____ Absence of interchange of employees
_____ Absence of loss of work from one company to the other
_____ Absence of loss of jobs from one company to the other
_____ Some independent shareholders in each of the two corporations
_____ Separate boards of directors with at least some different directors
_____ Different chief operating officers

_____ Separate authority for daily operations (officers having authority to make independent decisions necessary to run the businesses on a day-to-day basis).

These factors indicate that companies wishing to maintain or establish separate employer identities must avoid the following:

_____ All interchange of employees below the managerial level.

_____ Routine interchange of management or the establishment of a line of advancement from one company to another.

_____ Integration of operations to the extent that one company performs the work for which the other has contracted.

_____ The use of services made available by the parent company without adequate compensation.

_____ Consultation on routine items. (Of course, consultation on overall policy matters is permissible.)

_____ Operating in such a manner that one company loses business directly to the other.

_____ Operating in such a manner that the employees of one company lose jobs to the employees of the other company.

_____ Giving, in any way, the appearance of using the second corporation to evade the obligations of a collective bargaining contract.

_____ Direct competition for business on more than an infrequent basis. The NLRB has looked upon frequent or direct competition as an indication that the two businesses are shams.

These same NLRB factors indicated that the following actions have not been sufficient to destroy separate employer status when other factors are not present.

1. Common use of staff or contract services such as accounting, bookkeeping, engineering, and estimating, if the decision to use these services is made by the operating officers of each company and fair market value is paid for these services.

2. Common use of equipment if there is a formal lease agreement for fair market value.

3. Consultation on policy or major problems so long as each company retains autonomous authority for daily operations.

4. The establishment of limits on the authority of the operating officers of each company so long as these limits do not restrict the officers' authority for daily operations.

CHAPTER 13

DEALING WITH HAZARDOUS WASTE AND ENVIRONMENTAL ISSUES

Jill Barson Gilbert
Douglas J. Hileman

Jill Barson Gilbert is a member of the Houston, Texas, firm of Pilko & Associates, Inc., where she consults to industry, attorneys, and investment bankers on regulatory and environmental issues. She holds an M.S. in environmental management from the University of San Francisco and an A.B. from Miami University. Her background includes site investigations, remediation, waste management programs, environmental audits, environmental policies and procedures, and regulatory analysis. Ms. Gilbert's credentials also include the permitting of projects such as chemical plants, land disposal operations, hazardous waste facilities, and PCB incinerators. She is active in the Air & Waste Management Association.

Douglas J. Hileman is a consultant with Pilko & Associates in Los Angeles, California, where his areas of expertise include client programs, site assessments, lender consulting, training programs, real estate, and litigation support. He is a registered professional engineer (chemical), a California registered environmental assessor, and has an M.B.A. He teaches environmental auditing in the certificate programs at the University of California Extension, Irvine. Mr. Hileman is a member of the steering committee of the Environmental Auditing Forum and the Association for Corporate Growth. He has facilitated workshops on environmental ethics at numerous professional associations, including the national Air and Waste Management Association conference.

§ 13.1 Introduction

A contractor demolishing an old shopping center fails to properly remove asbestos, causes a release of asbestos fibers to the atmosphere, and increases public exposure. The contractor is subsequently prosecuted, fined, and given jail time. Another contractor mixes contaminated soil with incoming fill, causing an entire site to become designated as "contaminated," bringing a major project to a screeching halt, and beginning a lengthy process of site investigation and cleanup. A third contractor removing an underground storage tank is not informed by the site owner of its previous contents; a worker is killed when an explosion occurs because of a failure to properly remove flammable vapors before scrapping the tank.

These are among the unpleasant situations in which contractors can find themselves if they are not aware of environmental, health, and safety issues. Regulatory agency enforcement policies are becoming increasingly aggressive, holding that ignorance is no excuse for noncompliance with regulations or standard industry practices.

The public demands a clean environment and a safe and toxic-free workplace. A 1989 New York Times survey found that over 85 percent of those polled agreed that "protecting the environment is so important that requirements and standards cannot be too high, and continuing environmental improvements must be made regardless of cost" (emphasis added).[1] Environmental issues affect not only the major oil and chemical companies, but also every company or business handling or working around any quantity of hazardous substances.

Smaller companies, including contractors, may be even more at risk because they seldom have access to internal staff specially trained in environmental, health, and safety regulations and procedures. The regulatory system addressing environmental issues has evolved in piecemeal fashion over the last 20 years and can be complicated and confusing to the non-environmental professional. "Bootstrapping" can lead to any of the unfortunate incidents mentioned above. In addition, if companies building or expanding facilities fail to obtain proper environmental permits, contractors can fall victim to significant delays.

This chapter discusses key environmental issues, situations, and procedures that may affect contractors, and provides topical information on regulatory framework and dynamics, transaction considerations, the property life cycle, and other issues that frequently confront contractors.

§ 13.2 Types of Environmental Risk

Environmental risk falls into four categories.

Residual risk. Residual risk is inherent in real property and improvements. If the operations or tenant(s) were gone, this type of risk is what would be left. Typical residual risk concerns include contaminated soil or groundwater, and asbestos in building materials. These risks can affect contractors during the normal course of site work and are the focus of most standard real estate assessments.

Ongoing risk. Ongoing risk relates to maintaining operations, and includes compliance with rules and regulations that govern environmental areas. Examples of relevant concerns are obtaining proper permits for an

---

[1] R. Suro, *Grass-Roots Groups Show Power Battling Pollution Close to Home,* N.Y. Times, July 2, 1989, at 1, 18.

air pollution exhaust and limiting discharges of industrial wastewater into the city sewer. Examples of ongoing risks for a contractor's operations include removing an asbestos-containing roof and storing contaminated soil.

Personal injury risk.   Personal injury risk involves injury or sickness from exposure to toxic substances, either suddenly (from releases) or nonsuddenly (from long-term chronic exposure). These injuries can be sustained by individuals on-site or by neighbors. For example, a contractor employee may sustain injuries if an underground tank containing solvents is discovered and the chemicals are handled improperly.

Public policy risk.   Public policy risk cannot be cited in specific regulations, but often has powerful effects nonetheless. For example, zoning laws can change and preclude the development of a previously encouraged industrial park. Agency officials and elected politicians may take stands on certain issues, such as pollution controls or land use, that affect contractor operations.

Public expectations and demands create these risks, while Congress and state and local officials create numerous regulations to address key issues. The result is a complicated and confusing tangle of regulations governing environmental (and health and safety) issues. These regulations, and the common law interpretations of them through various court cases, can affect contractors in many ways. Consequences of violations or excursions from procedures mandated by the regulations include significant fines and penalties, restrictions on, or denials of, projects or land use, work slowdown or shutdown or, in some instances, criminal prosecution and possible imprisonment.

Congress periodically reauthorizes federal statutes such as the Clean Air Act and Superfund, often with substantial changes. The United States Environmental Protection Agency (EPA) or state agencies can make substantial changes, or changes of interpretation, in implementing regulations. Common law interpretations also influence how environmental issues are handled.

§ 13.3   Regulatory Framework

Sections 13.4 through **13.11** examine several federal environmental statutes with selected state counterparts, in conjunction with managing a contracting, development, or real estate-related business. Typically, each regulation was passed in reaction to a specific need or situation. Regulatory amendments and policy implementations contribute to growing, complex requirements that have corresponding effects on the entire regulated community, including contractors. There is an abundant supply of tutorials outlining regulatory requirements and procedures. Rather than attempting to present a tutorial on one or more regulations, individual sections examine the dynamics of the regulations, the goal being to outline the history and dynamics of regulatory policies and their effect on contractors, and areas currently requiring attention.[2]

§ 13.4   —Clean Air Act

The Clean Air Act, passed in 1963 with major amendments in 1970 and 1977, was the first major federal statute of the environmental movement as it is known.[3] The Act responded to visual public images of billowing smokestacks and smoking automobile tailpipes by creating a set of *national ambient air quality standards* for a variety of relatively common "criteria" pollutants. The Act includes a regulatory framework requiring various levels of air pollution control technology, and especially targets industrial sources. Air pollution sources in areas that fail to meet the air quality standards are required to install additional pollution control systems.

The Act also includes provisions to identify hazardous air pollutants. The *national emissions standards for hazardous air pollutants* (NESHAPs) set strict and explicit requirements for handling these hazardous air pollutants and for preventing exposure of workers and the public. Initial public and Congressional expectations were that scores of chemicals eventually would be subject to this strict regulation. However, several years after the program went into effect, the EPA had designated less than a dozen chemicals as NESHAPs pollutants. Among them are asbestos, commonly used in building materials until 1979; benzene, a constituent of gasoline; and formaldehyde, a component of some building insulation.

As the more obvious pollution sources were dealt with, health risk evolved as a growing concern driving air pollution regulations. Air toxics are now regulated with increasing stringency. The Clean Air Act Amendments of 1990[4] identify 189 *hazardous air pollutants,* mandate a broad new

---

[2] For further information regarding hazardous waste and environmental issues, *see* Environmental Dispute Handbook: Liability and Claims (D. Carpenter etal. eds., John Wiley & Sons 1991); J. Stensvaag, Hazardous Waste Law and Practice (John Wiley & Sons 1990); Hazardous Waste Disposal and Underground Construction Law (Cushman & Ficken eds., John Wiley & Sons 1987).

[3] Clean Air Act Amendments of 1970, Pub. L. No. 91-604, 84 Stat. 1676; Clean Air Act Amendments of 1977, Pub. L. No. 95–95, 91 Stat. 685 (codified in scattered sections of 42 U.S.C.).

[4] Clean Air Act Amendments of 1990, Pub. L. No. 101-549, 104 Stat. 2399 (codified in 42 U.S.C. §§ 7401–7671q); *see generally* J. Stensvaag, Clean Air Act 1990 Amendments: Law and Practice (John Wiley & Sons 1991).

permitting system, and introduce additional economic incentives for pollution control. Many severely polluted areas already have invented creative ways of regulating and controlling air pollution. California (particularly Southern California) has been especially thorough and may provide a glimpse of a national regulatory scenario for air pollution control in years to come. The 1991 Air Quality Management Plan specifies that proposed development projects in the South Coast Air Quality Management District must consider the air impacts not only of the factory or business itself, but also of mobile air emission sources such as traffic. If contaminated soil is uncovered during the construction of a project, it must be covered with impermeable plastic to prevent volatile substances from polluting the air. A great deal of attention is paid to recordkeeping and documentation of all air pollution-causing materials. For example, businesses repairing airplanes or repainting vehicles must keep running inventories of paint used, and must determine the air emissions by performing material balances on business operations.

It is fair to say that air pollution is still an overriding concern for the nation's voters, regulators, and politicians. Contractors can expect air pollution issues to become more stringent and to affect widening areas of the contractors' operations.

§ 13.5 —Clean Water Act

The Federal Water Pollution Control Act (Clean Water Act) was passed in 1972,[5] also in the early days of the current environmental movement, when the nightly news brimmed with images of sudsy, polluted rivers and dead fish. Rumors circulated about the death of Lake Erie. Regulations required polluters discharging directly to the nation's waterways to treat their wastewater streams to prescribed standards. As these "point sources" installed their treatment systems, regulators turned their attention to municipal systems and to the problems associated with the industries that discharged to them. Municipalities were required to "lower the boom" on any industries discharging to the municipal system, requiring the industries to limit their discharges by treatment or process modification and subjecting them to hefty surcharges or fines for excessive discharge of pollutants.

After a series of notable oil spills into the nation's waterways, the Clean Water Act was amended to require that measures be taken to prevent the release of any type of oil into a waterway. A written *Spill Prevention,*

---

[5] Federal Water Pollution Control Act, Pub. L. No. 92-500, 86 Stat. 816 (1972) (codified in scattered sections of 33 U.S.C.); Clean Water Act of 1977, Pub. L. No. 95-217, 91 Stat. 1566 (codified at 33 U.S.C.); Water Quality Act of 1987, Pub. L. No. 100-4, 100 Stat. 7 (codified in scattered sections of 33 U.S.C.).

Control and Countermeasure Plan is now required for all facilities that store 1,320 gallons or more of oil aboveground, or more than 660 gallons in a single tank. *Oil* is broadly defined under the Act and includes frequently used materials such as diesel fuel, dust suppression oil, fuel oil, machine oil, and others.

Stormwater is one focus of current regulatory activity for water pollution. Rainwater that comes in contact with hazardous substances can entrain them, and subsequent flow off-site can cause pollution of waterways, sediments, and groundwater. These hazardous substances may include roofing compounds, oil stains in parking lots, pesticides used in agriculture, or any number of other materials. Contractors may have to include extensive systems in building projects to handle stormwater and to prevent run-on from neighboring facilities. A scheme for obtaining permits is now under way, with the possibility of controls later on.

Another evolving focus is pesticide contamination of surface water sediments or groundwater. Contractors may need to incorporate special handling procedures to prevent public exposure, at the discretion of local health officials, if the contractors are involved in projects in which land is converted from agricultural to other uses.

§ 13.6   —Resource Conservation and Recovery Act

In the wake of public outrage about Love Canal, Congress passed the Resource Conservation and Recovery Act (RCRA) in 1976[6] with the goal of establishing a system to regulate wastes "from cradle to grave." It took nearly four years for the EPA to develop regulations to categorize over 400 commercial chemicals as "hazardous" if discarded, and to designate over 100 waste streams as hazardous by definition.

Hazardous waste generators must characterize all waste streams for proper disposal, requiring that generators know the source, composition, and chemical and physical attributes of every waste. Generators must determine whether the wastes are RCRA hazardous wastes, hazardous either by being listed or by showing certain characteristics. *Listed* wastes are hazardous by definition if they originate from a source described in the regulations. Two examples are spent halogenated (chlorinated) solvents from degreasing operations and leaded gasoline tank bottoms from petroleum refining. *Characteristic* wastes are hazardous if they meet one of four indicators: (1) ignitability, (2) corrosivity (pH less than or equal to 2.0 or greater than or equal to 12.5), (3) reactivity (explosive, reacts violently on contact with water, or can emit toxic gases such as sulfide or cyanide), and

---

[6] Resource Conservation and Recovery Act, Pub. L. No. 94-580, 90 Stat. 2795 (1976) (codified in scattered sections of 42 U.S.C.).

(4) toxicity (the waste extract exceeds specified concentrations of any one of eight heavy metals, six pesticides, or 25 organic compounds). The test defining RCRA toxic wastes was changed in 1990 from the *extraction procedure* (EP) test to the *toxicity characteristic leaching procedure* (TCLP). RCRA toxic wastes now include many waste streams with organic constituents that were not previously regulated. Testing performed on many waste streams before May 1990 may not suffice for current standards. Regardless of whether wastes are determined to be hazardous or nonhazardous, the waste generator must maintain documentation supporting the waste classification.

RCRA also categorizes entities that handle hazardous wastes as generators, transporters, or treatment, storage, and disposal (TSD) facilities. Generators are given responsibilities for EPA notification, testing, ensuring proper management, and recordkeeping. *Generators* include anyone who arranges for the transportation or disposal of wastes; generators also retain ultimate permanent responsibility for those wastes, wherever their final disposal may be. Transporters are required to register with the EPA and meet specific requirements for training, vehicle inspection and maintenance, recordkeeping, and work practices. TSD facilities are confronted with onerous permitting provisions, including extensive written management procedures, descriptions of activities that will be required at partial or complete facility closure, and proof of financial stability to cover all closure costs. The retention of wastes classified as hazardous for over 90 days triggers the full brunt of TSD permitting requirements. This RCRA provision has great potential to impact contractors who may inadvertently exceed this 90-day limit.

In 1984, the Hazardous and Solid Waste Amendments (HSWA) added a broad scheme to regulate underground storage tanks (USTs).[7] Requirements include phased-in technical standards for USTs, annual leak-testing of tanks and associated piping systems, installation and maintenance of leak detection systems, proof of financial ability to cover closure costs, and prompt reporting requirements and remediation of any leaks. These stiff requirements are a major factor contributing to the decrease in the number of corner gas stations.

Other changes in RCRA have focused on:

1. Minimizing waste
2. Restricting land disposal
3. Regulating smaller quantity generators (currently 220 pounds per month in some states; zero threshold in others)

---

[7] Hazardous and Solid Waste Amendments of 1984, Pub. L. No. 98-616, 98 Stat. 3221 (codified in scattered sections of 42 U.S.C.).

4. Handling empty containers
5. Regulating recyclers
6. Controlling boilers and industrial furnaces that burn regulated hazardous wastes
7. Regulating medical and infectious wastes
8. Restricting or banning hazardous waste exports.

Contractors may encounter hazardous wastes in their normal operations, such as during facility renovations or demolition, in subsurface contamination, or in other ways. It is possible to unwittingly become a generator of hazardous waste by arranging for its disposal or by signing a shipping manifest. A contractor need only carry hazardous wastes such as certain contaminated soil on any public thoroughfare—even if only moving it from one portion of a construction site to another—to be considered a hazardous waste transporter. Similarly, a contractor need only store hazardous wastes such as used degreasing solvents, waste paints, or qualifying contaminated soil for more than 90 days to be considered a TSD facility. Fines authorized by hazardous waste regulations are normally $500 to $5,000 per day of violation. Enforcement agencies can prove violation easily through documentation. It is entirely the generator's responsibility to determine both the nature of wastes being handled and the inclusion of any materials that meet the defined criteria of hazardous wastes.

§ 13.7   —Comprehensive Environmental Response, Compensation, and Liability Act

Despite the fact that regulations had "closed the loop" on air, water, and hazardous waste pollution by 1976, the public remained concerned about addressing abandoned hazardous waste facilities. Cost estimates for cleanups varied, but all were in the hundreds of billions of dollars. Which sector would provide the expertise and funds to handle the cleanups?

Congress passed the Comprehensive Environmental Response, Compensation and Liability Act (CERCLA or Superfund)[8] in the waning days of 1980 to address the issue of paying for cleanup of abandoned hazardous waste sites. Superfund includes strict liability provisions, exposing any owner of real property to all the risks thereof, including soil and groundwater contamination, even if the contamination originated off-site or was left by former owners or operators. Provisions allow for cost recovery from any *owner or operator,* terms with broad definitions that can include any

---

[8] Comprehensive Environmental Response, Compensation and Liability Act, Pub. L. No. 96-510, 94 Stat. 2767 (1980) (codified at 42 U.S.C. §§ 9601–9675 (1988)).

person or entity involved with placement, movement, or release of hazardous substances on the property.

Superfund also includes joint and several liability provisions, meaning that if a generator sends hazardous waste to a disposal site that requires cleanup at a later date, the generator could be held liable for any portion of the overall cleanup liability at that disposal site. A generator of waste placed in a disposal site that later requires cleanup may be designated a *potentially responsible party* (PRP) for that site, meaning significant litigation costs and contributions to clean up. This liability can be proportionally far greater for generators than their original contribution to the contamination. This deep pocket provision could affect contractors if they generate (or agree to stand in for a project proponent as a "generator") contaminated soil that is placed in a landfill that later requires cleanup. The EPA can force private parties to perform cleanup or the private parties may handle cleanup themselves. Government-managed cleanups typically cost two to three times those managed by the private sector.

Superfund also creates requirements for reporting to government agencies any release of broadly defined or listed "hazardous substances" into the environment. This is an effort to prevent the occurrence of additional abandoned waste sites. Reporting thresholds are specified for all chemicals; for many, spills in excess of one pound require reporting. Some states, including Texas, have a zero threshold for many chemical spill reporting requirements. These reporting obligations apply not only to property owners or operators, but also apply universally. They can easily apply to contractors in their own operations, or from the disturbance of hazardous substances on a site.

The Superfund Amendments and Reauthorization Act of 1986 (SARA) made significant changes to the Superfund program and reauthorized Superfund for another five years. SARA adds more stringent cleanup standards, with the focus on permanent remedies and the use of applicable federal or state regulations. SARA also establishes a fund for remediating petroleum and chemical product underground storage tanks.[9]

Several states have created their own Superfunds to augment the federal effort. The latitude of some of these programs goes well beyond Superfund in the ability to order investigation or cleanup of sites.

There are now nearly 1,200 designated Superfund sites, but Superfund has been responsible for the cleanup of disappointingly few of these sites since 1980. Superfund trends include:

1. Broader circle of PRPs in an effort to pay for cleanups of landfills and regional contamination

---

[9] Superfund Amendments and Reauthorization Act of 1986, Pub. L. No. 99-499, 100 Stat. 1613 (codified in scattered sections of 42 U.S.C.).

2. Protracted, costly, and complicated litigation
3. Increased political pressure for making sites cleaner, faster
4. Smaller businesses becoming involved without realizing it through improper management or documentation of small quantities of hazardous wastes
5. Spiraling costs
6. Continued restrictions imposed by financial institutions or investment or development firms (see § 13.14).

§ 13.8   —State Property Transfer and Disclosure Requirements

In addition to the federal regulatory framework with which entities, including contractors, must be familiar are various state property transfer and disclosure statutory provisions that require compliance. Among them are the following examples.

Environmental Cleanup Responsibility Act.   New Jersey passed the Environmental Cleanup Responsibility Act (ECRA) in 1983 to expedite the process of cleaning up contaminated sites.[10] Before the close of escrow on an industrial property, the seller must prove to the state's satisfaction that the site is acceptably clean. Regulated properties include Standard Industrial Classification Codes 22–39 inclusive, 46–49 inclusive, and some 51 or 76 as designated. Any excessive contamination discovered must be cleaned up, or funds provided to the state's satisfaction, before the close of escrow. The state's supervisory role is funded entirely by the parties to the transaction. Several other states, such as Indiana, Illinois, and Connecticut, have laws with similar goals, but none are as rigorous as New Jersey's.

Superlien.   Some states have the right to impose a lien on a property or a business to recover costs incurred by the state for site remediation. This "superlien" takes precedence over all other liens, including mechanic's liens that may be imposed by contractors for any type of work on a property.

Disclosure.   In many states, the impact of hazardous substances on the property, whether "known or should have been known," must be disclosed. This requirement applies both to property sellers and to tenants vacating the premises.

---

[10] Environmental Cleanup Responsibility Act of 1987, N.J. Stat. Ann. § 13:1K-6.

§ 13.9 —Toxic Substances Control Act

Congress passed the Toxic Substances Control Act (TSCA) in 1976[11] to prevent new substances from entering the marketplace without previous testing for potential hazards. Because of political convenience and timeliness, TSCA also includes a broad scheme to regulate the use, management, and disposal of polychlorinated biphenyls (PCBs), a group of compounds used extensively since the 1950s in electrical insulating fluids for transformers, capacitors, and other applications. The need to regulate asbestos was addressed by passing the Asbestos Hazard Emergency Response Act (AHERA) as Title II of TSCA in conjunction with the TSCA reauthorization in 1986.[12] AHERA prescribes testing for asbestos in schools and provides a framework for training requirements for persons engaged in sampling, managing, maintaining, or abating asbestos or any asbestos-containing materials (ACM). Title III was added to TSCA in 1988 to address radon.[13] TSCA requirements affect contractors every time building equipment or materials are encountered that may contain PCBs or asbestos.

The EPA currently is taking a more proactive and comprehensive role in environmental management by encouraging pollution prevention, rather than by focusing exclusively on controlling pollution that has already been generated or by cleaning up orphaned dump sites. In early 1991, the EPA indicated its intention to use the broad authority granted to it under TSCA and SARA (see § 13.7) to enforce its policies. TSCA also directs the EPA to develop model construction standards and techniques for controlling radon levels in new buildings. The EPA can be expected to enforce provisions on all entities within its regulatory net, so contractors will need to stay abreast of developments in this effort.

§ 13.10 —Federal Insecticide, Fungicide, and Rodenticide Act

Congress passed the Federal Insecticide, Fungicide and Rodenticide Act (FIFRA) in 1947 and amended it in 1988[14] to regulate virtually all uses of insecticides, fungicides and rodenticides, including

---

[11] Toxic Substances Control Act, Pub. L. No. 94-469, 90 Stat. 2003 (1976) (codified at 15 U.S.C. §§ 2601–2629 (1988)).

[12] Asbestos Hazard Emergency Response Act of 1986 (TSCA Title II), Pub. L. No. 99-519, 100 Stat. 2970 (codified in scattered sections of 15 U.S.C.); 40 C.F.R. §§ 763.80–763.126.

[13] 15 U.S.C. §§ 2661–2671.

[14] Federal Insecticide, Fungicide, and Rodenticide Act of 1947, *as amended by* Pub. L. No. § 2(b), 92-516, 86 Stat. 973 (1972) (codified at 7 U.S.C. §§ 136–136y (1988)).

1. Product labeling
2. Product uses
3. Methods of application
4. Licensing of persons applying or managing these substances
5. Worker protection during application
6. Holding times after application and before reentry into areas.

Contractors can encounter various provisions of FIFRA by spraying weed control products as a service, even on a small scale; by authorizing employees to enter a building after it has been sprayed for termites or insects; and by engaging in rodent or vector control as a service to shopping center owners.

The management of pesticide-contaminated soils, sediment, or residue that may be encountered in the development of agricultural land is regulated by RCRA or by Superfund or by both.

§ 13.11   —Occupational Safety and Health Act

Congress passed the Occupational Safety and Health Act (OSH Act) in 1970.[15] The Occupational Safety and Health Administration (OSHA) oversees the various provisions of the Act. The OSHA organization should be no stranger to contractors. In addition to the familiar procedures for worker safety around construction equipment and machinery, OSHA enforces regulations on employee exposure to hazardous substances and hazardous wastes.

OSHA sets worker *permissible exposure limits* for hazardous materials, including a *time-weighted average* (TWA) for a maximum 8-hour exposure and a *short-term exposure limit* (STEL) for a maximum 15-minute exposure. Employers must determine and implement administrative or engineering controls to meet these limits.

The Occupational Safety and Health Administration is the supervisory and enforcement agency for the *hazard communication standard.* Manufacturers of any chemical must evaluate and convey hazards of that chemical to distributors and to end users. Distributors and employers must relay hazard information to their customers and employees, respectively, to fulfill worker right-to-know requirements. *Material safety data sheets* (MSDS) have been compiled by the manufacturer of each chemical, and should be received by the user before purchase or with the receipt of the chemical itself. MSDS also are prepared for proprietary mixtures or for substances

---

[15] Occupational Safety and Health Act of 1970, Pub. L. No. 91-596, 84 Stat. 1590 (codified in scattered sections of 29 U.S.C.).

with trade names. All employers, including contractors, must provide training to employees concerning hazardous chemicals and must have MSDS available to employees on request. *Written hazard communication programs* must be prepared to address all of these issues. Contractors also are responsible for ensuring proper hazard communication to subcontractors for all hazardous substances provided for use by subcontractors.

There are additional OSHA standards for exposure to hazardous substances and hazardous mixtures, as broadly defined. These standards apply to virtually any site cleanup in which regulatory agencies are involved, to response to spills or emergency releases, and to many site assessments when there is the possibility of encountering hazardous materials or contaminated soils. OSHA requirements include specific training, medical monitoring, personal protection, and controls to reduce hazards.

OSHA standards have generally remained consistent in recent years. Changes that may affect contractors would include the new designation of a hazardous chemical or the lowering of permissible exposure limits in response to new information obtained from scientific studies.

§ 13.12   Transaction Considerations

As a property, building, or business goes through its life cycle, environmental risks change because of modifications in operations, regulatory requirements, public expectations, and the involvement of various parties. Environmental risks are of special interest if they are being transferred to a new party, which can occur in transactions such as:

1. Purchase or sale of a property, with new principals and financial backers

2. Purchase or sale of a business, with new principals and financial backers

3. Creation of a new subsidiary or joint venture with additional capital from a new investor

4. Involvement of a trust, whether through creation, change in management, or disbursement

5. Purchase of insurance policies to cover losses from environmental damages

6. Refinancing of existing operations or properties

7. Transfer of financial packages to the secondary market

8. Acquisition of property by eminent domain.

A methodology of assessing environmental risks has evolved to address these risks and to enable the business community to make more enlightened decisions.

§ 13.13   —Phase 1, 2, and 3
Environmental Assessments

Environmental reviews must address diverse considerations such as previous site use, proximity to landfills and schoolyards, soil chemistry, and many other factors. These reviews differ from a comparatively straightforward civil engineering analysis of soil load-bearing capability or an economic analysis of benefits presented by freeway access. To obtain reasonable information with limited effort, environmental investigations are performed in phases. Environmental reviews can include up to three phases, each phase summarized neatly in one word: research, test, and cleanup.

Phase 1 Research

Phase 1 investigations are requested as a fairly standard practice for any transaction of industrial and certain commercial real properties. Phase 1 reports assess several factors to determine the residual risk of a property:

1. Current and previous operations
2. Chemicals used on-site, and the practices used to manage the chemicals
3. Regulatory or enforcement activities
4. Possible effects of neighboring sites.

   This information is obtained by compiling research from a variety of sources, including site inspection, agency lists, building records, aerial photographs, and environmental permits.
   An experienced professional can evaluate these factors to highlight areas of known or potential problems or risks. Areas of possible concern could include the following situations:

1. Underground tanks have been removed but the status of remaining soil is uncertain
2. The facility is near a landfill known to have problems with contaminant migration
3. Previous tenants left various unused, outdated chemicals on-site
4. Structural materials may contain asbestos
5. A previous tenant is known to have been cited for improperly storing hazardous materials, but the residual impact to the property is unknown.

Phase 2 Testing

Phase 2 investigations involve physical testing of some kind and are generally undertaken to address known or potential problem areas identified in

Phase 1 research work. Phase 2 investigations may be initiated if required by law or regulation, agreed upon in terms of a contract, or at any time by an owner or operator seeking additional information.

Specific media that can be physically tested include soil (to any depth), soil vapor, groundwater, surface water, surface water sediment, drinking water supply, indoor air, ambient air, dust, building materials, and residues. Analytical parameters are selected to address the item(s) of concern. Sampling procedures must be followed and documented carefully; physical samples, once taken, have a specified shelf life or holding time and, if not analyzed promptly, may become worthless.

Perhaps the most important part of any Phase 2 investigation is the determination of a project's goals, scope, schedule, and budget. All four items must be compatible for a successful project. Constraints on any one of these can alter the project outcome significantly. An example of a compatible goal, scope, schedule, and budget follows:

1. Goal: determine the likelihood of residual contamination from a waste oil tank that was removed from a known location six years ago.
2. Scope: (a) install five soil borings to a depth of 30 feet; (b) take a total of 30 soil samples; (c) submit all soil samples for analysis of total petroleum hydrocarbons (general indicator for oil) and PCBs (possible contaminant to oil with strict requirements for cleanup); and (d) compile complete written report.
3. Schedule: complete project in eight weeks.
4. Budget: authorized up to $50,000.

As mentioned, if constraints are placed on any one aspect, the other aspects are affected. For example, if a budget of only $20,000 is authorized, then perhaps only selected soil samples are analyzed and conclusions may be less certain. If the constraint is a restriction of access to the site, fewer borings may be possible; this reduces the scope and budget and, again, narrows the assurance provided by any conclusions. Alternatively, if the project must be completed in 17 days, cost surcharges may be required for drillers, laboratories, and consultants.

Contractors generally are aware that field activities involve many uncertainties and can present challenges or impossibilities that affect costs or the overall viability of a project. Problems relating to the environmental project proposed above could include any of the following:

1. Presence of underground utilities, complicating proper placement of soil borings
2. Limited access because of structures or overhead wires
3. Permitting requirements for field activities

4.   Agency inspections or requirements during field activities
5.   Improper or incomplete documentation on required OSHA training for hazardous waste workers
6.   Discovery of contaminants, odors, or physical conditions not anticipated before commencement of field activities.

Phase 3 Cleanup

Phase 3 projects are instigated to remediate environmental contamination or to install preventive systems. Phase 3 projects are customized to each situation and require specific information on the following factors:

1.   Type(s) of contamination
2.   Extent of contamination
3.   Location of contamination (for example, whether impact has been on soil or on groundwater)
4.   Satisfactory levels for cleanup, whether established by regulations, informal discussions with agencies, on advice from counsel or consultants, or agreed upon in contract
5.   Appropriate technologies.

Satisfactory levels for cleanup should be understood well before any remediation activity begins.

The selection of appropriate remediation technology becomes especially challenging when:

1.   More than one contaminant is present, and treatment for both contaminants requires more than one treatment method
2.   Access to subsurface contamination is limited by structures, equipment, or traffic patterns on-site
3.   Contamination has migrated off-site
4.   Contamination originated from off-site.

Preventive measures may be selected when hazardous materials do not present an imminent hazard. An example of a preventive measure is a vapor barrier or passive vapor venting system for a building located in a risk area for subsurface accumulation of methane.

Contractors should be aware that many companies and consulting firms provide environmental assessment and remediation services. An experienced practitioner or consultant can focus very quickly on risks associated with technical, management, or potential third-party claims issues. An experienced professional will also design an overall program in phases so that only information specific to relevant risks is reviewed. This minimizes the risk of involvement in irrelevant contamination issues and unnecessary research projects. Practitioners and consultants vary considerably in experience, management philosophy, and technical capabilities. Contractors procuring environmental services or working with environmental consultants should invest the time and effort in an in-depth interview to establish confidence that the services rendered will be proficient, equitable, and appropriate to the need.

§ 13.14   —Lender Liability

Transactions involve the transfer of environmental risk along with the assets in question. All parties should have an interest in the accurate assessment of the risks and a reasonable and clearly-defined mechanism for risk apportionment. *Buyers* want to avoid acquiring liabilities associated with contamination. *Sellers* want to document preexisting conditions to minimize their exposure after the sale. *Brokers* want to keep their clients satisfied and want to avoid issues of nondisclosure. *Environmental agencies* want opportunities to prescribe a cleaner environment. *Municipalities and redevelopment agencies* want to avoid involvement in hazardous or environmentally-risky sites. *Developers* want to avoid excessive site design and permitting costs if environmental considerations make projects unfeasible. *Investors and financial institutions* want to determine the exposure of their own assets to environmental risks. *Contractors* want to avoid liabilities created by unknowingly generating or managing hazardous wastes or by excessive workplace exposure by employees.

Although Superfund provides for exemptions from environmental liabilities for secured creditors, the exact conditions for the exemptions have not been specified clearly. Lenders have been held liable for environmental costs through a variety of theories including the following:

1. Actual holding of title so that an investment constituted ownership
2. Taking ownership through foreclosure
3. Becoming involved sufficiently in site activities through loan policing or trust management so as to be considered an operator
4. Merely having the option to exercise the right to perform environmental inspections or make environmental recommendations.[16]

As a result, investors and financial institutions have taken the lead in determining the course of environmental investigations. There have been a number of proposals from the EPA and from Congress to define more

---

[16] *See* 42 U.S.C. § 9601(20)(A).

succinctly the secured lender exemption and to provide lenders with a modicum of relief. Contractors can look forward to a heightened awareness of environmental issues on the part of financial institutions. Lender involvement may mean initiation of several types of project requirements:

1. Phase 1 environmental assessment report
2. *New* Phase 1 environmental assessment report if the existing report is outdated
3. Disclosure of any and all documentation or records regarding environmental issues and the condition of the secured interest (property or otherwise)
4. Physical sampling and testing to determine the presence of asbestos
5. Other physical sampling and testing programs
6. Requirement to set aside sufficient escrow funds to address contamination remediation, with appropriate contingencies
7. Periodic inspections of site operations during the life of the loan to determine risks of environmental impact
8. Environmental agency documentation, when available, of acceptable site condition or remediation activities.

Lender liability is dynamic with regard to applicable regulations, agency policy statements, and evolving case law. Lender policies on environmental issues vary considerably among institutions and may be modified frequently to reflect new considerations. If the involvement of a lending institution is anticipated on any project, it is prudent to contact all possible lending sources ahead of time to obtain policies or requirements on environmental issues so that no critical issues are overlooked.

The proper interpretation of technical information into terms of risk, certainty, anticipated expenditure timing, and other terms of concern to lenders, is an important factor in smooth lender review of projects. Contractors should be aware that outside resources who specialize in lender management and consulting can provide benefits to project management, cost tracking and allocations, and expedited project scheduling.[17]

§ 13.15 —Innocent Landowner

Superfund created sweeping liability for company owners and operators, real estate investors, bankers, contractors, municipalities, and other entities. As a consequence, small businesses, such as one selling luggage out of a former gas station, were among those who found themselves liable for

---

[17] *See generally* O.T. Smith, Environmental Lender Liability (John Wiley & Sons 1991).

contamination. In 1986, amendments to Superfund (SARA) attempted to correct certain inequities by creating an "innocent landowner" clause, whereby purchasers of real property could be excused from financial responsibility for cleanups provided they had been duly diligent in performing investigations before acquisition. A buyer contemplating the purchase of a former gas station would be expected to assess the possible presence of fuels, oil, or other similar contamination. If the purchaser were duly diligent in investigating, and metal plating wastes that had no reason to be suspected were uncovered during site grading, the new owner may be able to defer cleanup costs to Superfund or to other government funding sources.

The innocent landowner clause has yet to be tested in court. Some relief also is provided to parties who inherit contaminated property. The standards for "due diligence" are not contained in regulatory guidelines and would be expected to vary with previous property use.

§ 13.16   Construction and the Property Life Cycle

The *property life cycle* begins when a developer improves raw or previously agricultural land. As the property matures, the land use and physical improvements often change. The life cycle ends with abandonment, demolition and site disposition; the cycle then may begin anew.

Unimproved, active, inactive, closed, and divested sites all can represent liabilities. Past operating practices, although commonly accepted and legal at the time, can impact the site or surrounding environment and may eventually require remediation. Current landowners or operators can be held liable for remediation if the past owners are not financially able or if clear allocation of environmental liability was not established at the time of transfer. The determination of the potential risks, effective management of the risks, and allocation of the appropriate resources can make the difference between profitable enterprises and unprofitable operations with major negative financial impacts.

Contractors conduct several activities at various stages of the property life cycle that often have hazardous waste and environmental impacts. Among the activities are developing raw land, expanding or modifying an existing facility, or demolishing a facility or razing a site for disposition. Hazardous waste and environmental issues differ depending on the types of contractor activities and the maturity of the property or its improvements. These issues impact land use, residual waste management, building design and operation, and the public image of both the contractor and the property user. At every stage, the contractor is exposed to the risk of unwanted involvement with environmental or worker health liabilities, or the risk of protracted work delays because of improper planning or management of environmental issues. Each stage of the property life cycle is discussed in §§ 13.17 through 13.19.

§ 13.17   —Developing Raw Land

Even undeveloped land can present liabilities that can hinder or halt site development if not managed properly. As at any transaction stage, a project proponent should conduct environmental due diligence studies to identify pending or latent liabilities. These studies are critical for the owner, operator, purchaser, or other proponent to identify potential deal killers or major expenditures. The level of detail in the due diligence review varies with the types of proposed operations and the sensitivity of the surrounding area.

Environmental Considerations

Environmental considerations of special interest on raw or previously agricultural land include hidden contamination originating off-site, pesticide residues, radon, wetlands, sensitive or endangered species, protected surface water or groundwater sources, and unauthorized dumping.

A Phase 1 site assessment to identify and evaluate environmental liabilities on raw or previously agricultural land may focus on the following list of factors:

1. Site tour to assess the condition of the property
2. Discussion with past property owner(s), if possible
3. Review of historical aerial photos and the property chain-of-title
4. Evidence of unauthorized dumping
5. Site security, current and historical
6. Stressed vegetation
7. Surface drainage patterns
8. Archaeological or historical designations
9. Underground oil or gas pipelines
10. Previous oil and gas exploration activity, including drilling mud disposal and the presence of abandoned wells
11. Environmental regulatory agency concerns with considerations regarding regional contamination
12. Endangered species
13. Review of neighboring operations for potential impacts on the site.

A Phase 2 site investigation may be undertaken to establish baseline physical property conditions or to further delineate any contamination or other uncertainties identified in Phase 1. Some Phase 2 site investigation activities that may be appropriate at this stage are the following:

1. Shallow soil sampling or soil borings
2. Surface water sampling

3. Sediment sampling
4. Groundwater sampling
5. Inventory of residual wastes from unauthorized dumping, if any
6. Geophysical survey for underground utilities
7. Site survey
8. Special site inspections for endangered species, botanical inventories, or archaeological considerations
9. Legal review to determine the extent of protection provided by indemnifications, warranties, and representations or other language in sales agreements.

Phase 3 remedial actions are less common on unimproved property than on developed property. Nonetheless, remedial actions or changes to proposed projects may be required as a result of Phase 2 findings. These corrections might include:

1. Removal of pesticide-contaminated stream sediment
2. Removal of drilling muds
3. Proper reabandonment of oil wells
4. Project redesign to accommodate site-specific or regionally-sensitive species or archaeological remains.

Project proponents also should be aware that the National Environmental Policy Act (NEPA)[18] and state counterparts frequently apply to proposed projects on unimproved property. NEPA provisions may require *environmental impact reports* (EIRs) to evaluate the environmental impacts in very broad terms. The impacts include possible effects on flora, fauna, traffic, noise, appearance, and overall community standards of living. EIRs have long lead times and can present considerable delays while the project undergoes review by regional development agencies, city councils, or citizens groups. Generally, EIRs are prepared by companies or professionals with differing areas of expertise than those discussed throughout this chapter.

Project Implementation

If the environmental due diligence effort does not identify "deal killers," and the project is determined to be worth pursuing, the next step is for the project proponent to identify and apply for any needed environmental permits and registrations for the project itself. Permits are often a critical

---

[18] National Environmental Policy Act of 1969, *as amended by* Pub. L. No. 94-52, §§ 2, 3, 89 Stat. 258 (1975) and Pub. L. No. 94-83, 89 Stat. 424 (1975) (codified in scattered sections of 42 U.S.C.).

path item and require lead time before construction or other site activities begin. Federal, state, and local agencies all can be involved in the permitting process, depending on the site location and the type of project proposed. Some activities requiring permits are air emissions, wastewater discharge (including stormwater runoff), discharge to sewers, solid or hazardous waste management, or the use of aboveground and underground storage tanks. As one might expect, chemical plants may require years to complete the permitting process. In addition, however, distribution centers, office buildings, and other relatively benign facilities may require one or more environmental permits.

Regulations are especially strict and require that air permits be obtained before construction can begin. The air emissions permit process is more complex in areas that fail to meet the national ambient air quality standards (nonattainment areas). The key pollutants of concern in these nonattainment areas are volatile organic compounds (VOCs), particulates, sulfur dioxide, carbon monoxide, and nitrogen oxides. The permitting of toxic air contaminant emissions is also more stringent today than in the past. Failure to obtain proper air permits for all equipment for the proposed project that will eventually be regulated may bring construction to a standstill, even in very early phases of site grading.

Wastewater permits may also be a prerequisite if the wastewater to be generated by the project will be discharged to a sensitive (or already over-polluted) waterway, or to a municipal treatment plant already strained to capacity.

Other permit applications and registrations should be applied for before construction, but usually do not pose an imminent threat of construction activity shutdown. UST registrations and RCRA hazardous waste permits must be approved and received before start-up of operations. If permits are not in hand early, however, agencies could change requirements, thus affecting project design and construction, and causing work slowdowns.

Public opinion influences the successful outcome of environmental permit applications. If the site operations are controversial or can affect the community, project proponents should begin working with community leaders early in the planning process to determine specific public concerns. Generally, close contact with the community throughout the planning, permitting, and construction processes can make the project run more smoothly.

Contractor Implications

Before beginning fieldwork, a contractor should review proposed site activities and develop environmental contingency plans to address the management of materials handled during construction or remediation. Plans should cover contingencies for spills, physical risks, and health risks from toxic or hazardous materials or wastes. If environmental permits are required for the construction activity, environmental contingency plans may have to be in written form. Regulations in some jurisdictions simply specify a general performance standard prohibiting pollution.

Spill contingencies.   Spill contingency planning should include a review of applicable regulations and the installation of the proper containment berms or dikes before materials arrive at the site. Spill contingency procedures also should address materials handling and containment strategies for day-to-day activities. For example, diesel fuel transfers from a delivery truck into a portable tank at the construction site should be conducted in a way to minimize the impact of any spills. The contractor also should plan to provide the equipment, capability, and employee training to respond properly if any materials are mismanaged or spilled.

Physical risks.   If site activities involve physical risks, such as welding, lasers, noise, or dangerous equipment, the contractor should train employees to recognize these hazards and abide by appropriate safety and inspection procedures. Once operations begin, the contractor should hold regular safety meetings and encourage employees to conduct their own inspections regularly. The safety procedures should follow applicable OSHA regulations, industry guidelines, and good operating practices to protect employee health and safety.

Health risks.   If toxic or hazardous materials will be used, contractors should develop plans to address areas including fire prevention, materials tracking, container labeling, worker exposure, air emissions, and management of hazardous wastes.

Procedures should follow guidelines from OSHA, RCRA, local codes or ordinances, or other appropriate industry standards. Contractors should be aware that they are responsible for the health and safety provisions of any subcontractors under their domain. If normal subcontractor safety procedures are insufficient, the contractor may elect to perform additional general and site-specific training or to seek other qualified subcontractors. If performing as a subcontractor, the contractor should expect and demand appropriate communication and training with regard to potential environmental or health hazards on the site.

§ 13.18   —Expanding or Modifying an
Existing Facility

The expansion or modification of an existing facility can present liabilities because of the impact from preexisting operations or the nature of proposed activities. Plant changes involving modifications to existing equipment, for example, can change the nature or amount of emissions to the environment or may pose new risks to workers during construction or after modification. Physical plant expansion can impact the environment and the local population with effects that include air emissions, stormwater runoff, emergency evacuation routes, and noise.

Environmental Considerations

Project proponents generally conduct environmental due diligence assessments before facility expansion or modification to minimize the environmental impacts and liabilities. Environmental due diligence studies at this stage of the property life cycle can indicate whether past practices have resulted in contamination or whether special precautions must be taken in project design or construction as a result of preexisting conditions. Environmental due diligence for expansions or modifications may include one or more phases as described in § **13.13**.

Phase 1 site assessments usually are performed for site modification or expansion. Special emphasis may be placed on the following factors:

1. Review of the potential environmental impact to soil or groundwater from existing operations
2. Review of the potential environmental impact to soil or groundwater from any known previous operations
3. Changes in land use that may trigger different environmental standards
4. Changes in regulatory standards for cleanup levels that may resurrect previously "completed" site remediation
5. Asbestos that may be disturbed during construction
6. Discussions with federal, state, and local environmental agency officials to review the overall compliance history of site operations.

Phase 2 site investigations become more important at the expansion or modification stage of the property life cycle, serving as baseline studies to document conditions at the time of expansion, reducing the possibility of future enforcement problems. This benchmarking is especially important if a new owner or operator is entering the picture. It is also critical when the proposed project will continue to use hazardous materials on the site, creating the possibility of commingling liability for soil or groundwater contamination. Phase 2 investigations that might be especially appropriate at the expansion/modification stage of the property life cycle could include (1) soil gas survey, (2) soil samples from shallow subsurface or deeper borings, (3) groundwater samples, (4) sampling of building materials for asbestos, and (5) geophysical surveys for underground utility lines.

Phase 3 site remediation projects may be required before, or in conjunction with, site expansion or modification. If the presence of residual materials or site contamination is identified in Phase 2, the proper allocation of responsibilities, risk, and liabilities is critical. Selection of the appropriate remediation technologies is a factor in implementing Phase 3 projects and must consider aspects of the project that include

1. The chemical nature of the contaminant
2. The lateral and vertical extent of contamination
3. Whether soil or groundwater has been impacted
4. Whether site process operations will continue throughout construction activities
5. The ease of obtaining permits from relevant environmental agencies.

Some remediation technologies, such as the excavation of soil contaminated with heavy metals, are disruptive to existing site operations and construction activities. Other technologies, such as vapor extraction of dry cleaning solvents from soil, may be installed and operated with very little disruption of continuing operations.

Project Implementation

Changes to an existing facility can alter the nature or amount of air emissions, wastewater discharges, and solid or hazardous waste generation. If the environmental due diligence does not identify project killers, the project proponent must determine if permits are needed and apply for them. As in the development of raw land, permits are often a critical path item and require considerable lead time before construction or modification can begin.

Regulations for air permit modifications are especially explicit in requiring the completion of all aspects of permit applications and approval *before* building or structure modification can begin, even at existing facilities. The expansion of an existing facility may trigger more stringent controls for the entire plant, particularly in air nonattainment areas, to offset the proposed expansion. As discussed in § 13.17, permits for changes in project wastewater discharges may also be a critical path item in locations with receiving streams or municipal treatment plants that have limited capacities for additional pollutant loading from wastewater.

If hazardous substances will be disturbed during site modification activities, regulatory agencies may require the submittal of written plans detailing the exact procedures and plans for the activities. The regulators may elect to send agency inspectors to observe the activities and verify compliance with the written plan. For example, local agency representatives may take soil samples during a contaminated soil cleanup to verify that all designated contaminated soils are being removed. Agency inspectors may wish to observe the removal of asbestos-containing materials to verify that appropriate procedures are being followed to prevent fibers from becoming airborne and escaping into the ambient atmosphere. The failure to submit proper notifications and plans may expose the project proponent or contractor to fines, or to an excessive burden of proof in verifying that proper procedures were followed during the course of the project.

Contractor Implications

As with development of raw land, if site activities during construction involve physical risks such as welding, lasers, noise, or dangerous equipment, the contractor must train employees to recognize risks and implement safety procedures to ensure employee safety and health. If employees will handle toxic or hazardous materials or wastes, contractors should develop safety and material handling procedures, and maintain inspection logs, as described in § **13.17**.

If the contractor generates waste during site expansions or modifications, the contractor must determine whether the wastes are hazardous or non-hazardous and handle them accordingly. Generally, hazardous waste disposal is more tightly regulated than nonhazardous waste disposal. RCRA sets specific requirements for hazardous waste generation, handling, and disposal. Rules and regulations require permits and registrations for some contractor activities and allow the disposal of hazardous wastes only in permitted facilities, which are not as plentiful as municipal waste facilities.

If sites are to be expanded or modified while existing facilities continue to operate, contractors must pay special attention to the compatibility of their own operations with ongoing site activities. Ongoing process activities may present any of the following situations that demand extra precautions on the part of a contractor:

1. Generation of air emissions or fumes that may impact the health of contractor workers
2. Generation of fumes that may cause explosions or fires if welding or other flames are used nearby
3. Management of hazardous substances that require special precautions to avoid fire, spills, or releases
4. Site configurations that require special care for contractor access or egress

5. Normal process hazards that require all personnel at the facility to use safety glasses or other additional safety equipment

6. Specific evacuation procedures for emergencies or drills.

Environmental, health, and safety emergencies can occur during expansions and modifications, so contractors should develop appropriate emergency, contingency, and spill plans. Effective emergency response training can often make the difference between a minor and a major incident, and is required by some environmental permits. Contractors should review release reporting requirements because they can differ depending on the type and circumstances of a release. Adequate preparation for emergencies can minimize environmental liabilities. Emergency responders need to know the types of operations and materials they might encounter. The contractor should also develop lists of emergency equipment, cleanup contractors, transporters, and disposal sites, and conduct periodic drills with employees.

§ 13.19   —Demolition, Razing, and Site Disposition

At the end of the property life cycle, the contractor often is involved in demolition or razing to prepare for site disposition. Environmental due diligence is once again required at this stage of the property life cycle.

Environmental Considerations

Ideally, environmental due diligence is performed while the facility is still in operation. Phase 1 and 2 activities depend heavily on the firsthand observations by an environmental specialist of process operations, materials management, and environmental management systems. The availability of facility personnel who are familiar with current and previous operations and the identity of chemicals used contribute significantly to the proper due diligence investigation. All too often, however, environmental investigations are not initiated until after operations have ceased. Environmental investigators are left to guess at important information such as the location and types of equipment, chemicals, and procedures used for the previous removal of USTs.

Demolition or razing activities have many of the same concerns as those for new construction, expansion, or modification. In addition, these activities can expose toxic or hazardous wastes or materials that would otherwise not be a concern. Some materials, such as asbestos, do not meet today's construction and environmental standards and have special handling and disposal requirements. Contractors should know if these materials are present before starting demolition, and should conduct any required inspections, sampling, and testing of the building components or wastes. Prudent management reduces liability, positively affects the property value, and reduces waste management costs.

Phase 1 assessments at the demolition/disposition phase of the property life cycle include special consideration of the following issues:

1. Presence of asbestos-containing materials in portions of the building to be razed
2. Documentation of previous site investigations or tank removals
3. Presence of in-ground tanks, sumps, oil/water separators, clarifiers, or floor drains that may trigger regulatory requirements for abandonment
4. Facility plans for discontinuing operations and disposing of leftover materials and other residual wastes.

Phase 2 investigations at this stage of the property life cycle are similar to those for an expansion/modification project. The testing of building materials for asbestos and of electrical equipment for PCBs would be expected to be particularly aggressive. Leftover materials, tank bottoms, and other residual wastes would also require testing (see § 13.20). Some residuals become hazardous waste after a specified period.

Phase 3 remediation programs include those efforts expected during expansion/modification. Removal or remediation of residual wastes can be a major concern at this time.

§ 13.20   Other Issues That May Affect Contractors

Contractors may encounter many issues during their involvement on various projects. Common factors of concern include:

1. Asbestos
2. PCBs
3. Leftover raw materials and other residual wastes
4. USTs, sumps, clarifiers, or oil/water separators
5. Active or inactive waste disposal sites
6. Soil and groundwater contamination
7. Importation or disposal of fill or rubble.

Each of these issues is discussed in more detail in §§ 13.21 through 13.27. Table 13–1 provides a timeline overview of when these issues can arise and require assessment or management during the property life cycle.

Table 13–1

Overview of Potential Contractor Environmental Concerns

Environmental Issue	Stage of Property Life Cycle		
	Unimproved Land	Expansion/ Modification	Demolition/ Disposition
Asbestos	no	yes	important
PCBs	no	possibly	yes
Leftover materials residual wastes	no	yes	important
UST, clarifier, oil/ water separator	no	yes	important
Waste disposal sites	unauthorized dumping	yes	yes
Soil/goundwater contamination	possibly	yes	yes
Fill import or rubble disposal	yes—fill	possibly	yes

§ 13.21   —Presence of Asbestos

Inhalation of asbestos poses the hazard of asbestosis or mesothelioma, diseases provoked by small asbestos fibers lodging in the lungs and causing the formation of scar tissue, sharply reducing lung capacity. Strict regulations have been adopted to prevent worker exposure to asbestos and to prevent asbestos from becoming airborne through disintegration of building materials or improper removal or demolition. The term *friable* describes asbestos that can be crushed into a powdery form (the small fibers most susceptible to lodging in lung tissue).

The presence of asbestos qualifies many construction materials as *asbestos containing materials* (ACM), and triggers a host of regulatory, procedural, and documentation requirements. Asbestos was introduced as a component of some building materials as early as the 1920s and was in widespread use by the 1950s. ACM may be present in any of the following building materials if they were installed before 1979:

1. Ceiling tile
2. Floor tile, tile backing, or tile adhesive
3. Spray-on "cottage cheese" acoustical ceilings
4. Thermal insulation on pipes, boilers, or refrigerators
5. Roofing or flashing materials

6. Fire doors
7. Transite TM siding.

Federal regulations require the proper removal of asbestos before any demolition or renovation activities that would break up the material. Some asbestos regulatory requirements that apply to contractors include (1) worker and agency notification, (2) inspector training and certification, (3) worker training, (4) personnel protection and monitoring, and (5) ACM-waste handling, packaging, labeling, and disposal.

Regulations require a written asbestos removal plan and notice to the EPA and other appropriate agencies before removal. Contractors must ensure the use of protective clothing and equipment for all workers engaged in abatement. They also must use proper work area isolation procedures and monitor the ambient area for airborne asbestos during abatement. In addition, contractors must properly handle, package, label, and dispose of asbestoscontaining materials, including workers' discarded protective clothing suits and respirators. ACM wastes must be disposed of in approved waste disposal facilities. State and local standards may be even more strict than federal standards for issues such as worker protection, airborne fiber limits, definitions of ACM, or notification procedures to regulatory agencies or to the public.[19]

§ 13.22   —Management of PCBs

In a quirk of regulatory framework, PCBs are not regulated by RCRA as hazardous wastes, but are strictly regulated under TSCA (see § 13.9). PCBs typically are found in hydraulic fluids and older electrical equipment, such as transformers and capacitors. If electrical transformers supplying a facility are located off-site and are owned by a local utility, there is minimal concern to the project proponent for PCB management regulations. PCBs do present troublesome environmental liabilities in the event of a fire or explosion of a PCB-containing electrical component. Heavy smoke from such a fire will contact and contaminate building materials and contents, rendering all damaged materials as potentially hazardous wastes. This scenario actually occurred shortly after a brand new state office building was opened in Binghamton, New York. Employees were forced to evacuate the premises, including all furniture, files, and personal effects, and were prevented from reentry for several years.

PCBs also may be encountered in waste oils. Oil recycling companies did not segregate various waste oil streams before PCBs were known to be a hazard. This resulted in the commingling of PCB-laden transformer oils

---

[19] See 40 C.F.R. §§ 763.80–763.126; see also Cal. Health & Safety Code, div. 20, ch. 10.4, § 25,915; South Coast Air Quality Management Dist. (Cal.) R. 1403.

with other oils for reprocessing and distribution to customers as reclaimed oils. Discovery of waste oil tanks, spills, or impact to soil or groundwater (dating from the 1970s or before) during the course of a project also raises the concern for the presence of PCBs.

In addition, PCBs are known to have been used in fluorescent lighting ballasts. Since PCBs were removed from the market in 1978, alternate materials have been used, and fluorescent lights are labeled as being non-PCB. If large numbers of fluorescent lights are slated for removal during a facility modification or demolition, PCB management requirements may apply.

Knowledge of the PCB status of electrical equipment through site audits or by inventory or documentation from the local utility can help to minimize liabilities in case of a spill or fire. PCB regulations could apply during site modification or demolition for the use, storage, or disposal of PCBs or PCB-containing items. Contractors should also watch out for unlabeled electrical equipment containing liquids, especially during the demolition/remodeling portion of the property life cycle. Federal standards under TSCA stipulate that materials containing PCBs in concentrations of 500 parts per million (ppm) or greater must be incinerated; 50 to 500 ppm may be landfilled; and less than 50 ppm generally is not regulated. State standards in California require incineration of materials in excess of 50 ppm PCBs.

§ 13.23   —Leftover Materials and Other Residual Wastes

Leftover materials and other residual wastes may be encountered as any of the following:

1. Unusable process raw materials
2. Unusable laboratory chemicals
3. "Last batch" wastes from discontinued processes or operations
4. Tank bottom sludge
5. Condensate from steam cleaning
6. Miscellaneous containers of cleaners or maintenance materials.

Cleaning residues may be encountered in facility modification or expansion. The issue of leftover materials is encountered most frequently, however, at a facility shutdown or at property demolition or redeployment.

Project proponents all too frequently overlook the fact that, upon discontinuation of operations, small quantities of many different types of materials that formerly had commercial value may become designated as "wastes." If containers are unlabeled, or if facility personnel are unavailable to describe the origins of waste streams, then expensive full-spectrum analytical characterization may be required. Project proponents should undertake a thorough inventory of chemicals and hazardous substances well before operational shutdown, with a focus on the nonroutine items mentioned above.

Disposal options for these materials, as with all wastes, vary. Ideally, raw materials no longer suitable for use on the site may be returned to the vendor, or sold for recycling or reclamation. Waste materials with sufficient heat content may be suitable for use as a supplemental fuel in an approved boiler or industrial furnace. The beneficial reuse of leftover materials (and the corresponding economic benefit) depends on the proper identification and segregation of the materials; the unintentional commingling of reusable materials with wastes can result in additional expense for disposal of the entire inventory.

Treating hazardous wastes to render them less hazardous or nonhazardous is also possible, but may fit the definition of "treatment" under RCRA and expose the project proponent or contractor to unwanted permitting requirements or liabilities. Some specialized contractors have obtained appropriate permits from regulatory agencies to perform chemical treatment, fixation, lab-packing, or soil treatment on-site. In other instances, the only answer may be to remove materials for proper off-site disposal.

RCRA regulations for hazardous waste treatment, storage, and disposal (see § 13.6) are becoming increasingly stringent. Many wastes must now be treated in some form before placement into any landfill. Hazardous "liquids," including liquid-containing materials such as sludges, may not be placed directly into landfills. Taxing schemes have been imposed in many jurisdictions to provide market-based incentives away from landfill disposal and toward recycling, reclamation, or reuse.

Contractors involved in facility demolition or redeployment should be assured that the project proponents have adequate plans in place to properly identify and dispose of residual wastes. The contractor should understand the full liability scheme of generating, owning, or disposing of hazardous wastes, and avoid doing "favors" that consist of accepting wastes from project proponents. If contractors will be working with or adjacent to any of these materials, they should incorporate appropriate health and safety provisions to protect their own workers and to prevent the release of any of the materials into the environment. Contractors should also implement their own security provisions to avoid the unauthorized placement of hazardous materials into dumpsters or roll-off boxes, or unsolicited "gifts" of leftover hazardous materials that may require costly disposal.

§ 13.24   —Underground Storage Tanks

Many formerly operating sites have USTs that are removed as site operations change or cease. Other USTs previously unknown to any site operator may be discovered during site activities or closure. Leaks from USTs or associated piping systems, or overflow from UST filling, can contaminate the soils or groundwater, with potential off-site impacts. Contractors removing USTs should be aware that regulations require advance notification, affecting the lead time before UST closure can begin. If the USTs have stored chemicals, soil borings or other assessment activities may be required before tank removal. Removal of flammable vapors is required by tank degassing or icing with dry ice. Regulations also require UST registration, agency notifications, reporting of contamination associated with USTs, spill response procedures, investigation activities, verification of site conditions, and notification upon closure.

Contractors should be aware that special registrations may be required to legally participate in UST removals. Special employee training may be required and documentation of this training may be required to be available on-site.

If they are involved in the excavation of a UST, contractors should check the integrity of the UST and piping after removal for holes, corrosion, or evidence of leaks or overfills. Contractors also should check the excavation for visual or olfactory signs of leaks, and may use a portable organic vapor analyzer to screen for contamination. Even if not required by the agencies, contractors should collect soil samples for analysis to ensure that the excavation is clean before backfilling and restoring the original contours. Removed tanks should be cut apart or perforated to prevent subsequent reuse. A receipt verifying proper disposal should be maintained to minimize future liabilities.

Other structures or facility features may be regulated as USTs in some jurisdictions and may include inground clarifiers, inground oil/water separators, piping systems connected to USTs, and inground trenches or floor drains. These units may be encountered as part of industrial wastewater collection systems, near discharges to city sewers, or as parts of pits used for auto maintenance or waste oil collection. Requirements for investigation, treatment, and remediation may apply in these situations. The features are most typically encountered at facility demolition. For example, if the land use is being changed from commercial auto maintenance to residential, then requirements for investigation and remediation may be even more stringent.

§ 13.25 —Active or Inactive Waste Sites

During site demolition or razing, contractors may work in or around active or inactive waste disposal sites, and should be aware of potential hazards and special requirements. Discontinued operations can include hazardous waste or other solid waste landfills, surface impoundments (ponds), waste treatment units, or drum or tank storage areas.

Hazardous and solid waste management units usually are associated with industrial activities. Waste treatment units include incinerators and biological or chemical treatment systems. Some common waste storage areas are drum storage, roll-off container storage, tank farms, and surface impoundments. Surface impoundments commonly are used to manage cooling water, stormwater, wastewater, and mining overburden. Waste disposal activities include landfarming for biological degradation and landfills. Landfills may be used for wastes ranging from innocuous trash and debris to hazardous wastes; at older industrial facilities, hazardous materials may have been disposed of according to practices of earlier days.

Site owners or operators may hire contractors to develop closure protocol or to close hazardous or solid waste management facilities per predetermined plans and specifications. RCRA closure plans address closure of RCRA-regulated areas, including hazardous waste inventory removal, equipment decontamination, and site remediation. Closure plans are part of RCRA permits at TSD facilities, but should be reviewed thoroughly as actual closure activities are being contemplated.

"Clean" closures involve the removal of all wastes and residual contamination to background levels or to cleanup levels acceptable to federal, state, or local agencies. Some closures involve leaving the wastes in place. For example, a clay cap and grassy cover may be added to a landfill. Surface impoundment closure often involves dewatering sludges and stabilizing residues in place rather than excavating all contaminated materials for off-site disposal. Closure with hazardous wastes remaining may require a note in the property deed record that hazardous waste activities occurred, whereas clean closure may not require deed recordation.

Contractors should be aware that rigorous requirements apply if their work involves hazardous wastes. In addition, the requirements vary from state to state and are growing more stringent over time. Before beginning work on any project involving wastes, contractors should be satisfied that the site owner or operator has performed the appropriate tests or evaluations and that it is safe to proceed.

Hazardous and solid waste regulations can impact the contractor's scheduled field activities, and can be a critical path item. RCRA closures must follow a regulatory-driven timetable, including the time allowed for waste removal and for site decontamination and final closure. The regulations also dictate procedures for agency notifications. Non-RCRA closures may require similar timetables, depending on the agencies involved.

At major milestones in waste site closure, the site owner or operator should conduct sampling and analysis to verify the level of decontamination achieved, whether or not the facility managed hazardous wastes during its lifetime. The contractor may wish to review the sampling and laboratory data or collect samples independently to minimize future liability from unknowingly disturbing or moving materials and aggravating the problem.

§ 13.26 —Soil and Groundwater Contamination

During site demolition or razing, contractors may find signs of soil and groundwater contamination from past operations, disposal practices, or substances entrained in stormwater runoff. These factors can contribute to both on-site and off-site impacts. Contractors should look out for soil staining or discoloration, distressed vegetation, and odors.

Contractors may conduct activities such as cleaning process equipment, and removing USTs or sumps which, if improperly performed, could cause soil or groundwater contamination. If a release occurs, several federal regulations require immediate spill and incident reporting for spills or releases that have the potential to impact human health or the environment.

During site demolition or razing, contractors may remove contaminated soil and debris for off-site disposal. RCRA regulates the management of soil or debris that is hazardous waste. The project proponent would need to obtain an EPA *generator identification number* to dispose of RCRA-regulated materials (see § 13.6). Currently, federal regulations exempt oil- or fuel-impacted UST cleanup debris from the hazardous waste rules, but some states make no distinction between the regulation of petroleum-contaminated soils and other hazardous wastes.

If soil or groundwater cleanup is being performed, the definition of "clean" is a key question. There are few established federal cleanup standards for soil or groundwater contamination. State cleanup standards vary, and even states with established contaminant cleanup levels usually treat cleanup on a case-by-case basis.

Contractors may encounter groundwater monitoring wells during demolition or razing. Contractors should take precautions not to disturb these wells, as the wells may need to remain in place for many years after site closure. Unknowing or improper demolition at the surface of a groundwater monitoring or extraction well can provide a pathway for contamination to migrate from the surface into the groundwater. Also, contractor employees should be trained not to dispose of waste oils or solvents in drinking water or groundwater monitoring wells, exposing the contractor to significant liability for cleanup.

§ 13.27 —Importation of Fill or Disposal of Rubble

Contractors frequently import fill to level or stabilize a site before construction. Contractors should be aware that many unscrupulous or unknowing parties continue to balk at the increased costs associated with complying with current environmental regulations, and they should make certain that imported fill is not contaminated soil from a UST excavation or spill, metal-bearing filter coke, tank bottoms, or other materials that would contaminate the project site. Even a sizable accumulation of grass clippings may raise agency concerns about residual pesticides and may designate a proposed project site as a "landfill," thus thwarting the best-laid plans of project proponents. Contractors should also implement site security measures when fill is being imported. Multiple piles of fill dirt on an isolated, unsecured site may present a tempting option to haulers or owners of contaminated soil.

Disposal of construction rubble poses the risk of commingling hazardous wastes with nonhazardous rubble, causing the mixture to be regulated as hazardous and requiring expensive disposal. This commingling could occur inadvertently on-site, or by sending nonhazardous rubble to another site that is accepting hazardous or contaminated soils. These risks raise the possibility of joint and several liability for cleanups.

Contractors should be certain that the imported fill they obtain and place on-site is not hazardous waste or contaminated soil. Similarly, the contractor should ensure that construction rubble remains nonhazardous on the job-site and is sent off-site only to locations that do not commingle contaminated soils or hazardous wastes.

§ 13.28   Summary and Conclusions

Virtually every aspect of a construction project in which a contractor may become involved is impacted in some way by federal, state, or local environmental, health, and safety regulations. Regulations continue to be a moving target, changing requirements and contractor exposure on a continuing basis. Environmental or hazardous materials management aspects that are not specifically regulated demand good management procedures to minimize overall risks and hazards to workers, the public, and the environment.

Environmental due diligence investigations are critical at every stage of construction, transactions, and the property life cycle. Leftover materials and residual materials such as steam-cleaning condensate and building debris present special risks that contractors unwittingly may become involved with liabilities associated with the improper management of hazardous wastes.

Contractor knowledge of requirements imposed by regulations for training, testing, recordkeeping, agency notification, and general workplace procedures is critical. The contractor should not assume blindly that project proponents, contracting entities, or subcontractors have addressed all environmental, health, and safety issues adequately. The contractor should not do any unsolicited or improper favors for other parties in any project with regard to environmental or hazardous waste management.

In spite of these seemingly formidable obstacles, risks can be identified, managed, and minimized. The contractor may develop resources in-house, rely on proficient outside consultant expertise, or use some combination of both options. Addressing environmental, health, and safety issues properly and early can enhance a well-run and profitable business.

PART IV

RIGHTS, LIABILITIES, AND REMEDIES

CHAPTER 14

BID PROTESTS AND MISTAKES IN BID

Sandra Lee Fenske*
W. Bruce Shirk

Sandra Lee Fenske is an associate attorney with the law firm of Seyfarth, Shaw, Fairweather & Geraldson in Washington, D.C. She specializes in federal government contract issues. Ms. Fenske received her B.A. degree from Colgate University and J.D., with honors, from the National Law Center, George Washington University. She is vice chair of the Bid Protest Committee of the Public Contracts Section, American Bar Association.

W. Bruce Shirk is a partner in the law firm of Seyfarth, Shaw, Fairweather & Geraldson in Washington, D.C. He specializes in construction and government contract litigation. He received his A.B. and J.D. degrees from Harvard University. As an active member of the American Bar Association, Mr. Shirk has served as chair of various committees and is currently chair of the Suspension and Debarment Committee of the Public Contracts Section. He has lectured and written widely on various matters related to government and construction contracting.

*Ms. Fenske gratefully acknowledges the invaluable assistance of Norma Leftwich and Marietta Geckos in preparing this chapter.

§ 14.1   Function of Bid Protests

A contractor responding to a solicitation from a public sector agency, whether that agency is local, state, or federal, usually invests significant time, effort, and money in the preparation of the bid or proposal. The contractor, therefore, has a sizable investment in the outcome of the award process, and rightfully desires assurance both that the solicitation is fairly written, not giving any undue advantage to competitors, and that the proposed or actual award of the contract is fair and not made on the basis of error, bias, or favoritism on the part of the contracting agency.

Protests are a means by which such contractors can assert their written objections to the terms of a solicitation for the acquisition of supplies or services or to a proposed award or award of such a contract.[1] In short, protests are a means by which actual and prospective bidders can attempt to assure themselves of a level playing field when competing for public sector construction work.

In addition to providing assurances to businesses competing for public work of the fairness of the contracting process, the existence of the protest remedy serves the public interest in safeguarding the integrity of each procurement. By vindicating their own self-interests in the fairness and equity of the process, protesters ensure that the acquisition of construction services in the public sector is based on fair and open competition for all qualified competitors. Taxpayers benefit when the government purchases low-cost, high-quality goods and services in a competitive market place policed by the competitors, thus avoiding favoritism and arbitrary decision making that may lead to "gold plating," extensive cost overruns, or shoddy workmanship.

Prospective contractors should be aware of procedural requirements for public sector procurement and the availability of bid protests whenever they pursue contracting opportunities. Federal, state, and local governments all purchase construction services. Not surprisingly, this presents a number of protest procedures almost as numerous as the jurisdictions that procure those services. Unfortunately, this brief chapter cannot begin to address those entities in all their variety.

---

[1] 31 U.S.C. § 3551 (1988); FAR 33.101; ABA Model Procurement Code for State and Local Governments Recommended Regulations, 1981 [hereinafter Model Procurement Code] § R1-301.01.25. The FAR is found at Title 48 of the Code of Federal Regulations.

Nevertheless, virtually every contracting entity in the public sector will entertain protests made directly to the procuring or purchasing agency, although procedures for prosecuting protests at the agency level vary from somewhat general and informal to fairly refined.

Many states and localities have developed their own procurement regulations relating to protests. Each is different and should be consulted individually. However, some uniformity has been imposed by the adoption at the state and local levels of the American Bar Association (ABA) Model Procurement Code for States or Model Procurement Ordinance for Local governments. The aim of the ABA is to encourage uniform procurement standards in all states and localities. As of this writing, 18 states and 21 localities have adopted some form of the Model Code or Ordinance. This chapter refers to the Model Procurement Code and Model Procurement Ordinance when discussing state and local procedures.

On the federal level, the Federal Acquisition Regulation (FAR), various agency supplements, the rules and precedents of the General Accounting Office (GAO), and case law precedent in the United States Claims Court and federal district courts and courts of appeals all govern procedures for bid protests.

§ 14.2   Available Forums for Bid Protests

Once a contractor determines that it has a valid basis for protest, the contractor must consider where to bring that protest. At the state level, the alternatives vary but may include the chief procuring official, the head of the purchasing agency, or the courts.[2] At the local level, the alternatives also may include the city council, mayor, or manager.[3] Although most states have a central purchasing office, and some 34 states have through statute for regulation or through other operating procedure a legal basis for written protests, the authority of the central purchasing office and the characteristics of the protest procedure vary from jurisdiction to jurisdiction.

At the federal level, the disappointed bidder can file a protest directly with the procuring agency or with the GAO on an administrative level. The protester may also file a protest at the United States Claims Court or a federal district court.

The following analysis discusses the various forums available to protesters, the procedures used in the forums, and the pros and cons associated with each.

---

[2] *See* Model Procurement Code § R9-101.03, R9-101.09.

[3] *See* Model Procurement Ordinance for Local Governments [hereinafter Model Procurement Ordinance] § R9-101(1).

§ 14.3   Concept of Standing to Protest

One of the chief principles of the American legal system is the concept of standing. *Standing* means that only a party with a real interest in litigation may bring suit before a court or board. Each administrative forum or court has its own standing requirements. In bid protests, standing is often determined by whether a protester is an "interested party." The FAR provides a useful guide to standing for the contractor considering a protest:

> *Interested Party for the purpose of filing a protest,* as used in this subpart, means an actual or prospective offeror whose direct economic interest would be affected by the award of a contract or by the failure to award a contract.[4]

Similarly regarding the "right to protest," the Model Procurement Code provides:

> Any actual or prospective bidder, offeror, or contractor who is aggrieved in connection with the solicitation or award of a contract may protest to the Chief Procurement Officer or the Head of a Purchasing Agency.[5]

In order to have standing to protest in the United States Claims Court, a party must have submitted a bid or offer thus having entered into an "implied contract for good faith consideration" of its bid or offer with the federal government.[6] Standing in federal district court requires first that a party have suffered an economic injury, such as loss of profits from the lost award or the fruitless expenditure of bid and proposal costs, and second that the party be within the "zone of interest" to be protected by a federal procurement statute. This includes but is not limited to having submitted a bid or offer in response to a solicitation.[7]

In sum, the general requirement for standing to bring a protest is that the contractor filing the protest have a genuine economic interest in the contract to be awarded by the public sector entity and have been actually hurt by the government's failure to follow its own rules in the solicitation and evaluation of bids and the award of the contract.

---

[4] FAR 33.101.

[5] Model Procurement Code § R9-101(1).

[6] Heyer Prods. Co. v. United States, 135 Ct. Cl. 63, 140 F. Supp. 409 (1956); Keco Indus., Inc. v. United States, 192 Ct. Cl. 773, 428 F.2d 1233 (1970).

[7] Scanwell Lab., Inc. v. Shaffer, 424 F.2d 859 (D.C. Cir. 1970).

§ 14.4   Protests to Procuring Agencies

Contractors who believe they have grounds for a bid protest should always first consider protesting to the agency. Resolution at this level tends to be both inexpensive and expeditious. Despite a skepticism that some contractors may have about having a procuring agency judge its own actions, many procurement decisions have been reversed over the years by state and federal agencies on the grounds that an agency erred in establishing the terms of a solicitation or that an agency has improperly awarded a contract.

At the federal level, the FAR encourages an interested party wishing to protest to seek resolution at the agency level before filing a protest with the GAO.[8] The contracting officer is obligated to consider all protests, whether submitted before award to protest the terms of solicitation or after award to protest the award itself.[9] The objective of the agency protest procedures outlined in the FAR is to enable the effective resolution of protests, to build confidence in the government's acquisition system, and to reduce protests to the GAO or the General Services Board of Contract Appeals (GSBCA).[10]

The objective of protest procedures at the state and local levels also should be to assure effective resolution of questions regarding the terms of solicitation and disputes over contract awards. This is the case in those jurisdictions that have adopted the Model Procurement Code or the Model Procurement Ordinance for Local Governments. Nevertheless, a prospective offeror should, as part of the decision to bid or propose, assess the availability of protest procedures in any local or state jurisdiction where the offeror is considering doing business.

§ 14.5   —Place, Time, and Form of Filing in Agency Protest

A potential protester must understand the requirements for place and time of filing protests, whether at the agency or other levels. Failure to do so could result in dismissal of the protest without a decision.

Location Requirements

At the federal agency level, interested parties must file their protests with the individual or at the location designated in the service of protest clause

---

[8] FAR 33.102(c)(1).

[9] *Id.* 33.102(a).

[10] *Id.* 33.103(a)(1). The GSBCA is a specialized forum that only considers protests against the procurement of automatic data processing equipment and services. Thus, GSBCA will not be considered further in this chapter.

in the solicitation.[11] In most cases, this will be either the contracting officer or the cognizant contract specialist. If the solicitation does not designate an official for receipt of an agency protest, the protester should submit the protest to the contracting officer. At the state and local levels the protest must be filed as prescribed in applicable statute, regulation, or procedure or in the solicitation itself.[12]

Time Requirements

The time for filing a protest is determined by the improprieties on the face of the solicitations, what the protester knew about the solicitation, and when the protester knew or should have known it. Thus, at the federal level, a protest that alleges a solicitation impropriety or error "which [is] apparent prior to bid opening or the closing date for receipt of proposals shall be filed prior to bid opening or the closing date for receipt of proposals."[13] Examples of protests based on alleged solicitation improprieties include overly restrictive specifications, inappropriate geographical restrictions, errors or omissions in specifications, or ambiguous requirements. In other words, the improprieties are problems with the solicitation that are evident from reading the solicitation and nothing more. If a prospective contractor does not protest these improprieties prior to the date for submission of bids or offers, the contractor cannot raise them later. It is essential that a prospective bidder review the solicitation as early as possible to identify any valid grounds for protests.

In other cases, protests are to be filed not later than "10 working days after the basis of the protest is known, or should have been known."[14] Examples of "other" protests include the responsiveness of another's bid or the alleged nonresponsiveness of a contractor's bid; the agency's failure to comply with the evaluation criteria in the solicitation; or any impropriety, inequity, or unfairness in the agency's review of bids or contract award. A potential protester must be keenly aware of events that could start the protest clock running. Thus, a protester may have knowledge of its alleged nonresponsiveness on the date of the *notice of award,* rather than on the date of a later debriefing. Waiting too long waives a contractor's right to protest.

At the state and local levels, the timing requirements vary by jurisdiction and may, in fact, be nonexistent. For Model Procurement Code jurisdictions the protest must be filed within 14 days "after the protester knows or

---

[11] *See* FAR 52.233-2.

[12] *See* Model Procurement Code § R9-101.03.

[13] FAR 33.103(b)(2).

[14] *Id.*

should have known of the facts giving rise thereto."[15] Model Procurement Ordinance for Local Governments places a slightly different emphasis on the knowledge requirement, requiring that a protest regarding the terms of a solicitation be submitted prior to the opening date for bids or the closing date for proposals "unless the aggrieved person did not know and should not have known of the facts giving rise to such protest prior to bid opening or the closing date for proposals."[16]

Form Requirements

The FAR and the Model Procurement Code have similar procedural requisites for filing a protest. First, the protest must be in writing.[17] Although a protest is an informal nonlegalistic document usually in the form of a letter, it should contain all relevant information available to the protester, including:

1. Name, address, and telephone number of the protester
2. Clear identification of the solicitation or procurement, by number if available
3. If a contract has been awarded, the contract number
4. A detailed statement of the legal and factual grounds for the protest
5. Copies of all relevant documents and supporting exhibits.

If the documents and exhibits are not available at the filing, then the protest should include a statement of the expected availability date.[18] The protest also should specifically request a ruling by the agency and state the relief requested,[19] that is, whether the protester desires the agency to revise the terms of the solicitation, direct award of the contract to other than the proposed awardee, resolicit the work, or provide such other remedy as is appropriate to the circumstances of the procurement. FAR states that failure to comply with any of these procedural requirements could result in dismissal of the protest.[20]

It is critical to the success of a contractor's protest that it be presented coherently so that the agency can conduct its review of the merits without having to engage in a lengthy process of decoding the presentation to understand the grounds of the protest. The protest must, in the words of the FAR,

---

[15] Model Procurement Code § R9-101.03.1.

[16] Model Procurement Ordinance § R9-101(1).

[17] FAR 33.101; Model Procurement Code § R9-101.03.1.

[18] *See* FAR 33.103(b)(3); Model Procurement Code § R9-101.03.3.

[19] FAR 33.103(b)(3)(iv), (v).

[20] *Id.* 33.103(b)(4).

"be concise, and logically presented."[21] Although declamations such as "it just isn't fair" and "I know my rights" are doomed to failure, a well-reasoned protest that presents the facts and arguments succinctly has a much greater chance of success.

§ 14.6   —Agency Protest Procedure

The protester has very little involvement in the agency protest procedure beyond writing the initial letter. The contracting officer reviews the protest and generally requests a review by counsel. If the protest has merit, the contracting officer grants the protester's requested remedy or makes another appropriate change in the procurement. If the contracting officer, with the advice of counsel, determines that the protest has no merit, the officer continues to process the procurement as originally intended.

When a protest is filed with the agency at the federal level, the contracting officer is not to make award of the work until a written decision is issued or the protest is otherwise resolved. Award may be made absent a written decision or resolution only if the contracting officer states in writing that the construction work is urgently required, that performance will be unduly delayed by failure to make prompt award, or that a prompt award will otherwise be advantageous to the government.[22]

The Model Procurement Code and Model Procurement Ordinance contain similar procedural protection for protesters. Thus, for example, the Model Procurement Ordinance provides that award will not be made "until all administrative and judicial remedies have been exhausted or until the [City Council] [Mayor] [City Manager] makes a determination on the record that the award of a contract without delay is necessary to protect substantial interests of the [City]."[23]

When a protest is filed before award with a federal agency and award is to be withheld pending disposition or resolution of the matter, other potentially eligible offerors are to be notified and requested to extend the time for acceptance to avoid the need for resolicitation.[24] When a protest is filed after award, the contracting officer is not obligated to suspend performance or terminate the procurement, unless it appears likely that the award will be invalidated.[25] The other potentially eligible offerors are, of course, interested parties, and have standing to submit comments on protests that have been filed by competitors, whether the protests are filed before or

---

[21] *Id.*

[22] *Id.* 33.103(a)(2).

[23] Model Procurement Ordinance § R9-101(2).

[24] FAR 33.103(a)(3).

[25] *Id.* 33.103(a)(4).

after award. This is true both at the federal level and in those state and local jurisdictions that have enacted one of the Model Codes.

Thus, a prospective contractor competing for a contract award should monitor the award process closely to determine whether a competitor has filed a protest. At the federal level, and usually at the state and local levels, it is possible to obtain a copy of the protest filed by one's competitor so as to intervene in the protest and make an appropriate response. In some instances, information related to the protest that is not proprietary or confidential may be obtained on written request submitted to the agency. It is wise to obtain all available information regarding a protest filed by a competitor.

§ 14.7   —Remedies Resulting from Agency Protests

The remedies that may result from an agency protest are limited only by the procurement statutes and regulations. When a protester files a protest with the agency, the protester does so with the intent of changing the contracting officer's mind about a procurement decision. Revised decisions can range from terminating an award and awarding to the protester or canceling the solicitation and resoliciting.

There is no provision at the federal level for either bid and proposal costs or attorneys' fees. Under the Model Procurement Code, however, the chief procurement officer or the head of the purchasing agency is directed by statute to award bid and proposal costs, other than attorneys' fees, to a successful protester who was not awarded the contract under the solicitation but who should have been the awardee.[26] The Model Ordinance also provides for bid and proposal costs in this situation.[27]

§ 14.8   —Appeal Rights after Agency Decisions

The decision of the contracting officer in a federal agency protest may be appealed directly to the GAO.[28] Such an appeal must be taken within 10 working days of when the protester knew or should have known about the adverse agency action.[29] Although a protester does not have a direct right of appeal to the courts, a protester can bring a separate court action at any time before or after the contracting officer makes a decision.

---

[26] Model Procurement Code § R9-101.07.2.

[27] Model Procurement Ordinance § R9-101(7).

[28] 4 C.F.R. § 21.2(a)(3) (1991).

[29] *Id.*

The Model Procurement Code provides for a formal process to request reconsideration of a final decision in a protest.[30] Any interested party who submitted comments during the protest may request reconsideration.[31] Although the Model Procurement Code does not provide expressly for court review of a challenged procurement, a protester may find that state courts will review the procurement actions of the state agency independently.

The Model Ordinance provides that a dissatisfied protester can appeal to either the city council or a court of competent jurisdiction. Otherwise the decision of the purchasing agent is conclusive and final.[32]

§ 14.9 —Pros and Cons of Agency Protest

An agency level protest is the quickest, simplest, and least expensive avenue for a potential protester. It can take the form of a letter and may be resolved in a day.

However, there are several disadvantages to the agency protest. First, a protester is asking the decision maker to modify or reverse a decision. The contracting officer has a lot at stake and may not be willing to reverse him- or herself. Second, the contractor may have a continuing business relationship with the procuring agency that the contractor feels may be jeopardized by an adversarial action. Finally, a protester's participation in an agency level protest is limited to submitting the protest and waiting for a decision. There is no opportunity for discovery, hearing, or briefing. All of the relevant facts are within the hands of the agency and the contractor usually does not have access to them, thereby making a complete, forceful argument difficult.

§ 14.10 Protests to General Accounting Office

The United States GAO, headed by the Comptroller General, has been involved for over 70 years in resolution of bid protests, first under the Comptroller General's authority to settle public accounts and now under the Competition in Contracting Act (CICA), which grants the GAO specific, though not exclusive, jurisdiction over "a protest concerning an alleged violation of a procurement statute or regulation."[33] GAO is required by statute

---

[30] Model Procurement Code § R9-101.08.

[31] Id.

[32] See Model Procurement Ordinance § R9-102(5).

[33] 31 U.S.C.A. § 3552 (West Supp. 1991).

to provide "inexpensive and expeditious" resolution of bid protests under CICA.[34]

The standing requirements before the GAO are, like those of the agencies discussed in § 14.3, based on the concept of interested party. Under CICA, as implemented by GAO's rules, an *interested party* for the purpose of filing a protest means "an actual or prospective bidder or offeror whose direct economic interest would be affected by the award of the contract or by the failure to award the contract."[35] This definition is applicable to both pre-proposal protests of solicitation terms and conditions and pre-award and post-award protests of the propriety of the government's evaluation. However, a protester will not be considered to be an interested party if it would not be in line for the protested award even if GAO sustained the protest.[36] An example of this would be if the bidder who was fourth in line for award protested the government's evaluation of the awardee but not of the second and third low bidder. In that case, the protester would not be an interested party because, even if the GAO sustained the protest, the second low bidder, not the protester, would get the award.

GAO has an alternative definition of interested party for those who wish merely to participate in a protest that has already been filed. An *interested party* for participation in a protest includes the awardee for protests after award is made and "all bidders or offerors who appear to have a substantial prospect of receiving an award if the protest is denied" for other protests.[37] An interested party can limit its participation to receiving copies of all of the material filed with GAO or can participate fully by submitting briefs and attending hearings.

§ 14.11   —Limitations on Protests before GAO

An interested party may protest the violation of statute or regulation in the procurement of goods or services by a federal agency at the GAO. The protest may concern the propriety of the terms of a solicitation, the government's evaluation of bids or offers prior to award, or the actual award of a government contract. Some of the most common grounds for protest are addressed below.

In its rules, however, the GAO has expressly declined to consider certain matters that a contractor may wish to protest.[38] In those cases, a more appropriate party or forum usually is available for resolving the issue, or the

---

[34] *Id.* § 3554(a)(1).

[35] *Id.* § 3551(2); 4 C.F.R. § 21.0(a) (1991).

[36] Brunswick Corp. & Brownell & Co., B-225784.2, 87-2 CPD ¶ 74.

[37] 4 C.F.R. § 21.0(b).

[38] 4 C.F.R. § 21.3(m) (1991).

matter is otherwise inappropriate for GAO's consideration. Potential areas of protest that GAO will dismiss without consideration include matters of contract administration, including whether an awardee is capable of or intends to perform.[39] Once an agency makes an award, the performance or nonperformance by the contractor is a dispute between the parties to the contract, not involving an outside third party, to be settled in accordance with the Contract Disputes Act.[40]

The GAO will not, absent a showing of bad faith or fraud, undertake to review a determination of the Small Business Administration (SBA) to issue a *certificate of competency* to a small business.[41] Nor may the GAO under any circumstances review a size determination made by the SBA.[42] In addition, absent bad faith or fraud, the GAO will not review an SBA determination regarding a contractor's qualifications under § 8(a) of the Small Business Act.[43] All these determinations are under the exclusive jurisdiction of the SBA; offerors should be aware that procedures exist within the SBA for review of determinations to issue certificates of competency and to protest or appeal size determinations.[44]

GAO generally will not review an affirmative determination of responsibility by the contracting officer.[45] Under FAR, the contracting officer may only award a contract to a responsive, responsible bidder. A prospective contractor will be determined to be *responsible* if it:

1. Has adequate financial resources to perform the contract or the ability to obtain them
2. Will be able to perform the contract if awarded
3. Has a satisfactory record of both performance and business ethics
4. Has the necessary organization, experience, accounting and operational controls, and technical or construction capability, or the ability to obtain such attributes
5. Is otherwise eligible under applicable laws and regulations.[46]

GAO considers such a determination to be based in large measure on the subjective judgments of the contracting officer, thus not readily susceptible to reasoned review.[47] GAO will, however, consider protests of a

---

[39] *Id.* § 21.3(m)(1).

[40] 41 U.S.C. 601–613 (1988).

[41] 4 C.F.R. § 21.3(m)(3).

[42] *Id.* § 21.3(m)(2); 15 U.S.C. § 637(b)(6); *see* 13 C.F.R. § 121.301(b).

[43] 4 C.F.R. § 21.3(m)(4); 15 U.S.C.A. § 637(a) (West Supp. 1991).

[44] FAR 19.301, 19.302, 19.601, 19.602-3.

[45] 4 C.F.R. § 21.3(m)(5).

[46] FAR 9.104-1.

[47] 4 C.F.R. § 21.3(m)(5).

responsibility determination based on definitive responsibility criteria stated in the solicitation (such as obtaining specialized certifications or licenses); and protests involving allegations of fraud or bad faith by the contracting officer in making an affirmative determination of responsibility.[48]

The GAO also will not consider protests of a subcontractor,[49] challenges to the legal status of a firm as a regular dealer or manufacturer under the Walsh-Healey Act,[50] protests of automated data processing procurements brought to the GSBCA,[51] and protests "where the matter involved is the subject of litigation before a court of competent jurisdiction, unless the Court requests a decision by the General Accounting Office.[52]

§ 14.12   Place, Time, and Form of Filing in GAO Protest

The timeliness requirements for filing a protest before the GAO are the same as the timeliness requirements for protesting to federal agencies. Thus protests relating to alleged improprieties in solicitations that are apparent on the face of the solicitation must be filed prior to bid opening or the time set for receipt of initial proposals.[53] If an impropriety does not exist in the initial solicitation but is incorporated by an amendment or modification, the protest must be filed by the closing date for submission of the next responsive submission.[54] In other cases protests must be filed not later than 10 days after the grounds for the protest are known or should have been known.[55]

If a contractor has filed a timely protest with the contracting agency, the contractor can file a subsequent protest with the GAO if the outcome of the agency protest is unfavorable. Such a protest must be filed within 10 days of the protester's actual or constructive notice of an adverse agency action.[56] It must be kept in mind that an adverse agency action need not be a written denial of the contractor's protest. It can be *any* action by the contracting officer that is inconsistent with granting a contractor's protest. For example, if a contractor protests a term of the solicitation as being overly restrictive, and the contracting officer subsequently awards the contract without issuing a modification to the solicitation or a written denial of the protest,

---

[48] *Id.*

[49] *Id.* § 21.3(m)(10).

[50] *Id.* § 21.3(m)(9); 41 U.S.C.A. § 35(a) (West 1987).

[51] *Id.* § 21.3(m)(6).

[52] *Id.* § 21.3(m)(11).

[53] 4 C.F.R. § 21.2(a)(1) (1991).

[54] *Id.*

[55] *Id.* § 21.2(a)(2).

[56] *Id.* § 21.2(a)(3).

contract award would be an adverse agency action beginning the running of time for filing a protest at GAO.

As a practical matter, these timing requirements mean that a contractor must be alert to the possibility that filing a protest may be necessary to protect the contractor's investment in the procurement from issuance of the solicitation through award of contract. To do so, the contractor must establish internal procedures to assure that the contractor's organization conducts timely reviews of solicitations for errors and improprieties so that, if grounds for protest exist, the filing can be made prior to bid opening. After contract award, the contractor's company must be organized to assess the award process and the responses of other offerors carefully to assure that any grounds for protest are identified and a protest filed within the relevant time evaluation. As with agency protests, protests that are untimely filed may be dismissed.[57]

Protests to GAO, like those to a federal agency, generally take the form of a letter. No specialized legal forms or pleadings are required and a protester may file a protest without representation by counsel. The form and content of the protest before the GAO is substantially the same as that discussed in § 14.5 for agencies. The protest must:

1.   Include the protester's name, address, and telephone number
2.   Identify the contracting agency and contract or solicitation number
3.   Set forth a detailed statement of the legal and factual grounds for the protest, including relevant documents
4.   Include a specific request for a ruling by the Comptroller General
5.   State the form of relief requested.[58]

The protester must submit a signed original and at least one copy to the GAO.[59] A copy of the protest must be filed with the cognizant contracting officer within one day of filing the protest at the GAO.[60]

§ 14.13   —Automatic Stay Provision

The contracting agency may not award a contract during the pendency of a protest.[61] If a protester files a protest and the cognizant contracting officer is so notified within 10 calendar days of award of a protest, the contracting

---

[57] *Id.* § 21.3(m)(7).

[58] *Id.* § 21.1(c).

[59] 4 C.F.R. § 21.1(c)(2). Protests must be addressed to the General Counsel, General Accounting Office, 441 G. Street, N.W., Washington, D.C., 20548; Attn: Procurement Law Control Group.

[60] 4 C.F.R. § 21.1(d).

[61] 31 U.S.C.A. § 3553(c)(1) (West Supp. 1991); 4 C.F.R. § 21.4(a) (1991).

agency must immediately direct the contractor to stop work and to suspend any related activities that may result in additional obligations being incurred by the United States under the contract.[62] This is known as the *automatic stay provision* of the CICA or the "29¢ injunction," as it has power to stop contract performance for the price of a postage stamp.

The contracting agency may only make an award or continue performance on a contract in the face of a protest if the head of the procuring activity for the agency makes a written finding that "urgent and compelling circumstances" significantly affecting the interests of the United States will not permit awaiting the Comptroller General's decision in the protest and, in the case of continued performance, that performance of the contract is in the best interests of the United States.[63]

The automatic stay provision avoids a "Pyrrhic victory" for a successful protester. Before CICA, a protester could show that the government blatantly violated the rules, but by the time the Comptroller General rendered a decision, the contract had been fully performed. In such cases, GAO took the position that it was too late to provide any relief to the protester or that it would be too costly to the government to remedy the flaw. The automatic stay avoids this result by maintaining the status quo pending resolution of the protest. In that way, a protester can obtain meaningful relief, such as contract award, if the protester shows that the procurement was improper.

§ 14.14   —GAO Protest Procedure

In the event that a disappointed bidder files a protest with the GAO, the bidder can expect a proceeding that varies in formality from submission of letters by the protester and the agency, to a full, transcribed, fact-finding hearing preceded by limited discovery. The GAO recently changed its protest procedures to make them more "trial-like" but still sufficiently accessible to a litigant without representation by counsel in accordance with its mandate to provide for "inexpensive and expeditious" resolution of protests.[64] Thus the protester controls the complexity of the proceeding.

When a disappointed bidder files a protest, GAO immediately notifies the contracting agency of the protest.[65] The agency then has 25 days to submit a complete report of the protested procurement, including all relevant documents, to the GAO.[66] The agency must simultaneously provide a

---

[62] 31 U.S.C.A. § 3553(d)(1); 4 C.F.R. § 21.4(b).

[63] 31 U.S.C.A. § 3553(c), (d); 4 C.F.R. § 21.4.

[64] 31 U.S.C.A. § 3554(a)(1) (West Supp. 1991).

[65] *Id.* § 3553(b)(1); 4 C.F.R. § 21.3(a) (1991).

[66] 31 U.S.C.A. § 3553(b)(2); 4 C.F.R. § 21.3(i).

copy of the report to the protester and any interested parties who have expressed an interest in participating in the protest with GAO.[67]

The *relevant documents* submitted by the agency in conjunction with its report are those documents considered to be relevant *by the agency*. This may not include all of the documents that the protester would consider to be relevant. In order to provide GAO with a more evenly balanced record of potentially relevant documents, the protester may submit limited requests for production of documents to the agency. The protester must make this request for specific documents that may be relevant to the protest simultaneously with filing a protest or later if the existence of such documents subsequently becomes known.[68]

If the government or the protester believes that either the protest or the protest file contains either source-selection sensitive or commercial, proprietary material, either party may request a protective order, thus limiting the individuals who can review the documents.[69] The GAO generally limits access to protected material for those individuals not involved in the competitive decision-making process of the protester.[70] Thus, in most cases, only outside counsel will be permitted to view protected material. GAO may impose sanctions for failure to comply with the terms of the protective order.[71]

After submission of the agency report, the protester has an opportunity either to request a fact-finding hearing with regard to the contested procurement or to submit a response to the agency report without having a hearing.[72] A hearing is conducted by a GAO hearing officer and consists of the examination of witnesses and review of documents in an attempt to establish uncontested facts.[73] The hearing normally is recorded or transcribed and held either at GAO in Washington, D.C., or at another appropriate location.[74]

The Comptroller General has 90 working days from the date that the protest was filed to render a written decision in the protest, based on the parties' submissions and the facts ascertained from the hearing.[75] The Comptroller General may be required to render a decision in 45 working days if the parties have requested the "express option." This procedure

---

[67] 4 C.F.R. § 21.3(i).

[68] *Id.* § 21.3(e).

[69] *Id.* § 21.3(d).

[70] *See* U.S. Steel Corp. v. United States, 730 F.2d 1465 (Fed. Cir. 1984).

[71] 4 C.F.R. § 21.3(d)(5).

[72] *Id.* §§ 21.3(j); 21.5(h), (i).

[73] *Id.* § 21.5(c).

[74] *Id.* § 21.5(f), (c).

[75] 31 U.S.C.A. § 3554(a)(1); 4 C.F.R. § 21.7.

provides for a less formal consideration of the protest and may be used only when deemed appropriate by the GAO.[76]

§ 14.15 —Remedies Resulting from GAO Protests

If the protester is successful and the Comptroller General determines that the procuring agency has not complied with statute or regulation, GAO may recommend several courses of action to the agency. The Comptroller General may recommend, as appropriate, that the federal agency:

1. Refrain from exercising any options under the contract
2. Recompete the contract immediately
3. Issue a new solicitation
4. Terminate the contract
5. Award a contract consistent with statute or regulation, including direct award to the protester
6. Implement any combination of these recommendations
7. Implement such other regulations as the Comptroller General determines are necessary.[77]

The decisions of the Comptroller General are only recommendations and need not be followed by the procuring agency. Nevertheless, if the agency decides not to implement a recommendation, it must make a report to Congress as to why it failed to do so.[78] Most agencies do, however, implement the recommendations of the Comptroller General.

§ 14.16 —Attorneys' Fees and Bid and
Proposal Costs

If a protester is successful at showing that an agency violated statute or regulation in the contested procurement, GAO may direct the agency to pay the protester or other interested party the costs of filing and pursuing the protest, including attorneys' fees and bid and proposal preparation costs.[79] Attorneys' fees may be appropriate in any situation in which the protester prevails. However, bid and proposal preparation costs will only be awarded if the successful protester did not receive the award but had a

---

[76] 4 C.F.R. § 21.8.

[77] 31 U.S.C.A. § 3554(b)(1) (West Supp. 1991); 4 C.F.R. § 21.6(a) (1991).

[78] 31 U.S.C.A. § 3554(e).

[79] 31 U.S.C.A. § 3554(c)(1) (West Supp. 1991); 4 C.F.R. § 21.6(d) (1991).

substantial chance to receive the award or if the protester was unreasonably excluded from competition.[80]

As of this writing, the United States Department of Justice has filed suit for declaratory relief with respect to the constitutionality of the attorneys' fees provision of the CICA. In the pending case, GAO directed the procuring agency to pay attorneys' fees to a successful protester. The Department of Justice intervened stating that it believed that the attorneys' fees provision of CICA violated the separation of powers doctrine of the United States Constitution and asked a court to decide the issue.[81] Pending the court's decision, the government is amending FAR to make payment of attorneys' fees discretionary with the agency and subject to recoupment should the Department of Justice prevail in the current suit.[82] Until there is a final determination by the court, it appears as though federal agencies will not be paying attorneys' fees under CICA even if directed to do so by the Comptroller General.

§ 14.17   —Appeal Rights after GAO Decisions

If a protester or other interested party is dissatisfied with the decision of the GAO in a bid protest, the party may request that the GAO reconsider that decision.[83]

The protester who is still not satisfied may file suit in the United States Claims Court or federal district court challenging the GAO's decision or requesting an independent review of the contested procurement. The prior decision of the GAO is not binding on the court.[84] If GAO has not as yet rendered a decision, the court may defer to GAO and request an advisory opinion. The court challenge is not a direct appeal of the GAO decision but is an alternate route for contesting the procurement.

§ 14.18   —Pros and Cons of GAO Protest

There are a number of tactical reasons why a contractor would choose to protest a procurement at GAO. First, the contractor may feel that a disinterested third party will give the contractor a fairer hearing than will the

---

[80] *See* International Limousine Serv., B-206708, 82-2 CPD ¶ 77; Tracor Marine, Inc., B-207285, 83-1 CPD ¶ 604.

[81] United States v. Instruments, S.A., Fisons Instruments/VG Instruments, No. 91-1574 (D.D.C. filed June 26, 1991).

[82] *See generally* 56 Fed. Reg. 28,652 (1991) (to be codified at 48 C.F.R. pt. 33) (proposed June 21, 1991).

[83] 4 C.F.R. § 21.12 (1991).

[84] *See* Meisel Rohrbau GmbH & Co. Kg, B-228152.3, 88-1 CPD ¶ 371.

procuring agency. It may appear to the contractor that the agency has hardened its view on the merits and will only deny a direct agency protest. Likewise, the agency may have already denied the initial protest and the contractor may wish to exercise the contractor's right of appeal to GAO. The determining factor in the decision may even come down to a matter of personalities in that the contractor has dealt with the contracting officer before and believes that any protest will fall on deaf ears.

Probably the most significant reason for filing a protest with GAO is the availability of the automatic stay. For the price of a postage stamp, a protester can stop performance of a contract. By preserving the status quo and leaving the agency the option of resoliciting or awarding to the protester, the automatic stay prevents the protester's victory from being a hollow one. Before the existence of the automatic stay, GAO usually would not recommend a protest before GAO as the best course of action in the event that the contract had been fully performed.

Another reason to choose GAO over the procuring agency is the existence of limited discovery. Document production is limited but at least the protester is able to see some of the material upon which the contracting officer bases its decision. This can be extremely helpful to the protester in arguing the protester's position. Alternatively, it may give a protester sufficient confidence in the contracting officer's decision to withdraw the protest. In any event, a review of relevant documents should give a protester greater faith in the process than a mere "trust me" from the contracting officer.

Finally, a protester may choose GAO over the courts because GAO provides a fast, inexpensive remedy. If a protester does not opt for any of the documentary discovery or hearing rights and files the protest on the protester's own behalf, the GAO option is, like an agency protest, almost without cost. However, if the protester chooses to engage an attorney to represent the protester in the presentation to GAO, either to enhance the protest through reasoned legal argumentation, to gain access to otherwise protected material, or to take advantage of an attorney's expertise at a fact-finding hearing, the cost of the protest goes up. Even when most formal, however, the cost of a proceeding at the GAO is unlikely to reach the level of a suit filed in court.

Some tactical reasons not to file a protest at GAO include the possibility of a favorable outcome at the agency level; the expense of the protest if protected material or an extended hearing is involved; or simply the fear of compromising business relations with the contracting agency. Needless to say, a contracting agency is not permitted by regulation to retaliate against a contractor for filing a protest, but the contractor should still assess the possible changes in relationships that may result from an adversarial proceeding. Finally, the contractor may believe that it needs a "bigger stick" wielded by either the United States Claims Court or federal district court in the form of an injunction and is not reluctant to pay the price.

§ 14.19   Protests to United States Claims Court

A disappointed bidder may file a bid protest in the United States Claims Court if the agency has not, as yet, awarded the contract.[85] The Claims Court, which is headquartered in Washington, D.C., is authorized to sit in other locations in order to minimize inconvenience and expense to litigants.[86] It is a specialized court, but is similar in authority to United States District Courts located around the country.

The Claims Court considers protests of violations of statute and regulation based on an "implied contract" between the government and the bidder to consider the bid fairly.[87] The implied contract arises when a bidder submits a responsive bid.[88] Thus, the Claims Court will not consider a protest against the terms of a solicitation that is filed prior to submission of a bid.[89] Likewise, a party that did not submit a bid in response to a solicitation cannot protest at the Claims Court.[90] Furthermore, the bid must have been responsive,[91] and the bidder must be eligible for award (that is, neither suspended nor debarred) in order to file a protest.[92] If the above preliminary criteria are unmet, the Claims Court has determined that no "implied contract" has arisen between the government and the would-be protester and thus, the Claims Court has no jurisdiction.

§ 14.20   —Place, Time, and Form of Filing in Claims Court

The United States Claims Court can hear and decide only those bid protests that are filed before contract award.[93] Post-award protests must be filed elsewhere. Nevertheless, the procuring agency cannot prevent the United States Claims Court from hearing and deciding a protest merely by awarding the contract that is the subject of that protest.[94] Finally, the Claims

---

[85] 28 U.S.C.A. § 1491(a)(3) (West Supp. 1991).

[86] *Id.* § 173.

[87] Heyer Prods. Co. v United States, 135 Ct. Cl. 63, 140 F. Supp. 409 (1956); Keco Indus., Inc. v. United States, 192 Ct. Cl. 773, 428 F.2d 1233 (1970); Marine Power & Equip. Co. v. United States, 5 Cl. Ct. 795 (1984).

[88] *Id.*

[89] Eagle Constr. Corp. v. United States, 4 Cl. Ct. 470 (1984).

[90] Hero, Inc. v. United States, 3 Cl. Ct. 413 (1983).

[91] Yachts Am., Inc. v. United States, 3 Cl. Ct. 447 (1983).

[92] ATL, Inc. v. United States, 735 F.2d 1343 (Fed. Cir. 1984).

[93] 28 U.S.C.A. § 1491(a)(3) (West Supp. 1991); Ingersoll-Rand Co. v. United States, 2 Cl. Ct. 373 (1983); United States v. John C. Grimberg Co., 702 F.2d 1362 (Fed. Cir. 1983).

[94] *See* F. Alderete Gen. Contractors, Inc. v. United States, 2 Cl. Ct. 184, *rev'd on other grounds,* 715 F.2d 1476 (Fed. Cir. 1983).

Court cannot hear or decide a protest if it has already been filed in another federal court.[95]

A protest at the Claims Court results in standard federal court litigation. As such, any corporation filing a protest must be represented by counsel.[96] In form, the protest is initially filed as a request for a temporary restraining order, preliminary injunction, and request for declaratory relief.

§ 14.21   —Claims Court Protest Procedure

In a bid protest at the Claims Court, the initial filing is usually a motion for a temporary restraining order (TRO). This is a request to the court to direct the federal government not to award the contract due to a violation of statute or regulation or a breach of the implied contract of fair consideration. The TRO is a mandatory directive of the court to the agency to take a certain action. However, the TRO only lasts 10 days.[97] The TRO is an emergency measure intended to maintain the status quo while the court decides on the merits of the case. It may be followed by a preliminary injunction that continues to maintain the status quo, usually stopping all action on the procurement until the hearing on the merits of the protester's case is concluded.

Prior to the hearing on the merits of the protest, the parties may engage in various forms of discovery to assist in establishing the facts in the case. Discovery may include depositions upon oral examination or written questions of parties or third-party witnesses, written interrogatories, requests for production of documents, physical inspection of land or other property, and requests for admissions.[98] This discovery is considerably more extensive than that provided by the GAO and, although it is intended to be consensual, discovery can be ordered by the court if the parties refuse to comply.[99]

As with protests before the GAO, a protest at the Claims Court may entail review of documents that are sensitive to the procurement process or may contain commercially-sensitive or proprietary data. In such cases, the court can issue a protective order limiting access to such material.[100]

After the parties have completed discovery sufficient to establish the facts of the case, the Claims Court provides for an evidentiary trial to a judge

---

[95] 28 U.S.C.A. § 1500.

[96] U.S. Claims Ct. R.81(d)(8).

[97] Id. 65(b).

[98] Id. 26(a).

[99] See, e.g., id. 37(c), (d).

[100] Id. 26(c).

sitting without a jury based on the standard federal trial court rules.[101] The parties present their case to a judge in either Washington, D.C., or another appropriate location.[102]

Upon conclusion of the hearing, the judge provides the parties with an opinion from the bench or a written decision and opinion.[103] If the protester prevails, the preliminary injunction is modified as appropriate and made permanent, thereby directing the procuring agency how to proceed with the procurement. If the protester is unsuccessful, the court dissolves the injunction and the agency most likely awards the contract as the agency originally intended.

§ 14.22   —Remedies Resulting from
Claims Court Protests

The Claims Court may craft its remedies as it sees fit in order to correct the violation of statute or regulation or breach of the implied contract of fair consideration that resulted in the protest. Remedies can include a directed award, reevaluation of the bids or proposals, revision of the solicitation and subsequent reevaluation, or any combination of actions. The court also may grant declaratory relief, which is a determination as to whether an action that the government will be taking is improper. A protester usually requests an injunction in combination with a request for declaratory relief whereby the court directs the government to do what is right.

§ 14.23   —Attorneys' Fees and Bid and
Proposal Costs

The Claims Court awards a protester bid and proposal costs if the protester prevails but does not receive the award.[104] The protester must, however, have had a substantial chance for award.[105] The court will not award a protester lost profits if it fails to receive the award.[106]

As a general matter, parties to a lawsuit in the U.S. courts bear their own costs.[107] However, the Equal Access to Justice Act provides for attorneys'

---

[101] *Id.* 1(b).

[102] *See generally* U.S. Claims Ct. R. 39.

[103] *Id.* 52(a).

[104] *See* Keco Indus., Inc. v. United States, 192 Ct. Cl. 773, 428 F.2d 1233 (1970).

[105] Morgan Business Assocs. v. United States, 223 Ct. Cl. 325, 619 F.2d 892 (1980); Tracor Marine, Inc., B-207285, 83-1 CPD ¶ 604.

[106] Rockwell Int'l Corp. v. United States, 8 Cl. Ct. 662 (1985).

[107] 32 Am. Jur. 2d *Federal Practice* § 169 (1982).

fees and costs to a prevailing party in litigation against the federal government under certain circumstances.[108] The most significant limitation on the award of attorneys' fees is that only businesses who have a net worth of less than $7 million and fewer than 500 employees are eligible.[109]

The protester who prevails and meets the size limitations in the statute must submit an application to the court.[110] The court will award attorneys' fees and costs as limited by the statute unless it finds that the position of the United States during the litigation was substantially justified or that special circumstances exist that would make an award of attorneys' fees unjust.[111]

§ 14.24   —Appeal Rights after Claims Court Decisions

Either party may appeal the decision of the Claims Court to the Court of Appeals for the Federal Circuit.[112] This is an appeal of right. An appeal can be taken from a decision of the Court of Appeals for the Federal Circuit to the United States Supreme Court, which the Supreme Court may review in its discretion.[113] The Court usually will not review the decisions of the Claims Court or the Court of Appeals for the Federal Circuit, but instead will defer to the expertise of these courts in the area of government contracts.

§ 14.25   —Pros and Cons of Claims Court Protest

There are a number of jurisdictional considerations that eliminate the Claims Court as a viable forum for a bid protest. First, the action must be filed prior to award of the contract. Thus, if the contract has been awarded already, the Claims Court is no longer an option. Second, if the protest is based on a flaw in the solicitation, the Claims Court has stated that it has no jurisdiction. Finally, a potential protester must have submitted a responsive bid in order to have entered into the "implied contract of fair consideration" in order for the Claims Court to have jurisdiction over the protest.

If a protester meets the jurisdictional tests, the protester may choose the Claims Court because it has the power to stop an award and to direct an

---

[108] 28 U.S.C.A. § 2412(a) (West Supp. 1991).

[109] *Id.* § 2412(d)(2)(B).

[110] 28 U.S.C.A. § 2412(d)(1)(B); U.S. Claims Ct. R. 81(e)(1) app. E.

[111] 28 U.S.C.A. § 2412(d)(3) (West Supp. 1991).

[112] 28 U.S.C.A. § 1295(a)(3) (West Supp. 1991).

[113] *See id.* § 1254.

agency to take action. This authority is unlike that of the GAO whose opinions are advisory and whose stay of the procurement can be overridden by an agency determination. Furthermore, litigants at the Claims Court have greater discovery rights than at the GAO. Due to its national character, the Claims Court also has a broader geographical scope for discovery than federal district courts. One reason for a small business to choose the Claims Court is the availability of attorneys' fees and costs under the Equal Access to Justice Act. Finally, the Claims Court is a specialized court that arguably has a specific expertise in the government contracts area.

An obvious drawback of litigating at the Claims Court is the cost. A protester requires counsel. The procedures at the Claims Court are formal and legalistic and consequently require costly legal assistance. In addition, a review of the cases coming before the Court shows that the Claims Court has identified many jurisdictional limitations that prevent it from deciding cases. As a result, a protester may find itself out of court without a decision on the merits due to a jurisdictional technicality. Another reason why a protester may not want to file a protest at the Claims Court prior to award is that the agency may, in fact, make an award to the would-be protester. Surely a contractor would not want to risk sacrificing an award to itself by filing a protest, if award by the agency is a real possibility.

§ 14.26   Protests to Federal District Court

A disappointed bidder may file a protest in one of 90 federal district courts located throughout the United States, Puerto Rico, and the District of Columbia.[114] If a party can show that it has been injured by the arbitrary and capricious acts of the contracting officer and that it is entitled to the protection of the procurement statues and regulations, the party has standing to bring a bid protest in the federal district courts.[115] The procedures and remedies are similar to those available to protesters in the United States Claims Court.

The district courts, with the exception of the United States District Court for the District of Columbia, have considerably less expertise in government procurement issues than the Claims Court or the GAO. Each district court is bound by legal precedent in the judicial circuit in which it is located. Each circuit and thus each district court may have slightly different case law with respect to any issue, on substantive law as well as procedural matters. A would-be protester must look carefully at case law in the circuit where the protester intends to file in order to maximize chances for success in the matter.

---

[114] *Id.* §§ 81–131.

[115] Scanwell Lab., Inc. v. Shaffer, 424 F.2d 859 (D.C. Cir. 1970).

§ 14.27 —Place, Time, and Form of Filing in District Court

The time for filing a protest in a federal district court varies according to the circuit in which the district court sits. All district courts hear protests filed after a contract has been awarded. However, due to anomaly in the statute granting bid protest jurisdiction to the United States Claims Court, some district courts, including the United States District Court for the District of Columbia, will not hear pre-award protests.[116] Thus, prior to filing a bid protest in a federal district court, it is imperative to determine the law in the jurisdiction. Some district courts will hear a pre-award bid protest and some will not. All, however, will hear protests filed after award of the contract.

Federal courts are courts of limited jurisdiction. A party cannot file a lawsuit in any district court it chooses. The court must have the authority to hear the matter, which often depends upon the identity of the parties. In a bid protest, the U.S. government or one of its officers will always be the defendant in the case; thus, the United States District Court for the District of Columbia is an appropriate forum. The protester also may bring an action in a district court within the jurisdiction where the contract action occurred or in the district where the protester has its principal place of business.[117]

Once a protester has decided when and where to file its protest, the form of filing is similar to that in the United States Claims Court. All district courts are governed by the Federal Rules of Civil Procedure.[118] Most district courts also have "local rules" that supplement the federal rules. Together, the federal and local rules instruct the protester how to file its action.

As in the Claims Court, a protest generally is commenced by filing a request for a TRO, a request for a preliminary injunction, and sometimes a request for declaratory relief. Also, as in the Claims Court, a corporation must be represented by counsel.

---

[116] See 28 U.S.C.A. § 1491(a)(3) (West Supp. 1991); Opal Mfg. Co. v. UMC Indus., Inc., 553 F. Supp. 131 (D.D.C. 1982) (holding that there is no pre-award jurisdiction in federal district court); J.P. Francis & Assocs. v. United States, 902 F.2d 740 (9th Cir. 1990) (same); Rex Sys., Inc. v. Holiday, 814 F.2d 994 (4th Cir. 1987) (same); B.K. Instrument, Inc. v. United States, 715 F.2d 713 (2d Cir. 1983) (same in dicta); Ulstein Maritime, Ltd. v. United States, 833 F.2d 1052 (1st Cir. 1987) (concurrent pre-award jurisdiction in both Claims Court and federal district court); Coco Bros. v. Pierce, 741 F.2d 675 (3d Cir. 1984) (same); see also Cubic Corp. v. Cheney, 914 F.2d 1501 (D.C. Cir. 1990) (analysis of state of circuits regarding jurisdiction under 28 U.S.C.A. § 1491(a)(3)).

[117] 28 U.S.C.A. §§ 1331, 1391.

[118] Fed. R. Civ. P. 1.

§ 14.28   —District Court Protest Procedure

The protest procedure in a federal district court is similar to that in the United States Claims Court. Discovery is permitted under the Federal Rules of Civil Procedure.[119] However, it is limited in geographical scope.[120] Protesters are permitted to have a hearing with a judge sitting without a jury in proceedings for injunctive and declaratory relief. The court's decision generally is accompanied by a written decision.

§ 14.29   —Remedies Resulting from
District Court Protests

The remedies available to a protester in federal district court essentially are the same as those provided by the Claims Court. The court has the power to grant a TRO for a period of 10 days to maintain the status quo.[121] This can mean stopping the government from awarding the contract or directing the contracting officer to stop work on a contract already awarded. If the protester makes the proper showing, the court can grant a preliminary injunction to maintain the status quo until the court decides on the merits of the case. Finally, a court can grant a successful protester a declaratory judgment and permanent injunction that directs the contracting officer how to proceed. If the protester is unsuccessful, however, the court will dissolve the injunction and the contracting officer is most likely to proceed in the manner originally intended.

Again, as with the Claims Court, the federal district court is only limited by statute and regulation as to the type of relief that it can offer to a protester. The relief can include direction to terminate a contract already awarded, directed award to the protester, reevaluation of some or all of the bids and offers, cancellation of the solicitation, or any combination of remedies.

§ 14.30   —Attorneys' Fees and Bid and
Proposal Costs

Like the Claims Court, the federal district court can award attorneys' fees and costs under the Equal Access to Justice Act to a successful protester meeting the statutory size limitations.[122] The successful protester must

---

[119] *See* Fed. R. Civ. P. 26.

[120] *See id.* 45.

[121] Fed. R. Civ. P. 65(b).

[122] 28 U.S.C.A. § 2412 (West Supp. 1991).

apply to the court after completion of the litigation.[123] The court will not award attorneys' fees and costs if it decides that the position of the United States during the litigation was substantially justified or that special circumstances exist that would make an award of attorneys' fees unjust.[124]

Unlike at the Claims Court, the amount of bid and proposal preparation costs available to a protester at the federal district court is limited to $10,000.[125] Under the Tucker Act, a litigant can only claim $10,000 in a suit against the United States filed in federal district court. In some cases, this amount may be sufficient to cover all of the expenses that a contractor may incur in submitting a bid for a construction project. However, in some cases, bidding on a federal contract may cost much more. If suit is filed in federal district court, a protester expending more than the $10,000 jurisdictional amount is limited in its recovery.

§ 14.31   —Appeal Rights after District Court Decisions

A protester who is dissatisfied with the result at the federal district court level may bring an appeal to the federal court of appeals for the circuit in which the district court is located.[126] There are 12 circuits that are located throughout the United States. The Court of Appeals for the Federal Circuit, the thirteenth circuit court, is located in Washington, D.C., but unlike the other circuit courts whose jurisdiction is primarily geographical, the jurisdiction of the Federal Circuit is limited to appeals from specialized courts such as the Claims Court. The appellate court will consider an extension of the original injunction pending appeal if the unsuccessful protester has initially filed its request with the district court.[127] The court of appeals does not grant additional fact-finding or a new trial, but limits its review to the decision of the federal district court.

If the court of appeals denies the protester's appeal, the protester may petition the United States Supreme Court to hear its further appeal. Such review is discretionary with the Supreme Court and is seldom granted in bid protest cases.

---

[123] *Id.* § 2412(d)(1)(B).

[124] *Id.* § 2412(d)(3).

[125] *Id.* § 1346(a)(2).

[126] *See* 28 U.S.C.A. §§ 1291, 1294(1) (West Supp. 1991).

[127] Fed. R. App. P. 8.

§ 14.32   —Pros and Cons of District Court Protest

A protester may choose to file its protest in federal district court for several reasons. First, the clout of a TRO and injunction are much greater than the advisory recommendations of the GAO. This is the same reason that a protester would choose the United States Claims Court. Second, the protester may feel that the "home field advantage" is beneficial in its case. The federal district court will be located in the place where the protester's company is located. The judge may be sympathetic to the local concern and the number of jobs that the federal contract would create for the region. Obviously, this is more of a psychological advantage and should have no legal impact on the decision of the judge. Third, the federal district court (with the exception of the United States District Court for the District of Columbia) is probably less familiar with federal procurement issues. It may be easier to make an argument based on fairness and equity rather than on the technicalities of the procurement process. Finally, it is less likely that a protester will be dismissed on jurisdictional grounds in the federal district court than in the Claims Court.

Another major reason for choosing federal district court over the Claims Court is the status of the protester. As noted earlier, the Claims Court only hears protests by those parties that have actually submitted bids. The district court is not so limited. Thus, a major subcontractor may file a protest in federal district court whereas the subcontractor may not be able to file the same protest at the Claims Court. Likewise, a party wishing to protest a provision of the solicitation as overly restrictive, but who has not as yet submitted a bid, may find itself out in the cold at the Claims Court but within the jurisdiction of the federal district court. A large business may wish to question a small business set aside that neither the GAO nor the Claims Court would consider.

The major reasons not to file a protest at the federal district court are the expense and the stage of the procurement. Clearly, an action for injunctive relief in federal court will be expensive, considerably more so than at the agency or the GAO. Filing a protest at the district court may, however, be less expensive than at the Claims Court because the protester's principals and witnesses will not have to travel to Washington, D.C., for hearings and are likely to lose fewer workdays on protest.[128] The second major obstacle to a protest in federal district court may be timing. The best practical time to protest may be prior to contract award. As noted earlier, some jurisdictions will not hear a protest before award of the contract. In that case, a protester will be limited to the Claims Court or to waiting until after award.

---

[128] The Claims Court will travel to the protester's locale on some occasions.

In addition, the district court's relative lack of familiarity with federal procurement issues may be a good a reason not to bring suit there. A protester may be able to prevail using novel theories with an emphasis on fairness and equity when protesting in a federal district court lacking in procurement expertise. Nevertheless, the protester may find itself in a situation in which its protest is based on the government's failure to adhere strictly to the procurement regulations, making the outcome of the protest hang on a technicality. In that case, the protester would benefit from specialized procurement expertise. This expertise would most likely be found at the GAO, the Claims Court, or the United States District Court for the District of Columbia.

Finally, a would-be protester will have to consider the business implications of an adversarial proceeding on its relationship with the government. Although the government is not permitted to retaliate for any actions a protester takes to preserve its rights, a seller must always consider the practical implications of litigation on carefully cultivated customer relations.

§ 14.33 Typical Grounds for Bid Protests

Federal, state, and local governments must comply with certain statutes and regulations in procuring goods and services. State and local procurement regulations vary from jurisdiction to jurisdiction, but as a general matter, most locales consider protests based on the government's failure to comply with the regulations, to consider a bid in accordance with the terms of the solicitation, or to make an award to the lowest responsive, responsible bidder.

The CICA requires the federal government to award contracts based on "full and open competition."[129] Solicitations must enhance competition and can include restrictive provisions only to the extent that those provisions are required to meet the agency's minimum needs.[130] Finally, agencies can evaluate bids and offers based solely on the factors specified in the solicitation.[131] The FAR provides an elaborate system for implementing these statutory mandates.[132]

A bidder may wish to file a bid protest if it believes that the government has failed to comply with statute or regulations or has not evaluated a bid in accordance with the solicitation. The range of possible protests is limited only by the actions of the government and the terms of the statute,

---

[129] 41 U.S.C.A. § 253(a)(1)(A) (civilian agencies) (West Supp. 1991); 10 U.S.C.A. § 2304(a)(1)(A) (West Supp. 1991) (Department of Defense).

[130] 41 U.S.C.A. § 253a(a)(1)(A), (a)(2)(B); 10 U.S.C.A. § 2305(a)(1).

[131] 41 U.S.C.A. § 253b(a); 10 U.S.C.A. § 2305(b)(1).

[132] Title 48, Code of Federal Regulations.

regulations, and solicitation. However, there are some issues that frequently arise as the basis for protest. They can be grouped in three categories, including:

1. Pre-bid protests challenging the terms of the solicitation
2. Protests challenging the government's failure to comply with the governing procurement statutes and regulations
3. Protests challenging the government's award of the contract based on factors other than those established by the solicitation.

Some possible grounds for protest are discussed further in §§ **14.34** through **14.36**. These are not exhaustive but will provide the reader with some examples of potential bid protests.

§ 14.34   —Pre-Bid Protests Challenging Terms of Solicitation

In federal contracting for construction services, the CICA requires that the government conduct the procurement in order to obtain full and open competition.[133] One of the key factors in "full and open" competition is specifications that do not overly restrict a bidder's ability to bid. To enhance competition, the FAR requires that plans, drawings, specifications, standards, or purchase descriptions state only the government's minimum needs.[134] In construction contracting, the contracting officer must ensure, whenever possible, that references in specifications are to widely-recognized standards or specifications promulgated by governments, industries, or technical societies.[135]

The development of specifications and the determination of the agency's minimum needs are technical and economic judgments that are within the discretion of the agency.[136] However, a protester may prevail if it can show that the government has abused that discretion by writing the specifications in an overly restrictive manner.[137]

Some types of overly restrictive specifications are the inclusion of an arbitrary additional requirement in the specification not related to the agency's needs.[138] This is sometimes known as *goldplating*. Specifications also may contain an impermissible geographical restriction. A protester

---

[133] 41 U.S.C.A. § 253(a)(1)(A) (West Supp. 1991); 10 U.S.C.A. § 2304(a)(1)(A) (West Supp. 1991).

[134] FAR 10.004(a)(1); *see also id.* 36.202(a).

[135] *Id.* 36.202(b).

[136] GE Am. Communications, Inc., B-233547, 89-1 CPD ¶ 172.

[137] North Am. Reporting, Inc., B-198448, 80-2 CPD ¶ 364.

[138] Transmission Structures, Ltd., B-230855.2, 88-2 CPD ¶ 50.

will prevail if it can show that there is no rational basis for a contractor to have a facility within a specified distance of a government construction project when that requirement only serves to limit the number of qualified firms.[139] A specification also may be unduly restrictive if it is written around a specific product.[140]

Other types of defective specifications that may provoke a bid protest are ambiguous specifications, and errors and omissions in specifications. A specification is ambiguous if it is susceptible to more than one reasonable interpretation.[141] This unduly restricts competition because various bidders could have various interpretations and essentially would be bidding on different projects. An ambiguous specification will be considered to be an infirmity when it appears in a contract for construction services.[142] As with ambiguous specifications, a contractor may protest any errors or omissions in specifications that make submitting a cogent bid difficult or impossible.[143]

A restrictive specification usually will be apparent on the face of the solicitation and thus must be raised at the agency level or at GAO prior to submission of bids.[144] A restrictive specification, especially a mistake or omission, may become apparent after the site inspection that is provided in most construction solicitations.[145] If such an omission would have been apparent to a potential bidder at the site inspection, but the bidder chooses not to make that inspection, the potential bidder may lose its opportunity to protest. In such a case, the protest clock would start to run on the date of the inspection and would end 10 days later. If the potential bidder does not attend the inspection but discovers the omission much later, the protest is no longer timely.

A solicitation may also be determined to be restrictive if potential bidders are not permitted sufficient time to respond.[146] The FAR requires that invitations for bids for construction contracts allow sufficient time for bid preparation to allow potential bidders to prepare and submit their bids.[147]

---

[139] Space Age Surveyors, Inc., B-198952, 81-1 CPD ¶ 467.

[140] 39 Comp. Gen. 101 (1959).

[141] HEC Elec. Constr., B-233111, 89-1 CPD ¶ 143.

[142] Maron Constr. Co., B-193106, 79-1 CPD ¶ 169; Allied Contractors, Inc., B-186114, 76-2 CPD ¶ 55.

[143] 50 Comp. Gen. 50 (1970).

[144] See FAR 33.103(b)(2); 4 C.F.R. § 21.2(a)(1) (1991).

[145] FAR 36.503, 52.236-3.

[146] Compare Vicksburg Fed. Bldg. Ltd. Partnership, B-230660, 88-1 CPD ¶ 515 (agency admitted that 11-day period between mailing of solicitation and proposal due date was short; however, unusual and compelling urgency did not allow normal 30-day response time).

[147] FAR 36.303(a).

In determining a reasonable period, the contracting officer must consider the construction season and the time necessary for bidders to inspect the site, obtain subcontract bids, examine data concerning the work, and prepare estimates based on plans and specifications.[148]

§ 14.35   —Government's Failure to Comply with Procurement Laws

Pre-award bid protests generally relate to the procurement process as it impacts the evaluation of the protester's bid. These protests can be distinguished, to some extent, from post-award protests in which the protester believes that either (1) but for the improper evaluation it would have been the awardee or (2) but for the improper evaluation the purported awardee would not have received the award. Pre-award protests usually raise the contracting officer's failure to comply with the procurement regulations in evaluating the protester's bid.

Most federal construction contracts are awarded using sealed bidding.[149] *Sealed bidding* is a method of contracting whereby contractors submit bids based on specifications publicized by the contracting agency. After submission, the agency publicly opens all the bids and awards a contract to the responsible bidder whose bid, conforming to the invitation for bids, is most advantageous to the government, considering only price and price-related factors.[150] Most state and local procurement of construction is done by sealed bidding and the same issues arise.

Bid Responsiveness

Responsiveness, often the subject of bid protests, requires that a bid comply with the terms of the solicitation in all material respects.[151] This requirement enables all bidders to be on a level playing field when being considered for award.[152] A protester can question either the contracting officer's decision that the protester's bid was nonresponsive, thus improperly eliminating the protester from the competition, or that the awardee's bid was responsive, thus improperly causing an award to a nonresponsive bidder.

A bid must conform exactly with the literal requirements of the invitation for bids. If a bid takes exception to any material requirement in the

---

[148] *Id.*

[149] FAR 36.103(a).

[150] *Id.* 14.101.

[151] *Id.* 14.301(a).

[152] *Id.*

invitation, it cannot be considered to be responsive.[153] A bid's responsiveness is determined from the face of the bid at the time of bid opening.[154]

Some nonconformities, however, are not considered to be material and the contracting officer may award in the face of the nonconformity. A minor nonconformity is one that is merely a matter of the form of the bid and not its substance.[155] A minor nonconformity can be corrected or waived without prejudice to other bidders.[156] The contracting officer will consider the defect in the bid to be immaterial when the defect's effect on price, quantity, quality, or delivery is negligible when contrasted with the total cost or scope of the construction services being procured.[157] If, for instance, a protester fails to acknowledge an amendment to the invitation that increased a wage rate determination, the bid will be considered to be nonresponsive.[158] Examples of minor nonconformities include failure to:

1. Return the number of copies required by the invitation
2. Furnish the required information concerning number of employees
3. Sign the bid, but only if there is some evidence of the firm's intent to be bound
4. Acknowledge the receipt of an amendment under some circumstances
5. Execute certain certifications in the invitation.[159]

The contracting officer must either give the bidder an opportunity to cure the nonconformance or waive it.[160]

A bid will not be considered to be responsive if the bidder elects not to cure a defect and the government cannot waive it.[161] The contracting officer may ignore a material nonconformity and award the contract if the award will not prejudice any of the bidders, as in the case in which both bids received in response to the invitation were nonresponsive for the same material nonconformity. The GAO has held that an award in this case is proper as long as the resulting contract satisfied the government's needs.[162]

---

[153] AAA Roofing Co., B-240852, 90-2 CPD ¶ 485.
[154] Luther Constr. Co., B-241719, 91-1 CPD ¶ 76.
[155] FAR 14.405.
[156] *Id.*
[157] *Id.*
[158] North Santiam Paving Co., B-241062, 91-1 CPD ¶ 18.
[159] FAR 14.405.
[160] *Id.*
[161] Grade Way Constr. Co. v. United States, 7 Cl. Ct. 263 (1985).
[162] Singleton Contracting Corp., B-211259, 83-2 CPD ¶ 270.

Responsiveness versus Responsibility

As a rule, the GAO will not consider protests based on a contractor's responsibility unless the protester alleges fraud or bad faith or a failure to meet definitive responsibility criteria.[163] However, this issue may be protested in either the United States Claims Court or federal district court.[164]

Responsiveness and responsibility are closely related. One of the major procedural differences between the two is that responsiveness is determined at the time of bid opening from the face of the bid and responsibility is determined at the time of award and can be based on extraneous information provided by the bidder. The GAO will consider protests when the contracting officer improperly rejects a bidder as nonresponsive when the issue actually is one of responsibility, the theory being that a responsibility issue can be cured through additional contractor proof.[165]

Other Grounds for Protest

Most construction contracts require bidders to provide performance and payment bonds.[166] The provision of such bonds is a material requirement of the invitation for bids and the failure to provide them can render a bid nonresponsive. Protesters often raise the failure to provide bonds or the failure of a bond to comply with the requirements of the solicitation.[167]

Another ground for protest is a bidder's failure to submit a timely bid. Each solicitation must include a designated time and place for bid opening, and each bid must be received prior to that time.[168] Timeliness is often a subject of protest.[169] A protester may raise either the government's failure to accept its late bid or the acceptance of the late bid of another bidder.

Some protestable violations of statute or regulation not related to the evaluation of a specific proposal include: the government's failure to prepare a realistic cost estimate,[170] the cancellation of invitation for bids,[171]

---

[163] 4 C.F.R. § 21.3(m)(5) (1991).

[164] See, e.g., PNM Constr., Inc. v. United States, 13 Cl. Ct. 745 (1987).

[165] Burtch Constr., B-240695, 90-2 CPD ¶ 423; Luther Constr. Co., B-241719, 91-1 CPD ¶ 76.

[166] 40 U.S.C.A. §§ 270a–270f (West Supp. 1991); FAR 28.102-1(a).

[167] Eagle Asphalt & Oil Co., B-240340, 90-2 CPD ¶ 395; Maytal Constr. Corp., B-241501, 90-2 CPD ¶ 476.

[168] FAR 14.302(a).

[169] Carothers Constr. Co. v. United States, 18 Cl. Ct. 745 (1989); Barnes Elec. Co., B-241391.2, 91-1 CPD ¶ 10.

[170] Bean Dredging Corp. v. United States, 19 Cl. Ct. 561 (1990).

[171] Caddell Constr. Co. v. United States, 7 Cl. Ct. 236 (1985).

and the conversion of a procurement from one restricted to a small, disadvantaged business to an unrestricted procurement.[172]

§ 14.36　—Government's Failure to Follow Solicitation in Award

The CICA requires that award of contracts be based only on the factors specified in the solicitation.[173] Protests based on the government's failure to follow its evaluation criteria are more particularly appropriate in the area of negotiated contracts than they are in sealed bids.

The federal government is beginning to use competitive negotiation more and more in the procurement of construction services. The Model Procurement Code also provides for similar procedures that it refers to as *competitive sealed proposals.*[174] In this type of procurement, the solicitation will include the specifications, terms and conditions, and evaluation factors specifying the basis for award. The evaluation factors can include price and price-related factors as well as non-price-related factors.[175] After submission of proposals, the agency conducts discussions with offerors in the competitive range and provides those offerors with a chance to revise their proposals based on those discussions.[176] The government then awards the contract to the responsible offeror whose offer is most advantageous to the government, considering only cost or price and the other factors included in the solicitation.[177]

The government's use of competitive negotiation rather than sealed bidding in construction contracting has been upheld by GAO under certain circumstances.[178] However, the government must show that the proposed repair or construction work is more complex than routine construction.[179]

In negotiated procurements, protests can include the government's failure to include a protester in the competitive range,[180] failure to conduct "meaningful discussions,"[181] and failure to evaluate a proposal in

---

[172] RNJ Interstate Corp., B-241946, 91-1 CPD ¶ 219.

[173] 41 U.S.C.A. § 253b(a) (West Supp. 1991); 10 U.S.C.A. § 2305(b)(1) (West Supp. 1991).

[174] Model Procurement Code § 3-203.

[175] 41 U.S.C.A. § 253a(b); 10 U.S.C.A. § 2305(a)(2).

[176] 41 U.S.C.A. § 253b(d); 10 U.S.C.A. § 2305(b)(4).

[177] 41 U.S.C.A. § 253b(d)(4); 10 U.S.C.A. § 2305(b)(4)(B); *see generally* Contracting by Negotiation, FAR pt. 15.

[178] Claude E. Atkins Enters., Inc., B-241047, 91-1 CPD ¶ 42.

[179] Northeast Constr. Co., B-234323, 89-1 CPD ¶ 402.

[180] Adams Corporate Solutions, B-241097, 91-1 CPD ¶ 24.

[181] Virginia Technology Assocs., B-241167, 91-1 CPD ¶ 80.

accordance with the terms of the solicitation.[182] In the last instance, a protest usually is filed after award of the contract and can be filed by a disappointed offeror who would have received the award but for the failure to comply with the evaluation criteria or by an offeror claiming that the awardee would not have received the award had the contracting officer evaluated the awardee's proposal properly.

A competitively negotiated procurement probably provides more opportunities for protest due to the fact that it is more complex than a standard sealed bid. A potential offeror should be aware of any such opportunities that may be present during the procurement process.

§ 14.37 Tips for Successful Bid Protests

A contractor can take a number of steps in order to maximize its probability of success in winning bid protests. First, it is essential that the contractor know the rules governing the procurement. All the states and localities have different rules for procurement and for the filing of protests. Most have not adopted the Model Procurement Code or Model Ordinance. If a contractor is to be successful, it must not only know where to go to file a protest, but also know what rules the government must follow in order to detect a protestable violation.

Second, a contractor must constantly monitor the procurement process to identify in a timely manner any improper actions taken by the government. A contractor must review the solicitation shortly after its issuance to detect any protestable improprieties. Furthermore, a contractor must keep itself fully informed of the government's actions at all stages of the procurement in order to preserve its right to protest.

Third, the contractor must assess the viability of the protest, with legal counsel if necessary, in order to avoid filing a useless protest in an area of settled law. This could prove to be a waste of time and effort for a contractor and could delay the procurement process needlessly.

Fourth, if the contractor decides to protest, the contractor should make sure that its submission is a concise, logical presentation of the facts and the law. The more carefully the protest is written, the better the contractor's likelihood of success. The contractor should keep in mind, however, that some of the forums discussed in this chapter require an attorney to file a protest. In other instances, counsel may be appropriate to enhance the protester's likelihood of success.

Fifth, a contractor must carefully consider its options for filing a protest and choose the option that is most beneficial. Determinations will include consideration of factors such as jurisdiction, precedent, and expense. If an

---

[182] Cygna Project Management, B-236839, 90-1 CPD ¶ 21.

agency protest will yield the desired results, it is foolish to spend the time and money on a claim for injunctive relief at the United States Claims Court.

Finally, a contractor must consider the business realities in deciding whether to protest. If the contractor has cultivated a long-standing business relationship with the government, it may not be worth entering into an adversarial relationship for a protest that has little merit. Again, although the government cannot retaliate against a protester for filing a protest, such an action may nevertheless impact day-to-day working relationships.

Bid protests present a maze of rules, regulations, and forums that may at times seem impenetrable. Nevertheless, a well-timed, thoughtful protest may be the difference between winning and losing a contract award. A protest may be financially beneficial to the protester, but it is also of tremendous worth in maintaining the integrity of the procurement system.

§ 14.38   Mistakes in Bid

Mistakes in bids may be disclosed either before or after award of a contract.[183] Those mistakes that are disclosed before award may influence the ultimate award of the contract. Mistakes disclosed after award will probably not impact award, but may affect substantially a contractor's ability to perform for the agreed upon price and, thus, are a matter of contract administration. This chapter discusses the issues associated with mistakes disclosed before the award of the contract that may have an impact on the award process.

If a bidder makes a mistake in its bid that is discovered after bid opening[184] but before award of the contract, it is likely that the bidder will either request the correction or withdraw its bid. The government usually is cautious in permitting a bidder to withdraw or correct a bid, as such an action could compromise the integrity of the procurement system.[185]

The government only provides relief from a mistake in bid if the mistake is a clerical rather than a judgmental one.[186] Clerical mistakes include

---

[183] Mistakes in bid generally are found in procurements by sealed bidding. If there is a mistake in an offer submitted pursuant to a negotiated procurement, the government may hold further negotiations in order to correct that mistake, thus rendering mistake in bid procedures unnecessary. *See* Energy Container Corp., B-235595.2, 89-2 CPD ¶ 414; FAR 15.607(a), 15.610. This section focuses on mistakes in sealed bids that are governed at the federal level by FAR subpt. 14.406.

[184] Prior to bid opening, a bid may be modified or withdrawn by an authorized representative of the bidder without the permission of the contracting officer. FAR 14.303; Model Procurement Code § R3-202.13.2.

[185] Black Diamond Energies, Inc., B-241370, 91-1 CPD ¶ 119.

[186] Ruggiero v. United States, 190 Ct. Cl. 327, 420 F.2d 709 (1970); Model Procurement Code § R3-202.13.1.

arithmetic errors, apparent misreading of the specification, misplaced decimal points, obviously incorrect discounts, obvious reversal of the price of FOB (free on board) destination and price of FOB origin, and obvious mistakes in designation of units.[187] Errors in business judgment result from a bidder's failure to assess adequately the requirements of the solicitation and to determine the cost and effort required to perform the contract.[188]

If the contracting officer detects an apparent mistake in a bid, the officer must inform the bidder immediately and either verify that the bid is correct or invite the bidder to make a correction or to withdraw its bid.[189] The rationale for verification is that it would be unfair for the government to hold a bidder to a bargain that it did not mean to make. Bids that are obviously erroneous cannot be accepted by the government.[190] However, a bidder has no standing to question the government's failure to verify an error in the bid of another bidder.[191]

Once the contracting officer or the bidder has identified a mistake, the contracting officer has a variety of options: (1) permit the bidder to correct the mistake; (2) deny the bidder the opportunity to correct the mistake; (3) permit the bidder to withdraw the bid; or (4) reject the bid.

§ 14.39   —Correction of Bid

The contracting officer can either correct or permit a bidder to correct an apparent clerical error in a bid.[192] Clerical errors include typographical errors, errors in extending unit pricing, transposition errors, and arithmetic errors.[193] An example of a clerical error is one that is obvious from the face of the bid, that is verified by the bidder, and that is corrected readily by a standard mathematical formula.[194]

If the error is one that is not an apparent clerical error, the contracting officer may grant the bidder the opportunity to correct the mistake if the bidder can show by clear and convincing evidence (1) the existence of the mistake and (2) the intended bid.[195] A bidder can make this showing by presenting evidence of bid preparation, including sworn statements or

---

[187] Ruggiero v. United States, 190 Ct. Cl. 327, 420 F.2d 709 (1970), F.A.R. § 14.406-2(a).

[188] See Aydin Corp. v. United States, 229 Ct. Cl. 309, 669 F.2d 681 (1982); Oregon Elec. Constr., Inc., B-232419, 88-2 CPD ¶ 512.

[189] FAR 14.406-1; Model Procurement Code § R3-202.13.3.

[190] Pamfilis Painting Inc., B-237968, 90-1 CPD ¶ 355.

[191] Diesel Sys., Inc., B-237333, 89-2 CPD ¶ 451.

[192] FAR 14.406-2(a).

[193] Model Procurement Code § R3-202.13.4(b).

[194] North Landing Line Constr. Co., B-239662, 90-2 CPD ¶ 60.

[195] FAR 14.406-3(a); Raymond L. Crawford Constr. Co., B-211516, 83-2 CPD ¶ 239.

affidavits;[196] the bidder's file copy of the bid;[197] original worksheets;[198] other data used in bid preparation;[199] subcontractor quotes;[200] published price lists; and other evidence.[201] GAO will reverse a contracting officer's decision to permit correction of a bid if the evidence that the contracting officer used to make its determination does not clearly and convincingly show the existence of the mistake and the intended bid.[202]

As a general rule, the contracting officer will not permit correction of a mistake if doing so will replace a low bidder.[203] The only exception to the rule is if the existence of the mistake and the bid actually intended are apparent from the bid itself without resort to the review of extrinsic evidence.[204]

Because contracting officers will not often permit a correction to displace the low bidder, a bidder will usually request a correction when its bid is low but would have been higher but for the mistake. This may be viewed by the contracting officer as an attempt to avoid "leaving money on the table," thereby contravening the competitive bidding process. In order to protect the integrity of the procurement system, the contracting officer will give closer scrutiny to the evidence of mistakes in those cases in which the correction brings the bid close to the next low bidder.[205]

The contracting officer will likewise not permit correction of a bid if the purpose of the correction is to make a nonresponsive bid responsive.[206] However, if the correction is merely a matter of mathematical calculation, the correction will not be considered to affect bid responsiveness.[207]

§ 14.40   —Withdrawal of Bid

A bidder may make a request to the contracting officer to withdraw rather than to correct its bid.[208] The degree of proof required to permit a bidder to withdraw its bid is not as high as that required for correction. The burden

---

[196] FAR 14.406-3(g)(2); States Roofing & Metal Co., B-237900, 90-1 CPD ¶ 353.

[197] FAR 14.406-3(g)(2).

[198] *Id.;* Shoemaker & Alexander, Inc., B-241066, 91-1 CPD ¶ 41.

[199] *Id.*

[200] *Id.*

[201] *Id.*

[202] Weather Data Serv., Inc., B-241621, 91-1 CPD ¶ 185.

[203] FAR 14.406-3(a); R.C. Constr. Co., B-241176.2, 91-1 CPD ¶ 118.

[204] *Id.*

[205] Northwest Builders, B-228555, 88-1 CPD ¶ 200.

[206] FAR 14.406-3; Atlantic Co. of Am., Inc., B-241697, 91-1 CPD ¶ 49.

[207] Haag Elec. & Constr., Inc., B-240974, 91-1 CPD ¶ 29.

[208] FAR 14.406-3(c); Model Procurement Code § R3-202.13.4(c)

may be sustained if the bidder can demonstrate the existence of the mistake, which may be shown by a significant difference between the mistaken bid and the next low bidder or government estimate.[209] If the evidence of the existence of the mistake and the intended bid is clear and convincing, and the bid, both corrected and uncorrected, is low, the head of the agency may decide to accept the bid and permit correction rather than permit the bidder to withdraw.[210]

§ 14.41   —Rejection of Bid

The contracting officer must reject the bid if it is so far out of line with the other bids or the agency estimate so as to appear unreasonable or if there are other clear indications of a major error justifying the conclusion that acceptance of the bid would be unfair to the bidder or other bona fide bidders.[211] Rejection is further required if it is not clear that the bid would have remained low absent the correction.[212]

If the evidence submitted by the bidder does not justify correction, withdrawal, or rejection, the contracting officer, at the direction of the agency head, will consider the bid as it stands.[213]

---

[209] American Block Co., B-235053, 89-2 CPD ¶ 90.

[210] FAR 14.406-3(b).

[211] FAR 14.406-3(g)(5).

[212] Black Diamond Energies, Inc., B-241370, 91-1 CPD ¶ 119.

[213] FAR 14.406-3(d). For further information on bid protests and mistakes in bid, *see generally* Construction Bidding Law (R. Cushman & W. Doyle eds., John Wiley & Sons 1990).

CHAPTER 15

CONTRACTOR RIGHTS AND REMEDIES AGAINST OWNERS

Mark J. Coleman
Ruth E. Gaube

Mark J. Coleman joined Pillsbury, Madison & Sutro in San Francisco, California, in 1984 and became a partner in 1991. He has extensive experience in the development and construction of industrial and urban (office tower) projects, with particular emphasis on the financing of such projects. He received his bachelor's degree in 1980 from Pomona College, after study at Oxford University, England, and he received his law degree from the University of California at Berkeley's Boalt Hall in 1983. Mr. Coleman is a member of the UCC Committee of the Business Law Section of the California bar, is on the editorial board of the *Business Law News,* and is also a member of the San Francisco and American Bar Associations.

Ruth E. Gaube joined Pillsbury, Madison & Sutro in San Francisco, California, in 1989, specializing in real estate and commercial law. She received her B.A., summa cum laude, in English from San Francisco State University, and her J.D., summa cum laude, from the University of Minnesota. Ms. Gaube is a member of the California, San Francisco, and the American Bar Associations.

§ 15.1   Introduction

Problems arise during the course of performance of many construction contracts that make it difficult for contractors to complete construction projects as contemplated in the construction contracts. Such problems can arise either from the failure of the contractor or the owner to perform properly its obligations under the construction contract or from the occurrence of unanticipated events that are the fault of neither the contractor nor the owner. When such problems arise, it becomes necessary to determine which party to the contract—the contractor or the owner—must take financial responsibility for any losses arising from the delay in or difficulty of performance of the contract. This chapter deals with situations in which the owner must compensate the contractor for losses suffered by the contractor as a result of problems arising during the course of performance of the construction contract or in which the contractor may be excused from its performance due to the owner's failure to perform. The chapter first examines the options available to a contractor when the owner breaches the construction contract. Then a variety of specific situations are discussed that may give rise to a claim by the contractor against the owner for losses suffered during the course of performing the construction contract. Some of those situations, however, depending on the terms of the construction contract, may not involve breaches of the contract by the owner but rather may result in the contractor's having the right to collect compensation from the owner based on the terms of the contract.

The rules of law this chapter discusses are generally applicable to all construction contracts and provide an introduction to the various rights and remedies contractors have against owners. The law of each individual state and the federal law governing contracts with federal governmental entities as owners, however, may contain variations on the general rules discussed in the chapter. The state or federal law that governs a particular contract controls the rights and remedies available to a contractor with respect to that contract.

Although a discussion of the rules for determining which state's law governs a particular contract is beyond the scope of the chapter, generally the law of the state with the most connections with the contract governs the contract. For example, if the site of the construction project is located in California and the contractor is a California corporation with its principal office in California, California law likely will govern the contract. In addition, many construction contracts contain a provision whereby the owner and the contractor select the law of a particular state to govern the contract. Such a provision generally is enforceable, as long as the state whose law is chosen to govern the contract has a reasonable connection with the contract. If the owner on the construction project is a federal governmental entity, the contract probably will be governed by federal law, not state law.

BREACH BY OWNER

§ 15.2 Remedies for Breach

Common types of breaches of construction contracts by owners include the following:

1. Failure of the owner to pay the contractor according to the schedule included in the construction contract
2. Failure of the owner to provide the contractor with adequate access to the jobsite
3. Interference by the owner with the contractor's performance of the contract
4. Failure of the owner to approve or inspect items that the construction contract requires the owner to approve or inspect in a timely fashion
5. Provision of defective plans and specifications for the work
6. Failure to provide equipment or other items the contract requires the owner to provide
7. Wrongful termination of the construction contract by the owner.

Determining whether a breach of a construction contract by an owner has occurred requires careful examination of the contract. Once the contractor has determined that the owner has breached the contract, it is important for the contractor to examine the contract carefully again to determine whether the contract contains a specific remedy designed to compensate the contractor for the particular breach by the owner. Such a specific remedy is enforceable in most situations and may, if the contract so provides, be the only remedy available to the contractor for the particular breach. **Sections 15.10, 15.14,** and **15.24** dealing with particular types of breaches by owners discuss standard contract provisions that often are included in construction contracts to address particular breaches by owners.

If the contract does not contain a specific remedy for the breach, the contractor generally is entitled to damages from the owner in an amount equal to the losses suffered or extra expenses incurred by the contractor as a result of the owner's breach. **Sections 15.12, 15.17, 15.21, 15.26,** and **15.29** dealing with particular types of breaches by owners discuss specific methods of calculating damages for those types of breaches. In addition, a breach by the owner may excuse performance by the contractor of the contractor's duties under the contract that are affected by the breach. For example, if the contract obligates the contractor to complete the project by a certain date but the owner's breach delays the contractor's ability to construct the project, the requirement that the contractor complete the project by the date in the contract may be excused and the contractor may be granted an extension of the time in which the contractor must complete the contract.

Material versus Minor Breach

It is important for contractors to be aware that minor breaches of a construction contract by an owner do not give the contractor the right to cease performance under the construction contract until the contractor is compensated for the loss caused by the breach unless the construction contract explicitly gives the contractor the right to cease performance. Rather, in a situation in which the owner's breach is minor, the contractor generally is obligated to continue performing under the construction contract while the contractor pursues its remedies for the breach provided either by the terms of the contract or by applicable statutory or common law.

On the other hand, when the breach by the owner is a material breach of the contract, the contractor may cease work under the construction contract without thereby breaching the contract itself. Whether a particular breach by an owner is a material breach depends on the construction contract and the facts of the situation. As a general rule, a breach is material only if the owner fails to perform a substantial portion of its duties under the construction contract or under one of the contract's essential conditions or if the effect of the breach is substantially to deny the contractor the benefit the contractor expected to obtain from performance of the contract.[1] An example of a material breach is the termination of the construction contract by the owner when the contractor is not in material breach of the contract and when the contract does not contain a provision allowing the owner to terminate the contract in the absence of such a breach by the contractor. An example of a breach that would be a minor breach in most situations is the failure of the owner to make a progress payment until three days after the payment was due under the construction contract.

If the owner materially breaches the construction contract, the contractor has a choice of two basic alternatives, each of which involves a different method for calculating the damages to the contractor for which the owner is liable as a result of the breach. Those two alternatives are discussed in § 15.3. The goal of each of the methods of damage calculation is to compensate the contractor for the breach by putting the contractor in as good a position as the contractor would have been in if the breach had not

---

[1] For a more detailed discussion of the elements of material breach and factual situations that can constitute material breach, *see* 1 S. Stein, Construction Law ¶ 4.14 (1990).

occurred. That goal is the general goal upon which all calculations of damages in contract actions are based. In addition, the foreseeable indirect consequences of the owner's breach—termed *consequential damages*—and the damages resulting from the contractor's attempts to mitigate its losses after breach by the owner—termed *incidental damages*—may be available in specific situations. Damages designed to punish the wrongdoer—termed *punitive damages*—generally are not available in breach of contract actions, although they may be available in special cases, such as when the owner fraudulently refuses to pay the contractor amounts due under the contract or when the owner fraudulently misrepresents important information to the contractor.

§ 15.3   Measure of Damages for Material Breach

If the owner has materially breached the construction contract, there are two basic alternative courses of action available to the contractor. The alternative that the contractor chooses will depend upon a variety of factors, including the amount of work the contractor has done on the project, the value to the owner of the work completed, and the profitability of the construction contract from the contractor's perspective. The contractor must select the appropriate alternative carefully because once the contractor chooses to pursue the first alternative involving rescission of the contract, the law automatically forecloses the contractor from later choosing the second alternative involving collection of damages pursuant to the contract and the converse is also true.

Rescission of the Contract

The first alternative available to the contractor when the owner has materially breached the construction contract is to treat the construction contract as rescinded and to recover from the owner an amount equal to the value of the work performed by the contractor up to the date of the breach. This method of calculating damages is known as *quantum meruit.* The goal of this method of damage calculation is to put both the owner and the contractor in the positions they were in prior to entering into the construction contract by rescinding the contract or, in other words, treating the contract as if it never existed, and then compensating the contractor for the benefit the owner received from having the work performed.

Because the contract is viewed as never having existed in this method of damage calculation, the value of the work performed by the contractor is not measured by the price for the work contained in the contract. Rather, the value of the work is calculated by determining the reasonable value of the services and materials provided by the contractor. Because the contract price is not considered in determining the amount the contractor can recover, this method of damage calculation is the most beneficial to the contractor when performance under the contract and payment of the contract price would have resulted in a loss or a lesser recovery for the contractor.

Collection of Damages Pursuant to Contract

The second alternative available to the contractor when the owner materially breaches the construction contract is to view the breach as terminating the contractor's obligation to continue performing under the contract but to keep the contract in effect for determining the proper measure of damages for the breach. The goal of this second method is to put the contractor in the position it would have been in had the contract been performed fully without requiring full performance.

There are several different formulas available for calculating the amount of damages under this second method. One formula is to award the contractor the full contract price (less any progress payments made by the owner to the contractor) minus the costs that would have been incurred by the contractor to finish performing the work under the contract. A second formula is to award the contractor all costs incurred by the contractor in performing the work up to the date of the breach plus the profit the contractor anticipated receiving if the contract had been performed fully minus any progress payments made by the owner to the contractor. The second alternative is probably the best alternative for a contractor that had anticipated receiving a reasonable profit from performance of the construction contract. In addition, this second method is the appropriate method to use when the contractor has not performed any work under the contract prior to the breach by the owner. In such a case, the contractor would have incurred either no costs or minimal costs and the main portion of the recovery would be for the profits the contractor anticipated receiving upon completion of the contract.

§ 15.4   Calculation of Damages

The contractor's remedy for many of the breaches by an owner discussed in this chapter is the recovery of additional costs incurred by the contractor in connection with the owner's breach. The preferred method for establishing the amount of those additional costs is for the contractor to present evidence of amounts actually incurred by the contractor for each item of additional cost.[2] For example, if the contractor is claiming an amount for

---

[2] *See, e.g.,* Dawco Constr., Inc. v. United States, 930 F.2d 872, 882 (Fed. Cir. 1991); State Highway Comm'n v. Brasel & Sims Constr. Co., 688 P.2d 871, 879 (Wyo. 1984).

additional labor costs incurred as a result of removing an unexpected storage tank uncovered at the work site, and the owner is liable to the contractor for the amount of such costs pursuant to the differing site conditions provision in the contract as discussed in §§ **15.8** through **15.12,** the contractor should present evidence of the extra payments the contractor actually made to the workers over and above the amounts the contractor needed to pay the workers to complete the work as originally contemplated. Whenever the contractor believes that it may have a claim against the owner for which it intends to seek damages, the contractor should keep careful records of each cost incurred by the contractor in connection with the extra work or delays for which the contractor believes the owner should be liable.

Total Cost Method

If the contractor fails to keep careful records or if multiple breaches by the owner make it difficult for the contractor to segregate the individual costs attributable to each breach from the general cost of completing the contract, it may be possible for the contractor to recover damages based on the total cost method of calculating damages. Under the *total cost method,* the contractor calculates damages for the owner's breach or multiple breaches by subtracting the total of all costs incurred by the contractor in completing the work from the original contract price or bid estimate. The contractor should avoid reliance on the total cost method if at all possible, however, because courts generally limit use of the method to situations in which the contractor can demonstrate the following:

1. That the contractor incurred all of the additional costs as a result of a breach or multiple breaches by the owner
2. That itemizing costs incurred would be extremely difficult or impossible
3. That the original contract price or bid estimate was reasonable
4. That the extra costs incurred were reasonable.[3]

Some courts have expressed a willingness to apply modified versions of the total cost method in situations in which the contractor cannot meet the requirements for use of the total cost method but is unable to itemize each

---

[3] *See, e.g.,* Servidone Constr. Corp. v. United States, 931 F.2d 860, 861 (Fed. Cir. 1991); Moorhead Constr. Co. v. City of Grand Forks, 508 F.2d 1008, 1016 (8th Cir. 1975); J.D. Hedin Constr. Co. v. United States, 347 F.2d 235, 246–47 (Ct. Cl. 1965); Department of Transp. v. Hawkins Bridge Co., 457 So. 2d 525, 528 (Fla. Dist. Ct. App. 1984); John F. Harkins Co. v. School Dist., 313 Pa. Super. 425, 460 A.2d 260, 263–64 (1983); State Highway Comm'n v. Brasel & Sims Constr. Co., 688 P.2d 871, 877–78.

type of cost incurred. Under one such version of the total cost method—the *modified total cost method*—the contractor either limits the calculation of total cost to a segregated portion of the work or deletes from the total cost calculation the costs that the contractor can demonstrate are not attributable to breaches by the owner.[4] Under the other generally-recognized version of the total cost method—the *jury verdict method*—the contractor presents evidence of the amount of damages based on the total cost method and the court modifies the amount based on the court's determination as to the proportion of the total damages caused by the owner's breach or breaches and the reasonableness of the contractor's costs.[5]

§ 15.5   Limitations on Damages

The amount of damages a contractor is able to collect for a breach by the owner may be limited by various rules of law applicable to contract damages generally or by contract clauses placing limitations on damages either for specific breaches or for any breach.[6]

The law governing contract damages generally requires that the amount of damages claims be proven with reasonable certainty. If the amount of damages claimed by a contractor is too speculative, a court will not grant recovery for that amount. The law governing contract damages generally also requires that after breach of a contract has occurred, the injured party mitigate its damages, or, in other words, do everything reasonably possible to reduce the amount of the damages arising from the breach.[7] Typical mitigation actions could include, depending on the circumstances, laying off unneeded workers, selling materials purchased for the project that are no longer necessary as a result of the breach, or canceling orders for materials. If the contractor does not mitigate its damages, the amount that it can recover will be reduced by any amounts the owner can prove could have been reduced by mitigation. The law does not, however, require that the contractor's mitigation actions actually reduce its damages. In fact, the law allows a contractor to recover costs incurred in mitigating damages even if

---

[4] *See, e.g.,* Servidone Constr. Corp. v. United States, 931 F.2d 860, 861–62; Delco Elec. Corp. v. United States, 17 Cl. Ct. 302, 324–29 (1989), *aff'd,* 909 F.2d 1495 (Fed. Cir. 1990).

[5] *See, e.g.,* S.W. Elec. & Mfg. Corp. v. United States, 655 F.2d 1078, 1086–89 (Ct. Cl. 1981); Meva Corp. v. United States, 511 F.2d 548, 557–59 (Ct. Cl. 1975); State Highway Comm'n v. Brasel & Sims, 688 P.2d 871, 880.

[6] For a more detailed description of various types of limitations on damage recovery by contractors, *see* 2 S. Stein, Construction Law ¶ 11.05[5].

[7] *See, e.g.,* 5 A. Corbin, Corbin on Contracts §§ 1039, 1044 (1962); 11 W. Jaeger & S. Williston, Williston on Contracts §§ 1053–1054 (3d ed. 1968).

the mitigation does not reduce the contractor's damages as long as the mitigation actions are reasonable under the circumstances.

In addition to limitations on damage recovery imposed by the law governing contracts generally, some construction contracts contain provisions limiting the amount of damages the contractor can recover either for specified breaches or for any breach. These provisions usually are enforceable, although courts generally interpret them narrowly and may refuse to apply them in some circumstances.

§ 15.6   Methods of Recovery

In the absence of a contract provision specifying the method of recovery, a contractor that has a claim against an owner that the owner disputes or refuses to pay will need to sue the owner to obtain recovery.

Many construction contracts, however, contain explicit procedures for a contractor to follow in presenting a claim to the owner for specific types of breaches. In addition, many construction clauses contain a general provision requiring the parties to arbitrate any disputes that arise under the contract.[8] The provision may specify the number of arbitrators who will resolve the disputes and the method for selecting them or may simply refer to standard rules for the selection of arbitrators and the conduct of the arbitration process. Provisions requiring arbitration usually state that the decision of the arbitrators is binding on both the owner and the contractor. Arbitration provisions generally are enforceable and the decision of the arbitrators, if the contract so specifies, generally is viewed as final in the absence of fraud or coercion in the arbitration process.

The main advantage of including an arbitration provision in contract clauses is that the amount of time it takes to complete the arbitration process and reach a decision generally is less than the amount of time necessary to complete the litigation process. In addition, arbitrators often are experts in the construction field who are less likely to make errors based on a misunderstanding of the factual situation than jurors might be. On the other hand, the panel of arbitrators may be less impartial than a judge or jury would be.

§ 15.7   Collection of Damages

Once the contractor establishes a claim against the owner, the contractor is faced with the task of collecting the damages from the owner. In some

---

[8] For a detailed discussion of the statutes governing arbitration and the arbitration process, *see id.* ch. 12.

situations, a recalcitrant owner may refuse to pay the damages or may be unable to pay the damages as a result of financial difficulties.

Mechanic's Liens

In addition to the various methods of collecting damages that are available generally, statutes or state constitutions in all 50 states and the District of Columbia give contractors a special lien, known as a *mechanic's lien,* to assist the contractor in collecting the amount due from the owner.[9] Although each of the various statutes or constitutional provisions are based on the same general principle of granting a contractor a lien on the structures constructed by the contractor in order to secure payment of the price under the construction contract, each state's statute or constitutional provision varies significantly regarding the procedures that a contractor must follow to establish a lien, the duration of the lien, and the property that the lien will cover. If a contractor desires to establish a mechanic's lien, the contractor should examine carefully the requirements for establishing such a lien that exist in the state where the contractor is performing the construction contract.

Generally, a contractor that contributes to the performance of construction work is entitled to assert a lien against that work if the contractor is not paid for the work. In order to establish a mechanic's lien, the contractor generally must give the owner notice that the contractor intends to assert a lien against the structure being constructed and thereafter must record a claim for a mechanic's lien with the appropriate governmental office, generally the office where documents affecting real property must be recorded in the county where the construction project is located. Most states require that contractors give owners notice and file claims for liens within a specified time period after performance of the work. The duration of a mechanic's lien depends entirely on the time period set forth in the applicable statute or constitutional provision. Because the right to a mechanics' lien arises solely as the result of a statute or pursuant to a state constitution, it is important for the contractor to comply strictly with all the various procedural requirements set forth in the applicable statute or constitutional provision in order for the lien to be enforceable.

If the contractor properly creates and perfects a mechanic's lien against property of the owner by following the procedures set forth in the applicable statute or constitutional provision, the lien of the contractor against the property will generally have priority over any further liens subsequently asserted against the property, but will be subordinate to properly created and perfected liens existing against the property at the time the contractor

---

[9] For a more detailed description of mechanic's liens, *see id.* ch. 9.

creates and perfects the mechanic's lien. In some states, mechanic's liens will be deemed to relate back to the date the construction commences and thus will have priority over liens recorded against the property between the date construction commences and the date the contractor records the mechanic's lien. If the contractor decides to enforce the lien as the method of collecting the damages owed to the contractor by the owner, the contractor will have to file an action for judicial foreclosure in the appropriate court to obtain a court order for the sale of the property upon which the contractor has created and perfected the lien. The contractor then can collect the amount owed from the proceeds of the sale, after payment of the expenses of the sale and payments to any senior lienholders. Before instituting an action to foreclose a mechanic's lien, the contractor should determine whether the amount received from the sale of the property will be sufficient to pay the senior lienholders as well as to cover the expenses of the sale and the amount owed to the contractor.

Stop Notices

In order to protect contractors when the amount received from the sale of the property likely will not be sufficient to pay the senior lienholders and cover the expenses of the sale, some states, such as California, have enacted statutes giving a contractor the right to serve a stop notice on the bank or other financial institution lending money to the owner to finance the construction of the project.[10] Statutes in some states, such as California, Mississippi, New Jersey, and Texas, also give subcontractors the right to serve a stop notice on the owner or construction lender.[11] Once the lender or owner receives a stop notice that is properly served in accordance with the applicable state statute, the lender or owner generally must reserve a portion of the undisbursed proceeds of the loan or, in the case of an owner, the amount due the prime contractor, to pay the contractor or subcontractor, although some states require the contractor or subcontractor to post a bond before the stop notice is enforceable. Because the right to a stop notice, similar to the right to a mechanic's lien, arises solely as the result of a statute, it is important for the contractor to comply strictly with all the various procedural requirements set forth in the applicable statute to ensure that the stop notice is enforceable.

---

[10] *See, e.g.,* Cal. Civ. Code §§ 3158, 3160–3175 (1991).

[11] *See, e.g.,* Cal. Civ. Code §§ 3159–3175 (1991); Miss. Code Ann. § 85-7-181 (1990); N.J. Stat. Ann. §§ 2A:44-77 through 2A:44-80; Tex. Prop. Code Ann. §§ 53.081–53.084 (1991).

DIFFERING SITE CONDITIONS

§ 15.8   Recovery under Common Law

One common problem that arises in the course of performing construction contracts that makes it difficult to complete the contract in the manner originally contemplated by the parties is the discovery of unusual physical conditions at the work site that were not known to the parties at the time of contracting. Unexpected physical conditions often consist of unexpected obstructions under the surface of the work site discovered during excavation, such as unusual rock formations, unanticipated storage tanks, remnants of earlier construction, or even the discovery of important archaeological artifacts that are protected by local law. In the absence of a provision in the construction contract dealing with the rights and remedies of the contractor when the contractor discovers such unexpected conditions, under the common law the contractor usually must absorb any losses associated with the increased expense of constructing the project caused by the unexpected condition.[12] The contractor may, however, be able to recover from the owner the extra expense incurred in dealing with the unusual site conditions even if the construction contract does not contain a clause governing unusual site conditions if the contractor can prove that the owner either misrepresented the condition of the site or failed to disclose knowledge possessed by the owner of the unusual site condition.

In order for the contractor to recover based on a misrepresentation theory, the contractor must show each of the following:

1. That the physical condition of the site was materially different from the condition represented to the contractor by the owner
2. That the contractor was justified in relying on the representations by the owner instead of conducting its own investigation
3. That the owner knew of the unusual site conditions and purposefully misrepresented the condition of the site
4. That the extra costs claimed by the contractor were actually caused by the unexpected site conditions.

---

[12] *See, e.g.,* Eastern Tunneling Corp. v. Southgate Sanitation Dist., 487 F. Supp. 109, 113 (D. Colo. 1980). For a more detailed description of recovery for unexpected physical conditions under the common law, *see* Hannan & Maloney, *What's Different About Differing Site Condition Claims?,* 1990 Def. Couns. J. 304, 310–11; Cushman et al., *The Contractor and Subcontractor as Claimants,* Construction Contracts and Litigation 1988, at 519, 546–557 (1988) [hereinafter Cushman].

In order to recover on a failure-to-disclose theory, the contractor must show the following factors:

1. That the owner failed to disclose the existence of unusual site conditions
2. That the owner had a duty to disclose the unusual site conditions
3. That the owner knew the contractor would rely on the owner's silence as an indication that the unusual site conditions did not exist
4. That the contractor actually did rely on the owner to disclose information about the site rather than conduct its own investigation
5. That the extra costs incurred by the contractor were actually caused by the unusual site conditions.[13]

The difficulty with both the common law theories of recovery is that, in the ordinary situation, both the owner and the contractor are unaware of the unusual site conditions until the conditions are discovered during the performance of the work. In addition, even if the contractor can prove that the owner was aware of the unusual site conditions, in the absence of a special relationship between the contractor and the owner, it may be difficult for the contractor to prove that it was reasonable for the contractor to rely on the owner's description of the work site rather than conduct a careful investigation of the site itself.

Because of the difficulty of recovering increased costs incurred as a result of unusual site conditions under the common law, it is generally beneficial for contractors to insist on a contract clause governing the discovery of unusual site conditions. Contractors may protect themselves by including generous estimates in their bids for dealing with unexpected physical conditions in situations in which the contractor will be forced to bear any additional expense incurred as a result of the discovery of unusual physical conditions. Therefore, it is also generally beneficial for an owner to agree to a provision in the contract dealing with differing site conditions that will make it easier for the contractor to recover such additional expenses and thus to reduce the amounts of its bid.

---

[13] For examples of when a governmental entity acting as owner under a construction project has a duty to disclose information to a contractor, *see, e.g.,* McCormick Constr. Co. v. United States, 18 Cl. Ct. 259, 265–67 (1989), *aff'd,* 907 F.2d 159 (Fed. Cir. 1990); American Ship Bldg. Co. v. United States, 654 F.2d 75, 79–80 (Ct. Cl. 1981); Hardeman-Monier-Hutcherson v. United States, 458 F.2d 1364, 1371–72 (Ct. Cl. 1972); Helene Curtis Indus., Inc. v. United States, 312 F.2d 774 (Ct. Cl. 1963); Morrison-Knudsen Co. v. State, 519 P.2d 834, 839–42 (Alaska 1974); Annotation, *Public Contracts: Duty of Public Authority to Disclose to Contractor Information, Allegedly in its Possession, Affecting Cost or Feasibility of Project,* 86 A.L.R.3d 182 (1978).

§ 15.9   Typical Provisions for Differing Conditions

The standard federal contract form and the standard American Institute of Architects (AIA) contract form each contain a provision dealing with unusual site conditions.[14] The two provisions are substantially similar and allow recovery for two different types of unusual site conditions.[15] The first type of unusual site condition for which the standard provisions allow recovery, commonly known as a *Type 1 condition,* is a subsurface or latent physical condition at the site that differs materially from the physical conditions indicated in the contract documents. In order for a physical condition to qualify as *latent* for purposes of the differing site condition provision, it must be concealed or dormant and undetectable in a reasonable site investigation. An example of a Type 1 condition would be a subsurface rock formation discovered during excavation when the plans showed that no rock formation existed.

The second type of unusual physical condition for which the standard contract provisions allow recovery, commonly known as a *Type 2 condition,* is an unknown and unusual physical condition at the site that materially differs from the type of physical condition ordinarily encountered and generally recognized as inherent in work of the character provided for in the construction contract. An example of a Type 2 condition would be the discovery of underground storage tanks at the site when no such storage tanks were known to exist.

An example of an unusual physical condition that would not qualify as either a Type 1 or Type 2 condition is unprecedented weather, such as a drought, a hurricane, or a flood.[16] Nevertheless, unprecedented weather can interact with latent or unknown physical conditions at the work site that are themselves Type 1 or Type 2 conditions but that might not have generated an additional expense in the absence of the unprecedented weather, thereby giving rise to a claim under the differing site conditions clause.[17] In addition, delays caused by unprecedented weather are generally excusable, as discussed in § **15.13**.

The key difference between Type 1 and Type 2 conditions is that in order for a condition to qualify as a Type 1 condition, it must be either subsurface

---

[14] 48 C.F.R. § 52.236-2 (1990); AIA Doc. A201, General Conditions of the Contract for Construction, para. 4.3.6 (1987).

[15] For a more detailed discussion of both types of physical conditions, *see* Laedlein, *Differing Site Conditions,* 19 A.F. L. Rev. 1 (1977). For a collection of cases applying a differing site conditions clause to various factual situations, *see* Annotation, *Construction and Effect of "Changed Conditions" Clause in Public Works or Construction Contract with State or its Subdivision,* 56 A.L.R.4th 1042 (1987).

[16] *See, e.g.,* Turnkey Enters., Inc. v. United States, 597 F.2d 750, 754 (Ct. Cl. 1979); Hardeman-Monier-Hutcherson v. United States, 458 F.2d 1364, 1370–71 (Ct. Cl. 1972).

[17] *See, e.g.,* Phillips Constr. Co. v. United States, 394 F.2d 834, 836–38 (Ct. Cl. 1968).

or latent and must be of a type indicated in the *contract documents,* a term that includes the bidding documents as well as the actual contract and any exhibits to the contract or other material incorporated into the contract. In order for a physical condition to be indicated in the contract documents for purposes of establishing a Type 1 condition, the contract documents must contain either express representations regarding the condition or material from which a reasonable and prudent contractor could imply representations regarding the condition.[18] Type 2 conditions, on the other hand, need only be unknown; but the contractor has the more difficult burden of showing that the conditions differ from the type of conditions ordinarily encountered and generally inherent in completing the type of work contemplated by the contract.

§ 15.10   Site Investigation Clauses

Many construction contracts contain a site investigation clause that requires the contractor to acknowledge that the contractor has investigated the physical condition of the site. Such site investigation clauses impose a duty on the contractor to conduct an investigation of the physical conditions of the site using the care that a reasonable and prudent contractor would exercise under the circumstances.[19] If the contractor fails to conduct the site investigation or conducts a site investigation that is not as careful or complete as the site investigation a reasonable and prudent contractor would conduct under the circumstances, the contractor will be held deemed to have knowledge of all the physical conditions that would have been disclosed by a reasonable and competent site investigation.[20]

Site investigation clauses may limit the conditions for which the contractor can recover from the owner under a differing site conditions clause; however, site investigation clauses will not bar a contractor from recovering for conditions that were not disclosed by a reasonable and competent site investigation and were not foreseeable by a reasonable and prudent contractor from the physical conditions disclosed by such an investigation. In

---

[18] *See, e.g.,* P.J. Maffei Bldg. Wrecking Corp. v. United States, 732 F.2d 913, 916–19 (Fed. Cir. 1984); Erickson-Shaver Contracting Corp. v. United States, 9 Cl. Ct. 302, 304–306 (1985); J.F. Shea Co. v. United States, 4 Cl. Ct. 46, 51–52 (1983); Mojave Enters. v. United States, 3 Cl. Ct. 353, 357–58 (1983); Pacific Alaska Contractors, Inc. v. United States, 436 F.2d 461, 469–70 (Ct. Cl. 1971).

[19] *See, e.g.,* North Slope Technical Ltd., v. United States, 14 Cl. Ct. 242, 253–54 (1988); Stock & Grove, Inc. v. United States, 493 F.2d 629, 637–39 (Ct. Cl. 1974); Foster Constr. C.A. & Williams Bros. Co. v. United States, 435 F.2d 873, 884–88 (Ct. Cl. 1970); Kaiser Indus. Corp. v. United States, 340 F.2d 322, 330 (Ct. Cl. 1965).

[20] *See, e.g.,* McCormick Constr. Co. v. United States, 18 Cl. Ct. 259, 263–65 (1989), *aff'd,* 907 F.2d 159 (Fed. Cir. 1990).

addition, despite the presence of a site investigation clause in the construction contract, the contractor may still recover for physical conditions that would have been revealed by a reasonable and competent site investigation if the owner either prevented the contractor from conducting a reasonable and competent site investigation or misled the contractor about the condition of the site either through affirmative misrepresentations about site conditions upon which the contractor reasonably relied or by failing to disclose information about the site that the owner had a duty to disclose.

§ 15.11   Other Barriers to Contractor Recovery

Many construction contracts contain disclaimer clauses that purport to limit the liability of owners for subsurface or other concealed physical conditions at the site and place all responsibility for any such conditions on the contractor.[21] Courts often refuse to enforce such provisions or interpret them narrowly to avoid rendering differing site conditions clauses meaningless.[22] Nonetheless, it is possible that a court could construe a disclaimer clause to bar recovery by the contractor for an unusual site condition despite the presence of a differing site conditions clause in the contract.

In addition, many construction contracts that contain differing site conditions clauses provide a notice procedure for the contractor to follow in order to collect additional compensation for an unusual site condition. Failure to comply with such notice requirements may bar the contractor from recovering additional compensation for the unusual site condition, although a contractor that fails to comply with the notice requirements may still be able to recover if the owner had actual knowledge of the site condition or was not prejudiced by the contractor's failure to comply with the notice requirements.

§ 15.12   Remedies for Unusual Conditions

The usual remedy for discovery of an unusual site condition by a contractor for which recovery is available either based on a differing site conditions clause or one of the common law theories discussed in § 15.8 is the

---

[21] For a more detailed discussion of the various types of disclaimer clauses and the effect courts give such clauses, *see* Annotation, *Construction and Effect of "Changed Conditions" Clause in Public Works or Construction Contract with State or its Subdivision*, 56 A.L.R.4th 1055–60 (1987).

[22] *See, e.g.,* United Contractors v. United States, 368 F.2d 585, 598 (Ct. Cl. 1966); Morrison-Knudsen Co. v. United States, 345 F.2d 535, 539 (Ct. Cl. 1965); Metropolitan Sewerage Comm'n v. R.W. Constr., Inc., 72 Wis. 2d 365, 241 N.W.2d 371, 382–83 (1976).

difference between the amount it cost the contractor to complete the project and the amount that it would have cost had the unusual site condition not existed.[23] In addition, if the existence of the differing site condition created a delay in the completion of the project, the contractor generally is entitled to an extension of the time within which the contractor must complete the project.

Before seeking recovery for a differing site condition, however, the contractor should consult the construction contract because many construction contracts contain provisions that specify the method by which the amount of the contractor's costs incurred in dealing with the unusual site condition are to be calculated. In addition, some construction contracts may contain a clause limiting the contractor's recovery for differing site conditions to an extension of the time allotted for completion of the work under the construction contract. Such a limitation is unfavorable to the contractor because dealing with unexpected site conditions generally not only delays the performance of the work, but also requires the contractor to incur extra costs to deal with the condition.

DELAY AND DISRUPTION

§ 15.13 Excusable Delays

Another common problem that arises in the course of performing construction contracts that makes it difficult to complete the contract in the manner originally contemplated by the parties is the occurrence of an unanticipated event that causes a delay in the contractor's performance of the work under the contract. Most construction contracts include a clause that excuses the contractor from liability to the owner for delays in the completion of the work caused by events outside the control of the contractor; both the standard federal contract form and the standard AIA contract form contain such a provision.[24] Events creating delays in the completion of the project that the provisions generally include as excusable are delays caused by actions of the owner and delays caused by actions beyond the control of either the owner or the contractor. The latter type of event generally includes tornadoes, hurricanes, floods, earthquakes, other unusually severe

---

[23] *See, e.g.,* North Slope, 14 Cl. Ct. 242, 261–62.

[24] 48 C.F.R. § 52.249-14 (1991); AIA Doc. A201, General Conditions of the Contract for Construction, para. 8.3.1 (1987).

weather conditions, strikes, and the acts of a public enemy, such as bombing damage in wartime.[25]

If the construction contract does not contain an express provision excusing the contractor from the liability for delays caused by circumstances beyond the contractor's control, the traditional common law rule imposes liability on the contractor for such delays unless the delays are caused by the owner. The modern common law trend, however, is to excuse the contractor from delay caused by circumstances beyond the contractor's control as long as the event causing the delay was not reasonably foreseeable by the contractor at the time of contracting.[26]

§ 15.14 Compensable Delays

All compensable delays are excusable; however, not all excusable delays are compensable. The important distinction between excusable and compensable delays is that the remedy for an excusable delay is an extension of time to perform under the contract while the remedy for a compensable delay also includes an award of damages for losses suffered by the contractor as a result of the delay.

Compensable delays are delays resulting from the actions of the owner. Events that give rise to a compensable delay include any type of interference by the owner in the progress of the work and any delay by the owner in completing obligations the owner has under the construction contract, such as delays in furnishing appropriate plans and specifications, delays in approving change orders or drawings, delays in making progress payments, delays in making inspections or furnishing materials, and delays in providing the contractor access to the work site.[27] In addition, some construction contracts contain provisions making other types of delays, such as delays caused by unprecedented weather, compensable.

Many construction contracts contain an explicit provision making delays caused by the actions of the owner compensable delays. Even if the construction contract does not contain such a provision, delays caused by the owner, although not other types of delays, will be compensable based on

---

[25] For a collection of cases applying an excusable delay clause to various types of severe weather, *see* Annotation, *Construction Contract Provision Excusing Delay Caused by "Severe Weather,"* 85 A.L.R.3d 1085 (1978).

[26] For a more detailed discussion of recovery for delays caused by circumstances beyond the control of either the contractor or the owner under the common law, *see* B. Bramble & M. Callahan, Construction Delay Claims (John Wiley & Sons, 2d ed. 1992); 2 S. Stein, Construction Law ¶ 6.09[1].

[27] For a more detailed discussion of the various types of compensable delays, *see* 2 S. Stein, Construction Law ¶ 6.11[1].

common law principles requiring all parties to a contract to perform their obligations under the contract and implying a duty not to interfere with the performance of the other parties to the contract.[28]

§ 15.15 Concurrent Delays

Delays caused by the contractor are neither excusable nor compensable and the contractor will be liable to the owner for such delays. In some situations, however, a delay is caused both by the contractor and by an event beyond the contractor's control that would otherwise be an excusable delay. Under the traditional rule, that type of delay—known as a *concurrent delay*—will not entitle either the owner or the contractor to damages for the delay.[29] Recently, however, some courts have expressed a willingness to apportion the damages caused by the delay between the owner and the contractor based on the proportion of the entire delay that was caused by the excusable delay and proportion that was caused by the nonexcusable delay when those proportions can be determined with reasonable certainty.[30]

§ 15.16 Barriers to Recovery for Delay

Many construction contracts contain a provision that bars the contractor from obtaining any damages for compensable delays and limits the contractor's remedy for compensable delays to an extension of time to perform under the contract. Those provisions are referred to as no damages for delay provisions. No damages for delay provisions are generally enforceable although they are strictly construed by courts and are not enforceable in certain situations. **Chapter 20** discusses the scope and enforceability of no damages for delay provisions in greater detail.

In addition, many construction contracts that contain excusable delay provisions provide a notice procedure for the contractor to follow in order

---

[28] *See, e.g.,* Luria Bros. & Co. v. United States, 369 F.2d 701, 708 (Ct. Cl. 1966); Kenworthy v. State, 236 Cal. App. 2d 378, 382, 46 Cal. Rptr. 396 (1965); Champagne-Webber, Inc. v. City of Fort Lauderdale, 519 So. 2d 696, 697–98 (Fla. Dist. Ct. App. 1988).

[29] *See, e.g.,* CCM Corp. v. United States, 20 Cl. Ct. 649, 659 (1990); Acme Process Equip. Co. v. United States, 347 F.2d 509, 535 (Ct. Cl. 1965), *rev'd on other grounds,* 385 U.S. 138 (1966); J.A. Jones Constr. Co. v. Greenbriar Shopping Ctr., 332 F. Supp. 1336, 1349 (N.D. Ga. 1971), *aff'd,* 461 F.2d 1269 (5th Cir. 1972); Lee Turzillo Contracting Co. v. Frank Messer & Sons, 23 Ohio App. 2d 179, 261 N.E.2d 675, 679 (1969).

[30] *See, e.g.,* United States v. William F. Klingensmith, Inc., 670 F.2d 1227, 1231 (D.C. Cir. 1982); Blinderman Constr. Co. v. United States, 695 F.2d 552, 559 (Fed. Cir. 1982); Pathman Constr. Co. v. Hi-Way Elec. Co., 65 Ill. App. 3d 480, 382 N.E.2d 453, 458–60 (1978).

to obtain an extension of time for performance under the contract because of the excusable delay. Failure to comply with such notice requirements may prevent the contractor from obtaining an extension of time for the excusable delay, although a contractor that fails to comply with the notice requirements may still be able to recover if the owner had actual knowledge of the excusable delay or was not prejudiced by the contractor's failure to comply with the notice requirements.

§ 15.17   Remedies for Delay

As discussed in § **15.13**, the remedy for excusable delays is an extension of time to perform under the contract. Compensable delays also entitle the contractor to an extension of time to perform but in addition entitle the contractor to recover from the owner the losses incurred by the contractor as a result of the delay. The most common types of losses experienced by contractors as a result of delays are extra costs for idle labor and equipment, additional home office overhead expenses, inefficiency and lost productivity in performance of the work, and increased cost for material, equipment, labor, and subcontractors due to an escalation in those costs from the time period in which the contractor originally intended to perform the contract.[31]

Although the calculation of the amount for most of the losses suffered by the contractor as a result of compensable delay is relatively straightforward, the calculation of additional expenses for home office overhead deserves special mention.[32] The case of *Eichleay Corp.*,[33] decided in 1960, established the most widely-used formula for calculating such losses. Under the *Eichleay* formula, extra home office overhead expense is calculated as follows:

1. Determine the total overhead allocable to the contract on the basis of a ratio of the total billings of the contractor under the contract to the

---

[31] For a more detailed discussion of the various types of losses for which the contractor can recover from the owner as a result of compensable delays and a general discussion of compensable delay claims, *see* B. Bramble & M. Callahan, Construction Delay Claims (John Wiley & Sons, 2d ed. 1992); Asselin & Harris, *How to Recognize, Preserve, Prevent, and Prosecute Construction Contractor's Delay Claims,* 40 S.C. L. Rev. 943 (1989); Phillips et al., *Construction Disputes and Time,* Issues in Construction Law 49, 66–72 (1988) For a discussion of the methods for calculating loss of efficiency damages, *see* Shea, *Searching for the Standard of Productivity: Loss of Efficiency Damages in Construction Cases,* 15 Ohio N.U. L. Rev. 225 (1988).

[32] For a more detailed discussion of the various methods of calculating home office overhead expenses, *see* Cushman, Construction Contracts and Litigation 1988, at 620–68.

[33] Eichleay Corp., ASBCA No. 5183, 60-2 B.C.A. (CCH) ¶ 2688 (1960).

total billings of the contractor for the period during which the contractor administers the contract

2. Determine the total overhead expense per day of contract performance by dividing the total overhead expense allocable to the contract determined in step 1 by the total number of days of contract performance

3. Determine the extra home office overhead caused by the compensable delay by multiplying the amount of daily home office overhead determined in step 2 by the total number of compensable delay days.

Although a number of courts have rejected the *Eichleay* formula,[34] most courts have embraced the formula as the standard method of calculating losses for extra home office overhead expenses incurred as a result of compensable delays.[35]

§ 15.18   Claim for Disruption

A claim for disruption arises when the owner breaches its implied duty not to interfere with the contractor's performance under the contract, a duty that § **15.14** dealing with compensable delays discusses, and the breach disrupts the contractor's intended schedule for performing the work. Although both a disruption claim and a compensable delay claim are based on the same type of breach by the owner, the important distinction between the two types of claims is that in a disruption claim the owner's interference creates a loss in efficiency for the contractor but does not delay the completion of the work.[36] The types of losses for which a contractor can recover from the owner under a disruption claim include increased labor and material costs due to unanticipated rescheduling of the work and other types of damages for loss of efficiency.[37]

---

[34] *See, e.g.,* Berley Indus. Inc. v. City of N.Y., 45 N.Y.2d 683, 385 N.E.2d 281, 283–84, 412 N.Y.S.2d 589 (1978); Manshul Constr. Corp. v. Dormitory Auth., 79 A.D.2d 383, 436 N.Y.S.2d 724, 729–30 (1981).

[35] *See, e.g.,* Nebraska Pub. Power Dist. v. Austin Power, Inc., 773 F.2d 960, 972 (8th Cir. 1985); Capital Elec. Co. v. United States, 729 F.2d 743, 745–47 (Fed. Cir. 1984); Golf Landscaping, Inc. v. Century Constr. Co. 39 Wash. App. 895, 696 P.2d 590, 592–94 (1985).

[36] For a more detailed discussion of disruption claims, *see* K. Gibbs, California Construction Law 93–97 (9th ed. 1987).

[37] For a more detailed discussion of calculating loss of efficiency damages, *see* Shea, *Searching for the Standard of Productivity: Loss of Efficiency Damages in Construction Cases,* 15 Ohio N.U. L. Rev. 225 (1988).

ACCELERATION

§ 15.19   Actual Acceleration

Another common problem that arises during the course of performing a construction project is that the contractor may need to increase the rate at which the work is completed either because the owner requests that the contractor complete the work ahead of schedule or because delays have occurred and the owner has requested that the contractor increase the rate of performance to complete the work on schedule. Such an increase in the rate of the contractor's performance is known as *acceleration.* Actual acceleration occurs when the owner expressly orders the contractor to accelerate the rate of completion of the work. In the absence of a contract provision giving the owner the right to accelerate the contractor's performance, the contractor is under no obligation to follow such an order and should not accelerate performance under the contract before reaching an agreement with the owner as to the amount of extra compensation the owner will pay the contractor for the acceleration.[38]

Some construction contracts, however, contain provisions expressly granting the owner the right to accelerate the contractor's performance. If the contract contains such a provision, the contractor must follow the owner's order and should examine the contract carefully to determine if the contract contains specific provisions governing the right of the contractor to extra compensation for such acceleration.

In addition, an order from the owner to accelerate the work may fall within the scope of a changes provision, a provision that most contracts contain and which §§ 15.22 through 15.26 discuss. If the acceleration order constitutes a valid change order under the contract, the contractor must accelerate the work in accordance with the order and pursue a claim for the extra costs the contractor incurs in connection with the acceleration under the dispute resolution provisions of the contract.

§ 15.20   Constructive Acceleration

Constructive acceleration does not involve an express order from the owner to the contractor requesting the contractor to accelerate the contractor's performance. Rather, *constructive acceleration* occurs when an excusable delay exists for which the contractor has requested an extension in the time for performance in a timely fashion, but the owner refuses to acknowledge

---

[38] *See, e.g.,* Northway Decking & Sheet Metal Corp. v. Inland-Ryerson Constr. Prods. Co., 426 F. Supp. 417, 429–30 (D.R.I. 1977).

the existence of the excusable delay and demands completion of the work within the original performance period contained in the construction contract.[39]

Although the owner in a constructive acceleration situation does not expressly order acceleration, because the delay has interrupted performance of the contract the contractor must, as a practical matter, accelerate its performance in order to complete the work in accordance with the original contract schedule. In order to establish a claim for constructive acceleration, it is crucial for the contractor to demonstrate that the existence of the excusable delay made it impossible for the contractor to complete the work in accordance with the original contract schedule without acceleration and that the owner required completion within the original schedule in order to prevent a court from finding that the contractor voluntarily agreed to accelerate.

§ 15.21   Remedies for Acceleration

If the contractor can establish a claim for acceleration, either actual or constructive, unless the contract provides otherwise, the contractor is entitled to recover from the owner the expenses incurred by the contractor in completing the work on an accelerated schedule that the contractor would not have otherwise incurred. The most common types of extra expenses incurred by contractors in connection with acceleration include overtime wage payments to workers, additional equipment expenses, increased cost for materials the contractor must procure through unusual sources in order to obtain the materials on an accelerated basis, extra overhead expenses, and loss of efficiency.[40]

CHANGES

§ 15.22   Changes to Construction Contract

In order to deal with the various unexpected problems that arise during the course of performance of a construction contract that make it difficult to complete the contract in the manner originally contemplated by the parties,

---

[39] *See, e.g.,* Envirotech Corp. v. Tennessee Valley Auth., 715 F. Supp. 190, 192 (W.D. Ky. 1988); Nello L. Teer Co. v. Washington Metro. Area Transit Auth., 695 F. Supp. 583, 589–92 (D.D.C. 1988); Norair Eng'g Corp. v. United States, 666 F.2d 546, 548–50 (Ct. Cl. 1981).

[40] For a more detailed discussion of the types of expenses recoverable in connection with acceleration claims, *see* 2 S. Stein, Construction Law ¶ 6.12[3] (1990).

a practice has developed in the construction industry of including a provision in construction contracts that gives the owner the right to order minor changes to the work to be performed by the contractor without obtaining the consent of the contractor to the changes. The law governing contracts generally requires that both parties to a contract agree to a change to the contract before that change will bind the parties.

Requiring the consent of both parties to every change in the construction contract setting, however, could significantly delay the completion of the work because of the large number of minor changes that typically are required during the construction of a large project to accommodate unexpected problems. In order to avoid such delays, the law enforces changes ordered by an owner pursuant to a changes provision in a construction contract even though the contractor does not agree to each change. Unless the contract provides otherwise, if the owner orders a change pursuant to the changes provision, the contractor must perform the change even if the contractor and the owner disagree on the amount of extra compensation the contractor should receive for the change, the amount by which the owner should extend the time for performance as a result of the change, or the propriety of the change. The contractor may, during the performance of the change, resolve the disagreement by pursuing a claim through the dispute resolution provisions of the contract.

Changes provisions give the owner the flexibility the owner needs to accommodate unexpected problems without having to engage in frequent negotiations with the contractor over changes necessary to deal with those problems. Nevertheless, giving the owner the right to make any type of change to the work that the contractor must perform under the contract without having to obtain the contractor's consent would give an owner the right to order changes that result in the contractor's obligations under the construction contract being substantially different than the contractor agreed to perform when the contractor entered into the contract.

Limits on Types of Changes

In order to prevent the owner from making such substantial changes without the contractor's consent, the law limits the types of changes an owner can order under the changes provision to changes that are within the scope of the original contract. Whether a particular change or series of changes goes beyond the scope of the original contract—often described as a *cardinal change*—depends on the construction contract and the facts of the situation; however, the general rule for determining when a change or series of changes goes beyond the scope of the contract is whether the change or series of changes results in the project the contractor is to construct being substantially different from the project the contractor agreed to construct in the original contract.[41] An example of a change that a court is unlikely to consider outside the scope of the original contract would be a change in the type of floor covering contemplated in the original contract to a similar type of floor covering available at a similar price because the original floor covering was either unavailable or unsuitable for some unanticipated reason. An example of a change that a court likely would consider to be outside the scope of the original contract would be a change in the material used for the exterior of a building to be constructed under a construction contract from brick to wood.

Compliance with Change Order

If the owner orders a change that the contractor believes falls outside the scope of the original contract, the changes provision does not obligate the contractor to comply with the change order. In fact, the law deems the ordering of a change outside the scope of the original contract, which converts the work the contractor must perform under the contract into an undertaking that is substantially different from the original undertaking, as a repudiation of the original contract by the owner, an event that constitutes a material breach of contract by the owner and gives the contractor the rights discussed in §§ 15.2 and 15.3 of this chapter dealing with material breach by the owner.

The contractor should be extremely cautious when evaluating change orders, however, because, as discussed previously, changes provisions require the contractor to proceed with the ordered change while the contractor and the owner resolve any disputes as to the appropriateness of the change. If the contractor refuses to perform the change and a court or arbitrator later determines that the change was within the scope of the original contract, the contractor's refusal to perform the change will constitute a breach of the construction contract by the contractor.

Because the determination as to whether a particular change is within or outside of the scope of the original contract is based to a large degree on the particular facts of the situation, making it difficult to predict in advance how a court or arbitration panel would view the change, it is generally advisable for the contractor to perform the requested change order and pursue a claim for extra compensation for the performance of the changed work under the appropriate dispute resolution provisions of the construction contract unless the contractor is confident that the change is outside the scope of the contract. The contractor should be aware that performance of the change may operate as a waiver of any right the contractor may have had to view the change as a material breach of the contract by the owner

---

[41] *See, e.g.,* Wunderlich Contracting Co. v. United States, 351 F.2d 956, 965–66 (Ct. Cl. 1965); J.D. Hedin Constr. Co. v. United States, 347 F.2d 235, 257–58 (Ct. Cl. 1965).

and pursue remedies for material breach as discussed in § 15.2. In most situations, however, a contractor can avoid the implication that the contractor is waiving the right to protest the change by expressly reserving the right to protest in a written notice delivered to the owner prior to commencing the changed work.

§ 15.23   Performance of Extra Work

Changes to the work the construction contract requires the contractor to perform that fall outside the scope of the original contract are known as *extras*. As discussed in § 15.22, such changes do not fall within the scope of an owner's right to unilaterally order changes under a change provision and the contractor has no duty to perform them. If the contractor wishes to perform the extras, the contractor should enter into a modification of the original contract with the owner that sets forth the scope of the extra work the contractor is to perform and the additional compensation and extension of time for performance under the contract, if any, the contractor will receive in consideration for performance of the extra work.

The usual formula for determining the amount of compensation a contractor should receive for performing extra work is the reasonable value of the work plus a reasonable amount for overhead and profit; however, some construction contracts contain a formula for calculating the amount a contractor will be entitled to receive for performing any extra work the owner may request in connection with the construction project. If the contractor does not enter into an agreement with the owner that outlines the extra work to be performed and the compensation the contractor will receive for performance of the work, the contractor takes the risk that a court or arbitrator will decide the contractor undertook the extra work voluntarily and that the owner is not liable for the work.[42]

§ 15.24   Typical Changes Provisions

The AIA standard contract form contains a changes provision that provides for three different types of changes.[43]

Minor changes.   The simplest type of change for which the form provides is an order for a minor change in the scope of the work. Only the architect

---

[42] For a discussion of the various theories used by courts to hold owners liable for extra work performed by contractors in the absence of a written agreement with the owner, *see* Galligan, *Extra Work in Construction Cases: Restitution, Relationship and Revision,* 63 Tul. L. Rev. 799 (1989).

[43] AIA Doc. A201, General Conditions of the Contract for Construction, Art. 7 (1987).

has the authority to order such minor changes that are binding on both the owner and the contractor. In order for a change to qualify as a minor change, it must not be inconsistent with the intent of the original contract and must not involve adjustments to the contract price or the time for completion of the contract.

Change orders. Change orders, in contrast to orders for minor changes, are used when a material change is contemplated. The change order is a written agreement between the owner, the contractor, and the architect, signed by all three parties, that sets forth the agreement of the parties with respect to a specific change and the amount of adjustment in the contract price and time of completion for the contract, if any, to be made as a result of the change.

Construction change directive. The final type of change under the AIA form is a construction change directive. *Construction change directives* are written orders signed by both the owner and the architect that direct a change in the work and include a proposed basis for adjustments to the contract price and time for the completion of the contract to be made as a result of the change. The changes provision requires the construction contractor to proceed with the change ordered under a construction change directive, subject to the limitation that the change must be within the general scope of the contract. If the contractor agrees with the proposed basis for adjustments to the contract price and completion date set forth in the construction change directive, the contractor signs the directive, thereby converting it into a change order. If the contractor does not agree with the proposed basis for adjustments set forth in the directive, the provision calls for the architect to determine the appropriate adjustment based on the reasonable expenditures and savings to the contractor attributable to the change, including a reasonable allowance for overhead and profit if the change order results in an increase to the work. If the contractor disputes the determination made by the architect, the contractor must nonetheless continue to perform the change and pursue further claims through the dispute resolution provisions of the contract form.

Federal Government Form

The changes provision in the standard federal government form allows the owner to make changes in the work the contract requires the contractor to perform by written change order as long as the changes are within the general scope of the contract.[44] The provision requires that an equitable

---

[44] 48 C.F.R. § 52.243-4 (1991).

adjustment be made for increases or decreases in the cost of or time for performance of the contract by the contractor as a result of the changes.

§ 15.25   Necessity of Written Order

Unless the construction contract expressly requires that a change order or order for extra work be in writing to be enforceable, an oral change order or order for extra work will most likely be enforceable, although the statute of frauds in some states may require that such orders be in writing to be enforceable. Even if state law does not require such orders to be in writing, it is always in the contractor's best interest to obtain such orders in writing because the existence of a writing will make it easier to prove the existence of the order if the owner disputes the order.

Most construction contracts contain a clause that requires change orders and orders for extra work or any other modification of the contract to be in writing. Contractors should be careful to comply with such provisions, as they are generally enforceable. If the contract requires a change order or order for extra work to be in writing, but the contractor proceeds with changes in the work based on an oral order from the owner, the oral order may not be enforceable and the contractor may be unable to recover any additional costs or receive any extensions of time for the extra work or change performed under the order.[45]

Waiver of Writing Requirement

If the contractor has proceeded based on an oral change order or order for extra work and the contract requires the order to be in writing, the contractor may nonetheless be able to recover for the change or extra work if the contractor can demonstrate that the owner waived the requirement of a writing.[46] One method a contractor can use to show waiver of the writing requirement is to demonstrate that in the course of performance of the construction contract, the owner has routinely ordered changes or extras

---

[45] For a compilation of cases discussing the enforceability of clauses requiring change orders or orders for extras to be in writing, *see* Annotation, *Effect of Stipulation, in Private Building or Construction Contract, that Alterations or Extras Must Be Ordered in Writing,* 2 A.L.R.3d 620 (1965) [hereinafter Private Contract Changes]; Annotation, *Effect of Stipulation, in Public Building or Construction Contract, that Alterations or Extras Must Be in Writing,* 1 A.L.R.3d 1273 (1965) [hereinafter Public Contract Changes].

[46] For a compilation of cases discussing the various ways a contractor can demonstrate that the owner waived the requirement of a writing, *see* Private Contract Changes, 2 A.L.R.3d 654–85; Public Contract Changes, 1 A.L.R.3d 1297–1312.

orally.[47] Another method of demonstrating that the owner has waived the writing requirement is to demonstrate that the owner knew of the extra work or change being performed by the contractor and agreed that the contractor should receive additional compensation for the work.[48]

The owner's knowledge of the performance of the change or extra work by the contractor without objection is generally not sufficient to demonstrate waiver on the part of the owner of the writing requirement; however, knowledge of the performance of the work together with affirmative acquiescence in the changes or extra work may be sufficient.[49] In addition, courts use the doctrine of equitable estoppel to impose liability on the owner for additional compensation to the contractor as a result of the changes or extra work performed in the absence of a writing if the contractor can demonstrate that the owner promised to pay for the change or extra work and the contractor reasonably relied on that promise in performing the change or extra work. If the owner received a benefit from the performance of the work and the work is extra work outside the scope of the contract, the contractor also may be able to recover from the owner the reasonable value of the extra work performed on a quantum meruit theory of recovery.[50]

§ 15.26   Remedies for Extras and Changes

The basic measure of the amount that a contractor is entitled to receive for performance of extras or changes that involve additional work is the actual cost incurred by the contractor in connection with performing the additional work plus a reasonable amount for the contractor's overhead expenses incurred in connection with performance of the additional work and a reasonable profit for the contractor. If the change involves a significant deletion of work from the contract, the contract price may be decreased by the amounts the contractor will save as a result of not having to perform the deleted work.

---

[47] *See, e.g.,* Brookhaven Landscape & Grading Co. v. J.F. Barton Contracting Co., 676 F.2d 516, 522 (11th Cir. 1982); Northway Decking & Sheet Metal Corp. v. Inland-Ryerson Constr. Prods. Co., 426 F. Supp. 417, 430–31 (D.R.I. 1977); Doral Country Club, Inc. v. Curcie Bros., 174 So. 2d 749, 750–51 (Fla. Dist. Ct. App.), *cert. denied,* 180 So. 2d 656 (Fla. 1965).

[48] *See, e.g.,* United States *ex rel.* Falco Constr. Corp. v. Summit Gen. Contracting Corp., 760 F. Supp. 1004, 1010 (E.D.N.Y. 1991); V.L. Nicholson Co. v. Transcon Inv. & Fin. Ltd., 595 S.W.2d 474, 482 (Tenn. 1980); Texas Constr. Assocs. v. Balli, 558 S.W.2d 513, 521–22 (Tex. Ct. App. 1977).

[49] *See, e.g.,* Universal Builders, Inc. v. Moon Motor Lodge, Inc., 430 Pa. 550, 244 A.2d 10, 15–16 (1968).

[50] *See, e.g.,* Brookhaven Landscape & Grading Co. v. J.F. Barton Contracting Co., 676 F.2d 516, 522.

Many contract provisions governing changes or orders for extra work, such as the standard federal government and AIA forms discussed in this chapter, contain more specific formulas for determining the amounts to which the contractor is entitled as a result of performing the change or extra work. The contractor should examine the construction contract carefully when a claim for additional compensation arises in connection with the performance of the change or extra work to determine the appropriate measure of the amount of the claim. In addition, many contracts also provide notice requirements or procedures for submitting claims for extra compensation or time extensions with which a contractor must comply in asserting a claim for additional compensation or time extension for work performed in connection with a change order or order for extra work. Failure to comply with such requirements and procedures may bar the contractor from recovering additional compensation or time extensions for the change or extra work.

As discussed in § **15.23**, when the contractor agrees with the owner to perform extra work outside the scope of the original contract, the contractor and the owner should agree, prior to the contractor beginning performance of the extra work, to the additional compensation or extension of time that the owner is to receive in consideration for the contractor's performance of extra work. In addition, the agreement concerning payment or time extension should be incorporated into the writing that contains the agreement on the part of the contractor to perform the extra work.

OWNER'S WARRANTY OF PLANS AND SPECIFICATIONS

§ 15.27   Owner's Implied Warranty of Accuracy

The final problem this chapter examines arising during the course of performance of a construction project that makes it difficult to complete the project as originally intended is a defect in the plans or specifications. The law of most states and the law governing contracts with federal government entities implies in every construction contract a warranty by the owner of the accuracy of the plans and specifications provided by the owner for construction of the project.[51] That warranty covers two different situations.

---

[51] For a more detailed discussion of the implied warranty of the accuracy of plans and specifications and the exceptions to the warranty, *see* Harrington et al., *The Owner's Warranty of the Plans and Specifications for a Construction Project,* 14 Pub. Cont. L.J. 240 (1984).

First, the owner warrants that the conditions of the work site shown on the plans and specifications are correct.[52] For example, if the plans and specifications show easy access to the work site off a major road, and that access is unavailable at the time for the contractor to begin construction, the lack of access represents a breach of the owner's warranty.

Second, the owner warrants that if the contractor constructs the project strictly in accordance with the plans and specifications, the project will function correctly. If the contractor constructs the project strictly in accordance with the plans and specifications but the project does not function correctly because of a defect in the plans and specifications and the contractor must perform corrective work on the project to remedy the problem, the defect represents a breach of the owner's warranty.[53]

§ 15.28   Exceptions to Implied Warranty

Many construction contracts contain broad exculpatory clauses that purport to disclaim the implied warranty of the accuracy of the plans and specifications. Another common exculpatory clause requires the contractor to acknowledge review of the plans and specifications and to verify the suitability of those plans and specifications for the project. Courts do not favor broad exculpatory clauses, however, and in many situations the owner will not be able to enforce those clauses to escape liability for defects in the plans and specifications.[54] Despite the general rule that broad exculpatory clauses are not enforceable, courts generally enforce narrowly tailored exculpatory clauses in which an owner discloses a particular potential defect in the plans and specifications and the contractor agrees to accept any problems that may arise during construction from that defect.[55]

Minor defects in the plans and specifications generally do not fall within the scope of the implied warranty. Minor defects should be dealt with by a change order to the contract. Glaring defects in the plans and specifications

---

[52] *See, e.g.,* Carl M. Halvorson, Inc. v. United States, 461 F.2d 1337 (Ct. Cl. 1972); Souza & McCue Constr. Co. v. Superior Court, 57 Cal. 2d 508, 370 P.2d 338, 20 Cal. Rptr. 634 (1962); Alpert v. Commonwealth, 357 Mass. 306, 258 N.E.2d 755, 763–66 (1970); *see also* Annotation, *Right of Public Contractor to Allowance of Extra Expense Over What Would Have Been Necessary if Conditions Had Been as Represented by the Plans and Specifications,* 76 A.L.R. 268 (1932).

[53] *See, e.g.,* Neal & Co. v. United States, 19 Cl. Ct. 463, 467–69 (1990); John McShain, Inc. v. United States, 412 F.2d 1281, 1283 (Ct. Cl. 1969); J.L. Simmons Co. v. United States, 412 F.2d 1360, 1363–80 (Ct. Cl. 1969); Laburnum Constr. Corp. v. United States, 325 F.2d 451, 457 (Ct. Cl. 1963).

[54] *See, e.g.,* Teledyne Lewisburg v. United States, 699 F.2d 1336 (Fed. Cir. 1983); Condon-Cunningham, Inc. v. Day, 22 Ohio Misc. 77, 258 N.E.2d 264 (Ohio C.P. 1969).

[55] *See, e.g.,* Rixon Elec., Inc. v. United States, 536 F.2d 1345 (Ct. Cl. 1976).

that would be obvious to a reasonable and prudent contractor also do not fall within the scope of the implied warranty.[56] If the contractor executes and proceeds to perform the contract despite such glaring defects in the plans and specifications, the contractor may in essence be agreeing to accept a known risk even though the contract does not contain a clause pursuant to which the contractor expressly agrees to accept the risk.

Another exception to the implied warranty arises when the plans and specifications are silent as to the suitability of a particular method of construction adopted by the contractor.[57] The warranty will not apply in such a situation unless the suitability of the method can be reasonably inferred from items contained in the plans and specifications.

§ 15.29   Remedies for Breach of Warranty

Unless the contract provides otherwise, if the owner breaches the implied warranty of the accuracy of the plans and specifications, the contractor will be entitled to recover from the owner an amount equal to the additional costs incurred by the contractor as a result of the defect in the plans and specifications.

Many construction contracts contain specific procedures for the contractor to follow in asserting a claim for additional costs incurred as a result of a defect in the plans and specifications. In addition, many contracts contain provisions requiring the contractor to give the owner notice of defects in the plans and specifications within a prescribed time after the contractor discovers the defect. Contractors should be careful to comply with those provisions because failure to comply could prevent the contractor from recovering for the breach unless the contractor can show that the owner knew of the defect or was not prejudiced by the failure to receive notice within the time period specified in the contract.

---

[56] Bromley Contracting Co. v. United States, 14 Cl. Ct. 69, 72–73 (1987), aff'd, 861 F.2d 729 (Fed. Cir. 1988); Highway Prods., Inc. v. United States, 530 F.2d 911, 919–21 (Ct. Cl. 1976); Wickham Contracting Co. v. United States, 546 F.2d 395, 397–401 (Ct. Cl. 1976); L.W. Foster Sportswear Co. v. United States, 405 F.2d 1285, 1290–91 (Ct. Cl. 1969).

[57] See, e.g., Stuyvesant Dredging Co. v. United States, 11 Cl. Ct. 853, 859–61, aff'd, 834 F.2d 1576 (Fed. Cir. 1987).

CHAPTER 16

CONTRACTOR LIABILITY TO THE OWNER

Steven T. Graham
Diane R. Smith

Steven T. Graham is a partner in the law firm of Snell & Wilmer in Irvine, California, where he heads the firm's California construction law practice. He handles construction disputes on behalf of owners, developers, contractors, and lending institutions in state and federal court, and through arbitration.

Diane R. Smith is a partner in the law firm of Snell & Wilmer in Irvine, California. She heads the firm's California environmental law practice, handling matters involving federal, state, and local environmental regulatory agencies; cost recovery for environmental cleanups; publicly and privately funded cleanups of contaminated properties; environmental compliance; client counseling on regulatory matters/permitting; environmental due diligence for real estate and business transactions; and defense of civil and criminal enforcement actions.

CONTROLLING EXPOSURES AND PROVIDING PROTECTION

§ 16.1 Overview of Potential Liability Concerns

The potential liability of the construction contractor to the owner of the facility under construction expands far beyond obvious liability to finish the work. A contractor's liability exposure to the owner includes all of the conventional risks of completing the work in accordance with the plans and specifications, within the bid amount (plus approved extras and plus or minus changes), and of bringing the project to completion within the allowable time. Nevertheless, there are also significant exposures for consequential damages, work in progress, loss of or damage to existing property of the owners and property of others, bodily injury, and even diminished value of the completed project (resulting, for example, from the market effects of ineffective, inefficient, or environmentally-unacceptable operational characteristics).

Each of these areas of potential exposure and liability, as well as approaches to appropriately allocate risk and liability, are discussed in §§ 16.2 through 16.10.

§ 16.2   Completing Work in Accordance with Contract

The conventional risks of contractual exposure for completion of the work on time, within budget, and in accordance with the contract are usually the major, and for the unwary, the only matters addressed in negotiations. The contractor's liability for correction of defects, cost overruns, and delay damages, which constitute a large percentage of contractor liability, is determined largely by the form of contract. Because most form contracts are drafted by organizations with their own agendas and biases, negotiations usually are critical to a workable arrangement.

§ 16.3   —Not-to-Exceed Arrangements

"Not-to-exceed" contracts are by far the contractor's financial worst case. A contractor who performs so well that it does not require the entire budget for completion "leaves money on the table" (assuming at least some profit factor in unexpended costs). A contractor who overruns the budget "eats it." The effects of the not-to-exceed arrangement can be ameliorated significantly if the need for some price or schedule adjustments is expected at the outset, the owner is informed of the uncertainties, the owner's approval is obtained for any additional costs incurred, and schedule impacts are documented prior to proceeding. This converts the not-to-exceed arrangement to a level of effort, not to be exceeded without approval basis, that, though requiring conscientious project management attention, does provide an avenue for relief from unworkable constraints.

The other major liability areas, such as responsibility for bodily injury, property damages, consequential losses, and work in progress, are still crucial liability concerns, as in other contract forms. One area in which not-to-exceed contractors should have fewer concerns than fixed-price performers is with respect to warranty (reperformance and correction of defects). If the contractor has costed the job properly, the cost of corrections should have been included as a contingency in the basic budget for establishment of the not-to-exceed price; that is, a contingency for errors should be present in the budget at the outset.

§ 16.4 —Fixed-Price Arrangements

"Hard money" ("fixed-price or lump sum") contractors are the next high-risk category for conventional price and schedule issues. The very nature of the fixed contractual arrangement requires that the contractor accept the risk of bid and schedule requirements and correction of defects. There are, of course, negotiable issues such as allowance items and escalation formulas that, if properly addressed in the contract, can ease the contractor's burden greatly and facilitate the relationship with the owner. For example, through negotiation, the contractor may be able to obtain relief from unworkable cost escalation in prices and from late definitization of quantity requirements.

Other relief valves that should be considered when negotiating modifications to a conventional fixed-price, fixed-completion-date arrangement are:

1. Direct hire by owner of specialty or high-risk subcontractors
2. Owner reliance on subcontractor guarantees or indemnities
3. Liquidated damages arrangements between the owner/contractor and subcontractors
4. Limitations on performance guarantee liability
5. Carefully drafted force majeure and change order terms referring specifically to potentially troublesome potential events or circumstances
6. Unknown or differing site conditions and economic benefit clauses (especially overseas)
7. Shared responsibility arrangements with respect to defects, arranging incentives for cooperative and realistic project administration.

Though fixed-price arrangements conventionally impose unlimited rework liability on the contractor, there is nothing to stop parties from negotiating some limitation on such exposure for errors in performance. Under appropriate circumstances, such an arrangement can prevent both risk to the contractor and the possibility that an error-free job will increase the contractor's profit (with retained contingencies for unrealized error) to no benefit to the owner. When the contractor accepts unlimited liability for rework and corrections, as in most fixed-price arrangements for projects that are not high tech or industrial, any serious contractor includes a realistic contingency for errors, which, if not utilized, can greatly enhance the contractor's profit picture upon completion.

Liquidated damages provisions (especially coupled with bonus arrangements) are good stop loss arrangements that can both serve as incentivizing arrangements for good performance and yet eliminate the contractor's exposure to unlimited liability.

§ 16.5   —Cost Reimbursement Contracts

Contractors working under reimbursable cost arrangements, in which profit is determined as a percentage of costs expended, generally have the fewest possible risks and liabilities associated with contract price, time for performance, and warranty (rework), as such contracts normally are utilized in circumstances in which scope and other matters are uncertain and not capable of effective estimate at the outset of the contract. Warranty (rework) exposure must still be specifically addressed in the agreement, but logical and persuasive arguments exist for rework at cost (without profit) because a cost reimbursable arrangement contains no contingency for errors in pricing (except the usually separately stated profit fee).

Many conventional risks still must be appropriately allocated among the contractor, designer, owner, and others, even in a cost reimbursable contract (for example, liability for existing property, indemnities, and liability for consequential damages). Furthermore, project management attention and cost control are essential to protect the client's interests, maintain the contractor's relationship with the client, and manage the project cash flow (especially if payment is in arrears). Still, cost reimbursable arrangements are by far the preferred choice of contractors with the market strength, good cost control, project qualifications, reputation, and clientele necessary for this rather sophisticated method of project performance. Many of the high-risk aspects of construction become much more manageable when working on a reimbursable basis.

Nevertheless, because most construction projects are carried out on some sort of a not-to-exceed or fixed-price basis due to client concern about "blank check" contracting, this chapter focuses on the two more usual forms of contractual arrangements, but discusses, when appropriate, the implications of certain exposures when a cost reimbursable arrangement is employed.

§ 16.6   Liability for Consequential Damages

Liability for consequential damages is another area of high risk for contractors. Consequential damages may include such items as damages for delay, business interruption, loss of interest, loss of use, loss of profits, downtime, and loss of value from failure to perform as promised.

Basically, there are two ways to write a consequential damages article: (1) *broadly* ("Contractor shall have no liability for consequential damages of any nature whatsoever, howsoever arising"), or (2) *narrowly* ("Contractor shall have no liability for consequential damages comprising [for example: loss of use of the project, loss of interest, or failure of financing]). From the contractor's standpoint, the more broadly written the consequential damages exclusion, the better.

In some instances, particularly in contracts pertaining to hotels and mining industry facilities, some acceptance of exposure to consequentials is customary. In those industries, all exclusions of consequentials should detail clearly the nature of the damages for which the contractor accepts responsibility, and from which the contractor is excused from responsibility. Because of the extremely high potential levels of liability imposed by acceptance of responsibility for consequentials, prudence dictates that an exclusionary provision be included in every contract. To the extent that the consequential damages result from an actual occurrence in the field, the contractor's general liability policy may respond to and cover the loss, though paying the claim may later result in additional insurance costs or an obligation on the part of the contractor to repay amounts paid on its behalf by the insurer.

§ 16.7   Liability for Construction Work in Progress

Responsibility for the actual construction work as it progresses as well as for goods and materials in transit to the construction site is one of the more conventional risks normally accepted by contractors and covered by an all risk builders' risk insurance policy. Such policy normally names the contractor, subcontractor, owner, and others as additional insureds as their interests may appear. Assuming adequate coverage of the builders' risk policy (including, when necessary, coverage for "hot work" or startup), the only financial exposure of the parties is or should be for deductibles (which can be substantial) and uninsured risks.

§ 16.8   Liability for Damage to
Owner's Existing Property

Sometimes builders' risk policies are particularly useful when the owner wishes for the contractor to accept responsibility for any damage to the owner's existing property at or adjacent to the construction site. Some builders' risk policies will have a "Part B" coverage providing property damage protection for a specified level of property at the construction site other than the construction work in progress. The Part B coverage provides some degree of protection to both the contractor and owner when damage to existing property occurs due to the construction activity.

The insurance carried by many large contractors is quoted with the understanding that the contractors will not accept liability for an owner's property (which is usually already, and more economically, protected by the owner's first party property policy). Owners often expect or demand that contractors accept exposure to at least the level of liability evidenced by the owner's property coverage deductible.

Obviously there is enhanced risk to property in the proximity of the construction site. Many contractors have *retro* programs, whereby the actual premium paid for insurance coverage in prior years is determined retroactively based on claims made or processed and paid for each policy year. The contractor agrees in advance to a particular yearly premium based on amounts paid in prior years. The premium may be adjusted downward (by refund or credit of premium for future years) if claims experience is better, in retrospect, than anticipated. If expectations are exceeded, future premiums will be higher, to recoup amounts paid in excess of expectations in prior years. The net result of retro programs is exposure for certain varying amounts of claims paid by insurers, resulting in some bottom-line impact whenever an occurrence is experienced. Exposure for owner's property is, therefore, a heavily negotiated contractual provision. Occasionally the existence of the Part B coverage facilitates easy resolution of this issue because the contractor is able to cover (at least part of) the owner's uninsured (deductible) risk via the Part B. The owner frequently is willing to accept the remaining exposure until the threshold for property coverage is reached. (The owner had intended to self-insure this portion anyway through establishment of the deductible.)

When the owner does not take responsibility for protection of its own existing property, or at least minimize the contractor's risk by contract, the contractor's commercial general liability insurance is exposed to the risk, to the extent of the contractor's legal liability or to the extent the risk is within any contractual liability clause. Further, the owner may have required that the contractor name the owner as an additional insured, which may also, unless drafted otherwise, provide coverage for owner's negligence. Again, such responsibility on the part of the contractor's insurer results in a hit to the contractor's bottom line with every occurrence, in most cases.

Unless the contract provides otherwise, any loss over the limits of the liability policy (as well as any self-retained amounts due to the existence of a retro or other retained risk mechanism) for which the contractor is liable becomes a potential claim against the contractor, to the extent that the contractor is liable as a matter of law or is liable under the contract.

§ 16.9   Liability for Third-Party Property Damage

Liability for loss of or damage to the property of third parties is either established by contract through the indemnity article or arises as a result of operation of common law. The indemnity article may make the contractor liable for damages suffered by others due to the contractor's negligent performance of the work; some contracts make the contractor liable for all damages even if the owner or other individuals were partly at fault. Contractors usually resist strongly the imposition of vicarious liability for the negligence of others.

Many states prohibit by statute the imposition of liability for the negligence, sole or gross negligence, or willful misconduct of others. Nevertheless, even if the indemnity is drafted so as to impose liability only for the negligence of the contractor, if the insurance article is not crafted properly, and names the owner (or other otherwise legally liable party) as an additional insured, the contractor again may find itself paying for the liability of others through a charge to the bottom line. In a fixed-price arrangement, the contractor is usually held responsible for all loss of or damage to third-party property to the extent that the damage arises out of the contractor's negligence. One way of limiting this exposure is to provide that the contractor's liability will be limited to amounts recoverable from the contractor's insurance policy, after which the owner will assume responsibility.

An arrangement limiting exposure in this way is not unusual in cost reimbursable contracts, in which the owner is paying for costs incurred plus a separately calculated fee. As there is no unstated "contingency for error or loss" in a cost reimbursable bid, the cost of uninsured casualty losses (on the part of the contractor's liability) and the owner's portion of liability (which may be within the owner's coverage) are properly included in the owner's account. Without such an arrangement, the contractor would be in the position of being liable for matters for which no contingency was possible.

§ 16.10   Liability for Bodily Injury and Death

Construction projects are dangerous activities, and the risk of injury or death to workers or to the public is substantial. Liability for bodily injury to and for death of persons usually is addressed in the indemnity article. The risk that an employee of the contractor will be injured or killed is, in most instances, more significant than the risk of injury or death of other parties. The contractor has the protection of the workers' compensation program; the injured employee cannot recover other damages from the employer.

However, if the employee sues the owner, a large judgment may be obtained on some theory such as nondelegable duty of the landowner, negligence of the owner, or vicarious liability. If the contractor has agreed to indemnify the owner under the contract, except to the extent of the owner's sole negligence, the contractor may find itself in the position of paying any judgment that the employee gets against the owner, despite the fact that the contractor cannot be sued by the employee directly. This result may ensue because the owner tenders the employee's claim to the contractor for payment under the contractor's indemnity. In such event, the contractor's general liability policy usually will respond, with the usual hit to the contractor's bottom line for any self-retained risk.

CONSIDERING CONSTRUCTION CLAIMS

§ 16.11   Types of Construction Claims

The most commonly made construction claims involve defects (quality of performance), delay (timely completion), and claims for contractual indemnity. **Sections 16.16** through **16.22** cover the available defenses to defect and delay claims.

§ 16.12   —Claims for Contractual Indemnity

Claims for contractual indemnity arise from obligations assumed by the contractor in the contract with the owner. Indemnity claims can arise during and after performance of the contract in the form of owner demands for defense and indemnity as well as in the forms of stop notice and mechanic's lien claims made by subcontractors and suppliers. The best way to prevent these types of claims is to have in place a system of payment that provides for the proper use of vouchers, joint checks, and other methods of payment to be exchanged for the proper statutory or industry practice releases from the subcontractors and suppliers.

Another common type of claim arises from a contractual indemnity provision that provides, in essence, that the contractor will defend and indemnify the owner, architect, engineers, and others from and against any and all claims for property damage or personal injury in connection with the work of improvement. Often, these provisions require the general contractor to fully indemnify the owner and others against such claims unless the claims have been proven to result from the indemnitee's sole negligent or willful misconduct. A contractor must be aware of its own state's statutes as many states provide anti-indemnity protection to contractor's, prohibiting an owner from requiring that a contractor indemnify and defend against the owner's (or the owner's agent's) sole negligence or misconduct.[1]

Personal injury claims commonly arise from jobsite workers, including those employed by the general contractor itself. When a contractual indemnity provision is in the contract, the normal statutory protection provided by the workers' compensation laws may be contractually abrogated by the indemnity article. The result is that the general contractor's own employees

---

[1] *See, e.g.,* Cal. Civ. Code § 2782 (West 1990).

are able to make indirect claims through the owner to the contractor/employer due to the contractor's duty to indemnify the owner, which frequently covers claims by the contractor's employees.

If limitations on the contractual indemnity provision cannot be negotiated, then it is incumbent upon the general contractor to obtain insurance coverage for the resulting exposure. The contractor must read and understand the contracts to ensure full comprehension of the planning for the risks being assumed.

§ 16.13   —Claims of Defect or Delay

Most claims of defect or delay can be stated as actions for breach of contract or negligence. The respective rights and obligations involved in a breach of contract action are those stated by the terms of the contract. Usually, the terms involve specific requirements for time of completion, quality of performance, or other specific contractual requirements.

In most states, an owner adds to the breach of contract action a claim for common law negligence. Irrespective of contractual terms, as long as the owner can establish the general contractor owed a duty of care, that a breach of the duty occurred, and that a breach of the duty proximately caused damages, a general contractor is potentially liable.[2] It is possible, however, to adequately draft an *exclusive remedies* provision, extending contractual limits and protection to the common law negligence cause of action. To avoid the possibility of a suit at common law negating negotiated contractual liability terms, use of an exclusive remedies clause is essential.

There are significant jurisdictional differences with regard to the applicable statutes of limitations, measures of damages, and the availability of certain defenses. Although most states permit an owner to proceed on both contractual and tort theories, a few jurisdictions limit the owner to a breach of contract cause of action in the face of a negotiated contract.[3] With regard to the measure of damages, breach of contract damages usually are limited to those within the contemplation of the parties at the time the contract was signed, whereas the more liberal standard in a negligence claim allows recovery of all damages proximately caused by the contractor's negligence.

---

[2] 257 Am. Jur. 2d *Negligence* § 32 (1964).

[3] *See, e.g.,* Worthington Constr. Corp. v. Moore, 266 Md. 19, 291 A.2d 466 (Ct. App. 1972) (Maryland); Battista v. Lebanon Trotting Ass'n, 538 F.2d 111 (6th Cir. 1976) (applying Ohio law).

§ 16.14   Checklist for Claim
Evaluation and Investigation

After a claim has been made or upon notice of a potential claim, the most prudent course is to start investigating immediately. Clearly, the scope of any investigation depends on the size of the project, the nature of the claim, and the dollar amount involved. The following is a checklist of items to follow when investigating a claim:

_____ Assemble all relevant written records including the contract, plant specifications, job logs, correspondence, and any documentation related to the claim.

_____ Consider the retention of a technical consultant to evaluate the claim and contractor's performance. Again, depending on the size and nature of the claim, this evaluation can be made by the contractor's in-house staff, or through the retention of technical consultants that make their living evaluating such claims.

_____ Seriously consider the retention of an experienced construction lawyer to coordinate the investigation. Although the obvious disadvantage in dealing with lawyers is the expense involved, there are numerous advantages. A significant advantage is that most, if not all, of the investigation conducted at the direction of the lawyer is likely protected from disclosure through the attorney-client privilege or work product rule. Knowing that the information provided is protected from disclosure often facilitates more candid responses from those interviewed. Also, in certain types of defect cases, the contractor can maintain the confidentiality of certain compliance and performance tests as long as the tests are performed at the direction of the lawyer.

_____ Whether done at the direction of the lawyer or performed by the lawyer personally, have interviews conducted with the key employees to establish conclusively how and why the work was performed as it was. Many significant changes in design, methodology, and scope of work are agreed upon as the result of conversations. These conversations, if established, can result in important defenses to the contractor, including those of waiver of specific contractual provisions requiring written modifications to the contract.

_____ Consider documenting the current condition of the work of improvement through photographs or videotape.

_____ Begin evaluating claims against others, for example, against the owner, architect, engineers, subcontractors, and material suppliers. Delay claims are most often very complicated and result from a confluence of factors. Defect claims are often traceable directly to an engineer that did the design work or to a subcontractor that performed it.

§ 16.15   Reading and Understanding the Contract

Unfortunately, the first time many contractors read and understand their contracts is after a claim has been made. From the owner's perspective, the contractual provisions provide an opportunity to allocate risk to the contractor for harm arising from foreseeable events commonly or even rarely encountered in construction projects. In every jurisdiction, the law is clear that a party to a contract is bound by the contract's terms as long as those terms do not violate public policy. Not to appreciate and understand the contract fully is to give an undue advantage to the owner (and indirectly to competitors who theoretically can produce lower bids through minimized risk).

The best preventative medicine is a careful and thoughtful analysis and drafting of contractual terms during the negotiation stage so the contractor understands where it is at risk and how best to minimize the potential financial harm inherent in the contract of work.

DEFENSES TO OWNERS' DEFECT
AND DELAY CLAIMS

§ 16.16   Compliance with Plans and Specifications

Almost universally, courts hold that when a contractor follows the plans and specifications provided by the owner and does so in a workmanlike manner, the contractor will not be held liable for damages that result from deficiency in the plans and specifications.[4]

As such, the owner impliedly warrants that the plans and specifications created by it (or its architects and engineers) are fit for the intended purpose of constructing the work of improvement.[5] In like fashion, the contractor warrants that it will exercise good workmanship and will follow the plans faithfully. To require more is to make the general contractor a guarantor of the sufficiency of the plans.

---

[4] United States v. Spearin, 248 U.S. 132, 39 S. Ct. 59 (1918). *See also* Harrington, *The Owner's Warranty of the Plans and Specifications for a Construction Project,* 14 Pub. Cont. L.J. 240 (1984).

[5] Souza & McCue Constr. Co. v. Superior Court, 57 Cal. 2d 508, 370 P.2d 338, 20 Cal. Rptr. 634 (1962).

When, however, the general contractor expressly warrants that a performance standard will be met, the contractor is bound by that warranty and will be held liable if the work of improvement fails to perform as warranted.[6]

Depending on the type of claim, it may be necessary for the contractor to bring a third-party action against the architect or engineer that designed the improvement. A lack of privity will bar any breach of contract action, but most states provide for equitable indemnity claims against those that contributed to the damage. Although acts and omissions by the architects and engineers employed by the owner can be raised as a defense, raising the issue by way of affirmative defense often is easier, relying upon the vicarious liability of the owner for insufficiencies in the plans and specifications.[7]

§ 16.17 Substantial Performance

The rule has long been that a contractor may recover the agreed-upon contract price as long as the contractor has rendered a good-faith and substantial performance of the requirements of the contract, even if the performance of that contract does not meet the technical specifications. The owner's damages are limited to the difference between the agreed-upon contract price and the value of the work of improvement as completed, or the cost of repairing the technical deficiency, depending on the measure that provides the greatest equity.[8] Nearly the entire body of law surrounding substantial performance has been stated in a California Supreme Court footnote as follows:

> [I]t is settled, especially in the case of Building Contracts where the owner has taken possession of the building and is enjoying the fruits of the contractor's work in the performance of the contract, that if there has been a substantial performance thereof by the contractor in good faith, where the failure to make full performance can be compensated in damages to be deducted from the price or allowed as a counterclaim, and the omissions and deviations were not willful or fraudulent and do not substantially affect the usefulness of the building for the purposes for which it was intended, the contractor may, in an action upon the contract, recover the amount paid of his contract price, less the amount allowed as damages for the failure in strict performance.[9]

---

[6] Fidelity & Deposit Co. v. City of Sheboygan Falls, 713 F.2d 1261 (7th Cir. 1983).

[7] Berkel & Co. Contractors v. Providence Hosp., 454 So. 2d 496 (Ala. 1984).

[8] 13 Am. Jur. 2d *Building and Construction Contracts* § 42 (1964).

[9] Thomas Haverty Co. v. Jones, 185 Cal. 285, 288–289, 197 P. 105, 108 (1921).

This, of course, assumes that the contractor's performance must meet a reasonable standard adhered to by contractors similarly situated.[10]

The primary issue in establishing the substantial performance defense is to establish that the discrepancy is essentially cosmetic or immaterial rather than one that goes to the utility or safety of the structure itself.

§ 16.18 Impossibility and Impracticability

Absent a contractual provision allocating risk for circumstances that make performance of the contract impossible or impractical, the court attempts to make an objective determination as to whether performance is impossible, impractical, or merely "very difficult." Some direction is given by the Restatement of Contracts when it provides:

> Where, after a contract is made, a party's performance is made impracticable without his fault by the occurrence of an event, the non-occurrence of which was a basic assumption of which the contract was made, his duty to render that performance is discharged, unless the language or the circumstances indicate the contrary.[11]

There seems to be no consistent theme upon which one can rely in determining how a given court will rule. In California, for example, an excavating contractor agreed to level a large plot of land by a given date. Soon after the work commenced, the plot of land was flooded unexpectedly, making further performance impossible. The contractor was not relieved of its obligations.[12] Numerous cases have held that true impossibility is an excuse for nonperformance.[13] Possibly the one consistent strain of cases is that "extreme difficulty," even if unforeseen, will not excuse performance.[14]

§ 16.19 Owner-caused Delays

In response to an assessment of liquidated damages or to a direct claim for consequential damages as a result of delays, the general contractor should evaluate carefully the owner's responsibilities in causing or contributing to the delays.

---

[10] Bause v. Anthony Pools, Inc., 205 Cal. App. 2d 606, 23 Cal. Rptr. 265 (1962).

[11] Restatement (Second) of Contracts § 261 (1981).

[12] Caron v. Andrews, 133 Cal. App. 2d 402, 284 P.2d 544 (1955).

[13] *See, e.g.,* Restatement (Second) of Contracts § 261 illus. (1981).

[14] Kennedy v. Reece, 225 Cal. App. 2d 717, 37 Cal. Rptr. 708 (1964); Associated Grocers, Inc. v. West, 297 N.W.2d 103 (Iowa 1980); Monroe Piping & Sheet Metal, Inc. v. Edward Joy Co., 138 A.D. 2d 941, 526 N.Y.S.2d 279 (1988).

A common problem occurs when an excessive number of changes or changes late in the job are made by the owner or its representatives and these changes result in difficulty of performance, scheduling problems, and related delays.[15]

To the extent that the plans and specifications are defective and those defects cause delays in the construction process, the contractor is entitled to relief.[16] This is true also for delays occasioned by correcting the defects in the plans.[17]

As with every defense discussed in §§ **16.16** through **16.22**, it is necessary to review the contract documents carefully for provisions that express the intention of the parties with regard to responsibility for acts or omissions that have given rise to the delay claims.

§ 16.20   Owner Waiver of Contractual Provisions

Waiver is defined as the intentional or voluntary relinquishment of a known right or conduct warranting an inference of the relinquishment of such right.[18]

It is increasingly commonplace for contracts drafted by owners to contain provisions requiring written waivers and other provisions stipulating that any acts or statements by the owner will not constitute a waiver of any contractual provision. Although the owner may waive such clear contractual provisions, the waiver must be proved by clear and convincing evidence.[19]

To the extent the contractor can establish that the owner accepted the work of improvement with full knowledge of defects, the acceptance constituted a waiver of the right to require technical compliance.[20] Clearly, there cannot be a knowing waiver when the alleged defects are latent.[21]

As a general proposition, final payment by the owner, in and of itself, does not amount to a knowing waiver. It is simply one of many factors that aids the trier of fact in determining whether the owner has knowingly waived a patent defect.[22]

---

[15] HTC Corp. v. Olds, 486 P.2d 463 (Colo. 1971).

[16] Laburnum Constr. Corp. v. United States, 325 F.2d 451 (Ct. Cl. 1963).

[17] Carl M. Halvorson, Inc. v. United States, 461 F.2d 1337 (Ct. Cl. 1972).

[18] Black's Law Dictionary 1417 (5th ed. 1979).

[19] Broadway Maintenance Corp. v. Rutgers, 90 N.J. 253, 259, 447 A.2d 906, 912 (1982).

[20] Havens Steel Co. v. Randolph Eng'g Co., 613 F. Supp. 514 (W.D. Mo. 1985).

[21] 13 Am. Jur. 2d *Building and Construction Contracts* § 55 (1964).

[22] 13 Am. Jur. 2d *Building and Construction Contracts* §§ 58–59 (1964).

§ 16.21   Liquidated Damages Provisions

The enforceability of liquidated damages provisions has been litigated frequently in almost every jurisdiction of the United States. There is a great body of evolving case authority as well as more frequent treatment by state legislatures.[23]

Generally speaking, liquidated damages provisions will be enforced if they are found to be reasonable in light of the anticipated or actual damages caused by the breach, taking into consideration the difficulty of proving actual loss, that is, if they are not perceived as a penalty.[24]

Although the court generally inquires into what was reasonably anticipated by the parties at the time of entering into the contract, the courts routinely compare the amount of actual damages with the liquidated damages in determining the reasonableness of the anticipated damages.[25] Thus, in common cases in which the actual damages are significantly less than the liquidated damages, the provision may well be held unenforceable.

Assuming that the owner can meet its burden of establishing that the liquidated damages provision is enforceable, there is a significant split in jurisdictions with regard to whether the liquidated damages provision will be enforced if the owner is partially at fault for the delays or whether the liquidated damages will be apportioned.[26] Clearly, the modern trend with most courts is to allow apportionment of fault for liquidated damages, especially in light of the number of jurisdictions enacting or authorizing principles of comparative fault in standard negligence analysis.

Knowledgeable and prudent general contractors will make certain that all subcontractors have express notice of any liquidated damages provisions with the relevant provisions providing for an apportionment of fault to those subcontractors to the extent those subcontractors (or their sub-subcontractors or suppliers) contributed to any delays. At a minimum, most general contractors should be sure to incorporate the prime contract

---

[23] *See, e.g.,* Cal. Civ. Code § 1671 (1990), Governing Liquidated Damages in Construction Contracts, providing that:

> [Except as provided in Subdivision (c), a provision in a contract liquidating the damages for the breach of the contract is valid unless the party seeking to invalidate the provision establishes that the provision was unreasonable under the circumstances existing at the time the contract was made.

[24] Restatement (Second) of Contracts, § 356(1). *See also* Annotation, *Contractual Provisions for Per Diem Payments for Delay in Performance as One for Liquidated Damages or Penalty,* 12 A.L.R.4th 891 (1982) and cases cited therein.

[25] Ogden Dev. Corp. v. Federal Ins. Co., 508 F.2d 583 (2d Cir. 1974).

[26] *See, e.g.,* E.C. Ernst, Inc. v. Manhattan Constr. Co., 551 F.2d 1026 (5th Cir. 1977), *cert.* denied, 434 U.S. 1067, 98 S. Ct. 1246 (1978); *compare* Peter Kiewit Sons', Co. v. Pasadena City Junior College Dist., 59 Cal. 2d 241, 379 P.2d 18, 28 Cal. Rptr. 714 (1963).

provisions into each and every subcontract to ensure that the courts will apportion fault for liquidated damages.

§ 16.22   Statutes of Limitations

As the name implies, limitations on the time within which a claim can be made against a contractor are determined by statute. The applicable statute of limitations depends on the nature of the claim being made. In California, for example, there is a two-year statute for breach of oral contract,[27] a three-year statute for injury to real property,[28] a four-year statute for breach of written contracts or written warranties,[29] and a ten-year statute of repose for actions against developers, architects, and contractors for latent deficiencies in works of improvement to real property.[30] In the event courts are faced with the decision to apply different periods of limitations, the courts generally apply the longer statute.[31]

Once a determination has been made on the appropriate statute of limitations, the question arises about when the statutory period begins to run. The cases and jurisdictions vary in their approaches to the question, some starting the clock at the earliest point when the wrongful act occurred, others at the time a project was completed, with some jurisdictions not commencing the statutory period until the plaintiff knew or should have known of the damage.[32]

Given the facts necessary to determine when the cause of action accrues will not be known until after discovery has commenced, prudent counsel should state every possible applicable statute of limitations as an affirmative defense because failure to raise a statute of limitations as an affirmative defense constitutes a waiver of the right to do so.[33]

---

[27] Cal. Civ. Proc. Code § 339 (Deering 1990).

[28] *Id.* § 338.

[29] *Id.* § 337.

[30] *Id.* § 337.15.

[31] Annotation, *What Statute of Limitations Governs Action by Contractee for Defective or Improper Performance of Work by Private Building Contractor,* 1 A.L.R.3d 914 (1965).

[32] Velotta v. Leo Petrozonio Landscaping, Inc., 69 Ohio St. 2d 376, 433 N.E.2d 147 (1982).

[33] Fed. R. Civ. P. 8(c).

CHAPTER 17

RIGHTS AND REMEDIES AGAINST OTHER PARTIES TO THE PROCESS

John W. Bakas, Jr.
J. Bert Grandoff

John W. Bakas, Jr., is a partner in the Tampa, Florida, law firm of Lawson, McWhirter, Grandoff & Reeves. He practices in the areas of construction litigation and local government. Mr. Bakas has represented contractors in claims against architects and other parties in the construction process. He has authored a chapter on bids and bid disputes in a Florida bar book on Florida construction law. In addition to lecturing on the construction process to contractors, architects, and owners, he is an adjunct professor at the Stetson College of Law, where he teaches construction law.

J. Bert Grandoff is a senior partner in the Tampa, Florida, law firm of Lawson, McWhirter, Grandoff & Reeves, and concentrates his practice in the area of construction litigation. Mr. Grandoff is a founding member of the American College of Construction Lawyers, and has lectured and written widely on the subject for meetings of the American and the Florida Bar Associations. He is the editor of *Florida Construction Law and Practice* published by the Florida bar, and he is a former division chairman of the Forum Committee on the Construction Industry of the ABA. He is also an adjunct professor at the Stetson University College of Law, where he teaches construction law.

ANALYZING CONTRACTOR
CAUSES OF ACTION

§ 17.1   Commonly Found Relationships
Between Parties

Most contractors find themselves in a construction project after the owner has previously executed a contract with an architect or other design professional. Subsequently the owner, often as the result of competitive bidding, enters into an agreement with the contractor to build the project using the drawings and specifications and the contract prepared by the architect or other design professional.

An owner may have signed contracts with several contractors, each contractor obligated for a portion of the work. Again, most often in these multi-prime or co-prime models, the contractor does not have a contract with the other contractors but is impacted if the other contractors do not coordinate properly or if the work of other contractors on the site causes damage or delay.

A construction manager also may have a contract with the owner but not with the contractor. Projects that benefit by the added coordination of a construction manager may use an organizational model in which the owner enters into a contract with the construction manager and the construction manager then contracts directly with one or more contractors to perform the work. Each such contractor is considered a prime contractor because of the direct contractual relationship with the construction manager. The construction manager may only have a contract with a single general contractor who will in turn contract with the speciality subcontractors.

Even without a contractual relationship with the architect or the construction manager, as is frequently the case, the contractor is directly affected by the actions of those parties. Indeed, damages may occur because the contractor has many of the burdens but none of the reciprocal benefits of a direct contract. Although not a relationship based in contract, the contractor is in a confining relationship with those who wield ultimate power over performance and payment.

§ 17.2 Determining Nature of Damage and Cause of Action

When a contractor incurs damage by the action or inaction of an architect, construction manager, or other contractor, the nature of the damage and cause of action must be an initial determination. The American legal system recognizes distinct causes of actions, each with particular elements that must be proved. A contractor's civil cause of action most often will be based in contract, in tort, or on some statutory right. In analyzing the rights of the contractor, the legal concept of *privity of contract,* the relationship created when two or more parties enter into a contract, shapes the remedies a contractor can use to recover damages. Although the privity concept is easily understood, its effect is the tinder that fuels much of the in-court defenses used to block a contractor's recovery.

When the criminal law is violated, the cause of action is brought by the state or a federal governmental entity whose remedies include prison, fines, restitution to the victim, or community service. As a result, when an architect, construction manager, or other contractor commits a crime, the cause of action is not brought by the contractor who was the victim. Nevertheless, the same wrong that gave rise to the criminal cause of action also may allow the contractor to bring a civil action. Moreover, federal and state RICO (Racketeer Influenced and Corrupt Organizations) laws offer an arsenal of statutory remedies including treble damages, attorneys' fees, and estoppel.

§ 17.3   Initial Checklist for Pursuit of Rights and Remedies

The contractor pursuing potential causes of action against architects, construction managers, and other contractors should continue its analysis and pursuit of the action by following certain steps, each of which is described briefly in §§ 17.4 through 17.9.

____ In an action for breach of contract, give the notice required by the contract

____ In an action based on tort or contract, file the lawsuit within the time allowed by the applicable statute of limitations

____ Question whether the suit is for damages incurred by a subcontractor

____ Consider any existing settlement with the owner

____ Determine who is the real party in interest to bring the lawsuit

____ Decide whether facts state proper cause of action.

§ 17.4   —Giving Notice Required in Action for Breach

When the contractor has a contractual relationship with the architect, construction manager, or other contractor who caused damage, the contractor must follow the notice provisions of the contract carefully. The notice provisions usually are prerequisites to filing a lawsuit or a demand for arbitration. Contractual notice provisions can be technical, but their technicality and apparent insignificance will not cause a court to overlook a contractor's failure to comply. For example, when a steel fabricator failed to follow the contract's dual notice provisions that required notice first to the owner and then to the construction manager, the court rejected the contractor's claim that the contractor should be relieved from the notice provisions because the owner was not prejudiced by the contractor's noncompliance.[1]

---

[1] Paterson-Leitch Co. v. Massachusetts Elec., 840 F.2d 985 (1st Cir. 1988).

Sometimes a contractor will claim the other party to the contract waived the notice requirement. Establishing a waiver defense is difficult because waiver must be based on clear and unambiguous conduct by the other party. Courts are reluctant to imply waiver in the absence of such specific conduct.[2]

§ 17.5   —Filing Within Applicable Statute of Limitations

Although actions by contractors based on tort principles rather than on a breach of contract will not be subject to the contractually-imposed notice provisions found in contracts, both tort and contract actions are subject to statutes of limitation. Most states have statutes that limit the time in which a contractor or other claimant can file a lawsuit against the responsible party.

In applying the statute of limitations, a contractor must know when any of the contractor's employees first learned of the defective plans, the delay, or other damage. This knowledge usually starts the clock of the statute of limitations.[3] Such statutes usually require the contractor to bring an action within two to five years after the cause of action accrues. A contractor's right to sue (when the cause of action accrues) comes into existence when the contractor knows it has been damaged by the wrongful act of another. Because the knowledge element is objective, the statute of limitations in most instances begins when the contractor knew or should have known with the exercise of due diligence that the would-be defendant caused damage to the contractor. If the action is not filed within the specified number of years after the action accrues, it is barred.

Contractor actions based on delays caused by the wrongful acts of the architect, construction manager, or other contractor may pose serious problems for a contractor. If a contractor knows that another party is allowing activities to occur on the job that will delay completion, the contractor's right to sue may begin at that point. For example, when a contractor filed suit for delay of completion after the statute of limitations period had run, the suit was untimely. The court concluded that the contractor's claim regarding the failure of the construction manager to enforce a project labor agreement was time-barred because the contractor knew during construction that long coffee breaks were being permitted by the

---

[2] *Id.*

[3] Farrell Constr. Co. v. Jefferson Parish, 693 F. Supp. 490 (E.D. La. 1988). *But see* same case 896 F.2d 136 (5th Cir. 1990).

construction manager and that the practice would mean the steelwork could not be finished on time.[4]

§ 17.6 —Dealing with Suits for Subcontractor Damages

Another factor the contractor should consider before going ahead with a lawsuit is whether the suit is for damages that actually were incurred by a subcontractor. If the contractor has not suffered the damages, the contractor may need an assignment of the subcontractor's claim.[5]

§ 17.7 —Handling Contractor Settlement with Owner

If the contractor has settled with the owner, the contractor should examine settlement documents to determine whether the documents clearly express the intent not to release the architect, the construction manager, or other contractors. Any one of these parties, and especially the architect, may be an agent of the owner included in standard release forms that release the actual party to the document as well as the party's officers, employees, and agents.[6]

§ 17.8 —Determining Real Party in Interest to Bring Lawsuit

Defaulting contractors face special problems in bringing lawsuits. For example, if the contractor had a surety bond and the surety completes work, the contractor may have assigned all of its rights to the surety. Such assignment may preclude a subsequent lawsuit by the contractor.[7] One of the rights of a surety is to take over construction and complete the work. To assist in such completion activities, the surety may require the contractor's rights to be assigned to the surety automatically if the contractor is not able to finish

---

[4] Paterson-Leitch Co. v. Massachusetts Elec., 840 F.2d 985 (1st Cir. 1988); Bowen & Bowen, Inc. v. McCoy-Gibbons, 185 Ga. App. 298, 363 S.E.2d 827 (1987).

[5] Farrell Constr. Co. v. Jefferson Parish, 693 F. Supp. 490 (E.D. La. 1988). *But see* same case 896 F.2d 136 (5th Cir. 1990).

[6] Tri-City Constr. v. A.C. Kirkwood & Assoc., 738 S.W.2d 935 (Mo. Ct. App. 1987); Malta Constr. Co. v. Henningson, Durham & Richardson, Inc., 694 F. Supp. 902 (N.D. Ga. 1988).

[7] James McKinney v. Lake Placid 1980 Olympic Games, Inc., 92 A.D.2d 991, 473 N.Y.S.2d 960 (1984).

the contract or files a petition in bankruptcy. A surety also may require the contractor to give the surety the right to settle, compromise, and issue any releases that may be necessary to protect the surety under the indemnification agreement. Contractors should be aware of all such provisions in their agreements with surety companies to prevent a settling surety from cutting off the contractor's rights to proceed against the architect or other parties.[8]

§ 17.9   —Deciding Whether Facts State Proper Cause of Action

After a contractor files a lawsuit, the defendant to the suit has several procedural weapons that may defeat the contractor's claim even before it can be heard by the trier of fact.

Motion to Dismiss

The first is a motion to dismiss, which is a pleading filed by the defendant. In the motion, the judge is asked to rule that the contractor's complaint, even assuming all of the facts to be true, does not contain the elements or allegations necessary to state a valid cause of action. For instance, in a tort action based on negligence, the elements of this cause of action are:

1. The defendant had a duty to protect the contractor from the damage or loss for which the contractor is suing.
2. The defendant failed to act or perform in accordance with the duty.
3. The contractor suffered loss or damage as a direct result of the defendant's actions.

In a motion to dismiss, the defendant will claim that the contractor failed to allege one of the elements listed above. If the contractor's complaint is dismissed for failure to state a cause of action, most often the dismissal will be without prejudice. This means the contractor has another opportunity to plead, and the defendant has the corresponding opportunity to file another motion to dismiss.

For example, if a contractor sues an architect for cost overruns but merely states in the contractor's complaint that the project cost more than expected, the complaint is subject to a motion to dismiss because it does not allege the necessary elements of a valid negligence action. Even if the contractor suffered damages because of the cost overruns, the complaint did not allege that the architect had any duty to prevent such costs overruns

---

[8] *Id.*

nor did it allege how additional costs were directly caused by the architect's negligent acts.

Motion for Summary Judgment

If the contractor's complaint withstands the defendant's motion to dismiss, there is a more deadly obstacle likely to confront the contractor: the defendant's motion for summary judgment. Unlike a motion to dismiss that tests whether the contractor has alleged the necessary elements of a cause of action, a motion for summary judgment tests whether there are any disputed issues of fact that would necessitate the trier of fact hearing evidence to resolve the dispute. The trier of fact can either be the jury or judge. However, if the facts that might be used to support the contractor's complaint are established without dispute, there is no need for witnesses to describe the facts to the jury or to a judge. The trial is not needed because the principal purpose of a trial is for witnesses to describe facts disputed by the parties. After hearing the witnesses, the jury or judge, sitting as the trier of fact, decides which facts have been established by a preponderance of the evidence.

Either party to a lawsuit may file a motion for summary judgment. The judge reviews all of the alleged facts and if none are disputed, the judge must decide the case based on those undisputed facts and the applicable law. Although the contractor may also file a motion for summary judgment, it is usually the defendant who files, hoping the contractor will be unable to demonstrate a dispute on some essential fact. Motions for summary judgment also are filed when defendants believe contractors cannot present facts necessary to support the elements of the cause of action. Thus, when the contractor is unable to offer the required facts, even after any permitted amendment to the complaint, the judge will enter a judgment dismissing the contractor's complaint with prejudice.

The operation of a motion for summary judgment will illustrate its power. A contractor sued an architect because allegedly the architect wrongfully induced the owner to terminate the contractor. The defendant/architect filed a motion for summary judgment, arguing that there were no facts on the issue of whether the owner breached its contract. In response, the contractor filed an affidavit of its president who claimed the owner's wrongful suspension of the contractor's work was a breach of the owner-contractor contract. The affidavit of the contractor's president established a reasonable inference that the owner's suspension was a breach of contract. Thus, the contractor avoided an adverse summary judgment on that basis. But the architect had another argument. The architect claimed there were no disputed issues of fact regarding whether the architect acted with actual malice, a required element in the tort of intentional interference with a contractual relationship. In fact, the architect claimed that there were no facts to prove or even reasonably to infer actual malice. The contractor failed to present any evidence from which a reasonable inference could be drawn that the architect's actions regarding the suspension were done maliciously. Although reasonable inferences from facts would be allowed, the court would not allow inferences to be built on other inferences. Thus, the court affirmed the granting of summary judgment in favor of the architect, dismissing the contractor's complaint.[9]

§ 17.10   Significance of Contract Documents to Contractor's Suit

In the private sector, the standard forms of agreement published by the American Institute of Architects (AIA) are used widely. Although the AIA documents are the basis for much of the construction industry, one court has noted that the AIA contract "is replete with ambiguities, contradictions, and is an attempt to give all things to both parties."[10] Of the many paragraphs in the AIA documents, certain provisions are particularly significant in any contractor's action. For example, both AIA Document B141, *Standard Form of Agreement Between Owner and Architect* (1987), and AIA Document A201, *General Conditions of the Contract for Construction* (1987), obligate the contractor to supervise and direct the work. The architect does not have control of the construction means, methods, techniques, sequences, or procedures.[11] Similarly, the architect's role in reviewing shop drawings, product data, samples, and similar submittals is "only for the limited purpose of checking for conformance with information given and the design concept expressed in the contract documents."[12] Further, the architect's approval of a shop drawing or submittal that contains an error or deviation from the contract documents does not relieve the contractor from liability.[13]

In addition to the foregoing limitations on the architect's role, in any action by the contractor against the architect, the provisions in the standard AIA document that purport to limit the architect's on-site responsibilities are in constant tension with the inherent role of the architect as designer, with the actual practice of architect's visiting the site on behalf of the

---

[9] Certified Mechanical Contractors v. Wight & Co., 162 Ill. App. 3d 391, 515 N.E.2d 1047 (1987).

[10] Fletcher v. Laguna Vista Corp., 275 So. 2d 579 (Fla. Dist. Ct. App.), *cert. denied,* 281 So. 2d 213 (Fla. 1973).

[11] AIA Doc. A201, General Conditions of the Contract for Construction, para. 3.3.1 (1987); AIA Doc. B141, Standard Form of Agreement Between Owner and Architect, para. 2.6.6 (1987).

[12] *Id.* para. 2.6.12.

[13] *Id.*

owner, and with the architect's substantial authority to reject work that does not conform to the contract documents.[14] The realities of construction necessitate the active involvement of an architect in clarifying, interpreting, and approving the work performed by the contractor, but the standard AIA documents do not give the architect the express responsibility to supervise construction. The omission is intentional. Typically, no contractual relationship exists between the contractor and architect. Therefore, the contractor's cause of action against the architect is often for negligence, which requires an allegation of some duty owed by the architect to the contractor. If the contract between the owner and architect directs the architect to supervise construction, courts often recognize a duty in that supervisory obligation.[15] On the other hand, if the AIA documents lack any reference to supervision, an architect may argue that the basis for the contractor's negligence action also has been eliminated. Regardless of that argument's validity, the AIA documents still vest the architect with considerable power during construction.

Under AIA A201 and B141, the architect's attempts to limit involvement are shadowed by pervasive controls given the architect over the contractor's work:

1. Compare subparagraph 4.2.3 of AIA A201,[16] disavowing architect control over the means and methods of construction, with Article 2 of AIA B141,[17] giving the architect authority and responsibility to prepare the size and character of the project as to architectural, structural, mechanical, and electrical systems, and as to materials, and to prepare the construction documents consisting of drawings and specifications, setting forth in detail the requirements for construction.

2. Interpret the subparagraph 4.2.2[18] limitations on the architect's need to make thorough inspections to check work quality or quantity alongside subparagraph 4.2.6,[19] giving the architect the express power to reject work not conforming to the contract documents.

3. Notice that subparagraph 4.2.7,[20] which limits the architect's review of shop drawings to a check for agreement of the drawings with given information and design concept and which does not extend the review

---

[14] *Id.* para. 2.6.11.

[15] United States v. Rogers & Rogers, 161 F. Supp. 132 (S.D. Cal. 1973); Hanberry Corp. v. State Bldg. Comm'n, 390 So. 2d 277 (Miss. 1980).

[16] AIA Doc. A201, General Conditions of the Contract for Construction, para. 4.2.3 (1987).

[17] AIA Doc. B141, Standard Form of Agreement Between Owner and Architect, art. 2 (1987).

[18] AIA Doc. A201, General Conditions of the Contract for Construction, para. 4.2.2 (1987).

[19] *Id.* para. 4.2.6.

[20] *Id.* para. 4.2.7.

to detail accuracy and completeness, loses some of its significance when read with subparagraph 3.12.6,[21] which prevents the contractor from performing any work described in submittals until the architect has approved them.

In addition, the AIA documents give architects the following types of authority and responsibility:

1. Authorization to review and certify the amounts due the contractor[22]
2. Permission to require additional inspection or testing of the work[23]
3. Requirement to conduct inspections to determine the date of substantial completion and final completion[24]
4. Power to analyze contract performance matters and contract document requirements when requested in writing by the owner or contractor[25]
5. Responsibility to render a decision on a matter before arbitration or litigation between the contractor and owner may occur, with certain exceptions[26]
6. Authority to investigate differing site conditions and the responsibility to recommend any equitable adjustment in the contract sum or contract time[27]
7. Power to review contractor claims[28]
8. Authorization to issue construction change directives along with the owner[29]
9. Permission to determine the method for the adjustment in the contract sum if the contractor does not respond promptly or disagrees[30]
10. Authority to deny a certificate for payment[31]
11. Authority to direct the contractor not to cover work and to uncover work for the architect's observation.[32]

---

[21] *Id.* para. 3.12.6.

[22] AIA Doc. A201, General Conditions of the Contract for Construction, para. 4.2.5 (1987).

[23] *Id.* para. 4.2.6.

[24] *Id.* para. 4.2.9.

[25] *Id.* para. 4.2.11.

[26] *Id.* para 4.3.2.

[27] *Id.* para. 4.3.6.

[28] AIA Doc. A201, General Conditions of the Contract for Construction, para. 4.4.1 (1987).

[29] *Id.* para. 7.3.1.

[30] *Id.* para. 7.3.6.

[31] *Id.* para. 9.5.1.

[32] *Id.* para. 12.1.1.

In addition to the controls given architects over the contractor's work, AIA documents place some restrictive requirements on the contractor. For example, even when the contractor disputes the price charged or time involved for changes in work, the AIA document requires that the contractor continue with the work, proceeding promptly with the change in the work involved.[33]

APPLYING LEGAL PRINCIPLES IN CONTRACTOR ACTIONS

§ 17.11   Direct Breach of Contract Actions

When a contractor has a contractual relationship with an architect, construction manager, or other contractor, and the contractor is damaged by the breach of the contract by the other contracting party, the contractor has a cause of action for breach of contract. In stating the claim against the architect, construction manager, or other contractor, the contractor must identify the contract, the portion of the contract that has been breached, the damages that the contractor has suffered as a result of the breach, and the contractor's own performance prior to the breach of the other party.

Sometimes the economic loss rule (discussed in § **17.16**) has been applied to prevent parties in privity of contract from suing in tort for economic damages if there is no personal injury or property damage.[34] Consequently, if a contractor has a contractual relationship with an architect, the contractor's only remedy may be in contract rather than in both contract and tort. This situation could arise if the contractor and the architect were part of a joint venture and the architect was negligent.

§ 17.12   Lack of Privity as Bar to Actions for Breach

Construction industry practice usually does not find a contractor entering into a contract with the architect or construction manager. At common law only parties to a contract could sue for breach of the contract. Thus, if an architect failed to carry out a duty imposed by the owner-architect contract, such as the duty to provide proper drawings, the contractor would

---

[33] *Id.* para. 7.3.4.

[34] Florida Power & Light v. Westinghouse Elec. Corp., 510 So. 2d 899 (Fla. 1987); AFM Corp. v. Southern Bell Tel. & Tel. Co., 515 So. 2d 180 (Fla. 1987).

have no cause of action against the architect if the drawings proved to be defective. Recognizing that a remedy should follow a wrong, contractors sought exceptions to the privity requirement. At the same time, architects sought to preserve and strengthen their privity defense. The exceptions permitted by modern courts describe the body of law applicable to a contractor's rights and remedies against architect, the construction manager, or other contractors.[35]

§ 17.13   —Third-Party Beneficiary Status as Exception to Rule

Parties to a contract can intend their agreement to confer a benefit on a nonparty. Such individuals, if intended to receive a benefit, are known as *intended* or *third-party beneficiaries*. An intended or third-party beneficiary of a contract can recover damages that flow as a result of the breach of contract.

Co-prime contractors generally are held to be intended or third-party beneficiaries of contracts between the owner and other contractors.[36] Consequently, co-prime contractors will find the burden of alleging a cause of action against another co-prime contractor for breach of contract much less than the burden required to establish a single prime contractor as an intended or third-party beneficiary of the owner-architect contract. A co-prime contractor also may have an action against a co-prime contractor's surety bond.[37] Owners seeking to avoid getting caught in the cross fire frequently include express language in each co-prime contractor's contract requiring harmonious relations with the other co-prime contractors. In striving for peace, the owner also helps the co-prime contractors because damage that one co-prime contractor suffers as a result of another co-prime contractor's failure to coordinate its work is the very damage such contract clauses, which bestow beneficiary status in the owner-co-prime contractor contract, are intended to prevent. Thus, a co-prime contractor is clearly an intended beneficiary of such provisions.[38]

Exculpatory Clauses

A good sword for the contractor may actually be a better shield for the architect. The owner-contractor contract may contain clauses benefiting

---

[35] United States v. Rogers & Rogers, 161 F. Supp. 132 (S.D. Cal. 1958).

[36] Moore Constr. v. Clarksville Dep't of Elec., 707 S.W.2d 1 (Tenn. Ct. App. 1985).

[37] Hanberry Corp. v. State Bldg. Comm'n, 390 So. 2d 277 (Miss. 1980).

[38] *Id.*

the architect or construction manager. For example, an owner may include a no damages for delay clause in the contract between owner and contractor. Although architects normally desire to stay detached from the owner-contractor relationship, they will quickly accept the benefit of the no damages for delay clause. Courts may find architects or construction managers to be third-party beneficiaries of exculpatory clauses, such as no damages for delay clauses, when the following exists:

1.   The contractor's exculpatory clause recognizes that delays may be caused by the architect
2.   The architect is named as an owner's representative
3.   The contractor's only compensation for delay is an extension of time
4.   The architect exercises extensive management and oversight of the project
5.   The owner relies on the expertise of the architect in the operation of the project
6.   The architect's independence to act might be restricted by the threat of delay suits from the contractor.[39]

Applying the same principles, construction managers may be found to be third-party beneficiaries of no damages for delay clauses.[40]

Consequently, because of the no damages for delay clause in the owner-contractor contract, contractors may have difficulty avoiding the third-party beneficiary principles that protect the project architect. For example, the contractor on the construction of a sewage treatment plant argued that its damages were not delay damages and thus that the architect could not benefit by the no damages for delay clause in the owner-contractor contract. The contractor claimed damages because there was no electrical service furnished to the site for more than a year, the contractor was denied access to the site, and the engineer was negligent in designing electrical switch gear and for requiring a redesign of switch gear after the original switch gear had been ordered from the supplier. As a result of the engineer's alleged negligence, the contractor suffered cost overruns and lost profits. Reduced to its most common elements, the contractor's claim was for additional cost of labor and supervision caused by delays in providing adequate electrical switch gear due to the engineer's alleged negligence. The contractor failed to give any other characterization of the damages and, even during discovery, attributed its damages to delays. The court held in favor of the architect. The contractor's "own characterization of the damages

---

[39] L.K. Comstock & Co. v. Morse/UBM Joint Venture, 153 Ill. App. 3d. 475, 505 N.E.2d 1253 (1987).
[40] *Id.*

incurred as the result of delays compels the conclusion that such damages are covered by the no-damage-for-delay clause."[41]

Sufficient Intent

The language in statutory performance bonds may not show sufficient intent to benefit a separate co-prime contractor to permit that separate co-prime contractor to sue the surety of another co-prime contractor who caused delay.[42] Likewise when the owner-architect contract specifically excludes conferring any benefit on a third party, courts will refuse to bestow intended or third-party beneficiary status on the contractor.[43]

§ 17.14   —Duty of Cooperation with Multiple Prime Contractors

On projects with more than one contractor in privity with the owner, in which none of the contractors have been given the specific authority to direct the sequence of the other contractor's work, and even in cases in which a contractor does have such responsibility, a contractor may find its work hindered by the actions of another contractor. Work at the site is especially prone to these failure to cooperate situations.

As an illustration, for construction of the Washington metropolitan area subway system, Shea—S&M Ball (Shea) contracted with the owner to construct the tunnel south of the Foggy Bottom Metro Station. Massman-Kiewit-Early (MKE) contracted with the owner to construct the tunnel north of the station. MKE was alleged to have allowed surface water to flood onto Shea's portion of the work.

The contract between MKE and the owner required MKE to submit complete drawings of the dewatering system it proposed to use and to modify the drainage facilities if they caused damage to existing buildings, structures, utilities, or facilities. MKE also was obligated by its contract with the owner to conduct operations so as not to interfere with the sewers and laterals from adjoining properties. Shea's worksite was flooded when a steel, corrugated sewer built by MKE overflowed. The court held that Shea was a third-party beneficiary of the contract between MKE and the owner. Thus, even though Shea was not a party to the MKE-owner contract, Shea was entitled to sue for breach of the contract.[44]

---

[41] Bates & Rogers Constr. v. Greeley & Hansen, 109 Ill. 2d 225, 486 N.E.2d 902 (1985).

[42] MGM Constr. v. New Jersey Educ. Facilities Auth., 220 N.J. Super. 483, 532 A.2d 764 (1987).

[43] Edward B. Fitzpatrick v. Suffolk, 138 A.D. 446, 525 N.Y.S.2d 863 (1988).

[44] Shea—S&M Ball v. Massman-Kiewit-Early, 606 F.2d 1245 (D.C. Cir. 1979).

The AIA *Standard Form of Agreement Between Owner and Contractor* entered into by three co-prime contractors was found to be sufficient to allow the electrical contractor to sue as a third-party beneficiary on the contracts of the other two co-prime contractors.[45]

§ 17.15 —Abolition of Requirement for Contractual Privity

The requirement of privity or a contractual relationship as an element in a cause of action based on someone's nonperformance of a contractual duty was first widely litigated in cases arising out of personal injury to consumers of manufactured products.[46] As the law regarding personal injuries from products evolved, liability shifted from negligence to strict liability in tort. No longer were plaintiffs required to prove that the manufacturer of the product was negligent. The next step in the evolution of these nonprivity actions saw claims for losses that did not have accompanying personal injury or property damage. In these cases, plaintiff sought recovery for economic losses caused by defective products. American jurisdictions are split on the subject, some allowing a plaintiff to recover economic losses for defective products.[47] Other courts hold that strict liability in tort should not be extended to purely economic losses.[48]

Actions Against Architects

The leading early construction case in this area arose out of a school construction project in California. A concrete supplier sued the general contractor, Rogers & Rogers, for the unpaid price of the concrete. Rogers & Rogers counterclaimed against the government's architect because of the architect's alleged negligence in interpreting test data regarding the concrete. Rogers & Rogers also alleged the architect negligently interpreted test reports regarding the concrete installed as part of the building's skeleton. According to Rogers & Rogers, the architect should have known the concrete did not meet specifications. In analyzing the architect's potential

---

[45] Barth Elec. Co. v. Traylor Bros., 553 N.E.2d 504 (Ind. Ct. App. 1990); AIA Doc. A101, Standard Form of Agreement Between Owner and Contractor (1987).

[46] MacPherson v. Buick Motor Co., 217 N.Y. 382, 111 N.E. 1050 (1916).

[47] Moorman Mfg. Co. v. National Tank Co., 91 Ill. 2d 69, 435 N.E.2d 443 (1982); Berg v. General Motors Corp., 555 P.2d 818 (Wash. 1976); City of La Crosse v. Schubert, Schroeder & Assocs., 240 N.W.2d 124 (Wis. 1976).

[48] Midland Forge, Inc. v. Letts Indus., Inc., 395 F. Supp. 506 (N.D. Iowa 1975); Hiigel v. General Motors Corp., 190 Colo. 57, 544 P.2d 983 (1975); Hawkins Constr. Co. v. Matthews Co., 209 N.W.2d 643 (Neb. 1973).

liability, the court held the architect could be liable in tort for the negligent breach of duties assumed by the architect in the contract with the owner.

The architect argued that without a contractual relationship with Rogers & Rogers, there was no duty that could give rise to an actionable claim. According to the architect, the failure to perform the contractual obligations in the contract with the owner gave the owner the right to sue, but did not give a similar right to the contractor who was not a party to the contract.

In rejecting this argument, the court fixed its analysis on the terms of the owner-architect contract. The architect had the authority to:

1. Prepare plans and specifications
2. Supervise the construction
3. Stop work.

The court stated "the power of the architect to stop the work alone is tantamount to a power of economic life or death over the contractor." Along with such authority, the court held it was only fair to recognize a corresponding responsibility.[49]

A similar result has been reached by the Florida courts. A supervising architect may be liable to a general contractor who may foreseeably suffer economic loss by the architect's negligence in performing duties under the owner-architect contract.[50] Construction managers are held to a similar standard of care if they supervise the work.[51]

Even in the absence of specific supervisory responsibilities in the owner-architect contract, the aggregate inspection and on-site responsibilities of the architect may be sufficient to establish the duty of due care to the contractor. Architects may be liable to the contractor if the architects are permitted by the contract documents to:

1. Provide a field representative or field inspector for the project
2. Inspect to determine if the contractor laid pipe according to the specifications
3. Determine if the contractor's applications for payment were correct
4. Require the contractor to correct work
5. Check invert elevations of installed pipe.[52]

---

[49] United States v. Rogers & Rogers, 161 F. Supp. 132 (S.D. Cal. 1958).

[50] A.R. Moyer, Inc. v. Graham, 285 So. 2d 397 (Fla. 1973).

[51] Gateway Erectors Div. v. Lutheran Gen. Hosp., 102 Ill. App. 3d. 300, 430 N.E.2d 20 (1981).

[52] Magnolia Constr. v. Mississippi Gulf S. Eng'g, 518 So. 2d 1194 (Miss. 1988).

Other courts state the rule somewhat differently, requiring a relationship "sufficiently intimate to be equated with privity."[53] Again, however, the factors of preparation of the drawings, responsibility for reviewing and approving change orders, recommending equitable adjustments during construction, and supervision of the work are sufficient to require the architect to carry out such duties reasonably toward the contractor.[54]

Actions Against Multiple Prime Contractors

In projects in which multiple prime contractors are used, a contractor who suffers economic damage because of the interference or delays caused by another prime contractor may have a cause of action in tort. The same principles applicable to whether an architect is liable apply in an action against another contractor who is in privity with the owner.

A state statute may enable one prime contractor to sue another prime contractor for the latter's failure to coordinate the work.[55]

In actions by a contractor against another prime contractor, the architect may serve as an important asset in the contractor's claim because of the architect's responsibility to determine claims between contractors.[56] An issue that may be raised is the finality that should be accorded the architect's decision. Typically, finality is limited to matters of artistic effect. The authority of the architect to decide disputes between contractors, even absent a contractual provision for finality, may be read by the court to give the architect's decision prima facie validity unless it is shown that the architect's decision was based on fraud or mistake.[57]

§ 17.16 Privity as Bar to Tort Action for Economic Loss

Although the privity wall may have fallen on one side of the fortress, it has not completely collapsed. Many jurisdictions still prevent tort actions for economic damages if no personal injury or property damage has been sustained. This is the economic loss rule. Some courts reason that if the contract defines the duties an architect owes the contractor, an action for negligence is still inappropriate because there was no common law duty to

---

[53] Northrup Contracting v. Village of Bergen, 139 Misc. 2d 435, 527 N.Y.S.2d 670 (Sup. Ct. 1986).

[54] See also Credit Alliance Corp. v. Anderson & Co., 65 N.Y.2d 536, 483 N.E.2d 110, 493 N.Y.S.2d 435 (1985).

[55] Bolton Corp. v. T.A. Loving Co., 380 S.E.2d 796 (N.C. Ct. App. 1989).

[56] Id.

[57] Id.

"protect the contractor from purely economic losses."[58] These jurisdictions also place greater emphasis on the function of tort law to protect against personal injury and property damage. If loss of an expected monetary gain is the only damage, the jurisdictions view tort principles as being inappropriate.

For example, when the general contractor suffered economic losses because of delays in the construction of post-tension bridges on the South Atlanta Freeway, the contractor sued the architect claiming that the loss was caused by the architect's slow approval of shop drawings. The general contractor sued in tort and also as a third-party beneficiary to the owner-engineer contract.

The engineering firm defended by arguing that a contractor could not sue in tort in the absence of privity and when the contractor only suffered monetary damages. The court agreed; the general contractor's allegations that the design professional failed to review shop drawings promptly or adequately fit within the general economic loss rule and thus were barred.[59] Other courts are similarly reluctant to extend the design professional's tort liability arising out of the owner-architect contract when the contractor has suffered only economic losses.[60]

Jurisdictions that apply the economic loss rule to prevent tort actions for economic loss may nevertheless recognize an exception when the economic loss to the contractor is caused by false information given by the architect. Allegations that the architect supplied deficient drawings that resulted in delays came within the false information exception to the economic loss rule.[61]

In jurisdictions that do not follow the economic loss rule, allegations that an architect was aware its drawings would be used by a structural steel subcontractor and that the architect intended the structural steel erector to rely on such drawings should be sufficient to establish a duty to the subcontractor on the part of the architect even in absence of privity. At first a court held that such allegations sufficiently alleged a duty to act reasonably.[62] Later, however, after a ruling by the Court of Appeals for the Second Circuit,[63] the lower court reversed its decision. In the Second Circuit case, a subcontractor alleged that a landscape architect had caused economic loss

---

[58] Blake Constr. Co. v. Alley, 353 S.E.2d 724 (Va. 1987).

[59] Malta Constr. v. Henningson, Durham & Richardson, 694 F. Supp. 902 (N.D. Ga. 1988).

[60] Floor Craft v. Parma Community Gen. Hosp., 54 Ohio St. 3d 1, 560 N.E.2d 206 (1990); Widett v. United States Fidelity & Guar. Co., 815 F.2d 885 (2d Cir. 1987).

[61] Malta Constr. v. Henningson, Durham & Richardson, 694 F. Supp. 902 (N.D. Ga. 1988).

[62] Morse/Diesel, Inc. v. Trinity Indus., Inc., 655 F. Supp. 346 (S.D.N.Y. 1987).

[63] Widett v. U.S. Fidelity & Guar. Co., 815 F.2d 885 (2d Cir. 1987).

to the subcontractor by negligently preparing site plans. The court found that the architect only had a duty under the architect-owner contract to make "casual inspections" of the subcontractor's work. The court said that a subcontractor could not maintain an action against an architect in the absence of privity or "extraordinary circumstances."[64] Thus, the court that had first allowed the negligence claims, reversed its decision and dismissed the actions.[65]

§ 17.17   Negligent Misrepresentation as Basis for Liability

States that still use the lack of privity as a defense may allow a claim for negligent misrepresentation, possibly serving as an additional basis of liability.[66] Therefore, as a separate cause of action, contractors may be able to state a claim for negligent misrepresentation. The elements of this cause of action are:

1. A duty of the defendant to act reasonably in communicating the information
2. Negligence in communicating information upon which others can be reasonably expected to rely
3. Reliance on such information by the affected party
4. Damage to the affected party as a result of such misrepresentation.[67]

§ 17.18   Intentional Interference with Contractual Relationships

To establish a cause of action against an architect for tortious interference with a contractual relationship most courts will require the contractor to present evidence to prove the following elements:

1. A valid contract between the contractor and a third party
2. The architect's knowledge of the established contractual relationship

---

[64] *Id.*

[65] Morse/Diesel, Inc. v. Trinity Indus., Inc., 664 F. Supp. 91 (S.D.N.Y. 1987), *rev'd on other grounds,* 859 F.2d 242 (2d Cir. 1988).

[66] Harbor Mechanical, Inc. v. Arizona Elec., 496 F. Supp. 681 (D. Ariz. 1980).

[67] Morse/Diesel, Inc. v. Trinity Indus., Inc., 655 F. Supp. 346 (S.D.N.Y. 1987); Donnelly Constr. Co. v. Oberg/Hunt/Gilleland, 139 Ariz. 184, 677 P.2d 1292 (1984).

3. The architect's intentional and unjustified inducement of the third party to breach or terminate the contractual relationship with the contractor

4. A finding that the third party breached or terminated the contractor's contract because of the architect's intentional and unjustified acts

5. The contractor's suffering of damages because of the breach or termination.[68]

Courts that apply the privity defense to defeat a contractor's tort claim for economic loss may be amenable to an action against the architect for intentional interference with the contract between the owner and contractor.[69]

In the tort of intentional interference with contractual relationships, the law seeks to protect economic interests. Consequently, the rationale used to insulate architects for the negligent performance of their contractual duties that causes economic damages to a contractor is distinguishable.[70]

Conditional Privilege Defense

Against the contractor's claim for intentional interference with a contractual relationship, architects may raise the defense of a conditional privilege. The architect will argue that the special relationship existing between the architect and the owner excuses interference. To establish such a conditional privilege, the architect must prove that the interference is to protect a conflicting interest "that is considered under the law to be of a value equal to or greater than the [contractor's] contractual rights."[71] Second, the architect's interference must be through legal means. Third, the architect's acts must not be unreasonable in the circumstance.[72]

In establishing the contractor's claim for intentional interference, the contractor, in addition to alleging the specific acts and damages also may have to allege that the architect's actions were not justified.[73]

One way to overcome an architect's conditional privilege to interfere in the contractor-owner contract is for the contractor to establish that the interference was undertaken with actual malice. An architect acts with actual malice when the architect's interference in the owner-contractor

---

[68] Certified Mechanical Contractors v. Wight & Co., 162 Ill. App. 3d. 391, 515 N.E.2d 1047 (1987).

[69] Santucci Constr. Co. v. Baxter & Woodman, Inc., 151 Ill. App. 3d. 547, 502 N.E.2d 1134 (1986), *cert. denied*, 511 N.E.2d 437 (Ill. 1987).

[70] *Id.*

[71] *Id.*

[72] *Id.*

[73] *Id.*

contract is with the specific desire and intention to annoy or injure the contractor. Thus, with the architect's specific desire to harm the contractor, the conditional privilege that may exist allowing the architect to protect the interest of the owner is eliminated. The courts and jury will find that the architect's actions were all taken beyond the orbit of the conditional privilege.[74]

Contractors who attempt to state a cause of action for intentional interference with a contract may have difficulty if they cannot also allege and establish a resulting breach. For example, in one case a contractor alleged that in the construction of an outpatient clinic, the architect and owner tortiously interfered with the contractual relationship the general contractor had with its subcontractors. Although the architect's and owner's actions allegedly included publication of false statements concerning cost increases, malicious reduction of amounts shown on payment requests, and meeting with the contractor's subcontractors to encourage them to stay with the project even though the general contractor would be replaced, the allegations were insufficient. The allegations amounted to hindrance perhaps, an adverse impact on the contract, but the contractor did not allege that the architect induced the subcontractors to breach their contracts with the general contractor. Because of this omission, the complaint failed to state a cause of action and was dismissed.[75]

On the other hand, not all tortious interference cases require the contractor to show that a contract has been terminated or that a party has been induced to breach its contract with the general contractor. It is sufficient if the other party to the contractor's contract was wrongfully induced to make performance impossible.[76]

For instance the project engineer for the construction of two wastewater treatment facilities could be liable for tortiously interfering with the contractor-owner contract if the project engineer maliciously enforced literal compliance with contract specifications when such enforcement was not justified to protect the owner's interest. Rather the action was taken with the intent "to further his personal goals or to injure the [contractor] which is thereby forced to breach its contract with the [owner]." During the construction of the wastewater treatment facilities, the project engineer allegedly specified sledge dewatering equipment specifications that could be met by only one manufacturer. According to the contractor, project engineer intended to use the specific equipment "to the exclusion of other

---

[74] Certified Mechanical Contractors v. Wight & Co., 162 Ill. App. 3d. 391, 515 N.E.2d 1047 (1987).

[75] George A. Fuller Co. v. Chicago College of Osteopathic Medicine, 719 F.2d 1326 (7th Cir. 1983).

[76] Certified Mechanical Contractors v. Wight & Co., 162 Ill. App. 3d. 391, 515 N.E.2d 1047 (1987).

manufacturers" and the engineer's decision was a "conscious" and "deliberate disregard for environmental protection agency regulations requiring fair competition." Further, the contractor claimed the project engineer had no reasonable basis for requiring the unique equipment. Although acknowledging the conditional privilege, the court did not allow the conditional privilege in the situation in which the architect's interference was not necessary to "protect the Sanitary District's best interest."[77]

A contractor who has properly pleaded a claim for tortious interference by an architect may still be unable to prove the allegations. If the evidence of tortious interference is inadequate and does not overcome the claims of conditional privileges, the case will be subject to a directed verdict by the judge.[78]

§ 17.19 Architect's Standard of Care to Contractors

As a professional, an architect must abide by the following standard of care: "[a]n architect must exercise his judgment, skill and ability reasonably and without neglect."[79] The architect, however, is not a guarantor of a perfect project or even a project that meets the owner's needs unless the architect has undertaken such responsibility as an additional obligation. Consequently, if the architect exercises reasonable judgment and in a manner consistent with the practice of other architects, the architect will have met the standard of care. This standard of care may be contrasted with the contractor's duty that, in most instances, is to build the project in accordance with the plans and specifications.

The following is an illustration of the effect an architect's duty of care may have on a contractor. In a levee failure case,[80] the architect's duty arose out of the owner-architect contract. Even though the contractor did not have a contract with the architect, it was reasonably foreseeable that failure of the architect to exercise reasonable care in the design of the method by which the collars were placed on the pipes and by which the pipes were installed into the levee would cause economic loss to the contractor.[81]

Construction managers owe the same types of duties to contractors when the construction managers are directly involved in overseeing the site work.[82]

---

[77] Waldinger Corp. v. CRS Group Eng'rs, Inc., 775 F.2d 781 (7th Cir. 1985).

[78] V.M. Solis Underground Util. v. Laredo, 751 S.W.2d 532 (Tex. Ct. App. 1988).

[79] Bayshore Dev. Co. v. Bonfoey, 75 Fla. 455, 78 So. 507 (1918); Coombs v. Beede, 36 A. 104 (Me. 1896).

[80] Mayor & City Council v. Clark-Dietz, 550 F. Supp. 610 (N.D. Miss. 1982), *leave to appeal denied,* 702 F.2d 67 (5th Cir. 1983).

[81] *Id.*

[82] R.S. Noonan, Inc. v. Morrison, Knudsen Co., 522 F. Supp. 1186 (E.D. La. 1981).

§ 17.20   —Architect's Design Responsibility

The contractor's obligation to build in accordance with the drawings and specifications prepared by the architect can be the source of damage when those drawings and specifications are inadequate for the work and cause delays and disruptions to the contractor.[83]

Courts that allow negligence actions against an architect recognize the architect's duty to provide adequate drawings and specifications and to oversee the project without neglect.[84] In those states that recognize such actions, the architect should reasonably foresee that a contractor will suffer added costs if there are errors in the drawings and specifications.[85]

One case has illustrated that, in pursuing an architect for faulty drawings, the contractor may avoid the defense that the architect is a third-party beneficiary of exculpatory clauses in the owner-contractor contract if the contractor can show the errors occurred in an architect's work prepared prior to the signing of the owner-contractor contract.[86] The case held that an exculpatory clause in the contract did not cover acts prior to the owner-contractor contract.

Language in the owner-contractor contract that insulates the architect from liability for inaccurate plans and specifications prepared for the work may not protect the architect's subconsultant who prepares soil reports that are not part of the contract documents and that are documents upon which the contractor reasonably relies.[87]

§ 17.21   —Architect's On-Site
Responsibility to Contractor

The on-site relationship of the architect with the contractor should be distinguished from other relationships in which one party to the construction process claims economic damage by the failure of the other party to carry out a contractual duty but there is lack of oversight exercised by architects.

The supervision of actual construction is an important element in the finding by most courts that an architect may be liable in tort for the

---

[83] Farrell Constr. Co. v. Jefferson Parish, 693 F. Supp. 490 (E.D. La. 1988).

[84] Donnelly Constr. Co. v. Oberg/Hunt/Gilleland, 139 Ariz. 184, 677 P.2d 1292 (1984); Prichard Bros. v. Grady Co., 407 N.W.2d 423 (Minn. Ct. App. 1987), *rev'd,* 428 N.W.2d 391 (Minn. 1988).

[85] Donnelly Constr. Co. v. Oberg/Hunt/Gilleland, 139 Ariz. 184, 677 P.2d 1292 (1984); Davidson & Jones v. County of New Hanover, 41 N.C. App. 661, 255 S.E.2d 580, *petition for discretionary review denied,* 259 S.E.2d 911 (N.C. 1979).

[86] Farrell Constr. Co. v. Jefferson Parish, 693 F. Supp. 490 (E.D. La. 1988).

[87] M. Miller Co. v. Central Contra Costa Sanitary Dist., 199 Cal. App. 2d, 18 Cal. Rptr. 13 (1962).

economic losses of the contractor.[88] A court stated "a supervising engineer must be held to know that a general contractor will be involved in a project and will be directly affected by the conduct of the engineer."[89]

The distinction between design professionals who consult with the owner and those who supervise construction is important. Courts are much more likely to find potential liability for design professionals when there are supervisory powers than when a professional's responsibilities are more limited.[90] A contractor on a Commonwealth Edison facility entered into a contract with the manufacturer of precipitator units that were to be installed at the facility. The manufacturer "provided plans and specifications for the electrical work on the precipitator."[91] The contract also incorporated a manual prepared by the manufacturer. The manufacturer, pursuant to the incorporated manual, was obligated to inspect the work and to notify the contractor of any deviations. The manufacturer allegedly required the subcontractor's work to be redone even though it was performed properly. The manufacturer in some respects occupied the same position to the subcontractor as an architect occupies in a typical construction project. The court held that the subcontractor could not recover economic losses in tort. The court distinguished cases in which economic losses are recoverable in tort when "'one who is in the business of supplying information for the guidance of others in their business transactions makes negligent representations;'"[92] in such cases, the suppliers of information may be liable if representations are negligently made to the economic loss of another.

The economic loss rule does not prevent recovery of economic losses when there is property damage.[93] When a contractor alleged that an engineer failed to properly inspect roof trusses that collapsed after they were installed, the contractor properly stated a cause of action, the supervising architect's alleged negligence caused defective trusses to be installed. The day after the roof trusses were installed, the roof structure collapsed.[94]

When a levee that was intended to protect the Columbus Wastewater Treatment Plant broke, flooding the nearly complete treatment plant site, the City of Columbus, Mississippi, sued the architect/engineer and the contractor for the damage. The general contractor cross-claimed against the architect/engineer, alleging that the city's loss was caused by negligent design and negligent supervision of the project. The architect/engineer's

---

[88] Normoyle-Berg & Assoc. v. Village of Deer Creek, 39 Ill. App. 3d 744, 350 N.E.2d 559 (1976).

[89] Id.

[90] Shoffner Indus. v. W.B. Lloyd Constr. Co., 42 N.C. App. 259, 257 S.E.2d 50 (1979).

[91] Anderson Elec., Inc. v. Ledbetter Erection Corp., 503 N.E.2d 246 (Ill. 1986).

[92] Id.

[93] Shoffner Indus. v. W.B. Lloyd Constr. Co., 42 N.C. App. 259, 257 S.E.2d 50 (1979).

[94] Id.

design of the levee specified pipes to pass through the levee. Collars around the pipes were to act as seepage collars. The exact placement of the seepage collars and the interface of the collar with a slurry wall that was to be poured around them was at the center of the controversy. The architect/ engineer possessed a graph from which the architect/engineer could have computed the slurry's unconfined compressive strength, but the architect/ engineer failed to do the computation. Based on expert testimony, the court found that a prudent architect/engineer would have checked the interface of the slurry wall and collars as part of proper design. The architect/engineer's failure to "properly evaluate characteristics of the cement-bentonite slurry was" negligence.[95]

In the case, during the installation of the pipes through the levee and the necessary backfill, the architect/engineer's on-site inspector supervised the contractor's work. The architect/engineer's on-site inspector approved the use of pneumatic hand tamps, required work to be removed and re- placed, visually inspected all backfilling of which the inspector was aware, and approved the contractor's work as it progressed. In restoring the cuts in the levee, in installing the pipes, and in backfilling, the contractor fol- lowed the "explicit instructions of the architect/engineer's inspector." As such, the general contractor was not responsible for the breaks in the levee but, instead, the architect/engineer's defective design was the sole proxi- mate cause.[96]

§ 17.22   —Architect's Responsibility for Delay, Disruption, and Interference

An architect was liable for delay that cost the contractor a $100,000 early completion bonus. The House of Representatives of the State of Louisiana contracted for the construction of a large committee room as part of reno- vations to the state capitol.[97] The architect's drawings for the project did not show a metal X-brace within an interior wall. The X-brace was part of the capitol's wind-bracing system and was shown on the original drawings maintained in the state archives. The architect had discovered a similar X-brace in the basement of the Senate during work on that side of the capitol but apparently missed locating the wind-bracing drawings for the House. When the contractor began to remove the interior walls, he

---

[95] Mayor & City Council v. Clark-Dietz, 550 F. Supp. 610, 616 (N.D. Miss. 1982), *leave to appeal denied,* 702 F.2d 67 (5th Cir. 1983).

[96] *Id.*

[97] M.J. Womack, Inc. v. State House of Representatives, 509 So. 2d 62 (La. Ct. App. 1987).

discovered the X-brace that would have interfered with a spectator's view of the committee proceedings. The obstruction necessitated a redesign and caused a 66-day delay. In exercising the duty to use reasonable skill and care, the architect was required to reasonably investigate the original plans to discover potential conflicts with the renovations. The court charged the $100,000 bonus to the architect who caused the delay.

An architect who negligently interpreted specifications and responded to the contractor's shop drawing submittals was liable to the general contractor for delay damages in accordance with the total cost method. This measure of damage is based upon the "'reasonable value of the work done including actual costs, overhead and profits.'"[98]

§ 17.23   —Architect's Responsibility for Measuring Quantities and Approving Pay Requests

In the typical construction triangle, there is no contractual relationship between the contractor and the architect. Moreover, the contractual relationships by the contractor and the architect with the owner may be viewed as complementary functions.[99] But when the supervising architect negligently fails to determine quantities, due in a pay request, a contractor may have a cause of action for negligence. For example, the contractor had a cause of action against the architect when a contractor was required to remove rock and boulders from the project site and the architect's alleged failure to measure the quantities and to reflect them in its pay request resulted in the owner denying the pay request.[100]

§ 17.24   —Architect's Implied Warranty of Accuracy of Work

Architects do not warrant the accuracy of their work. Architects, being professionals, are held to the requirement of exercising their skill and ability reasonably and without neglect.[101] An express guarantee, however, by the architect regarding the accuracy of the drawings and specifications may create a cause of action for breach of implied warranty.[102]

---

[98] Prichard Bros. v. Grady Co., 436 N.W.2d 460 (Minn. Ct. App. 1989).

[99] Forte Bros. v. National Amusements, Inc., 525 A.2d 1301 (R.I. 1987).

[100] *Id.*

[101] Donnelly Constr. Co. v. Oberg/Hunt/Gilleland, 139 Ariz. 184, 677 P.2d 1292 (1984).

[102] *Id.*

§ 17.25 —Architect's Quasi-Judicial Immunity

An architect who is charged with the responsibility of resolving disputes between the owner and the contractor and who acts in such a quasi-judicial capacity doing so is immune from liability as to its decisions concerning the disputes. Significantly, it is only the acts in the quasi-judicial capacity that are cloaked with immunity. There is no quasi-judicial immunity for the architect's performance as an architect.[103]

§ 17.26 Existence of Requirement for Expert Testimony

Expert testimony may or may not be required to establish an architect's negligence in the breach of the architect's standard of care. In those jurisdictions that do not strictly require the use of expert testimony, the jurisdictions will, nevertheless, usually apply the following guidelines:

1. Is the question one that can be understood by a layperson?
2. Can the jury apply its common sense to the facts to determine whether an architect has used reasonable skill?
3. Is the subject of the alleged negligence and the architect's failure capable of being understood by the jury without expert testimony?[104]

In one case, expert testimony was not required when the negligence alleged involved activities in supervision rather than in preparing drawings.[105] Similarly, it was not error for the trial court to allow a professional estimator and certified engineering technician to testify regarding the architect's failure to properly interpret specifications and review shop drawings.[106]

§ 17.27 Documentation, Proof, and Recovery of Damages

In a tort action, the contractor is entitled to be restored to its prior position. The knowledge of the contractor's position is not significant. The negligent architect is liable for the damages that follow as a direct or proximate result

---

[103] *Id.*

[104] M.J. Womack, Inc. v. State House of Representatives, 509 So. 2d 62 (La. Ct. App. 1987).

[105] Bartak v. Bell-Galyardt & Wells, Inc., 629 F.2d 523 (8th Cir. 1980); Jaeger v. Henningson, Durham & Richardson, Inc., 714 F.2d 773 (8th Cir. 1983); Nelson v. Commonwealth, 368 S.E.2d 239 (Va. 1988).

[106] Prichard Bros. v. Grady Co., 436 N.W.2d 460 (Minn. Ct. App. 1989).

of the wrongful conduct so the contractor will be placed in the same position occupied before the tort.

An intended or third-party beneficiary of a contract can recover damages that flow as a result of the breach of contract intended for benefit of the beneficiary. The damages that can be recovered usually are those that are "normal and foreseeable."[107] Third-party beneficiary damages may include, but are not limited to, the following damages:

1. Employee costs
2. Material costs
3. Costs from the inefficient use of equipment
4. Bonding and insurance costs
5. Overhead reasonably related to the work that was affected by the breach.

In all actions, the contractor must establish the amount of damages incurred as a result of the wrongful acts. Damages will not be awarded if based on speculation or mere estimates. On the other hand, if the contractor has established that damages have in fact been suffered, courts consistently hold that damages need not be proved with mathematical exactness.

An architect who negligently responds to shop drawing submittals may face the total cost method of damages that are based upon the "'reasonable value of the work done including actual costs, overhead and profits.'"[108] The AIA standard documents discussed previously attempt to restrict the architect's liability for interpretation of specifications and shop drawing review. When such oversight is undertaken negligently in such a way as to cause damage to the contractor, the architect will be liable to the contractor.[109] In one case, a school district had contracted with the architect using the AIA standard documents. The owner subsequently entered into a contract with a general contractor also using the AIA standard general conditions. After a trial the architect was found to be negligent in the "interpretation of specifications and response to shop drawings."[110]

A contractor might be obligated to the owner for damages but be entitled to recover from the architect. In one case, a contractor's cross-claim against the architect for indemnification and contribution arising out of defects in the exterior masonry of a school building yielded a partial victory for both the architect and the contractor. The court held that as a matter of law, the

---

[107] Moore Constr. v. Clarksville Dep't of Elec., 707 S.W.2d 1 (Tenn. Ct. App. 1985).

[108] Prichard Bros. v. Grady Co., 436 N.W.2d 460 (Minn. Ct. App. 1989).

[109] *Id.*

[110] *Id.*

contractor's indemnification claim could not stand, but that the contractor could seek recovery by way of contribution.[111]

§ 17.28   Doctrine of Mitigation of Damages

Defendants who face the prospect of defending damage claims will seek to avoid some or all of the damages by invoking the doctrine of *mitigation of damages*. Under this requirement, every person who has suffered damage is required to take reasonable steps to mitigate or avoid the harm caused by the wrongful act of another. Thus, a contractor may not allow damages to accumulate when the contractor can avoid the damages by taking reasonable mitigating steps. When Shea claimed that another contractor on-site, MKE, was causing flooding, MKE defended on the ground that Shea could have done the simple act of building a dike at the point where the flood waters entered the Shea site. MKE argued that if Shea could have avoided the flooding by the relatively inexpensive method of constructing a dike, Shea's inaction amounted to failure to mitigate.[112] The court disagreed, holding that the doctrine of mitigation of damages does not apply when both the plaintiff and the defendant have the equal opportunity to avoid the harm.[113] Thus, when there is equal opportunity to prevent the harm, the mitigation doctrine will not shift the burden from the wrongdoer to the innocent party.[114]

---

[111] Board of Educ. v. Mars Assocs., 133 A.D.2d 800, 520 N.Y.S.2d 181 (1987). *See also* Chicago College of Osteopathic Medicine v. George A. Fuller Co., 719 F.2d 1335 (7th Cir. 1984) (holding that the contractor failed to state a cause of action against the architect for indemnification).

[112] Shea—S&M Ball v. Massman-Kiewit-Early, 606 F.2d 1245 (D.C. Cir. 1979).

[113] *Id.*

[114] *Id.*

CHAPTER 18

RIGHTS AND REMEDIES OF THE CONSTRUCTION MATERIAL SUPPLIER

Brian C. Carter
Patrick L. Rendon

Brian C. Carter is a litigation associate with Jones, Day, Reavis & Pogue, in its Irvine, California office. He received a B.A. degree in economics from the University of California at Berkeley in 1982 and his J.D. degree from King Hall School of Law, University of California at Davis, in 1988. He clerked in Anchorage for the Alaska Supreme Court during the 1988 term, and joined Jones, Day in 1989. Mr. Carter has litigated numerous lawsuits involving mechanics' lien, stop notice, and contract claims against lenders and owners of construction projects. He is a member of the California and Orange County Bar Associations.

Patrick L. Rendon practices in the areas of construction and environmental law within the Los Angeles office of Jaffe, Trutanich, Scatena & Blum. He has experience in drafting and negotiating contracts for the performance of environmental services and advising clients on environmental issues associated with remedial actions, real estate, and corporate transactions. He also has considerable experience in drafting and negotiating domestic and international contracts, including joint venture and project finance documentation, related to the construction of substantial industrial facilities for companies, infrastructure projects for government entities, and alternative energy facilities for developers. He is a member of the bars of California, Colorado, and the District of Columbia.

§ 18.1 Introduction

This chapter addresses both the effect of the Uniform Commercial Code (UCC) on transactions involving construction materials and the supplier's rights under the UCC to prescribe in the contract the rights and remedies that are available to a buyer. The first part of the chapter briefly discusses the affirmative, proactive role that a supplier should take in order to attempt to control the risks that it assumes under a particular purchase order.

The second part addresses certain statutory remedies, both under and outside the UCC, that a supplier may rely on in the event a contractor or subcontractor is unable or unwilling to pay for the materials it receives. The discussion includes a brief explanation of the certain remedies available under the UCC and the procedures available outside the UCC to perfect rights accruing to a supplier that attains the status of a materialman on a construction project.

The discussion is not intended to be an exhaustive discussion of the supplier's and materialman's remedies, but rather is designed to familiarize both suppliers and materialmen with the basic concepts and procedural steps upon which ultimate recovery may depend. With these concepts and procedures in mind, the supplier should be able to draft a contract and perform under it with appropriate attention to those matters that may prove critical to the ultimate enforcement of its rights. The careful supplier, by fulfilling all of the prerequisites to the perfection of the statutory rights, and by aggressively and creatively prosecuting the common law claims, will be well-armed in the courtroom against all contingencies.

NEGOTIATING RIGHTS UNDER THE PURCHASE ORDER

§ 18.2 Uniform Commercial Code

Article 2 of the UCC establishes a uniform law for transactions involving goods, and the article has been enacted, with some variations, in 49 of the 50 states.[1] The UCC defines *goods* as "all things . . . which are moveable

---

[1] Unless indicated otherwise all references to the UCC in this chapter are to the 1978 official text of the Uniform Commercial Code.

at the time of identification to the contract for sale."[2] Construction materials generally fall within this category.[3] Therefore, a supplier should be familiar with how the UCC affects transactions involving such materials.

§ 18.3   Freedom to Contract

Under the UCC, the parties to a transaction are free to agree on the rights and remedies available to the nonbreaching party. These rights and remedies will govern the relationship between the parties.[4] Although a supplier should address many issues in a contract, one of the more important issues involves the liability that a supplier may face in performing its obligations under a purchase order. **Sections 18.4** through **18.9** address the right a supplier has under the UCC to limit its liability in two important areas: (1) limiting or excluding consequential damages and (2) disclaiming warranties and establishing the remedies that are available to a buyer for defective materials.

§ 18.4   —Limiting Consequential Damages

A supplier who repudiates or otherwise fails to perform its obligations may be subject to a buyer's action for consequential damages.[5] Consequential damages include such damages as lost profits, loss of production, or business interruption.[6] Because these damages may be substantial, prudence dictates that a supplier routinely request and successfully negotiate contractual language that limits, if not excludes, the supplier's liability for consequential damages.

---

[2] U.C.C. § 2-105(1).

[3] *See, e.g.,* Huff v. Hobgood, 549 So. 2d 951, 10 U.C.C. Rep. Serv. 2d (Callaghan) 856 (Miss. 1989); Wehr Constructors, Inc. v. Steel Fabricators, Inc., 769 S.W.2d 51, 9 U.C.C. Rep. Serv. 2d (Callaghan) 488 (Ky. Ct. App. 1988).

[4] U.C.C. § 1-102(3) specifically states as follows:

The effect of provisions of [the UCC] may be varied by agreement, except as otherwise provided [by the UCC] and except that the obligations of good faith, diligence, reasonableness and care prescribed by [the UCC] may not be disclaimed by agreement but the parties may by agreement determine the standards by which the performance of such obligations is to be measured if such standards are not manifestly unreasonable.

[5] For a discussion on consequential damages, *see* 1 J.J. White & R.S. Summers, Uniform Commercial Code 307–311 (3d ed. 1988).

[6] *Id.* at 309.

The right to contractually settle on language that limits or excludes damages is provided for by the UCC, which states in part that the parties to an agreement "may limit or alter the measure of damages recoverable"[7] and "[c]onsequential damages may be limited or excluded unless the limitation or exclusion is unconscionable."[8] Nevertheless, a supplier should note that any language of limitation included in the contract will be construed strictly by the courts and the "failure to state an attempted exculpation . . . in plain, unambiguous and clear terminology will result in an interpretation that the clause was not intended to exempt the actor from liability."[9]

The following limitation of liability clause is an example that contains plain language:

a. The total cumulative liability of the Supplier with respect to the services, equipment and material furnished under this purchase order, arising from or in any way connected with the performance or breach of this purchase order, whether in contract, in tort (including negligence and strict liability) or otherwise shall in no event exceed $_____.

b. Neither party shall be liable to the other in contract, in tort (including negligence and strict liability) or otherwise for any special, indirect, punitive, incidental or consequential loss or damage whatsoever, including, without limitation, claims based on loss of use, lost profits or revenue, interest, work stoppage or other loss based on shut-down or non-operation, or lost goodwill.

§ 18.5   —Warranties Associated with Materials

Another area in which a supplier can attempt to control the risk it assumes under a contract is in the area of warranties. As discussed in **Chapter 7**, under the UCC, there are three warranties of quality associated with goods such as construction materials: (1) the express warranty; (2) the implied warranty of merchantability; and (3) the implied warranty of fitness for a particular purpose.[10] A supplier may limit or exclude these warranties from a transaction, and a supplier also may specify the particular remedies that will be available to a buyer in the event that the materials provided prove to be defective.

---

[7] U.C.C. § 2-719(1)(a).

[8] U.C.C. § 2-719(3).

[9] Delta Airlines v. Douglas Aircraft Co., 238 Cal. App. 2d 95, 100, 47 Cal. Rptr. 518, 521 (1965).

[10] U.C.C. §§ 2-313, 2-314, 2-315.

§ 18.6 —Limiting Express Warranties

The only warranties that a supplier should provide are those that are expressly agreed to by contract. Because express warranties may be created by a supplier's statements or affirmations of facts or through a supplier's use of samples or models of the goods that are to be delivered under a purchase order, a supplier should enact policies or guidelines that limit or avoid altogether statements, promises, or descriptions, or the use of products or samples, that are inconsistent with the warranties set forth in a purchase order or with the products that are to be delivered under a purchase order. For example, a supplier should ensure that sales brochures and promotional materials contain statements that are consistent with the express warranties found in the purchase order.

An aggrieved buyer is likely to introduce evidence of additional warranties, including any documents, notes, and statements, that were made or provided by a supplier. Thus, a supplier may want to ensure that the final, negotiated contract contains a merger clause that may bar admission of such evidence.[11] The following is an example:

COMPLETE AGREEMENT: This purchase order constitutes the entire agreement between the parties. Any and all prior negotiations, proposals, writings and representations relating to this purchase order or the subject matter thereof, including any statements or representations which may have been made and which are not a part of this purchase order, are superseded by the terms contained herein, and have not been relied upon by the Buyer. The terms of this purchase order shall only be amended by a writing executed by both parties.

§ 18.7 —Disclaimer of Other Warranties

The purchase order also should contain a statement that clearly disclaims the warranties of merchantability and of fitness for a particular purpose that may apply to materials.

The warranty of merchantability is created in every sale of goods that involves suppliers who are considered merchants under the UCC—that is, they deal in the types of goods involved in the transaction or they hold themselves out as having knowledge as to such goods—and provides that the goods are fit for the ordinary purposes for which they are produced.[12]

---

[11] *See, e.g.,* Session v. Chartrand Equip. Co., 133 Ill. App. 3d 719, 479 N.E.2d 376 (1985); Agristor Leasing v. Meuli, 634 F. Supp. 1208 (D. Kan. 1986).

[12] There are six nonexclusive definitions for the warranty of merchantability. *See, e.g.,* U.C.C. § 2-314(2). *See, e.g.,* DeKalb Agresearch, Inc. v. Abbott, 391 F. Supp. 152 (N.D. Ala. 1974), *aff'd,* 511 F.2d 1162 (5th Cir. 1975); Barr v. S-2 Yachts, Inc., 7 U.C.C. Rep. Serv. 2d (Callaghan) 1431 (E.D. Va. 1988).

The warranty of fitness for a particular purpose provides that the materials are fit for the specific use that a buyer intends for such materials; however, the warranty of fitness for a particular purpose arises only if, at the time of contracting, the supplier has reason to know of the purpose for which the materials are to be used and also has reason to know that the buyer is relying on the supplier's experience in selecting the materials.[13] Although there is no particular form for disclaiming such warranties, language that is intended to exclude or modify the implied warranty of fitness for a particular purpose must be in writing.[14] The implied warranty of merchantability can be excluded in writing or orally; however, either form of disclaimer must use the word "merchantability."[15]

All disclaimers also must be conspicuous. A provision is conspicuous if it is written in such a manner "that a reasonable person against whom it is to operate ought to have noticed it. . . . Language in the body of a form is 'conspicuous' if it is in larger or other contrasting type or color."[16] Accordingly, suppliers should place any disclaimer or general limitation in large type to avoid having it disregarded by a court. The language may be enforceable in certain cases even if it is not in large type, such as when both parties are sophisticated businesspersons, as opposed to consumers, who are represented by attorneys.[17]

§ 18.8   —Remedies Available for Nonconformance

Another practice that a supplier should follow in order to quantify the risk it is assuming under a contract, and in the process perhaps decrease the likelihood of a dispute, is to set forth in the purchase order the particular remedy available to a buyer in the event the materials do not conform to the standard agreed to in the purchase order. For example, a purchase order may limit a buyer's remedy to requiring a supplier to repair or replace defective materials for a limited time period only. The purchase order may further provide that following the expiration of such time period, the supplier would have no further obligations to incur any liability on account of nonconforming materials.

In drafting the remedy provisions to a purchase order a supplier should bear in mind that the UCC creates "a presumption that clauses prescribing

---

[13] U.C.C. § 2-315; *see, e.g.,* Barrington Corp. v. Patrick Lumber Co., 447 So. 2d 785, 38 U.C.C. Rep. 744 (Ala. Civ. App. 1984); DeLamar Motor Co. v. White, 249 Ark. 708, 460 S.W.2d 802 (1970).

[14] U.C.C. §§ 2-316(2), 2-316 cmt. 4.

[15] *Id.* § 2-316(2).

[16] *Id.* § 1-201(10).

[17] *See, e.g.,* American Elec. Power Co. v. Westinghouse Elec. Corp., 418 F. Supp. 435 (S.D.N.Y. 1976).

remedies are cumulative rather than exclusive."[18] Therefore, the remedy provision should clearly state that it sets forth the exclusive remedy available if the materials fail to meet the agreed upon warranty standard. For example, the remedy provision could provide:

> The Supplier's sole obligation, and Buyer's sole and exclusive remedy, in the event the material fails to conform to the standard of performance set forth in this section shall be limited to the repair or replacement, in the sole discretion of and at the sole cost of Seller, of the material. The Supplier's obligation under this section shall continue for a period of one (1) year from the date of Buyer's receipt of the material after which time the Supplier shall have no further obligation to repair or replace such non-conforming material.

If a supplier is acting in the capacity of a distributor of materials, it may add language that states:

> With respect to equipment, parts and work not manufactured or performed by Supplier, Supplier's sole and exclusive obligation to Buyer under this purchase order shall be to assign to Buyer whatever warranty Supplier receives from the manufacturer.

The supplier who acts as a distributor may negotiate the inclusion of such language on grounds that the supplier is in no better position than the buyer to ensure that the materials it supplies conform with the warranty standard.

§ 18.9   —Consolidating Warranties

To avoid having provisions in other parts of the purchase order or statements contained in other documents construed to be additional warranties, a supplier also may wish to consolidate into one section all provisions relating to the warranties, disclaimers, and remedies that have been agreed to. The supplier also should add to the end of such section a clause similar to the following:

> SOLE WARRANTIES. THE WARRANTIES AND REMEDIES SET FORTH IN THIS SECTION ARE IN LIEU OF ALL OTHER WARRANTIES AND REMEDIES, WHETHER STATUTORY, EXPRESS OR IMPLIED, AND ANY OTHER WARRANTIES, INCLUDING, BUT NOT LIMITED TO, ANY IMPLIED WARRANTIES OF MERCHANTABILITY OR FITNESS FOR A PARTICULAR PURPOSE AND ALL WARRANTIES ARISING FROM COURSE OF DEALING OR USAGE OF TRADE ARE HEREBY EXPRESSLY EXCLUDED AND WAIVED.

---

[18] *See* U.C.C. § 2-719 cmt. 2.

STATUTORY REMEDIES OF THE SUPPLIER

§ 18.10   Remedies of Supplier under the UCC

The discussion in §§ **18.4** through **18.9** focuses on the supplier's ability to limit its liability by contract. **Sections 18.10** through **18.16** address certain statutory remedies that are available under the UCC to a supplier that is confronted with a breaching buyer. As with the liability provisions, a supplier may modify these rights by the terms of a contract.[19]

During the course of performance of a purchase order, a supplier may find that a buyer has wrongfully rejected or revoked acceptance of materials that have been tendered, has repudiated all or part of the purchase order, or has failed to make a payment that is due on or before delivery of the goods. In these cases, U.C.C. § 2-703 lists the remedies that are available to a supplier as follows:

(a) withhold delivery of such goods;

(b) stop delivery by any bailee as hereafter provided (Section 2-705);

(c) proceed under the next section respecting goods still unidentified to the contract;

(d) resell and recover damages as hereafter provided (Section 2-706);

(e) recover damages for non-acceptance (Section 2-708) or in a proper case the price (Section 2-709);

(f) cancel.[20]

These remedies are "cumulative in nature"[21] and, therefore, an aggrieved supplier may, for example, elect to cancel a purchase order and then proceed to recover damages it incurs from a buyer's breach.

The following discussion is divided into two parts: (1) §§ **18.11** through **18.15** address those provisions in U.C.C. § 2-703 that enable a supplier to retain control over its materials; and (2) § **18.16** addresses those provisions that determine the amounts to which a supplier is entitled to recover from a buyer who has breached. The first part also includes a discussion of U.C.C. §§ 2-702 and 2-507, which address a supplier's right to reclaim materials in credit sales and cash sales, respectively.

---

[19] U.C.C. § 1-102(3).

[20] U.C.C. § 2-703.

[21] *Id.* § 2-703 cmt. 1.

§ 18.11   —Withholding Delivery of Materials

A supplier who has possession of materials has the right to withhold delivery of the materials when a buyer fails to make payments that are due on or before the date of delivery of the materials.[22] Accordingly, when feasible, it would be prudent for a supplier to require by the terms of a purchase order that payments for particular materials be made on or before the time such materials are delivered. For example, one court held that a general contractor who had not been paid by an owner for prefabricated metal buildings that remained in the possession of the general contractor was entitled to retain possession of such buildings until it received payment from the buyer, when the buyer had not made payments that were due on or before the delivery of such buildings.[23]

In exercising the right to withhold delivery, a supplier must proceed in good faith. This obligation may require a supplier who is exercising its right to withhold delivery to provide a buyer with notice of such action.[24] In addition, it would be prudent to provide such notice in writing and to specify in such notice the steps that are requested of a buyer in order for the buyer to receive the materials.

§ 18.12   —Stopping Delivery of Materials

A supplier also may stop the delivery of materials that are in the possession of a bailee such as a carrier or a warehouseman. This right is triggered in any of the following circumstances:

1. When the supplier learns that a buyer is insolvent and the materials are in the possession of a carrier or bailee
2. When the supplier has learned that the buyer has either repudiated the contract or failed to make payments that were due prior to the time of delivery of materials and delivery is by "carload, truckload, planeload or larger shipments of express or freight"
3. When the supplier is entitled to withhold or reclaim materials under the UCC.[25]

---

[22] *Id.* § 2-703(a).

[23] Skinny's Inc. v. Hicks Bros. Constr. Co., 602 S.W.2d 85 (Tex. Ct. App. 1980).

[24] Indussa Corp. v. Reliable Stainless Steel Supply Co., 369 F. Supp. 976 (E.D. Pa. 1974) (court found that reasonable commercial standards of fair dealing required seller to notify buyer of seller's decision to stop delivery of aluminum on account of buyer's insolvency).

[25] U.C.C. § 2-705(1).

However, a supplier's right to stop the delivery of materials in such cases ceases after any of the following events occur:

(a) receipt of the goods by the buyer; or

(b) acknowledgment to the buyer by any bailee of the goods except a carrier that the bailee holds the goods for the buyer; or

(c) such acknowledgment to the buyer by a carrier by reshipment or as warehouseman; or

(d) negotiation to the buyer of any negotiable document of title covering the goods.[26]

In other words, a supplier's right to stop delivery of goods continues until circumstances indicate that either the materials have been received by a buyer or a buyer has taken constructive possession of the materials, or circumstances are such that a carrier or other bailee is no longer in a position in which it can effectively stop a delivery of materials.[27] For example, one court has held that a supplier's right to stop delivery of goods ceased when a buyer resold goods that were in the possession of a carrier and the buyer then proceeded to instruct the carrier to ship the goods to the new buyer and the carrier acknowledged to the original buyer that the goods would be reshipped to the new buyer.[28]

§ 18.13   —Reclaiming Materials

Another remedy that is available to a supplier is the right to reclaim materials that are delivered on credit or in cash sale transactions. In cases in which a supplier extends credit to a buyer, as, for example, when a buyer agrees to pay for materials it receives within a given period of time after delivery, a supplier's right to reclaim the delivered materials is addressed in U.C.C. § 2-702. In a cash sale transaction, when payment for materials is due and demanded upon the delivery of materials, a supplier's right to reclaim the delivered materials is addressed in U.C.C. § 2-507. Typically, this UCC section is resorted to when a supplier delivers materials and is paid with a check that is later dishonored. As discussed below, both of these UCC sections are subject to the reclamation provision of the Bankruptcy Code if the buyer files bankruptcy. In addition, a supplier's right to reclaim materials may be affected by a third party who purchases the materials from the buyer without having knowledge of the supplier's claim or from a

---

[26] *Id.* § 2-705(2); *see, e.g.,* Ceres Inc. v. Acli Metal & Ore Co., 451 F. Supp. 921 (N.D. Ill. 1978).

[27] *In re* Brio Petroleum, Inc., 800 F.2d 469 (5th Cir. 1986).

[28] Butts v. Glendale Plywood Co., 710 F.2d 504 (9th Cir. 1983).

creditor who has a security interest in the materials.[29] Although a discussion of such third-party rights is beyond the scope of this chapter, it would be prudent for a supplier to follow the procedures set forth in Article 9 of the UCC for retaining a security interest in materials delivered in the described circumstances.

Reclaiming Materials to be Delivered on Credit

A buyer may agree in a purchase order to pay for materials it receives within a given period after delivery. If the supplier learns, before delivering the materials, that the buyer is insolvent, the supplier may refuse delivery of, and in effect reclaim, such materials, unless the buyer agrees to pay for the materials in cash.[30] The supplier also may demand that a buyer make a cash payment of all amounts due on those materials that had previously been delivered under the particular purchase order.[31]

Under the UCC, a buyer is deemed insolvent if it "either has ceased to pay [its] debts in the ordinary course of business or cannot pay [its] debts as they become due or is insolvent within the meaning of the federal bankruptcy law."[32] The courts have interpreted this definition of insolvency broadly, giving a supplier the right to refuse delivery in a broad range of situations.[33]

Reclaiming Materials Previously Delivered on Credit

In cases in which the materials already have been delivered on credit to a buyer, a supplier's ability to reclaim the materials rests on whether the supplier is able to show (1) that the supplier did not discover that the buyer was insolvent until after the materials were delivered and (2) that a demand for reclamation was made within the required time period.[34]

Discovery, under the UCC, is based on actual knowledge. Therefore, the fact that the supplier could have reasonably discovered the buyer's insolvency does not preclude a supplier from reclaiming the materials. However, the supplier only has a 10-day period after delivery within which to assert this right to reclaim, unless, within the three months preceding delivery of the materials, the buyer had provided the supplier with

---

[29] *See, e.g., In re* Bosley Supply Group, 74 B.R. 250 (Bankr. N.D. Ill. 1987).

[30] U.C.C. § 2-702(1).

[31] *Id.*

[32] *Id.* § 1-201(23).

[33] Indussa Corp. v. Reliable Stainless Steel Supply Co., 369 F. Supp. 976 (E.D. Pa. 1974).

[34] U.C.C. § 2-702(2).

a writing, such as a financial statement, that misrepresented the buyer's financial condition.[35]

Because a supplier who does not know that a buyer is insolvent when the supplier delivers its materials is unlikely to learn of a buyer's solvency within this 10-day time period, it is prudent for the supplier to request that a buyer periodically provide reports that update the buyer's financial condition.

Before exercising its right to reclaim materials under U.C.C. § 2-702, a supplier should note that if it reclaims materials from a buyer successfully, the supplier will be precluded from recovering any other damages.[36] For example, in one case in which a buyer of equipment failed to tender payment to an auction company and the auction company exercised self-help to reclaim the equipment, the court held that the auction company was precluded by U.C.C. § 2-702(3) from any other remedies.[37]

Reclaiming Materials Delivered for Cash

A cash sale transaction requires that payment be due and demanded upon the delivery of the materials to the buyer.[38] In cash sale transactions, it is important to note that, unlike under U.C.C. § 2-702, a supplier that exercises the right to reclaim materials under U.C.C. § 507(2) may seek to reclaim the materials under this UCC section without forfeiting the right to recover certain damages the supplier may incur on account of the buyer's breach.[39]

U.C.C. § 2-507(2) does not address whether a supplier is required to demand the return of materials within any certain period of time; however, Comment 3 to § 2-507 states that "The provision of this Article for a 10 day limit within which the seller may reclaim goods delivered on credit to an insolvent buyer is also applicable here." Accordingly, the same time limitation applies to cash sale transactions and credit sale transactions.

Reclaiming Materials from a Buyer in Bankruptcy

Despite compliance with the pertinent reclamation provisions of the UCC, a supplier's right to reclaim materials under the UCC will be subject to the more stringent reclamation procedures of the Bankruptcy Code[40] in the

---

[35] *Id.*

[36] *Id.* § 2-702(3).

[37] Bullock v. Joe Bailey Auction Co., 580 P.2d 225 (Utah 1978).

[38] U.C.C. § 2-507(2).

[39] Burk v. Emmick, 637 F.2d 1172, 1175 (8th Cir. 1980).

[40] References to the Bankruptcy Code in this chapter are to the Bankruptcy Reform Act of 1978, codified beginning at 11 U.S.C.A. § 101.

event a buyer files bankruptcy.[41] Section 546(c) of the Bankruptcy Code provides in pertinent part that:

> [T]he rights and powers of a trustee . . . are subject to any statutory or common-law right to a seller of goods that has sold goods to the debtor, in the ordinary course of such seller's business, to reclaim such goods if the debtor has received such goods while insolvent, but—
>
> (1) such a seller may not reclaim any such goods unless such seller demands in writing reclamation of such goods before ten days after receipt of such goods by the debtor; . . .

This provision requires a supplier to follow similar but not identical reclamation procedures as those that are set forth in U.C.C. §§ 2-507(2) and 2-702(2) if the seller is to be successful in recovering the materials in cases in which the buyer files bankruptcy.[42] The greatest difference between these UCC sections and § 546 of the Bankruptcy Code is that a demand for reclamation under the Bankruptcy Code must be made in writing and it must be asserted within 10 days after the buyer/debtor's receipt of the materials. If a reclaiming supplier follows the appropriate reclamation procedures of § 546 of the Bankruptcy Code, its right of reclamation will continue to exist, though, as mentioned above, such right may be subject to the rights of certain third parties.[43]

§ 18.14 —Dealing with Unfinished Materials

Occasionally a material supplier such as a manufacturer is in the process of completing the manufacture of materials when it learns of the buyer's breach or repudiation of the purchase order. In these cases, a supplier has the right to:

1. Complete the manufacture of the materials, identify the materials that are covered by the purchase order and pursue its other remedies under the UCC, for example, by reselling the materials and recovering the damages discussed in § **18.16**
2. Stop the manufacture of the materials and proceed to resell the unfinished materials for scrap or salvage value and, again, recover certain damages that are incurred
3. Proceed in any other reasonable manner.[44]

---

[41] *See, e.g., In re* Energy Coop., Inc., 94 B.R. 975 (Bankr. N.D. Ill. 1988).

[42] *In re* Rozel Indus., 74 B.R. 643 (Bankr. N.D. Ill. 1987).

[43] *In re* Bosley Supply Group, 74 B.R. 250 (Bankr. N.D. Ill. 1987).

[44] U.C.C. § 2-704.

In deciding which of these options to pursue, a supplier must exercise "reasonable commercial judgment."[45] In order to protect a supplier from a buyer's claims that damages would have been minimized had the supplier pursued the option not selected, the comments to the UCC state that the commercial reasonableness of a supplier's actions is based on "the facts as they appear at the time" the supplier learned of the breach. In addition, the buyer has the burden of showing that a supplier failed to meet the required standard.[46] Another factor to which courts have looked in determining whether a supplier acted reasonably in its decision to complete the manufacture of material is whether a market existed for the finished materials. In neither case is the reasonableness of a supplier's decision based on a hindsight evaluation of which course of action would have resulted in the least damages.

If a supplier is able to show that it acted in a commercially reasonable manner, it may stop manufacture of the materials and, pursuant to U.C.C. § 2-708, seek to recover its lost profits, for example. In the event the supplier elects to complete the materials, it would have the right to resell the materials and recover its incidental damages pursuant to U.C.C. § 2-706. Both of these UCC sections are discussed in § 18.16.

§ 18.15   —Canceling the Contract

An additional remedy available to a supplier that learns of a buyer's breach or repudiation of a contract is to cancel the contract.[47] The supplier that properly exercises this right is relieved of its obligations to further perform the contract and may pursue other remedies available to it under the UCC.

A supplier may be justified in exercising the right to cancel if a buyer's breach substantially impairs the value of the contract.[48] In order to avoid being second-guessed on whether a buyer's failure to perform a particular obligation constitutes a material breach of a contract, a supplier should identify in its purchase order those events that a supplier considers "material."

---

[45] *See, e.g.,* Modern Mach. v. Flathead County, 202 Mont. 140, 656 P.2d 206 (1982).

[46] *See* U.C.C. § 2-704 cmt. 2.

[47] *Id.* § 2-703(f).

[48] *See, e.g.,* Nora Springs Coop. Co. v. Brandau, 247 N.W.2d 744 (Iowa 1976); Glenville Elevators, Inc. v. Beard, 284 S.C. 335, 326 S.E.2d 185 (Ct. App. 1985).

§ 18.16 —Recovering the Contract Price and Damages

The goal of the UCC is to place an aggrieved supplier in as good a position as it would have been had a breach not occurred.[49] In keeping with this general principle, a supplier left holding materials that it intended to sell to the breaching buyer may resort to U.C.C. §§ 2-706 and 2-708 to measure the monies it is entitled to recover from the breaching buyer and, in the event these UCC provisions are unable to compensate the supplier adequately, the supplier may rely on U.C.C. § 2-709 to recover the full contract price from the buyer. If a buyer fails to pay the amounts due under a purchase order, the supplier may have the right to recover the full contract price when (1) the materials have been accepted by buyer; (2) the risk of loss passed to buyer and the materials were lost or damaged within a reasonable time thereafter; or (3) the supplier has been unable to resell the materials that were supplied or manufactured under the purchase order.[50]

This right to recover the contract price reflects the goal of the UCC of placing the aggrieved supplier in as good a position as it would have been in had full performance of a contract occurred when events or circumstances are such that only a recovery of the contract price would adequately compensate the supplier.

Like the other remedies available under U.C.C. § 2-703, a supplier that institutes an action for the full contract price is also entitled to recover incidental damages arising from the buyer's breach, such as costs associated with caring for and transporting the unsold materials.[51]

Resale of Materials

Under U.C.C. § 2-706 a supplier may resell the materials it holds and recover the difference between the contract price and the resale price.[52] The supplier also is entitled to recover any incidental damages, less any savings it realizes from the breach.[53]

A resale of materials pursuant to § 2-706 can be carried out through public or private sale, but the resale must be performed in good faith and in a commercially reasonable manner.[54] Procedurally this may require, for

---

[49] U.C.C. § 1-106(1).

[50] Id. § 2-709.

[51] Id. §§ 2-709(1), 2-710.

[52] Id. § 2-706.

[53] Id.

[54] See, e.g., Meadowbrook Nat'l. Bank v. Markos, 3 U.C.C. Rep. Serv. (Callaghan) 854 (N.Y. Sup. Ct. 1966); Uganski v. Little Giant Crane & Shovel, Inc., 35 Mich. App. 88, 192 N.W.2d 580 (1971).

example, that in a private sale a supplier provide a buyer with reasonable notice of the supplier's intent to sell the materials. In a public sale, this may require that the supplier provide potential bidders with an opportunity to inspect the materials. The procedures for conducting either form of sale are addressed by statute and should be referred to in each jurisdiction where the sale is to take place.

Although the term *commercially reasonable* is not defined by the UCC, the types of factors that courts look to in evaluating the commercial reasonableness of a supplier's resale include the materials or products that are in issue, the industry or type of trade that is involved, and the timing of the resale.[55] For example, the supplier of computer terminals may not be found to have acted in a commercially reasonable manner if it waits for six months to resell terminals that face obsolescence if not sold quickly or if pricing in the computer industry is relatively volatile.[56]

Alternate Recovery of Damages

A supplier that fails to conduct a commercially reasonable sale is relegated to recovering damages in accordance with U.C.C. § 2-708. In addition, certain suppliers who would not be adequately compensated under U.C.C. § 2-706 may rely on this section for calculating their damages. This section establishes two separate rules for measuring the damages to which a supplier is entitled: (1) the difference between the market price at the time and place of tender and the unpaid contract price;[57] or (2) the profit (including reasonable overhead) that a supplier would have made had the buyer performed its obligations.[58] A supplier may also recover incidental damages under either measure of damages, less any expenses that are saved due to the breach.[59]

A significant detriment associated with the first measure of damages is that the supplier must establish the market price for the materials at the time and place of tender. This issue is resolved in an action for recovery under U.C.C. § 2-706 by simply referring to the price obtained from the resale of the materials. The second measure of damages generally is available to a supplier who falls within one of the following categories: (1) a lost volume seller; (2) a component seller; or (3) a jobber.[60] A supplier who

---

[55] *See, e.g.,* Servbest Foods v. Emessee Indus., Inc., 82 Ill. App. 3d 662, 403 N.E.2d 1 (1980).

[56] *See, e.g.,* City Univ. v. Finalco, Inc., 129 A.D.2d 494, 514 N.Y.S.2d 244 (1987).

[57] U.C.C. § 2-708(1).

[58] *Id.* § 2-708(2).

[59] *Id.*

[60] For a discussion on lost volume sellers, component sellers, and jobbers, *see* 1 J.J. White & R.S. Summers, Uniform Commercial Code 357–361 (3d ed. 1988).

asserts damages under U.C.C. § 2-708(2) has the burden of showing that it falls within one of these categories and that the damages calculated under § 2-708(1) are inadequate to put the supplier in as good a position had performance occurred.[61]

A *lost volume seller* is generally a supplier that would have made two sales, instead of one, had the buyer performed.[62] Therefore, in order to recover lost profits, such a supplier must show that it could have supplied the materials required by the contract. For example, one court found that a company that had entered into an agreement to provide coal was not entitled to recover damages under U.C.C. § 2-708(2) because at the time of the buyer's breach, one of the two principal mines of the company was out of service and the company had a history of falling behind in its delivery schedule.[63]

A *competent seller* is one who assembles goods pursuant to a contract either through the manufacture of the goods or through obtaining the goods from third parties. A *jobber* is similar; however, it effectively acts as a middleman under a contract by reselling finished materials or goods. In both cases, the other provisions of the UCC for measuring damages may be inappropriate because the acquisition of components or finished materials by the component seller or jobber when it learns of a buyer's breach would not be commercially reasonable. Therefore, the only measure of damages available is the lost volume, and corresponding profit, of the lost sale.

Incidental Damages

Under the UCC, a supplier is entitled to recover incidental, but not consequential,[64] damages arising from a buyer's breach. Incidental damages include "any commercially reasonable charges, expenses or commissions incurred in stopping delivery, in the transportation, care and custody of goods after the buyer's breach, in connection with the return or resale of goods or otherwise resulting from the breach."[65]

Because the distinction between incidental and consequential damages may not always be clear, any supplier who would bear particular damages

---

[61] *See, e.g.,* Bill's Coal Co. v. Board of Pub. Utils., 887 F.2d 242 (10th Cir. 1989); R.E. Davis Chem. Corp. v. Diasonics, Inc., 826 F.2d 678 (7th Cir. 1987).

[62] National Controls, Inc. v. Commodore Business Machs., Inc., 163 Cal. App. 3d 688, 209 Cal. Rptr. 636 (1985).

[63] Bill's Coal Co. v. Board of Pub. Utils., 887 F.2d 242 (10th Cir. 1989).

[64] *See, e.g.,* Afram Export Corp. v. Metallurgiki Halyps, S.A., 592 F. Supp. 446 (E.D. Wis. 1984).

[65] U.C.C. § 2-710.

that are not referenced in U.C.C. § 2-710 should expressly identify in its contract any such damages.

MECHANIC'S LIENS AND RELATED
REMEDIES OF THE MATERIALMAN

§ 18.17   Goals of the Laws on Recovery

In addition to a material supplier's rights under the UCC, the law gives a material supplier that attains the status of "materialman" on a work of improvement a variety of tools with which to enforce a claim. These tools reflect society's judgment that a person contributing labor or materials that permanently improve the property of another and thus increase its value should be able to recover the value of its services or materials or both. However, in addition to protecting the materialman's rights, the law also must protect owners' and lenders' rights to receive advance notice of potential claims, and the law must promote the policy of promptly eliminating clouds on the titles to real property. As a result of the multiple goals of the laws on recovery, the procedural prerequisites to the perfection of the statutory remedies are detailed and complex: a materialman must use considerable care to protect all of its rights.

Courts, in pursuing the conflicting goals, have interpreted broadly the remedial statutes creating mechanic's liens, stop notices, and surety bonds, and are hesitant to defeat a claim when the purposes of the various statutes (especially notice to owners and lenders of potential claims) have been achieved. At the same time, courts have denied claims when a basic procedural step in the perfection of such claims has not been performed. **Sections 18.18** through **18.37** discuss the various procedures that must be followed to preserve and perfect a materialman's right to a mechanic's lien, stop notice, or surety bond. The sections also briefly discuss common law breach of written or oral contract, common count, and unjust enrichment claims that may be asserted concurrently with the statutory claims, and issues that may arise in connection therewith.

To illustrate the procedural requirements of typical statutory provisions, the discussion is based upon California law; but similar rights accrue to materialmen in other states. Nevertheless, procedures for perfecting the various rights in other states may differ in several material respects. Therefore, the materialman should review the statutes of its jurisdiction carefully prior to commencing performance in order to discern the exact procedural requirements applicable in its jurisdiction. The discussion is limited to privately-owned works of improvement. The right to assert certain claims, and the procedures required to do so, on public works also may differ materially from those discussed herein.

§ 18.18   Persons Entitled to Assert Claims

In California, a materialman is entitled to assert mechanic's lien, stop notice, or surety bond claims with respect to a work of improvement.[66] A *materialman* is defined as one who provides materials directly to a contractor, subcontractor, or other person "having charge of a work of improvement," for use on a particular work of improvement.[67] One who supplies a materialman, however, is not entitled to assert such claims. The critical question is thus whether the person to whom a person provides materials is a subcontractor, in which case lien and related rights will accrue, or a materialman, in which case these rights will not accrue.[68]

§ 18.19   Materials Used or Consumed in
Work of Improvement

The right to assert a claim based on a mechanic's lien, stop notice, or surety bond accrues whenever a materialman supplies materials specifically for use in a work of improvement and the materials are in fact "used or consumed" in the construction of the work of improvement.[69] A *work of improvement* is defined broadly under California law to include the construction, alteration, addition to, or repair of any building, bridge, road, and the like, the filling, leveling, or grading of land, and the demolition or removal of buildings. Work of improvement refers to the entire structure or scheme of improvement as a whole.[70]

Under the more strict test applied by some California courts, lien and related rights arise only when the materials furnished are contained in the finished structure. Nevertheless, the current trend is to grant lien rights when materials supplied are used or consumed in the course of construction, whether or not they are actually embodied in the finished structure. Thus, explosives and form lumber, though not actually embodied in the final structure, have been held to be consumed in and instrumental to

---

[66] Cal. Civ. Code §§ 3085, 3110, 3158, 3159.

[67] *Id.* § 3110.

[68] *See* Theisen v. County of Los Angeles, 54 Cal. 2d 170, 352 P.2d 529, 5 Cal. Rptr. 161 (1960); Vaughn v. De Kreek, 2 Cal. App. 3d 671, 677, 83 Cal. Rptr. 144 (1969).

[69] Cal. Civ. Code § 3110.

[70] *Id.* § 3106.

the construction of a work of improvement and thus a proper subject of a mechanic's lien.[71]

§ 18.20   —Proof of Use

The materialman's mere delivery of materials to a subcontractor does not satisfy the materialman's burden of proof, notwithstanding the subcontractor's stated intention to use the materials on a given work of improvement. The materialman must prove that the materials were actually used or consumed in the particular work of improvement. Although circumstantial evidence is sufficient proof in many cases, situations arise in which a materialman will be unable to make the necessary showing, and will thereby lose its statutory claim. The materialman's contract or invoices can provide useful evidence in this regard. A clause in the materialman's contract should identify specifically the project for which the subcontractor purchases, and the materialman provides, the subject materials.

Of even greater value are invoices or other documents on which the purchasing subcontractor states, after the fact, that the provided materials were in fact used or consumed at the particular work of improvement. Thus, the materialman should create an extra copy of the subject invoice and request the subcontractor to sign statements to the above effect as performance progresses. The above documents should provide strong evidence at any trial, and if not sufficient for this purpose, will provide an ample basis for a claim against the subcontractor for intentional or negligent misrepresentation.

MECHANIC'S LIENS

§ 18.21   Definition of Mechanic's Lien

A *mechanic's lien* is a lien upon real property, given to those who provide materials at the request of an owner or an agent of the owner, for use in a particular permanent work of improvement, and which are used or consumed in the course of constructing the work of improvement. The mechanic's lien gives the materialman a security interest in the improved

---

[71] *See* Stimpson Mill Co. v. Los Angeles Traction Co., 141 Cal. 30, 74 P. 357 (1903) (strict test; temporary structure, later removed, does not give rise to lien rights); Pacific Sash & Door Co. v. Bumiller, 162 Cal. 664, 124 P. 230 (1912) ('used or consumed' test; materials used for pipe threading, temporary lighting, and wire pulling give rise to lien rights).

property itself and the right to foreclose upon the property. The mechanic's lien right is embodied in the statutes or constitutions of the various states. For example, in California, the right to a mechanic's lien is contained in Article XIV, Section 3, of the Constitution and is implemented by statute.[72]

§ 18.22   Preliminary 20-Day Notice for Lien

The materialman's initial procedural step in perfecting a mechanic's lien is the giving of the statutorily mandated preliminary 20-day notice to the necessary parties. This notice is a prerequisite to enforcement of a mechanic's lien.[73]

Timing

The preliminary notice may be given prior to the materialman's commencement of performance of the contract, and should be given, at the latest, within 20 days of such commencement of performance. This will ensure that the mechanic's lien right attaches to all of the materials the materialman supplies to the project. The materialman may, however, file a 20-day notice at a later time, but in that case the lien will not attach to materials provided more than 20 days prior to service of the notice.

Although an owner or lender may, in certain extreme cases, be estopped to rely on the lack of a preliminary 20-day notice, or be held to have waived the materialman's failure to give it, these are the exceptional cases and depend on facts clearly showing that the intent of the statutes was in fact achieved. California courts have held, however, that the preliminary 20-day notice is an absolute prerequisite to enforcement of a mechanic's lien. Failure to give a preliminary 20-day notice is thus a gamble, and rarely worth the risk. Additionally, the giving of a preliminary 20-day notice is a prerequisite to the enforcement of a stop notice, and is therefore doubly important.

Recipients

A materialman must give the preliminary 20-day notice to all parties with whom the materialman is not in privity of contract, thereby providing notice of potential claims to parties that might not otherwise be aware of the materialman's involvement in the project. In a typical construction project, a materialman contracting with a subcontractor should deliver a

---

[72] Cal. Civ. Code §§ 3082–3267.

[73] Cal. Civ. Code § 3114.

preliminary 20-day notice to the construction lender, the owner, and the general contractor.[74] When the materialman is not certain as to the identity of the parties involved in the project, California law provides for service of the preliminary 20-day notice to those "purported" to be the lender, owner, and contractor. The materialman would be well-advised, however, to conduct reasonable investigation as to the identity of these parties. In California, the name and address of these persons must be included in the prime construction contract between the general contractor and the owner, and the general contractor is required by law to give the materialman access to this contract on request.[75]

The materialman normally need only give one preliminary 20-day notice to each of the required parties, even if the initial contract is subsequently modified. However, the notice requirement must be satisfied for each contract that the materialman performs on a project. Thus, if the materialman delivers materials to two subcontractors under two separate contracts, the materialman must serve two preliminary 20-day notices, one for each contract, to each recipient discussed above.

Contents

The preliminary notice must contain the following information:

1. General description of the materials furnished or to be furnished (the construction lender is also entitled to an estimate of the total price of the materials to be provided)
2. Name and address of the materialman
3. Name of the person with whom the materialman has contracted
4. Description of the jobsite sufficient for identification (the street address is a good start)
5. Specific statutory statement, in boldfaced type, containing explicit notice to the property owner of the fact that if bills go unpaid, the owner may lose the property in a mechanic's lien foreclosure suit.[76]

The materialman should exercise great care to ensure that its preliminary 20-day notice contains the exact language and form required by the relevant statute. The failure to comply has been held fatal to a mechanic's lien claim.[77] Thus, if the form used is mass-produced and pre-printed, the

---

[74] *Id.* § 3097.

[75] *Id.* § 3097(l), (m).

[76] *Id.* § 3097(c).

[77] *See* Harold James, Inc. v. Five Points Ranch, Inc., 158 Cal. App. 3d 1, 204 Cal. Rptr. 494 (1984).

materialman should review it carefully to confirm that it has been updated to reflect any recent statutory changes.

Service

Under California law, the preliminary 20-day notice containing the above information must be properly served upon the persons entitled to receive the notice, and the materialman must be able to prove that this was done. Such service may be by (1) personal service, by leaving it with some person in charge at the residence or place of business of the person to be notified, or by (2) first-class registered or certified mail, postage prepaid, mailed to the residence or place of business of the person to be notified.[78]

When service of the notice is by personal service, the materialman should obtain an affidavit of proof of service. This affidavit must be a sworn statement by the person effecting the service, stating the time, place, and manner of service and facts showing that the service complied with the statutory requirements. When the service is by registered or certified mail, a return receipt, to be signed by the recipient, should be requested. The materialman should retain all return receipts and other evidence that service was made or attempted.[79]

§ 18.23   Proper Claim of Lien

A materialman that has delivered materials but has not been paid in accordance with the terms of its contract must timely record a proper claim of lien to activate its mechanic's lien.

Contents

In California, the claim of lien is a written statement, signed and verified by the materialman or its agent, that contains the following:

1. Statement of the amount owing after deducting all just credits and offsets
2. Name of the owner or reputed owner
3. General statement of the kind of materials furnished
4. Name of the person with whom the materialman contracted and to whom it furnished materials
5. Description of the real property sufficient for identification.[80]

---

[78] *Id.* § 3097(f).
[79] Cal. Civ. Code § 3097.1.
[80] *Id.* § 3084.

The materialman or its agent verifies the claim of lien by signing a statement thereon to the effect that he or she knows the contents of the claim of lien and believes them to be true. The willful inclusion in the claim of lien of the price of materials not actually used in the work of improvement can lead to the forfeiture of the mechanic's lien.[81] This claim of lien must be recorded in the office of the county recorder in the county in which the land is situated.

Timing

Extreme care should be exercised to ensure that the claim of lien is timely recorded. Statutes establish very short time periods after the project is completed or construction is ceased for the filing of claims of lien. Thus, in California, when no notice of completion or cessation of the project is recorded, the materialman has 90 days after completion of the project to record its claim of lien. When the owner records a notice of completion or notice of cessation, however, the materialman has only 30 days from the recordation of such notice in which to file its claim of lien.[82] The failure to meet these deadlines usually is fatal to a mechanic's lien claim.

A materialman may, however, record successive claims of lien, as in the case when suit is not timely brought upon the first claim of lien but the above time frames have not expired. In that case, another claim of lien can be filed and suit brought upon this latter claim of lien, an approach that involves serious risks. Under California law, if the materialman has not filed an action to foreclose the lien within the 90-day period after the filing of the initial claim of lien, an owner may petition the court for an order that not only expunges the lien created by the initial claim of lien, but also destroys the materialman's right to file a subsequent claim of lien.[83] The materialman should therefore be certain to record any subsequent claim of lien within 90 days of filing the initial claim of lien.

§ 18.24   Release of Lien

Upon the recordation of a claim of lien in California, if the owner, general contractor, or subcontractor "disputes the correctness or validity of any claim of lien," each may record on the public records a release bond that releases the improved property from the effect of the lien and becomes the security for the materialman's claim.[84] This bond must be (1) in an amount

---

[81] Cal. Civ. Code § 3118.

[82] *Id.* § 3116.

[83] *Id.* § 3154; Coast Cent. Credit Union v. Superior Court, 209 Cal. App. 3d 703, 257 Cal. Rptr. 468 (1989).

[84] Cal. Civ. Code § 3143.

one and one half times the amount of the claim of lien, (2) issued by a corporate surety licensed by California to issue such bonds, and (3) conditioned for the payment of any amount the claimant may recover on the lien claim, plus costs of suit. As discussed in § **18.34** on release bonds, upon learning of the recordation of such a bond, the materialman should promptly take the necessary steps to perfect its claim against the principal and surety on this bond.

§ 18.25   Action to Foreclose Lien

The materialman must file a lawsuit to foreclose the lien activated by the filing of the claim of lien. The foreclosure cause of action may be asserted concurrently with several other claims.

Timing

In California, the materialman has 90 days from the filing of the claim of lien in which to file the foreclosure suit in court. The suit must be brought in the county in which some or all of the improved property is located.[85] This 90-day period may be extended up to 365 days after completion of the project if the materialman grants the subcontractor credit for the amount owing, and notice of the giving of credit and the terms of the credit is recorded in the county recorder's office prior to the expiration of the 90-day period.[86] If no suit is filed within the relevant time period, the lien becomes "null and void and of no further force and effect."[87]

Parties

Under California law, (assuming no credit is given) the materialman must, within these 90 days, name as a defendant all persons who possess an interest in the property as of the date the complaint is filed and whose interest the materialman seeks to subject to the lien. The naming of one such interested party does not satisfy the statute of limitations as to other parties not named, and the interest of parties not named within the relevant time period becomes senior to the materialman's claim for all purposes.[88] Therefore, the materialman should conduct a reasonable investigation (such as obtaining a title report) to determine the identity of the construction lender, the owner, and any other persons that may have an interest in the

---

[85] *Id.* § 3144(a).

[86] *Id.*

[87] *Id.* § 3144(b).

[88] Paramount Sec. Co. v. Daze, 128 Cal. App. 515, 517, 275 P.2d 816 (1933).

property on the date the complaint is filed. The beneficiaries, and not simply the trustees, of all deeds of trust on the property are essential parties to the suit unless the materialman concedes the seniority of such deed of trust over its mechanic's lien. The materialman should also utilize Doe pleading to avoid the running of the statute of limitations on its claim against parties of whose identity the materialman is ignorant at the time the complaint is filed.[89]

Notice of Action

Notice of the pendency of the foreclosure suit should also be recorded in the county recorder's office promptly upon the filing of the complaint. This notice, known as a *lis pendens,* provides constructive notice of the materialman's claim to all persons who may acquire an interest in the property during the pendency of the suit. If this is not done, any purchaser of the property who lacks actual knowledge of the materialman's claim may take title to the property free and clear of the materialman's lien.

Trial

At trial, the materialman must prove its compliance with all of the above statutory prerequisites, including the timely and proper service of a proper preliminary 20-day notice, the timely filing of a proper claim of lien, the date of the completion of the work, that the materials provided by the materialman were in fact used on that particular work of improvement, and the reasonable value of the materials provided. The materialman will be well-served by having obtained verifications from the subcontractor during the course of performance of the contract stating that the materials provided under the contract were in fact used in the particular work of improvement. To facilitate proof of all of the above, the materialman should carefully retain and segregate all documentary evidence relevant to the items.

Seniority of Lien

The mechanic's lien rights of all contractors and materialmen on a California construction project are deemed to arise at the moment the first member of the construction team commences the work of improvement. The liens of all persons involved in the work of improvement are given equal priority, regardless of the date on which they actually performed work on or

---

[89] *See* Sobeck & Assocs., v. B&R Invs. No. 24, 215 Cal. App. 3d 861, 867, 264 Cal. Rptr. 156 (1989); Grinnell Fire Protection Sys. Co. v. American Sav. & Loan Ass'n, 183 Cal. App. 3d 352, 228 Cal. Rptr. 292 (1986).

provided materials to the work of improvement. All encumbrances on the property, such as deeds of trust, that are recorded after the work of improvement is commenced are subordinate to the mechanic's liens arising from the work of improvement.[90] Thus, if subcontractor S commences the work of improvement on Monday, a construction deed of trust on the property is recorded on Wednesday, and materialman M commences its performance on Friday, M's lien will be effective as of Monday, as will S's, and both will be senior to the deed of trust recorded on Wednesday. Thus, upon foreclosure of the mechanic's liens, M's and S's interests in the improved property will be senior to the deed of trust, and will therefore be more likely to result in a full recovery by M and S.

Judgment

If successful at trial, the materialman will obtain a judgment imposing the mechanic's lien upon the improved property and ordering foreclosure of the lien. The materialman will also be entitled to a deficiency judgment against the subcontractor with whom the materialman contracted.[91] The decree of foreclosure will lead to the public auction and sale of the improved property. The proceeds of the sale, if insufficient to satisfy all lien claims in full, will be shared by the successful lien claimants on a pro rata basis.

§ 18.26   Weaknesses of Mechanic's Lien

The mechanic's lien is a valuable tool in the materialman's repertoire, as owners and lenders are averse both to clouds on their title and to the loss of the property through foreclosure. However, sophisticated construction lenders generally refuse to lend unless their construction deeds of trust are recorded prior to the commencement of the work of improvement, and are therefore senior to all mechanic's liens. The failure of a construction project frequently leads to the construction lender's foreclosure of its construction deed of trust, thereby destroying all mechanic's liens. This is an increasingly frequent phenomenon that represents a significant threat to a materialman.

Additionally, when the construction deed of trust is senior but is not foreclosed, and the materialman seeks only to foreclose the owner's interest in the property, the proceeds of the sale will not exceed the value of the owner's equity. Thus, if the value of the property does not exceed the amount of the

---

[90] Cal. Civ. Code § 3134.

[91] *Id.* § 3151.

construction loan by a sufficient amount, the proceeds of the foreclosure sale will not fully satisfy all lien claimants' claims.

For the above reasons, a mechanic's lien is subject to defeat in a relatively high proportion of those projects that experience difficulty, notwithstanding the materialman's full and satisfactory performance of its contract. As a result, legislatures have created the stop notice (alternatively known as a *notice to withhold*), a remedy which gives materialmen access to a much more liquid source of repayment.

STOP NOTICES

§ 18.27   Stop Notice Remedy

The stop notice is a statutory weapon that can require a person holding any construction funds to retain such funds for the benefit of the stop notice claimant. The failure to withhold funds when so required subjects the stop notice recipient to personal liability for the amount of the stop notice claim. The stop notice is thus superior to a mechanic's lien, for it is not defeated by the foreclosure of a senior construction deed of trust, and is not dependent on the extent of the owner's equity in the project. Additionally, courts have interpreted these statutes broadly, such that stop notices "catch" funds previously disbursed into the lender's own coffers. The stop notice is thus a very effective remedy.

Stop notice rights accrue to a materialman for the provision of the same materials that give rise to mechanic's lien rights. Thus, in a nutshell, the materialman must provide materials, at the request of an owner or a statutory agent of the owner, for use in a particular permanent work of improvement, and the materials must be used or consumed in the course of the construction of the work of improvement.[92]

§ 18.28   Preliminary 20-Day Notice for Claim

The giving of a preliminary 20-day notice is a prerequisite to the enforcement of a stop notice in California.[93] The requirements for the timing, contents, and service of the preliminary 20-day notice on a stop notice claim are the same as those for a mechanic's lien preliminary 20-day notice.[94] Indeed, these two separate remedies both flow from the materialman's

---

[92] *Id.* §§ 3158, 3159.

[93] *Id.* § 3160.

[94] *Id.* §§ 3097, 3097.1.

giving of one preliminary 20-day notice. The materialman need not give two separate notices.

§ 18.29 Other Prerequisites to Enforcement

Service of the stop notice itself is required to activate the right to serve and enforce a stop notice. Unlike the claim of lien, which is recorded, the stop notice is delivered to the owner or to the lender and need not be recorded.

Contents

The stop notice is a written notice, signed and verified by the materialman or its agent, that contains a general statement of the following:

1. Kind of materials furnished or agreed to be furnished by the materialman
2. Name of the party to whom or for whom such materials were furnished
3. Amount in value of the materials already furnished and the total value of the materials agreed to be furnished
4. Name and address of the claimant.[95]

The willful inclusion in the stop notice of the price of materials not actually used in the work of improvement can lead to the forfeiture of the stop notice.[96] Defects in the form of the stop notice will not, however, render the stop notice invalid if the contents of the stop notice substantially inform the owner or lender of the information required.[97]

Timing

A stop notice may be given at any time prior to the expiration of the period during which a claim of lien may be recorded, but may be given only for materials or equipment already furnished by the materialman.[98] This period may be shortened by the recordation of a notice of completion or notice of cessation.[99]

---

[95] Cal. Civ. Code § 3103.
[96] *Id.* § 3168.
[97] *Id.* § 3103.
[98] *Id.* § 3159.
[99] *Id.* § 3116.

Recipients

A materialman may give a stop notice to the owner or to the construction lender.[100] An owner is entitled to demand in writing that a materialman serve a stop notice on the owner, and failure to comply will result in the forfeiture of the materialman's mechanic's lien rights.[101] By doing this, the owner will be entitled upon receipt of the stop notice to withhold funds in its possession from the general contractor when the owner suspects that certain members of the construction team have not been paid.

Service

The stop notice must be delivered to the owner personally or left at its residence or place of business with some person in charge, or delivered to the owner's architect.[102] If given to the construction lender, the stop notice must be delivered to the manager or other responsible officer of the lender, or sent to such office by registered or certified mail.[103] If the lender has branch offices, the stop notice must be delivered to the office or branch actually administering or holding the construction funds.[104]

Action on Stop Notice

Once a stop notice has been served, a lawsuit must be filed to enforce the claim. Under California law, this action must be filed with the court no earlier than 10 days after service of the stop notice and no later than 90 days after the expiration of the period during which a claim of lien could have been filed.[105] The materialman must name as defendants the person or persons upon whom the stop notice was served. Also, the materialman must, within five days of filing the action on the stop notice, give a notice of commencement of the action "to the same persons and in the same manner as" the stop notice itself was given.[106]

At trial, the materialman must prove the following:

1. Its timely and proper service of a proper preliminary 20-day notice
2. Timely and proper service of a proper stop notice

---

[100] *Id.* §§ 3158, 3159.

[101] Cal. Civ. Code § 3158.

[102] *Id.* § 3103.

[103] *Id.* § 3103.

[104] *Id.* § 3083.

[105] *Id.* § 3172.

[106] *Id.*

3. Recipient's possession, at the time of service of the stop notice, of construction funds adequate to meet the claim

4. Materialman's provision of materials that actually were used or consumed in the work of improvement

5. Reasonable value of such materials.

If successful at trial, in the absence of a payment bond or release bond, the materialman will be entitled to a decree ordering the holder of such funds to pay the same to the materialman. If several persons perfect stop notice claims, and the captured funds are insufficient to pay all claims in full, the funds will be shared among the successful claimants on a pro rata basis.[107]

§ 18.30   Bonded Stop Notice

The critical distinction in the realm of stop notices is between a bonded and an unbonded stop notice. Whereas an unbonded stop notice will be effective to require an owner to withhold funds, stop notices are not frequently given to owners due to the fact that owners rarely hold construction funds. The construction lender is the primary target of stop notices. In California, for a stop notice to be effective against a construction lender, the stop notice must be *bonded.* [108] This means that the stop notice must be accompanied by a bond with "good and sufficient sureties" in a sum equal to one and one quarter times the amount of the stop notice claim, and conditioned upon the payment of "all costs that may be awarded against the owner, original contractor, construction lender, or any of them, and all damages that [these parties] may sustain by reason of the equitable garnishment effected by the claim" if the recipient of the stop notice prevails on the claim.[109] The construction lender, upon receipt of a bonded stop notice, is entitled to object to the sufficiency of the sureties on such bond if the surety is not a corporate surety licensed by California.[110]

§ 18.31   Funds Caught by the Stop Notice

California courts have interpreted the stop notice statutes broadly, with the result that a stop notice not only "catches" undisbursed construction loan funds in the owner's, lender's, or contractor's possession, but also may

---

[107] Cal. Civ. Code § 3167.

[108] *Id.* §§ 3159, 3162.

[109] *Id.* § 3083.

[110] *Id.* § 3163.

catch funds previously assigned by the owner or general contractor to the lender, such as interest, points, and administrative expenses.[111]

The stop notice is thus a potent weapon that frequently can produce prompt payment from a liquid construction lender without the necessity of extensive litigation. This is especially true when the materialman is able to provide thorough and convincing documentation that all the necessary procedures have been followed.

As discussed in § 18.33, however, the lender may elect not to withhold funds pursuant to a stop notice if a payment bond has previously been recorded. Similarly, the lender, owner, or contractor may record a release bond that frees the funds caught by the materialman's stop notice and that replaces these funds as the security for the materialman's claims. These and other bonds that may be recorded with respect to a work of improvement enhance rather than detract from the materialman's prospects of recovery.

STATUTORY SURETY BONDS

§ 18.32   Overview of Surety Bonds

Surety bonds provide a materialman an alternative and reliable means of recovery. These bonds basically guarantee the payment of amounts owing to the materialman, and in the case of release bonds, replace the improved property or the construction loan fund as the security for the materialman's claim, freeing the property or loan fund from the effect of the materialman's claim. The statutory surety bonds of primary interest to a materialman are payment bonds and mechanic's lien or stop notice release bonds. A materialman may, if it satisfies the necessary prerequisites, recover against a release or payment bond in an action independent of a mechanic's lien or stop notice enforcement action. Alternatively, the materialman may recover against such bonds in the same action in which it seeks to enforce its mechanic's lien or stop notice.

§ 18.33   Payment Bonds

A payment bond guarantees payment to the materialman (among others) of the amount of its valid claims.[112] Thus, if a materialman is not paid under its contract, it may recover the amount owed by proceeding against

---

[111] *Id.* § 3166; Familian Corp. v. Imperial Bank, 213 Cal. App. 3d 681, 262 Cal. Rptr. 101 (1989).

[112] Cal. Civ. Code § 3096.

the payment bond. If timely and properly recorded, a payment bond also (1) protects an owner of improved property from the risk of paying more than the amount of its contract with the general contractor[113] and (2) allows a construction lender to disregard a bonded stop notice given by a materialman.[114]

On a private work of improvement in California, the owner or lender may require the general contractor to obtain and record a payment bond that protects the owner from "any failure of the . . . contractor to perform his contract and make full payment for all work done and material furnished thereunder."[115] For this payment bond to have the desired effects, the prime construction contract between the owner and general contractor must be recorded in the county recorder's office prior to the commencement of the work of improvement. The payment bond, which must be in an amount not less than one half of the contract amount, must also be recorded, but this may be done after the work of improvement is commenced.

When the above steps are taken, and a materialman proves its mechanic's lien claim, the materialman will be granted judgment against the payment bond rather than against the owner's land.[116] Similarly, when the construction contract is timely recorded and the payment bond is recorded prior to the receipt of the first stop notice, the owner or lender may disregard a stop notice or bonded stop notice from a materialman, as the stop notice claimants will be granted judgment against the payment bond.[117]

When giving a lender a bonded stop notice, the materialman should always request notice of the lender's election whether or not to withhold funds. This requires the lender to give the materialman, in addition to notice of its election, a copy of the recorded payment bond.[118]

Upon learning that a payment bond has been recorded on a work of improvement, the materialman should (1) carefully review the bond to ensure that it meets the statutory requirements and that the surety or sureties are adequate, and (2) take the necessary steps to assert a cause of action against the principal and surety on the bond. In California, when a payment bond is recorded prior to the completion of the work of improvement, the materialman must either (1) file a claim of lien or (2) give the surety, within the time during which a claim of lien could be recorded, a written

---

[113] Id. § 3235.

[114] Id. §§ 3159, 3162.

[115] Id. § 3236.

[116] Id. § 3235.

[117] Id. §§ 3161, 3162.

[118] Cal. Civ. Code § 3162.

notice of the materialman's claim.[119] This notice must contain a statement of the following:

1. Kind of equipment or materials furnished or agreed to be furnished
2. Name of the person to whom or for whom these items were furnished
3. Value of the equipment or materials furnished
4. Value of the entire amount agreed to be furnished.[120]

This notice must be delivered to the surety personally or by registered or certified mail.[121] A recorded payment bond may reduce the applicable statute of limitations for a suit on the payment bond to as little as six months from the date of completion of the work of improvement.[122]

Payment bonds also may be acquired and recorded in California to give junior encumbrances priority over mechanic's liens for work of improvement[123] or mechanic's liens for site improvement.[124]

§ 18.34   Release Bonds

A release bond may be posted by a person who wishes to release the property or loan fund from the effect of the lien or stop notice. The release bond replaces the property or loan fund as the security for the materialman's claim.[125] These bonds guarantee payment to the materialman of any sum it may recover on its claim, plus costs of suit, if it prevails upon its claim. These bonds, being merely substitute security and guaranteeing payment only on valid claims, do not relieve the materialman from proving the validity of its mechanic's lien or stop notice claim.

The mechanic's lien release bond must be in an amount equal to one and one half, and the stop notice release bond must be in an amount equal to one and one quarter, times the amount of the claim. The mechanic's lien release bond must be recorded in the office of the county recorder where the claim of lien was recorded, and the person recording the bond must give notice of its recordation to the lien claimant by mailing a copy of the bond to the claimant at the address appearing on the claim of lien, by

---

[119] *Id.* § 3240.

[120] *Id.* § 3240.

[121] *Id.* § 3241.

[122] *Id.* §§ 3239, 3240.

[123] *Id.* § 3138.

[124] Cal. Civ. Code §§ 3137, 3139.

[125] *Id.* §§ 3143, 3171.

registered or certified mail, return receipt requested.[126] The stop notice release bond, on the other hand, need not be recorded, but rather must be filed with the stop notice recipient. No provision requires the recipient of the bond to give the materialman notice of its receipt.[127]

In California, an action on the mechanic's lien release bond must be filed within six months of the bond's recordation, but failure by the person recording the bond to give notice of its recordation will toll the statute of limitations.[128] No minimum statute of limitations for an action on the stop notice release bond appears in the statute.

Upon learning of the recordation or filing of any of the above bonds, the materialman should (1) carefully review the bond to ensure that it meets the statutory requirements and that the surety or sureties are adequate and (2) take the necessary steps to assert a cause of action against the principal and surety on the bond.

§ 18.35   Contractor's License Bond

Another bond that bears mentioning, though it may not be large in amount, is the license bond of the general contractor. This bond normally provides for recovery by any person damaged by the general contractor's fraud or diversion of funds in the course of performance of the general contractor's contract. The bond need only be in the amount of $5,000, however, unless the contractor has previously had its license suspended, in which case the amount of the bond will be greater. The materialman should therefore always consider this bond as a potential source of recovery.

COMMON LAW CLAIMS

§ 18.36   Breach of Contract Claim

A supplier, whether or not a materialman, may assert a breach of contract claim against its vendee. The contract claim may prove the materialman's only means of recovery, and offers the considerable advantage of allowing the recovery of attorneys' fees, if the contract so provides. The supplier should insist on the inclusion of an attorneys' fees provision in all its contracts, and should execute written contracts whenever possible. The supplier also may assert oral contract or common count claims against parties

---

[126] *Id.* § 3144.5.

[127] *Id.* § 3171.

[128] *Id.* § 3144.5.

with whom no written contract exists. However, written contracts are much easier to prove than are oral contracts.

Pay When Paid Clauses

Many contractors insert pay when paid clauses in their contracts. These clauses generally provide that the contractor will have no obligation to pay the supplier unless and until the contractor is paid by the owner. Under California law, however, in the absence of language very explicitly shifting the risk of nonpayment or failure of the project to the materialman, the pay when paid clause will not be enforced. The clause will generally be construed, not as a condition precedent, but rather as requiring the general contractor or subcontractor to pay the materialman within a reasonable time after the materialman has performed.[129]

§ 18.37   Unjust Enrichment Claim

California courts have frequently stated that the general intent of the mechanic's lien statutes is to prevent the unjust enrichment of property owners. Thus, a materialman may seek to obtain judgment against the owner of a project by way of an unjust enrichment claim. Such a claim is based on a "quasi-contract," that is, a contract "implied in law." This is an obligation "created by the law without regard to the intention of the parties, and is designed to restore the aggrieved party to his former position by return of the *thing* or its equivalent in money."[130] This claim therefore appears to offer the materialman the best chance of recovering from a party with whom the materialman is not in privity of contract.

It has been stated that to prevail on an unjust enrichment claim, the defendant must have accepted the benefits of the materialman's work with full knowledge of the facts, the materialman must have diligently attempted to exercise its other statutory remedies, and the defendant would be unjustly enriched if allowed to escape liability because it has not paid for the work or materials.[131] However, unjust enrichment claims generally do not lead to the recovery of attorneys' fees and are not entitled to priority on the court's calendar.

---

[129] Henry Yamanishi v. Bleily & Collishaw, Inc., 29 Cal. App. 3d 456, 105 Cal. Rptr. 580 (1972).

[130] 1 Witkin, *Contracts,* Summary of California Law § 91 at 122 (9th ed. 1987).

[131] Rogers v. Whitson, 228 Cal. App. 2d 662, 39 Cal. Rptr. 849 (1964). *See also* Truestone Inc. v. Simi W. Indus. Park II, 163 Cal. App. 3d 715, 209 Cal. Rptr. 759 (1984); Annotation, *Building And Construction Contracts: Right Of Subcontractor Who Has Dealt Only With Primary Contractor to Recover Against Property Owner In Quasi Contract,* 62 A.L.R.3d 288 (1988).

CHAPTER 19

PAY WHEN PAID CLAUSES

John M. Rubens

John M. Rubens is a member of the Redwood City, California, law firm of Ropers, Majeski, Kohn, Bentley, Wagner & Kane. Mr. Rubens graduated from the University of California at Berkeley and Hastings College of Law, University of California. He was admitted to the California bar in 1962 and has been practicing in the area of fidelity and surety law for several years. Mr. Rubens is a member of the International Association of Defense Counsel, and he is also a member of the California and American (Fidelity and Surety Committee and Forum on the Construction Industry) Bar Associations.

§ 19.1 Overview

Commentators have observed that most litigation in construction cases involves payment claims for services rendered.[1] Within this area, there is

---

[1] M. Simon, Construction Claims and Liability § 9.12 (John Wiley & Sons 1989); A. Farnsworth, Contracts § 8.4 (1982).

probably no more confounding question than how a court will enforce a contract clause that on its face appears to call for payment to a subcontractor by the prime contractor only when the latter receives payment from the owner. This contractual provision is referred to as a *pay when paid* clause.

Pay when paid clauses attempt to shift the risk of payment failure by the owner to the subcontractor.[2] The effect of the clause is to assist the prime contractor with its cash flow[3] and, in return, the subcontractor makes allowance for the contingency by factoring the risk into its own price.[4]

A typical pay when paid clause may look like this:

> Contractor shall pay Subcontractor for work performed by Subcontractor at such time as Contractor receives payment from Owner.

It is well-settled that all courts in the United States will enforce this contract provision.[5] Before a court can enforce the clause, however, the court must determine what the parties intended the clause to mean. The analysis requires that the clause be reread and that the perspectives of the contractor, the subcontractor who has performed but has not been paid, and the judge before whom the case is being argued be considered. Does the provision mean that the subcontractor is out of pocket until the owner pays the prime contractor? If the owner never pays the prime contractor, has the subcontractor's claim similarly vanished into eternity?[6] Conversely, does the absence of a specific time period mean that the contractor has impliedly agreed to pay the subcontractor within a "reasonable time" notwithstanding the owner's nonpayment?[7] What would be the influence of the terms of the referenced general contract if the contract between the owner and prime contractor was "cost-plus," which required the prime contractor to pay the subcontractors before the owner would reimburse the prime contractor?[8] Furthermore, what about the terms of the prime contractor's surety bond, which may contain payment terms different from the contract between the prime contractor and its subcontractors?[9] Alternatively, suppose the subcontract and bond have the same pay when paid

---

[2] Peacock Constr. Co. v. Modern Air Conditioning, 353 So. 2d 840 (Fla. 1977).

[3] A. Farnsworth, Contracts § 8.4.

[4] A. Corbin, Corbin on Contracts § 733 (1960).

[5] Thos. J. Dyer Co. v. Bishop Int'l Eng'g Co., 303 F.2d 655 (6th Cir. 1962); Mascioni v. I.B. Miller, Inc., 261 N.Y. 1, 184 N.E. 473 (1933); W.H. Page, The Law of Contracts § 2100 (2d ed. 1920).

[6] Mascioni v. I.B. Miller, Inc., 261 N.Y. 1, 184 N.E. 473 (1933).

[7] Henry Yamanishi v. Bleily & Collishaw, Inc., 29 Cal. App. 3d 457, 462, 105 Cal. Rptr. 580 (1972).

[8] OBS Co. v. Pace Constr. Corp., 558 So. 2d, 404, 405 (Fla. 1990).

[9] *Id.* at 405.

terms?[10] Finally, what if there were change orders issued, some falling within the scope of the contract containing the pay when paid clause and some outside of it?[11]

These questions are intended to illustrate that there can be factual ambiguities that make uncertain just what the parties intended when they signed a contract with a pay when paid clause. Whether the objective is to draft a pay when paid clause having the best chance of holding up through the rigors of litigation and judicial scrutiny, or to knock down the seemingly impregnable Maginot Line, it is essential to understand how courts approach the clause, an understanding that, in turn, requires an appreciation of some of the principles that underlie contract law.

§ 19.2 Contract Performance

A contract describes the duties to be performed by the respective parties to the contract. Often the duties described are conditioned on the occurrence of some event that may or may not happen. If the event materializes, the condition precedent is satisfied and the duty of the party to perform arises. If the party fails to so perform, then the party is in breach.

If the condition precedent is not satisfied because the event never occurred, then the party has no duty to perform. This last point is subject to two important qualifications that should be kept in mind when a party is faced with a pay when paid clause. First, under certain circumstances the occurrence of the condition precedent may be excused, in which case the party's duty arises whether or not the condition precedent is satisfied. Second, what may appear to be a duty contingent upon fulfillment of a condition precedent may in fact be an absolute duty, with satisfaction or failure of the condition representing only a guidepost fixing the time of payment.

This matrix of possibilities is especially important when one considers that a court reviewing a pay when paid clause ultimately is going to select one of three boxes in its determination of what the parties intended. The three interpretation possibilities are that the clause is:

1. An absolute bar to payment until such time as payment is received from the owner

2. An absolute duty by the prime contractor to pay the subcontractor at the time of the party's performance notwithstanding nonpayment by the owner

---

[10] Schuler-Haas Elec. Corp. v. Aetna Casualty & Sur. Co., 49 A.D.2d 60, 371 N.Y.S.2d 207 (1975), aff'd, 40 N.Y.2d 883, 357 N.E.2d 1003, 389 N.Y.S.2d 348 (1976).

[11] Thos. J. Dyer Co. v. Bishop Int'l Eng'g Co., 303 F.2d 655 (6th Cir. 1962).

3. A duty of the prime contractor to pay its subcontractor within a reasonable time after the subcontractor's performance regardless of the timing of the owner's payment.

Parties to the contract should heed the following word of caution—it is not surprising to find identically worded pay when paid clauses ending up in any of the three boxes.

§ 19.3 Contract Interpretation

Litigation of the pay when paid clause typically arises in a situation in which a subcontractor substantially completes its work under the contract. The prime contractor does not pay the subcontractor because the prime contractor has not been paid by the owner. The subcontractor then sues the prime contractor for payment. When the parties are at the courthouse, the judge attempts to determine the answers to two questions. First, was the prime contractors duty to pay the subcontractor conditional or not?[12] Second, if the duty to pay was conditional, upon what event was it conditioned?[13] The judge seeks answers by trying to discover just what the parties intended when they inserted the clause into the contract.[14]

Identification of intention is carried out through a process of contract interpretation. The process is shaped by both important procedural and policy considerations, and an understanding of these interpretational components is critical in assessing how a pay when paid clause may fare in court.

A court investigates the purpose of the clause intended by the parties by looking at the words of the clause itself in an attempt to discover what each party subjectively[15] or objectively[16] expected the clause to mean. The court may seek additional assistance by looking to the parties' preliminary negotiations, or to how the clause is customarily applied in the trade or how the parties have conducted themselves under the clause in the present contract or in their past dealings.[17]

In certain situations, a party may seek to introduce evidence of oral agreements between the parties or writings with a third party. When this

---

[12] A. Farnsworth, Contracts § 8.4 (1982).

[13] *Id.*

[14] Thos. J. Dyer Co. v. Bishop Int'l Eng'g Co., 303 F.2d 655 (6th Cir. 1962).

[15] Restatement (Second) of Contracts §§ 201–203 (1980).

[16] Restatement (First) of Contracts §§ 230, 233, 235, 236 (1932).

[17] A. Farnsworth, Contracts § 8.4.

evidence is introduced for the purpose of explaining the meaning of the clause, there is no obstacle to its admission.[18]

In a recent Florida case, *OBS Co. v. Pace Construction Corp.*, a general contract between the prime contractor and the owner was incorporated by reference into a contract between the prime contractor and the subcontractor.[19] The incorporation purported to bind the subcontractor to all of the provisions contained in the prime contractor-owner contract.[20] The prime contractor-owner contract contained straight reimbursement provisions.[21] These clauses meant that the owner was required to pay the prime contractor only after the prime contractor had paid its subcontractors. Meanwhile, the subcontract contained a pay when paid clause. Not surprisingly, the Florida Supreme Court found the payment provisions, when read together, ambiguous.[22]

Courts may resolve an ambiguity in situations like this by employing certain rules of interpretation. Most familiar of the rules are those that require any ambiguity of a contract to be strictly construed against the party who prepared the contract.[23] The courts reason that because the drafter has more control over the contract drafting process, the drafting party should therefore take due care in preparation of the contract. This rule for resolving ambiguity is most often applied to interpreting adhesion or form contracts prepared by only one of the parties. In the *OBS* case the Florida Supreme Court placed responsibility for the ambiguity with the general contractor for other reasons that may be better understood after a discussion of some fundamental policies that guide contract law.

§ 19.4   —Effect of Policies

The pay when paid clause triggers two competing policies of contract law. The first is freedom of contract, which takes tangible form in the express provisions of the contract. In the payment term context, a noted author has observed that "[a]n express provision that payment shall not be made until a certain event occurs, leaves no room for construction and is given full force and effect."[24]

---

[18] Comment note, Annotation, *The Parol Evidence Rule and Admissibility of Extrinsic Evidence to Establish and Clarify Ambiguity in Written Contract*, 40 A.L.R.3d 1384, 1396 (1990).

[19] 558 So. 2d 404 (Fla. 1990).

[20] *Id.* at 406.

[21] *Id.*

[22] *Id.* at 406–07.

[23] Henry Yamanishi v. Bleily & Collishaw, Inc., 29 Cal. App. 3d 457, 463, 105 Cal. Rptr. 580 (1972); Cal. Civ. Code § 1654 (West 1970).

[24] W.H. Page, The Law of Contracts § 2100 (2d ed. 1920).

In matters of interpretation, however, the breadth of this statement may be limited by a court's concern with the risk of forfeiture. The policy regarding risk of forfeiture holds that when a party has substantially performed its obligations under a contract, the party should not be asked to forgo compensation for its labor unless it is clear the party assumed that risk.[25] The law of contracts finds forfeiture abhorrent. Most contractors are familiar with the customer who refused to pay anything because the "living room is a foot too narrow or the house is five feet too far back on the lot, or the pipe in the walls is not the brand specified" when the contract called for full conformance with the specifications.[26] Not only would it be inequitable to leave the contractor with nothing for its efforts, but also it would be an economic waste of resources to force the contractor to rebuild the house.[27] A variation of this rationale is carried into interpretation of pay when paid clauses. Courts have noted that "a contract will not be construed so as to place one party at the mercy of another," and that "[c]ourts should avoid an interpretation which will make a contract 'unusual, extraordinary, harsh, unjust or inequitable.'"[28]

The inequity resulting from pay when paid clauses arises because the subcontractor is at the mercy of payment by the owner to the prime contractor. If the owner does not pay, and the subcontractor has substantially performed its own contractual duties, a forfeiture may result. In the absence of a clear provision in the contract, uncontroverted by evidence that may be extrinsic to the contract itself, the modern trend of authority is to construe a pay when paid clause as merely fixing the time for payment by the prime contractor to the subcontractor and not as an absolute condition precedent to the contractor's duty to pay.[29]

A court's interpretation of a pay when paid clause as either a requirement that payment be made by the owner as a condition precedent to the prime contractor's duty to pay the subcontractor, or a provision calling for

---

[25] A. Farnsworth, Contracts § 8.4 (1982).

[26] G. Schaber & C. Rohwer, Contracts in a Nutshell § 156 (3d ed. 1990).

[27] Id.

[28] Henry Yamanishi v. Bleily & Collishaw, Inc., 29 Cal. App. 3d 457, 463, 105 Cal. Rptr. 580, 583 (1972).

[29] Peacock Constr. Co., Inc. v. Modern Air Conditioning, 353 So. 2d 840 (Fla. 1977); OBS Co. v. Pace Constr. Corp., 558 So. 2d 404 (Fla. 1990); Bentley Constr. Dev. & Eng'g Inc. v. All Phase Elec. & Maintenance, Inc., 562 So. 2d 800 (Fla. Dist. Ct. App. 1990); A.J. Wolfe Co. v. Baltimore Contractors, Inc., 355 Mass. 361, 244 N.E.2d 717 (1969); Thos. J. Dyer Co. v. Bishop Int'l Eng'g Co., 303 F.2d 655 (6th Cir. 1962); Henry Yamanishi v. Bleily & Collishaw, Inc., 29 Cal. App. 3d 457, 105 Cal. Rptr. 580 (1972); Action Interiors, Inc. v. Component Assembly Sys., 144 A.D.2d 606, 535 N.Y.S.2d 55 (1988); Schuler-Haas Elec. Corp. v. Aetna Casualty & Sur. Co., 49 A.D.2d 60, 371 N.Y.S.2d 207 (1975), aff'd, 40 N.Y.2d 883, 357 N.E.2d 1003, 389 N.Y.S.2d 348 (1976); Sturdy Concrete Corp. v. NAB Constr. Corp., 65 A.D.2d 262, 411 N.Y.S.2d 637 (1978).

payment at the time of performance or a reasonable time thereafter, often turns on subtle circumstantial and semantic distinctions. Although an appreciation of the distinctions is essential for drafting and litigation purposes, the process is incomplete without understanding the fundamental policies that shape the judicial interpretations of the pay when paid clause. Because each of the judicial approaches is sound in its own right, the extent to which a pay when paid clause may be enforced as a condition precedent will largely reflect the policy justification adopted by a court in giving or not giving effect to a particular pay when paid provision.

§ 19.5 —Minority Rule

Prior to the early 1960s, courts usually adhered to the doctrine that "freedom of contract generally requires that the parties' agreement be honored even if forfeiture results."[30] Although some early case law endeavored to mitigate or avoid the harsh results engendered by forfeiture,[31] for the most part the courts required complete and literal compliance with the pay when paid clause.[32] Sweeping away the sometimes subtle fine distinctions employed by courts to avoid forfeiture, Judge Lehman of the New York Court of Appeals, in *Mascioni v. I.B. Miller, Inc.,* admonished, "Whether the defendant's express promise to pay . . .'if' payment is made by the owner or 'when' such payment is made, 'the result must be the same; since, if the event does not befall, [or time does not arrive], in neither case may performance be expected.'"[33]

The rule enunciated in the *Mascioni* case holds that when an express promise to pay is conditioned on receipt of payment from an owner, a finder of fact may reasonably infer that it was not the intention of the parties that the subcontractor be paid in any event other than payment by the owner to the prime contractor.[34] Today, this view represents the position of a minority of jurisdictions in the United States.[35] Although not explicitly overruling *Mascioni,* New York has since joined the majority approach that bears little

---

[30] A. Farnsworth, Contracts § 8.4 (1982); *see also* Garner v. Edwards, 119 N.C. 566, 26 S.E. 155, 156 (1896).

[31] Nunez v. Dautel, 86 U.S. 560, 562–63 (1873) (holding that literal enforcement of provision providing for payment as soon as certain events occurred would be mockery of justice; finding the clause provided for payment within reasonable time after nonoccurrence of events specified in the clause); Crass v. Scruggs, 115 Ala. 248, 22 So. 81, 82 (1897) (in noting the ambiguity of the clause, court held that the clause created an absolute duty of the contractor to pay the subcontractor within a reasonable time).

[32] Standard Asbestos Mfg. v. Kaiser, 316 Ill. App. 441, 45 N.E.2d 75 (1942).

[33] 261 N.Y. 1, 184 N.E. 473, 473 (1933).

[34] *Id.* at 474.

[35] Peacock Constr. Co. v. Modern Air Conditioning, 353 So. 2d 840, 841–42 (Fla. 1977).

resemblance to the rule applied in the earlier cases interpreting the pay when paid clause.[36]

§ 19.6 —Majority View

The following statement represents the rule for interpreting pay when paid clauses in a majority of states today:[37] "[a]bsent a clear expression to the contrary, a contract provision that payment is not due the subcontractor until the owner has paid the general contractor does not establish a condition precedent for payment but merely fixes the time for payment."[38]

The leading case espousing this view is *Thos. J. Dyer Co. v. Bishop International Engineering Co.*[39] Bishop had contracted with the Kentucky Jockey Club to construct a horse racing track. Bishop, in turn, subcontracted with Dyer to supply plumbing work. The contract between Bishop and Dyer provided that "no part [of the subcontract price] shall be due until five (5) days after Owner shall have paid Contractor."[40] The subcontract had been priced at $115,000 and in mid-August, 1958, Dyer was paid in full for this work after payment had been received by Bishop from the Jockey Club.[41]

At issue in the case was payment for change orders Bishop had placed with Dyer during the course of the job. The value of these change orders amounted to approximately $113,000. After the Jockey Club filed for reorganization under the Federal Bankruptcy Act in December 1959, Dyer sued Bishop for payment.[42]

Bishop and its surety defended primarily through the express provisions of the subcontract's pay when paid clause.[43] The court framed the issue this way:

[W]hether [the pay when paid clause] is to be construed as a conditional promise to pay, enforceable only when and if the condition precedent has taken place, which in the present case has not occurred, or . . . it is to be construed as an unconditional promise to pay with the time of payment

---

[36] Schuler-Haas Elec. Corp. v. Aetna Casualty & Sur. Co., 49 A.D.2d 60, 371 N.Y.S.2d 207 (1975); Sturdy Concrete Corp. v. NAB Constr. Corp., 65 A.D.2d 262, 411 N.Y.S.2d 637 (1978).

[37] Peacock Constr. Co. v. Modern Air Conditioning, 353 So. 2d 840, 841–42 (Fla. 1977).

[38] Action Interiors, Inc. v. Component Assembly Sys., 144 A.D.2d 606, 535 N.Y.S.2d 55, 56 (1988).

[39] 303 F.2d 655 (6th Cir. 1962).

[40] *Id.* at 656.

[41] *Id.* at 657.

[42] *Id.*

[43] *Id.* at 658.

being postponed until the happening of a certain event, or for a reasonable period of time if it develops that such event does not take place.[44]

After reviewing the relevant case law and differing interpretational views of pay when paid clauses, the court held that the payment clause merely postponed Bishop's duty to pay for a reasonable period after work was completed, but not indefinitely.[45] Accordingly, judgment was entered for subcontractor Dyer.

An appreciation of the reasoning employed by the Sixth Circuit is important because courts adhering to the majority view incorporate one form or another of the *Dyer* rationale.[46] The court initially observed that the prime contractor goes into a job with the expectation of being paid in full by the owner. Without such an intention, the prime contractor would not remain in business long. The credit risk of the owner, then, is with the prime contractor. The prime contractor may seek protection in the form of installment payments or through mechanic's liens to reduce its exposure. These measures, the court noted, evidence the intention of the parties that the contractor be paid even though the owner may ultimately become insolvent.[47] In turn, the subcontractor looks primarily to the solvency of the prime contractor and mitigates this primary credit exposure with mechanic's liens.

The *Dyer* court then noted the role of the pay when paid clause. The court reasoned that, because the prime contractor assumed the credit risk of the owner, the effect of the clause was merely to supplement the prime contractor's cash flow on a particular project. The clause operated in this way by postponing payment to the subcontractor for a reasonable period after the subcontractor's work was completed. During the interim period, the prime contractor would seek the opportunity to procure from the owner the funds necessary to pay the subcontractor.[48] In the framework of this analysis, the appellate court concluded that to construe the pay when paid clause as requiring the subcontractor to wait to be paid for an indefinite period until payment was received by the owner would be an "unreasonable construction" of the clause given the parties' intent upon entering the subcontract.[49]

All courts in jurisdictions that follow the majority approach recognize that a prime contractor and a subcontractor may transfer the owner's credit risk to the subcontractor. The only obstacle to the shifting of the risk is that it be contained in an express condition clearly showing this result to be the

---

[44] *Id.* at 659.

[45] Thos. J. Dyer Co. v. Bishop Int'l Eng'g Co., 303 F.2d 655, 661.

[46] *Id.* at 660–61.

[47] *Id.*

[48] *Id.* at 661.

[49] *Id.*

intention of the parties.[50] How express and clear the clause must be in order for a majority view court to find that a prime contractor has no duty to pay the subcontractor in the event of nonpayment by the owner is addressed in §§ 19.7 through 19.9.[51]

§ 19.7 Drafting the Clause

The extent to which a court will interpret a pay when paid clause as requiring payment by the owner as a condition precedent to the prime contractor's duty to pay the subcontractor is guided by the general principles that courts have established in interpreting these clauses.[52] In addition, a review of case law on pay when paid clauses reveals that the clauses that are held to require payment by the owner before any duty on the part of the prime contractor to pay the subcontractor arises share two characteristics.

§ 19.8 —Language Used

First, in conditioning payment to the subcontractor on receipt of payment by the owner, the clause must be worded so that there is no doubt that, in entering the contract with the prime contractor, the subcontractor knowingly accepted the credit risk of the owner. This wording is in accord with the holding of the Court of Appeals for the Sixth Circuit in *Dyer*, which requires such provision, if intended to act as a condition precedent, to express in unequivocal terms the possible insolvency of the owner.[53]

Clauses that do not explicitly allude to owner insolvency also have been upheld as valid conditions precedent.[54] Nevertheless, perhaps a more prudent approach to drafting the clause is to make explicit reference to

---

[50] *Id.;* W.H. Page, The Law of Contracts § 2100 (2d ed. 1920); Peacock Constr. Co. v. Modern Air Conditioning, 353 So. 2d 840 (Fla. 1977).

[51] For a variation of the majority approach, *see* Henry Yamanishi v. Bleily & Collishaw, Inc., 29 Cal. App. 3d 457, 463, 105 Cal. Rptr. 580, 583 (1972). In holding that the pay when paid clause required payment at the time of performance or a reasonable time thereafter, the California court refused to interpret the clause as a condition precedent. The approach taken by the court was to interpret the purpose of the clause as a means to assure that the contractor would not divert funds it received, but rather would faithfully apply the funds to the subcontract.

[52] See §§ 19.5–19.6.

[53] Thos. J. Dyer Co. v. Bishop Int'l Eng'g Co., 303 F.2d 655 (6th Cir. 1962); *see* DEC Elec., Inc. v. Raphael Constr. Corp., 558 So. 2d 427, 428 (Fla. 1990).

[54] *See* Dyser Plumbing Co. v. Ross Plumbing & Heating, Inc., 515 So. 2d 250, 252 (Fla. Dist. Ct. App. 1987).

"condition precedent" and "owner insolvency." The following is a form to consider:

> Payment to the Subcontractor by the Contractor is expressly and entirely conditioned upon the Contractor's receipt of payment from the Owner. It is a condition precedent to the Contractor's duty to pay the Subcontractor that the Contractor must first be paid in full by the Owner. The Subcontractor acknowledges that if the Owner does not pay the Contractor, the Subcontractor has remedies available against the Owner through mechanic's lien laws or other legal procedures.[55]

No Conditions Precedent

By contrast, it is useful to observe those clauses that courts have found not to create conditions precedent. Examples of clauses that were inadequate and so merely gave rise to a duty to pay within a reasonable time after subcontractor's performance, notwithstanding the owner's nonpayment, include:

1. "Subcontractor shall be entitled to receive all progress payments and the final payment within ten working days after contractor receives payment for such from the owner."[56]
2. "[Payment to Subcontractor will be made] within 30 days after the completion of the work included in this subcontract, written acceptance by the architect and full payment therefor by the Owner."[57]
3. "[P]ayment will be made on monthly requisitions for progress payments within 10 days after . . . (the Owner's) payment of such monthly progress payments . . . (has) been received by [Contractor]."[58]
4. "Contractor will pay Subcontractor when full payment for this subcontract is received [by the Contractor] from the Owner."[59]

---

[55] *See* S.M. Siegfried, Introduction to Construction Law § 2.04 (1987); DEC Elec., Inc. v. Raphael Constr. Corp., 558 So. 2d 427, 428 (Fla. 1990).

[56] Bentley Constr. Dev. & Eng'g Inc. v. All Phase Elec. & Maintenance, Inc., 562 So. 2d 800, 802 (Fla. Dist. Ct. App. 1990).

[57] Peacock Constr. Co. v. Modern Air Conditioning, 353 So. 2d 840, 841 (Fla. 1977).

[58] A.J. Wolfe Co. v. Baltimore Contractors, Inc., 355 Mass. 361, 244 N.E.2d 717, 720 (1969).

[59] Schuler-Haas Elec. Corp. v. Aetna Casualty & Sur. Co., 49 A.D.2d 60, 371 N.Y.S.2d 207 (1975); Sturdy Concrete Corp. v. NAB Constr. Corp., 65 A.D.2d 262, 411 N.Y.S.2d 637 (1978).

§ 19.9   —Absence of Ambiguity

The second characteristic of a pay when paid clause that creates a condition precedent to the contractor's duty to pay the subcontractor is the absence of ambiguity. This requirement goes beyond any textual ambiguity within the clause itself and extends to documents that may be referenced elsewhere in the subcontract. Because most courts desire to avoid forfeiture in construction cases, the drafter of the clause should not overlook the effect of incorporating external agreements into the subcontract. The references often arise when terms of the prime contractor-owner contract are incorporated into the subcontract or when the existence of a prime contractor's surety bond referencing subcontractor payment is noted in the contract between the prime contractor and subcontractor.

In *OBS Co. v. Pace Construction Corp.* the subcontract stated that "[f]inal payment shall not become due unless and until the following conditions precedent to Final Payment have been satisfied . . . [plus] receipt of final payment for Subcontractor's work by Contractor from Owner."[60] Standing alone, the clause would probably have been interpreted as requiring a payment to the prime contractor from the owner before the subcontractor was entitled to payment. Although the clause may have been adequate for this purpose, other provisions of the contract incorporated by reference portions of the prime contractor-owner contract.

Because the payment terms of the prime contractor-owner contract were cost-plus, calling for reimbursement of the prime contractor by the owner after the prime contractor's payment to the subcontractor, there was ambiguity with the subcontract's pay when paid provision. Applying the rule of construction that ambiguity would be resolved against the drafter, the court determined the pay when paid clause to fix a reasonable time for payment after the subcontractor performed and not to make payment to the prime contractor a condition precedent to payment to the subcontractor.[61]

In *Schuler-Haas Electric Corp. v. Aetna Casualty & Surety Co.,* the subcontract provided that payment would be made to the subcontractor "when full payment for this subcontract work is received (by the general contractor) from the Owner."[62] The surety bond, on the other hand, authorized suit by a claimant who had not been paid before the expiration of 90 days after the work was performed.[63] Aetna defended against the subcontractor's pay claim on grounds that the bond and contract should be read together and that it was the intent of the parties that payment to the subcontractor would

---

[60] 558 So. 2d 404, 405 (Fla. 1990).

[61] *Id.* at 407.

[62] 49 A.D.2d 60, 371 N.Y.S.2d 207, 209 (1975).

[63] *Id.*

not be triggered until payment was made by the owner. The New York court, citing *Dyer*, [64] held that Aetna was liable to pay the subcontractor and that the subcontract's pay when paid clause merely fixed a time for payment and did not create a condition precedent. [65] The different payment terms between the subcontract and the bond enabled the court to determine that the required clear expression of condition precedent was absent in the case. [66]

The problem posed to the pay when paid clause by external document reference or incorporation can be overcome by care in review and selective incorporation of only those provisions of outside agreements that do not conflict, or otherwise create ambiguity, with the pay when paid clause. A properly drafted merger clause, although not barring the admission of extrinsic evidence in resolving interpretational issues, may provide some evidence that the parties intended to be bound only by the payment terms in their contract, and not by those embodied in any external writing or oral understanding. [67]

---

[64] Thos. J. Dyer Co. v. Bishop Int'l Eng'g Co., 303 F.2d 655 (6th Cir. 1962).

[65] Schuler-Haas Elec. Corp. v. Aetna Casualty & Sur. Co., 49 A.D.2d 60, 371 N.Y.S.2d 207, 211–12 (1975).

[66] *Id.* at 210.

[67] *See* J. White & R. Summers, Uniform Commercial Code §§ 2–23 (3d ed. 1988).

NO DAMAGES FOR DELAY CLAIMS

Robert A. Rubin*

Robert A. Rubin is a partner in the law firm of Postner & Rubin, New York, New York. Mr. Rubin is an attorney in private practice concentrating in construction matters. He is a fellow of the American Society of Civil Engineers, a fellow of the American Bar Foundation, a fellow of the American College of Construction Lawyers, and a member of The Moles. Mr. Rubin received a B.S. in civil engineering from Cornell University and a J.D. from Columbia University.

*The author expresses appreciation to Alison Freed, law student and Note and Comment Editor of the Albany Law Review, for her assistance in the preparation of this chapter.

§ 20.1   Introduction

In an effort to relieve owners of the expense of damages due to delay, many construction contracts contain no damages for delay clauses.[1] Basically, these exculpatory clauses allow owners to escape contractual liability on account of delays caused by the owner, the contractor, or the contractor's agents or employees. In order to provide an outlet to the contractor faced with a strict no damages provision, most contracts that contain the clause also contain a provision providing that the delays to which the no damages clause refers shall be compensated for by an extension of time.[2]

---

[1] Parts of this chapter have been adapted from Postner & Rubin, *New York Construction Law,* to be published by Shepard's/McGraw-Hill in 1992. Reprinted by permission of Shepard's/McGraw-Hill, Inc. All rights reserved.

[2] Annotation, *Validity and Construction of "No Damage" Clause with Respect to Delay in Building or Construction Contract,* 74 A.L.R.3d 187, 200 (1976) [hereinafter Annotation, 74 A.L.R.3d 187].

§ 20.2   Enforceability of No Damages Clause

As the law now stands, as long as the basic requirements for a valid contract are present, no damages clauses are valid and enforceable in most jurisdictions. The legislatures of Washington, Oregon, Colorado, California, Missouri, and Louisiana have either expressly or impliedly declared such clauses to be against public policy.[3]

The difference between jurisdictional approaches lies in how broadly or narrowly each jurisdiction interprets the clause. For example, the Massachusetts courts[4] tend to adhere to a literal reading of the clause and are reluctant to recognize exceptions to the general rule. Other jurisdictions, however, are restrained in their approval of this type of provision because of its harsh implications, and in most cases the clause will be strictly construed against the owner, who is usually the drafter of the clause.[5] In addition, courts tend to hold that clauses containing especially broad language, for example, excusing owners from paying damages resulting from delays occurring "from any cause whatsoever," will not be interpreted literally in all cases.[6] The burden of proof rests on the party wishing to avoid operation of the clause.[7] Each case, however, must be evaluated individually and according to its own particular facts. Nevertheless, because the clauses now are accepted universally and have not been held to be void as against public policy, a contractor cannot simply render meaningless an express condition of a contract that the contractor knowingly and freely agreed to.[8]

Jurisdictions that are wary of the potential injustice the no damages clause may work on the contractor hold the clause subject to various exceptions.[9] These exceptions include delay not provided for in the no damages

---

[3] Wash. Rev. Code § 4.24.360 (1988); Or. Rev. Stat. § 279.063 (1989); Cal. Pub. Cont. Code § 7102 (West 1990); Mo. Ann. Stat. § 34.058 (Vernon 1990); La. Rev. Stat. Ann. § 38:2216 (1990); *see generally* Walker, *Statutory Responses to "No Damage For Delay Clauses,"* 6 Construction Law. No. 3, at 9 (ABA Apr. 1986).

[4] *See* Charles T. Main v. Massachusetts Turnpike Auth., 347 Mass. 154, 196 N.E.2d 821 (1964); Wes-Julian Constr. Corp. v. Commonwealth, 351 Mass. 588, 223 N.E.2d 72 (1967).

[5] *See, e.g.,* **Illinois:** L.K. Comstock & Co., Inc. v. Morse/UBM Joint Venture, 153 Ill. App. 3d 475, 505 N.E.2d 1253 (1987). **Michigan:** Phoenix Contractors, Inc. v. General Motors Corp., 135 Mich. App. 787, 355 N.W.2d 673 (1984). **Ohio:** Carrabine Constr. Co. v. Chrysler Realty Corp., 25 Ohio St. 3d 222, 495 N.E.2d 952 (1986). **Pennsylvania:** Gasparini Excavating Co. v. Pennsylvania Turnpike Comm'n, 409 Pa. 465, 187 A.2d 157 (1963); **Washington:** Christensen Bros. v. State, 90 Wash. 2d 872, 586 P.2d 840 (1978).

[6] Annotation, 74 A.L.R.3d 187, 201 & n.4.

[7] Vanderline Elec. Corp. v. City of Rochester, 54 A.D.2d 155, 388 N.Y.S.2d 388 (1976).

[8] Annotation, 74 A.L.R. 187, 205 & n.70.

[9] *See* Charles T. Main v. Massachusetts Turnpike Auth., 347 Mass. 154, 196 N.E.2d 821 (1964); Wes-Julian Constr. Corp. v. Commonwealth, 351 Mass. 588, 233 N.E.2d 72 (1967).

clause[10] or delay not within the contemplation of the parties;[11] delay due to certain tortious, wrongful, or willful action by the owner,[12] particularly fraud or bad faith;[13] and direct or active interference with the work of the contractor.[14] Some jurisdictions even provide exceptions for delay due to the negligence of the owner,[15] breach of contract,[16] or arbitrary or capricious action,[17] or unreasonable delay by the owner.[18]

§ 20.3   —General Contractors and Subcontractors

General contractors who are faced with no damages clauses in a prime contract often include the clauses in their contracts with subcontractors, either by way of the inclusion of the clause itself, or by a specific incorporation-by-reference of the prime contract's delay damages provisions.[19] Whereas ordinarily the law places the contractor under an obligation to reimburse the subcontractor for all losses resulting from the delays for which the subcontractor is not at fault, the no damages for delay clause of a contract may override the contractor's duty.[20]

§ 20.4   —Government Contracts

No damages clauses found in government contracts are generally governed by the same rules of construction that apply to other contracts, except for the added rule that in the absence of fraud or mistake, the contract entered into by the parties must be upheld no matter how unfair it may be to one side. However, whether the no damages clause applies to a particular situation is still determined by an evaluation of the particular facts of the case, the objectives of the parties, the nature of the delay, and any other circumstances deemed to be of importance in the case.[21]

---

[10] Annotation, 74 A.L.R.3d 187, 201 & n.44.

[11] *Id.* at 201 & n.45.

[12] *Id.* at 201 & n.46.

[13] *Id.* at 201 & n.47.

[14] *Id.* at 201 & n.48.

[15] Annotation, 74 A.L.R.3d 187, 201 & n.49.

[16] *Id.* at 201 & n.50.

[17] *Id.* at 201 & n.51.

[18] *Id.* at 201 & n.52.

[19] Martin Mechanical Corp. v. Mars Assocs., 132 A.D.2d 688, 550 N.Y.S.2d 681 (1990); *see* 13 Am. Jur. 2d *Building & Construction Contracts* § 52 (1964).

[20] Annotation, 74 A.L.R.3d 187, 201 & n.38.

[21] *Id.* at 202 n.54.

§ 20.5   Construction of the Clause

Although courts have the power to construe and interpret contracts when the contract and its provisions are clearly and expressly stated, courts are required to take them as they find them.[22] Courts are constrained from attempting to compensate a businessperson who is the victim of a seemingly one-sided commercial contract.[23] The same applies to a no damages clause. Such clauses should not be rendered meaningless when their objectives are clear. Nevertheless, when a provision of this type is ambiguous, it is open to interpretation.[24]

Clauses containing broad language are especially susceptible to being found ambiguous, but courts have gone both ways in interpreting them.[25] A Virginia court has construed broad no damages clauses as not covering a situation in which the delay was caused by the owner's direct interference with the contractor's work because the clause was found to be ambiguous.[26] On the other hand, a court in New York found that a no damages provision was not ambiguous and that the delays that could have been reasonably foreseen could have been provided for in the contract and therefore the clause was included to cover those delays that were unforeseen.[27] When interpreting the meaning of a no damages clause, the court tends to place great weight on the intent of the parties.[28] Parol evidence may be admitted to assist the court in the interpretation of an ambiguous clause,[29] for example, to prove as a matter of law that a particular cause for delay is not encompassed by a broad no damages clause.[30] In determining the intent of the parties, the court will look to the language of the contract,[31] and the whole contract read in the light of the existing facts with reference to which it was framed.[32]

§ 20.6   —General versus Specific Clauses

No damages for delay clauses may be general or specific. General clauses contain broad exclusionary language and attempt to excuse owners from

---

[22] *Id.* at 207.

[23] *Id.*

[24] *Id.*

[25] Annotation, 74 A.L.R.3d 187, 208.

[26] *Id.* at 208 & n.88.

[27] *Id.* at 208.

[28] *Id.* at 209 & n.95.

[29] *Id.* at 209 & n.96.

[30] Annotation, 74 A.L.R.3d 187, 208 & n.93.

[31] *Id.* at 209 & n.97.

[32] *Id.* at 209 & n.98.

paying delay damages for both contemplated and uncontemplated delays. However, the courts have generally interpreted the general clauses to apply only to contemplated delays. Nevertheless, even when the delay is determined to be contemplated, a contractor may still be entitled to delay damages if the delay was caused by the owner's willful or grossly negligent conduct.

Courts are more lenient in enforcing specific no damages provisions. These clauses prevent the recovery of damages due to specified causes, such the owner's failure to acquire title to the property in a timely manner,[33] the owner's failure to make the work site available in time,[34] or the owner's failure to coordinate work schedules properly.[35] However, a no damages provision cannot be limited by its title of "Delay in Commencing Work" if it is shown that the intent of the parties was for the clause to apply to delays occurring after the performance of the contract has begun as well as delays in the commencement of the work.[36]

§ 20.7 —Typical Clauses

No damages for delay clauses come in a variety of forms. One typical clause appears in Article 13 of the City of New York's public works contract:

> The contractor agrees to make no claim for damages for delay in the performance of this contract occasioned by an act or omission to act of the City or any of its representatives, and agrees that any such claim shall be fully compensated for by an extension of time to complete performance of the work as provided herein.[37]

The City of New York Board of Education has used this clause:

> If the work is delayed by an act or omission of the City or the Board, or for any reason that the City or the Board does not own, or has not obtained possession of, or the right to enter upon, the land upon which the work is to be performed, or because of any act or omission of any employee or agent of the City or of the Board . . . the Board . . . shall then extend the time for

---

[33] See John T. Brady & Co. v. Board of Educ., 222 A.D. 504, 226 N.Y.S. 707 (1928).

[34] Thomason & Perry, Inc. v. State, 38 A.D.2d 609, 326 N.Y.S.2d 246 (1971), aff'd, 30 N.Y.2d 836, 286 N.E.2d 465, 335 N.Y.S.2d 81 (1972).

[35] Id.

[36] Annotation, 74 A.L.R.3d 187, 210.

[37] Corinno Civetta Constr. Corp. v. City of N.Y., 67 N.Y.2d 297, 493 N.E.2d 905, 502 N.Y.S.2d 681, 685 n.1 (1986); Kalisch-Jarcho, Inc. v. City of N.Y., 58 N.Y.2d 377, 448 N.E.2d 413, 461 N.Y.S.2d 746, 747 (1983); Buckley & Co. v. City of N.Y., 121 A.D.2d 933, 505 N.Y.S.2d 140, 142 (1986).

the completion of the work for such period as the Superintendent shall certify that the work has been delayed. No allowance whatsoever, as damages or otherwise, shall be claimed by or made to the contractor because of any such delays.[38]

The North Shore Sanitary District in Illinois has used this clause in their contracts:

The contractor agrees to make no claim for damages for delay in the performance of this Contract occasioned by any act or omission to act of the District or any of its representatives, or because of any injunction which may be brought against the District or its representatives, and agrees that any such claim shall be fully compensated for by an extension of time to complete performance of the work as provided herein.[39]

§ 20.8   Exceptions to Enforcement

When parties negotiate a construction contract containing a no damages for delay clause, it is assumed that the contractor itself will bear the burden of delays resulting from ordinary types of delays.[40] No damages for delay clauses, however, are not an absolute bar to recovery and will not be enforced under all circumstances regardless of the cause of the delay. Courts have held that certain exceptions may prevent the enforcement of the clause. Included among the exceptions are the following:

1. Delays that do not fall within the parameters of the no damages clause[41]
2. Delays not contemplated by the parties[42]
3. Unreasonable delays
4. Delays resulting from wrongful conduct of the owner such as fraud or bad faith
5. Direct or active interference by the owner
6. In some cases, delays caused by the owner's negligence or breach of contract by the owner.[43]

---

[38] John T. Brady & Co. v. Board of Educ., 222 A.D. 504, 505, 226 N.Y.S. 707, 709 (1928).

[39] Bates & Rogers Constr. Corp. v. Greeley & Hanson, 109 Ill. 2d 225, 486 N.E.2d 902 (1985).

[40] Ace Stone, Inc. v. Township of Wayne, 47 N.J. 431, 221 A.2d 515 (1966).

[41] Cauldwell-Wingate Co. v. State, 276 N.Y. 365, 12 N.E.2d 443 (1938); O'Connor v. Smith, 84 Tex. 232, 19 S.W. 168 (1892).

[42] Annotation, 74 A.L.R.3d 187, 224–226 & nn.91–99.

[43] *Id.* at 214.

There have even been cases in which contractors have been able to recover for damages for delays caused by the ignorance and incompetence of engineers in their issuance of unreasonable or unnecessary orders to the contractor.[44]

One of the leading cases in establishing exceptions to enforcement of no damages clauses is *Corinno Civetta Construction Corp. v. City of New York.*[45] In *Corinno Civetta,* a case that comes from the highest court in New York, the Court of Appeals stated:

> Generally, even with such a clause, damages may be recovered for: (1) delays caused by the contractee's bad faith or its willful, malicious, or grossly negligent conduct, (2) uncontemplated delays, (3) delays so unreasonable that they constitute an intentional abandonment of the contract by the contractee, and (4) delays resulting from the contractee's breach of a fundamental obligation of the contract.[46]

The *Corinno Civetta* case seems to expand somewhat the exceptions set forth three years earlier in the well-known New York Court of Appeals case, *Kalisch-Jarcho, Inc. v. City of New York,*[47] in which the court held that a contractor could recover delay damages despite the presence of a no damages clause if the owner's conduct caused the delay and amounted to "active interference." A more recent Connecticut Supreme Court case, *White Oak Corp. v. Department of Transportation,*[48] adopted the reasoning in *Corinno Civetta* and held that a no damages for delay clause, although generally valid and enforceable, is subject to certain exceptions. The court went on to list those exceptions as they appeared in *Corinno Civetta.*

§ 20.9 —Uncontemplated Delay

A no damages clause will not be enforced when it is found that the cause of the delay was not contemplated by the parties at the time the contract was executed. "[C]ontemplation involves only such delays as are reasonably foreseeable, arise from the contractor's work itself during performance, or others specifically mentioned in the contract."[49] In determining whether a

---

[44] *Cf.* Bates & Rogers Constr. Corp. v. Greeley & Hansen, 109 Ill. 2d 225, 486 N.E.2d 902 (1985) (engineers not permitted to invoke no damages clause when they were not parties to the agreement nor third-party beneficiaries).

[45] 67 N.Y.2d 297, 493 N.E.2d 905, 502 N.Y.S.2d 681 (1986).

[46] *Id.* at 682.

[47] 58 N.Y.2d 377, 448 N.E.2d 413, 461 N.Y.S.2d 746 (1983).

[48] 217 Conn. 281, 585 A.2d 1199 (1991).

[49] Peckham Road Co. v. State, 32 A.D.2d 139, 300 N.Y.S.2d 174 (1969), *aff'd,* 28 N.Y.2d 734, 269 N.E.2d 826, 321 N.Y.S.2d 117 (1971).

delay was contemplated, some courts have established an objective test. Courts generally study the agreement itself as well as its relevant clauses and related documents. In addition, the relationship between the parties and their objectives are examined. All of the factors are then viewed in light of the circumstances surrounding the particular case.

If it is found that the delay was one that was contemplated, sometimes the no damages clause is enforced no matter how subjectively implausible it would have seemed to be at the time the contract was signed. Application of the objective test has led to some harsh results. For example, in *John E. Gregory & Sons, Inc. v. A. Guenther & Sons Co.,* [50] the Wisconsin court held that a delay not contemplated by the parties is not necessarily an exception to the enforcement of a no damages for delay clause because the very adoption of the clause shows that the parties can mutually agree to the clause without contemplating in particularity all possible causes for delay. [51] Only those delays that are the result of "unforeseeable" causes are the ones to which the broad language of the no damages clause applies. [52]

Also, in a case arising out of the Court of Special Appeals in Maryland, the court followed what they termed the "literal enforcement approach" as set forth by the Wisconsin case when the Maryland court held that "the 'not contemplated by the parties' exception is not recognized by the courts of this state." [53] The court noted, however, that this reasoning does not apply to the situation in which there is intentional wrongdoing or gross negligence on the part of the owner. [54] Under those facts, a no damages provision would be enforced. [55]

Use of Changed Conditions Clause

Some construction contracts that involve underground work contain a changed conditions clause that provides a method for modifying the contract should additional work be necessary due to "unanticipated subsurface" conditions. [56] Several courts have read the changed conditions clause as an intention by the parties to prepare for the possibility that, although the

---

[50] 147 Wis. 2d 298, 432 N.W.2d 584 (1988).

[51] *Id.*

[52] *Id.*

[53] State Highway Admin. v. Greiner Eng'g Sciences, Inc., 83 Md. App. 621, 577 A.2d 363 (1990).

[54] *Id.*

[55] *Id.*

[56] Buckley & Co. v. City of N.Y., 121 A.D.2d 933, 505 N.Y.S.2d 140 (1986). *See also* Edwin J. Dobson, Jr., Inc. v. State, 218 N.J. Super. 123, 526 A.2d 1150 (App. Div. 1987) (reading the no damages for delay clause and the unchartered obstacle provision together, the court held that the parties intended to bar delay damages even when unchartered obstacles were discovered).

specific conditions themselves may not have been expressly provided for, the parties have implicitly accepted the fact that the conditions may arise.[57]

An illustration of the use of the changed conditions clause is presented in *Buckley & Co. v. City of New York.*[58] Buckley (the contractor) sued the City of New York for delay damages because of the city's improper design of a cofferdam. Originally the cofferdam was supposed to prevent seepage into the excavation site. It proved ineffective, however, causing extensive delays in construction. The court noted that unanticipated subsurface problems were specifically mentioned in the contract. The court stated: "Thus, while the conditions themselves may not have been anticipated, the possibility, however unlikely, of their arising was contemplated and addressed by the parties in their agreement. Plaintiff may not then avoid the bar to delay damages posed by the contract . . . by claiming that the delay was uncontemplated."[59]

One interpretation of the reasoning employed in the case is that it is fallacious, belying a lack of understanding of the construction process. The rationale supporting the inclusion of changed conditions clauses in construction contracts is to induce bidders not to include contingency sums in their bids in order to cover the risk of encountering adverse subsurface conditions.[60] Following the logic of *Buckley,* a contractor should not include a contingency sum in its bid to cover the direct costs of encountering adverse subsurface conditions, but must include a contingency sum in its bid to cover the cost of delay caused by encountering such conditions, an illogical result.

Use of Change Order Clause

A clause with a similar effect is a change order clause. Several courts have ruled that because a change order clause appeared in the contract and provided compensation for extra work required by change orders, all change orders were contemplated by the parties, even ones that delayed the project significantly.[61]

These cases can be seen to be as illogical as the adverse subsurface cases following the *Buckley* rationale. How is a contractor to contemplate how many changes an owner will make and what the impact of those changes will be on the construction schedule?

---

[57] Buckley & Co. v. City of N.Y., 121 A.D.2d 933, 505 N.Y.S.2d 140 (1986).

[58] *Id.*

[59] *Id.* at 142.

[60] Metropolitan Sewerage Comm'n v. R.W. Constr., Inc., 72 Wis. 2d 365, 241 N.W.2d 371 (1976).

[61] Blau Mechanical Corp. v. City of N.Y., 158 A.D.2d 373, 551 N.Y.S.2d 228 (1990).

§ 20.10   —Uncontemplated versus
Contemplated Delay

In *W.L. Waples Co. v. State,*[62] the contractor was responsible for cleaning, painting and waterproofing the State Capitol Building in Albany. The project was delayed for two reasons. First, the state delayed in testing the waterproofing the contractor was to use. Although the contract provided delay damages for delays due to any acts of state authorities, the court found that a reasonable delay was "within the contemplation of the parties" and delay damages were denied. The second delay was caused when the contractor was forced to stop sandblasting procedures because the noise was interfering with a legislative impeachment hearing. The court held that damages were recoverable in this case by the contractor because this type of delay was not contemplated, although it was technically due to an act of state authorities.[63]

Causes of delay that have been held to be uncontemplated include the following:

1. City's delay in securing necessary rights-of-way, thereby causing the plaintiffs' equipment to remain idle, forcing the plaintiffs to complete the project under adverse weather conditions[64]

2. City's failure to obtain excavation permits it was required to obtain by contract[65]

3. General contractor's improper field measurements and faulty grading, paving, and curb work as well as the contractor's disregard for certain subcontract provisions[66]

4. Owner's failure to provide necessary rights-of-way, provide required materials, and furnish bridge plans on time as required by contract[67]

5. Contractee's failure to notify owners of utility facilities to remove or relocate the facilities within a specified time[68]

6. City's delay in procuring a right-of-way to permit the construction of a street[69]

---

[62] W.L. Waples Co. v. State, 178 A.D. 357, 164 N.Y.S. 797 (1917).

[63] *Id.*

[64] McGuire & Hester v. San Francisco, 113 Cal. App. 2d 186, 247 P.2d 934 (1952).

[65] Earthbank Co. v. City of N.Y., 145 Misc. 2d 937, 549 N.Y.S.2d 314 (1989).

[66] Quaker-Empire Constr. Co. v. D.A. Collins Constr. Co., 88 A.D.2d 1043, 452 N.Y.S.2d 692 (1982).

[67] Wilson & English Constr. Co. v. New York Cent. R.R., 240 A.D. 479, 269 N.Y.S. 874 (1934).

[68] Grant Constr. Co. v. Burns, 92 Idaho 408, 443 P.2d 1005 (1968).

[69] Sheehan v. Pittsburgh, 213 Pa. 133, 62 A. 64 (1905).

7. States's failure to furnish temporary heat required by contract so the contractor could work through the winter[70]
8. Defective plans and specifications[71]
9. Occupation of the building and monopolization of the elevator before the building was complete, despite a contract clause providing for pre-completion occupation[72]
10. Work stoppage due to the city's failure to furnish necessary funds to complete the project.[73]

Delays found to have been contemplated include:

1. Cessation of work when contract allowed cessation if it was in the best interests of the city[74]
2. Delays caused by other contractors[75]
3. Delays resulting from the presence of underground power lines when the contractor's duty was to check for underground obstructions[76]
4. State's failure to obtain title to properties when bid documents warned that the state was engaged in eminent domain proceedings[77]
5. Delay caused by hospital operations when the contract stated that the contract work was not to interfere with hospital services[78]
6. Delay in highway construction as the result of the gas company's failure to move a gas line.[79]

§ 20.11 —Active Interference

Most courts will not enforce a no damages provision when the contractee in some part is found to have caused the delay in the contractor's work through

---

[70] De Riso Bros. v. State, 161 Misc. 934, 293 N.Y.S. 436 (Ct. Cl. 1937).

[71] Cauldwell-Wingate Co. v. State, 276 N.Y. 365, 12 N.E.2d 443 (1938).

[72] Seglin-Harrison Constr. Co. v. State, 30 N.Y.S.2d 673 (Ct. Cl. 1943), *modified on other grounds,* 264 A.D. 466, 35 N.Y.S.2d 940 (1944).

[73] Johnson v. City of N.Y., 191 A.D. 205, 181 N.Y.S. 137, *aff'd,* 231 N.Y. 564, 132 N.E. 890 (1920).

[74] Mechanic's Bank v. City of N.Y., 164 A.D. 128, 149 N.Y.S. 784 (1913).

[75] F.N. Lewis Co. v. State, 132 Misc. 688, 230 N.Y.S. 517 (Ct. Cl. 1928).

[76] Davis Constr. Corp. v. County of Suffolk, 149 A.D.2d 404, 539 N.Y.S.2d 757, *appeal denied,* 74 N.Y.2d 615, 549 N.Y.S.2d 960, 549 N.E.2d 151 (1989).

[77] Peckham Road Co. v. State, 32 A.D.2d 139, 300 N.Y.S.2d 174 (1969), *aff'd,* 28 N.Y.2d 734, 269 N.E.2d 826, 321 N.Y.S.2d 117 (1971).

[78] Phoenix Contracting Corp. v. New York City Health & Hosp. Corp., 118 A.D.2d 477, 499 N.Y.S.2d 953 (1986), *appeal denied,* 68 N.Y.2d 606, 498 N.E.2d 151, 506 N.Y.S.2d 1031 (1986).

[79] White Oak Corp. v. Department of Transp., 217 Conn. 281, 585 A.2d 1199 (1991).

"active interference."[80] Interference can be termed direct,[81] active[82] or willful.[83] Active interference requires some affirmative act or combined acts by the owner that are "reprehensible," "unreasonable," and in bad faith.[84] The interference must also be in collusion with or run at cross-purposes to the work of the contractor.[85]

The active interference exception to the enforcement of the no damages for delay clause originates from the uncontemplated delay exception; however, the delay through interference does not have to be uncontemplated for the contractor to recover damages. Many cases discuss both exceptions in the same opinion.[86] Every contract contains an implied obligation that neither party will interfere with the completion of the work. This especially applies to interference by the owner or contractee.[87] Therefore, it follows that any active interference by the owner will be deemed to be not contemplated by the parties and the contractor will not be barred from recovery as a result of the no damages clause.

Active interference requires more than a simple mistake or error in judgment. Bad contract administration,[88] or inaction, faulty work, or lack of complete diligence are not enough to constitute active interference.[89] Active interference is also not found when an owner underestimates the time needed to complete a job or when the owner refuses to grant a contractor an extension of time.[90]

---

[80] Gasparini Excavating Co. v. Pennsylvania Turnpike Comm'n, 409 Pa. 465, 187 A.2d 157 (1963). *See* Wright & Kremers, Inc. v. State, 263 N.Y. 615, 189 N.E. 724 (1934), *modifying,* 238 A.D. 260, 264 N.Y.S. 393 (1983), *as explained in* Shore Bridge Corp. v. State, 186 Misc. 1005, 61 N.Y.S.2d 32, *aff'd,* 271 A.D. 811, 66 N.Y.S.2d 921 (1946).

[81] Grant Constr. Co. v. Burns, 92 Idaho 408, 443 P.2d 1005 (1968); Cauldwell-Wingate Co. v. State, 276 N.Y. 365, 12 N.E.2d 443 (1938); Shore Bridge Corp. v. State, 186 Misc. 1005, 61 N.Y.S.2d 32, *aff'd,* 271 A.D. 811, 66 N.Y.S.2d 921 (1946); Algernon Blair, Inc. v. Norfolk Redevelopment & Hous. Auth., 200 Va. 815, 108 S.E.2d 259 (1959).

[82] Grant Constr. Co. v. Burns, 92 Idaho 408, 443 P.2d 1005 (1968).

[83] Norman Co. v. County of Nassau, 27 A.D.2d 936, 278 N.Y.S.2d 719 (1967), *on remand,* 63 Misc. 2d 965, 314 N.Y.S.2d 44 (1970).

[84] Corinno Civetta Constr. Corp. v. City of N.Y., 67 N.Y.2d 297, 493 N.E.2d 905, 502 N.Y.S.2d 681 (1986).

[85] Cunningham Bros. v. Waterloo, 245 Iowa 659, 117 N.W.2d 46 (1962); Peter Kiewit Sons' Co. v. Iowa S. Utils. Co., 355 F. Supp. 376 (S.D. Iowa 1973).

[86] *See* W.L. Waples Co. v. State, 178 A.D. 357, 164 N.Y.S. 797 (1917).

[87] Shalman v. Board of Educ., 31 A.D.2d 338, 297 N.Y.S.2d 1000 (1969).

[88] Martin Mechanical Corp. v. P.J. Carlin Constr. Co., 132 A.D.2d 688, 518 N.Y.S.2d 166 (1987).

[89] Peter Kiewit Sons' Co. v. Iowa S. Utils. Co., 355 F. Supp. 376 (S.D. Iowa 1973) (holding neglect and delay by other contractors in itself did not constitute active interference by the contractee or engineer).

[90] Taylor-Fichter Steel Constr. Co. v. Niagara Frontier Bridge Comm'n, 261 A.D. 288, 25 N.Y.S.2d 437, *aff'd,* 287 N.Y. 669, 39 N.E.2d 290 (1941).

On the other hand, active interference has been found in the following instances:

1. Owner failed to provide temporary heat on the jobsite when required to by contract[91]

2. Owner occupied and used the building prior to the completion of the work[92]

3. Owner gave another contractor priority in completing its work, thereby preventing the plaintiff contractor from finishing its work on time[93]

4. Order was given to proceed in spite of a delay in other work[94]

5. Misleading plans and specifications were submitted[95]

6. Owner opened the road on which the plaintiff contractor was working so it could be used by other contractors and the nearby college.[96]

Although single acts by themselves sometimes are sufficient in invoking the active interference exception to the enforceability of a no damages clause, at other times several acts combined are required to enforce this exception. A good example of combined acts amounting to active interference is found in *Blake Construction Co. v. C.J. Coakley Co.*[97] In the case, Blake Construction, the general contractor on a major construction project to build a hospital, obtained a bid from Coakley, a subcontractor, for $570,000 for the spray fire-proofing work called for under the contract.[98] Contained in the agreement was a no damages for delay clause that precluded the subcontractor from claiming damages for delays caused by reasons beyond the subcontractor's control.[99] The contract also required Coakley to proceed in its work according to schedules established by Blake, allowing for the possibility that the schedules may be altered occasionally, but provided that Coakley be allowed to request an extension of time under these circumstances.[100] Blake then prepared a Critical Path

---

[91] De Riso Bros. v. State, 161 Misc. 934, 293 N.Y.S. 436 (Ct. Cl. 1937).

[92] Seglin-Harrison Constr. Co. v. State, 30 N.Y.S.2d 673 (Ct. Cl. 1943), *modified other grounds,* 264 A.D. 466, 35 N.Y.S.2d 940 (1944).

[93] Phoenix Contractors, Inc. v. General Motors Corp., 355 N.W.2d 673 (Mich. Ct. App. 1984).

[94] American Bridge Co. v. State, 245 A.D. 535, 283 N.Y.S. 577 (1935).

[95] Cauldwell-Wingate Co. v. State, 276 N.Y. 365, 12 N.E.2d 443, (1938).

[96] Johnson v. State, 5 A.D.2d 919, 172 N.Y.S.2d 41 (1958).

[97] Blake Constr. Co. v. C.J. Coakley Co., 431 A.2d 569 (D.C. 1981).

[98] *Id.* at 571.

[99] *Id.* at 572.

[100] *Id.*

Method (CPM) work progress and sequence plan and gave it to Coakley.[101] That was when the trouble began.

It was soon apparent that the work sequence on the project was taking a different route than that projected by the CPM.[102] Due to delays in the receiving of materials, other subcontractors on the job started either later than planned or before others that they were supposed to follow. The overcrowding of workers and equipment in the work areas resulted in Coakley having to schedule its work during available time in available work areas. This caused work to proceed at an erratic pace. Unfinished walls and roofs allowed rain to enter the building. Because of that and incidents of other subcontractors in striking against sprayed areas, some of the waterproofing that did get done was destroyed.

If that were not bad enough, several of Coakley's workers ended up striking for several months in protest of the unworkable conditions they were forced to endure, including insufficient heat and heaters; when heaters were provided, they were stolen by other subcontractors.

The trial court found no evidence that Blake ever attempted to coordinate the work of the other subcontractors with Coakley's work. Also, although Coakley requested change orders, many orders that were sent never reached Coakley. Finally Coakley stopped its work on the project. Blake responded by stating that Coakley was in breach of contract.

The trial court also determined that:

> Blake did not provide a reasonably clear and convenient work area to Coakley, thus impeding Coakley's work and increasing Coakley's cost of performance; that Blake failed to sequence reasonably the work so as to permit Coakley to perform under the subcontract; and that Blake was remiss in its supervision of its other subcontractors when they were allowed to "steal" space heaters and damage the in-place fireproofing due to Blake's failure to schedule work reasonably; thereby breaching implicit provisions of its subcontract with Coakley.[103]

The District of Columbia Court of Appeals affirmed the trial court's findings and held that the delays involved were not contemplated by the parties to the subcontract and resulted from "conduct amounting to active interference, largely due to Blake's improper work sequencing."[104]

---

[101] 431 A.2d 569, 573 (D.C. App. 1981).

[102] *Id.*

[103] *Id.* at 575.

[104] *Id.* at 579.

§ 20.12 —Unreasonable Delay and Abandonment

Another exception to enforcement of a no damages for delay clause arises when "the delays are so unreasonable as to constitute an intentional abandonment of the contract by the owner."[105] This type of delay can also fall within the previously discussed exception that the delay was not within the contemplation of the parties. The unreasonable delay exception does not unequivocally apply in all instances in which there is unreasonable delay, as no damages clauses do allow for some unreasonable behavior.[106] Also, the fact that a delay was extensive does not in itself justify a finding that the parties had abandoned the contract.[107] Basically, the exception only applies in situations in which delays are so unreasonably lengthy that it is apparent that the owner has completely abandoned the contract with no intent of resuming it.[108]

There have been some cases, however, in which a no damages clause has precluded a claim for damages due to delay even though the act of the contractee in causing the delay was unreasonable.[109] These cases concentrate on the fact that had there not been a no damages clause to begin with, the contractee would be liable for any delays it could have reasonably avoided had it not abandoned the contract, and that the purpose of the no damages clause is to avoid the question of whether delays are reasonable or unreasonable by placing all risk on the contractor.[110]

No bright line rule exists for determining how much time constitutes an unreasonable amount of time. The determination all depends on the particular facts in the case. When a contractor was ordered not to continue work in constructing a sewer line and three manholes until receiving revised plans for manholes, and in the meantime the contractor completed all excavation work necessary and then waited for two months for the revised orders, the court held this to be an unreasonable delay on the part of the contractee because the contractee was aware that the excavation work

---

[105] Corinno Civetta Constr. Corp. v. City of New York, 67 N.Y.2d 297, 309, 493 N.E.2d 905, 502 N.Y.S.2d 681, 686 (1986).

[106] Mack v. State, 122 Misc. 934, 203 N.Y.S. 436 (Ct. Cl. 1937).

[107] F.D. Rich Co. v. Wilmington Hous. Auth., 392 F.2d 841 (3d Cir. 1968).

[108] *Id.;* Kalisch-Jarcho, Inc. v. City of New York, 58 N.Y.2d 377, 448 N.E.2d 413, 461 N.Y.S.2d 746 (1983); Foulke v. New York Consol. R.R., 228 N.Y. 269, 127 N.E. 237 (1920).

[109] Charles I. Hosmer, Inc. v. Commonwealth, 302 Mass. 495, 19 N.E.2d 800 (1939); Coleman Bros. Corp. v. Commonwealth, 307 Mass. 205, 29 N.E.2d 832 (1940); Wes-Julian Constr. Corp. v. Commonwealth, 351 Mass. 588, 223 N.E.2d 72 (1967).

[110] Siefford v. Housing Auth., 192 Neb. 643, 223 N.W.2d 816 (1974); Gherardi v. Board of Educ., 53 N.J. Super. 349, 147 A.2d 535 (1958); Mack v. State, 122 Misc. 86, 202 N.Y.S. 344, *aff'd,* 211 A.D. 825, 206 N.Y.S. 931 (1923); Psaty & Fuhrman, Inc. v. Housing Auth., 76 R.I. 87, 68 A.2d 32 (1949).

would be ruined if it stood unprotected for too long a period of time.[111] When the Board of Education failed to clear structures from a school site for over a year thereby preventing the contractor from commencing work, the court held the delay to be so unreasonable as to strike at the heart of the contract.[112] Similarly, when it took over three years to complete a job that was to take only 120 days, the court held the unreasonable delay exception to apply.[113]

However, when it took two years to remedy a problem that was delaying the contractor, the court found that this was not an unreasonable amount of time.[114] Also, a period of approximately six months, during which time the contractor was prevented from continuing construction of a highway because of the gas utility's failure to move gas lines, was not found to be unreasonable.[115]

Strict Standard

Meeting the "unreasonable delay" can prove to be difficult. Even when other independent prime contractors are involved in the project and are permitted by the owner to proceed at a slow pace and when the owner is not quick to attend to problems causing work slowdown, it cannot be said that there has been unreasonable delay because the work did actually continue and was not abandoned.[116]

An example of this strict standard is reflected in the *Honeywell, Inc. v. City of New York*[117] portions of the *Corinno Civetta* case. In August 1973, Honeywell contracted with the city to install and maintain a complex computer system at the city's sewage treatment plants. The contract called for a completion date of February, 1977. In February 1979, Honeywell terminated its work with unfinished installation work still remaining. Honeywell, hoping to avoid the operation of the contract's no damages for delay clause, sued the city for damages for abandonment and breach of contract and not for damages due to delay. The New York Court of Appeals did not reject this attempt outright; it recognized the abandonment exception to enforcement of a no damages clause and stated that: "[T]o avoid the risk of the exculpatory clause and recover on the ground of abandonment, a contractor must establish that the contractee is responsible for delays which are

---

[111] 74 A.L.R.3d 187, 226 & n.99.

[112] John T. Brady & Co. v. Board of Educ., 222 A.D. 504, 226 N.Y.S. 707 (1928).

[113] Wells & Newton Co. v. Craig, 232 N.Y. 125, 133 N.E. 419 (1921).

[114] Corinno Civetta Constr. v. City of New York, 67 N.Y.2d 297, 493 N.E.2d 905, 502 N.Y.S.2d 681 (1986).

[115] White Oak Corp. v. Department of Transp., 217 Conn. 281, 585 A.2d 1199 (1991).

[116] *Cf.* Wells & Newton Co. v. Craig, 232 N.Y. 125, 133 N.E. 419 (1921).

[117] 67 N.Y.2d 297, 493 N.E.2d 905, 502 N.Y.S.2d 681 (1986).

so unreasonable that they connote a relinquishment of the contract by the contractee with the intention of never resuming it."[118]

Honeywell based its claims on the city's failure to correct wiring problems at two of the sewage plants Honeywell was working on. These problems, caused primarily by another city contractor, were still present when Honeywell walked off the job two years after its original completion date. The wiring problems still existed almost one year after Honeywell left the job, although the city estimated that the problems would be attended to "in the near future." Wiring was finally completed in August, 1979, two and one-half years after the contract's completion date. The court determined that because the city attempted to resolve the wiring problems throughout contract performance and because the contract provided that Honeywell would look to the source of problem (other contractors) and not to the city if Honeywell was damaged because of delays, the claim for delay damages should be denied. The court held that the wiring problems were not uncontemplated; that the city's conduct was not malicious, in bad faith, or grossly negligent or so unreasonable that it connoted abandonment or avoided operation of the no damages clause; and that the city had not breached the contract.[119]

Questionable Result

Following the logic of *Honeywell,* so long as an owner makes some effort, albeit minimal, to continue a project, a contractor will be precluded from claiming abandonment or breach of contract in the face of a no damages for delay clause. Although it is difficult to state with precision just how long a contractor must endure owner-caused delay, under the facts in *Honeywell* two years is well beyond any reasonable limit.

§ 20.13   —Willful or Gross Negligence

Another exception to enforcement of a no damages for delay clause occurs when the delays are caused by the owner's wrongful,[120] willful,[121]

---

[118] Corinno Civetta Constr. Co. v. City of N.Y., 67 N.Y.2d 297, 313, 493 N.E.2d 905, 912, 502 N.Y.S.2d 681, 688 (1986).

[119] *Id.*

[120] Lichter v. Mellon-Stuart Co., 196 F. Supp. 149 (W.D. Pa. 1961), *aff'd,* 305 F.2d 216 (3d Cir. 1962).

[121] Corinno Civetta Constr. Co. v. City of N.Y., 67 N.Y.2d 297, 493 N.E.2d 905, 502 N.Y.S.2d 681 (1986); W.C. James, Inc. v. Phillips Petroleum Co., 347 F. Supp. 381 (D. Colo. 1972), *aff'd,* 485 F.2d 22 (10th Cir. 1973); Anthony P. Miller, Inc. v. Wilmington Hous. Auth., 165 F. Supp. 275 (D. Del. 1958); Southern Gulf Utils., Inc. v. Boca Ciega Sanitary Dist., 238 So. 2d 458 (Fla. Dist. Ct. App. 1970).

deliberate,[122] or arbitrary and capricious[123] conduct or delay due to conduct of the owner that indicates tortious intent.[124] For example, when an owner wrongfully refused the contractor a time extension to complete the work and later wrongfully terminated the entire contract, the contractor was able to recover damages for delay despite the presence of a no damages clause in the contract.[125]

This exception, like the others, is narrowly construed. Not every wrongful act by the contractee will support the use of the willful negligence exception. Delays caused by an owner's poor administration of the contract,[126] or by its failure to coordinate contractors' work to ensure prompt and proper performance by all contractors,[127] or by the city's improper design of a cofferdam and their incorrect assessment of subsurface conditions,[128] or by the Department of Transportation's failure to effectuate timely relocation of gas lines by the gas company[129] are delays that have all been held not to meet the requirements for the willful negligence exception.

The no damages clause itself has been interpreted broadly, thereby further limiting the application of the willful negligence exception. A no damages clause covering damages for delay from any cause in the progress of the work, whether the delay was avoidable or not, exempted the contractee from liability for all delays regardless of fault.[130] Also, the clause has been held to preclude a claim for damages from the result of injunction proceedings, even though the proceedings were the direct result of the fault of the contractee.[131] The courts have even gone so far as to hold that a contractee whose actions were otherwise negligent, unreasonable, or due to indecision, or were arbitrary, willful, and capricious, was still protected by the no damages clause contained in the contract.[132]

Few cases could be found in which an owner's conduct fit the standard required by the willful negligence exception. Nevertheless, the New York

---

[122] *See* Sandel & Lastrapes v. Shreveport, 129 So. 2d 620 (La. Ct. App. 1961).

[123] People *ex rel.* Wells & Newton Co. v. Craig, 232 N.Y. 125, 133 N.E. 419 (1921).

[124] Gherardi v. Board of Educ., 53 N.J. Super. 349, 147 A.2d 535 (1958); Lichter v. Mellon-Stuart Co., 196 F. Supp. 149 (W.D. Pa. 1961), *aff'd,* 305 F.2d 216 (3d Cir. 1962).

[125] Northeast Clackamas County Elec. Coop., Inc. v. Continental Casualty Co., 221 F.2d 329 (9th Cir. 1955).

[126] Novak & Co. v. New York City Hous. Auth., 108 A.D.2d 612, 485 N.Y.S.2d 166 (1987).

[127] Blau Mechanical Corp. v. City of N.Y., 158 A.D.2d 373, 551 N.Y.S.2d 228 (1990).

[128] Buckley & Co. v. City of N.Y., 121 A.D.2d 933, 505 N.Y.S.2d 140 (1986).

[129] White Oak Corp. v. Department of Transp., 217 Conn. 281, 585 A.2d 1199 (1991).

[130] Annotation, 74 A.L.R.3d 187, 218 (citing Anthony P. Miller, Inc. v. Wilmington Hous. Auth., 165 F. Supp. 275 (D. Del. 1958)).

[131] *Id.* (citing Dietrich v. Seattle, 95 Wash. 654, 164 P. 251 (1917)).

[132] Annotation, 74 A.L.R.3d 187, 218 & n.52.

Court of Appeals, in the infamous *Kalisch-Jarcho*[133] case, recognized the willful negligence exception and indicated that gross negligence would be established if, on retrial, the contractor could prove that the city's misconduct caused an extraordinarily lengthy delay, an inordinate amount of drawing revisions, and lack of coordination of contractors. The court stated that if these facts could be proven, the contractor would "have to establish that the city's conduct amounted to gross negligence. . . ," even in the absence of any evidence of malice.[134]

§ 20.14   —Fraud or Bad Faith

Every contract implies good faith and fair dealing between parties.[135] When there is fraud or bad faith, the necessary meeting of the minds is absent. A no damages for delay clause will not be enforced when there has been fraud,[136] concealment or misrepresentation,[137] or bad faith,[138] on the part of the contractee who seeks the benefit of the clause.[139]

Although in most states the fraud or bad faith exception is generally recognized, Massachusetts is unwilling to apply it. In *Marsch v. Southern New England Railroad Corp.,* a contract for the construction of a railroad provided that the railroad would have the right to suspend the contractor's work at any time for an undetermined period of time.[140] The contractor in that case would have no claim for delay damages against the railroad. The court held that the contractor could not recover delay damages from the railroad, even though the railroad delayed the contractor solely for the purpose of harassing and embarrassing the contractor in order to induce the contractor to abandon the project.

Generally, however, the fraud or bad faith exception is accepted by the courts. A contractor won its delay damages claim by alleging that the owner misrepresented that it had obtained a wetland excavation permit, when in fact it had not.[141] Similarly, a contractor avoided dismissal by summary

---

[133] Kalisch-Jarcho, Inc. v. City of New York, 58 N.Y.2d 377, 448 N.E.2d 413, 461 N.Y.S.2d 746 (1983).

[134] *Id.* at 385, 448 N.E.2d at 417, 461 N.Y.S.2d at 750.

[135] Annotation, 74 A.L.R.3d 187.

[136] Anthony P. Miller, Inc. v. Wilmington Hous. Auth., 165 F. Supp. 275 (D. Del. 1958); Cunningham Bros. v. Waterloo, 254 Iowa 659, 117 N.W.2d 46 (1962).

[137] Gherardi v. Board of Educ., 53 N.J. Super. 349, 147 A.2d 535 (1958); Psaty & Fuhrman, Inc. v. Housing Auth., 76 R.I. 87, 68 A.2d 32 (1949).

[138] Peter Kiewit Sons' Co. v. Iowa S. Utils. Co., 355 F. Supp. 376 (S.D. Iowa 1973); Christhilf v. Baltimore, 152 Md. 204, 136 A. 527 (1927).

[139] Annotation, 74 A.L.R.3d 187, 216.

[140] 230 Mass. 483, 120 N.E. 120 (1918).

[141] Earthbank Co. v. City of New York, 145 Misc. 2d 937, 549 N.Y.S.2d 314 (1989).

judgment of its claim by its allegations that the county misrepresented ground water condition, drainage systems, and the presence of underground electrical lines.[142] In addition, the court awarded delay damages to a contractor when the state's engineers misrepresented subsurface conditions causing the state to provide erroneous subsurface information, leading to an increase in excavation time from an estimated three weeks to nearly a year.[143]

§ 20.15   —Breach of Contract

The final exception to enforcement of a no damages for delay provision arises if the delay results from the owner's breach of a fundamental contract obligation.[144] This exception is applied to an "especially narrow range of circumstances."[145] Some cases hold that even a breach of contract by the contractee is not sufficient grounds to override a no damages clause.[146] It has been held that a no damages clause did not apply when the owner breached its contract without justification.[147]

In *Corinno Civetta,* the New York Court of Appeals explained that the reason for such a narrow exception is because the purpose of a no damages clause is to protect the owner from "claims for delay damages resulting from its failure of performance in ordinary, garden variety ways."[148] An example of this set forth by the court is the owner's failure to obtain title to the worksite or to make the site available to the contractor so it can begin its work.[149]

Often, cases allowing for recovery for breach of contract also refer to other recognized exceptions to the enforcement of the no damages clause. Some examples include: when an owner failed to furnish temporary heat as required by contract so that the contractor could work through the

---

[142] J.R Stevenson Corp. v. County of Westchester, 113 A.D.2d 918, 493 N.Y.S.2d 819 (1985).

[143] Cauldwell-Wingate Co. v. State, 276 N.Y. 365, 12 N.E.2d 443 (1938).

[144] Corinno Civetta Constr. Corp. v. City of New York, 67 N.Y.2d 297, 309, 493 N.E.2d 905, 910, 502 N.Y.S.2d 681, 686 (1986). *See* Hawley v. Orange County Flood Control Dist., 211 Cal. App. 2d 708, 27 Cal. Rptr. 478 (1963) (recognizing rule).

[145] Corinno Civetta Constr. Corp. v. City of N.Y., 67 N.Y.2d 297, 312, 493 N.E.2d 905, 912, 502 N.Y.S.2d 681, 688.

[146] Humphreys v. J.B. Michael & Co., 341 S.W.2d 229 (Ky. 1960), *overruled on other grounds in* Foley Constr. Co. v. Ward, 375 S.W.2d 392 (Ky. 1963).

[147] Northeast Clackamas County Elec. Coop., Inc. v. Continental Casualty Co., 221 F.2d 329 (9th Cir. 1955).

[148] Corinno Civetta Constr. Corp. v. City of New York, 67 N.Y.2d 297, 313, 493 N.E.2d 905, 912, 502 N.Y.S.2d 681, 688 (1986).

[149] *Id.; see also* Carlo Bianchi & Co. v. State, 17 A.D.2d 38, 230 N.Y.S.2d 471 (1962), *aff'd,* 28 N.Y.2d 536, 268 N.E.2d 121, 319 N.Y.S.2d 439 (1971).

winter (the court also called this active interference);[150] when an owner failed to obtain a wetland excavation permit (the court also called this misrepresentation and uncontemplated cause of delay);[151] and when an owner failed to obtain the necessary funds for the project, thereby delaying its completion.[152]

§ 20.16   Application of Clause to Contractee-Caused Delay

Although the exceptions to the no damages for delay clause generally apply to acts or omissions of the owner or contractee, many clauses do not associate the delay with a particular person but instead refer to delay resulting "from any cause." Generally courts hold that these clauses apply to acts of the contractee anyway, even if not specifically stated. Nevertheless, one court has held that the clause did not apply to acts of the contractee.[153] The court held that a clause precluding a claim by the contractor for damages resulting from a delay "from any cause," did not include delay caused by the failure of the contractee to perform an express provision in the contract.[154]

§ 20.17   —Delay in Commencement of Work

Some contracts specifically exempt contractees from liability for delays that occur prior to the commencement of work. Sometimes, however, the timing of the delay creates a question as to the coverage of the clause. A provision that the state could delay commencement of the work without liability for damages has been held applicable to delays occurring after, as well as before, commencement of the work.[155] Also, these delay clauses have been held to encompass all delays that occurred in relation to the contract.[156]

On the other hand, some cases have held that a delay occurring early on in the work was not covered by a clause precluding damages for delay "in the progress of work."[157] Conversely, a delay before the work began was

---

[150] De Riso Bros. v. State, 161 Misc. 934, 203 N.Y.S. 436 (Ct. Cl. 1937).

[151] Earthbank Co. v. City of New York, 145 Misc. 2d 937, 549 N.Y.S.2d 314 (1989).

[152] Johnson v. City of New York, 191 A.D. 205, 181 N.Y.S. 137, aff'd, 231 N.Y. 564, 132 N.E. 890 (1920).

[153] McGuire & Hester v. San Francisco, 113 Cal. App. 2d 186, 247 P.2d 934 (1952).

[154] Id.

[155] Charles I. Hosmer, Inc. v. Commonwealth, 302 Mass. 495, 19 N.E.2d 800 (1939).

[156] Nelson v. Eau Claire, 175 Wis. 387, 185 N.W. 168 (1921).

[157] Dallas v. Shortall, 87 S.W.2d 844 (Tex. Civ. App. 1935), rev'd on other grounds, 131 Tex. 368, 114 S.W.2d 536 (1938).

held to be not "during the progress of the work" and therefore not within the operation of the clause.[158]

§ 20.18   Contractor's Perspective

Although courts generally have held that no damages for delay clauses are not violative of public policy,[159] the courts' strict application of the clauses indicates their hesitancy in applying the clauses in just any circumstance in which they happen to appear in a construction contract. Courts' reluctance to enforce the clause no matter what the cause of delay is shown by the existence of the various exceptions to the clause. It is true that, through the use of a no damages clause, an owner may be able to insulate itself from liability that will inevitably arise. Nevertheless, use of the clause can be burdensome to the contractor in the way of increased construction costs from owner-caused delay over which the contractor has no control and which the contractor cannot foresee at the time of the bid.

Construction delay falls into several different categories.[160] **Sections 20.19** through **20.24** discuss the categories and explain why many feel that it is both inequitable and unwise to make the contractor liable for all categories of construction delay. The sections illustrate how the no damages clause works to destabilize construction costs, unnecessarily drive up bid prices, and foster an adversarial relationship between owners and contractors. An evaluation is made of the public's interest in holding the government responsible for its own conduct versus the government's interest in shielding itself from liability via a unilaterally-drafted exculpatory clause.

The discussion then examines the contractor's sole remedy in the case of delays that are covered by the no damages clause—the time extension—and explains how the nature of construction delay renders this so-called remedy inadequate. In addition, a no damages clause is compared with a liquidated damages clause and, finally, the no damages-time extension scheme is compared with other construction contract clauses that seek to establish an equitable allocation of risks.

---

[158] Nelson v. Eau Claire, 175 Wis. 387, 185 N.W. 168 (1921).

[159] Annotation, 74 A.L.R.3d 187, 203 & nn.63–64; *but see* Mo. Rev. Stat. § 34.058 (1990) (The statute states: "Any clause in a public works contract that purports to waive, release, or extinguish the rights of a contractor to recover costs or damages, or obtain delay is caused in whole, or in part, by acts or omissions within the control of the contracting public entity or persons acting on behalf thereof, is against public policy and is void and unenforceable").

[160] *See generally* J. O'Brien, Construction Delay (1976).

§ 20.19   —Types of Delay

Basically, types of delay can be divided into six categories:[161]

1. Contractor-caused delay
2. Inherent (foreseeable) delay
3. Delay caused by act of God
4. Owner-caused delay
5. Delay caused by other contractors on the project
6. Architect-caused delay.

Upon examination of these categories, it appears inequitable to hold the contractor liable for all types of delay listed. Normally the contractor should be liable for Types 1 and 2 because they are delays over which the contractor has control or has some reasonable basis for predicting. It is inappropriate, however, for the owner to hold the contractor liable for delay Types 4, 5, or 6. Instead, the owner should take responsibility in these cases. A Type 3 delay, however, presents a case in which neither the owner or the contractor can control or predict its happening. It would seem logical that in Type 3 situations, each party should bear its own costs; the contractor should receive an extension of time to complete the work but not receive damages from the owner.

§ 20.20   —Adverse Consequences of Clause

When a contract containing a no damages clause is competitively bid, the contractor, in calculating its bid, is forced to increase the contingency factor. Any contract price given by the contractor must take into account foreseeable contingencies such as inclement weather, increased heating costs during winter months, occasional late delivery of materials, among other factors. To the extent that such uncertainties can be foreseen and reasonably quantified, the contractor's bid can reflect their cost. Contractors are in the business of pricing risks and contingencies that the contractors can foresee or can control. When contractors are asked to price risks they cannot foresee or control, the bidding process is turned into a gambling transaction.[162]

Some contractors simply will not engage in the competition when asked to price unforeseeable or uncontrollable risks. These are often the most

---

[161] *See* Vance, *Fully Compensating the Contractor for Delay Damages in Washington Public Works Contracts,* 13 Gonzaga L. Rev. 410, 447 (1978).

[162] *See* J. Reiss, *Kalisch-Jarcho, Its Effect on Construction Industry,* 189 N.Y. L.J. No. 71, at 1 (1983).

desirable contractors from the owner's standpoint, in terms of competence and experience. Among the contractors who do engage in the competition, the winner frequently is the one who will ultimately lose the most money because the winner has taken the biggest gamble and underestimated the risks.

But the real loser in such a transaction is most often the owner. The field of willing contractors has been reduced, frequently by the elimination of the most desirable contractors. The risk of contractor default is increased significantly if delays for which compensation is barred are actually experienced. If contractor default does not occur, certainly the contractor can be expected to try to make up the loss in other ways, such as reduced quality control, increased claims, and general uncooperativeness, often further delaying the project.

Most construction contracts are let through the process of competitive bidding, not through negotiation.[163] Indeed, federal, state, and local authorities often are required to let construction contracts by competitive bidding.[164] It follows that a contractor who is awarded such a contract has no genuine opportunity to negotiate or draft the terms of its agreement.[165] The contractor has no choice but to enter into a contract with an owner who starts off with an unfair advantage.

If a contractor knows that its liability for delays will extend to all types of unforeseeable[166] and unreasonable delays, it will be forced to provide a bigger contingency factor.[167] Professor Justin Sweet argues that the no damages clause will act as a bid inflator. Either contractors will have to increase their bid prices to make up for later losses, or they will make claims for reasons other than delay later on in order to recoup expenses.[168] Because

---

[163] J. Sweet, Legal Aspects of Architecture, Engineering, and the Construction Process 257 (2d ed. 1984).

[164] See, e.g., N.Y. Pub. Bldgs. Law § 8 (McKinney Supp. 1991).

[165] Kendall, *Changed Conditions as Misrepresentation in Government Construction Contracts,* 35 Geo. Wash. L. Rev. 978, 987 (1967). A primary difference between government contracts and commercial contracts is the absence of real negotiation. The contractor may either accept the contract with all its boilerplate or leave it. There is no real give-and-take nor any "meeting of the minds" as to the inclusion of or the meaning of exculpatory language.

[166] See Comment, *No Damage Clauses in Construction Contracts: A Critique,* 53 Wash. L. Rev. 471, 486 n.67 (1978) [hereinafter Critique]. "An owner's negligence, its noncooperation, and its arbitrary changes in the work are not susceptible to reasonable calculation at the time a contractor submits its bid." *Id.*

[167] See id. at 486 n.66. "The unforeseeability of this potential liability puts the contractor in the impossible situation of attempting to include in its bid an extra sum great enough to cover any possible delay damages, yet small enough so as not to sacrifice its competitive edge." *Id. See also,* Nash & Cibinic, *The Changes Clause in Federal Construction Contracts,* 35 Geo. Wash. L. Rev. 906 (1967).

[168] J. Sweet, Legal Aspects of Architecture, Engineering, and the Construction Process 257, 410 (2d ed. 1984).

competitive bidding forces contractors to operate on such a narrow profit margin, the no damages clause wreaks havoc on the bidding process by forcing an increase in bidding contingencies, driving up the owner's cost, at no real benefit to the owner and often to the owner's detriment. In the final analysis, no damages clauses, more often than not, are contrary to the public interest.

Some commentators, in support of no damages clauses in public contracts, argue that it is the public body who is at the mercy of private contractors and that the competitive bidding scheme puts the government at a disadvantage. It is difficult to see how the public body is at the mercy of contractors when the contract documents, drafted by the public body, stack the deck entirely in the public body's favor. Although it is true that competitive bidding requirements limit a public body's choice of contractors, it is difficult to understand why this is a justification for imposition of a no damages clause.

If strictly construed no damages clauses are routinely used by a major contracting entity having a dominant position in a particular geographic area, what can be expected to occur over a period of time is instability of the local construction industry through contractor defaults and large financial losses, a reduced field of willing bidders (often the least qualified or reliable), unnecessarily high bid prices, a multitude of claims and litigation, overall reduced quality of construction, and many projects long delayed in completion.

§ 20.21 —Case for Responsible Government

Enforcing no damages clauses is unwise for another reason: namely, it reduces the incentive of a public owner's employees to resolve job problems expeditiously. Absent a no damages clause, the party responsible for the delay is responsible for the cost. When an owner, particularly a large public owner, has the "benefit" of a no damages clause, the incentive of the owner's employees to respond quickly to construction problems is reduced because the urgency that accompanies responsibility no longer exists.

Private owners function with an ever-present profit motive. The faster a job is completed, usually the greater the profit will be. Employees of private owners are given strong incentives to resolve problems quickly to facilitate project completion. Decision-making authority is often bestowed on field level employees to achieve that end.

By contrast, it often appears that employees of public owners are given strong disincentives to resolve problems quickly and decision-making authority most often resides only in the seniormost administrative levels. The reason appears to be an almost paranoic fear of graft, kickbacks, corruption, and ineptitude in public employees. It sometimes appears that under the guise of protecting the public weal, government officials will spend, in relative order of magnitude, $1,000 to possibly save the $100 that might result from the possible improvidence of a public employee. Checks and balances and administrative red tape often slow to a snail's pace the decision-making process in public works contracting. Another view of the decision-making process in public works projects is that, not only is the objective aimed at protecting the public weal, but also it is directed toward shielding public officials from the embarrassment of scandals arising from possible corruption or improvidence in public works construction.

Whatever the motivation, there often exists a clear distinction between public construction and private construction in relation to the ability and motivation of field level employees to quickly resolve the problems that inevitably arise during construction. In private construction, field level employees generally believe they will be rewarded for making decisions to resolve problems that threaten to hold up progress of the work. In public construction the opposite is generally true; the public employee often feels criticism will result if the employee makes the wrong decision, and efforts will be unnoticed if the employee makes the right decision. Moreover, superiors may second-guess the employee's decision. Making no decision at all is often perceived by the employee to be the best course of action to protect the job and further the career.

Viewed in this context, a no damages clause mainly serves to reinforce the public employee's attitude that no decision is the best course of action, because no decision will not expose the public owner to liability and therefore no decision will further insulate the employee from criticism.

Public policy should enjoin a public body from exculpating itself from its own negligence, breach, or misrepresentation. In *Kalisch-Jarcho*,[169] the court states that one purpose of a no damages clause is "avoidance of vexatious litigation as to whether delays are reasonable or unreasonable or, for that matter, real or fancied."[170] But is not the public's interest in avoiding costly litigation countered by its equally strong interest in holding public officials responsible for their conduct? This is especially true when the public entrusts public funds to these officials. If the exculpation of a public official's breach or negligence results in the squandering of public money, then the clause is clearly counterproductive. At the very least, the clause is imprudent for removing a public body's incentive to perform a contract expeditiously.

Because the clause is not actually negotiated when the contract is competitively bid, the argument against exculpation gains added force. When a

---

[169] Kalisch-Jarcho, Inc. v. City of N.Y., 58 N.Y.2d 377, 448 N.E.2d 413, 561 N.Y.S.2d 746 (1983).

[170] *Id.*

contract is negotiated at arm's length between two parties, whether or not the parties are of relatively equal bargaining power, normally there is less impropriety in an agreement to allocate and assume certain risks. In the case, however, of a competitively-bid public contract, whose terms are unilaterally drawn by the public body and accepted by the contractor on a "take it or leave it" basis, the public body should not be able to dictate its own immunity. Fundamental justice militates against one party to a contract, especially a public entity, insulating itself from liability for its own breaches of contract.

§ 20.22 —Time Extension as Sole Remedy

The no damages clause is patently inequitable in providing that a "time extension" will be the contractor's sole remedy for any delay, especially owner-caused delay. In reality, a time extension is no remedy at all. A contractor's damages in the event of delay are such that an extension of time fails to alleviate such damages.[171] A time extension does allow a contractor to avoid termination for default or an assessment of liquidated damages for late completion; however, this so-called remedy does not acknowledge the fact that almost any delay will render a contractor's performance more expensive.[172] It is consummate chutzpah for an owner to hold out as complete relief to a contractor that the owner will not terminate the contract or assess liquidated damages in the event the contractor is unable to complete the job on time because of owner-caused delay.

---

[171] Professor Sweet cites these examples of delay damage items:
1. Idleness and underemployment of facilities, equipment, and labor
2. Diminished productivity
3. Increased cost and scarcity of labor and materials
4. Utilization of more expensive modes of operation
5. Stopgap work needed to prevent deterioration
6. Shutdown and restarting costs
7. Maintenance
8. Supervision
9. Equipment rentals and cost of handling and moving
10. Site and home office overhead
11. Travel
12. Bond and insurance premiums
13. Interest

J. Sweet, Legal Aspects of Architecture, Engineering, and the Construction Process 257, 410 (2d ed. 1984).

[172] Id.

§ 20.23   —No Damages versus Liquidated Damages

It has been argued that a no damages clause is analogous to a liquidated damages clause, [173] which sets the contractor's damages at zero, in the event of the owner's breach.[174] Liquidated damages clauses are enforceable only if the amount so fixed is a reasonable forecast of just compensation for the harm that is caused by the breach. Therefore, no damages clauses should be unenforceable because they are not reasonable pre-estimates of the harm caused by an owner's breach.

An illustration may be helpful. A contractor's performance is delayed because the owner's plans are defective and require revision. Additional delays result from the owner's insistence that the contractor accept unreasonable schedule changes. Such unreasonable owner-caused delays constitute the breach of two implied warranties: (1) implied warranty of specifications and (2) implied duty not to hinder the contractor.[175] Both of these warranties are enforceable by an action at law for damages. However, when the construction contract contains a no damages clause, the effect of such clause is to fix contractor's recovery in advance of breach at zero. This is clearly unreasonable.

§ 20.24   —Benefit from Other Clauses

Owners and contractors mutually benefit from other construction contract clauses that equitably allocate risks.

It is often the case, at the time of bidding, that the risk of unforeseen subsurface conditions seriously threaten to affect the cost of a project. Such a contingency has the potential to devastate the contractor's time cost structure. Because owners recognize the potential detrimental effects on bids, it has become widespread practice to customarily include differing site conditions (also known as changed conditions) clauses in construction contracts. The now familiar clause provides that, should the contractor encounter unusual subsurface conditions or those differing from information contained in the bid documents, the contractor shall notify the proper authority and be entitled to an "equitable adjustment" in the contract price. Because of these

---

[173] *See* C. McCormick, Damages § 146, at 599 (1935):

> *Liquidated damages* are a sum which a party to a contract agrees to pay or a deposit which he agrees to forfeit, if he breaks some promise, and which, having been arrived at by a good-faith effort to estimate in advance the actual damage which would probably ensue from the breach, are legally recoverable or retainable as agreed damages if the breach occurs.

[174] Critique at 491 (1978).

[175] *Id.* at 493.

provisions, neither the owner nor the bidders must suffer the consequences of attempting to put a price on an unforeseeable contingency.

Absent such a provision for equitable adjustment, the bidder is forced to inflate its bid and an owner is free to avoid the costs of incomplete or inaccurate geotechnical investigations. Thus, the differing site conditions clause averts these consequences and creates a fair allocation of risks, while enforcement of the no damages-time extension scheme serves to inflate bids and foist upon the contractor the risk of delays that are beyond the contractors control and responsibility.

Another useful example, which is not yet as prevalent as the differing site conditions clause, is the "bonus for early completion" coupled with a liquidated sum for each day of unexcused delay beyond the completion date. Should the contractor finish construction before the completion date, it receives a bonus and the owner gets early occupation of the premises or compensation in the event of a delay. The advantages of such a system of incentives and disincentives, by contrast, serves to further illustrate the deficiencies of the no damages clause.

As the changed conditions and bonus for early completion schemes demonstrate, all parties benefit when rights, duties, and risks are equitably distributed. Use of the no damages clause works to diminish and eliminate the benefits and to perpetuate an inefficient and inequitable system that is to the ultimate detriment of owners who embrace such a contracting philosophy.

§ 20.25   Owner's Perspective

There are those however, who believe that no damages for delay clauses are a necessary and positive aspect of a construction contract.[176] **Sections 20.26** through **20.31** are devoted to presenting the arguments for the inclusion of a no damages clause in construction contracts.

§ 20.26   —Public Contracts

Although no damages provisions are frequently employed by private owners, they are particularly important to governmental entities. This is because public entities, unlike private owners, are prevented by law from exercising sound business judgment to protect themselves. Public entities must

---

[176] Parts of this section have been adapted from Grubin, *"No-Damage-For-Delay" Clauses: Fair or Foul—The Owner's Perspective,* 78 Mun. Engineer's J. 1 (1990).

follow certain rules and often must endure much bureaucratic red tape[177] in regard to the public bidding process. Rules require that public entities accept the contractor with the lowest responsible bid,[178] not the one that is the most qualified or the one with the best reputation. As a result, the public contractor is not under pressure to lay the foundation for a good working relationship with its employer in order to establish the possibility for another job. In other words, the contractor has no economic motive to perform as expeditiously as possible to produce high quality work, or to forbear from making countless, frivolous or otherwise, claims for delay. The only requirement needed to get the job the next time is for the contractor to once again be the low bidder. Human nature dictates that if delays are not discouraged by economic or other motivation, they will occur.

§ 20.27 —Policy Bases Underlying Clauses

Several purposes are fulfilled by the use of the no damages clause. Among these are, first, the achievement of fiscal stability and integrity by ensuring that the owner knows at the outset substantially the full cost it will incur on any construction project. In exchange for this certainty and the avoidance of a multitude of claims, the owner is willing to accept, if it must, the possibility of higher bids.

Second, such clauses attempt to deflect vexatious litigation over whether delays were reasonable or unreasonable, or over who was at fault and by how much. Delay cases tend to be time-consuming, which of course leads to high litigation costs. For example, on retrial *Kalisch-Jarcho*[179] took four months and ended in a hung jury.

Third, no damages clauses are intended to protect the public bidding process by ensuring that the "lowest" bid is actually the lowest bid. If contractors take into account the cost of delays in their bid price, they will not later have the need to compensate (by imposing numerous other claims) for the bid they used only to underbid the competitors. Otherwise, if the owner refuses to give in to the frivolous demands of the contractor, absent a no damages clause the contractor may stop or slow down, causing further delays at no additional cost to itself; in fact, the contractor may add a delay claim to its lawsuit for extra work. The contractor also is aware that once in

---

[177] *See, e.g.,* N.Y. Gen. Mun. Law § 101 (McKinney 1986) (The law governing public contracts in New York City, also known as the Wicks Law, requires the city draw up four different sets of plans and hire four different contractors for every job costing more than $50,000).

[178] *See, e.g.,* N.Y. Gen. Mun. Law § 103 (McKinney 1986).

[179] Kalisch-Jarcho, Inc. v. City of N.Y., 58 N.Y.2d 377, 448 N.E.2d 413, 461 N.Y.S.2d 764 (1983).

the midst of the project, the owner will probably not default the contractor, because removal of the contractor from the job will only cause the owner further delays. Additionally, more delays may prompt the contractor to impose yet another claim against the owner.

Finally, perhaps the most important purpose of no damages provisions is the discouragement of delay itself. If a contractor knows that it alone will bear the cost of delay regardless of fault, it may think twice about delaying the job itself and later attempting to extract delay claim money from the owner. The no damages provision provides incentive to all contractors on the job to cooperate with one another in the expeditious completion of the project.

§ 20.28   —Fairness of Enforcement

No damages clauses have been universally upheld as valid and not violative of public policy.

> Practically without exception, a "no damage" clause which exculpates a contractee from liability for damages suffered by a contractor by reason of his being delayed in the performance of his work is held or recognized to be valid, and not void as against public policy. Such a clause, it is said, is now universally accepted as valid and has been upheld as against the claim that it constituted an adhesion contract. Thus, it has been declared that such stipulations are obviously conceived in the public interest in protecting public agencies contracting for large improvements on the basis of fixed appropriations or loan commitments against vexatious litigation based on claims, real or fancied, that the agency has been responsible for unreasonable delays.[180]

In *Kalisch-Jarcho*,[181] the New York Court of Appeals stated "[P]ublic policy is not undermined by a frank recognition of such a perfectly common and acceptable business practice, by which an entrepreneur may provide protection against its own fault."

The applicability of the clause however, is not unlimited. Checks are imposed by courts to prevent the clause's inequitable application. Outer limits are imposed to the circumstances in which the clauses may be enforced. These limits include acts or omissions by the owner that occur through intentional wrongdoing, willful misconduct, fraud, malice, and bad faith. Although these exceptions to the enforcement of the no damages clause exist, they have nothing to do with the intention of the parties upon entering into the contract. They exist because the courts believe that

---

[180] Annotation, 74 A.L.R.3d 187, 203–04.

[181] Kalisch-Jarcho, Inc. v. City of N.Y., 58 N.Y.2d 377, 385, 461 N.Y.S.2d 746, 749, 448 N.E.2d 413, 416 (1983).

enforcement under such circumstances would contravene acceptable notions of morality.[182]

Courts also may find an exception when the delay was not contemplated by the parties at the time they entered into the contract. Contemplated delays generally either (1) are reasonably foreseeable, (2) arise from the contractor's work during performance, or (3) are provided for in the contract.[183] So, a delay may be contemplated without being reasonably foreseeable, for example, if the delay is provided for in the contract. There are cases such as *Buckley,* discussed in § **20.9**, in which the court found that including a clause in the contract such as the one providing for "changed conditions," effectively demonstrates that the parties did contemplate that problems concerning subsurface conditions would arise.

§ 20.29   —Unfairness of Nonenforcement to Honest Contractor

Failure to enforce valid exculpatory provisions provides a competitive advantage to those contractors who attempt to underbid their competitors and then attempt to make up the difference later through unfounded delay claims. This type of behavior virtually encourages litigation. With the enforcement of the no damages clause, valid delay claims such as delays occurring from the willful misconduct of the owner can be heard, while claims made just to supplement the contractor's low bid can be weeded out.

§ 20.30   —Unfairness of Nonenforcement to Contractee

As has been stated, the no damages clause protects the owner from vexatious litigation. Some argue that the owner is at an advantage in perceiving potential delays; however, the statement of the Supreme Court of the United States over 68 years ago still rings true:

> Men who take $1,000,000 contracts for government buildings are neither unsophisticated nor careless. Inexperience and inattention are more likely to be found in other parties to such contracts than the contractors, and the presumption is obvious and strong that the men signing such a contract as

---

[182] *See id.,* 58 N.Y.2d 377, 385, 448 N.E.2d 413, 416, 461 N.Y.S.2d 746, 750 (1983).

[183] Corinno Civetta Constr. Corp. v. City of New York, 67 N.Y.2d 297, 310, 493 N.E.2d 905, 910, 502 N.Y.S.2d 681, 686 (1986); Peckham Road Co. v. State, 32 A.D.2d 139, 141, 300 N.Y.S.2d 174, 176 (3d Dept. 1969), *aff'd,* 28 N.Y.2d 734, 269 N.E.2d 826, 321 N.Y.S.2d 117 (1971).

we have here protected themselves against such delays as are complained of by the higher price exacted for the work.[184]

§ 20.31   —Answers to Arguments Against the Clause

It has been argued that the no damages clause should not be enforced because the clause is not negotiated. However, especially in the case of publicly-bid projects, no contractor is forced to do business with a public entity that supposedly injures the contractor job after job; rather, it is the public agency that must do business with the contractor every time the contractor again submits the "lowest" bid.

Also, the argument is made that no damages clauses seem to elicit higher bids from contractors who claim that with the enforcement of the clause they will be forced to compensate for the inevitable delays that will occur. Nevertheless, contractors must consider other factors in deciding how much to bid. In determining a bid price in the absence of no damages provisions, the contractor must also consider: (1) the expenses of the litigation following most major projects; (2) the size of any judgments or settlements; and (3) the cost to the owner of delayed project acquisition caused by problems that contractors bearing the risk of delays would have avoided. In addition, the enforcement of the no damages clause deprives the claims-conscious contractor of its advantage.

Finally, some say that public policy dictates that there is a strong interest in holding public officials responsible for their conduct. However, lawsuits for delay, which come to fruition years after the conduct complained of has occurred, rarely result in the "responsible" individual being held accountable for anything. When a municipality is sued, trial preparation may take months, or even years. At the same time much money is expended with the cost going to the taxpayer. Most actions end up being settled though, with both sides exchanging releases that declare the mutual recognition by each side that neither side admits of having done anything wrong. People blame public officials for many of the problems that exist in public contracting. If this is the case, the public should not be taxed; instead, new officials should be elected.

§ 20.32   Weighing Both Sides

No damages for delay clauses are conceived in the public interest. They promote the achievement of fiscal stability, the avoidance of endless litigation,

---

[184] Wells Bros. Co. v. United States, 254 U.S. 83, 87 (1920).

the integrity of public bidding, and the discouragement of delay itself. They also prevent those responsible for large government projects from conveying additional public moneys to construction contractors as an alternative to proper job administration.

Existing law makes it clear that no damages provisions are valid and not violative of public policy. They protect the owner from frivolous litigation, and especially benefit the public entity who is not free to choose the parties with whom it does business.

Nevertheless, no damages for delay clauses benefit neither the contractor nor the owner by destabilizing construction costs, unnecessarily driving up bid prices, and fostering litigation and adversarial relationships to the detriment of construction time and quality. In public works, such clauses provide a disincentive to timely and responsible action by public employees in resolving construction problems. Therefore, it is strongly recommended that such no damages clauses be avoided.

CHAPTER 21

SUBCONTRACTOR PERFORMANCE AND DISPUTES

Stephen G. Walker
Ronald L. Shumway
Stephen D. Butler

Stephen G. Walker is senior counsel of the Bechtel Corporation in San Francisco, California, and is a member of the legal department's claims group. He received a degree in civil engineering from the Catholic University of America, followed by a law degree from Duquesne University. He is admitted to the bars of Pennsylvania, New York, and California, and is a registered professional engineer in Pennsylvania. Mr. Walker is a member of the American Bar Association's Forum on the Construction Industry and the Construction Contracts Committee of the American Society of Civil Engineers, the Legal Advisory Committee of the Associated General Contractors of California, and the American Arbitration Association and its Northern California Construction Industry Advisory Committee. He speaks and writes frequently about construction law topics.

Ronald L. Shumway is currently acting as claims counsel in Eurotunnel's London, England, office, seconded there from the Bechtel Legal Department in San Francisco. He is a 1966 graduate of Brigham Young University, and in 1969 received his J.D. degree from the Duke University School of Law. Mr. Shumway is a member of the American Bar Association Forum Committee on the Construction Industry and the Legal Advisory Committee of the Associated General Contractors of California, and speaks frequently on construction topics.

591

Stephen D. Butler is principal counsel in Bechtel Corporation's Legal Department, San Francisco, California. He is head of the Litigation Group and is responsible for managing all of Bechtel's litigation. He is a graduate of the University of Arizona, having received degrees in economics and law. Mr. Butler is a member of the American Bar Association's Forum on the Construction Industry and a member of the Center for Public Resources Construction Industry Task Force. He is also a member of the Construction Industry Panel of Arbitrators of the American Arbitration Association.

§ 21.1   Introduction

The amount of subcontracting involved in a particular project varies from one project to another, depending on the type of project, any restrictions in the prime contract, and the contractor's own capabilities to perform the various work segments. The potential for problems and disputes between contractor and subcontractor easily outweighs that between contractor and owner.

This chapter is devoted to subcontractor performance problems and disputes, bringing together all of the post-contract formation issues between the prime contractor and its subcontractors.[1] Other chapters in the book deal collaterally with many of the topics covered in this chapter, and will be referred to here as appropriate.

PERFORMANCE

§ 21.2   Precontract Performance

In theory, subcontractor performance begins only after execution of the subcontract and pursuant to an agreed schedule. As with the case of owners, occasionally the contractor may encourage a subcontractor to commence work despite the fact that the subcontract may not have been finally negotiated or executed, particularly when the subcontractor is performing some of the early activities critical to a smooth project start.

The implications of an early start on contract formation issues and later contract interpretation problems are covered in **Chapter 6**. Of greater

---

[1] Although this chapter is intended to provide comprehensive treatment of subcontract performance and dispute issues, particularly as seen from the viewpoint of the prime contractor, a recent book in the Wiley Construction Law Library covers the entire subcontracting area and encompasses the subcontractor's position as well. Construction Subcontracting: A Legal Guide for Industry Professionals (Currie et al. eds., John Wiley & Sons 1991).

concern in this chapter is the possibility that the subcontractor will begin performance without a contract. When that happens, essential subcontract terms are uncertain and both parties take on additional, unquantifiable risks.

A contractor may believe that it gains when the subcontractor spends money on performance, thus possibly enhancing the contractor's negotiating position. A subcontractor may believe that it "gets a lock on the job" by being on-site and working. In fact, both parties are right and both parties are wrong. If subcontract negotiations turn sour, the parties ultimately may find out in court that a contract was formed when actual performance had begun, binding both parties to what perhaps is an unsatisfactory deal.

The better view is for the prime contractor to avoid permitting (or encouraging) a subcontractor to begin work before the subcontract is executed. If certain critical work must be started, a short agreement[2] covering the essential points of agreement—the principal risk-sharing clauses—can be made to cover short-term performance. Short-term performance is the key: the work to be performed under the precontract agreement should be defined specifically to avoid the temptation of dawdling too long on the subcontract itself.

§ 21.3   —Enforcing Bonding Requirements

Even when the subcontract has been finalized and executed, certain prerequisites should be fulfilled before the subcontractor is permitted to commence work at the site. If bonds are required by the subcontract, they normally must be furnished before work can begin. This requirement should be strictly enforced because the surety on the bond may refuse to respond to a demand to discharge the unperformed obligations of the subcontractor upon later discovery that work, particularly risky work such as excavation, had already been performed when the bonds were issued.

Other reasons for strict enforcement of bonding requirements are that it emphasizes to the subcontractor the importance of the requirements, minimizes arguments over whether they are required at all, and establishes at an early, critical time whether the subcontractor can actually meet minimal start-up requirements.

When the bonds are received, they should be inspected to make sure that the obligations contained in the documents are consistent with those

---

[2] This is not to be understood as endorsing in any form the "letter of intent" approach. This approach has been (mis)used to allow subcontract performance to begin when the subcontract terms cannot be agreed to in a timely way. Use of letters of intent generally, when disputes arise, simply leads back to the court, where the parties will for the first time learn the contents of their legally-imposed subcontract terms.

contained in the subcontract. Particular note should be made of any exceptions that water down an unconditional obligation to stand behind the subcontractor's payment and performance requirements under the subcontract. Extended notice and "cure" periods for defaults are not uncommon, and can be extremely damaging to a prime contractor when a subcontractor with work on the critical path is in default, but cannot be budged in a timely fashion without losing the all-important performance bond coverage.

The surety on the bond should be investigated if not otherwise known to the contractor to be responsible. A common source of comfort is the United States Treasury's list of bonding companies acceptable on U.S. government projects. Although better than nothing, complete reliance on the Treasury list can be misplaced. The list, published annually, should not be taken as a guarantee of the creditworthiness of listed firms. It does not reflect the insurer's total bonding capacity versus assets nor the surety's reputation for making good on legitimate bond claims.

Like many other reliable sources of information in the construction industry, information about the adequacy of a surety is likely to be informal, that is, from "flesh and blood" sources such as the contractor's own surety company, other contractors, industry organizations, and street talk. Of that lot, the contractor's own surety is generally the best source of information, because of its own exposure to the same risks that the contractor faces. These sources should not be ignored.

§ 21.4   —Obtaining Insurance Certificates

As important as it is to make sure that bonds are furnished prior to beginning work, it is absolutely critical for the contractor to obtain insurance certificates from the subcontractor before work at the site is commenced. The financial consequences to the contractor resulting from an uninsured subcontractor can be many multiples of the loss caused by insufficient bonding.

For example, without correctly-specified insurance coverage, a suit by an adjacent property owner against the owner, the prime contractor, and an uninsured subcontractor for property damage caused by the subcontractor will likely be defended (and probably settled and paid) by the contractor. The majority of subcontractors are small, and do not have the resources to defend or settle significant litigation without insurance coverage. In addition, although in most states a subcontractor who does not provide workers' compensation insurance violates the law, that is little consolation to a contractor who consequently must bear the economic brunt of that obligation.

Some contractors simply file away the insurance certificates upon receipt, a mistake more likely to be made during the flurry of activity surrounding project start-up. The certificates should be examined carefully:

the amount and types of coverage, the expiration dates, the parties included as additional named insureds, and even the name of the insurer.

The insurance certificate is no guarantee that all of the required coverage has actually been provided or that the insurer is reputable. As to the former, the contractor should resolve any doubt by requesting a copy of the policy itself.[3] Regarding the latter, the A.M. Best Company Key Rating Guide reflects the financial responsibility of the listed companies by two types of rating: Classes 1 through 15, and C through A+. Although a Best rating is not an absolute guarantee of solvency or financial responsibility, the industry generally places reliance on the grading system: the higher the class and grade, the more likely that the insurer will be there when the contractor needs it.

As with sureties, informal inquiries around the industry may also be fruitful sources of the reputation of the insurer to respond promptly to legitimate claims. Given the contractor's exposure when a subcontractor works "bare," these sources should be investigated if any doubt exists about the responsibility of the subcontractor's insurer.

§ 21.5   Jobsite Issues

Once performance begins, the adequacy of the contractor's planning and the paperwork and the on-site supervision and contract administration is tested. A project that proceeds with only minor hiccups benefits from good planning and a lot of luck. But most projects have their share of problems that stem as much from the perfectly human failing to perfectly specify the scope of the work and the refusal to apportion risks fairly as from the parties' on-site contentiousness and failure to keep costs within budget.

Given that disputes will undoubtedly arise, early recognition of problems is important to resolving them quickly or, failing that, to preparing for a successful prosecution or defense in a lengthier process of disputes resolution, including litigation as the last resort. Part of that recognition is familiarity with the issues that can arise during performance.

§ 21.6   —Coordinating Flow-Down

Many of the issues that arise during performance are the result of the flow-down of rights and obligations from the prime contract into the subcontract.[4] Thus, very often the rights of the subcontractor under a

---

[3] Resistance to this request from the subcontractor can be minimized by putting the requirement to provide the policy at the contractor's request in the subcontract.

[4] See **Ch. 6**.

subcontract provision are congruent with those the contractor has under the same (if incorporation by reference is used) or similar provision in the prime contract.

It is particularly important that the contractor follow the notice, documentation, and other requirements of the prime contract when such disputes arise to preserve the right to pass subcontractor claims and disputes along to the owner. If the prime contract contains time periods within which notice must be given or information furnished, the subcontractor must furnish that notice or information in time for the contractor to discharge its correlative obligation to the owner within the prime contract's time limits.

§ 21.7   —Interpreting Contract Scope

Probably the most frequent source of contractor-subcontractor problems is the language of the contract itself: its errors, ambiguities, and omissions. To be sure, other motives may impel one of the parties to be more keenly aware of these contract deficiencies: mistakes in the bid, unexpected low productivity, or an unpleasant owner-contractor relationship. But human errors, including those that show up in the preparation of drawings, specifications, and contract documents for a typical construction project, quite naturally lead to finger pointing and disputes.

Although issues will arise under clauses granting specific relief, a well-drafted and properly-administered contract change procedure will be particularly helpful in identifying and resolving disputes as they arise. Because most scope issues arise out of deficiencies in the prime contract documents, it will be particularly important to request timely clarification from the owner's architect or engineer and pass that response back to the subcontractor. If the subcontractor claims that the interpretation requires work outside the scope of the subcontract, notice of this fact can be timely passed along to the owner.

§ 21.8   —Providing Site Access

As the owner owes the contractor a place to work, the contractor owes the subcontractor access to the site sufficient to perform the obligations under the subcontract.[5] Failure to provide access can be total or partial, and can lead to a delay or disruption claim from the subcontractor.[6]

---

[5] Manhattan Fireproofing Co. v. Thatcher & Sons, 38 F. Supp. 749 (E.D.N.Y. 1941).

[6] *Id.*

The contractor needs to be aware of site conditions and requirements and possible obstructions or interferences before entering into the subcontract. When known and applicable to the work of a specific subcontractor, potential site interferences and access limitations should be stated in the subcontract.

If jobsite interferences are not known until performance has started, affected subcontractors should be notified immediately. Early notification helps minimize disruption to the schedule and may provide an opportunity to resequence the work and provide maximum use of available float, thus lessening the chance for unresolvable claims.

§ 21.9 —Coordinating Subcontractors

Another common site problem arises from the contractor's obligation to coordinate the work of the several subcontractors on the site. In the absence of a subcontract clause that exculpates the contractor from liability to a subcontractor who is damaged or delayed by another subcontractor,[7] the contractor will be liable for the consequences of the acts of one subcontractor to another.[8]

A significant and effective tool to help the contractor coordinate the work is a weekly meeting with subcontractors. At this meeting the contractor can review the current schedule with all principal subcontractors and fairly allocate work areas and dictate work sequence that minimizes disruption, if any, on the progress of the work and that of each subcontractor. If conflicts or interferences occur, the contractor can monitor the effects and promptly resolve any ensuing dispute.

Good site supervision and awareness of the potential for conflict will help to anticipate coordination disputes before they arise. When such disputes do arise, the contractor should immediately investigate claims of subcontractors and document them fully. Claims administration will be discussed in §§ **21.24** through **21.26** in more detail.

§ 21.10 —Investigating Differing Site Conditions

Differing subsurface or latent physical conditions at the site of the work may affect a subcontractor's work directly or indirectly. Because of the

---

[7] See **Ch. 6.**

[8] *See* Annotation, Building and Construction Contracts: Prime Contractor's Liability to Subcontractor for Delay in Performance, 16 A.L.R.3d 1252 § 2 (1967 & Supp. 1991). The burden of coordinating subcontractors should remain with the prime contractor as the only party with the authority and contractual protection to carry out that duty. Nevertheless, monumental disclaimers may be sufficient to avoid that responsibility and leave the subcontractors to handle coordination among themselves.

potential for project delay and disruption, these conditions should be investigated immediately when they are discovered. Because they are likely to occur early in the project during foundation and utility excavation, subcontractors who are engaged in this work should be alerted about the importance of early detection during daily and weekly meetings to discuss the work.

It is an unusual differing site condition that does not result in a claim. Even if the prime contract does not contain a clause providing for additional time and compensation resulting from differing site conditions, claims may be brought on the basis of the owner's failure to disclose pre-bid data that would have indicated the conditions, or to reveal superior knowledge about the conditions because of other work the owner might have done in the area.

As with other potential scope changes, notice should be given to the owner promptly upon discovery of a differing site condition, particularly if the prime contract contains a clause granting relief. In addition, the condition needs to be examined thoroughly, and may necessitate the use of a geologist or soils expert, whose credibility will be enhanced if the conditions are observed at the time they are discovered.

§ 21.11   —Handling Delay, Acceleration, and Schedule Issues

Site availability, coordination, and differing site condition problems can lead to delay and disruption, which will affect the prime contractor's direction of the work. The extent of that effect will depend on the seriousness and legitimacy of the reason for the delay, and on the prime contractor's right to pass along the economic consequences of these problems to the owner.

If the subcontract mirrors the relief under the prime contract, then the latter must be examined to determine what direction the contractor must give the subcontractor. If a clause in the prime contract bars time extensions for all but "unusually severe weather," a subcontractor's request for additional time because normal rainfall made the site unaccessible will be denied. But if the subcontractor replies that the failure of the contractor to coordinate other subcontractors prevented the building from being closed in (and thus making weather irrelevant), the contractor will look to the subcontract itself to see whether it limits the subcontractor's remedy to a claim directly against the responsible subcontractors.

Most prime contractor-subcontractor time and schedule issues involve the prime contract. Assuming proper flow-down of all time-related clauses, the prime contract will dictate the direction to be given to subcontractors concerning their rights to time extensions and damages. Only when the subcontract is more restrictive (or, unthinkably, more liberal), or when the contractor's own actions cause delay, will the subcontract alone determine the contractor's direction to the subcontractor.

A few words should be said about schedule. **Chapter 6** counseled against the use of two schedules, that is, one submitted to the owner and a more aggressive schedule to be shown only to subcontractors. A contractor may do this to ensure that a sluggish subcontractor meets the "real" schedule, or perhaps to earn an early completion bonus. Although both of these objectives are valid, the risk is that a compensable delay to the subcontractor's critical path may not be a critical path delay on the schedule submitted to the owner. Thus this deviousness earns the contractor the right to pay for delay damages to the subcontractor despite the fact that the damages are unrecoverable from the owner. The problem is compounded, of course, when multiple (and different) subcontractor schedules are used.

The best policy is for the prime contractor to maintain a single uniform schedule for the owner and all subtrades. Strict enforcement of this schedule with each trade by invoking contractual remedies for delay or by sharing bonuses for early completion will avoid incurring unrecoverable delay damages.[9]

§ 21.12   Suspicion of Default

Most jobsite disputes deal with disagreements concerning someone's scope of work or entitlement to relief under a specific clause. During most of these disputes the work goes on while occasional threats of stopping the work (by the subcontractor) or of defaulting the subcontractor's performance (by the contractor) may punctuate the controversy. Certain events, however, are the first indicators of much more serious problems.

§ 21.13   —Indicators of Problems

The first indication of a subcontractor's potential default might be a call to the prime contractor from an equipment lessor, material supplier, or lower-tier subcontractor of the subcontractor, complaining of nonpayment for labor, material, or other services supplied to the project. The subcontractor's likely response will be either that the amount demanded or the quality of the services are in dispute, or perhaps, in a moment of extreme candor, an admission of "temporary" cash flow problems.

---

[9] The temptation to insert a no damages for delay clause in the subcontract should be avoided, as the enforceability of these clauses in the face of delays caused by the owner or the contractor is questionable. See **Ch. 20.**

Although the latter response should be an immediate cause for concern, the real alarm often is not sounded until several such calls or letters are received. By then the subcontractor will have declined further until, in the extreme case, bankruptcy protection from creditors is sought under Chapter 11 of the Bankruptcy Code (attempting to restructure the business) or under Chapter 7 (asking for liquidation of the business).

The effects of bankruptcy are discussed further in § 21.22. Short of that, what should the contractor do when faced with a financially-strapped subcontractor?

§ 21.14   —Remedies to Consider

Although throwing the subcontractor off the project incident to a default is one possible alternative, it may not be the best one if the subcontractor is still able to perform the work (and particularly if changing subcontractors would cause intolerable delay and other performance problems).[10] Instead, other remedies should be explored to minimize the contractor's already-existing exposure to mechanic's lien and payment bond claims, and yet obtain the benefit of the subcontractor's continued performance.

Most of the remedies are reviewed in **Chapter 6** from the viewpoint of a contractor who is considering what security should be required to assure the subcontractor's performance. Those sections should be read in conjunction with the discussion that follows.

It is difficult at best to obtain bonding after performance has commenced. It becomes virtually impossible after a subcontractor has evidenced problems that suggest the unavailability of assets that a surety would be expected to rely on as its own security for guaranteeing the subcontractor's performance. Consequently, bonding is almost never a realistic remedy for a contractor concerned about a financially-shaky subcontractor.

Other forms of security discussed in **Chapter 6** should be met with similar pessimism. A letter of credit, like a bond, depends on the subcontractor's creditworthiness. Real or personal property that otherwise might be available as security probably is already encumbered by mortgages or security interests.

Nevertheless, the occasional miracle rescue may turn up. It is not unknown for a financially-sound parent company or the subcontractor to appear on the scene and provide a guarantee covering subcontractor obligations. In the same sense, banks finding themselves suddenly owning a subcontractor may offer a letter of credit to the prime contractor so as to keep the payments flowing under a (profitable only) subcontract.

---

[10] Termination for default is discussed in § 21.28.

Even without a miracle rescue, the prime contractor is well-advised to begin acting like a creditor of the subcontractor. Inquiry into the availability of real or personal property assets should be made. Organizations exist that will search the records in any state to determine whether and to what extent the subcontractor's assets are encumbered, at least those evidenced by public filing.[11]

The most fruitful source of prime contractor protection against further default of a struggling subcontractor will likely be financial controls. **Chapter 6** cautioned against increasing retention as a mechanism to provide additional security to the prime contractor. However, because the contractor's biggest exposure is to unpaid creditors of the subcontractor, payments to suppliers and lower-tier subcontractors controlled by the prime contractor can often help minimize claims from those parties.

Controlling payments means making sure that those who are potential claimants against the contractor are paid out of payments to be made by the contractor to the subcontractor.[12] Releases from each of these parties should be obtained no later than the time of payment (preferably no earlier than the previous payment, but further back in time if the facts require).[13] Joint checks are another method of making sure that payment is directed to potential claimants.[14]

---

[11] One type of security not necessarily in the public domain is a general assignment given to a financial institution covering all accounts receivable of the subcontractor. This is why a contractor may receive a notice from a bank requesting that all further payments to a subcontractor (who made such an assignment to the bank) be sent directly to the bank.

[12] Subcontractors, sub-subcontractors, labor, and suppliers of the subcontractor may have rights to payment under the payment bond furnished by the contractor to the owner or conferred under state or federal law. See §§ **21.18–21.21; Ch. 6.**

[13] It is common practice to require such waivers prior to making the payment covered by the waivers. However, some states recognize the effectiveness of such waivers only when payment is actually received by the party granting the waiver. *See, e.g.,* Cal. Civ. Code § 3262 (Deering 1984 & Supp. 1991).

[14] Even these methods are not foolproof, and the jurisdictions vary as to whether lower-tier subcontractors and suppliers are bound by joint checks or releases given under one of these methods. As an example of law favorable to the joint check procedure, Yoder v. Post Bros. Constr. Co., 20 Cal. 3d 1, 569 P.2d 133, 141 Cal. Rptr. 28 (1977), extended to multiple suppliers (and presumably sub-subcontractors) the California rule that a joint check payable to a subcontractor and its supplier, when endorsed by the supplier, discharges the prime contractor's obligation to the supplier. On the other hand, liability can attach even if net payroll checks are paid jointly to the subcontractor and the individual employees. *See* 26 U.S.C.A. § 3505 (West 1989 & Supp. 1991). In Deer v. United States, 498 F. Supp. 337 (W.D. Wis. 1980), the contractor was held liable for unpaid withholding taxes resulting from the use of this procedure, even though the checks were given to the subcontractor for distribution.

CLAIMS BETWEEN PARTIES

§ 21.15   Claims of Subcontractors, Suppliers, and Others

As the night follows the day, so will claims arise on construction projects in today's environment. As with jobsite difficulties, claims can be better handled when they are anticipated and when, accordingly, both the jobsite and home office staffs are equipped to handle them.

Fortunately, the general rules with respect to claims administration and disputes between the general contractor and the owner[15] apply equally to disputes between the prime contractor and those below the prime contractor in the contracting process. However, the bases for entitlement in the latter category of disputes are often different because of differences both in contract language and applicable law.[16]

§ 21.16   Contractual Bases of Entitlement

Most construction contract disputes involve the prime contractor and those with a direct contractual relationship with the prime contractor. Occasionally, contractual rights may arise in more remote parties. For example, a lower-tier subcontractor or supplier might take advantage of a clause flowed down from the subcontract that states that money paid by the prime contractor to the subcontractor for work performed is expressly for the benefit of those who supply labor and material to the subcontractor for the work.[17] A prime contractor might make promises to lower-tier subcontractors or suppliers or otherwise engage in conduct that confers a right in those parties to receive payment directly from the prime contractor.[18]

Entitlement based on contract is evaluated, of course, by reviewing the contract clauses that relate to the relief sought.[19] In addition, however, implied obligations arise that cannot be determined from the subcontract

---

[15] See **Chs. 15–16**.

[16] Claims by suppliers are dealt with in **Ch. 18**. However, claims against a general contractor by suppliers of a subcontractor will be addressed in this chapter.

[17] *See* United States *ex rel.* Hargis v. Maryland Casualty Co., 64 F. Supp. 522 (S.D. Cal. 1946).

[18] *Id.;* United States *ex rel.* Greenwald Indus. Prods. Co. v. Barlows Commercial Constr. Co., 567 F. Supp. 464 (D.D.C. 1983).

[19] Rules of contract interpretation regarding, for example, ambiguities in language are beyond the scope of this chapter. *See, e.g.,* 4 Williston, Contracts §§ 277–325, 696–729 (Law. Co-op. 1979).

itself. For example, a contractor has an implied duty not to interfere with the subcontractor's work, unless otherwise disclaimed by contract.[20]

§ 21.17   Statutory Bases of Entitlement

The federal government and virtually all of the states have legislated relief for subcontractors and others furnishing labor and material on public and private construction projects. Generally speaking, these potential claimants have lien rights on private projects and payment bond protection on public projects. **Sections 21.18** through **21.23** discuss various types of statutes that give rise to payment rights for labor, material, and other creditors.

It sounds elementary, but is often misunderstood even by counsel for lower-tier subcontractors and suppliers, that lien rights (and other statutory equivalents) do not actually improve the merits of the claim being advanced. They merely give access to more solvent parties when merit has been (or will later be) established and the primary debtor is (or may be) insolvent.

§ 21.18   —Miller Act and State Counterparts

The dominant statutory scheme for protection of those furnishing labor and material on public projects is the federal Miller Act.[21] Many states providing similar protection draw their provisions from the Miller Act. These statutes require that a payment bond be furnished by the general contractor for the benefit of certain stated persons. A bond is required as security because public lands are not subject to liens. Generally, the rights of claimants against these bonds are not as broad as those under state mechanic's lien acts.

Under the Miller Act, those who supply labor or material on federal contracts of $25,000 or more are protected to the level of the second tier below the general contractor.[22] In other words, subcontractors, sub-subcontractors, and all others who furnish labor and material directly to a subcontractor may recover for nonpayment by claiming against the payment bond.[23] Disappointed subcontractors and suppliers below this level have no bond rights, and can only proceed directly against the party with whom they have a contract; or against a bond posted by the

---

[20] See **Ch. 6**. Disclaimers are not always effective. See, e.g., **Ch. 20**, which discusses the validity of no damages for delay clauses.

[21] 40 U.S.C.S. §§ 270a–d (Law. Co-op. 1978 & Supp. 1991).

[22] *Id.* § 270b (Law. Co-op. 1978 & Supp. 1991).

[23] The rights of suppliers under a payment bond are discussed in **Ch. 18**.

party with whom they have a contract; or attempt to "create"[24] contractual rights directly against the contractor.

Costs recoverable under the bond are for labor and material used "in the prosecution of the work."[25] Generally, the labor and material must be used on, or must be reasonably intended for use on, the work itself.[26] Tools capable of being used on other projects are not claimable.[27] The cost of leased equipment is recoverable;[28] but capital expenses of owned equipment and the purchase price of new equipment are not.[29] Legal fees are not recoverable unless provided by contract or statute.[30] The cases are split on whether delay damages may be claimed against a Miller Act bond.[31]

Time limits contained in the Miller Act are critical to preserve the rights against the bond. The first deadline is 90 days after the claimant last furnished labor or material for which the claim is made. By that point, written notice of the amount of the claim and the party for whom the work was performed or to whom the material was provided must have been given by registered mail to the general contractor.[32] However, written notice by registered mail is often excused by the court when the contractor has actual notice of the substance and amount of the claim and notice that the claimant intends to seek the remedy of the bond.[33]

If the claimant has not been satisfied by the general contractor or its surety, suit must be brought no later than one year after the date on which the last labor or material was furnished.[34] These time periods overlap for the first 90 days, and thus in most cases the time for filing suit will be less than one year.

---

[24] *See* United States *ex rel.* Hargis v. Maryland Casualty Co., 64 F. Supp. 522 (S.D. Cal. 1946); United States *ex rel.* Greenwald Indus. Prods. Co. v. Barlows Commercial Constr. Co., 567 F. Supp. 464 (D.D.C. 1983).

[25] 40 U.S.C.S. § 270a(2) (Law. Co-op. 1978 & Supp. 1991).

[26] United States *ex rel.* Westinghouse Elec. Supply Co. v. Endebrock-White Co., 275 F.2d 57 (4th Cir. 1960).

[27] Ibex Indus., Inc. v. Coast Line Waterproofing, 563 F. Supp. 1142 (D. Colo. 1983).

[28] United States *ex rel.* Carlisle Constr. Co. v. Coastal Structures, Inc., 689 F. Supp. 1092 (M.D. Fla. 1988).

[29] Ibex Indus., Inc. v. Coast Line Waterproofing, 563 F. Supp. 1142 (D. Colo. 1983).

[30] See **Ch. 6**.

[31] *Pro:* United States *ex rel.* Mariana v. Piracci Constr. Co., 405 F. Supp. 904 (D.D.C. 1975); *contra:* United States *ex rel.* Mobile Premix Concrete, Inc., 515 F. Supp. 512 (D. Colo. 1981).

[32] 40 U.S.C.S. § 270b(a) (Law. Co-op. 1978 & Supp. 1991).

[33] Houston Casualty Ins. Co. v. United States, 217 F.2d 727 (5th Cir. 1954); United States *ex rel.* Greenwald Indus. Prods. Co. v. Barlows Commercial Constr. Co., 567 F. Supp. 464 (D.D.C. 1983).

[34] 40 U.S.C.S. § 270b(b) (Law. Co-op. 1978 & Supp. 1991).

Again, state payment bond rights may vary from each other and from the Miller Act, and local counsel should be consulted in each.

§ 21.19   —Davis-Bacon Act and State Counterparts

The Davis-Bacon Act insures the payment of prevailing wages to any craftsman working on a federal project.[35] The method by which wages are determined as "prevailing" is determined by a statutory formula,[36] but in areas where union labor predominates, the prevailing wage is usually the union rate. Prevailing wages in each geographical area are set by the Secretary of Labor.[37]

Federal law protects any labor on a federal project, regardless of tier, not only as to the base wage rate, but also on health and fringe benefit payments. Labor unions are permitted to act on behalf of their members with respect to the trust funds that they manage, and are frequently prime movers asserting Davis-Bacon rights.

The distinction between coverage under the Miller Act and the Davis-Bacon Act is important. Although the Miller Act provides relief to those within two tiers of the general contractor, the Davis-Bacon Act goes all the way down through the site organization, regardless of tier or distance from the prime contractor, and makes the prime contractor responsible for substandard wages paid by subcontractors at all levels.[38] Consequently, claims may come from remote sources well down in the subcontracting chain.

The Davis-Bacon Act protects those furnishing labor "directly upon the site of the work."[39] This term includes sites proximate to the work and dedicated solely to the project.[40] Thus labor performed at a concrete batch plant established near the site of the work to produce concrete for the project is covered under the Act.[41]

---

[35] *Id.* § 276a.

[36] *Id.* § 276a(b).

[37] *Id.*

[38] *Id.*

[39] *Id.* § 276a(a).

[40] O.G. Sansone Co. v. Dep't of Transp., 55 Cal. App. 3d 434, 127 Cal. Rptr. 799 (1976); Re ATCO Constr., Inc., WAB No. 86-1 (CCH) ¶ 26,901.42 (1986).

[41] Regulations under the Davis-Bacon Act provide as follows:

> [F]abrication plants, mobile factories, batch plants, borrow pits, job headquarters, tool yards, etc., are part of the 'site of the work' provided they are dedicated exclusively, or nearly so, to performance of the contract or project, and are so located in proximity to the actual construction location that it would be reasonable to include them.

29 C.F.R. § 5.2(1)(2) (1991).

§ 21.20   —Mechanic's Lien Statutes

Virtually every state has laws securing payment to those who furnish labor or material on or for private construction projects. The laws vary among the states with respect to the persons and types of costs covered and the notices that must be given before a lien may be filed. Because liberal construction is usually required,[42] local counsel must be consulted unless the contractor is very familiar with the lien laws of the jurisdiction in which the work is being performed.

As with the Miller Act, notice requirements are critical, for a claimant who fails to follow them may lose their protection on what otherwise may be a legitimate claim. For this reason, a contractor who receives a notice of lien or a claim preparatory to the filing of a lien will want to scrutinize carefully whether the requirements of the law have been followed.

§ 21.21   —Other State Statutes

Forms of security other than bonds and liens for suppliers of labor and material may be part of a state's protection mechanisms. For example, in California a claimant on either public or private projects may stop payment to a prime contractor by serving on the owner (and, in the case of private construction, the lending institution) a notice of nonpayment for labor or material.[43] After receiving that notice, the owner must withhold the amount of the claim plus an amount to cover the costs of pursuing the claim.[44] This stop notice must have been preceded by a notice to the contractor that such labor and material is being furnished.[45]

Another example is Massachusetts, where a notice to the owner can result in a direct payment from the owner to the claimant, though the contractor has an opportunity to object to and prevent the payment.[46] Other states may have similar procedures for further protection of those furnishing labor and material.

§ 21.22   —Bankruptcy Act

A trustee in bankruptcy or "debtor in possession" after a bankruptcy filing may initiate an unwelcome quest at some point in the construction claims

---

[42] Cal. Mechanics' Liens and Other Remedies § 1.3 (California Continuing Educ. of the Bar 1988 & Supp. 1990).

[43] Cal. Civ. Code §§ 3158 (private), 3181 (public) (Deering 1986 & Supp. 1991).

[44] Id. §§ 3161 (private), 3186 (public).

[45] Id. §§ 3097 (private), 3098 (public).

[46] Mass. Ann. Laws ch. 30, § 39F (Law. Co-op. 1990 & Supp. 1991).

process.[47] This party comes armed with powers beyond the humble (and insolvent) subcontractor, granted by the Bankruptcy Act.[48]

One of the first communications from the subcontractor's new manager (under Chapter 11) or bankruptcy trustee (under Chapter 7) will be an inquiry about assets or receivables the contractor holds that are the alleged property of the subcontractor. Prime contractor responses and payments to complete the bankrupt subcontractor's work will require careful monitoring and documentation, because one of the letters from the bankrupt subcontractor will demand the entire unpaid balance under the subcontract from the prime contractor. That obviously puts the contractor under the obligation to show that every penny paid out to complete the work and satisfy the bankrupt's unpaid subcontractors and suppliers were properly paid.

It should be apparent that the contractor will have to satisfy claims from subcontractors and suppliers of the bankrupt subcontractor who have lien rights against the contractor or the owner (which become the contractor's because of the prime contract indemnity obligation to the owner). It becomes equally obvious that this contractor should not make payment to those lower tiers who have no lien or other rights against the contractor or the owner, because any gratuitous payments ("we like to keep our lower tiers satisfied") will not count in the bankruptcy proceeding, and will have to be paid a second time to the estate of the bankrupt or reorganized debtor.

Prudence requires consultation with counsel when a subcontractor files for bankruptcy, as there are many wrinkles in bankruptcy practice beyond the scope of this chapter. Nonetheless, a few words of caution are appropriate here.

First and foremost, because the job of a bankruptcy trustee is to collect the assets of the bankrupt and pay debts according to the priority set out in the bankruptcy law, the right of the trustee to the property of the bankrupt is no greater than the right of the bankrupt itself. Accordingly, after the trustee has requested an accounting from the contractor of the assets of the bankrupt subcontractor, the first inquiry that the contractor should make is what property, if any, the contractor holds (paying particular care before describing any sum as "retention"). The proper response to that inquiry often depends on the exact language of the subcontract with respect to the subcontractor's right to payment.

A well-drafted subcontract will entitle a subcontractor to payment for work performed and material supplied only upon assurance or certification that those to whom the subcontractor owes money for such work and

---

[47] See **Ch. 31** for further discussion about bankruptcy considerations.

[48] The bankruptcy law gives the trustee or debtor in possession the power to "reject", that is, quit performing, executory contracts. This power is obviously not invoked when the subcontract is profitable, and is invoked when it is not. 11 U.S.C.S. § 365 (Law. Co-op. 1985 & Supp. 1991).

material have been paid. It is not uncommon for a subcontractor in bankruptcy to have listed as creditors in the bankruptcy filing others on the project who are owed money for labor and material. These creditors, recognizing the limitations of recovery through bankruptcy, are the ones who will seek to enforce their rights against the contractor's bond and other forms of security discussed in §§ **21.16** through **21.21**. Consequently, the contractor will want to use money withheld from the subcontractor, particularly including the retention, to pay the claims of these creditors.

Even if the language of the subcontract is vague, the contractor may be well-advised to consult with counsel about asserting the right of offset, by which any of the subcontractor's money (and unencumbered property, if the subcontract gives the prime contractor the right to take it over to complete the work) can be held and used to satisfy the prime contractor's obligations caused by the subcontractor's bankruptcy and default.

One reasonable (and innocuous) response to the trustee is that, because the work is not yet complete, the final cost (and damage to the prime contractor) cannot be determined until completion of the work. However, under no circumstances should the prime contractor offer to send retention or any other payment to the trustee until the subcontractor's work is completed and all labor and material suppliers have been paid.

Even in the absence of a controlling contractual provision, some state laws impose a trust on payments received by the prime contractor from the owner for the benefit of all those furnishing labor and material on the project.[49] Because this money is in trust, it is not the property of the subcontractor and thus not attachable by a bankruptcy trustee.

§ 21.23   —Internal Revenue Code

The U.S. government occasionally calls on prime contractors regarding amounts due a subcontractor that are held by the prime contractor. The Internal Revenue Service may seek to recover the subcontractor's unpaid taxes and, unlike some third-party claims, tax liens have an absolute priority under the law.[50] However, the rules that apply to the prime contractor's obligation to disgorge payments withheld from the subcontractor are much the same as those applying to the trustee in bankruptcy.

Like other liens, tax liens attach only to "property" of the subcontractor,[51] and retention should not be characterized as such property until all

---

[49] New York is one such state. N.Y. Lien Law § 71 (McKinney 1966 & Supp. 1991).

[50] Even certain previously-secured liens, which do retain some priority status in the face of a tax lien, lose much of their force. 26 U.S.C.S. § 6323 (Law. Co-op. 1991).

[51] 26 U.S.C.S. § 6321 (Law. Co-op. 1991); Slodov v. United States, 436 U.S. 238, 98 S. Ct. 1778 (1978), *on remand,* 579 F.2d 400 (6th Cir. 1978).

possible claims arising out of the subcontractor's work have been satisfied. If the subcontractor is not entitled to the withholding until claims of labor and material suppliers have been paid, or if a right of offset can be asserted, then the government must wait until a final determination is made.[52]

§ 21.24   Administration of Claims

Determination of entitlement is one facet of the claims process; administration of claims is another. Claims may include those solely against the contractor by the subcontractor or lower tiers; by the contractor against the subcontractor; or by the subcontractor through the contractor to the owner. Claims in the last category are often referred to as *pass-through* claims.

§ 21.25   —Pass-Through Claims

Claims from subcontractor (a portion of which may be flowed up from lower tiers) for which responsibility rests, if at all, with the owner are often combined with the contractor's own claims against the owner. A number of steps should be taken both to maximize the opportunity for the subcontractor's recovery and to avoid personal (or sole) liability of the prime contractor for the subcontractor's claim.

Claims often arise after some prolonged dispute, during which at times the parties may be vociferous in stating their respective positions. Excessive finger pointing should be avoided, however, because allegations that may upon later examination prove to be untrue, or that the parties may want to retract for the purpose of providing a united front against the owner, will provide fuel for an owner who obtains the correspondence and memoranda containing these allegations during discovery if litigation ensues.

Another important caveat is to avoid an unconditional release or settlement of a claim that the parties intend to assert against the owner. If the prime contractor has no liability to the subcontractor, then neither will the owner be liable, because the owner has no direct contractual relationship with the subcontractor. Therefore, the contractor must maintain at least an obligation to press the subcontractor's claim and to pay over to the subcontractor money received from the owner, if any, related to the subcontractor's claim.

The contractor should provide support to the subcontractor and the maximum opportunity to be heard by the owner. This will lessen the possibility of a later assertion by the subcontractor that the contractor comprised the subcontractor's right to the owner's full review, an argument that might be

---

[52] *Id.;* Scott v. Zion Evangelical Lutheran Church, 75 S.D. 559, 70 N.W.2d 326 (1955).

persuasive because the subcontractor's only access to the owner for resolution of the claim is through the prime contractor.

Disputes over the procedure to be followed in presenting joint claims to the owner and over the method of determining the ultimate amount due, if any, can be minimized by agreeing in writing in advance of the preparation of the claim. Usually called *liquidating agreements,* the agreements address such matters as the following:

1. Extent of sharing of services, such as legal advice, delay analyses, and claim preparation
2. Timing and method of presentation
3. Approval authority of final claim document and claim settlement offers
4. Manner of apportioning amounts received from the owner, such as pro rata based on respective claim amounts, unless specific allocation to individual claim items is made
5. Amount of contractor markup.

§ 21.26   —Dispute Resolution

A program of contract administration that does not have as its principal goal the resolution of disputes is doomed to failure. Early identification of problems, maintenance of a reasonable, logical, and regularly updated project schedule, prompt investigation and documentation of events and occurrences likely to lead to claims, and a fair and timely procedure for resolving the parties' differences are all essential to a successful dispute resolution program.

Opinions abound as to the best means and methods for ultimate resolution of disputes. In the case of pass-through claims, of course, the owner already has determined in the prime contract how disputes are to be resolved, and it is critical that the subcontract reflect that process for claims that are to be flowed up to the owner. However, for claims solely between the contractor and the subcontractor, the contractor has flexibility in determining how the disputes should be resolved.[53]

---

[53] The prime contract's disputes mechanism and procedures must still be kept in mind when establishing time periods for notices. It is rare that a subcontractor will (or should) know at the outset which claim(s) might be passed through by the prime contractor to the owner, in whole or in part; but failure to give timely notice under the prime contract may make it impossible for the prime contractor to preserve the subcontractor's rights. Therefore, the subcontractor should be required to meet time limits—with luck, backed up by a subcontract provision—that will enable the contractor to comply with the notice provisions of the prime contract.

Regardless of whether litigation or binding arbitration is chosen to ultimately resolve disputes, other less drastic methods should be pursued in advance. A procedure that has found overwhelming success in settling claims is alternative dispute resolution (ADR), discussed in detail in **Chapter 23**. Even if not the subject of a subcontract clause,[54] ADR can be voluntarily implemented at almost any time during the dispute process. It is quick, inexpensive, confidential, and can in many cases restore the parties' business relationship.

Claims arising from statutorily-granted rights[55] are generally against the general contractor or its surety and usually cannot be passed on to the owner. Although claims from lower tiers can often be passed back to the subcontractor, relief may not be forthcoming when the subcontractor's financial problems were the cause of the statutory claim to begin with. Litigation is usually the means provided for resolving statutory claims, but ADR is nonetheless an attractive preliminary step.

TERMINATIONS

§ 21.27   Termination in General

For one reason or other the subcontractor may fail to complete the subcontract, partially or totally. Involuntary incompletion may result from what is often called a termination for convenience—either because the owner (via a flow-down clause from the prime contract) or the contractor has elected to reduce or eliminate the subcontract scope, or because a default termination was later determined to be improper and was converted into a convenience termination.

Most reasons for termination, however, relate to the subcontractor's breach of its obligations under the subcontract, and result in terminations for default. Understandably, a default termination is likely to evoke an emotional and antagonistic response and, as further discussed in § **21.28** should not be undertaken lightly or as a mere threat.

§ 21.28   —Termination for Default

The contractor's entitlement to declare a default termination is often based on a subcontract clause setting forth the grounds for a default. Independent of a contractual basis, however, a contractor has a common law right to terminate a subcontractor's right to perform and recover the resulting

---

[54] See **Ch. 6.**

[55] See § **21.17.**

damages under the subcontract[56] or, in limited cases, to rescind (treat as a nullity) the subcontract and pay the subcontractor the value of the work performed.[57]

The decision to terminate a subcontract for default must be made carefully, requiring a weighing of the benefits to be gained against the possible detriments. The contractor has every reason to use caution. If a court later decides the termination for default was wrongful, the contractor will be fortunate if a subcontract clause converts the default termination into one for convenience (a provision that normally excludes profit on the uncompleted portion of the work). However, if the court applies the "benefit of the bargain" rule to calculate the subcontractor's damages, the contractor may well pay the subcontractor's profit on the portion of the work that the subcontractor was not allowed to complete.[58]

Both the timing and the correctness of the decision must be examined closely. A termination made too early will involve the contractor in needless expense and aggravation, because a subcontractor who has the ability to ultimately complete the subcontract, even with the contractor's increased monitoring and supervision, is often a better choice than a new (and almost always more expensive) subcontractor and the threat of a long and bitter battle defending against the disappointed subcontractor's suit for wrongful termination. A contractor who terminates too late, however, may encounter a powerful adversary in the bankruptcy trustee. The trustee or "debtor in possession" (under a Chapter 11 proceeding) comes into the fray armed with potent court processes that can easily block any action by the contractor that would adversely affect the subcontractor's assets.[59]

In assessing when defaulting a subcontractor might be defensible, remember that few jobsite disputes are so clear as to be without good arguments on both sides. For example, a contractor contemplating a subcontractor default for delay in performance should be reasonably sure that the subcontract provides a basis for the claimed time of performance; that the contractor's schedule is current, accurate as to logic and duration, and

---

[56] Restatement (Second) of Contracts § 253 (1981).

[57] *See* 12 Williston, Contracts § 1455 (1970 & Supp. 1988). This remedy is rarely invoked, as it would require the contractor to pay the subcontractor the value of the work performed. Because rescission treats the contract as if it never existed and creates an independent measure of damages under the law, the contractor is not entitled under this theory to apply the usual contractual offsets to this payment, such as the costs of defective work and reprocurement of the performance remaining under the subcontract.

[58] Restatement (Second) of Contracts §§ 243, 347 (1981).

[59] Once a bankruptcy petition is filed, termination of the subcontract may not result because of the bankruptcy itself. However, termination may be made for the reasons that might have, not coincidentally, given rise to the bankruptcy. Nevertheless, the timing of the default is still critical, and counsel should be consulted in making this decision. 11 U.S.C.S. § 362 (Law. Co-op. 1985 & Supp. 1991).

shows the subcontractor actually behind schedule; and that the subcontractor has no excusable (or, worse yet, compensable) bases for the delay. Hard scrutiny must be made of the reasons for a default termination; the cost of consulting experienced construction counsel is money well spent.

Other practical considerations must be studied carefully, not the least being the financial impact of a termination on the project. Often, little is gained by replacing a subcontractor with hard-to-find expertise. Even if more money must be spent to keep afloat a financially-strapped and un-bonded subcontractor with little hope of recouping the additional expense, in the long run this may be less costly than the delay and extra expense in finding a suitable replacement. The same is true when prime contract commitments involve disadvantaged businesses, or when reprocurement of long lead items (such as structural steel already in process) is involved.

An important distinction must be made between termination of the sub-contract and termination of performance. If the contractor terminates the subcontract, all of the subcontract "dies," including relief-granting clauses and procedures under the subcontract. In the worst case, the subcontractor's common law remedies may be more disadvantageous to the contractor than the subcontract terms. Termination of the subcontract may also bring to an end warranty and indemnity obligations that would otherwise survive the subcontract. Common law obligations vary from state to state (and may be amended statutorily), and may not provide sufficient protection to the contractor.

Termination of performance, on the other hand, has the effect of merely reducing the scope of the work or removing the subcontractor from the jobsite. The contractor can exercise important contract rights, such as taking over the subcontractor's equipment and tools still on the site and completing the work. All of the subcontract provisions still apply and may be enforced.

Once the decision to terminate is made, it is critical to establish a baseline from which the scope of reprocurement can be measured. If a partial termination (though uncommon) is made, then the value of the work deleted will have to be determined.[60] A complete termination, however, requires a careful analysis of the subcontract work completed at the time of termination to minimize later arguments that the costs of reprocurement include additional scope or unreasonable charges—arguments made by suspicious bankers and other creditors of the subcontractor, unfamiliar with construction practices and procedures, who see their precious few attachable assets dwindling.

---

[60] This is essentially a pricing exercise, and has much in common with a deductive change order. In fact, the contractor with a weak case on termination for default and a well-crafted subcontract may be better off using either the changes clause to issue a change order deleting the remainder of the work or the termination for convenience clause.

§ 21.29   —Termination for Convenience

Terminations for convenience are less controversial than default terminations because the reputation and character of the subcontractor is not called
into question, especially when the termination is only partial.[61] Convenience terminations are solely a matter of contract, which sets forth the reasons for which the subcontract may be terminated and the payment to
which the subcontractor is entitled.

Permissible reasons for convenience terminations are usually broad. A
portion of a termination for convenience clause usually flowed down from
federal prime contracts is the following:

> The Government may terminate performance of work under this contract in
> whole or, from time to time, in part if the Contracting Officer determines
> that a termination is in the Government's interest.

The remainder of the clause specifies the duties to be undertaken by the
contractor in terminating the work, the rules and procedure for determining the payment to which the contractor is entitled, and the manner in
which disputes over such payment will be resolved.[62] Although the clause
gives the government (and thus the contractor) wide discretion to terminate, this discretion will not permit termination merely to arbitrarily or
capriciously obtain a replacement contractor or for reasons not related to
legitimate business considerations.[63]

Disputes during convenience terminations almost always revolve around
the amount of final payment. The more strict the payment provisions, the
more likely arguments will develop over entitlement. For example, a clause
that limits recovery to the value of the work in place at the time of termination necessarily ignores legitimate windup costs like demobilization, termination of sub-subcontracts and material suppliers, and equipment or material in fabrication intended for incorporation in the work.

---

[61] Remember that a subcontractor will normally have lenders, insurers, and a bonding
company, the written agreements with which probably require notice of any actual or
alleged defaults in the course of the subcontractor's business. In the extreme (but not at
all unusual) case, an uncured default under any subcontract may also constitute a
default under a bank or other lending agreement, insurance policy, or bonding company
indemnity agreement. This may have the effect of putting the subcontractor in peril of
losing its line of credit, the ability to bond or insure on projects, and—ultimately—its
entire business.

[62] FAR 52.249-2(a).

[63] Torncello v. United States, 681 F.2d 756 (Ct. Cl. 1982); Tamp Corp., 84-2 B.C.A. (CCH)
¶ 17,460 (ASBCA 1984).

CHAPTER 22

FEDERAL CONTRACT DISPUTES

James F. Nagle

James F. Nagle, a partner in the Seattle, Washington, firm of Oles, Morrison & Rinker, received his Bachelor's degree from the Georgetown University School of Foreign Service, his J.D. from Rutgers Law School, and his LL.M. and S.J.D. in government contracts from the National Law Center at George Washington University. A frequent lecturer, he has written numerous books and articles on government contracts, including *Federal Construction Contracting* for John Wiley & Sons (1992). He has extensive experience in all phases of government contracts, stemming from his 20 years with the Defense Department. Mr. Nagle is on the board of governors of the Boards of Contract Appeals Bar Association and is the editor of its newsletter. He also serves on the Board of Editors of the National Contract Management Association.

§ 22.1   Introduction

Federal contract disputes are handled pursuant to the Contract Disputes Act (CDA) of 1978.[1] In general terms, the CDA provides for the contracting

---

[1] Contract Disputes Act of 1978, Pub. L. No. 95-563, 92 Stat. 2383 (codified at 41 U.S.C. §§ 601-613 (1988)). For further discussion concerning federal contract disputes, *see generally* J. Nagle, Federal Construction Contracting (John Wiley & Sons 1992); J. Nagle, Claims and Disputes (Educational Services Inst. 1991).

officer to issue a final decision on a claim. The contractor may appeal this decision to an agency board of contract appeals, or the contractor may completely bypass the board of contract appeals and file suit directly in the United States Claims Court. If either the contractor or the government is dissatisfied with the decision of those forums, it may appeal the board of contract appeals or United States Claims Court decision to the United States Court of Appeals for the Federal Circuit. These rights are subject to time limits, elections, and various procedural requirements.

Disputes Clause

The CDA and FAR 33.214 require the contracting officer to insert the Disputes clause[2] in all contracts unless exempted by the head of the agency under 41 U.S.C. § 603(c). Among the provisions included in the clause are the following:

1. Definition of claim
2. Requirement that the claim be in writing and submitted to the contracting officer for a written decision
3. For claims over $50,000, a requirement of certification that the claim is accurate and complete
4. Those responsible for executing the certification
5. Time requirements for rendering a decision
6. Interest payment requirements
7. Requirement that contractor proceed diligently with performance and comply with the contracting officer's decision.

§ 22.2   Claims Subject to Disputes Process

The CDA encompasses both claims arising under and claims relating to a contract.

FAR 52.233-1 defines a claim *arising under a contract* as a claim that can be resolved under a contract clause that provides for the relief sought by the claimant. Examples of such clauses include the Changes clause, the Suspension of Work clause, the Differing Site Conditions clause, or the Termination for Convenience clause.

Claims *relating to a contract* are claims that arise out of a government contract that are not addressed by a clause in the contract. Such claims include breach of contract claims alleging the failure of the government to perform an express or implied duty for which no remedy is provided under

---

[2] *See* FAR 52.233-1, 52.233-1I.

the contract[3] and mistake claims in which the contractor alleges that the contract should be reformed because it was created under a mistake shared by both parties.[4]

§ 22.3   Matters Outside Disputes Process

For claims to be subject to the contract disputes process, the subject matter of the dispute must fall within the jurisdiction of the CDA. **Sections 22.4** through **22.10** address those issues to which jurisdiction does not extend in the process.

§ 22.4   —Issues of Fraud

Jurisdiction under the CDA does not extend to fraud matters. Agency heads cannot "settle, compromise, pay or otherwise adjust any claim involving fraud."[5] This does not necessarily prevent a board or court from hearing contract claims that are separate from the fraud allegations.[6] Generally, the judge will permit the other contract claims to proceed unless they are directly related to an ongoing, active fraud investigation and the Department of Justice requests a suspension of the proceedings.[7]

§ 22.5   —Matters Within Jurisdiction of
Another Agency

The contracting officer's decisional authority does not extend "to a claim or dispute for penalties or forfeitures prescribed by statute or regulation which another federal agency is specifically authorized to administer, settle or determine."[8]

For example, contracting officers cannot resolve aspects of the Davis-Bacon Act because claims under that Act are within the province of the Department of Labor.

---

[3] *E.g.,* Globe Eng'g Co., ASBCA No. 23934, 83-1 B.C.A. (CCH) ¶ 16,370.

[4] Gentex Corp., ASBCA No. 24040, 80-2 B.C.A. (CCH) ¶ 14,732.

[5] 41 U.S.C. § 605(a) (1988); United States v. Medico Indus. Inc., 685 F.2d 1273 (Fed. Cir. 1985).

[6] Fidelity Constr. Co., DOT CAB No. 1113, 80-2 B.C.A. (CCH) ¶ 14,819.

[7] *Id.*

[8] 41 U.S.C. § 605(a) (1988).

§ 22.6   —Requests for Relief under Public Law No. 85-804

Requests for relief under Public Law No. 85-804 are not considered to be claims within the CDA or the Disputes clause, and should continue to be processed under FAR Part 50, *Extraordinary Contractual Actions.*

§ 22.7   —Contract Award Controversies

The Claims Court and the General Services Administration Board of Contract Appeals do have jurisdiction over protests. The other boards of contract appeals, however, have consistently refused to take jurisdiction of contract award controversies because the boards' authority under the Disputes clause extends only to disputes "arising under an existing contract."[9]

§ 22.8   —Tort Claims

Neither the CDA nor its legislative history specifically addresses tort claims, but the boards and courts have ruled that they have no jurisdiction to hear pure tort claims.[10] Nevertheless, the CDA does provide jurisdiction for contract claims that involve tortious conduct, such as a claim that a contractor was induced to enter into a contract with the government by fraudulent misrepresentations.[11]

To determine whether the disputes process covers tort claims, torts connected with a contract must be distinguished from those that are independent of the contract. For example, in *Chain Belt Co. v. United States,*[12] the court stated:

> Inasmuch as we have found that defendant's removal methods resulted in unnecessary and excessive damage to the floors, we discuss briefly defendant's contention that this claim is beyond the court's jurisdiction because it sounds in tort. While it is true that this court does not have jurisdiction over claims sounding primarily in tort, an action may be maintained in this court which arises primarily from a contractual undertaking regardless of the fact that the loss resulted from the negligent manner in which the defendant performed its contract . . . a tortious breach of contract is not a

---

[9] *See* Hoel-Steffen Constr. Co., IBCA No. 634-4-67, 67-2 B.C.A. (CCH) ¶ 6,673.

[10] Western Pine Indus., Inc. v. United States, 231 Cl. Ct. 885 (1982).

[11] Kolar, Inc., ASBCA No. 28482, 84-1 B.C.A. (CCH) ¶ 17,044.

[12] 127 Ct. Cl. 88, 115 F. Supp. 701 (1953).

tort independent of the contract so as to preclude inaction under the Tucker Act.[13]

Torts will be within the CDA to the extent that they relate to the contract. However, if the tort is independent of the contract, the tort claim will not be covered by the disputes procedure under the Act.[14]

In *Asfaltos Panamenos, S.A.,*[15] the contractor claimed for damages to its foreman's pickup truck caused when a military helicopter blew a construction sign into the truck. The board of contract appeals held that the claim sounded in tort and was therefore outside the jurisdiction of the board because the damage to the vehicle arose independently from the performance of the contract. To recover for a purported tort, a contractor must demonstrate a direct nexus between the government's alleged tortious conduct and its obligations under the contract.

§ 22.9   —Nonappropriated Fund Activities

The CDA applies only to the military exchanges such as the Army and the Air Force Exchange Service. Other nonappropriated fund activities normally will not be within the jurisdiction of the CDA.[16] A foreign military sales contract performed in Saudi Arabia was subject to the CDA because the Saudi funds were held in trust by the United States and took on the character of appropriated funds.[17]

§ 22.10   —Other Matters

The courts or boards of contract appeals have no jurisdiction to order that an option be exercised[18] or to order an accounting.[19] In one case[20] a board of contract appeals ruled that, contrary to the appellant's wishes, the board did not have jurisdiction to direct the government's project leader to write a letter of apology to the contractor or to order the replacement or reassignment of program managers or staffs. The board lacks authority under the CDA to grant injunctive relief.[21]

---

[13] *Id.* at 711–712.

[14] *See* Jay Rucker, AGBCA No. 79-211A CDA, 80-2 B.C.A. (CCH) ¶ 14,513.

[15] ASBCA 39425, 91-1 B.C.A. (CCH) ¶ 23,315.

[16] *See* Wolverine Supply, Inc. v. United States, 17 Cl. Ct. 190 (1989).

[17] Saudi Tarmac Co., Ltd. ENGBCA No. 4841, 89-3 B.C.A. (CCH) ¶ 22,036.

[18] Marvin R. Iseminger, PSBCA No. 2537, 90-1, B.C.A. (CCH) ¶ 22,262.

[19] Tom Shaw, Inc., DOT CAB Nos. 2100–2115, 2124–2128, 90-1 B.C.A. (CCH) ¶ 22,286.

[20] Chung-Ho Chiao, DOT CAB No. 2264, 91-1 B.C.A. (CCH) ¶ 23,404.

[21] M&T Co., ASBCA No. 38128, 90-3 B.C.A. (CCH) ¶ 23,091.

§ 22.11   Contracting Parties

Not only must the subject matter of the dispute be within the jurisdiction of the CDA but also the dispute must be brought by one of the contracting parties.

§ 22.12   —Subcontractors

Subcontractors do not have the right to file a direct appeal against the government unless they are in "privity of contract" with the government. Privity will occur if the prime contractor is an agent of the government, but establishing such an agency relationship is very difficult.[22] At one time, agencies would occasionally include language in a contract permitting a subcontractor to proceed with direct appeals against the government.[23] However, this practice is now precluded by FAR 44.203(b)(3). As a result, a subcontractor must process its claim under the sponsorship of the prime contractor.[24] The prime contractor must sponsor even if the prime contractor had advised the government to deny the claim.[25]

Nevertheless, Small Business Administration Act § 8(a) subcontractors have been held to be in privity with the government and thus are contractors within the meaning of the CDA and can pursue their claims directly against the government.[26]

§ 22.13   —Sureties, Assignees, and Contractor Employees

A contractor's surety has been found not to be a contractor within the meaning of the CDA and thus has no authority to bring a dispute.[27] However, if the surety has entered into a completion agreement with the government and has completed the performance, the surety does have authority to bring a dispute.[28] An assignee under the Assignment of Claims Act of

---

[22] *E.g.,* Johnson Controls, Inc. v. United States, 713 F.2d 1541 (Fed. Cir. 1983).

[23] A&B Foundry, Inc., EBCA No. 118-4-80, 81-1 B.C.A. (CCH) ¶ 15,161.

[24] JMC Mechanical, Inc., ASBCA No. 26750, 82-2 B.C.A. (CCH) ¶ 15,878; Agnew Constr. Co., GSBCA No. 4178, 75-1 B.C.A. (CCH) ¶ 11,086.

[25] United States v. Turner Constr., 827 F.2d 1554 (Fed. Cir. 1987).

[26] Decorma Painting, Inc., ASBCA No. 25299, 81-1 B.C.A. (CCH) ¶ 14,992, *modified on other grounds,* 82-1 B.C.A. (CCH) ¶ 15,746; North Chicago Disposal Co., ASBCA No. 25535, 81-1 B.C.A. (CCH) ¶ 14,978.

[27] United States Fidelity & Guar. Co., IBCA No. 1645-12-82, 83-2 B.C.A. (CCH) ¶ 16,572.

[28] Fidelity & Deposit Co. of Md. v. United States, 2 Cl. Ct. 137 (1983).

1940[29] also is not considered a contractor.[30] Contractor employees have no right under the CDA to appeal to the boards in their own names.[31]

§ 22.14   Government Claims

The CDA makes all government claims against a contractor subject to the disputes process, providing that "all claims by the Government against a contractor should be the subject of a decision of the contracting officer."[32]

No procedure is specified in the CDA, and there is no statutory requirement for written or certified governmental claims against the contractor. Just as the contractor must properly identify its claim before the contracting officer is required to issue a decision, the contracting officer must apprise the contractor of a government claim and provide it the opportunity to respond before the officer can properly issue the decision required by § 6(a) of the Act.[33] This requirement encompasses questions of fact and law, including breach of contract claims.

A contracting officer's failure to advise a contractor of the government's claim and to provide an opportunity for response before issuing a final decision asserting the claim will deprive the board of contract appeals of jurisdiction over the government's counterclaim.[34]

It is often difficult to determine when a claim is a government claim and, therefore, does not have to be certified by the contractor. For example, in one case[35] a government request for reimbursement of funds already paid was ruled to be a government claim as long as the contractor was simply trying to retain funds. As a result, no certification was required. Similarly, an appeal from the disallowance of costs is a government claim.[36] So also is an assessment of liquidated damages[37] or the exercise of an option at a price the contractor has declared to be nonbinding.[38]

---

[29] Assignment of Claims Act of 1940, Oct. 9, 1940, ch. 779, 54 Stat. 1029 (codified as amended at 31 U.S.C. § 203, 41 U.S.C. § 15 (1988)).

[30] Tolson Oil Co., ASBCA No. 28324, 84-3 B.C.A. (CCH) ¶ 17,576.

[31] Matthew v. Close, AGBCA No. 84-120-1, 84-2 B.C.A. (CCH) ¶ 17,458 (claim for wages by employee of defaulted contractor).

[32] 41 U.S.C. § 605(a) (1988).

[33] See Woods Hole Oceanographic Inst. v. United States, 677 F.2d 149 (1st Cir. 1982); LTV Aerospace & Defense Co., ASBCA No. 36036, 88-2 B.C.A. (CCH) ¶ 20,752.

[34] Blaze Constr. Co., IBCA No. 2668-A, 90-1 B.C.A. (CCH) ¶ 22,522.

[35] LTV Aerospace Defense Co., ASBCA No. 36036, 88-2 B.C.A. (CCH) ¶ 20,752.

[36] General Dynamics Corp., ASBCA No. 31359, 86-3 B.C.A. (CCH) ¶ 19,008.

[37] Evergreen Int'l Aviation, Inc., PSBCA No. 2468, 89-2 B.C.A. (CCH) ¶ 21,712.

[38] Boeing, ASBCA No. 37579, 89-3 B.C.A. (CCH) ¶ 21,992.

§ 22.15   —Submission of Claim to Contracting Officer

The preferred method of settlement is by agreement of the parties.[39] If they fail to agree, however, the first step in the disputes procedure is for the claim to be submitted to the contracting officer for decision.[40]

§ 22.16   —Elements of the Claim

Even if the claim involves a matter within the subject matter jurisdiction of the CDA and is brought by one of the contracting parties, other elements of the statute must be met before a claim arises.

Writing.   The claim must be in writing. Oral "claims" are not claims under the Act.

Demand.   The claim must be a demand or written assertion, seeking as a matter of right the payment of money in a sum certain, the adjustment or interpretation of contract terms, or other relief arising under or relating to the contract.[41] Thus, a letter merely stating "Your prompt payment will be appreciated," in response to a government rejection of a progress payment request did not constitute a claim.[42] Some cases indicate that as long as the contractor's submission manifests an intent to seek relief, there is no requirement to specifically demand a decision from the contracting officer;[43] but other cases clearly state that a specific demand is a requirement of a claim.[44] Consequently, to avoid confusion, contractors should always specifically request a final decision.

Detail.   The claim must give sufficient details to permit the contracting officer to give meaningful consideration to the claim.[45] The claim must notify the contracting officer of the basic factual allegations upon which the claim is premised so as to allow the contracting officer to exercise discretion properly in making an informed decision.[46] Some leeway is

---

[39] FAR 33.204, 33.210; *see* System Dev. Corp., Comp. Gen. Dec. B-191195, Aug. 13, 1978, 78-2 CPD ¶ 159; August Perez & Assocs., 56 Comp. Gen. 289 (1977).

[40] FAR 33.206.

[41] Essey Electro Eng'rs, Inc., 702 F.2d 998 (Fed. Cir. 1983).

[42] Jones, Inc., GSBCA No. 1708, 84-2 B.C.A. (CCH) ¶ 17,382.

[43] J.G. Enters., Inc., ASBCA No. 27150, 83-2 B.C.A. (CCH) ¶ 16,808; Mendenhall v. United States, 20 Cl. Ct. 28 (1990).

[44] *See* West Coast Gen. Corp., 19 Cl. Ct. 98 (1989).

[45] Harris Management Co., ASBCA No. 27291, 84-2 B.C.A. (CCH) ¶ 17,378.

[46] Westclox Military Prods., ASBCA No. 25592, 81-2 B.C.A. (CCH) ¶ 15,270.

allowed, however. In *Blake Construction Co.,*[47] a contractor's claim that reserved the right to submit a later claim for accelerated costs was sufficiently complete to require the contracting officer to render a final decision.

Sum certain. The sum certain means exactly that. Merely stating that the contractor is entitled to an amount not less than a specific sum is not a sum certain for the purpose of the CDA.[48] Nevertheless, there is no need for the claim to state a specific amount if the amount can be determined through the use of simple arithmetic.[49] For example, if the claim is based on an extra three dollars per cubic yard, the government can determine the amount of the claim by multiplying that amount by the number of cubic yards.

Disputed. The matter must be in dispute and not merely a routine request for payment. The Disputes clause states that a voucher, invoice, or other routine request for payment that is not in dispute when submitted is not a claim under the CDA. The submission may be converted to a claim under the Act, by complying with the submission and certification requirements of the Disputes clause, if the submission is disputed either as to liability or amount or is not acted upon in a reasonable time.

Although the Disputes clause cites supporting data, there is no formal requirement that the claim be accompanied by supporting data as long as sufficient information is provided to enable the contracting officer to understand what is claimed.[50]

§ 22.17 —Certification of Claims over $50,000

One of the most important requirements in drafting a claim over $50,000 is to ensure that the claim is properly certified. The CDA requires that the contractor certify that the claim is made in good faith, that the supporting data are accurate and complete to the best of the contractor's knowledge and belief, and that the amount requested accurately reflects the contract adjustment for which the contractor believes the government is liable.[51]

A contractor cannot avoid the certification requirement by splitting one claim in excess of $50,000 into several sub-$50,000 claims.[52] However, truly separate claims no greater than $50,000 each do not require

---

[47] ASBCA No. 39937 et al., 90-3 B.C.A. (CCH) ¶ 23,196.

[48] Atlantic Indus., Inc., ASBCA No. 34832, 88-1 B.C.A. (CCH) ¶ 20,244.

[49] Dillingham Ship Yard, ASBCA No. 27458, 84-1 B.C.A. (CCH) ¶ 16,984.

[50] Bridgewater Constr. Corp., VACAB No. 2866 et al., 90-2 B.C.A. (CCH) ¶ 22,764.

[51] 41 U.S.C. § 605(c) (1988); Newell Clothing Co., ASBCA No. 24482, 80-2 B.C.A. (CCH) ¶ 14,774.

[52] Walsky Constr. Co. v. United States, 3 Cl. Ct. 615 (1983).

certification, even though the amount totals more than $50,000 and all are in the same appeal.[53]

Because the certification requirement is mandatory for all claims exceeding $50,000, no claim exists until certification is made.[54] The certification requirement is absolute and cannot be waived by the contracting officer.[55]

A claim that was properly uncertified when submitted to the contracting officer need not be certified if it increases in value to over $50,000 during the disputes process, such as when the amount of the claim grows after the government exercises an option.[56] But the boards of contract appeals lack jurisdiction to hear an uncertified matter that had begun as a claim for less than $50,000, but was presented as an appeal for an amount exceeding $50,000, with no explanation why a certification was not required.[57]

Besides the certification requirement, the CDA makes a contractor liable to the government for an amount equal to any unsupported part of the contractor's claim plus the government's costs in reviewing the claim, if it is determined that the inability to support the claim is attributable to "misrepresentation of fact or fraud" on the part of the contractor.[58] The Act defines a *misrepresentation of fact* as a "false statement of substantive fact, or any conduct which leads to a belief of a substantive fact material to proper understanding of the matter in hand, made with intent to deceive or mislead."[59] *Fraud* is not defined by the Act, but a reasonable assumption would be to use its common law meaning. Thus, although a fraudulent intent of the contractor must be found, this burden is eased by the requirement, in claims exceeding $50,000, that the contractor certify the good faith of its claim and its knowledge and belief that the supporting data are accurate and complete. Thus, a claim for $100,000 that is found to be fraudulently inflated by $20,000 would be granted only to the extent of $60,000—the amount legitimately due the contractor ($80,000) less a penalty for fraud of $20,000.

§ 22.18   —Who Can Certify

If the claimant is not an individual, FAR 33.207(b)(2) requires that the certifying official be a senior company official in charge at the contractor's plant or location involved or an officer or a general partner of the contractor

---

[53] B.D. Click Co., ASBCA No. 25609, 81-2 B.C.A. (CCH) ¶ 15,394.

[54] FAR 52.233-1(c).

[55] Paul E. Lehman, Inc. v. United States, 673 F.2d 352 (Cl. Ct. 1982).

[56] Tecom, Inc. v. United States, 732 F.2d 935 (Fed. Cir. 1984).

[57] *E.g.,* 4-J Technologies, Inc., VACAB Nos. 3218, 3219, 90-3 B.C.A. (CCH) ¶ 23,161.

[58] 41 U.S.C. § 604.

[59] *Id.* § 601(7).

having overall responsibility for overall conduct of the contractor's affairs.[60] This requirement has created a great deal of confusion as the government routinely challenges the authority of various individuals. It is clear that the individual's title is not dispositive because the same title in two different companies might mean vastly different authority. What is paramount is the individual's authority.

In *Newport News Shipbuilding & Drydock Co.*,[61] the board of contract appeals held that the contractor's marketing director was not a proper certifying official. In another Newport News case,[62] the board held that the executive vice-president did possess requisite responsibility over the contractor's affairs to be a proper certifying official. An acting president had no authority to certify contract claims under the CDA because there was no showing that he was a corporate officer or that the company's president was authorized to designate him as a corporate officer as required by FAR 33.207.[63] In *Fireman's Fund Insurance Co.*,[64] a certification of a subcontractor's claim by an assistant vice-president of the surety division of a surety company was inadequate because the assistant vice-president did not qualify as an individual authorized by the regulations to certify the subcontractor's claim. In *Ball & Brosamer, Inc. v. United States*,[65] the chief contract engineer was not a proper official even though he served as the senior contract claims manager.

Unique questions arise when the contractor is a joint venture. In *Boeing Co.*,[66] a certification by one corporate member of a joint venture was not a certification by the contractor. In *Sun Cal, Inc. v. United States*,[67] a limited partnership whose general partner is a corporation could validly have its claim certified by an official of the general partner.

Whoever is the certifier must certify to all the required elements. The statutes and certification requirement cannot be satisfied by piecemeal statements executed by two different individuals even if each individual had authority to certify claims on a contractor's behalf.[68]

---

[60] Tracor, Inc. ASBCA No. 29912, 87-2 B.C.A. (CCH) ¶ 19,808.

[61] ASBCA No. 36751, 90-2 B.C.A. (CCH) ¶ 22,937.

[62] Newport News, ASBCA No. 32289, 90-2 B.C.A. (CCH) ¶ 22,859.

[63] BMY-Combat Sys., ASBCA No. 39495, 90-3 B.C.A. (CCH) ¶ 23,089.

[64] ASBCA No. 38284, 91-1 B.C.A. (CCH) ¶ 23,439.

[65] 878 F.2d 1426 (Fed. Cir. 1989).

[66] ASBCA No. 36612, 89-1 B.C.A. (CCH) ¶ 21,421.

[67] 21 Cl. Ct. 31 (1990).

[68] Tech Dyn Sys. Corp., ASBCA No. 38727, 91-2 B.C.A. (CCH) ¶ 2,374.

The court or board of contract appeals will have to be satisfied with proof that the individual fits the criteria—bare allegations by the contractor will not suffice. The legend "authorized signature" appearing below the signature on a certification for a contract claim was not sufficient to establish that the signer was a senior company official in charge of its affairs, or that the signer had authority from the other members of a joint venture to act on behalf of the venture.[69] In another case,[70] the board held that the contractor did not meet the requirement by merely alleging that the contractor's "managing claims attorney" was the senior company official in charge at the plant location involved. The contractor had the burden of proving the truth of the allegation and failed to do so in that case.

The leading case in the area is *United States v. Grumman Aerospace Corp.,*[71] in which the Court of Appeals for the Federal Circuit dismissed a claim for lack of jurisdiction, ruling that the certification by Grumman's senior vice-president and treasurer was not sufficient. The court first found that the individual was not "in charge" within the meaning of the applicable FAR clause because he reported to the Grumman Comptroller, who "made the ultimate decision" to present the claim. Nor, in the court's view, was the individual qualified to certify under another paragraph in the clause because he lacked "overall responsibility for the conduct of [Grumman's] affairs." "Responsibility limited to financial affairs is not enough," the court concluded.

In another Grumman Aerospace case,[72] the board ruled that the certifying official does not have to be the senior official in charge of everything at the location involved, but that the clause does require that the senior official be in charge of "all activities relevant to the claim." In that case, the certifying official was in charge of contract formation and administration, but was not in charge of the engineering and production activities relating to the contract claim. The board, therefore, held that certification was ineffective.

Several cases have indicated that because the statutory certification requirement applies to the submission of claims to the contracting officer, a certification unauthorized at that submission time cannot be cured by the later ratification of an appropriate contractor official.[73]

---

[69] Intercontinental Equip., Inc., ASBCA No. 38444, 90-1 B.C.A. (CCH) ¶ 22,501, at 94,934. *See also* Triax Co. v. United States, 17 Cl. Ct. 653 (1989), *rev'd,* 20 Cl. Ct. 507 (1990).

[70] Fidelity & Deposit Co. of Md., ASBCA No. 40327, 91-1 B.C.A. (CCH) ¶ 23,312.

[71] 927 F.2d 575 (Fed. Cir. 1991).

[72] Grumman Aerospace, ASBCA No. 33091, 91-2 B.C.A. (CCH) ¶ 2,375.

[73] *See, e.g.,* Building Sys. Contractors, Inc., VABCA No. 2749 89-2 B.C.A. (CCH) ¶ 21,678.

§ 22.19   —What Must Be Said

Even if a determination is made concerning the appropriate person to sign the certification, the certification language must meet statutory requirements.[74] The specific statutory words need not be used if the certificate contains the essence of the statutory requirements.[75] However, anyone who deviates from the language of the statute in even the minutest degree risks a judgment that a proper claim was not submitted. For example, in *WSCON Corp.,*[76] a certification stating that the contractor certified to his knowledge that the supporting data were accurate and complete was defective because the statute demands that the supporting data be certified to the contractor's knowledge and belief. The certificate of current cost or pricing data required by the Truth in Negotiations Act does not satisfy the certification requirements of the CDA.[77] Furthermore, although the requirements may be met in a series of letters,[78] incorporating the applicable language by reference is not enough.[79]

The certification requirement can be especially burdensome on prime contractors who often certify their subcontractor's claims. In *Century Construction Co. v. United States,*[80] the court ruled that when a prime contractor certifies a claim on behalf of the subcontractor, the prime contractor must certify its own belief in the accuracy and legitimacy of the claim. It is not enough to certify the subcontractor's belief.

The Department of Defense Appropriations Authorization Act of 1979 requires that, for contract claims in excess of $100,000, "a senior company official in charge at the plant or location [certify] at the time of submission of [the] contract claim . . . that such claim . . . is made in good faith and that the supporting data are accurate and complete to the best of such official's knowledge and belief."[81] Like the CDA, the regulations implementing the Appropriations Authorization Act require that the certification stipulate that "the amount requested accurately reflects the contract adjustment for which the contractor believes the government is liable."

---

[74] W.H. Moseley Co. v. United States, 677 F.2d 850 (Ct. Cl.), *cert. denied,* 549 U.S. 836 (1982).

[75] United States v. General Elec. Corp., 727 F.2d 1567 (Fed. Cir. 1984).

[76] ASBCA No. 39502, 90-3 B.C.A. (CCH) ¶ 23,169.

[77] ReCon Paving, Inc., ASBCA No. 27836, 83-2 B.C.A. (CCH) ¶ 16,658.

[78] A&J Constr. Co., IBCA No. 2376-F, 88-2 B.C.A. (CCH) ¶ 20,525; *but see* Echo W. Constr., VACAB No. 3186, 90-3 B.C.A. (CCH) ¶ 23,106 (contractor tried to incorporate prior communications of supportive data in certification document; it failed because the attempted certification did not simultaneously make all assertions required by Contract Disputes Act).

[79] Schwartz, VACAB No. 2856, 89-2 B.C.A. (CCH) ¶ 21,681.

[80] 22 Cl. Ct. 63 (1990).

[81] Pub. L. No. 95-457, 92 Stat. 1231 (1978).

DFARS 252.233-7000 provides that the CDA certification will also satisfy the 1979 Appropriations Authorization Act certification if the request for payment is made at the same time as the inception of the dispute. The Appropriations Authorization Act certification may also satisfy the CDA requirements,[82] but contractors should submit both certificates to be sure.

Because almost all monetary claims relate to the resolution of nonmonetary issues, such as the meaning or effect of a contract clause, contractors will, at times, try to present monetary claims as requests for nonmonetary relief to avoid the certification requirements of the CDA. Contracting officers are not required to adjudicate contractors' nonmonetary claims when the recovery of money is primarily sought, with resolution of the nonmonetary issues being ancillary to monetary relief, but the claim has not been submitted properly.[83]

§ 22.20   Role of the Contracting Officer

In the last few years, an issue has developed regarding how directly the contracting officer must receive the claim.

In *West Coast General Corp. v. United States,*[84] the contractor had alleged in letters to the Resident Officer in Charge of Construction (ROICC) that the government had constructively changed the contract. Later, the contractor submitted an estimate for the constructive change and stated that the change proposal was being submitted in accordance with the Disputes clause. The ROICC informed the contractor that its "claim package . . . has been forwarded to Western Division Naval Facilities Engineering Command for a contracting officer's final decision." After the contracting officer's final decision denied the contractor's claim, the contractor appealed to the U.S. Claims Court. The court found a variety of problems with the "claims" submitted by the contractor, specifically that the claim was not submitted directly to the contracting officer. The court reiterated the statutory language that "all claims by a contractor against the government relating to a contract shall be in writing and shall be submitted to the contracting officer for decision."[85] The contractor admitted that it had not sent the letters directly to the contracting officer, but portrayed the strict language of the statute as a "meaningless formality" because the ROICC had properly and customarily transmitted the claim to the contracting officer. The Claims Court rejected that argument and ruled instead that strict compliance with the CDA is important so that the contracting

---

[82] Stencel Aero Eng'g Corp., ASBCA No. 28654, 84-1 B.C.A. (CCH) ¶ 16,951.

[83] Newell Clothing Co., ASBCA No. 24482, 80-2 B.C.A. (CCH) ¶ 14,744.

[84] 19 Cl. Ct. 98 (1989).

[85] 41 U.S.C. § 605(a) (1988).

officer will know what he or she is dealing with and what must be done. The court concluded that it would be "inappropriate for a court to permit correspondence sent to the ROICC to substitute for the requirement that the claim be submitted to the contracting officer who is, by statute, the person responsible for deciding contract disputes."[86] The court argued that if it countenanced such behavior, this would allow contractors to send claims to any government employee in the hope that the claim eventually would be forwarded to the contracting officer having authority to decide the claim. Because a proper claim had not been submitted, the contracting officer could not issue a final decision. The purported final decision was a nullity.

The court then granted the government's motion to dismiss the complaint. That case was decided on December 18, 1989.

Seven and one-half months later, the Claims Court decided another Navy case with very similar facts, but reached a diametrically opposed conclusion. In *American Pacific Roofing Co. v. United States,*[87] the contractor had submitted two claims to the Navy. Both claims had requested a final decision from the contracting officer and were for specific amounts that the contractor alleged the Navy owed it for constructive changes and improperly withheld charges. The contractor submitted these claims to the ROICC, who forwarded both claims to the contracting officer, who denied both claims.

After the contractor had filed suit in the Claims Court, the Navy moved for dismissal because the contractor had not submitted its claims directly to the contracting officer. Not surprisingly, the Navy relied heavily on the *West Coast General Corp.* case.

However, in this case, the Claims Court stated that the CDA does not state that the contractor must send a claim directly to the contracting officer. Rather, it merely requires that the written claim "be submitted" to the contracting officer. After looking to the dictionary definition of *submit,* the court concluded that submit does not mean the same as *address* or *directly send.* Thus, the court concluded that a contractor may submit a claim without necessarily sending papers directly to the contracting officer. Looking at the facts in that case, the court concluded that the contractor had submitted its claim to the contracting officer for decision under the wording of the statute.

The court distinguished *West Coast General Corp.* by pointing out that in *West Coast,* the contractor submitted several letters to the ROICC, but never requested a final decision from the contracting officer. Moreover, the contractor in *West Coast* failed to assert any specific basis for monetary relief and had not properly certified its claim, unlike the contractor in *American Pacific Roofing Co.*

The court's attempt to distinguish *West Coast* is an admirable attempt by one judge to avoid the clear contradiction of another judge on the same

---

[86] West Coast Gen. Corp. v. United States, 19 Cl. Ct. 98, 101 (1989).

[87] 21 Cl. Ct. 265 (1990).

court. A fair reading of both cases, however, leaves no doubt that the *West Coast* court viewed the failure to submit the claim directly to the contracting officer as a separate and distinct ground upon which to dismiss for lack of jurisdiction, while the *American Pacific Roofing Co.* judge unequivocally ruled otherwise. As the court stated in *American Pacific Roofing Co.,* neither the statute nor its legislative history dictates any requirement that the claim be sent directly to the contracting officer.

In *Robert Irsay Co. v. United States Postal Service,*[88] the court followed the *West Coast General* case and held that a contractor's letters to the contract manager, which were later fortuitously received by the contracting officer, were not claims because the indirect receipt of claims by the contracting officer does not satisfy the requirements of the CDA.

In *McGinnis & Co.,*[89] the ASBCA refused to follow *West Coast General* and held that a claim transmittal letter submitted to a district legal office without specifically addressing either the contracting officer or the district engineer was an adequate claim submission. Even though the contractor had been directed to submit all correspondence to the office of the area engineer, the contractor's claim was submitted in a manner reasonably calculated to be received by the contracting officer authorized to decide the claim.

Fortunately, the Court of Appeals for the Federal Circuit resolved the issue in *DAWCO Construction, Inc. v. United States* by ruling that the *American Pacific* decision had correctly interpreted the statutory requirements.[90]

§ 22.21   Duties of the Contracting Officer

The submission of a properly certified claim imposes several duties on the contracting officer. Initially, FAR 33.204 requires the contracting officer to try to resolve the claim through negotiation. The contracting officer has authority to reach binding agreements with contractors conclusively disposing of claims through contract modifications.[91]

Accordingly, FAR 33.210 authorizes contracting officers to decide or settle all claims arising under, or relating to, a contract except claims involving fraud, penalties, or forfeitures prescribed by statute for determination by another federal agency. The contracting officer can do this through binding contract modifications. One technique the contracting officer can use is alternate dispute resolution (ADR).

ADR is the process of resolving disputes by consent of the parties rather than by submitting the dispute through the formal process of the CDA and

---

[88] 21 Cl. Ct. 502 (1990).

[89] ASBCA Nos. 40004, 40005, 91-1 B.C.A. (CCH) ¶ 23,395.

[90] 930 F.2d 872 (Fed. Cir. 1991).

[91] Peters v. United States, 694 F.2d 687 (Fed. Cir. 1982).

pursuing a final decision from the board of contract appeals BCA or the Claims Court. Some of the techniques involve settlement judges, disputes panels agreed to by the parties at the start of the contract, nonbinding arbitration, or minitrials.[92]

Both the boards and the Claims Court encourage the use of ADR,[93] and in 1990 Congress passed the Administrative Dispute Resolution Act.[94] FAR 33.204 includes the following suggestion relative to ADR:

> In appropriate circumstances, the contracting officer, before issuing a decision on a claim, should consider the use of informal discussions between the parties by individuals who have not participated substantially in the matter in dispute, to aid in resolving the differences.

The suggestion recognizes the benefits of an objective evaluation by those not directly involved in creating or perpetuating the dispute. Many cases are settled even after appeal because the government and contractor counsel provide a new and detached assessment of the case. Sometimes particular individuals can be so enmeshed in the dispute that their positions become nonnegotiable and unchangeable. For example, the contracting officer and the contractor may have developed such an adversarial relationship that no settlement is possible. In such cases, a detached, informed appraisal is well worth the effort.

Besides the reference to an objective evaluation in FAR 33.204, FAR 33.211(a) requires the contracting officer to do the following:

1. Review the facts pertinent to the claim
2. Secure assistance from legal and other advisers
3. Coordinate with the contract administration officer and others as appropriate
4. Prepare a written decision.

§ 22.22   —Contracting Officer's Decision

The decision must be the contracting officer's personal and independent judgment on the merits of the contractor's claim.[95] If the decision is made or directed by another, it will not be considered a decision under the

---

[92] See Ch. 23.

[93] See Alternative Dispute Resolution in the Construction Industry (Cushman et al. eds., John Wiley & Sons 1991).

[94] Administrative Dispute Resolution Act of 1990, Pub. L. No. 101-552, 104 Stat. 2736.

[95] Byrd Foods, Inc., VACAB No. 1679, 83-1 B.C.A. (CCH) ¶ 16,313; Dames & Moore, IBCA No. 130810-79, 81-2 B.C.A. (CCH) ¶ 15,418.

Disputes clause.[96] The decision may be invalid if it results from a direction from the contracting officer's superior.[97]

Normally a contracting officer should seek, and rely on, the opinions and conclusions of technical and legal advisers in arriving at the final decision. The contracting officer complies with the law if the final decision is the contracting officer's own by adoption.[98] Moreover, the contracting officer's decision can be reviewed by the officer's superiors.[99] The requirement for a personal and independent decision does not prevent the government from replacing the original contracting officer unless the contract specifically designates a particular government official to make the decision.[100]

The contracting officer's authority and opportunity to settle the claim do not end with the final decision and the filing of an appeal. The contracting officer may continue to negotiate the claim even after issuing a final decision[101] and can negotiate a settlement during litigation before the boards of contract appeals.[102] However, the contracting officer's authority to settle claims does not extend to cases in which litigation has commenced in a court, because federal law grants the United States Attorney General sole authority to settle cases being litigated in the courts.[103] Nevertheless, the contracting officer can, and usually does, strongly influence the outcome by assuring that the contracting officer's position is known and understood. Consequently, the contracting officer must keep abreast of the case as it winds its way through the appeals process to determine when settlement is in the government's best interests.

§ 22.23   —Time Limits for Contracting Officer's Decision

The contracting officer is under a duty to issue a decision on any claim of $50,000 or less within 60 days from the receipt of a written request from the contractor that a decision be rendered within that period.[104] The

---

[96] Pacific Architects & Eng'rs Inc. v. United States, 203 Ct. Cl. 499, 491 F.2d 734 (1974); Systems Technology Assocs., 81-1 B.C.A. (CCH) ¶ 14,934; Edmund Leising Bldg. Contractor, Inc., VACAB No. 1428, 81-1 B.C.A. (CCH) ¶ 14,925.

[97] John A. Johnson Contracting Corp. v. United States, 132 F. Supp. 698 (Ct. Cl. 1955).

[98] FAR 33.211(a); AFARS 1.697; Pacific Architects & Eng'rs, Inc. v. United States, 203 Ct. Cl. 499, 491 F.2d 734 (Ct. Cl. 1974).

[99] Jacob Schlesinger, Inc. v. United States, 94 Ct. Cl. 289 (1941).

[100] New York Shipbuilding Corp. v. United States, 385 F.2d 427 (Ct. Cl. 1967).

[101] Pervis Constr. Co., GSBCA No. 905, 69-1 B.C.A. (CCH) ¶ 7,723.

[102] E-Systems, Inc., ASBCA No. 12091, 79-1 B.C.A. (CCH) ¶ 13,806.

[103] United States v. Newport New Shipbuilding & Dry Dock Co., 571 F.2d 1283 (4th Cir.), cert. denied, 439 U.S. 875 (1978).

[104] 41 U.S.C. § 605(c)(1) (1988).

contracting officer is further obliged to decide all claims exceeding $50,000 within 60 days of receipt of the claim or to notify the contractor of the time within which a decision will be issued.[105] If the latter option is chosen, the decision must be issued within a reasonable time,[106] in accordance with agency regulations, taking into account factors such as the size and complexity of the claim and the adequacy of the information supplied by the contractor in support of the claim.[107]

If a contractor believes that the time set by the contracting officer is unreasonable, or in the event of undue delay by the contracting officer in issuing a decision, the contractor can apply to the agency board of contract appeals for an order directing the contracting officer to issue a final decision within a specific time.[108] If the contracting officer fails to comply with the 60-day limitation or with the times established by the officer or by the board, the contractor may treat the failure to issue a decision as a decision denying the claim and may commence an appeal.[109] In such cases, however, the tribunal to which the appeal is taken may, at its option, stay the proceedings to obtain a decision on the claim by the contracting officer.[110] Should a board of contract appeals grant a contractor's request for an order directing the contracting officer to render a decision, pursuant to 41 U.S.C. § 605(c)(4), the request does not bind the contractor to file the subsequent appeal to a board.[111]

§ 22.24   —Form of Decision

The contracting officer must issue a decision in writing and mail or otherwise furnish a copy to the contractor. Although specific findings of fact are not required (and, if made, will not be binding in any subsequent proceeding), the contracting officer must state the reasons for the decision and inform the contractor of the contractor's rights under the CDA.[112] The decision must specifically advise the contractor that the decision is final and that the contractor has a right to appeal the decision.[113] The paragraph

---

[105] *Id.* § 605(c)(2); John R. Handley, Inc., ASBCA No. 26689, 82-1 B.C.A. (CCH) ¶ 82,467.

[106] 41 U.S.C. § 605(c)(3).

[107] *Id.*

[108] *Id.* § 605(c)(4).

[109] *Id.* § 605(c)(5).

[110] 6800 Corp., GSBCA No. 5880, 81-2 B.C.A. (CCH) ¶ 15,388.

[111] *See* WNJ Constr. v. United States, 12 Cl. Ct. 507 (1987); Vemo Co. v. United States, 9 Cl. Ct. 217 (1985).

[112] 41 U.S.C. § 605(a) (1988); FAR 33.211(a)(4).

[113] FAR 33.211(a).

suggested at FAR 33.211(a)(4)(v) should be included verbatim in the final decision. Doing so ensures that the decision will include the proper requirements. If the contractor is not properly advised, the decision may not be considered final for purposes of starting the time period during which the contractor has the right to appeal.[114]

The main issue arising is whether a determination is "meant to be a final decision." If it was meant to be a final decision, then it is appealable even though the required format has not been followed.[115] For example, a government notice regarding audit findings and inviting contractor comments on those findings was held not to be a final decision and, therefore, not appealable.[116] Procedural deficiencies will not normally be held against the contractor. In *Terrace Apartments Ltd.,*[117] the board of contract appeals ruled that, although a contractor did not file its appeal within 90 days of receipt of a letter from the contracting officer terminating the contractor for default, the government's motion to dismiss the appeal as untimely was denied because the terminating letter did not advise the contractor of its appeal rights.

§ 22.25 —Interest on Contractor Claims

Simple interest, calculated at rates established by the Secretary of the Treasury, is payable on unpaid amounts found due to contractors from the date the contracting officer received a valid claim until payment thereof.[118] Interest is calculated based on Treasury rates in effect for each segment of the overall period for which interest is given.[119]

§ 22.26 —Finality of Contracting Officer's Decision

Unless an appeal or suit is timely commenced as authorized by the CDA, the contracting officer's decision on a claim is considered final, conclusive, and binding on both parties and is not subject to review by any other

---

[114] Imperator Carpet & Interiors, Inc., GSBCA No. 6156, 81-2 B.C.A. (CCH) ¶ 15,248; VEPCO, Inc., ASBCA No. 26993, 82-2 B.C.A. (CCH) ¶ 15,824. See DFARS 233.211.

[115] Technical Support Servs., Inc., ASBCA No. 37976, 89-1 B.C.A. (CCH) ¶ 21,518.

[116] United Indians of All Tribes Found., GSBCA No. 9679-ED, 89-2 B.C.A. (CCH) ¶ 21,716.

[117] ASBCA No. 40125, 90-3 B.C.A. (CCH) ¶ 23,240.

[118] 41 U.S.C. § 611 (1988); FAR 52.233-1, para. (g).

[119] Brookfield Constr. Co. & Baylor Constr. Corp. (AJV) v. United States, 661 F.2d 159 (Ct. Cl. 1981). See FAR 32.614 (regarding interest on government claims).

forum, tribunal, or government agency.[120] After receipt of a contracting officer's final decision, the contractor has 90 days to appeal to an agency's board of contract appeals[121] or 12 months to appeal to the United States Claims Court.[122]

However, a final decision favoring the contractor could be rescinded and another final decision denying the contractor's claim could properly be issued so long as this was done within the CDA appeal period.[123] If a final decision is withdrawn with prejudice after an appeal, the contractor's appeal will be sustained.[124] Also, contractors must remember that the boards of contract appeals and the Claims Court will review the final decision de novo and can reduce the amount given to the contractor in the final decision.[125]

§ 22.27   Contractor's Performance During Litigation

The Disputes clause states that the contractor shall diligently proceed with performance of the contract in accordance with the contracting officer's decision while the dispute is being resolved.[126] FAR 43.201(b) reiterates that rule but notes that in cost-reimbursement or incrementally-funded contracts, the contractor is not obligated to continue performance or incur costs beyond the limits established in the Limitation of Cost or Limitation of Funds clause.

The regular subparagraph (h) of the Disputes clause requires the contractor to continue performance of the contract pending resolution of an appeal only if the claim in question arose under the contract. However, if the dispute is the result of a claim relating to a contract—for example, a cardinal change (breach)—the contractor could stop work. This is the rule as it existed before the CDA.

Alternate I of the Disputes clause substitutes a different subparagraph (h), which obligates the contractor to proceed even after a breach. This alternate is used only in important cases, however, in accordance with agency regulations. In the Defense Department, Alternate I must be used

---

[120] 41 U.S.C. § 605(b) (1988); FAR 52.233-1, para. (f); 41 U.S.C. 609(a); United States v. Holpuch, 328 U.S. 234 (1946).

[121] 41 U.S.C. § 606.

[122] *Id.* § 609(a).

[123] Daniels & Shanklin Constr. Co., ASBCA No. 37102, 89-3 B.C.A. (CCH) ¶ 22,060.

[124] McDonnell Douglas Astronautics Co., ASBCA No. 36770, 89-3 B.C.A. (CCH) ¶ 22,253.

[125] Assurance Co. v. United States, 813 F.2d 1202 (Fed. Cir. 1987); B&K Constr. Co., ASBCA No. 37713, 89-3 B.C.A. (CCH) ¶ 22,247.

[126] *See* FAR 52.233-1(h)

when acquiring aircraft, spacecraft, launch vehicles, naval vessels, missile systems, tracked combat vehicles, and related electronic systems.[127]

DFARS 233.214 states that Alternate I may also be used:

> when the performance of the contract is so vital to the national security or to the public health and welfare that performance must be guaranteed even in the event of a dispute that may be characterized as a claim relating to, as opposed to arising under the contract.

In recognition of this increased burden on contractors, FAR 33.213(b) states that the contracting officer "shall consider providing, through appropriate agency procedures, financing of the continued performance; provided that the government's interest is properly secured."

Thus, the current rule is that contractors can be forced to perform a cardinal change only in very narrow circumstances, and then only when the contract signed by the parties gives the contractor notice of this obligation. In the absence of Alternate I, contractors are on the horns of a dilemma as to how, or whether, to proceed regarding a government action that may be a change within the scope of the Changes clause or a cardinal change. A contractor who is terminated for default for refusal to comply with what the contractor regards as a cardinal change is liable for the increased costs incurred by the government in completing the contract with another contractor if it is ultimately held that the ordered change was within the scope of the Changes clause.

This dilemma is illustrated by *Yukon Services, Inc.*,[128] a case involving a contract for the construction of a road in Alaska. When the road could not be constructed in accordance with the specifications, the government changed the specifications by requiring that the roadbed be excavated to a lower grade in a rocky area so as to provide fill material for the troublesome swampy area. The contractor refused to proceed as directed under the changed specifications, alleging that the government had breached the contract. The government then terminated the contract for default. On appeal, the board of contract appeals upheld the default termination, finding that performance under the changed specifications was possible and that the change in specifications was not a cardinal change.

§ 22.28   —Duty to Proceed Diligently

Unless the contractor wants to risk a default termination, it should proceed with the work. Merely proceeding, however, will not preclude a default termination. There is a duty to proceed "diligently." In *American Dredging*

---

[127] DFARS 233.214.

[128] AGBCA No. 213, 69-2 B.C.A. (CCH) ¶ 7,843.

Co. v. United States,[129] a default termination was upheld when the contractor proceeded with easier dredging work while inexcusably putting off the drilling and blasting of hard rock, pending resolution of its claim of a differing site condition.

Furthermore, the Court of Claims has held that a contractor must proceed with the work after oral notice of a change when that is the customary practice. If a contractor wishes to dispute the change order and stops performance, it cannot subsequently use the absence of a written change order as a basis for a delay claim.[130]

§ 22.29 —Election of Forum

A decision on whether to appeal to a board of contract appeals or to the Claims Court must be made carefully because the contractor is precluded from changing forums after electing to appeal to a specific forum.[131] However, the filing of an appeal with an appropriate board of contract appeals is not a binding election if it is determined by the board that the contractor's appeal was untimely and hence the subsequent filing of a claim in the Claims Court is not barred.[132] A contractor may choose a different forum for each of several claims arising out of the same contract,[133] but the Claims Court can consolidate appeals filed both in the boards and before the Claims Court in either the board or the Claims Court. In *Giuliani Contracting Co. v. United States,*[134] the Claims Court granted a government motion to transfer the appeal to the Armed Services Board of Contract Appeals (ASBCA) because two claims from the same contract were pending before that board, which had already resolved the other claims arising out of the contract. The ASBCA was the contractor's principal forum and, given the current stage in the litigation, a transfer to the Claims Court would have had the overtones of forum shopping.

The ASBCA has decided that unless the appeal notice specifically elects a forum (that is, board of contract appeals or Claims Court), it is not a valid appeal.[135] Nevertheless, shortly before that decision, the ASBCA reached a different conclusion in another case.[136] The lesson for contractors, however,

---

[129] 207 Ct. Cl. 1010, 521 F.2d 1405 (1975).

[130] Ardelt-Horn Constr. Co. v. United States, 207 Ct. Cl. 995, 521 F.2d 1406 (1975).

[131] Tuttle/White Constructors, Inc. v. United States, 656 F.2d 644 (Ct. Cl. 1981).

[132] National Neighbors, Inc. v. United States, 839 F.2d 1539 (Fed. Cir. 1988).

[133] American Nucleonics Corp., ASBCA No. 27894, 83-1 B.C.A. (CCH) ¶ 16,520.

[134] 21 Cl. Ct. 81 (1990).

[135] Stewart-Thomas Indus., Inc., ASBCA No. 38773, 90-1 B.C.A. (CCH) ¶ 22,481.

[136] McNanara-Lunz Vans & Warehouses, Inc., ASBCA No. 38075, 89-2 B.C.A. (CCH) ¶ 21,636.

is to make a clear election in the notice of appeal. Deciding whether to go to the board of contract appeals or to the Claims Court is a decision that must be made on a case-by-case basis.

The boards of contract appeals have some advantages that will be explained in detail. First, they can hear cases all around the world; the Claims Court can hold hearings only throughout the United States. The boards of contract appeals have specific rules for expediting small-dollar-value cases. The boards are less formal and do not require strict adherence to the Federal Rules of Evidence or the Federal Rules of Civil Procedures. So, if a contractor is going to appeal without an attorney, the contractor might be well-advised to appeal to the board of contract appeals. Although the Claims Court permits individuals or partnerships to appear pro se, the Court requires that an attorney represent a corporation. Normally, the board of contract appeals administrative judges will be more knowledgeable in public contract law. The CDA requires that board of contract appeals judges have five years of public contract law experience. Claims Court judges, on the other hand, need not be well-versed in public contract law before gaining appointment to the bench and, once appointed, must concentrate on a greater range of disciplines that fall within the Court's jurisdiction. Furthermore, Claims Court judges render one-judge decisions as opposed to the collegial decisions reached by the boards of contract appeals. This can lead to more conflicts within the Claims Court's precedents. There will be instances in which the Claims Court will have adopted a different approach, in an area of the law, from the ASBCA, for example. However, this does not occur any more or less frequently than the ASBCA may differ from the Agriculture Board or the General Services Board.

Advantages at the Claims Court are that the government is represented by the Justice Department, which will undoubtedly give a fresh look to the merits of the case, rather than the agency attorneys who, depending on the agency, might have been the ones advising the contracting officer from the beginning. Furthermore, if the relief sought is a break from tradition, the lone Claims Court judge deciding the case is more likely to break from tradition than the panel of board of contract appeals judges.

One significant difference between the boards of contract appeals and the Claims Court involves jurisdiction to hear appeals from default terminations. In *Overall Roofing, Inc. v. United States,* [137] the Court of Appeals for the Federal Circuit ruled that the jurisdiction of the Claims Court depended on the existence of a money claim in connection with an appeal from a default termination, but that the boards of contract appeals did not need such a money claim for their jurisdiction. Consequently, contractors appealing a default termination can appeal directly to the boards as soon as they receive the letter of termination, but an action in the Claims Court

---

[137] 929 F.2d 687 (Fed. Cir. 1991).

requires a money claim, normally a termination for convenience or breach claim.

§ 22.30 Boards of Contract Appeals

The boards of contract appeals are designated by the heads of the executive agencies to hear contract disputes. The Armed Services Board of Contract Appeals (ASBCA) has the largest caseload and, therefore, has the largest staff. In addition to appeals arising from the Department of Defense, it hears cases from organizations such as the State Department and the Central Intelligence Agency. It also hears cases from the Corps of Engineers for appeals arising from contracts for construction on military bases. The Corps of Engineers Board of Contract Appeals (ENGBCA) hears appeals arising from the Corps' civil projects. The next largest board after the ASBCA is the General Services Administration Board of Contract Appeals (GSBCA). The remaining boards are the Agriculture Board of Contract Appeals (AGBCA), the Department of Housing and Urban Development Board of Contract Appeals (HUDBCA), the Labor Department Board of Contract Appeals (LBCA), the Department of Transportation Contract Appeals Board (DOT CAB), the Energy Department Board of Contract Appeals (EBCA), the National Aeronautics and Space Administration Board of Contract Appeals (NASABCA), the Postal Service Board of Contract Appeals (PSBCA), the Department of Interior Board of Contract Appeals (IBCA), and the Department of Veterans Affairs Contract Appeals Board (VABCA).[138]

§ 22.31 —Time Limit for Appeal to Boards

Written notice of an appeal must be mailed or delivered to the board of contract appeals within 90 days after receipt of the contracting officer's decision. A copy also must be furnished to the contracting officer. In computing the 90-day period, the date the contractor receives the decision is excluded.[139] The government must prove that the contractor received the final decision and the date of receipt.[140] If the last day falls on a Saturday, Sunday, or federal holiday, the period for appeal is extended to the next

---

[138] *See* Nagle, How to Review a Federal Contract and Research Federal Contract Law (ABA Press 1990).

[139] Pyramid Van & Storage Co., ASBCA No. 14257, 69-2 B.C.A. (CCH) ¶ 7,952.

[140] Pleasant Logging & Milling Co., AGBCA No. 79-172, 80-1 B.C.A. (CCH) ¶ 14,290; Joseph Morton Co., GSBCA No. 4707, 77-1 B.C.A. (CCH) ¶ 12,320 (actual notice); San Col Mar Indus., ASBCA No. 16897, 73-1 B.C.A. (CCH) ¶ 9,812 (constructive notice); Alco Mach. Co., ASBCA No. 38183, 89-3 B.C.A. (CCH) ¶ 21,955.

business day.[141] The appeal time starts when the contractor receives the decision even if the subcontractor will file the appeal.[142] The running of the 90-day limitation period stops on the day the contractor mails or personally delivers a written notice of appeal to the appropriate board of contract appeals.[143] If the appeal is late because of a commercial courier, it is still untimely.[144]

An appeal not filed within the statutory period is untimely and the board lacks jurisdiction to hear it.[145] The boards have embraced a liberal policy regarding misdirected appeal notices. Appeals have been held to be filed within the time limits even though sent to the secretary of the agency through the contracting officer,[146] or directly to the contracting officer.[147] The Agriculture Board, however, has taken a harder view and cited that such appeals have not been timely made.[148]

The contracting officer may not revive the right to appeal by reconsidering the contractor's claim after the time has expired.[149] However, the contracting officer may reconsider its own decision within the 90-day period, and if so, the contractor will have 90 days to appeal after receipt of the contracting officer's decision.[150]

A peculiar rule has developed in termination for default cases. Under what is known as the "Fulford Doctrine," the contractor may question the validity of its default and have this issue determined on an appeal from an assessment of excess costs, even though it did not submit a timely appeal from the default termination itself.[151] When there is an appeal from a

---

[141] *E.g.,* ASBCA R. of Prac. 33.

[142] Arctic Glazing Contractors, ASBCA No. 38288, 90-1 B.C.A. (CCH) ¶ 22,350.

[143] Micrographic Technology, Inc., ASBCA No. 25577, 81-2 B.C.A. (CCH) ¶ 15,357; Pyramid Van & Storage Co., ASBCA No. 14257, 69-2 B.C.A. (CCH) ¶ 7,952.

[144] Kirchhan Indus., Inc., ASBCA No. 39260, 90-1 B.C.A. (CCH) ¶ 22,340; North Coast Remfg., Inc., ASBCA No. 38599, 89-3 B.C.A. (CCH) ¶ 22,232.

[145] Western Pac. Enters., ASBCA No. 25822, 81-2 B.C.A. (CCH) ¶ 15,217.

[146] Contraves-Goerz Corp., ASBCA No. 26317, 83-1 B.C.A. (CCH) ¶ 16,309.

[147] Yankee Telecommunications Lab., Inc., ASBCA No. 25240, 82-1 B.C.A. (CCH) ¶ 15,515.

[148] Doris Bookout, AGBCA No. 89-147-1, 89-1 B.C.A. (CCH) ¶ 21,570.

[149] McGraw-Hill Book Co., ASBCA No. 4500, 58-2 B.C.A. (CCH) ¶ 1,858.

[150] Roscoe-Ajax Constr. Co. & Knickerbocker Constr. Corp., 198 Ct. Cl. 133, 458 F.2d 55 (1972). The court in *Ajax* found that the reconsideration by the contracting officer kept the matter open and necessarily destroyed the finality that the decision theretofore had. A new final decision in proper form would be required to start a new appeal period running. McCotter Motors, Inc., ASBCA No. 21046, 77-2 B.C.A. (CCH) ¶ 12,642; Precision Tool & Eng'g Corp., ASBCA No. 16652, 73-1 B.C.A. (CCH) ¶ 9,878.

[151] Fairfield Scientific Corp., ASBCA No. 21151, 78-1 B.C.A. (CCH) ¶ 13,082; Racon Elec. Co., ASBCA No. 8020, 1962 B.C.A. (CCH) ¶ 3,528; Metimpex Corp., ASBCA No. 4658, 59-2 B.C.A. (CCH) ¶ 2,421; Fulford Mfg. Co., ASBCA Nos. 2143, 2144 (May 20, 1955); 44 Comp. Gen. 200 (1964).

default termination, a subsequent assessment of excess costs may be contested in the default appeal without filing an additional notice of appeal from the assessment of excess costs.[152] The United States Claims Court has adopted the Fulford Doctrine.[153] The Fulford Doctrine does not apply to the imposition of liquidated damages.

§ 22.32   —Form of Appeal

The notice of an appeal must be in writing and mailed or otherwise furnished to the board and the contracting officer from whose decision the appeal is taken. Dispatch by mailing of the appeal is a filing.[154] Providing an appeal to the contracting officer is a filing.[155] The contents of the notice of appeal should indicate that an appeal is being taken and should identify the contract (by number), the department or agency involved in the dispute, the decision from which the appeal is taken, and the amount in dispute, if known. The notice should be signed by the contractor taking the appeal or by the contractor's duly authorized representative or attorney.[156]

A contractor should explicitly indicate in the notice that an appeal from the contracting officer's decision is being taken. However, the boards have been liberal in some cases in finding that a contractor has expressed an intent to appeal,[157] holding, for example, that the contractor's letter stating "Would you please look into this matter?" was sufficient to show a present intent to appeal.

§ 22.33   —Procedures

To the fullest extent practicable, an agency board must provide "informal, expeditious, and inexpensive resolution of disputes."[158] As discussed in §§ 22.40 and 22.41, special procedures must also be provided for the accelerated disposition of claims of $50,000 or less and small claims of $10,000 or less.[159]

The boards of contract appeals conduct trials at locations most convenient to the parties. The general procedure is for the hearing to be conducted

---

[152] AIRCO, Inc., IBCA No. 1074-8-75, 76-1 B.C.A. (CCH) ¶ 11,822; El-Tronics, Inc., ASBCA No. 5457, 61-1 B.C.A. (CCH) ¶ 2,961.

[153] D. Moody & Co. v. United States, 5 Cl. Ct. 70 (1984).

[154] Micrographic Technology, Inc., ASBCA No. 25577, 81-2 B.C.A. (CCH) ¶ 15,357.

[155] Yankee Telecommunications Lab., Inc., ASBCA No. 25240, 82-1 B.C.A. (CCH) ¶ 15,515.

[156] E.g., ASBCA R. of Prac. 2.

[157] E.g., Erwin D. Judkins, GSBCA No. 6164, 81-2 B.C.A. (CCH) ¶ 15,350.

[158] 41 U.S.C. § 607(e) (1988).

[159] Id. § 607(f).

by a single administrative judge, who normally writes the decision. The decision is then adopted by a panel of three to five judges as a decision of the full board. Normal board prehearing instructions explain that quantum will not be tried unless the board expressly agrees to hear it; complete cost schedule and support information have been furnished; and, if it is a contractor claim, the government has had an opportunity to audit.

As a policy matter, the boards separate entitlement from quantum whenever practicable. Several factors must be considered in deciding whether to separate or bifurcate quantum and entitlement. In some disputes, the facts relating to entitlement may prove relatively simple, although quantum issues are extremely complex. In such cases, it may prove more efficient to try entitlement first. If the contractor loses its appeal, the board and the parties need not waste time and energy in the trial of a complex monetary issue. If the contract prevails and the appeal is sustained, parties can attempt to negotiate a settlement of the quantum issues or, should that fail, proceed to a second action. Few appeals remanded to the parties for negotiation require additional participation by the boards for resolution. If the contractor believes it has a strong case on entitlement but a relatively weak case on quantum, it may prove advantageous to separate the two issues for trial.

§ 22.34 —Pleadings

Within 30 days after receipt of notice of docketing of the appeal, the appellant must file with the board a complaint setting forth simple, concise, and direct statements of each of its claims. Appellant also must set forth the basis, with appropriate reference to contract provisions, of each claim and the dollar amount claimed to the extent known. No particular form is required. Upon receipt of the complaint, the board serves a copy of it upon the government.[160]

Within 30 days of receipt of the complaint, the government must prepare and file an answer with the board. The answer must set forth simple, concise, and direct statements of the government's defenses to each claim asserted by the appellant, including any affirmative defenses available, such as accord and satisfaction. Upon receipt of the answer, the board serves a copy upon the appellant.[161] Each party must then advise the board whether a hearing is desired or whether submission of the case on the record, without a hearing, is more appropriate.[162]

---

[160] *E.g.,* ASBCA R. of Prac. 6(a).

[161] *E.g., id.* R. 6(b).

[162] *E.g., id.* R. 8.

Upon its own initiative, or upon application of either party, the board may arrange a conference—either by telephone or before an administrative judge or examiner—to consider the following:

1. Simplification, clarification, or severance of the issues
2. Possibility of obtaining stipulations, admissions, agreements, and rulings on admissibility of documents, understandings on matters already of record, or similar agreements that avoid unnecessary proof
3. Agreements and rulings to facilitate discovery
4. Limitation of the number of expert witnesses or avoidance of similar cumulative evidence
5. Possibility of agreement disposing of any or all of the issues in dispute
6. Such other matters as may aid in the disposition of the appeal.[163]

While this is going on, the government is required to file the appeal file within 30 days of docketing. This file is commonly known as the *Rule 4 File* because it is filed pursuant to Rule 4 of the various boards. Basically, the file consists of the contracting officer's decision that is being appealed, the contract itself, and the relevant correspondence and documents that were generated during the period of the contract. The file may also contain any additional information deemed relevant. Within 30 days of receipt of its copy of the Rule 4 File, the contractor has the right to supplement the file with any additional relevant documents. Each party has the right to object to the inclusion of documents in the Rule 4 File submitted by the other party, giving the reasons for the objections. Documents in the Rule 4 File, other than those to which an objection is sustained, constitute part of the record upon which the board will base its decision.

§ 22.35   —Discovery

The boards encourage the parties to participate in voluntary discovery procedures. Should voluntary participation not be successful, the board may issue orders to either party to compel compliance and participation.[164]

Depositions

After an appeal has been docketed and a complaint filed, the parties may mutually agree to (or the board may, upon application of either party, order) the taking of testimony of any person by deposition (oral examination

---

[163] *E.g., id.* R. 10.

[164] *E.g.,* ASBCA R. of Prac. 14.

or written interrogatories) before any officer authorized to administer oath at the place of examination for use as evidence or for purposes of discovery. No testimony taken by deposition will be considered as part of the evidence in the hearing of the appeal until such testimony is offered and received in evidence at the hearing. The deposition ordinarily will not be received in evidence if the deponent is present and can testify at the hearing. In such instances, however, the deposition may be used to contradict or impeach the testimony of the deponent given at the hearing. Each party bears its own expenses associated with the taking of any deposition.

Other Discovery Methods

After an appeal has been docketed and a complaint filed, a party may serve on the other party:

1. Written interrogatories to be entered separately, signed under oath, and answered or objected to within 30 or 45 days depending on the board

2. Request for the admission of specified facts or the authenticity of any documents answered or objected to within 30 or 45 days after service

3. Factual statements or the authenticity of the documents to be deemed admitted upon failure of the party to respond to the request

4. Request for the production, inspection, and copying of any documents or objects not privileged, which reasonably may lead to the discovery of admissible evidence, to be answered or objected to within 30 or 45 days after service.[165]

§ 22.36   —Rule 11 Cases

Rule 11 provides for a record submission; in other words, the case is decided without a hearing on the basis of the documents and briefs.[166] This is best suited for relatively uncomplicated factual situations in which there was ample documentary evidence that could be adequately described in a written brief. The key question for the parties to consider is whether they can be as persuasive in writing as the witnesses would be in testifying. Either party may elect, under Rule 11, to waive a trial and to submit its case on the written record before the board. This record consists of the appeal file as well as any affidavits, admissions, answers to interrogatories,

---

[165] *E.g., id.* R. 15.

[166] *E.g.,* ASBCA R. of Prac. 11.

or stipulations that the parties may have accumulated. It is particularly important for Rule 11 parties to distinguish between bare allegations that will not benefit their case and substantiated facts that will play an important role in persuading the judge.

§ 22.37 —Hearings

The boards conduct hearings at locations determined by the boards to best serve the interests of the parties and the board. So, although the boards are headquartered in the Washington, D.C., area, they may hold hearings worldwide.

Hearings will be as informal as may be reasonable and appropriate under the circumstances. Appellant and the government may offer such evidence as they deem appropriate and as would be admissible under the Federal Rules of Evidence or in the sound discretion of the presiding judge or examiner. Witnesses before the board will be examined orally—under oath or affirmation—unless the presiding judge or examiner otherwise orders.

The testimony or arguments at hearings are recorded verbatim. Transcripts of the proceedings are then given to each party. Posthearing briefs may be submitted as directed by the presiding judge or examiner. Decisions of the judges of the boards will be made in writing, and authenticated copies of the decision will be forwarded simultaneously to both parties. In the ASBCA, for example, unless the claim was below $50,000, the decision will be signed by three judges—the presiding judge, the chair, and the vice-chair.[167]

§ 22.38 —Subpoenas

Board judges have the power to "administer oaths to witnesses, authorize depositions and discovery proceedings, and require by subpoena the attendance of witnesses, and production of books and papers, for the taking of testimony or evidence by deposition or in the hearing of an appeal by the agency board."[168] Subpoenas are enforced, upon application of the board or the Attorney General, by orders of a federal district court having jurisdiction over the person refusing to obey the subpoena, with power to punish continuing disobedience by contempt proceedings.

---

[167] *E.g.,* ASBCA R. of Prac. 17.
[168] 41 U.S.C. § 610 (1988).

§ 22.39   Procedures for Handling Claims

The CDA provides the boards with accelerated procedures for handling claims of $50,000 or less,[169] and an expedited procedure for claims of $10,000 or less.[170] Both procedures are available solely at the election of the contractor.

§ 22.40   —Expedited Procedure for Small Claims

The expedited procedure is available for the disposition of any appeal from a decision of the contracting officer when the amount in dispute is $10,000 or less.[171] The Office of Federal Procurement Policy (OFPP) Administrator may adjust the $10,000 level based on a study of economic indexes every three years. This procedure shall be available at the sole election of the contractor. Decisions may be reached under this expedited procedure by a single member of a board, and such decisions are final and conclusive except in cases of fraud. Thus, neither the contractor nor the government may seek judicial review of a decision made in accordance with the small claims procedure. The limitation on appeal does not preclude the filing of a motion for reconsideration before a board of contract appeals.[172] In addition, such decisions do not have value as precedent for future cases. The procedures shall be simplified to facilitate the decision, which shall be made, whenever possible, within 120 days from the date on which the contractor elects to use the small claims procedure.

The board rules[173] provide for the contractor to elect the small claims (expedited) procedure by written notice to the board within 60 days after receipt of the notice of docketing. Time limits are imposed on the government and the board personnel at various stages of the process; and pleadings, discovery, and other prehearing activities are allowed only to the extent that they are consistent with a simplified procedure and expedited hearing schedule, if any hearing is to be held. The decision will be rendered by a single administrative judge who will issue a short written decision containing only summary findings of fact and conclusions, or who may, as a matter of discretion, render an oral decision on the appeal, with copies to be furnished to the parties subsequently.

---

[169] 41 U.S.C. § 607(f) (1988).

[170] *Id.* § 608.

[171] 41 U.S.C. § 608 (1988).

[172] *See, e.g.,* ASBCA R. of Prac. 12.4.

[173] *E.g., id.* R. 12.1, 12.2.

§ 22.41   —Accelerated Procedure

For appeals involving $50,000 or less, the CDA also requires the boards of contract appeals to provide an accelerated procedure, which will result in a decision within 180 days whenever possible.[174] This procedure is also available at the sole election of the contractor, and the 180-day period runs from the date of its election. Unlike the expedited procedure, there is no limitation on the right of appeal or judicial review for claims appealed under the accelerated procedure. This means that a contractor appealing a decision involving $10,000 or less has three choices:

1. Normal board of contract appeals procedures and rights of judicial review
2. Small claims (expedited) procedure resulting in a nonreviewable board decision within 120 days
3. Accelerated procedure, resulting in a judicially-reviewable decision within 180 days.

The implementing rules adopted by the boards for contractor elections under the expedited procedure also apply to the accelerated procedure.

To accelerate a decision, the parties are encouraged, if consistent with adequate presentation of factual and legal positions, to waive pleadings, discovery, and briefs. The decision normally will be rendered by a single administrative judge with concurrence of a vice-chairperson, or a majority among those two and the chairperson, in case of disagreement between the former.[175] If the amount in dispute is $10,000 or less, the administrative judge may render an oral decision, with copies to be furnished to the parties subsequently.

§ 22.42   Direct Action in United States Claims Court

The United States Claims Court, created pursuant to the Federal Courts Improvements Act of 1982,[176] and organized pursuant to Article I of the Constitution, is composed of 16 judges, appointed for 15-year terms by the President. As Article I judges, the Claims Court judges are vested with authority to "enter dispositive judgments," including orders on motions for summary judgment.

---

[174] 41 U.S.C. § 607(f) (1988).

[175] *E.g.,* ASBCA R. of Prac. 12.3.

[176] Federal Courts Improvement Act of 1982, Pub. L. No. 97-164, 96 Stat. 25.

By providing that, in lieu of appealing a decision of a contracting officer, a contractor may bring an action directly on the claim in the United States Claims Court, the CDA has eliminated the traditional requirement that the contractor exhaust any available administrative remedies before seeking judicial relief.[177]

A suit brought by a contractor directly in the Claims Court must be filed within one year of the date of receipt by the contractor of the contracting officer's decision concerning the claim.[178] This appeal time, as with the time for appealing decisions to the boards of contract appeals, is considered jurisdictional and cannot be waived by the Claims Court.[179] The six-year statute of limitations[180] for civil actions against the government is expressly made inapplicable to suits brought under the CDA.[181]

Unlike the boards of contract appeals, the date of receipt of the complaint by the Claims Court is controlling in determining whether an appeal has been filed within the statutory time limits.[182] Nevertheless, an otherwise untimely complaint still may be considered if it was mailed by certified or registered mail in sufficient time to be received before the due date.[183]

Pursuant to 28 U.S.C. § 2503(b), the proceedings of the Claims Court are conducted according to the Federal Rules of Evidence. The court is not bound by the Federal Rules of Civil Procedure, but has incorporated them "to the extent that they appropriately can apply to the proceedings."[184]

The Claims Court sits in Washington, D.C., but will hold trials at any location within the United States necessary for the convenience of the parties and witnesses.[185] Cases before the Claims Court are heard and decided by one judge.[186] The 16 judges of the Claims Court have not hesitated in refusing to follow each other's decisions.[187] Conflicts between the individual decisions of the Claims Court judges are resolved by the Court of Appeals for the Federal Circuit.

---

[177] United States v. Holpuch Co., 328 U.S. 234 (1946); United States v. Lair, 321 U.S. 730 (1944); Henry E. Wile Co. v. United States, 144 Ct. Cl. 394 (1959).

[178] 41 U.S.C. § 609(a)(3) (1988).

[179] Cosmic Constr. Co. v. United States, 697 F.2d 1389 (Fed. Cir. 1982).

[180] 28 U.S.C. §§ 2401, 2501.

[181] *Id.* § 2401.

[182] U.S. Claims Ct. R. 3.

[183] *Id.* R. 3(b)(2)(C).

[184] *Id.* R. 1(b).

[185] 28 U.S.C. § 173; *In re* United States, 877 F.2d 1568 (Fed. Cir. 1989).

[186] 28 U.S.C. § 174(a).

[187] *Compare* Big Bud Tractors, Inc. v. United States, 2 Cl. Ct. 195, *aff'd,* 727 F.2d 118 (Fed. Cir. 1983) *with* Dean Forwarding Co. v. United States, 2 Cl. Ct. 559 (1983).

The Tucker Act jurisdiction of the United States Claims Court extends to civil actions based on an express or implied-in-fact contract with the government, for liquidated or unliquidated damages.[188] Suits based on quasi-contracts, or contracts implied-in-law, are not authorized. In order to give the Claims Court jurisdiction to give judgment against the government an implied contract must be implied-in-fact and not one based merely on equitable considerations and implied in law.[189] Actions sounding in tort likewise are not authorized. The Comptroller General has ruled that, except as provided by statute, "the United States is not responsible for the negligence of its officers, employees, or agents and such liability cannot be imposed upon it by an attempt on the part of the contracting officer to make it a part of the consideration of a contract."[190]

The court can grant money judgments and appropriate equitable relief such as injunctions.[191] Also, the court may enter a money judgment based on the contract as reformed to accord with the actual intention of the parties.[192] As previously noted, the CDA authorizes the payment of interest on amounts found to be due a contractor from the date the contracting officer receives the claim until it is paid.[193] This is simple, not compound, interest.[194]

§ 22.43 —Process Before United States Claims Court

A suit in the Claims Court is initiated by filing a complaint with the Clerk of the Court, who then serves the complaint on the government by delivering a copy to the Department of Justice, which represents the government before the Claims Court. The government has 60 days from the date of service of the complaint to file its answer. Claims Court pretrial proceedings are governed by Appendix G to the Rules of the Court, although the judge has discretion to change the pretrial proceedings, if felt appropriate. Within 15 days after the government answers the complaint or the plaintiff replies to a government counterclaim, the attorneys for the parties are

---

[188] 28 U.S.C. §§ 1491–1507.

[189] United States v. Minnesota Mut. Inv. Co., 271 U.S. 212 (1926); Dean Prosser & Crew, IBCA No. 1471-6-81, 81-2 B.C.A. (CCH) ¶ 15,294.

[190] 16 Comp. Gen. 803, 804 (1937).

[191] United States v. Jones, 131 U.S. 1 (1889); Chas. Hummel Co., AGBCA No. 81-147-4, 81-1 B.C.A. (CCH) ¶ 14,968; 28 U.S.C. § 1491.

[192] United States v. Milliken Imprinting Co., 202 U.S. 168 (1906); Paragon Energy Corp. v. United States, 645 F.2d 966 (Ct. Cl. 1981); Quality Elec. Serv., ASBCA No. 25811, 81-2 B.C.A. (CCH) ¶ 15,380.

[193] 41 U.S.C. § 611.

[194] ACS Constr. Co. v. United States, 230 Cl. Ct. 845 (1982).

required to confer and discuss preparation of a joint preliminary status report. In this context, attorneys are required, among other things, to address each party's factual and legal contentions, their respective discovery needs, and the proposed discovery schedules. They also are required to discuss settlement of the action. Next, parties must submit the joint preliminary status report no later than 30 days after the attorneys confer. The parties are required to advise the court on a number of points relevant to the conduct of the case, including whether there are any jurisdictional issues in the case, whether a trial of liability and damages should be bifurcated, and whether either party intends to file a dispositive motion. The rules for discovery in front of the Claims Court are similar to those before the boards of contract appeals.

The trials and judgments are similar to those before the federal district courts. The applicable rules are Claims Court Rules 39–68.

§ 22.44   Appeal to Court of Appeals for the Federal Circuit

If the parties are dissatisfied with the decision of the board of contract appeals or the Claims Court, they may appeal the decision to the United States Court of Appeals for the Federal Circuit, which hears appeals from both forums.

The CDA authorizes the United States Court of Appeals for the Federal Circuit to review the decisions of a board of contract appeals, providing as follows:

> [N]otwithstanding any contract provision, regulation, or rules of law to the contrary, the decision of the agency board on any question of law shall not be final or conclusive, but the decision on any question of fact shall be final and conclusive, and shall not be set aside unless the decision is fraudulent, or arbitrary, or capricious, or so grossly erroneous as to necessarily imply bad faith, or if such decision is not supported by substantial evidence.[195]

This provision restates essentially the same standards of, but does not expressly repeal, the Wunderlich Act,[196] which sets out the scope of review standards for government contract cases.[197] That Act was passed to overcome limits placed on review as the result of *United States v. Wunderlich*.[198] In the case, the Supreme Court held that a decision under a Disputes clause was conclusive unless actual fraud were alleged and proved.

---

[195] 41 U.S.C. § 609(b) (1988).

[196] *Id.* §§ 321–322.

[197] *E.g.*, Systems Technology Assocs. v. United States, 699 F.2d 1383 (Fed. Cir. 1983).

[198] 342 U.S. 98 (1951).

The contractor's right to judicial review of decisions under a Disputes clause thus became extremely limited.

Consistent with the general policy of the 1978 legislation to afford the government, as well as the contractor, the right to adjudicate its claims, the CDA specifically authorizes the government to appeal from a decision of a board of contract appeals.[199] An agency head who determines that an appeal should be taken must first secure the approval of the Attorney General and then transmit the board decision to the United States Court of Appeals for the Federal Circuit for judicial review. As with contractor appeals, the judicial review must be invoked by the government within 120 days of the agency's receipt of a copy of the board of contract appeals decision.[200]

The head of an executive department or agency should exercise discretion to seek judicial review only when it has concluded that the board of contract appeals decision is not entitled to finality under the review standards of the CDA. These standards are the same for government and contractor appeals. That is, an agency board decision on questions of law is not considered final (but a finding of fact is) unless the decision is fraudulent, arbitrary, capricious, so grossly erroneous as to necessarily imply bad faith, or is not supported by substantial evidence.[201]

The CDA provides that, in an appeal from an agency board, the Court of Appeals for the Federal Circuit "may render an opinion and judgment and remand the case for further action by the agency board or by the executive agency as appropriate, with such direction as the court considers just and proper."[202] This includes the taking of additional evidence. This authority to remand the case applies to judicial review sought by the government or a contractor.[203]

The Court of Appeals for the Federal Circuit also has exclusive jurisdiction to hear appeals from final decisions of the United States Claims Court.[204] These appeals must be received by the Clerk of the Court within 60 days of entry of the Claims Court's judgment.[205] The Claims Court's findings of fact will be set aside only if "clearly erroneous."[206]

A decision of the United States Court of Appeals for the Federal Circuit may be reviewed upon application for a writ of certiorari to the United

---

[199] 41 U.S.C. § 607(g)(1)(B), 28 U.S.C. § 2510(b).

[200] Id.

[201] 41 U.S.C. § 609(b).

[202] Id. § 609(c), in conjunction with 28 U.S.C. § 1295(b), (c).

[203] 41 U.S.C. § 609(c).

[204] 28 U.S.C. § 1295(a)(3).

[205] Id. § 2107; accord Sofarelli Assocs., Inc. v. United States, 716 F.2d 1395 (Fed. Cir. 1983).

[206] Milmark Servs., Inc. v. United States, 731 F.2d 855 (Fed. Cir. 1984).

States Supreme Court, but such writs are infrequently granted in government contract cases.

§ 22.45   Equal Access to Justice Act

The Equal Access to Justice Act (EAJA),[207] has substantial implications for small businesses contracting with the government because it provides certain parties with limited resources the opportunity to litigate unreasonable governmental action when finances would normally deter such litigation. The EAJA provides that agencies will award to a prevailing party, other than the United States, reasonable fees and other expenses (in-house as well as outside assistance) incurred by that party during the proceedings unless the position of the agency is found to be substantially justified. This means that eligible parties who prevail over the government in certain civil actions brought by or against the government may be awarded reasonable attorneys' fees and other expenses, unless the government acted reasonably during the conduct of a genuine dispute or special circumstances make an award unjust.

A prevailing party under the EAJA excludes any individual whose net worth exceeds $2 million and any sole owner of an unincorporated business, or any partnership, corporation, association, or organization with a net worth exceeding $7 million or with more than 500 employees. In determining the eligibility of applicants, the net worth and number of employees for affiliated entities may be aggregated. There is no EAJA relief for a small, otherwise eligible subcontractor who is involved in litigation with the government in the name of a large (not eligible) prime contractor with whom the government has privity.[208]

Fees and Expenses

The EAJA specifies that an application for fees and expenses must be submitted within 30 days of final judgment, with an itemized statement that shows actual time expended and rates used in computations. The definition of fees of expenses requires that expenses of expert witnesses and attorneys' fees be "reasonable." The amount of fees is to be based on prevailing market rates for the kind and quality of the services furnished. Attorneys' fees shall not be awarded in excess of $75 per hour unless the agency determines by regulation (or the court determines) that an increase in the cost of living

---

[207] Equal Access to Justice Act, Pub. L. No. 99-80, 99 Stat. 186 (Aug. 5, 1985).
[208] Teton Constr. Co., ASBCA Nos. 27700, 28968, 87-2 B.C.A. (CCH) ¶ 19,766.

or a special factor, such as the limited availability of qualified attorneys for the proceedings involved, justifies a higher fee.[209]

The court should compensate counsel for the time reasonably expended[210] but prelitigation expenses are not allowed.[211] The EAJA requires the court to award "reasonable" attorneys' fees and this might be accomplished by reducing the hours claimed to a figure the court deems to have been reasonably expended.[212] The court will strike hours when it appears that the time expended was inordinately high for the work performed.[213] A court will also reduce an award for inadequately documented (as well as excessive) hours, duplicated work by another attorney, incurred hours due to inexperience, work unrelated to the claim, and work not normally performed by an attorney (for example, work normally performed by paralegals, even when paralegals are not employed).

A pro se litigant cannot collect attorneys' fees, but (like any other litigant) can request an award of costs and other allowable expenses. Other allowable expenses are defined to include the reasonable expenses of expert witnesses (except that no expert witness shall be compensated at a rate in excess of the highest rate of compensation for expert witnesses paid by the agency) and the reasonable cost of any study, analysis, engineering report, test, or project found by the agency or court to be necessary for the preparation of the party's case.[214] Work performed by paralegals and computer researchers are compensable under the Act.[215]

Prevailing Party

A party does not have to prevail on all issues; however, the party is a prevailing party under EAJA if it succeeds on any significant issue in the litigation that achieves some of the benefits sought in bringing the suit.[216] A contractor who was successful on appeal on one of two claims denied by the government was entitled to 75 percent of its total attorneys' fees and

---

[209] 5 U.S.C. § 504(b)(1)(A) (1988) applies to agency adjudications. A $75 hourly rate for attorneys' fees is also provided in 28 U.S.C. § 2412(d)(2)(A) for judicial actions. Even though attorneys' fees may exceed $75, they must still be reasonable. Any fee-setting inquiry begins with the number of hours reasonably expended multiplied by a reasonable hourly rate.

[210] Copeland v. Marshall, 641 F.2d 880 (D.C. Cir. 1980).

[211] Bailey v. United States, 721 F.2d 357, 359 (Fed. Cir. 1983).

[212] St. Paul Fire & Marine Ins. Co. v. United States, 4 Cl. Ct. 762, 771-772 (1984) (hours were reduced to avoid the possibility of overcompensation).

[213] Photo Data v. Sawyer, 533 F. Supp. 348, 353, (D.D.C. 1982).

[214] 28 U.S.C. § 2412(d)(2)(B).

[215] Hiorschey v. FERC, 760 F.2d 760 (D.C. Cir. 1985).

[216] Austin v. Department of Commerce, 742 F.2d 1417 (Fed. Cir. 1984).

costs incurred in prosecuting the appeal because that ratio affected the ratio between the total claim and the amount actually awarded.[217] The judge may award attorneys' fees for the particular "phase" of the litigation in which the plaintiff did prevail.[218] The fact that the case was terminated by stipulation for dismissal does not in itself foreclose an application for fees and expenses.[219] A party may even be deemed prevailing under EAJA if it obtains a settlement of it case. A victory following a full trial on the merits is not required.[220]

An agency or court shall award fees and other expenses unless the "position of the agency (United States)" was substantially justified. The Court of Appeals for the Federal Circuit initially held that it would not reexamine the government's position prior to the litigation proceeding, but would only look to the government's litigation position.[221] The amendments to the EAJA expanded the definition of *position* and imposed a broader and stricter standard of liability on the government. The original Act provided that fees would not be awarded if the government's position was "substantially justified." The new Act replaces this language and now provides the following:

> Whether or not the position of the agency was substantially justified shall be determined on the basis of the administrative record as a whole, which was made in the adversary adjudication for which fees and other expenses are sought.[222]

The Court of Appeals for the Federal Circuit has now adopted the rule that substantial justification requires the government to show that it was clearly reasonable in asserting its position, including its position at the agency level, in view of the law and the facts. The government must show that it has not "persisted in pressing a tenuous factual or legal position, albeit one not wholly without foundation." It is not sufficient for the government to show merely "the existence of a corollary legal basis for the government's case."[223]

The EAJA allows recovery of fees and expenses incurred both before and after its effective date if the action was pending on the effective date or initiated thereafter.

Under EAJA, an award of costs is a discretionary matter for the court and is not governed by the "substantially justified" test. Court costs (for

---

[217] Sardis Contractors, ENGBCA No. 5256-F, 90-3 B.C.A. (CCH) ¶ 23,010.

[218] Ellis v. United States, 711 F.2d 1571, 1576 (Fed. Cir. 1983).

[219] Gould v. United States, 3 Cl. Ct. 693, 695 (1983).

[220] St. Paul Fire & Marine Ins. Co. v. United States, 4 Cl. Ct. 762 (1984).

[221] Ellis v. United States, 711 F.2d 1571, 1575 (Fed. Cir. 1983).

[222] 5 U.S.C. § 504(a)(1) (Supp. III 1991).

[223] Schuenemeyer v. United States, 776 F.2d 329, 330 (Fed. Cir. 1985).

example, filing fees) are not usually recoverable under 28 U.S.C. § 2412(c) in accordance with the long-standing policy of the United States Court of Claims.[224] Under the EAJA, cost and fees and other expenses are expressly authorized but under different subsections and different standards.[225]

Burden of Proof

The burden of proof is always on the applicant to prove entitlement to fees and expenses.[226] To prove its fees and expenses, the applicant must submit an application accompanied by sufficiently detailed supporting documents (for example, affidavits, time sheets, or contemporaneous time records).[227] The prevailing party must request fees and expenses within 30 days of final judgment.[228] A judgment is final when it is no longer appealable. For example, a CDA appeal to a board of contract appeals becomes final if the court's decision is not appealed within 120 days after receipt of the decision. That 30 days is statutory and cannot be waived. Thus, an applicant for fees and expenses must file within 150 days after receipt of a board decision.

---

[224] Schuenemeyer v. United States, 7 Cl. Ct. 417, 421-22 (1985).

[225] 28 U.S.C. § 2412(a) (costs), (d)(2)(A) (fees and other expenses).

[226] National Ass'n of Concerned Veterans v. Screen, 675 F.2d 1319, 1337 (D.C. Cir. 1982).

[227] *Id.*

[228] 28 U.S.C. § 2412(d)(1)(B).

CHAPTER 23

TECHNIQUE OF ALTERNATIVE DISPUTE RESOLUTION

Douglas W. Sullivan
Michael E. Olsen

Douglas W. Sullivan is a partner in the San Francisco, California, office of Folger & Levin. He is a 1979 graduate of the University of Virginia Law School, and has been primarily involved in resolving and litigating construction industry disputes. He has represented a wide variety of interests on major commercial and power-related projects, including the interests of owners, contractors, engineers, and sureties. Mr. Sullivan is an arbitrator for the American Arbitration Association and is a member of the ABA sections on Litigation and Public Contract Law.

Michael E. Olsen is an associate in the San Francisco, California, office of Folger & Levin and a 1989 graduate of the Georgetown University Law Center. Since the completion of a federal district court clerkship, his practice has focused on construction and real estate litigation.

§ 23.1   Introduction

Attorneys and their clients realize that the investment of time and money required by litigation can make losers out of both sides in a dispute. Alternatives to litigation, therefore, often serve the client's interests better than litigation. As discussed in this chapter, virtually every case can benefit from alternative dispute resolution (ADR), at least at some stage of the litigation.

What is ADR? Simply put, ADR includes any method by which parties settle a dispute without resorting to formal litigation in the courts. ADR encompasses a broad range of alternate methods, including nonbinding mediation, binding mediation, minitrials, court-ordered settlement conferences, use of special masters or independent experts to further settlement, and the more formal process of arbitration.

Statistics demonstrate the rising popularity of ADR. For example, the American Arbitration Association reports that the number of construction cases arbitrated by the American Arbitration Association rose from 2,831 in 1980 to 5,132 in 1989.[1] This represents an 81 percent increase. Although the numbers are substantial, they represent just the tip of the iceberg; these statistics do not include cases arbitrated by other tribunals, nor do they include disputes resolved by other means, such as mediation.

---

[1] 1989–1990 Am. Arb. Ass'n Gen. Couns. Ann. Rep.

The reason for this surge in ADR usage is simple. Increasingly, clients recognize that almost all cases can benefit from ADR. Specifically, ADR can:

1. Save the client time and money by providing an alternative to the burdensome demands of litigation
2. Encourage each party to assess the strengths and weaknesses of its own positions in the dispute
3. Provide each party and its attorney an opportunity to assess the other side's case
4. Help the parties focus on the heart of the dispute
5. Help the parties communicate, thereby increasing the likelihood of settlement and offering the opportunity for creative methods of settlement
6. Help preserve the business relationships between the parties
7. Help the parties structure the proceedings and discovery so that they proceed more efficiently, even if ADR is not successful in resolving the dispute fully.

§ 23.2   Advantages of ADR

The impetus for ADR is particularly high in the construction industry, where disputes are common, time-consuming, and costly.[2] Years ago, arbitration clauses became a standard component of construction contracts. Now, however, dissatisfied with the lengthy processes and costs involved even in formal arbitration, parties are looking for more streamlined approaches for resolving their differences. ADR is designed to settle cases earlier than they otherwise would be resolved, thereby serving to curtail litigation costs.

Handling Multiple Issues and Parties

Although ADR offers a flexible mechanism with which to begin the process toward settlement, it is up to the parties and their lawyers to decide how best to deal with the issues and the participants in ADR so as to effectuate settlement. ADR can benefit complex construction cases by providing a way to handle cases with multiple factual disputes and parties, as is typical in defect and delay claims in construction litigation in which the owner,

---

[2] *See generally* Alternative Dispute Resolution in the Construction Industry (R. Cushman et al. eds., John Wiley & Sons 1991).

architect/engineer, contractors, and material suppliers are all involved. Joint presentations can be made. Alternatively, limited parties can participate in ADR and thereafter attempt to reach accommodations with the other parties. For example, in a dispute between an owner and a contractor (with numerous subcontractors also involved), the owner and contractor may wish to undertake ADR separately and reach common grounds before addressing the particular subcontractors.

Similarly, the parties (including, for example, an owner, contractor, and subcontractor) may pursue ADR jointly with respect to isolated defects, rather than confront all the defects together. By bifurcating or trifurcating the issues related to the defects, the parties may resolve important issues first, bringing the problems into focus and the parties to the settlement table.

ADR also can be used to bring third parties (including insurers) into the negotiations even though those third parties are not named parties in the court or arbitration proceedings. In construction disputes involving condominium projects and homeowners' associations, ADR can be particularly helpful given that numerous entities are often involved and given the necessity of participation of insurers in any ultimate resolution.

Educating Parties

Through ADR, lawyers may also educate their clients early in the process. Parties often possess a too rosy view of their positions. By the same token, lawyers may be reluctant to voice too strongly the weaknesses of their clients' positions, lest the lawyers alienate their clients. In ADR, lawyers may forcefully advocate their clients' positions, to the pleasure of the clients, while at the same time achieving the benefit of having third parties advise the clients of the strengths and weaknesses of the clients' cases. Then the clients are in a position to make informed decisions about the economic wisdom of settling for a particular result or proceeding with litigation. Of course, as is true with any settlement process, the success of ADR depends on the participation of competent and appropriate decision makers for the clients.

In addition, many clients are skeptical whether the lawyers are unnecessarily increasing the level of litigation activity or hindering settlement. Even if unsuccessful, ADR educates the clients and allows them to evaluate whether the opposing parties (rather than the lawyers) are being unreasonable, and, if so, how to proceed in light of the economics. If litigation continues, lawyers will also have the comfort of knowing that their clients appreciate the need to undertake litigation with the resulting costs.

Concomitantly, a properly structured ADR serves to enlighten the opposing parties in the formative stages of the litigation. Although the parties may fail to be persuaded by arguments of opposing parties and counsel, a respected mediator should be substantially more persuasive in offering a nonbiased view.[3]

Encouraging Creative Settlement

Unlike the more formal processes of court litigation and arbitration, non-binding ADR offers the opportunity for creative settlement methods. ADR can lead to settlements not involving simply the exchange of money. In a construction defect-related case, through ADR the parties can be encouraged to compromise on the nature of the corrective work, if any. In particular, ADR offers a forum for frank discussions between experts, including architects, engineers, and contractors, rather than through attorneys. Once the scope of corrective work is agreed upon, the contractor may be willing to undertake the work. This process is not unlike the dispute resolution procedures set out in the standard American Institute of Architects' Document A201, *General Conditions.* Unlike the AIA procedures, however, ADR generally involves the use of a neutral mediator who has not had any involvement with the project.

  In the construction industry, where business relationships often are continuing with other projects, a settlement through ADR could also involve an agreement to conduct business on another project rather than simply to pay money. When continuing business relationships are involved, ADR may also be beneficial in avoiding any deterioration of the relationships. ADR can be conducted in a much less adversarial context and with confidentiality agreements.

Preserving Confidentiality

There obviously are many instances when the client would like to keep the details of the dispute, or even the mere existence of a dispute, private. The need for confidentiality may be desired when knowledge of the dispute potentially might affect other business or relationships. Although court proceedings are a matter of public record, ADR can be confidential if the parties so agree.[4] This confidentiality is reinforced by many states' statutes. For example, California Evidence Code § 1152 makes all statements in

---

[3] *See also* W. Brazil et al., *Early Neutral Evaluation: An Experimental Effort to Expedite Dispute Resolution* 69 Judicature 279 (1986) (discussing a program instituted by the courts to assure early evaluation of cases by the clients).

[4] The American Arbitration Association Construction Industry Mediation Rules (1988) [hereinafter AAA Mediation R.] provide that the "parties shall maintain the confidentiality of the mediation." AAA Mediation R. 12.

"settlement discussions," including discussions in a properly structured ADR, inadmissible in court.[5]

Narrowing the Dispute

Even if unsuccessful, ADR may lead to a narrowing of the dispute so as to minimize costs. In addition, with at least a rudimentary understanding of the other side's case early in the process, the parties may be more willing to set limits on discovery. Even in the arbitration context, in which various types of discovery, such as depositions, are not permitted, the parties may determine that limited depositions of key experts on particular issues, within time constraints, are worthwhile. The limited depositions may well narrow the disputes or at least curtail the time necessary for hearing evidence and testimony.

Perhaps most importantly, ADR can be used effectively when one of the parties has adopted an unrealistic position and is recalcitrant in that position. Having a third party in the ADR process, whom the recalcitrant party respects, to advise the resisting party of the weaknesses of its positions can be a useful tool in furthering settlement. If the recalcitrant party is reluctant to participate in ADR, that reluctance can be alleviated in a number of ways, including letting the party choose the mediator.

Shortcomings

Nevertheless, ADR will not be productive at every stage of the litigation or in every case. For example, in cases in which information is largely in the hands of one party, ADR may be handicapped until there is a sharing of information. Of course, this shortcoming may be overcome by structuring limited discovery to correct the imbalance, whether it be formal or informal discovery. Unfortunately, however, the party possessing the information may conclude that the benefits from its informational advantage outweigh any advantages to be gained from ADR.

In some cases, it may be difficult to convince the other party to try ADR because the financial situation of that party precludes a fair settlement. ADR is particularly hampered when the financial condition of one party dictates an all-or-nothing strategy.

§ 23.3   Types of ADR

In considering the various types of ADR, one should be careful not to view them as completely separate concepts but rather should see the overlap

---

[5] *See also* Fed. R. Evid. 408; Fed. R. Civ. P. 68.

between the types. It is more important to concentrate on shaping a method of ADR that will best serve the client than it is to adhere blindly to the standard features of any one ADR method.

The discussion of the types of ADR in §§ 23.4 through 23.8 includes only a brief description and catalog of considerations. In reviewing the alternatives, the lawyer and client should remember that none of the formats is static. The parties may blend, eliminate, or substitute features to form the combination that most appeals to the participants and that best fits the nature of the dispute.

§ 23.4   —Nonbinding Mediation

Sometimes described as "facilitated negotiation," nonbinding mediation involves an agreement between the parties to have a third-party mediator serve as an intermediary between the parties. The mediator does not resolve the dispute.[6] Rather, the mediator facilitates communication and moves the parties to a mutually agreeable resolution. Nonbinding mediation is available through a number of organizations, including the American Arbitration Association, which has published mediation rules specifically addressed to the construction industry.

An unwilling disputant may conclude that nonbinding mediation is futile and that expending time and resources on a mediation would be wasteful. Nevertheless, such a conclusion on the part of one of the disputants can be overcome.

Agreeing to Mediate

Nonbinding mediation provides an inexpensive opportunity for the parties to assess the disputes realistically. When the lawyer is reluctant to participate, direct contact between the parties, in which a request for mediation is made, may be useful. Rarely do clients turn down offers to avoid litigation expenses, in particular when the mediation is structured to cost little. In addition, by advising the opposing party that it is likely that the client will learn from the mediation process and reassess the case afterward, one can increase the likelihood of mediation.

A reluctant adversary also can be urged toward mediation by the courts and by arbitration panels. If the dispute is already in litigation or arbitration, a lawyer should not hesitate to request that the judge or arbitrator order or urge nonbinding mediation. Most court rules allow a judge to order settlement conferences, and nonbinding mediation is simply part of the settlement process. Although arbitrators do not get involved directly in

---

[6] *See, e.g.,* AAA Mediation R. 10.

settlement, they often encourage settlement conferences and mediations at the request of one party. The American Arbitration Association oversees both arbitrations and mediations, and a party desiring nonbinding mediation may request that a representative from the American Arbitration Association approach the other side and attempt to obtain an agreement to mediate.[7]

Selecting the Mediator

Once the parties agree in concept to pursue nonbinding mediation, the mediator must be selected. The mediator can be appointed or selected pursuant to the agreement of the parties or by the mediation organization. The American Arbitration Association has a Construction Mediation Panel.[8] The American Arbitration Association (AAA) Mediation Rules evidence a strong preference for neutral mediators, but parties may stipulate otherwise.[9]

The parties must, after appointing the mediator, decide what authority that mediator will have. Under the AAA Mediation Rules, the mediator has the authority "to conduct joint and separate meetings with the parties and to make oral and written recommendations for settlement."[10] The mediator is also empowered to seek expert advice concerning "technical aspects of the dispute."[11]

Choosing the Procedure

The nonbinding mediation itself is malleable. The format of the presentation, the participants, the length, and the form of decision are some of the considerations that the parties must address in advance.

In many mediations, the parties simply choose to make succinct factual presentations to the mediator through the equivalent of an opening statement without resort to direct testimony or voluminous document submissions. The parties may wish to stipulate that these statements suffice and leave it to the mediator to request additional evidence to iron out the disputes. This process avoids the cost of over-presentation, focusing the mediation on the real disputes. When the dispute is largely legal, the parties may

---

[7] *Id.* R. 2.

[8] *Id.* R. 5.

[9] *Id.*

[10] *Id.* R. 10.

[11] The rules provide that a mediator may call upon an expert to be compensated by the parties. AAA Mediation R. 10.

wish to present their entire case to the mediator and allow the mediator to request further briefing on the more troublesome issues.[12]

Although nonbinding mediations typically do not involve the live testimony of witnesses, such testimony may be helpful in certain instances.

Example.   A and B agree to hold a nonbinding mediation to resolve a dispute over the interpretation of a contract term. Each side realizes that the case will turn on the credibility of the testimony of the people involved in negotiating the contract. Because presentation by the attorneys will do little to educate either side, the parties agree to a limited amount of direct examination by the key witnesses. This process allows the parties to assess the credibility of the witnesses and educates each side as to the potential weaknesses in their cases.

There is no limit to the creativity that can be infused into the presentation. The parties simply may wish to have private discussions with the mediator and then allow the mediator to explore possible ways to settle the dispute after fully understanding the parties' positions and desires. The American Arbitration Association encourages such a process by providing for private hearings and for confidentiality of shared information.[13] In addition, statements and evidence presented in the mediation are not to be used in any arbitral or judicial proceeding.[14]

During the course of the presentation, the parties should feel free to confer with each other, with the mediator, and among themselves. The purpose of ADR is to resolve disputes, and resolution cannot be achieved without deliberation. A good mediator will be particularly helpful in coaxing the parties toward a middle ground, pointing out strengths and weaknesses during the course of the proceeding. The mediator should be discouraged from issuing an ultimate opinion because that may polarize the parties. It is usually best to have the mediator withhold any decision on the dispute until the possibilities for resolution have been exhausted.

Generally speaking, nonbinding mediation ends when a settlement is reached or one of the parties terminates the mediation. To avoid hasty terminations, the AAA Mediation Rules provide for the continuation of the mediation until execution of a written settlement agreement, until the parties have terminated the mediation in writing, or until the mediator executes a written declaration stating that in the mediator's view further efforts at mediation are no longer worthwhile.[15]

---

[12] These issues are discussed in greater detail in §§ **23.10–23.14.**

[13] AAA Mediation R. 11, 12.

[14] AAA Mediation R. 12; *see also* Fed. R. Evid. 408, advisory committee's notes.

[15] AAA Mediation R. 14.

§ 23.5   —Minitrial

An increasingly popular subset of nonbinding mediation is the minitrial, which is usually nothing more than a preformatted nonbinding mediation. In a minitrial, the parties present their cases before a neutral adviser, who renders an advisory opinion at the end if settlement discussions are unsuccessful in the interim. Because its format is sometimes structured like a shortened trial, with testimony of witnesses, attorneys are almost always involved in minitrials.

Each party should have present a representative who has both settlement and decision-making authority. If the party's representative has only settlement authority, creative settlements, involving something other than the exchange of money, are unlikely.

Procedure

The American Arbitration Association has a standard procedure for the minitrial.[16] The purpose of the minitrial is to permit the exchange of information and views and to provide a forum to negotiate toward settlement.[17] The AAA Minitrial Rules provide that the minitrial may be initiated by the consent of the parties, with the details governed by their agreement.[18] Generally speaking, counsel for each party is to prepare its "best case" and then to sit down, with properly empowered representatives of each side, and work toward settlement.[19] A neutral adviser is in attendance to decide questions of procedure and to advise party representatives when requested to do so.

The American Arbitration Association has a pool of potential neutral advisers, but this pool does not exhaust the potential candidates; the parties may choose anyone.[20] If the parties to a minitrial cannot agree upon an adviser, they may ask the American Arbitration Association to select an adviser.[21]

The American Arbitration Association Rules, however, are only a starting point. They can be changed, supplemented, or eliminated; indeed, the AAA Minitrial Rules themselves provide that issues of evidence, discovery, and length are left to agreement.[22]

---

[16] AAA Minitrial Proc. (1986).

[17] AAA Minitrial R. 3.

[18] *Id.* R. 1, 2.

[19] *Id.* R. 4, 5, 6.

[20] *Id.* R. 7.

[21] *Id.*

[22] *See, e.g.,* AAA Minitrial R. 2, 8, 10.

§ 23.6   —Binding Mediation

Like nonbinding mediation, the parties have great flexibility in structuring binding mediation. For example, in a dispute between an architect and contractor regarding whether a particular defect is the fault of one or both of them, the mediation structure may dictate simply allowing an independent expert to resolve the dispute based on written reports. Alternatively, a binding mediation could involve the equivalent of a formal trial on one issue, with limited witnesses for set periods of time. In such an instance, the parties must agree on percipient and expert testimony, and the nature and presentations of any evidence at the hearing.

Limiting the Risk

Because the decision is binding, and because the process is a shortened one, binding mediation is often perceived as risky. For example, lawyers and clients may be reluctant to request a dispositive ruling based on only a partial display of their cases, and brief presentations may not permit full attention to credibility issues. The risks can be ameliorated, however, in several ways.

One method of limiting risk is to bracket the award. Bracketing requires the parties to reach a tentative settlement as to the range of their respective claims. The parties then use this range to "cap" the mediator's discretion.

Example.   Contractor (C) sues project owner (O) seeking $10 million for work performed on a project. Because of certain delays and defects in the construction, C concedes that it is possible that O does not owe the full amount. C does believe, however, that O owes at least $8 million and has offered to settle for that amount. O, on the other hand, has offered to settle for only $4 million. C fears binding mediation because of the risk of an award under $4 million; O fears binding mediation because of the risk of an award above the $8 million figure for which C has offered to settle. The parties therefore structure the mediation using a "high-low" format. Under this format, it is agreed that even if the final award is less than $4 million, C will receive $4 million. Conversely, even if the award is over $8 million, O only pays $8 million. Of course, the binding mediator should not be advised of the caps, lest knowledge of the caps encourages the mediator to split the difference.

Another alternative is to use the "last best offer" method, which is currently used by Major League Baseball in its salary arbitration.

Example.   In the scenario above, O and C each agree to submit a final settlement offer immediately before mediation. If each side rejects the other's final offer, mediation will commence, with the award being in the amount of the more reasonable of the last offers by the parties. This method encourages the parties to submit reasonable settlement offers.

As with nonbinding mediation, the selection of the right mediator is important. However, unlike the nonbinding mediation, the mediator's neutrality is of paramount concern in binding mediation. Parties should also keep in mind that it is possible to stipulate that the judge sit as a binding mediator, bringing to bear the judge's knowledge of the facts and law applicable to the dispute. The judge may be willing to participate in this role if it means avoiding a more lengthy trial.

Other Considerations

Although not every case is susceptible to binding mediation, there are those for which it holds particular promise. For example, in construction disputes involving hundreds of relatively minor defects in design and construction, the cost of litigating the plethora of defects may dwarf the substantive claim. In such a circumstance, a 15-minute-per-defect presentation to a mediator for binding resolution may result in a net savings to both parties, regardless of the outcome.

The outcome of binding mediation will be enforceable by the terms of the parties' contract. For example, the parties may wish to stipulate that the award be enforced by the court in which an action is currently pending. Both parties should also take care in specifying under what limited circumstances an award may be vacated, if at all.

§ 23.7 —Binding Arbitration

In binding arbitration, the parties agree either in the original contract or after the dispute arises to submit their claims to a third party who will hear evidence and resolve the claims.[23] Because arbitration is contractual, the parties are free to structure the arbitration however they see fit.

Typically, disputes are submitted to bodies such as the American Arbitration Association, which has arbitration procedures specially fashioned for construction disputes. The rules provide the following:

1. Groundwork for submitting a dispute[24]
2. Selection of one or more arbitrators[25]

---

[23] American Arbitration Association, Construction Industry Arbitration Rule 5 (1991) [hereinafter AAA Arb. R.].

[24] *Id.*

[25] *Id.* R. 12–17.

3. Preliminary hearings (if desired or necessary, though usually useful)
4. Admissibility of evidence[26]
5. Procedures for the hearing[27]
6. Posthearing submissions[28]
7. Inspections[29]
8. Reopening the hearing[30]
9. Form of award.[31]

These rules are general and can be supplemented or replaced by the agreement of the parties.

The American Arbitration Association has panels of potential arbitrators who are experienced in various fields, including construction. In the construction context, the arbitrators include lawyers, retired judges, professors, architects, engineers, contractors and other businesspersons involved in the industry. Under AAA Arbitration Rules, each party is provided with a list of potential arbitrators and then given the opportunity, in confidence, to strike those arbitrators who are deemed to be unacceptable to that party.[32] Following the striking, should there be no remaining acceptable arbitrators, the American Arbitration Association reserves the right to appoint an arbitrator.[33] Unfortunately, this process may lead to the appointment of an arbitrator who does not necessarily have the full respect of all parties. To avoid this possibility, the parties should be encouraged mutually to agree upon an arbitrator or arbitrators. The American Arbitration Association typically accommodates the parties and is generally agreeable to the appointment of any arbitrator stipulated to by the parties, even if the arbitrator is not part of the American Arbitration Association panels.

Limits on Discovery

Most states' statutes as well as the AAA Arbitration Rules provide for subpoenas to compel the appearances of witnesses and productions of documents at the arbitration hearing itself, but these subpoenas do not aid in the discovery process.[34] Document exchanges among the parties themselves,

---

[26] *Id.* R. 31–33.

[27] *Id.* R. 21–26.

[28] *Id.* R. 32.

[29] AAA Arb. R. 33.

[30] *Id.* R. 36.

[31] *Id.* R. 40–43.

[32] *Id.* R. 13.

[33] *Id.*

[34] *Id.* R. 31.

however, generally can be compelled by the arbitrators in advance of the hearing.[35] Additional discovery is largely consensual. Although the arbitrator's urging carries some influence with the parties, the arbitrator lacks the power to compel most prehearing discovery.

Vacation of Award

In most states there are few grounds for vacating an arbitrator's award. For example, under § 1286.2 of the California Code of Civil Procedure, a court may vacate an arbitration award only if (1) it was procured by fraud or corruption, (2) there was corruption in any of the arbitrators, (3) there was misconduct of a neutral arbitrator, (4) the arbitrators exceeded their powers, or (5) the arbitrators wrongfully refused to postpone the hearing or refused to hear material evidence.[36] The last ground often leads arbitrators to accept all kinds of evidence that the parties wish to provide, including duplicative and irrelevant testimony. To avoid this result, the parties should contemplate stipulating to the applicability of the rules of evidence or should put time limits on the presentation of evidence. In addition, the parties should not be reluctant to request preliminary hearings, at which the issues can be narrowed and the scope of evidence addressed.[37] Even if the arbitrators do not issue orders precluding certain issues or evidence, the statements of the arbitrators at the preliminary hearing may tend to curtail the proceedings.

§ 23.8 —Court-Ordered Settlement Conference

Most courts have developed rules under which they may order the parties to participate in a settlement conference. These orders usually are made at the eleventh hour, right before commencement of the trial. These settlement conferences have several drawbacks.

One problem is the involuntary nature of court-ordered settlement conferences. Because this form of ADR is imposed by the court, many parties to the dispute will view the conference as a mere formality to be observed before beginning the trial. With this frame of mind, the parties are ill-prepared to reach a meaningful resolution of the dispute. Furthermore, this

---

[35] AAA Arb. R. 10.

[36] Errors such as mistake of law or the rendering of a decision not supported by the evidence are generally not grounds for reversal. *See, e.g.,* Lindholm v. Galvin, 95 Cal. App. 3d 443, 157 Cal. Rptr. 167 (1979); Abbott v. California State Auto Ass'n, 68 Cal. App. 3d 204, 137 Cal. Rptr. 580 (1972).

[37] AAA Arb. R. 10.

form of ADR often comes too late, after the parties have already expended considerable time, effort, and money to prepare for litigation. Thus two of the principal benefits of ADR—speed and savings—are lost.

The judge, presiding over a court-ordered settlement conference, may also be a less effective mediator. Unlike a professional mediation service, a judge may have no professional incentive to see that the parties are satisfied with the resolution of the dispute. Professional mediators, on the other hand, have this incentive, as they will want to encourage the parties to bring any future disputes to their services. Furthermore, the court's crowded docket may prevent the court from devoting sufficient time to resolving the dispute.

The parties may consider requesting that the court—when ordering a pretrial settlement conference—refer the parties to a third-party mediator who can devote the time necessary to facilitate settlement. Any of the various nonbinding types of ADR are useful at this juncture.

§ 23.9   Presentations in Nonbinding and Binding Mediation

The methods for presenting cases in court and jury trials and in binding arbitrations are generally well-known to attorneys. Nevertheless, given the relatively recent development of ADR, parties and counsel often are not acquainted with the different ways in which ADR may be structured, whether the method used by nonbinding or binding mediation.

In structuring ADR, parties and their counsel should be creative. Because most of the types of ADR discussed in §§ 23.4 through 23.8 are voluntary and contractual in nature, the structure can be molded to fit the situation. The need to be creative will be especially great when the other side is reluctant to utilize ADR. In such a situation, an astute attorney can suggest features that will allay the other sides' fears and concerns.

It is difficult to describe a set format for nonbinding or binding mediation because a primary advantage of ADR is its flexibility. However, generic suggestions can be made for the mediation, keeping in mind the need for the parties and their counsel to decide which issues and which parties should be involved to further the goal of settlement.

Before proceeding to discuss the method of presentation, one prefatory remark is in order. Regardless of whether the mediation is binding or nonbinding, counsel should not be reluctant to make an elaborate presentation. To achieve favorable results, a party and its counsel must necessarily be persuasive. Given the nature of ADR, the mediator must be convinced in a relatively short period of time. Visual aids, blowups, charts, summaries of evidence, and models are invaluable. As the saying goes, "a picture is worth a thousand words." This axiom should not be forgotten.

§ 23.10   —Use of Opening and Closing Statements

When the ADR merely involves a factual, nonlegal dispute, it may be possible simply to have ADR proceed with experts or the parties alone, and without attorneys. However, in virtually all other instances, it is best to have the lawyer act as the lead spokesperson and master of ceremonies. Because the training and function of the lawyer are to persuade, it is often a mistake to delegate the role to others. Thus, organized opening and closing statements by counsel, within set time frames, are effective tools. Similarly, written statements of positions are essential to crystallize the issues for the mediator, although limitations on the length of the statements are again advisable.

Summaries of positions and evidence should be highlighted by counsel in the course of these activities with the use of all forms of visual aids. This process should assist counsel in impressing on the mediator and the opposing party the seriousness with which counsel view the dispute. Equally as important, this procedure allows counsel to demonstrate to their clients their abilities, both in terms of persuasion and in terms of synthesis of the facts and issues at hand.

Although attorneys may be reluctant to disclose all of their clients' positions and supporting evidence, it is a mistake not to do so. If positions and supporting evidence are withheld, counsel will not obtain as favorable a result in the mediation, and, once concluded, the results of the mediation form the normative basis for future negotiations. Failure to argue the facts and theories fully can also lead to disappointment by the client; conversely, rarely will a client be disappointed by disclosure of supportive facts and theories in a mediation. In addition, the downside of disclosure of information is generally exaggerated, with the only result being prolonged litigation.

§ 23.11   —Use of Presentations and Testimony by Witnesses

Although binding and nonbinding mediation can take any form that may be agreed upon by the participants pursuant to a contract, it is a mistake not to have witnesses and representatives of the parties participate directly in the proceedings, whether it be by way of testimony, statements, or other presentations. The reason is that lawyers are viewed as advocates, not as bearers of evidence. The credibility of a party's position can be greatly enhanced through direct presentations by the client. Thus, even in a nonbinding mediation in which a party is simply allotted time to make whatever presentation it desires, it is useful to structure the presentation to include witnesses, not just arguments of counsel.

The methods for presentations by clients can vary. For example, to keep appropriate control over the organization, the lawyer may want to undertake the equivalent of direct examination, with questions and answers. Alternatively, the lawyer, as the master of ceremonies, may simply wish to introduce limited topics for the witnesses to speak about during a set period of time.

Cross-examination is rarely useful in the nonbinding mediation. It only tends to polarize the parties and defeat the common goal of accommodation. If, however, the credibility of a particular witness is at issue, the attorney may want to structure the mediation so that the mediator is at least apprised of discrepancies or inaccuracies in the story. Questions can even be suggested for the mediator to ask the opposing party. In such a manner, the adversarial nature of cross-examination can be avoided.

Full disclosure of witnesses and the topics on which they will make presentations is essential. Surprise is rarely useful at a mediation, and, instead, only tends to spur antagonism.

In binding mediation, limited examination and cross-examination may be indispensable elements of the proceeding. Of course, whenever ADR involves a binding decision, the parties are less concerned about the adverse consequences of cross-examination. This may not be the case, however, when continuing business relationships are involved.

§ 23.12   —Use of Exhibits

Because mediations generally are for a limited duration, large numbers of exhibits should be avoided. In particular, duplicative exhibits can be counterproductive.

When exhibits are required to prove particular points, copies should be provided to the mediator and the opposing parties in advance. During the mediation, blowups of the key exhibits may be best to maintain the flow of the presentation. To the extent possible, joint exhibits should be prepared. Again, the less surprise there is in mediation, the more likely the parties will resolve their differences.

§ 23.13   —Use of Legal Briefs

If legal issues are involved, the parties should not be reluctant to file memoranda of law. This is true regardless of the type of ADR employed. The briefs should be succinct, and they should be exchanged so that all parties are given an opportunity to respond, an important element of mediation. Of course, to the extent that legal issues are involved in the ADR, the use of a judge or lawyer as the mediator generally is required.

§ 23.14   —Length of ADR

Absent limitations on the length of the presentations of ADR, not only may it be difficult to persuade the other side to engage in ADR in the first instance, but, in addition, it defeats the purpose of ADR—namely, savings of time and money. As long as the issues are sufficiently narrowed, there is little reason that significant time limits cannot be imposed. In a non-binding mediation, the process can effectively occur in one or two days at most.

There may be occasions, however, when it is best for the parties to agree to leave the length of the mediation to the discretion of the mediator. This, of course, presumes the use of a mediator with whom all participants in ADR have confidence. An example would be a dispute in which there are a host of alleged construction defects on a project, with the parties leaving it to the mediator to determine the nature and degree of further evidence (potentially including presentations or testimony by experts) required for resolution. Even in such circumstances, however, outer limitations can be placed on the process, whether it be binding or nonbinding mediation.

In the nonbinding context, the parties will want to reserve sufficient time following any presentations for the mediator to conduct appropriate settlement discussions. Although an initial estimate of that time is useful, the ultimate length of the mediator's participation will undoubtedly depend on the success with which ADR is proceeding.

§ 23.15   Selecting the Right Person to Assist in ADR

Parties opting to utilize ADR have a wide range of people available to them to assist in the process. First, retired judges are becoming more and more prevalent in ADR. Retired judges understand the drawbacks of formal litigation. They also recognize that return business is dependent on the success of ADR, and, therefore, they are often willing to labor to get the parties to resolve their differences. Throughout the country, organizations of retired judges have formed, providing easy access for litigants. Second, many lawyers, both retired and practicing, serve as mediators and arbitrators. Third, parties often use construction consultants and experts to serve as mediators. However, when legal issues are involved, the parties should be cautious in using only experts. Finally, there are many organizations that specialize in ADR. The American Arbitration Association is perhaps the most prominent of these organizations.

Considerable attention should be given to the selection of the person to assist in ADR (the assistant). The success of all forms of ADR depends on the ability of the assistant to bring the parties to an appropriate accommodation or to issue the correct decision. It is essential that the assistants be willing to work hard and that they be creative. For this reason, it is often best to utilize assistants who have been involved in the process before.

The assistant must also be respected by the parties on the particular issues involved. Absent respect, ADR is not likely to be successful.

It is common to have three neutral parties serve as the assistants.[38] Supporters of the use of three assistants argue that the practice is more likely to result in an award or settlement weighted toward moderation than when only a single decision maker is used, who may have idiosyncratic or arbitrary views. However, the use of three assistants necessarily involves added expense because it is common for assistants (whether they be mediators, arbitrators, or judges) to charge for their time. In nonbinding mediation, it is generally unnecessary to have more than one well-qualified and respected mediator.

One strategy sometimes used by parties when engaging three assistants is to have one neutral and two nonneutral assistants. This method is usually undertaken by allowing each party to select its own assistant, and then having those assistants select a third. Although the use of a panel of this sort may have some academic appeal, in practice the results are disappointing. This process removes control from the attorneys. The biased assistants quickly become the true advocates, a result that often is not anticipated by the clients. Moreover, although nonneutral assistants may be well-versed in a particular field, they often are not trained to be advocates.

When deciding on an assistant, one must keep in mind the goal of ADR: resolution of the dispute. This goal militates in favor of neutral assistants. Engaging a nonneutral assistant rarely serves this goal, as such an assistant will be trusted by only one party. But there are times when a nonneutral decision can be used creatively to bring home a point in a case.

Example.   In a dispute with a subcontractor, a contractor is convinced, rightfully so, that it has an airtight case. For some reason, the subcontractor mistakenly believes the contractor's case to be weak. This belief has precluded any productive settlement discussions. The contractor offers to submit to a nonbinding mediation and allows the subcontractor to select the mediator. After being informed of the strength of the contractor's case by a mediator whom the subcontractor trusts, the subcontractor becomes more amenable to settlement discussions.

---

[38] Thus, the American Arbitration Association generally appoints three arbitrators if over $100,000 is in dispute.

§ 23.16   Arbitration or Mediation
Clauses in Contracts

It is now common practice to insert arbitration clauses into construction contracts. At first glance, this practice appears to be a good idea as it guarantees the use of ADR. Unfortunately, however, binding arbitration by itself does not assure a less expensive or less time-consuming dispute than in court or jury trials. Although a hearing is generally obtained at any earlier date through arbitration than through the courts, the overall expense of arbitration can be just as great as or greater than that of litigation. This is true even though depositions, interrogatories, requests for admissions, and the like are not a matter of right in arbitration. The reason is threefold.

First and foremost, because the rules of evidence do not apply in arbitration,[39] and because one of the primary bases for overturning arbitrations is the refusal of the arbitrators to hear evidence, arbitrators are inclined to allow the introduction of irrelevant, duplicative, and time-consuming evidence. In fact, there are horror stories in which relatively simple issues have taken as long as a year to arbitrate. To minimize these risks, parties should consider limiting arbitrations to disputes involving only a certain monetary amount.

Second, in arbitration, the parties obviously have to compensate the arbitrator or arbitrators for their time. Although jury trials involve compensation for the jurors, court trials do not require compensation for the judge. In a protracted proceeding, the costs in arbitration can run very high.

Third, because arbitration is a consensual matter and can only be compelled when the parties have agreed to arbitration,[40] problems often arise in joining all the necessary parties in one proceeding. As a result, a party may find itself litigating both in court and in arbitration. For example, if an owner has an arbitration clause in its contract with the architect but not in its contract with the general contractor, the owner may be forced to litigate with these parties separately even when there is an overlap of issues.

Thus, in construction projects that have multiple parties, as is often the case, parties should make sure that either all or none of the contracts have arbitration clauses in them. Unfortunately, it is not always possible to assure the inclusion of arbitration clauses in all contracts, given the number of participants.

In the abstract, it might seem beneficial to have provisions in contracts calling for mediation. However, because the format of the mediation needs to be molded to the dispute, and because the mediation is only successful when the parties are willing to participate at the particular time with respect

---

[39] *See* AAA Arb. R. 31.

[40] *See, e.g.,* Cal. Civ. Proc. Code §§ 1281–1281.8 (West Supp. 1991).

to a particular issue, it is unlikely that the parties will be able to craft an appropriate mediation provision at the time of contracting. Nevertheless, a general provision calling for mediation does at least offer an opportunity for getting the parties together and beginning negotiations. Thus, there is rarely a downside to including a nonbinding mediation clause.

§ 23.17   Checklist of Issues to Consider

The following is a sample checklist of questions and concerns that the parties should ask themselves in the course of evaluating whether to enter into ADR and, if so, the process they should follow in ADR:

_____ What type of ADR is best suited to the parties' dispute?

_____ Can the parties live with a binding decision, with limitations on the scope of discovery, evidence, presentations, or time?

_____ Can the parties live with a binding decision if upward and downward limitations are placed on the amount of the award?

_____ If the parties stipulate to upward and downward limitations on any award, should the decision maker be so apprised?

_____ Should the parties exchange final settlement offers prior to the ADR?

_____ If the parties do exchange final settlement offers, do they wish to structure the ADR such that there is a decision by the decision maker in favor of one or other offers?

_____ If the more formal process of binding arbitration is to be used, can there be limitations on the number of witnesses, the time for examination, the time for cross-examination, or the number of exhibits or other evidence?

_____ If the dispute is currently pending before the courts, should the parties request assistance in setting up an ADR?

_____ If the parties are involved in a binding arbitration, should they request the arbitration organization or the panel of arbitrators to encourage nonbinding mediation?

_____ Is it necessary to undertake discovery prior to engaging in the ADR?

_____ Will limited discovery prior to an ADR help educate the parties?

_____ What format should the ADR take once the type of ADR is agreed upon?

_____ Should there be opening and closing statements?

_____ Should there be memoranda of law?

_____ Should blowups, pictures, charts, graphs, models, or other visual aids be used?

_____ What representatives of the parties should attend the ADR?

____ What type of authority is necessary for the party representative to have in order to further settlement best?

____ Is it beneficial to have representatives from the parties directly participate in the ADR?

____ What role should the lawyer play in the ADR?

____ Is the credibility of any witness in issue?

____ Should examination or cross-examination be used?

____ Rather than use cross-examination, should the parties simply comment on inaccuracies in the stories of witnesses?

____ Should there be confidentiality of the ADR or particular aspects of the ADR?

____ How long should the presentations in the ADR take place?

____ What issues should be part of the ADR?

____ What parties should be joined to the ADR?

____ Are there persons or entities not involved in the dispute (such as insurers) that should also participate in the ADR?

____ Can the parties stipulate to the assistant in the ADR?

____ Should the assistant be neutral or nonneutral?

____ Would it be beneficial to obtain an advisory opinion from a nonneutral assistant so as to convince a recalcitrant party of the weakness of its positions?

____ How many assistants should there be in the ADR process?

____ How much will it cost to pay for the time of the assistants?

____ Should the assistant hold meetings in private?

____ What qualifications should the assistant have?

____ Should the assistant be a lawyer, judge, businessperson, or expert?

____ Are there potential bases for settlement that involve something other than the exchange of money?

____ What mechanism should be established to enforce any agreement or award in an ADR?

____ Even if unsuccessful, what limitations can be placed on the subsequent litigation in light of what has been learned during the ADR?

____ Even if unsuccessful, has ADR highlighted for the parties the key issues in dispute such that bifurcation of issues is appropriate?

PART V

DAMAGES AND COLLECTION

CHAPTER 24

ENFORCING AND AVOIDING LIQUIDATED DAMAGES

Charles E. Schwenck
Barry A. Weiss

Charles E. Schwenck is senior vice president and general counsel of LG & E Power Systems Incorporated, Irvine, California, and a former partner in the firm of Pillsbury, Madison & Sutro. He is a graduate of the University of California, Berkeley, and its Boalt Hall School of Law. He also has served as general counsel for Fluor Engineers, Inc., and as a division counsel in the Bechtel Group. Mr. Schwenck has been a lecturer at California State University, at various seminars on construction matters, and has authored or contributed to several publications on construction and related legal topics.

Barry A. Weiss is counsel to LG & E Power Systems Incorporated, Irvine, California, and serves as chief counsel to its engineering and construction subsidiaries. He graduated from Cornell University and the Cornell Law School, where he served on the board of editors of the *Cornell International Law Journal.* He represented several engineering and construction companies in his previous private practice. Mr. Weiss is on the Governing Committee of the California Continuing Education of the Bar (CEB) and has been a frequent consultant on CEB publications. He is a former law clerk in the Ninth Circuit U.S. Court of Appeals.

§ 24.1   Liquidated Damages in General

The use of liquidated damages in contracts involves an attempt by the parties to estimate the amount of actual changes that would be suffered by a party for a breach. The parties then stipulate in the contract that the aggrieved party will be entitled to recover such prescribed, or "liquidated," sum upon a breach. A predetermined measure of damages is thereby substituted in lieu of any proof of the actual damages suffered by the aggrieved party.

Provisions in contracts for liquidated damages may take several forms. Liquidated damages may be set as a fixed, prescribed sum or may be calculated in accordance with a predetermined formula, with the level of damages changing in accordance with the applicable variables. Liquidated changes also may be limited to specified breaches and may apply to one or more breaches of a contract. For example, in construction contracts there may be liquidated damages applicable for delays in completion, for shortfalls in performance of an operational facility, or for other breaches of the contract, and different sums or formulas may be used to calculate the different types of liquidated damages.

§ 24.2   Reasons for Using Provisions

Liquidated damages are most likely to be used in situations in which damages from a breach either are speculative in amount or difficult or impracticable to prove. By substituting certainty of outcome for the uncertainty that surrounds any attempt to persuade a third-party decision maker, parties to a contract can avoid what they consider inequities in the application of traditional rules of damages.

A properly drafted liquidated damages clause therefore avoids or reduces the expense, difficulty, and delay of proving damages at the time of breach and ensures that the aggrieved party has a compensatory remedy. The parties also avoid unnecessary fact-finding, discovery, and procedural posturing (and related legal expenditures) involved in proving causation and foreseeability of damages—issues often present in complex commercial cases. Further, because damages are set at the time of breach, the use of a liquidated damages clause allows prejudgment interest to begin to run against the breaching party immediately. The growing factual and legal complexity of modern-day business transactions, the rising cost of legal services, and the longer delays in reaching trial due to crowded court calendars only increase the incentive to provide certain, liquidated remedies in complex commercial contracts.

Certainty of Outcome

Certainty of outcome also acts as a clear incentive (or disincentive) in cases in which parties are tempted to "rationally" breach a contract. For example, a certain level of liquidated damages may, as a practical matter, deter a party from breaching a contract when otherwise the costs of compliance exceed the benefits of performance. Liquidated damages also may deter breaches in situations in which a party might otherwise breach because of a perceived inability or difficulty of the other party to prove damages. The amount of liquidated damages must not, however, be so large as to constitute a penalty for breach. The historical principle against enforcing penalties prohibits the imposition of liquidated damages in a penal amount.[1]

Allocation of Risk

Conversely, there are situations in which liquidated damages clauses are included in order to allocate risk between the parties and, in effect, limit liability. Thus, a party may be likely to breach a contract as a rational economic decision if the liquidated damages are less than the cost of performance. By so restricting the liability of the breaching party, a liquidated damages provision may act as a limitation on liability and as an exclusive remedy. Although at first blush it may appear that this is contrary to the intent behind the use of liquidated damages provisions—that is, to estimate the actual damages that will be caused by a breach—a closer look indicates that to the extent such intent is measured at the time of contracting, enforcement of a liquidated damages provision that reasonably estimates anticipated harm actually promotes the parties' intent. In addition, although some courts have shown a reluctance to enforce liquidated damages provisions in instances in which the liquidated amount is substantially less than the amount of damages actually suffered, most of these cases involve situations in which the amount of liquidated damages is so unreasonably small that enforcement would be unconscionable[2] or would operate to unjustly enrich one party at the expense of the other.[3]

Estimate versus Limitation

The Uniform Commercial Code (UCC), although less than a model of clarity on the subject, does illustrate the distinction between the use of liquidated damages as an estimate of liability and as a limitation on liability. Section 2-718(1) of the UCC governs liquidated damages clauses and § 2-719 governs clauses limiting or excluding remedies. Although § 2-719 contains language that expressly subjects § 2-719 to § 2-718, the source of the UCC's uncertainty is that comment one to § 2-718 indicates that unreasonably small liquidated damages provisions should be adjudged under the unconscionability standard set forth in U.C.C. § 2-302, which is the standard applicable under § 2-719. Given the high standard necessary to

---

[1] *See* U.C.C. § 1-106(1) (1978); Restatement (Second) of Contracts § 356(1), cmts. a, b (1979); Chicago House-Wrecking Co. v. United States, 106 F. 385 (1901); Equitable Lumber Corp. v. IPA Land Dev. Corp., 38 N.Y.2d 516, 344 N.E.2d 395, 381 N.Y.S.2d 463 (1976).

[2] *See, e.g.,* Seeman v. Biemann, 108 Wis. 365, 84 N.W. 490 (1900).

[3] *See, e.g.,* Massman Constr. Co. v. City Council, 147 F.2d 925 (5th Cir. 1945); Northwest Fixture Co. v. Kilbourne & Clark Co., 128 F. 256 (9th Cir. 1904).

demonstrate unconscionability under the UCC,[4] it would almost always follow that an unconscionably low liquidated damages clause also would be stricken under the § 2-718 reasonableness test.[5] Nevertheless, the converse proposition may not necessarily be true—a liquidated damages clause intended to act as a limitation on liability and which is conscionable under § 2-302 may nevertheless be unreasonable under § 2-718. Thus, by drafting a clause that the parties know may provide for a relatively small damages remedy as a limitation on liability rather than as a liquidated damages provision, the parties may be able to increase the likelihood of enforceability of a provision intended to act as an exclusive, limited remedy.

ENFORCEABILITY STANDARDS

§ 24.3   Common Law Approach to Enforcement

In early English legal history, penal bonds (or bonds setting sums due for nonperformance) were used to secure contract performance in cases in which no actual damages were suffered as a result of a breach.[6] Early United States courts emphasized freedom of contract and generally upheld liquidated damages clauses notwithstanding whether little or no damages actually occurred.[7] For example, in *United States v. Bethlehem Steel* the Court emphasized upholding freedom of contract in situations in which the parties attempted in advance to reasonably estimate the damages likely to result from a breach.[8]

This majority rule was, however, tempered in some cases in which actual damages resulting from a breach were small or nonexistent. Several courts used equitable principles, such as unjust enrichment, to avoid enforcing otherwise valid liquidated damages provisions,[9] which made case results

---

[4] *See* U.C.C. § 2-302, Official Comment 1 (1978); Anderson, *Liquidated Damages under the Uniform Commercial Code,* 41 Sw. L.J. 1083, 1106–08 (1988).

[5] See § **24.5**.

[6] *See* 3 S. Williston, Williston on Contracts § 774 (1920).

[7] *See, e.g.,* Wise v. United States, 249 U.S. 361 (1919); United States v. Bethlehem Steel Co., 205 U.S. 105 (1907); Sun Printing & Publishing v. Moore, 183 U.S. 642 (1902); *see also* Note, *Liquidated Damages Recovery under the Restatement (Second) of Contracts,* 67 Cornell L. Rev. 862, 863–66 (1982).

[8] 205 U.S. 105, 119 (1907); Bethlehem Steel Co. v. City of Chicago, 350 F.2d 649 (7th Cir. 1965); *see also* McCarthy v. Tally, 46 Cal. 2d 577, 297 P.2d 981 (1956).

[9] *See* Seeman v. Biemann, 108 Wis. 365, 373, 84 N.W. 490, 492 (1900); Massman Constr. Co. v. City Council, 147 F.2d 925 (5th Cir. 1945); Ward v. Haren, 183 Mo. App. 569, 167 S.W. 1064 (1914); Note, *Liquidated Damages Recovery under the Restatement (Second) of Contracts,* 67 Cornell L. Rev. 862, 866–67.

extremely unpredictable in situations in which little or no actual damages could be shown.

§ 24.4 Restatement of Contracts

The *Restatement of Contracts* (*Restatement*) perpetuated the common law focus on the parties' attempt to estimate damages at the time of contracting.[10] Section 339 of the *Restatement* set forth a two-part test for adjudging the validity of a liquidated damages provision:

> An agreement, made in advance of breach, fixing the damages therefor, is not enforceable as a contract and does not affect the damages recoverable for the breach, unless (a) the amount fixed is a reasonable forecast of just compensation for the harm that is caused by the breach, and (b) the harm that is caused by the breach is one that is incapable or very difficult of accurate estimation.[11]

In applying the *Restatement* test, courts typically focused on the first part—the "intent of the parties" test[12]—and used the time of contracting as the benchmark for analyzing the validity of the clause; the introduction of evidence at trial intended to show, in retrospect, that the estimate of actual damages was unreasonable most often was prohibited.[13] Although the illustrations and comments to the *Restatement* support this view,[14] some courts rejected the *Restatement* approach and looked at the lack of actual damages as critical.[15] In one case, a reasonably agreed upon liquidated damages clause was held unenforceable on the ground that the clause must be reasonable both at the time of contracting and at the time of enforcement.[16] Although commentators have noted this, the minority view

---

[10] Note, *Liquidated Damages Recovery under the Restatement (Second) of Contracts,* 67 Cornell L. Rev. 862, 867.

[11] Restatement of Contracts § 339 (1932).

[12] *See* 5 S. Williston, Williston on Contracts § 778 (1961); Note, *Liquidated Damages Recovery under the Restatement (Second) of Contracts,* 67 Cornell L. Rev. 862, 868.

[13] *See, e.g.,* Bethlehem Steel Co. v. City of Chicago, 350 F.2d 649 (7th Cir. 1965); McCarthy v. Tally, 46 Cal. 2d 577, 297 P.2d 981 (1956); United States v. J.D. Street & Co., 151 F. Supp. 469 (E.D. Mo. 1957); Byron Jackson Co. v. United States, 35 F. Supp. 665 (S.D. Cal. 1940).

[14] *See* Restatement of Contracts § 778 (1961); Note, *Liquidated Damages Recovery under the Restatement (Second) of Contracts,* 67 Cornell L. Rev. 862, 868.

[15] The case of Norwalk Door Closer Co. v. Eagle Lock & Screw Co., 153 Conn. 681, 220 A.2d 263 (1966) typifies this minority view. *See also* Massman Constr. Co. v. City Council, 147 F.2d 925 (5th Cir. 1945); Priebe & Sons v. United States, 332 U.S. 407 (1947).

[16] *Id.*

under the *Restatement* supported the basic compensatory principle of contract law and provides the best assurance that penal clauses are not enforced.[17] The minority view did not address the tension such equitable limitations created with freedom of contract principles.

§ 24.5   Uniform Commercial Code

The UCC sets forth a multifactor test to adjudge the reasonableness of a liquidated damages provision:

> Damages for breach by either party may be liquidated in the agreement but only at an amount which is reasonable in the light of the anticipated or actual harm caused by the breach, the difficulties of proof of loss, and the inconvenience or nonfeasibility of otherwise obtaining an adequate remedy. A term fixing unreasonably large liquidated damages is void as a penalty.[18]

The UCC test departs from the common law treatment of liquidated damages provisions; not only is the intention of the parties test abandoned, but the UCC test establishes that evidence of actual damages or the lack thereof may be relevant in determining the validity of the liquidated damages provision.[19]

Anticipated or Actual Harm

Most commentators agree that the first factor of the UCC test—anticipated or actual harm—is at the crux of the analysis.[20] This factor has been interpreted in two ways. Under one interpretation, the parties must both attempt at the time of contracting to provide a reasonable estimate of probable harm and be right in their estimate—that is, the sum specified also must be reasonable in light of the actual harm. Under this interpretation the lack of actual damages provides evidence of unreasonableness. Although this interpretation unites the two methods of analysis courts historically have used, it eviscerates one of the central purposes of liquidated

---

[17] 5 A. Corbin, Corbin on Contracts § 1062 (1964); Anderson, *Liquidated Damages under the Uniform Commercial Code,* 41 Sw. L.J. 1083, 1087. *See also* Restatement of Contracts § 339 cmt. e (1932), which seems to support this view.

[18] U.C.C. § 2-718-1 (1978).

[19] Note, *Liquidated Damages Recovery under the Restatement (Second) of Contracts,* 67 Cornell L. Rev. 862, 871. *But see* Macneil, *Power of Contract and Agreed Remedies,* 47 Cornell L.Q. 495, 505 (1962) for an opposite analysis.

[20] *See* Anderson, *Liquidated Damages under the Uniform Commercial Code,* 41 Sw. L.J. 1083, 1091; Note, *Liquidated Damages Recovery under the Restatement (Second) of Contracts,* 67 Cornell L. Rev. 862, 871.

damages clauses—to allow parties the freedom of contract to avoid expensive and difficult litigation over contract damages. This interpretation also renders the second sentence of the UCC provision meaningless; if all liquidated damages provisions that prove to be unreasonable at the time of trial are unenforceable, then the statement in the second sentence—"unreasonably large liquidated damages [are] void as a penalty"—adds nothing to the analysis.

An alternative interpretation of the anticipated or actual harm factor provides that a court may enforce a liquidated damages provision that either reasonably estimates the likely harm or accurately reflects the actual harm. Under this interpretation, a liquidated damages provision that is unreasonable at the time of contracting, but turns out to be reasonable after the breach, is upheld; the sole test is reasonableness. The Official Comment to the UCC supports this interpretation and indicates that the factors noted in the UCC text merely are elements to be considered in determining the reasonableness of the liquidated damages provision.[21]

Application to Construction Contracts

One should note, however, that the UCC test has not been applied or tested in many court cases. One reason for this is that Article 2 of the UCC literally only applies to fact situations involving sales of goods.[22] In such cases, general damages for breach are almost always ascertainable; liquidated damages typically are used in limited situations involving delays in delivery or other breaches involving unique or specially manufactured goods. Another reason is the courts' willingness to rely on the common law principles embodied in the *Restatement* in analyzing liquidated damages provisions. The UCC test often is referred to as requiring only a general "reasonableness" approach.[23]

Nonetheless, the application of the UCC in the context of construction contracts is particularly important. Although the UCC generally is not applicable to construction contracts,[24] most, if not all, construction projects involve the procurement of goods at some time during the construction schedule. Moreover, the types of goods procured for many construction projects typically are specialized or custom-made goods for which general "market" damages usually are not ascertainable; there may be no ready market for an aggrieved seller to dispose of such goods or for

---

[21] *See* U.C.C. § 2-718, Official Cmt. 1 (1978).

[22] *See* U.C.C. § 2-102 (1978).

[23] *See* Anderson, *Liquidated Damages under the Uniform Commercial Code,* Sw. L.J. 1083, 1091; Note, *Liquidated Damages Recovery under the Restatement (Second) of Contracts,* 67 Cornell L. Rev. 862, 871.

[24] Construction contracts primarily involve the sale of services, not goods.

an aggrieved buyer to "cover," by purchasing similar goods. Also, it is often difficult to demonstrate issues concerning the actual damages for delays in delivery of goods for the project, given the complex, intertwined nature of the procurement process as part of the construction schedule. For example, in a design/build contract the nondelivery of a critical component for a project may not actually delay the completion of the project (thereby not resulting in any discernible actual damages to the contractor), but may cause the contractor to accelerate or otherwise reschedule other portions of the work or to take other action to ameliorate the effects of the delay. This seems to be exactly the situation in which use of liquidated damages appears reasonable. The application of the UCC to construction contracts also is important in that some courts have indicated a willingness to apply the principles embodied in the UCC in non-UCC cases.[25]

To a large extent, however, the UCC treatment of liquidated damages has done little to resolve the major issue in adjudging the validity of a liquidated damages provision—that is, the role of actual damages resulting from the breach. Most courts, when analyzing liquidated damages provisions under the UCC test, resort to imposing a general reasonableness approach to all facets of the case and appear confused over the role of actual damages in the reasonableness evaluation.[26]

§ 24.6   Restatement (Second) of Contracts

Under the *Restatement (Second) of Contracts* (the *Second Restatement*) another two-fold test emerges: "Damages for breach by either party may be liquidated in the agreement but only at an amount that is reasonable in light of the anticipated or actual loss caused by the breach and the difficulties of proof of loss."[27] An either-or approach is created by the first factor:[28] the amount of liquidated damages must either be a reasonable (1) forecast of possible, anticipated damages or (2) an approximation of the actual harm. The second factor has no time orientation; the difficulty of proof of loss could be measured prospectively at the time of contracting or retrospectively at the time of breach or trial. The illustrations, however, seem to focus more on the retrospective approach, abandoning the perspective of

---

[25] *See, e.g.,* E.C. Ernst, Inc. v. Manhattan Constr. Co., 551 F.2d 1026 (5th Cir. 1977); Illingsworth v. Bushong, 297 Or. 675, 688 P.2d 379 (1984).

[26] *See* Note, *Liquidated Damages Recovery under the Restatement (Second) of Contracts,* 67 Cornell L. Rev. 862, 873–74.

[27] Restatement (Second) of Contracts § 356(1) (1979).

[28] *Id.* cmt. b.

estimating damages at the time of contract formation.[29] The comments suggest that both of the *Second Restatement* factors are to be balanced: the greater the difficulty in proving loss, the greater discrepancy is allowed between liquidated and actual damages, and vice versa.[30] Most importantly, under the *Second Restatement* a defense of "no actual damages" is allowed if the liquidated sum, measured at the time of trial, is unreasonably large.[31] Thus, even though the parties to a contract may fully intend to be bound by a liquidated damages provision at the time of contracting, the nonexistence of actual damages will, under the *Second Restatement,* provide relief from such bargain.

More than resolving any controversy, the *Second Restatement* approach perpetuates the major problem in analyzing liquidated damages provisions—the role of actual damages. The *Second Restatement* appears to uphold a provision specifying a damages amount that would be unreasonable if viewed prospectively from the time of contracting but that is reasonable at the time of trial because, fortuitously to the aggrieved party, the amount of actual damages was reasonably approximated. Conversely, the approach seems to invalidate a provision specifying a damages amount that would be reasonable if viewed prospectively from the time of contracting, but that is unreasonable at the time of trial because little or no actual damages were suffered. Although the intent of the parties is not violated by the first result because it enforces the agreement of the parties, a party is able to recover damages that were not contemplated at the time of the contract, raising independent questions of foreseeability of damages. The intent of the parties, however, is violated by the second result; freedom of contract between the parties is restricted in favor of principles.

At least one commentator has suggested that the *Second Restatement* approach is meant to promote the either-or interpretation of the UCC test—liquidated damages provisions are enforceable if they either reasonably estimate harm or reasonably reflect actual harm.[32] Whether or not this view is advanced by the courts, the *Second Restatement* does command the courts to analyze, on a case-by-case basis, the equities of individual liquidated damages provisions in light of actual damages.

---

[29] *See id.,* illus. 3, 4 (1979). *But see* Note, *Liquidated Damages Recovery under the Restatement (Second) of Contracts,* 67 Cornell L. Rev. 862, 877–78 for a criticism of this approach on the ground that, at least in contracts involving sale of goods, all liquidated damages provisions would be invalid because proof of loss at trial usually is not difficult.

[30] Restatement (Second) of Contracts § 356(1), cmt. b (1979).

[31] *Id.*

[32] *See* Note, *Liquidated Damages Recovery under the Restatement (Second) of Contracts,* 67 Cornell L. Rev. 862, 877.

§ 24.7   Burden of Proof under the Tests

As the discussion in §§ 24.3 through 24.6 illustrates, the burden of proving the validity or invalidity of a liquidated damages provision depends on the test used. Under both the common law and *Restatement* approaches, the majority rule was that the party seeking to enforce the liquidated damages provision had the burden of pleading and proving that the provision reasonably approximated the anticipated harm.[33] However, to the extent freedom of contract principles militated in favor of enforcement of such provisions and no evidence of actual damages was admissible under the majority rule, this burden of proof provided little obstacle to enforcement once the breach was demonstrated. Most parties to a contract could demonstrate easily that at the time of contracting they reasonably believed there would be harm caused by the breach; liquidated damages could then be used to predetermine or limit such reasonably anticipated harm. Because the parties' expectations were evaluated at the time of contracting, the reasonableness of the forecast of damages was virtually impossible to second—guess.

Under the UCC and *Second Restatement* tests, however, the burden appears to have been shifted; the weight of case law suggests that the defendant seeking to invalidate a liquidated damages provision must essentially prove that the clause was unreasonable.[34] This burden requires proof that the provision did not reasonably approximate the anticipated or actual harm—that is, the defendant must essentially demonstrate the amount (or absence) of the other party's damages. Although ostensibly this burden appears especially difficult to meet, requiring the defendant to prove the presence or absence of the other party's damages, at least one commentator has suggested that this burden should only require the defendant to raise credible evidence that the anticipated harm is well out of line with the actual loss.[35] Further, the burden of proving unreasonableness should not be difficult to meet in those jurisdictions that view the reasonableness of the damages at the time of trial.[36]

---

[33] *See, e.g.,* McCarthy v. Talley, 46 Cal. 2d 577, 297 P.2d 981 (1956).

[34] *See, e.g.,* Farmers Export Co. v. M/V Georgis Prois, 799 F.2d 159 (5th Cir. 1986). *See also* Cal. Civ. Code § 1671(b) (Deering Supp. 1991) and Law Rev. Com. Comment thereto, which codifies this burden of proof on the ground that the use of liquidated damages provisions should be encouraged.

[35] Anderson, *Liquidated Damages under the Uniform Commercial Code,* 41 Sw. L.J. 1083, 1102.

[36] *Id.*

DRAFTING THE PROVISION

§ 24.8   Exclusivity and Drafting Considerations

Properly drafted, a liquidated damages provision acts as an exclusive, limited remedy for a particular breach of a contract. This well-settled rule of common law[37] is quite logical in approach. Enforcing both a liquidated damages clause and enabling a party to recover actual damages for a breach not only would eviscerate the intent of the parties in using liquidated damages provisions—to preset damages definitively—but also would create a situation in which it is more likely that the liquidated amount is being enforced as a penalty. In other words, the provision of liquidated damages in a contract appears so inconsistent with any other damages remedy so as to presume exclusiveness. The current commentary and cases support this view.[38]

Nonetheless, even though a liquidated damages provision may be enforced as the exclusive damages remedy, parties may wish to enforce other nondamages remedies, such as termination, and equitable remedies, such as specific performance, for a breach. Although it may appear that equitable principles should not be altered by private agreement, a careful look at such types of remedies (which is beyond the scope of this chapter) indicates that enforcement may be inconsistent with the provision of liquidated damages, notwithstanding the existence or nonexistence of exclusivity language in the contract. For example, specific performance generally only is available when actual damages are impractical or difficult to ascertain and when a remedy at law would be inadequate. The existence of a liquidated damages provision not only negates the second factor, but the analysis used to adjudge the liquidated damages provision itself—whether or not the liquidated sum reasonably approximates the anticipated or actual harm—must necessarily invalidate the first factor in that the reasonable ascertainment of such damages is exactly what is being tested. At least one court has agreed with this analysis, refusing to specifically enforce a contract on the theory that the existence of a liquidated damages provision merely allows the breaching party the privilege of paying the agreed sum, rather than performing.[39] However, this view has been criticized on the theory that recourse to equitable remedies must be available to prevent injustice.[40]

---

[37] *Id.* at 1104 n.137.

[38] *Id.* at 1104; *see also* Northern Ill. Gas Co. v. Energy Coop., Inc., 122 Ill. App. 3d 940, 461 N.E.2d 1049 (1984) (exclusive remedy even if not expressly stated).

[39] *See* Carolinas Cotton Growers Ass'n v. Arnette, 371 F. Supp. 65 (D.S.C. 1974). *Cf.* United States v. American Sur. Co., 322 U.S. 96 (1944) (liquidated damages and termination are mutually exclusive alternative remedies for delayed performance).

[40] *See* Anderson, *Liquidated Damages under the Uniform Commercial Code,* 41 Sw. L.J. 1083, 1105; D. Calamari & J. Perillo, Contracts § 14-33 (1977). *Cf.* Rubinstein v.

Parties must recognize the concept of exclusivity when drafting liquidated damages provisions. Although many courts have held that the actual language used is not conclusive in determining the exclusivity or validity of a liquidated damages provision, careful draftsmanship should, in practice, be rewarded in that it will serve to clarify the parties' intent, avoiding the need for a court to interpose its own interpretation of such intent.

For example, because the courts have been reluctant to uphold liquidated damages provisions that specify one amount of damages for a variety of breaches, presumably under the theory that the liquidated sum cannot be a reasonable approximation of the harm from the particular breach,[41] care should be taken to draft the liquidated damages provision narrowly so as to apply only to the particular, specified breach for which it is intended. The parties also may wish to consider adjusting the amount of damages based on the extent of the breach, such as the duration of the delay or period of default. Further, clauses that give the aggrieved party the option to enforce liquidated damages or that try to establish actual damages for the same breach should be avoided. Courts clearly have held that liquidated damages provisions will not be upheld when intended solely to induce performance rather than to compensate for nonperformance.[42] Words such as *penalty* or *forfeit,* although not conclusive, also should be avoided so as not to taint the provision; conversely, it may be wise to include the word *liquidated* as evidence of the parties' intent to predetermine damages.

If the parties intend that liquidated damages be an exclusive remedy for a particular breach, this, too, should be spelled out in the contract. Specificity may provide a court with the basis for not enforcing other types of remedies, in essence permitting the liquidated damages provision to operate as a limitation or modification of remedies and enabling a party to pursue other remedies with regard to those other breaches for which damages have not been liquidated.[43]

§ 24.9   General Application in Construction Contracts

Liquidated damages clauses can be used in construction contracts to liquidate the damages payable by the contractor to the project owner by reason

---

Rubinstein, 23 N.Y.2d 293, 244 N.E.2d 49, 296 N.Y.S.2d 354 (1968) (specific performance not precluded in absence of exclusivity language).

[41] *See, e.g.,* Bradford v. New York Times Co., 501 F.2d 51 (2d Cir. 1974).

[42] *See, e.g.,* Loggins Constr. Co. v. Stephen F. Austin Univ. Bd. of Regents, 543 S.W.2d 682 (Tex. Ct. App. 1976); S.L. Rowland Constr. Co. v. Beall Pipe & Tank Corp., 14 Wash. App. 297, 540 P.2d 912 (1975).

[43] *See* cases collected in 2 Stein, Construction Law ¶ 6.10[2] (1991). *See also* Dunbar, *Drafting the Liquidated Damage Clause—When and How,* 20 Ohio St. L.J. 221, 234–36 (1959) for a discussion of the do's and don'ts of drafting liquidated damages provisions.

of virtually any breach of a duty owed to the project owner by the contractor.[44] For example, liquidated damages clauses have been used to compensate the project owner for the following:

1. Failure of the contractor to provide technical information in a timely manner when the owner needs such technical information for the purposes of completing related projects
2. Failure of the contractor to provide promised key personnel or required staffing levels
3. Failure of a completed project to perform in the manner intended
4. Deviations from the contractor's represented financial condition when such financial condition affects the costs of financing the project.[45]

Nevertheless, by far the most common type of damages liquidated in construction contracts are damages for delays in completion of the project. Therefore, the discussion hereinafter is limited to clauses that liquidate delay damages.

§ 24.10   —Liquidating Construction Delay Damages

Liquidated damages clauses are used more often in construction contracts than most other types of commercial contracts, and the differential in frequency of use is particularly apparent when comparing construction contracts to contracts for the sale of goods.[46] The reasons for the proliferation of liquidated damages clauses in construction contracts are several. Perhaps the most important is that there typically is a higher level of difficulty in predicting and establishing actual damages in construction contracts than in the average commercial transaction. The relationships between the parties are more complex and the difficulty of apportioning fault is greater in the construction setting. A delay may be contributed to concurrently by

---

[44] Theoretically, such clauses also can be used to liquidate damages for breaches of duties owed to the contractor by the project owner. However, such use of liquidated damages provisions is unusual, because change orders and other price adjustment mechanisms are more flexible tools for collecting such damages.

[45] The last mentioned use of liquidated damages occurs occasionally when nonrecourse or limited recourse project financing is used, but is most often found in contracts involving public financing in which the contractor has a long-term involvement in the project and the contractor's financial strength affects the bond rating.

[46] The courts and the commentators have judged the use of liquidated damages in sale of goods contracts harshly on the theory that the requisite difficulties of proof of loss are not present in such contracts: the "cost of cover" is usually readily calculable. *See* Anderson, *Liquidated Damages under the Uniform Commercial Code,* 41 Sw. L.J. 1083, 1088–1090.

the contractor, the project owner, the owner's other contractors, and circumstances beyond the control of any of them (for example, acts of God and changes in law). In addition, the line between direct and consequential damages often is blurred in construction contract situations, and there often are multiple elements of damages. For example, in a typical construction delay situation, damages are incurred as a result of increases in expenses (including financing costs) as well as of loss of revenues during the delay. All of these difficulties in predicting and establishing actual damages are exacerbated by the long time periods involved in construction projects. In contracts for large industrial construction projects, the parties often are attempting to predict damages that may occur five or more years after the contracting date.

§ 24.11   —Advantages to Project Owner and Lender

From the project owner's perspective, the uncertainty in predicting and proving actual damages raises the concern that the contractor will not see the threat of actual damages as a significant incentive to performance, believing instead that the difficult proof issues and the multitude of defenses and counterclaims available to the contractor will result in a settlement after the fact that is not economically significant to the contractor. Therefore, considerations of compensation for actual damages aside, a liquidated damages clause may be desired by the owner simply to provide clear incentives for performance.

In some cases, the project owner may have no choice but to require liquidated damages. This may be true if the owner is a public entity.[47] Alternatively, if the financing for the construction project is arranged so that a project lender does not have adequate recourse beyond project revenues to assure adequate debt coverage during construction delays or project outages caused by the contractor, the lender is likely to require liquidated damages in the construction contract at least sufficient to cover debt service in the event of such occurrences. In addition, if other increased costs and expenses or losses of revenues due to construction delays or performance shortfalls are not covered by other security devices such as reserve funds, the lender also may require liquidated damages sufficient to cover those items.

---

[47] *See, e.g.,* Cal. Pub. Cont. Code § 10,226 (Deering Supp. 1991), requiring liquidated damages for delay in certain public works contracts and providing that the liquidated damages amount is enforceable "unless manifestly unreasonable under the conditions arising at the time the contract was made."

§ 24.12　—Advantages to Contractor

There also may be significant advantages to the contractor in liquidating damages when actual damages are difficult to predict or prove. The contractor may find such lack of predictability to be unacceptable from a risk management standpoint and desire a liquidated damages provision as a means of achieving an acceptable level of risk by limiting liability. This incentive is most likely to occur in situations in which the contractor is unable to obtain a release from liability for indirect, incidental, or consequential damages or when the distinction between these types of damages and direct damages is unclear. In addition, the contractor may use liquidated damages to avoid costly delays in obtaining a release of retention funds at the end of the project. It is not unheard of for an owner to use the fact that the actual amount of damages is not readily determinable as justification for withholding the release of retention to the contractor, even when the actual damages are likely to be substantially less than the amount of the retention. Liquidation of such damages denies the project owner this leverage.

§ 24.13　Setting Amount of Damages for Delays

Given the propensity of courts to refuse to enforce liquidated damages provisions that set damages at levels that may turn out to be significantly different—especially if higher—than actual damages,[48] the care with which the amount of liquidated damages is set is at least as important as the care with which the clause is drafted. Therefore, it is critical that the amount of or formula for determining liquidated damages not be set by using "rule of thumb" numbers for gross damages for delay, but rather that it be built "from the ground up," by carefully identifying each element of potential damages and separately evaluating it. Per diem debt service costs for the construction loan should be estimated and other increased expenses (construction and otherwise) flowing from the delay should be separately analyzed and estimated, as should lost revenues and costs of providing interim substitutes for the use of the project.

§ 24.14　—Separating Elements of Delay Damages

In establishing the amount of liquidated damages, one should not assume that all damages flowing from the delay should be liquidated. It may be that one element of damages (for example, debt service) is readily calculable,

---

[48] See § 24.18.

whereas another (for example, cost of cover or lost revenues) is not. Under such circumstances it may be appropriate to liquidate only the latter, leaving the damages that are easily calculable outside the scope of the liquidated damages provision. This approach also will help avoid having the clause rendered unenforceable because it does not meet the requirement that the damages liquidated be "incapable or very difficult of accurate estimation"[49] or that liquidation be dictated by difficulties of proof of actual damages.[50]

Separating various elements of delay damages, and liquidating some and not others, should not run afoul of courts' abhorrence of nonexclusive liquidated damages provisions.[51] A clause that requires the contractor to pay liquidated damages in addition to all actual damages should and most probably will be stricken as a penalty provision, and a clause that gives the project owner the option of collecting liquidated damages or seeking actual damages raises concerns regarding enforceability in terms of the difficulties in proof of loss. Nevertheless, liquidating only that distinguishable portion of damages that is not readily capable of accurate estimation or proof, and leaving that portion of damages that readily lends itself to estimation and proof outside the scope of the clause, limits the use of the liquidated damages clause to the circumstances favored by the courts and the commentators, and should, therefore, decrease the likelihood of the clause being held unenforceable.[52] Nevertheless, to assure that the clause is not mistaken for one that allows the owner both liquidated and actual damages for the same element of damages, such a "partial liquidation" clause should include recitals designed to show that the unliquidated and liquidated portions do not overlap.[53]

§ 24.15   —Unreasonably Small Liquidated Damages

As noted above in § 24.2,[54] although unreasonably large liquidated damages are unenforceable as a penalty, it does not necessarily follow that courts will refuse to enforce liquidated damages that are unreasonably small as a limitation of remedies. Although some commentators have suggested that such clauses should be rendered unenforceable if it was the

---

[49] Restatement of Contracts § 339(1) (1932).

[50] Restatement (Second) of Contracts § 356(1) (1979).

[51] See 2 Stein, Construction Law ¶ 6.10[2] (1991); Dunbar, *Drafting the Liquidated Damage Clause—When and How,* 20 Ohio St. L.J. 221, 234–36 (1959). See § **24.8**.

[52] See J.E. Hathaway & Co. v. United States, 249 U.S. 460 (1918), Hillsborough County Aviation Auth. v. Cone Bros. Contracting Co., 285 So. 2d 619 (Fla. Dist. Ct. App. 1973). *See also* Stein, Construction Law ¶ 6.10[2] (1991).

[53] For example, a clause that liquidates all delay damages other than debt service should be accompanied by recitals that subject the owner to damages in event of delay.

[54] See § **24.1**.

intent of the parties in negotiating the clause to liquidate damages,[55] the courts have fairly consistently held that such clauses are enforceable if the parties' intent was to limit liability and the clause is not unconscionable.[56] Thus, the owner and the contractor can agree that the liquidated damages will be an amount significantly less than actual damages, at least if they clearly state their intention. This can be accomplished by specifically calling the clause a limitation of liability rather than a liquidated damages clause, and accompanying it with a recital that the contractor is entering into the contract on the express condition that contractor's liability be so limited and would not otherwise enter into the contract.

Bonus for Early Completion

Another method of decreasing the risk that a liquidated damages provision will be held to be unenforceable by virtue of a large discrepancy between the amount of damages specified in the clause and the actual damages incurred is to combine the liquidated damages provision with a provision requiring the payment of a bonus for early completion. Although the courts have been anything but consistent in their rationale, they have been reluctant to overturn clauses that provide for liquidated damages—or even amounts indicated to be penalties—when the contract also calls for a significant bonus for early completion. The primary reason for this attitude is probably a concern for mutuality of remedies. Because there is no convenient legal theory on which the project owner can attack a bonus provision that is overly generous, it would be unfair to allow the contractor to attack the penalty or liquidated damages provision that is presumably negotiated as an integral part of the incentive scheme.

The relative merits of such incentive clauses and their use in lieu of or in conjunction with liquidated damages provisions is beyond the scope of this chapter. It should be noted, however, that bonuses for early completion are only appropriate under circumstances in which the project owner obtains some discernible economic advantage from early completion. Extreme care must be taken to draft the provision so that it does not provide for payment of a bonus under circumstances in which the anticipated economic benefit does not exist.

---

[55] *See, e.g.,* Anderson, *Liquidated Damages under the Uniform Commercial Code,* 41 Sw. L.J. 1083, 1107; W. Hawkland, Uniform Commercial Code Series § 2-718.01 (1982).

[56] *See* Dow Corning Corp. v. Capitol Aviation, Inc., 411 F.2d 622, 627 (7th Cir. 1979); Better Food Markets v. American Dist. Tel. Co., 40 Cal. 2d 179, 253 P.2d 10 (1953).

§ 24.16   —Defining the Delay

Damages may be contractually liquidated for any delay in performance. For example, liquidated damages may be applied to failure of a design/ build contractor to provide engineering data required early in the project and to failure of a general contractor to provide foundations and footings necessary to allow a separate speciality contractor or supplier to install such items as equipment as well as to failure to achieve "substantial" or "final" completion by a specified date. However, provisions liquidating damages for preliminary project milestones may be held to be unenforceable penalties if delays in the preliminary milestones do not independently result in actual damages because the impact on the overall project can be overcome and the project completion schedule maintained without significant additional cost.[57] Therefore, provisions for liquidated damages for failure to meet early project milestones should be limited to situations in which damages from the failure to meet such milestones can be justified separately, such as when the meeting of the early milestone is essential to or will affect the cost of the activity of a party other than the contractor.

In fact, because the economic effect of delays tends to differ from one stage of construction project to another and the enforceability of the liquidated damages provision may depend on the extent to which a court finds that the liquidated damages provision is a reasonable attempt at estimating actual damages, it is useful in drafting liquidated damages provisions for construction delays to identify each event that affects the nature or amount of actual damages and apply separate levels of liquidated damages to each such event. In this way, the likelihood of a major discrepancy between actual and liquidated damages (and a resulting disallowance of the provision) can be minimized. Thus, if an intermediate project event such as completion of a portion of the project or substantial completion of the project would reduce the amount of ongoing damages by allowing another contractor to complete its work or allowing the project owner to begin beneficial use of the project or convert its construction loan to a term loan at a lower interest rate, the level of liquidated damages should be adjusted based on the event that causes the level of actual damages to change. Failure to do so may result in the entire liquidated damages provision being held to be unenforceable because it does not represent a reasonable attempt to estimate actual damages.

At the very least, a distinction should be made between damages for delays in substantial completion and damages for delays in final completion.[58] Even if the failure to make such a distinction does not render the

---

[57] See § 24.3–24.6 for a discussion on enforceability of liquidated damages provisions when there are no actual damages.

[58] *See* discussion in J. Sweet, Legal Aspects of Architecture, Engineering, and the Construction Process 407 (2d ed. 1977).

clause unenforceable, the courts are likely to hold that liquidated damages do not extend beyond substantial completion if the project owner did or could have obtained substantial beneficial use of the project at the point of substantial completion.[59]

§ 24.17   Enforcing or Avoiding the Provision

The ability of the project owner to avoid an undesirable (from the owner's perspective) liquidated damages provision is more limited than that of the contractor. The project owner, not being harmed by the penal nature of a delay clause, generally is not allowed to escape the effect of the clause on that ground.[60] Moreover, as a practical matter, a project owner would only seek invalidation of a liquidated damages provision if the provision acted to unduly limit the contractor's liability. In order for the project owner to argue successfully that a liquidated damages clause is invalid as an attempt to limit liability rather than to liquidate damages, the project owner must show that the limitation is unconscionable, and the grounds for such a showing are much more limited than the basis for invalidating a liquidated damages provision.[61]

Thus, the contractor has the advantage in terms of arguments available to render a liquidated damages provision invalid. The contractor may argue, for example:

1. That the clause is invalid because the actual damages were readily susceptible to estimation and proof and, therefore, liquidation is inappropriate[62]
2. That the provision is overly broad in that it covers elements of damages that are not difficult to estimate or prove as well as those that are[63]
3. More generally, that the liquidated damages provision is not a reasonable attempt to estimate actual damages.[64]

However, the contractor must exercise extreme caution in using the aforementioned arguments, because the effect of unenforceability of a liquidated

---

[59] *See, e.g.,* Hungerford Constr. Co. v. Florida Citrus Exposition, Inc., 440 F.2d 1229 (5th Cir. 1968), *cert. denied,* 391 U.S. 928 (1969); Continental Ill. Nat'l Bank & Trust Co. v. United States, 101 F. Supp. 755 (Ct. Cl.), *cert. denied,* 343 U.S. 963 (1952).

[60] X.L.O. Concrete Corp. v. John T. Brady & Co., 104 A.D.2d 181, 482 N.Y.S.2d 476 (1984); Mahoney v. Tingley, 85 Wash. 2d 95, 529 P.2d 1068 (1975) (*en banc*).

[61] *See* Restatement (Second) of Contracts § 208; U.C.C. § 2-719 (1977). See also § **24.2.**

[62] See § **24.3–24.6.**

[63] See § **24.14.**

[64] See § **24.3–24.6.**

damages provision is that it will be stricken from the contract and the intended beneficiary may prove and collect actual damages.[65] The contractor will, therefore, want to challenge the validity of the clause only when it is clear that actual damages are smaller than the liquidated sum or when there is a degree of uncertainty on that issue such as to give the contractor significant leverage in settlement discussions. The difficulty of the contractor's decision whether to challenge a liquidated damages provision is compounded by the fact that both the validity of the provision and the advisability of a challenge to it may depend on factors more readily provable by the project owner than by the contractor—namely, the project owner's actual damages.

§ 24.18   —No Actual Damages

Although the difficulties in assessing the effect of the decision to challenge a liquidated damages provision and the problems of proof with respect thereto are considerably less when it is clear that there are no actual damages, neither the courts nor the commentators as discussed in § 24.3 through 24.6 have been consistent with regard to whether the lack of any actual damages itself renders a liquidated damages provision invalid. Some early decisions held, on the basis of equity and unjust enrichment, that liquidated damages provisions should not be enforced under such circumstances.[66] Although comment e to § 339(1) of the *Restatement* suggests a defense of no actual damages based on mutual mistake of fact, the courts generally have interpreted the *Restatement's* emphasis on the parties' intent at the time of contracting as prohibiting the introduction of proof of actual damages.[67] The comments to § 356 of the *Second Restatement* expressly allow a defense of no actual damages, but a review of cases since the *Second Restatement* does not evidence a significant shift toward allowing introduction of evidence to support such a defense.

It is quite common in construction contract cases that there are no actual damages because, due to circumstances outside the contemplation of either party, the project owner would have been unable to use the work of the contractor even if the work had been completed on time. Both the courts

---

[65] *See* Dunbar, *Drafting the Liquidated Damage Clause—When and How,* 20 Ohio St. L.J. 221, 234–36 (1959).

[66] *See* Seeman v. Biemann, 108 Wis. 365, 84 N.W. 490 (1900); Massman Constr. Co. v. City Council, 147 F.2d 925 (5th Cir. 1945); Northwest Fixture Co. v. Kilbourne & Clark, 128 F. 256 (9th Cir. 1904). Government contract cases generally are to the contrary. *See, e.g.,* Ellicott Mach. Co. v. United States, 43 Ct. Cl. 232 (1908); Byron Jackson Co. v. United States, 35 F. Supp. 665 (S.D. Cal. 1940).

[67] *See* McCarthy v. Tally, 46 Cal. 2d 577, 297 P.2d 981 (1956); Note, *Contracts: Liquidated Damages: Necessity of Actual Damages,* 4 UCLA L. Rev. 126 (1956). See also discussion § 24.4.

and the commentators have struggled with this situation and the results reached by the courts have been based as often on equitable principles as on either the *Restatement* or the *Second Restatement*. For example, in the leading case of *California & Hawaiian Sugar Co. v. Sun Ship, Inc.,*[68] C&H contracted with Sun to build a barge to be towed by a tug and contracted separately with another company to build the tug. Sun breached the contract by not completing the barge by the required date, but the other company did not complete the tug until substantially after Sun completed the barge. Thus, the barge would have been of no use if it had been completed earlier than Sun actually completed it. In rejecting Sun's argument based on comment b of § 356 of the *Second Restatement* that "where it is clear that no loss at all has occurred, a provision fixing a substantial sum as damages is unenforceable," the court stated:

> The Restatement, however, deals with the case where the defaulting contractor was alone in his default. We deal with a case of concurrent defaults. If we were to be so literal minded as to follow the Restatement here, we would have to conclude that because both parties were in default, C&H suffered no damage until one party performed . . . . The continued default of both parties would operate to take each of them off the hook. That cannot be the law.[69]

Commentators have, however, criticized such analysis.[70]

§ 24.19   —Language and Excuse under the Provision

If the effect of the liquidated damages provision cannot be avoided by having the contractual provision declared invalid, it may be possible to have the provision declared inapplicable or at least to have its effects mitigated, either by a strict reading of its language or by reason of excuse. The most commonly alleged excuses are that the delay was caused or contributed to by the owner or someone for whom the owner is responsible. The English common law rule, which is reflected in the United States by such cases as *United States v. United Engineering & Contracting Co.*[71] and is often considered by commentators as the majority rule in the United States,[72] is that

---

[68] 794 F.2d 1433 (9th Cir. 1986), *cert. denied,* 108 S. Ct. 200 (1987).

[69] *Id.* at 1437.

[70] *See* Anderson, *Liquidated Damages under the Uniform Commercial Code,* 41 Sw. L.J. 1083; Note, *Contracts: Liquidated Damages: Necessity of Actual Damages,* 4 UCLA L. Rev. 126 (1956).

[71] 234 U.S. 236 (1941).

[72] *See, e.g.,* K. Cushman, Construction Litigation 192–200 (1981).

there should be no apportionment of fault between owner and contractor if the owner or its agents contributed to the delay. The liquidated damages provision fails and the owner must prove actual damages. This typically is contrasted with the minority rule that the delay should be apportioned in such circumstances.[73] However, a careful reading of the modern cases suggests a more complex analysis. The extent to which delays caused by the owner or its agents will defeat or mitigate a claim for liquidated damages depends on such factors as the specific language of the liquidated damages provision, the availability under the contract in question of specific procedures and remedies dealing with owner-caused delay, and the timing of the owner-caused delay, whether occurring before or after the scheduled completion date.

It appears obvious that the contractor will have a greater opportunity to mitigate or defeat, on the basis of owner-caused delays, an owner's claim for liquidated damages under a clause that provides for liquidated damages if the failure to meet a specified completion date is "due to the fault of the contractor" than under a clause that provides for such liquidated damages without reference to such fault. However, although a provision with the quoted language may be beneficial to the contractor in that it may require the owner to specifically show contractor fault, courts have allowed contractors to avoid or mitigate the effect of even the latter type of provision, at least when the owner's contribution to the delay takes the form of an unreasonable delay in acceptance of completion of the work.[74] The results have been the same when the delay in acceptance was by a third party (such as an architect) to whom the owner had delegated such authority.[75]

Unreasonable Delay in Acceptance

The cases dealing with unreasonable delay in acceptance have been the easiest for the courts to deal with, primarily because they represent the purest examples of an obvious distinction applied by courts in those cases involving owner contributions to contractor delays: the courts will apportion fault and mitigate the effects of the liquidated damages provision when it is clear that the contractor would have completed the work on the required date (or on some later date in cases in which the contractor is claiming owner interference after the required completion date) but for the owner delay or interference and, conversely, are less likely to do so when such "but for" causation is unclear. In order to obtain such apportionment, it is not necessary

---

[73] *See, e.g.,* American Eng'g Co. v. United States, 24 F. Supp. 449 (E.D. Pa. 1938).

[74] *See, e.g.,* Peter Kiewit Sons' Co. v. Pasadena City Junior College Dist., 59 Cal. 2d 241, 379 P.2d 18, 28 Cal. Rptr. 714 (1963).

[75] *See, e.g.,* Morgen & Oswood Constr. Co. v. Big Sky Inc., 171 Mont. 268, 557 P.2d 1017 (1976).

that the contractor show that it was without fault. The contractor need only show that, even in light of unexcused delays, there was a date after which the work clearly would have been complete but for the owner's interference or delay. The courts typically will find that no liquidated damages are payable after such date. It is the situation in which the fault of the owner and fault of the contractor are inextricably intermingled so as to make the application of the but for analysis impossible or very difficult with which the courts have struggled and have sometimes resorted to the majority rule, that there should be no apportionment of fault between owner and contractor if the owner or its agents contributed to the delay.

Delay Claim Provisions

The contractual analysis in the more difficult cases—when the but for analysis cannot be used—usually focuses not on the liquidated damages provisions of the contract, but rather on the provisions of the contract dealing with the contractor's rights and remedies in connection with delays in general. If the contract provides a particular procedure for delay claims, the contractor may have to show affirmatively that it complied with each and every prerequisite to a time extension under the contract,[76] to avoid the enforcement of a liquidated damages provision. On the other hand, the absence of any provision in the contract allowing the contractor to make a delay claim may in some cases be considered evidence of an intent that the contractor be strictly liable.[77]

Focus on the delay claim provisions of the contract can provide some interesting results. Such provisions often are part of the printed boilerplate, whereas liquidated damages provisions typically are not, so there is often the lack of coordination between the liquidated damages provisions and the delay claim provisions. For example, the delay claim provisions may provide for adjustments of specific schedule references in the boilerplate and fail to provide specifically for adjustment to the "target date" governing liquidated damages. The court may treat such an omission as merely an oversight to be corrected by the court, or it may, at one extreme, treat the admission as evidence of an intent that the contractor be strictly liable with respect to liquidated damages, or, at the other extreme, treat the omission as evidence that the contractor is not required to follow the procedures specified therein when seeking an adjustment of the target date.

When the delay claim provisions of the contract provide for unliquidated damages (or contract price adjustments) as well as for schedule adjustments in the event of delays caused by the owner, the interaction between such provisions and the liquidated damages provisions can become even more

---

[76] *See, e.g.,* Austin-Griffith, Inc. v. Goldberg, 224 S.C. 372, 79 S.E.2d 447 (1953).

[77] *See* United States v. United Eng'g & Contracting Co., 234 U.S. 236 (1941).

complex. In effect, the owner's damages are liquidated and the contractor's are not, and the contractor may use the delay claim provisions as an offensive weapon as well as a defense. If actual damages exceed the liquidated damages of the owner, the contractor may be in an advantageous offset position. Even if the contractor's actual damages do not exceed the liquidated damages, the contractor may be able to obtain an adjustment to the target date in addition to recovering actual damages. It is for these reasons that a sophisticated and well-advised project owner will seldom couple a provision allowing the contractor a contract price adjustment or unliquidated damages for owner-caused delays with a provision liquidating the contractor's damages for delays. The delay claims clause more typically will limit the contractor's relief to schedule adjustments only.

§ 24.20   —Effect of Termination

Cases in which the project is never completed by the contractor, either because the contractor abandons the project or because the contractor is terminated by the project owner, have produced mixed results.[78] Most courts have held that, at least when the termination occurs prior to the scheduled completion date, the owner waives the right to liquidated damages and must look to its damage remedies for termination for cause.[79] Even when the termination occurs after the scheduled completion date, liquidated damages usually do not continue for delays caused or contributed by the owner or its substituted contractor after termination of the original contractor.[80] However, some cases have held that liquidated damages provisions remain applicable regardless of how (or even if) the owner chooses to complete the work on the theory that a contractor that wrongfully breaches a contract may not object to the consequences of that action.[81] The courts

---

[78] *Compare* Continental Realty Corp. v. Andrew J. Crevolin Co., 380 F. Supp. 246 (S.D. W. Va. 1974) (liquidated damages inapplicable) *with* Austin-Griffith, Inc. v. Goldberg, 224 S.C. 372, 79 S.E.2d 447 (1953) (liquidated damages applicable).

[79] *See, e.g.,* National Am. Bank v. Southcoast Contractors Inc., 276 So. 2d 777 (La. Ct. App.), *writ refused,* 279 So. 2d 694 (La. 1973); Transamerica Ins. Co. v. McKeesport Hous. Auth., 309 F. Supp. 1321 (W.D. Pa. 1970); Continental Realty Corp. v. Andrew J. Crevolin Co., 380 F. Supp. 246 (S.D. W. Va. 1974). *But see* Oregon State Highway Comm'n v. DeLong Corp., 9 Or. App. 550, 495 P.2d 1215 (1972), *cert. denied,* 411 U.S. 965 (1973) (liquidated damages allowed for delay after termination for defective work and recovery of excess completion costs).

[80] *See* Austin-Griffith, Inc. v. Goldberg, 224 S.C. 372, 79 S.E.2d 447 (1953).

[81] Kasten Constr. Co. v. Anne Arundel County, 262 Md. 482, 278 A.2d 282 (1971). *See also* Grier-Lowrance Constr. Co. v. United States, 98 Ct. Cl. 434 (1943). *Cf.* 48 C.F.R. § 52.212-5 (1990) (the liquidated damages provision for federal construction contracts expressly allows the federal government to both assess liquidated damages until final completion and recover the increased costs incurred in completing the work).

consistently have held that the owner is subject to the obligation to mitigate—or at least not unreasonably increase—the damages incurred,
whether or not liquidated.

§ 24.21   —Waiver of Rights

The right to liquidated damages for delay may be waived by actions of the
owner after the delay.[82] Similarly, the contractor's actions occurring after
the delay may be held to constitute a waiver of a defense against liquidated
damages. In addition to failures to comply with specified contractual procedures, the contractor may be held to have waived its right to contest liability
for liquidated damages if the contractor accepts progress payments after the
scheduled completion date that include specific deductions for liquidated
damages for delay in meeting the scheduled completion date.[83] In such cases
the analysis focuses on the intent of the parties, so both the contractor and
the owner must take care not to commit an act or omission that might be
considered inconsistent with the exercise of their contractual rights.

§ 24.22   Effect on Subcontracting Strategy

Numerous considerations go into determining the extent to which the
prime contractor subcontracts work and the manner in which the contractor divides the subcontracted work among the various subcontractors, and
those considerations may conflict with each other. For example, considerations of relative expertise and access to resources may cause a prime contractor to subcontract on a "functional" basis, awarding subcontracts on
the basis of speciality areas such as soils, concrete, mechanical, ventilation,
and insulation, whereas considerations of schedule coordination and desire
for clear delineation of contractual responsibility and liability may result in
subcontracts being let to cover complete responsibility for separate, physically defined portions of a project, such as the "power island" in a power
plant, the "control house" in an industrial plant, or the exterior of a building. These decisions may also be affected by the firmness of scope definition in the prime contract; an evolving, undefined scope may require that
the prime contractor minimize subcontracting to avoid having to negotiate
numerous scope changes and extra work orders with subcontractors.

The existence of liquidated damages provisions in the prime contract
also affects the prime contractor's decision whether or not to subcontract.

---

[82] *See, e.g.,* Haggarty v. Selsco, 166 Mont. 492, 534 P.2d 874 (1975).

[83] Dahlstrom Corp. v. State Highway Comm'n, 590 F.2d 614 (5th Cir. 1979); McGillvray v.
Gross, 167 F. Supp. 373 (D. Alaska 1958).

Although it seems that a prime contractor subject to liquidated damages for delays in completion would most likely be able to "spread the risk" and make subcontractors whose performance it is dependent upon responsible for the liquidated damages caused by the subcontractors' delay in performance, the analysis and strategy applicable to subcontracting is not that simple. Because subcontracting involves a considerable loss of control over the scope of work, subcontracting certain aspects of the project (especially minor tasks), in cases in which the prime contractor is responsible for liquidated damages actually, may increase the prime contractor's risk of being subject to liquidated damages if, for example, such subcontractor's work is critical to the project schedule. In such instance, because the prime contractor may not be able to adequately manage its own risk of paying liquidated damages it may not make sense for the contractor to subcontract.

Conversely, a delay in performance by a subcontractor actually may not cause a delay in the prime contractor's performance if the subcontractor's work is not critical to the prime contractor's timely performance or if the prime contractor can otherwise rearrange the work or utilize other subcontractors to avoid such result. In such circumstance, the prime contractor is still able to manage the risk of delay and corresponding liquidated damages. Thus, in deciding whether to subcontract, the prime contractor must assess the contemplated scope of the subcontractor's work and the anticipated effect on the project schedule as well as the level of liquidated damages that the subcontractor is likely to agree to absorb.

Equally important as a practical matter, the prime contractor must assess the financial strength and reputation of each subcontractor in determining whether the use of a subcontractor is consistent with the prime contractor's risk profile. This assessment entails a subjective analysis of whether the existence and amount of liquidated damages will act as an adequate incentive to prevent subcontractor delays and an objective analysis of whether, if payable, such liquidated damages will be recoverable.

The following examples illustrate the foregoing considerations:

Example 1.   The prime contractor has a $20 million prime contract to build a new industrial facility. The prime contract requires the contractor to pay up to $5 million of liquidated damages if the facility is not substantially complete by a specified date. The concrete work on the project cannot be done in advance of other work because the configuration of the facility requires that the portions of the concrete be poured after as well as before certain key equipment is installed. The value of the concrete work is approximately $1 million. Given this set of facts, even the contractor who is accustomed to subcontracting all concrete work would be ill-advised to award such a "functional" subcontract. In light of the value of the subcontract, the prime contractor is unlikely to obtain coverage of the entire liquidated damages from the concrete subcontractor if the subcontractor causes a delay, because the subcontractor most probably will attempt to limit damages to the contract value. In addition, even if coverage is obtained, the determination of a reasonable liquidated damages amount in this situation will be extremely difficult given the schedule interdependence between the concrete work and other project activities such as equipment, supply, and installation. The prime contractor should consider either performing the concrete work itself or subcontracting various phases of the project in such a way that the subcontractor for each phase is responsible for its own concrete work.

Example 2. The prime contractor has a contract for a power plant, which contains liquidated damages based solely on the plant's ability to achieve a specified boiler and turbine output by a specified date. The boiler and turbine are in a separate "power island" from the remainder of the project, and the liquidated damages are not affected by the date of completion of other areas such as the administrative building and environmental systems. The boiler and turbine are being supplied by a single supplier and the value of supply and installation of the boiler and turbine are approximately 50 percent of the project value. Under these circumstances, functional subcontracts again make little sense; the logical choice is a separate contract for supply and installation of the power island. The division of responsibility will match the risk allocation under the prime contract and there is sufficient control and incentive to reasonably expect the subcontractor to cover the entire amount of liquidated damages assessable under the prime contract.

Example 3. Although the prime contractor has sufficient mechanical contracting skills within its own organization, it typically subcontracts all mechanical work in the St. Louis area to a local subcontractor because that subcontractor has local relationships that result in a price advantage. The prime contractor has a project in St. Louis that requires the payment of substantial liquidated damages for delay. The scope of the work is very preliminary and substantial evolution during the course of the project is expected, especially in the mechanical area. Under these circumstances, in spite of the price advantage of the local subcontractor, serious consideration should be given to not subcontracting the mechanical work. Because the combination of potential liquidated damages liability and an evolving scope requires a degree of control and flexibility not likely to be achieved in the contractor-subcontractor relationship, the price advantage is likely to be quickly lost by price concessions and delays resulting from negotiations with the subcontractor over scope changes.

As the foregoing examples illustrate, extreme caution must be taken in determining those packages of work to subcontract in a complex construction project. Although theoretically the concept of spreading risk by "passing through" liquidated damages is valid, more careful analysis is necessary to appropriately match subcontractor risk and responsibility with those allocations set forth in the prime contract.

§ 24.23   Coordinating Subcontract with Prime Contract

Once the decision has been made to subcontract a certain scope of work, it is important to coordinate, as between the prime contract and the subcontract, the critical elements of the liquidated damages provision. To the extent possible, the clauses should parallel one another, in order for the prime contractor to avoid the situation in which it is responsible for liquidated damages for late completion and is unable to pass through such liquidated damages to the subcontractor, even though the delay is attributable to the subcontractor.[84]

§ 24.24   —Coextensive Triggering Event

Most important, the event triggering liability for liquidated damages should be coextensive. Obviously, if a prime contractor is responsible for completion of a project by a certain date and would be liable for liquidated damages if it failed to do so, the subcontracts applicable to the project should provide for commencement of liquidated damages in sufficient time to allow the prime contractor either to rearrange the work or otherwise accelerate the schedule so as to avoid its own late completion (and recoup the costs of doing so) or to ensure that its own potential liquidated damages are covered. Less obvious is the all too common situation in which liquidated damages under the prime contract commence upon failure to reach "completion" and liquidated damages under the subcontract commence upon failure to reach "substantial completion." Given this discontinuity in the language, the prime contractor may be responsible for liquidated damages due to the subcontractor's own failure to reach completion (assuming, as is the case in most construction contracts, that in order for the contractor to reach completion, all subcontractor work must be complete), even when the subcontractor is not responsible for such

---

[84] P&C Thompson Bros. Constr. Co. v. Rowe, 433 So. 2d 1388 (Fla. Dist. Ct. App. 1983) (illustrating the importance of coordination). The court in that case refused to allow the prime contractor to both recover liquidated damages from the subcontractor and obtain indemnification for delay damages paid to the owner on the ground that such recovery would be inequitable and would allow the prime contractor to receive a windfall.

damages. Moreover, because the subcontractor will always reach substantial completion of its scope of work prior to completion by the prime contractor, any pass-through of liquidated damages is negated.

Another similar example of the importance of having a coextensive triggering date is the situation in which the prime contractor is responsible for the satisfactory completion of a particular technical test in order to avoid liquidated damages and that test is not part of the subcontract. In this situation, a subcontractor's nonperformance could cause a delay in the test, without the corresponding risk of liquidated damages being passed through for such nonperformance. Again, in such situations, the prime contractor must accurately assess the effect that nonperformance by such subcontractor will have on the prime contractor's ability to conduct the test and apportion liquidated damages accordingly.

§ 24.25   —Limit on Subcontractor Defenses

Equally important, the subcontract provisions must limit those defenses available to the subcontractor to avoid payment of liquidated damages, especially in situations in which the prime contractor is responsible for such damages. Not only must the amount of liquidated damages attributable to the subcontractor be a reasonable approximation of anticipated or actual harm, but also care should be taken to avoid other pitfalls that would make the contractor responsible for liquidated damages in situations in which the subcontractor is only responsible for actual damages, at least in situations in which the prime contractor expects that the liquidated amount will be greater than the amount of actual damages.

For example, in drafting liquidated damages provisions for subcontracts, a careful draftsman will pay close attention to the types of delays for which liquidated damages are payable under the prime contract. A prime contractor responsible for payment of liquidated damages for "all delays" should not enter into any subcontracts in which liquidated damages are payable only for "delays attributable to the subcontractor." This type of provision not only gives the subcontractor a defense to any enforcement action by the contractor, but also complicates the analysis of those factual situations involving delays by the prime contractor or owner in the acceptance of work.[85] However, in the converse situation, a prime contractor responsible for liquidated damages only for delays "attributable to it" would not necessarily give subcontractors the benefit of such provision. This not only permits the prime contractor to recover liquidated damages without showing subcontractor fault and therefore limits the subcontractors' defenses, but also avoids those difficulties relating to apportionment of responsibility in

---

[85] See § 24.19 for a related discussion.

complex factual situations involving multiple subcontractors performing interrelated work.

§ 24.26 —Excusable Delay

The extent to which delays are excusable under the prime contract also must be considered. Typical force majeure provisions, which may excuse a prime contractor's performance due to "circumstances beyond its control," may not provide adequate protection from all subcontractor-caused delays because the decision to subcontract and the terms and conditions thereof usually are within the contractor's control, and most, if not all, sophisticated owners will not allow a force majeure to be defined to include such subcontractor-caused delays. Nevertheless, to the extent that delays are excusable under the subcontract, thus preventing the enforcement of any liquidated damages or other remedy provided to the prime contractor thereunder, the prime contractor must ensure that the same excusable delays, whether due to force majeure or otherwise, also constitute excusable delays under the prime contract. For example, if a subcontractor supplying a piece of equipment is excused from performance due to delays in transportation (caused by a railroad strike, for example) the prime contractor must ensure that it, too, is excused from late performance due to the occurrence of such delay.

§ 24.27 —Delay Claims

As discussed in § **24.19**,[86] many contracts may contain specific provisions dealing with rights and remedies in connection with delays. Similar considerations apply in the context of subcontracting as to the interrelationship of liquidated damages and such delay claims provisions; the prime contractor should ensure that the language of such provisions in the subcontract are coextensive with those in the prime contract. For example, to the extent a delay claims provision in a subcontract provides the exclusive remedy for delays, the contractor again may be put in the untenable position of having to pay greater liquidated damages to the owner than those actual damages recoverable from the subcontractor under such provision. More important is the opposite situation; to the extent the delay claims provision of the subcontract provides for a subcontract price and schedule adjustment to the subcontractor and there also exists a liquidated damages provision, the prime contractor may be in a situation in which, to the extent there are owner- or contractor-caused or other excusable delays under the

---

[86] *Id.*

subcontract, the delay claim provision may be used offensively by the sub-contractor.[87] Again, to the extent delay claim provisions are included along with liquidated damages provisions in a subcontract, relief to the subcontractor thereunder should be limited to schedule adjustments.

§ 24.28 —Consequential Damages

The exclusion of provisions limiting consequential damages in the subcontract may mitigate the interrelationship between liquidated damages clauses in both the prime contract and subcontract and provide relief to the prime contractor from other defenses available for the subcontractor to contest the enforcement of a liquidated damages provision. Without any exclusion on recovery of consequential damages, the prime contractor may be able to argue that all damages that it suffers as a result of the subcontractor's breach, including all payments to the owner of liquidated damages provided in the prime contract, are consequential damages that it is entitled to recover. However, because the prime contractor must still overcome those difficult questions of proof and causation that it was trying to avoid by using a liquidated damages provision in the first place, reliance by the prime contractor on the exclusion of such provisions should not be over-stated; excluding provisions limiting consequential damages from the subcontract only gives the prime contractor additional backup protection in cases in which the liquidated damages provisions in the subcontract are inapplicable or unenforceable.

§ 24.29　Establishing Amount of Damages

The reluctance of some courts to enforce liquidated damages provisions setting damages at levels that turn out to be significantly different than actual damages, especially if no actual damages are shown,[88] is particu-larly important with respect to subcontracting. Again, it is imperative that such liquidated amount be developed "from the ground up" by identifying those elements of potential damages likely to result and separately evaluat-ing them for each subcontractor. The amount of liquidated damages should be relatively proportional to either the percentage of work that is to be completed by the subcontractor or the importance of such work in rela-tion to the performance of other aspects of the project, either by other subcontractors or by the prime contractor itself. Recitals should be used to reflect the role of each subcontractor with regard to the project. In light

---

[87] *Id.*

[88] See §§ **24.3–24.6, 24.13, 24.15, 24.18.**

of the enforceability standard that the parties should try to reasonably approximate the damages that will be caused by the breach, the contractor must analyze the potential effect on the project of a subcontractor's breach and limit the use of liquidated damages to those particular breaches for which actual damages are difficult to ascertain.

For example, although a prime contractor may be able to accelerate or otherwise rearrange work in order to avoid payment of liquidated damages to the owner, a delay by a subcontractor may still cause damages to the prime contractor (acceleration or overtime costs, for example), which the parties wish to liquidate. In this context it also may be possible to liquidate only certain damages flowing from a subcontractor's delay and to let others be the subject of proof at trial. If this approach is used, recitals again should be included to show that the unliquidated and liquidated portions do not overlap.[89]

As noted in § 24.25, the use of multiple subcontracts for a project only exacerbates the issues and concerns that need to be addressed in establishing liquidated damages amounts for each subcontract. The validity and enforceability of the liquidated damages clauses, from the contractor's perspective (and from the subcontractors' perspective to the extent the provisions are viewed as limitations on liability), must be analyzed separately for each subcontract. Also, the interrelationship between the work performed by the various subcontractors and the prime contractor's entire scope of work must be considered in terms of setting and establishing the amount of liquidated damages attributable to delays by each in order to ensure that the contractor's own risk of payment of liquidated damages for delays is appropriately covered by those subcontractors upon whose performance the prime contractor most depends.

---

[89] See § 24.14.

CHAPTER 25

RECOVERY OF INTEREST AND ATTORNEYS' FEES

Howard I. Gross
Craig S. Taschner

Howard I. Gross is a principal in the Farmington, Connecticut, law firm of Tarlow, Levy & Droney, P.C. He attended Amherst College and received his J.D. from the University of Connecticut School of Law in 1951. He has represented national construction industry companies and was instrumental in the early formation of the National Association of Credit Management in Connecticut. Mr. Gross is a panel member of the American Arbitration Association.

Craig S. Taschner is an associate in the law firm of Tarlow, Levy & Droney, P.C. of Farmington, Connecticut. He received his J.D. from New York Law School in 1987. He specializes in construction litigation in state and federal court as well as before various alternate dispute resolution forums. Mr. Taschner has represented contractors, subcontractors, and owners, including municipalities, in prosecuting and defending construction claims.

§ 25.1   Introduction

The question most frequently asked attorneys by contractors, subcontractors, and material suppliers (collectively referred to in this chapter as "contractors") who are considering bringing a claim for nonpayment is "How much is this going to cost?"

The answer to that question is made up of two components—time and attorneys' fees. When bringing a claim for nonpayment, time, however, translates directly into dollars in the form of interest—the time value of money.

This chapter discusses the rules governing recovery of interest and attorneys' fees. Regarding interest, the chapter only discusses the recovery of prejudgment interest—that is, interest on the monies the contractor claims to be due. Postjudgment interest, or interest on the amount of a judgment, running from the date of judgment, is usually set by state statute. The recovery of direct interest costs actually incurred by the contractor also is addressed.

As will be evident from reading the chapter, a common theme running throughout the rules governing recovery of interest and attorneys' fees is to provide for the recovery of each in the contract. Because many contractors, for several different reasons, fail to address specifically the recovery of interest and attorneys' fees in their contracts, the discussion begins with an analysis of the recovery of interest in the absence of a specific contractual provision.

§ 25.2   Recovery of Prejudgment Interest

As a general rule, interest may be charged by a creditor only when the contract between the debtor and creditor expressly provides for payment of interest or when, in the absence of a contract provision, a statute specifically authorizes the charging of interest notwithstanding such absence.

Recognizing the amount of time that may pass between the time an invoice or requisition for payment is submitted and the date a court may award an unpaid contractor an amount claimed due, courts have formulated rules governing and authorizing the recovery of prejudgment interest in the absence of a statutory or contractual provision. For purposes of this discussion, the term *prejudgment interest* means interest calculated on the amount found by the court to be due, but for a time period (also determined by the court) prior to the entry of judgment. Courts across the country and over the years have formulated and applied rules stated in many different ways. Those rules, however, can be broadly set forth in two categories: (1) the certainty of amount of principal claim rule and (2) the complete compensation rule.

§ 25.3   —Certainty of Amount of
Principal Claim Rule

The most widely-followed rule governing the recovery of prejudgment interest on a construction contract claim generally provides that the recovery of such interest should be awarded by a court (or jury) only when the contractor's claim is "liquidated" or "reasonably ascertainable."[1] This rule reflects a philosophy of the courts to award interest only based on sums that are certain, as in a claim on a promissory note. If the contractor's claim is "unliquidated" or "not reasonably capable of ascertainment," due to an honest dispute or uncertainty as to calculation of the amount due, courts adhering to the certainty of amount of principal claim rule deny recovery of prejudgment interest.[2] The rule recognizes that an owner (or other party

---

[1] *See, e.g.,* Peter Kiewit & Sons' Co. v. Summit Constr. Co., 422 F.2d 242 (8th Cir. 1969); United States *ex rel.* A.V. DeBlasio Constr., Inc. v. Mountain States Constr. Co., 588 F.2d 259 (9th Cir. 1978); Plantation Key Dev., Inc. v. Colonial Mortgage Co., 589 F.2d 164 (5th Cir. 1979); Shook & Fletcher Insulation Co. v. Central Rigging & Contracting Corp., 684 F.2d 1383 (11th Cir. 1982); United States v. Western States Mechanical Contractors Inc., 834 F.2d 1533 (10th Cir. 1987); Paul Hardeman, Inc. v. Arkansas Power & Light Co., 380 F. Supp. 298 (E.D. Ark. 1974); Singer Housing Co. v. Seven Lakes Venture, 466 F. Supp. 369 (D. Colo. 1979); Homes & Son Constr. Co. v. Bolo Corp., 22 Ariz. App. 303, 526 P.2d 1258 (1974); Bryan & Sons Corp. v. Klefstad, 265 So. 2d 382 (Fla. Dist. Ct. App. 1972); Marathon Oil Co. v. Hollis, 167 Ga. App. 48, 305 S.E.2d 864 (1983); Obray v. Mitchell, 98 Idaho 533, 567 P.2d 1284 (1977); Lystarczyk v. Smits, 435 N.E.2d 1011 (Ind. 1982); D.K. Meyer Corp. v. Bevco, Inc., 206 Neb. 318, 292 N.W.2d 773 (1980); Manshul Constr. Corp. v. Dormitory Auth., 79 A.D.2d 383, 436 N.Y.S.2d 724 (1981); Northwest Eng'g Co. v. Thunderbolt Enters., Inc., 301 N.W.2d 421 (S.D. 1981). *But see* Perry Roofing Co. v. Olcott, 744 S.W.2d 929 (Tex. 1988) (award of prejudgment interest based on equitable considerations to encourage settlement and discourage delays); Lester N. Johnson Co. v. City of Spokane, 22 Wash. App. 265, 588 P.2d 1214 (1978); Sime Constr. Co. v. Washington Pub. Power Supply Sys., 28 Wash. App. 10, 621 P.2d 1299 (1980).

[2] *See, e.g.,* General Ins. Co. v. Hercules Constr. Co., 385 F.2d 13 (8th Cir. 1967); E.C. Ernst, Inc. v. Manhattan Constr. Co., 551 F.2d 1026 (5th Cir. 1977); North Am. Life & Casualty Co. v. Wolter, 593 F.2d 609 (5th Cir. 1979); Marathon Oil Co. v. Hollis, 167 Ga. App. 48, 305 S.E.2d 864 (1983).

from whom damages are sought) should only be charged interest, as damages, when such person wrongfully or improperly detains monies due someone else. The detention is deemed wrongful or improper by this rule when the sum detained is fixed or certain. The rule goes on to recognize that a person should not be charged interest for a failure to pay an uncertain amount, because if the amount is uncertain, the failure to pay or the detention of such an amount cannot be considered wrongful.

The difficulty in applying the liquidated versus unliquidated analysis lies in attempting to determine whether, prior to trial, the sum claimed due was fixed or uncertain. This difficulty has resulted in a relaxation of the rule in some jurisdictions. To the extent that the amount can be considered capable of being ascertained, the detention or failure to pay is deemed wrongful and interest is properly recoverable.[3] For example, a contractor was found to be entitled to prejudgment interest on an amount found due under a cost-plus construction contract when the contractor provided the debtor, prior to litigation, with sufficient information to enable the debtor to determine the amount due with reasonable certainty.[4] Therefore, the liquidated-unliquidated rule has been relaxed somewhat in some jurisdictions to provide for the recovery of prejudgment interest when the amount, though unliquidated under a traditional analysis, is nevertheless capable of ascertainment through calculation pursuant to the terms of the contract or by reference to some other accepted standard of value. Such calculation or other standard of value may be found in the subject construction contract or by reference to market values for the same materials or services.[5] If, however, the calculation can only be made by a court based on conflicting evidence or if the claim is comprised of prospective or contingent damages (such as lost profit), the amount of the claim may be deemed incapable of ascertainment for purposes of awarding prejudgment interest.[6]

The court also may look to other factors in determining whether the amount claimed is reasonably ascertainable for purposes of deciding whether to award prejudgment interest. For example, a large disparity between an invoice submitted by the contractor prior to trial and the amount finally awarded by the court may lead a court to determine that the amount was not liquidated prior to trial and thus lead it to deny recovery of interest.[7]

---

[3] Peter Kiewit & Sons Co. v. Summit Constr. Co., 422 F.2d 242 (8th Cir. 1969); E.C. Ernst, Inc. v. Koppers Co., 520 F. Supp. 830 (W.D. Pa. 1981); E. Paul Kovacs & Co. v. Alpert, 180 Conn. 120, 429 A.2d 829 (1980); Parsons v. Henry, 65 Or. App. 627, 672 P.2d 717 (1983).

[4] Homes & Son Constr. Co., Inc. v. Bolo Corp., 22 Ariz. App. 303, 526 P.2d 1258 (1974).

[5] See, e.g., Ottinger v. United States, 230 F.2d 405 (10th Cir. 1956).

[6] See, e.g., Kraemer Bros. v. Prepakt Concrete Co., 432 F. Supp. 462 (W.D. Wis. 1977).

[7] See, e.g., Portage Ind. Sch. Constr. Corp. v. A.V. Stackhouse Co., 153 Ind. App. 366, 287 N.E.2d 564 (1972).

Another factor that a court may look to is the number and complexity of issues between the parties and whether the issues render calculation of the amount due prior to trial too difficult to ascertain.[8]

Suffice to say that, under the certainty of amount of principal claim rule, the more certain the amount of the contractor's principal claim prior to trial, the greater the likelihood that prejudgment interest may be awarded. A contractor that has failed to bargain for an interest provision in its contract can still help itself in its quest to recover interest through proper and complete documentation of its claim and presentation of that documentation to the target defendant by way of a formal demand together with backup documentation prior to institution of litigation. In that way, the target will be hard-pressed to claim lack of notice or inability to calculate the amount claimed due.

This effort should also be undertaken as early on as possible, because the date from which interest runs is often the date of demand of the amount due or the date the sum became due.[9]

§ 25.4   —Complete Compensation Rule

The "complete compensation" rule essentially leaves the issue of whether or not to award prejudgment interest to the sound discretion of the court or jury, and the court or jury applies traditional contract damages principles or equitable principles (depending on the nature of the cause of action sued upon) to make its decision. The test in such cases is usually stated as whether the detention of money is or is not wrongful "under all the circumstances,"[10] or whether, under traditional damages rules, interest should be awarded to fully compensate a contractor for the loss resulting from the delay in payment of the amount found due.[11]

Some jurisdictions have sought to clarify the complete compensation rule by specifically enacting statutes providing for the recovery of prejudgment interest pursuant to certain express standards. For example, in Connecticut, the prejugment interest statute provides that "interest at the rate of ten percent . . . may be recovered . . . as damages for the detention of money after it becomes payable."[12]

---

[8] *See, e.g.,* United Pac. Ins. Co. v. Martin & Luther Gen. Contractors, Inc., 455 P.2d 664 (Wyo. 1969); *but see* Chris Constr. Co. v. May Ctrs., Inc., 23 Conn. App. 453, 581 A.2d 748 (1990) (by claiming setoff, defendant acknowledged that some amount was due).

[9] *See, e.g.,* National Roofing & Siding Co. v. Gros, 433 So. 2d 403 (La. Ct. App. 1983).

[10] *See, e.g.,* Campbell v. Rockefeller, 134 Conn. 585, 59 A.2d 524 (1948).

[11] *See, e.g.,* E.I. DuPont de Nemours & Co. v. Lyles & Lang Constr. Co., 219 F.2d 328 (4th Cir. 1955), *cert. denied,* 349 U.S. 956, 75 S. Ct. 882 (1955).

[12] Conn. Gen. Stat. § 37–39 (1958); *see also* Walter Kidde Constructors, Inc. v. State, 37 Conn. Supp. 50, 434 A.2d 962 (1981).

Other jurisdictions have enacted statutes that make the recovery of prejudgment interest a matter of right from the date the contractor's cause of action accrues.[13]

§ 25.5   Bargaining for Prejudgment Interest

Although the preceding discussion is helpful in the absence of a contractual or statutory provision for the recovery of prejudgment interest, most of the guesswork involved in determining whether a contractor will be awarded prejudgment interest can be avoided by the negotiation and incorporation of a contract term providing for such recovery. The mere costs and often lengthy duration of construction litigation warrant proper planning during the contracting stage. This is true regardless of where the contracting party falls within the chain of project participants (that is, general contractor, subcontractor, sub-subcontractor, or material supplier).

Clear and comprehensive contract language should be incorporated into each contract and subcontract and even included on invoices or purchase orders.

The more specific the contractual terms, the less is left for a court to determine. The essential elements of any contractual provision regarding the payment of interest should include the following:

1. Rate of interest to be charged
2. Whether the rate contemplates simple or compound interest
3. If compounded, the frequency of the compounding (that is, weekly, monthly, or yearly)
4. Event(s) that trigger the running of interest (such as any default in payment or performance)
5. Date from which the interest will be calculated (for example, "30 days from invoice, requisition, or other demand" or "from the date payment is due under the contract").

The American Institute of Architects (AIA) publishes contract documents for purchase and use on construction projects. Most of these contract documents contain provisions for the recovery of interest. Specifically, the AIA documents include the following:

1. A101, *Agreement Between Owner and Contractor—Stipulated Sum,* Article 7, paragraph 7.2 (1987)

---

[13] *See, e.g.,* State v. Phillips, 470 P.2d 266 (Alaska 1970); Paradise Homes, Inc. v. Central Sur. & Ins. Corp., 84 Nev. 109, 437 P.2d 78 (1968). *See also* N.Y. Civ. Prac. L.&R. 5001, 5002 (1962).

2. A101, *Agreement Between Owner and Contractor—Stipulated Sum,* Article 5 (1980)

3. A107, *Abbreviated Owner-Contractor Agreement,* Article 4, paragraph 4.2 (1987)

4. A201, *General Conditions of the Contract for Construction,* subparagraph 13.6.1 (1987)

5. A401, *Contractor-Subcontractor Agreement,* Article 15, paragraph 15.2 (1987).

These AIA documents set forth, in broad terms, the conditions under which interest will be charged. They still require filling in the rate of interest, or if none, dictate that the rate shall be the legal rate (usually defined by state statute). The parties should fill in a specific rate so it is clear to a court that interest was specifically addressed and, therefore, definitely part of the bargain.

On projects not utilizing AIA forms, the parties should incorporate in the contract documents an adequate contract clause pertaining to interest. The following provision is illustrative:

> Interest at the rate of _____% per year shall be charged on all payments due and unpaid under the contract documents, including any change orders, for work performed or materials provided, including approved extra work or material, from the date payment became due under the contract documents. Interest will be compounded monthly but shall never exceed the maximum amount permitted by law in the State of _____.

This provision is merely an example of a contractual provision that attempts to clarify that interest will be charged in all cases of nonpayment. It should be noted that state and federal Usury and Truth-In-Lending laws should be consulted, as they may affect the validity and enforceability of any interest provision. The rate set should also be a reasonable rate, one in line with rates charged to contractors borrowing money in the same or similar jurisdictions.

§ 25.6   Recovery of Actual Interest Costs

Another type of interest that contractors may seek to recover is interest on monies borrowed by the contractor during or for the project. Interest costs such as this are usually presented as an integral part of a delay damages claim or extra work claim. These interest costs can be characterized at least two different ways: (1) additional interest costs as a result of an extended borrowing term incident to a delay claim or claim for extra time incident to extra work; and (2) increased interest costs due to increased interest rates during the extended borrowing term.

Claims for such interest costs can arise in a variety of situations: owner-caused delay, unforeseen site conditions or changed conditions, extra work claims, or labor escalation charges (resulting in increased borrowing to meet payroll). Reasons for borrowing by a contractor are only limited by the wide range of business considerations incident to the specific project or specific company as a whole. The question is whether the contractor can recover those additional interest payments.

Generally, such interest costs are recoverable in accordance with traditional rules of damages in contract, negligence, and other common causes of action relating to construction projects. As a broad statement, the interest costs are recoverable if they were a reasonably foreseeable element of the contractor's loss.[14] An example of this type of recovery is for interest paid on borrowings to finance expenses incurred as a result of delay or extra work.[15] When the interest paid, however, results from unexcused delay, no recovery of such interest will be allowed.[16]

Again, an important element of recovering this type of loss is proper documentation of the claim. The contractor must carefully and fully document compensable reasons for the additional borrowings or extended terms of borrowings. Charges for such costs should be included in requests for change orders, in monthly requisitions, and in correspondence between the parties. Claiming the costs contemporaneously on the job as opposed to in court for the first time lends credibility and support to the claim.

§ 25.7 Recovery of Attorneys' Fees

Similar to the rules governing recovery of prejudgment interest, the general rule pertaining to the recovery of attorneys' fees is that the fees are only recoverable if provided for by contract or by a specific statute—regardless of the outcome of litigation.[17] This rule is generally referred to as the "American Rule." In stark contrast is the "English Rule," which affords a prevailing party or successful litigant the right to recover attorneys' fees and litigation expenses from the other party as items of costs. Although no American jurisdiction has adopted the English Rule in its entirety, several have cut out exceptions to the American Rule and have allowed recovery of attorneys' fees.

Generally, in actions based in fraud, courts may allow attorneys' fees as an element of punitive damages or may, in fact, define punitive damages

---

[14] Metropolitan Transfer Station, Inc. v. Design Structures, Inc., 328 N.W.2d 532 (Iowa 1982).

[15] Bell v. United States, 186 Ct. Cl. 189, 404 F.2d 975 (1968).

[16] Roanoke Hosp. Ass'n v. Doyle & Russel, Inc., 215 Va. 796, 214 S.E.2d 155 (1975).

[17] See, e.g., Gionfriddo v. Avis Rent A Car Sys., Inc., 192 Conn. 280, 297, 472 A.2d 306 (1984).

as attorneys' fees.[18] To the extent, therefore, that a contractor may have an action against an owner based in fraud, attorneys' fees may be recovered by the successful contractor.

In the construction litigation context, however, it should be noted that fraud claims usually arise against contractors in situations involving allegations that the contractor concealed construction defects or fraudulently misled the owner into believing the project was constructed properly.[19] To the extent that the work was done by a subcontractor or other party down-the-line of project participants, the same claim may be asserted by the prime contractor or general contractor against the subcontractor and so on down the line.

Another situation in which attorneys' fees may be recovered is that in which one party's breach of contract or negligent performance of work places the contractor in breach of its own contract(s) with others. Courts may consider the legal fees incurred by the contractor in defending the claims by subcontractors or other third parties as part of the damages in the contractor's case against the owner or prime/general contractor.[20]

In order to recover this type of attorneys' fee, the contractor must show the following:

(1) that the plaintiff had become involved in a legal dispute either because of a breach of contract by the defendant, or because of defendant's tortious conduct, that is, that the party sought to be charged with the fees was guilty of a wrongful or negligent act or breach of agreement; (2) that the litigation was with a third party, not with the defendant from whom the fees are sought to be recovered; (3) that the attorneys' fees were incurred in that third-party litigation; and (4) whether the fees and expenses were incurred as a result of defendant's breach of contract or tort, that they are the natural and necessary consequences of the defendant's act, since remote, uncertain, and contingent consequences do not afford a basis for recovery.[21]

If the only reason the contractor was involved in litigation with its subcontractors, however, was to delay paying them in the hopes of receiving payment from the owner in the interim, a court may be reluctant to reimburse the contractor for such legal fees.[22]

---

[18] *See* Moffa v. Perkins Trucking Co., 200 F. Supp. 183 (D. Conn. 1961); Triangle Sheet Metal Works, Inc. v. Silver, 154 Conn. 116, 222 A.2d 220 (1966). *See also* Markey v. Santangelo, 195 Conn. 76, 485 A.2d 1305 (1985).

[19] *See, e.g.,* Morris Clark v. W.L. Aenchbacher, 143 Ga. App. 282, 238 S.E.2d 442 (1977).

[20] *See, e.g.,* Waldinger Corp. v. Ashbrook-Simon-Hartley, Inc., 564 F. Supp 970 (C.D. Ill. 1983).

[21] Uyemura v. Wick, 57 Haw. 102, 551 P.2d 171, 176 (1976).

[22] *See, e.g.,* Norin Mortgage Corp. v. Wasco, Inc., 343 So. 2d 940 (Fla. Dist. Ct. App. 1977).

§ 25.8   Bargaining for Attorneys' Fees

Due to the limited situations in which attorneys' fees are awarded in the absence of contractual or statutory provisions, and because of the cost involved in litigating construction claims, great care should be taken to incorporate a contractual provision for the recovery of attorneys' fees.

Unlike bargaining for interest in the construction context, when only one party to the contract is usually responsible for paying, attorneys' fees possibly may be recovered by either party, depending on who is ultimately found to have been correct.

This is the reason many contracts are entered into without provisions for recovery of attorneys' fees. Notwithstanding that, some jurisdictions simply do not permit parties to contract for the recovery of attorneys' fees and strike down such provisions as unenforceable.[23]

Most jurisdictions, however, provide for a rule that attorneys' fees provisions in contracts are enforceable if the contract is enforceable and not against a contrary statute or public policy.[24]

Reference to AIA Document A201, *General Conditions* (1987), reveals attorneys' fees provisions concerning indemnities (subparagraph 3.18.1), owner's receiving discharges of subcontractors' liens after payment to the contractor (subparagraph 9.10.2), and indemnification pertaining to asbestos and PCB (polychlorinated biphenyl) (subparagraph 10.1.4). There appears to be no reference to recovery of attorneys' fees in the event of nonpayment from the owner to the contractor.

A traditional clause for the recovery of such fees reads as follows:

> Contractor shall be entitled to recovery of all costs of any action brought to recover any amounts due under the Contract Documents including *reasonable attorneys' fees.*

The words "reasonable attorneys' fees" are highlighted because, although this is language traditionally found in such clauses, an alternate use of language may be preferable. The words "all attorneys' fees incurred" may save the contractor from an often difficult and time-consuming burden of proving, through an expert witness, that the attorneys' fees sought are, in fact, reasonable.

In the latter case, the clause is meant to be self-executing, and a court may be bound to award all attorneys' fees incurred provided the amount is reasonable on its face.[25] In the former instance, the court may base its

---

[23] *See, e.g.,* Missouri Pac. R.R. v. Winburn Tile Mfg. Co., 461 F.2d 984 (8th Cir. 1972).

[24] *See, e.g.,* United States *ex rel.* Micro-King Co. v. Community Science Technology, 574 F.2d 1292 (5th Cir. 1978).

[25] *See* Storm Assocs. v. Baumgold, 186 Conn. 237, 246, 440 A.2d 306 (1982).

award on factors other than the actual expense incurred by the prevailing party and may require an evidentiary showing of reasonableness.[26]

Of course, all of this presumes that the contractor is the prevailing party in the litigation on the contract. A recovery of the value of materials and services provided by the contractor may not result in an award of attorneys' fees based on a clause in the contract to a plaintiff/contractor who has substantially performed, but whose own breach of the contract precipitates the litigation.[27]

§ 25.9   Statutory Awards for Attorneys' Fees

Many jurisdictions have enacted statutes providing for the recovery of attorneys' fees in certain specific instances applicable to the construction industry. Examples include:

1. Mechanic's lien foreclosures[28]
2. Actions under state Equal Access to Justice Acts[29]
3. Defense of mechanic's lien suits[30]
4. Bond claims on public works projects[31]
5. Unfair trade practice claims.[32]

Contractors working pursuant to federal government construction contracts also should be aware of the federal Equal Access to Justice Act.[33] This Act permits small businesses (defined as having less than 500 employees and less than $7 million in net worth) to recover attorneys' fees, upon application within 30 days after final disposition of the case and upon a showing that the government's position was not "substantially justified."[34] Attorneys' fees under the Act are generally limited, however, to $75 per hour.[35]

---

[26] *See* Bizzoco v. Chinitz, 193 Conn. 304, 310, 476 A.2d 572 (1984); Appliances, Inc. v. Yost, 186 Conn. 673, 680, 443 A.2d 486 (1982).

[27] *See, e.g.,* Simonetti v. Lovermi, 15 Conn. App. 722, 726, 546 A.2d 331 (1988).

[28] *See, e.g.,* Conn. Gen. Stat. §§ 49-33(h), 49-7 (1958); *see also* Sime Constr. Co. v. Washington Pub. Power Supply Sys., 28 Wash. App. 10, 621 P.2d 1299 (1980).

[29] *See* Mission Hardwood Co. v. Registrar of Contractors, 149 Ariz. 12, 716 P.2d 73 (1986).

[30] *See* Marshall v. Karl F. Schultz, Inc., 438 So. 2d 533 (Fla. Dist. Ct. App. 1983).

[31] Conn. Gen. Stat. § 49-42.

[32] Conn. Gen. Stat. § 42-110a–42-110g. Mass. Gen. L. ch. 93A (1988).

[33] 5 U.S.C. § 504 (1988).

[34] *See* Hill v. United States, 3 Cl. Ct. 428 (1983).

[35] 5 U.S.C. § 504(b)(1)(A).

CHAPTER 26

INDEMNIFICATION AND THE ANTI-INDEMNIFICATION STATUTES

Susan Rogers Brooke*

Susan Rogers Brooke is a partner with the law firm of Dutton Overman Goldstein Pinkus, P.C., in Indianapolis, Indiana. She has extensive experience in construction law in both contract negotiations and dispute resolution. She is a frequent speaker on construction law topics. Ms. Brooke is a member of the American Bar Association, Section of Labor and Employment Law, and the Forum on the Construction Industry, where during the forum year 1991–1992, she is serving as Chairperson of Division 4 Construction Management, Design/Build and Related Concepts. She graduated from the University of Delaware and from Indiana University Law School at Indianapolis.

*The author expresses appreciation to Michael D. Kerr, Esquire, Ice, Miller, Donadio & Ryan, for his research into the Indiana Anti-indemnification Statute, and to Krisandra Kukesh who patiently worked through all the revisions to the manuscript.

§ 26.1   Introduction

A construction contract contains many provisions, such as scope of the work, cost of the work, and payment terms. Although indemnification is an important and necessary requirement on any construction site, the existence or absence of an indemnification provision in a contract may be given no real consideration by the contractor. To *indemnify* is to save harmless, to secure against loss or damage, to give security for the reimbursement of a person in case of an anticipated loss falling upon the person, or to make reimbursement to one for a loss already incurred. An indemnification clause shifts some or all of the risk from the person seeking indemnification, such as the owner on a construction project, to the person giving the promise of indemnification, the contractor.

The most familiar construction documents for the contractor are the documents issued by the American Institute of Architects (AIA). AIA Document A201, *General Conditions of the Contract for Construction,* subparagraph 3.18.1 (1987), provides for indemnification consistent with the applicable laws for the owner and the owner's design professionals from the contractor for claims that originate totally or partially in the negligence of the contractor and the contractor's construction team.

The contractor does not know the full impact of subparagraph 3.18.1 until the contractor determines the extent to which applicable laws permit indemnification. Because no one law governs, a prudent contractor must know what the law permits and must verify the current status of any anti-indemnification legislation in each state in which the contractor does business before drafting the indemnification provision. Only then should the contractor make the risk-shifting "bet-the-company" decision.

§ 26.2   General Rules on Indemnification

The right to indemnity and the corresponding obligation to indemnify generally spring from contract, express or implied. In absence of an expressed or implied contract, a right to indemnity generally does not exist.[1] Express contractual provisions greatly aid in determining indemnity rights. A contract of indemnity should be construed to cover all losses and damages to which it reasonably appears that the parties intended it to

---

[1] McClish v. Niagara Mach. & Tool Works, 266 F. Supp. 987 (S.D. Ind. 1967); Elcona Homes Corp. v. McMillan Bloedell, Ltd., 475 N.E.2d 713 (Ind. Ct. App. 1985).

apply.[2] The burden of proof is on the indemnitee to prove all of the material elements of its cause of action by a preponderance of the evidence. The indemnitor must prove any affirmative defenses.[3] Want of consideration and failure of consideration are valid defenses to a contract of indemnity. Once the indemnitor has raised the affirmative defense of want of consideration, the indemnitee has the burden of making a prima facie case on the element of consideration. The agreement itself may be sufficient to satisfy the indemnitee's burden.[4]

Contract clauses providing for indemnification for one's own negligence are strictly construed and are not held to provide indemnification unless expressed in clear and unequivocal terms.[5] The applicable provision must make explicit reference to the indemnitee's negligence to qualify for enforcement.[6] General liability policies are one form of an express indemnity contract. Subject to the express terms of the insurance contract, the insurance carrier will pay for losses or damage caused by the insured's own negligence. Because this form of indemnity is socially useful and responsible,[7] the rules change: a court will find that the insurance contract does provide coverage (indemnification) in favor of the policyholder and named insureds (indemnitees) and against the insurer unless the coverage is *excluded* in clear and unequivocal terms.

A more difficult legal question arises when the right of indemnity is an implied right, not an express contractual provision. The doctrine of implied indemnity is equitable in nature. The right to indemnity may be implied in favor of one whose liability to a third party is solely derivative or constructive, and only implied against one who has by wrongful act caused such derivative or constructive liability to be imposed on the indemnitee.[8] In Indiana, to claim the common law right of indemnity, the indemnitee must be without fault.[9] In other words, indemnity will not be allowed when the party seeking indemnity is guilty of actual negligence, be it malfeasance, misfeasance, or nonfeasance.[10] Further, under traditional common law, joint tortfeasors who are in pari delicto are not entitled to contribution from each other.

---

[2] Zebrowski Assocs. v. City of Indianapolis, 457 N.E.2d 259, 261 (Ind. Ct. App. 1983).

[3] *Id.*

[4] Seaboard Sur. Co. v. Harbison, 304 F.2d 247, 250 (7th Cir. 1962).

[5] Sink & Edwards, Inc. v. Huber, Hunt & Nichols, Inc., 458 N.E.2d 291, 294 (Ind. Ct. App. 1984).

[6] Indiana State Highway Comm'n v. Thomas, 169 Ind. App. 13, 22, 346 N.E.2d 252, 263 (1976).

[7] U.S. Steel Corp. v. Emerson-Comstock Co., 141 F. Supp. 143, 145 (N.D. Ill. 1956).

[8] McClish v. Niagara Mach. & Tool Works, 266 F. Supp. 987, 991 (S.D. Ind. 1967).

[9] Coca Cola Bottling Co.-Goshen, Inc. v. Vendo Co., 455 N.E.2d 370 (Ind. Ct. App. 1983).

[10] *Id.* at 373.

§ 26.3   Debate over Indemnification on
Construction Projects

If a trend exists at all, the trend among states who struggle with the use of indemnity agreements on construction projects is to limit indemnification on the projects. Various courts suggest that the need to enhance safety on construction projects voids indemnification under those circumstances.[11] An Illinois court stated that the Illinois Legislature, in enacting § 1 of the Illinois Structural Work Act, may have considered that the widespread use of indemnity and hold harmless agreements in the construction industry may have removed or reduced the incentive to protect workers and others from injury; persons having charge of the work and, thus, persons liable for violations of the Structural Work Act are able to escape the consequences of this liability by requiring indemnifying agreements from general contractors or subcontractors. The court concluded that those persons who avoid the burdens of liability no longer have the same motivation to lessen the extent of the danger.[12]

With the great risks attendant to work in the construction industry, workers generally would work under even more hazardous conditions because of the existence of an indemnification agreement. Without any empirical evidence to support the statements, the Court of Appeals for the Seventh Circuit argued that if the general contractor can shift the financial burden of liability, the contractor may have less incentive to take measures to make the construction site safe. Of course, the contractor will have to compensate the subcontractors because of the imposition of a greater risk of liability on them, and thus will pay a price for the subcontractors' carelessness; but in just the same way, a person who becomes more careless by having liability insurance may in the end have to pay for greater carelessness in a form of higher premium for insurance. The court then concluded that the buffering of liability by the insurance company could result in some additional carelessness.[13]

Other jurisdictions disagree on the relationship between indemnity and carelessness. In 1956, Chief Judge Duffy of the Seventh Circuit stated that there is nothing unconscionable or illicit involved in an individual or private corporation contracting for protection against its own negligence. Chief Judge Duffy was not convinced that motorists as an example, as a class, become reckless or negligent because they have taken out a policy

---

[11] Fort Wayne Cablevision v. Indiana & Mich. Elec. Co., 443 N.E.2d 863 (Ind. Ct. App. 1983).

[12] Davis v. Commonwealth Edison Co., 61 Ill. 2d 494, 336 N.E.2d 881, 884 (1975); Ill. Ann. Stat. ch. 48, paras. 59.90–69 (Smith-Hurd 1989).

[13] McMunn v. Hertz Equip. Rental Corp., 791 F.2d 88, 92 (7th Cir. 1986).

of automobile liability insurance.[14] Likewise, the Supreme Court of Texas has held:

> Only a few jurisdictions, and Texas is not one of them, hold that a contract of indemnity against the results of one's negligence is contrary to public policy in that such contracts tend to encourage careless conduct. This theory or doctrine is not regarded as being sound and has been described as being somewhat fanciful. From a public policy standpoint an indemnity agreement against one's negligence issued by an insurance company would be as objectionable for encouraging carelessness as would an indemnity contract issued by any other form of indemnity or by a natural person.[15]

Even judges and legislators disagree. In 1975, specifically saying that there is nothing unreasonable, unjust, or inconsistent with public policy, the Supreme Court of Rhode Island stated that no significant distinction exists between a general contractor who secures indemnification for its own negligence through subcontractors and who obtains insurance to cover the negligence of subcontractors, and the insured who is allowed to insure itself against all losses, from any perils not occasioned by the insured's own personal fraud.[16] In 1976 the legislature of Rhode Island promptly passed an anti-indemnification statute.[17]

A second reason advanced for voiding indemnification on construction projects is the simple unfairness of indemnifying a party for its own misdeeds. This is particularly acute when the entity demanding indemnity is a well-financed owner and the indemnitor is a marginal subcontractor. As a result, many states restrict the right of the parties to contract for indemnity in the construction industry. Some states prohibit indemnity for one's own negligence.[18] Other states prohibit indemnity for one's sole negligence in construction contracts.[19] A third set of states allow some indemnity agreements provided certain statutory requirements are met.[20] Some states have no specific statutory restrictions against contractual indemnification on construction projects. Although courts in these states may be reluctant to enforce indemnity clauses and may seek ways to avoid them, the courts do enforce the clauses,[21] as a contractor in Pennsylvania recently learned. A court ordered the contractor, pursuant to an indemnity agreement, to

---

[14] Indemnity Ins. Co. v. Koontz-Wagner Elec. Co., 233 F.2d 380, 383 (7th Cir. 1956).

[15] Spence & Howe Constr. Co. v. Gulf Oil Corp., 365 S.W.2d 631, 632 (Tex. 1963), *overruled for other reasons by* Ethyl Corp. v. Daniel Constr. Co., 725 S.W.2d 705 (Tex. 1987).

[16] DiLonardo v. Gilbane Bldg. Co., 114 R.I. 469, 471, 334 A.2d 422, 424 (1975).

[17] R.I. Gen. Laws § 6-34-1 (1990).

[18] See § **26.4**.

[19] See § **26.5**.

[20] See § **26.6**.

[21] See §§ **26.7–26.10**.

indemnify an owner for damages paid by the owner to an employee of contractor injured on the job. The indemnification was not contrary to the public policy of Pennsylvania, even though the contractor's direct liability to the injured employee was limited by workers' compensation.[22]

§ 26.4 —Prohibiting Indemnification for One's Own Negligence

Representative of the states that restrict the right of parties to contract for indemnity in the construction industry are those, set forth in **Table 26–1**, that prohibit indemnity for one's own negligence, whether it be sole or partial negligence.

A typical statute having broad application to many facets of the building and construction industry is that of North Carolina.[23] The statute applies to design as well as construction, thus applying as much to the architect and

Table 26–1

States Prohibiting Indemnity in Construction Contracts for One's Own Negligence

California	Cal. Civ. Code § 2782 (West 1991)
Delaware	Del. Code Ann. tit. 6, § 2704 (1990)
Illinois	Ill. Ann. Stat. ch. 29, para. 61 (Smith-Hurd 1990)
Louisiana	La. Rev. Stat. Ann. § 38:2216 (West 1991) (Note: Statute applies to public contracts only.)
Massachusetts	Mass. Gen. Laws Ann. ch. 149, § 29C (West 1991) (Note: Limitations apply to contractor-subcontractor agreements only. Presumably an owner could demand an indemnity for the owner's negligence. The contractor, however, clearly could not "pass through" such a covenant to its subcontractors.)
Minnesota	Minn. Stat. Ann. § 337.01 (West 1991)
Nebraska	Neb. Rev. Stat. § 25-21,187 (1990)
New York	N.Y. Gen. Oblig. Law § 5-322.1 (McKinney 1991)
North Carolina	N.C. Gen. Stat. § 22B-1 (1990)
Ohio	Ohio Rev. Code Ann. § 2305.31 (Page 1990)
Rhode Island	R.I. Gen. Laws § 6-34-1 (1990)
Wisconsin	Wis. Stat. Ann. § 895.49 (West 1990)
Wyoming	Wyo. Stat. § 30-1-131 (1990)*

* Note: Statute does not apply generally to construction; statute governs oil, gas, and water wells, and mines and construction associated with such activity.

---

[22] Fulmer v. Duquesne Light Co., 374 Pa. Super. 537, 543 A.2d 1100 (1988).

[23] N.C. Gen. Stat. § 22B-1 (1990).

engineers of record as to the contractor and subcontractors. It applies to buildings and structures, but also applies to roads and highways. It applies to the preliminary site work that is usually done, such as moving, demolition, and excavating, even if the project itself never matures. Not unexpectedly, the statute applies to the repair of buildings, structures, highways, roads, appurtenances, and appliances. However, it also applies to the maintenance of those listed items.

AIA Document A201, subparagraph 3.18.1, would not be enforceable in jurisdictions such as this, absent modification. Under the terms of subparagraph 3.18.1, the contractor is obligated to indemnify and hold harmless, among others, the owner. In the language of the North Carolina statute, the owner is one of the promisees. Subparagraph 3.18.1 extends to claims whether or not such claim is made in part by a party indemnified by subparagraph 3.18.1. In North Carolina, the promise contained in subparagraph 3.18.1 is against public policy and is void and unenforceable.

§ 26.5   —Prohibiting Indemnification for One's Sole Negligence

Among other states restricting the right of parties to contract for indemnity in the construction industry are those, listed in **Table 26–2**, that prohibit indemnity for one's sole negligence.

The statute in Maryland is typical, stating that contract provisions purporting to indemnify certain individuals against their sole negligence are void, unenforceable, and against public policy.[24] The statute expressly excludes insurance contracts and workers' compensation contracts so there is no ambiguity about the efficacy of jobsite insurance or the application of workers' compensation to the project.

Alaska and Indiana, in addition to prohibiting indemnification for one's sole negligence, also prohibit indemnification for willful misconduct by the promisee. Assuming at least one other party was negligent, the indemnitee will be able to enforce the indemnification provision in these two states when the indemnitee has engaged in acts of simple negligence. Presumably a willful finding by the Occupational Safety and Health Administration (OSHA) or its state equivalent will negate any indemnification in Alaska and Indiana.[25] A "serious" violation may or may not constitute willful misconduct within the meaning of the statute.

A comparison of subparagraph 3.18.1 to Maryland's provision yields the conclusion that the AIA provision would be valid in Maryland. Subparagraph 3.18.1 applies only to the extent that the contractor or persons

---

[24] Md. Cts. & Jud. Proc. Code Ann. § 5-305 (1990).
[25] *See* 29 U.S.C.A. § 658 (West 1991).

Table 26–2

States Prohibiting Indemnity in Construction
Contracts for One's Sole Negligence

Alaska	Alaska Stat. § 45.45.900 (1990) (Note: Statute also bars indemnity for willful misconduct by promisee, the promisee's agents, or independent contractors who are directly responsible to the promisee.)
Arizona	Ariz. Rev. Stat. Ann. § 34-226 (1990)
Connecticut	Conn. Gen. Stat. Ann. § 52-572k (West 1991)
Idaho	Idaho Code § 29-114 (1990)
Indiana	Ind. Code Ann. § 26-2-5-1 (West 1991) (Note: Statute also bars indemnity for willful misconduct by promisee, the promisee's agents, or independent contractors who are directly responsible to the promisee.)
Maryland	Md. Cts. & Jud. Proc. Code Ann. § 5-305 (1990)
Michigan	Mich. Comp. Laws Ann. § 691.991 (West 1991)
New Jersey	N.J. Stat. Ann. § 2A:40A-1 (West 1991)
South Carolina	S.C. Code Ann. § 32-2-10 (Law. Co-op. 1990)
South Dakota	S.D. Codified Laws Ann. § 56-3-18 (1991)
Tennessee	Tenn. Code Ann. § 62-6-123 (1990)
Utah	Utah Code Ann. § 13-8-1 (1990)
Virginia	Va. Code Ann. § 11-4.1 (Michie 1990)
Washington	Wash. Rev. Code Ann. § 4.24.115 (West 1991)
West Virginia	W. Va. Code § 55-8-14 (1990)

working through the contractor, such as subcontractors, are negligent. Because the contractor or those working through the contractor must be negligent, then the owner is not seeking indemnification for the owner's sole negligence, which is the only activity prohibited under the Maryland statute.

In Alaska and Indiana, subparagraph 3.18.1 would be valid unless the conduct of the owner or named indemnified parties was considered willful. An indemnity clause first stating that the contractor was obligated to indemnify the owner whether or not due in whole or in any part to any act, omission, or negligence of the owner clearly violated the Indiana statute.[26] The drafters of this contract clause, however, saved the clause from being void and unenforceable by adding language providing that, in the event the indemnity protecting the owner from the owner's sole negligence was against the local laws, then that portion of the indemnity was void and unenforceable and the remander of the indemnity obligating the contractor to indemnify the owner was valid and enforceable.[27] The Indiana Court of Appeals enforced the indemnity.

---

[26] Ind. Code Ann. § 26-2-5-1(4) (West 1991).

[27] Progressive Constr. & Eng'g Co. v. Indiana & Mich. Elec. Co., 533 N.E.2d 1279, 1286 (Ind. Ct. App. 1989).

§ 26.6   —Allowing Indemnification
If Requirements Are Met

The following **Table 26–3** lists those states that restrict the right of parties to contract for indemnity in the construction industry by allowing indemnification only if certain requirements are met.

The states of Florida and New Mexico, although disliking indemnification statutes, have addressed the issues in a different manner.

The Florida statute appears to bar indemnification for the acts of the indemnitee, but then creates two conditions under which indemnifications can be valid.[28] The conditions allowing indemnification if the contract sets a monetary limitation or if the person being indemnified gives a specific consideration are so broad that they devour the rule.

All a party seeking indemnification in Florida must do to get indemnification for its own negligence is to state in the contract that the parties have allocated a certain portion of the contract amount to the specific indemnification clause. Effectively this becomes a mere recital, but that mere recital shifts a burden from the indemnitee to the indemnitor. Parties to such a contract are unlikely to set a monetary limitation as permitted by § 725.06(1) when the requirements of § 725.06(2) are so simple to meet.

A Florida Appellate Court held that a project owner complied with this statute when the owner included in the construction contract "one percent (1%) of the contract price represents specific consideration to Contractor for the indemnification set forth in this contract."[29] The contractor failed to convince the court that the 1 percent was a "mere empty recital."[30] The Appellate Court specifically found that the contract was for approximately $1 million and 1 percent of that figure was adequate consideration.

In New Mexico, the pertinent provision allows for indemnification for "passive negligence" of the contractor, provided that the agreement is clear and unambiguous.[31] A New Mexico contractor who wants to include this indemnity in subcontracts should consider specific reference to § 56-7-1(b) in the indemnification clause.

Table 26–3
States Allowing Some Indemnity Agreements
Provided Certain Requirements Are Met

Florida	Fla. Stat. Ann. § 725.06 (West 1991)
New Mexico	N.M. Stat. Ann. § 56-7-1 (Michie 1990)

---

[28] Fla. Stat. Ann. § 725.06 (West 1991).

[29] Peoples Gas Sys., Inc. v. RSH Constructors, Inc., 563 So. 2d 107 (Fla. Dist. Ct. App. 1990).

[30] *Id.*

[31] N.M. Stat. Ann. § 56-7-1 (1990).

§ 26.7   Scope of the Indemnity

The contractor still has to worry about specific contract language even in states in which indemnification has not been partially or totally banned. Montana and North Dakota have by statute defined the meanings of certain frequently-used terms to which contractors need pay particular attention.

Under Montana and North Dakota law, if the contract provides for an *indemnity against liability,* the person indemnified is entitled to recover upon becoming liable to pay damages.[32] In other states it is widely accepted that under an indemnity against liability, the indemnitor is obligated to pay the indemnitee when the indemnitee demonstrates its liability; the indemnitee does not have to establish that it has made any payments or paid any judgments.[33] Frequently, the indemnity provision includes a hold harmless pledge. AIA Document A201, subparagraph 3.18.1, provides indemnification from "claims, damages, losses and expenses . . . ," and it also obligates the contractor to "hold harmless" the indemnified parties. A *hold harmless agreement* is a contractual arrangement whereby one party assumes the liability inherent in a situation, thereby relieving the other party of responsibility.[34] The obligation contained in subparagraph 3.18.1 to hold harmless requires the contractor to pick up and defend on demand from the owner, architect, and their agents.

The Montana and North Dakota statutes provide that under an *indemnification against claims, demands, damages, or costs,* the person indemnified is not entitled to recover without payment thereof.[35] Minnesota has held that an agreement to indemnify against "claims" for damages is a contract of indemnity against liability as opposed to one against loss or damage;[36] the Minnesota Supreme Court specifically rejected a contention that the contractor was not entitled to indemnity merely because the contractor had suffered no loss or damage. *Indemnification against claims, demands or liability,* as defined in the Montana and North Dakota statutes, embraces the costs of defense against such claims, demands, or liability incurred in good faith and in exercise of reasonable discretion.[37] Costs of defense may be owed by the indemnitor regardless of whether such costs were incurred

---

[32] Mont. Code Ann. § 28-11-314 (1989).

[33] B&G Elec. Co. v. G.E. Bass & Co., 252 F.2d 698 (5th Cir. 1958), *cert. denied,* 357 U.S. 931, 78 S.Ct. 1372 (1958); Spurr v. LaSalle Constr. Co., 385 F.2d 322 (7th Cir. 1967).

[34] Black's Law Dictionary 658 (5th ed. 1979).

[35] Mont. Code Ann. § 28-11-314(2) (1989).

[36] Christy v. Menasha Corp., 279 Minn. 334, 211 N.W.2d 773 (1973), *overruled for other reasons by* Farmington Plumbing & Heating Co. v. Fischer Sand & Aggregate, Inc., 281 N.W.2d 838 (Minn. 1979).

[37] Mont. Code Ann. § 28-11-315 (1989).

before or after the indemnified party demanded that the indemnitor defend the action.[38]

If the person obligated to indemnify fails to do so, recovery against the indemnitee suffered in good faith will be conclusive.[39] A Wisconsin court found that a subcontractor need only show potential, not actual, liability to recover for contribution made in connection with a judgment against the general contractor for injuries sustained by an employee of the second contractor on faulty equipment.[40] However, the indemnitee must give the indemnitor reasonable notice or any judgment obtained by the indemnitee may be rebutted in a subsequent action.[41] Generally, the same rule applies if the indemnitee settles a claim or suit before trial or arbitration.[42]

Finally, although Montana does not require that contracts provide for recovery of attorneys' fees by the prevailing party, if the contract provides that one party will receive attorneys' fees if it prevails, the court will read that provision as reciprocal regardless of any protestation in the contract to the contrary.[43] North Dakota is very similar to Montana with the exception of the reciprocity on attorneys' fees.[44] AIA Document A201, subparagraph 3.18.1, includes attorneys' fees under its indemnification language. If a dispute arose in Montana over the application of subparagraph 3.18.1, the loser would pay the fees.

§ 26.8   —Express Contractual Language

Although indemnification clauses may be lawful in many jurisdictions, the courts are reluctant to enforce the clauses. A court will not order a party to indemnify another for the latter's own negligence unless such an indemnity is expressed in clear and unequivocal terms.[45] If an indemnification clause is ambiguous, the court will construe the clause against the purported indemnitee when the result otherwise would be to allow the drafter of the clause to recover for its own negligence.[46]

---

[38] Monical & Powell, Inc. v. Bechtel Corp., 404 S.W.2d 911 (Tex. Ct. App. 1966), writ *ref'd n.r.e*).

[39] Mont. Code Ann. § 28-11-316 (1989).

[40] Barrons v. J.H. Findorff & Sons, 89 Wis. 2d 444, 278 N.W.2d 827 (1979).

[41] Mont. Code Ann. § 28-11-317 (1989).

[42] Mills v. Zapata Drilling Co., 722 F.2d 1170 (5th Cir. 1983).

[43] Mont. Code Ann. § 28-3-704 (1989).

[44] N.D. Cent. Code § 9-08-02 (1991).

[45] Sweetman v. Strescon Indus., Inc., 389 A.2d 1319 (Del. Super. Ct. 1978); Farmington Plumbing & Heating Co. v. Fischer Sand & Aggregate, Inc., 281 N.W.2d 838 (Minn. 1979).

[46] Jones v. Strom Constr. Co., 84 Wash. 2d 518, 527 P.2d 1115 (1974); Ruhland v. John W. Cowper Co., 72 A.D.2d 907, 422 N.Y.S.2d 182 (1979).

A trade contractor in Minnesota owed indemnification to a construction manager under a clause providing that the contractor indemnify and hold harmless the owner, the architect, and the construction manager from and against all claims, losses, and expenses, including attorneys' fees arising out of or resulting from performance of the work regardless of whether or not the claims, losses, or expenses were "caused in part by a party indemnified hereunder."[47] The clause used clear and express language; one can only speculate whether the contractor understood the risk being taken at the time the contractor signed the contract. AIA Document A201, subparagraph 3.18.1, contains the same phrase: "caused in part by a party indemnified hereunder."

A contractor learned to its detriment that a broad indemnification clause required the contractor to indemnify the owner's engineer when certain safety issues should have been discovered by the engineer. The indemnity clause required that the contractor indemnify and hold harmless the owner and engineer from any and all claims, suits, or judgments, based on damage to property or injury or death to persons arising out of, or connected with, the work covered by the contract, regardless of the cause.[48] The court concluded that the language in subparagraph 11.3.1 of the Supplemental Conditions related only to the contractor's work and not to any negligence of the owner.[49]

The Supreme Court of Texas refused to order full indemnification for an owner from a contractor because the purported indemnification clause did not make explicit reference to indemnification for the owner's own negligence.[50] That court enforced an indemnity clause in a subsequent case in which the contractor agreed to indemnify the owner for "any negligent act or omission" of the latter.[51] It found that the indemnity clause clearly expressed the obligation of the contractor to indemnify the owner for the owner's own negligence.

Courts must find a clear expression of the risk-shifting. The Supreme Court of Massachusetts found that there was no express agreement between a contractor and its subcontractor for indemnification and barred the contractor's claim.[52] The contractor had been sued by an employee of the subcontractor who was injured in a scaffolding accident. The language of the purported indemnification did not clearly express that the subcontractor was to indemnify the contractor for the contractor's own negligence. A New Jersey court similarly refused to find that the contract between an owner

---

[47] Oster v. Medtronic, Inc., 428 N.W.2d 116 (Minn. Ct. App. 1988).

[48] Apel Mach. & Supply Co. v. J.E. O'Toole Eng'g Co., 548 So. 2d 445 (Ala. 1989).

[49] *Id.* at 478.

[50] Ethyl Corp. v. Daniel Constr. Co., 725 S.W.2d 705 (Tex. 1987).

[51] Atlantic Richfield Co. v. Petroleum Personnel, Inc., 768 S.W.2d 724 (Tex. 1989).

[52] Larkin v. Ralph O. Porter, Inc., 405 Mass. 179, 539 N.E.2d 529 (1989).

and its contractor expressed the parties' intent to indemnify the owner against its own negligence. The contract between owner and contractor provided that the contractor would indemnify the owner for claims that arose partially or completely from the contractor's actions.[53]

The contract documents between the contractor and the owner contained other indemnification provisions, but none of the provisions specifically mentioned that the contractor was indemnifying the owner for acts or omissions of the owner or the owner's agents. The court concluded the the contractor could only be responsible for its own negligence, but recovery against contractor was barred by the exclusive remedy of workers' compensation.

§ 26.9   —Integration of Contract Documents

The prudent contractor must integrate all the contract documents so that an indemnification in general conditions applies to a separate contract document. Versions of AIA Document A111, *Standard Form of Agreement Between Owner and Contractor,* prior to 1987 did not explicitly incorporate AIA Document A201. A Kansas court generously concluded that the older version of A111 did incorporate A201, and as a result the court required a contractor to indemnify a project owner for money expended in correcting a warranty item after the project was completed. The 1987 edition of A111 identifies A201 by its full correct name, expressly incorporates it by reference, and therefore should avoid the problem if those documents are used.[54]

§ 26.10   —Incorporation of Obligations in Subcontracts

To maximize its contractual protections, the contractor should verify that its subcontractors owe the contractor a duty of indemnification no less than the duty that the contractor owes to the owner. In its contract with the contractor, not only did a subcontractor agree to such a flow-through clause, the subcontractor further agreed to indemnify the contractor for claims arising from the subcontractor's negligence.[55] When an employee of the subcontractor stepped off the back of a roof that should have had a railing or other safety protection device, the subcontractor owed indemnification to the

---

[53] Meder v. Resorts Int'l Hotel, Inc., 240 N.J. Super. 470, 478, 573 A.2d 922, 926 (1989) (emphasis added).

[54] Southwest Nat'l Bank v. Simpson & Son, 14 Kan. App. 763, 799 P.2d 512 (1990), *review denied* (Jan. 29, 1991).

[55] Indenco, Inc. v. Evans, 201 Cal. App. 2d 369, 20 Cal. Rptr. 90 (1962).

contractor and the owner. Key in the decision was the express language in the contract documents that the subcontractor assumed all of the obligations and responsibilities that the contractor assumed toward the owner.

§ 26.11   —Implied Indemnification in Construction

Courts may yet imply an indemnification when the indemnitee has not been negligent, but due to (1) the relationship of the indemnitee and indemnitor or (2) the conduct of the indemnitor, the courts award indemnification.

California prohibits indemnity for one's own negligence, be it sole or partial, in construction contracts. A contractor was required to indemnify an architect for attorneys' fees under an indemnification clause in the contract between the contractor and owner. The architect had been totally exonerated from any liability in a separate proceeding. Therefore, the finding of nonliability of the architect allowed the architect to assert and prevail on a claim of indemnity.[56] North Carolina also bars contractual indemnity for one's own negligence. In a case in North Carolina, a contractor directed its subcontractor to install cracked glass. Before the glass could be reglazed, it broke and struck a worker who was employed by neither. The subcontractor was entitled to indemnification from the contractor.[57] The court used an implied indemnity theory.

A contractor in Indiana was held to owe indemnification to an owner who paid one of the contractor's subcontractors monies due and owing the subcontractor from the contractor on the project.[58] In arriving at this conclusion, the court does not refer to Indiana's anti-indemnification statute, but rather bases its conclusion on common law principles: "It is axiomatic that where a person who, without fault, has been compelled to pay damages because of the wrongful conduct of another primarily liable may recover from such other for expenditures properly made in the discharge of such liability."[59]

---

[56] Hillman v. Leland E. Burns, Inc., 209 Cal. App. 3d 860, 257 Cal. Rptr. 535 (1989).

[57] Hartrick Erectors, Inc. v. Maxson-Betts, Inc., 98 N.C. App. 120, 389 S.E.2d 607, *review allowed,* 327 N.C. 482, 397 S.E.2d 218 (1990), *review dismissed,* 328 N.C. 326, 401 S.E.2d 359 (1991).

[58] Complete Elec. Co. v. Liberty Nat'l Bank & Trust Co., 530 N.E.2d 1216 (Ind. Ct. App. 1988).

[59] *Id.* at 1219.

CHAPTER 27

COLLECTION PROCEDURES IN THE CONSTRUCTION INDUSTRY

Michael S. Greene

Michael S. Greene is a partner in the Fort Lauderdale, Florida, office of the law firm of Holland & Knight. He graduated from the University of Florida School of Building Construction in 1978 and from the University of Florida College of Law in 1981. Mr. Greene's practice concentrates on real estate development and construction law, involving projects ranging from residential developments to airports and convention centers. He has lectured to the Associated Builders and Contractors, American Institute of Architects, the Construction Specifications Institute, and the American Association of Cost Engineers. He is a member of the Florida bar, the American Bar Association, including the Forum Committee on the Construction Industry, and the Construction Specifications Institute.

§ 27.1   Introduction

To those uninitiated in the experience of lengthy litigation, the collection process may be viewed as the nasty business of collection agents, demand letters, and attorneys' fees that all too often result when an individual is not paid. Those in the construction industry who have endured several years in prosecuting a lawsuit while attempting to collect their rightful due regrettably learn that the collection process should begin the day an order for material or equipment is received, or an invitation to bid or request for proposal is received. Those who cling to the belief that they will collect later have a better than even chance of discovering the least desirable method of recovering payment: litigation.

If the collection process is viewed as a mechanism for obtaining payment for work performed, it must include the prospective analysis of a customer's ability to pay and the utilization of all reasonable measures to maximize ability to get paid. The goal should be to accomplish these tasks while minimizing the costs expended in collection efforts.

This chapter addresses, in the form of general guidelines, the basic steps necessary to maximize collections in typical construction industry projects, and, particularly, the preventative and protective measures that may be applied by general contractors, subcontractors, and suppliers of labor, material, and equipment. In most cases, with the noted exception of claims against a payment bond, measures that a general contractor may apply with respect to an owner may also be applied by a subcontractor or supplier with respect to a general contractor. The chapter often uses the term *contractor* to describe measures that need to be considered by each of these parties.

This chapter does not recap local laws or regulations, because they vary greatly from state to state, nor does it address the limitations on debt collection practices imposed by federal, state, or local laws or explore the use of outside collection agencies. Instead it is intended to alert the reader to a range of practices designed to increase the likelihood of obtaining payment.

§ 27.2   Collection Problems in the Construction Industry

The unique nature of the construction industry, particularly the oft-cited fragmented nature of doing business, and the number of companies, businesses, and persons, each separately under contract to do work, complicates collection efforts. Unlike the manufacturing and selling of automobiles, toasters, or widgets, each construction project is its own unique enterprise with its own collection problems, bringing together contractors, subcontractors, and suppliers that may never work together again.

Because the work moves to the site of each new project, accounting and cost controls are more difficult to maintain. Contractors that keep accounting and billing practices in a central location must put procedures in place to collect and monitor documents, particularly delivery receipts, change or field orders, time slips, and the like, and to process in a timely manner payment information through a central billing office. Surprisingly often, payments are withheld or never made because of a general contractor's or subcontractor's inability to deliver timely bills, requisitions, or invoices, and most importantly, adequate and detailed backup information. This becomes particularly problematic when claims for delay or concealed conditions, or extra or changed work, are involved.

Contractors also suffer from the impact of adverse tax consequences when payments are not timely (or never) received. The percentage of completion method of accounting generally recognizes income when work, under a particular contract, progresses and is partially completed. Thus, recognized income may include costs and income not yet invoiced, an advantage on long-term jobs that extend over more than one accounting period in order to avoid unrealistically skewing income into one period. However, because of the dependence on estimates of costs and income, the results of the accounting may also become skewed if that income is not collected.

The completed contract method of accounting recognizes income only when work is substantially completed. Therefore, the method avoids some of the undesirable results from a failure to collect revenues, but creates other tax issues if the work continues for longer than a single tax accounting period.

MINIMIZING THE RISKS

§ 27.3   Analysis of Customer's Financial Condition

In these times when even gasoline stations require up-front payment, the first question that must be asked before undertaking work for an owner, or before performing for a contractor, or before shipping or delivering materials or equipment to any party, is simply: "Can my customer afford to pay me?" The answer to the question coming from an analysis of a customer's position and reliability should greatly influence the decision to accept the work or to impose requirements for additional security or alternative sources of payment.

Because bonding companies regularly perform credit analyses of their clients, the ability of a customer to obtain a bond from a reliable, financially-sound surety may be a significant factor to consider in the analysis. However, the mere existence of a bonding line, is itself not dispositive. The customer may have pledged significant collateral as security for the bonding line and personal indemnities of the principals may have tied up their personal net worth. These factors should be taken into account in the review.

A determination also should be made concerning the percentage of a customer's projects that have been bonded. The greater the portion of total work that is bonded, the greater the risk that a customer's surety will be first to collect that customer's assets in the event of the customer's untimely financial demise.

Perhaps more important than the bondability of a customer is the application of the methods of analysis that sureties apply to their customers. The so-called three C's—capital, capacity, and character—that factor into a surety's decision to issue a bonding line should also factor into every decision to accept work or an order from a customer. The three C's may be addressed by the following questions:

1. Does the customer have sufficient capital (cash) available or is the customer overextended and spread too thin?
2. Does the customer have the capacity (skill, expertise, equipment, and personnel) to perform the work, or has the customer undertaken more than it can handle?
3. Does the customer exhibit the character necessary to trust that future payments will be made in a timely manner or is the customer's reputation for payment unacceptable?

If a small- or medium-sized contractor has signs on jobs all over town or has undertaken out-of-state work, does the contractor have the capacity to perform on the project at hand and avoid the trap of shifting money from a profitable job to unprofitable jobs? The customer's bonding company may, with the customer's permission, identify the available bonding capacity and identify the projects for which bonds have been issued. Beware the customer who refuses to allow communication with its surety or other financial sources.

An analysis of the contractor's track record, the size of its work force, and its experience in the industry provides meaningful insight into the capacity of the contractor to handle the work. Past work will indicate whether the contractor is currently handling work beyond its scope, that is, projects that are too large and outside the experience of the contractor, or specialty construction such as health care or utility facilities that the customer has not handled in the past. Shifts in types of work without the addition of experienced personnel may indicate desperation on the part of a customer to take on any available work.

Complete credit applications should be required of every new customer and credit information of existing customers should be updated periodically, at least once per year. All credit information should be certified as true and correct and should be cross-checked with credit agencies whenever possible. The advent of the personal and microcomputer and on-line information services simplifies the process of obtaining credit information. Many credit services now exist that can provide credit histories on prospective customers through computer access.

Making inquiries of others who have worked for the customer and of local trade organizations, obtaining and investigating references, and checking the local public records for recent lawsuits or judgments against the customer will tell much about that customer's reputation. If a project or an owner typically has numerous lien foreclosure actions against it or a contractor has been subject to numerous actions for payment by subcontractors or suppliers, a pattern of behavior may be in evidence.

§ 27.4   —Determining Customer's Organization

The first step in preparing a financial analysis should be to determine the entity through which the customer works. Most general contractors and subcontractors wisely operate through an investment vehicle that provides the best shield against liability, whether liability incurred from accident to property or persons or incurred for payments under a contract. Although limited partnerships and several other types of operating entities may provide this liability shield, most individuals in the construction industry choose to operate through corporations. Typically, the assets of officers, directors, or shareholders of a corporation are not reachable by a creditor of the corporation and only the assets of the corporation itself should then be considered in making the analysis.

For example, it is not unusual for developers to hold each separate parcel of land in a different limatated partnership, each with a so-called "shell" corporation as general partner, thereby limiting the developer's assets that may be subject to a judgment lien held by that partnership. A claim against a shell entity or a lien against property encumbered by a first-priority mortgage (subject to those few jurisdictions in which mechanic's liens may enjoy superior priority by law) is difficult at best. Contractors and subcontractors using a shell corporation as their primary operating vehicle often lease or rent all equipment, furniture, and furnishings, and lease their office and construction yard space, leaving few assets to support payment claims. If a contractor or subcontractor owned its valuable equipment, the equipment may be found to be subject to security interests in favor of purchase money lenders or owned by an affiliated corporation that then leases the equipment to the customer.

Although the likelihood of piercing the corporate shell varies from jurisdiction to jurisdiction, leaving this to the courts to determine later is an expensive, and usually losing, proposition. The key to protection lies in identifying those customers with assets to back up the corporation or other entity and making them responsible for payment.

§ 27.5   Reducing the Credit Risks

Although contractors always find it difficult to turn down work, they should give serious thought to accepting a project from a prospective client whose credit analysis reveals an unacceptable risk. Before plunging ahead with the work, the contractor should ask: (1) whether there is a great risk that the contractor will not be paid for its work after performing the work, and (2) whether there are ways the credit risk can be reduced to an acceptable level.

Obviously the only thing worse to a contractor than turning down work is accepting work and not getting paid for it. Work capacity is used up, the contractor may be on the hook to others for subcontracted work, wages and workers' compensation insurance will likely have been paid, and other opportunities may have been lost.

Use of guaranty. If the customer itself does not have the financial wherewithal to make the project acceptable, perhaps a parent corporation, or, as mentioned in § 27.4, the true party in interest does. A guaranty of that party may be a solution if adequate assets are available. An attorney should always be consulted to draft the guaranty. One-line guaranties at the bottom of a credit application should not be considered sufficient. A guaranty is a separate independent legal document, and unless properly drafted, the contractor might find that it has lost benefits provided to it in a contract, vis-à-vis the guarantor.

Many states protect the assets of one spouse from judgments that may attach to the assets of the other and some provide protection from levy for the primary residence or jointly-owned assets. Therefore, the local laws must be considered in the financial analysis. If a principal of a company agrees without question to a personal guaranty, an asset check of the principal's spouse, and the possible joinder of the spouse in the credit guaranty, may be appropriate.

Use of lien. Reliance on lien rights as a substitute for having a creditworthy customer will likely result in additional cost and a reduction in a claimant's ability to collect all sums owed to it. Collection efforts against a third-party owner, particularly by a remote-tier subcontractor or supplier, should be thought of as backup protection only, and not as a substitute for payment by the customer. The use of liens in the collection process is discussed in § 27.11.

Parties in the chain. The analysis of a customer should also include a review of the project itself, the claimant's remoteness from the ultimate source of funding (that is, owner or lender) and, on a large dollar volume contract, a review of the financial ability of the parties in the chain, from the source of funding down to the claimant. The combined impact of a paid when paid clause and a credit risk in the chain may result in nonpayment even with a credit-worthy customer. The claimant's remoteness in the chain also increases the risks involved in collection procedures against third parties because lien laws and bond statutes typically provide for a limit to the number of tiers of parties that may claim a lien. If the claimant is too remote in the chain, it may not have access to the land or the bond as backup security in the event of nonpayment.

§ 27.6 Governmental Agencies

Contracts with governmental agencies can be the proverbial "double-edged sword" when it comes to payments. A governmental entity is not thought of as subject to the same credit analysis as would be a private owner, yet the 1990s may see a return of the financial difficulties suffered by cities, and even states, during the 1970s. Public works departments often are extremely thorough in their review of payment applications, sometimes to the point that a nominal cost item may hold up for months the processing of a requisition for tens of thousands of dollars while additional backup is sought. Final payment may be tied to and delayed until the governing board of the company has accepted the work.

In addition, standard governmental contracts and local laws and ordinances may prohibit or limit reimbursement for certain types of expenses. Documentation requirements are usually greater and the audit process more time-consuming.

Because government work is typically the subject of competitive bids, prices for work leave no room for contingencies, and losses must be made up through careful monitoring of charges from or inconsistencies within the contract documents and careful documenting of the resultant extra claims. Although claims are not the main thrust of this chapter, claims are a particular problem when it comes to payment, the result being greater time and cost involved in collections.

Although payment bonds are usually required for governmental projects, smaller projects may be exempted, leaving the claimant without a bond claim or lien rights. Large government projects likely will be bonded; however, the projects may have many tiers of contractors and those contractors on the bottom may have no claim against the bond under applicable law.

Knowing the rights of claimants under lien laws, having adequate contracts, documenting the work, backing up cost data, and knowing the customer are vital to getting paid.

§ 27.7 Contract Protections

Although it is not the intent of this chapter to be the definitive guide to the preparation of form contracts, subcontracts, purchase orders, and other typical construction documents, an understanding of certain aspects, terms, and conditions of these instruments is critical to the collection process. Nothing generates disputes more quickly than an oral construction contract, although some poorly-crafted written contracts may come close. The mere existence of the written agreement is not the important factor, but what the agreement stands for is important, that is, the "bottom-line" agreement of the parties. In its simplest concept, the contract or purchase order sets forth two interdependent ideas: the work to be performed, or the material, equipment, or labor to be supplied; and the price to be paid for that work, material, equipment, or labor.

Clear, unambiguous documents reduce disputes and eliminate defenses that could be raised by the customer. Complete documentation entered into based on an analysis of the customer's financial condition may avoid the later shifting or hiding of assets to avoid payment should problems arise.

§ 27.8   —Proper Description of Scope of Work

Beginning with the simple concepts mentioned above, the contract or purchase order, and especially postcontract change orders, should clearly, and in detail, describe the scope of work and the corresponding price to be paid for that work. From the perspective of the general contractor vis-à-vis the owner, and a subcontractor or supplier vis-à-vis the general contractor, a more specific and detailed description, and not a broad general description, reduces the chances of an unanticipated item being considered as within the price to be paid. Some typical provisions, such as those relating to claims for additional costs arising from concealed or unknown conditions or relating to inconsistencies in plans and specifications, relate to elements of work that a contractor or a subcontractor may not reasonably foresee as part of the defined scope of work and therefore would not be included in the price. The contractor or subcontractor for a particular job, in order to maintain profitability or, at a minimum, to prevent losses on the job, must contemplate payment for work not anticipated by the contractor or subcontractor. Not being paid for extras is no different than not being paid for anticipated work.

If a more expansive interpretation of the scope of the work can be made because of a too general or unclear description, the contractor or subcontractor may be required to absorb the cost of these extras. In preparing a contract, the contractor or subcontractor should review the scope of work carefully with the expectation that nonconstruction professionals (that is, lawyers, judges, and juries) may ultimately decide what items may be included or excluded, and thereby determine whether the claimant is entitled to payment.

§ 27.9   —Documentation of Change Orders

The corollary to defining the initial scope of work is the documentation of change orders that add or delete work, whether from a change directed by the owner or from a change resulting from an ambiguity or omission in plans and specifications or in the scope of work description. (A related concept, the backcharge, presents a similar result. If a party is not properly backcharged or if the backup or basis of the backcharge is incomplete or unclear, or made in an untimely manner, a contractor or subcontractor may not recoup payments already made, the result being the same as if the contractor had never received payment for the work performed.) More disputes arise and more legal fees are spent in prosecuting or defending claims based on payments for change orders than for almost any other cause.

The obvious recommendation is that no work should be performed until a written change order, which must adequately detail and describe the change and its effect on the contract price and time, is signed by all of the required or appropriate parties. Contractors concerned about the reality of field changes and lost time in waiting for signatures always cringe when their attorneys recommend this course of action. Therefore, attorneys cannot assume that their construction clients can or will be able to negotiate and execute change orders before the work is needed. Nevertheless, clients must understand that by not doing so, they increase their risk of not collecting full payment for the change work.

The contract must incorporate a mechanism by which some certainty can be provided to a contractor or subcontractor that reasonable compensation will be received for the change work. A contractor, or subcontractor, should document to the owner, or contractor, respectively, the change work it will undertake and its expectation of payment for that work, whether by reasonable negotiation or pursuant to the terms of the written agreement. This avoids the question as to whether the work was intended as a change, and acknowledges that the claimant was proceeding reasonably, relying on eventual and reasonable, compensation.

The 1987 editions of the American Institute of Architects (AIA) general construction contract documents provide mechanisms for determining costs involved in change work. These provisions, however, may not reflect all costs for which a contractor or subcontractor would expect to be paid. Therefore, the contractor and subcontractor must carefully review and analyze these provisions to determine whether or not additional costs should be reimbursable.[1]

It is important to note a few contract concepts and the questions to which they give rise in the collection process:

1. Payment schedule
   ____ When are requisitions to be submitted?
   ____ When are payments to be received?
   ____ If payments are not timely, are interest charges or late fees assessed?
   ____ Does the schedule for receipt of payments coordinate with payments out to subcontractors and suppliers? (Often suppliers are

---

[1] *See* AIA Doc. A201, General Conditions of the Contract for Construction, Art. 7 (1987).

on a net/30 days; lower tier subcontractors may not receive payment within that time frame as payments flow down.)

2. Retainage

____ How much retainage is to be held?

____ Is the retainage to be reduced at particular defined stages? (The contractor should not forget to request reduction in its requisitions, as the other customer may not be likely to give a reminder.)

____ Does retainage stand as security for punch-list items? May payment of the retainage be withheld or the retainage kept for any reason?

____ Is the percentage of retainage great enough to trigger nonpayment notices under lien or bond laws, or under the terms of the payment bond?

3. Attorneys' fees and costs

____ Does the contract or purchase order provide that the contractor may recover its reasonable attorneys' fees and costs if it employs an attorney to collect payment? (This is of vital importance in states that do not provide for attorneys' fees to the prevailing party in a construction dispute or that only award the same in the event of court action.)

4. Right to stop work

____ Does the contract grant the contractor the right to stop work if the contractor is not paid?[2]

5. Flow-down (pass-through) terms

____ Does the contract or purchase order grant the contractor the same remedies that the contractor has against the owner, and conversely grant the contractor the same rights as the owner has against the contractor? (The existence of the so-called pass-through provision should be pre-conditioned on a review of the prime contracts, the terms of which will be passed through.)

6. Work through dispute provisions.

§ 27.10 —Standardization of Procedures

The adoption of standardized forms and procedures reduces the administrative burden of creating a paper trail. Although some situations do not fit within standardized procedures, the risk of nonpayment is greatly reduced by having instituted procedures to make timely demands for payment, by maintaining and providing detailed backup information, and by keeping records of meetings, discussions, and telephone calls. The strict adherence

---

[2] *See id.* para. 9.7. The AIA General Conditions grant the right to stop work after certain conditions are satisfied.

to a program of recordkeeping and administrative procedures will create for the claimant the better trail. As litigants' memories may become more selective as time goes by and as witnesses may become difficult to locate, a well-documented file may be the only evidence for a claimant's right to payment. Whether the weight given to the paper trail is valid or not, it does factor into the contractor's ability to prevail against the offending party.

The other side of the "forms" coin is knowing when forms do not go far enough or when a homemade change can have broader implications. It is far less costly to call an attorney and request assistance in modifying a form, or in inserting and writing a phrase, than to have a judge or an arbitrator provide the interpretation. The contractor's job is to provide materials or equipment, or perform construction work; the lawyer's is to write the contract. All of the lawyer's efforts, and the legal fees incurred in preparing forms and creating systems, may be wasted because of a change in one sentence or the insertion of a new provision.

§ 27.11   Construction Liens

Those in the construction industry rely too heavily on the protection of lien laws and not enough on the credit analysis of customers and projects. This occurs because often the timing of a job does not permit the full examination of the financial picture. It should be expected, however, that the 1990s will see a return of more thoughtful and time-consuming construction loan underwriting and a potential corresponding delay in project start-ups, providing the claimant with additional time to undertake its credit analysis.

The right to put a lien on property and related improvements in order to recover payment should be viewed as one part of the whole collection process and not as a substitute for a credit analysis or adequate contracts and documentation. For all but the general contractor, foreclosing on a construction lien means a suit against a third-party owner, who may not be familiar with the nature of any dispute between the claimant and the offending party or who may have, by law or by contract, certain defenses. If a customer is a tenant in a building, some states may not permit the landlord's interest to be subjected to a lien. The value of a lien on a lease in default is minimal.

§ 27.12   —Attaching and Perfecting Liens

Lien laws in most jurisdictions mandate very specific requirements for attaching and perfecting construction liens.[3] Preliminary lien notices often

---

[3] As an example, in Florida a claimant must serve a preliminary notice, called a Notice to Owner, within 45 days of first furnishing labor, materials, or services. Fla. Stat. Ann.

must be delivered to the owner, surety, lender, or other parties within specified time parameters and must contain certain required information. Liens
themselves generally must be filed within a specified time after completing
the work or after a failure to receive a payment. Providing notices and
complying with the lien laws generally means additional costs and administrative burden at the start of a project when there do not appear to be any
problems. Small contractors and subcontractors often believe they do not
have the staff to obtain the necessary information to send preliminary lien
notices or sufficient profit in each job to use notice services. Viewed in the
context of one's company-wide collection efforts, the cost and time involved is, more often than not, worth the investment in order to preserve
and prosecute available lien rights.

Because lien laws and the protection they provide vary from state to state,
it is important to consult an attorney before entering into contracts or beginning work in a new jurisdiction. The ability of an owner to require
prospective lien waivers, the timing, form, and content of preliminary notices and liens, the identity of a party's entitlement to lien, and the relative
priorities of liens should be determined and built into forms, checklists, and
administrative procedures to be used in that state.

Contractors, and subcontractors in particular, feel uncomfortable sending preliminary notices, filing liens, and possibly upsetting a customer. Although a customer may be upset, it is not often that a contractor or subcontractor actually loses work for filing a valid lien.

The timing of the lien filing is important, not just to meet statutory requirements, but to maintain priority of the lien vis-a-vis other lien
claimants. Some states render all liens to be of equal priority or provide a
date (such as the date of recording of an owner's notice of commencement
or similar document, or the visible commencement of construction) to
which liens relate back and take priority. If the lien of numerous other
lienors have priority over the claimant's lien, the claimant's chances of recovery in a foreclosure action may be greatly reduced. Significant delay in
filing a lien can therefore diminish the protection the lien provides.

Realistically, however, it is the infrequent case in which a lienor ultimately forecloses and takes title to the property. The greater likelihood for
receiving payment as a result of a lien and the action to foreclose that lien is
the necessity on the part of an owner to maintain clear title before construction proceeds are disbursed by the lender, or before a permanent

---

§ 713.06(2)(a) (West 1991). Failure to serve the notice in a timely manner results in an
absolute bar to enforcement of a claim of lien. The claim of lien must be filed of record
within 90 days after the final furnishing of labor, materials, or services and served
within 15 days thereafter. *Id.* § 713.08 (West 1991). On bonded jobs, the notices are
slightly different in form (being a Notice to Contractor instead of a Notice to Owner, and
a Notice of Nonpayment instead of a claim of lien), but the prerequisites are similar. *Id.*
§ 713.23 (West 1991).

mortgage is obtained or recorded. The owner will apply pressure to a contractor in these situations to settle (or transfer to bond) a lien to avoid losing
the funding.

§ 27.13   —Foreclosing the Lien

The filing of the lien itself does not always result in immediate collection.
Aggressive enforcement is usually necessary if a lien is to be effective to
obtain payment. Typically waiting more than a reasonable period of time
to commence an action to foreclose the lien diminishes the chance of a
complete recovery. This is particularly true when the lienor is a subcontractor or supplier not in direct contract with the owner. The practical result is
that the longer one waits, the less likely the chance of recovery. Aggressively
pursuing lien actions makes it more likely that a claimant will be able to
obtain some reimbursement, while those claimants who are less aggressive
may recover nothing.

Some jurisdictions provide mechanisms by which an owner can shorten
the statutory period in which a lien may be foreclosed.[4] The unwary may be
caught in this trap and lose the ability to foreclose. All notices and written
correspondence should be read carefully and an attorney's advice sought if
a question or response is required.

One decided advantage enjoyed by a lienholder is the priority granted the
holder of a perfected security interest versus that given a general unsecured
creditor under the Bankruptcy Code.[5] The party who holds contract claims,
accounts receivable, and actions in progress may be deemed a general unsecured creditor under the current Bankruptcy Code. Those holding a perfected security interest will likely be paid before general unsecured creditors, and, assuming some assets of a bankrupt owner remain, the chances of
recovery are more likely. Additionally, as the lien claim is against a third-
party owner, some protection may be provided in the event of a bankruptcy
of a customer other than the owner.

---

[4] As an example, in Florida an owner can shorten the time period in which a suit to
enforce the lien must be commenced from one year to 60 days by filing of record a
document called a notice of Contest of Lien. Fla. Stat. Ann. § 713.22(2) (West 1991). In
Florida, an owner can also eliminate certain lien rights by making a demand for a sworn
statement of account from a claimant. *Id.* § 713.16(2) (West 1991). If the claimant fails
to deliver the sworn statement within 30 days after the demand or if the claimant
furnishes a false or fraudulent statement, the claimant loses its lien as to the payment to
be made by the owner to the contractor. *Id.*

[5] Section 506 of the Bankruptcy Code, beginning at 11 U.S.C. § 101, defines and describes the rights of secured creditors with respect to the enforcement of their liens or
security interests in the property of the debtor. *See also* G. Treister et al., Fundamentals
of Bankruptcy Law § 6.0 (A.L.I., A.B.A. Comm. on Continuing Prof. Educ., 2d ed.
1988).

§ 27.14   —Describing the Lien

Once the decision has been made to file a lien, the lienor must verify that the property to be subject to the lien properly reflects the property that was improved. If the applicable jurisdiction provides for a prework notice of commencement by the owner, that notice may set forth an adequate legal description. Placing a lien on too much property could expose the lienor to an action or counterclaim for slander of title by an owner. Having too little subject to the lien results in diminished protection. When improvements are made under a single general contract to several parcels of property, some states allow all to be covered under a single claim of lien. This is less expensive than filing several liens and may have the desirable effect of forcing payment if the parcels (particularly if residential units) are to be immediately sold.

The amount of the lien is also important. In some jurisdictions care must be taken to avoid "overliening" and creating a resultant fraudulent lien.[6] States vary in the remedies available to an owner if a fraudulent lien is filed, but possible repercussions may include loss of the entire lien and even punitive damages. Some jurisdictions provide liens in the full contract amount prior to work being performed. If work is being performed in a state that permits such a prospective lien, there may be a disadvantage vis-a-vis other parties if the lien is filed late in the project.

§ 27.15   Payment Bonds

The bond typically issued to protect subcontractors and suppliers from nonpayment by those above them in the tiers of claimants is known as a payment bond. The best protection is provided by jurisdictions having a statutory form of bond, which is intended to protect subcontractors and suppliers in exchange for exempting the owner's property from liens.

The lienor must generally comply with statutorily mandated preliminary notice and notice of nonpayment procedures similar to those for filing a lien against real property. As failure to comply with these requirements could result in a complete defense by the surety to a claim against the bond,

---

[6] As an example, Florida law provides that if the amount of the lien has been willfully exaggerated or amounts have been included in a claim for work not performed or materials provided, or if the claim has been compiled with such willful and gross negligence as to amount to a willful exaggeration, the lien is considered fraudulent. Fla. Stat. Ann. § 713.31(2)(a) (1990). A fraudulent claim may be found to be unenforceable (*see id.* § 713.31(2)(b)), and an owner, contractor, or subcontractor that suffers damages thereby may have a right to recover for those damages, including certain punitive damages. *Id.* § 713.31(2)(c).

a review of the prerequisites mandated by the state for preserving one's right against a bond should be determined.

Some jurisdictions impose conditions on an owner in order to consider a bond as being "statutory." For example, if a state requires that a bond be recorded in the public records to be an effective statutory bond, and an owner fails to do so, the terms of the bond would control and the owner's real property would not have been exempted from being subject to the lien. This has two effects on the lienor: one, the lienor would have to look to the terms of the bond itself to determine whether the bond protects subcontractors and suppliers, rather than just the owner, and, if so, the lienor would have to determine the conditions for collecting against the bond; and, two, if the lienor failed to determine in a timely manner whether the bond met statutory requirements, the lienor may not be able to place a lien on the now nonexempted real property. Unless local law prohibits both filing a lien and claiming against what may appear to be a proper statutory bond (as is typically the case on a government or public project), caution dictates that procedures for both be followed.

Bonds, like liens, should be considered as backup security and not a substitute for a careful credit analysis of the customer.

The financial health of the surety is also a concern, as in these economic times it is not uncommon for sureties to become bankrupt. If an owner has properly complied with all requirements necessary for a statutory bond, and if the jurisdiction does not have financial criteria for its statutory bonds, then the lienor may have no real recourse against either the bond or the real property. In the event of the bankruptcy of a surety, a lienor should check with the state's insurance regulatory agency to determine if a fund has been created to make at least partial recompense to claimants.

Rating systems, such as the Best's Key Rating Guides, provide some indication as to the financial well-being of a particular surety.[7] Many lenders and owners will establish minimum criteria for sureties, the rating A+ XII under the Best's Key Rating System being not unusual as a minimum for an acceptable surety.

Some bonding companies have developed reputations among subcontractors and sureties as only paying proper claims when and if they are sued. Although reputations can be deceiving, and one subcontractor's proper claim is a surety's good faith dispute, the likelihood of collecting from the surety with that reputation without the expense of a suit should be calculated into the up-front financial analysis.

---

[7] Contractor's insurance agent or lender may be able to identify the rating of a particular insurer or the local public library should have a copy of the most recent edition of the Best's Key Rating Guide.

§ 27.16   Other Sources of Payment

In analyzing the financial abilities of the customer, a contractor, subcontractor, or supplier may look to determine whether sources of payment other than the customer also may be available. In trying to find other sources of payment, the parties should consider all of the potential players in the construction process.

Owners

As discussed in § **27.11**, an owner ultimately may become liable to a subcontractor or supplier by virtue of the subcontractor's or supplier's right to lien the owner's property. An owner also may become liable if the owner has agreed to a joint-pay agreement by which checks will be made jointly payable to the contractor and a subcontractor or supplier. This is an avenue that may be used by a major subcontractor or supplier who is concerned about the viability of a contractor, or by a sub-subcontractor or a supplier to a subcontractor.

Lenders

In the past, some construction lenders have been willing to enter into joint-pay arrangements when an owner does not have the financial wherewithal that the contractor has. Whether this willingness will diminish with current loan underwriting standards remains to be seen. If the owner (or lender) has failed to comply with the joint-pay agreement, there may be an independent right to damages for breach of that agreement. Of course, the joint-pay agreement itself provides some protection from misappropriation of funds by the contractor or other party.

Construction lenders are an important part of the collection process. Laws vary from state to state as to the responsibility of a lender for construction liens or the priority of a construction mortgage versus construction liens. The lender's goal is to insulate itself from liability to contractors, subcontractors, and suppliers, and from claims by its borrower. Lenders therefore become a difficult target for third-party claims. Lenders do, however, enter into loan disbursement agreements or institute mechanisms through which the lender can monitor payments to the contractor, and subcontractors and suppliers, on a project. In some states, lenders commonly enter into disbursement agreements with title companies or other escrow agents in order to ensure that payments ultimately reach those who provide preliminary lien notices. Even in states in which a lender can foreclose out construction liens because of the priority of the mortgage, a foreclosing lender prefers to own a completed, lien-free, project, but with all contractor warranties.

Before commencing work, it is important to confirm the availability of funds for the project. The lender will typically confirm the available construction budget; however, some lenders are hesitant to confirm available funds because of the possibility that an error as to the amount of funds could result in a claim for fraudulent inducement to enter into the construction contract.

Insurers

Although not truly part of the collection process, insurers, in addition to the sureties who issue payment bonds, are a source of funds for a project. If negligent workmanship has been performed by a third party providing work to another party, the latter may find that insurance is available to cover the cost if the owner or contractor has refused to pay for the same. Special coverages such as force majeure insurance or rent interruption insurance may be available to offset claims by another party. Although not generally available as a source of payment recovery, potential claims under insurance policies should be reviewed to determine whether or not additional costs may be covered.

State Funds

As a last resort in the event an insurance company becomes defunct or bankrupt, state funds may be available to compensate those individuals with claims against a bond or policy issued by an insurance company. As this has become more common in the 1990s, these funds will become stretched to the limit.

METHODS OF COLLECTION

§ 27.17   Methods of Collection Generally

When the worst happens and payments are not received, the timing and method of collection will ultimately determine the claimant's genuine ability to fully recover all monies due. Understanding the reasons for nonpayment is important in determining the best course of action. For example, if nonpayment is due to the financial problems of the customer, then third parties may become the only source of payment. If the underlying problem is a project in trouble or the failure of an owner, then full recovery of all sums is more difficult and further questions may need to be answered.

§ 27.18   —Demanding Payment

In general, there must be in place a system of standardized procedures in the event a payment is not timely received. By standardizing practices in collection, the claimant avoids having a nonpayment "slipping through the cracks." Once a payment is not received after a certain defined period of time pursuant to a contract, a written demand should be made on the customer. The demand should note the time payment was due, the claimant's right to collect payment, and additional damages that may be recoverable such as attorneys' fees and interest, and if the situation and contract rights warrant, a notice of intent to stop work. It is usually counterproductive to make specific threats of a suit unless the suit would be filed as threatened. Promises for action that are not actually acted upon lose credibility.

Providing copies of the demand to third parties, whether they be contractors, sub-subcontractors, suppliers, subcontractors, or owners, can also get action. When mailing demands on third parties, care must be taken that the facts are stated clearly and that defamatory remarks are excised.

§ 27.19   —Delivering Notice

At the time a nonpayment is noticed, it is also important to make sure that all preliminary lien notices to the customer under lien laws or bond laws have been delivered. As discussed in § 27.11, all such procedures must be followed strictly to avoid losing lien rights. If a notice service is not being utilized, then procedures must be established in-house to ensure that all notices are delivered on time. A checklist should be prepared for each project noting the dates by which each notice must be sent.

§ 27.20   —Filing and Serving the Lien

Once the claimant has consulted its attorney and identified the applicable lien laws in the local jurisdiction, there should be no reason to wait until the last day possible to file and serve the lien. It is always important to verify the requirements of lien and bond claim laws in each state in which work is being performed and prepare a checklist to identify when the time periods will run out in each instance. Some states tie the outside date for filing of the lien to completion of the work for a particular trade, or to the date a payment was due (and not made), or to some more uncertain event. It is important that issues such as the timely filing of the lien be eliminated in order to minimize possible defenses by the owner or bonding company. The more defenses available to an opponent, the more expensive and time-consuming the collection efforts. Waiting until the last minute to file increases the risk that an owner can challenge the lien as being untimely, particularly if the owner can show that the trigger event happened earlier than claimed by the lienor.

In almost all cases, states require that the lien, or other affidavit that effectively constitutes the lien, be served on certain defined parties. Typically, the lien would be served on the owner and parties in the claim that are not in privity with the lienor. Sometimes it is useful to serve parties who are not required to be served by statute, such as a lender, to let them know, prior to their next title examination, that a lien has been filed.

Form.   The lien itself generally must be in the form mandated by statute. Stationery store forms sometimes pose a risk in that an old version may not have been replaced, or the form may not give a complete explanation of how to complete, file, and serve the document. Each jurisdiction may apply different rules as to who can sign on behalf of the lienor on the lien. Money spent to have an attorney prepare the appropriate lien documents and a time frame checklist is usually money well spent and avoids the outlay of more money as the claimant tries to defend the validity of its lien at a future date. Form preparation is less expensive than legal research and the possible loss of lien rights.

Description.   Caution also must be taken and questions should be addressed to an attorney before filing the lien if there is any confusion regarding the legal description of the property to be liened or the amount of the lien. In states in which the building permit application, a notice of commencement, or other device would contain a legal description of the property being improved, a ready source for the property description is available. Otherwise, an examination of the public records by an attorney or a notice service may be necessary in order to identify the property adequately. In that case, the claimant must be careful not to "over-lien" property that was not improved. If an owner believes that the land has been "over-liened," the owner may seek to collect damages in an action for slander of title. Slander of title may occur if title to the real property has been encumbered by a lien that is not related to the work that was done. In most cases, if the lienor acted in good faith, it would be difficult for an owner to prove and prevail under a slander of title action. However, the addition of any defenses or counterclaims by an owner creates more issues to dispute (and to ultimately litigate) and makes the action more expensive and full collection less likely.

Amount.   The amount of the lien must also be carefully addressed. As mentioned earlier, some jurisdictions prevent a lienor from including in the lien any lost profits or accrued interest and allows only the value of the work and improvements made to the property to be included. Other states allow the amount to be determined on a percentage of completion basis, including profits earned and not paid. Some states grant a lien in the total contract amount before any work has been completed. Because of the possibility of the loss of one's lien or other resultant damages if a lien is for a greater amount than appropriate, it is not helpful to overstate the amount of the lien for more than one is entitled to by law. Often liens are filed for the full contract amount or for other damages that are suffered by a claimant in the belief that the greater the amount the more likely the owner will settle. If a claimant tries this in a state that prohibits liens other than for the value of improvements, or that deems such liens to be fraudulent, the owner likely will not settle. If the owner can readily determine that the amount of the lien does not represent the work performed and is fraudulent or overstated, then the owner may have a complete defense to the lien and may even have the right to institute an action for damages on its own.

§ 27.21   —Collecting Payment

In attempting to collect payment, a validly executed lien on the correct property for the maximum amount that may lawfully be liened is the best way to collect. Deviating from clear legal requirements only provides defenses to an owner and results in greater legal fees.

The complaint most often heard from members of the construction industry is that a lien was filed and nothing happened. Some react in disgust and do not bother filing liens in the future. Liens are generally only effective as a source of immediate payment, without undertaking litigation to enforce the lien, in several scenarios.

If the construction loan is about to be paid off by a permanent lender or if the property, such as a residential housing unit, is about to be sold, the likelihood of getting paid by merely filing a lien is much greater. If title cannot be cleared of the lien, or the title insurer will not insure title without exception for the lien, the permanent financing will not be obtained and the buyer would not close. If the nonpayment has resulted from significant cost overruns on the project, the owner will attempt to settle out liens for less than full value in exchange for a quick payment. This is particularly true if the funds left in the construction loan are not sufficient to cover the full amount owed to all lien claimants whether due to claims for extra work, change orders, or the misappropriation of funds by the contractor. It typically comes down to a business decision as to how much each lienor will accept for partial payment in order to satisfy its lien, the trade-off being expensive litigation.

In states that provide for different priorities of lien claimants, it is important for the contractor to know its position vis-a-vis other lien claimants in order to determine its likelihood of success. If another lien claimant could successfully sue and foreclose and eliminate the contractor's lien because of the claimant's priority in time, accepting a reasonable settlement may be appropriate. Sometimes, however, commencing an action will result in a more advantageous settlement because the owner knows that the contractor intends to take the matter seriously and is willing to spend money to collect.

In states that permit priority of the construction mortgage over construction liens, title companies will insure that the liens are subordinate to the mortgage. In that event, unless the liens are numerous and thereby evidence a job in trouble, a construction lender may continue to fund notwithstanding the existence of the lien. The decision must then be made by the lienor as to whether to wait for a "trigger" event, such as permanent financing or sale of the property, to ultimately achieve payment under the lien or to foreclose. The concern should be addressed in the context of the particular state in which the work is located, the length of time that a claim of lien may exist before an action must be filed, and the steps an owner may have taken to accelerate that statutory time period.

If the owner has used a statutory device to accelerate the time in which an action in foreclosure must be commenced, the action must be filed in order to preserve lien rights.

Additionally, construction loans that automatically roll into the permanent financing, and properties (such as apartments) that ultimately are not intended to be sold in the short term may mean that the lien will be allowed to expire. It is surprising how often that, at the completion of a project, one can examine the public records and identify the large number of liens never acted upon and ultimately lost. The best course of action for collection is usually the aggressive approach, and if payment is not otherwise immediately anticipated, an action to foreclose the lien may be the only way to achieve some payment. In projects that may be in trouble, especially office and retail projects during the 1990s, the results can sometimes be that the "early bird gets the worm." By aggressively seeking to collect under a lien, a claimant may achieve some payment, while waiting until the last minute may cause the claimant to be in line behind a foreclosing lender.

§ 27.22 Cost-Benefit Analysis

There are also some times when enforcement of a lien is hopeless. If a lender with a priority position mortgage is foreclosing on the project, if there is no bond, and if every other lien claimant is simultaneously foreclosing, an attorney may advise the contractor that foreclosure efforts will be futile. In most states, when the lender completes its foreclosure of a priority position mortgage, all other lien claimants will be eliminated.

Sometimes winning the foreclosure action could be a lien claimant's biggest headache. The status of title to the property and existence of pricing position mortgages and other encumbrances on the property should be determined before the claimant becomes a property owner. The point is this: if the claimant expects to own the property by completing the foreclosure process and obtaining title, the claimant will inherit any prior mortgages and encumbrances on the property and will be obligated to pay the loan and liens or lose the property after completing expensive litigation. It is rare that a lien goes this far, and usually only in the instance of individual single family residences, or renovations or interior improvements; both are situations in which an owner may have run out of cash. The purpose of undertaking a foreclosure action is to convince an owner to pay, not necessarily to complete foreclosure. The owner does not desire to lose its property to a construction lienholder.

A decision to undertake litigation also requires a cost-benefit analysis. The first question that should always be asked is: "Will the claimant be able to collect from the defendant if the claimant wins in litigation?" There are general avenues to help answer that question.

There are services that perform asset investigations of particular defendants. Existing judgments usually can be checked in the public records, and property searches can be checked by name through the tax rolls. Bank accounts and other assets are, unfortunately, usually only identified after a judgment has been obtained and appropriate depositions-in-aid-of-execution have been held. Financial institutions are generally reticent to release information on their depositors unless directed to do so by a court. It is possible to garnish, or collect upon, salaries and debts owed to a customer once a judgment has been obtained, but ultimately the ability to do so depends on how many other persons are also likely to obtain judgments or have already obtained judgments against the same parties. Many properties are also exempt under state laws from levy under judgments, particularly residences and certain other types of personal property. Some states also exempt property held in joint names from being levied upon by judgment against one party. In addition, contractors who have made themselves judgment-proof by shifting assets to the spouse or children may also be difficult to collect from.

§ 27.23   Appropriate Forum

Once a decision to litigate has been made based on the belief that funds or assets will be available to collect upon, the determination of the appropriate court in which to file must be made. If an action involves a demand that is small enough, the action may be brought in a local small claims court, which will have expedited and simplified procedures that do not always require an attorney to be present. The process is more like arbitration in that the judge hears a presentation from each side and makes a decision based on the facts presented without extensive testimony. There is usually a dollar limit on the cases that may be brought before a small claims court, but the expedited process may make it worthwhile. Parties have been known to drop several hundred dollars from a claim in order to bring the action in small claims court rather than have a more expensive action in a higher court.

In foreclosing a lien or seeking to collect against a bond, there may be jurisdictional requirements to bring the case in a specific court regardless of the size of the claim. If the lien is small, and would otherwise be capable of being brought in a small claims court (and if a customer has assets against which a judgment could be collected), it may be more expeditious to forgo the lien and seek to collect in small claims court. However, this is generally the exception to the rule as lien rights may be more valuable when preserved against an owner.

Some cases may be brought in federal court if the appropriate "diversity" jurisdiction is available. This would more likely be raised or used by a person defending a claim than by someone seeking to collect payment, because bringing an action in federal court is extremely time-consuming, and if one expects to collect payment before retirement age, it is a forum best avoided.

§ 27.24   Costs of Litigation

The problems and shortcomings of litigation may themselves be used as a weapon if one is willing to put up with the time and dollar investment. If a defendant is not willing to, or if it is economically disadvantageous for the defendant to, sit through depositions and spend an inordinate sum on defense, an adequate settlement may be reached.

The expense of bringing an action can be overwhelming and may not be justified unless attorneys' fees and costs are recoverable. For attorneys' fees to be recoverable, there must be a right under contract or by statute. If the contractor is litigating without a lien, or in a jurisdiction that does not provide statutory legal fees to the prevailing party, or under a contract that does not provide for recovery of attorneys' fees, the cost of litigation could exceed the recovery. It is very possible in today's dollars to spend anywhere between $20,000 and $40,000 in taking even a small case to trial. If a contractor could spend more in legal fees than its claim warrants, the claim likely is not worth pursuing.

Some costs of litigation are difficult to calculate. In addition to the legal fees and out-of-pocket costs, there is the lost time spent in depositions, completing interrogatories, and sitting through a trial. That time may be better spent bringing in new work or managing existing jobs and collecting on more recoverable payments.

Often attorneys are requested to take cases on a contingency fee. The ability of an attorney to take a case on a contingency fee is generally related to the ability to collect on the final judgment. This does not necessarily mean that if the case is meritorious, an attorney will rush to join a claimant in sharing in the fruits of the claim. There must still be assets available to collect. Because of unknown factors, such as the availability of bank accounts or other assets that may not be discovered by an investigator, most attorneys are not willing to take cases on a contingency fee unless there is a bond or unencumbered assets available. Having the security of a bond (and, perhaps, even a solvent surety) generally means that if a case is meritorious, then the claimant has a source of funds for collection. Additionally, contingency fees are dependent on the size of the claim. If a lawyer takes a percentage of the winnings, but the winnings would be too small to cover the attorney's reasonable fees charged in bringing the action, the case would not likely be taken on a contingency fee.

§ 27.25   Arbitration

Arbitration has the reputation of being an expedited process that is less expensive and time-consuming than litigation. Nevertheless, in complex cases, even with relatively small amounts in dispute, attorneys are still necessary in order to adequately present the legal issues involved. A primary advantage of arbitration, unless, as is sometimes the case, the contract provides a detailed procedure or adopts the rules of civil procedure, is accelerated discovery.

Discovery is likely the most expensive and time-consuming aspect of litigation except for direct trial preparation. The discovery process generally includes depositions, interrogatories, requests for admission, and requests to produce documents. Typically, arbitration bypasses most of this process, although the arbitrator is usually granted the authority to request documents and subpoena witnesses. The arbitration proceeding itself is more of a tribunal than a court process; each side presents its case and the arbitrator may ask questions of each. The arbitrator then issues a decision. Decisions in most states are final and binding.

Before including arbitration in a contract form for a particular state, several questions should be asked of local counsel:

1. Is arbitration final and binding or may a new action (an action de novo) be instituted by either party?
2. Must the contract clause contain specific language in order for the arbitrator's decision to be final and binding, and enforceable?

3. What is the court process to enforce the arbitrator's decision? Is it inexpensive and expedited?

4. What grounds are available for an appeal of an arbitrator's decision? Is the standard high, such as the decision must have been arbitrary and capricious, or does a lesser standard apply, making appeals by the loser more likely and reducing the benefits of having undertaken arbitration to begin with?

5. Do the contract or local laws provide for some discovery process to minimize possible surprises at the hearing?

6. Is only the American Arbitration Association (AAA) type of arbitration recognized or may individually created dispute resolution mechanisms be utilized and decisions enforced?

§ 27.26   Mediation

Mediation, whether privately undertaken or court ordered, differs from arbitration in that, instead of a decision being rendered, the parties are cajoled into moving closer to a settlement of their dispute. The mediator generally is not granted the ability to end the dispute but only to convince the parties to settle. If the parties have no predisposition or inclination to settle before the mediation proceeding, a successful result is not likely. However, mediators skilled in the court process—retired judges in particular—can help the participants to see the weaknesses in their own cases that could affect the outcome at trial. In this case, mediation can reveal how a presiding judge may rule and thereby be an incentive for settlement.[8]

SPECIAL RIGHTS AND SPECIAL PROBLEMS

§ 27.27   Pay When Paid Clauses

One of the most important questions to be asked of local counsel before contracting to do work in a particular jurisdiction is whether or not the pay when paid clause is enforceable. This clause, when included in a contract, means that unless the paying party has itself received payment, it is not obligated to make payment to the party it has employed.[9] Obviously, if enforceable in the applicable jurisdiction, this provision is of great benefit in a contract when one is the payor; however, it is not desirable if one is the

---

[8] See **Ch. 23** for further discussion on these two methods of alternative dispute resolution.

[9] See **Ch. 19** for discussion on pay when paid clauses.

payee. If a subcontractor or other party is in the position of having to accept the pay when paid condition in order to receive the work, then an assessment of the risks of getting paid must be determined and care must be taken to ensure that all contracts for work entered into contain a similar clause. Generally, material suppliers do not accept pay when paid clauses as modifications to their purchase order forms, and the risk of liability for payment without having been paid would exist. A paid when paid clause undermines the financial and credit analysis of a customer by making it irrelevant if that customer is not paid.

§ 27.28 Stop Work Provisions

Having the right and ability pursuant to contract to stop work or refuse to ship materials or equipment can be more effective than litigation, liens, or other demands for payment. A subcontractor or supplier can quickly get an owner's attention if the owner's project is stopped because a critical element of work cannot be completed. An owner may be able to ignore a lien for some time before having to deal with it, but must act to keep its project moving to completion. Pressure can then be applied to the customer party to bring payments current. The same principle can work if the contractor has not received payment from the owner.

Stopping work can, however, be riskier than filing a lien or a lawsuit. If the lack of payment is the result of a good faith dispute by the party obligated to make payment, stopping work can result in an action for damages caused in the delay of the project. Documentation of the basis for stopping work and the corresponding right to payment, and a clear and unambiguous contract right to stop work are prerequisites to taking this action. An attorney should always be contacted before stopping work.

§ 27.29 Improper Withholding of Funds

Some states provide civil and criminal remedies against parties improperly withholding funds. The "trustee" concept imposes a fiduciary duty on the part of one who receives funds to see that the funds are paid to the proper parties. A higher standard is thus imposed than a mere contractual agreement to make payment and, in some cases, individuals may be subject to an action for damages. Third parties also may be subject to an action under this concept if provided by state statute or if developed in case law in the pertinent jurisdiction.

The misappropriation concept is similar, and may also provide criminal penalties for a party that improperly withholds payment. With drug wars and gang violence, hallmarks of these times, it is not likely that contractors and subcontractors will be imprisoned for every unpaid claim. Neverthe-less, filing the appropriate action can often result in payment. The threat of filing a criminal complaint must be used with great caution, as making such a threat to obtain an advantage, that is, payment, can be deemed extortionate.

§ 27.30   Handling Worthless Checks

Most states have enacted laws that may punish, or provide recompense, or both, for the writing of a worthless check, that is, a check returned for insufficient funds, written on a closed account, or returned for an improper "stop payment" order. Assuming that the check writer has assets to back up its empty checking account, an additional avenue for collection may be provided, like with misappropriation of funds statutes, the risk of criminal punishment may be a motivation to make payment. For small sums, law enforcement agencies may not be inclined to take action or even to file a report. Some states provide special damages for actions for worthless checks and could make this a valuable route for collection.

§ 27.31   Negotiations and Workouts

In reaching a settlement on payment, all of one's rights should be reviewed and preserved to the extent possible and practicable. If an action is already in litigation, the settlement documents should be enforceable by the court in the event the defendant fails to meet a payment obligation. If possible, a final judgment should be entered and perfected against the defendant, par-ticularly if lien rights against property or claims against a bond are being released. Holders of a perfected security interest receive preferential treat-ment under the Bankruptcy Code versus unsecured creditors, and giving up a security interest may add to the risk of collection if the debtor files for bankruptcy.

Workouts are sometimes made among multiple claimants and all must agree to the pre-offered settlement terms before the payor will settle and pay. This is seen most often at the completion or abandonment of a proj-ect—a time when the payor itself has a limited source of funds. Multiple-party settlement agreements often result in the largest claimants determin-ing the payments to smaller claimants. If the settlement agreement is all-encompassing and intended to avoid bankruptcy, the claimants may ob-tain a greater yield than they would have from the bankruptcy court, and without a long wait. Generally, waivers of lien rights and other claims by all parties are appropriate conditions to such agreements.

CHAPTER 28

CLAIMS AGAINST BONDING COMPANIES

Laurence Schor*

Laurence Schor is a member in the Washington, D.C., firm of Miller & Chevalier, Chartered, where he concentrates his practice in construction and government contract law. He holds a Bachelor's degree in business administration from Southern Methodist University, a law degree from the University of Texas, Austin, School of Law, and a Master of Laws degree from George Washington University. He has authored articles, book chapters, and manuals, and lectures regularly for professional groups on complex construction law issues. Mr. Schor is a member of the American Bar Association, Public Contracts Section, where he was chairman of the Construction Committee and now serves on the governing council, and the Forum Committee on Construction. He is a founding member and on the Board of Directors of the American College of Construction Lawyers.

*The author expresses appreciation to Penrose Wolf, Esquire, of Hartford, Connecticut, and to Thomas D. Dinackus of Miller & Chevalier, Chartered, for their assistance.

§ 28.1   Basic Introduction

How and when to file a claim on a construction surety bond is a topic of interest to all subcontractors and suppliers of material and certain services to public and private construction projects. Therefore, some preliminary facts concerning bonds are provided in §§ 28.2 through 28.6 as useful guidance.

Although suretyship has been in use since ancient times, performance bonds and labor and material payment bonds have come into widespread use since about the turn of the twentieth century, at approximately the same time the federal government began imposing bonding requirements on public projects. The first statutory requirements imposed on the federal level were contained in the Heard Act (1894), followed by the Miller Act, enacted in 1935, still the primary federal statute in this area. Presently, every state requires that contractors on certain public work projects furnish a bond to protect labor and material suppliers. Although the statutory requirements vary somewhat from state to state, the intent generally is to require contractors both to furnish a performance bond to ensure completion of the work pursuant to the construction prime contract plans and specifications, and to furnish a labor and material payment bond to ensure payment to subcontractors and other creditors for work, labor, and materials actually furnished or intended to be furnished to the project. Courts at the federal and state levels are inclined to interpret the bond laws liberally and extend coverage of the bond in order to protect the mechanic, who furnishes labor and the material or service supplier to the project.

The purpose of this chapter is not to summarize the federal and state statutory requirements, but rather to discuss the essential elements of how and when to file a claim and explain the types of surety bonds normally furnished on public and private projects. A general discussion on recoverable costs under the payment bond is also included; however, the discussion will not include reference to claims by the owner/obligee on the performance bond.

§ 28.2   Definition of a Bond

Essentially, a contract bond is a guarantee of performance by the contractor, assuring the owner/obligee that the contractor to whom the construction contract has been awarded will perform the contract in accordance with plans and specifications and that the labor and material bills incurred in performance of the contract will be paid, but with certain limitations. The bond is not a contract of insurance. Unless specially conditioned, and certainly as encountered in most standard bond forms, the bond does not cover all the contingencies, such as delays and lost profits, that can occur on a construction project.[1]

§ 28.3   Parties to the Bond

Briefly, the terms encountered when reading a bond include "principal," "obligee," and "surety." The principal is the contractor or subcontractor who has the obligation to perform the underlying construction contract or subcontract. The obligee, who sometimes is the owner and who also may be the general contractor, is the other party to the construction contract and the party to whom the obligations on the performance and payment bonds run. In other words, the obligee is the party to whom the duty of performance is owed in the event of default by the principal and the party to be protected in the event of nonpayments by the principal. The surety, the third party to the bond, is, in effect, the guarantor, whose assurance the obligee holds that, if the principal fails in the obligation of performance, the surety will assume that obligation.

TYPES OF BONDS

§ 28.4   Bid Bonds

A bid bond protects the owner by guaranteeing that the bidder who is eligible to be awarded the contract will execute the contract documents and provide the performance and payment bonds and meet other precontract conditions that are required. Failure to execute the contract and provide the required bonds and other data usually leaves the bidder liable for money

---

[1] For further discussion about and examples of construction forms for sureties, *see generally* 2 Construction Industry Forms (R. Cushman & G. Blick eds., John Wiley & Sons 1988).

damages—either actual (usually the difference between the contract award amount and the next low bid or the amount of the contract then awarded) or liquidated (for example, 20 percent of the value of the submitted bid or proposal), depending on the governing bond provisions, the applicable statutes, or the regulations promulgated pursuant to those statutes. Bid bonds are also available to protect a general contractor by guaranteeing that the low bidders for key subcontracts will enter into their subcontracts and provide any necessary performance or payment bonds or other data.

The bid bond usually is only required on public contracts although no limitation on the use of the bond exists other than by practice or habit. In public contracts, bid bonds are intended to ensure that the public receives the benefit of the low bid. Even those contractors who cannot be awarded a contract are entitled to the protection a bid bond gives.

Contractors who are required to furnish bid bonds should make certain that the surety is bound for more than the time frame within which the owner must make award. If a specific number of days is mentioned, the owner may take the full time reserved to make award, and then the awardee will have at least 10 days to furnish the requisite bonds. Hence, there would be no "call" on the bid bond until the awardee's inability to comply manifested itself, perhaps 70 days after bids were submitted. If, on the other hand, no time frame for award by the owner is mentioned, the law requires that the bid remain open a "reasonable" time (each state's laws may differ) and, therefore, the bid bond should have no time limits. Owners and prime contractors requiring bid bonds also should take heed of this precaution.

Typical Examples

Figure 28–1 is an example of a bid bond issued by a private company, but approved by the American Institute of Architects. The obligation language contained in a typical bid bond commits the principal (including the surety) to pay the obligee (usually the owner or general contractor) the difference between the amount specified in the bid and such larger amount for which the obligee may in good faith contract with another party to perform the work covered by the bid. What is, or is not, "good faith" may be open to legal challenge.

Figure 28–2 is a bid bond form for federal government use which is found in the Federal Acquisition Regulation, commonly referred to as the FAR. Note that the federal form identifies time periods for contract award and submissions of required bonds, which periods can be extended for up to 60 days without notice to the bid bond surety.[2] The general time frames for the life of the bid bond are identified in this form.

---

[2] FAR 53.228(a) (GSA Standard Form No. 24, Bid Bond) (all FAR references can be located in Title 48 of the Code of Federal Regulations).

BOND NO._____

**Bid Bond
SURETY DEPARTMENT**

THE HARTFORD

KNOW ALL MEN BY THESE PRESENTS,

That we,

as Principal,

a corporation created and

hereinafter called the Principal, and the

existing under the laws of the State of   , whose principal office is in

as Surety, hereinafter called the Surety, are held and firmly bound unto

as Obligee, hereinafter called the Obligee,

in the sum of

Dollars ($),

for the payment of which sum, well and truly to be made, the said Principal and the said Surety, bind ourselves, our heirs, executors, administrators, successors and assigns, jointly and severally, firmly by these presents.

Whereas, the Principal has submitted a bid for

NOW, THEREFORE, if the Obligee shall accept the bid of the Principal and the Principal shall enter into a contract with the Obligee in accordance with the terms of such bid, and give such bond or bonds as may be specified in the bidding or contract documents with good and sufficient surety for the faithful performance of such contract and for the prompt payment of labor and material furnished in the prosecution thereof, or in the event of the failure of the Principal to enter such contract and give such bond or bonds, if the Principal shall pay to the Obligee the difference not to exceed the penalty hereof between the amount specified in said bid and such larger amount for which the Obligee may in good faith contract with another party to perform the work covered by said bid, then this obligation shall be null and void, otherwise to remain in full force and effect.

Signed and sealed this................ ....day of ....A.D. 19..........

Witness.. (SEAL)
(If Individual)   (Principal)

By ....(SEAL)
                                                                              (Title)

Attest .... (SEAL)
(If Corporation)

.... (SEAL)

Attest ....   By ....(SEAL)
                                                                              (Title)

(Approved by The American Institute of Architects.
A.I.A. Document No. A-310, Feb., 1970 Edition)

Form S-3266-4   Printed in U.S.A. 12-'70 .

Figure 28–1. Bid bond. Reprinted with permission.

BID BOND *(See Instructions on reverse)*	DATE BOND EXECUTED *(Must be same or later than bid opening date)*	
PRINCIPAL *(Legal name and business address)*	TYPE OF ORGANIZATION *("X" one)*	
	☐ INDIVIDUAL	☐ PARTNERSHIP
	☐ JOINT VENTURE	☐ CORPORATION
	STATE OF INCORPORATION	
SURETY(IES) *(Name and business address)*		

PERCENT OF BID PRICE	PENAL SUM OF BOND				BID IDENTIFICATION	
	AMOUNT NOT TO EXCEED				BID DATE	INVITATION NO.
	MILLION(S)	THOUSAND(S)	HUNDRED(S)	CENTS		
					FOR *(Construction, Supplies or Services)*	

OBLIGATION:

We, the Principal and Surety(ies) are firmly bound to the United States of America (hereinafter called the Government) in the above penal sum. For payment of the penal sum, we bind ourselves, our heirs, executors, administrators, and successors, jointly and severally. However, where the Sureties are corporations acting as co-sureties, we, the Sureties, bind ourselves in such sum "jointly and severally" as well as "severally" only for the purpose of allowing a joint action or actions against any or all of us. For all other purposes, each Surety binds itself, jointly and severally with the Principal, for the payment of the sum shown opposite the name of the Surety. If no limit of liability is indicated, the limit of liability is the full amount of the penal sum.

CONDITIONS:

The Principal has submitted the bid identified above.

THEREFORE:

The above obligation is void if the Principal — (a) upon acceptance by the Government of the bid identified above, within the period specified therein for acceptance (sixty (60) days if no period is specified), executes the further contractual documents and gives the bond(s) required by the terms of the bid as accepted within the time specified (ten (10) days if no period is specified) after receipt of the forms by the principal; or (b) in the event of failure so to execute such further contractual documents and give such bonds, pays the Government for any cost of procuring the work which exceeds the amount of the bid.

Each Surety executing this instrument agrees that its obligation is not impaired by any extension(s) of the time for acceptance of the bid that the Principal may grant to the Government. Notice to the surety(ies) of extension(s) are waived. However, waiver of the notice applies only to extensions aggregating not more than sixty (60) calendar days in addition to the period originally allowed for acceptance of the bid.

WITNESS:

The Principal and Surety(ies) executed this bid bond and affixed their seals on the above date.

PRINCIPAL			
Signature(s)	1.	2.	Corporate Seal
	(Seal)	*(Seal)*	
Name(s) & Title(s) *(Typed)*	1.	2.	

INDIVIDUAL SURETIES		
Signature(s)	1.	2.
	(Seal)	*(Seal)*
Name(s) *(Typed)*	1.	2.

CORPORATE SURETY(IES)					
SURETY A	Name & Address		STATE OF INC.	LIABILITY LIMIT $	Corporate Seal
	Signature(s)	1.	2.		
	Name(s) & Title(s) *(Typed)*	1.	2.		

NSN 7540-01-152-8059
PREVIOUS EDITION USABLE

24-104

STANDARD FORM 24 (REV. 10-83)
Prescribed by GSA
FAR (48 CFR 53.228(a))

Figure 28–2. Bid bond.

CORPORATE SURETY(IES) *(Continued)*

				STATE OF INC.	LIABILITY LIMIT	
SURETY B	Name & Address			STATE OF INC.	LIABILITY LIMIT $	Corporate Seal
	Signature(s)	1.		2.		
	Name(s) & Title(s) (Typed)	1.		2.		
SURETY C	Name & Address			STATE OF INC.	LIABILITY LIMIT $	Corporate Seal
	Signature(s)	1.		2.		
	Name(s) & Title(s) (Typed)	1.		2.		
SURETY D	Name & Address			STATE OF INC.	LIABILITY LIMIT $	Corporate Seal
	Signature(s)	1.		2.		
	Name(s) & Title(s) (Typed)	1.		2.		
SURETY E	Name & Address			STATE OF INC.	LIABILITY LIMIT $	Corporate Seal
	Signature(s)	1.		2.		
	Name(s) & Title(s) (Typed)	1.		2.		
SURETY F	Name & Address			STATE OF INC!	LIABILITY LIMIT $	Corporate Seal
	Signature(s)	1.		2.		
	Name(s) & Title(s) (Typed)	1.		2.		
SURETY G	Name & Address			STATE OF INC.	LIABILITY LIMIT $	Corporate Seal
	Signature(s)	1.		2.		
	Name(s) & Title(s) (Typed)	1.		2.		

INSTRUCTIONS

1. This form is authorized for use when a bid guaranty is required. Any deviation from this form will require the written approval of the Administrator of General Services.

2. Insert the full legal name and business address of the Principal in the space designated "Principal" on the face of the form. An authorized person shall sign the bond. Any person signing in a representative capacity (e.g., an attorney-in-fact) must furnish evidence of authority if that representative is not a member of the firm, partnership, or joint venture, or an officer of the corporation involved.

3. The bond may express penal sum as a percentage of the bid price. In these cases, the bond may state a maximum dollar limitation (e.g., 20% of the bid price but the amount not to exceed _____ dollars).

4. (a) Corporations executing the bond as sureties must appear on the Department of the Treasury's list of approved sureties and must act within the limitation listed herein. Where more than one corporate surety is involved, their names and addresses shall appear in the spaces (Surety A, Surety B, etc.) headed "CORPORATE SURETY(IES)". In the space designated "SURETY(IES)" on the face of the form, insert only the letter identification of the sureties.

(b) Where individual sureties are involved, two or more responsible persons shall execute the bond. A completed Affidavit of Individual Surety (Standard Form 28), for each individual surety, shall accompany the bond. The Government may require these sureties to furnish additional substantiating information concerning their financial capability.

5. Corporations executing the bond shall affix their corporate seals. Individuals shall execute the bond opposite the word "Corporate Seal"; and shall affix an adhesive seal if executed in Maine, New Hampshire, or any other jurisdiction requiring adhesive seals.

6. Type the name and title of each person signing this bond in the space provided.

7. In its application to negotiated contracts, the terms "bid" and "bidder" shall include "proposal" and "offeror".

STANDARD FORM 24 BACK (REV. 10-83)

☆ GPO : 1984 0 – 421-526 (20)

Figure 28–2. *(continued)*

§ 28.5　Performance Bonds

Performance bonds protect the owner from a default by the general contractor, or the general contractor from a default by a subcontractor. These bonds are usually required on all significant construction projects, public and private. Performance bonds only protect the owner or obligee on the bond. They cannot serve as the basis for a claim against the surety by subcontractors or other creditors of the general contractor.

To trigger the surety's liability on a performance bond, the contractor must be in default and the owner must notify the surety. It is always good policy for owners to put the surety on notice as soon as problems that portend default manifest themselves. A default may exist when the contractor's performance is seriously deficient. However, no default exists when the problem was caused by factors beyond the contractor's control, when the problem resulted without the contractor's fault or negligence, or when the problem is minor, unless the contract or local common law places the risk of the particular occurrence on the contractor whether or not the contractor is at fault. What constitutes default usually is defined in the construction contract or the bond.

When the owner invokes the performance bond successfully, the surety ensures completion of the project by utilizing one or more of the following alternatives.

Financing.　The surety can provide financing to the contractor who is the principal on the bond if it appears that the contractor will be able to complete the project. Financing is accomplished by the provision of funds or payment of performance costs directly by the surety or to the contractor for the purpose of completing the project, or by the surety's guarantee of a bank loan. Under most circumstances, the general contractor signs a joint control agreement for its company operations with the surety and assigns contract progress payments either to the surety, which becomes a financing institution, or to the lending bank.

Takeover agreement.　The surety can sign a takeover agreement with the owner and, in effect, become the owner's contractor for payment and contractual responsibility purposes, such as for claims under warranties. Subcontractors and suppliers would look to the surety, then, in the same manner they looked to the defaulted prime contractor and also would retain all their contract rights and remedies for claim purposes. Sureties usually arrange for a substitute construction company to finish the work and the surety is responsible to the owner, the subcontractors, and the suppliers for any funding shortfalls between the funds remaining to be paid by the owner under the contract and the costs of completion.

Payment of bond penalty.   A third option for the surety is to pay the bond penalty to the owner. By so doing, the surety obtains a complete release of all future obligations under the bond and the owner assumes the risk of contract completion. This option may become complicated if (1) the surety has also issued the payment bond and claims have been or may be made under that bond, or (2) the remaining work scope is significantly less than the value of the full bond penalty as a result of work performed by the defaulted general contractor. In the first instance, the defaulted general contractor should insist that the surety attempt to gain a complete release under both bonds should the surety tender the full bond penalty. Only then can those people within the contractor's organization who may be responsible as indemnitors to the surety establish with some certainty what their ultimate liability may be. In the second situation, the defaulted general contractor should object to the owner receiving a potential windfall as their indemnitor's obligations will be directly affected by the amounts paid out by the surety.

In **Figure 28–3**, a private performance bond form approved by the American Institute of Architects the surety is given the option to complete the contract work itself, or to arrange for a takeover contractor to complete the work. In the latter option, the surety makes available sufficient funds to complete the work less an amount reflecting the balance of the contract price that does not exceed other costs and damages for which the surety may be liable hereunder, or alternatively provides the total amount of the bond.

Figure 28–4 is the most recent Subcontract Performance Bond form approved and issued by the Associated General Contractors (AGC) of America. This form contains much the same language as the one for prime contractors discussed above except that specific reference is made to a number of costs for which the defaulted subcontractor may be liable.[3] These costs include correction of defective work, legal and design professional costs, and liquidated damages. It should be noted that these are examples only and that other reasonably incurred costs may be recoverable.

In the federal form, **Figure 28–5**, the surety obligates itself to pay the full amount of the penal sum in the event of default.[4] It is interesting to note that the federal form provides for multiple sureties, each with a limit on its liability, and for specific recognition by the surety of the need to pay all taxes due from the defaulted contractor.

A special concern for performance bond sureties in the 1990s and possibly beyond is the area of environmental cleanups. The issue is the potential liability of the surety to indemnify or compensate the obligee for loss or

---

[3] AGC Doc. 606, Subcontractor Performance Bond (1988).

[4] FAR 53.228(b) (GSA Standard Form No. 25, Performance Bond).

BOND No. ....

Performance Bond
(NOTE: THIS BOND IS ISSUED SIMULTANEOUSLY
WITH PAYMENT BOND ON PAGE 2, IN FAVOR OF THE
OWNER CONDITIONED FOR THE PAYMENT OF LABOR
AND MATERIAL.)

THE HARTFORD

Know All Men By These Presents:
That ....
(Here insert the name and address, or legal title, of the Contractor)

as Principal, hereinafter called Contractor, and the..., a
corporation organized and existing under the laws of the State of.., with
its principal office in the City of ...., as Surety, hereinafter called
Surety, are held and firmly bound unto..
....
(Here insert the name and address, or legal title, of the Owner)

as Obligee, hereinafter called Owner, in the amount of..
.... Dollars ($....................................),
for the payment whereof Contractor and Surety bind themselves, their heirs, executors, administrators, successors,
and assigns, jointly and severally, firmly by these presents.
  Whereas, Contractor has by written agreement dated ....
entered into a contract with Owner for..
....

in accordance with drawings and specifications prepared by ....
(Here insert full name, title and address)

....

which contract is by reference made a part hereof, and is hereinafter referred to as the CONTRACT.

  Now, Therefore, the condition of this obligation is such that, if Contractor shall promptly and faithfully
perform said CONTRACT, then this obligation shall be null and void; otherwise it shall remain in full force and
effect.

  The Surety hereby waives notice of any alteration or extension of time made by the Owner.

  Whenever Contractor shall be, and declared by Owner to be in default under the CONTRACT, the Owner
having performed Owner's obligations thereunder, the Surety may promptly remedy the default, or shall promptly

  (1) Complete the CONTRACT in accordance with its terms and conditions, or

  (2) Obtain a bid or bids for completing the Contract in accordance with its terms and conditions, and upon
      determination by Surety of the lowest responsible bidder, or, if the Owner elects, upon determination by the
      Owner and the Surety jointly of the lowest responsible bidder, arrange for a contract between such bidder
      and Owner, and make available as Work progresses (even though there should be a default or a succes-
      sion of defaults under the contract or contracts of completion arranged under this paragraph) sufficient funds
      to pay the cost of completion less the balance of the contract price; but not exceeding, including other costs
      and damages for which the Surety may be liable hereunder, the amount set forth in the first paragraph
      hereof. The term "balance of the contract price," as used in this paragraph, shall mean the total amount
      payable by Owner to Contractor under the Contract and any amendments thereto, less the amount properly
      paid by Owner to Contractor.

  Any suit under this bond must be instituted before the expiration of two (2) years from the date on which final
payment under the CONTRACT falls due.

  No right of action shall accrue on this bond to or for the use of any person or corporation other than the Owner
named herein or the heirs, executors, administrators or successors of the Owner.

Signed and sealed this   day of   A. D. 19

	PRINCIPAL	(Corporate Seal)
Witness (If Individual/Partnership)	Name	
Attest (If Corporation)	Signature	
	By:	
	Typed Name and Title	
	SURETY	(Corporate Seal)
Attest	Name	
	Signature	
	By:	
	Typed Name	
		Attorney-in-fact

Form S-3213-5 **Page 1.** Printed in U.S.A.
(A.I.A. Form — Document No. A-311, February, 1970 Edition Approved by The American Institute of Architects)

Figure 28–3. Performance bond. Reprinted with permission.

THE ASSOCIATED GENERAL CONTRACTORS OF AMERICA

SUBCONTRACT
PAYMENT BOND

TABLE OF ARTICLES

1. SCOPE OF BOND

2. EFFECT OF OBLIGATION

3. CLAIMANT

4. AMOUNT OF BOND

5. ALTERATION NOTICE WAIVER

SAMPLE

This document has important legal and surety consequences. AGC encourages consultation with an attorney and surety consultant when completing or modifying this document.

AGC DOCUMENT NO. 607 • SUBCONTRACT PAYMENT BOND • 1988   1

Figure 28–4. Subcontract payment bond. Represented with permission of the Associated General Contractors of America (AGC). Copies of current forms may be obtained from AGC's Publications Department, 1957 E Street, NW, Washington, D.C. 20006, (202) 393-2040.

Special Instructions

NAMES AND ADDRESSES: The legal name and address of the Principal should be filled in. The Principal is the Subcontractor who provides the Subcontract Payment Bond to the Obligee who is the Contractor.

The legal name and address of the Obligee, who is the Contractor, should be filled in.

The legal name of the Surety should be filled in along with the address of the Surety's office after "Surety (Name and Address of Surety Company Office)." This name and address of the Surety is **not** the name and address of the surety agent.

In the blank for information on the Subcontract, the effective date of the Subcontract should be filled in with the day, month and year when the Subcontract is to become effective. The amount of the Subcontract, stated in both Arabic numerals and words, should be filled in after "Amount." After "Description of Project," the name and address of the project where the Subcontract will be performed should be filled in.

In the blank for information on the Bond, the date blank should be filled in with the day, month and year the Bond is to become effective. This date is not to be earlier than the effective date of the Subcontract. After "Penal Amount," fill in the amount, stated in both Arabic numerals and words, for which the Principal and Surety will be obligated.

In the blank "Subcontractor as Principal," fill in the company name of the Subcontractor after "Company." The signature of the person representing the firm should be placed on the line entitled "Signature." Below the signature line, the person's name who placed their signature on the signature line should be typed or printed in along with their business title. The signature of the witness to the signature for the "Subcontractor as Principal" should be placed on the line entitled "Witness."

In the blank entitled "Surety," fill in the company name of the Surety after "Company" (not the name of the surety agent). The signature of the person representing the firm should be placed on the line entitled "Signature." Below the signature line, the person's name who placed their signature on the signature line should be typed or printed in along with their business title. It is most important that the Surety's Power of Attorney be attached. The signature of the witness should be placed on the line entitled "Witness."

In both the cases of the blanks for the signatures for the "Subcontractor as Principal" and "Surety," any additional signatures should be included on an attached sheet and this fact should be noted in the space below the line "(Any additional signatures appear on page attached)."

In the blank entitled, "For Information Only," fill in with the name, address and telephone number of the surety agent of the Subcontractor.

Figure 28–4. *(continued)*

THE ASSOCIATED GENERAL CONTRACTORS OF AMERICA

SUBCONTRACT PAYMENT BOND

Any singular reference to Principal, Surety, Obligee or other party shall be considered plural where applicable.

PRINCIPAL (SUBCONTRACTOR)   SURETY (Name and Address of Surety
(Name and Address):   Company Office):

OBLIGEE (CONTRACTOR)
(Name and Address):

SUBCONTRACT
    Date:
    Amount: $
    Description of Project (Name and Location):

BOND
    Date (Not earlier than Subcontract Date):
    Penal Amount: $

SUBCONTRACTOR AS PRINCIPAL   SURETY
Company: (Corporate Seal)   Company: (Corporate Seal)

Signature: _____   Signature: _____
Name and Title: Name and Title:
                                         Attach Power of Attorney

Witness:_____   Witness:_____
(Any additional signatures appear on page attached)

FOR INFORMATION ONLY
AGENT or BROKER:
(Name, Address and Telephone)

AGC DOCUMENT NO. 607 • SUBCONTRACT PAYMENT BOND • 1988

Figure 28–4. *(continued)*

Articles

1. **SCOPE OF BOND.** The Principal and the Surety, jointly and severally, bind themselves, their heirs, executors, administrators, successors and assigns to the Obligee to pay for labor, materials and equipment furnished for use in the performance of the Subcontract, which is incorporated in this bond by reference and pursuant to which this bond is issued. In no event shall the Surety's total obligation exceed the penal amount of this bond.

2. **EFFECT OF OBLIGATION.** If the Principal shall promptly make payment directly or indirectly to all Claimants as defined in this bond, for all labor, material and equipment used in the performance of the Subcontract, then this bond shall be null and void; otherwise it shall remain in full force and effect, subject, however, to the following conditions:

   2.1 **TIME FOR CLAIM.** The Principal and Surety hereby jointly and severally agree with the Obligee that every Claimant, who has not been paid in full before the expiration of a period of ninety (90) days after the date on which the last of such Claimant's work or labor was done or performed, or materials were furnished by such Claimant, for which claim is made, may have a right of action on this bond. The Obligee shall not be liable for the payment of any costs or expenses including attorneys' fees which the Obligee may incur in connection with its defense of any such right of action.

   2.2 **RIGHT OF ACTION.** No suit or action shall be commenced on this bond by any Claimant:

      2.2.1 Unless Claimant, other than one having a direct contract with the Principal, shall have given written notice to any two of the following: Principal, Obligee, or the Surety above named, within ninety (90) days after such Claimant did or performed the last of the work or labor, or furnished the last of the materials for which said claim is made, stating with substantial accuracy the amount claimed and the name of the party to whom the materials were furnished, or for whom the work or labor was done or performed. Such notice shall be served by mailing the same by registered mail or certified mail, postage prepaid, in an envelope addressed to the Principal, Obligee or Surety, at any place within the United States where an office is regularly maintained for the transaction of business, or served in any manner in which legal process may be served in the state in which the aforesaid Project is located, however, such service need not be made by a public officer.

      2.2.2 After the expiration of one (1) year from the date (1) on which the Claimant gave the notice required by Subparagraph 2.2.1, or (2) on which the last labor or service was performed by anyone or the last materials or equipment were furnished by anyone on the Project, whichever first occurs. Any limitation embodied in this bond, which is prohibited by any law controlling the Project, shall be deemed to be amended so as to be equal to the minimum period of limitation permitted by such law.

      2.2.3 Other than in a state court of competent jurisdiction in and for the county or other political subdivision of the state in which the Project, or any part thereof, is situated, or in the United States District Court for the district in which the Project, or any part thereof, is situated, and not elsewhere.

3. **CLAIMANT.** A Claimant is defined as an individual or entity having a direct contract with the Principal to furnish labor, materials or equipment for use in the performance of the Subcontract or any individual or entity having valid lien rights which may be asserted in the jurisdiction where the Project is located. The intent of this bond shall be to include without limitation in the terms "labor, materials or equipment" that part of water, gas, power, light, heat, oil, gasoline, telephone service or rental equipment used in the Subcontract, architectural and engineering services required for performance of the work of the Principal, and all other items for which a mechanic's lien may be asserted in the jurisdiction where the labor, materials or equipment were furnished.

4. **AMOUNT OF BOND.** The amount of this bond shall be reduced by and to the extent of any payment or payments made in good faith by the Surety.

5. **ALTERATION NOTICE WAIVER.** The Surety waives notice of any alteration or extension of the Subcontract, including but not limited to the Subcontract price and/or time, made by the Obligee. This waiver shall not apply to the time for suit provided by Paragraph 2.2 hereunder.

AGC DOCUMENT NO. 607 • SUBCONTRACT PAYMENT BOND • 1988

Figure 28–4. *(continued)*

PERFORMANCE BOND *(See Instructions on reverse)*	DATE BOND EXECUTED *(Must be same or later than date of contract)*			

PRINCIPAL *(Legal name and business address)*

TYPE OF ORGANIZATION ("X" one)

☐ INDIVIDUAL ☐ PARTNERSHIP

☐ JOINT VENTURE ☐ CORPORATION

STATE OF INCORPORATION

SURETY(IES) *(Name(s) and business address(es))*

PENAL SUM OF BOND

MILLION(S)	THOUSAND(S)	HUNDRED(S)	CENTS

CONTRACT DATE	CONTRACT NO.

OBLIGATION:

We, the Principal and Surety(ies), are firmly bound to the United States of America (hereinafter called the Government) in the above penal sum. For payment of the penal sum, we bind ourselves, our heirs, executors, administrators, and successors, jointly and severally. However, where the Sureties are corporations acting as co-sureties, we, the Sureties, bind ourselves in such sum "jointly and severally" as well as "severally" only for the purpose of allowing a joint action or actions against any or all of us. For all other purposes, each Surety binds itself, jointly and severally with the Principal, for the payment of the sum shown opposite the name of the Surety. If no limit of liability is indicated, the limit of liability is the full amount of the penal sum.

CONDITIONS:

The Principal has entered into the contract identified above.

THEREFORE:

The above obligation is void if the Principal —

(a)(1) Performs and fulfills all the undertakings, covenants, terms, conditions, and agreements of the contract during the original term of the contract and any extensions thereof that are granted by the Government, with or without notice to the Surety(ies), and during the life of any guaranty required under the contract, and (2) perform and fulfills all the undertakings, covenants, terms conditions, and agreements of any and all duly authorized modifications of the contract that hereafter are made. Notice of those modifications to the Surety(ies) are waived.

(b) Pays to the Government the full amount of the taxes imposed by the Government, if the said contract is subject to the Miller Act, (40 U.S.C. 270a-270e), which are collected, deducted, or withheld from wages paid by the Principal in carrying out the construction contract with respect to which this bond is furnished.

WITNESS:

The Principal and Surety(ies) executed this performance bond and affixed their seals on the above date.

PRINCIPAL			
Signature(s)	1.	2.	Corporate Seal
	(Seal)	*(Seal)*	
Name(s) & Title(s) *(Typed)*	1.	2.	

INDIVIDUAL SURETY(IES)			
Signature(s)	1.	2.	
	(Seal)	*(Seal)*	
Name(s) *(Typed)*	1.	2.	

CORPORATE SURETY(IES)				
SURETY A	Name & Address		STATE OF INC.	LIABILITY LIMIT $
	Signature(s)	1.	2.	Corporate Seal
	Name(s) & Title(s) *(Typed)*	1.	2.	

NSN 7540-01-152-8060
PREVIOUS EDITION USABLE

25-106

STANDARD FORM 25 (REV. 10-83)
Prescribed by GSA
FAR (48 CFR 53.228 (b))

Figure 28–5. Performance bond.

CORPORATE SURETY(IES) *(Continued)*

			STATE OF INC.	LIABILITY LIMIT	
SURETY B	Name & Address			$	Corporate Seal
	Signature(s)	1.	2.		
	Name(s) & Title(s) *(Typed)*	1.	2.		
SURETY C	Name & Address		STATE OF INC.	LIABILITY LIMIT $	Corporate Seal
	Signature(s)	1.	2.		
	Name(s) & Title(s) *(Typed)*	1.	2.		
SURETY D	Name & Address		STATE OF INC.	LIABILITY LIMIT $	Corporate Seal
	Signature(s)	1.	2.		
	Name(s) & Title(s) *(Typed)*	1.	2.		
SURETY E	Name & Address		STATE OF INC.	LIABILITY LIMIT $	Corporate Seal
	Signature(s)	1.	2.		
	Name(s) & Title(s) *(Typed)*	1.	2.		
SURETY F	Name & Address		STATE OF INC.	LIABILITY LIMIT $	Corporate Seal
	Signature(s)	1.	2.		
	Name(s) & Title(s) *(Typed)*	1.	2.		
SURETY G	Name & Address		STATE OF INC.	LIABILITY LIMIT $	Corporate Seal
	Signature(s)	1.	2.		
	Name(s) & Title(s) *(Typed)*	1.	2.		

BOND PREMIUM ▶	RATE PER THOUSAND $	TOTAL $

INSTRUCTIONS

1. This form is authorized for use in connection with Government contracts. Any deviation from this form will require the written approval of the Administrator of General Services.

2. Insert the full legal name and business address of the Principal in the space designated "Principal" on the face of the form. An authorization person shall sign the bond. Any person signing in a representative capacity (e.g., an attorney-in-fact) must furnish evidence of authority if that representative is not a member of the firm, partnership, or joint venture, or an officer of the corporation involved.

3. (a) Corporations executing the bond as sureties must appear on the Department of the Treasury's list of approved sureties and must act within the limitation listed therein. Where more than one corporate surety is involved, their names and addresses shall appear in the spaces (Surety A, Surety B, etc.) headed "CORPORATE SURETY(IES)". In the space designated "SURETY(IES)" on the face of the form insert only the letter identification of the sureties.

(b) Where individual sureties are involved, two or more responsible persons shall execute the bond. A completed Affidavit of Individual Surety (Standard Form 28), for each individual surety, shall accompany the bond. The Government may require these sureties to furnish additional substantiating information concerning their financial capability.

4. Corporations executing the bond shall affix their corporate seals. Individuals shall execute the bond opposite the word "Corporate Seal"; and shall affix an adhesive seal if executed in Maine, New Hampshire, or any other jurisdiction requiring adhesive seals.

5. Type the name and title of each person signing this bond in the space provided.

STANDARD FORM 25 BACK (REV. 10-83)
☆ GPO : 1984 O – 421-526 (94)

Figure 28–5. *(continued)*

liability arising from personal injury or property damage incurred by the defaulted contractor in the course of performing a site cleanup contract. Congress recognized the potential problem and included a provision in the FY 1992 and 1993 Defense Authorization Act by: (1) making surety bonds a requirement for any direct federal procurement of a contract for a response action under the Defense Environmental Restoration Program, and (2) providing that the performance bond surety is not liable for personal injury or property damage whether or not caused by a breach of the bonded contract.[5]

§ 28.6 Labor and Material Payment Bonds

A labor and material payment bond is a guarantee to the owner that the tradespeople hired by the prime contractor to work on the project, the subcontractors, and certain material suppliers (to first tier subcontractors, for the most part) on a project will be paid if they are not paid by the prime contractor, regardless of the payment status or problems between the general contractor and owner. In addition to benefiting the subcontractors and suppliers, payment bonds can protect the owner from liens that would otherwise be initiated by subcontractors or suppliers who were not paid by the general contractor. The protection of a payment bond is also available to general contractors and subcontractors.

The payment bond forms must be read carefully and in conjunction with applicable federal or state laws by anyone wishing to submit a claim thereunder. **Figure 28–6**, a private Labor and Material Payment Bond form, also sanctioned by the American Institute of Architects, addresses who may be a claimant, who may sue, where and when, and what conditions on time of action apply.

Figure 28–7, the Associated General Contractors' Subcontract Payment Bond, contains essentially the same provisions dealing with time limits for entitlement and action, who may claim, and where suit may be brought.[6] Due to the evolution of the law over the past decade or more, both payment bond forms identify utility and rental equipment suppliers as having rights to claim under the payment bonds.

The federal form, **Figure 28–8**, appears to be more restrictive in limiting claimants to "all persons having a direct relationship with the Principal (General Contractor) or a subcontractor of the Principal."[7] Again, the federal form provides specifically for multiple sureties.

---

[5] Defense Authorization Act for FY 1992 & 1993, Pub. L. No. 102-190, § 336 (1991) (to be codified at 10 U.S.C. § 2701(h)-(j)).

[6] AGC Doc. 607, Subcontractor Payment Bond (1988).

[7] FAR 53.228(c) (GSA Standard Form No. 25-A, Payment Bond).

Labor And Material Payment Bond

(NOTE: THIS BOND IS ISSUED SIMULTANEOUSLY WITH
PERFORMANCE BOND ON PAGE 1, IN FAVOR OF THE
OWNER CONDITIONED FOR THE FULL AND FAITHFUL
PERFORMANCE OF THE CONTRACT.)

THE HARTFORD

KNOW ALL MEN BY THESE PRESENTS:

That ....
(Here insert the name and address, or legal title, of the Contractor)

as Principal, hereinafter called Principal, and the..., a
corporation organized and existing under the laws of the State of.. , with
its principal office in the City of .... , as Surety, hereinafter called
Surety, are held and firmly bound unto...

....
(Here insert the name and address, or legal title, of the Owner)

as Obligee, hereinafter called Owner, for the use and benefit of claimants as hereinbelow defined, in the amount
of ....
(Here insert a sum equal to at least one-half of the contract price)

.... Dollars ($..................................),
for the payment whereof Principal, and Surety bind themselves, their heirs, executors, administrators, successors,
and assigns, jointly and severally, firmly by these presents.

    Whereas, Principal has by written agreement dated...
entered into a contract with Owner for ....
....
in accordance with drawings and specifications prepared by ....
....
(Here insert full name, title and address)

which contract is by reference made a part hereof, and is hereinafter referred to as the CONTRACT.

    Now, therefore, the condition of this obligation is such that, if the Principal shall promptly make payment to
all claimants as hereinafter defined, for all labor and material used or reasonably required for use in the performance of the CONTRACT, then this obligation shall be void; otherwise it shall remain in full force and effect,
subject, however, to the following conditions:

1. A claimant is defined as one having a direct contract with the Principal or with a sub-contractor of the
   Principal for labor, material, or both, used or reasonably required for use in the performance of the contract,
   labor and material being construed to include that part of water, gas, power, light, heat, oil, gasoline,
   telephone service or rental of equipment directly applicable to the CONTRACT.

2. The above named Principal and Surety hereby jointly and severally agree with the Owner that every claimant as herein defined, who has not been paid in full before the expiration of a period of ninety (90) days
   after the date on which the last of such claimant's work or labor was done or performed, or materials were
   furnished by such claimant, may sue on this bond for the use of such claimant, prosecute the suit to final
   judgment for such sum or sums as may be justly due claimant, and have execution thereon. The Owner
   shall not be liable for the payment of any costs or expenses of any such suit.

3. No suit or action shall be commenced hereunder by any claimant,

(a) Unless claimant, other than one having a direct contract with the Principal, shall have given written notice to
    any two of the following: The Principal, the Owner, or the Surety above named, within ninety (90) days after
    such claimant did or performed the last of the work or labor, or furnished the last of the materials for which
    said claim is made, stating with substantial accuracy the amount claimed and the name of the party to
    whom the materials were furnished, or for whom the work or labor was done or performed. Such notice
    shall be served by mailing the same by registered mail or certified mail, postage prepaid, in an envelope
    addressed to the Principal, Owner or Surety, at any place where an office is regularly maintained for the
    transaction of business, or served in any manner in which legal process may be served in the state in which
    the aforesaid project is located, save that such service need not be made by a public officer.

(b) After the expiration of one (1) year following the date on which Principal ceased work on said CONTRACT,
    it being understood, however, that if any limitation embodied in this bond is prohibited by any law controlling
    the construction hereof, such limitation shall be deemed to be amended so as to be equal to the minimum
    period of limitation permitted by such law.

(c) Other than in a state court of competent jurisdiction in and for the county or other political subdivision of the
    state in which the project, or any part thereof, is situated, or in the United States District Court for the
    district in which the project, or any part thereof, is situated, and not elsewhere.

4. The amount of this bond shall be reduced by and to the extent of any payment or payments made in good
   faith hereunder, inclusive of the payment by Surety of mechanics' liens which may be filed of record against
   said improvement, whether or not claim for the amount of such lien be presented under and against this
   bond.

Signed and sealed this   day of   A. D. 19

	PRINCIPAL	(Corporate Seal)
Witness (If Individual/Partnership)	Name	
Attest (If Corporation)	Signature	
	By:	
	Typed Name and Title	
	SURETY	(Corporate Seal)
Attest	Name	
	Signature	
	By:	
	Typed Name	
		Attorney-in-fact

Form S-3213-5   **Page 2**   Printed in U.S.A.
(A.I.A. Form — Document No. A-311. February, 1970 Edition. Approved by The American Institute of Architects)

Figure 28–6. Labor and Material Payment bond. Reprinted with permission.

THE ASSOCIATED GENERAL CONTRACTORS OF AMERICA

SUBCONTRACT PERFORMANCE BOND

TABLE OF ARTICLES

1. SCOPE OF BOND

2. EFFECT OF OBLIGATION

3. ALTERATION NOTICE WAIVER

4. PRINCIPAL DEFAULT

5. TIME FOR SUIT

6. RIGHT OF ACTION

This document has important legal and surety consequences. AGC encourages consultation with an attorney and surety consultant when completing or modifying this document.

Figure 28–7. Subcontract Performance bond. Represented with permission of the Associated General Contractors of America (AGC). Copies of current forms may be obtained from AGC's Publications Department, 1957 E Street, NW, Washington, D.C. 20006, (202) 393-2040.

Special Instructions

NAMES AND ADDRESSES: The legal name and address of the Principal should be filled in. The Principal is the Subcontractor who provides the Subcontract Performance Bond to the Obligee who is the Contractor.

The legal name and address of the Obligee, who is the Contractor, should be filled in.

The legal name of the Surety should be filled in along with the address of the Surety's office after "Surety (Name and Address of Surety Company Office)." This name and address of the Surety is **not** the name and address of the surety agent.

In the blank for information on the Subcontract, the effective date of the Subcontract should be filled in with the day, month and year when the Subcontract is to become effective. The amount of the Subcontract, stated in both Arabic numerals and words, should be filled in after "Amount." After "Description of Project," the name and address of the project where the Subcontract will be performed should be filled in.

In the blank for information on the Bond, the date blank should be filled in with the day, month and year the Bond is to become effective. This date is not to be earlier than the effective date of the Subcontract. After "Penal Amount," fill in the amount, stated in both Arabic numerals and words, for which the Principal and Surety will be obligated.

In the blank "Subcontractor as Principal," fill in the company name of the Subcontractor after "Company." The signature of the person representing the firm should be placed on the line entitled "Signature." Below the signature line, the person's name who placed their signature on the signature line should be typed or printed in along with their business title. The signature of the witness to the signature for the "Subcontractor as Principal" should be placed on the line entitled "Witness."

In the blank entitled "Surety," fill in the company name of the Surety after "Company" (not the name of the surety agent). The signature of the person representing the firm should be placed on the line entitled "Signature." Below the signature line, the person's name who placed their signature on the signature line should be typed or printed in along with their business title. It is most important that the Surety's Power of Attorney be attached. The signature of the witness should be placed on the line entitled "Witness."

In both the cases of the blanks for the signatures for the "Subcontractor as Principal" and "Surety," any additional signatures should be included on an attached sheet and this fact should be noted in the space below the line "(Any additional signatures appear on page attached)."

In the blank entitled, "For Information Only," fill in with the name, address and telephone number of the surety agent of the Subcontractor.

Figure 28–7. *(continued)*

THE ASSOCIATED GENERAL CONTRACTORS OF AMERICA

SUBCONTRACT
PERFORMANCE BOND

Any singular reference to Principal, Surety, Obligee or other party shall be considered plural where applicable.

PRINCIPAL (SUBCONTRACTOR)   SURETY (Name and Address of Surety
(Name and Address):   Company Office):

OBLIGEE (CONTRACTOR)
(Name and Address):

SUBCONTRACT
    Date:
    Amount: $
    Description of Project (Name and Location):

BOND
    Date (Not earlier than Subcontract Date):
    Penal Amount $

SUBCONTRACTOR AS PRINCIPAL   SURETY
Company: (Corporate Seal) Company: (Corporate Seal)

Signature: _____   Signature: _____
Name and Title: Name and Title:
                                             Attach Power of Attorney

Witness: _____   Witness: _____
(Any additional signatures appear on page attached)

FOR INFORMATION ONLY
AGENT or BROKER:
(Name, Address and Telephone)

AGC DOCUMENT NO. 606 • SUBCONTRACT PERFORMANCE BOND • 1988

Figure 28–7. *(continued)*

Articles

1. **SCOPE OF BOND.** The Principal and the Surety, jointly and severally, bind themselves, their heirs, executors, administrators, successors and assigns to the Obligee for the performance of the Subcontract, which is incorporated in this bond by reference. In no event shall the Surety's total obligation exceed the penal amount of this bond.

2. **EFFECT OF OBLIGATION.** If the Principal performs the Subcontract, then this bond shall be null and void; otherwise it shall remain in full force and effect.

3. **ALTERATION NOTICE WAIVER.** The Surety hereby waives notice of any alteration or extension of the Subcontract, including but not limited to the Subcontract price and/or time, made by the Obligee. This waiver shall not apply to the time for suit provided by paragraph 5 hereunder.

4. **PRINCIPAL DEFAULT.** Whenever the Principal shall be, and is declared by the Obligee to be in default under the Subcontract, with the Obligee having performed its obligations in the Subcontract, the Surety may promptly remedy the default, or shall promptly:

   4.1 **COMPLETE SUBCONTRACT.** Complete the Subcontract in accordance with its terms and conditions; or

   4.2 **OBTAIN NEW CONTRACTORS.** Obtain a bid or bids formally, informally or negotiated for completing the Subcontract in accordance with its terms and conditions, and upon determination by the Surety of the lowest responsible bidder, or negotiated proposal, or, if the Obligee elects, upon determination by the Obligee and the Surety jointly of the lowest responsible bidder, or negotiated proposal, arrange for a contract between such party and the Obligee. The Surety will make available as work progresses sufficient funds to pay the cost of completion less the balance of the contract price. The cost of completion includes responsibilities of the Principal for correction of defective work and completion of the Subcontract; the Obligee's legal and design professional costs resulting directly from the Principal's default, and; liquidated damages or actual damages if no liquidated damages are specified in the Subcontract. The term "balance of the contract price," as used in this paragraph, shall mean the total amount payable by the Obligee to the Principal under the Subcontract and any amendments to it, less the amount properly paid by the Obligee to the principal; or

   4.3 **PAY OBLIGEE.** Determine the amount for which it is liable to the Obligee and pay the Obligee that amount as soon as practicable; or

   4.4 **DENY LIABILITY.** Deny its liability in whole or in part and notify and explain to the Obligee the reasons why the Surety believes it does not have responsibility for this liability.

5. **TIME FOR SUIT.** Any suit under this bond must be instituted before the expiration of two (2) years from the date of substantial completion as established by the contract documents.

6. **RIGHT OF ACTION.** No right of action shall accrue on this bond to or for the use of any person or entity other than the Obligee named herein, its heirs, executors, administrators or successors.

AGC DOCUMENT NO. 606 • SUBCONTRACT PERFORMANCE BOND • 1988

Figure 28–7. *(continued)*

PAYMENT BOND *(See Instructions on reverse)*	DATE BOND EXECUTED *(Must be same or later than date of contract)*			
PRINCIPAL *(Legal name and business address)*	TYPE OF ORGANIZATION ("X" one)			
	☐ INDIVIDUAL ☐ PARTNERSHIP			
	☐ JOINT VENTURE ☐ CORPORATION			
	STATE OF INCORPORATION			
SURETY(IES) *(Name(s) and business address(es))*	PENAL SUM OF BOND			
	MILLION(S)	THOUSAND(S)	HUNDRED(S)	CENTS
	CONTRACT DATE	CONTRACT NO.		

OBLIGATION:

We, the Principal and Surety(ies), are firmly bound to the United States of America (hereinafter called the Government) in the above penal sum. For payment of the penal sum, we bind ourselves, our heirs, executors, administrators, and successors, jointly and severally. However, where the Sureties are corporations acting as co-sureties, we, the Sureties, bind ourselves in such sum "jointly and severally" as well as "severally" only for the purpose of allowing a joint action or actions against any or all of us. For all other purposes, each Surety binds itself, jointly and severally with the Principal, for the payment of the sum shown opposite the name of the Surety. If no limit of liability is indicated, the limit of liability is the full amount of the penal sum.

CONDITIONS:

The above obligation is void if the Principal promptly makes payment to all persons having a direct relationship with the Principal or a subcontractor of the Principal for furnishing labor, material or both in the prosecution of the work provided for in the contract identified above, and any authorized modifications of the contract that subsequently are made. Notice of those modifications to the Surety(ies) are waived.

WITNESS:

The Principal and Surety(ies) executed this payment bond and affixed their seals on the above date.

		PRINCIPAL		
Signature(s)	1.	2. (Seal)	(Seal)	*Corporate Seal*
Name(s) & Title(s) (Typed)	1.	2.		
		INDIVIDUAL SURETY(IES)		
Signature(s)	1.	2. (Seal)		(Seal)
Name(s) (Typed)	1.	2.		
		CORPORATE SURETY(IES)		
SURETY A	Name & Address		STATE OF INC.	LIABILITY LIMIT $
	Signature(s)	1.	2.	*Corporate Seal*
	Name(s) & Title(s) (Typed)	1.	2.	

NSN 7540-01-152-8061
PREVIOUS EDITION USABLE

25-204

STANDARD FORM 25-A (REV. 10-83)
Prescribed by GSA
FAR (48 CFR 53.228(c))

Figure 28–8. Payment bond.

CORPORATE SURETY(IES) *(Continued)*

			STATE OF INC.	LIABILITY LIMIT	
SURETY B	Name & Address		STATE OF INC.	$	Corporate Seal
	Signature(s)	1.	2.		
	Name(s) & Title(s) *(Typed)*	1.	2.		
SURETY C	Name & Address		STATE OF INC.	$	Corporate Seal
	Signature(s)	1.	2.		
	Name(s) & Title(s) *(Typed)*	1.	2.		
SURETY D	Name & Address		STATE OF INC.	$	Corporate Seal
	Signature(s)	1.	2.		
	Name(s) & Title(s) *(Typed)*	1.	2.		
SURETY E	Name & Address		STATE OF INC.	$	Corporate Seal
	Signature(s)	1.	2.		
	Name(s) & Title(s) *(Typed)*	1.	2.		
SURETY F	Name & Address		STATE OF INC.	$	Corporate Seal
	Signature(s)	1.	2.		
	Name(s) & Title(s) *(Typed)*	1.	2.		
SURETY G	Name & Address		STATE OF INC.	$	Corporate Seal
	Signature(s)	1.	2.		
	Name(s) & Title(s) *(Typed)*	1.	2.		

INSTRUCTIONS

1. This form, for the protection of persons supplying labor and material, is used when a payment bond is required under the Act of August 24, 1935, 49 Stat. 793 (40 U.S.C. 270 a–270e). Any deviation from this form will require the written approval of the Administrator of General Services.

2. Insert the full legal name and business address of the Principal in the space designated "Principal" on the face of the form. An authorized person shall sign the bond. Any person signing in a representative capacity (e.g., an attorney-in-fact) must furnish evidence of authority if that representative is not a member of the firm, partnership, or joint venture, or an officer of the corporation involved.

3. (a) Corporations executing the bond as sureties must appear on the Department of the Treasury's list of approved sureties and must act within the limitation listed therein. Where more than one corporate surety is involved, their names and addresses shall appear in the spaces (Surety A, Surety B, etc.) headed "CORPORATE SURETY(IES)". In the space designated "SURETY(IES)" on the face of the form, insert only the letter identification of the sureties.

(b) Where individual sureties are involved, two or more responsible persons shall execute the bond. A completed Affidavit of Individual Surety (Standard Form 28), for each individual surety, shall accompany the bond. The Government may require these sureties to furnish additional substantiating information concerning their financial capability.

4. Corporations executing the bond shall affix their corporate seals. Individuals shall execute the bond opposite the word "Corporate Seal"; and shall affix an adhesive seal if executed in Maine, New Hampshire, or any other jurisdiction regarding adhesive seals.

5. Type the name and title of each person signing this bond in the space provided.

STANDARD FORM 25-A BACK (REV. 10-83)

☆ GPO : 1984 O – 421-526 (97)

Figure 28–8. *(continued)*

TYPES OF OWNER

§ 28.7   Federal Government

Federal construction projects are covered by the Miller Act,[8] which requires performance and payment bonds on all projects that involve construction, alteration, or repair of a "public building" or "public work" in excess of $25,000.[9] Demolition contracts are not included in this definition. The Act's performance bond protects only the government, not subcontractors or other creditors.

§ 28.8   State Government and Private Party Owners

Each state has adopted a statute that is based on the Miller Act. These "Little Miller Acts," however, differ from the federal statute in many ways. A contractor should check the current version of the statute in effect in the state where the prime contract is to be performed in order to determine the terms that will apply to the contractor's project. For example, some statutes only apply to contracts with the state government, while others also cover contracts with other political entities within the state.

Private party owners generally are free to adopt whatever terms for a project that they feel are appropriate to provide the protection they feel is necessary.

MAKING A CLAIM ON PAYMENT BOND

§ 28.9   Filing the Claim

When a subcontractor or supplier concludes that the prime contractor has failed to honor its contractual obligation to pay for work done on a construction project, and the appropriate time frames for action exist, the subcontractor should file a claim against the payment bond.

---

[8] 40 U.S.C. §§ 270a-270f (1988).
[9] *Id.* § 270a(a).

Investigation

First, the subcontractor should investigate the matter. This investigation should include collecting key documents and identifying all the individuals who know the relevant facts—those employed by the subcontractor, the prime contractor, and any other involved parties. This investigation should be done as soon as possible after the claimant realizes it may have a claim under the bond because of the tendency of people in the construction industry to relocate.

Copy of the Bond

The next step in the process is to obtain a copy of the bond and to become familiar with its terms. There is no longer a requirement for the party requesting a copy of the bond to submit an affidavit in a specific format, but the particular contracting office may have its own requirements for information that it may want to see or be furnished before furnishing a copy of the bond. The requesting party should ask about what is needed upon making the request. There may be a charge involved for a certified copy.

If a Miller Act contract is involved, to obtain a copy of the payment bond it is necessary to contact the contracting officer or legal counsel at the federal agency that awarded the contract. For example, the contracting officer's representative under GSA contracts is charged by that agency to maintain copies of the bonds. The Office of the Comptroller General of the United States, which was the repository of bonds in prior years, is no longer responsible for providing copies.

Notice Requirements

The subcontractor or supplier should then initiate its claim by notifying the surety in writing. Careful review should be made of the bond requirements concerning who must be given notice of claim, because notice, if required, generally must be given to more than one party, such as the surety and owner or principal. To the extent possible, the material submitted at this time should include a fairly detailed explanation of the claim, paying particular attention to the facts that prove the subcontractor or supplier is entitled to recover and that prove the amount of damage that has been sustained. Copies of all the relevant documents and submitted invoices should be included.

Including each of these items in the notice is the ideal. In reality, however, and depending upon the size of the claim in dispute, gathering all this information may well require a significant amount of time and effort. Bond claims are subject to important time limits that, if ignored, could destroy the claimant's right to recover. Therefore, subcontractors and suppliers must balance the advantages of presenting a comprehensive claim package initially against the time constraints involved. It is clearly more important to assert the claim in a timely manner. As long as all the basic information is covered, that should be sufficient. Therefore, the claimant should submit as much material as possible within the time available and then supplement this initial submission, if necessary, as more information becomes available. The notice requirement will have been met if the surety or principal (the general contractor) or owner is aware of the minimum information. This basic data are addressed further under the discussion of notice in § 28.12.

Generally, no special format for notice is required. The claim, however, should be submitted in such a way that the contractor can prove receipt by the surety, such as by certified mail, return receipt requested. Hand delivery is also a good method of delivery, so long as the claimant can prove the date the surety and the others received the claim. A stamped receipt or copy of the transmittal letter is sufficient.

Examination of the Claim

Once the surety and owner or general contractor receives the claim, it either denies liability, or accepts liability, pays the claimant any amount that it concedes is due, and usually enters into negotiations directly or confers with the general contractor about resolving any disputed amounts of the claim. In any event, the surety may request additional information from the claimant. In addition to responding to these requests, the claimant should, on its own initiative, supplement its initial claim with additional materials (such as copies of documents or updated calculations on the damages sustained) as these become available. If the claim is particularly complicated or a large sum of money is involved, the claimant should consider retaining an attorney experienced in construction claims to prepare the claim and negotiate or litigate, as appropriate.

If the surety refuses to pay the claimant, or the amount offered in settlement negotiations is insufficient, the subcontractor should consider bringing a lawsuit against the surety. Some states have statutes that require the surety to make a good faith examination of the claim and not summarily dismiss it. A failure to do so could subject the surety to treble damages.

§ 28.10   Potential Claimants

Although payment bonds provide important protection for subcontractors and suppliers, there are certain defined limits to the categories of potential claimants who can bring a claim under a bond.

Under the Miller Act

The Miller Act for federal contracts differentiates between first tier, second tier, and third tier claimants. Generally, all first tier claimants—subcontractors and suppliers that have a contract directly with the prime contractor as well as the prime contractor's employees—can bring a claim. At the third tier level, the general rule is that no person or company is allowed to bring a claim, although there are some very limited exceptions. At the second tier level, the rules are somewhat complicated.

First, it is clear that subcontractors and suppliers of a first tier *supplier* have no right to bring a claim under a Miller Act payment bond. The Miller Act defines *subcontractor* as an entity to which the prime contractor has assigned responsibility for a specific portion of the project, whereas a *supplier* is an entity that provides material or labor to the prime contractor to enable the prime contractor to perform.[10] A key factor is responsibility for work on the site. When the prime contractor has delegated overall responsibility for the actual performance of some aspect of the project to a subordinate entity, that entity is a subcontractor. When the prime contractor has retained responsibility, the entity is a supplier. The following factors, among others, have been used by the courts to determine whether a claimant was a subcontractor or supplier:

1. How the entity with whom the prime contractor has a contract is referred to in the contract document, as a subcontractor or supplier
2. Whether actual work is to be done on the site
3. Whether some clauses in the contract document are only applicable to a subcontractor. For example, scheduling, coordination with other trades, qualified superintendents, and wage minimums such as those required by the Davis-Bacon Act normally would be applicable only to subcontracts.

Second, it is clear that subcontractors and suppliers of a first tier *subcontractor* are entitled to bring a claim on a Miller Act payment bond. Nevertheless, it is unclear whether employees of a first tier subcontractor are entitled to bring a claim, although one Supreme Court case suggests that these employees would be entitled to bring a claim.[11] There have been a number of recent attempts to broaden the scope of those entitled to claim under the federal Miller Act bonds. However, these attempts have not been successful. Contractors and bonding companies should review individual state laws to determine which people and entities are covered by payment bonds at the state level.

---

[10] *See id.* § 270b(a).

[11] *See* J.W. Bateson Co. v. United States *ex rel.* Bd. of Trustees, 434 U.S. 586 (1978).

Under the Little Miller Acts

State statutes provide varying degrees of protection for subcontractors and suppliers. Although some follow the federal Miller Act, many others differ to one extent or another. A solid understanding of the state statute that applies, as interpreted by the courts of that state, is therefore critical.

Many state statutes differ in how they define subcontractors. Some require a claimant to have performed some work at the jobsite in order to be protected. In addition, the "tier" issue, which plays such an important role under the Miller Act, also applies at the state level. Although the tier analysis that has developed under the Miller Act generally applies under state Little Miller Acts, many variations exist that allow many other tiers to be protected. People or entities covered by state payment bond requirements are those having a direct contract with the principal or subcontractor of the principal to provide labor or materials or both required in the performance of the contract, including companies providing water, power, light, gasoline, and telephone service.

Under a Private Bond

Because private parties generally are free to adopt whatever terms they feel are appropriate to provide the protection they feel is necessary, the terms of their bond determine whether a potential claimant will be able to recover if the prime contractor fails to pay the parties for work done. It is therefore critical for all subcontractors and suppliers to obtain a copy of the applicable payment bond at the beginning of their involvement on a project, perhaps even before they have submitted their bid in order to assure that they have some protection in their bid price in the event they are not covered by the bond.

The subcontractor or supplier should closely analyze the bond and its requirements as early in the process as possible, preferably before problems arise or shortly thereafter. Strict compliance with the terms of the bond must be a top priority if the claimant hopes to recover under the bond. Claimants under private bonds frequently have an advantage, however, because they may have additional ways to obtain relief, such as filing a claim under the state's mechanic's lien statute.

§ 28.11   Time Frame for Filing Claim

There is no hard and fast rule about the earliest date on which a subcontractor or supplier can file a claim. However, the language contained in the Miller Act and in most labor and material bonds identifies the 90-day period after the last labor has been performed or material furnished to the project site as the critical period for notice to the surety, principal, or owner. When installments are involved, for which separate performance and billing are done, some jurisdictions hold that a separate claim and notice must be submitted for each unpaid installment or the right to pursue the bond is waived. This is not the federal law, however.

§ 28.12 Notice for Bringing Claim

A claimant may be required to notify one or more parties in order to bring a claim. These parties are usually two of the three directly affected by the proposed action on the bond—the surety, the principal, or the owner. Failure to satisfy the applicable notice provisions makes it impossible for the claimant to recover under the bond, that is, against the surety and the public owner.

Under the Miller Act

The Miller Act does not require a claimant who has a contract directly with the prime contractor to give notice in order to make a claim under the bond or to institute litigation against the surety. Claimants that do not have a direct contract with the prime contractor, however—such as sub-subcontractors—are required to provide notice of their claims not later than 90 days after they complete work on the project, as noted in § **28.11**. Notice cannot be given, however, prior to completion of the claimant's portion of the project.

Notice must be given in writing. The writing should clearly identify the contract, project, and parties involved, and should include a concise discussion of the facts that establish the claimant's entitlement. It must state that the claimant may assert a claim, and must include the following information:

1. Amount owed the claimant, identified as precisely and accurately as possible. Calculations that produced the amount owed should be included, for example, total contract price, prior amounts paid, and retainage withheld.
2. Relationship between the claimant and the prime contractor.
3. Fact that the claimant may pursue payment from the prime contractor or surety.

Note that there are no standard forms required to file a claim, and that the notice does not have to meet the precise formality of a mechanic's lien claim. In most cases the claim under the bond will not come as a surprise to the parties, as there will probably have been extensive correspondence and other communications regarding nonpayment by the time formal notice is given.

The Miller Act requires that notice be given by registered mail. Some courts have held that other methods (such as regular mail) are sufficient; however registered mail should be used in order to ensure that the method used to give notice is not an issue and to confirm receipt of the notice, to the extent possible.

Under the Little Miller Acts

If a state project is involved, the contractor must check the applicable state statute. Some state statutes follow the provisions of the Miller Act closely; others vary greatly from the federal statute. Many only require notice to the prime contractor; others require notice to several parties.

Some states use a "dual notice" approach. Under this system, a subcontractor (or supplier) typically must notify the prime contractor at about the time the project begins that the subcontractor intends to rely on the payment bond for protection. If the prime contractor fails to pay, the subcontractor must then provide a second notice, which is similar to the single notice provided under the Miller Act.

Under a Private Bond

For private construction projects, the contractor must check the bond itself for notice requirements because its terms will control. Many private bonds require second tier subcontractors and suppliers to give notice to any two of the following: the prime contractor, the owner, and the surety.

§ 28.13   Initiating a Lawsuit

If the surety refuses to honor the claim, or the parties are unable to reach a mutually acceptable result through negotiation, the claimant must initiate a lawsuit to recover the funds it is owed by the prime contractor. An attorney must be retained to initiate a suit on behalf of any corporation, if that becomes necessary. It is suggested that an attorney also be retained to evaluate the merits of the lawsuit before it is filed because frivolous suits can cause courts to award sanctions, including attorneys' fees, against a party who brings such a suit. Note that the subcontractor can sue the surety directly and that the subcontractor is not required to involve the prime contractor in any way.

When Can You Sue?

Under the Miller Act, a claimant can initiate a lawsuit if it has not been paid in full for the work it did on a construction project once 90 days have passed from the date the claimant completed work on the project.[12] State Little Miller Acts vary widely, however. Although some follow the Miller Act, others use the same basic approach but have a different time period that must pass before a suit can be filed. Other states have adopted a completely different approach, using completion of the project as the milestone that must pass before a suit can be initiated. For private bonds, the terms of the bond will be controlling.

When Must You Sue?

Under the Miller Act, the subcontractor must file its lawsuit not later than one year from the date that it completed work on the project.[13] The Little Miller Acts vary tremendously from the federal statute; both the time period for filing suit and the date the period starts running can differ from the federal law. For private bonds, the time period and date the limitations period begins to run may be specified in the bond. Otherwise, the general state statute of limitations for actions based on a contract applies.

Where Can You Sue?

Under the Miller Act the suit must be brought in the United States District Court closest to the location of the project. A suit on a state project under the state's Little Miller Act should be brought in the court specified in that state's statute. This will typically be the state court of general jurisdiction.

A bond covering a private construction project may specify the court(s) in which a suit can be initiated. For example, the standard form payment bond published by the American Institute of Architects (AIA) specifies that a suit can be brought in a state or federal court that has jurisdiction over the area where all or part of the work was performed.[14]

If the bond does not address this issue, the claimant may have some choices concerning where it can sue, subject to certain rules. Under the "sue them where you find them" concept, the claimant may be able to initiate a lawsuit in the state court of general jurisdiction that is responsible for any geographic area in which the defendant surety operates. At a minimum, this will include the area in which the construction project is

---

[12] 40 U.S.C. § 270b(a).

[13] *Id.* § 270b(b).

[14] AIA Doc. A311, Labor and Material Payment Bond, para. 3(c) (Feb. 1990).

located; the surety's agreement to provide a bond for this project constitutes "presence" that justifies adjudicating a lawsuit in this area. "Presence" would be defined by the particular state's statutes and these statutes should be consulted before a suit is initiated.

Alternatively, the claimant may be able to sue the surety in another area in which the surety does business. The claimant also may have the option of bringing its suit in a federal district court, provided there is diversity between the parties. A construction litigation attorney should be consulted to determine what options are available and the advantages and disadvantages of each. Normally, any limitation in the contract between the prime contractor and the claimant (subcontractor or supplier) concerning where a lawsuit could be brought will apply only to suits between those parties and will not limit the claimant's choice of where to sue the surety. Federal and state statutes that mandate the use of payment bonds make provision for court jurisdiction should suits be brought against sureties that have provided bonds pursuant to those statutes.[15]

§ 28.14   Types of Recoverable Damages

The general rule is that a claimant can recover all costs of labor, material, equipment, and supplies it incurred that were necessary and required for completion of its contract or subcontract.

Under the Miller Act

Under the Miller Act, the claimant can only recover for the cost of labor or material that was used "in the prosecution of the work" on the project.[16] The courts have applied a liberal standard here, however, and the claimant must only prove that it provided the labor or material with the reasonable expectation that it would be used by the recipient on the project at issue— the claimant does not need to prove that the labor or material it provided was actually used on the project at issue.[17]

The cost of equipment purchased specifically for the project at issue can be recovered only if it was "substantially consumed" on the project. Similarly, the cost of repairing equipment that was damaged during the project is recoverable, but only if the repairs enabled the equipment to be used on the project. If the repairs were done primarily to enable the claimant to use

---

[15] *See, e.g.,* 40 U.S.C. § 270b(b).

[16] *Id.* § 270b(a).

[17] United States *ex rel.* Consol. Pipe & Supply Co. v. Morrison-Knudson Co., 687 F.2d 129 (5th Cir. 1982); United Bonding Ins. Co. v. Catalytic Constr. Co., 533 F.2d 469 (9th Cir. 1976).

the equipment on subsequent projects, the cost will not be recoverable. The cost of rental equipment used in the performance of the contract is usually recoverable under most payment bonds.[18]

The general rule is that delay damages are not recoverable. A few court decisions, however, have allowed claimants to recover delay damages. Only the District Court for the District of Columbia has allowed claimants to recover delay damages in situations in which the subcontract did not specifically provide for such a recovery.[19]

Attorneys' fees and lost profits are not recoverable unless the contract or a relevant statute specifically authorizes them. Extended overhead costs that result from a change in the work done under the contract should be recoverable unless the contract with the federal government clearly prohibits the prime contractor from recovering this type of expense. An example of this situation would be certain contracts issued by the GSA that permit overhead percentage markups only.

Under the Little Miller Acts

The Little Miller Acts generally follow the federal statute in allowing recovery for the cost of labor and of material that was delivered to the jobsite and which the claimant believed would be used on the project, even if the material was not actually used on the project. The Little Miller Acts vary substantially with regard to the types of costs that are recoverable. Two of the most significant areas in which state laws diverge from the Miller Act are interest on the claim and attorneys' fees. Many Little Miller Acts allow claimants to recover some or all of these costs, at least under certain circumstances, although the federal Act does not.

Under a Private Bond

Unless prohibited by the bond itself, the claimant should be able to recover all costs of labor and material that the claimant reasonably incurred in performing its subcontract. The language of the bond is not precise in this area and it is appropriate to review the applicable decided cases to determine if the cost category in question has been the subject of a prior decision.

---

[18] *See* AIA Doc. A311, Labor and Material Payment Bond, para. 3(c) (Feb. 1990).

[19] *See, e.g.,* United States *ex rel.* Heller Elec. Co. v. William F. Klingensmith, Inc., 670 F.2d 1227, 1231–32 (D.C. Cir. 1982); United States *ex rel.* Mariana v. Piracci Constr. Co., 405 F. Supp. 904 (D.D.C. 1975).

§ 28.15 Summary Checklist

If a contractor's company is a claimant or potential claimant on a construction project, it should take the following steps, in light of the discussion in this chapter:

_____ Obtain a copy of the labor and material payment bond or bonds (depending on the contractor's status in the respective tiers of contractors) and become thoroughly familiar with the requirements

_____ Send the requisite notice to all necessary parties

_____ Be certain that the notice is as specific and detailed as the facts permit and be aware of the costs that can and cannot be the subject of a payment bond claim

_____ Be certain to observe the time limitations imposed by the bond or the statutes

_____ Be aware of the limitation in the bond or statutes within which suit may be filed

_____ Refer the matter to counsel well ahead of all applicable deadlines.

PART VI

FACING FINANCIAL DIFFICULTIES

CHAPTER 29

OBTAINING FINANCIAL AID FROM THE SURETY

R. Earl Welbaum

R. Earl Welbaum received his undergraduate degree from the University of Miami and his LL.B. from the University of Miami School of Law. He was admitted to the Florida bar in 1969, and after a clerkship in the Third District Court of Appeal, entered the private practice of law, and is now a partner with the Miami, Florida, law firm of Welbaum, Zook & Jones. He specializes in fidelity, surety, and construction law, and is a past chairman of the Fidelity and Surety Committee of the International Association of Defense Counsel. He is also a member of the Fidelity and Surety Committee of the Insurance and Tort Section of the American Bar Association.

§ 29.1   Introduction

A surety has no contractual or other legal obligation to finance its principal or to otherwise provide funds to a principal encountering financial difficulties. As often recited by surety's representative, "we are not a bank or a lending institution." Nevertheless, lending financial support to a contractor, who is the surety's principal, is a valuable tool available to a surety company in mitigating potential losses. A number of excellent articles[1] describe the procedures and documentation of surety financing. The purpose of this chapter is to discuss the circumstances surrounding surety financing and to afford to those in the construction industry an insight into this little-understood alternative available to a performance bond surety.

§ 29.2   When Does a Surety Finance?

The most effective use of financing arises when the surety is able to determine the need and desirability for an infusion of funds before the contractor's financial difficulty has caused the contractor's operation to degenerate beyond the point of effective and efficient performance.

Clearly, the legal obligation of a performance bond surety does not generally arise until the contractor is in default and, in fact, has been defaulted by the obligee. Nevertheless, at the point of declared default, the contractor's financial problems may be beyond salvaging and, therefore, it behooves a prudent contractor to keep the surety advised of financial difficulty even at the risk of adversely affecting future bonding.

The impact of financial difficulty on the liability of the contractor is marked and becomes increasingly apparent as time passes. A contractor becomes forced to look to immediate cash expenditures at the expense of long-term savings. The contractor's cash flow condition frequently dictates, in an effort to save immediate cash, that the contractor sacrifice substantial dollars down the road. Further, the contractor becomes vulnerable to economic persuasion not only from subcontractors and suppliers but

---

[1] Britt, *The Surety's Investigation,* 17 Forum 1151 (Summer 1982); Carruth, *A Guide to Actions: Contract Defaults,* 17 Forum 328 (Fall 1981); Connally, *The Principal Is in Default: What Does the Surety Do Now?,* Int'l Ass'n Ins. Counsel J. (1986); Joyce & Haug, *Financing the Contractor,* Bond Default Manual 21 (1987); Kirwan, *Miscellaneous Problems Including Whether to Finance the Contractor,* 1964 A.B.A. Sec. Ins., Negl. & Compensation L. Proc. 70; J. Petro, *Rights and Responsibilities of the Contractor Surety-What Happens when the Contractor Defaults,* Construction Contracts C. 15 (1978); Schroeder, *Providing Financial Support to the Contractor,* 17 Forum 1190 (Summer 1982); Webster, *The Surety's Decision on What to Do,* 17 Forum 1168 (Summer 1982); Young, *When To Finance and When Not to Finance a Defaulted Contractor,* 1966 A.B.A. Sec. Ins., Negl. & Compensation L. Proc. 317.

also from obligees. Economic difficulty is a malady that ultimately results in loss of key personnel, delays, work stoppages, and (at the time of the ultimate declaration of default) claims directed at the surety company from the obligee for liquidated damages and delay damages from subcontractors. Furthermore, the surety confronts the subcontractors' and suppliers' unwillingness to perform except after renegotiation of subcontracts and purchase orders. The surety will find that the morale of the work force has deteriorated, adversely affecting the quality of the work.

Faced with the foregoing, a surety, although not a lender and although not legally obligated to do so, may well exercise its business judgment to enter into a financing arrangement with the contractor.

§ 29.3   Factors Considered by a Surety

The factors considered by a prudent surety, of course, depend on the time available to the surety and involve many of the factors discussed in §§ **29.4** through **29.12**.

§ 29.4   —Extent of Contractor Need

A contractor's financial difficulties arise from many causes even though the effects generally may be characterized as the same. A single bad job may be the cause of immediate, albeit temporary, cash deficiencies. The financial difficulty may result from an uninsured loss or, in today's economy, from a shrinking of operating lines of credit resulting, at times, from the failure or closing of lending institutions. The historical data on profitability and a rational explanation of the immediate cash flow need weigh heavily in a surety's decision on whether to provide financial aid. A surety should consider the cause of the contractor's financial difficulty and should be influenced by its own determination of the extent of the financial need, not only in immediate dollars but in projected time of repayment.

§ 29.5   —Nature of Contractor's Work in Force

A surety looks at the nature and extent of the work in force and is influenced greatly by the extent to which that work is bonded by a single surety. Complicating the equation is the existence of substantial uncompleted unbonded work or the existence of several sureties with conflicting interests and exposures. A surety's decision to finance is simplified when the financially-strapped contractor's work in force is bonded and those bonds are all issued by a single surety.

Although the surety is interested in and to some extent is influenced by the projected profits and losses as to each of the uncompleted jobs, whether they are bonded or unbonded, the greater concern of the surety is that it will be forced to finance the completion of unbonded work as a condition to securing completion of the work to which its own bond is conditioned.

§ 29.6 —Extent and Condition of Nonbonded Obligations

In addition to a surety's consideration of its exposure to financing the completion of unbonded work or work bonded by another surety, the proposed financing surety is extremely interested in determining the extent of the financially-strapped contractor's other nonbonded obligations. Although these nonbonded obligations may be evaded by a carefully drafted and prosecuted financing arrangement, the likelihood is that the nonbonded obligations will undermine the ability of the contractor to carry out a plan of completion and certainly a successful financing plan that would include factors such as the existence and extent of federal, state, and local tax obligations. Liens and levies for such taxes pose severe impediments to a surety's decision to finance.

The existence and extent of trade union obligations or Davis-Bacon exposure also threaten the survival of the financially-strapped contractor and weigh against the decision of a surety to finance.

The existence and extent of secured and unsecured bank loans create exposure to the successful financing of a contractor.[2] Certainly, sophisticated bankers recognizing their priorities should be inclined to enter into standby or subordination arrangements. However, the realities of today's banking climate frequently precipitate an entirely different response.

§ 29.7 —Nature of Contractor's Work

The unique expertise or specialized techniques of construction of the contractor and its employees tend to justify a decision by surety to finance. This decision is simplified by the lack of availability or excessive cost of securing a completing contractor in a relatively noncompetitive area of construction. Likewise, a qualified and well-trained work force and an in-place management team bolster a surety's confidence and further tend to justify a surety's decision to finance.

---

[2] Lacy v. Maryland Casualty Co., 32 F.2d 48 (4th Cir. 1929); Indemnity Ins. Co. v. Lane Contracting Corp., 227 F. Supp. 143 (D. Neb. 1964).

§ 29.8   —Existence of Assignments

The existence of recorded assignments, perfected under state statutes including the Uniform Commercial Code, as well as the existence of unrecorded agreements, influences the surety's decision. A surety will investigate the filings of record as well as the nature of the recorded assignments and security agreements and will attempt to determine the extent and willingness of the secured parties to participate in a financing program.

§ 29.9   —Real and Personal Assets

A contractor seeking financial assistance from its surety must be prepared to furnish to the surety accurate records concerning the extent and nature of the contractor's assets, including its contracting equipment and office equipment as well as all real property owned by the contractor or upon which the contractor may have mortgages or other liens. A surety expects a forthright representation of not only the existence but also the physical condition of the assets, and the contractor should anticipate that the surety will engage a qualified consultant for the purpose of identifying, inspecting, and cataloging all such equipment.

Furthermore, a contractor seeking financing from its surety should approach the surety as though approaching a lender for long-term financing. All pending and anticipated litigation should be disclosed with an evaluation of the potential of that litigation furnished to the surety by counsel for the contractor. The evaluation should be in substantially the same form required for submission to an auditing certified public accountant.

§ 29.10   —Management Record

A surety contemplating financing will attempt to evaluate the honesty of the contractor's management. A forthright approach to the surety is most often more effective than an approach by a contractor who feels that the contractor and its company are indispensable to the surety's financial well-being and the economic completion of the bonded work. Certainly there are circumstances in which that indispensability may play a significant role; however, a contractor seeking financial assistance should anticipate that the surety will recognize the need without the threat of abandonment, destruction of records, bankruptcy, or some other less than forthright approach. A surety will be concerned with any eventuality that might render the contractor unable to complete the bonded work or to perform the financing undertaking, even to the extent of being concerned about the personal relations of the company principals, and the commitment of managers, project managers, superintendents, and foremen to the contractor and to the completion of the work. Because a surety is expected to finance the contractor, the salary and wage structures in place as well as the perquisites enjoyed by management and senior supervisors will be the subject of discussions and negotiation.

§ 29.11   —Relationship with Obligee

Of course, the technical performance of the work must be satisfactory, but the relationship of the contractor with the owner/obligee is significant in the surety's decision to finance. An owner who is aware of the contractor's difficulties, but whose relationship with the contractor has not deteriorated to the point that the owner's dissatisfaction with performance has reached personal disenchantment, is a persuasive consideration to the surety's decision. Such a relationship results most often from direct hands on management by the contractor and its principals. A good relationship between contractor and owner cannot be created after financial difficulties arise, but must result from a long-standing management philosophy of the contractor. A surety contemplating financing must consider the status of receivables, extra work performed that has been reduced to change orders, and extra work and disputes that remain in controversy. Obviously, the contractor's continuing involvement facilitates both the pursuit of compensation for authorized extra work and the preparation and presentation of claims for equitable adjustment and additional compensation as well as provides a defense to claims and disputes from the owner/obligee.

§ 29.12   —Financial Records

A surety contemplating financial assistance will be spooked by a contractor's lack of adequate financial records, including inaccurate or incomplete job records of payables and receivables, and nonexistent or improperly maintained current job cost and historical information on previous jobs. A contractor seeking financial assistance should anticipate that the surety's consultants will be knowledgeable and that their review of the financial records will be thorough. In making its determination, the surety looks for the extent of front-end loading, realistic costs of completion, and the status of retainage due to the contractor and due from the contractor. The surety investigates the status of subcontractors and material suppliers, together with their willingness and ability to perform and the extent to which their relationship with the contractor has deteriorated because of the financial condition of the contractor. The surety investigates the contractor's policy concerning subcontracting, including any requirement for bonding, the shopping of subcontract prices, the use in all instances of the lowest bid, and the spread between bids and the financial relationship, if any, between the contractor and the various subcontractors.

§ 29.13   Continuing Relationship Between the Parties

Ideally, the relationship between a financing surety and its principal results in the continued viability of the contractor and the passing of the contractor's critical cash flow deficiency. Nevertheless, the financing of a contractor is generally the beginning of an orderly liquidation or change in the size or direction of the contractor. A contractor who is consistent with its own idea of continued viability is most often seeking, in addition to an infusion of funds, a continued bond line. Such a request is not unrealistic and the surety may well perceive that its best interests are served by underwriting additional bonds or by subordinating its interest so that the contractor can secure bonding from others. The dichotomy in the surety industry between claim and underwriting renders the surety emotionally ill-equipped to consider a further bond line for a contractor in claim. Nevertheless, a surety may be induced to extend a further bond line by additional indemnity, by adequate collateralization of the financing arrangement, or by the simple need for an orderly liquidation.

§ 29.14   Security to the Financing Surety

A surety generally is disinclined to consider financial assistance without a clear and unequivocal reaffirmation of the principal's obligation to indemnify and a reaffirmation of the previous indemnity obligations by the individual indemnitors. The surety will likewise anticipate a subordination by other creditors to the rights of the surety, including, but not limited to, the surety's rights to unpaid contract funds including retainages, to chattel mortgages, and to security interests in contractor's equipment, and including, when appropriate, the recognizing of collateral mortgages on real property and chattel mortgages on personal property.

The surety may consider direct financing of the contractor or indirect financing through a lending institution collateralized by the surety's guarantee of payment.[3] This latter method of financing is frequently used when a contractor is engaged in federal projects and the surety seeks the protection of the Assignment of Claims Act of 1940.[4] In any event, the surety will

---

[3] Postula, *The High Cost of Financing a Defaulted Contractor and How To Avoid It,* 1966 A.B.A. Sec. Ins., Negl. & Compensation L. Proc. 323.

[4] 41 U.S.C.A. § 15 (West 1987).

demand assignments or irrevocable letters of direction to the owners and obligees directing that funds be paid either to the surety or to a controlled account. The surety will insist that all funds received and disbursed be handled through a controlled account or a zero balance account that will be secure from the claims of other creditors or from lien and levy by taxing authorities. The contractor should anticipate that the surety will retain the right, in its sole discretion, to cease funding and will have in its hands from the contractor letters of voluntary default, which may be used at any time in the surety's discretion.

A financing surety will be concerned over a misinterpretation of the financing arrangement as one of partnership, joint venture, or domination.[5] Thus, the contractor, its principals, and its indemnitors will be required to acknowledge that the relationship is not a partnership or a joint venture. The agreements should be drafted to reflect that, although the surety has certain controls, including joint control of the bank accounts, and may have a representative in the offices of the contractor, these controls are intended solely for the surety's benefit and do not constitute domination by the surety. A concern by the surety that its actions may be deemed domination will result in a surety's refusal to undertake financing of a distressed contractor.

§ 29.15 Other Considerations

A surety may insist on financing through an entirely new entity created by the surety or created jointly by the surety and the principals (indemnitors) of the contractor. Such an arrangement is clearly not the financing usually desired by the contractor but affords the financing surety a higher degree of protection and also affords the contractor an opportunity for continuity of a construction business.

The prospect of a Chapter 11 bankruptcy filing must also be considered.[6] Ideally the filing of Chapter 11 petition by the principal/contractor should not adversely affect the financing surety's right to remaining contract funds. Therefore, the surety's exposure should be limited to the amount above the contract balances necessary to conclude the work. Assuming that the surety has been successful in securing prepetition cooperation of the

---

[5] Wilcon Inc. v. Travelers Indem. Co., 654 F.2d 976 (5th Cir. 1981); Texasteel Mfg. Co. v. Seaboard Sur. Co., 158 F.2d 90 (5th Cir. 1946); John G. Lambros Co. v. Aetna Casualty & Sur. Co., 468 F. Supp. 624 (S.D.N.Y. 1979); Lambert v. Maryland Casualty Co., 403 So. 2d 739 (La. Ct. App. 1981); Dwelle-Kaiser Co. v. Aetna Casualty & Sur. Co., 241 N.Y. 464, 150 N.E. 517 (1926); Copeland Sand & Gravel, Inc. v. Insurance Co. of N. Am., 288 Or. 325, 607 P.2d 718 (1980).

[6] Leo, *The Financing Surety and the Chapter 11 Principal,* ABA F. Comm. on Construction Industry & Fidelity & Surety L. Comm. Joint Program (Jan. 26, 1989).

contractor's secured lenders and unsecured major creditors, the assistance of the other creditors in the Chapter 11 proceedings becomes indispensable. Nevertheless, the surety's concern over the event of bankruptcy is amply justified by the apparent willingness of bankruptcy courts to ignore or distinguish *Pearlman v. Reliance Insurance Co.*[7] and its legacy.[8] Among the cases that have created concern for the financing surety are those that distinguish between earned and unearned contract balances.[9]

Obtaining financial aid from a surety that considers financing a last resort requires that the contractor consider all of the foregoing in the presentation and request for aid. A business approach with the recognition that the surety is not a lender, but like a lender, is concerned with the bottom line, is the primary approach. Because the expectation of loss is clear, the consideration is minimization of that loss. A difficult decision by the surety will be eased by the contractor's ability to address the surety's concerns.

---

[7] Pearlman v. Reliance Ins. Co., 371 U.S. 132, 83 S. Ct. 232 (1962).

[8] *In re* J.V. Gleason Co., 452 F.2d 1219 (8th Cir. 1971); National Shawmut Bank of Boston v. New Amsterdam Casualty Co., 411 F.2d 843 (1st Cir. 1969); *In re* Dutcher Constr. Corp., 378 F.2d 866 (2d Cir. 1967).

[9] *In re* Universal Builders, Inc., 53 B.R. 183 (Bankr. M.D. Tenn. 1985); *In re* Glover Constr. Co., 30 B.R. 873 (Bankr. W.D. Ky. 1983).

CHAPTER 30

RIGHTS OF THE SURETY TO COLLECT ITS LOSSES FROM THE CONTRACTOR

John S. Bevan
Andrew J. Ruck

John S. Bevan is a partner in the Philadelphia, Pennsylvania, law firm of Duane, Morris & Heckscher. He is a graduate of Princeton University (B.A. 1963) and Temple University (J.D. 1966). Mr. Bevan concentrates his practice in fidelity, surety, and construction contract litigation, and he has authored and co-authored numerous papers in these areas.

Andrew J. Ruck is a partner in the Philadelphia, Pennsylvania, law firm of Duane, Morris & Heckscher. Mr. Ruck concentrates his practice in fidelity, surety, and construction contract litigation. A graduate of LaSalle University (B.A. 1952) and Temple University (J.D. 1955), he is general counsel to the National Association of Surety Bond Producers.

§ 30.1   Introduction

This chapter focuses on the surety's right to recover losses arising from payments made on claims under its bid, payment, or performance bonds. The recovery rights of the surety come from two different sources: first, from equitable principles,[1] such as the doctrine of equitable subrogation; and second, from express contract rights. As an example, under the proper circumstances, the surety has the right to recover its losses from contract balances held by the owner because of alleged breaches by the general contractor of the contractor's contractual obligations. The surety's assignment right to these sums is set forth in the *General Indemnity Agreement* (GIA), a contract between the surety and its bonded contractor or its indemnitors. This same right to contract balances is also available to the surety under the time-honored right of equitable subrogation. The focus of this chapter is not on the surety's equitable rights, which will only be dealt with in passing; but

---

[1] See § **30.3**.

rather, on contractual remedies that the surety may pursue in order to recover its losses directly from the bonded contractor and the surety's indemnitors pursuant to the terms of the GIA.[2]

The intent of the discussion is to acquaint the reader with pertinent features of the GIA and to explain the effect and power of such provisions, as
well as their limitations, usually manifested by defenses raised by indemnitors. It is important to note, however, that this discussion is not intended to
be comprehensive, but rather illustrative of the array of choices the surety
may employ in seeking to recover its losses. It is also important to remember that different courts may interpret essentially identical clauses of the
GIA in diametrically opposite ways.[3] In any given situation, it is thus necessary to look to the applicable law of the state involved.

§ 30.2   Trigger Mechanisms for Surety Rights

A surety agrees to issue bid, payment, and performance bonds in exchange
for a specified premium and the execution by the contractor, and frequently other indemnitors as well, of the GIA. The surety's indemnity
agreement is a fairly standard document, although variations may appear
as a function of the surety involved and occasionally the circumstances of
the transaction. Almost invariably, however, the GIA is written in such a
way as to maximize the protection afforded to the surety in the event it
suffers, or risks suffering, any loss in connection with its issuance of a bond
for the benefit of a particular contractor.

The signing of a GIA by the indemnitors is part of the consideration the
surety receives in exchange for its issuance of one or more of its bonds.[4] In

---

[2] In order to induce a surety to issue bid, payment, or performance bonds, the surety will
require the contractor to sign a GIA in favor of the surety. Frequently, particularly when
small or medium-sized construction companies are involved, the surety will require
others to sign the GIA as well. Most commonly, these other indemnitors will be the
principal officers of the contractor and their spouses. For the sake of convenience, all
these parties shall sometimes be collectively referred to as the "indemnitor." The reader
should bear in mind that this term may only refer to a contractor, or to the contractor
and others as well. Further discussion of this requirement is set forth in §§ 30.3 and
30.4.

[3] For purposes of this chapter, the bond "obligee" is referred to as "owner" and the bond
"principal" is referred to as "contractor." In actual practice, however, these terms may
describe other entities. For example, a general contractor may be the bond obligee and
its subcontractor the bond principal.

[4] *See, e.g.,* United States v. Tilleraas, 709 F.2d 1088, 1091 (6th Cir. 1983) ("[B]enefit
flowing to the debtor by virtue of the surety's promise [to pay] places that debtor under a
implied legal obligation to make good any loss incurred by any payment the surety must
ultimately make to the creditor.").

other words, the GIA has tangible value and is a basis of the bargain between the principal and the surety. The contractor should realize that the GIA is not simply a pro forma document of little import, but rather is a contract like any other and that each clause has a specific meaning, with significant and oft-times substantial consequences to those who sign it.

At the same time, any contractor who is hesitant about signing a GIA faces a substantial, if not insurmountable, barrier to being awarded a construction contract of any size. If the contractor does not or cannot procure the requisite bonds, the owner, prior to awarding its contract, will, as an alternative, require the contractor to post an irrevocable letter of credit in the amount of the contract price, or possibly to provide fully-marketable, readily saleable collateral in that same amount. It is a simple matter of economic reality that few, if any, small or medium-sized construction companies have sufficient resources to secure or escrow collateral in such an amount. Thus, the contractor almost inevitably is compelled to sign a GIA or forgo bidding and seeking an award of the construction contract.

The purpose of the GIA is clear; it is designed and drafted with one goal in mind: to protect the surety or, in legal terms, to hold it harmless for any losses it sustains or might sustain as the result of its issuance of one or more bonds for a given contractor.

Principal's Actual or Claimed Default under the Contract

The surety's obligations under the bonds and its rights under the GIA are generally triggered by the contractor's actual or claimed default under the construction contract.[5] A default occurs whenever the bonded contractor fails, or is alleged to have failed, to satisfy a condition of performance under its construction contract with the owner. Events of default are frequently specified in the construction contract. Some typical examples of a default under the contract include the following:

1. Contractor's failure to perform within the time set forth in the contract
2. Contractor's failure or refusal to comply with the contract specifications or to perform its work in a timely, workman-like manner
3. Contractor's failure to make progress in its performance under the contract as determined by the owner or the owner's construction

---

[5] Anderson v. United States, 561 F.2d 162, 167 (8th Cir. 1977) (citing Pearlman v. Reliance Ins. Co., 371 U.S. 132, 141, 83 S. Ct. 232 (1962); Henningsen v. United States Fidelity & Guar. Co., 208 U.S. 404, 411, 28 S. Ct. 389 (1908); Prairie State Bank v. United States, 164 U.S. 227, 232–33, 17 S. Ct. 142 (1896)) ("Default is the operative fact, and it is the general rule that default operates to vest the interest in such [retainage] funds in the surety to the exclusion of the principal.").

manager or other representatives, such as its engineering or architectural firms

4. Contractor's failure to pay other parties performing work on the project, including laborers, material suppliers, subcontractors, or other suppliers

5. Contractor's abandonment of the project or its explicit repudiation of a significant part of the contract.[6]

A default may be declared by either the owner or the contractor. Except in rare situations, however, the owner will be the one that declares the contractor to be in default, resulting primarily from the owner's objective or subjective perception of how the contractor is performing the contractor's contractual obligations.

The contractor may admit voluntarily that it is or shortly will be in default due to its deteriorated financial condition, making its performance under the contract impossible to complete. The contractor may also refuse further performance based on its belief that the owner is in breach of the construction contract, which, if true, will discharge the contractor from its obligation to perform. If it is the owner who declares a default, the contractor will frequently dispute that declaration and will assert that it is the owner who in reality has breached the contract. A contested default will often be employed as a contractor's defense to the surety's claim for reimbursement under the GIA.[7]

Surety's Available Options on Default

Once a proper and valid default has been declared, the surety's liability matures and the surety is required to discharge its bond obligations by one of several methods. Specific provisions in the construction contract or bond itself may, however, attempt to circumscribe the surety's options.[8] Absent such limitations, the surety is traditionally viewed as having four options available to it on default of the contractor:

1. Finance the defaulted contractor with the surety's own funds

2. Obtain a takeover contractor, which results in the surety entering into a completion contract with a new contractor

---

[6] *See, e.g.,* First Ala. Bank of Birmingham v. Hartford Accident & Indem. Co., 430 F. Supp. 907, 911 (N.D. Ala. 1977) (citing Fidelity & Deposit Co. of Md. v. Scott Bros. Constr. Co., 461 F.2d 640 (5th Cir. 1972)) (default is a factual matter occurring "either when a contractor declares default or when it materially fails in contract performance.").

[7] See § **30.15**.

[8] For instance, the construction contract may require the surety to finance the defaulted contractor.

3. Tender a new contractor to the owner, resulting in a new contract between the owner and the replacement contractor, to which the surety is not a party

4. Permit the owner to complete the project and then reimburse the owner for any additional costs of completion that have been incurred.

Regardless of which option it elects to utilize, it is likely that the surety will incur some loss in discharging its bond obligations. Having done so, the surety then has the right, among others, to attempt to recover its losses from the indemnitors under the terms of the GIA.

§ 30.3 Equitable Recourse Against Contractor after Default

As previously stated in § **30.1**, the surety has both equitable and legal remedies available to it to recover from the contractor losses the surety has sustained, or which it anticipates that it will sustain, as a result of its issuance of bid, payment, or performance bonds for the contractor.[9] The surety's equitable remedies against the contractor are briefly described here in order to place its legal remedies in the proper context.

Exoneration

The first such equitable remedy is that of exoneration. *Exoneration* is an equitable principle that allows the surety to compel the contractor or indemnitors to pay the outstanding obligation, or to remedy any breach declared by the owner. This remedy is available to the surety once the surety's obligation has matured.[10] Under the doctrine of exoneration, a surety is not required to first pay the obligation and then seek reimbursement from the principal. Exoneration relieves the surety of its obligation to the owner or to payment bond claimants by requiring the contractor to satisfy the obligation before the surety expends any of its own funds.[11]

The terms *exoneration* and *reimbursement* are often used interchangeably. This is technically incorrect. Although both concepts represent transactions that ultimately discharge the surety's bond obligations, exoneration allows the surety to avoid first having to pay claims out of its own funds, while the concept of reimbursement requires the surety to make payment

---

[9] The surety, under appropriate circumstances, also may have the right to recover contract balances from the owner, pursuant to the doctrine of equitable subrogation.

[10] *See, e.g.,* Borey v. National Union Fire Ins. Co., 934 F.2d 30, 32–33 (2d Cir. 1991).

[11] *Id.*

first, to discharge the legal obligation, and then recover its payments from the contractor and its indemnitors, to make the surety whole. The right of a surety to compel a contractor to pay the obligation when due is referred to as the "equity of exoneration."[12] The usual question that arises in connection with this remedy is at what point does the contractor's obligation become so fixed so as to require the surety to discharge its payment obligation, that is, whether a default must first be formally declared by the owner against the contractor before the surety may seek exoneration, or whether it is sufficient for the surety to establish only that there is a reasonable risk that the surety will be required to make such a payment.[13]

Quia Timet

Quia timet is a second equitable remedy. Quia timet is a Latin phrase meaning "because he fears." This right arises when the surety believes it has a claim against the contractor for an anticipated loss.[14] A surety may file a bill quia timet whenever it fears that the contractor will be unable to satisfy an obligation that is about to come due, leaving the surety with no legal ability to be made whole after it satisfies the third-party obligation. In such a case, the surety may bring an action quia timet in a court of equity, seeking, inter alia, a preliminary injunction compelling the contractor to deposit sufficient funds into court to cover the anticipated claim. Quia timet is thus a mechanism by which a court orders the contractor to refrain from utilizing a specified amount of money or assets that may be needed to satisfy a claim or judgment in the future.[15]

Specific Performance

The surety also may request that a court of equity order the contractor and the indemnitors to comply with the terms of the GIA. This is known as an action for specific performance.[16] Often, however, the court will not grant specific performance in equity because the surety is considered to have an adequate and proper remedy at law under its indemnity contract.[17]

---

[12] Western Casualty & Sur. Co. v. Biggs, 217 F.2d 163, 165 (7th Cir. 1954).

[13] *See, e.g.,* Abish v. Northwestern Nat'l Ins. Co., 924 F.2d 448 (2d Cir. 1991) (one of a series of opinions in the *In re Gas Reclamation* litigation, involving financial guarantee bonds).

[14] *See, e.g.,* Borey v. National Union Fire Ins. Co., 934 F.2d 30, 32–33 (2d Cir. 1991).

[15] *Id.*

[16] Great Am. Ins. Co. v. Geris, 3 Pa. D. & C.4th 211, 225 (1987).

[17] *Id.* at 225–26.

§ 30.4   Surety's Rights under the GIA

Before a surety issues any bonds, it will inevitably require the contractor to sign an indemnity agreement as a condition to issuing such bonds for the contractor's benefit. The indemnity agreement is necessarily designed to protect the surety against any and all loss and liability in the event claims are or might be asserted against it. The GIA thus shifts the possible financial obligations of the surety to the indemnitor, or provides the mechanism by which the surety may seek to recover any losses it has sustained. With this goal in mind, it is hardly surprising to note that the GIA is designed, to the extent possible, to fully protect the surety by placing only the assets of the indemnitors, rather than those of the surety, at risk. In essence, the GIA enables the surety to expand its already existing legal and equitable rights so that it has the maximum flexibility to attempt to recover its losses from the indemnitors, or to be provided with protection against incurring future losses. Under the law of contracts, a principal may be "bound not simply to indemnify the surety but to keep it unmolested, and this before the surety has paid the principal's debt."[18] This then is the intent and purpose of the GIA.

§ 30.5   —Identifying the Indemnitors

The indemnitors are simply parties that agree to hold the surety harmless in the event the surety must make payments or otherwise incur any risk, liability, or loss under the bond.

Invariably, the contractor will be one of the surety's indemnitors, and, depending on the construction company's size, the length of the company's involvement with the surety, its history of claims, and its present and past financial condition, others may be required by the surety to sign the GIA as well. More specifically, if the surety, through its bond producer or insurance agent, is presented with a small or medium-sized construction company having approximately five years of construction experience, having adequate, but not spectacular, financial success, and having no previous bonding history, the surety may well require additional financial security before it agrees to issue any bonds on behalf of the contractor. This additional security most frequently takes the form of a requirement that the principal officers or shareholders of the construction company and their spouses also

---

[18] Fidelity & Deposit Co. of Md. v. Bristol Steel & Iron Works, Inc., 722 F.2d 1160, 1165 (4th Cir. 1983) (citing Almi, Inc. v. Dick Corp., 31 Pa. Commw. 26, 375 A.2d 1343, 1348 (1977)).

execute the GIA. The surety will require those individuals to supply it with copies of their tax returns and personal financial statements for several years preceding the proposed transaction, with such information preferably prepared by a CPA or outside auditor. The extent to which such information is required, analyzed, or evaluated generally will vary and is a function of the surety underwriter involved.

An indemnitor who signs a GIA is contractually bound by its terms and conditions. The liability of the indemnitors is joint and several, meaning that the surety may collect part or all of its losses from any one of the indemnitors or any combination of them.[19] Obviously, this is important to the surety because the assets of each indemnitor, available at any given time, will vary.

As noted, the bond principal, that is, the contractor, is the first party that the surety will require to sign the indemnity agreement. This is obvious because the contractor is the one that has exclusive control over the construction contract and, therefore, will do whatever is necessary, not only to obtain the bonds, but also to control the bidding on and performance of the contract. Because, from the surety's perspective, the contractor is the initiator of the request for surety credit, it is only reasonable for the surety to look to the contractor for indemnification. When a contractor enters into an indemnity agreement, it accepts potential liability on two fronts: first, to the owner under the construction contract, and, second, to the surety under the GIA. Even if an express indemnity agreement is lacking, the common law obligation of the contractor to indemnify the surety for any payment made by the surety in compliance with the surety's bond obligations is at least some motivation for the contractor to complete the project according to the contract specifications.[20] Obviously, the surety attempts to insulate itself from potential losses when it issues a bond by obtaining as much protection as possible in the form of requiring additional indemnitors on the GIA. This is akin to a bank's requirement that an additional party cosign a loan application or that persons or entities, in addition to the debtor, guarantee an extension of credit. The individuals who serve as indemnitors assume the same obligations under the GIA as does the contractor, that is, they agree to indemnify the surety should the surety sustain any loss, or run the risk of incurring a loss: "[T]he fact that [the indemnitor] is not a principal and did not sign the bond is irrelevant."[21]

---

[19] See § **30.21** (first WHEREAS clause).

[20] *See, e.g.,* Federal Ins. Co. v. Community State Bank, 905 F.2d 112 (5th Cir. 1990); International Fidelity Ins. Co. v. United States, 745 F. Supp. 578 (E.D. Mo. 1990) (regarding surety's equitable rights to funds).

[21] Thomas v. Reliance Ins. Co., 617 F.2d 122, 128 (5th Cir. 1980).

Spouses of the contractor's key officers and shareholders who have a material interest in the existence of the construction company frequently are required to sign the GIA as individual indemnitors. The surety's objective here is to ensure that all of the property shown on the contractor's balance sheet, all property acquired after the documents are signed, and all property held jointly by those officers or shareholders and their spouses will be available to the surety if claims are later asserted against the surety. Other persons or entities who have a significant and substantial financial interest in the project or in the contractor's future success may also be requested to sign the GIA as indemnitors, particularly if the surety perceives that the inclusion of those other parties will significantly diminish its risk of incurring any liability or of ultimately recouping its losses and expenses.

Thus, if a newly formed subsidiary corporation is to be the bond principal, its corporate parent may well be required to sign the GIA, because the parent corporation is generally the source of the financial strength of the subsidiary.

Nature of Indemnitor Liability

As previously stated, all such firms and persons signing the GIA are jointly and severally liable under the GIA, regardless of the degree of their involvement or responsibility with the company or the performance of the construction contract.

Moreover, it has often been noted that "once an indemnitor, always an indemnitor," because such liability continues until all of the bond liability of the surety is terminated. A change in marital status or even the death of an indemnitor will not relieve that indemnitor or the indemnitor's estate of the obligations under the GIA. In the case of a claim that exists at the time of an indemnitor's death, the surety may recover from the indemnitor's estate or from distributees of the assets of that estate or from both.[22]

Similarly, even if the indemnitors are subsequently divorced or separated, such a change in their legal status will not excuse them from discharging their respective obligations as indemnitors. A surety is entitled to be indemnified by an ex-spouse if, at the time the ex-spouse signed the GIA,

---

[22] *See, e.g.,* Colonial Trust Co. v. Fidelity & Deposit Co. of Md., 144 Md. 117, 123 A. 187, 191 (1923)

> ("[S]urety was entitled to be reimbursed by the principal and, if at the time the right to reimbursement accrued the principal was dead, the right could have been asserted against her estate, and if the estate had been distributed when the right accrued, it could have been . . . asserted against the distributees of her estate.").

See also Schirm v. Auclair, 597 F. Supp. 202 (D. Conn. 1984) (claim against estate based on decedent's indemnity agreement held proper).

he or she was married to another indemnitor. This is also true notwithstanding the fact of a subsequent change in a spouse's marital status or a legal change of name as on remarriage.[23] The rationale behind this principle is that the courts, as well as the surety, treat the GIA just like any other contract: if it was valid when each of the parties entered into it, then none of the parties is relieved of the legal consequences of signing that document simply because of an unrelated change in his or her legal identity or status.

As stated above, an indemnity agreement is continuing in nature and does not terminate even after a project is completed. A GIA may, however, contain a provision permitting an indemnitor to withdraw from the agreement upon proper notice to the surety. This procedure necessarily must be set forth in the GIA and must be strictly followed by the contractor or other indemnitor.[24] A notice of termination is effective only with respect to bonds executed by the surety after the effective date of the withdrawal of the indemnitor. It is important to understand that the indemnity agreement is still binding on the indemnitors, even though they may have given notice to the surety of their withdrawal on all bonds executed prior to the effective date of their withdrawal.[25]

INDEMNITY AGREEMENT PROVISIONS

§ 30.6 Sampling of Important GIA Provisions

General indemnity agreements are standardized, form documents and invariably contain certain key provisions. These include:

1. The indemnitor's undertaking to indemnify the surety, as discussed in § **30.4**
2. Provisions that grant the surety the exclusive right to settle or litigate any or all claims asserted against it without the need for the indemnitor's consent
3. An assignment of all of the contractor's rights to contract balances, whether or not arising from bonded contracts

---

[23] *See, e.g., In re* Lapp, 66 B.R. 67 (Bankr. D. Colo. 1986) (wife's obligation as cosigner is separately binding).

[24] A typical withdrawal provision requires written notice to the surety at least 30 days in advance of the date of the withdrawal and must be delivered by registered or certified mail to the surety.

[25] See § **30.21** (typical example of a GIA currently in use in the construction industry).

4. An agreement to pay the surety for all attorneys' fees and costs it incurs in connection with the issuance of its bonds

5. An express contractual agreement, coupled with appropriate procedural mechanisms, to enable the surety to pursue the legal and equitable remedies such as those previously discussed, for example, exoneration, quia timet, and the like.

Sections **30.7** through **30.14** set forth some standard GIA provisions that may be asserted by the surety against the indemnitors, together with some clarifying comments.

§ 30.7 Indemnification

Clearly, the core of the agreement between the indemnitors and the surety is the following provision:

> [The contractor agrees] to indemnify and keep indemnified, and hold and save harmless the Surety against all demands, claims, loss, costs, damages, expenses and attorneys' fees whatever, and any and all liability therefor, sustained or incurred by the Surety by reason of executing or procuring the execution of any said Bond or Bonds, or any other Bonds, which may be already or hereafter executed on behalf of the Contractor, or renewal or continuation thereof; or sustained or incurred by reason of making any investigation on account thereof, prosecuting or defending an action brought in connection therewith, obtaining a release therefrom, recovering or attempting to recover any salvage in connection therewith or enforcing by litigation or otherwise any of the agreements herein contained. Payment of amounts due Surety hereunder together with legal interest shall be payable upon demand.[26]

It is drafted broadly enough to ensure that indemnitors are contractually responsible for any losses the surety might incur as the result of its issuance of one or more bonds.[27] Many of the other provisions of the GIA are drafted to enable the surety to enforce this provision as efficiently as possible and without unnecessary cost or delay.

---

[26] See § **30.21** (para. second).

[27] *See, e.g.,* Fireman's Fund Ins. Co. v. Nizdil, 709 F. Supp. 975, 977 (D. Or. 1989) (quoting Commercial Ins. Co. v. Pacific-Peru Constr. Co., 558 F.2d 948, 953 (9th Cir. 1977)) ("[T]here can be no question that a surety is entitled to stand upon the letter of his contract.") (fidelity bond case).

§ 30.8   Assignment of Collateral and Contract Balances

Under the assignment clause, the contractor and indemnitors assign virtually all of their assets to the surety as collateral for the surety's protection. This assignment includes all the contractor's rights in any of its construction contracts, whether those contracts are bonded by the surety or not:

> [The indemnitor agrees] to assign, transfer and convey, . . . as of the date of execution of said Bond or Bonds, as collateral security for the full performance of the . . . agreements herein contained and the payment of any other indebtedness or liability of the undersigned to the Surety, whether heretofore or hereafter incurred, the following:
>
> a) All right, title and interest . . . to all machinery, equipment, plant, tools and materials which are . . . upon the site of work to be performed under the contract . . . [or will be used on the job, or are chargeable to it];
>
> b) All rights of the undersigned in, or growing . . . out of, said contract or any extensions, modifications, changes or alterations . . . thereto.
>
> c) All rights, actions, causes of action, claims and demands . . . [of] the undersigned . . . in any subcontract . . . or against any subcontractor . . . [in connection with the contract].
>
> d) All right, title and interest of the undersigned in and to any and all percentages retained by the obligee under said contract, any and all estimates, payments, extras, final payment and other sums that . . . may be due or may become due.[28]

This provision serves as a legal complement to the surety's equitable right of subrogation, at least in respect to the contract balances in the contracts bonded by the surety. With respect to the assignment of collateral, this provision potentially gives the surety priority over other unsecured creditors and will generally be enforced for the benefit of the surety, so long as the surety acts in good faith.[29]

Under the law of secured transactions, the surety must follow certain procedures set forth in the Uniform Commercial Code (UCC) to perfect its security interest in those assets and to enforce the assignment against creditors of the bonded contractor. The surety must perfect its assignment rights by proper public filing, in accordance with the terms of Article 9 of the UCC. In actual practice, however, because of the drastic effect such a recording normally has on the contractor's ability to obtain financing in

---

[28] See § **30.21** (para. fourth).

[29] *See, e.g.,* Federal Ins. Co. v. Community State Bank, 905 F.2d 112 (5th Cir. 1990) (surety's rights superior to those of other creditor).

the future, sureties rarely, if ever, record such an assignment until there are warning signs making the contractor's default appear likely.[30]

§ 30.9   Demand and Deposit

Another provision of the GIA is that of demand and deposit under the terms of which the indemnitor agrees:

> That if Surety shall be required or shall deem it necessary to set up a reserve in any amount to cover any claim, demand, liability, expense, suit, order, judgment or adjudication under or on any Bond or Bonds or for any other reason whatsoever, to immediately upon demand deposit with Surety an amount of money sufficient to cover such reserve and any increase thereof, such funds to be held by Surety as collateral, in addition to the indemnity afforded by this instrument, with the right to use such funds or any part thereof, at any time, in payment or compromise of any liability, claims, demands, judgment, damages, fees and disbursement or other expenses.[31]

The obvious purpose of this provision is to compel the indemnitors to provide the surety with financial reserves before the surety actually has to make any payments. The *reserve* is a requirement that funds or other readily-marketable collateral be set aside, whether for accounting purposes or otherwise, in an amount sufficient to discharge an obligor's liability with respect to any particular potential or actual claim. The purpose then for requiring the indemnitors to set up a reserve is to ensure that ample and necessary funds are available to the surety should the surety become obligated to make any payment; and to enable the surety to discharge that obligation using the funds of the indemnitors, rather than the surety's own funds.

---

[30] As a rule, and because of strictly competitive considerations, no surety will seek to perfect its security interest until the contractor is perceived by the surety to be in real financial difficulty. In consequence, the contractor's construction lender will invariably have a security interest in all the contractor's assets, tangible and intangible, superior in priority to any security interest held by the surety. The counterblance to this is the performing surety's equitable right of subrogation, which is superior to the lender's security interest on a bonded project. *See* National Shawmut Bank of Boston v. New Amsterdam Casualty Co., 411 F.2d 843 (1st Cir. 1969); *see also* First Ala. Bank of Birmingham, 430 F. Supp. 907, 910 (N.D. Ala. 1977) (holding "that the surety's failure to record its indemnity agreement does not defeat its equitable right to subrogation.").

[31] See § **30.21** (para. seventh).

§ 30.10   Attorneys' Fees and Other Expenses

In addition to protecting the surety against losses from claims, another purpose of the GIA is to insulate the surety from any indirect, unreimbursed losses as a consequence of having issued its bond. Therefore, not only does the indemnification requirement apply to amounts paid out by the surety on claims, but also it applies to indirect expenditures such as attorneys' fees, costs of suit, and the like incurred by the surety in investigating, in litigating, or in settling claims.[32] The contractor may assume the defense of a particular claim asserted against the surety, thus providing the indemnitors with the potential for reducing the aggregate costs, expenses, and attorneys' fees associated therewith. Not infrequently, however, the contractor declines or is unable to assume the surety's defense. In such an event, the contractor and the other indemnitors are exposed to duplicate costs, expenses, and attorneys' fees associated with the defense of the suit.

If the surety defends the action, the indemnitors are of course liable not only to reimburse the surety for the attorneys' fees it incurs as well as related costs and expenses, but also to reimburse it for the amount of any negotiated settlement or judgment that might ultimately be rendered against the surety.

Moreover, if the surety loses the suit, the indemnitors are generally barred from challenging that outcome or from contending that the surety failed to raise any substantive or procedural defenses.[33] The indemnitor is also generally precluded from claiming that the surety settled the litigation for too great an amount or from arguing that the surety should have appealed an adverse judgment.[34]

Conversely, if the surety elects to appeal an adverse judgment, the indemnitors will be liable for the attorneys' fees and costs incurred by the surety in connection with that appeal, regardless of the ultimate outcome

---

[32] *See, e.g.,* Reliance Ins. Co. v. Romine, 707 F. Supp. 550, 553, (S.D. Ga. 1989), *aff'd,* 888 F.2d 1344 (11th Cir. 1989) (indemnitors liable to surety for settlement of disputed amount plus prejudgment interest and attorneys' fees); *see also* Fidelity & Deposit Corp. of Md. v. Bristol Steel & Iron Works, Inc., 722 F.2d 1160, 1167 (4th Cir. 1983).

[33] *See, e.g.,* Continental Casualty Co. v. Guterman, 708 F. Supp. 953, 954 (N.D. Ill. 1989) ("[T]he indemnity agreement between the parties expressly provides for indemnification . . . regardless of whether [the surety] asserts [the bond principal's] equitable claims. Thus, even if [the surety] paid off claims [when the principal] was not liable, the indemnity contract entitles [the surety] to full reimbursement.") (citing Fidelity & Deposit Co. of Md. v. Bristol Steel & Iron Works, Inc., 722 F.2d 1160, 1163 (4th Cir. 1983) and Commercial Ins. Co. v. Pacific-Peru Constr. Corp., 558 F.2d 948, 953 (9th Cir. 1977)).

[34] *See, e.g.,* Hill Bros. Chem. Co. v. Grandinetti, 123 Ariz. 84, 597 P.2d 987 (Ct. App. 1979).

of the appeal or the indemnitors' wishes with respect to taking the appeal in the first place.[35]

Because of the potential for such liability, it is usually in the best interest of the indemnitors to assume the defense of the surety, if they have the financial resources to do so.

§ 30.11   Confession of Judgment

In the event the contractor defaults under its contract and the indemnitors fail to honor their indemnity obligation or otherwise cure the default, the GIA provides:

> [That the indemnitors] hereby authorize and empower any attorney of any court of record . . . to appear for them . . . and to confess judgment against them . . . for any sum or sums of money up to the amount of any or all Bond or Bonds, with costs, interest and reasonable attorneys' fees.[36]

A confession of judgment provision thus entitles the surety, in those states that permit the entry of a judgment by confession, to apply to the court and have the court enter judgment against one or more of the indemnitors in the amount the surety demands. The process occurs without the need for the surety to file a lawsuit or to go through a formal trial. The confession of judgment is an agreement between the parties pursuant to which the indemnitors commit themselves to voluntarily submit to the jurisdiction of any court designated by the surety and to permit that court to enter a final judgment against the indemnitors, without a trial, and in such amount as to which the surety is entitled. Moreover, the confession of judgment provision includes a specific representation by the indemnitors that the surety is to act, or is in fact acting, as the indemnitors' own attorney-in-fact for this purpose.[37]

The purpose of the confession of judgment provision is to enable the surety to expeditiously proceed against the contractor and the surety's indemnitors and to avoid the risk, expense, and time required for the surety to obtain a judgment against the indemnitors after litigation on the merits. Of course, after the judgment by confession is entered against the indemnitors, the surety is still required to follow the statutory execution procedures to

---

[35] *See, e.g.,* Republic Ins. Co. v. Culbertson, 717 F. Supp. 415, 420 (E.D. Va. 1989) ("The majority of the courts . . . award appellate fees based on the rule that the contract controls and that appellate fees are covered by the contract.").

[36] See § **30.21** (para. seventh).

[37] *Id.*

obtain possession of assets from the indemnitors or third parties such as banks, trustees, and escrow agents.[38]

Most courts construe confessions of judgment very strictly and, in consumer goods situations, refuse to uphold the provisions as being contrary to public policy.[39] Further, even when such provisions are considered valid, courts generally view confessions of judgment with disfavor and set them aside if there are grounds upon which the entry of judgment was improper.[40]

§ 30.12   Exclusive Right of Surety to Settle Any Claims

Although the settlement provision in a GIA is not actually a method of financial recovery for the surety, the right to settle provision directly influences the amount of recovery the surety may seek from the indemnitors. This provision grants to the surety the exclusive right "at its option and in its sole discretion" to adjust, settle, defend, or compromise any claim, demand, or suit; and further provides that the surety has the exclusive right "to decide and determine whether any claim . . . shall on the basis of liability, expediency, or otherwise be paid, settled, defended or appealed."[41]

Thus, under the GIA the surety can recover from the indemnitors all amounts the surety expends in paying, settling, defending, or appealing a claim or judgment, together with attorneys' fees, costs, expenses, and interest. The courts generally apply these provisions as written, leaving the indemnitors with little room for challenging the validity of this section.[42] In

---

[38] All states have execution procedures that must be utilized by a judgment creditor, such as the surety. These laws are written to protect the debtor from an unwarranted taking of property. *See, e.g.,* Pa. R. Civ. P. §§ 3101–3149.

[39] *See, e.g.,* Swarb v. Lennox, 314 F. Supp. 1091 (E.D. Pa. 1970), *aff'd,* 405 U.S. 191, *reh'g denied,* 405 U.S. 1049 (1972) (confession of judgment in consumer purchase situation impermissible unless, among other things, it is shown that the individual made an intelligent and knowing waiver of his or her right to a trial on the merits and has an annual income in excess of $10,000).

[40] *See, e.g.,* Beckett v. Laux, 395 Pa. Super. 563, 577 A.2d 1341 (1990) (due to inherent potential for oppression, court did not permit execution due to the creditor's noncompliance with procedural rules).

[41] See § **30.21** (paras. ninth(c), tenth). The surety's use of this provision may be conditioned upon a request, in writing, by an indemnitor that the surety defend the action, together with the deposit of money or readily-marketable collateral in an amount satisfactory to the surety.

[42] See §§ **30.15–30.20.** *See generally* Employers Ins. v. Able Green, Inc., 749 F. Supp. 1100, 1103 (S.D. Fla. 1990) ("[C]ourts have consistently held that the surety is entitled to reimbursement pursuant to an indemnity contract for any payments made by it in a good faith belief that it was required to pay, regardless of whether any liability actually existed.") (citations omitted).

one case, for instance, the surety settled a claim that the indemnitors disputed. The surety then sought indemnification under the terms of GIA.[43] The court found in favor of the surety on its indemnification claim and the indemnitors appealed. The appellate court affirmed the lower court's decision, holding that the surety was entitled not only to receive the indemnification award but also to recover attorneys' fees and costs the surety incurred in opposing the indemnitors' appeal.[44]

§ 30.13 Indemnitors' Waiver of Exemptions

Under the waiver of exemption provision, the indemnitors theoretically relinquish any right to retain property that they would otherwise be entitled to keep under state execution-law exemptions.

> [The indemnitor] does hereby waive all right to claim any property, including homestead, as exempt from levy, execution, sale or other legal process under the law of any state . . . as against the rights of the Surety to proceed against the same for indemnity.[45]

Most states permit certain enumerated assets of the debtor, such as small amounts of personal property, land (homestead), or forms of income, for example, wages and workers' compensation benefits, to remain free from execution proceedings.[46] Further, many states have enacted specific laws that provide that these exemptions cannot be waived by the debtor.[47] Thus, in those states that have such nonwaiver statutes, the surety is prohibited from enforcing the waiver-of-exemptions clause in the GIA. Such a waiver provision therefore may in reality have little or no value to the surety. Moreover, even in the absence of a statute precluding such a waiver by the debtor, there is a strong public policy against it, and that alone may dissuade the surety from employing this provision. Nevertheless, the provision remains in most GIAs, even if only as a matter of tradition or leverage in negotiations with the indemnitors; and naturally it may be used in those jurisdictions that still permit its enforcement.

---

[43] Republic Ins. Co. v. Culbertson, 717 F. Supp. 415 (E.D. Va. 1989).

[44] *Id.*

[45] See § **30.21** (para. fourteenth).

[46] *See, e.g.,* 42 Pa. Cons. Stat. Ann. §§ 8121–8127 (1982).

[47] *See, e.g., id.* § 8122 (1982) (providing, in pertinent part: "Exemptions from attachment or execution may not be waived by the debtor by express or implied contract.").

§ 30.14   Recovery by Surety of Transferred Assets

Most states have laws that provide several different mechanisms by which the surety may seek to recover assets or property transferred by an indemnitor to other persons, including creditors, family members, or third parties. Although a comprehensive discussion of the surety's rights with respect to such asset transfers is beyond the scope of this chapter, it is important to know of the existence and nature of such laws and the interrelationship of the laws with the GIA.

For example, numerous states have enacted the Uniform Fraudulent Conveyance Act (UFCA)[48] or similar statutes.[49] The UFCA generally provides that certain transfers by an indemnitor to another party, whether or not the indemnitor actually intends to defraud the surety, are deemed to be fraudulent, and the surety has the right to seek to set the transfers aside and to recover the transferred assets. One such section of the UFCA provides, in pertinent part, that:

> Every conveyance made and every obligation incurred by a person who is or will thereby be rendered insolvent, is fraudulent as to creditors without regard to his actual intent, if the conveyance is made or the obligation is incurred without a fair consideration.[50]

Because courts generally accept and enforce the UFCA's broad definitions and remedies, the UFCA is generally interpreted to apply to the transfer of any assets regardless of the intent of the transferor or whether insolvency has or has not been declared. For instance, insolvency is defined as existing when the present fair value of the transferor's "assets is less than the amount that will be required to pay his probable liability on his existing debts as they become absolute and matured."[51] Thus, the transferor may have substantial wealth, but will still be considered "insolvent" under the UFCA if the debt at issue, that is, the amount demanded by the surety under the indemnity agreement, exceeds the transferor's current assets.

Similarly, the term *debt* is defined broadly and includes "any legal liability, whether matured or unmatured, liquidated or unliquidated, absolute, fixed or contingent."[52] It is not difficult to see that an indemnitor may incur a legal liability under the GIA, even though that liability is unmatured, unliquidated, or contingent at the time of the indemnitor's transfer of assets to another. Thus, if an indemnitor transfers assets to a family member for a

---

[48] *See, e.g.,* Pa. Stat. Ann. tit. 39, §§ 351–359 (1954); Del. Code Ann. tit. vi, §§ 1301–1312 (1975).

[49] *See, e.g.,* Pa. Stat. Ann. tit. 39, §§ 351–363 (1954).

[50] *See, e.g., id.* § 354 (1954).

[51] *See, e.g., id.* § 352 (1954).

[52] *See, e.g., id.* § 351 (1954).

nominal sum or as a gift, the surety may recover those assets because the transfer is presumed to be fraudulent under the law.[53]

Similarly, federal bankruptcy law allows a trustee to recover property transferred by a bankrupt indemnitor to others, even if that transfer occurred prior to the filing of the bankruptcy petition or the time that a bankruptcy was otherwise declared.[54]

The UCC also provides that transfers of the majority of an indemnitor's materials, supplies, merchandise, or inventory, other than in the ordinary course of business, may be set aside.[55]

Finally, certain transfers by an indemnitor may be illegal under state criminal statutes.[56]

DEFENSES TO CLAIMS

§ 30.15   Defenses of Indemnitors to Surety's Claim Against Them

When the surety seeks to recover its losses from the indemnitors under the GIA, the indemnitors may challenge the validity of the surety's claim against them and may raise one or more defenses to the surety's claims. Such a dispute may eventually result in a lawsuit between the surety and the indemnitors, which in turn will require the court to decide which party prevails under the terms of the GIA. The indemnitors, by asserting such defenses, seek to avoid their contractual liability to the surety. In consequence, the defenses are difficult to establish. Courts generally enforce the terms of the GIA, as written, provided that the surety has not acted in bad faith or with manifest disregard of the indemnitors' interests. Some of the more common examples of defenses routinely asserted by indemnitors are set forth in §§ 30.16 through 30.20.[57]

---

[53] *See, e.g., id.* § 352 (1954).

[54] *See, e.g.,* 11 U.S.C.A. §§ 544, 548, 550 (West 1979 & Supp. 1991).

[55] *See, e.g.,* 13 Pa. Cons. Stat. Ann. §§ 6101–6111 (1984).

[56] *See, e.g.,* 18 Pa. Cons. Stat. Ann. § 4111 (1983).

[57] *See, e.g.,* United States *ex rel.* IBEW Local 449 v. United Pac. Ins. Co., 697 F. Supp. 378 (D. Idaho 1988) (citing Martin v. Lyons, 98 Idaho 102, 358 P.2d 1063, 1066 (1977)) ("It is a well-established principle of surety law in regard to indemnification that the 'surety will . . . be permitted to rely on the exact terms of the agreement.'").

§ 30.16   —Surety Acted as a Volunteer

As discussed in §§ 30.16 through 30.20, the surety's obligations under its payment or performance bonds do not arise until the contractor is declared to be in default by the owner. Accordingly, the indemnitor may defend the surety's suit against it by contesting the validity of the owner's initial declaration of default. The indemnitor thus argues that if the contractor was not in default and the surety paid claims asserted against it or the owner anyway, the surety made such payments as a "volunteer," and the indemnitor is relieved of any obligation to indemnify the surety under the GIA.

The outcome of this defense depends in large measure on the terms and conditions of the GIA as well as on the reasonableness of the surety's actions under the circumstances. If, for example, the construction contract clearly defines an event of default and the conduct of the contractor is within the meaning of that provision, then it will be difficult, if not impossible, for the contractor to successfully assert this defense.[58]

§ 30.17   —Surety Acted in Bad Faith

A second, and closely related, defense is the assertion by the indemnitor that the surety paid claims when, based on an evaluation of the merits of the claims, there was no legal obligation to do so. In essence, the indemnitors assert that, even if the contractor was in default, the surety should not have paid the claim for any of a variety of reasons. For example, the indemnitors may make one of the following arguments:

1. The claim was not timely filed under the law
2. The claim itself was fictitious, inflated, inaccurate, or duplicative
3. The claimant had no standing to sue, that is, the claimant was not a proper party to the lawsuit
4. The claim was not ripe, that is, it was merely a potential liability as opposed to one that had accrued already
5. The surety had no obligation to pay the claim until the claim was reduced to a judgment against the surety.

Although such defenses sound promising for the indemnitor, they are, in actuality, very difficult to prove. General indemnity agreements, almost without exception, contain a clause granting the surety complete and

---

[58] *See, e.g.,* Continental Casualty Co. v. Guterman, 708 F. Supp. 953, 954 (N.D. Ill. 1989) (indemnitor contended surety voluntarily paid debt); *see also* Federal Ins. Co. v. Community State Bank, 905 F.2d 112, 115 (5th Cir. 1990) (volunteer defense defeated because surety did "that which the situation prudently required.").

exclusive authority to settle, litigate, pay, or defend any claim in whole or in part, whether for the sake of expediency or otherwise.[59] This provision is fundamental to the efficacy of the agreement between the surety and indemnitors and its absence would produce substantial delay and inefficiency in the resolution of disputes and payment to legitimate creditors. Without it, every decision of the surety could be second-guessed or disputed by the indemnitors. The end result of this would only lead to more litigation and greater costs to all parties.

Under the law, the presence of the "exclusive right to settle" provision results in a presumption that the surety's exercise of this right is made in good faith.[60] In order to rebut that presumption the indemnitors must come forward with clear and convincing evidence that the surety acted in "bad faith," which is, at best, a very difficult burden for the indemnitors to bear. Indeed, courts consistently recognize that "lack of diligence or negligence is not the equivalent of bad faith and even gross negligence is not the same as bad faith."[61] Thus, the very act of the surety in settling a claim may be "indicative of good faith where litigation would far exceed the expense of settling the claim out of court."[62]

One index of the surety's good faith is whether the surety thoroughly investigated the claim before paying the third-party claimant. One court has held that under the express terms of the GIA the surety has no duty even to make such an investigation.[63] Other courts have held that the common law of suretyship supersedes the written GIA and requires a jury to determine whether the surety acted in "utmost good faith,"[64] thus implying the existence of such a duty. Indeed, at least one court has held that a surety occupies a "fiduciary relationship" with the indemnitor and thus must adhere to the highest standards of good faith in protecting the indemnitors' interests.[65] Needless to say, such decisions are rare, and generally the surety needs only to present reasonable evidence that it acted in good faith in order to prevail.

The indemnitor might also attempt to establish the surety's bad faith by showing that it failed to assert the contractor's defenses to the claim. This argument, however, has not been well-received by the courts.[66]

---

[59] See § **30.12**.

[60] *See, e.g.,* Employers Ins. v. Able Green, Inc., 749 F. Supp. 1100, 1103 (S.D. Fla. 1990); Fidelity & Deposit Co. of Md. v. Wu, 150 Vt. 225, 552 A.2d 1196, 1199 (1988).

[61] *See, e.g.,* Employers Ins. v. Able Green, Inc., 749 F. Supp. 1100, 1103.

[62] *Id.*

[63] *Id.*

[64] *See* Windowmaster Corp. v. Morse Diesel, Inc., 722 F. Supp. 1532, 1535 (N.D. Ill. 1988).

[65] *Id.*

[66] *See, e.g.,* United States *ex rel.* IBEW Local 449 v. United Pac. Ins. Co., 697 F. Supp. 378, 381 (D. Idaho 1988) ("[Indemnitor] not bound, as it would be at common law, to pay

§ 30.18   —Surety Tortiously
Interfered with Contract

Another defense raised by indemnitors is that the surety's conduct wrongfully interfered with the construction contract between the owner and the contractor. This usually occurs after the owner has made a formal declaration of default and, upon demand, the surety has notified the owner of the surety's intention to complete performance of the construction contract and collect the contract balances. If the contractor objects to the declaration of default or to the surety's assumption of the contractor's obligations, the cautious owner may decide to stop all payments until the conflict between the surety and the contractor has been resolved.[67] Once the owner stops those payments, the contractor's cash flow halts and thereby jeopardizes the financing and timely completion of the project. In consequence, the contractor may bring an action against the surety for interfering with the owner-contractor construction contract.[68] The surety then asserts its rights under the GIA to protect its interests.

§ 30.19   —Terms of the GIA Are Unconscionable

The indemnitor may also argue that the terms of the GIA are unconscionable and oppressive. This is basically a fairness argument and as such is difficult for the indemnitor to win. Courts have consistently rejected this defense, holding that, as a matter of law, the GIA is "not unconscionable because it is in no manner oppressive, harsh or shocking. To the contrary, the indemnity agreement was given [in exchange for the surety's] execution of the bonds."[69]

Moreover, the surety may well argue that the contractor was free to purchase its bond from another surety, or to obtain a personal guarantor. The surety will further argue that the contractor could have protected the surety in other ways, for instance by providing the surety with a satisfactory letter of credit.

---

only amounts for which the principals were legally liable. Upon the express terms of the Agreement, the Indemnitors are liable to indemnity [the surety] no matter what the legal defenses or other avenues of resolution may have been.").

[67] By this time, it should be fairly apparent to the reader that any conflict between the surety and the contractor is not likely to be resolved overnight because of the numerous competing considerations, claims, defenses, and the like.

[68] See, e.g., Gerstner Elec., Inc. v. American Ins. Co., 520 F.2d 790 (8th Cir. 1975) (on principal's claim for wrongful interference with contract the court held that "it was 'appropriate' for [the] surety to request the [owner] to withhold further payments pending a resolution of the dispute.").

[69] See Employers Ins. v. Able Green, Inc., 749 F. Supp. 1100, 1104 (S.D. Fla. 1990).

Notwithstanding the above, the contractor is entitled to be discharged from its obligations under the GIA if the contractor proves it was induced to execute the GIA by fraud, deception, misrepresentation, or mutual mistake. Proof of this defense is at best difficult and, as a consequence, such cases rarely reach the stage in which a court opinion is handed down and published.[70] Precedents in this area are therefore "few and far between."

§ 30.20   —Miscellaneous Defenses

The following additional defensive maneuvers have been attempted, but have not been particularly successful. One or more of them, however, may still be viable in some courts.

Additional bonds not issued.   The indemnitor may claim that surety would not issue additional bonds for the contractor.[71] If the GIA specifically provides that the surety is under no obligation to issue additional bonds, which it almost invariably does, then the indemnitor is bound by such language.

Signature missing.   The contractor did not sign the bond.[72] Case law and the GIA specifically state that the contractor's signature on the bond is not required in order for it to be valid and enforceable. All that is required is that the contractor sign the GIA or assume the obligations thereunder.

Damages not mitigated.   The surety has failed to mitigate its damages.[73] Under the terms of the GIA the surety is not required to mitigate damages, although some courts may impose this duty on the surety, regardless of the language of the GIA.

---

[70] *See, e.g.,* United States *ex rel.* IBEW Local 449 v. United Pac. Ins. Co., 697 F. Supp. 378 (D. Idaho 1988) (citing Fidelity & Deposit Co. of Md. v. Bristol Steel & Iron Works, Inc., 722 F.2d 1160, 1163 (4th Cir. 1983) ("[A]n indemnitor is excused if a surety makes a payment through fraud."); *see also* Fidelity & Deposit Co. of Md. v. Bristol Steel & Iron Works, Inc., 722 F.2d 1160, 1163 (4th Cir. 1983).

[71] *See, e.g.,* Charles H. Tompkins Co. v. Lumbermens Mut. Casualty Co., 732 F. Supp. 1368 (E.D. Va. 1990) (GIA specifically negated duty of surety to issue bonds subsequent to those already posted); United States Fidelity & Guar. Co. v. R.W. Lutz Elec. Contractor, Inc., 3 Pa. D. & C.4th 278 (1989).

[72] *See, e.g.,* United States *ex rel.* IBEW Local 449 v. United Pac. Ins. Co., 697 F. Supp. 378, 381 (D. Idaho 1988) (contractor not required to sign the bond).

[73] *See, e.g.,* Continental Casualty Co. v. Guterman, 708 F. Supp. 953 (N.D. Ill. 1989) (GIA guaranteeing obligations on financial bond).

Counterclaims not asserted. The surety failed to assert the contractor's counterclaims or setoffs that would have lessened the surety's losses.[74] Courts have held that the surety has no duty under the GIA to do so.

Notice not provided. The surety failed to provide notice to the indemnitor that the surety was about to settle or pay a claim.[75] This is contrary to the practice of experienced sureties, and courts may well ignore it, absent a persuasive showing of prejudice by the indemnitor, or of a manifest disregard of significant, substantial, and pertinent information, supplied to the surety by indemnitors in sufficient time for the surety to evaluate that information before the surety itself sustains some prejudice.

Contract terms limit relief. A potentially successful, although rarely used, defense for the indemnitors is that the terms of the indemnity agreement itself limit the surety's relief. Thus, the indemnitors may argue that they owe no additional obligations to the surety because the surety has been indemnified to the extent of the indemnity contract, even if, through the exercise of its rights under the GIA, the surety has not been made whole.[76]

§ 30.21   Continuing Agreement of Indemnity

It should be evident that the contract surety has a wide variety of options available to it to secure the recovery of its losses and expenditures resulting from the issuance of one or more of its bonds. Many of those remedies are significantly biased in favor of the surety and, to that extent, indemnitors must beware. In reality, however, the efficacy of the surety's arsenal of rights and remedies depends on the financial health of the indemnitors. In consequence, underwriting decisions and evaluations made prior to the execution of the GIA or the issuance of any bonds may well be rendered moot before even coming into effect. A solvent and reliable contractor is usually of far greater significance to the surety than a court's interpretation of any given provision of the GIA.

---

[74] *Id.*

[75] *See, e.g.,* United States *ex rel.* IBEW Local 449 v. United Pac. Ins. Co., 697 F. Supp. 378, 381 ("[N]o notice was required under the terms of the Agreement; [the surety's] right was exclusive."); *cf.* United States Fidelity & Guar. v. Lipsmeyer Constr. Co., 754 F. Supp. 81, 85 (M.D. La. 1990) (statute requires that surety take reasonable steps to notify principal).

[76] *See, e.g.,* Surety Managers, Inc. v. Stanford, 633 F.2d 709, 712 (5th Cir. 1980), *cert. denied,* 454 U.S. 828 (1981) (surety "limited its remedies under the [indemnity] agreement, and because we find no other remedy pursuant to that agreement . . . Surety has no further claim against [indemnitors].").

Nevertheless, the following sample Contractor's Continuing Agreement of Indemnity[77] will give the surety contractual remedies to pursue in collecting losses from the contractor:

THIS AGREEMENT is made by the Undersigned for continuing benefit of the Surety for the purpose of saving it harmless and indemnifying it from all loss and expense in connection with any Bonds executed on behalf of any one or more of the following persons, firms or corporations:

[Contractor's name inserted below]

WITNESSETH,

WHEREAS, the Contractor, individually or jointly with others, may desire or be required from time to time to give certain bonds, undertakings, or instruments of guarantee (all of which will hereinafter be included within the term "Bond" or "Bonds"), and WHEREAS, upon the express condition that this instrument be executed, the Surety has executed or procured the execution of, and may hereafter execute or procure the execution of such Bonds.

NOW THEREFORE, in consideration of the execution of any such Bond or Bonds and as an inducement to such execution, we, the Undersigned, agree and bind ourselves, our heirs, executors, administrators, successors and assigns, jointly and severally, as follows:

FIRST: To pay all premiums on said bonds computed in accordance with the Surety's regular manual of rates in effect on the date said Bonds are executed.

SECOND: To indemnify, and keep indemnified, and hold and save harmless the Surety against all demands, claims, loss, costs, damages, expenses and attorneys' fees whatever, and any and all liability therefor, sustained or incurred by the Surety by reason of executing or procuring the execution of any said Bond or Bonds, or any other Bonds, which may be already or hereafter executed on behalf of the Contractor, or renewal or continuation thereof; or sustained or incurred by reason of making any investigation on account thereof, prosecuting or defending any action brought in connection therewith, obtaining a release therefrom, recovering or attempting to recover any salvage in connection therewith or enforcing by litigation or otherwise any of the agreements herein contained. Payment of amounts due Surety hereunder together with legal interest shall be payable upon demand.

THIRD: To furnish money to the Contractor or to the Surety as needed for the prompt payment of labor, materials, and any other costs or expenses in connection with the performance of contracts when and as requested to do so by the Surety.

---

[77] Continuing Agreement of Indemnity—Contractor's Form, reprinted with permission of Reliance Insurance Co./United Pacific Insurance Co.

FOURTH: To assign, transfer and convey, and each of the Undersigned does by these presents assign, transfer and convey to the Surety, as of the date of execution of said Bond or Bonds, as collateral security for the full performance of the covenants and agreements herein contained and the payment of any other indebtedness or liability of the Undersigned to the Surety, whether heretofore or hereafter incurred, the following:

(a) All right, title and interest of the Undersigned in and to all machinery, equipment, plant, tools and materials which are, on the date of execution of any such Bond or Bonds, or may thereafter be, about or upon the site of the work to be performed under the contract referred to in and guaranteed by such Bond, or elsewhere for the purpose thereof, including as well materials purchased for or chargeable to said contract which may be in process of construction or in storage elsewhere or in transportation to said site;

(b) All rights, of the Undersigned in, or growing in any manner out of, said contract or any extensions, modifications, changes or alterations thereof or additions thereto;

(c) All rights, actions, causes of action, claims and demands whatsoever which the Undersigned or any of them may have or acquire in any subcontract in connection with said contract, and against any subcontractor or any person, firm or corporation furnishing or agreeing to furnish or supply labor, materials, supplies, machinery, tools or other equipment in connection with or on account of said contract, and against any surety or sureties of any such materialmen, subcontractor, laborer or other person, firm or corporation.

(d) All right, title and interest of the Undersigned in and to any and all percentages retained by the Obligee under said contract, and any and all estimated payments, extras, final payments and other sums that, at the time of abandonment, forfeiture or breach of said contract or such Bond or Bonds or of the terms of this Agreement or at the time of any advance, payment or guaranty by the Surety for the purpose of avoiding such abandonment, forfeiture or breach, may be due or may thereafter become due under said contract to or on behalf of the Undersigned, together with any and all sums due or which thereafter become due under or on all other contracts, bonded or unbonded, in which any or all of the Undersigned have an interest.

FIFTH: Each of the Undersigned does hereby irrevocably nominate and appoint any officer of the Surety the true and lawful attorney-in-fact of the Undersigned, with full right and authority, in the event the Contractor fails or is unable to complete the work called for by the contract guaranteed by any Bond or in the event of the breach of any provision of this Agreement to execute on behalf of, and sign the names of each of the Undersigned to, any voucher, release, satisfaction, check, bill of sale of all or any property by this Agreement assigned to the Surety or any other paper or contract necessary or desired to carry into effect the purposes of this Agreement; with full right and authority also, in such event, to dispose of the performance of said contract by subletting the same in the name of the Contractor or otherwise; and each of the Undersigned does hereby ratify and confirm all that such attorney-in-fact or the Surety may lawfully do in the premises and further authorizes and empowers the Surety and such attorney-in-fact and each of them to enter upon and take possession of the tools, plant, equipment, materials and subcontracts and all other collateral security mentioned in this Agreement and enforce, use, employ and dispose thereof for the purposes set forth in this Agreement. Each of the Undersigned specifically agrees to protect, indemnify and hold harmless the Surety and such attorney-in-fact against any and all claims, damages, costs and expenses that may in any way arise or grow out of the exercise of the assignments contained in this Agreement and the powers herein granted, specifically waiving any claim which any Undersigned has or might hereafter have against the Surety or such attorney-in-fact on account of anything done in enforcing the terms of this agreement, assignments and power-of-attorney.

SIXTH: That the entire contract price of any contract referred to in a Bond or Bonds, whether in the possession of the Undersigned or another, shall be and hereby is impressed with a trust in favor of Surety for the payment of obligations incurred for labor, materials and services in the performance of the contract work for which Surety would be liable under such Bond or Bonds and for the purpose of satisfying the conditions of the Bond executed in connection with the contract.

SEVENTH: That if Surety shall be required or shall deem it necessary to set up a reserve in any amount to cover any claim, demand, liability, expense, suit, order, judgment or adjudication under or on any Bond or Bonds or for any other reason whatsoever to immediately upon demand deposit with Surety an amount of money sufficient to cover such reserve and any increase thereof, such funds to be held by Surety as collateral, in addition to the indemnity afforded by this instrument, with the right to use such funds for any part thereof, at any time, in payment or compromise of any liability, claims, demands, judgment, damages, fees and disbursements or other expenses; and the Undersigned, in the event of their failure to comply with such demand, hereby authorize and empower any attorney of any court of record of the United States or any of its territories or possessions, to appear for them or any of them in any suit by Surety and to confess judgment against them or any of them for any sum or sums of money up to the amount of any or all Bond or Bonds, with costs, interest and reasonable attorneys' fees; such judgment, however, to be satisfied upon the payment of any and all such sums as may be found due by the Undersigned Surety under the terms of this Agreement. Demand shall be sufficient if sent by registered or certified mail to the Undersigned at the address or addresses given herein or last known to Surety, whether or not actually received. The authority to confess judgment as set forth herein shall not be exhausted by any one exercise thereof, but may be exercised from time to time and more than one time until all liability of the Undersigned to Surety shall have been paid in full.

EIGHTH: All collateral security held by or assigned to the Surety may be used by the Surety at any time in payment of any claim, loss or expense which the Undersigned have agreed to pay hereby, whether or not such claim, loss or expense arises out of or in connection with such Bond or contract under which such collateral is held. The Surety may sell or realize upon any or all such collateral security, at public or private sale, with or without notice to the

Undersigned or any of them, and with the right to be purchaser itself at any such public sale, and shall be accountable to the Undersigned only for such surplus or remainder of such collateral security or the proceeds thereof as may be in the Surety's possession after it has been fully indemnified as in this Agreement provided. The Surety shall not be liable for decrease in value or loss or destruction of or damage to such security, however caused.

NINTH: The Surety shall have the right, at its option and in its sole discretion:

(a) To deem this Agreement breached should the Contractor become involved in any agreement or proceeding of liquidation, receivership, or bankruptcy, voluntarily or involuntarily, or should the Contractor if an individual die, be convicted of a felony, become a fugitive from justice, or for any reason disappears and cannot immediately be found by the Surety by use of usual methods.

(b) To take possession of the work under any contract and at the expense of the Undersigned to complete or to contract for the completion of the same, or to contest to the reletting of the completion thereof by the obligee in said contract Bond or Bonds, or to take such other steps as in the discretion of the Surety may be advisable or necessary to obtain its release or to secure itself from loss thereunder.

(c) To adjust, settle or compromise any claim, demand, suit or judgment upon said Bond or Bonds, or any of them, unless the Undersigned shall request in writing the Surety to litigate such claim or demand, or defend such suit, or appeal from such judgment, and shall deposit with the Surety, at the time of such request, cash or collateral satisfactory to the Surety in kind and amount to be used in paying any judgment or judgments rendered with interest, costs and attorney's fees.

All damage, loss or expense of any nature which the Surety may incur under Section Ninth shall be borne by the Undersigned.

TENTH: The Surety shall have the exclusive right for itself and for the Undersigned to decide and determine whether any claim, demand, suit or judgment upon said Bond or Bonds shall, on the basis of liability, expediency or otherwise, be paid, settled, defended or appealed, and its determination shall be final, conclusive and binding upon the Undersigned (except as provided in Section Ninth(c) hereof); and any loss, costs, charges, expense or liability thereby sustained or incurred, as well as any and all disbursements on account of costs, expenses and attorneys' fees, deemed necessary or advisable by the Surety, shall be borne and paid immediately by the Undersigned, together with legal interest. In the event of any payment, settlement, compromise or investigation, an itemized statement of the payment, loss, costs, damages, expenses or attorneys' fees, sworn to by any officer of the Surety's or the voucher or vouchers or other evidence of such payment, settlement or compromise, shall be prima facie evidence of the fact and extent of the liability of the Undersigned to the Surety in any claim or suit hereunder and in any and all matters arising between the Undersigned and the Surety.

ELEVENTH: The Surety is further authorized and empowered to advance money or to guarantee loans to the Contractor which the Surety may see fit to advance to said Contractor for the purpose of any contract referred to in or guaranteed by said Bond or Bonds; and all money so loaned or advanced and all costs, attorneys' fees and expenses incurred by the Surety in relation thereto, unless repaid with legal interest when due, shall be conclusively presumed to be a loss by the Surety for which each and all of the Undersigned shall be responsible, notwithstanding said money or any part thereof so loaned or advanced to the Contractor for the purpose of any such contract should not be so used by the Contractor. The Undersigned hereby waive all notice of such advance or loan, or of any default or any other act or acts giving rise to any claim under any said Bond or Bonds, and waive notice of any and all liability of the Surety under any said Bond or Bonds or any and all liability on the part of the Undersigned to the effect and end that each of the Undersigned shall be and continue liable to the Surety hereunder notwithstanding any notice of any kind to which the Undersigned might have been or be entitled and notwithstanding any defenses which the Undersigned might have been or be entitled to make.

TWELFTH: No assent, assignment, change in time or manner of payment or other change or extension in the terms of any Bond or of any contract referred to in such Bond or in the general conditions, plans or specifications incorporated in such contract, granted or authorized by the Surety or the refusal to so grant or authorize, shall release, discharge or in any manner whatsoever affect the obligations assumed by the Undersigned in executing this Agreement of indemnity. This Agreement shall apply to any and all renewal, continuation or substitution bonds executed by the Surety. The Surety shall not be required to notify or obtain the approval or consent of the Undersigned prior to granting, authorizing or executing any assent, assignment, change or extension.

THIRTEENTH: Until the Surety shall have been furnished with competent legal evidence of its discharge without loss from any and all Bonds, the Surety shall have the right at all times to free access to the books, records and accounts of each of the Undersigned for the purpose of examining the same. Each of the Undersigned hereby authorizes and requests any and all depositories in which funds of any of the Undersigned may be deposited to furnish to the Surety the amount of such deposits as of any date requested and any person, firm or corporation doing business with the Undersigned is hereby authorized to furnish any information requested by the Surety concerning any transaction. The Surety may furnish copies of any and all statements, agreements and financial statements and any information which it now has or may hereafter obtain concerning each of the Undersigned, to other persons or companies for the purpose of procuring co-suretyship of reinsurance or of advising interested persons or companies.

FOURTEENTH: Each of the Undersigned does hereby waive all right to claim any property, including homestead, as exempt from levy, execution, sale or other legal process under the law of any state, province or other government as against the rights of the Surety to proceed against the same for indemnity hereunder.

FIFTEENTH: The Surety shall have right and remedy which a personal surety without compensation would have, including the right to secure its discharge from the suretyship and nothing herein contained shall be considered or construed to waive, abridge or diminish any right or remedy which the Surety might have if this instrument were not executed. The Undersigned will, on request of the Surety, procure the discharge of the Surety from any Bond or Bonds, and all liability by reason thereof. Separate suits may be brought hereunder as causes of action may accrue, and the pendency or termination of any such suit shall not bar any subsequent action. The Surety shall be notified immediately by the Undersigned of any claim or action which may result in a claim against the Surety, such notice to be given by registered mail to the Surety at its Home Office. In the event of legal proceedings against the Surety, upon or on account of any said Bond or Bonds, the Surety may apply for a court order making any or all of the Undersigned parties defendants, and each Undersigned hereby consents to the granting of such application and agrees to become such a party defendant and to allow judgment, in the event of judgment against the Surety, to be rendered also against such Undersigned in like amount and in favor of the Surety, if the Surety so desires.

SIXTEENTH: The Surety reserves the right to decline to execute any such Bond; and if it shall execute any proposal Bond, and if the Contractor is awarded the contract, the Contractor shall not be obligated to obtain any Bond or Bonds required by the contract from the Surety nor shall the Surety be obligated to execute such Bond or Bonds.

SEVENTEENTH: The Undersigned warrant that each of them is specifically and beneficially interested in the obtaining of each Bond or Bonds, or any of them, or executing at that request of the Surety said Bond or Bonds, or any of them as well as any company or companies assuming co-suretyship or reinsurance thereon.

EIGHTEENTH: The Undersigned warrant that each of them is specifically and beneficially interested in the obtaining of each Bond. Failure to execute, or defective execution, by any party, shall not affect the validity of this obligation as to any other party executing the same and each such other party shall remain fully bound and liable hereunder. Invalidity of any portion or provision of this Agreement by reason of the laws of any state or for any other reason shall not render the other provisions or portions hereof invalid. Execution of an application for any Bond by the Contractor, or of any other indemnity agreement by any Undersigned for the Contractor shall in no way abrogate, waive or diminish any rights of Surety under this Agreement. The Undersigned acknowledge that the execution of this Agreement and the undertaking of indemnity was not made in reliance upon any representation concerning the financial responsibility of any Undersigned, or concerning the competence of the Contractor to perform.

NINETEENTH: Each of the Undersigned expressly recognizes and covenants that this Agreement is a continuing obligation applying to and indemnifying the Surety and that the rights of indemnification of each Surety signatory to this Agreement shall be individual and not joint with those of the other signatory Sureties as to any and all Bonds (whether or not covered by any application signed by Contractor—such application to be considered between the parties hereto as merely supplemental to this Continuing Agreement of Indemnity) heretofore or hereafter executed by Surety on behalf of Contractor (whether contracting alone or as a Co-adventure) until this Agreement shall be canceled in the manner hereinafter provided. Any of the Undersigned may notify the Surety(ies) at its Head Office, of such Undersigned's withdrawal from this Agreement; such notice shall be sent by certified or registered mail and shall state when, not less than thirty days after receipt of such notice by the Surety, such withdrawal shall be effective. Such Undersigned will not be liable under this Agreement as to any Bonds executed by the Surety after the effective date of such notice; provided, that as to any and all such Bonds executed or authorized by the Surety prior to effective date of such notice and as to any and all renewals, continuations and extensions thereof or substitutions therefore (and, if a proposal or Bid Bond has been executed or authorized prior to such effective date, as to any contract Bond executed pursuant thereto) regardless of when the same are executed, such Undersigned shall be and remain fully liable hereunder, as if said notice had not been served. Such withdrawal by any Undersigned shall in no way affect the obligation of any other Undersigned who has given no such notice of termination.

TWENTIETH: That this Agreement shall constitute a Security Agreement to Surety and also a Financing Statement, both in accordance with the provisions of the Uniform Commercial Code of every jurisdiction wherein such Code is in effect, but that the filing or recording of this Agreement shall be solely at the option of Surety and that the failure to do so shall not release or impair any of the obligations of the Undersigned under this Agreement or otherwise arising, nor shall such failure be in any manner in derogation of the rights of Surety under this Agreement.

CHAPTER 31

BANKRUPTCY ALTERNATIVE

Brian T. Moore
John K. Sherwood

Brian T. Moore is a partner with Arthur Andersen & Co., in Roseland, New Jersey, and is in charge of the Reorganization and Bankruptcy Practice for New Jersey. Mr. Moore is a graduate of the College of William & Mary and is a certified public accountant. He is a member of the American Institute of Certified Public Accountants, New Jersey Society of Certified Public Accountants, Association of Insolvency Accountants, American Bankruptcy Institute, and an associate member of the American Bar Association. He provides loan workout services to a number of banks, and has been involved in the numerous bankruptcies as financial consultants to debtors and creditors. In addition, he has substantial experience in litigation consulting to the construction industry.

John K. Sherwood, is an associate with the Roseland, New Jersey, law firm of Ravin, Sarasohn, Cook, Baumgarten, Fisch & Baime. Mr. Sherwood received his J.D. from Seton Hall University School of Law in 1986. He specializes in real estate and construction bankruptcy matters. He is the former law secretary for the Honorable Daniel J. Moore, United States Bankruptcy Judge for the District of New Jersey. He has lectured before several professional groups on the subject of bankruptcy law.

§ 31.1   Introduction

Recent years have shown a tremendous increase in the number of troubled companies requiring restructuring and reorganization. The construction industry has made, and continues to make, its contribution to the list of companies seeking alternatives to operate effectively in the current economic environment. Construction activities covering both the public and private sectors have been affected by many factors. Budgetary constraints and tremendous competition are affecting the volume and the pricing of work in the public sector. Private sector work, whether it be commercial, industrial, or residential, is being affected by a number of supply and demand factors. These factors include excess office space, the absence of continued economic growth, decrease in consumer demand for housing, changes in consumer preference for types of housing (condominiums, townhomes, and cooperatives), and the decrease in industry demand for warehousing and distribution facilities.

A significant factor affecting the ability of a company to survive is the condition of the banking industry. The banking industry is experiencing the effect of regulatory pressure and requirements, nonperforming assets, and liquidity problems. The availability of new or continued credit to both contractors and owners is affecting the ability of the contractor to complete existing projects and to gain new work where available. Contributing factors to a troubled situation need to be analyzed by the contractor to properly evaluate the alternatives, if any, that are available.

One of the alternatives available to the contractor is the bankruptcy process. One of the purposes of this chapter is to highlight some of the legal principles of bankruptcy and to identify common issues encountered while operating a construction business under the bankruptcy laws. Given current economic conditions, it is imperative that contractors understand the bankruptcy process as an alternative.

§ 31.2   Bankruptcy Process

The bankruptcy process is governed by complex legislation known as the United States Bankruptcy Code,[1] which was enacted in its present form in 1978. Generally, the Bankruptcy Code is designed to protect the following interests: (1) the interest in providing the honest debtor[2] with a fresh start; (2) the interest in giving the honest debtor the opportunity to reorganize its business affairs; and (3) the interest in treating creditors of the same class equally. These interests are often in competition with one another. Not only is there the obvious tension between the debtor and its creditors, but also there is competition between the creditors themselves in their efforts to protect their share of the debtor's estate.

Virtually all bankruptcies confronted by the contractor fall in the subcategory of either Chapter 7 liquidation or Chapter 11 reorganization.

§ 31.3   —Chapter 7 Liquidation

Chapter 7 is the process of liquidating the debtor's assets and distributing the proceeds to creditors according to class or priority. This process is carried out under the supervision of the bankruptcy court. The proceedings usually begin with the filing of a Chapter 7 petition by the debtor. A Chapter 7 petition can also be filed by a relatively small group of creditors against the debtor. These are referred to as "involuntary" Chapter 7 proceedings.

Shortly after the Chapter 7 petition is filed, a trustee is appointed who is responsible for collecting and liquidating the debtor's assets and distributing the proceeds to the creditors according to the priority of the creditors under the law. Classes of creditors are formed according to their order of priority, which is as follows:

1. Administrative or priority claims—generally, claims arising after the bankruptcy petition is filed and other pre-petition claims defined by statute, including certain taxes and obligations to secured lenders[3]
2. General unsecured claims—claims arising before the filing of the bankruptcy petition

---

[1] 11 U.S.C. §§ 101–1330 (1988).

[2] The entity filing bankruptcy is referred to as the "debtor" herein.

[3] *See* 11 U.S.C. §§ 503, 507.

3. Equity interests—claims arising due to an ownership interest in the debtor.

Because creditors of senior class must be paid in full before junior creditors receive any distribution, creditors strive for administrative or priority claim status. The objective of the Chapter 7 trustee is to minimize the number of creditors in the administrative or priority class. If a claim is collateralized by a valid pre-petition lien or security interest in the debtor's property, such property must be used by the Chapter 7 trustee to satisfy the claim of the holder of the lien or security interest.

In a Chapter 7 case, the debtor's ongoing responsibilities are minimal because the liquidation and distribution process is carried out, for the most part, by the Chapter 7 trustee. Also, the Chapter 7 process normally does not involve the continuation of the debtor's business. This alternative is appropriate for the contractor whose business cannot be reorganized and who has little or no risk as a result of the failure of the business. The risk factor is important because, although the Chapter 7 case operates to discharge the debtor from all claims arising prior to the filing date, it does not operate to discharge principals or other parties that have guaranteed corporate obligations or that are potentially liable to the surety.

§ 31.4 —Chapter 11 Reorganization

By contrast, a Chapter 11 reorganization is a complex process that involves a great deal of effort on the part of the debtor and its employees due to the fact that the debtor remains in control of its business, which continues to operate in the normal course, but under the jurisdiction of the court. A debtor in control of its business under Chapter 11 is known as a "debtor-in-possession" and inherits an assortment of rights, powers, and duties under the Bankruptcy Code.[4] One of the goals of the Chapter 11 case is to preserve the going concern value of the debtor's business. The underlying rationale is that the going concern value of a business is worth more than its liquidation value. Although the debtor is entitled to maintain control of the business operations, its financial affairs are open to inspection by creditors and other parties in interest who have the right to object and be heard by the court on issues that arise during the reorganization process. General unsecured creditors normally are represented in a Chapter 11 case by an official committee of unsecured creditors that may retain counsel and be heard on any issue in the case.[5]

---

[4] See id. § 1107.
[5] See id. § 1103.

Creditor Dividend

The ultimate goal under the Chapter 11 proceedings is the approval or "confirmation" of a plan of reorganization that provides a debtor a new start and pays creditors a fair dividend. The amount of the dividend varies depending on the circumstances of each case; however, the dividend must exceed the value that unsecured creditors would receive if the debtor's assets were liquidated under Chapter 7.[6] In both Chapter 7 and Chapter 11 cases, the dividend that a creditor receives depends on the creditor's classification or priority. Thus, the Chapter 11 case also involves a struggle between the debtor and its creditors over classification. Again, the creditors seek administrative or priority status while the debtor, in order to decrease the cost of reorganization, seeks to minimize the number of claims within the administrative or priority class.

Automatic Stay

One of the well-known and key protections the debtor immediately receives under Chapter 11 is the "automatic stay."[7] The automatic stay precludes creditors with claims against the debtor arising prior to the filing of bankruptcy from proceeding on those claims outside the bankruptcy court. Thus, the debtor is afforded a "breathing spell" from the lawsuits, levies, and other measures taken by creditors to enforce their claims. This breathing spell is designed to relieve the debtor from the pressure of defending multiple claims and afford the debtor the opportunity to concentrate on the formulation of a plan of reorganization. Moreover, the debtor is temporarily relieved from the obligation of paying its pre-petition debt. The contractor must be aware that the protection of the automatic stay is not everlasting. As set forth in **§ 31.15**, parties may obtain relief from the automatic stay in certain circumstances.

Plan of Reorganization

The debtor is afforded a period of 120 days from the filing (plus such additional time as the court allows) during which time it has the exclusive right to present its plan of reorganization to the court for approval.[8] After the plan of reorganization is confirmed, the debtor is essentially out of bankruptcy and its debts arising prior to confirmation are discharged. Nevertheless, the debtor is still bound to comply with the provisions for

---

[6] *See id.* § 1129(a)(7).

[7] *Id.* § 362.

[8] *Id.* § 1121(b).

repayment of creditors as set forth in the plan, which may include the issuance of new debt.

§ 31.5   Prefiling Considerations and Planning

There are many issues that need to be addressed in the consideration of the business decision to file bankruptcy. The decision to file bankruptcy is one of significance that requires an understanding of the process and careful planning. Bankruptcy planning should not begin on the date the petition is filed. The filing of a Chapter 11 case carries with it a basic representation that there is a likelihood of a successful reorganization within a reasonable period of time. The contractor, therefore, needs to evaluate itself as a reorganizable entity before the petition is filed and, subsequent to the filing, be prepared to demonstrate this to the court. This is difficult in an industry in which business is dominated by so many contractual relationships. A contractor, despite its history and reputation, can be viewed as limited in life to its existing contracts and not necessarily reorganizable.

Evaluation of Assets

The ability to reorganize first requires an evaluation of the contractor's assets, tangible and intangible, around which the contractor believes it can reorganize. The most important aspect of the evaluation is the availability of cash and the ability to generate cash flow. The contractor must analyze its sources of future cash from existing assets and the expected uses of such cash. Without cash flow, there simply will be no reorganization. The contractor needs to plan to have as much cash as possible within its control at the date of the filing of a petition. The ability to gain financing or other infusions of capital will be limited after a bankruptcy filing. The ability of the contractor to use cash from the future collection of existing receivables and future billings may also be contested by various parties in interest.

Effects of Filing on Relationships

If the contractor depends on bonding to maintain existing construction contracts and to obtain new contracts, it must also evaluate the effect that a bankruptcy filing will have on its relationships with bonding companies. Before the petition is filed, there should be dialogue between the contractor and the bonding companies to explore terms and conditions under which existing bonds can be maintained and new bonds can be provided.

Once the determination is made that the contractor is reorganizable in concept, the contractor needs to plan for the process. The contractor also needs to evaluate the effect of a filing on its relationship with owners, sureties, subcontractors, contract suppliers, open bids, and its own employees. The effect of the filing on the contractor's ability to bid new work must be evaluated. The filing of a bankruptcy will cause a degree of chaos between the contractor and most of the parties involved in the business. A plan to communicate effectively with the various parties in interest is essential to minimizing the chaos so that the contractor can continue to operate with the least amount of disruption. The contractor, having analyzed the problems that lead to the filing of the petition, should provide creditors with some insight as to the plans of the business in the short term. The contractor needs to gain the support of its creditors and other parties in interest to effect a reasonably smooth reorganization. Debtors sometimes feel that because the filing gives them the protection of the automatic stay, they need not deal with their creditors. Ignoring one's creditors can have a significant impact on the contractor's reorganization efforts.

Business Plan

To communicate effectively, the contractor should prepare a short-term business plan to demonstrate, primarily to the court, where the contractor thinks it is going. This business plan should include cash flows on a project-by-project basis, giving consideration to the overhead structure. Hopefully, these cash flows will demonstrate that it is more beneficial to go forward than to cease construction. This can be a complex assignment. The gathering of information for estimated costs to complete, future billings, change orders, and retainage releases requires time and effort. The contractor needs to perform this effort before the filing. A well-thought-out and prepared business plan and cash flow projections will probably put the contractor in a favorable light with the court at the outset of the proceeding and help gain credibility.

Executory Contracts and Leases

The bankruptcy process provides the debtor with methods to relieve itself of financial burdens. As discussed in detail in § **31.12** below, one of the significant options available to a debtor is the ability to assume or reject executory contracts and leases.[9] An evaluation of the existing contracts and leases to determine the ones to be rejected or assumed must be made in the planning process. The debtor will then avoid undue administrative costs from the outset of the case. Examples of executory contracts and leases to be evaluated include equipment leases, car leases, truck leases, building or

---

[9] *See* 11 U.S.C. § 365.

office leases, yard leases, phone leases, furniture leases, employment agreements, construction contracts, subcontracts, and purchase commitments. The rejection of executory contracts and leases gives rise to new liabilities (rejection claims) against the debtor. However, these liabilities will be categorized as general unsecured claims and may be dealt with in the context of the eventual plan of reorganization. Proper study and planning will allow the debtor both to accomplish the assumption and rejection process quickly after the commencement of the bankruptcy and to increase the cash flow for reorganization.

Administrative Responsibilities

Probably the most underestimated aspect of a Chapter 11 proceeding is the additional administrative responsibilities the contractor and its management must assume. The filing requires the contractor to operate under the jurisdiction of the bankruptcy court and imposes significant reporting requirements to the court as well as to the Office of the United States Trustee. Shortly after the filing, the contractor is required to submit lists of creditors, schedules of assets, and liabilities as well as a statement of its financial affairs. These documents are extremely detailed and require, at a minimum, a complete analysis of all assets and liabilities of the contractor as of the petition date.

The ability of the debtor to generate such information is often affected by its resource of people and its accounting system. This increased work load usually occurs after overhead has been reduced to a minimum. Extensions of the reporting deadlines established by the Bankruptcy Rules are often given but are not automatic. The debtor must also file monthly reports of operations to the Office of the United States Trustee. They are generally due by the 10th day after the close of the month on which a report is due. All of these reporting requirements will consume the time of key management personnel, primarily the financial group.

Creditors' Committee

Subsequent to the filing, under the supervision of the United States Trustee, a creditors' committee will be formed. This committee represents the entire creditor body and acts in a fiduciary capacity on their behalf. The creditors' committee will select counsel and probably accountants. The committee, through its professionals, will put increased demands for information on the debtor, requiring further attention of management. The contractor can also expect information requests from its lenders, owners, and bonding companies. To avoid duplication, the contractor should formulate a reporting vehicle that is satisfactory to all parties.

§ 31.6 Common Issues Arising in the Bankruptcy Process

Sections 31.7 through **31.17**, provide an overview on various issues that the contractor normally encounters in bankruptcy proceedings. An understanding of these issues will help the contractor to analyze its alternatives properly. The issues discussed are by no means exhaustive. Indeed, due to the fact that the bankruptcy court is a court of equity, and in light of the policies underlying the Bankruptcy Code, bankruptcy courts tend to implement creative solutions to problems when justice requires.

§ 31.7 —Property of the Estate

A major aspect of the Chapter 11 process is the continued ability of the debtor to use its assets to fund its reorganization. In order to use assets for this purpose, the assets must be property of the estate. *Property of the estate* is defined in the Bankruptcy Code as all legal or equitable interests of the debtor in property as of the date the case is commenced.[10] The determination of property interests in bankruptcy is governed by state law.[11] Thus, the creditor that has perfected its lien or security interest under state law before the bankruptcy petition is filed is not necessarily hurt when the debtor commences a bankruptcy case. Collectively, all of the property of the estate is referred to as the estate that is liquidated for the benefit of creditors under a Chapter 7 case or preserved for the benefit of creditors and the reorganization of the debtor's business in a Chapter 11 case.

The contractor's estate may consist of property such as leases, equipment, vehicles, real estate, office furniture, and perhaps certain causes of action against third parties. The contractor's most precious assets, however, usually are its cash and accounts receivable. Receivables usually consist of progress payments earned on a monthly basis based on services performed on construction projects. The contractor relies on its progress payments to fund its cost of operations and to pay its subcontractors for work performed on a monthly basis. If progress payments are cut off, the contractor's business is in deep trouble. Indeed, the cessation of progress payments on one or more of the contractor's construction projects is usually the cause of bankruptcy.

---

[10] *Id.* § 541(a)(1).

[11] *In re* Bevill, Bressler & Schulman Asset Management Corp., 67 B.R. 557, 585 (Bankr. D.N.J. 1986).

Accessing Progress Payments

In order to fund the reorganization process in Chapter 11, therefore, it is necessary to access these progress payments. Unfortunately, by the time the bankruptcy proceedings are filed, the debtor is usually not the only one asserting a claim against the progress payments and no party is willing to surrender its claim voluntarily. The contractor may have pledged its accounts receivable as collateral for bank financing; the contractor's surety may claim that it has the superior right to the progress payments under a theory of subrogation; and subcontractors or material suppliers may assert lien claims against the progress payments or claim that such payments are held in trust for the payment of their claims. Thus, it is quite possible that the debtor's efforts to release progress payments from the possession of the project owners will involve a struggle.

The bankruptcy laws give the debtor certain advantages in this struggle that it otherwise would not have. For example, most bankruptcy judges are extremely sensitive to a debtor's need in certain cases to have issues resolved quickly and efficiently rather than through the drawn-out process of construction litigation. The ease of access to the bankruptcy courts may also provide a better environment for compromise. Another advantage is found in 11 U.S.C. § 544, known as the "strong arm" clause of the Bankruptcy Code. As of the commencement of the case, the debtor is afforded the rights and powers of a judicial lien creditor. This hypothetical status gives the debtor the ability to avoid mortgages or liens that are not perfected under state law prior to filing, despite the fact that the debtor may have agreed to recognize such security interests or liens before filing bankruptcy.

It is recognized that progress payments and retainage due on an uncompleted construction project are part of the debtor's estate and the debtor is allowed to use such progress payments to pay post-petition expenses, including its operating costs, as well as obligations to subcontractors and material suppliers.[12] When property of the estate is in the form of a debt due and payable to the debtor, it must be turned over to the debtor by the entity owing such debt for use in the reorganization.[13]

---

[12] *See In re* Hughes-Bechtol, Inc., 117 B.R. 890, 898 (Bankr. S.D. Ohio 1990); *In re* Universal Builders, Inc., 53 B.R. 873 (Bankr. W.D. Ky. 1983); *In re* Shore Air Conditioning & Refrigeration, Inc., 18 B.R. 643 (Bankr. D.N.J. 1982).

[13] United States v. Whiting Pools, Inc., 462 U.S. 198, 103 S.Ct. 2309 (1983); Georgia Pac. Corp. v. Sigma Serv. Corp., 712 F.2d 962, 965–66 (5th Cir. 1983).

Arguments Against Free Use of Payments

Notwithstanding the above, subcontractors, sureties, and other creditors of the debtor argue that the debtor/contractor must not be granted free use of progress payments. For example, the contractor's surety may oppose the contractor's efforts to obtain the use of progress payments. This is especially true when the proposed use of the progress payments will not have the effect of reducing the surety's exposure under its bond. In *Pearlman v. Reliance Insurance Co.,* [14] the Supreme Court of the United States held that the surety's equitable right of subrogation was superior to any right of the contractor to certain retainages held by the owner of a construction project that the contractor claimed were part of the bankruptcy estate. The holding in *Pearlman,* however, does not stand for the wholesale proposition that a contractor cannot use progress payments on a bonded construction project over the objection of the surety. Indeed, various bankruptcy courts have not hesitated to distinguish *Pearlman* or to limit the scope of its holding. [15] In any event, the potential claims of a surety against progress payments must be taken seriously and the contract documents between the surety and the contractor must be analyzed in detail to determine whether the surety's claims to the progress payments take precedence over the debtor's rights to use such funds in the reorganization.

Another potential barrier to the use of progress payments by the contractor may be found in the general contract itself. Construction contracts often provide that the contractor must demonstrate to the owner that the contractor is paying its subcontractors on a current basis before the contractor is entitled to receive the next progress payment. In the case of a troubled construction company, however, subcontractors are often not paid on a current basis. Thus, the United States Bankruptcy Court for the Eastern District of Pennsylvania held in *In re Temp-Way Corp.,* [16] that when the language of the contract required that the debtor certify full performance of all obligations to its vendors before receiving payment, such was an enforceable condition of payment. The bankruptcy court authorized payment directly from the contractor to the material suppliers despite the argument by the debtor/subcontractor that it was entitled to use of the progress payments.

The result in *Temp-Way* runs contrary to the fundamental premise in bankruptcy, which provides that creditors of the same class shall be treated

---

[14] 371 U.S. 132, 83 S. Ct. 232 (1962).

[15] *See In re* Diversified Transp. Resources, Inc., 88 B.R. 635 (Bankr. D.N.J. 1988); *In re* Universal Builders, Inc., 53 B.R. 183, 186 (Bankr. M.D. Tenn. 1985); *In re* Bagwell Coatings, Inc., 34 B.R. 193 (Bankr. N.D. La. 1983).

[16] 82 B.R. 747 (Bankr. E.D. Pa. 1988).

equally. Obviously, the suppliers that were paid directly by the contractor in *Temp-Way* fared much better than the other creditors of the bankrupt subcontractor.[17] Pre-petition creditors are to be paid only pursuant to a plan proposed to creditors and confirmed by the bankruptcy court.[18] Arguably, the debtor is precluded by law from paying subcontractors or suppliers on their pre-petition claims. Under 11 U.S.C. § 549, post-petition payments by a debtor on pre-petition debts are subject to avoidance.[19] Thus, the contractor may argue that progress payments should be turned over for use by the debtor in reorganization despite contractual language to the contrary.

Finally, subcontractors and suppliers may argue that progress payments are held in trust by the contractor for payment of those who have actually toiled on the project. These trust fund claims are supported by statute in some states.[20] The existence of a trust fund statute under state law could create problems for the contractor in its attempt to access the progress payments.

Absent a statutory trust provision in favor of subcontractors and suppliers, it is difficult for a subcontractor or supplier to argue that progress payments are held in "constructive trust." In *Georgia-Pacific Corp. v. Sigma Service Corp.*,[21] the Fifth Circuit Court of Appeals held that, in order to succeed on a trust fund claim, the creditor must establish that the debtor and the owner intended to create a trust by showing that the debtor and owner mutually agreed that the subcontractor or supplier should receive a nonrevocable property interest in the funds due from the owner to the contractor.[22]

These are some of the methods used by subcontractors, suppliers, and bonding companies to prevent the general contractor from obtaining free use of progress payments due from the project owner. Prior to the filing of the Chapter 11 petition, it is incumbent upon the general contractor to analyze potential competing claims to progress payments and other assets so that the debtor will know whether it can count on these assets as sources of cash.

---

[17] *Id.* at 753.

[18] *See In re* B&W Enters., Inc., 19 B.R. 421, 425 (Bankr. N.D. Ohio 1982).

[19] *See In re* Isis Food, Inc., 37 B.R. 334, 338 (W.D. Mo. 1984).

[20] *Compare In re* Sun Belt Elec. Constructors, Inc., 56 B.R. 686 (Bankr. N.D. Ga. 1986), *with In re* Esteves Excavation, 56 B.R. 802 (Bankr. D.N.J. 1985).

[21] 712 F.2d 962 (5th Cir. 1983).

[22] *Id.* at 972. *See also In re* Nami Bros., Inc., 63 B.R. 160, 162 (Bankr. D.N.J. 1986) ("Absent actual proof of a trust fund, same does not exist and there is no authority to impose it within the framework of the Bankruptcy Code.").

Review of Pre-Petition Transfers

Related to the "property of the estate" question is the review of pre-petition security interests and other pre-petition transfers of property. As set forth in § 31.7, § 544 of the Bankruptcy Code provides that, as of the commencement of the bankruptcy case, the debtor is afforded the rights and powers of a judicial lien creditor. Because the debtor takes on a new status when it files bankruptcy, the debtor can challenge the validity of a security interest that it granted prior to the filing of the case. In the event that the holder of the security interest has not properly documented and perfected the interest in accordance with state law, the debtor may avoid the security interest. The result is that the debtor and its estate has free use of property that, prior to the filing of the petition, was encumbered by a security interest. In the event that the debtor is able to set aside a pre-petition security interest, the debtor's ability to reorganize probably will be enhanced due to the fact that it will have more unencumbered property at its disposal with which to structure its financial reorganization.

Another potential source of cash for the debtor is through the avoidance of certain transfers that occurred prior to the filing of the petition. In order to promote the basic policy of equality of treatment among creditors, § 547 of the Bankruptcy Code gives the trustee the power to avoid preferential transfers. Generally, preferential transfers are made shortly before the bankruptcy and give one creditor an unfair advantage over the other. The elements necessary to find that a transfer is *preferential* are set forth in 11 U.S.C. § 547:

1. Transfer must have been to or for the benefit of a creditor
2. Transfer must have been on account of an antecedent debt
3. Debtor must have been insolvent at the time of the transfer
4. Transfer must have been made within 90 days or, in the case of an insider, within 1 year before bankruptcy
5. Transfer must enable the creditor to receive more than it would receive in a liquidation case.

Another type of transfer that can be avoided by the debtor is a fraudulent transfer. Section 548 of the Bankruptcy Code grants the debtor (or trustee) the power to set aside such transfers. Generally, transfers with actual fraudulent intent, transfers for less than reasonably equivalent value while insolvent, transfers for less than reasonably equivalent value that render the debtor insolvent, and transfers for less than reasonably equivalent value when the debtor is undercapitalized are among those considered "fraudulent" under the Bankruptcy Code.[23] Pre-petition transfers

---

[23] *See* 11 U.S.C. § 548.

may also be set aside if such transfers are considered to be fraudulent under applicable state law.[24]

The debtor should examine all significant pre-petition transfers as well as the extent and validity of the security interests alleged by its creditors. Either of these causes of action may produce unencumbered funds for the estate's use, which will increase the likelihood of a successful reorganization.

§ 31.8 —Use of Cash Collateral

When the debtor's accounts receivable or progress payments are subject to a lien or security interest, the proceeds are known as "cash collateral."[25] The debtor may use cash collateral in a Chapter 11 bankruptcy case only if: (1) the creditor that has an interest in the cash collateral consents to such use, or (2) the court finds that the entity having an interest in the cash collateral is adequately protected.[26] By imposing these requirements, the Bankruptcy Code guards against the impairment of a secured creditor's interest. Section 361 of the Bankruptcy Code offers methods by which the debtor can provide creditors with adequate protection of their interest in cash collateral. These methods include, but are not limited to: (1) periodic cash payments; (2) additional or replacement liens; and (3) other methods by which the creditor will realize the equivalent of its security interest.

Simply stated, a lien or security interest is a property interest that is worthy of protection under the Bankruptcy Code. The debtor cannot use property subject to a lien, that is, cash collateral, without demonstrating to the court that the use of such property will not impair the right of the creditor holding the lien or security interest. In the construction arena, a contractor may offer any of the above forms of adequate protection. The following is one common example. Assume that a creditor has a lien or security interest in the contractor's progress payments. Progress payments are due on a $5 million construction project that is 60 percent complete. The debtor has approximately $2.5 million of future billings on this project alone. The debtor offers the secured party a replacement lien in new accounts receivable on this project as adequate protection. The debtor's argument is that, although existing receivables will be used to maintain overhead, pay subcontractors, and pay suppliers, the expenditure of these funds will generate future receivables from the owner on the project that will exceed the value of the existing receivables. Thus, the creditors' interest in the existing accounts receivable is adequately protected.[27]

---

[24] *Id.* § 544(b).

[25] *Id.* § 363(a).

[26] *Id.* § 363(c)(2).

[27] *See In re* Thomas Parker Enters., Inc., 8 B.R. 207 (Bankr. D. Conn. 1981).

As a result of the filing of a petition by a contractor, owners are reluctant to release existing progress payments that are due. This puts the contractor in the position of having inadequate means to complete the project. The contractor, as a matter of practicality, can take the position that if it is permitted to receive payment of receivables and use the cash to continue the project, it will generate new value (adequate protection) by virtue of a new receivable. In addition, the contractor has provided the owner with a project that is moving closer to completion.

Due to the fundamental bankruptcy policy in favor of reorganization, the bankruptcy court is more likely to allow the use of cash collateral when there is a showing that a successful reorganization is likely.[28] However, to see that the rights of creditors are not trampled upon, the bankruptcy courts generally subject the use of cash collateral to various terms and conditions and require that the debtor continue to demonstrate to the court on a periodic basis that the use of cash collateral is appropriate.[29]

§ 31.9   —Post-Petition Financing

An alternative to the use of cash collateral is post-petition financing from a new lender. Post-petition financing is governed by § 364 of the Bankruptcy Code. Commonly, third parties providing a debtor with post-petition financing require that their new loan be adequately collateralized. The debtor can obtain post-petition credit in any of the following forms:

1. On an unsecured basis
2. Secured by (a) a superpriority administrative claim; (b) a lien on property of the estate that is not otherwise subject to a lien; or (c) a junior lien on property of the estate that is already subject to a lien
3. Secured by a lien, senior or equal to property of the estate that is already subject to a lien.

In the case of number 3 above, the debtor must show that the interest of the existing lienholder that is being "primed" by the new financing is adequately protected and that the debtor is unable to obtain credit otherwise. Take the following example. The debtor has machinery and equipment with a fair market value of $200,000 that is subject to a lien of $50,000. The debtor needs $100,000 to "prime the pump" of its business that has been idle for some time due to trouble on certain construction projects. The debtor finds a bank that is willing to lend it $100,000 only if said bank can

---

[28] *See* United States v. Timbers of Inwood Forest, 484 U.S. 365, 375–76, 108 S. Ct. 626 (1988).

[29] *See* Bankwest N.A. v. Todd, 49 B.R. 633 (Bankr. D.S.D. 1985).

be granted a first priority security interest on the machinery and equipment. Theoretically, the debtor can offer this type of security interest to the new lender due to the fact that there is sufficient value or equity in the machinery and equipment to secure not only the new advance, but also the existing lien against the machinery and equipment.

§ 31.10　—Injunctive Relief

Bankruptcies involving contractors have enormous potential for litigation. This is due to the nature of the construction business. The contractor often has various projects in progress and does business with numerous subcontractors, sureties, and banks. All these parties may have conflicting claims to the progress payments that are due on a construction project and also may have conflicting opinions as to whether a construction project should continue. The problem may be compounded due to the fact that a contractor may have projects pending in various parts of the country and may be faced with the possibility of participating in massive litigation on several fronts. The contractor may be engaged in so many legal disputes that it no longer has the time to run an efficient business. Thus, it is quite possible that the contractor's business may fail, not due to business, economic, or market forces, but due to the fact that it is unable to attend to its business.

As indicated in § 31.4, one of the benefits of bankruptcy is the protection of the automatic stay from the continuation of these proceedings. However, there are circumstances in which a party can affect the affairs of the contractor although such party is not proceeding directly against said contractor. For example, this situation arises when subcontractors, material suppliers, and other creditors of the debtor proceed against project owners for payment on account of monies due from the contractor. Project owners faced with these competing claims for progress payments are reluctant to turn over any monies because of the owners' inability to determine who is entitled to the funds. There must be a way to remobilize the debtor that is crippled by these competing claims. The Bankruptcy Code may offer the contractor some relief in these circumstances. Pursuant to 11 U.S.C. § 105(a), the bankruptcy court "may issue any order, process or judgment that is necessary or appropriate to carry out the provisions of its title."

In the case *In re Wynne Enterprises, Inc.,*[30] the bankruptcy court entered an injunction pursuant to § 105(a) of the Bankruptcy Code preventing subcontractors, laborers, and material suppliers from filing mechanic's liens against various properties or the owners of such properties. The court reasoned that in the event an injunction was not entered, the owners of the properties would stop making progress payments to the debtor on its

---

[30] 40 B.R. 311 (Bankr. S.D. Fla. 1984).

construction projects and the debtor would not be able to effectively continue to operate its business. The court's holding was supported, in part, by the fact that there was a substantial likelihood of a successful reorganization within a reasonable time and that successful reorganization was in the public interest.[31]

Injunctions such as the one in *Wynne Enterprises, Inc.,* may be the only means by which a contractor can operate its business in bankruptcy. With the increased number of construction bankruptcies, bankruptcy courts are becoming less reluctant to provide injunctive relief to keep a bankruptcy case under control. The exercise of this type of authority by the bankruptcy court is supported by the opinion of the Fifth Circuit Court of Appeals in *In re Timbers of Inwood Forest Associates, Ltd.:*[32]

> The principal goal of the reorganization provisions of the Bankruptcy Code is to benefit the creditors of the Chapter 11 debtor by preserving going concern values and thereby enhancing the amounts recovered by all creditors.
>
> * * *
>
> Early and ongoing judicial management of Chapter 11 cases is essential if the Chapter 11 process is to survive and if the goals of reorganizability on one hand and creditor protection on the other are to be achieved. In almost all cases, a key to avoiding excessive administrative costs which are born by the unsecured creditors, as well as excessive interest expense, which is born by all creditors, is early and stringent judicial management of the case. We recognize that Congress, in 1978, amended the bankruptcy laws with the intention of removing bankruptcy judges from the administration of the debtor's estate. The purpose of this amendment was to ensure the impartiality of the bankruptcy judge. We do not believe, however, that Congress thereby intended to relieve the bankruptcy judge of the responsibility of managing the cases before him in such a way as to promote the objectives and goals of the Bankruptcy Code.[33]

The contractor's bankruptcy case often requires the type of judicial management referred to by the court in *Timbers.* Without this type of judicial management, the excessive court proceedings and litigation costs could be the sole reason that a contractor's bankruptcy fails.

§ 31.11 —Payment of Pre-Petition Claims

It may be that the contractor's financial problems are not spread throughout the entire company. The contractor may be engaged in one or several

---

[31] *Id.* at 312; *see also In re* Cardinal Indus., Inc., 109 B.R. 748 (Bankr. S.D. Ohio 1989); *In re* Monroe Well Serv., Inc., 67 B.R. 746 (Bankr. E.D. Pa. 1986).

[32] 808 F.2d 363 (5th Cir. 1987).

[33] *Id.* at 373.

construction projects that are proceeding forward without a hitch and that represent a source of revenue that will assist the reorganization of the business. A contractor may anticipate that the interruption of payment to subcontractors on such projects may cause turmoil among subcontractors and suppliers. Thus, the contractor may decide that it would be less of a burden to pay these suppliers and subcontractors than to interrupt the progress of a healthy project.

One alternative, if affordable in the context of an anticipated filing, is to make sure that the contractor's critical subcontractors and suppliers are paid up-do-dately before the case is filed. There are methods subsequent to the filing that can give the contractor the ability to satisfy the pre-petition claims of subcontractors or suppliers. First, the contractor can apply to the court for an order under § 105(a) of the Bankruptcy Code, permitting the payment under the "Necessity of Payment Doctrine."[34] The second alternative is to treat the subcontract as an executory contract and assume it. Section 365(b) of the Bankruptcy Code provides that the debtor cannot assume an executory contract unless it cures all existing defaults. Therefore, the debtor will be able to pay the subcontractor in question when the assumption of the subcontract is authorized by the court. Other creditors may object to the special treatment of the subcontractor whose contract is being assumed. However, as long as there is a business justification for assuming the contract, it will be approved by the court.[35]

The above alternatives to nonpayment can be urged upon the contractor by the subcontractor or supplier as a means by which they can receive payment. Whether the contractor wishes to comply with a subcontractor's demand for payment on its pre-petition debt boils down to a question of business judgment. The debtor must consider whether keeping the subcontractor or supplier on the project is more important than having the cash available to pay the debtor's expenses in going forward.

§ 31.12   —Assumption or Rejection of Executory Contracts and Leases

One of the features of Chapter 11 reorganization is the ability of the debtor to assume or reject executory contracts and leases. This gives the debtor the option to reject leases or executory contracts that are burdensome to the estate. An *executory contract* is one in which performance is due to some extent on both sides. It would appear that executory contracts include the

---

[34] *In re* Gulf Air, Inc., 112 B.R. 152 (Bankr. W.D. La. 1989) (bankruptcy court may authorize Chapter 11 debtor to pay pre-petition debt when such payment is essential to reorganization efforts).

[35] *See In re* Sun Belt Elec. Constructors, Inc., 56 B.R. 686, 689 (Bankr. N.D. Ga. 1986).

general construction contract and subcontracts thereunder.[36] When determining whether to permit a debtor to reject a lease or executory contract, the bankruptcy court will defer to the debtor's sound business judgment.[37]

The debtor is given 60 days from the date of the filing of bankruptcy to assume or reject a lease of nonresidential real property. Other executory contracts and leases may be assumed or rejected at any time up to confirmation of the debtor's plan. Thus, the debtor is given ample opportunity to assume or reject its leases and executory contracts. During the period between filing and assumption or rejection of the lease or executory contract, the debtor is obligated to stay current on at least the post-petition portion of the lease or executory contract. Thus, once the debtor decides that a lease or executory contract will be rejected, it should immediately apply for a court order authorizing rejection so that administrative expenses and the overall costs of administration are minimized. This decision should be made in the planning process.

The rejection of a lease or executory contract gives rise to a general unsecured claim in the amount of the damages caused by such rejection.[38] In order to assume a lease or executory contract, the debtor must cure any existing defaults and provide adequate assurance that it is capable of performing under the lease or executory contract in the future.[39]

§ 31.13   —Transactions Outside the Ordinary Course of Business

The debtor is entitled to conduct its ordinary business affairs under Chapter 11. However, any time a transaction is considered to be outside the ordinary course of the debtor's business, it must be approved by the court on notice to parties in interest.[40] Examples of transactions outside the ordinary course of business include sales of equipment and bulk sales of inventory. In determining whether or not to approve a transaction outside the ordinary course of business, the bankruptcy court analyzes, among other things, whether the transaction is proposed in good faith, whether the transaction serves a sound business purpose, and whether the proposed transaction is in the best interests of the estate.[41] The contractor's opinion of what

---

[36] See id. at 686.

[37] In re Constant Care Community Health Ctr., Inc., 19 Bankr. Ct. Dec. (CRR) 275 (Bankr. D. Md. 1989).

[38] 11 U.S.C. § 365(g)(1).

[39] Id. § 365(b)(1).

[40] Id. § 363(b).

[41] See In re Lionel Corp., 722 F.2d 1063 (2d Cir. 1983); In re Industrial Valley Refrigeration & Air Conditioning Supplies, Inc., 77 B.R. 15 (Bankr. E.D. Pa. 1987).

constitutes ordinary course of business may be different than that of the court. Thus, the debtor should consult with counsel prior to engaging in most transactions.

§ 31.14 —Utility Service

The debtor's flow of utility service is protected under § 366 of the Bankruptcy Code. This section provides that a utility may not discontinue service to the debtor solely on the basis of the commencement of the bankruptcy case. If the debtor refuses to post adequate assurance of payment within 20 days of the date of the bankruptcy filing, the utility may discontinue service. The amount of each security deposit is negotiable. Thus, another prefiling consideration for the contractor is the ability to post adequate security deposits. An inventory should be taken of the existing security deposits. In the event that security deposits have been drawn upon, the debtor should plan to post additional security deposits early in the case. This requirement applies to utility service provided to the project site, which is the responsibility of the contractor.

§ 31.15 —Relief from the Automatic Stay

The protection afforded to the debtor by the automatic stay may be terminated. A creditor precluded from proceeding against the debtor by the automatic stay may seek relief from the automatic stay pursuant to 11 U.S.C. § 362(d). Relief from the automatic stay is granted "for cause including lack of adequate protection of an interest in property" or with respect to a stay of an act against property "if the debtor does not have equity in such property and such property is not necessary to an effective reorganization." Again, the major concept is adequate protection. If a secured creditor persuades the court that its security interest in the debtor's property is being eroded, it may obtain relief from the automatic stay to proceed against its collateral.

The debtor should anticipate motions for relief from the automatic stay if the debtor has defaulted on scheduled payments to secured creditors. In this situation, the secured creditor will insist on either some form of adequate protection[42] or access to its collateral.

---

[42] *See* 11 U.S.C. § 361.

§ 31.16   —Conversion and the
Appointment of a Trustee

Conversion is governed by 11 U.S.C. § 1112, which provides that a case can be converted from Chapter 11 to Chapter 7 for "cause," including the following:

1. Continuing loss or diminution of the estate and absence of a reasonable likelihood of rehabilitation
2. Inability to effectuate a plan
3. Unreasonable delay by the debtor that is prejudicial to creditors
4. Failure to propose a plan within any time fixed by the court
5. Denial of confirmation of a proposed plan
6. Revocation of an order of confirmation
7. Inability to consummate a confirmed plan
8. Material default by the debtor with respect to a confirmed plan
9. Termination of a plan by reason of the occurrence of a condition specified in the plan
10. Nonpayment of any fees or charges required under chapter 123 of title 28.

The appointment of a trustee is governed by 11 U.S.C. § 1104. Grounds for the appointment of a trustee include fraud, dishonesty, incompetence, and gross mismanagement by the debtor. A trustee will also be appointed if such appointment is in the interest of creditors, equity security holders, or other interests of the estate.

From the debtor's standpoint, conversion and the appointment of a trustee have certain major consequences. First, another layer of administrative expense (the trustee's fees and expenses) is added to the case, making reorganization more costly. Obviously, in the case of conversion to a Chapter 7 liquidation, reorganization is no longer an option. Second, the debtor is no longer in complete control of the affairs of its business. In the Chapter 11 case, the trustee will be involved in the day-to-day business decisions. In Chapter 7, the debtor and creditor must rely on the trustee to realize the maximum value for the estate's assets.

§ 31.17   Plan of Reorganization

At some point in time during the bankruptcy process, the contractor will focus on its plan to emerge from bankruptcy. Hopefully, the bankruptcy will have allowed the contractor to eliminate financial burdens and position its business as one that is viable and capable of carrying out a feasible financial reorganization. Often during the bankruptcy process, the contractor will be negotiating plan concepts and terms regarding the payment of its pre-petition obligations. Agreements in concept with creditors before a plan is formerly prepared will assist in a swift confirmation process. However, complete agreement before a plan is filed is unusual. The contractor must go forward with what it believes to be a viable plan of reorganization that treats creditors fairly. As indicated in § **31.4**, only the debtor may file a plan during the 120 days following the date of the filing. This is referred to as the *period of exclusivity.* Debtors often get extensions of this period depending on the performance of the business and other factors such as the complexity of the case. However, extensions are not automatic and may be contested by the various parties in interest and may lead to a court hearing regarding extensions. The importance of the period of exclusivity is it allows the debtor to maintain control of the reorganization process and the structure of its plan. If the debtor fails to file a plan within the 120-day period, or any extended period, then any party in interest may file its own plan.

A plan is not a simple proposal, but a detailed document dealing with many contingencies that must comply with statutory guidelines. Section 1123 of the Bankruptcy Code sets forth the necessary contents for a plan of reorganization and § 1129 sets forth the requirements for confirmation of the plan.

Disclosure Statement

Together with the plan, the debtor must also file a disclosure statement that contains adequate information regarding the contractor's business to enable a reasonable hypothetical investor to make an informed judgment about the plan.[43] The disclosure statement will include items such as financial projections, background information, a summary of the plan, implementation strategies, management structure, corporate structure, and other matters necessary to give parties in interest "adequate information." The disclosure statement is similar to a prospectus and requires the gathering of a great deal of information and tremendous effort by the debtor and its professionals. Once the adequacy of the disclosure statement is approved by the court, both the disclosure statement and plan are distributed to creditors together with a ballot so that creditors may vote on whether to accept or reject the plan.

---

[43] *Id.* § 1125.

Impaired Classes of Creditors

The plan must designate the different classes of claims that are based on the nature of the claim (that is, secured or unsecured). A class of claims is deemed to have accepted the plan if more than two-thirds in amount and one-half in number of the creditors voting on the plan have accepted.[44]

A significant factor in the confirmation process is whether impaired classes of creditors have accepted the plan. Indeed, one impaired class of creditors must accept the plan in order for it to be confirmed. Generally, a creditor's claim is *impaired* if such creditor receives something less than the full amount of its claim in cash at confirmation.[45] Thus, the determination of the impairment is a significant step in the plan process, and disputes may arise over the classification of certain creditors as impaired or unimpaired.

Basically, the plan should be confirmed if acceptances of all the impaired classes designated in the plan are obtained. If there is a class or classes of impaired creditors that reject the plan, there are "cram down" provisions that allow the court to confirm a plan despite rejection by an impaired class. The ability to cram down a particular class or classes, however, requires acceptance of the plan by at least one impaired class if the plan is to be confirmed.

The ability to cram down certain class or classes of creditors requires proof that these classes are receiving value under the plan at least equal to the amount they would have received in liquidation. This proof may require the use of valuation experts such as investment bankers, accountants, or appraisers. For example, the determination of "value" of common stock in the new reorganized entity issued to creditors may require a valuation opinion of an investment banker.

Confirmation of Plan

The confirmation of a plan requires the approval of the court and may require a great deal of trial preparation if full acceptance was not achieved through the ballot process. The contractor needs to be prepared to fully defend the classification of creditors and the consideration given.

Once a plan is confirmed, it sets forth the binding terms and conditions upon the debtor, creditors, and shareholders. The confirmation is the end of the bankruptcy process. It discharges the debtor from its liabilities that existed at the filing. Nevertheless, these pre-petition liabilities usually are replaced by new liabilities with terms and conditions by which the

---

[44] *Id.* § 1126(c).

[45] *See id.* § 1124.

reorganized company is bound. These may include restructured bank debt, periodic cash payments to creditors, or other payout schemes based on the future performance of the reorganized entity.

§ 31.18   Summary

Bankruptcy can be an effective alternative for the contractor to deal with its current and anticipated operating problems. In order to maximize the benefits that bankruptcy can offer, the contractor and its professionals must have an understanding of the bankruptcy process. For instance, the protection of the automatic stay, the ability to reject executory contracts, and the ability to avoid certain liens and security interests may improve current operating results dramatically.

The contractor must weigh these benefits against the effect of operating a business under the jurisdiction of the bankruptcy court. The contractor must consider the effect that bankruptcy will have on the relationship it has with project owners and other clients, bonding companies, subcontractors, suppliers, employees, and prospective clients. The effect of the filing on the debtor's ability to compete in the marketplace and the reactions of competitors in the industry should also be considered before the petition is filed.

The contractor must realize that once the petition is filed, the contractor will be conducting its business affairs in a totally new environment. It must develop a strategy beforehand to operate in this environment. The bankruptcy process can have a different pace than that to which the contractor is accustomed. Because the business is operated under the supervision of the bankruptcy court, which must consider the rights of creditors as well as the debtor's right to reorganize, court approval is sometimes required for transactions proposed by the debtor. Thus, the contractor must be prepared to support all business decisions and demonstrate how they benefit the reorganization.

All of the above factors and issues suggest that bankruptcy is an extremely complex and difficult process. Nevertheless, a thorough understanding and analysis may lead the contractor to selecting the bankruptcy alternative. The contractor's chances of successfully reorganizing its business affairs will be greatly increased if it is prepared to operate in the Chapter 11 environment from the outset.

TABLE OF CASES

Case	*Book §*
Grier-Lowrance Constr. Co. v. United States, 98 Ct. Cl. 434 (1943)	§ 24.20
Griggs v. Duke Power Co., 401 U.S. 424 (1971)	§ 10.1
Grinnell Fire Protection Sys. Co. v. American Sav. & Loan Ass'n, 228 Cal. Rptr. 292 (Ct. App. 1986)	§ 18.26
Grumman Aerospace, ASBCA No. 33091, 91-2 B.C.A. (CCH) ¶ 2375	§ 22.18
Grumman Aerospace Corp., ASBCA No. 27476, 86-3 B.C.A. (CCH) ¶ 19,091	§ 8.6
Guaranteed Constr. Co. v. Gold Bond Prods., 395 N.W.2d 332 (Mich. Ct. App. 1986)	§ 7.14
Guardians Ass'n of the N.Y. City Police Dep't v. Civil Serv. Comm'n, 630 F.2d 79 (2d Cir. 1980), *cert. denied,* 452 U.S. 940 (1981)	§ 10.1
Gulf Air, Inc., *In re,* 112 B.R. 152 (Bankr. W.D. La. 1989)	§ 31.11
Gulf Oil Corp. v. Clark County, 575 P.2d 1332 (Nev. 1978)	§ 5.6
Guy F. Atkinson v. Schatz, 161 Cal. Rptr. 436 (Ct. App. 1980)	§ 6.36
Haag Elec. & Constr., Inc., B-240974, 91-1 CPD ¶ 29	§ 14.39
Haggarty v. Selesco, 534 P.2d 874 (Mont. 1975)	§ 24.21
Hallett Constr. Co. v. Iowa State Highways Comm'n, 154 N.W.2d 71 (Iowa 1967)	§ 5.19
Hamilton v. 1st Source Bank, 895 F.2d 159 (4th Cir.), *modified,* 928 F.2d 86 (4th Cir. 1990)	§ 10.6
Hanberry Corp. v. State Bldg. Comm'n, 390 So. 2d 277 (Miss. 1980)	§ 17.13
Harbor Mechanical, Inc. v. Arizona Elec., 496 F. Supp. 681 (D. Ariz. 1980)	§ 17.17
Hardeman-Monier-Hutcherson v. United States, 458 F.2d 1364 (Ct. Cl. 1972)	§§ 15.8, 15.9
Harold James, Inc. v. Five Points Ranch, Inc., 204 Cal. Rptr. 494 (Ct. App. 1984)	§ 18.22
Harris Management Co., ASBCA No. 27291, 84-2 B.C.A. ¶ 17,378	§ 22.16
Hartrick Erectors, Inc. v. Maxson-Betts, Inc., 389 S.E.2d 607 (N.C. Ct. App.), *review allowed,* 397 S.E.2d 218 (N.C. 1990), *review dismissed,* 401 S.E.2d 359 (N.C. 1991)	§ 26.11
Haskell v. Kaman Corp., 743 F.2d 113 (2d Cir. 1984)	§ 10.6
Haughton Elevator Div. v. Louisiana, 367 So. 2d 1161 (La. 1979)	§ 5.6
Havens Steel Co. v. Randolf Eng'g Co., 613 F. Supp. 514 (W.D. Mo. 1985)	§ 16.20
Hawkins Constr. Co. v. Matthews Co., 209 N.W.2d 643 (Neb. 1973)	§ 17.15
Hawley v. Orange County Flood Control Dist., 27 Cal. Rptr. 478 (Ct. App. 1963)	§§ 5.19, 20.15
Hayes v. McIntosh, 604 F. Supp. 10 (N.D. Ind. 1984)	§ 10.10
Hazelwood Sch. Dist. v. United States, 433 U.S. 299 (1977)	§ 10.1
HEC Elec. Constr., B-233111, 89-1 CPD ¶ 143	§ 14.34
Helene Curtis Indus., Inc. v. United States, 312 F.2d 774 (Ct. Cl. 1963)	§ 15.8
Henepin, County of v. AFG Indus., 726 F.2d 149 (8th Cir. 1984)	§ 7.14
Henningsen v. United States Fidelity & Guar. Co., 208 U.S. 404, 28 S. Ct. 389 (1908)	§ 30.2

Case	*Book §*
Shore Bridge Corp v. State, 61 N.Y.S.2d 32, *aff'd,* 66 N.Y.S.2d 921 (App. Div. 1946)	§ 20.11
Siefford v. Housing Auth., 223 N.W.2d 816 (Neb. 1974)	§ 20.12
Sime Constr. Co. v. Washington Pub. Power Supply Sys., 621 P.2d 1299 (Wash. Ct. App. 1980)	§§ 25.3, 25.9
Simonette v. Lovermi, 546 A.2d 331 (Conn. Ct. App. 1988)	§ 25.8
Singer Hous. Co. v. Seven Lakes Venture, 466 F. Supp. 369 (D. Colo. 1979)	§ 25.3
Singleton Contracting Corp., B-211259, 83-2 CPD ¶ 270	§ 14.35
Sink & Edwards, Inc. v. Huber, Hunt & Nichols, Inc., 458 N.E.2d 291 (Ind. Ct. App. 1984)	§ 26.2
6800 Corp., GSBCA No. 5880, 81-2 B.C.A. (CCH) ¶ 15,388	§ 22.23
Skinner v. Railway Labor Executives Ass'n, 489 U.S. 602 (1989)	§ 11.16
Skinny's Inc. v. Hicks Bros. Constr. Co., 602 S.W.2d 85 (Tex. Ct. App. 1980)	§ 18.11
S.L. Rowland Constr. Co. v. Beall Pipe & Tank Corp., 540 P.2d 912 (Wash. Ct. App. 1975)	§ 24.8
Slodov v. United States, 436 U.S. 238, 98 S. Ct. 1778 (1978), *on remand,* 579 F.2d 400 (6th Cir. 1978)	§ 21.23
S&M Plumbing Co. v. Commissioner, 55 T.C. 702 (1971)	§ 4.13
Smith v. Evening News Ass'n, 371 U.S. 195 (1962)	§ 11.23
Sobeck & Assocs. v. B&R Invs. No. 24, 264 Cal. Rptr. 156 (Ct. App. 1989)	§ 18.26
Soble v. University of Md., 778 F.2d 164 (4th Cir. 1985)	§ 10.8
Socar, Inc. v. St. Paul Fire & Marine Ins., 341 S.E.2d 822 (S.C. Ct. App. 1986)	§ 6.2
Sofarelli Assocs., Inc. v. United States, 716 F.2d 1395 (Fed. Cir. 1983)	§ 22.44
Solberg v. Inline Corp., 740 F. Supp. 680 (D. Minn. 1990)	§ 11.14
South Prairie Constr., 231 N.L.R.B. 76 (1977), *enforced,* 595 F.2d 844 (D.C. Cir. 1979)	§ 12.11
South Prairie Constr. Co. (Peter Kiewit Sons' Co.) v. Local 627, Int'l Union of Operating Eng'rs, 425 U.S. 800 (1976)	§ 12.11
South W. Bell Tel. Co. Maternity Benefits Litig., *In re,* 602 F.2d 845 (8th Cir. 1979)	§ 10.4
Southern Cal. Acoustics Co. v. C.V. Holder, Inc., 456 P.2d 975 (Cal. 1969)	§§ 6.6, 6.7
Southern Concrete Servs. v. Mabelton Contractors, 407 F. Supp. 581 (N.D. Ga. 1975)	§ 7.18
Southern Gulf Utils., Inc. v. Boca Ciega Sanitary Dist., 238 So. 2d 458 (Fla. Dist. Ct. App. 1970)	§ 20.13
Southern Pac. Co. v. Gila River Ranch, Inc., 454 P.2d 1010 (Ariz. Ct. App.), *vacated,* 460 P.2d 1 (Ariz. 1969)	§ 6.36
Southport Petroleum Co. v. NLRB, 315 U.S. 100 (1942)	§ 12.10
Southwest Nat'l Bank v. Simpson & Son, 799 P.2d 512 (Kan. Ct. App. 1990), *review denied,* _____ P.2d _____ (Jan. 29, 1991)	§ 26.8
Souza & McCue Constr. Co. v. Superior Court, 370 P.2d 338 (Cal. 1962)	§§ 15.27, 16.16
Space Age Surveyors, Inc., B-198952, 81-1 CPD ¶ 467	§ 14.34
Spagnuolo v. Whirlpool Corp., 717 F.2d 114 (4th Cir. 1983)	§ 10.6
Spence Bros., B-243766, 91-1 CPD ¶ 428	§ 8.9
Spence & Howe Constr. Co. v. Gulf Oil Corp., 365 S.W.2d 631 (Tex. 1963), *overruled for other reasons,* 725 S.W.2d 705 (Tex. 1987)	§ 26.3

Case	*Book §*
Upton v. Fidelity Standard Life Ins. Co., 185 So. 2d 297 (La. Ct. App. 1966)	§ 5.2
U.S. Air, Inc. v. OSAHRC, 689 F.2d 1191 (4th Cir. 1982)	§ 9.1
U.S. Steel Corp. v. Emerson-Comstock Co., 141 F. Supp. 143 (N.D. Ill. 1956)	§ 26.2
U.S. Steel Corp. v. United States, 730 F.2d 1465 (Fed. Cir. 1984)	§ 14.14
Utility Workers v. Southern Cal. Edison Co., 852 F.2d 1083 (9th Cir. 1988)	§ 11.19
Uyemura v. Wick, 551 P.2d 171 (Haw. 1976)	§ 25.7
Vanderline Elec. Corp. v. City of Rochester, 388 N.Y.S.2d 388 (App. Div. 1976)	§ 20.2
Vaughn v. De Kreek, 83 Cal. Rptr. 144 (Ct. App. 1969)	§ 18.19
Velotta v. Leo Petrozonio Landscaping, Inc., 433 N.E.2d 147 (Ohio 1982)	§ 16.22
Vemo Co. v. United States, 9 Cl. Ct. 217 (1985)	§ 22.23
VEPCO, Inc., ASBCA No. 26993, 82-2 B.C.A. (CCH) ¶ 15,824	§ 22.24
Vermont Marble Co. v. Baltimore Contractors, Inc., 520 F. Supp. 922 (D.D.C. 1981)	§ 6.23
Vicksburg Fed. Bldg. Ltd. Partnership, B-230660, 88-1 CPD ¶ 515	§ 14.34
Virginia Technology Assocs., B-241167, 91-1 CPD ¶ 80	§ 14.36
V.L. Nicholson Co. v. Transcon Inv. & Fin. Ltd., 595 S.W.2d 474 (Tenn. 1980)	§ 15.25
V.M. Solis Underground Util. v. Laredo, 751 S.W.2d 532 (Tex. Ct. App. 1988)	§ 17.18
Waldinger Corp. v. Ashbrook-Simon-Hartley, Inc., 564 F. Supp. 970 (C.D. Ill. 1983)	§ 25.7
Waldinger Corp. v. CRS Group Eng'rs, Inc., 775 F.2d 781 (7th Cir. 1985)	§ 17.18
Wallace Indus. Constructors v. Louisiana Elec. Coop., 348 F. Supp. 675 (M.D. La. 1972), *aff'd,* 472 F.2d 1407 (5th Cir. 1973)	§ 5.5
Walsky Constr. Co. v. United States, 3 Cl. Ct. 615 (1983)	§ 22.17
Walter Kidde Constructors, Inc. v. State, 434 A.2d 962 (Conn. Super. Ct. 1981)	§ 25.4
Ward v. Haren, 167 S.W. 1064 (Mo. Ct. App. 1914)	§ 24.3
Wards Cove Packing Co. v. Atonio, 490 U.S. 642, 109 S. Ct. 2115 (1989)	§ 10.1
Watson v. Fort Worth Bank & Trust, 108 S. Ct. 2777 (1988)	§ 10.1
W.C. James, Inc. v. Phillips Petroleum Co., 347 F. Supp. 381 (D. Colo. 1972), *aff'd,* 485 F.2d 22 (10th Cir. 1973)	§ 20.13
Weather Data Serv., Inc., B-241621, 91-1 CPD ¶ 185	§ 14.39
Wehr Constructors, Inc. v. Steel Fabricators, Inc., 769 S.W.2d 51 (Ky. Ct. App. 1988)	§ 18.2
Wells Bros. Co. v. United States, 254 U.S. 83 (1920)	§ 20.30
Wells & Newton Co. v. Craig, 133 N.E. 419 (N.Y. 1921)	§ 20.12
Wes-Julian Constr. Corp. v. Commonwealth, 223 N.E.2d 72 (Mass. 1967)	§§ 20.2, 20.12
West Coast Gen. Corp., 19 Cl. Ct. 98 (1989)	§§ 22.16, 22.19, 22.20
Westclox Military Prods., ASBCA No. 25592, 81-2 B.C.A (CCH) ¶ 15,270	§ 22.16

INDEX

917